Communications
in Computer and Information Science 250

Vinu V Das Nessy Thankachan (Eds.)

Computational Intelligence and Information Technology

First International Conference, CIIT 2011
Pune, India, November 7-8, 2011
Proceedings

Springer

Volume Editors

Vinu V Das
The IDES
Ouderkerk aan de Amstel
1191 GT Amsterdam, Netherlands
E-mail: vinuvdas@theides.org

Nessy Thankachan
College of Engineering
Trivandrum, Kerala, India
E-mail: nessythankachan@gmail.com

ISSN 1865-0929 e-ISSN 1865-0937
ISBN 978-3-642-25733-9 e-ISBN 978-3-642-25734-6
DOI 10.1007/978-3-642-25734-6
Springer Heidelberg Dordrecht London New York

Library of Congress Control Number: Applied for

CR Subject Classification (1998): C.2.4, C.2, H.3-4, I.2.11, C.1.4, D.4.7, D.2, I.4

Typesetting: Camera-ready by author, data conversion by Scientific Publishing Services, Chennai, India

Printed on acid-free paper

Springer is part of Springer Science+Business Media (www.springer.com)

Preface

International Conference on Computational Intelligence and Information Technology (CIIT 2011), sponsored and organized by The Association of Computer Electronics and Electrical Engineers (ACEEE), was held during November 7–8, 2011, in Pune, India. The mission of the CIIT conference is to bring together innovative academics and industrial experts in the field of computer science, information technology, computational engineering, mobile communication and security to a common forum, where a constructive dialog on theoretical concepts, practical ideas and results of the state of the art can be developed. In addition, the participants of the symposium have a chance to hear from renowned keynote speakers.

CIIT 2011 received 483 submissions overall. Only 157 papers were accepted and registered for these proceedings. We thank Alfred Hofmann, for the constant support and guidance in publishing the proceedings in the Springer CCIS series. We would like to express our gratitude to the Springer LNCS-CCIS editorial team, especially Leonie Kunz, for producing such a wonderful quality proceedings book.

The conference would not be successful without the help of so many people. First, we would like to express our deep gratitude to Janahanlal Stephen, Yogesh Chaba, and Gylson Thomas. Together with their Program Committee, they assembled a strong program from submissions and invited papers. We would like to thank the Program Chairs, organization staff, and the members of the Program Committees for their hard work. We would like to thank all our colleagues who served on different committees and acted as reviewers to identify the set of high-quality research papers presented at CIIT 2011.

September 2011 Vinu V. Das

CIIT 2011 - Organization

Technical Chairs

Pascal Lorenz	University of Haute Alsace, France
Abdelhamid Mellouk	University of Paris Est, France

Technical Co-chairs

R. Vijayakumar	MG University, India
Ford Lumban Gaol	Bina Nusantara University, Indonesia
William M. Mongan	Drexel University, USA

Organizing Chairs

Janahan Lal	ILAHIA College of Engineering, India
P.M. Thankachan	Mar Ivanious, India

Organizing Co-chairs

Srinivasa K.G.	M.S. Ramaiah Institute of Technology, India
Hatim A. Aboalsamh	King Saud University, Saudi Arabia

General Chair

Vinu V. Das	The IDES

Publicity Chair

Mohammad Hammoudeh	University of Wolverhampton, UK

Publication Chair

Mohamed Jamaludeen	SRM University, India

Advisory Committee

Sudarshan T.S.B.	BITS Pilani, India
Sumeet Dua	Louisiana Tech University, USA
Ansari Nirwan	

Program Committee

Volume Editors

Editors-in-Chief

Vinu V. Das (vinuvdas@theides.org) – contact person
Nessy Thankachan (nessythankachan@gmail.com)

Associate Editors

Janahanlal Stephen (drlalps@gmail.com)
G.R. Sinha (ganeshsinha2003@gmail.com)
Sunil Manvi (sunil.manvi@revainstitution.org)

Table of Contents

Full Paper

Short Paper

Poster Paper

Parallel Coupled Microstrip Bandpass Filter for Short Range UWB Applications

K. Thirumalaivasan and R. Nakkeeran

Department of Electronics and Communication Engineering
Pondicherry Engineering College, Puducherry - 605014, India
{thirumalaivasank,rnakeeran}@pec.edu

Abstract. Bandpass filter is presented based on parallel coupled line microstrip structure suitable for short range Ultra-Wideband (UWB) applications. Chebyshev filter of order 4 and 0.2 dB passband ripple with fractional bandwidth of 86 % is designed using insertion loss method. The proposed filter demonstrates -10 dB bandwidth over the range 3.9 GHz to 9.8 GHz and has linear phase response in the operating band. The analysis of the filter is performed by using MoM based electromagnetic solver, IE3D. With the above functional features the overall dimension of the filter is 31 mm (height) × 4 mm (length) × 1.6 mm (breadth). It is not only compact but also delivers excellent scattering parameters with the magnitude of insertion loss, $|S_{21}|$ lower than -0.5 dB at center frequency, 6.85 GHz and return loss better than -32.67 dB. In the passband, the computed group delay is well within the tolerable variation of 0.02 ns.

Keywords: Ultra-wideband, bandpass filter, parallel coupled line, microstrip, group delay.

1 Introduction

The ultra-wideband (UWB) technology has brought tremendously increasing research interests since the Federal Communications Commission (FCC) in USA released its unlicensed use for indoor and hand-held systems in 2002 [1], [2]. Much effort has been made in the past eight years towards exploring various UWB components and devices. As one of the essential component blocks, the researchers are attempting to design the UWB bandpass filter (BPF) with 120% fractional bandwidth centered at 6.85GHz. With the rapid developments of wireless systems, a lot of attention is being given to the design of bandpass as it is inevitable elements of UWB receivers [3], [4], [5]. In the recent years, the market pays much attention towards miniaturization of receiver system. Contemporary researchers have been working for the development of small size and cost effective filters [6], [7], [8].

Parallel coupled-line microstrip filters have been found to be one of the most commonly used microwave filters in many practical wireless systems for several decades [9], [10]. In addition to the planar structure and relatively wide bandwidth, the major advantage of this kind of filter is that its design procedure is quite simple. Based on insertion loss method, filter functions of maximally flat and Chebyshev type

V.V. Das and N. Thankachan (Eds.): CIIT 2011, CCIS 250, pp. 1–5, 2011.

can be easily synthesized. Moreover, the filter performance can be improved in a straightforward manner by increasing the order of the filter. When these filters are to be realized by parallel coupled microstrip lines, one of the main limitations is the small gap size of the first and the last coupling stages. To increase the coupling efficiency, more fractional bandwidth and smaller gap size are required. Obviously, shrinking the gap size is not only the way to increase the coupling of coupled lines.

The proposed bandpass filter in this paper is based on parallel coupled line microstrip structure. The filter is designed to cover the entire UWB range. The obtained scattering parameter characteristics of UWB bandpass filter convey an optimal performance in terms of insertion and return loss. It is distinctive in its structure and it has simple design with less number of design parameters compared to the existing filter designs in the literature [11], [12], [13].

The paper is organized as follows: In Section 2, the UWB bandpass filter design using parallel coupled line is presented. Simulation results and analysis are discussed in Section 3. Section 4 concludes the paper.

2 Parallel Coupled Bandpass Filter Design

Fig. 1 shows one possible circuit arrangement of bandpass filter using parallel coupled line microstrip structure for UWB range. It consists of transmission line sections having the length of half wavelength at the corresponding center frequency. Half wavelength line resonators are positioned so that adjacent resonators are parallel to each other along half of their length.

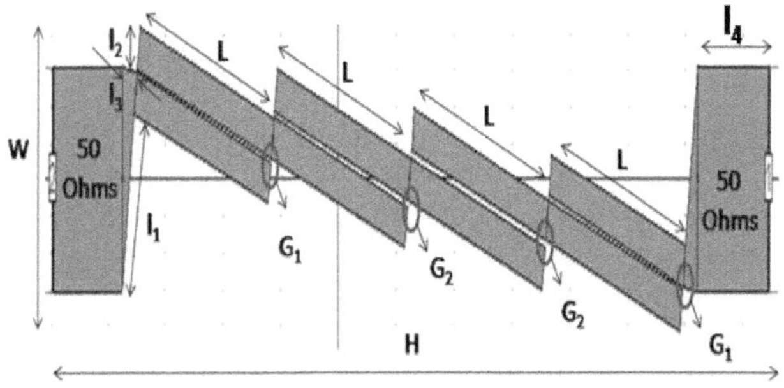

Fig. 1. Geometry of the proposed UWB bandpass filter

This parallel arrangement gives relatively large coupling for the given spacing between the resonators, and thus, this filter structure is particularly convenient for constructing filters having larger bandwidth as compared to the other structure. The gap between the resonators is introducing a capacitive coupling between the resonators, which is represented by a series capacitance.

The physical parameters of the proposed bandpass filter are optimized to the following values, $L = 5.8$ mm; $G_1 = 0.05$ mm; $G_2 = 0.1$ mm; $l_1 = 1.5$ mm; $l_2 = 0.5$ mm; $l_3 = 0.6$; $l_4 = 3$ mm; $W = 4$ mm and $H = 31$ mm to cover the entire UWB range between 3.1 GHz and 10.6 GHz. Using this configuration, higher coupling is obtained and therefore wider bandwidth is achieved. This structure is used to generate a wide passband and expected to achieve a tight coupling, and lower insertion by reducing both strip and slot width.

3 Results and Discussion

The proposed filter is designed to provide a wide passband, low insertion loss and return loss, linear phase over the passband, flat group delay and high fractional bandwidth. The simulation S parameters of the proposed UWB bandpass filter using parallel coupled line are shown in Fig. 2. It is clear from the response that the proposed filter has better insertion loss of -0.5 dB and the low return loss of about -32.67 dB at 6.3 GHz. The -10 dB fractional bandwidth computed from the response is about 86 %.

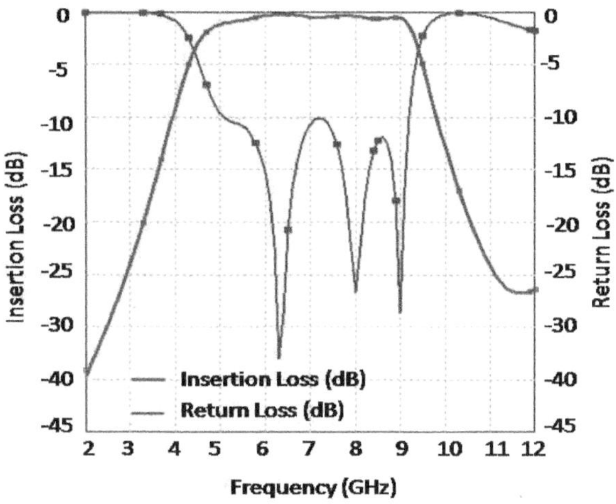

Fig. 2. Simulation S- Parameters of the proposed bandpass filter

For wideband applications, the examination of the flat group delay is essential and required. The simulation group delay for the proposed filter is shown in Fig. 3, which exhibits a flat group delay response below 0.02 ns over the whole passband. It implies that this proposed UWB filter has a very good linearity of signal transfer and would ensure the minimum distortion to the input pulse when it is implemented in the UWB system. The response of the Fig. 4 shows that the phase of S_{21} throughout the -10 dB passband between 3.9 GHz and 9.8 GHz of designed filter is acceptably linear.

In order to evaluate the performance of the proposed UWB bandpass filter, the filter is simulated through the simulation tool, IE3D [14]. The filter is designed based on microstrip substrate FR4 with dielectric constant of 4.4 and thickness of 1.6 mm for easy integration with Printed Circuit Board (PCB). Comparisons of some of the bandpass filters based on parallel coupled line with respect to their performances are tabulated in Table 1.

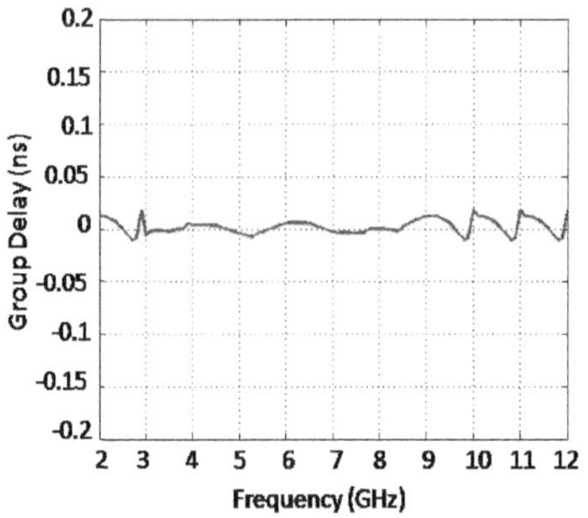

Fig. 3. Simulation group delay of the proposed bandpass filter

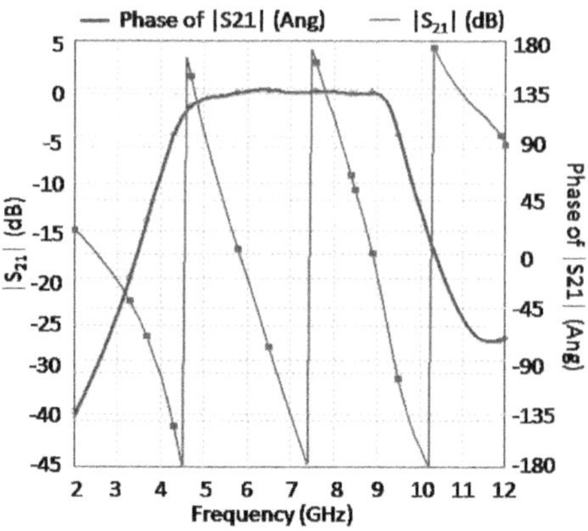

Fig. 4. Simulation of phase of S_{21} of the proposed bandpass filter

Table 1. Comparison of the filter with best reported parallel coupled UWB bandpass filters in the literature

Parameters/Ref.	[13]	[5]	[11]	This Work
S_{21} (dB)	1±0.3	- 1.19	< -1.5	-0.5
S_{11} (dB)	< -37	--	> -10	-32.67
Passband (GHz)	3.22-7.87	1.4-4.68	3.1-4.8	3.9-9.8
GD (ns)	0.3-1.5	0.5	0.6-0.7	0.01

4 Conclusion

In this paper, a bandpass filter based on parallel coupled line microstrip structure is presented. The proposed filter demonstrated an excellent ultra-wide bandwidth from 3.9 GHz to 9.8 GHz. Total size of the filter is 31 mm (height) × 4 mm (length) × 1.6 mm (breadth) and the fractional bandwidth of the Ultra-Wideband bandpass filter is about 86 %. Simulation of bandpass filter delivers excellent scattering parameters with the magnitude of insertion loss, $|S_{21}|$ lower than -0.5 dB at 6.85 GHz and return loss better than -32.67 dB. The obtained group delay for this filter is below 0.02 ns. The scattering parameters of UWB bandpass filter provide optimal performance in terms of insertion and return loss and group delay.

References

1. FCC NEWS (FCC 02-48): FCC News release (2002)
2. Hong, J.S., Lancaster, M.J.: Microstrip Filters for RF/Microwave Application. Wiley, New York (2001)
3. Mattaei, G., Young, L., Jones, E.M.T.: Microwave Filters, Impedance-Matching Networks, and Coupling Structures. Artech House, Norwood (1980)

4. Shaman, H., Hong, J.S.: Asymmetric Parallel-Coupled Lines for Notch Implementation in UWB Filters. IEEE Microw. Wireless Compon. Lett. 17(7) (2007)
5. Wang, X.-H., Xue, Q., Chai, W.-W.: A Novel Ultra-Wideband Differential Filter Based on Double Sided Parallel Strip Line. IEEE Microw. Wireless Compon. Lett. 20(8), 471–473 (2010)
6. Fathelbab, W.M., Jaradat, H.M.: New Stepped-Impedance Parallel Coupled Line (PCL) Filters for Ultra-Wideband (UUB) Application. In: Proceedings of IEEE 38th European Microwave Conference, Amsterdam (2008)
7. Carro, P.-L., Mingo, J.: Analysis and Synthesis of Double-Sided Parallel-Strip Transitions. IEEE Trans. Microw. Theory Tech. 58(2), 372–380 (2010)
8. Karthikeyan, S.S., Kshetrimayum, R.S.: Harmonic suppression of parallel coupled microstrip line bandpass filter using CSRR. Progress in Electromagnetics Research, PIER 7, 193–201 (2009)
9. Phromloungsri, R., Chongcheawchamnan, M., Robertson, I.D.: Inductively Compensated Parallel Coupled Microstrip Lines and Their Applications. IEEE Trans. on Microwave Theory and Tech. 54(9) (2006)
10. Kuo, J.T., Hsu, W.-H., Huang, W.T.: Parallel Coupled Microstrip Filters with Suppression of Harmonic Response. IEEE Microw. Wireless Compon. Lett. 12(10) (2002)
11. Chen, C.-P., Ma, Z., Takakura, Y., Nihei, H., Anada, T.: Novel Wideband Bandpass Filer Using Open-Ended Stub Loaded Parallel Coupled Short-Circuited Three-Line Unit. In: Proceedings IEEE IMS (2009)
12. Chen, C.-P., Ma, Z., Anada, T.: Synthesis of Ultra-Wideband Bandpass Filter Employing Parallel Coupled Stepped Impedance Resonators. IET Microwave Antennas and Propagation 2(8), 766–772 (2008)
13. Ye, C.S., Su, Y.K., Weng, M.H., Hung, C.Y., Yang, R.Y.: Design of the Compact Parallel-Coupled Lines Wideband Bandpass Filters Using Image Parameter Method. Progress in Electromagnetics Research, PIER 100, 153–173 (2010)
14. IE3D 14, Zeland Software, Ins., Fremont, USA

Speed Control of Switched Reluctance Motor Using Artificial Neural Network Controller

Brwene Salah Ali, Hany M. Hasanien, and Yasser Galal

Electrical and Computer control Department
Arab Academy for Science and technology
Ain Shams University

Abstract. Switched reluctance motors (SRMs) have an intrinsic simplicity and low cost that makes them well suited to many applications. However, the motor has doubly salient structure and highly non-uniform torque and magnetization characteristic. Since it was hard to determine the accurate mathematical model of (SRM) .The Artificial Neural Networks (ANNs) solve the problem of non-linearity of SRM drive. It ensures fast, accurate, less overshoot and high precision dynamic response with perfect steady state performance. In the simulation analysis, this paper tests the (SRM) motor adopting two different control modes at starting process under full load torque with a reference speed of 2000 rpm, and the load disturbance under full load torque with a reference speed 2250 rpm. Simulation results show that speed control is better using (ANN) controller than using the (PID) controller. Matlab/Simulink tool is used for the dynamic simulation study.

Keywords: Switched relcutance motor (SRM), proportional plus integrator plus diffrrential controler (PID), artificial neural network controller (ANN).

1 Introduction

Switched reluctance motors (SRMs) and drives have received growing interest recently. Their simple structure and low cost of manufacture make (SRMs) potentially attractive for various general purposes adjustable speed applications [1]. However, the motor has many drawbacks due to the doubly salient structure and the extremely comprehensive mathematical modeling which is complicated due to its highly non-linear torque output and magnetization characteristic [2][3]. This due to the fact that (SRMs) primarily operate in magnetic saturation and hence the developed torque is a non-linear function of rotor position and stator current [4].The non-linearity of (SRM) uses the general feedback theory or the conventional PID controller, but it is impossible to obtain good control performance. It required applying the advanced control strategy to the SR drive to improve the system performance. Several drive control methods for SRM have been proposed in literatures in the last decade: sensorless control using a mechanical position sensor [5], [6], fuzzy logic control [7], State-switching control technique [8], Speed control of SRM powered by a fuel cell [9] , Speed Control of Switched Reluctance Motor Drive Powered by A Fuel Cell [10],.etc. Among them the sensorless control strategy reduces overall cost and dimension of the

V.V. Das and N. Thankachan (Eds.): CIIT 2011, CCIS 250, pp. 6–14, 2011.

drive and improves the product reliability, although all other methods have their own pros and cons depending on the principles of operation applied.

Simple logic controller is used between steady and transient state to achieve the desired performance of various control approaches including PID and ANN controllers [11].It is found that the artificial neural network ANN has better adaptability, stability, less overshoot, faster response and high precision than PID controller. The dynamic response of the SRM with the proposed controller is studied during the starting process and load disturbance under full load torque. The effectiveness of the proposed ANN controller is then compared with that of the conventional PID controller [12][13].

The proposed methodology solves the problem of non-linear ties of SRM drive. ANN controller based SRM control has become popular due to simple calculation, easy implementation. It also ensures fast and accurate dynamic response with an excellent steady state performance. Matlab/simulink tool is used for the dynamic simulation study.

2 Mathematical Model of SRM

The switched reluctance motor is a rotating electric machine where both, the stator and rotor have salient poles. Hence, the machine is referred to as a doubly salient machine. It consists of a stator with exciting winding and magnetic rotor, both carries a set of salient pole. Permanent magnet is not required because torque is produced by the tendency of rotor poles to align with the excited stator poles, such as to minimize the stator flux linkages that results from a given applied stator current. To produce a torque: the stator winding inductance varies with the position of rotor, because torque in this machine is directly proportion to variation of winding inductance with angular position and square of motor phase current [14] [15].

$$Torq.\alpha i^2 \frac{dl}{d\theta} \quad , \quad T \sim i^2 \frac{l_{\max} - l_{\min}}{\Delta\theta} \tag{1}$$

where

$l_{\max}$: occurs when a pair of rotor is exactly aligned with excited stator pole.

$l_{\min}$: occurs when rotor pole is moving away from the aligned position.

i : Motor phase current.

θ : Angular position.

The terminal voltage equation for one phase could be written in the form:

$$V = iR + \frac{d\psi}{dt} \tag{2}$$

Since the flux ψ is a function of both current I and rotor angle θ.

$$V = iR + \frac{d\psi}{d\theta}\frac{d\theta}{dt} + \frac{d\psi}{di}\frac{di}{dt} \tag{3}$$

$$V = iR + \omega I \frac{dL}{d\theta} + L \frac{di}{dt} \tag{4}$$

$$V = iR + e + L \frac{di}{dt} \tag{5}$$

$$\psi = N\,\phi = LI \tag{6}$$

$$\psi = \psi(i, \theta) \tag{7}$$

Where L is the incremental inductance (the slope of the magnetization curve), and e is the back emf. (it depends on the angular rotor speed ω)

At high speed the back emf value is high, and in turn it limits the phase current from reaching undesirable values. At low speeds the back emf is low and the current may exceed the maximum allowed values. The mathematical model of the SRM consists of three basic groups of equations, which are the motor phase equations, the mechanical equation, and the angular speed equation. The motor phase equations describe the electrical behavior of the SRM. The mathematical representation of the motor phase equations are written relative to time in order to study the dynamic behavior of the motor.[15][16]

The motor phase equations can be written as follows:-

$$\frac{d\psi_k(\theta_k, i_k)}{dt} = \pm V - R\, i_k \tag{8}$$

The mechanical equation which describes the mechanical motion of the motor can be written as follows:-

$$\frac{d\omega}{dt} = \frac{1}{J}\left(\sum_{k=1}^{q} T_k(\theta_k, i_k) - T_\ell\right) \tag{9}$$

Where:

ω is the rotor speed, (rad./s),

J is the moment of inertia of both the rotor and load, (kg.m^2),

T_ℓ is the load torque, (N.m),

q is the number of phases, $T_k(\theta_k, i_k)$ is the torque produced by the Kth phase and θ_k is the rotor position as seen by the Kth phase.

3 Steady State Performance

The steady state performance of a switched reluctance motor is a complex interdependent influence between motor parameters and excitation.. The model of an SRM for static analysis includes the set of phase circuit and mechanical differential equations. In integrating these equations, the problem focused on handling the data (flux-linkage/theta/current) used to describe the magnetic nature of the SR machine. Fig.1 evaluates the steady state performance by showing the flux and current at θ on = 45° and θ off = 75° .

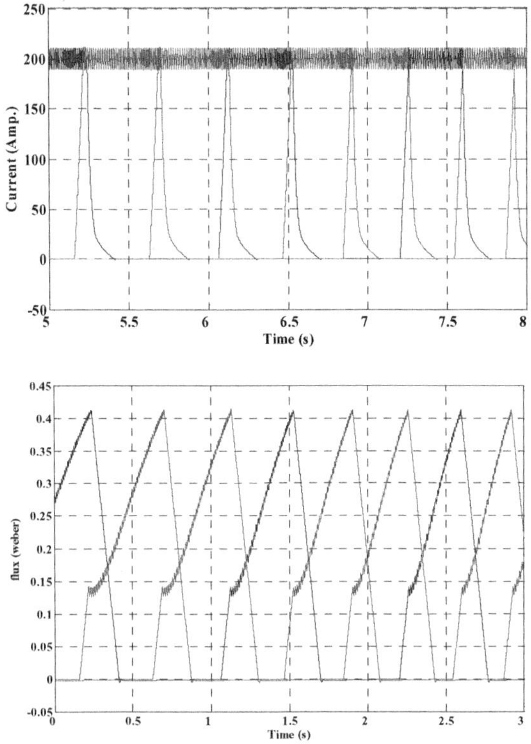

Fig. 1. The motor performance at speed 2000rpm, θ on = 45° and θ off = 75° for the flux and current with respect to the time

4 Speed Control of SRM Using PID

The system under study consists of a SRM fed from a dc supply via an inverter. The data of the motor is given in the Appendix. The drive is tested under the following condition. First the motor is started against its full load torque (382 N m) until the motor reaches the steady state speed (2000 rpm). Then, the motor is subjected to a speed reference (2250 rpm) under full load torque.The proportional plus integral plus differential PID controller is one of the famous controllers that are used in a wide range in the industrial applications. The output of the PID controller in time domain is defined by the following equation:-

$$V_c(t) = Kp\,e(t) + \frac{Ki}{Ti}\int_0^t e(t)\,dt + Kd\,\frac{de(t)}{dt} \tag{10}$$

$V_c(t)$ is the output of the PID controller,
K_p is the proportional gain,
K_i is the integral gain,

Kd is the differential gain,
T_i is the integral time constant,
And e(t) is the instantaneous error signal

The final output of the controller is used to regulate the switching-on angle of the SRM to regulate the motor shaft speed, while the input of the controller is the speed deviation.

The motor speed deviation (e_w), in p.u is given by the following equation:-

$$e_{\omega} = \frac{\omega_{ref} - \omega}{\omega_{ref}} \tag{11}$$

The new turn-on switching angle θ_{on}(new), which is obtained from the controller output is calculated by the following equation:-

$$\theta_{on}(new) = \theta_{on}(old) - [K_p e_w(t) + \frac{Ki}{Ti}\int_0^t e_w(t)dt + K_d \frac{de(t)}{dt}] \tag{12}$$

The simulation results will be classified into two zones by varying the PID controller parameters. Each zone will have three cases according to varying the PID variables.

Zone I : This zone will study the dynamic response at starting process under the full Load torque and ω_{ref} = 2000 rad./sec.

Zone II : This zone will study the dynamic response at a speed reference disturbance under full load torque and ω_{ref} = 2250 rad./s.

The SRM used is simulated using MATLAB/SIMULINK. The model consists of the SRM motor block, a power electronics converter which is fed from a 240 V DC source. A speed controller block is proposed to generate firing signals for the converter. Fig.2 shows the MATLAB/SIMULINK model.

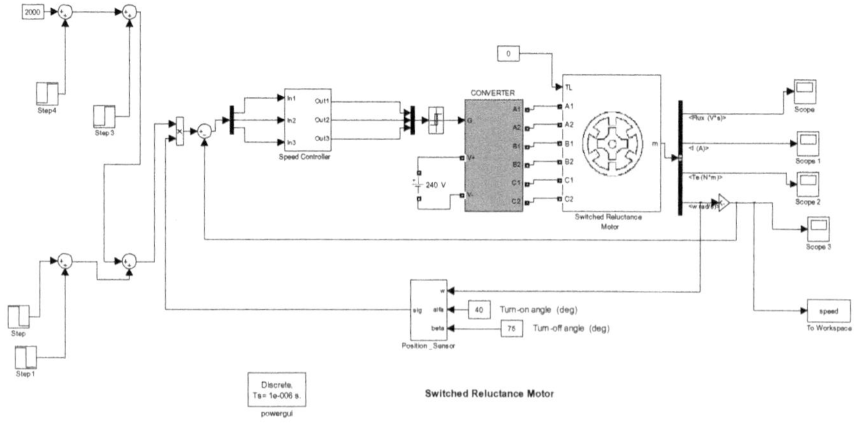

Fig. 2. MATLAB/SIMULINK model of the used SRM

5 Speed Control of SRM Using ANN Controller

Classical control theory suffers from some limitations due to the assumptions made for the control systems such as linearity, and time-invariance. These problems can be overcome by using artificial intelligence based control techniques. The main advantages of the artificial neural networks (ANNs) controllers are as follow:

- A neural network can perform tasks that a linear program can not.
- When an element of the neural network fails, it can continue without any problem by their parallel nature.
- A neural network learns and does not need to be reprogrammed.
- It can be implemented in any application and without any problems.
- They may require less tuning effort than conventional controller.

6 Description of ANN

A three layer (2*5*1) feed forward structure with two nodes in the input layer is used. The output layer of the ANN consists of only one neuron, while the number of neurons in the hidden layer is five. The input vector consists of the motor speed error, and the previous output of the ANN. The previous output of the ANN is added to the input vector as a stabilizing signal. The activation function used is the sigmoid function in both hidden and output layer. Increasing the number of neurons in the hidden layer has the advantages of reducing the rising time (Tr) and the maximum overshoot (M.O.S) during load variation[17][18].

The output of a single neuron can be represented by the following equation:

$$a_i = f_i\left(\sum_{j=1}^{n} w_{ij} x_j(t) + b_i\right) \tag{12}$$

Where f_i is the activation function, w_{ij} is the weighting factor, x_j is the input signal, and b_i is the bias. The most commonly used activation functions are non-linear, continuously varying types between two asymptotic values -1 and +1. They are called tansigmoid function.

The activation function used is the tansigmoid function in both hidden and output layers.

The simulation results will be classified in to two zones by varying the ANN matrix gains G1, G2, G3 (Weight factors)

Zone I : This zone will study the dynamic response at starting process under the full load torque and ω_{ref} = 2000 rad. /s.

Zone II : This zone will study the dynamic response at a speed reference disturbance under full load torque and ω_{ref} =2250 rad./s.

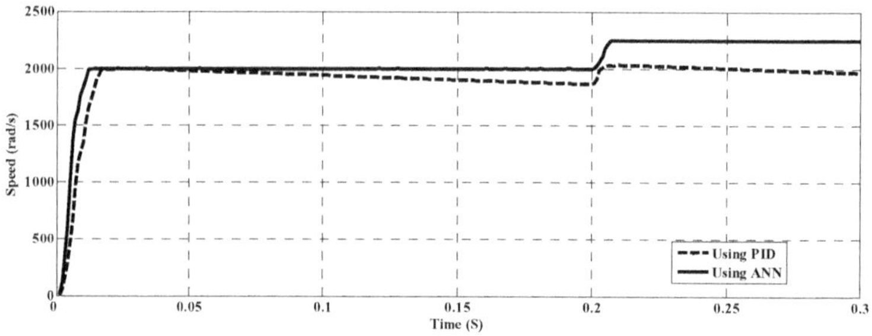

Fig. 3. Comparison of the Speed results using the two methods of control

Fig.3 shows the SRM output speed of the PID and ANN controllers. Table 1 shows an analysis of the speed response results in case of using the PID and ANN controllers and different parameters of the two controllers. It is clear from Table 1 and Fig.3 that the ANN performance is much better that of the PID controller due to the reduced M.O.S and rising time.

7 Conclusion

This paper has presented an ANN controller, which is applied to the switched reluctance motors for the purpose of regulating its speed. The application of the proposed controller for SRM drives is investigated through analysis and simulation results. The dynamic response of the switched reluctance motor with this proposed controller is obtained and analyzed at the starting process and under full load torque disturbance. By inspection of the dynamic response, it can be realized that, the dynamic response of SRM when provided with the ANN controller is improved in compared with that of the conventional PID controller. Simulation results have shown that the proposed control structure can achieve better damped speed response than that of the conventional PID controller. Therefore, simulation results have verified the validity and effectiveness of the proposed control scheme.

Table 1. Output speed results of PID and ANN controllers

Element	PID	ANN
Controller parameters	Kp=0.8 Ki=0.8 Kd=0.0005	G1=0.18 G2=1000 G3=100 C=95
Speed at zone I	2001 rad/s	2001.5 rad/s
M.O.S at zone I	100.5 %	100.075 %
Tr at zoneI	0.0223 s	0.0146 s
Speed at zone II	2037 rad/s	2253 rad/s
M.O.S at zone II	-	100.133 %
Tr at zone II	-	0.0207 s

Appendix

Table 2. SRM specifications

Symbol	Quantity	Value
P	Rated power	60 kW
V	Dc voltage	240 V
N	Rated speed	1500 rpm
I	Rated phase current	250 A
T	Rated torque	382 N m
R	Stator resistance	0.005 ohms
L	Inductance	0.00015 H
J	Motor inertia	0.05 kg m^2
B	Fricition coefficient	0.02 N m s
N_r	No. of rotor poles	4

References

1. Zhang, Z., Pian, Z., Feng, G.: Research on New Control Model for Switched Reluctance Motor. In: ICCASM (2010)
2. Xu, L., Ruckstadter, E.: Direct modeling of switched reluctance machine by coupled field-circuit method. IEEE Trans. Energy Conv. 10, 446–454 (1995)
3. Nagel, N.J., Lorenz, R.D.: Modeling of a saturated switched reluctance motor using an operating point analysis and the unsaturated torque equation. IEEE Trans. Ind. Applicat. 36, 714–722 (2000)
4. Garside, J.J., Brown, R.H., Arkadan, A.A.: Switched Reluctance Motor Control With Artificial Neural Networks
5. Bose, B.K., Miller, T., Szczensny, P.M., Bicknell, W.H.: Microcomputer Control of Switched Reluctance Motor. IEEE Trans. on Industry Applications IA-2, 708–715 (1986)
6. Hossain, S.A., Husain, I., Klode, H., Lequesne, B., Omekanda, A.M., Gopalakrishnan, S.: Four-quadrant and zero-speed sensorless control of a switched reluctance motor. IEEE Trans. on Industry Applications 39(5), 1343–1349 (2003)
7. Rodrigues, M.G., Suemitsu, W.I., Branco, P., Dente, J.A., Rolim, L.G.B.: Fuzzy logic control of a switched reluctance motor. In: Proc. of the IEEE International Symposium on Industrial Electronics (ISIE 1997), vol. 2, pp. 527–531 (1997)
8. Lukic, S.M., Emadi, A.: State-Switching Control Technique for Switched Reluctance Motor Drives: Theory and Implementation. IEEE Transactions on Industrial Electronics 57(9) (September 2010)
9. Hudson, C.A., Lobo, N.S., Krishnan, R.: Sensorless Control of Single Switch-Based Switched Reluctance Motor Drive Using Neural Network. IEEE Transactions on Industrial Electronics 55(1) (January 2008)
10. Chen, X., Salem, M., Das, T., Gopalswamy, S.: Speed Control of Switched Reluctance Motor Drive Powered by A Fuel Cell. In: American Control Conference, June 8-10 (2005)
11. Hanselman, D.C.: Mastering Matlab 7, reference book, 3rd ed., USA (2007)

12. Singh, B., Sharma, V.K., Murthy, S.S.: Comparative study of PID, sliding mode and fuzzy logic controllers for four quadrant operation of switched reluctance motor. In: International Conference on Power Electronic Drives and Energy Systems for Industrial Growth, pp. 99–105 (1998)
13. Rahman, A.S.B.F., Taib, M.N.B.: Simulation of PID and fuzzy logic controller for the newly developed switched reluctance motor program. In: Student Conference on Digital Object Research and Development SCOReD 2002 (2002)
14. Miller, T.J.E.: Switched reluctance motor and their control. Magna physics publishing and clarendon press, Oxford (1993)
15. Stephenson, J.M., Corda, J.: Computation of torque and current in a doubly salient reluctance motors from nonlinear magnetization data. IEE proceeding 126(5), 393–396 (1979)
16. Miller, T.J.E.: Switched reluctance motor drives, a reference book of collected papers, pp. 1–69. Interec communications Inc., Ventura (1988)
17. Krose, B.J.A., van der Smagt, P.P.: An introduction to neural Networks, 5th edn. University of Amsterdam (January 1993)
18. Abbas, E.H., El Sayad, M.A., El Saied, F.H.: Artificial Neural Network based control of switched reluctance motor, M.sc Thesis (2003)

Sliding Mode Control of Active Suspension Systems Using an Uncertainty and Disturbance Estimator

V.S. Deshpande[1] and S.B. Phadke[2]

[1] S.V.C.P, Sinhagad Technical Education Society, Pune
[2] College of Engineering Pune

Abstract. In this paper a novel active suspension scheme that can estimate the unknown road profile is proposed. The proposed scheme is a sky-hook model following scheme, based on the sliding mode control strategy augmented by an uncertainty and disturbance estimator. The model following is implemented without using an explicit model to simplify the implementation of the controller. The efficacy of the method is illustrated by simulation for an automobile vehicle suspension system.

1 Introduction

Active suspension systems have attracted the attention of researchers for a long time. The main function of vehicle suspension systems is to provide comfort to the passengers while maintaining a firm contact between the road and the tyres. The suspension system should tackle parametric uncertainties and irregular road profile under different load conditions. Unfortunately, the requirements of a good suspension systems can be conflicting. To follow the track and to support the weight of the car body, a stiff suspension is needed but to reduce the acceleration of the body caused by the road disturbance- thereby improving the ride comfort- a soft suspension is needed.

In an active suspension system, actuators are used to produce a force to reduce the displacement and acceleration of the body. An active suspension system is capable of providing better road holding ability and ride quality. Several diverse control strategies such as optimal, adaptive, model reference adaptive, sliding mode control, fuzzy control , neural network, genetic algorithm are used in the literature on active suspension systems. In general it is difficult to find an accurate model of a physical suspension system used in model based control design. Chen and Haung [1] proposed an adaptive SMC along with function approximation, of active suspension systems with time- varying loadings. Sliding mode control (SMC) is a type of variable structure system. Sliding mode control can guarantee invariance if the bound on uncertainty is known and matching conditions are satisfied. The desired behavior of the system can be obtained by making suitable choice of control surface. SMC in combination with model reference is used in [4], [3]. Kim and Ro [2] proposed a sliding mode controller for vehicles with nonlinearities.

In this paper, we propose an active suspension system that follows a sky-hook model using the sliding mode control along with an uncertainty disturbance estimator

V.V. Das and N. Thankachan (Eds.): CIIT 2011, CCIS 250, pp. 15–20, 2011.

(UDE), first proposed in [6] and extended to sliding mode control in [5]. We employ the uncertainty and disturbance estimator to estimate the nonlinear spring force, damping force and the effect of unknown road disturbance. The main contributions of this paper are as follows: (a)The proposed active suspension can give a response that is as good as the sky-hook suspension system irrespective of the road condition. (b) No knowledge of bounds on uncertainties and disturbances is required. (c) Unlike other sky-hook reference model schemes proposed in the literature, our scheme does not need real time integration of an explicit sky-hook model, reducing the controller complexity considerably. (d) The scheme proposed here can give the same performance under different passenger loading without any change in the controller.

2 Problem Statement

Consider a nonlinear quarter car suspension system using the modified reference model as shown in Fig. 1 as described in [2]. The sprung mass m_s represents the mass of the car body, frame and passengers that are supported above the suspension.

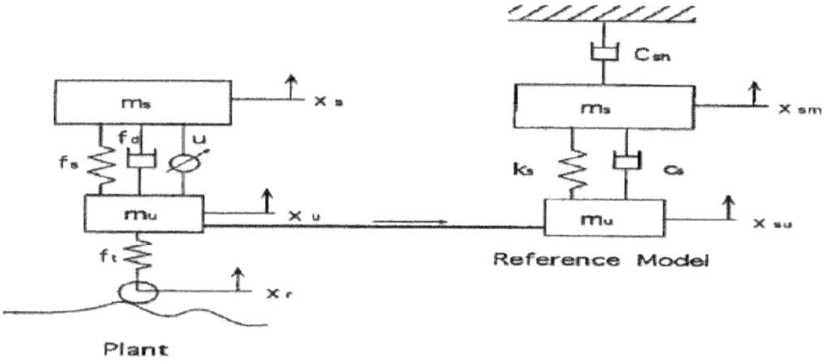

Fig. 1. Quarter car suspension model

The unsprung mass m_u is the mass of the assembly of axel and wheel, f_s and f_d are unknown nonlinear spring and damping forces between the sprung and the unsprung masses, f_t is the tyre force between unsprung mass and the road, u is the control force generated by actuator connected between sprung and unsprung masses, x_s is the displacement of the sprung mass, x_u is displacement of the unsprung mass and x_r denotes the road profile. The equations of motion of the plant are as follows:

$$m_s\ddot{x}_s = -f_s - f_d + u - m_s g; \quad m_u\ddot{x}_u = f_s + f_d + f_t - u - m_u g \tag{1}$$

$$f_s = k_0 + k_1\Delta x + k_2\Delta x^2 + k_3\Delta x^3, \quad f_d = c_1\Delta\dot{x} + c_2\Delta\dot{x}^2 \tag{2}$$

where g is acceleration due to gravity and the coefficients k_0, k_1, k_2, k_3, c_1 and c_2 are constants and $\Delta x = (x_s - x_u)$ is the rattle space. Let the state variables be denoted as, $x_1 = x_s$, $x_2 = \dot{x}_s$, $x_3 = x_u$ and $x_4 = \dot{x}_u$. Equations (1) can be expressed in the the state variable form as follows:

$$\dot{x}_1 = x_2, \quad \dot{x}_2 = \frac{1}{m_s}(-f_s - f_d + u) - g \tag{3}$$

$$\dot{x}_3 = x_4, \quad \dot{x}_4 = \frac{1}{m_u}(f_s + f_d + f_t - u) - g \tag{4}$$

The sky-hook damping system is chosen as reference model as described in reference [2] is shown in Fig. 1. The sky-hook linear damping coefficient is c_{sh}, m_s is the sprung mass of the reference model, x_{sm} is the displacement of the sprung mass of the reference model, the meaning of other symbols is as per [2]. Defining $x_m = [x_{sm}\ \dot{x}_{sm}]^T$ as the state vector, $f_{sm} = k_s(x_{sm} - x_u)$ and $f_{dm} = c_s(\dot{x}_{sm} - \dot{x}_u)$, the dynamics of the sky-hook reference model is given by

$$\dot{x}_m = f_m(x_{sm}, x_u, t); f_m = [\dot{x}_{sm}\ \frac{1}{m_s}(-f_{sm} - f_{dm} - c_{sh}\dot{x}_{sm}) - g]^T \tag{5}$$

3 Sliding Surface and Control Design

We select the sliding surface given by $\sigma = x_2 + z$, $z(0) = -x_2(0)$. The auxiliary variable z is defined as

$$\dot{z} = \frac{-1}{m_s}(-k_s(x_1 - x_u) - c_s(x_2 - x_u) - c_{sh}x_2) + g \tag{6}$$

Differentiating σ and using (3) and (6) and with $e = -f_s - f_d$ is the lumped uncertainty.

$$\dot{\sigma} = \frac{1}{m_s}e + \frac{1}{m_s}u + \frac{-1}{m_s}(-k_s(x_1 - x_u) - c_s(x_2 - x_u) - c_{sh}x_2) \tag{7}$$

Assumption 1. The lumped uncertainty e is such that $|\frac{de}{dt}| < \mu$, where μ is a small number.

Now, we design the control u, where u_n is the component that takes care of uncertainty in (7). Let

$$u = \frac{m_s}{m_s}(-k_s(x_1 - x_u) - c_s(x_2 - x_u) - c_{sh}x_2) - m_s K\sigma + u_n \tag{8}$$

where K is a positive number. Using (8) in (7)

$$\dot{\sigma} = \frac{1}{m_s}e - K\sigma + \frac{1}{m_s}u_n \tag{9}$$

Let $\hat{e}$ be the estimate of uncertainty e. Define the estimation error as

$$\tilde{e} = e - \hat{e} \tag{10}$$

Now selecting

$$u_n = -\hat{e} \tag{11}$$

and substituting (11) in (9), we get

$$\dot{\sigma} = -K\sigma + \frac{1}{m_s}\tilde{e} \tag{12}$$

If the estimate $\hat{e}$ is such that $\tilde{e}$ goes to zero asymptotically, sliding condition will be satisfied and thereby model following can be assured.

4 Uncertainty and Disturbance Estimatior

The UDE based control uses the system information in the recent past to get an estimate of the uncertainty e. The lumped uncertainty e can be estimated as

$$\hat{e} = G_f(s)e; \quad G_f(s) = \frac{1}{1+s\tau} \tag{13}$$

where $G_f(s)$ is a filter where τ is a small positive constant. From equations (13) and (12), after some calculation we get

$$\hat{e} = \frac{m_s\sigma}{\tau} + \frac{m_s K}{\tau}\int_0^t \sigma\, dt \tag{14}$$

From equations (10), (13), one can obtain the following expression

$$\dot{\tilde{e}} = \frac{-1}{\tau}\tilde{e} + \dot{e} \tag{15}$$

Revisiting the dynamics of the sliding surface (12),

$$\dot{\sigma} = -K\sigma + \frac{1}{m_s}\tilde{e} \tag{16}$$

It is easy to see that for stability, the design parameters K and τ need to be chosen so that $K > 0$ and $\tau > 0$ It can be seen that the estimation error $\tilde{e}$ can be made arbitrarily small by choosing the design parameters K and τ.

5 Illustrative Example

The efficacy of the proposed control is verified through computer simulations of the suspension model shown in Fig.1 for a variety of road profiles and sprung mass loadings. The system parameters are as as taken in [2] *Control Parameters:* $K = 2000, \quad \tau = 0.001$. Consider Case 1. The road excitation is assumed to be sinusoidal with frequency about 1.5 Hz which is close to the natural frequency of the sprung mass in bouncing mode. The road profile is considered as $x_r = 0.05 sin(2\pi 1.5t)$. For this case sprung mass was taken as $m_s = 240kg$. In Case 2. we consider a more rough road profile given by $x_r = 0.025 sin(1\pi 1.5t) + 0.025 sin(2\pi 1.5t)$ and the sprung mass m_s to be 320 kg. Responses for Case 1 and 2 are shown in Fig.2 and 3. The displacement of sprung mass of plant and model are shown in Fig. 2. The sprung mass follows the sky-hook model very closely. Perfect model following indicates the efficacy of the proposed control. The graph of uncertainty and its estimate for Case 1 is shown in Fig. 2. It shows that uncertainty and disturbance estimator, estimates the uncertainty accurately. The sprung mass acceleration is also moderate in Case 2 as shown in Fig. 3. The control effort required shown in Fig. 3 is almost same as first case.

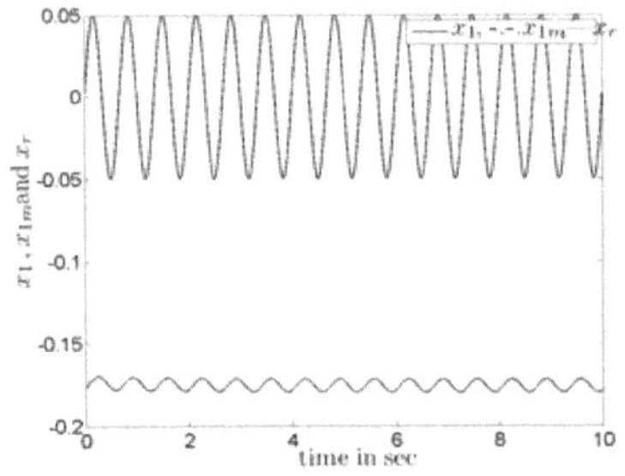

(a) Case1- Sprung mass deflections, road profile

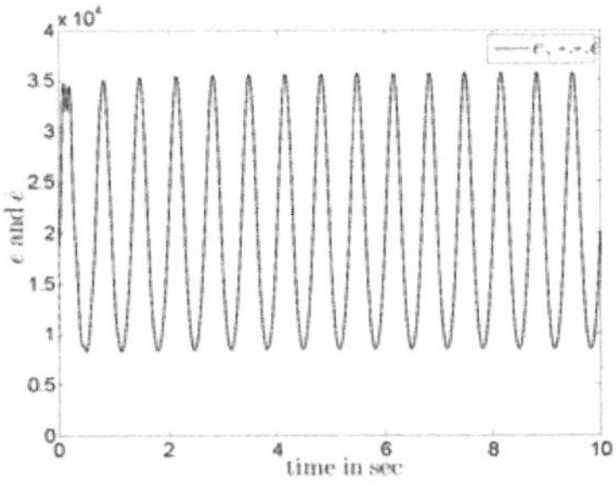

(b) Case1-Uncertainty and its estimate

Fig. 2. Responses of Case1

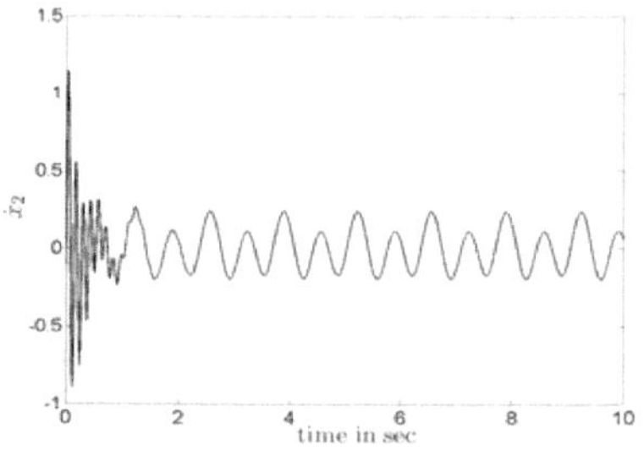

(a) Case2-Acc. of sprung mass

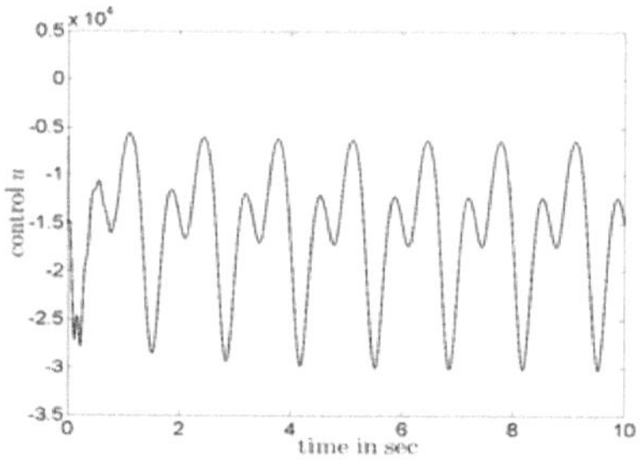

(b) Case2-Control

Fig. 3. Responses of Case2

6 Conclusion

In this paper, an active suspension system that can estimate the uncertainties and the effect road profile is proposed. The proposed control is a sliding mode control based on the uncertainty and disturbance estimator and overcomes the drawback of conventional sliding mode control which requires the bounds of uncertainty and disturbances. The control is simpler than other sky-hook suspensions from the implementation point of view and can accommodate changes in passenger loading without any change in control. The simulation results verify the efficacy of the control.

References

1. Chen, P.C., Huang, A.C.: Adaptive sliding mode control of non-autonomous active suspension systems with time-varying loading. Jnl of Sound and Vibration 282, 1119–1135 (2005)
2. Kim, C., Ro, P.I.: A sliding mode controller for vehivle active suspension systems with non-linearities. Proc. IMechE Part D 212, 79–92 (1998)
3. Mohan, B., Modak, J., Phadke, S.B.: Vibation control of vehicles using model reference adaptive variablestructure control. Advances in Vibration Engineering 2(4), 343–361 (2003)
4. Mohan, B., Phadke, S.B.: Variable structure active suspension system. In: Intl Conf. IEEE IECON, pp. 1945–1948 (1996)
5. Talole, S.E., Phadke, S.B.: Model following sliding mode control based on uncertainty and disturbance estimator. ASME J. Dyn. Syst. Meas. Control 130(3), 34501 (2008)
6. Zhong, Q.C., Rees, D.: Control of uncertain lti systems based on an uncertainty and disturbance estimator. ASME J. Dyn. Syst. Meas. Control 126(4), 905–910 (2004)

Rayleigh Fading MIMO Channel Prediction Using RNN with Genetic Algorithm

G. Routray and P. Kanungo

Department of Electronics and Telecommunication Engineering,
C.V. Raman College of Engineering, Bhubaneswar, Odisha, India
{gyanajyotiroutray,pkanungo}@gmail.com

Abstract. The spectral efficiency and reliability of Multi-Input Multi-Output (MIMO) systems greatly depends on the prediction result of channel state information (CSI), such that the transmitter and/or the receiver have perfect knowledge of CSI. The employment of linear predictors used for narrow-band prediction has produced poor results in prediction of correlation coefficients of the channel in the presence of received data that has undergone non-linear distortions. Hence, one of the potential solutions to this challenge is artificial neural networks (ANN). In this paper we used fully connected recurrent neural network to predict the Rayleigh fading channel coefficients using genetic algorithm based learning, which is compared with split complex real time and fully complex real time based recurrent learning process.

Keywords: Multi-Input Multi-Output (MIMO), Neural Network, Split Complex Real Time Recurrent Learning (SCRTRL), Fully Complex Real Time Recurrent Learning (FCRTRL), Genetic Algorithm (GA).

1 Introduction

The combination of ubiquitous cellular phone service and rapid growth of the Internet has created an environment where consumers desire seamless, high quality connectivity at all times and from virtually all locations. Though perhaps unrealistic, this is, in essence, a desire to replicate, and perhaps even surpass the wired experience in a wireless fashion. Theoretically 1Gbps link speed in a standard single-input single-output (SISO) wireless link can be achieved by employing sufficiently high bandwidth along with coding and modulation [1]. However such simplest designs faces the problem such as, transmit power and received signal-to-noise ratio (SNR) constraint limits the maximum achievable spectral efficiency in SISO link. In a SISO system 1Gbps data rate can be achieved by utilizing a spectral efficiency of 4b/s/Hz over 250 MHz bandwidth. But 250 MHz bandwidth is not possible on frequency band below 6 GHz, where non line of sight (NLOS) network are feasible. However 250 MHz bandwidth can be easily obtained in 40 GHz frequency range. Still difficulties persist at frequencies higher than 6 GHz, as increases in frequency band shadowed by obstructions in the propagation path make the NLOS links unusable. Again a high bandwidth results in reduction in range and frequency diversity, which reduces the

V.V. Das and N. Thankachan (Eds.): CIIT 2011, CCIS 250, pp. 21–29, 2011.

fade margin. This clearly places impossible bandwidth demand on SISO wireless system to achieve data-rate in the order of 1 Gbps [1]. On the contrary multiple-input multiple-output (MIMO) system provides high data rate in NLOS wireless network but which increases transmitter and receiver complexities. These results however are based on the assumption that the transmitter and/or receiver have perfect knowledge of the CSI. An alternative is to estimate the channel at the receiver and send the CSI back to the transmitter. This approach suffers when the transmitted CSI has become outdated due to channel fluctuation. It may be possible to improve performance by feedback arrangement of predicted CSI [2].

Many linear predictors are used in the literature [3-5] to predict these channel state information but they fails when the data undergoes nonlinear distortions. In such situation, Artificial Neural Network (ANN) produces some satisfactory result. As the channel undergone Rayleigh fading which is complex and stochastic in nature, complex learning algorithms are considered for the training of the neural network. Many solutions are reported in literature based on SCRTRL and FCRTRL [6-8], but they failed to provide the accurate measurement of the CSI. In this work a recurrent neural network (RNN) is chosen and a Genetic algorithm (GA) based learning algorithm is developed for narrow band channel prediction to overcome the premature convergence of RNN-SCRTRL and RNN-FCRTRL.

2 Modeling MIMO Receiver

In a MIMO system with N_T transmit antennas and N_R receive antennas as shown in Fig.2, we denote the equivalent low pass channel impulse response between the jth transmit antenna and the ith received antenna as $h_{ij}(\tau; t)$, where τ is the delay variable and t is the time variable [3]. Thus, the randomly time-varying channel is characterized by $H(\tau; t)$, defined as

$$H(\tau;t) = \begin{bmatrix} h_{11}(\tau;t) & h_{12}(\tau;t) & \cdots & h_{1N_T}(\tau;t) \\ h_{21}(\tau;t) & h_{22}(\tau;t) & \cdots & h_{2N_T}(\tau;t) \\ \vdots & \vdots & \cdots & \vdots \\ h_{N_R1}(\tau;t) & h_{N_R2}(\tau;t) & \cdots & h_{N_RN_T}(\tau;t) \end{bmatrix}_{N_R \times N_T} \tag{1}$$

Suppose that the signal transmitted from the jth transmit antenna is $x_j(t), j = 1, 2, ..., N_T$, then the signal received at the ith antenna in the absence of noise can be represented as

$$r_i(t) = \sum_{j=1}^{N_T} \int_{-\infty}^{\infty} h_{ij}(\tau;t) x_j(t-\tau) d\tau = \sum_{j=1}^{N_T} h_{ij}(\tau;t) * x_j(\tau), i = 1,2,...,N_R. \tag{2}$$

Then the received signal vector is

$$r(t) = H(\tau;t) * s(\tau) + \eta(t) \tag{3}$$

Where $\eta(t)$ is additive zero mean Gaussian noise and $s(t)$ is an N_Tx1 vector and $r(t)$ is a N_Rx1 vector. H denotes the channel state matrix.

3 Recurrent Neural Network for MIMO Channel Prediction

For channel prediction, it is necessary for the RNN to learn the statistics of the fading process. This achieved by supplying the RNN with previously obtained channel estimates. From the literature [9-11], the channel is written in terms of its minimum mean square error (MMSE) estimate

$$\tilde{H}(t) = H(t) + \eta(t) \tag{4}$$

Where $\tilde{H}(t)$ and $\eta(t)$ are uncorrelated with $\tilde{h}_{N_T N_R}(t) \sim \mathcal{CN}(0, \sigma_{\tilde{h}}(t)^2)$, and $\eta_{N_T N_R}(t) \sim \mathcal{CN}(0, \sigma_w(t)^2)$. In our simulation we considered a 2x2 MIMO communication system which is shown in Fig.2. The RNN structure used for prediction is shown in Fig.1. The outputs of the activation function are

$$d_j(k) = \varphi_j\left(\sum_{i=1}^{m+q+1} w_{j,i}\mathbf{x}_i(k)\right), \quad j = 1,2,\ldots, m. \tag{5}$$

Where,

$$\mathbf{x}(k) = [d_1(k-1),\ldots,d_m(k-1), b, \tilde{h}_{11}(k),\ldots,\tilde{h}_{1N_R}(k),\ldots,\tilde{h}_{N_T 1}(k),\ldots,\tilde{h}_{N_T N_R}(k)]^T$$

is the RNN input, b is the complex bias and set to $1+i$. $\varphi_j(.) = \tanh(.)$, $j = 1,\ldots,m$ are the non-linear activation functions. The RNN predictor is implemented in two stages. During the 1st stage $d_1(k-1),\ldots,d_m(k-1)=0$. The outputs are then feedback to form $\mathbf{x}(k)$. In the 2nd stage, the RNN predicts the N_TxN_R channel status for $(k+1)$ instant.

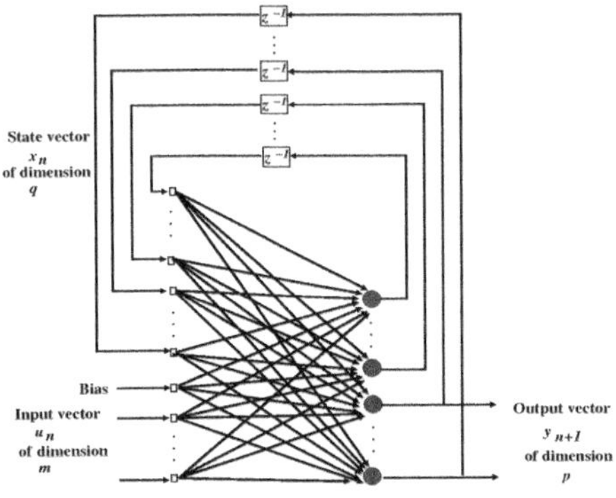

Fig. 1. RNN channel predictor

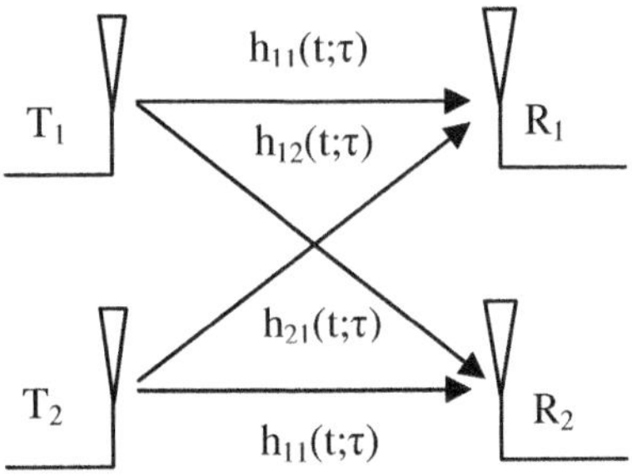

Fig. 2. A 2x2 MIMO communication

The RNN learning is carried using the real time recurrent learning (RTRL) algorithm [12]. As the channel undergoes Rayleigh fading the coefficients of CSI are complex and we considered the complex learning algorithms.

3.1 Split Complex RTRL for RNN Learning

The mostly used algorithm used for training RNN is RTRL algorithm proposed by Williams et al. [12]. The inputs, outputs, weights, and activation functions in RTRL algorithm are assumed to be real valued. This algorithm is stable and able to do continuous processing in order to implement dynamical systems described by the temporal stream of their inputs and outputs. In case of Rayleigh fading channel, the input to the RNN predictor is complex, hence we need to use an RNN with complex weights and activation functions to approximate the behavior of the dynamic system [6]. In SCRTRL algorithm the real and complex part of a complex number W is denoted as w_R and w_I. The weights of the RNN are complex numbers W_{ij} and that the external inputs and desired outputs are complex valued as well. The total input to a unit $\boldsymbol{x}_k$ is complex, and also the activation function $\varphi(.)$ is complex. Ideally activation function is analytic and bounded, but Liouville's theorem states that only such function is constant function. Hence the activation function defined [13] as:

$$\varphi(Z) = \varphi(Z_R) + \varphi(Z_I). \tag{6}$$

The objective function is defined as

$$J[t] = \frac{1}{2}\sum_{k=1}^{N} |E_k[t]|^2. \tag{7}$$

Where $E_k[t]$ is complex error of the unit k at time t. Since $J[t]$ is a non-constant real-valued function, its complex derivatives is not defined and therefore we compute its gradient with respect to W_{ij} .The gradient can be represented as [6]

$$\nabla W_{ij} J[t] = \sum_{k=1}^{N} \left(\begin{bmatrix} e_{Rk} & e_{Ik} \end{bmatrix} \begin{bmatrix} P^k_{RRij} & P^k_{RIij} \\ P^k_{IRij} & P^k_{IIij} \end{bmatrix} \begin{bmatrix} 1 \\ j \end{bmatrix} [t] \right). \tag{8}$$

And the weight update is given as

$$W_{ij}[t+1] = W_{ij}[t] + \alpha \nabla W_{ij} J[t]. \tag{9}$$

After each iteration the sensitivities terms are updated as

$$\begin{bmatrix} P^k_{RRij} & P^k_{RIij} \\ P^k_{IRij} & P^k_{IIij} \end{bmatrix} [t+1] = \begin{bmatrix} \varphi'(s_{Rk}) & 0 \\ 0 & \varphi'(s_{Ik}) \end{bmatrix} [t+1] \times \left(\sum_{l=1}^{N} \begin{bmatrix} w_{Rkl} & -w_{Ikl} \\ w_{Ikl} & w_{Rkl} \end{bmatrix} \begin{bmatrix} P^k_{RRij} & P^k_{RIij} \\ P^k_{IRij} & P^k_{IIij} \end{bmatrix} [t] + \delta_{ik} \begin{bmatrix} x_{Rj} & -x_{Ij} \\ x_{Ij} & x_{Rj} \end{bmatrix} \right). \tag{10}$$

Where α is the learning rate and δ is the Kronecker delta matrix.

3.2 Fully Complex RTRL for RNN Learning

The split-complex algorithms cannot calculate the true gradient unless the real and imaginary weight updates are mutually independent [7]. The problem encountered with the split complex RTRL algorithm proposed by Kechriotis et al.[6] for nonlinear adaptive filtering are: (i) The solutions are not general since split-complex activation function are not universal approximators, (ii) Split-complex activation functions are not analytic and hence Cauchy-Riemann equations cannot be applied, (iii) Split-complex algorithms do not account for a "fully" complex nature of signal and such algorithms therefore underperform in application where complex signals exhibit strong component correlation, (iv) These algorithms do not have a generic form of their real-valued counterparts, and hence their signal flow graphs are fundamentally different. A complex-valued RTRL algorithm is proposed by Goh et al. [7], referred as fully complex real time recurrent learning (FCRTRL). In their work the weight updating is described as:

$$\Delta w_{s,t}(k) = \eta \sum_{l=1}^{N} e_l(k) \Pi_{s,t}^{l\,*}(k), 1 \le l, s \le N, 1 \le t \le p + N + 1. \quad (11)$$

With the initial condition $\Pi_{s,t}^{l\,*}(0) = 0$.

Where $\Pi^{l}_{s,t}$ is the sensitivity and the sensitivity is updated as follows

$$\Pi_{s,t}^{l\,*}(k) = [\varphi'(k)] \times [W_l^H(k) \Pi^*(k-1) + \delta_{sl} I_n^*(k)] \quad (12)$$

4 Genetic Algorithm Based Prediction

GAs are randomized search algorithms based on the mechanics of natural selection and genetics. They implement survival of the fittest among the string structures. The behavior of genetic algorithm can be subtle, but their basic construction and execution cycle is straight forward. GA is an iterative procedure maintaining a population structure that are candidate solutions to specific domain challenges. During each generation, the structures in the current population are rated for their effectiveness as domain solutions. On the basis of these evaluations, a new population of candidate solution is formed using specific genetic operators such as reproduction, crossover and mutation [14]. The numbers of weights are 104 in our RNN structure. Hence we consider a chromosome of 104 genes length. The crossover and mutation operation is shown in Fig.3. Each chromosome consists of two strings, one having real parts of the weights and the other string contains the imaginary parts of the weights. The crossover points of the real and imaginary strings of a chromosome are chosen randomly for a better exploration of the search space. The real and imaginary values are normalized values between (0, 1). Our aim is to minimize the average error function at the output of the RNN, i.e.,

$$\min_W E(k) = \min_W \sum_{n=1}^{N} \mathbf{w}(k)\mathbf{x}_n(k) - \mathbf{y}_n(k) \quad (13)$$

Here $\mathbf{w}_n$ is the weights of the RNN constituting the elements of the chromosome, $\boldsymbol{x}_n$ is the input to the network, and $\mathbf{y}_n$ is the desired output.

Hence, the fitness function considered as

$$f_n(k) = \mathbf{w}(k)\mathbf{x}_n(k) - \mathbf{y}_n(k) \tag{14}$$

Algorithm

- Step1: Choose N number chromosomes, containing the weights of RNN randomly as initial population.
- Step2: Calculated the fitness of all the chromosomes. In our algorithm the fitness functions chosen as the error function given as $f_n(k) = \mathbf{w}(k)\mathbf{x}_n(k) - \mathbf{y}_n(k)$.
- Step3: Randomly choose two chromosomes with a probability P_c for mating through the genetic operator crossover (exchange of genetic material between two selected candidates) to give offsprings. Also secondary operator mutation is applied to both the offsprings with a probability P_m.
- step4: Calculate the fitness of parents and the children; include the two highest fit chromosomes among these four into the next generation.
- step5: Repeat step 3 and 4 for a fixed number of generations till convergence criteria satisfied.
- step6: Use the converged solution as the optimal weight for the channel prediction.

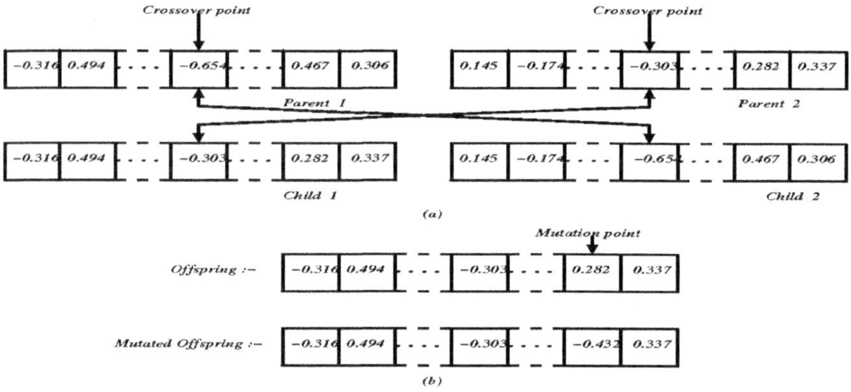

Fig. 3. (a) Crossover operation (b) Mutation operation for the real part of the chromosome

5 Simulation and Result

The simulation work is carried out using MATLAB 7.0 in Window XP platform with core2duo processor, 2Gb RAM, and 2Mb L2 cache. The parameters consider for GA are number of population N=100, the crossover rate P_c=0.8, mutation probability P_m=0.001 and the number of iteration 1000. Initially the gene of a single chromosome is assigned with a random value in the range $\pm$ 0.707.

We considered RNN-SCRTRL and RNN-FCRTRL convergence rate and prediction results to compare with our proposed RNN-GA based approach. The comparison of convergence rates are shown in Fig.4(a), which shows the iterations vs mean-square error. We observed from Fig.4(a) that for RNN-SCRTRL and RNN-FCRTRL have unstable convergence to local solution around 800 and 400 iterations respectively, where as GA based weight optimization converged with a faster rate and constant from 600 to 1000 iterations. The GA based error converged to approximately 0dB where as RNN-SCRTRL and RNN-FCRTRL converged to nearly 0.234dB.

We used the optimum weights for predict the channel. The channel model considered in our work is

$$CSI = L \times \left[\sqrt{\frac{1}{2}(X + iY)} \right] \tag{15}$$

Where L is correlation coefficient obtained from coloring matrix, X and Y are normalized random variables. From these set we used 25 numbers of state sets for training of the RNN and the used optimum weights for prediction of 100 state sets. Fig.5(a),(b), and (c) show channel coefficients (absolute value) prediction using SCRTRL, FCRTRL, and our proposed GA based RNN predictor respectively. From these results we observed that GA based RNN predictor predicts more accurately that the SCRTRL and FCRTRL based RNN prediction. To validate the results we used the predicted CSI information to calculate the bit error rate (BER). Fig.4(b) shows the comparison of theoretical BER, if the channel is known at the receiver, the channel predicted at receiver for RNN-SCRTRL, RNN-FCRTRL, and our proposed GA based predictor. We observed from Fig.4(b) that our proposed RNN-GA based approach

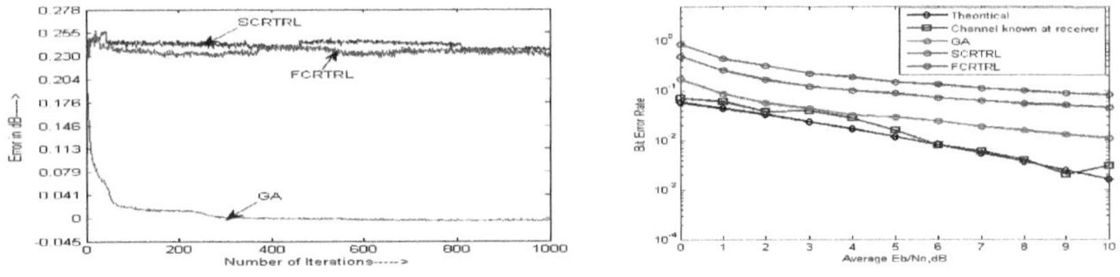

(a) (b)

Fig. 4. (a) Learning curves for SCRTRL, FCRTRL and GA; (b) Comparison between the BER in Rayleigh fading MIMO channel prediction using SCRTRL, FCRTRL, and Genetic Algorithm

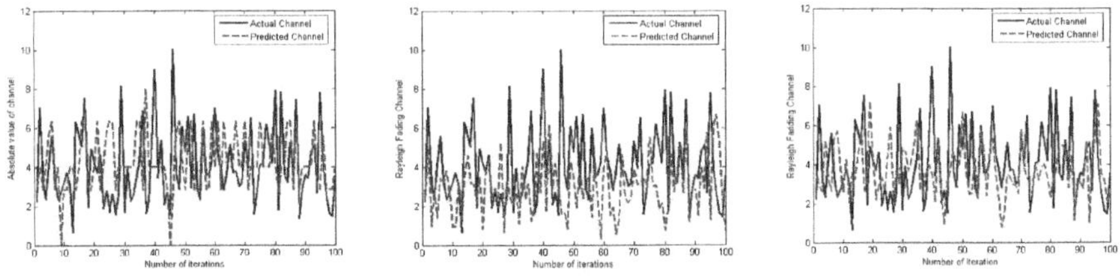

(a) (b) (c)

Fig. 5. Predicted CSI (absolute value) using (a) RNN-SCRTRL, (b) RNN-FCRTRL, (c) Proposed RNN-GA

BER is very closer to the theoretical and if the channel known at the receiver case. Whereas the RNN-SCRTRL and RNN-FCRTRL produces a much high BER than theoretical and our proposed RNN-GA based prediction approach.

6 Conclusion

CSI prediction at the receiver is an important problem for decrease the BER and increase the bandwidth in a MIMO channel. In this paper we assumed the MIMO channel as a Rayleigh fading channel whose channel matrix coefficients are complex in nature. Hence we used the RNN structure with SCRTRL and FCRTRL for the prediction of the CSI. We found that the SCRTRL and FCRTRL based learning algorithms failed to produce the optimum weight for the prediction of CSI. This is due to the loosing of the gradient during the optimization. Genetic algorithm is a soft-computing based optimization random search approach, which almost always produces a global solution by avoiding the local optimum points. Hence it motivated us to use GA for optimizing the weights; we observed that the convergence rate and BER outperforms the RNN-SCRTRL and RNN-FCRTRL. Our proposed method takes a longer time for each iteration than RNN-SCRTRL and RNN-FCRTRL. The differential GA may be the next solution to reduce the time complexity.

Acknowledgements. The research work is a part of the AICTE sponsored MODROBS project No: 8023/RID/BOR/MOD-288/2007-08 and Advance Communication Lab, Depart. Of Electronics & Telecommunication Engg., C.V.Raman College of Engineering, Bhubaneswar, Odisha.

References

1. Paulraj, A.J., Gore, D.A., Nabar, R.U., Bolcskei, H.: An overview of mimo communication-a key to gigabit wireless. In: Proceeding of the IEEE, vol. 92, pp. 198–218 (February 2004)
2. Potter, C., Venayagamoorthy, G.K., Kosbar, K.: RNN based MIMO channel prediction. Signal Processing 90, 440–450 (2010)
3. Proakis, J.G., Salehi, M.: Digital Communication, 5th edn. Mc Graw Hill (2008)
4. Huang, J., Winters, J.: Sinusoidal modelling and prediction of fast fading processes. In: Global Tel. Conf., pp. 892–897 (November 1998)
5. Andersen, J., Jensen, J., Jensen, S., Frederiksen, F.: Prediction of future fading based on past measurements. In: IEEE Vehicular Technology Conference, pp. 151–155 (1999)
6. Kechriotis, G., Manolakos, E.S.: Training fully recurrent neural networks with complex weights. IEEE trans.on Circuits and System-II:Analog and Digital, Signal Processing, 41(3), 235–238 (1994)
7. Goh, S.L., Mandic, D.P.: A complex-valued rtrl algorithm for recurrent neural networks. Neural computation 16, 2699–2713 (2004)
8. Sarma, K.K., Mitra, A.: Estimation of MIMO channels using complex time delay fully Recurrent Neural Network. In: 2nd National Conference on Emerging Trends and Applications in Computer Science (NCETACS), March 4-5 (2011)

9. Yoo, T., Goldsmith, A.: Capacity of fading mimo channels with channel estimation error. IEEE Commun. Soc., 808–813 (2004)
10. Yoo, T., Goldsmith, A.: Capacity and power allocation for fading mimo channels with channel estimation error. IEEE Trans. Inform. Theory 52(5), 2203–2214 (2006)
11. Yoo, T., Yoon, E., Goldsmith, A.: Mimo capacity with channel uncertainty: Does feedback help? In: Proceedings of IEEE GlobeCom, pp. 96–100 (2004)
12. Williams, R.J., Zipser, D.A.: A learning algorithm for continually running fully recurrent neural networks. Neural Computation 1(2), 270–280 (1998)
13. Laung, H., Haykin, S.: The complex backpropagation algorithm. IEEE Trans. on Signal Proc. 3(9), 2101–2104 (1991)
14. Goldberg, D.E.: Genetic Algorithms in search. Optimization and Machine Learning. Pearson Plc (2011)

A New Adaptive Algorithm for Two-Axis Sun Tracker without Sensor

Ahmad Parvaresh[1], Seyed Mohammad Ali Mohammadi[1], and Mohammad Mahdi Azimi[2]

[1] Department of Electrical Engineering, Shahid Bahonar University of Kerman, Iran
[2] Department of Electrical Engineering, University of Tafresh, Iran
ahmad.parvaresh@yahoo.com, a_mohammadi@mail.uk.ac.ir, mmahdi.azimi@gmail.com

Abstract. In recent years, sun tracking systems are being increasingly developed to improve the efficiency of PV panels. Due to problems of tracking methods which uses optical sensors, new methods with less practical problems are developing day by day. In this article, we suggest a new method to reduce the problems which exist with sun tracking. In this method, instead of using optical sensor, an adaptive algorithm is used, where recursive equations are employed to calculate Azimuth and Elevation angles of sun. We applied this method on a two-axis sun tracker system with fixed panel on 45° system. Then calculate the efficiency of PV panels. Finally, by comparing the Results of this method with respect to method of optical sensors, it has been shown that the efficiency of this method is higher than methods which used optical sensors.

Keywords: adaptive algorithm, optical sensor, two-axis sun tracker, azimuth angle, elevation angle.

1 Introduction

Nowadays, optimizing PV panel's efficiency by sun trackers is taken for account severally. In order to achieve these purposes, a lot of methods are presented such as one axis or two axis sun trackers [1], [2]. Moreover, controlling systems are considered to control and command motors. For instance, PLC controllers, AVR controllers or ARM controllers are the popular types of such control systems [2], [3]. In this method, incident data is received by an optical sensor like LDR, then tracking done according to achieving data. We encounter some systematic problems because sensor's characteristics such as sensitivity or repeatability change with time; hence, incident ray's data is not confident. In [3] is used from four optical sensors for receiving incident data.

In presented method, instead of optical sensors, we apply an adaptive algorithm to calculate Azimuth and Elevation angles. It is noteworthy that calculations are done in a central processor (AVR microcontroller) and its results command to motor.

It should be mentioned that presented tracker is of two axis type, and it can regulate solar panel in horizontal and vertical directions. In this system, at first, solar

V.V. Das and N. Thankachan (Eds.): CIIT 2011, CCIS 250, pp. 30–37, 2011.

panel sets on a special angle- usually in vertical direction- next output power of panel is measured. The measured Power is sent to microcontroller, and then the azimuth and elevation angles are calculated by the algorithm. These angles are applied as commands in order to rotate motors. A DC/DC BUCK-BOOST converter also is used which is located between solar panel and load. Presented system has several important advantages such as full automated tracking, low cost, needlessness of system to incident ray's data, less requirement to sensor and higher output efficiency.

2 Adaptive Algorithm

At first, two definitions should be considered:

- Azimuth angle: the angle between the projection of incident wave on a horizontal surface and south direction.
- Elevation angle: the angle between the direction of the geometric center of the sun's apparent disk and the horizon.

Additionally, these parameters which are shown in fig.1 should be defined as follows:

- α: the elevation angles of sun
- θ_S: the angle between solar panel and horizontal axis
- θ_I: the angle between perpendicular axis to solar panel and direction of radiation

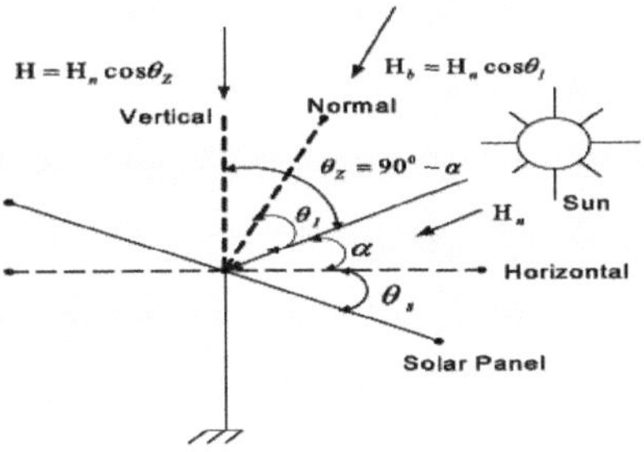

Fig. 1. Solar angles

Also according to fig.1 Eq.1 is derived.

$$\theta_S + \theta_I + \alpha = 90 \quad (1)$$

If tracking done correctly θ_I will be equal to zero; therefore:

$$\theta_S + \alpha = 90^\circ \quad (2)$$

The output power P of the PV panel is directly proportional to the incident direct beam solar radiation (H_b), given by the following relation:

$$P = H_b * A \quad (3)$$

Beside, H_b is obtained from:

$$H_b = H_n * A\cos(\theta_I) \tag{4}$$

Substituting (4) in (3) we obtained:

$$P = H_n * A\cos(\theta_I) * A * \cos(90 - (\theta_s + \alpha)) = H_n * A * \sin(\theta_s + \alpha) \tag{5}$$

It should be mentioned that recursive equation, which is applied to regulation of θ_s , is partial derivation of panel output power, according to following equation:

$$\theta_s(k+1) = \theta_s(k) + \mu(k) * \frac{\partial P(k)}{\partial \theta_s(k)} \tag{6}$$

Where, k is iteration index and $\mu(k)$ is step size.

We name $\theta_s + \alpha$ by θ_γ. Since we want to control α by change in θ_s, one can conclude in order to control α, θ_γ can also be changed. Hence, Eq. 6 can be rewrite as follows:

$$\theta_\gamma(k+1) = \theta_\gamma(k) + \mu(k) * \frac{\partial P(k)}{\partial \theta_\gamma(k)} \tag{7}$$

By calculating Taylor's series of output power with respect to θ_γ and combination with the Eq. 5, another equation is obtained:

$$\theta_\gamma(k+1) = \theta_\gamma(k) - \frac{H_n * A * \cos\theta_\gamma}{2 * H_n * A * \sin(\theta_\mu)} \tag{8}$$

We simply have from Eq. 5:

$$H_n * A * \cos(\theta_\gamma) = \sqrt{H_n^2 A^2 - P^2} \tag{9}$$

By substituting Eq.9 in Eq.8 we have:

$$\theta_s(k+1) = \theta_s(k) - \frac{\sqrt{P(k+1)^2 - P(k)^2}}{2 * P(k)} \tag{10}$$

In order to calculate $P(k+1)$ per every iteration of k, we use following equation:

$$\mathrm{P}(k+1) = \mathrm{P} + \left[sgn(P(k) - P(k-1))\right] * (P(k) - P(k-1) \tag{11}$$

By considering Eq. 10 we find that:

$$\begin{cases} if\ P(k) > P(k-1) \Rightarrow P(k+1) = 2 * P(k) - P(k-1) \\ if\ P(k) < P(k-1) \Rightarrow P(k+1) = P(k-1) \end{cases} \tag{12}$$

These recursive Eq. 10, 11 to be continued until $P(k+1) = P(k)$. At this last iteration, $\theta_s(k+1)$ is an angle which is applied to motor where moves panel in vertical direction.

By focusing on Eq. 10, an important problem is found. If we use Eq. 10 and 11 in microcontroller and run system at 90°, panel would rotate, yet it cannot turn back during reducing output power; therefore, system cannot be regulated.

Moreover, this practical problem can be derived from Eq. 10 According to m.file of MATLAB code in following section.

2.1 Program Code of Simulation

```
p=4;                          % line 1
pp=0;                         % line 2
teta=pi/2;                    % line 3
for i=1:100
  pf=p+((sign(p-pp))*(p-pp));        % line 4
  pu=sqrt((pf^2)-(p^2));             % line 5
  pd=pu/(2*p);                       % line 6
  tetaf=teta-pd;                     % line 7
  pp=p;                              % line 8
  teta=tetaf;                        % line 9
  p=-4.5*(tetaf^2-2.094*tetaf)+40;   % line 10
end
```

In order to accurate simulation of sun tracker by suggested algorithm, a function, which simulates received efficiency in any angle and in a particular tracking time, can be used.

We define such function as follows:

$$P = (-4.5)(tetaf^{2} - (2.094 * tetaf)) + 40 \tag{13}$$

Fig. 2 shows the curve of Eq. 13 Where angle (radian) versus output power, which is obtained from default PV panel with maximum output power of 45 watts is plotted.

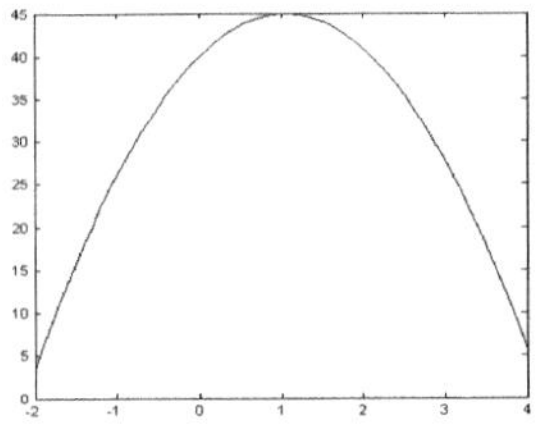

Fig. 2. Curve of default equation

In this code "p" is the measured power at the last search, while "pp" is that of previous search. "pf" is the derived power from default equation, "teta" is the system angle in the last search and "tetaf" is the angle that system must move to there.

Table 1. Explanation of above code

Line 1,2,3	Initializing of parameters "pp" it can be either percentage of measured power or zero for simulation. "p" first measured power after start. We assumed that it be 4.
Line 4	P (k+1) be calculated.
Line 5,6,7	$\theta_s(\mathrm{k}+1)$ is calculated by these equations, which is "tetaf" here.
Line 8,9	After calculating of $\theta_s(\mathrm{k}+1)$ and new power, system rotate toward next point and powers and angles is replaced.
Line 10	Measured power by sensor is simulated by this equation.

Table 2 shows the obtained results in term of iterations, i. it is apparent that by more and more increasing in iterations, calculated powers is not only severally lost but also in terms of 10 iterations, power and angle will be a complex number.

Table 2. Results of simulation for power and angle by using Eq. 10

Number of Iterations(i)	Power from Eq.10	Angle(tetaf)
1	44.4059	0.7048
2	38.9212	-0.1088
4	32.7314	-0.5997
8	7.5578	-1.8349
10	Complex number	Complex number

Results of Table.1 are obtained by use from Eq. 10. Now, by reforming Eq. 10 by Eq. 14 in terms of iteration, i, we obtain results that are shown in Table.3

Table 3. Results of simulation for power and angle by using Eq. 14

Number of Iterations(i)	Power from Eq.14	Angle(tetaf)
1	44.4059	0.7048
2	38.9212	-0.1088
4	39.8947	-0.0111
8	40.0904	0.0096
10	40.1072	0.0114

$$\theta_s(\mathrm{k}+1)=\theta_s(k)-\left[sign\left(P(k)-P(k-1)\right)\right]*\frac{\sqrt{P(k+1)^2-P(k)^2}}{2*P(k)} \tag{14}$$

Due to horizontal moving of panel that should cover left-right sides; it should be able to cover 180°. Hence, in order to providing horizontal moving of panel, equation 10 has to reform as follows:

$$\theta_s(\mathrm{k}+1)=2*(\theta_s(k)-\left[sign\left(P(k)-P(k-1)\right)\right]*\frac{\sqrt{P(k+1)^2-P(k)^2}}{2*P(k)}) \tag{15}$$

In order to obtain a correct performance of tracker, system should be calibrated according to angle for both vertical and horizontal movement.

3 Practical Results

In practice, we used Eq. 11 and Eq. 14 for calculate elevation angle and applied to vertical motor and used Eq. 11 and Eq. 15 for horizontal motor. This algorithm is tested on an electronic board, which is shown in Fig.4.a. Board includes a central microcontroller (atmega 32), a LCD monitor, two drivers (L298) to operate motors and also we use a BUCK-BOOST converter to save energy on battery.

Electrical characteristics of solar panel are shown in table 4.

Table 4. Characteristics of used solar panel

Name	Polycrystalline solar module, SP10-12P
Maximum power	10 W
Open circuit voltage	21-24 V
Optimum operation voltage	18 V
Short circuit current	0.61 A
Open operation current	0.56 A

Fig. 3 shows a flowchart which demonstrates how the presented system works.

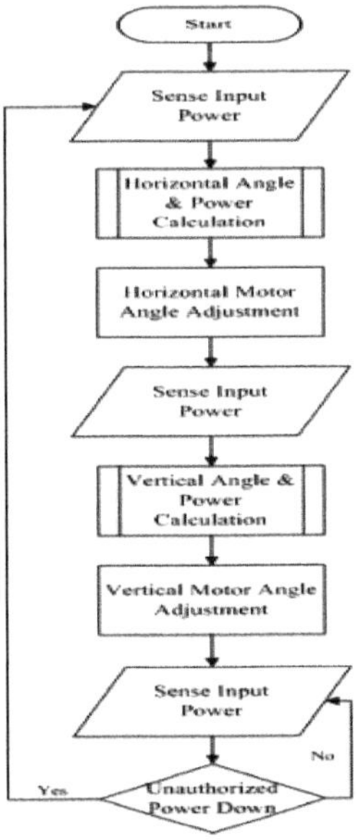

Fig. 3. Flowchart of system's operation

We show a photograph of sun tracker which is used in this research in Fig.4.b.

Fig. 5 shows a curve in which hours of a day set on horizontal axis and output power of system with optical sensor and also fixed system in 45 degree, set on vertical axis.

Fig. 6 shows a graph where hours of a day versus output power of adaptive two-axis system and fixed system in 45 degree.

Fig. 7 shows a graph where hours of a day versus optput power of system with optical sensor and adaptive two-axis system.

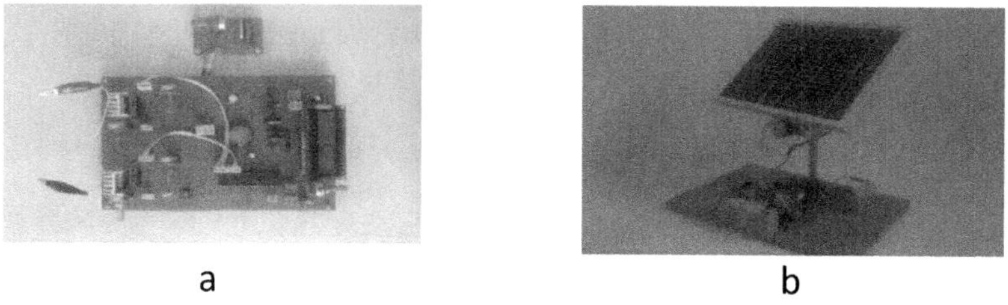

Fig. 4. a) Electronic board, used to test, **b)** Photograph of presented sun tracker

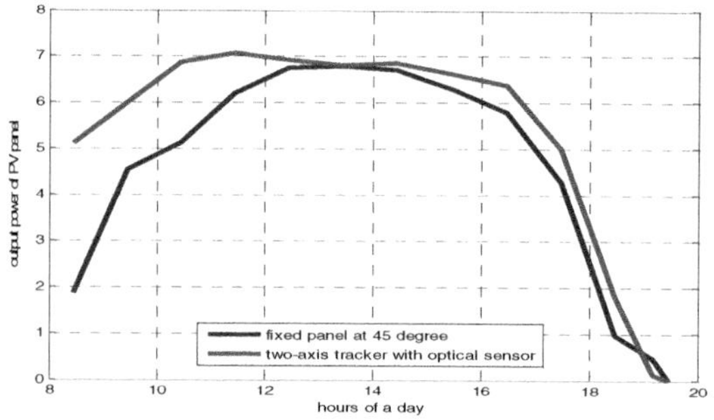

Fig. 5. Output power vs. hours of a day for fixed panel at 45 degree and two-axis tracker with optical sensor

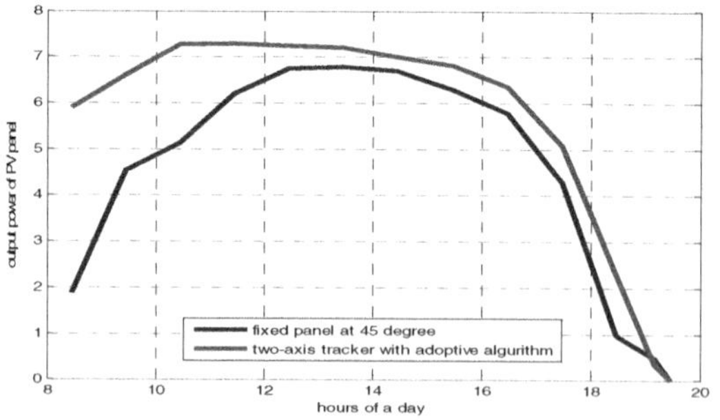

Fig. 6. Output power vs. hours of a day for fixed panel at 45 degree and two-axis tracker with adaptive algorithm

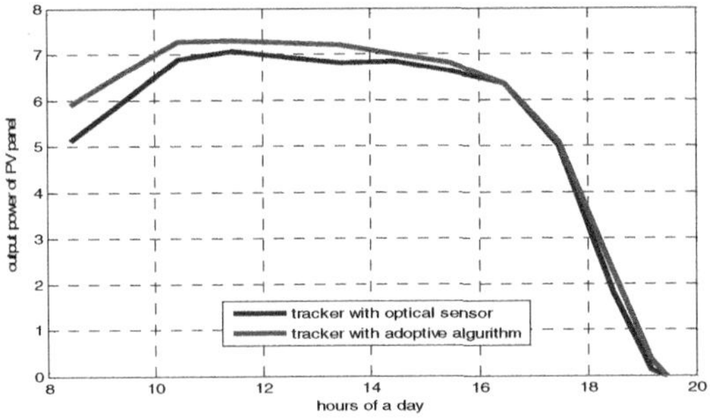

Fig. 7. Output power vs. hours of a day for tracker with optical sensor and two-axis tracker with optical sensor

4 Conclusion

In this article to track sun, an adaptive algorithm is suggested, which is applied on two-axis tracker. We compared the mentioned algorithm outputs with a system which works with optical sensor (LDR). Output results show that efficiency of PV panel in adaptive algorithm is more. Moreover, adaptive algorithm dose not involved practical problems, as we mentioned in introduction, of optical sensors.

References

1. Hossein, M., Alireza, K.: A review of principle and sun tracking methods for maximizing solar systems output. Renewable and Sustainable Energy Reviews (2009)
2. Raghuram, R., Wasfy, M.: Adaptive sun tracking algorithm for incident energy maximization and efficiency improvement of PV panels. Renewable Energy (2010)
3. Al-Mohammad, A.: Efficiency improvements of photo-voltaic panels using a sun tracking system. Applied Energy (2004)
4. Sungur, C.: Multi-axes sun-tracking system with PLC control for photovoltaic panels in Turkey. Renewable Energy (2009)
5. Barsoum, N., Vasant, P.: Simplified Solar Tracking Prototype. Global Journal on Technology & Optimization (2010)

A Self-Tuning Regulator by Using Bacterial Foraging Algorithm for Weight Belt Feeder

Behnaz Zare, Seyed Mohammad Ali Mohammadi, and Mohammad Kiani

Electrical Engineering Department, Shahid Bahonar University of Kerman, Kerman, Iran
behnaz_z00065@yahoo.com, A_Mohammadi@mail.uk.ac.ir,
M.kiani1984@gmail.com

Abstract. Industrial palnts are always exposed to environmenal changes and different disturbances. So producing a controller that can adapt with environmental changes and disturbances is an important issue. The weight belt feeder used in this research is a typical process feeder that is designed to transport solid materials into a manufacturing process at a constant feedrate and this feedrate should be controlled by a controller. A method to produce a controller with the ability to adapt with environmental changes is design and implementation of an indirect self-tuning regulator. At the end we can conclude that using this controller with an advanced heuristic algorithm based on bacterial foraging makes the performace of the system better.

Keywords: Adaptive Control, Indirect Self-Tuning Regulator, Weight belt feeder, bacterial foraging.

1 Introduction

Industrial palnts are always exposed to environmenal changes and different disturbances. Here we need to enter environmental changes into the control system. The weight belt feeder used in this research is a typical process feeder that is designed to transport solid materials into a manufacturing process at a constant feedrate and this feedrate should be controlled by a controller. In this paper first we used a self-tuning regulator. The plant is very sensitive to the initial values of $\hat{\theta}$ and the matrix P. By changing the initial values and observing the response, we chose the best choice for the initial values. Then by using an advanced heuristic algorithm based on bacterial foraging we calculated the initial values. By comparing the responses it was clear that using this controller with the so called algorithm for its tuning makes the performance of the system becomes better.

2 Weight Belt Feeder System Specifications

The weight belt feeder used in this research is produced by Merrick industrial and typically is used for food, chemical or plastic manufacturing process. However because of changes in environmental conditions and materials it is better to use a self

V.V. Das and N. Thankachan (Eds.): CIIT 2011, CCIS 250, pp. 38–43, 2011.

tuning regulator that can change parameters with changes in conditions. However the self-tuning controller is considered in many cases because it is flexible, easy to understand and easy to implement with microprocessors. In this research, all of the experiments were conducted under a constant belt load. Thus, only control of the belt speed is considered. To control the feedrate, the feeder has a shuntwound dc motor and a silicon controlled rectifier (SCR) motor controller combination. The belt speed and hence the overall system feedrate is controlled by varying the rotational rate of the motor.

2.1 Proposed Self-Tuning Controller

The order of the dynamic model of the weigh belt feeder must be determined to use pole placement design. A simple model is preferred to reduce the on-line parameter estimation effort. First-order system can reasonably approximate the observed step responses. Then, $\theta = [a_1, b_0]^T$is the parameter vector to be estimated. By using the STR method we use a recursive estimation method (RLS) to estimate real-time parameters. For simplicity, the reference model was chosen as the first-order model:

$$H_m(q) = \frac{b_{m_0}}{q+a_{m_1}} \tag{1}$$

In particular the continuous-time reference model was chosen as:

$$H(s) = \frac{1}{0.03s + 1} \tag{2}$$

Corresponding to a time constant of 0.03 sec which is a fast response for the weigh belt feeder. By discretizing this model at a sample period T=0.01s, the discretized model is

$$H(q) = \frac{0.2835}{q - 0.7165} \tag{3}$$

Based on the MDPP algorithm for the case in which all process zeros are canceled, we get the diophantine equation:

$$AR + BS = AC \tag{4}$$

$$(q + a_1)r_0 + b_0(s_0) = q + a_{m0} \tag{5}$$

Hence the control law becomes

$$u = \frac{T}{R}r - \frac{S}{R}y = \frac{b_{m0}}{b_0}r - \frac{a_{m1} - a_1}{b_0}y \tag{6}$$

Choosing proper initial values before imlementing the so called algorithm is a very important issue. Because of nonlinear behavior of the system these initial values are different for different setpoints. By changing the initial values and observing the response, the best choice for initial values can be chosen. One method to choose proper initial values of $\hat{\theta}$ is to use an advanced heuristic algorithm based on bacterial foraging. It is observed that using this controller with the proposed heuristic algorithm for its tuning makes the system performance better. P matrix initial values are considered as $P = 0.00012 * I_2$ in all set points. These choices were made to achieve transient responses with fast rise times and small overshoot and to avoid motor saturation.

3 Bacterial Foraging Optimization Algorithm

The original BFOA that was proposed by K.M.Passino includes three major operations: Chemotaxis, Reproduction and Elimination-dispersal. [11-12]

3.1 Chemotaxis

The behavior of the bacteria toward the nutrient sources is interpreted as chemotaxis. An E.coli bacterium moves in two different ways: tumble and swim. Tumble is a unit walk in a random direction and always continues by another tumble or a swim. If random direction results in a better position, it will be followed by a swim, else another tumble will be taken. In fact swim is a unit walk in a previous random direction. In each tumble unit walk position of bacterium is updated based on (7):

$$\theta^{i}(j+1,k,l) = \theta^{i}(j,k,l) + c(i)\varphi(i) \tag{7}$$

Where i is the index of bacterium and $\theta^{i}(j,k,l)$ is the position of ith bacterium in the jth step of chemotaxis and kth stage of reproduction and lth stage of elimination-dispersal. C is the step size of chemotaxis operation. The cost function of the ith bacterium is determined based on its position and is represented with $J(i,j,k,l)$. $J_{\min}$ represents the minimum fitness value. In the swim stage if at $\theta^{i}(j+1,k,l)$ the cost function becomes better than $\theta^{i}(j,k,l)$ then another step will be taken in a same direction. This sequence will continue until Ns steps are taken in swim. [11-12]

3.2 Reproduction

The basic idea of this operation is that nature tends to eliminate animals with poor foraging strategies and keep those which have better ones. Half of the population which has the worse cost function is eliminated. Each of the remained ones which have a better fitness is reproduced to two children bacteria to keep the population size.

3.3 Elimination and Dispersal

To increase the ability of bacteria for global searching and to prevent them from involving in local optimums, randomly some of the bacteria are eliminated and some of them are dispersed.[11-12]

4 Simulation

In this system we used an indirect self-tuning regulator explained in the previous sections and we used bacterial foraging optimization algorithm to choose initial values of estimation parameters. Ofcourse without using this algorithm and by trial and error we can achieve initial values which provide proper response, too but by using bacterial foraging algorithm we can achieve better responses. In figure 2 we can compare the response to the unit step,unit pulse with and without using bacterial foraging algorithm.

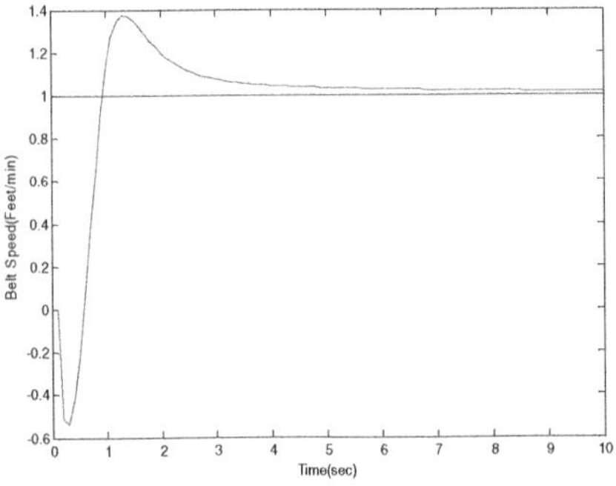

a

Fig. 1. a. The unit step response without using bacterial foraging algorithm

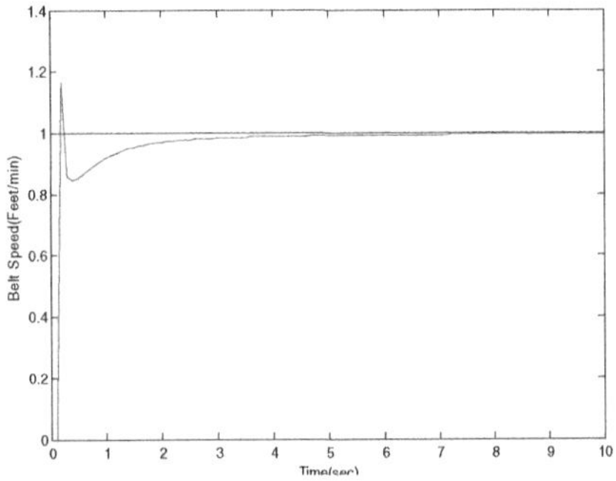

b

Fig. 1. b. The unit step response with using bacterial foraging algorithm

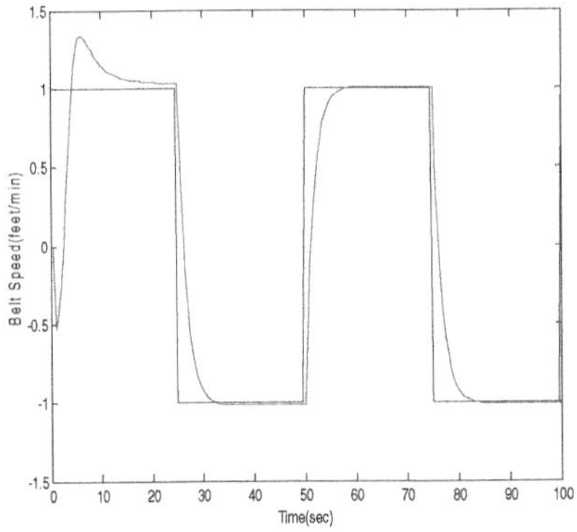

a

Fig. 2. a. The unit pulse response without using bacterial foraging algorithm

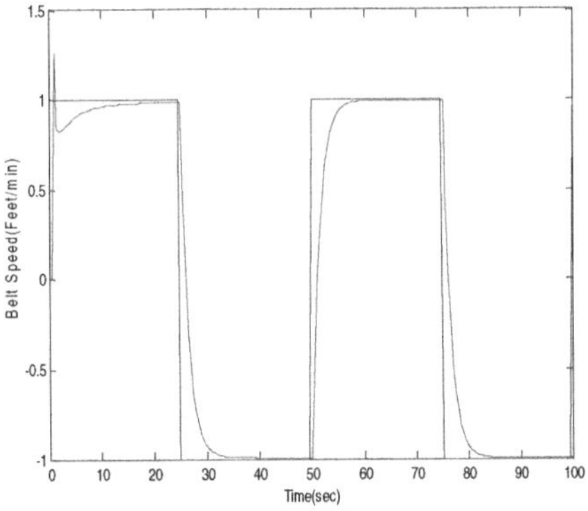

b

Fig. 2. b. The unit pulse response with using bacterial foraging algorithm

As we see by using the bacterial foraging algorithm the overshoot and the steady state error have decreased and the response speed has become better.

In the table bellow the specificathions of the system response in two cases are compared.

Table 1. Specificathions of the system response

	Overshoot		Settling time		Steady state error	
	Without algorithm	With algorithm	Without algorithm	With algorithm	Without algorithm	With algorithm
Unit step input	38%	18%	12	7.5	2%	0
Unit pulse input	35%	25%	10	8	0	0

5 Conclusion

By considering the results of the researching self-tuning regulators have good performancefor control of the weight belt feeder. The system is very sensitive to parameters initial values. One method to achieve proper initial values is trial and error. This method may give good results but is not a reliable method and cannot guarantee the optimal performance.Anader method for initial values estimation is bacterial foraging algorithm.As it is shown in the researches, using this mothod makes the performance of the self-tuning regulator and whole system better.

References

1. Zhao, Y., Collins Jr., E.G., Cartes, D.A.: Self-tuning adaptive control for an industrial weigh belt feeder. ISA Transactions 42 (2003)
2. Collins, E.G., Zhao Jr., Y., Millett, R.: A genetic search approach to unfalsified PI control design for a weigh belt feeder. Int. J. Adapt. Control Signal Process. 15, 519–534 (2001)
3. Zhao, Y., Collins Jr., E.G.: Fuzzy PI control of an industrial weigh belt feeder. In: Proceedings of American Control Conference, Anchorage, AK, pp. 3534–3539 (2002)
4. Astrom, K.J.: Theory and applications of adaptive control—A survey. Automatica 19, 471–486 (1983)
5. Astrom, K.J., Wittenmark, B.: Adaptive Control, 2nd edn. Addison-Wesley Publishing Company, Reading (1995)
6. Astrom, K.J.: Tuning and adaptation. In: Proceedings of the 13th World Congress of IFAC, San Francisco, CA, vol. K, pp. 1–18 (1996)
7. Yang, T.C., Yang, J.C.S., Kudva, P.: Loadadaptive control of a single-link flexible manipulator. IEEE Trans. Syst. Man Cybern. 22, 85–91 (1992)
8. Ji, J.K., Sul, S.K.: DSP-based self-tuning IP speed controller with load torque compensation for rolling mill DC drive. IEEE Trans. Ind. Electron. 42, 382–386 (1995)

9. Tsai, C.C., Lu, C.H.: Multivariable self-tuning temperature control for plastic injection molding process. IEEE Trans. Ind. Appl. 34, 310–318 (1998); Eng. Pract. 8, 1285–1296 (2000)
10. Astrom, K.J., Wittenmark, B.: Self-tuning controllers based on pole-zero placement. IEE Proc.-D: Control Theory Appl. 127, 120–130 (1980)
11. Passino, K.M.: Biomimicry of bacterial foraging for distributed optimization and control. IEEE Control Systems Magazine 22, 52–67 (2002)
12. Liu, Y., Passino, K.M.: Biomimicry of social foraging bacteria for distributed optimization: Models, principles, and emergent behaviors. J. Optimization Theory Applicat. 115(3), 603–628 (2002)

Extending the Operating Range of Linear Controller by Means of ESO

A.A. Godbole* and S.E. Talole

Department of Aerospace Engineering,
Defence Institute of Advanced Technology, Girinagar, Pune-411 025, India
aa_godbole@hotmail.com, setalole@hotmail.com

Abstract. This work presents a novel approach to extend the operational range of linear controllers designed for nonlinear systems using its linearized model. The higher order terms assumed to be negligible in linearization are estimated using Extended State Observer and compensated by augmenting the linear controller. Extended State Observer is an integrated state and disturbance estimator. Illustrative example of a planar pendulum is presented to demonstrate the efficacy of the approach.

Keywords: Linearization, Extended State Observer, Robust control.

1 Introduction

Controllers for nonlinear systems are often designed by linearizing the dynamics. In general, the dynamics is linearized about certain operating/equilibrium points and then using the linearized model, controllers are designed by employing well known linear control techniques. The success of the resulting controller hinges on the assumption that the controlled system operates close to the operating point so that the higher order terms (HOTs) arising in Taylor series expansion in the process of linearization are negligible. When such is not the case, i.e., if the system happens to operate significantly far from the operating point, the performance of the controller may degrade as the HOTS may not be negligible. For systems, where the operating conditions are likely to deviate significantly, gain scheduling is normally employed to address the issue. However, even in this case, some degradation in performance is expected as the system never operates at the operating point for which the gains are scheduled.

One approach to address the issue is to employ disturbance rejection control approach by considering the effect of HOTs as a disturbance. In ref [1], Neural Network based estimation of these effects has been presented and linear controller is augmented to compensate the same. Similarly, in ref [2] a robust trajectory following controller for autonomous underwater vehicle is presented by using similar approach.

Following this line of thinking, this work treats the effect of HOTs as a disturbance acting on the system. The disturbance is estimated by using Extended State Observer (ESO) and used to compensate the effects of HOTs by augmenting the linear controller

* The author would like to acknowledge the support extended to her by Bharati Vidyapeeth COE Pune-411043 during the course of this work.

V.V. Das and N. Thankachan (Eds.): CIIT 2011, CCIS 250, pp. 44–49, 2011.

designed using the linearized model. In effect, the operating range of the linear controller is increased by recovering the controller performance in off-nominal operating conditions. The concept is illustrated by considering a problem of control of pendulum. The remaining paper is organized as follows. The pendulum model used to illustrate the concept is introduced in Section 2. In Section 3, a brief introduction to ESO theory is presented. The ESO based control is presented in Section 4 and simulations and results are presented in Section 5. Lastly, section 6 concludes the work.

2 Pendulum Model

To illustrate the new concept presented in this work, we consider a problem of controlling a planar pendulum wherein the objective is to force the pendulum to track a desired angular position history. The model considers a spherical mass connected through a string at pivot. The string is considered as mass less. A motor provided at pivot generates torque which acts as the input to the system. The example is chosen because the mathematical model provides an analytical expression for the HOTs in linearization. The equations of motion of the planar pendulum after taking the moments about the pivot are given by

$$ml^2\ddot{\theta} = -mgl\sin(\theta) - b\dot{\theta} + T \tag{1}$$

Where m = 0.1 kg is the mass of bob, g = 9.81 m/s ^{2} is the acceleration due to gravity, l = 1 m is the length of the string, b = 0 is the friction co-efficient, T (Nm) is the input torque and θ (rad), $\dot{\theta}$ (rad/s) are the angular position and velocity respectively of the string. Defining the states as $x_1 = \theta, x_2 = \dot{\theta}$ and control input u = T and by considering the operating point as (0,0) and following the linearization procedure in OGATA [3], the linearized dynamics is obtained as

$$\begin{aligned} \dot{x}_1 &= x_2 \\ \dot{x}_2 &= -\frac{g}{l}x_1 - \frac{b}{ml^2}x_2 + \frac{1}{ml^2}u + HOTs \end{aligned} \tag{2}$$

Where it is easy to verify that the HOTs are given by $HOT = \frac{g}{l}(x_1 - \sin x_1)$ ·

When the system operates close to the operating point, the HOTs are negligible and hence are neglected in designing of controllers. Following this, a pole placement controller is designed as

$$u = \frac{1}{b_0}\left(\frac{g}{l}x_1 + \frac{b}{ml^2}x_2 + \ddot{\theta}_r + K_1(\dot{\theta}_r - \dot{\theta}) + K_0(\theta_r - \theta)\right) \tag{3}$$

Where $b_0 = \frac{1}{ml^2}$ and θ_r is the reference position. Substitution of (3) in (2) results into tracking error dynamics as $\ddot{e} + K_1\dot{e} + K_0 e = HOT$ where $e = \theta_r - \theta$ is the tracking error. When angle θ is small, the HOTs are negligible achieving asymptotic tracking of the reference trajectory. However when θ is large, the HOTs may not be negligible and thus the tracking performance will degrade. In this work, the HOTs are estimated by using ESO and are compensated by augmenting the controller (3) as described in the next section.

3 Extended State Observer

In literature, one can find various methods employed for design of robust control systems based on uncertainty and disturbance estimation and cancellation. The Time Delay Control [4], the Uncertainty and Disturbance Estimation technique [5] and the Disturbance Observer approach [6] are some such techniques to mention. The Extended State Observer [7] employed in this work is one such techniques that can be used to estimate the uncertainty and disturbances acting on the system. The ESO also provides estimate of system state apart from the uncertainty. Several diverse applications of ESO in designing robust controllers have been reported in literature [8], [9], [10], [11]. A brief introduction to the theory of ESO is presented here for the sake of ready reference and completeness.

For simplicity, consider a 2nd order, single input-single output nonlinear dynamical system described by

$$\ddot{y} = a(y, \dot{y}, w) + bu \tag{4}$$

Where a(.) represents the dynamics of the plant and the disturbance, w(t) is an unknown disturbance, u is the control signal, and y is the measured output. Let $a(.) = a_0(.) + \Delta a$ and $b = b_0(.) + \Delta b$ where $a_0(.)$ and b_0 are the best available estimates of a and b respectively and Δa and Δb are their associated uncertainties. Defining the uncertainty to be estimated as d = Δa + Δb u + w and designating it as an additional state, x_3, the dynamics given by (4) is re-written in a state-space form as

$$\begin{aligned}
\dot{x}_1 &= x_2 \\
\dot{x}_2 &= x_3 + a_0 + b_0 u \\
\dot{x}_3 &= h \\
y &= x_1
\end{aligned} \tag{5}$$

Where h is the rate of change of the uncertainty, i.e., h = $\dot{d}$ and is assumed to be unknown but bounded function. By making, d, a state, however, it is now possible to estimate it by using a state estimator. To this end, consider an observer of the form

$$\begin{aligned}
\dot{\hat{x}}_1 &= \hat{x}_2 + \beta_1 e_{o1} \\
\dot{\hat{x}}_2 &= \hat{x}_3 + \beta_2 e_{o1} + a_0 + b_0 u \\
\dot{\hat{x}}_3 &= \beta_3 e_{o1} \\
\hat{y} &= \hat{x}_1
\end{aligned} \tag{6}$$

Where $e_{o1} = y - \hat{x}_1 = x_1 - \hat{x}_1$ and $\hat{x}_3$ is the estimate of the uncertainty, d. The quantities β_i are the observer gains which need to chosen to ensure that the observer error dynamics is stable. The observer (6) is known as linear ESO and is employed in this work for the estimation of the HOTs.

4 ESO Based Controller

Following the procedure stated in earlier section, an ESO is designed for the dynamics (2) by considering the HOTs alone as the uncertainty, d. Using the estimated HOTs, the control law (3) is augmented as

$$u = \frac{1}{b_0}\left(\frac{g}{l}\hat{x}_1 + \frac{b}{ml^2}\hat{x}_2 + \ddot{\theta}_r + K_1(\dot{\theta}_r - \hat{x}_2) + K_0(\theta_r - \hat{x}_1) - \hat{x}_3\right) \quad (7)$$

It can be easily verified that if $\hat{x}_3 \approx$ HOTs, the controller (7) offers asymptotic tracking of the reference trajectory.

5 Simulation Results

Simulations are carried out by applying the linear controller (3) and the augmented ESO controller (7) to the nonlinear plant (1). The controller gains K_1 and K_0 are chosen to achieve settling time of 1 sec and damping of 0.9. The observer poles are

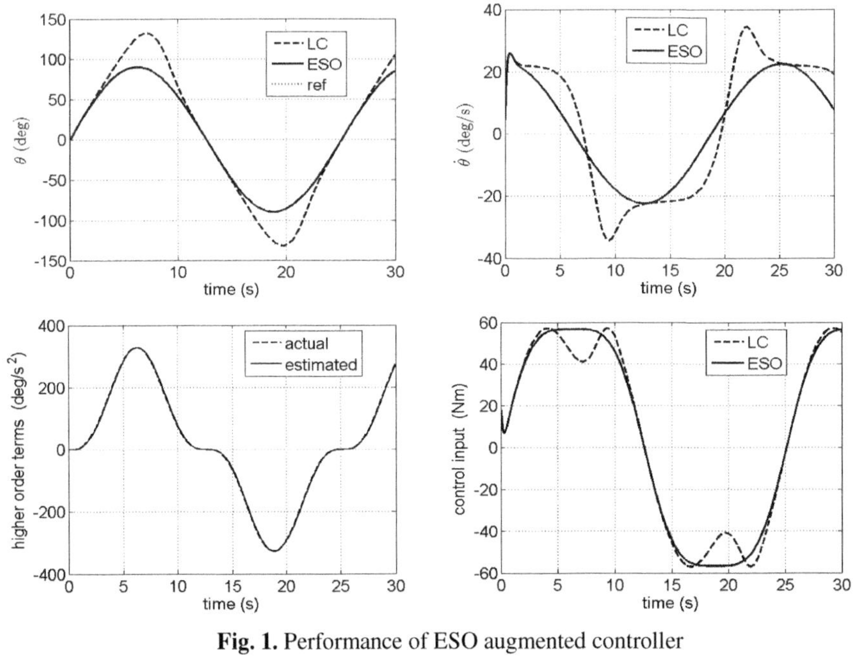

Fig. 1. Performance of ESO augmented controller

placed to ensure that its time constant is 1/3rd that of controller. The reference trajectory to be tracked is taken as $\theta_r = 90\ \sin(0.25t)$ and it may be noted that as the magnitude of θ_r is large, the HOTs are not negligible. The results are as shown in Fig.1 wherein LC denotes linear control whereas ESO denotes ESO augmented linear control. From the results, it can be clearly seen that the performance of the linear controller is restored when it is augmented by ESO estimated uncertainty.

6 Conclusion

This paper presents an ESO based control law to compensate the effects of HOTs arising in linearization when the system operates away from the equilibrium point. The higher order terms are estimated by ESO and this estimate is used in control to negate their effect. Simulations demonstrate the effectiveness of the controller and indicate the ability of ESO in estimation of higher order terms enabling enhancement of the operating range of controller designed for the linearized model.

Acknowledgement. This work is financially supported by the Defence Institute of Advanced Technology, Pune, India.

References

1. Sharma, M., Calise, A.J.: Neural Network Augmentation of Existing Linear Controllers. Journal of Guidance, Control and Dynamics 28(1) (January-February 2005)
2. Campa, G., Sharma, M., Calise, A.J.: Neural Network Augmentation of Existing Linear Controllers With Application to Underwater Vehicles. In: Proc. of the American Control Conference, Chicago, Illinois, pp. 75–79 (June 2000)
3. Ogata, K.: Modern Control Engineering, 4th edn. PHI Learning Pvt. Ltd., New Delhi (2009)
4. Youcef-Toumi, K., Ito, O.: A Time Delay Controller for Systems with Unknown Dynamics. Transactions of the ASME, Journal of Dynamic Systems, Measurement, and Control 112(1), 133–142 (1990)
5. Zhong, Q.C., Rees, D.: Control Of Uncertain LTI Systems Based On an Un certainty and Disturbance Estimator. Transactions of the ASME, Journal of Dynamic Systems, Measurement, and Control 126(4), 905–910 (1990)
6. Chen, W.: Nonlinear Disturbance Observer Enhanced Dynamic Inversion Control of Missiles. Journal of Guidance, Control, and Dynamics 26(1), 161–166 (2003)
7. Wang, W., Gao, Z.: A Comparison Study of Advanced State Observer Techniques. In: Proc. of the American Control Conference, Denver, Colorado, USA, pp. 4754–4759 (2003)
8. Godbole, A.A., Talole, S.E.: Robust Feedback Linearization Approach to Pitch Autopilot Design. In: International Conference on Control, Robotics and Cybernetics, vol. I, New Delhi, India, pp. 76–80 (2011)

9. Talole, S.E., Godbole, A.A., Kolhe, J.P., Phadke, S.B.: Robust Roll Autopilot Design for Tactical Missiles. Journal of Guidance, Control and Dynamics 34(1) (January-February 2011)
10. Talole, S.E., Kolhe, J.P., Phadke, S.B.: Extended State Observer Based Control of Flexible-Joint System with Experimental Validation. IEEE Transactions on Industrial Electronics 57(4), 1411–1419 (2010)
11. Huang, Y., Xu, K., Han, J., Lam, J.: Flight Control Design Using Extended State Observer and Non-smooth Feedback. In: Proc. of the 40th IEEE Conference on Decision and Control, Orlando, Florida, USA, pp. 223–228 (December 2001)

Analysis of Novel Window Based on the Polynomial Functions

Mahdi Nouri[1], Sajjad Abazari Aghdam[2] and Somayeh Abazari Aghdam[3]

[1] Department of Electrical Engineering, University of Science & Technology
[2] Department of Electrical Engineering, Islamic Azad South Tehran University
Tehran, Iran
[3] Department of Electrical Engineering, Islamic Azad University
Mahabad, Iran
mnuri@elec.iust.ac.ir,
{sajjadabazarei,somayeh.abazary}@gmail.com

Abstract. A simple form of a window function with application to FIR filter design is implemented two parts, that is using polynomial functions with grade two and three and computational complexity becomes unavoidable. The spectral characteristic of proposed window is studied in details, and its performance is compared with traditional windows such as Kaiser Window. This is performed in ripple ratio and sidelobe roll-off ratio for the same window length and normalized mainlobe width. Simulation results show that proposed window presents better ripple ratio for the both narrower and wider mainlobe width and larger sidelobe roll-off ratio, The new window is almost quasi equi-ripple. The other advantages for our window are ability to use in various applications by changing two parameters this window can change it's time frame and spectrum and want smaller window length compared with other windows.

Keywords: window functions, Filter Complexity, Spectral efficiency, Ripple Ratio.

1 Introduction

This Window functions are widely used in digital signal processing for many various applications such as digital filter design and speech processing [1-2]. As observed in literature on windows they are mostly as suboptimal solutions, and the best window is depending on the appropriate applications design an ideal FIR filter impulse response following equations and multiplication of them:

$h_d[n]$ is an ideal filter impulse response, w[n] is the desired window and M=N+1 is the window length.

$$\begin{cases} h[n] = h_d[n]w[n] \\ w[n] = \begin{cases} f(n) & 0 \le n \le M \\ 0 & otherwise \end{cases} \end{cases} \tag{1}$$

V.V. Das and N. Thankachan (Eds.): CIIT 2011, CCIS 250, pp. 50–54, 2011.

For different applications, a particular window has to be designed and is introduced to the DSP systems. Two desirable specifications for a window function are smaller main lobe width and good side lobe rejection (smaller ripple ratio) [3-5]. Special windows are used in spectral analysis to reduce the effect of spectral leakage. Windows with low side lobe amplitude are necessary for the detection of small signals when highly dynamic spectra are concerned. However, as we know, these two requirements are contradictory, this can be realized by a given window length and that window with a narrow main lobe has a poor side lobe rejection and vice versa. Sidelobe roll-off ratio is another spectral parameter and it is important for many applications, like for beam forming applications [6]. Various shapes of window functions have been introduced which have different characteristics; such as: Kaiser and Tukey windows [7-10]. For an equal length of M=N+1, the first three windows have approximately the same main lobe width. The Kaiser window is tunable function and offers the property that its main lobe width and side lobe peaks, in a trade-off, can be customized. The Kaiser window has the disadvantage of higher computational complexity due to the use of Bessel functions in the calculation of the window coefficients. There has been great interest into the design of new windows to meet the desired specification for different applications [11-13]. In this paper, a new window based on the polynomial function is proposed to provide higher sidelobe roll-off ratio than traditional windows, to be useful for some applications.

1.1 Proposed Window

As described earlier, a function with two parts are utilized, the proposed window time frame is divided into two Parts to provide high flexibility. Using polynomial function with grade two and three will provide a lower computational complexity than any introduced window. The Proposed window has the following shape:

$$w[n] = \begin{cases} \beta\left(n + \frac{(1+\alpha)N}{2}\right)^3 & , \frac{RN}{2} \le |n| \le \frac{N}{2} \\ \left(\left(\frac{N}{2}\right)^2 - n^2\right) + \gamma & , 0 \le |n| \le \frac{RN}{2} \end{cases} \tag{2}$$

where N is number of window coefficient, R is division coefficient for dividing time frame, α is a coefficient that is used for determine the starting point in window these two parameters can be achieve by equaling the derivation of two parts and own two parts of window function. β and γ are two coefficient that is used for connecting two parts of time frame and make them equal with the same line slope in connecting point. These two parameters β, γ could calculate by these equations:

$$R = 0.85(N/4)^2 + 0.07(N/4) + 0.035 \tag{3}$$

$$\alpha = 0.05R^2 + 0.046R \tag{4}$$

$$\beta = \frac{2R}{(3(\frac{N(1+\alpha)}{2} - R)^2)} \tag{5}$$

$$\gamma = \beta(\frac{N(1+\alpha)}{2} - R)^3 - \left((\frac{N}{2})^2 - R^2\right) \tag{6}$$

In the proposed method, as small changes in time frame can produce a big alternation in frequency spectrum . Based on following given below, by changing two parameters of this window α and R , mainlobe width ,shape of sidelobes and sidelobe ratio will change. α can be displaced sidelobe ratio And by R that is N/4 in parzen window with the static structure allocation period and having a constant change in the frequency spectrum, but in this window can be dynamic changed. These changes create a lot of frequency spectrum changes. By these two parameters can create the desired frequency spectrum for the proper application.

1.2 Performance Analysis

In this section, we compare the performance of the proposed window with several commonly used windows.

1.2.1 Kaiser Window. The Kaiser Window has the Following Shape:

$$w[n] = \begin{cases} \frac{I_0[\frac{2\beta}{N}(n(N-n))^{0.5}]}{I_0(\beta)} & , \quad 0 \leq n \leq N \\ 0 & , \quad else \end{cases} \tag{7}$$

Where β is the tuning parameter of the window to obtain the desired "main lobe width – side lobe peak" tradeoff, and $I_0(.)$ is the zero order modified Bessel function of the first kind. From Fig. 1.a, it is observed that for β=3.55, the two windows have the same window length and mainlobe width The simulation result given in table 1 shows that the proposed window provides a better ripple ratio than Kaiser window. If we want to increase β to 5.1 for the same N; while the proposed window gives less mainlobe width the proposed window has worse side lobe peak as can be seen from Fig. 1.b

Table 1. Data For The Comparisons Between The Proposed And Kaiser Windows

Window	*N*	w_R	*S*	*R*
Proposed	50	0.135	19	-30
Kaiser	50	0.135	21.3	-27.7
Proposed	50	0.147	16.3	-36.2
Kaiser	50	0.157	22.2	-38.1

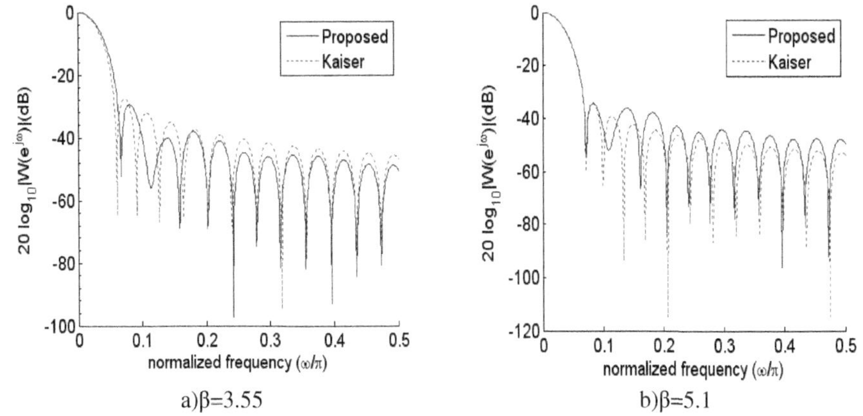

Fig. 1. Fourier transforms of the proposed and Kaiser Windows for the comparisons

2 Computational Analysis

This section is for considering that how many computations are done to reach to window results, and show that how much cost that we must pay for these results, the first consideration is about Kaiser window, The Kaiser window equation makes use of another function I_0, for this section we use Taylor expansion, although it expands to infinity the denominator quickly becomes very large. These two algorithms are implemented using MATLAB running on a personal computer with a Pentium IV 2.66 GHz processor and 3 GB RAM. The proposed window has reduced so many computations especially for Kaiser Window, calculations reduced without any cost for this, the execution time of the two algorithms is plotted in Fig. 2, it shows the time required to compute the window coefficients for the proposed and Kaiser Windows. The elapsed time for the proposed window changes from 0.07 to 0.18ms, while it changes from 0.4 to 0.75 ms for the Kaiser window. As it is obvious from this figure, the proposed window is computationally efficient compared to the Kaiser window due to having no power series expansion in its time domain representation.

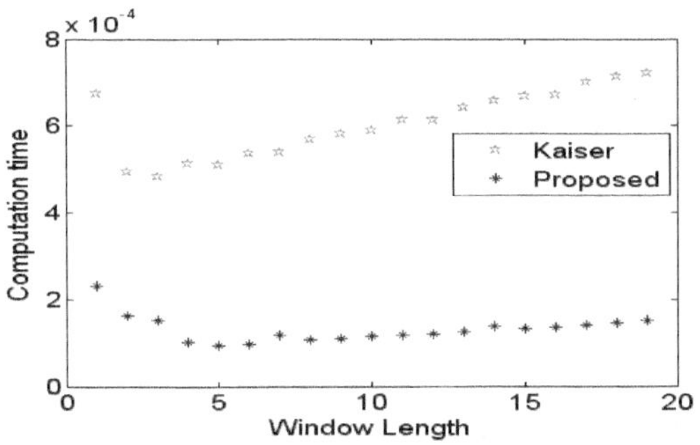

Fig. 2. Computation time comparison between the proposed and Kaiser windows for various window length

3 Conclusion

In this paper, a novel efficient window is proposed based on the polynomial functions with grade two and three. The frequency spectrums are compared with Kaiser Window. For the same window length, if the proposed window has the same main lobe like the other windows, then it offers less side lobe peak and for the case of near the same side lobe peak, the new window gives less main lobe width. The comparisons show that proposed window decrease time computation and time delay against Kaiser Window. This window can has less length against other windows that means reduction in cost and better cost effects because of lower length. By changing two parameters window frequency spectrum could change and can reach to results that is require. Finally some advantages of proposed window are using simple polynomial functions, few computational complexity, narrower main lobe, better cost effect, the ability for using in many applications.

References

1. Antoniou, A.: Digital signal processing: Signal, systems, and filters. McGraw-Hill (2005)
2. Kaiser, J.F., Schafer, R.W.: On the use of the Io-sinh window for spectrum analysis. IEEE Trans. Acoustics, Speech, and Signal Processing 28(1), 105–107 (1980)
3. Kaiser, J.F.: Nonrecursive digital filter design using I0-sinh window function. In: Proc. IEEE Int. Symp. Circuits and Systems (ISCAS 1974), San Francisco, Calif., USA, pp. 20–23 (April 1974)
4. Dolph, C.L.: A Current Distribution for Broadside Arrays Which Optimizes the Relationship Between Beamwidth and Side-lobe Level. In: Proc. IRE, vol. 34, pp. 335–348 (June 1946)
5. Saramaki, T.: A class of window functions with nearly minimum sidelobe energy for designing FIR filters. In: Proc. IEEE Int. Symp. Circuits and Systems (ISCAS 1989), Portland, Ore., USA, vol. 1, pp. 359–362 (1989)
6. Bergen, S.W.A., Antoniou, A.: Design of Ultraspherical window functions with prescribed spectral characteristics. EURASIP Journal on Applied Signal Processing (13), 2053–2065 (2004)
7. Oppenheim, A., Schafer, R., Buck, J.: Discrete-Time Signal Processing, 2nd edn. Prentice-Hall (1999)
8. Proakis, J., Manolakis, D.G.: Digital Signal Processing, 4th edn. Prentice-Hall (2007)
9. Antoniou, A.: Digital Filters. McGraw-Hill Inc., N.Y (1993)
10. Tukey, J.W.: An introduction to the calculations of numerical spectrum analysis. Spectral Analysis of Time Series, 25–46 (1967)
11. Deczky, A.G.: Unispherical windows. In: Proceedings IEEE ISCS, vol. II, pp. 85–89 (2001)
12. Jascula, M.: New windows family based on modified Legendre polynomials. In: Proceedings IEEE IMTC, pp. 553–556 (2002)
13. Zierhofer, C.M.: Data window with tunable side lobe ripple decay. IEEE Signal Processing Letters 14(11) (November 2007)

Cryptographic Key Management Using Fuzzy Vault Based on Statistical Analysis of Iris

Mrunal Fatangare[1] and K.N. Honwadkar[2]

[1] MIT Sri Savitribai Phule Polytechnic,
Paud Road, Pune-411038, Maharashtra, India
[2] D.Y. Patil College of Engg, Pune University
Akurdi, Pune-411044, Maharashtra, India
mrunalfatangare@gmail.com, knhonwadkar@yahoo.com.in

Abstract. We can make a blend of cryptography and biometric to achieve a upcoming security tool. Using unique biometric identity of a person the keys for cryptosystem can be made secure. Within biometric cryptosystems the advantages of biometric authentication are introduced to generic cryptographic key management systems to enhance security.Iris is one of the proven and accurate means to identify person and it does not change throughout life of a person. This paper presents a biometric solution to cryptographic key management problem using iris based fuzzy vault.

Keywords: Biocryptosystem, iris, fuzzy vault, polynomial reconstruction.

1 Introduction

Randomness of fuzziness is not entertained by the traditional cryptography. Biometric systems requires to deal with the fuzzy data, fuzziness means while encrypting or decrypting system should allow a key to be released using a nearer biometric feature extraction. A intermingle of these two techniques can produce a high level security system. This system can be called as a biocrypto system or Fuzzy vault [2].

There are different ways to achieve the bio crypto system [9]

1. Biometric based key release
2. Biometric key generation

2 Related Work

A number of research works have been reported toward effective combination of biometrics with cryptography. Juels and Wattenberg [1] proposed a fuzzy commitment scheme to combine CRC of Polynomial and Key. Juels and Sudan [2][5] introduced the basic fuzzy vault scheme. Karthik Nandakumar, A.K. Jain [4][6][7] had worked a lot on the fingerprint based fuzzy vault.. E.S.Reddy etal [9][10] have worked on iris based fuzzy vault. In the system, they carry on work using iris data as

V.V. Das and N. Thankachan (Eds.): CIIT 2011, CCIS 250, pp. 55–59, 2011.

password. Mrunal etal [13] had carried the work on color iris based fuzzy vault. Further in this paper we have implemented the work with storage criteria modification.

3 Proposed Method

Proposed method [13] that is iris based fuzzy vault involves two phases 1. Iris Feature extraction and 2. Fuzzy Vault construction (encoding and decoding).

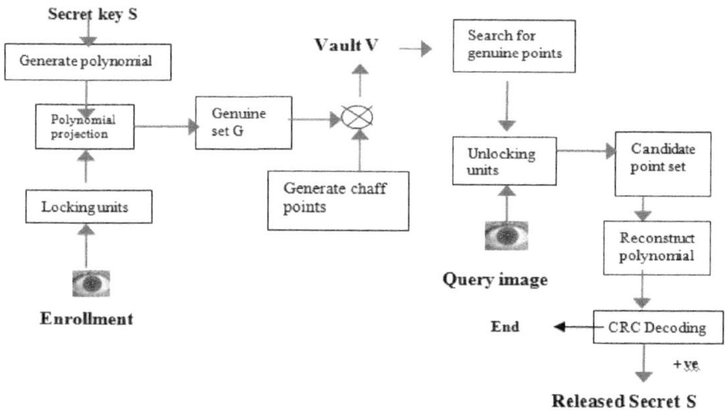

Fig. 1. Overall fuzzy vault encoding and decoding architecture

Statistical feature analysis is used to extract locking and unlocking elements. Fig. 1 depicts diagrammatic representation of overall fuzzy vault scheme.

A. Iris Preprocessing

First eye image is taken and from the eye image iris image is taken out. The output of this step results in storing the radius of inner and outer circles.Using canny edge detection iris from eye and pupil from iris is separated. Fig 2 shows the process of iris preprocessing. Color histogram analysis is performed to get y, u, v features. From these y is omitted and u, v is used to avoid the drawbacks caused due to light effect. [12], [13].

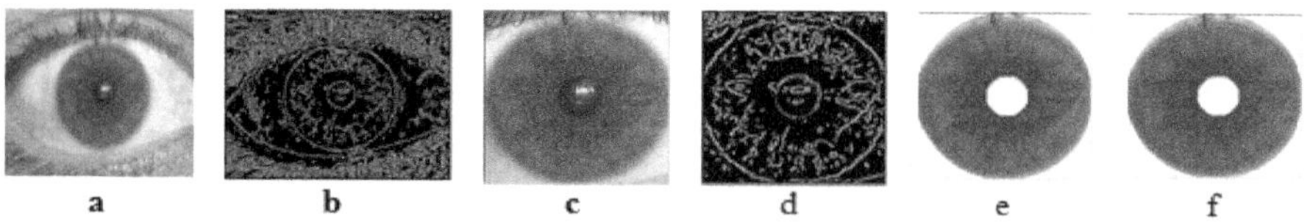

Fig. 2. Iris preprocessing a. Original image b. Iris marked after result of canny edge detection c. Iris separated d. Pupil marked e. Iris separated from pupil f. red circles marked on iris

B. Iris Feature Extraction

It has been proven that the statistical data about iris can be used for iris recognition system [11]. For which mean, median, mode, variance and standard deviation are calculated. On the iris image the circles are marked at the distance of 5 pixels each as shown in fig. 2(f). Using these features, an image can be viewed as a feature vector. These statistical features are used for extracting the locking and unlocking elements from the iris.

C. Matching Iris Framework

Byte pattern is decided for storing the mode and standard deviation values of u and v.

Bit no	Meaning	Bit no	Meaning
0	Always 0	4	V
1	M mode	5	Ring No
2	S standard deviation	6	Concentric circle Number
3	U	7	

Maximum 24 values are possible from the above bit pattern. Hence 24 locking units at the time of encoding can be extracted from the iris. So locking unit is defined as Byte from above table | value of respective unit. For example: 80 | mode value of u of ring 1 **2.** 73 | mode value of v of ring 2 Afterwards chaff points 1:10 are added to make a framework. While decoding, from iris 24 unlocking units are extracted in the same manner. First byte of every unit is compared with first byte of locking units in vault. 24 matching points are extracted from that vault. Then these genuine points from vault are compared with query unlocking points using hamming distance.

$$HD = \frac{1}{N}\sum_{j=1}^{N} C_A(j) \oplus C_B(j)$$

Where *CA* and *CB* are the coefficients of two iris images and N is the size of the feature vector. The $\oplus$ is the known Boolean operator (XOR).

For hamming distance threshold is decided as 0.2 and then it is decided that whether the query image is genuine or not.

Due to process of matching advantage achieved are

1. Instead of matching only (D + 1) points we are matching more number of points and it increases the GAR and reduces FAR.
2. Generally in biometric matching 75% match is considered as genuine match. Here by including matching process we are reducing the possibility of FAR.

4 Experimental Results

The implementation of proposed work has been carried out on UBIRIS color iris database. Database is composed of 1877 Images collected from 241 persons Camera A 128-bit secret S IS randomly generated, and after appending the 16 CRC bits, the resulting 144-bits are converted to the polynomial $p(u)$ as $p(u) = 28271u^8 + 29800u^7 + 26990u^6 + 26400u^5 + \ldots\ldots\ldots + 17208$. 144-bit data is divided into 16-bit chunks, and each one of these chunks determines one of the 9 coefficients of $p(u)$. Chaff set C is found by randomly assuming M points c1, c2, ...which do not overlap with u1, u2, ... Another set of random points d1, d2,, ..., are generated , with a constraint that pairs (cj, dj), j=1,2,...M do not fall onto the polynomial p(u). Chaff set C is then C={ (c_1,d_1), (c_2,d_2)....}.One hundred eye images (5 images of one eye of 100 users) from UBIRIS database are used for locking and unlocking the vaults with the following parameters: number of genuine points in a set G are N = 24 (generally 6 concentric circles are marked ,4 locking elements from each concentric circle selected so that the number of candidate points will be enough for reconstruction), number of chaff points M = 10 times the locking units (this directly affect on the security of the system against attackers, The ratio of chaff points and original points is taken as 10:1 so that the combinations are large in giving high security. To collect more points at the time of encoding/decoding the concentric circles could be marked at the lesser distance. It is observed that, during decoding, CRC performed with 100% accuracy: it signaled an error if and only if there is an error in the decoded polynomial. For evaluating the corresponding False Accept Rate (FAR), we tried to unlock the vaults with iris images that were not the mates of the templates that locked the vaults. For this small database, experimental FAR is 0%. For hamming distance we observed the values for unlocking with the mate image and non mate image. Which directely influences the GAR and FAR. The hamming distance threshold was kept as 0.2 and then the framework is matched.

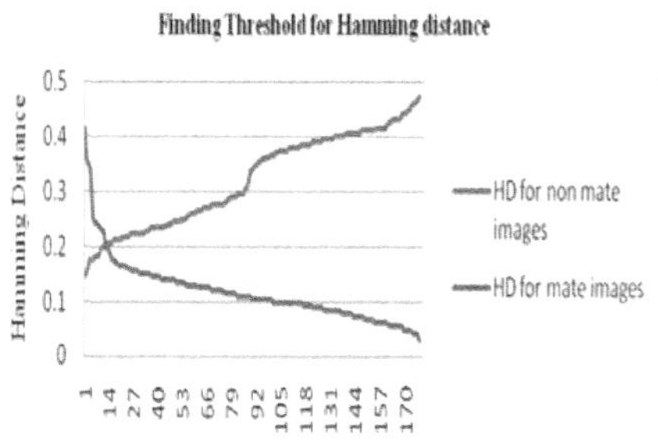

HD	FAR	GAR	FRR
0.18	2.7	92.09	7.344633
0.19	4.4	92.65	7.344633
0.2	6.7	93.22	6.779661
0.21	8.379888	93.78531	6.214689
0.22	13.40782	93.78531	6.214689

Assume that an attacker who does not use genuine iris to unlock the vault; instead he tries to separate genuine points from vault using brute-force. The vault has 264 points (24 genuine, 240 chaff); hence there are a total of C (264, 9) combinations with 9 elements. Only C (24, 9) of these combinations will disclose the secret (unlock the vault). So, it will take an average of C (198, 9)/C (18, 9)) $\approx 2.2^{10}$ evaluations for an attacker to crack the vault. From the analysis of graph above following information shown in side table could be obtained that FAR of the system is decreased at a satisfactory level at the cost of a little degradation in GAR.

5 Conclusion

Fuzzy vault is one of the most comprehensive mechanisms for secure biometric authentication and cryptographic key protection. We have discussed a fully automatic and practical fuzzy vault system based on iris that can easily secure secrets such as 128-b AES encryption/decryption keys. In this paper we have elaborated the fuzzy vault based on statistical analysis of color iris. From the ring wise statistical analysis of iris it becomes easy to capture locking and unlocking elements. Also it improves the FAR of system. However the proposed method can be used for other biometric also. The performance of the fuzzy vault can be further improved by using multiple biometric sources, such as multiple modalities (e.g., iris and face, iris and fingerprint).

References

1. Juels, Wattenberg, M.: A fuzzy commitment scheme. In: Proc. of Sixth ACM Conf. on Computer and Communication Security, pp. 28–36 (1999)
2. Jules, Sudan, M.: A fuzzy vault scheme. In: Proc. IEEE Int. Symp. Inform. Theory, Lausanne, Switzerland, p. 408 (2002)
3. Uludag, U., Pankanti, S., Prabhakar, S., Jain, A.K.: Biometric cryptosystems: Issues and challenges. In: Proc. IEEE (Special Issue Multimedia Security for Digital Rights Management), vol. 92(6), pp. 948–960 (June 2004)
4. Jain, A.K., Pankanti, S., Uludag, U.: Department of Computer Science and Engineering, "Fuzzy vault for fingerprint", Michigan State University, East Lansing, MI, 48824 2. Exploratory Computer Vision Group, IBM T.J. Watson Research Center, Yorktown Heights, NY, 10598
5. Juels, A.: RSA laboratories, 174 middlesex turnpike, bedford, ma 01730, USA, Madhu Sudan Massachusetts Institute of Technology, 32 Vassar street, Cambridge, MA 02139, USA, "A Fuzzy Vault Scheme", RSA Lab, Received November 27, 2002; Revised January 12, 2005; Accepted February 16, 2005
6. Nandakumar, K., Jain, A.K., Pankanti, S.: Fingerprint-Based Fuzzy Vault: Implementation and Performance. IEEE Transactions on Information Forensics and Security 2(4) (December 2007)
7. Nandakumar, K., Nagar, A., Jain, A.K.: Hardening Fingerprint Fuzzy Vault using Password. In: International Conference on Biometrics, pp. 927–938 (2007)
8. Jain, A.K., Nandakumar, K., Nagar, A.: Biometric Template Security. EURASIP Journal on Advances in Signal Processing, Special Issue on Biometrics (January 2008)
9. Srinivasa Reddy, E., Babu, R.: Performance of Iris Based Hard Fuzzy Vault. IJCSNS International Journal of Computer Science and Network Security 8(1) (January 2008)
10. Srinivasa Reddy, E., Babu, R.: Authentication using fuzzy vault based on iris texture. In: Second Asia international Conference on Modeling & Simulation, pp. 361–368 (2008)
11. Kyaw, K.S.S.: Iris recognition system using statistical features for Biometric identification. In: International Conference on Electronic Computer Technology, pp. 554–556 (2009)
12. Gonzalez, R.C., Woods, R.E.: Book- digital Image Processing, p. 522. Pearson Education
13. Fatangare, M., Honwadkar, K.N.: A Biometric Solution to Cryptographic Key Management Problem using Iris based Fuzzy Vault. International Journal of Computer Applications (0975 – 8887) 15(5) (February 2011)

Relay Feedback Based Improved Critical Point Estimation for Process Control Systems

D. Simhachalam, S. Talukder*, and R.K. Mudi

Dept. of Instrumentation & Electronics Engg, Jadavpur University, Kolkata, India
{chalamju10,santanu.809}@gmail.com, rkmudi@yahoo.com

Abstract. Relay feedback auto-tuning test is used for estimation of critical point i.e. ultimate gain and ultimate period for designing process control systems. An experimental technique is proposed for improved estimation of the critical point by conducting the relay feedback test for two different hysteresis bands. Simulation results show that the critical point estimation by our proposed method is superior to standard relay feedback method, and very close to the actual one. Usefulness of the proposed method is demonstrated through close-loop control performance for both set-point change and load disturbance.

1 Introduction

The performance of most of the control systems used for process industry depends on its controller design and tuning. In process industries, according to [1], more than 95% of the controllers are of PID type, because of its simplicity and ease of use [2, 3]. The designed controller should reject the disturbance to improve the performance of the process control. The most crucial phase of a successful controller design is its tuning. More than 60 years ago, in 1942 Ziegler and Nichols [4] proposed the ultimate cycling method for controller tuning. The PID controller tuning parameters are dependent on two factors, ultimate gain K_U and ultimate period T_U. However, this iterative tuning method is often difficult to apply in practice because it is time consuming, particularly for a process with large time constant. On the other hand, for designing model based controller, like internal model control (IMC), it is need to identify the process model, which is often based on the critical point, i.e., Ku and Tu. Therefore, estimation of critical point plays an important role on the performance of process control systems. Åström and Hägglund (1984) [5] have developed an attractive and simple experimental Relay feedback method to determine K_U and T_U. The conventional relay feedback consists of a relay of height μ in the feedback loop as shown in Fig.1. The loop starts to oscillate around the set-point. The maximum amplitude of the process response A is used to calculate the ultimate gain K_U using eq (1). The period of the output curve is the ultimate period, T_U.

$$K_U = 4\mu / A\pi \tag{1}$$

* Corresponding Author.

V.V. Das and N. Thankachan (Eds.): CIIT 2011, CCIS 250, pp. 60–64, 2011.

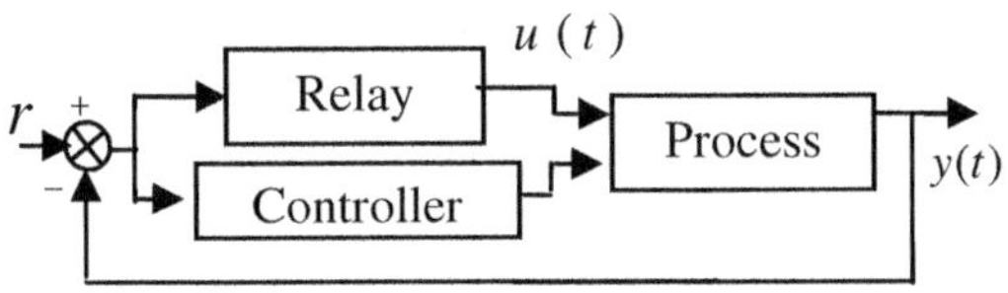

Fig. 1. Relay feedback system

The relay feedback test has many positive features that led to its widespread use: i) Only one parameter has to be specified (relay height), ii) The time it takes to run the test is short, iii) The test is a closed loop, so the process is not driven away from the set-point. However, the precision of this technique for normal processes is not very accurate. Many research works on modifying the relay feedback auto tuning method have been reported in the literature [6-8]. In 1995 T.H. Lee et. al [6] proposed a modification rule by using a mapping function with the normal on-off relay. In the same year S.W. Sung et al [7] reported a modification rule by using a six step relay in place of the normal relay. In 1996, S.Shen et al [8] introduced saturation relay to modify the relay auto-tuning rule. In 1997, Q.G. Wang et. al [9] proposed a method to determine exact expressions for the amplitudes and periods under relay feedback test for more accurate identification of first-order plus dead-time dynamics. Recently, attempts have been made [2, 11] to improve PID auto-tuning rules. Based on the analytical expressions derived in [9], here, a method is proposed to improve the accuracy of critical point estimation by conducting relay feedback test for two different hysteresis bands ε_1 and ε_2. Simulation results revealed that the actual critical point (*i.e.*, K_U and T_U) closely match with those obtained by our proposed method. It is also demonstrated that the PID controller tuned by proposed method exhibits better performance than that of standard relay feedback, in particular for disturbance rejection. The rest of the paper is presented in the following three sections:

2 Proposed Technique

A large number of practical processes can be characterized by the first order plus dead time model as,

$$G(s) = \frac{Ke^{-LS}}{Ts+1} \tag{2}$$

where, k = process gain, T = time constant, L = Dead time.

According to Q.G. Wang et al [9], for the above process model (eq 2) under the relay feedback (Fig.2a), the limit cycle oscillation is symmetric and characterized by the amplitude A and period T_U as expressed by eq (3) and eq (4) that could precisely yield the critical point. The unbiased relay and its response are shown in Fig.2.

$$A = \mu K\left(1 - e^{-L/T}\right) + \varepsilon e^{-L/T} \tag{3}$$

$$T_U = 2T \ln \frac{2\mu K e^{L/T} - \mu K + \varepsilon}{\mu K - \varepsilon} \tag{4}$$

Where, y = response, μ = relay amplitude, ε = hysterisis.

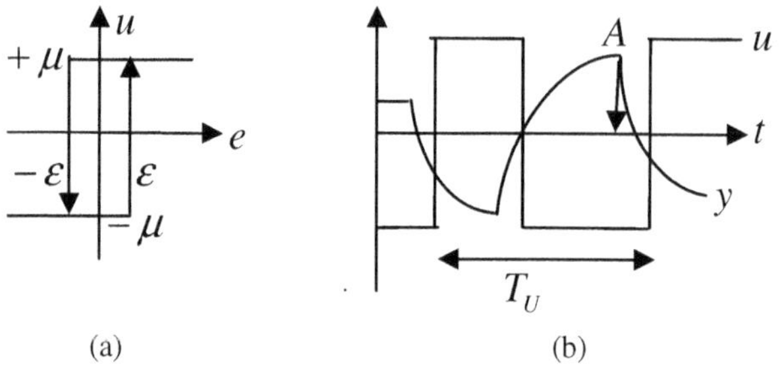

Fig. 2. a) Unbiased Relay, **b)** Oscillatory waveform under unbiased relay

The relay test is repeated for two different hysteresis bands ε_1 and ε_2, and then A_1, T_U for ε_1 and A_2 for ε_2 are recorded. First the model parameters, K, T, and K_I ($= e^{-L/T}$) are calculated by putting $A = A_1$ for $\varepsilon = \varepsilon_1$, and $A = A_2$ for $\varepsilon = \varepsilon_2$ in eq (3) and eq (4), *i.e.*,

$$A_1 = \mu K\left(1 - e^{-L/T}\right) + \varepsilon_1 e^{-L/T} \quad \text{and} \quad A_2 = \mu K\left(1 - e^{-L/T}\right) + \varepsilon_2 e^{-L/T}.$$

From the above expressions

$$K_I = e^{-L/T} = \left|\frac{A_2 - A_1}{\varepsilon_2 - \varepsilon_1}\right| \tag{5}$$

and from eq (5) and eq (3)

$$K = \frac{A - \varepsilon e^{-L/T}}{\mu\left(1 - e^{-L/T}\right)} = \frac{A - \varepsilon K_I}{\mu(1 - K_I)} \tag{6}$$

Now, putting K_I and K in eq (4)

$$\mathrm{T} = \frac{T_U}{2\ln\left[(2\mu K / K_I - \mu K + \varepsilon)/(\mu K - \varepsilon)\right]} \tag{7}$$

Next, to calculate the actual critical point, the Z-N ultimate cyclic method is conducted for the First Order plus Dead time (FOPDT) systems as given in eq (2) with the controller gain K_U in series for different values of process parameters (K, L, T) as shown in Table1. For the modification, loop gain $K_P = K_U{*}K$ and $Temp = 1/(1 - e^{-L/T})$ is plotted as shown in Fig.3. Fig.3 shows a linear relationship between K_P and $Temp$, so the expression for K_P can be expressed as $K_P = K_U K = C/(1 - e^{-L/T})$, where C is the gradient of the plot, which is found to be 1.55. Hence, the ultimate gain K_U can be obtained from the following relation:

$$K_U = \frac{1.55}{K(1 - K_I)} \tag{8}$$

And the ultimate period T_U can be derived from the stability condition [10]:

$$\left|\frac{K_U K e^{-L/T}}{Ts + 1}\right| = 1 \quad \Rightarrow \frac{4\Pi^2}{T_U^2} = \frac{K_U^2 K^2 - 1}{T^2} \qquad \therefore T_U = \frac{2\Pi T}{\sqrt{K^2 K_U^2 - 1}} \tag{9}$$

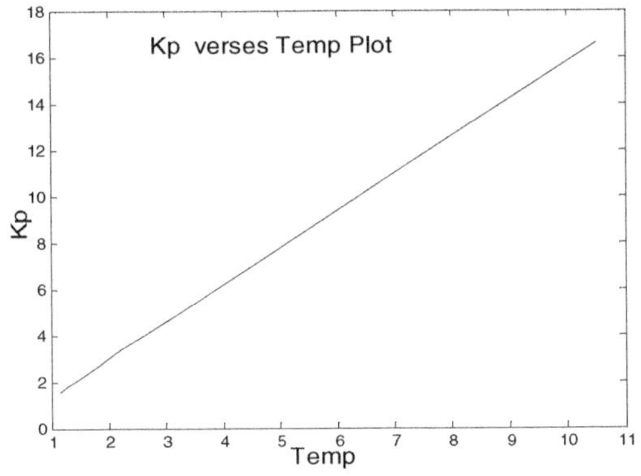

Fig. 3. Plot between K_P and *Temp*

Table-1. K_P for various L/T

S.No	*L/T*	*Kp*
1	0.1	16.6
2	0.15	11.3
3	0.2	8.59
4	0.3	5.98
5	0.4	4.65
6	0.5	3.86
7	0.6	3.38
8	0.7	2.95
9	0.8	2.68

3 Results

To study the effectiveness of the proposed method for critical point (K_U, T_U) estimation, seven systems with different process parameters (K, L, T) are simulated. Here, $K_{U\text{-}a}$, $T_{U\text{-}a}$, $K_{U\text{-}R}$, $T_{U\text{-}R}$ and $K_{U\text{-}M}$, $T_{U\text{-}M}$ represent the critical point for Z-N cyclic, standard relay feedback, and proposed methods, respectively. The results are recorded in Table2, which reveals that the critical point of the proposed method is very close to the actual one.

Table 2. Ultimate gain and Period for proposed, actual, and relay mthods

S.No	*K*	*L*	*T*	$K_{U\text{-}R}$	$K_{U\text{-}a}$	$K_{U\text{-}M}$	$T_{U\text{-}R}$	$T_{U\text{-}a}$	$T_{U\text{-}M}$
1	1	1	10	12.2	16.5	16.3	6.07	3.8	3.9
2	1	3	20	8.62	11.3	11.2	15.6	11.41	11.41
3	1	1	5	6.72	8.59	8.56	4.72	3.75	3.77
4	1	1	4	5.56	7.03	7.05	4.42	3.65	3.60
5	1	3	10	4.78	5.98	5.98	12.6	10.91	10.63
6	1	2	5	3.79	4.65	4.70	7.8	7.01	6.74
7	1	1	2	3.18	3.86	3.93	3.69	3.43	3.3

Next, it is demonstrated how the accuracy of critical point estimation influences the control performance. Fig.4 shows performances of PID controllers due to both set-point change and load disturbance. Table3 recorded its various performance indices. From Table3 and Fig.4, it is observed that the proposed method provides significantly improved overall performance compared to conventional relay feedback method. Most important point is that there is a remarkable performance improvement in the load disturbance, which is vital for most of the industrial processes.

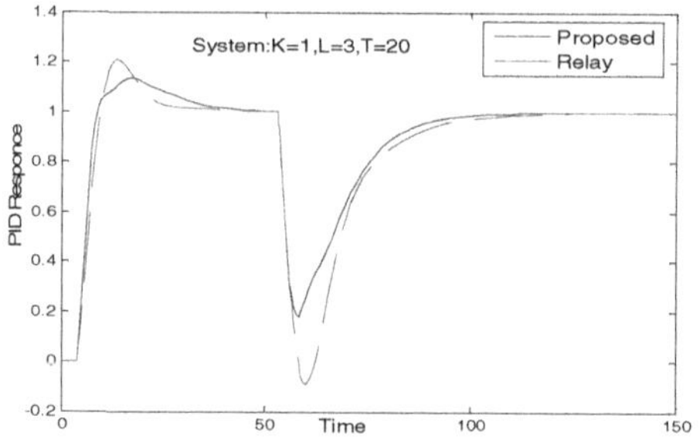

Fig. 4. Set point and load disturbance responses under PID controllers

Table 3. Performance indices for the proposed and standard relay methods

	System: *K=1,L=3, T=20*		
Method	*Overshoot*	*IAE*	*ITAE*
Proposed	13.73	55.63	1180
Relay	20.85	61.50	1490

4 Conclusion

In this study, a method is proposed for improved critical point estimation through simple relay feedback experiment. Results proved that the critical point estimation by the proposed method is superior to standard relay feedback method and very close to the actual one.

References

1. Astrom, K.J., Hagglund, T.: PID controller: Theory, Design and Tuning, USA. Instru ment Society of America (1995)
2. Dey, C., Mudi, R.K.: An improved auto-tuning scheme for PID controllers. ISA Transactions 48(4), 396–409 (2009)
3. Astrom, K.J., Hagglund, T.: Revisiting the Ziegler-Nichols step response method for PID control. Journal of Process Control 14(6), 635–650 (2004)
4. Ziegler, J.G., Nichols, N.B.: Optimum settings for automatic controllers'. ASME Transactions 64, 759–768 (1942)
5. Astrom, K.J., Hagglund, T.: Automatic Tuning of Simple Regulators with Specifications on Phase and Amplitude Margins'. Automatica 20, 645–651 (1984)
6. Lee, T.H., Wang, Q.G., Tan, K.K.: A modified relay based technique for improved critical point estimation in process control. IEEE Transactions on Control Systems Tech. 3(3), 330–337 (1995)
7. Sung, S.W., Park, J.H., Lee, I.: Modified relay feedback method. Industrial Engineering and Chemistry Research 34(11), 4133–4135 (1995)
8. Shen, S., Yu, H., Yu, C.C.: 'Use of the saturation relay feedback for autotune identification. Chem. Eng. Sci. 51(8), 1187–1198 (1996)
9. Wang, Q.G., Hang, C.C., Zou, B.: Low-Order Modeling from Relay Feedback. Industrial Engineering and Chemistry Research 36(2), 375–381 (1997)
10. Choudhury, D.R.: Modern Control Engineering. Prentice Hall of India, New Delhi (2006)
11. Mudi, R.K., Dey, C., Lee, T.T.: An improved auto-tuning scheme for PI controllers. ISA Transactions 47(1), 45–52 (2008)

Framework to Reduce the Hiding Failure Due to Randomized Additive Data Modification PPDM Technique

P. Kamakshi[1] and A. Vinaya Babu[2]

[1] Department of Information Technology, Kakatiya Institute of Technology and Science Warangal, Andhra Pradesh, India
[2] Department of Computer Science, J.N.T.U. Hyderabad, Andhra Pradesh, India
kamakshi_chiku@yahoo.co.in

Abstract. The development of technology in different domains facilitated organizations to collect huge amount of data for analysis purpose. Such data is analyzed by data mining tools to find trends, relationships and outcomes to enhance business activities and discover new patterns that may allow them to serve their customers and society in a better way. The data collected from various sources also consists of sensitive information. The application of data mining techniques on such databases may violate the privacy of an individual by revealing the information which is private and confidential. The threat of privacy due to data mining results has triggered development of many privacy-preserving data mining techniques.. In this paper we discussed the negative side of randomized additive perturbation technique and proposed a framework SARP which protects privacy by integrating basic data modification techniques. The experimental results shows that better privacy protection can be achieved with this framework than randomized additive perturbation technique.

Keywords: Data mining, Privacy, Privacy preserving data mining, swapping.

1 Introduction

In our day to day activities most of the data which is regularly collected [6]and recorded belongs to bank transactions, purchases, credit card information, filling of loan applications, health records, insurance policies etc. The main motivation behind the collection of such huge data by different government and commercial organization is to utilize such historical information for future decision making and increase companies' profits. When powerful data mining tools are applied on such data, will produce not only useful and interesting patterns but also reveal the results containing the sensitive data available in collected data base. Thus the data mining which aims to efficiently discover valuable information from large databases is also sensitive to privacy concerns. Threat to privacy from the data mining results became the most challenging issue to be solved in next coming years. Suppression of private information to protect privacy is not an effective technique because in some situation the privacy can be compromised by the identifiers which are not actually very

V.V. Das and N. Thankachan (Eds.): CIIT 2011, CCIS 250, pp. 65–71, 2011.

sensitive but can be used to link up with other identifiers and reveal actual sensitive information. PPDM is the new forthcoming research direction in data mining which furnish the desired data mining result and also protect the privacy of sensitive information in collaborative environment. Basically the privacy preserving data mining techniques modify the original sensitive data before releasing it to the outside world for the analysis purpose.

2 Related Work

Privacy preserving data mining techniques can be classified according to different protection methods. The first approach adopts data modification technique, which ensures the privacy by modifying the original information of a database that is sensitive and to be shared. The data is modified in such a way that privacy is protected in data mining results. The second approach is based on Cryptographic methods and is developed for distributed environment where two or more parties want to conduct a computation based on their private inputs. The computation is performed in such a way that no party knows anything except its own input [8] and the results. Another approach called query auditing method preserves the privacy by modifying or restricting the results of a query. This paper explores the major drawback of randomized additive data modification technique. It was found that the original information can be approximated [1] from the perturbed data obtained from additive perturbation technique. The main goal of this paper is to propose a novel framework SARP i.e. Swapping and Rotation on Perturbed data. This framework rectifies the problem due to additive data modification method and also reduces the hiding failure to a great extent.

3 A Brief Review of Data Modification Techniques

The productive side of data mining is marvelous benefits the businesses, governments, and society enjoys. But the downside of data mining results is threat of privacy due to misuse of personal information [10] and violation of privacy laws. Confining the data mining results may instigate pessimistic impact on businesses profits, national security and can be obstacle in the field of medical research. This has led to the development of PPDM algorithms that aim to extract the data patterns without directly accessing the original sensitive data and ensure that the mining process does not get sufficient information to reconstruct the original data. In this section we discuss the basic data modification technique which modifies the original information before it is released for analysis purpose. The proposed SARP framework is based on additive perturbation, swapping and rotation techniques.

3.1 Randomized Additive Perturbation

One approach to PPDM is based on perturbing the original data, then providing the perturbed dataset as input to the data mining operstions. Privacy is achieved by distorting the identifiable values and revealing the modified version for analysis purpose. In randomization approach the privacy [3] of the sensitive data is protected by adding small amount of noise ie. a random number derived from well known distribution is added to the value of a sensitive attribute. For example, if P is the original value of a sensitive attribute than, Pi+r will appear in the modified database, where r is a random value drawn from some distribution. The data modification is performed in such a way [7] that aggregate properties of the data can be recovered with sufficient precision while individual record values are distorted considerably. Generally the server keeps a complete and precise original database and makes a modified version of this database available to the public to work with.

3.2 Data Swapping Technique

Data swapping technique ensures confidentiality by selectively switching sensitive variable values between selected record pairs. Data swapping [13] limits the statistical disclosure of the individual data available at the record level. As all the records are altered to the maximum extent, it is challenging task for an intruder to recognize the identity of an individual in database. The most desirable property of swapping technique is that it is simple and can be used only on sensitive data without disturbing non sensitive information. In Table 1 example shows that the original values of gender of record 2 are swapped with record 3 and record 2 is swapped with 4. The swapped data does not resemble the original data but frequency counts are preserved.

Table 1. Table shows an example of original database with attributes transaction id, gender, job, income. The last column indicated the data after performing swap operation on gender.

TID	Gender	Job	Income	swap_ gender
1	F	Supervisor	2000	M
2	F	Supervisor	2200	F
3	M	Supervisor	2100	M
4	M	Supervisor	2000	F

3.3 Data Rotation Technique

Rotation based transformation technique is another interesting data modification technique which protect statistical properties of the sensitive data and also meet privacy requirements. In this technique noise is represented [14] with angle theta. The transformation is applied to the selected confidential attribute values by rotation angle theta. .The transformation is performed by observing the rotation of a point about the coordinate axes, and this transformation affects the values corresponding to X and *Y* co-ordinates. The rotation technique can be applied more than once to some confidential attributes promising better privacy protection than perturbation technique. Table 2 below shows an example of modified values of income after applying 3 degrees of rotation.

Table 2. The table below shows an example of database after the application of rotation technique on the attribute income

S.no.	Place	Age	Income	3 degrees rotation on perturbed income data
1	A	19	20000	22000
2	B	33	30000	33000
3	C	22	45000	42000
4	D	22	50000	48000

4 Proposed Framework

We discussed the major problem of additive perturbation technique in the previous section. The issue was raised [11] about utility of randomized additive perturbation method. It is found that different techniques like random matrix-based spectral filtering techniques can be used to retrieve the original information from the perturbed dataset. The main objective of this framework called as SARP ie. swap and rotate operation on perturbed data is to improve the performance of additive perturbation technique. This framework gives fruitful results in a collaborative environment [10] where number of parties wants to share the data for their mutual benefit but want to protect the privacy of sensitive information in their database. Three components in this architecture are the client, data miner and data provider. The role of data provider and client are interchangeable in collaborative environment. Initially the client submits the query to the data miner related to the information he desires to obtain from the other parties or data owners. The data miner then cooperates with other parties and find the data owner who are ready to share their database. After this

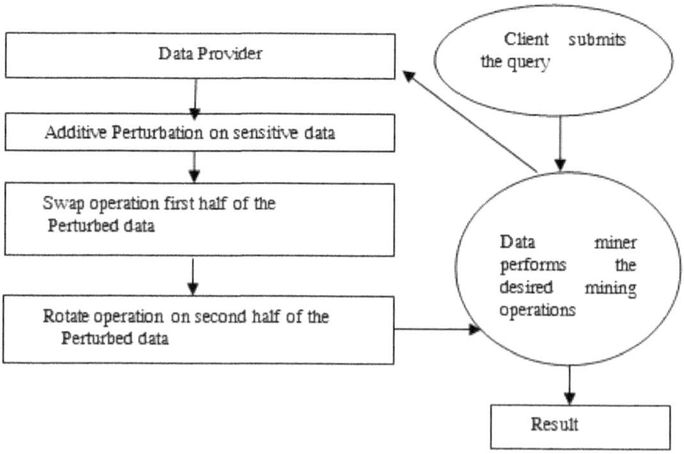

Fig. 1. Privacy Preservation by SARP architecture

negotiation, the data owner modifies the original sensitive information in three steps and put forward the transformed database to the data miner. In the first step data modification is performed by applying randomized additive data perturbation technique on sensitive information. Small amount of noise derived from Gaussian distribution is added to the sensitive information .The transformed dataset preserve the statistical properties of the dataset. In the second step the complete perturbed information is partitioned into two parts. Swap operation [12]is performed on the first half of perturbed data and rotation technique [14] is applied on other half of perturbed database. In the third step the complete modified set is supplied to data miner to perform various data mining operation. The novel framework which integrates the basic data modification techniques is shown in Fig. 1.

4.1 Experimental Results

In Table 3 the original freight charges are considered as sensitive data. After receiving query form data miner the data owner modifies the freight charges with additive perturbation technique.

Table 3. Shows the results after performing perturbation on freight attribute and then swap and rotation on each half of the perturbed freight data

Custid	freightcharge	perturbed Freightcharges	swap and rotate operation on perturbed data	hiding failure
1	28	28	29	FALSE
2	13	12	12	FALSE
3	62	62	62	**Match**
4	48	47	49	FALSE
5	67	69	66	FALSE
6	54	53	53	FALSE
7	24	24	23	FALSE
8	139	139	141	FALSE
9	10	11	8	FALSE
10	73	73	72	FALSE
11	202	202	204	FALSE
12	64	64	64	**Match**
13	4	4	7	FALSE
14	145	144	146	FALSE
15	4	5	6	FALSE
16	87	86	81	FALSE
17	75	77	80	FALSE
18	6	7	4	FALSE
19	38	36	37	FALSE
20	9	9	7	FALSE

After partitioning the perturbed records in to two sets, we applied swapping operation on the first set and rotation operation on the remaining second set. The results show that after performing randomized additive perturbation 8 records out of 20 records are matched with original values. Whereas only 2 records of freight values are matched with the original 20 records after performing swap and rotate operation on two sets of perturbed data. Hiding failure is the process of identifying the number of modified record values matching with original record values. In this Framework it is observed that the hiding failure is reduced noticeably when compared to application of only additive perturbation. In Table 3 FALSE under the column hiding failure, represents the final modified data submitted to data miner whose value doesn't matches with original data values. The term 'Match' represents the status where modified record values matches with original values.

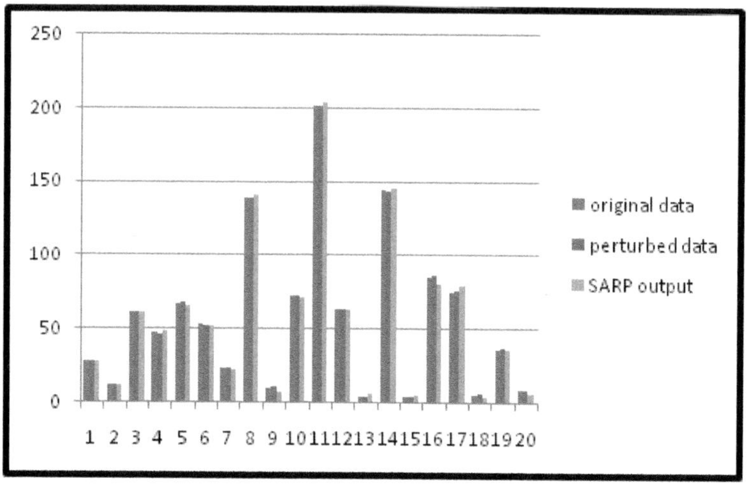

Fig. 2. The graph shows the variation shows the variation of freight charges in original, perturbed form and after applying SARP operation

5 Conclusion

The different aspects and application of data mining techniques show that remarkable benefits can be achieved by businesses, governments, and society. But, in recent years, preserving the privacy in data mining activities became an important issue in many applications due to sensitive information available in the databases. This paper illustrates the challenges faced by randomized additive perturbation technique. It is observed that under certain conditions it is possible to violate the privacy from the results obtained by additive perturbation technique. In this paper the proposed SARP framework gives improved performance over actual additive perturbation technique. The experimental results show the improvement in privacy preservation of sensitive data by reducing the hiding failure.

References

1. Agrawal, D., Aggawal, C.C.: On the design and quantification of privacy preserving data mining algorithms. In: Proceedings of the 20th ACM SIMOD Symposium on Principles of Database Systems, Santa Barbara, pp. 247–255 (2001)

2. Agrawal, R., Srikant, R.: Privacy-preserving data mining. In: Proceeding of the ACM SIGMOD Conference on Management of Data, pp. 439–450. ACM Press, Dallas (2000)
3. Muralidhar, K., Sarathi, R.: A General additive data perturbation method for data base security. Journal of Management Science, 1399–1415 (2002)
4. Agrawal, D., Aggarwal, C.C.: On the Design and Quantification of Privacy Preserving Data mining algorithms. In: ACM PODS Conference (2002)
5. Canny, J.: Collaborative filtering with privacy. In: IEEE Symposium on Security and Privacy, Oakland, pp. 45–57
6. Jiawei, H., Kamber, M.: Data Mining: Concepts and Techniques. China Machine Press, Beijing (2006)
7. Kargupta, H., Datta, S., Wang, Q., Sivakumar, K.: On the Privacy Preserving Properties of Random Data Perturbation Techniques. In: Proceedings of the 3rd International Conference on Data Mining, pp. 99–106 (2003)
8. Lindell, Y., Pinkas, B.: Privacy Preserving Data Mining. In: Bellare, M. (ed.) CRYPTO 2000. LNCS, vol. 1880, pp. 36–54. Springer, Heidelberg (2000)
9. Liu, L., Thuraisingham, B., Kantarcioglu, M., Khan, L.: An Adaptable Perturbation Model of Privacy Preserving Data Mining. In: ICDM Workshop on Privacy and Security Aspects of Data Mining, Huston, TX US (2005)
10. Fienberg, S.: Privacy and Confidentiality in an e-Commerce World. In: Data Mining, DataWarehousing, Matching and Disclosure Limitation. Statistical Science, 143–154 (2006)
11. Souptik, D., Kargupta, H., Sivakumar, K.: Homeland Defense, Privacy-Sensitive Data Mining, and Random Value Distortion. In: SIAM Workshop on Data Mining for Counter Terrorism and Security (2003)
12. Fienberg, S.E., McIntyre, J.: Data Swapping: Variations on a Theme by Dalenius and Reiss. In: Domingo-Ferrer, J., Torra, V. (eds.) PSD 2004. LNCS, vol. 3050, pp. 14–29. Springer, Heidelberg (2004)
13. Chen, K., Liu, L.: A random rotation perturbation approach to privacy preserving data classification. In: International conference on Data Mining, ICDM (2005)
14. Liu, K., Kargupta, H., Ryan, J.: Random Projection-based Multiplicative Perturbation for Privacy Preserving Distributed Data Mining. IEEE Transactions on Knowledge and Data Engineering (TKDE) 18, 92–106 (2006)

Optimum Power Loss in Eight Pole Radial Magnetic Bearing: Multi Objective Genetic Algorithm

Santosh N. Shelke and R.V. Chalam

National Institute of Technology Warangal, Andhra Pradesh, India

Abstract. Weight optimization of coil in eight pole radial magnetic bearings (RMB) has been carried out using multi-objective genetic algorithms (MOGAs). The coil weight of RMB and copper loss has been selected as the minimization type objective function. The maximum space available, saturation flux density, the maximum current densities that can be supplied in the coil and the maximum electromagnetic force have been chosen as constraints. The coil space radius, the pole tip radius, radial length of coil, number of poles has been proposed as design variables. Apart from the comparison of performance parameters in the form of figures and tables, designs are also compared through line diagrams. Post-processing has been done on the final optimized 100 populations by studying the variation of different parameters with respect to objective functions. A criterion for the choice of one of the best design based on the minimum weight of coil showing optimum copper loss.

Keywords: Radial Magnetic Bearings, Genetic Algorithms, Optimum Design, Multi-Objective Optimization.

1 Introduction

A radial magnetic bearing supports a rotating shaft, without any physical contact by suspending the rotor in the air, with an electrically controlled magnetic force. In magnetic bearings, first, the electrical energy transformed into the magnetic energy, and then it transforms into the mechanical energy.

Optimal design using GA of radial active magnetic bearings integrated with their control was studied by Chang and Chung (2002). R.T.marler, J.S.Arora (2004) suggested that decision making can be done on the basis of "a priori' or posteriori approach. In this method one needs prior knowledge of trade-off for taking decision. Rao and Tiwari (2006) attempted to optimize the physical parameters of design of thrust magnetic bearings by using single objective genetic algorithms.Bakay L., and Dubois M. (2007) studied effect of Cu and Iron losses of optimized eight pole radial AMB on discharge time of no load long term flywheel energy storage. NSSN configuration is used. . Rao and Tiwari (2008) attempted to optimize the physical parameters of design of thrust magnetic bearings and rolling element bearing by using single objective genetic algorithms. Bakay L., Dubois M., and Ruel J. (2009) optimized AMB to minimize Cu and Iron loss for different magnitude of external force.

V.V. Das and N. Thankachan (Eds.): CIIT 2011, CCIS 250, pp. 72–77, 2011.

2 Geometry of Radial Magnetic Bearing

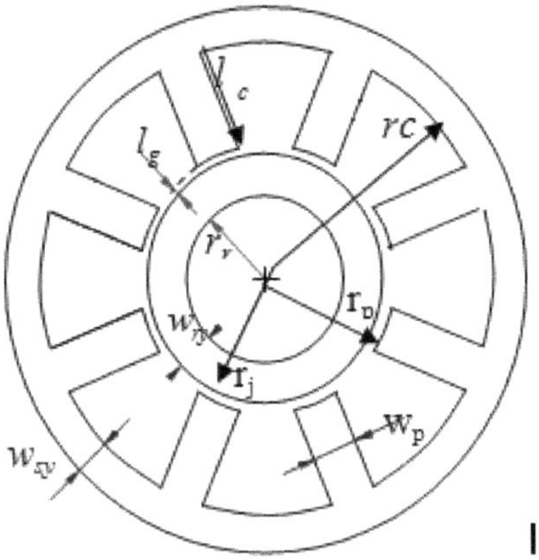

Fig. 1. Radial Magnetic Bearing

Where, l_g - Air gap, t_c–Thickness of coil, , t_c–Thickness of coil, l_c–radial length of coil on pole , t_c–Thickness of coil, l_c– length of coil, coil space radius - r_c, r_j - Radius of journal, r_r–Radius of rotor, r_p – pole tip radius, w_{sy} – width of stator yoke, w_{ry} – width of rotor yoke. Gap area, $A_g = w_p.l_p$, (w_p-width of pole, l_p-length of pole) , n_p-Number of poles.

3 Multi-objective Optimization Problem

The multi-objective optimization problem consists of objective functions to be optimized by design variables while satisfying certain constraints.

3.1 Input Parameters

Permeability of vacuum, $\mu_0 = 4\pi \times 10^{-7} H / m$; Resistivity, $\rho = 2\times10^{-5}\,\Omega m$; air gap length, $l_g = 0.001m$; radius of journal, $r_j = 0.03m$; width of stator yoke, $w_{sy} = 0.01m$; saturated flux density, $B_{sat} = 1.2T$; minimum flux density, $B_{\min} = 0.2T$; coil mmf loss factor, $K_i = 1.394$; actuator loss factor, $K_a = 1.072$; coil packing factor, $\eta = 0.85$; Electromagnetic force, $F = 350N$; Maximum volume of coil, $V_{\max} = 0.00039m^3$; maximum copper loss, $P_{\max} = 500W$; Iron saturation factor, $\alpha = 0.5$; weight densities of stator and coil, $\rho_s = 7770kg / m^3$; $\rho_c = 8910kg / m^3$; current density, $J_{ub} = 600000A / m^2$; Basic seed=0.1;crossover 0.6;Mutations=0.01.

3.2 Bounds for the Variables

$r_{c_{min}} = 0.3m, r_{c_{max}} = 0.8m, r_{p_{min}} = 0.03m, r_{p_{max}} = 0.08m, l_{c_{min}} = 0.2m, l_{c_{max}} = 0.8m, \quad n_{p_{min}} = 4, n_{p_{max}} = 12;$

3.3 Objective Functions

When the genetic algorithm is applied to two objective functions, namely the copper power-loss in the magnetic coil and the weight of the magnetic bearing, , it is observed that these are mutually conflictive [6], i.e. with the decrease in the power-loss causes an equivalent increase in the weight and visa versa.

3.3.1 Power-Loss in the Coil

The standard form of expression of the power-loss in the coil is given as

$$P = \rho \eta J^2 A_c V_c \tag{1}$$

3.3.2 Weight of the Magnetic Bearing

The overall weight of the magnetic bearing, W , could be expressed as

$$W = W_c + W_s \tag{2}$$

Where, Weight of coil and stator is

$$W_c = \rho_c V_c \text{ and } W_s = \rho_s V_s \tag{3}$$

3.4 Constraints

The maximum and minimum magnetic flux densities of the stator that are required to support the maximum and minimum loads. Hence electromagnetic force are expressed as

$$F_{max,min} = (0.25 \mu_0 A_g) \left(\frac{K_i n_p i_{max,min}}{K_a l_{g_{max,min}}} \right) \tag{4}$$

$$n_p i_{max,min} = \eta A_c J_{max,min} \tag{5}$$

$$J_{max,min} = \left(\frac{K_a l_{g_{max,min}}}{K_i \eta A_c} \right) \sqrt{\frac{4 F_{max,min}}{\mu_0 A_g}} \tag{6}$$

Hence, constraint becomes,

$$J_{sat} \geq J_{max} ; J_{min} \geq 0 \tag{7}$$

The summary of the formulation of the magnetic bearing design for the multi-objective optimization

Minimize $f_i(x_i) = 1,2$ where, x = $\{r_c, r_p, l_c, n_p\}$

Subject to ; $g_i(x) \geq 0$; $j = 1,2\ldots6$; $h_k(x) = 0$, $k = 1,2$; $x^p \leq x_p \leq x^p; p = 1,\ldots,3$.

Where $f_1(x) = p_{cu}$; $f_2(x) = W$. $g_1(x) = J_{sat} - J_{\max}$; $g_2(x) = J_{\min}$;

$g_3(x) = \alpha_{\max} B_{sat} - B_{\max}$; $g_5(x) = V_{\max} - V_c$; $g_4(x) = B_{\min} - \alpha_{\min} B_{sat}$;

$g_6(x) = P_{\max} - P$; $h_1(x) = F_{\max} - F(l_{g_{\max}}, i_{\max})$; $h_2(x) = F_{\min} - F(l_{g_{\min}}, i_{\min})$;

4 Results and Discussions

In this paper, a multi-objective optimization of magnetic bearings for 100 population, 100 runs and 1000 generation have been presented and illustrated. The non-dominated sorting genetic algorithm-II (NSGA-II) [6] is implemented. The algorithm involves the single point crossover and the bitwise mutation for binary variables, the simulated binary crossover (SBX) and the polynomial mutation for real coded variables, and the parameter-less approach is used to handle constraints.

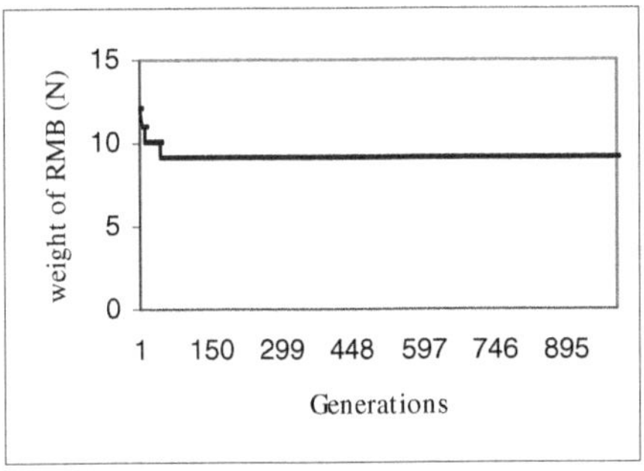

Fig. 2. Optimized power loss

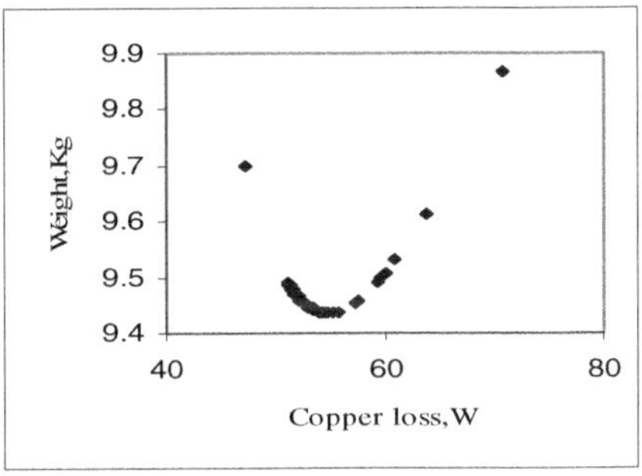

Fig. 3. Copper loss versus bearing weight

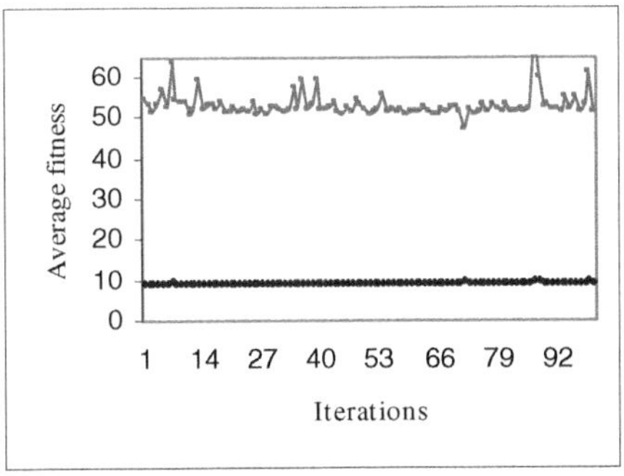

Fig. 4. Average loss and weight for 100 runs

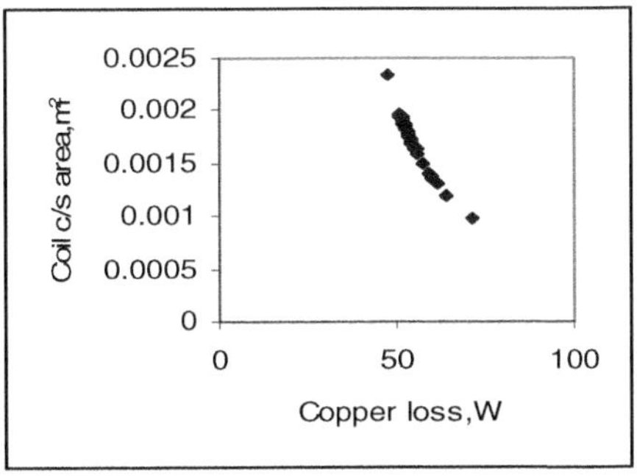

Fig. 5. Copper loss versus coil area

From fig.3 it is observed that decrease in the power-loss causes an equivalent increase in the weight and visa versa. It is found that optimum weight of bearing is 9.44 Kg where as optimum copper loss is 53.51W.

Fig.4 shows average values for loss and weight for different iterations. Fig. 5 shows with increase in coil area copper loss decreases.

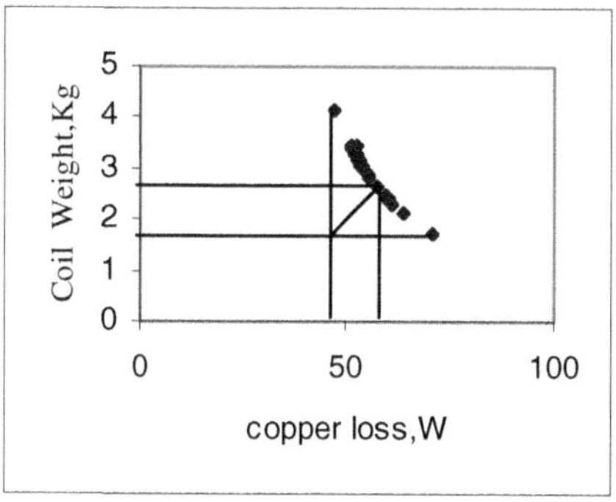

Fig. 6. Copper loss versus coil weight

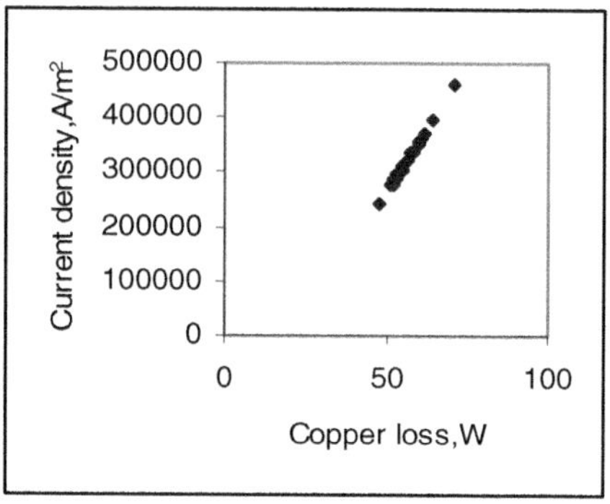

Fig. 7. Copper loss versus current density

5 Conclusion

The optimum values of variables are found at run 98.Optimum values of the coil space radius, pole tip radius, coil length, number of poles are 0.437m, 0.032m, 0.203m and 8 poles respectively. These are at 27.4%, 4%, 19.4% and 12.5% of feasible ranges, respectively. All the variables are near the lower limit of the feasible range. Fig.6 shows an increase of 43.72 % in the power-loss generated a decrease of 37.19 % in the coil weight. Also fig.7 shows copper loss increases with increase in current density in coil.

References

1. Chang, H., Chung, S.C.: Integrated Design of Radial Active Magnetic Bearing Systems using Genetic Algorithms. Mechatronics 12(1), 19–36 (2002)
2. Marler, R.T., Arora, J.S.: Survey of multiobjective optimization methods for engineering, vol. 26, pp. 369–395. Springer, Heidelberg (2004)
3. Rao, J.S., Tiwari, R.: Design Optimization of Thrust Magnetic Bearings Using Genetic Algorithms. In: 7th IFTOMM-Conference on Rotor Dynamics, Vienna, Austria, pp. 25–28 (September 2006)
4. Bakay, L., Dubois, M.: Losses in an optimized 8-pole radial magnetic bearing for long term flywheel energy storage. IEEE Transaction on Magnetic, 3–5 (2007)
5. Rao, B.R., Tiwari, R.: Optimum design of rolling element bearing using genetic algorithm. Mechanism and Machine Theory, 233–250 (2007)

6. Rao, J.S., Tivari, R.: Optimum design and analysis of thrust magnetic beating using genetic Algorithm. International Journal for Computational Methods in Engineering Science and Mechanics 9, 223–245 (2008)
7. Bakay, L., Dubois, M., Ruel, J.: Mass-Loss relationship optimized 8-pole AMB for long term flywheel energy storage. IEEE, 2–3 (2009)
8. Maslen, E.H.: Text book on Magnetic Bearings. University of Virginia 36(4), 1009–1013 (2000)

Dynamic Modelling and Control of Doubly Fed Induction Generator Variable Speed Wind Turbine

Seyed Zeinolabedin Moussavi and Reza Atapour

Faculty of Electrical and Computer Engineering,
Shahid Rajaee Teacher Training University, Tehran, Iran
smoussavi@srttu.edu, atapour2002@yahoo.com

Abstract. Tendency to erect ever more wind turbines can be observed in order to reduce the environmental consequences of conventional power generation. As a result of this, in the near future, wind turbines may start to influence the behavior of the power systems. Therefore, wind turbine models that can be integrated into power system simulation software are needed. Even more the wind farms are today required to participate actively in grid operation by an appropriate generation control scheme. In this paper, the modelling and dynamic behavior of a variable speed wind turbine with pitch control capability is explained in detail and the turbine performance characteristics are simulated in the MATLAB/SIMULINK. The paper also presents a comparative study on the performance of two control strategies for variable speed wind turbines.

Keywords: Doubly Fed Induction Generator (DFIG), Modelling, Wind Turbine Control System , Variable Speed Wind Turbine(VSWT).

1 Introduction

One way of addressing the rising energy demands and growing environmental concerns, is to harness green sources of power. Among these, tapping wind energy with wind turbines (WT) appears to be the most promising source of renewable energy. Wind energy conversion systems are used to capture the energy available in the wind to convert into electrical energy. A wind energy conversion system is a complex system in which knowledge from a wide array of fields comprising of aerodynamics, mechanical, civil and electrical engineering come together. The principle components of a modern wind turbine are the tower, the rotor and the nacelle, which accommodates the transmission mechanisms and the generator. The wind turbine captures the wind's kinetic energy in the rotor consisting of two or more blades mechanically coupled to generator [1]. The main component of the mechanical assembly is the gearbox, which transforms the slower rotational speeds of the wind turbine to higher rotational speeds on the generator side. The rotation of the generator's shaft driven by the wind turbine generates electricity, whose output is maintained as per specifications, by employing suitable control and supervising techniques. Besides monitoring the output, these control systems also include protection systems to protect the overall system. However, a tendency to maximize the amount of electricity generated from

V.V. Das and N. Thankachan (Eds.): CIIT 2011, CCIS 250, pp. 78–86, 2011.

wind can be observed. The increase of wind power penetration on power systems has led to a gradual substitution of conventional power plants by the current wind farms. Therefore, the wind farms are today required to participate actively in the power system operation as conventional power plants. Thus, the power system operators have revised the grid connection requirements for wind turbines and wind farms [3–5], demanding an operational behavior with several control tasks similar to those of conventional power plants. One of these control tasks is the capability of generation control, both active and reactive powers of a wind turbine. In this case, the system operator defines the operating requirements to be followed by the wind farms ensuring a reliable and safe power system operation.

Therefore, the penetration of wind turbines in electrical power systems will increase, they may begin to influence overall power system behavior and it will no longer be possible to run a power system by only controlling large scale power plants. It is therefore important to study the behavior of wind turbines in to the power system and their interaction with other generation equipment and with loads. Most of the control strategies for DFIG wind turbines referred in literature [6–10] are based on producing the maximum power for the best conditions of economic exploitation, when all the produced energy can be delivered to the grid. In this case, the wind turbine operates with optimum power efficiency for a wide range of wind speeds, without exceeding the rated power and with the desired power factor or generation voltage. However, as commented before, the wind turbines are today demanded to regulate both active and reactive powers according to the power set points ordered by the wind farm control system, which are defined considering the generation capability (related to the wind speed) and the grid power needs. Therefore, the present article focuses on the study of the control systems for DFIG wind turbines when regulating power. The main purpose of this work is to perform a comparative study of these control systems for DFIG wind turbines when regulating power, both the active and reactive powers, by means of simulations of DFIG wind turbines integrated in a wind farm with centralized control system.

The paper is organized as follows: On the first paragraph system is described, followed by system modelling of a DFIG on the next paragraph. Two control systems for DFIG wind turbines are explained in the last forth paragrath. The model and the control systems for DFIG wind turbines used in this work have been validated and comparison have been made with the DFIG wind turbine model included in the Sim Power Systems library of MATLAB/Simulink on the fifth paragraph and finally conclusion is provided.

2 DFIG Wind Turbine Model

2.1 Rotor Modelling

A simplified way of modelling the wind turbine rotor is normally used when the electrical behavior of the system is the main point of interest. An algebraic relation between wind speed and mechanical power extracted is assumed,which is described by the following equation:

$$P_w = \frac{1}{2}\rho A_r C_p(\lambda,\theta)v_w^3 \tag{1}$$

Where $\boldsymbol{P_w}$ is the power extracted from the wind [W]; $\boldsymbol{\rho}$ is the air density [kg/m]; $\boldsymbol{C_p}$ is the performance coefficient or power coefficient; $\boldsymbol{\lambda}$ is the tip speed ratio; $\boldsymbol{\theta}$ is the pitch angle of rotor blades [deg]; and $\boldsymbol{A_r}$ is the area covered by the rotor [m]. Numerical approximations have been developed to calculate $\boldsymbol{C_p}$for given values of $\boldsymbol{\lambda}$ and $\boldsymbol{\theta}$. Here, the following approximation is used:

$$C_p(\lambda,\theta) = 0.73\left(\frac{151}{\lambda_i} - 0.58\theta - 0.002\theta^{2.14} - 13.2\right)e^{-\frac{18.4}{\lambda_i}} \tag{2}$$

With

$$\lambda_i = \frac{1}{\frac{1}{\lambda - 0.02\theta} - \frac{0.003}{\theta^3 + 1}} \tag{3}$$

The maximum value of cp (c_{pmax}) is achieved for $\boldsymbol{\theta}$ = 0 degree.

2.2 Modelling of the Generator/Converter

When modelling the DFIG, the generator convention will be used, which means that the currents are outputs instead of inputs and real power and reactive power have a positive sign when they are fed into the grid. Using the generator convention, the following set of equations results,

$$v_{d(q)s} = R_s i_{d(q)s} \pm \Psi_{q(d)s} + \frac{1}{\omega_s}\frac{d\Psi_{d(q)s}}{dt} \quad , \quad v_{d(q)r} = R_r i_{d(q)r} \mp s\Psi_{q(d)r} + \frac{1}{\omega_s}\frac{d\Psi_{d(q)r}}{dt} \tag{4}$$

with v the voltage [V], R the resistance [ ], i the current [A], $_s$ the stator electrical frequency [rad/s], Ψ the flux linkage [VS] and s the rotor slip.

The indices d and q indicate the direct and quadrature axis components . s and r indicate stator and rotor quantities. All quantities are functions of time. The d-q reference frame is rotating at synchronous speed with the q-axis 90° ahead of the d-axis. The position of the d-axis coincides with the maximum of the stator flux, which means that V_{qs}, equals the terminal voltage , and V_{ds} equals zero. The flux linkages can be calculated using the following set of equations in per unit:

$$\Psi_{q(d)s} = X_s i_{q(d)s} + X_m i_{q(d)r} \, , \quad \Psi_{q(d)r} = X_r i_{q(d)r} + X_m i_{q(d)s} \tag{5}$$

with X_m the mutual reactance , X_s and X_r the stator and rotor leakage reactances respectively. The active power P and reactive power Q generated by the DFIG is equal with:

$$P = v_{ds}i_{ds} + v_{qs}i_{qs} + v_{dr}i_{dr} + v_{qr}i_{qr} \quad , \quad Q = v_{qs}i_{ds} - v_{ds}i_{qs} + v_{qr}i_{dr} - v_{dr}i_{qr} \tag{6}$$

The following equation gives the electro mechanical torque generated by the DFIG:

$$T_e = \psi_{dr} i_{qr} - \psi_{qr} i_{dr} \tag{7}$$

The mechanical torque can be calculated by dividing the power extracted from the wind that results from equations (1) to (7) by the mechanical generator frequency ω_m.The changes in generator speed that result from a difference in electrical and mechanical torque can be calculated using the generator equation of motion:

$$\frac{d\omega_m}{dt} = \frac{1}{2H}(T_m - T_e) \tag{8}$$

in which H is the inertia constant [s] and T_m is the mechanical torque.

3 Wind Turbine Control Systems

The aims of the control system of a DFIG wind turbine are the following:

- -maximize the power extracted from the wind for a wide range of wind speeds (also known as power optimization),
- - limit the output power to the rated power for high winds (power limitation),
- - adjust both active and reactive powers to a set point ordered by the wind farm control system (power regulation) when trying to adjust the wind farm production to the settings specified by the power system operator. In a DFIG wind turbine, this power control is performed by an appropriate control of the power converter and the blade pitch angle. Hence, to work effectively, the power converter must be controlled in collaboration with the blade pitch angle control.The converter is controlled by acting on the direct and quadrature components of the rotor voltage. This allows the decoupled control of active and reactive powers. Two control approaches are presented in this paper. The first approach is based on controlling the active power with the blade pitch angle, the rotational speed by the quadrature component of rotor current, and the reactive power with the direct component of rotor current. The second approach is based on controlling the active power with the quadrature component of the rotor voltage, the rotational speed by the blade pitch angle and the reactive power with the direct component of the rotor voltage. For the reactive power control, the two control systems present the same controller, based on controlling the direct component of the rotor voltage u_{dr}. The u_{dr} controller determines the direct component of rotor voltage, enabling the wind turbine operation with the desired reactive power. It includes three control loops, as shown in Fig. 1 Regarding the control of active power and generator speed, which has been performed by the quadrature component of the rotor voltage u_{qr} and the pitch angle , the control systems 1 and 2 present a different control scheme. In the design of the active power control for the two control systems described below and both for the power optimization and power limitation strategies, it is assumed that whenever the wind turbine can deliver all the available energy to the grid, the active power set point will be set up to its rated value.

3.1 Control System 1

This control system presents the following characteristics: (1) the speed is controlled by acting on the quadrature component of the rotor voltage; (2) the active power is controlled by acting on the pitch angle. The u_{qr} controller (Fig. 2a) is a rotational speed controller. It controls the generator speed in order to maximize the power extracted from the wind (power optimization) without exceeding the rated power of the generator (power limitation) or to adjust the output power to the power set point ordered by the wind farm control system when a reduction of power is demanded (down power regulation). The pitch angle controller (Fig.2b) acts as an active power controller, adjusting the pitch angle . Thus, the power coefficient and the power extracted from the wind are reduced. This controller keeps the blade pitch angle at its optimal value with power optimization strategy. Likewise, the controller enables the wind turbine to adjust the output power to a set point (rated power for high winds or the reference power required with down power regulation). When the output power goes up to the reference power, the controller acts adjusting the pitch angle and thus limiting the output power to the reference value. The controller includes the rate and angle limiters for the pitch angle movement.

3.2 Control System 2

In the second control system, (1) the active power is controlled by the quadrature component of the rotor voltage and (2) the speed control adjusts the rotational speed to a reference speed derived from the optimum power–speed curve by acting on the blade pitch angle. The u_{qr} controller (Fig. 3a) is an active power controller that controls the output power by acting on the quadrature component of the rotor voltage. As described before, it is assumed that the wind turbine operates autonomously with power optimization and power limitation, receiving the rated power as a power set point from the wind farm control system. This controller uses the actual rotational speed to define the reference power according to the power–speed curve. The controller adjusts the output power to the value derived from the power–speed curve and the actual rotational speed. In the wind turbine control system, the available power is derived from the power–speed control curve and sent out to the wind farm control system. Therefore, the active power controller does not include the power–speed control curve to define the reference power, as it is proposed here.

The blade pitch angle controller (Fig. 3b) acts as a speed controller adjusting the pitch angle to reduce the power coefficient and the power extracted from the wind. The speed reference is generated from the optimum power–speed curve and the power reference. When the wind turbine operates with power optimization and power limitation strategies, the power reference is set up at the rated power and this controller acts limiting the rotational speed to the rated speed. In winds below rated and power optimization strategy, the generator speed is smaller than the rated speed, and thus the controller keeps the blade pitch angle at its optimal value. On the other hand, this controller acts on the blade pitch angle assuring the rated speed with power limitation strategy and winds above rated. With down power regulation, the rotational speed reference is derived from the power–speed curve and the reference power ordered by the wind farm control system, and the controller acts on the blade pitch angle assuring the rotational speed.

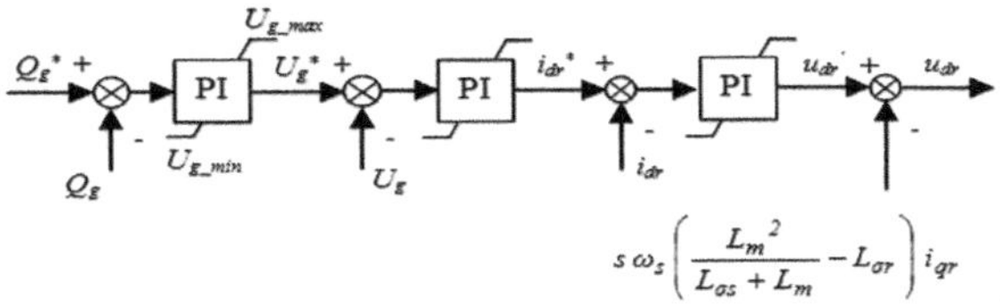

15

Fig. 1. Reactive power controller

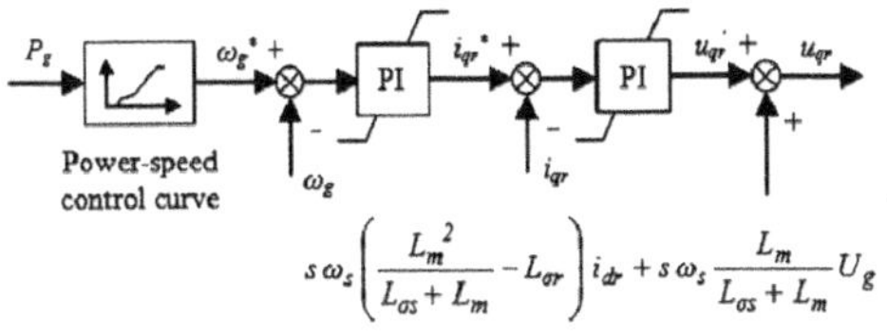

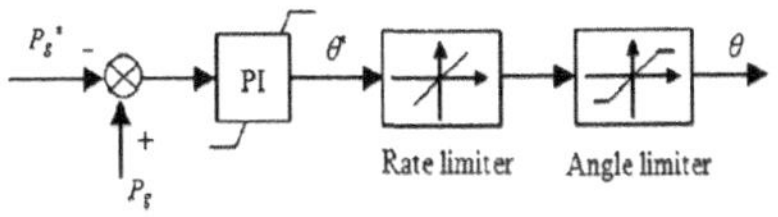

Fig. 2a. **Fig. 2b.**

Fig. 2. Control system 1

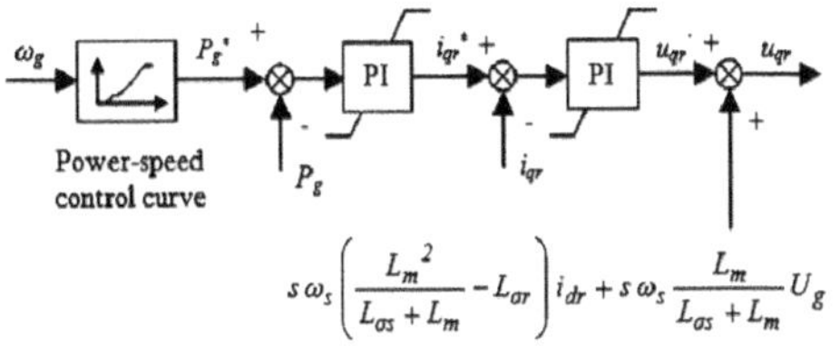

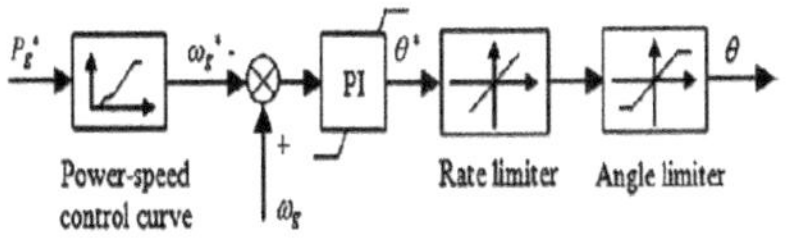

Fig. 3a. **Fig. 3b.**

Fig. 3. Control system 2

4 Validation of the Wind Turbine Model and Control Systems

The wind turbine model and control systems used in this work have been validated by comparison of the simulated responses with the one obtained by the built-in model for the DFIG wind turbine included in the SimPowerSystems library of MATLAB/Simulink. The DFIG wind turbine considered in this work presents a rated power of 1.5 MW and 525 V. To evaluate the control systems, two wind turbines have been simulated in MATLAB/Simulinks environment. Each wind turbine is controlled by one of the proposed control systems. The wind turbines have been simulated operating with the unity power factor (zero reactive power). Their responses are compared with the one obtained by the simulation of the built-in model included in SimPowerSystems.This comparison analysis is illustrated in Fig. 4,5,6. where the active power , the rotational speed, the pitch angle are presented. When the responses are compared, the following conclusions can be inferred: The responses show a high degree of correspondence for all the variables shown. In winds below rated , the wind turbine generates below rated power, it operates at variable speed and the pitch angle is kept at a minimum degree . In winds above rated, the control system adjusts the output power to the rated power, limits the rotational speed to the rated speed and acts on the pitch angle limiting the power extracted from the wind. Furthermore, the wind turbine operates with zero reactive power (unity power factor) during all the simulation. Fig.7 shows the response of DFIG and control system to wind speed's change and disturbance. Assume that at time 25s wind speed is increased from 10 m/s to 18 m/s.The generated active power starts increasing smoothly (together with the turbine speed) to reach its rated value of 1 pu in approximately 15s. Over that time frame the turbine speed will have increased from 0.8 pu to 1.21 pu. Initialy, the pitch angle of the turbine blades is zero degree and the turbine operating point follows the turbine power characteristics up to point nominal value. Then the pitch angle is increased from zero deg in order to limit the mechanical power.

5 Conclusion

The present paper presents a comparative study on the performance of two control strategies for DFIG wind turbines when they operate with power regulation, both active and reactive power to a set point ordered by the wind farm control system. The power control of a DFIG wind turbine is achieved by an appropriate control of the direct and quadrature components of the rotor voltage, performed through the power converter, in collaboration with the blade pitch angle control. In this work, two possible ways to control these variables have been investigated. For the reactive power control, the two control systems present the same controller, based on controlling the direct component of the rotor voltage u_{dr}. Regarding the control of the active power and the generator speed, performed by the quadrature component of the rotor voltage u_{qr} and the pitch angle , the control systems 1and 2 present a different control scheme.In the control system 1, the speed control is performed acting on the quadrature component of the rotor voltage, and the active power is controlled by the pitch angle. In the control system 2, the active power is controlled by the quadrature component of the rotor voltage, and the rotational speed is controlled to a speed reference derived from the power–speed curve control by acting on the pitch angle. The simulation results illustrate the capability of the described control systems to control the power production, both active and reactive powers, of a DFIG wind turbine in any operating conditions.

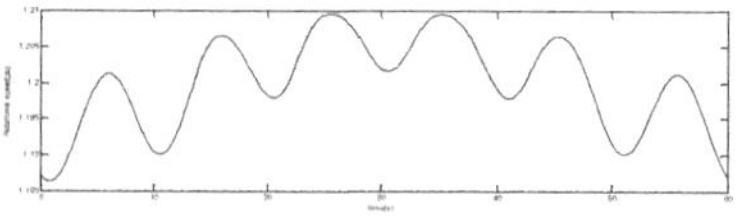

Fig. 4a.

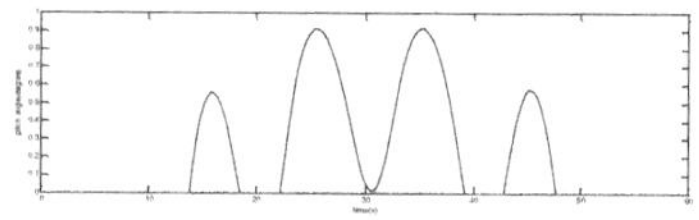

Fig. 4b.

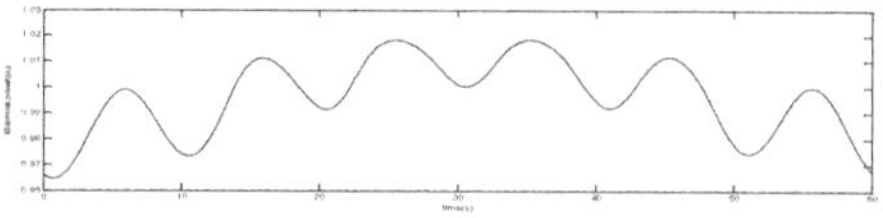

Fig. 4c.

Fig. 4. Validation of the model and the control system 1: respectively: rotational speed, pitch angle, active power

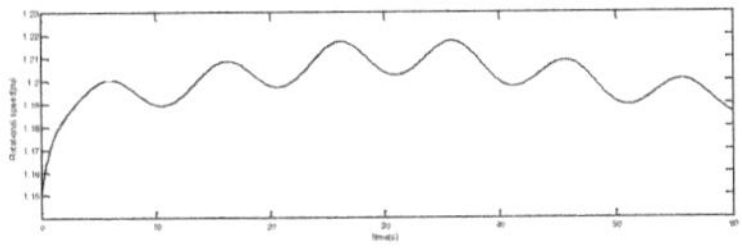

Fig. 5a.

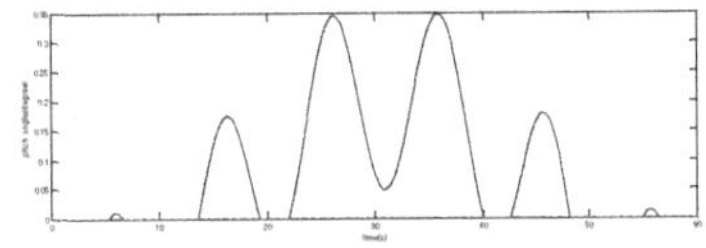

Fig. 5b.

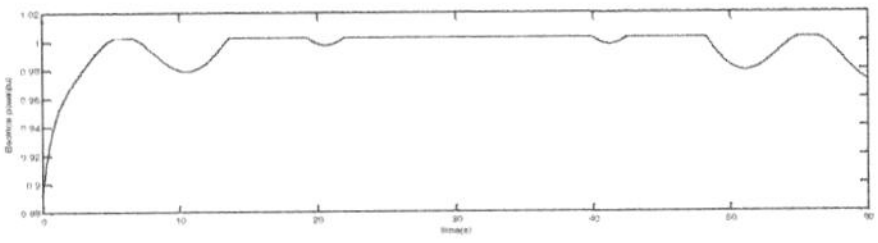

Fig. 5c.

Fig. 5. Validation of the model and the control system 2: respectively: rotational speed, pitch angle, active power

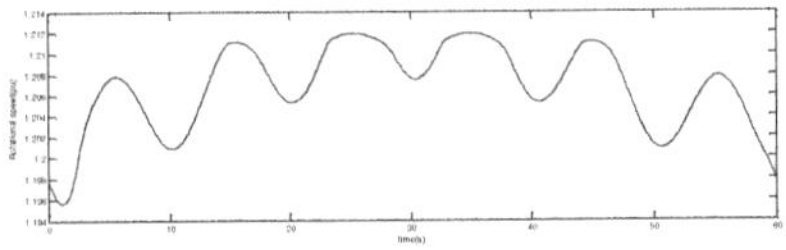

Fig. 6a.

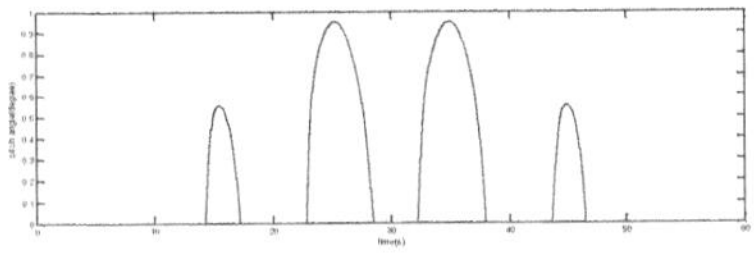

Fig. 6b.

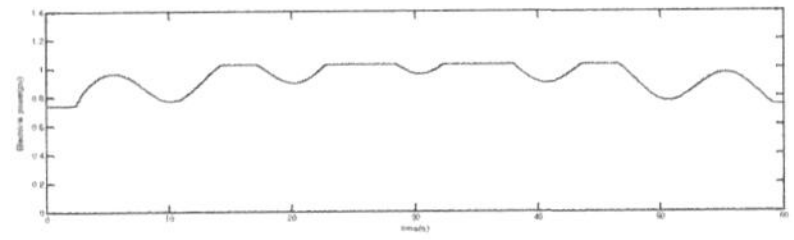

Fig. 6c.

Fig. 6. Validation of the model and the control system included in the SimPowerSystems library of MATLAB/Simulink: respectively: rotational speed, pitch angle, active power

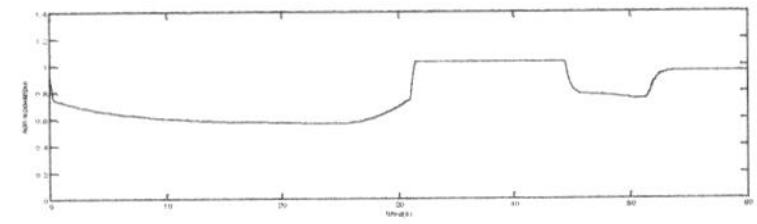

Fig. 7a.

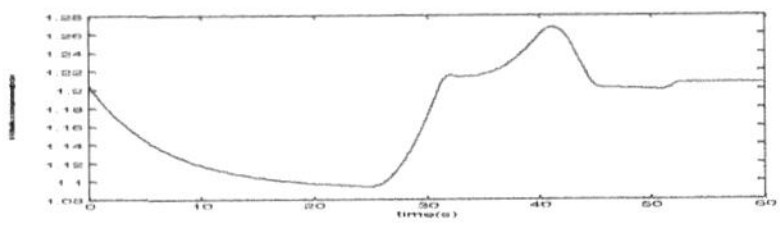

Fig. 7b.

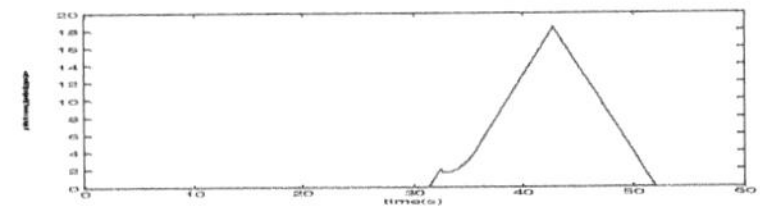

Fig. 7c.

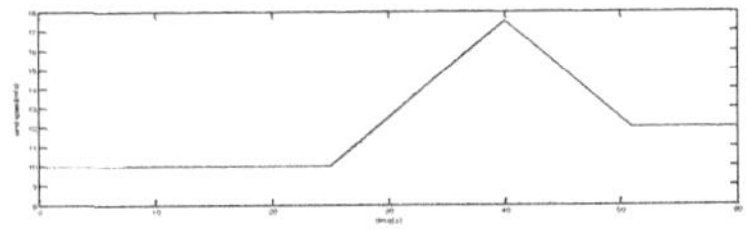

Fig. 7d.

Fig. 7. Response of DFIG when wind disturbance is occurred, respectively: active power, rotational speed, pitch angle, wind speed

References

1. Moussavi, S.Z., Kashkooli, F.R.: Stability assessment of wind power generation into the power system. In: 4th IEEE International Conference and Information Technology (2011)
2. Slootweg, J.G., Polinder, H., Kling, W.L.: Representing wind turbine electrical generating systems in fundamental frequency simulations. IEEE Trans. Energy Convers 18(4), 516–524 (2003)
3. Tapia, A., Tapia, G., Ostolaza, J.X., Saenz, J.R.: Modelling and control of a wind driven doubly fed induction generator. IEEE Trans. Energy Convers 18(2), 194–204 (2003)
4. Ekanayake, J.B., Holdsworth, L., Wu, X., Jenkins, N.: Dynamic modelling of doubly fed induction generator wind turbines. IEEE Trans. Power Syst. 18(2), 803–839 (2003)
5. Nunes, M.V.A., Pec-as, J.A., Zürn, H.H., Bezerra, U.H., Almeida, R.G.: Influence of the variable-speed wind generators in transient stability margin of the conventional generators integrated in electrical grids. IEEE Trans. Energy Convers 19(4), 692–701 (2004)
6. Lei, Y., Mullane, A., Lightbody, G., Yacamini, R.: Modelling of the wind turbine with a doubly fed induction generator for grid integration studies. IEEE Trans. Energy Convers 21(1), 257–264 (2006)
7. Rodriguez-Amenedo, J.L., Arnalte, S., Burgos, J.C.: Automatic generation control of a wind farm with variable speed wind turbines. IEEE Trans. Energy Convers 17(2), 279–284 (2002)
8. Hansen, A.D., Sørensen, P., Iov, F., Blaabjeg, F.: Centralised power control of wind farm with doubly fed induction generators. Renewable Energy 31(7), 935–951 (2006)
9. Sørensen, P., Hansen, A.D., Iov, F., Blaabjerg, F., Donovan, M.H.: Wind farm models and control strategies, report Risø-R-1464(EN). Risø National Laboratory, Roskilde (2005)
10. De Almeida, R.G., Castronuovo, E.D., Lopes, J.A.P.: Optimum generation control in wind parks when carrying out system operator requests. IEEE Trans. Power Syst. 21(2), 718–725 (2006)
11. Fernandez, L.M., Jurado, F., Saenz, J.R.: Aggregated dynamic model for wind farms with doubly fed induction generator wind turbines. Renewable Energy 33(1), 129–140 (2008)
12. Flores, P., Tapia, A., Tapia, G.: Application of a control algorithm for wind speed prediction and active power generation. Renewable Energy 30(4), 523–536 (2005)
13. Slootweg, J.G., Polinder, H., Kling, W.L.: Dynamic modelling of a wind turbine with doubly fed induction generator, 0-7803-7173-9/01/$10.00 © 2001 IEEE
14. Fernandez, L.M., Garcia, C.A., Jurado, F.: Comparative study on the performance of control systems for doubly fed induction generator (DFIG) wind turbines operating with power regulation. Energy 33, 1438–1452 (2008)
15. Heier, S.: Orid integration of Wind Energy Conversion Systems. John Wiley& Sons Ltd., Chicester (1998)

Ultra Low Power 50 nm SRAM for Temperature Invariant Data Retention

H.P. Rajani[1] and Shrimannarayan Kulkarni[2]

[1] K.L.E. Society's College of Engineering & Technology, Belgaum, India
hprajani@yahoo.com
[2] NMAM Institute of Technology, Nitte, India
sy_kul@yahoo.com

Abstract. Power efficient SRAM cell with temperature invariant data retention is very vital component in the design of deep-submicron Static memories. A novel ultra low power stable 8T-SRAM cell for 50 nm CMOS technology is analyzed for data retention property in this paper. It exhibits power reduction both in active mode and standby modes of operation and ideal data retention at operating temperature range of -50^{0}C to 150^{0}C. Two additional NMOS transistors, one each in the pull down path the two inverters of standard 6-T SRAM cell utilize self correcting feedback to provide this performance. During the active mode one of the inverters (OFF) utilizes stack effect and the other inverter (ON) uses cascode amplification property to reduce power dissipation. Sub threshold leakage power is reduced by utilizing stack effect in the idle mode. Simulations using BSIM 4 models for 50nm technology and supply voltage value of 0.5V, indicate about 23X power savings in active mode and 28 X times in stand-by(data-retention) mode at 50^{0}C. The logic 1 data of the SRAM cell is retained at 499.74 mV for V_{DD} of 500mV during standby (data retention) mode.

Keywords: subthreshold leakage power, stack effect, active mode power, data retention, cascode amplification, static random-access memory (SRAM).

1 Introduction

The performance as well as power dissipation of processors and System on Chips (SoCs) has phenomenally increased due to ever increasing levels of on chip integration. Reducing Static Random Access Memory (SRAM) power is critical to improve energy efficiency of mobile multimedia systems performing video/audio processing applications since larger portions of processors are being devoted to cache and memory structure [1]. Power consumption of Complementary Metal Oxide Semiconductor (CMOS) circuits consists of dynamic and static components. Dynamic power depends upon number of actively switching transistors and static power, especially subthreshold leakage power is consumed even when the transistors are not switching. However recent studies [2] indicate that dynamic power is a greater concern in some SoC designs, while leakage power dominates in others. A good VLSI

V.V. Das and N. Thankachan (Eds.): CIIT 2011, CCIS 250, pp. 87–92, 2011.

design should be aiming at both static and dynamic power reduction. Minimization of power both in active and stand-by modes while maintaining state retention at the entire operating temperature range are major design issues for current low power systems and SRAMs.

This paper discusses a novel 8-Transistor (8-T) SRAM cell which minimizes active mode power dissipation as well as the leakage power dissipation while providing ideal data state retention for large variations in temperature from -50 ^{0}C to 150 ^{0}C.

2 Related Work

Clock gating, Multi-V_{DD}, Dynamic frequency voltage scaling (DFVS), adaptive voltage scaling (AVS), power gating, Body biasing, Multi-V_{th}, Transistor stacking are some of circuit and micro architectural techniques for active and leakage power reduction [3, 4,5].

Additional NMOS/ PMOS transistor is used to gate power in Gated-V_{DD} technique [6]. In Data Retention Gated-Ground (DRG)-Cache [7] the Gated-V_{DD} control is supplied by the word line; the stability of the gated- V_{DD} cells reduces substantially with lower V_{TH} transistors and the stored data may be deleted. In [8], a special standby mode, a sleep mode is introduced, to diminish the leakage in the cell and to retain memory cell data. In Drowsy Caches approach inactive cache lines are allocated to a low-power mode, where a low standby V_{DD} is used to reduce leakage [9].

Conventional 6-T SRAM cell with dual bit line architecture is shown Fig.1. Power utilization of this cell is large both during active and stand-by mode of operations. The Gated – power SRAM cell (using 7/8 transistors) proposed in [5], results in reduced subthreshold leakage power due to stack effect. Due to the absence of a discharge path, Gated – power SRAM cell is less stable in the face of process and environment variations and cell state gets corrupted. A 10-T SRAM cell structure called the quasi-power-gated-SRAM (QPG-SRAM) is proposed in [10], to overcome the problem of decreased stability. QPG-SRAM cell exhibits better power savings as well as data retention as compared to both previous circuits but uses 10 transistors resulting in more area. A novel 8-T SRAM for substantial active power reduction using self correcting feedback is discussed in [11].

3 Ultra Low Power 8-T SRAM Cell for Ideal Data Retention

Novel ultra low power stable 8-T SRAM cell at 50nm CMOS Technology consists of two additional NMOS transistors M7 and M8, one each in the pull down path of conventional SRAM cell driven by the data nodes QN & Q respectively (Fig.2). WL is Word Select signal and complementary bit lines are BIT and BITN.

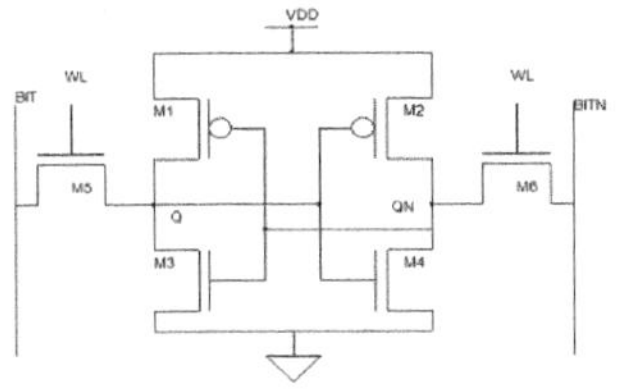

Fig. 1. Standard 6-T SRAM cell

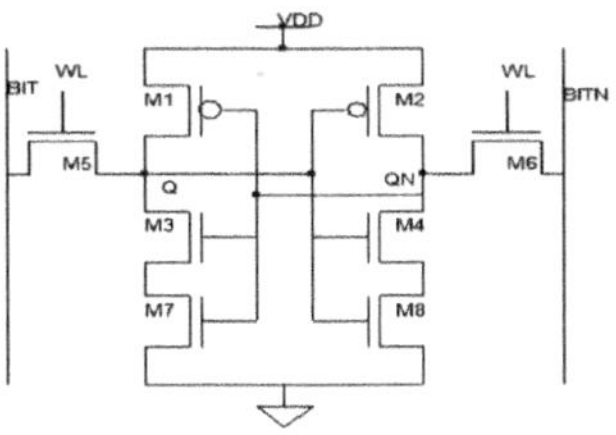

Fig. 2. Novel Ultra Low Power Stable 8-T SRAM Cell

3.1 Active Mode Operation

WRITE 1 operation: Word select signal WL =1, BIT =1 and BITN = 0. The access transistors M5 and M6 transmit BIT & BITN values to Q and QN. Transistors M4 and M8 are ON and M3 and M7 are OFF. Since the ON transistors M4 and M8 are in cascode configuration, the resistance is $r_{ds8}g_{m4}r_{ds4}$, where r_{ds8} is for M8, g_{m4} and r_{ds4} are for M4. The net current flowing through them will be lower than what it would be with a single ON transistors M4. Since serially connected transistors M3 and M7 are OFF, V_{SB} & threshold voltage increase while V_{GS} and V_{DS} of these transistors decrease which gives rise to sub threshold leakage current reduction due to stack effect. Thus current flowing through both inverters of SRAM is lowered and hence reduced power dissipation during active mode. Transistors M7and M8 do not hinder in the process of writing because

QN = 0 and Q =1, cause transistor M2 to be OFF and M1 to be ON. Thus Q is maintained at logic 1. The discharge path provided by the ON transistors M4 and M8 will help to drive node QN to logic 0 value. The logic 1 value written at node Q is prevented from getting discharged because both the transistors M3 and M7 are OFF, disconnecting the ground path. Since both the transistors M3 and M7 are off, due to the well-known stack property leakage current gets reduced.

WRITE 0 operation: Similarly while writing logic 0, Word select signal WL =0, BIT =0 and BITN = 1.This forces node Q = 0 and node QN = 1; the role of nodes Q and QN gets reversed and power dissipation gets reduced.

3.2 Standby Mode Operation

In the standby mode (idle mode), WL=0; bit lines BIT = BITN = 1(floating state).Both access transistors M5 and M6 are OFF and disconnect the SRAM cell from floating bit lines. Transistors M7 and M8 provide excellent feedback to retain the state of the SRAM cell to a good logic 1(0) value. The pull-up PMOS transistor driven by logic 0 storage node assists the node storing logic 1 in retaining that value. The ground discharge path provided by two series connected NMOS transistors aids the node storing logic 0 to retain the value. Stack effect is responsible to reduce subthreshold leakage power in the pair of OFF transistors; either (M3 or M7) or (M4 and M8) respectively for Q = 1 or Q = 0.

4 Simulation and Results

Simulations are performed using LTSPICE tool with advanced BSIM4 CMOS models for 50 nm technology. Active mode and Stand-by (state-retention) mode operations are simulated with word select signal WL, BIT and BITN values as given in section 3, for ultra low power stable 8-T SRAM cell for temperature range of -50^{0}C to 150 ^{0}C. Power dissipation and Logic 1 node voltage during both Active and Standby (data retention) mode are simulated for 6T SRAM, Gated SRAM and QPG SRAM also. 8-T SRAM cell results are compared with them. Steady-state leakage power dissipation of the stable 8-T SRAM Cell at 50^{0}C is considerably lower by about 28X, as compared to the standby leakage of the standard 6-T SRAM cell during idle(standby) mode with WL=0. Active mode power dissipation of the Stable 8-T SRAM Cell is also significantly lower by 23X, when WL=1. This 8-T SRAM cell is more stable in the face of process and environment variations, as observed in data retention voltage level at operating temperatures of -50°C, 100°C and 150°C. Fig.3 shows power dissipation and Fig.4 shows Logic 1 node voltage during both Active and Stand-by modes for different cells. Voltage at node Q, during write-1 and standby operation are depicted in Fig.5 and Fig.6 respectively at temperature=150^{0}C for WRITE pulse = 1ns and standby mode duration = 200ns.

Table 1. Power Dissipation in nW (VDD = 500mV)

Temp °C	6T SRAM		Gated SRAM		QPGSRAM		8TSRAM	
	Active	Standby	Active	Standby	Active	Standby	Active	Standby
-50	185.67	184.62	183.85	16.06	146.43	7.18	6.22	5.17
50	326.23	332.31	321.90	35.55	248.24	25.18	14.11	11.73
150	384.97	406.16	375.35	49.00	256.87	31.88	17.46	18.23

Table 2. Logic 1 Node Voltage in mV (VDD = 500mV)

Temp °C	6T SRAM		Gated SRAM		QPGSRAM		8TSRAM	
	Active	Standby	Active	Standby	Active	Standby	Active	Standby
-50	489.46	490.38	489.65	467.37	491.84	499.85	499.90	499.97
50	471.69	472.31	472.18	409.18	474.12	498.47	499.58	499.74
150	448.00	444.92	448.88	358.67	466.90	497.46	499.35	499.18

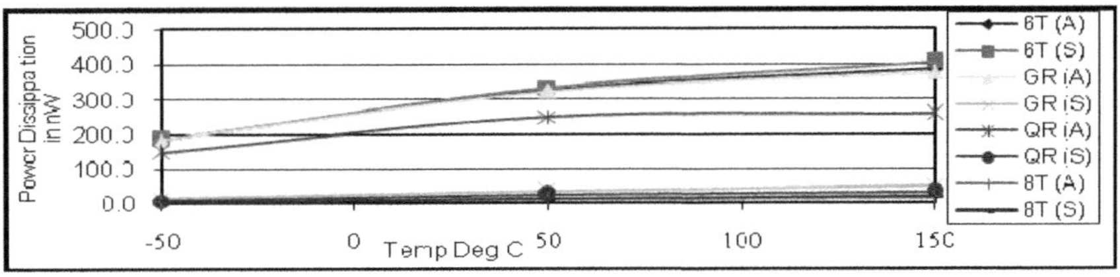

Fig. 3. Power dissipation during both Active and Stand- By modes

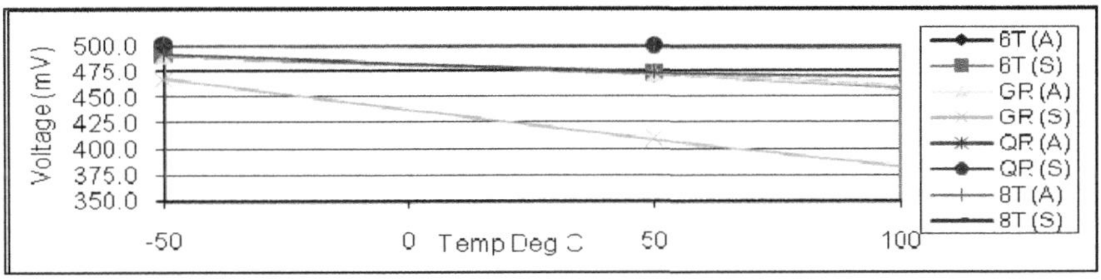

Fig. 4. Voltage at Logic 1 node during both Active and Stand- By modes

Key to legend: 6T-SRAM (6T), Gated–power SRAM (GR), 10–T QPG-SRAM (QR) 8-T SRAM (8T), Active mode (A) and standby mode (S)

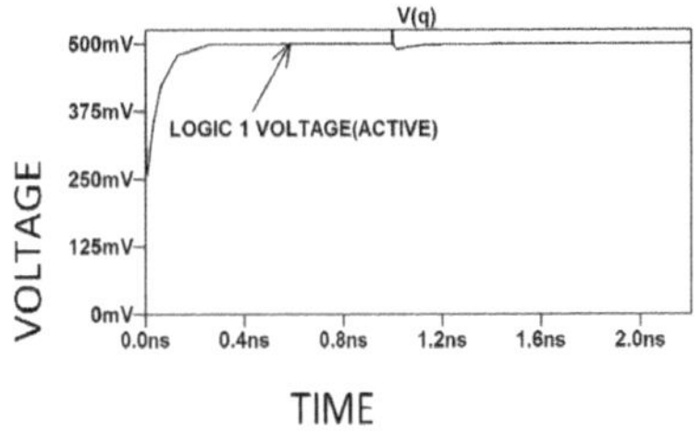

Fig. 5. Voltage at node Q during WRITE-1 Pulse = 1ns, temperature = 150°C

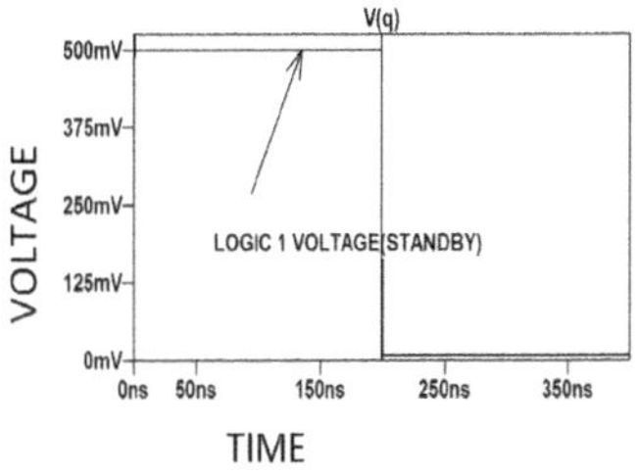

Fig. 6. Voltage at node Q during Standby Duration = 200ns, temperature =150°C

Active and Standby mode power dissipation in the novel 8-T SRAM cell is compared with all other cells in Table 1. Table 2 provides comparison of active and standby mode logic 1 state voltage level in the novel 8-T SRAM cell with other cells.

5 Conclusion

8 T SRAM cell resulted in about 24X power savings in active and 28X in idle mode. The logic 1 node voltage is at ideal value in temperature range of -50°C to 150°C.This cell exhibits stable data retention property. As compared to other representative low leakage power SRAM cells, 8-T SRAM cell achieves both active and leakage power savings using one circuit technique with only Word Select signal WL as the control signal.

References

1. Cho, M., Schlessman, J., Wolf, W., Mukhopadhyay, S.: Reconfigurable SRAM Architecture with Spatial Voltage Scaling for Low Power Mobile Multimedia Applications. IEEE Transactions on VLSI 19(1) (January 2011)
2. Goering, R.: Automating low power design– a progress report (September 2008), `http://www.SCD.source.com`
3. Roy, Mukhopadhyay, S., Mahmoodi, H., Meimand: Leakage Current Mechanisms and Leakage Reduction Techniques in Deep Sub micrometer CMOS Circuits. Proceedings of the IEEE 91(2) (February 2003)
4. Burd, T.D., Brodersen, R.W.: Design issues for dynamic voltage scaling. In: Proceedings of the 1998 International Symposium on Low Power Electronics and Design, pp. 9–14 (2000)
5. Park, J.C.: Sleepy Stack: a New Approach to Low Power VLSI Logic and Memory. A Thesis submitted at Georgia Institute of Technology (August 2005)
6. Powell, M.D., Yang, S.H., Falsafi, B., Roy, K., Vijaykumar, T.N.: Gated- VDD: A circuit technique to reduce leakage in cache memories. In: Proceedings of the 2000 International Symposium on Low Power Electronics and Design (July 2000)
7. Agarwal, A., Li, H., Roy, K.: DRG-Cache: A data retention gated-ground cache for low power. In: Proceedings of the 39th Design Automation Conference (June 2002)
8. Nii, K., et al.: A 90-nm low-power 32 KB embedded SRAM with Gate Leakage Suppression Circuit for Mobile Applications. IEEE J. Solid-State Circuits 39(4), 684–693 (2004)
9. Flautner, K., et al.: Drowsy caches: simple techniques for reducing leakage power. In: International Symposium on Computer Architecture, pp. 148–157 (May 2002)
10. Nair, P., Eratne, S., John, E.: A Quasi Power Gated Low Leakage Stable SRAM Cell. In: 53rd IEEE International Midwest Symposium on Circuits and Systems, MWSCAS 2010 (2010)
11. Rajani, H.P., Kulkarni, S.Y.: Novel Stable 8T SRAM for Power Minimization in Deep Submicron Cache Memories. In: Proceedings of International Conference on Emerging Trends in Engineering ICETE-II (May 2011)

An Optimum Checkpointing-Based Fault Tolerant Algorithm Using Mobile Agent in Distributed Systems

Farid Haji Zeinalabedin, Nassrin Eftekhari, and Abolfazl Torghi Haghighat

Computer & Electronic Department,
Islamic Azad University of Qazvin, Qazvin, Iran
{f.h.zeinalabedin,n.eftekhari,haghighat}@qiau.ac.ir

Abstract. Traditional message passing based checkpointing and rollback recovery algorithms perform well for tightly coupled systems. In wide area distributed systems these algorithms may suffer from large overhead due to message passing delay and network traffic. Mobile agent (MA) provides a new technology for implementing fault tolerant mechanism in distributed systems. MA has the merits of flexibility, low network traffic, efficiency, less communication latency, as well as highly asynchronous. So to design checkpointing and rollback recovery algorithms for wide area distributed systems, mobile agents are introduced. One of effective factors on performance of mobile agent based algorithms is number of migrations. In this paper we propose an optimum mobile agent based checkpointing protocol which attempts to eliminate useless migrations in different phases of checkpointing algorithm. The proposed algorithm will improve performance and network traffic greatly.

The effectiveness of proposed algorithms is evaluated by extensive simulation under a dataset including 7000 different connected graphs. Our results show a significant improvement in number of migrations and average execution time when these solutions are simulated.

Keywords: Fault Tolerant, distributed system, checkpointing, mobile agent, coordinated checkpointing, CGS, rollback recovery, non-blocking.

1 Introduction

The vast computing potential of distributed systems is often hampered by their susceptibility to failures. Therefore, many techniques such as rollback recovery have been developed to add reliability and high availability to these systems.Checkpointing with rollback recovery is a well-known method for achieving fault-tolerance in distributed systems. It gives fault tolerance without requiring additional efforts from the programmer [2].In checkpoint-based rollback recovery, recovery relies solely on saved checkpoints [3]. Upon a failure, checkpoint-based rollback recovery restores the system state to the most recent consistent set of checkpoints, i.e. the recovery line [5]. Checkpoint-based rollback-recovery algorithms can be classified into three categories: Coordinated (Synchronous) [1,2,4], Uncoordinated (Asynchronous) [1,4,5] and Communication Induced Checkpoints algorithms (CIC) and also called

V.V. Das and N. Thankachan (Eds.): CIIT 2011, CCIS 250, pp. 93–102, 2011.

Quasi-Synchronous [1,4].In this paper we propose an optimum mobile agent based checkpointing protocol which attempts to eliminate useless migrations in different phases of checkpointing algorithm. The proposed algorithm will improve performance and network traffic greatly. The rest of the paper is organized as follows: In the next section, we explain a checkpointing protocol. In section 3, we propose an improvement for checkpointing protocol. In section 4, we present simulation results.Finally, section 5 concludes the paper.

2 The Checkpointing Protocol

A set of checkpoints, with one checkpoint for every process, is said to be a *Consistent Global checkpointingState(CGS) or recovery line*. In the checkpointing algorithm [4], for each process, at most two checkpoints may have to be stored in the stable storage when checkpointing procedure is running; otherwise one checkpoint per process is enough to make a system consistent. Checkpoints have a one-bit version numbers (*v_no*). In the beginning all processes start by taking a permanent checkpoints with *v_no*= 0.This algorithm is non-blocking, i.e., even when a check-pointing process is running, processes are free to run their applications. To avoid orphan messages, every process tags the *v_no* of its latest checkpoint with each application message header. When a process receives an application message, it first compares application message's version no (*msg_v_no*) with its own current checkpoint *v_no*. If *msg_v_no* = (*v_no* + 1) mod 2 and *ckpt_state* = P then the receiver process decides that sender has taken a new checkpoint before sending the message and the checkpointing process is on. So the receiver first takes a checkpoint with *v_no* = *msg_v_no*. Then it sets *ckpt_state* = T and *msg_ckpt* = True before processing the message. Initially *msg_ckpt* is False for all processes. Each process has a list of all its neighbors (i.e., processes which are connected with this process by direct communication links). Each process may initiate checkpointing independently. The initiator creates a mobile agent, which travels across the network and creates a CGS. The mobile agent id (*agent_id*) is the same as the process id of its creator. The mobile agent moves to other processes following an execution path of depth-first search, starting from its creator. The agent maintains a stack and two lists. The stack, Stack, has the path to the root, as required by the DFS. The list *VL* (Visited List) is the list of processes which have been visited by this agent before any other agent in this checkpointing cycle. All these processes would thus have taken temporary checkpoints. Note that some of them may have taken the checkpoints induced by application messages, even before this agent reached them. *PLI* (Partial List of concurrent Initiators) is a list of processes who have initiated checkpointing. However, this list is not the complete list of initiators. If a process that has taken a check-point through another agent, is visited by our agent, the initiator of the other agent is added to *PLI*.

2.1 First Phase

Suppose, P_i is a checkpointing initiator.P_i creates a mobile agent with *agent_id* = i. The agent takes a temporary checkpoint (*ckpt_state*= T) and *v_no* equal to (*v_no*+1) mod 2. The *proc_id* of the current process, i, is pushed into the $Stack_i$. Then the agent leaves P_i and moves to a neighbor P_j.When an agent, MA_i, visits a process P_j , it halts the application process of *Pj* , adds its *agent_id (i)* to PLI_j . If it finds that the state of the current checkpoint of *Pj* is P ,MA_i takes a new temporary checkpoint for P_j with *ckpt_state* = T and *v_no* = (*v_no* + 1) mod 2. If any neighbor of P_j is yet to be visited, the agent moves to that neighbor and performs the same operation. Before leaving P_j, MA_i pushes j into Stack_i. If all neighbors of Pj have already been visited, then MAi moves back to the last process from which it came to Pj . The id of the last visited process is available at the top of $Stack_i$ (Top_Stack_i). Before leaving P_j ,MA_i puts j in VL_i.If P_j has already taken a temporary checkpoint (i.e., *ckpt_state* = T) then MA_i checks the flag *msg_ckpt*. If it is True then the current checkpoint was induced by an application message. MA_i sets *msg_ckpt* = False and adds j to VL_i. If *msg_ckpt* = False, then another agent, from a different initiator, has already visited this process. In both the cases, the information about the list of initiators available with the agent in PLI_i and the information on the same with P_j in PLI_j are merged and the updated information replaces both PLI_i and PLI_j . Finally, the agent leaves P_j and moves to either a yet unvisited neighbor of P_j (if *msg_ckpt* = True and such a neighbor exists) or to the process from which it came.At the end of first phase, mobile agent MA_i returns back to Pi and sets *CompletedFirstPhase* = True. Initially the flag was False. The topology of the graph is divided into clusters of processes such that processes in each cluster have taken checkpoints corresponding to one agent. The *PLI* of the agent, when it returns to its initiator, has the list of all the neighboring initiators. Whereas the *VL* of the agent, has the list of all the processes which have taken checkpoints induced by the agent.

2.2 Second Phase

In the second phase, the initiator with the minimum id generates the complete list of initiators. When an agent MA_i comes back to its initiator P_i, after the first phase, if PLI_i has an entry less than i, MA_i will remain at P_i. If all entries in PLI_i are greater than or equal to i, MA_i moves to a process, P_j in the list PLI_i.When MA_i, reaches P_j , it pushes j into $Stack_i$. If it finds that *CompletedFirstPhase* = False, then it waits for the return of MA_j . After MA_j returns, PLI_i and PLI_j are merged and the new list replaces both PLI_i and PLI_j . If the new list has an entry less than i, then MA_i is destroyed. If all entries in the list are greater than or equal to i, and if the list has a member so far not visited, MA_i moves to it. If all members have already been visited, it returns to the process it last came from. Before MA_i leaves P_j , the top of the $Stack_i$ is popped off.

2.3 Third Phase

In the third phase, the complete list of initiators is communicated to all other initiators by the minimum id initiator. They, in turn, now send agents to the processes which took checkpoints induced by their respective agents. Suppose process Pi is the minimum id initiator. It creates two different agents. The first one visits the processes in VL_i and confirms the temporary checkpoints, deleting the old permanent checkpoints. The second agent visits the processes in PLI_i. $P_j \in PLI_i$, when visited by this second agent, activates MA_j , which confirms the temporary checkpoints for processes in VL_j . All agents return to their creators and are destroyed.

3 Modified Chekpointing Protocol

One of effective factors on performance of mobile agent based algorithms is number of migrations. With decreasing migrations, the algorithm performance and network traffic will be improved. After studying algorithm [4], we found out that there are some excess and useless migrations in triple phases of algorithm. To remove this deficiency, we present an optimum method which will decrease the number of migrations intensively.

3.1 Improvement

In proposed method in this section, we aim to eliminate useless migrations in different phases of original algorithm.

3.2 Eliminating Additional Migrations in Phase I

First we concentrate on the first phase of algorithm. In phase one of original algorithm, each agent MA_imigrates to all nodes which has not met yet, In other words, it migrates to nodes which do not exist in its VL list, and when reaching a node, if agent MA_i realizes that the node has been met already by another initiator, it will move back to previous node after updating its PLI list. Hence, if we can update PLI list without migrating to these nodes, then we reduce number of migrations.

Here, we suppose that each agent MA_i besides having a stack and two VL and PLI lists, also keeps another list; EL (Explored List). Therefore in phase one, EL of one agent is a partial list of all nodes which at least one agent has taken checkpoint on it. (Nodes in VL list of an agent include nodes on which checkpoint has been taken by it.)Each MA_i agent shares its EL list with other agents, by updating EL list of nodes which it migrates to. So, other agents can prevent from migrating to those nodes by updating their EL list. Different phases of proposed algorithm are shown by an example. Table 1 shows executing steps of the proposed algorithm on the graph G#8 of the dataset (a dataset including of 7000 different connected graphs that because of its high volume just a small part of it has been shown in Table 2).Details of each agent activity are seen in Table 1. Suppose that operation done by each agent MA_i in each simulation step is displayed as follow:

Table 1. Details of each agent activities using improvedcheckpointingalgorithm on the graph G#8 of dataset

Agent	Operation
MA1	(1,1,CP-P1,{1},{1},{1})**,**(1,2,M-P6,CP-P6,{1},{1,6},{1,6})**,**(1,7,M-P4,CP-P4,{1},{1,6,4},{1,6,4})**,**(1,13,M-P7,U,{1,7},{1,6,4},{1,6,4,7,8,3,2,5,4})**,**(1,14,R-P4,{1,7},{1,6,4},{1,6,4,7,8,3,2,5,4})**,**(1,15,R-P6,{1,7},{1,6,4}, {1,6,4,7,8,3,2,5,4})**,**(1,16,R-P1,{1,7},{1,6,4},{1,6,4,7,8,3,2,5,4})**,**(2,16,S-Ph2,{1,7},{1,6,4},{1})**,**(2,19,M-P7,{1,7,8},{1,6,4},{1,7})**,**(2,20,M-P8,W-Ph1-P8,{1,7,8},{1,6,4},{1,7,8})**,**(2,20,Mrg-MA1-MA0,D-MA1,{1,7,8,0},{1,6,4},{1,7, 8,0})
MA7	(1,2,CP-P7,{7},{7},{7}),(1,3,M-P8,U,{7,8},{7},{7,8}),(1,4,R-P7,{7,8},{7},{7,8}),(1,5,M-P3,CP-P3,{7,8},{7,3},{7,8,3}),(1,6,M-P2,CP-P2,{7,8},{7,3,2} ,{7,8,3,2}),(1,7,M-P5,CP-P5,{7,8},{7,3,2,5},{7,8,3,2,5}),(1,8,M-P4,U,{7,8,1},{7,3,2,5},{7,8,3,2,5,4,1,6}),(1,9,R-P5, {7,8,1},{7,3,2,5},{7,8,3,2,5,4,1,6}) ,(1,10,R-P2,{7,8,1},{7,3,2,5},{7,8,3,2,5,4,1,6}),(1,11,R-3,{7,8,1},{7,3,2,5}, {7,8,3,2,5,4,1,6}),(1,12,R-P7,{7,8,1},{7,3,2,5},{7,8,3,2,5,4,1,6}),(2,12,S Ph2,{7,8,1},{7,3,2,5},{7}),(2,12,D-MA7,{7,8,1},{7,3,2,5},{7})
MA8	(1,1,CP-P8,{8},{8},{8}),(1,2,M-P0,U,{8,0},{8},{8,0}),(1,21,R-P8,{8,0,7},{8},{8,0,7}),(1,21,S-Ph2,Rst-MA0,{8,0,7},{8},{8})
MA0	(1,1,CP-P0,{0},{0},{0}),(1,2,M-P8,U,{0,8},{0},{0,8}),(1,3,R-P0,{0,8},{0},{0,8}),(2,3,S-Ph2,{0,8},{0},{0}),(2,4,M-P8,W-Ph1-P8, {0,8}, {0},{0,8}),(2,20,Mrg-MA1-MA0,D-MA1,{1,7,8,0},{0},{1,7,8,0}),(2,21,R-P0,S-Ph3,{1,7,8,0},{0},{1,7,8,0})
MA'0	(3,21,Cnf-CP-P0,{},{0},{0}),(3,21,D- MA'0 ,{},{0},{0})
MA''	(3,21, S-Ph3-P0,{1,7,8,0},{},{0}),(3,22, M-P8,S-Ph3-P8,{1,7,8,0},{},{0,8}),(3,23,M-P7,S-Ph3-P7,{1,7,8,0},{},{0,8,7}),(3,24, M-P1,S-Ph3-P1,{1,7,8,0},{},{0,8,7,1})
MA'8	(3,22,Cnf-CP-P8,{},{8},{8}),(3,22,D- MA'8 ,{},{8},{8})
MA'7	(3,23,Cnf-CP-P7,{},{7,3,2,5},{7}),(3,24,Cnf-CP-P3,{},{7,3,2,5},{7,3}),(3,25,Cnf-CP-P2,{},{7,3,2,5},{7,3,2}),(3,26,Cnf-CP-P5,{},{7,3,2,5},{7,3,2,5}),(3, 26,D-MA'7,{},{7,3,2,5},{7,3,2,5})
MA'1	(3,24, Cnf-CP-P1,{},{1,6,4},{1}),(3,25, Cnf-CP-P6,{},{1,6,4},{1,6}),(3,26, Cnf-CP-P4,{},{1,6,4},{}),(3,27,D- MA'1 ,{},{1,6,4},{1,6,4}

Notations: R-P_i = Return to P_i,**M-MA_i-P_j**=Migrate MA_i to P_i,**U**= Update Lists , **Cnf-CP-P_i**= Confirm Checkpoint at P_i / **S-Ph_i** =Start Phase$_i$, **S-Ph_i-P_i** =Start Phase$_i$ at P_i ,**W-Ph_i-P_i** =Wait to finish Phase$_i$ at P_i,**D-MA_i**= Destroy MA_i,
Mrg-MA_i-MA_j= Merge Lists of MA_i with MA_j, **CP-P_i** =Take Checkpoint at P_i , **Rst-MA_i**= Restart activation of MA_i
In parenthesis:
First Number=Phase Number, **Second Number**=Order, **First Bracket**=PLI, **Second Bracket**= VL, **Third Bracket**= EL

$MA_i(Phase\ Number, Order, Operation, PLI, VL, EL)$

Components have been separated from each other by comma. The components indicate phase No, time step of simulation, operation done by agent (which can include: R-Pi (Returning to node Pi), M-MAi-Pj (Migrating MA_i to node Pj), U (updating lists), Cnf-CP-Pi(Confirming Checkpoint at node Pi), S-Phi (Starting ith Phase), W-Phi-Pj (Waiting for ith Phase at node Pj), Rst-MAi (Restarting of the agent activity), S-Phi-Pi (Start Phasei at Pi), Mrg-MAi-MAj (Merging lists of agent MAi with agent MAj), D-MAi (Destroying of agent), CP-Pi (Checkpointing at node Pi)), PLI list, VL list and EL list, respectively. MA'': Mobile agent MA_i'' visits the processes in PLI_i.

$P_j \in PLI_i$, when visited by this agent, activates MA_i'', which confirms the temporary checkpoints for processes in VL_j. MA_i': Mobile agent MA_i' visits the processes in VL_i ($P_i \in PLI_i$)and confirms the temporary checkpoints, deleting the old permanent checkpoints.As an example, one of agent MA_1 activities at row 1 of Table 1 is as follow:(1, 14, R-P4, {1, 7}, {1, 6, 4}, {1, 6, 4, 7, 8, 3, 2, 5, 4})Which indicates that agent MA_1 is located at phase one, time step of simulation is 14, operation done by agent is R-P4 thatmeans MA1 returns to P4, and PLI, VL, EL lists are {1,7},{1,6,4,}, and {1,6,4,7,8,3,2,5,4}, respectively. As seen, although agent MA1 has not yet visited node P5 (node No. 5does not belong to VL list of agent MA1), but it does not migrate to P5, because when passing node P4 and updating EL, it realizes that node P5 has been met before at least by a parallel initiator and as a result migration to it is prevented. The details of first phase is given by the pseudocode in Algorithm1.

3.3 Elimination of Additional Migrations in Phase II

In the second phase of the original algorithm, we may have a situation in an initiator of a node such as Node x,which asecond phase agent (that we name it SPA from now) waits for the first phase agent (that we name it FPA from now) of Node x to be returned, so the first phase in this node ends and the SPA in this node can proceed algorithm. But when the FPA returns, the SPA that was waiting for the FPA, realizes that its own ID is larger than the FPA, as a result the SPA must destroy itself, that means the entire activities done by the SPA had been ineffective and these kinds of additional migrations only increase network traffic. While, if the SPA before destroying itself, presents list of nodes it has met along with its PLI list to the FPA, it prevents from wasting of tasks done by itself and the FPA can finish the SPA's task by using information presented and avoiding migration to nodes visited before by the destroyed agent. The details of second phase are given by the pseudo code in Algorithm2.

3.4 Elimination of Additional Migrations in Phase III

In the third phase of the original algorithm, after the SPA created two kinds of agents for beginning the third phase, it assigns one of them for migrating to all nodes located in its own PLI and this agent after migrating to all nodes, must move back to the source node and destroys itself there. While the agent does not need to move back to source node to destroy itself, instead it can destroy itself at node in which it is resident now. It is also true about the other agent which is responsible of confirmation. When it confirms checkpoints at all nodes in VL list, there is no need to move back to its source node to be destroyed. Therefore in this phase we can eliminate extra migration that occurred in useless move back to source nodes. The details of third phase are given by the pseudo code in Algorithm3.

Table 2. A dataset including of different connected graphs

Graph#	($Node_i$, $Node_j$, Weight of edge between i and j)
G#1	0 1 15,0 5 19,0 19 11,1 2 8,1 3 11,1 7 4,2 6 15,2 10 8,2 13 14,2 21 8,3 4 14,6 8 15,6 14 8,6 18 11,7 20 1,8 9 15,10 11 9,10 12 19,12 16 5,14 15 1,15 22 8,16 17 1
G#2	0 1 19,0 6 18,0 13 17,1 2 5,1 4 19,1 5 8,2 3 10,2 14 12,2 16 12,2 19 14,4 12 14,4 17 14,5 9 14,5 15 11,6 7 4,6 8 18,6 11 10,7 15 9,8 10 18,13 15 19,15 20 4,16 18 5
G#3	0 1 1,1 2 11,1 4 12,1 5 18,1 10 5,2 3 5,2 16 11,3 7 15,3 11 1,4 6 12,5 8 18,5 16 3,6 9 1,6 19 3,7 12 14,8 14 4,11 13 18,13 15 15,15 18 15,16 17 1,16 20 1,16 19 3
G#4	0 1 18,0 3 5,0 4 4,0 6 4,0 10 1,0 18 5,1 2 17,1 13 12,1 14 15,2 17 19,2 20 17,3 8 4,3 11 4,4 5 10,4 9 18,5 12 6,5 21 1,6 7 10,7 15 4,7 22 10,8 16 16,8 19 16,9 18 4
G#5	0 1 19,0 2 11,0 6 19,0 9 15,0 17 19,1 3 2,1 18 18,1 16 15,2 4 4,2 8 10,3 7 16,3 14 2,4 5 9,4 10 3,4 12 3,4 16 6,6 13 18,6 8 2,7 15 14,8 11 10,8 18 2,8 10 6
G#6	0 1 12,0 2 6,0 5 6,0 10 16,1 3 18,1 6 1,1 17 5,2 4 9,3 5 3,5 7 3,5 21 1,6 8 7,6 11 7,6 13 12,6 16 19,7 15 17,8 9 17,8 12 17,9 20 6,11 18 14,12 22 2,13 14 14,16 19 19
G#7	0 1 19,0 2 15,0 6 14,0 10 19,1 3 11,1 4 16,1 9 18,3 5 15,3 7 5,3 11 18,3 14 15,5 8 19,5 12 16,5 16 15,5 11 14,6 9 13,8 17 17,11 13 9,11 15 9,15 18 6
G#8	0 8 8,1 6 19,2 3 7,2 5 9,2 7 5,3 7 8,4 5 12,4 6 17,4 7 2,7 8 1

Improvement: First Phase

Algorithm1:MAi On being initiated

```
Initiator P_i
begin
    creates a mobile agent with agent id ← i
end
MobileAgentMA_i
begin
  Push i into the Stack_i
  TakeTemporaryCheckpoint(i,i)
  whileStack_i<>empty do
    if neighbor (P_j ) of Top_Stack_i<>null and
it is yet to be visited by MA_i and
        not in EL of MAi then
          move to the Pj
          TakeTemporaryCheckpoint(i,j)
          ifP_j is unvisited by any other agent
then
              Push j into Stack_i
          end if
          EL_j ← EL_j ∪ EL_i
          EL_i ← EL_j
    else
        Pop Stack_i and move to Top_Stack_i
    end if
  end while
end
TakeTemporaryCheckpoint(i,j)
Begin
  ifmsg_ckpt<> True ∧ ckpt_state<> T then
      take a new checkpoint
      ckpt_state ← T
      v_no ← (v_no + 1) mod 2
      PLI_j ← PLI_j ∪ {i} VL_i ← VL_i ∪ {l}
  else ifmsg_ckpt<> T rue ∧ ckpt_state = T then
          PLIi ← PLIi ∪ PLIj
          PLIj ← PLIi
      else {msg_ckpt = True ∧ ckpt_state = T }
          msg_ckpt ← False
          VLi ← VLi ∪ {j} PLIj ← PLIj ∪ {i}
      end if
end if
end
```

Improvement:Second Phase

Algorithm2:MAi Building the list of initiators

```
MA_i at P_i
begin
   if∃ a j∈ PLI_i such that j < i
then
        go to sleep
   else move to P_j such that j ∈ PLI_i
        and has shortest paths (cost) from P_i
        and not in EL2_i
        Push i into Stack_i
   end if
end
MA_j at P_i
Begin
   Push j into theStack_i
   whileCompletedFirstPhase= False do
       wait for return of MA_j{onMA_i's return}
       {set CompletedFirstPhase← True}
   end while
   whileStack_i<>do
       UpdateTheList(i,j)
   end while
end
UpdateTheList(i,j)
begin
   PLI_i←PLI_i ∪ PLI_j
   PLI_j←PLI_i
   if∃atleastone s∈PLI_i such that s < i then
       EL2_j←EL2_i
       MA_i is destroyed
   else if∈ a k ∈ PLI_i such thatP_k is unvisited
and
has shortest paths(cost) fromP_j and
         not in EL2_i then
             move to P_k
         else Pop Stack_i and move to Top_Stack_i
       end if
    end if
end
```

Improvement: Third Phase

Algorithm3: On completing the full list of initiators

```
MAi at Pi
begin
   Push i into Stacki
   MAi move to Pj such that j ∈ PLIi
   create a clone of MAi
   clone move to Pk such that k∈ VLi
end
MAi at Pj (j ∈ PLIi)
begin
   Push j into Stacki
      while Stacki<>empty do
         wake up MAj if it is asleep or recreate MAj
         if it is destroyed
            MAj move to Pk such that k ∈ VLj
         If∃ a k∈ PLIi such that Pk is unvisited then
            move to Pk
         else
            MAi is destroyed
         end if
      end while
end
MAi at Pj (j ∈ VLj )
begin
   Push j into Stacki
      while Stacki<>empty do
         delete old permanent checkpoint ckpt state ← P
         if∃ a k∈ V Iisuch that Pk is unvisited then
            move to Pk
         else
            MAi is destroyed
         end if
      end while
end
```

4 Performance Evaluation

To study the performance of improved checkpointing algorithms, we have developed a Java simulation environment using the J2SDK (Java2)1.6 with event processing method. We have simulated two cases of a checkpointing algorithm: the original mobile agent based checkpointing algorithm and its improvement. The effectiveness of proposed algorithm is evaluated by extensive simulation under a dataset including 7000 different connected graphs (because of its high volume just a small part of dataset has been shown in table 2) which is created based on presented code at [6]. The performance of the simulated system is assessed in the following criteria:

Average Execution Time: The average time during which one checkpoint epoch is executing.

Network Traffic: The overall communication overhead in the system, measured in total number of data (bytes) transferred by agent in migrations. Therefore network traffic of system is related to total number of migrations in the system and can be calculated as:

$$Network\,Traffic = N_{mig} * AVG\left(\sum_{agents\,i} TD_i\right) \tag{1}$$

Where

N_{mig} is the total number of migrations.

TD_i is data transferred by agent i.

Since there is relation between network traffic and number of migrations, then from now in each algorithm we only take the number of migrations into account. As a result, any algorithm which has smaller number of migrations, it will have smaller network traffic.

The details of simulation environment and algorithm parameters are given by the Table 3.Fig. 1 compares the number of migrations of original checkpointing algorithm and the proposed improvement. It shows that the improved algorithm has lower number of migration than the original algorithm.Fig. 2 compares the execution time of the original algorithm and the proposed improvement. It shows that the improved algorithm has lower execution time than the original algorithm.

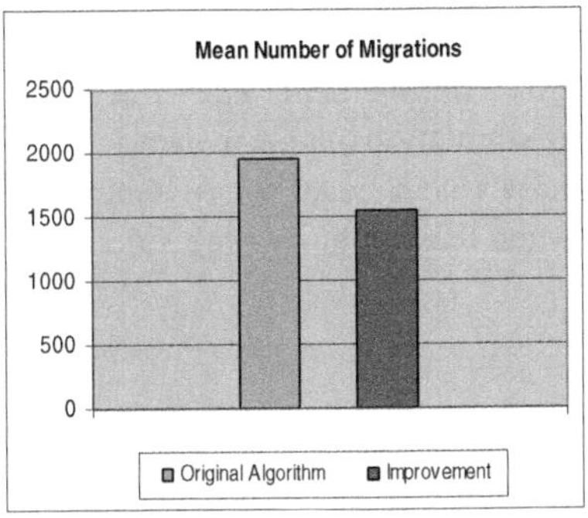

Fig. 1. Mean number of migrations of the rithm and its improvement

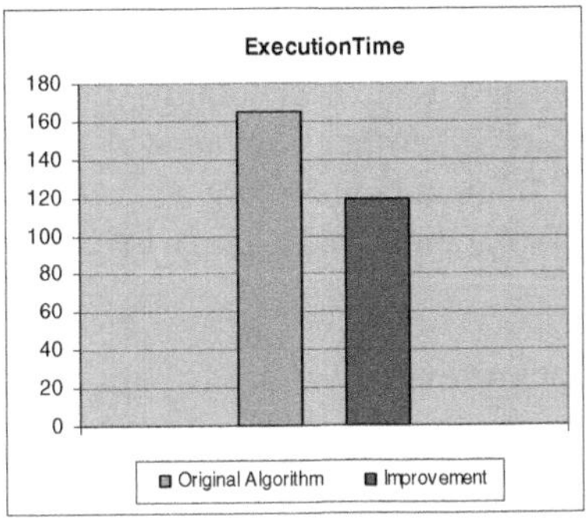

Fig. 2 Execution time of the original algo- original algorithm and its improvement

Table 3. Simulation Environment and algorithm parameters

Environment parameter	Default value
Checkpoint Epoch	100 epoch
Number of Graph in Dataset	7000 graph with different density
Checkpointing Interval	Exponential λ=0.04 Distribution
Migration Interval	Exponential Distribution $\lambda = 0.1$
Message Receiving Interval	Exponential Distribution $\lambda = 0.1$
Number of Simulation Run	7000 iteration

Table 4. Results of each simulation run for 100 checkpoint epochs on first five graphs of dataset

Graph #	Algorithm	Migration	AET
G#1	Original Algorithm	2104.00	183.18
	Improvement	1898.00	175.83
G#2	Original Algorithm	2009.71	170.92
	Improvement	1784.28	164.36
G#3	Original Algorithm	2200.57	166.13
	Improvement	2002.28	168.92
G#4	Original Algorithm	2031.71	195.62
	Improvement	1852.57	191.34
G#5	Original Algorithm	2008.42	162.44
	Improvement	1849.99	165.96

Table 4 shows results of each simulation run for 100 checkpoint epochs on first five graphs of dataset. It shows number of migrations and average execution time (AET) of original algorithm and its improvement explained in section 5.1.

5 Conclusion

In this paper we propose an optimum mobile agent based checkpointing protocol which attempts to eliminate useless migrations in different phases of checkpointing algorithm. The proposed algorithm will improve performance and network traffic greatly. We have simulated two cases of a checkpointing algorithm: the original mobile agent based checkpointing algorithm and its improvement. The effectiveness of proposed algorithm is evaluated by extensive simulation under a dataset including 7000 different connected graphs.Our results show a significant improvement in number of migrations and average execution time when these solutions are simulated.

References

1. Mandal, P. S., Mukhopadhyaya, K.: Checkpointing Using Mobile Agents in Distributed Systems. In: International Conference on Computing: Theory and Applications (ICCTA 2007). IEEE (2007)
2. Mandal, P.S., Mukhopadhyaya, K.: Checkpointing and recovery algorithms using mobile agents on a hamiltonian topology. In: The 6th International Conference on High Performance Computing in Asia Pacific Region (2002)
3. Cao, J., Chan, G.H., Dillon, T.S., Jia, W.: Checkpointing and rollback of wide-area distributed applications using mobile agents. In: The IEEE International Parallel and Distributed Processing Symposium (2001)
4. Mandal, P.S., Mukhopadhyaya, K.: Mobile Agent Based Checkpointing with Concurrent Initiators. International Journal of Foundations of Computer Science (2007)
5. Elnozahy (Mootaz), E.N., Alvisi, L., Wang, Y.M., Johnson, D.B.: A Survey of Rollback-Recovery Protocols in Message-Passing Systems (2002)
6. http://www.cse.ust.hk/graphgen

A Novel Threshold-Based Dynamic Load Balancing Algorithm Using Mobile Agent in Distributed System

Nassrin Eftekhari, Farid Haji Zeinalabedin, and Abolfazl Torghi Haghighat

Computer & Electronic Department,
Islamic Azad University of Qazvin, Qazvin, Iran
{n.eftekhari,f.h.zeinalabedin,haghighat}@qiau.ac.ir

Abstract. As a fundamental problem in distributed system, load balancing is important to achieving scalability, guarantee system fairness and avoid performance degradation. To efficient utilization of all available resources, we need the concept of load balancing to be added in this area. In message-passing based approaches, the nodes have to exchange messages of load information periodically in order to make decisions on load balancing. The message exchanges result in high communication latency and thus deteriorate the performance of the system. In this paper, we propose a novel threshold-based dynamic load balancing approach which uses mobile agent (MA) because MA based approaches have the merits of flexibility, low network traffic, efficiency, less communication latency, as well as highly asynchronous. The effectiveness of proposed load balancing approach is evaluated by extensive simulation under a dataset including 7000 different connected graphs. Our results show a significant improvement in network traffic compared with the traditional message passing based approach.

Keywords: Load Balancing, mobile agents, distributed system, load information, threshold, dynamic, network traffic.

1 Introduction

Because of heterogeneity of distributed systems, a large problem in this area is the efficient utilization of all available resources. So we need the concept of load balancing (LB) to be added in this area. Load balancing is a technique to enhance resources, utilizing parallelism exploiting, throughput improvisation, and to cut response time through an appropriate distribution of the application [1]. It is an active technology that provides the art of shaping, transforming and filtering the network traffic then routing and load balancing it to the optimal node. By adding the concept of load balancer we can distribute the traffic for preventing from failure in any case by having capabilities such as scalability, availability, easy to use, fault tolerant, quick response time [2, 3]. The strategy of load-balancing algorithms is based on the idea of transferring some processes from the heavily loaded nodes to lightly loaded nodes for processing. The load balancing strategies can be categorized according to whether they are centralized [4] or distributed [5, 6], local or global [7], static [1] or dynamic

V.V. Das and N. Thankachan (Eds.): CIIT 2011, CCIS 250, pp. 103–109, 2011.

[1, 4], sender-initiated [8] or receiver-initiated [6]. The rest of the paper is organized as follows: In the next section, we propose a novel threshold-based dynamic load balancing approach which uses mobile agents to balance system load. In section 3, we evaluate the performance of proposed load balancing approach with the message passing approach. Finally, section 4 concludes the paper.

2 Proposed Load Balancing Approach

In dynamic load balancing approaches, load balancing decisions are based on collected load information of system. Traditional message passing based Load balancing approaches involve frequent message exchanging between clients and servers for discovering and sharing load information. Because of frequent fluctuation of load information in distribution system, updating load information of system nodes is required, frequently. But because of vastness and high degree of dynamism of distribution systems, this usually results in enormous communication overhead and will increase network traffic. Mobile Agent-based methods can reduce this problem. Mobile agent provides a new technology for implementing load balancing mechanism in distributed systems. Proposed mobile agent based load balancing approach, balances system load and removes the above problems.

2.1 Threshold Value and Node Types

To balance system load the strategy of load balancing transfers some processes from overloaded nodes, i.e. heavy nodes, to under loaded nodes, i.e. light nodes, to be processed. The proposed load balancing algorithm uses the dynamic policy to determine whether a node is overloaded or under loaded. We define a threshold value T_{n_i} for each node n_i that is used to decide whether node n_i is overloaded or under loaded. Each task t_x that enters the system has its own specific load, and for running it needs amount of processor time to be served. The threshold value of node n_i is the limiting value of workload of node n_i and calculates as follows:

$$T_{n_i} = \left(\sum_{i=1}^{N} WL_i / N\right) * C_i \tag{1}$$

Where, WL_i is amount of workload of node n_i, N is number of node in the system, and C_i is capacity of node n_i, which shows processing capability of node n_i.

Each node n_i can be classified into two types:

- Heavy node, if $WL_i \geq T_{n_i}$;
- Light node, if $WL_i < T_{n_i}$.

When workload of a node exceed from its defined threshold, then it is considered as a heavy node, and is light otherwise. In fact, task assignment to nodes must be in a way that workload imposed by each node is not beyond its utilization. When number of overloaded nodes increase in the system, it will affect system performance.

2.2 Policy

The design of a load balancing mechanism should include the design of the following policies:

Information Gathering and Updating Policy **(IGUP):** It specifies the strategy of collecting and updating of load information about nodes, and includes the frequency of information exchange and method of information gathering and updating. There is a tradeoff between having accurate information and minimizing the overhead.

Job Transfer Policy **(JTP):** It decides when the initiator should consider re-allocate some requests to other servers. The decision can be made based on only local state or by exchanging global processor load information.

Node Selection Policy **(NSP):** Selects an appropriate node based on the load information to which the workload on an overloaded node can be reallocated. Different strategies can be used. The simplest strategy is to choose a node at random. The find-best strategy selects the first node whose load is below a threshold, i.e. the least loaded node. The find-first strategy selects very first node that is having the less threshold value.

Initiation Policy **(IP):** It determines who initiates the process of load balancing. The process can be initiated by an overloaded node (called sender-initiated) or by an under-loaded node (called receiver-initiated).

2.3 Agents

The proposed load balancing approach specifies three types of agents:

(1) ***Load Gathering and Updating Agent*** **(LGUA)** is a mobile agent that is responsible for load information gathering. An LGUA is not proprietary to a node where it is created, but it is shared among nodes and provides load information to them.

(2) ***Node Management Agent*** **(NMA)** is a stationary agent that is resident at a node, responsible for monitoring the workload on local node and executing job transfer policy if required. In sender-Initiated policy, when a node is overloaded, the NMA on it initiates the load reallocation process. The NMA selects the jobs from local job queue and dispatches the job to other nodes.

(3) ***Job Migrating Agent*** **(JMA)** is activated by the NMA on an overloaded node. A JMA executes the node selection policy to select another node to receive the reallocated job. Then, the JMA carries the reallocated job to that node.

2.4 Strategy of Load Balancing

The proposed load balancing approach is consisting of different agents with each agent has a specific role. Each LGUA moves to other nodes following an execution path of depth-first search, starting from its creator. Each LGUA maintains a stack, a list, and a table. The stack, *Stack*, has the path to the root, as required by the DFS. The list *VL* (Visited List) is the list of nodes which have been visited by this agent in each cycle. The table, includes the workload of all nodes and the time stamp in which the workload of nodes is collected or updated. Each row of table demonstrates workload value (*WL_Value*) and workload time stamp (*WL_TimeStamp*) of one node. If an LGUA has not yet visited node n_i, the *WL-Value* and *WL-TimeStamp* will be set to 0 (*WL_Value=0, WL_TimeStamp=0*).

Each NMA maintains a table and a counter. The table of an NMA has the same structure of the table belonged to each LGUA. The counter is valued by the last time stamp in which the workload of the node n_i is requested by one LGUA. In the beginning counter value of each NMA is set to 0, i.e. *counter_value* = 0. When an LGUA reaches a node n_i, it requests the resident NMA on node n_i the workload value of that node. The NMA first reports the workload to LGUA and increases its counter by 1, and then starts to update load information of both itself and the LGUA by comparing its table to the LGUA's table.

Table of LGUA

i	*TS*	*WL*
1	5	25
2	2	35
3	4	30
4	3	15
5	6	18
6	3	20
7	5	30
8	4	45
9	3	34
10	4	21

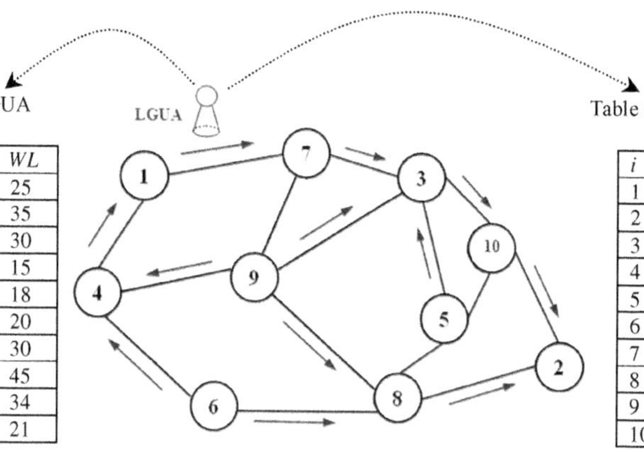

Table of NMA on Node7

i	*TS*	*WL*
1	3	20
2	2	35
3	6	26
4	1	20
5	5	15
6	3	20
7	8	24
8	5	41
9	2	30
10	3	32

Fig. 1. An example of collecting and updating load information in proposed approach. (TS(TimeStamp _Value),WL(WorkLoad_Value)).

If we have N nodes in the system, the table related to storing load information of all nodes will have N rows and three columns. The three columns demonstrate the *node_number*, the *TimeStamp_value (TS)* and *Workload_Value (WL)*, respectively. The workload of node with *node_number*=i will be stored in i^{th} row of table.

If the *TimeStamp_value* of node i in the LGUA's table is equal to the *TimeStamp_value* of node i in the NMA's table, then no action is taken. Else, if the *TimeStamp_value* of node i in the LGUA's table is greater than the *TimeStamp_value* of node i in the NMA's table , then the NMA should update load information of node i in its table according to the LGUA's table. Otherwise, the LGUA should update load information of node i in its table according to the NMA's table.

Each time that NMA of node n_i updates its table, it also updates the threshold value of node n_i by using the latest up-to-date table. Fig.1 shows that when LGUA reaches the node 7, load information of LGUA and NMA on node 7 should be updated. It shows that the LGUA has more updated load information of nodes 1,4,5,9 and 10 and the NMA has more updated load information of nodes 3,7 and 8. When an LGUA visited all nodes and backed to its creator node, then it will start a new round.

When a node receives new input tasks, the NMA on the node can immediately determine a node to process them. If local load is below the threshold value, the home node processes the incoming tasks itself. Otherwise, the local node is overloaded and cannot receive new tasks and should reallocate them to other nodes. Thus, the NMA initiates the load-balancing process by activating JMA to transfer some tasks to the nearest least loaded node such as node x as the best node.

If node x has also been overloaded, the JMA asks from the resident NMA on node x, the best node to receive the task. The NMA introduces to it the best node, using up-to-date load information in its table.

3 Performance Evaluation

To study the performance of proposed load balancing algorithm, we have developed a Java simulation environment using the J2SDK 1.6. The input tasks are randomly generated and sent to the nodes. The arrival interval of input tasks to each node follows exponential distribution with a mean of 0.1s. The processing time for an input task follows uniform distribution between 1s and 10000s. In each run of simulation, totally 500 tasks are generated and processed.

We have simulated three cases of a distributed system: using traditional load-balancing algorithm, using proposed load balancing algorithm, and running without load balancing. The effectiveness of proposed load balancing approach is evaluated by extensive simulation under a dataset including 7000 different connected graphs which is created based on presented code at [9].

The performance of the proposed approach is measured in the following criteria:

Load Distribution: The load on each of the nodes is measured at different time instants. The load on a node is denoted by the length of its job queue. The average deviation of the load distribution over all nodes is calculated to show the effect of load balancing.

System Throughput: The overall throughput of the system, measured in the number of jobs processed per second.

Network Traffic: The overall communication overhead, measured in the total number of data (bytes) transferred in the communication.

Table. 1 includes the average deviation of load by the proposed load balancing approach on 7000 different graph of dataset, using different number of LGUA agents. It shows that for the used dataset the lower bound of number of LGUA agent is about 5% of number of nodes. With this number of LGUA not only the Mean deviation didn't changed, but also the network traffic decreased greatly (Fig. 2).

In the message-passing-based approach, every node needs to periodically broadcast load information to other nodes. For totally N nodes, the broadcast incurs the communication overhead as high as $O(N^2)$. The high network traffic largely restrains the system performance. From the results of simulation, we can conclude that the proposed mobile agent-based approach is a communication-efficient approach to support load balancing (Fig. 3). Fig. 4 compares the system throughput of the proposed load balancing approach and the case without load balancing. The result shows that the proposed approach has the higher throughput.

We have also compared the network traffic of the proposed approach and message-passing approach (Fig. 5). The result shows that the proposed approach has the lower network traffic.

Table 1. Mean Deviation

Proposed Load balancing approach using different number of LGUAs for collecting load information			
Mean Deviation	Number of LGUA (x% of network nodes)	Mean Deviation	Number of LGUA (x% of network nodes)
10.5751	100.0%	10.5635	8.0%
10.5752	66.66%	10.5623	7.69%
10.5752	50.0%	10.5601	7.14%
10.5750	40.0%	10.5582	6.66%
10.5747	33.33%	10.5573	6.45%
10.5743	28.57%	10.5558	6.06%
10.5740	25.0%	10.5550	5.88%
10.5733	20.0%	10.5543	5.71%
10.5728	18.18%	10.5537	5.55%

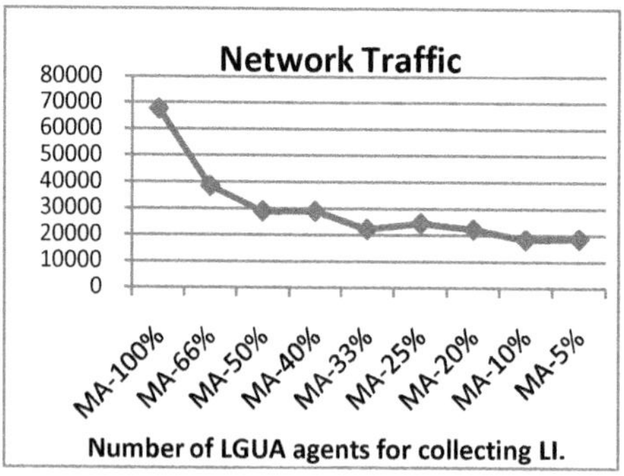

Fig. 2. Network traffic of proposed load balancing approach using different number of LGUA agents

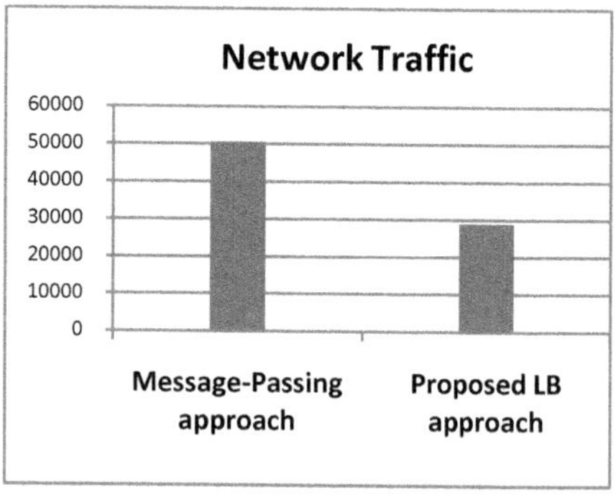

Fig. 3. Network traffic of proposed load b Balancing approach(number of LGUA agent is about 5% of number of nodes) and message passing approach

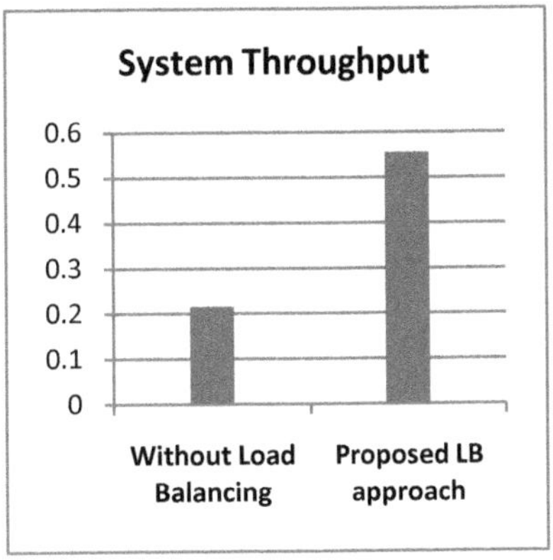

Fig. 4. The system throughput of proposed load balancing approach and the case without load balancing

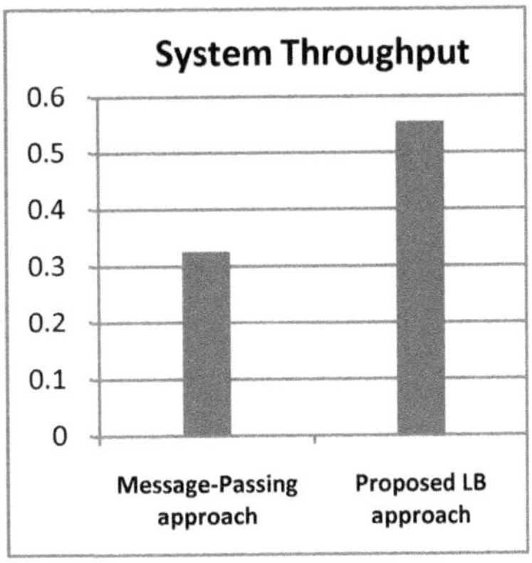

Fig. 5. The system throughput of proposed load balancing approach and message-passing approach

4 Conclusion

In this paper we proposed a novel threshold-based dynamic load balancing approach which uses mobile agent. To study the performance of proposed load balancing algorithm, we have developed a Java simulation environment using the J2SDK 1.6. The effectiveness of proposed load balancing approach is evaluated by extensive simulation under a dataset including 7000 different connected graphs. Our results show a significant improvement in network traffic compared with the traditional message passing based approach.

References

1. Jimenez, J.B.: Robin Hood: An Active Objects Load Balancing Mechanism for Intranet. In: 18th ACM Symposium on Applied Computing (2003)
2. Nehra, N., Patel, R.B., Bhat, V.K.: Load Balancing in Heterogeneous P2P Systems using Mobile Agents. World Academy of Science, Engineering and Technology (2006)
3. Patel, R.B., Aggarwal, N.: Load Balancing on Open Networks A Mobile Agent Approach. Journal of Computer Science (2006)
4. Cao, J., Wang, X., Das, S.K.: A framework of using cooperating mobile agents to achieve load sharing in distributed web server groups. Future Generation Computer Systems (2004)
5. Wen, Y.J., Wang, S.D.: Minimizing Migration on Grid Environments: An Experience on Sun Grid Engine. Journal of Information Technology and Applications (2007)
6. Renand, W., Beard, R.: Consensus seeking in multi agent systems under dynamically Changing interaction Topologies. IEEE Transactions on Automatic Control (2005)
7. Yagoubi, B., Lillia, H.T., Moussa, H.S.: Load Balancing in Grid Computing. Asian Journal of Information Technology (2006)
8. Huang, M.C., Hosseini, S., Vairavan, K.: A receiver-initiated load balancing method in computer networks using fuzzy logic control. In: IEEE Global Telecommunications Conference, GLOBECOM (2003)
9. `http://www.cse.ust.hk/graphgen`

Enhanced Spatial Mining Algorithm Using Fuzzy Quadtrees

Bindiya M. Varghese[1], A. Unnikrishnan[2], and K. Poulose Jacob[3]

[1] Department of Computer Science, Rajagiri College of Social Sciences, Kalamassery, India
[2] Naval Physical Ocenaographic Laboratory, Kakakkanad, India
[3] Department of Computer Science, CUSAT, Kochi, India

Abstract. Spatial Mining differs from regular data mining in parallel with the difference in spatial and non-spatial data. The attributes of a spatial object is influenced by the attributes of the spatial object and moreover by the spatial location. A new algorithm is proposed for spatial mining by applying an image extraction method on hierarchical Quad tree spatial data structure. Homogeneity of the grid is the entropy measure which decides the further subdivision of the quadrant. The decision for decomposition to further sub quadrants is based on fuzzy rules generated using the statistical measures mean and standard deviation of the region. Finally, the algorithm proceeds by applying low level image extraction on domain dense nodes of the quad tree.

Keywords: Fuzzy Quad Trees, Spatial Mining, Image Extraction, Spatial Clustering.

1 Introduction

Recent advances in sensing and storage technology have created many high-volumes, high dimensional data sets in pattern recognition, machine learning, and data mining. Spatial data mining is a demanding field since huge amounts of spatial data have been collected in various applications, ranging from remote sensing to geographical information systems, computer cartography, environmental assessment and planning. A spatial database contains objects which are characterized by a spatial location and/or extension as well as by several non-spatial attributes. The general problem of data clustering is concerned with the discovery of a grouping structure within a finite number of data points. Clustering is a descriptive task that seeks to identify homogeneous groups of objects based on the values of their attributes [1][2]. In spatial data sets, clustering permits a generalization of the spatial component like explicit location and extension of spatial objects which define implicit relations of spatial neighborhood.

2 Related Works

Different Spatial clustering algorithms such as DBSCAN [3], STING [4], CLIQUE [5], BIRCH [6], OPTICS [7] are based on either grid based or Density based clustering algorithms.

V.V. Das and N. Thankachan (Eds.): CIIT 2011, CCIS 250, pp. 110–116, 2011.

3 Quadtree

The term quad tree is used to describe a class of hierarchical data structures which are based on the principle of recursive decomposition of space. The differentiation of these data structures are based on the data they represent; the rules of decomposition and the resolution, i.e. the number of times the decomposition is applied [8]. The region quad tree is based on the successive subdivision of image array into four equal sized quadrants. If the region is not homogenous, each quadrant is subdivided into sub quadrants and so on. This process is represented by a tree of degree 4. The root node corresponds to the entire array. Each son of a node represents a quadrant, labeled in order NW, NE, SW, SE) of the region represented by that node. The application of quad tree can be traced in various algorithms.

4 Fuzzy Inference

A fuzzy set is a set containing elements that have varying degrees of membership in the set. Elements of a set are mapped to a universe of membership values using a function theoretic form. This function maps elements of a fuzzy set A to a real numbered value on the interval 0 to 1. An element x, is a member of fuzzy set A, then $\mu A\ (x) \in [0\ 1]$. The following operations are defined for fuzzy sets A and B for a given element x of the universe. Union: $\mu_{A \cup B}(x) = \max(\mu_{A(x)}, \mu_{B(x)})$; Intersection: $\mu_{A \cap B}(x) = \min(\mu_{A(x)}, \mu_{B(x)})$; Complement: $\mu_{\bar{A}}(x) = 1 - \mu_A(x)$ where μ is the membership function. A fuzzy system is characterized by a set of semantic statements based on expert knowledge. The expert knowledge is usually in the form of "if-then" rules. A fuzzy set A in X is characterized by a membership function which is implemented by fuzzy conditional statements. If the antecedent is true to some degree of membership, then the consequent is also true to that same degree. If antecedent Then consequent. The If part involves evaluating the antecedent, fuzzifying the input and applying any necessary fuzzy operators. The then part requires application of that result to the consequent, known as inference. Fuzzy inference is the process of devising a mapping from a given input to an output using fuzzy rules. Two types of fuzzy inference models are generally used; Mamdani and Takagi-Sugeno-Kang, method of fuzzy inference. Mamdani's fuzzy inference method is the most commonly seen fuzzy methodology [9].

5 The Proposed Framework

5.1 Quadtree Construction

Space based images has the characteristic to cover vast areas and have larger information quality. It is suitable for sustaining the locality information which is quite influential in spatial data. Spatial aggregation stored as minimum bounding rectangle may be obtained by constructing spatial hierarchy or combining neighboring spatial objects. Quad-tree is such a spatial data structure which is frequently used for raster data. Quadtree decomposition is an analysis technique that involves subdividing an image into blocks that are more homogeneous. The top-down approach will consist of successive non overlapping subdivisions of the original image blocks with dimensions 2h×2h by a factor of four. If a block is homogeneous, given some criterion it is not subdivided. If it is non-homogeneous, it is subdivided into non-overlapping four sub-blocks with dimensions 2h-1×2h-1. Quad tree encoding will segregate the image into equal 4 quadrants sub-blocks. All these sub-division of the non-homogeneous blocks will continue until the smallest block reaches a minimum pre-established block size. A sample quadtree is given as example in figure 1.

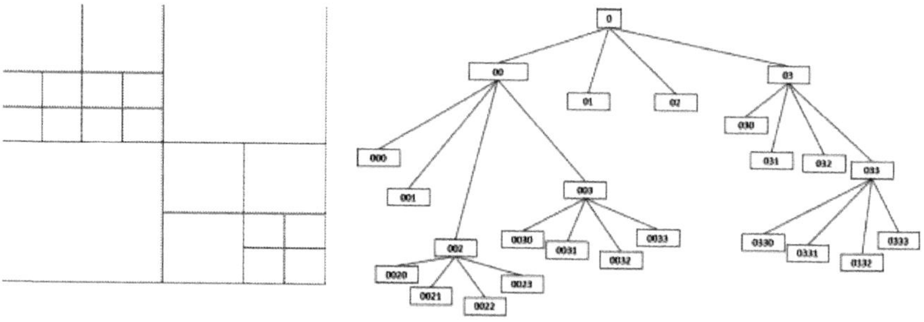

Fig. 1. Sample Quadtree decomposition

Without the loss of generality, assume the size of input image array is n x n, where n is power of two. An image is represented mathematically by a spatial brightness function f(x,y) where (x,y) denotes the spatial coordinate of a point in the image. A gray scale image pixel can be represented as f(x,y), 0< f(x,y) <255, is proportional to the gray level of the image at the point (x,y). The mean of any region of an image array is defined as $\frac{\Sigma f(x,y)}{N}$ where N=n.n; 0≤M≤255. The standard deviation is given by $S = \frac{1}{N}\sqrt{(f(x,y) - M)^2}$. For Computing, all attribute values are normalized into the unit interval [0, 1]. In order to preserve even the minor information that may get unnoticed when mean of region of a bigger size is taken, the mean of the parent region is passed over to the next iterative call. For the fuzzy inference the actual mean is taken as the difference between the parent mean and the sub quadrant mean.

5.2 Fuzzy Rules for Decomposition

The homogeneity criterion for decomposing Quadtree is based on fuzzy inference. The quadtree region can be considered homogeneous if, region satisfies the following intensity.

a. Pure black
b. Pure white

c. Highly Black
d. Highly white

If the region is in any other intensity range other than the above listed, say, intermediately gray, the region should be further decomposed to a level until which it satisfies any of the above intensity. For finding out the intensity level, we make use of mean and standard deviation of the pixels of the region to be considered. The rules are formulated as

R1. If M is low and S is low then region is highly black; info :=1
R2. If M is medium and S is low then the region is medium gray; decompose
R3. If M is high and S is low then the region is highly white; info:=0
R4. If M is low and S is high then region is scattered towards black; decompose
R5. If M is medium and S is high then the region is mixed; decompose
R6. If M is high and S is high scattered towards white; decompose

The consequence part is a decision whether to decompose the quadrant into further level or not.

The membership functions of mean M to be low, medium or high are specified as

$$\mu_{low}(M) = \frac{1}{(\frac{M}{0.07})^8 + 1} \qquad \text{(Fig2.a)}$$

$$\mu_{medium}(M) = e^{-\frac{(M-0.5)^2}{0.05}} \qquad \text{(Fig2.b)}$$

$$\mu_{high}(M) = 1 - \frac{1}{1 + (\frac{M}{0.9})^{55}} \qquad \text{(Fig2.c)}$$

The membership functions of standard deviation S to be low or high are specified as

$$\mu_{low}(S) = \frac{1}{1 + (\frac{S}{0.1})^9} \qquad \text{(Fig2.d)}$$

$$\mu_{high}(S) = 1 - \frac{1}{1 + (\frac{S}{0.9})^{11}} \qquad \text{(Fig2.e)}$$

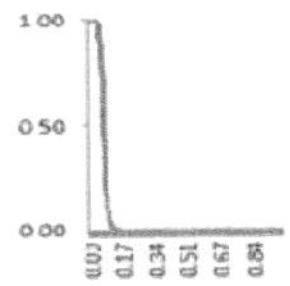

Fig. 2.a μlow(M)

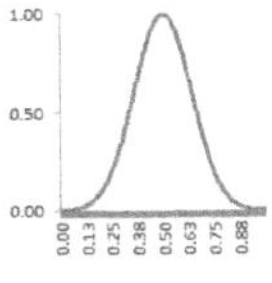

Fig. 2.b μmedium(M)

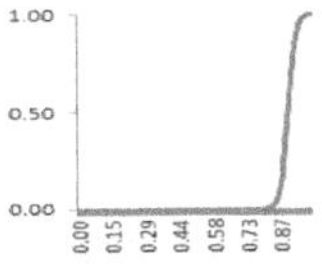

Fig. 2.c μhigh(S)

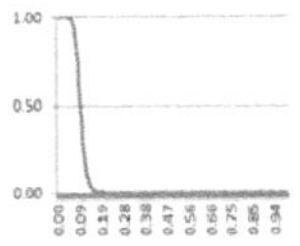

Fig. 2.d μlow(S)

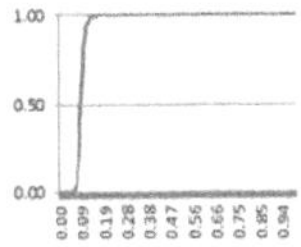

Fig. 2.e μhigh(S)

As per the Union rule of fuzzy inference system, the decision to decompose or not, can be stated as max [R1, R2, R3, R4, R5, R6] where each rule is given by

R1: μlow(M) .μlow(S)
R2: μmedium(M). μlow(S)
R3: μhigh(M). μlow(S)
R4: μlow(M) .μhigh(S)
R5: μmedium(M) . μhigh(S)
R6: μhigh(M) . μhigh(S)

If rule R1 is fired, the region is highly dense and its info bit is indicated as 1 and if rule R3 is fired, the region is devoid of information and its info bit is set to 0. The final output of the first phase of the algorithm is a Quadtree decomposed to a final level of leaf nodes whose info bit is either set to 0 or 1.In order to avoid pixel level subdivision, a threshold level for the size of block is predetermined. When the sub quadrant size reaches the threshold level, the algorithm probes the mean of the region and if it is less than 0.5 (normalized to the interval [0 1]), it takes the region as informative and sets its info bit to 1.

5.3 Image Extraction from MBR

The second phase of algorithm identifies the regions whose info bit is set to 0. These quadrants as a whole represents the clusters deduced from a spatial image. To form the boundaries of the clusters an image extraction algorithm is applied to these specific regions. Low-level Image information is represented by a feature vector, which contains a number of units associated with local spatially restricted interactions between neighboring pixels. The structure that can be perceived at low level is an edge structure [10]. An edge can be viewed as a discontinuity in spatial homogeneity. To extract the low level information content, we compute two components: a topological component and intensity information denoted by Itop (x, y) and Iint(x, y).. A measure of local information content Iloc (x, y) can be measured as a product of two constituting components:Iloc (x, y) = Itop (x, y). Iint(x, y)where Itop is the topological component and Iint in the intensity information. The calculation on Itop and Iint is clearly explained in the reference [10].

6 Implementation and Discussion

The algorithm is applied to different images from various disciplines. Fig 3 shows the weather image obtained from INSAT India. The intermediary image after the First Phase of the algorithm is shown as Fig 3.a. The final resultant image is shown as fig.3.b. Fig. 4 is the mammogram image of fibro adenoma of the breast (Copyrighted to Frontiers in Bioscience). Fig 5 is the Moonridge quadrangle, showing the mule deer locations copyrighted to GIS/LIS (1994), p647-657. The algorithm is coded and implemented using MATLAB. The images to which the algorithm is applied are 256 x 256 RGB JPEG images. The Quad tree construction helps in data focusing in a spatial image, by finding the Minimum Bounding rectangles using fuzzy quadtrees, which provides a closer fit to the actual data objects in the image. An MBR can be easily represented by the coordinates of the vertices. An earlier work by the authors [11][12] addressed the research problem using crisp boundaries for Mean given as HG factor (Q) = 1 if (Lp+•) < m (Q) < (Hp-•). The uncertainty in deciding the value of delta is being removed in this work by fuzzy rules. The issue which is not enunciated in this algorithm is noise that can alter the intensity of the information pixel and therefore its occurrence may influence the statistical measures of the image.

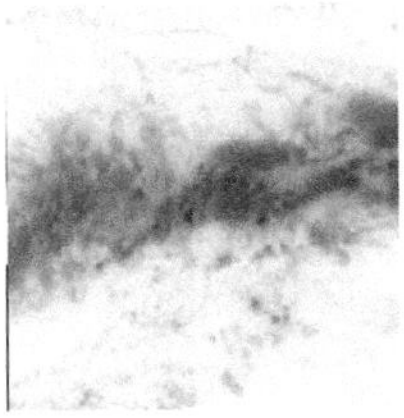

Fig. 3. Weather Image

Fig. 3a. MBR of Image

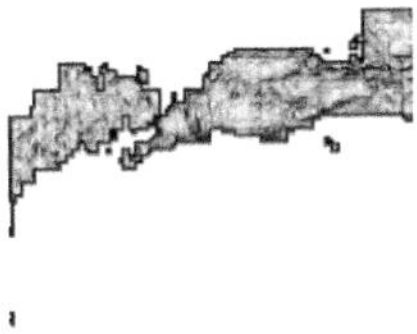

Fig. 3b. Resultant Image

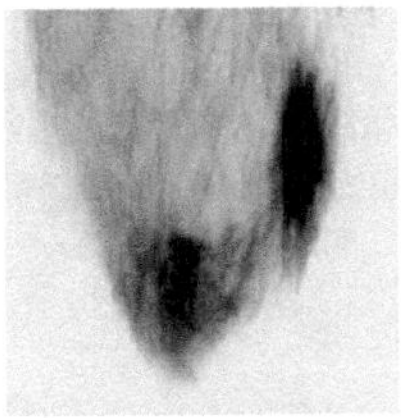

Fig. 4. Mamogram Image

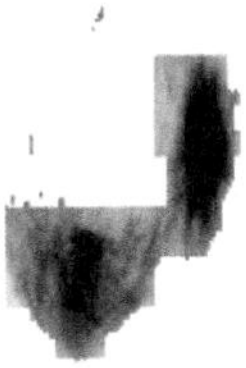

Fig. 4a. MBR of Image

Fig. 4b. Resultant Image

Fig. 5. Mule Deer Locations

Fig. 5a. MBR of Image

Fig. 5b. Resultant Image

7 Conclusion

Generally clustering algorithms are classified as partition based, hierarchical based, density based and grid-based methods. The proposed algorithm using fuzzy quadtree helps to focus on information dense areas and thereby reducing considerable amount of execution time. Subsequently the rules are generated using fuzzy inference; the uncertainty in specifying the threshold boundaries is avoided. Also, the Statistical measures of the parent region are passed down through the recursive call, so that any relevant information is not mislaid as an outlier.

Acknowledgement. The proposed work is funded by computer Society of India under research and development scheme.

References

1. Ester, M., Frommelt, A., Kriegel, H.-P., Sander, J.: Algorithms for characterization and trend detection in spatial databases. In: Proc. 4th Int. Conf. on Knowledge Discovery and Data Mining, New York City, NY, pp. 44-50 (1998)
2. Kaufman, L., Rousseeuw, P.J.: Finding Groups in Data: An Introduction to Cluster Analysis. Wiley Series in Probability and Statistics. Wiley-Interscience (March 2005)
3. Ester, M., Kriegel, H.-P., Jörg, S., Xu, X.: A density-based algorithm for discovering clusters in large spatial databases with noise. In: Proceedings of 2nd International Conference on Knowledge Discovery and Data Mining (KDD 1996), pp. 226–231 (1996)
4. Wang, W., Yang, J., Muntz, R.R.: STING: A Statistical Information Grid Approach to Spatial Data Mining. In: Proceedings of the 23rd International Conference on Very Large Data Bases, pp.186–195, August 25-29 (1997)
5. Agrawal, R., Gehrke, J., Gunopulos, D., Raghavan, P.: Automatic subspace clustering of high dimensional data for data mining applications. In: Proceedings of the 1998 ACM SIGMOD International Conference on Management of Data, Seattle, Washington, United States, June 01-04, pp. 94–105 (1998)
6. Zhang, T., Ramakrishnan, R., Livny, M.: BIRCH: an efficient data clustering method for very large databases. In: Proceedings of the 1996 ACM SIGMOD International Conference on Management of Data, Montreal, Quebec, Canada, June 04-06, pp. 103–114 (1996)
7. Samet, H.: Hierarchical Spatial Data Structures. In: Goos, G., Hartmanis, J. (eds.) Proc. SSD 1989, July 17-18 (1989)
8. Ankerst, M., Breunig, M.M., Kriegel, H.-P., Sander, J.: OPTICS: ordering points to identify the clustering structure. SIGMOD Rec. 28, 49–60 (1999)
9. Sugeno, M.: Industrial applications of fuzzy control. Elsevier Science Pub. Co. (1985)
10. Diamant, E.: Searching For Image Information Content, Its Discovery, Extraction And Representation. Journal of Electronic Imaging 14(1), 013016-1-1–013016-1-11 (2005)
11. Varghese, B.M., Unnikrishnan, A., Jacob, P.: Information Content Extraction on Quad Trees for Active Spatial Image Clustering. In: WRI World Congress on Computer Science and Information Engineering, CSIE, vol. 4, pp. 306–310 (2009)
12. Varghese, B.M., Unnikrishnan, A.: Recursive Decision Tree Induction Based on Homogeneousness for Data Clustering. In: 2008 International Conference on Cyberworlds, CW, pp. 754–758 (2008)

PAPR Reduction of SC-FDMA Based on Modified Tone Reservation Method

Neelam Dewangan, Suchita Chatterjee, and Mangal Singh

Chhatrapati Shivaji Institute of Technology, Durg (C.G), India
{neelamdewangan,suchitachatterjee,
mangalsingh}@csitdurg.in

Abstract. In wireless communication systems, peak–to-average power ratio (PAPR) is a performance measurement that indicates power efficiency of the transmitter. In this paper, an improved method based on tone reservation method for PAPR reduction was proposed. To improve PAPR reduction performance, the more appropriate magnitude of the time domain PAPR reduction signals was found by the proposed method. Simulation in single carrier frequency division multiple access (SC-FDMA) system demonstrates that PAPR reduction performance of the proposed method is better than that of the original approach when several PAPR reduction subcarriers were used.

Keywords: PAPR, Tone Reservation, SC-FDMA.

1 Introduction

Peak-to-average power ratio (PAPR) is indicative of the power efficiency of the mobile terminal. High PAPR at the transmitter can cause the transmitter high power amplifier (HPA) to go into non-linear regions and degrade the transmitter power efficiency. And low PAPR means longer battery life and cheaper output power amplifier for the same average transmitted power. To get lower PAPR, many PAPR reduction approaches for orthogonal frequency division multiplexing (OFDM) have been proposed [1], which can also be used to reduce PAPR in orthogonal frequency division multiple access (OFDMA) system, such as amplitude clipping, clipping and filtering, tone reservation (TR) and so on. In these methods, TR method is based on adding PAPR reduction signals to the data signals to reduce its peaks. TR method does not only eliminate the need for side information but also prevents the bit error rate (BER) degradation. In this paper, an improved method based on TR method for PAPR reduction is proposed. To improve PAPR reduction performance, the more appropriate magnitude of the time signals used to reduce PAPR was found by the proposed method. Simulations in single carrier frequency division multiple access (SC-FDMA) system demonstrate that the proposed method has better PAPR reduction performance than the original approach in [2].

V.V. Das and N. Thankachan (Eds.): CIIT 2011, CCIS 250, pp. 117–121, 2011.

1.1 PAPR of SC-FDMA Signals

SC-FDMA can be regarded as discrete Fourier transform (DFT) spread OFDMA, where time domain data symbols are transformed to frequency domain by DFT before going through OFDMA modulation [3].

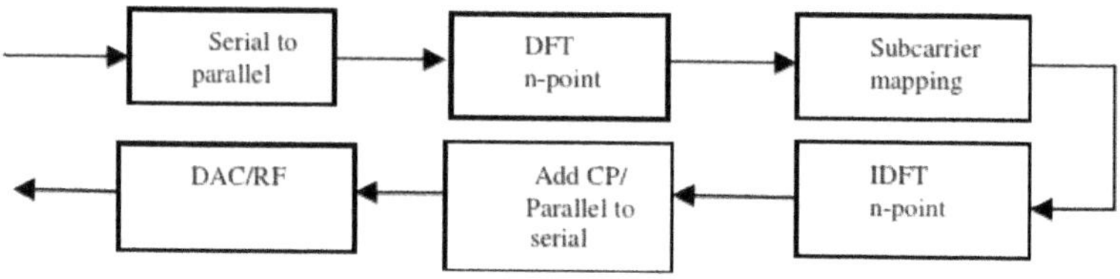

Fig. 1. Block diagram of SC-FDMA transmitter. x_m ($m = 0,1,, M\ 1$) are time domain symbols after SC-FDMA modulation. M is the total number of subcarriers, and N ($N < M$) is the number of subcarriers occupied by the input data.

Fig.1 shows the block diagram of an SC-FDMA transmitter, where M is the total number of subcarriers, x_m (m=0,1,∀, M-1) are time domain symbols after SC- FDMA modulation, and N ($N < M$) is the number of subcarriers occupied by the input data. SC-FDMA transmitter groups the modulation symbols into blocks each containing N symbols. Then each time domain data block was transformed to a frequency domain data block by an N-point DFT. Next it maps each of the N-point DFT outputs to one of the M orthogonal subcarriers. Then an M-point IDFT transforms subcarrier mapping outputs into a complex time domain signal x_m.

$$PAPR = \frac{\max_{m=0,1,\forall,M-1} |x_m|^2}{\frac{1}{M}\sum_{m=0}^{M-1}|x_m|^2} \tag{1}$$

1.2 Tone Reservation Method

Tone reservation (TR) method is based on adding time domain PAPR reduction signals to the time domain data signals to reduce its peaks. Both the transmitter and the receiver agree on reserving a small subset of tones for generating PAPR reduction signals. Those reserved tones are not used for data transmission. When TR method is used, the new time domain vector x can be represented as

$$x = x + c = IDFT(X + C) \tag{2}$$

where $\boldsymbol{c}$ is the corresponding time domain PAPR reduction vector of the frequency domain PAPR reduction vector $\boldsymbol{C}$, and $\boldsymbol{x}$ is the corresponding time domain data vector of the frequency domain data vector $\boldsymbol{X}$. $\boldsymbol{X}$ and $\boldsymbol{C}$ must lie in disjoint frequency subspaces. TR method does not need any side information and any receiver operation.

2 The Original Approach Based on TR Method

The approach based on TR method in [2] uses one reserved subcarrier to generate time domain PAPR reduction signals for reducing the first maximum peak magnitude of time domain data vector $\boldsymbol{x}$. First, the frequency domain PAPR reduction vector $\boldsymbol{C}$ has only one nonzero element C_k. k is the subcarrier index. The time domain PAPR reduction vector $\boldsymbol{c}$ is computed out as follows.

$$c = c[n] = \frac{1}{\sqrt{N}} C_k \exp j\frac{2\pi kn}{N} \in n = 0,1,\forall,N-1 \tag{3}$$

where N is the total number of subcarriers. c has a constant magnitude and a time varying phase for all n. To reduce the first maximum peak magnitude $[n_1]$, themagnitude and the phase of c must be modified. The phase of$c[n_1]$ must be modified into an opposite phase of $x[n_1]$, Where n_l is a time index of the l-th maximum peak.

3 The Proposed Improved Method

In this section, we proposed an improved method based on the original method in [2]. Let $\bar{c}$ be the time domain PAPR reduction vector which was generated by the original method, and $\hat{c}$ be the more appropriate time domain reduction vector which was generated by proposed improved method. The magnitude of $\hat{c}$ ($|\hat{c}| \geq |\bar{c}|$) was calculated out by the phase differences between$\hat{c}$ $[n_l] and$ $x[n_l]$, where n_l is time index of l-th maximum peak. When add $\hat{c}$ to x, because the magnitude of $\hat{c}$ is larger than that of $\bar{c}$, the first maximum peak magnitude $x[n_1]$ was suppressed further. So the improved method has better PAPR reduction performance. First, we used one reserved subcarrier to generate time domain PAPR reduction vector $\bar{c}$ by original method, whose magnitude and phases have been modified. Then normalize $\bar{c}$ as follow.

$$\hat{c} = \frac{\bar{c}}{|\bar{c}|} \tag{4}$$

And let$\hat{\theta}$ $[n_l] = \{\hat{\theta}[n_1], \hat{\theta}[n_2], \forall, \hat{\theta}[n_N]\}$ be a set of the phase differences between $\hat{c}\,[n_l]$ *and* $x\,[n_l]$. $\hat{\theta}\,[n_l]$ can be expressed as follow.

$$\hat{\theta}\,[n_l] = \angle\hat{c}[n_l] - \angle x\,[n_l] \tag{5}$$

Both original and proposed methods are to suppress $|x[n_1]|$ for PAPR reduction and to prevent other peak magnitudes larger than $|\bar{x}[n_1]|$ after PAPR reduction. So it is very important that $|\bar{x}[n_l]|$ must be always smaller than $|\bar{x}[n_1]|$ in both methods, i.e.

$$|\bar{x}\,[n_l]|^2 \leq |\bar{x}\,[n_1]|^2 \qquad l = 2,3,\forall,N, \tag{6}$$

Where

$$= |x[n_l]|^2 + |\hat{c}[n_l]|^2 + 2(\cos\hat{\theta}\ [n_l])|x[n_l]||\hat{c}[n_l]| \tag{7}$$

When l =1, since the phase of $\hat{c}\ [n_1]$ must be an opposite phase of $[n_1]$, i.e. $\hat{\theta}\ [n_1] = \pi$ then

$$\left|\overline{x[n_l]}\right|^2 = |x[n_l]|^2 + |\hat{c}[n_l]|^2 - 2|x[n_l]||\hat{c}[n_l]| \tag{8}$$

Next, since $\hat{c}$ has a constant magnitude, then ranges of $|\hat{c}[n_l]|$ for $l = 2,3,\forall, N$

$$|\hat{c}[n_l]| \leq \frac{|x\ [n_1]|^2 - |x[n_l]|^2}{2\{|x[n_1]| + |x[n_l]|(\cos\hat{\theta}\ [n_l])\}}, l = 2,3,\forall, N. \tag{9}$$

To reduce $|x[n_1]|$ further, $|\hat{c}|$ must be as large as possible. So let $|\hat{c}[n_l]|$ for $, l = 2,3,\forall, N$ be maximums, i.e.

$$|\hat{c}[n_l]| = \frac{|x\ [n_1]|^2 - |x[n_l]|^2}{2\{|x[n_1]| + |x[n_l]|(\cos\hat{\theta}\ [n_l])\}}, l = 2,3,\forall, N. \tag{10}$$

Then N -1 candidate magnitudes of $\hat{c}$ will be found by (10). Lastly, to make sure (6) for all l, the optimal magnitude of $\hat{c}$ i.e. must be the minimum of N -1 candidate magnitudes, i.e.

$$\begin{aligned} |\hat{c}| &= \min_{l=2,3,\forall,N} (|\hat{c}[n_l]|) \\ &= \min_{l=2,3,\forall,N} \frac{|x\ [n_1]|^2 - |x[n_l]|^2}{2\{|x[n_1]| + |x[n_l]|(\cos\hat{\theta}\ [n_l])\}} \quad € \end{aligned} \tag{11}$$

And $|\hat{c}|$ calculated out by (11) will be never smaller than $|\bar{c}|$, even though the phase $\angle\hat{c}[n_l]$ is same to $\angle x\ [n_l]$ for $l = 2,3,\forall, N$ (the worst case), i.e. $\hat{\theta}\ [n_l] = 0$. So the new vector $x + \hat{c}$ has low PAPR than$x + \bar{c}$. But the maximum PAPR reduction gain for the proposed method is the same as that for the original method, which is 6.02dB [2].

4 Conclusion

In this paper, an improved method for PAPR reduction based on the original approach in [2] was proposed. The proposed method improves PAPR reduction performance by finding out the optimal magnitude of PAPR reduction signals .Simulation results in SC-FDMA system shows that the PAPR reduction performance of the proposed improved method is better than that of the approach in [2] for using only one subcarrier and several subcarriers, respectively.

5 Simulation Results

Let method I be the original method in [2] and method II be the proposed improved method in this paper. Simulations are according to SC-FDMA system model in [4]. 10^4 uniformly random data points were generated to acquire the CCDF of PAPR which is calculated by Monte Carlo simulation. Subcarrier mapping modes is localized modes. The total number of subcarriers M was set to 256, input data block size N to 64 and the number of PAPR reduction subcarriers i to 1, 3 and 5. And 16QAM symbol constellations were considered.

References

[1] Jiang, T., Wu, Y.: An Overview: Peak-to-Average Power Ratio Reduction Techniques for OFDM Signals. IEEE Trans. On Broadcasting 54(2), 257–268 (2008)
[2] Son, Y., Nam, C.H., Lee, H.S.: An Approach for PAPR Reduction Based on Tone Reservation Method. In: IEEE Consumer Communications and Networking Conference, January 10-13 (2009)
[3] Myung, H.G., Lim, J., Goodman, D.J.: Single carrier FDMA for uplink wireless transmission. IEEE Vehicular Technology Mag. 1(3), 30–38 (2006)
[4] Myung, H.G., Lim, J., Goodman, D.J.: Peak-to-average Power Ratio of Single Carrier FDMA Signals with Pulse Shaping. In: IEEE International Symposium on Personal, Indoor and Mobile Radio Communications, September 11-14 (2006)

Reed-Solomon Decoder Architecture Using Bit-Parallel Systolic Multiplier

Suvarna K. Gosavi[1], U.S. Ghodeswar[1], and G.G. Sarate[2]

[1] Yeshwantrao Chavan College of Engineering, Nagpur
[2] Badnera College of Engineering, Amravati
suvarna.wakhare06@gmail.com,
sakharkar2002@yahoo.co.in,
ggs_anshu@rediffmail.com

Abstract. Reed-Solomon (RS) codes play an important role in providing error protection and data integrity. Design of a scalable RS decoder is implemented with Bit-Parallel Systolic Multiplier. This bit-parallel multiplier is defined from All-One Polynomial. This can perform higher data throughput rate with shorter latency. As compared to other decoder architecture design the proposed work consist of less arithmetic operations and gate count is also comparably less.

Keywords: RS Decoder, Bit-Parallel, All-One Polynomial.

1 Introduction

Reed-Solomon codec is a widely used Forward Error Correcting (FEC) technique. RS decoder can be implemented with a Bit-Parallel Systolic Multiplier using All-One Polynomial (AOP). Basic block diagram of RS decoder is shown in Fig.1. The three operations are syndrome calculation, key equation solving, and error correction.

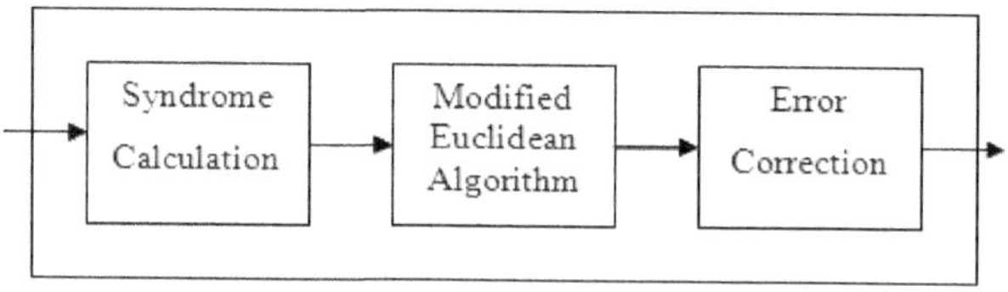

Fig. 1. Block diagram of a Reed-Solomon decoder

2 Syndrome Calculation

The syndrome calculation module receives codes from channel, denoted as r(x), and calculates syndrome polynomial S(x).

$$S(x) = \sum_{i=0}^{2t-1} S_i x^i \tag{1}$$

V.V. Das and N. Thankachan (Eds.): CIIT 2011, CCIS 250, pp. 122–126, 2011.

Where t is the error correcting capability, t = 4 and i= 0,1,2,……..,7. Also 2t = n-k. Then, the coefficients of syndrome polynomial can be calculated by,

$$S_i = r(\alpha^i) = \sum_{j=0}^{n-1} r_j \alpha^{ij}, i = 0,1,....,(2t-1) \tag{2}$$

Where n is the code length and α^0 , α^1 ,….., α^{2t-1} are the roots of the generation polynomial in encoding. Here, t = 4, n = 15 & k = 7.

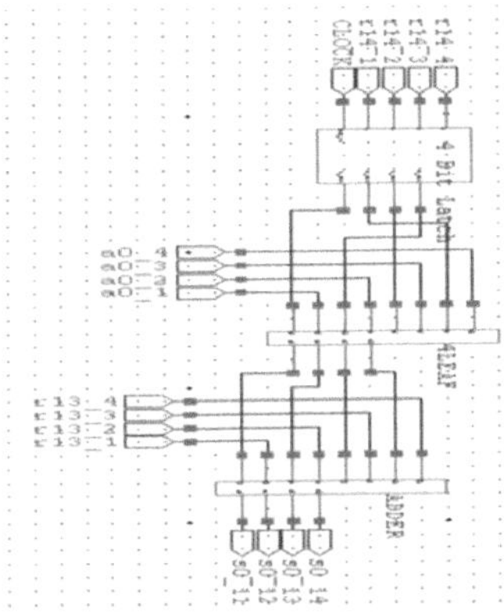

Fig. 2(a). Schematic of Syndrome Calculation

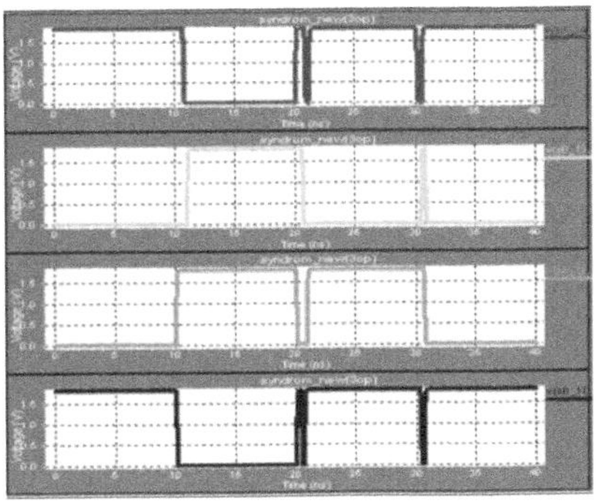

Fig. 2(b). Output Waveform of Syndrome Calculation

Table 1. I/P & O/P of Syndrome calculation for α^0

INPUTS			
r14	(0101)	(1110)	(0101)
r13	(0110)	(1010)	(0111)
a0	(1100)	(0110)	(1011)
OUTPUT			
S0_1	(1001)	(0110)	(1101)

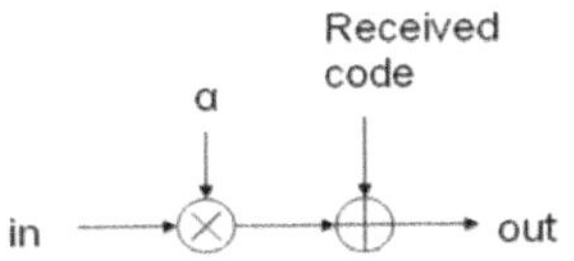

Fig. 2 (c). Processing unit of Syndrome Calculation

2.1 Bit- Parallel Systolic Multiplier

The Bit-Parallel Systolic Multiplier is the effective algorithm for computing multiplication over a class of fields $GF(2^m)$. This multiplier is composed of $(m)^2$ identical cells, each consist of one 2-input AND gate, one 2-input XOR gate and three 1-bit latches. A polynomial of the form $P(x) = p_0 + p_1x + p_2x^2 + \ldots + p_{m-1}\, x^{m-1}$ over

$GF(2^m)$ is called an all one polynomial (AOP) of degree m, if $p_i = 1$ for i = 0, 1, 2, …, m. For example, m = 4 i.e. $GF(2^4)$ the representation is $A = 1 + \alpha + \alpha^2 + \alpha^3$ For Multiplication, Let α be a root of the irreducible AOP of degree *m* over GF(2). Suppose that $A = A_0 + A_1\alpha + A_2\alpha^2 + \ldots + A_{m-1}\alpha^{m-1}$ and $B = B_0 + B_1\alpha + B_2\alpha^2 + \ldots + B_{m-1}\alpha^{m-1}$ are two elements in the field $GF(2^m)$. Therefore we obtained, $AB = (A_0 + A_1\alpha + \ldots + A_{m-1}\alpha^{m-1})(B_0 + B_1\alpha + \ldots + B_{m-1}\alpha^{m-1})$.

2.2 Properties

Let ⊗ and + denote the operations of a multiplication and addition over $GF(2^4)$ respectively. The product of the multiplication of A and B over $GF(2^m)$ can also be obtained from the following steps.

Step 1:

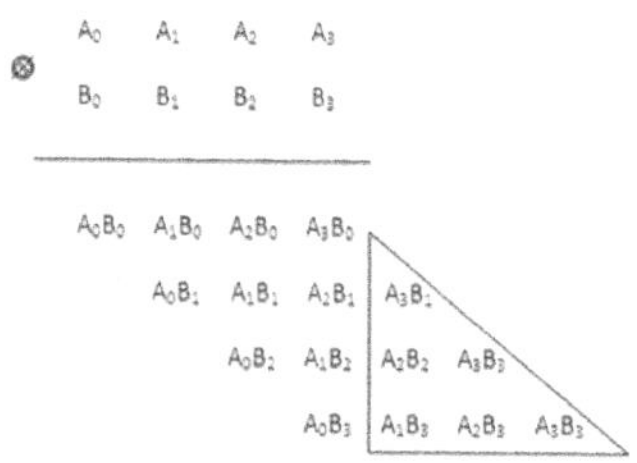

Step 2: Using the cyclic shift properties,

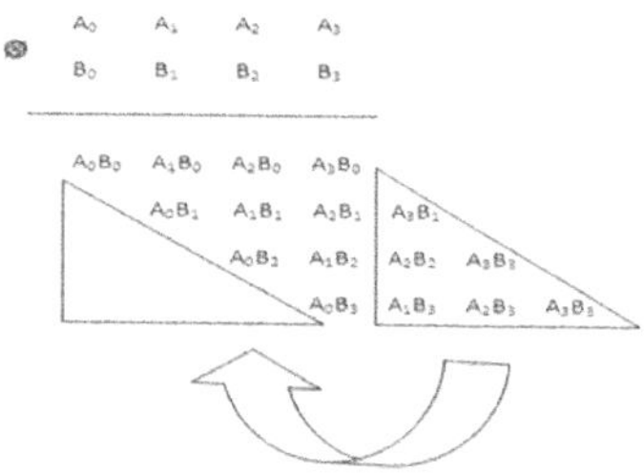

Step 3: After applying addition property

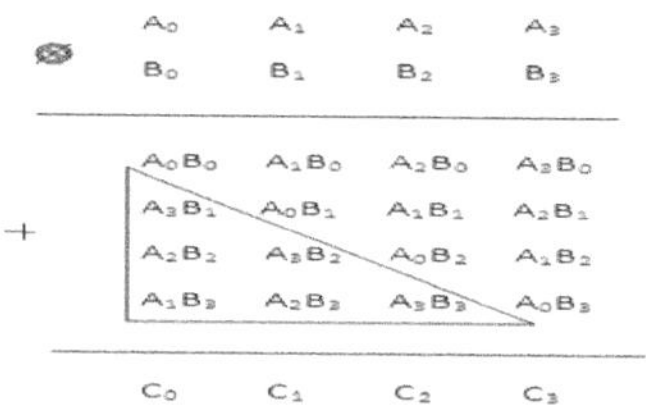

Fig. 3(a). Single cell multiplier

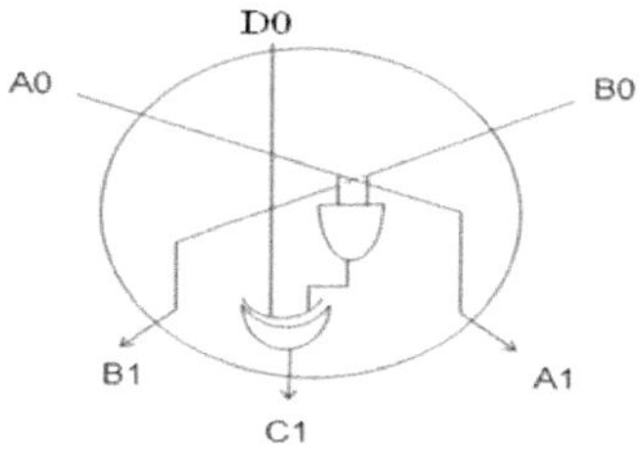

3 Modified Euclidean Algorithm

For key equation-solving module the modified Euclidean algorithm as it required low hardware complexity. We consider *σ(x)* as error location polynomial and *ω(x)* as error magnitude polynomial

$$S(x)\sigma(x) = \omega(x) \bmod(x^{2t}) \tag{4}$$

The modified Euclidean algorithm can be explained by following equations.

A. Initial Condition: $R_0(x) = x^{2t}$, $Q_0(x) = S(x)$, $L_0(x)$, $U_0(x) = 1$
B. Output Assignment: $\omega(x) = Q_{i-1}(x)$, $\sigma(x)$, $U_{i-1}(x)$

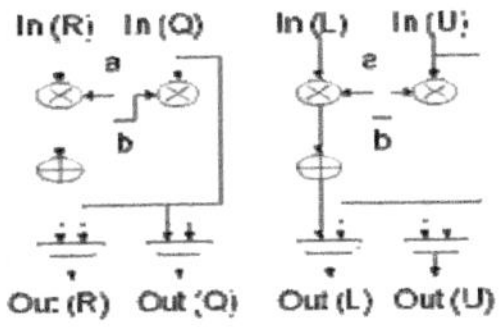

Fig. 4(a). Processing unit of solving key equation

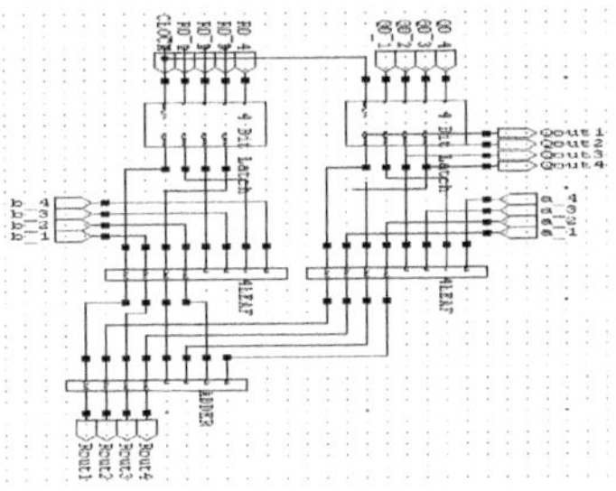

Fig. 4(b). Schematic of processing unit of solving key equation

Table 2. I/P & O/P of key solving equation

INPUTS		
RO	(1011)	(1100)
a	(1000)	(0100)
b	(1100)	(1010)
QO	(0010)	(0110)
OUTPUT		
Rout	(0010)	(1100)
Qout	(0100)	(0110)

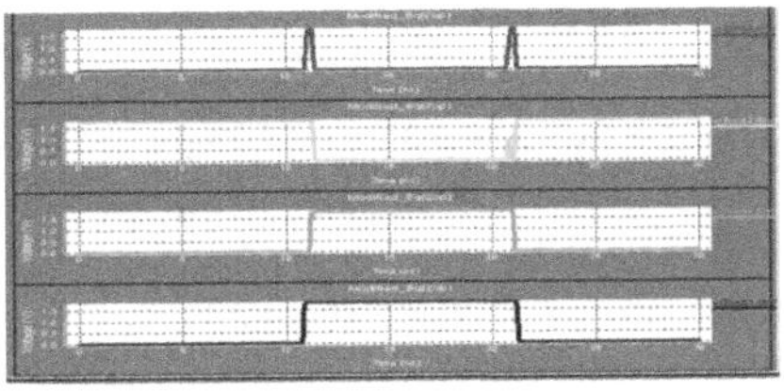

Fig. 4(c). Waveform of key solving equation

4 Error Correction

The error correction module finds the locations of errors by check if $\sigma(\alpha^{-k})=0$, from k = 0 to k = (n-1). This is called the Chien's search. Chien's search evaluates

$$\sigma(\alpha^{-k}) = \sum_{i=0}^{v} \sigma_i.(\alpha^{-i})^k, k = 0,1,\ldots,(n-1) \quad (5)$$

In this Forney algorithm is used for calculating the error values.

$$W_{ik} = W_{i(k+1)} * \alpha^i, i = 0, 1, \ldots, t\text{-}1.; \omega(\alpha^{-k}) = W_{0k} + W_{1k} + \ldots + W_{(t-1)k} \quad (6)$$

Table 3. I/P & O/P of Error correction

INPUTS		
D1	(1110)	(1010)
a0	(0111)	(0100)
e0	(0110)	(1001)
OUTPUT		
Out1	(0111)	(1100)

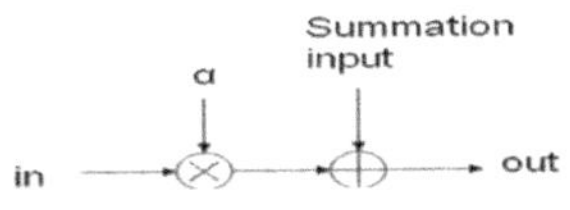

Fig. 5(a). Processing unit of error correction

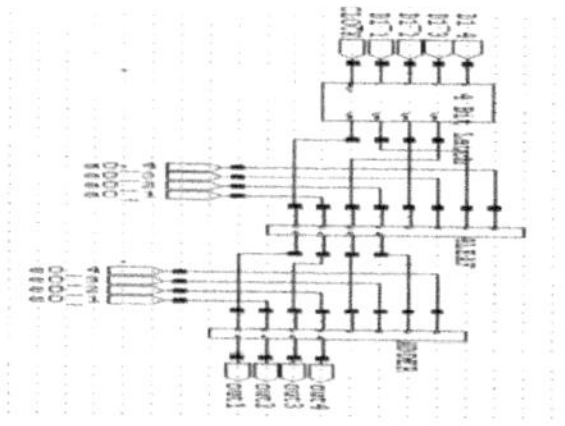

Fig. 5(b). Processing unit of error correction

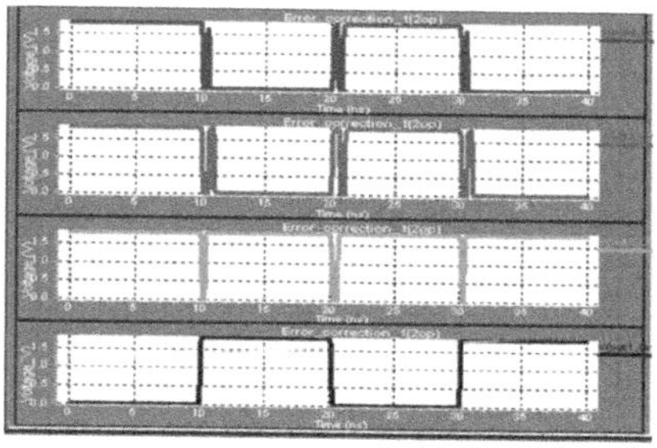

Fig. 5(c). Output Waveform of error correction

5 Conclusion

In this paper, we have design a scalable Reed-Solomon decoding processor based on Bit-parallel systolic multiplier using all one polynomial for GF (2^m). 4 bit Multiplier designed has a high throughput due to the low propagation delay in each cell. Moreover, the latency of the AOP-based multiplier is only m + 1 clock cycles to compute a multiplication in GF(2^m). Also RS decoder architecture has very good flexibility performing different data throughput rate from very low to very high, with acceptable power consumption on data path control. Table 4 shows the utilization of three blocks of the RS Decoder.

Table 4. Summery of utilization for various architecture

	Syndrome Calculation (S0)	Modified Euclidean Algorithm (R0) & (Q0)	Error Correction (σ0)
Gate Count	6048 MOSFET'S	808 MOSFET'S	2160 MOSFET'S
Simulation Time	1269.37 Sec.	4.94 Sec.	12.47 Sec
Average Power	8.0703e-003	2.5933e-004	5.9262e-004
Latency	0.25 nSec	0.9 nSec	0.2 nSec

References

1. Yeo, J.-C., Hsu, H.-Y., Wu, A.-Y.: A Scalable Reed-Solomon Decoding processor based on Unified finite-field processing element design. In: IEEE Workshop, pp. 148–151 (October 2004)
2. Lee, C.-Y., Lu, E.-H., Lee, J.-Y.: Bit-Parallel Systolic Multipliers for GF(2^m) Fields Defined by All-One Polynomials. IEEE Transaction on Computers 50(5) (May 2001)
3. Sklar, B.: Digital Communications, Fundamentals and Applications
4. Ilanchezhian, P., Parvathi, R.M.S.: Low Power Reed Solomon Codes Based Power Utilllization System

Significant Parametric Measures for Enhanced and Accurate Energy Management of Embedded Systems

R. Prabakaran[1], S. Arivazhagan[2], and X. Jennifer Viola[3]

[1] Department of Electrical and Electronics Engineering,
Anna University of Technology, Tiruchirappalli, Tamil Nadu, India
[2] Department of Electrical and Electronics Engineering, Mepco Schlenk Engineering College,
Sivakasi, Tamil Nadu, India
[3] M.E Pervaisve Computing Technology, Anna University of Technology,
Tiruchirappalli, Tamil Nadu, India
{hiprabakaran,xjenniferviola}@gmail.com, sarivu@yahoo.co.in

Abstract. The recent technological advancements of embedded gadgets is tremendous and they impose a wide gamut of challenges for their operation and maintenance. The biggest bottleneck however that remains is the power capacity of the devices. In this context, the measurement of energy of their peripherals and connectives has been gaining much importance. This work concentrates on bringing out the significant parameters and changeovers by scaling peripheral voltages and corresponding clock frequencies. This has the potential for important contributions in the gamut of ease of power measurement at voltage and frequency variations. The final conclusions of our analysis and measurement techniques can help researchers working in this area with flexibility and reliability of conceptual experimentation.

Keywords: Static power management, Dynamic power management, power and energy estimation, energy management, and embedded systems.

1 Introduction

The tremendous utilization of portable devices demands high performance with limited energy resource. The power management schemes in embedded systems are divided into two categories, namely static power management scheme and dynamic power management scheme. The recent advancement in the processor design allows dynamic scheduled power scheme based on voltage and frequency scaling. Initially high performance processors such as the Transmeta Crusoe, Intel StrongARM and XScale were designed to support these features, but now ARM 7, PIC microcontrollers and LPC900 series have been under use with dynamic power management capabilities.

As power consumption becomes a challenging task in design of the embedded device, the researcher needs efficient, accurate and low cost tools to evaluate the performance of their software and architectural innovations. Many attempts were made towards the characterization of power and energy measurement of the system but all involved only static power consumption techniques. Hence, there is a need to

V.V. Das and N. Thankachan (Eds.): CIIT 2011, CCIS 250, pp. 127–132, 2011.

measure and characterize dynamic power consumption and energy estimation of the embedded systems. Our paper gives details on developing a technique to measure the dynamic power of the embedded system by means of low cost measuring devices which may be further applicable to embedded system.

The authors in [1], introduced the technique for energy measurement of a zigbee based embedded systems. The authors in [2] described the method for model based embedded system, which gives detail about current consumption by using accurate and integrable energy meter. The measurement technique for data logging system with accurate estimation of energy was ascribed in [3], which will not affect normal operating condition of the core and peripheral modules. The methods suggested in [4 and 5] for measuring the digital circuit methods provided high accuracy. In [6], basic energy meter for all of the above heuristic measurements with the digital circuitry is introduced. The simulation based methodology for estimating the energy consumption in peripherals such as audio and video devices were explained in [7]. The approach for instantaneous current measurement technique was presented in [8]. In [9], the authors devised an instruction level energy model for the VLIW processor. The energy measurement from the control flow graph of the program which is applicable to non-pipelined processor was described in [10]. Further, a conceptual approach [11] was introduced which is applicable to both embedded systems & general purpose platforms. The authors [12, 13] developed the energy consumption by the use of java based portable devices. The energy measurement in [14] was calculated by means of number of instructions and machine cycles for the program to be executed.

2 Proposed Approach for Measurement of Energy

The Fig.1 gives the pseudo code for the measurement of the P89LPC936 microcontroller by varying the power level means of dynamic frequency scaling method. The experimental setup gives the details to implement the dynamic frequency scaling algorithm with the help of special function registers.

```
BEGIN
DEFINE the Initial Variables
SWITCH to Max/Required Power
SWITCH the UART Speed, Timer/Counter calculation etc., based on DIVM register
 value & Oscillator speed
IF Application Power=Need THEN SWITCH
IF NOT Brownout detection condition
RESET the controller
ELSE SWITCH
END
```

Fig. 1. Pseudo code

3 Experimental Setup for Measurement of Energy

The proposed methodology uses an energy meter which consists of the current mirror, a recording unit and the Target Development Board. The recording unit comprises of RS flip- flop and a microcontroller which acts as a counter and counts the number of discharges that takes place.

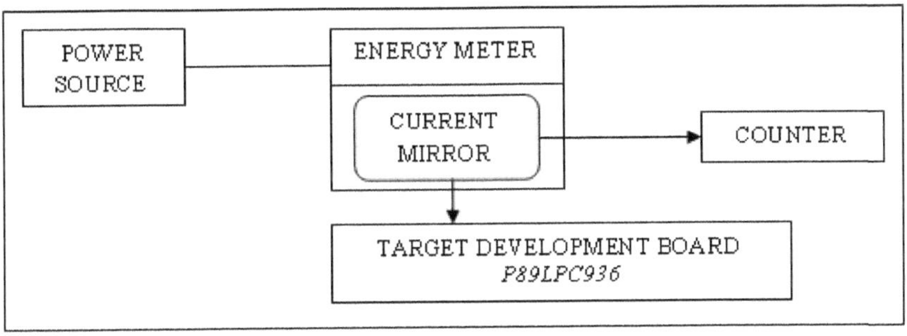

Fig. 2. Experimental Setup

The proposed approach is used to measure the power consumption of the processor, while scaling the frequency. The power consumption of the processor is given by the formula

$$P = CV^2f \quad (1)$$

By the above equation the power(P) consumption of the processor can be reduced or increased by three factors. Total switching capacitance(C), square of applied voltage(V) and clock frequency(f). In our paper we have used 89LPC936 processor in which the power consumption is reduced by scaling down the frequency.

"The oscillator frequency OSCCLK of the LPC936 can be divided down, by an integer, upto 510 times by configuring the dividing register DIVM. The output of the frequency CCLK of the divider is according the formula

$$CCLK = OSCCLK \ / \ (2 * N \ ) . \quad (2)$$

where N is the value of DIVM. The CCLK frequency can be in the range of OSCCLK to OSCCLK/510. For N = 0 CCLK = OSCCLK."

The frequency scaling is done by keeping the controller in the different modes such as ideal mode, active mode and in the power down mode. The current consumption of the controller is studied in various clock frequencies.

4 Results and Discussions

The experimental setup tried successfully, the following observations are made by varying the condition of Mode/DIVM. We have observed the current level of the microcontroller by varying f_{CCLK} values.

4.1 Measuring the Energy Consumption of Processor in Idle and Active Mode

In Idle mode, execution of instructions is suspended until either a reset or interrupt occurs. In active mode, the CPU is still running and the peripherals are turned off. The idle & active mode current consumption of our proposed system for different frequency is illustrated in the table 1 and figure 3.

Table 1. Current consumption in Idle & Active mode at varying frequencies

DIVM	fCCLK	I_{DD}(mA) at V_{DD} = 2.4V		I_{DD}(mA) at V_{DD} = 3.0V		I_{DD}(mA) at V_{DD} = 3.6V	
		IDLE	ACTIVE	IDLE	ACTIVE	IDLE	ACTIVE
DIVM = 00h	11.05 MHz	2.50	4.56	3.61	6.78	4.80	8.83
DIVM = 0Ah	553 kHz	0.71	0.85	1.09	1.41	1.45	1.70
DIVM = 64h	55.3 kHz	0.63	0.67	0.93	1.15	1.28	1.35
DIVM = FFh	21.7 kHz	0.62	0.65	0.92	1.14	1.27	1.34

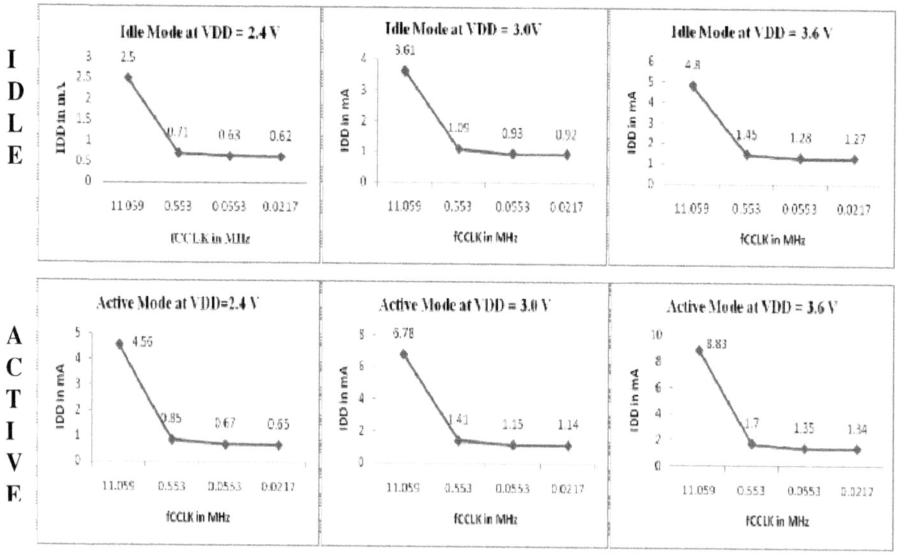

Fig. 3. Current waveforms at different frequencies in Idle & Active mode

4.2 Measuring the Energy Consumption of Processor in Power-Down Mode

In Power-down mode, the oscillator is shut down and the chip receives no internal clocks. The Power-down mode current consumption of our proposed system for different frequency is illustrated in the table 2 & 3 and figure 4.

Table 2. Current consumption in power-down mode

Power-Down Mode	IDD(μA) at VDD = 2.4V	IDD(μA) at VDD = 3.0V	IDD(μA) at VDD = 3.6V
Normal	51.9	54.6	58.1
Comparators are active	66.5	69.3	73.2

Table 3. Current consumption in Power-down mode at varying frequencies

DIVM	fCCLK (kHz)	IDD at VDD=2.4V	IDD at VDD=3.0V	IDD at VDD=3.6V
00h	32.768	105.1 μA	118.2 μA	138.9 μA
01h	16.384	96.2 μA	105.2 μA	116.5 μA
02h	8.192	96.0 μA	104.6 μA	116.3 μA
Total power-down	0.0	6.4 μA	10.2 μA	18.0 μA

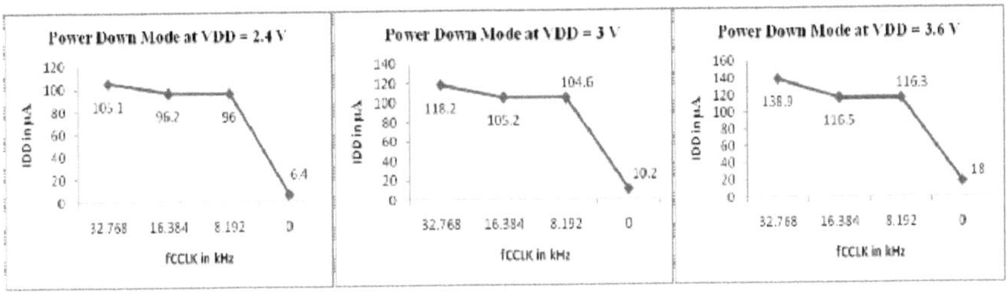

Fig. 4. Current waveforms at different frequencies in Power-down mode

In total Power-down mode the CPU and oscillator will be turned off. Only the System Timer / RTC and the WDT can still run (if enabled).

5 Conclusion

The measurement technique is verified with an experimental setup for different frequency by varying the core clock of the microcontroller. The frequency scaling clearly saves the energy consumption of the microcontroller. The results of the experiment will helpful for the researchers working in the area of embedded systems to study the critical power measurement techniques of the microcontroller with various operating conditions. The results also prove that total power down mode of the controller reduces the power consumption very significantly. Future work is planned to create the algorithm for and embedded systems to consume less energy with the help of the low power scheduler.

References

1. Konstantakos, V., Laopoulos, T.: Built-in energy measurements in zigbee systems. In: Proceedings on IEEE International Workshop on Intelligent Data Acquisition and Advanced Computing Systems: Technology and Applications, pp. 53–58 (2009)
2. Konstantakos, V., Laopoulos, T.: A power measuring technique for built-in test purposes. In: IEEE Instrumentation and Measurement Technology Conference, pp. 90–95 (2006)
3. Konstantakos, V., Laopoulos, T.: Self-Evaluation Configuration for Remote Data Logging Systems. In: IEEE International Workshop on Intelligent Data Acquisition and Advanced Computing Systems: Technology and Applications (September 2007)
4. Konstantakos, V., Kosmatopoulos, K., Nikolaidis, S., Laopoulos, T.: In-Chip Configuration for Monitoring Power Consumption in Micro-processing Systems. In: IEEE International Workshop on Intelligent Data Acquisition and Advanced Computing Systems: Technology and Applications (September 2005)
5. Kavvadias, N., Neofotistos, P., Nikolaidis, S., Kosmatopoulos, K., Laopoulos, T.: Measurement Analysis of the Software-Related Power Consumption in Microprocessors. IEEE Trans. on Instrumentation and Measurement 53(4) (August 2004)
6. Konstantakos, V., Chatzigeorgiou, A., Nikolaidis, S., Laopoulos, T.: Energy consumption estimation in embedded systems. IEEE Transactions on Instrumentation and Measurement 57(4), 797–804 (2008)
7. Celebican, O., Rosing, T.S., Mooney III, V.J.: Energy Estimation of Peripheral Devices in Embedded Systems. In: GLSVLSI 2004, April 26-28 (2004)
8. Konstantakos, V., Kosmatopoulos, K., Nikolaidis, S., Laopoulos, T.: Measurement of power consumption in digital systems. IEEE Transactions on Instrumentation and Measurement 55(5), 1662–1670 (2006)
9. Sami, M., Sciuto, D., Silvano, C., Zaccaria, V.: An Instruction-Level Energy Model for Embedded VLIW Architectures. IEEE Transactions on Computer-Aided Design of Integrated Circuits And Systems 21(9) (September 2002)
10. Chatzigeorgiou, Stephanides, G.: Energy Metric for Software Systems. Software Quality Journal 10(4), 355–371 (2002)
11. Rapaka, V.S.P., Marculescu, D.: Pre-characterization Free, Efficient Power/Performance Analysis of Embedded and General Purpose Software Applications. In: Proceedings of the Conference on Design, Automation and Test in Europe, vol. 1 (2003)
12. Seo, C., et al.: An Energy Consumption Framework for Distributed Java-Based Software Systems. In: ACM SIGSOFT 2006 / FSE 14 (2006)
13. Seo, C., Malek, S., Medvidovic, N.: An Energy Consumption Framework for Distributed Java-Based Systems. In: ASE 2007, Atlanta, Georgia, USA, November 5-9 (2007)
14. Zotos, K., Litke, A., Chatzigeorgiou, A., Nikolaidis, S., Stephanides, G.: Energy Complexity of Software in Embedded Systems. In: IASTED International Conference on Automation, Control and Applications (ACIT-ACA 2005), Novosibirsk, Russia, June 20-24 (2005)

Prediction of Productivity of Mustard Plant Using Variable Reduction and Artificial Neural Network Model

Satyendra Nath Mandal[1], J. Pal Choudhury[2], Debasis Mazumdar[3], Dilip De[4], and S.R. Bhadra Chaudhuri[5]

[1] Kalyani Govt. Engg College, Kalyani , Nadia (W.B), India
satyen_kgec@rediffmail.com
[2] Kalyani Govt. Engg College, Kalyani, Nadia (W.B), India
jnpc193@yahoo.com
[3] Dept. o f Agric. Statistics, B.C.K.V, Kalyani, Nadia (W.B), India
debstat@gmail.com
[4] Bidhan Chandra Krishi Viswavidyalaya, Kalyani, Nadia (W.B), India
dilipde.bckv@gmail.com
[5] BESU/Dept. of ETC , Howrah (W. B), India
prof_srbc@yahoo.com

Abstract. The productivity of mustard plant is dependent on huge number of time dependent parameters. But many of them are not significant or they are highly correlated with others parameters. Some parameters playing significant role in growth of the plant and give the information which is mandatory but not correlated with the others. So, same result can be produced by fewer parameters instead of considering all parameters. In this paper, an effect has been made to reduce the significant environmental parameters which have dominated the growth of mustard plant using principal component and factor analysis. These two methods have been used as variable reduction model. The artificial neural network has been applied on highly significant parameters to predict the shoot length of mustard plant. The linear equation has been used to find the shoot length at maturity. Finally, the productivity of the plant has been predicted based on shoot length of the plant at maturity.

Keywords: Environmental Parameters, Principal Component Analysis, Factor Analysis, Significant Parameters, Artificial Neural Network.

1 Introduction

The main application of principal component and factor analysis are (1) to reduce the number of variables and (2) to detect the structure in the relationship between variables. Factor analysis and principal component analysis are applied as data reduction or structure detection methods[2]. In this paper, an effort has been made to reduce the on environment parameters which are dominates the growth of mustard plant

V.V. Das and N. Thankachan (Eds.): CIIT 2011, CCIS 250, pp. 133–137, 2011.

using principal component and factor analysis. Using both methods, it has been proved that only few numbers of related factors have to consider predicting the growth of mustard plant. The shoot length has been predicted by applying artificial neural network (ANN) on few selected parameters. Linear equation has been used on predicted shoot length to find the shoot length at maturity. Finally, the productivity of plant has been predicted from shoot lengthy at maturity (after 95 days). Earlier, this sort of work has not been used in prediction of growth. That is the reason for selecting this work described in the paper.

2 Data Used in This Paper

Data used has been taken from a statistical survey conducted by a group of certain agricultural scientists on different mustard plants under the supervision of Prof. Dilip De, Bidhan Chandra Krishi Viswavidyalaya West Bengal, India.

3 Method

The proposed method which has been used in prediction of shoot length are described as follows

Step 1: Various components of environmental data that dominated the growth of mustard plant have been taken.

Step 2: The method of principal component analysis has to be applied to find the significant parameters as follows.

2.1. The correlation matrix has to be derived to find the correlation among the parameters using available data.

2.2. The eigen values, total variances, cumulative eigen vectors and percentage of contribution of component has to be found out.

2.3. The sum of the eigen values has to be computed from which the factors are extracted (computed). Those components where eigen value is greater than 1.0 has to be selected.

2.4. The eigen vector has to be derived and the components whose eigen values are greater than 1.0 has to be selected.

2.5. As principal component analysis, one component is linear combination of all variables; the variable for which the value of corresponding component is either maximum negative or maximum positive. To select the variables under the same component, 10% of the component value of the selected variable has to be reduced and all the variables which are greater than 10% of the value of selected variable has to be selected.

2.6. The 2.5 has to be repeated for all components whose eigen value is greater than or equal to 1.0.

2.7. The selected variables under 2.5 and 2.6 will be reduced variables among the all variables.

Step 3: The factor analysis has to be applied to find the significant parameter as follows.

3.1. Factor loading has to be calculated using original data set.

3.2. The number of factors has to be chosen from all those factors whose eigen value greater than 1.0.

3.2. One variable in factor analysis is linear combination of all factors. The factor value under one variable is greatest of all factors has to be marked. In each factor, the greatest value from all marks values has to be found; the corresponding variable has to be taken.

3.2. To select the other significant variables in factor analysis, 10% of the selected factor value has to be computed and select all the variables which is greater than 10% of the selected factor.

Step 4: The union of the selected variable under principal and factor component analysis will be selected as the significant variables.

Step 5: The tables in which the last column will be the target value i.e. shoot length will be restructured and rest columns will be significant environment parameters derived by step 4.

Step 6: The multi-layer neural network and setting the initial weights of input to hidden layer and hidden to output layer, bias, learning parameters and momentum parameters has to be designed.

Step 7: The shoot lengths will be predicted using training and testing of the network.

Step 8: The shoot length at maturity will be predicted by applying the linear equation on predicted data.

Step 9: The productivity i.e pod yield of mustered plant will be predicted based on shoot length at maturity.

4 Implementation

4.1 Principal Component Analysis

After the plantation, the environmental parameters have been collected during the harvest period of growing stage of parameters have been collected. Using Statistica 7 software package, the correlation matrix of data from fig 1 has been computed and furnished in table 1.

Table 1. Eigenvector computed from fig 1

variable	Eigenvector and number of components is 3			
	variable Number	Component1	Component2	Component3
Maxi Temp.	1	0.376844	0.351089	-0.049277
Min Temp	2	0.367258	0.368866	-0.057148
Rain Fall	3	0.278404	-0.335760	0.186305
Max Humidity	4	-0.255216	**-0.504113**	0.020553
Min Humidity	5	**-0.447332**	-0.114271	0.047172
D1	6	-0.362725	0.228962	-0.134402
D2	7	-0.354890	0.373221	0.023754
D3	8	-0.349858	0.387868	0.016830
Sun Shine	9	-0.021059	0.136358	**0.968523**

In principal component analysis, one component is linear combination of all variables. The particular variables on which the components mostly depend on have been shown by underline in the table 1.

4.2 Factor Analysis

The same data has been used in factor analysis and using statistica 7 software package, factor loading have been calculated using factor analysis based on eigen values greater than 1.0 is furnished in table 2.

Table 2. Factor Loadings (Unrotated)

Variable	Factor Loadings (Unrotated) (PCAapplication)		
	Factor1	Factor2	Factor3
Maxi Temp.	**-0.827782**	0.558140	-0.048038
MIN Temp	**-0.807268**	0.586862	-0.055871
Rain Fall	-0.599427	-0.544217	0.188404
Max Humidity	0.566025	**-0.805376**	0.017682
Min Humidity	**0.976464**	-0.176991	0.047259
D1	**0.785226**	0.373728	-0.132438
D2	**0.765244**	0.604171	0.025844
D3	**0.753988**	0.627647	0.018927
Sun Shine	**0.043168**	0.213214	**0.969636**

In factor analysis [3], one variable is linear combination of all factors. The factor value which is greatest of all factors has been marked in the row of all variables. In each factor, it has been found the greatest value from all marks values; the corresponding variable has been taken.

4.3 Artificial Neural Network (ANN)

Under artificial neural network system, a feed forward back propagation neural network is used which contain three layers. Using training and testing the predicted shoot length is furnished in table 3. The average error has been calculated as 1.47%.

Table 3. Predicted Shoot Length using ANN

Max Humidity	Min Humidity	Sun Shine	Shoot Length	Predicted Shoot Length
95.75	58.35	7.77	19.00	19.00
95.98	58.63	7.86	22.00	21.543
96.22	58.92	7.94	24.00	23.698
96.45	59.20	8.03	27.00	27.65
96.68	59.48	8.11	31.00	30.523
96.91	59.76	8.16	33.00	32.834
97.14	60.04	8.22	34.00	34.876
97.37	60.32	8.27	36.00	35.116
97.60	60.60	8.32	38.00	37.757
97.65	60.63	8.10	42.00	41.998
97.69	60.67	7.88	46.00	45.115
97.74	60.70	7.66	50.00	49.121
97.78	60.73	7.44	54.00	55.112

5 Result and Conclusion

Applying principal component and factor analysis, it has been proved that out of nine environmental parameters, three of them (max humidity, min humidity and sun shine) are plays significant role for growing the mustard plant. If these three parameters are available sufficiently, the growth of mustard plant will be healthy and they will be produced huge yields. The final shoot length can be predicted using predicted data by ANN which furnished table 3 and linear equations. The final shoot length after 95 days is 135.88 cm and the corresponding pod yield has been predicted 679gm. This result can be tested using fuzzy logic, genetic algorithms.

Acknowledgments. The authors would like to thank to the All India Council for Technical Education (F.No-1-51/RID/CA/28/2009-10) for funding this research work.

References

[1] Shashua, A.: Intor. to Machine Learning. Lecture 9: Algebraic Representation I: PCA (scribe), pp. 1–9 (2003)

[2] Anderson, T.W.: Principal Components. In: An Introduction to Multivariate Statistical Analysis, ch. 11, pp. 451–460

[3] Rammel, R.J.: Understanding Factor Analysis. A Summary of Rummel's Applied Factor Analysis (1970)

[4] Mandal, S.N., Pal Choudhury, J., De, D., Bhadra Chaudhuri, S.R.: A framework for development of Suitable Method to find Shoot Length at Maturity of Mustard Plant Using Soft Computing Model. International Journal of Computer Science and Engineering 2(3), 113–120

[5] Mandal, S.N., Pal Choudhury, J., Bhadra Chaudhuri, S.R., De, D.: A framework to Predict Suitable Period of Mustard Plant Considering Effect of Weather Parameters Using Factor and Principal Component Analysis. International Journal of Information Technology & Knowledge Management I(II), 303–309

Bio-inspired Algorithms to Reconstruct Stereoscopic Disparity

Sheena Sharma and C.M. Markan

Dept. of Phy. & Comp. Sc.
Dayalbagh Educational Institute
Agra, India
{sheenasharma11,cm.markan}@gmail.com

Abstract. Binocular disparity refers to the difference in image location of an object seen by the left and right eyes, resulting from the eyes' horizontal separation. Bio-inspired systems aim to extract some interesting features from living beings, such as adaptability and fault tolerance, for including them in human-designed devices. The biological vision systems routinely accomplish complex visual tasks such as object recognition, stereoscopic vision and many more, which continue to challenge artificial systems. If any cell in the brain is dead, other cell takes over the dead cell and brain works in the normal way. Any bio-inspired system must be any day superior to any artificial method. In this paper, this paper presents some algorithms which are motivated from biological functioning, such as Cepstral filtering technique, phase method, reaction-diffusion algorithm. Further, this paper compares cepstral filtering technique with phase method. These two algorithms are claimed as two different approaches, but in this paper we show that in essence they are same. Both the algorithms exploit only part of the functions used in the biological flow of data to reconstruct the depth perception. The algorithms look different as both follow different procedures and functions. If the computational steps are decomposed and compared then they are doing the same thing. Each step in both algorithms is same and only the functions used are different as they are just the mathematical way of representation. By comparing both the algorithms, the advantage of one can be benefited by the other. The equivalence condition has also been derived.

Keywords: Stereo vision, Cepstral filtering technique, Gabor filters.

1 Introduction

The reconstruction of three-dimensional disparity from stereoscopic image is a well known and intensively investigated research problem. Among the many cues which humans use for inferring the structure of a 3D scene, binocular stereopsis has been one of the most extensively investigated (both algorithmically and psychophysically). This cue is based on an (unknown) means of utilization of the slightly different views of a 3D scene, projected onto the right and a left retina. From a generic point of view, this problem reduces to a matching or correlation of two slightly different scenes, in order

V.V. Das and N. Thankachan (Eds.): CIIT 2011, CCIS 250, pp. 138–146, 2011.

to find the (vector) displacement of small corresponding patches of projected image. Stereo vision or stereoscopic vision probably evolved as means of survival. With this, we can see where objects are in relation to our own bodies with much greater precision especially when the objects are moving toward or away from us in the depth dimension. There are many models dedicated to find the stereoscopic disparity and out of the existing algorithms, some are bio-inspired algorithms. Examples of bio-inspired algorithms are Cepstral filtering technique, Reaction-Diffusion method, Phase method, Binocular Energy method and many more. This paper discusses two bio-inspired algorithms in detail: Cepstral technique and Phase method. Cepstral filtering technique [1] and [2] is a mechanism that applies Fourier transforms on interlaced portions on an image from the two eyes mapped on the cortex. Such interlacing naturally occurs in the visual cortex in the form of Ocular Dominance Maps. It has been shown that the chemical and biological systems have diffusion processes coupled with chemical and /or biological reactions, these systems are reaction-diffusion systems [3], [4] and [5]. Further, this paper compares Cepstral technique with Phase method [6] which is based on even and odd receptive fields found in the primary visual cortex. These two algorithms were compared and showed as two different algorithms. Qian [7] compared Cepstral technique with the Phase method and found that both are different as Cepstral uses “logarithmic transformation”. Another similar work has been done in [8], where it is shown that the Energy method is different from Cepstral as Cepstral contains complex logarithmic operation. This paper pin points the similarities between Phase method and Cepstral filtering technique and also shows that Phase method involves logarithmic transformation.

2 Reaction-Diffusion Algorithm

The reaction-diffusion algorithm is one of the way which deals with reconstructing the stereoscopic disparity, with two assumptions: continuity and uniqueness [3].

It consists of set of two reaction-diffusion equations with two variable u(x, y, t) and v(x, y, t),

$$\delta_t u = D_u \nabla^2 u + f(u,v) \qquad \delta_t v = D_v \nabla^2 v + g(u,v) \tag{1}$$

where f (u, v) and g (u, v) are reaction terms. The Fitz Hugh-Nagumo type reaction-diffusion equations have reaction terms [3] and [4], which is

$$\mathrm{f(u,v)} = \lambda[\mathrm{u}(1-\mathrm{u})(\mathrm{u}-\mathrm{a}) - \mathrm{v}] \text{ and } \mathrm{g(u,v)} = \mathrm{u} - \mathrm{bv} \tag{2}$$

where a and b are constants and λ is a positive large constant [3], [4] and [5].

The authors in the paper have used sophisticated methods, as numerical computation of the partial differential equation [3], [4] and [5]. They used finite difference method with Crank-Nicholson scheme to approximate partial derivatives and Gauss-Seidal method to solve linear equations. We implemented the algorithm by using simple and easy functions such as discrete definition of 2-D Laplacian operator to solve partial differential equations. Further the authors have used normalized cross-correlation as a similarity measure; this paper uses Gabor jet of Gabor wavelets.

The reaction-diffusion system with the Gabor filters makes the algorithm more close to biological system. In this scheme, each Gabor filter is convolved with the image and the response of each filter is combined to a vector representing the filters. This vector of Gabor filter responses is known as Gabor jet [9]. Comparison between different Gabor jets allows a measure of similarity between image regions to be computed. Below equation defines the jet similarity functions for two images (J and J').

$$s_a(J, J') = \frac{\sum_{j=1}^{G_f} a_j a'_j}{\sqrt{\sum_{j=1}^{G_f} a_j^2 \sum_{j=1}^{G_f} a'^2_j}} \quad (3)$$

where a_j is the magnitude of the result of the convolution between the real and imaginary part of Gabor filter 'j' and image [9].

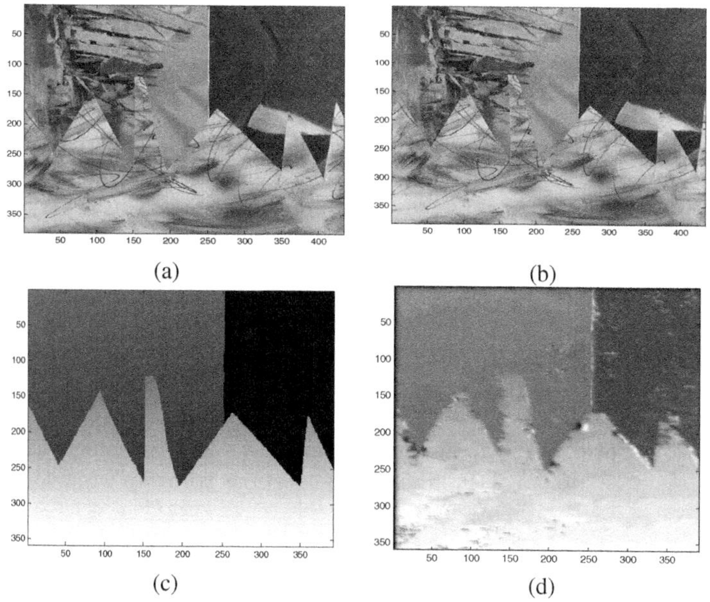

Fig. 1. Result of the modified reaction-diffusion algorithm, a) left stereo image, b) right stereo image, c) true disparity map, d) obtained dispatity map

We implement the proposed algorithm to stereo images, which has been widely utilized in other stereo algorithms. The website [10] provides the used stereo image and ground disparity map. The bad match percentage error for the test image (sawtooth) is 2.13 % whereas, in the rection-diffusion paper [3], it is 1.74%. The proposed algorithm has been tested on other images also.

3 Cepstral Filtering Technique

A windowed Cepstral filter, operating on an interlaced image format, is inspired by the structure of Ocular Dominance Columns [1]. The pattern presents the left and right images of the stereo pair in the form of thin strips of image. Each window is processed in parallel by Cepstral operator. The Cepstral is the Fourier transform of the log of its power spectrum.

Consider an interlaced image f (x, y) to be composed of a singular columnar pair. Data consists of an image patch s (x, y) (left image) and the shifted image (right image) placed next to it, and the columnar width is D.

We can mathematically represent the image as follows:

$$f\,(x,y) = s(x,y) * \{\delta(x,y) + \delta(x-D,y)\} \tag{4}$$

Cepstrum is defined as:

$$Cepstrum = |F\left(\log\left\{\left|F\big(f(x,y)\big)\right|^2\right\}\right)|^2 \tag{5}$$

The spectrum of the above equation will have a prominent term located at a magnitude of the shift (D, 0). The Cepstrum is the inverse transform of the log of the forward transform of the autocorrelation function [11]. Without the logarithm step, therefore, the algorithm would simply compute the autocorrelation function. The Cepstrum can be thought of as autocorrelation with an adaptive (non-linear) prefilter. The prefilter is compressive in the frequency domain-it tends to make the power spectrum more nearly uniform, reducing the contribution of narrowband signals while leaving broadband signals relatively unaltered. The periodic part of the signal is largely suppressed, while parts of the image that have unique matches are enhanced. The main features of Cepstrum analysis are: forward transformation to un-correlate the data, smooth the spectrum by applying a logarithmic function and inverse transformation to return to the Cepstrum.

3.1 Working

In the working of the Cepstral, first the sample windows of size h x w from left and right images are extracted. The sample windows are then spliced together along one edge to produce an image of size h x 2w. This results in the formation of peaks at the centre and at the left and right to it. The central peak is due to the autocorrelation, which is not taken into account.

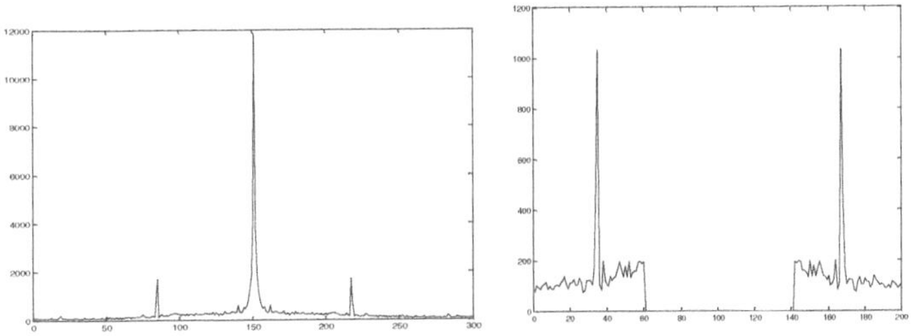

(a) (b)

Fig. 2. a) Cepstral applied to the image results in three peaks. The central peak is due to the autocorrelation, which is truncated. b). These peaks give the information related depth.

The main body of cepstral contains a 2-D FFT (FFT of Log of FFT). The DFT of size h x 2w can only handle frequencies in the range -h/2 to +h/2 vertically and –w to +w horizontally. Since DFTs are circular, positive disparities will wrap around to the opposite ends of the horizontal frequency axis transform [11]. The results is that disparities of (dh, dv) and (-dh, -dv) will be indistinguishable. The standard solution to this problem is to widen the input (the spliced input) by padding with zeros. This would increase the computational time.

3.2 Experiment and Result

Fig. 3. Stereo image (left and right eye view)

We will try to understand in the steps with the help of an example: size of total image: 300 x 400. The Input fed to the cepstral is a stereo image (left image and right image).

Step 1: Break the stereo image in small portion of size, say, 50x50:
Step 2: Whole image is broken down into 48 (left image) + 48 (right image) small images. Each small image from left is placed with the corresponding small image from right. And this forms a window consists of a spliced image, where in left and right images are placed adjacent to each other in the same pattern like Ocular Dominace pattern.
Step 3: Cepstral is applied to each image in parallel; independent of the adjacent window. The value of Disparity is obtained from each window.

Disparity for the whole image and its 3-D view are shown below:

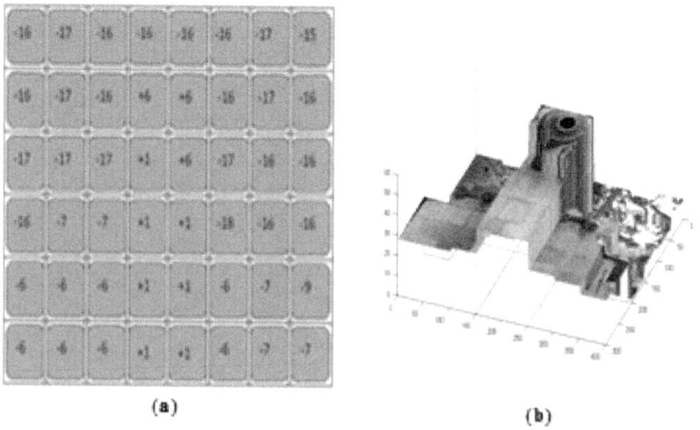

Fig. 4. a) Disparity values of each extracted window from image. b) 3-D view of 2-D picture

4 Other Bio-inspired Algorithms

Other method is Phase [6] and Energy method [12, 13and 14], which involve Gabor filters to decode disparity. The Gabor filters are the band pass filters [15, 16] which has both limited spatial width and finite bandwidth and whose space is similar to the receptive field profile of simple cells in primate visual cortex.

The Phase method is based on computing disparity in the image from the two eyes by means of relative responses of even and odd receptive fields found in the Primary Visual Cortex. This method is based on the computation of the differences between the Phases of the convolutions of two stereo images with the complex band pass filters [6].

Gabor filters, is represented as:

$$h(x,k) = e^{-x^2/\sigma^2} e^{ikx} = h_c(x,k) + ih_s(x,k) \tag{6}$$

where k is the peak frequency of the filter and σ determines the spatial extension. The resulting convolutions of image (I) and Gabor filter (h(x, k)) can be expressed as:

$$Q(x) = I * h(x,k) = \rho(x)e^{i\varphi(x)} = C(x) + iS(x) \tag{7}$$

where $\rho(x)$ and φ(x) denote their amplitude and phase components. Binocular disparity is related to the phase difference [17] by:

$$\delta(x) = \{\varphi_{left}(x) - \varphi_{right}(x)\}/k \tag{8}$$

5 Comparison between Cepstral Technique and Phase Method

Phase method is different from Cepstral in several ways. First of all, the Phase method applies the Gabor filters which depict the receptive fields while Cepstral does not use receptive field to compute disparity. Second, the binocular information from two different eyes is combined in the first step in Cepstral, on the other hand in Phase method, the interaction is delayed until the last step. Despite of the above mentioned differences, we show that Cepstral and Phase method follow the same steps to extract disparity, only the function they follow are different. Let us compare each step used in the algorithm and prove the similarities.

5.1 First Step

Cepstral uses Fast Fourier Transform in the first step which transforms the input to frequency domain from the spatial domain. In the Phase method, the images are convolved with the Gabor filters. The Gabor filters are closely related to the Fourier Transform. The complex exponential component of the filter is actually identical to the kernel of the Fourier Transform [18]. Further, the Gaussian window improves the Cepstral output [19]. Hence, the Fourier Transform of the Gaussian window would be similar to the Gabor filtering.

5.2 Second Step

Second step in the Cepstral, is to take log of absolute of the FFT and Phase method involves phase calculation. In the second step, the signals would be a complex number, let us consider a complex number, say,

$$c = a + bi \tag{9}$$

Log of complex number, by definition is:

$$\log(c) = \log|c| + i\arg(c) \tag{10}$$

This implies that the second step in both the methods is to take log. Cepstral involves the real part of log and Phase method involves the imaginary part of log. Therefore, both the methods involve logarithmic transformation. Further, again consider the equation (10), since log is a non-linear compressive function, it can be replaced with other functions such as arc tangent (atan (), atan2 ()) or fourth root, which would produce results that do not differ greatly [11]. Atan2 () are Atan () are mathematical functions to calculate the Phase (angle). The difference between two functions is the number of argument required, in atan2 (), it is two whereas in atan (), it is one. But both the functions would be same in the first quadrant.

Equation (10) can also be written as:

$$\log(c) = \text{atan}|c| + i\,\text{atan2}(b, a) \tag{11}$$

or,

$$\log(c) = \text{atan}\left(\sqrt{a^2 + b^2}\right) + i\,\text{atan}(b, a) \tag{12}$$

Now, the 2nd step for both the algorithms would be similar if real and imaginary parts of equation (12) are equal. By solving the same equation, we obtain that real and imaginary part of equation (12) would be same for

$$b \approx \sqrt{a^4/(1 - a^2)} \tag{13}$$

Therefore, both the algorithms would be similar, for

a. $b \approx \sqrt{a^4/(1 - a^2)}$
b. Small arguments i.e. when a and b are small numbers.
c. Both a and b lie in positive domain. Or when both correspond to first quadrant.

5.3 Third Step

The third step includes the transformation to spatial domain from frequency domain to find the disparity. Cepstral uses FFT (which is equivalent to IFFT) to transform back to spatial domain. Further, in Cepstral, both the signals are subtracted to get the disparity. On the other hand, in Phase method, the phase difference is divided by spatial frequency to transform to spatial domain to obtain disparity. The unit of spatial frequency is radian per meter and phase is radian, so on dividing the phase by spatial frequency, it will be: radian/ (radian/meter) =meter, which is in spatial domain. Now, if we rearrange the terms used in 2nd and 3rd step of the Phase method, which is to find the difference of phases { = (left) – (right)} and to divide the difference of phases by frequency { /freq} respectively, we get:

$$\text{disparity} = \{\Delta\varphi\ /\text{freq}\} = \{\varphi_{\ left}/\text{freq}\} - \{\varphi_{\ right}/\text{freq}\} \qquad (14)$$

This means that instead of computing disparity by:disparity = $\{\Delta\varphi\ /\text{freq}\}$, it can be computed using:

$$disparity = \{\varphi_{\ left}/\text{freq}\} - \{\varphi_{\ right}/\text{freq}\} \qquad (15)$$

The left and right phases can be subtracted after being divided by frequency to get disparity. Therefore, the third step in both the methods is the transformation into the spatial domain to obtain the disparity and subtract to get down to disparity.

5.4 Fourth Step

According to the Cepstral technique and to the Phase method the disparity is obtained from subtracting two signals present in the equations. Therefore, the fourth and the last step in both methods are to get the disparity.

6 Conclusion

This paper discusses some bio-inspired algorithms. Further, this paper has compared two different looking methods and showed that they follow same set of steps. The use of complex and complicated mathematical functions make the algorithms look different. If the input and output of all the algorithms are same, then there has to be a way to make them fall under the same line or the basic steps that are used by stereo algorithms.Authors in [20] and [21] have presented a set of algorithms or "building blocks", which are performed in general by stereo algorithms. But many algorithms like: Cepstral, Phase method, Energy method do-not comprise of the given building blocks. Future work will involve comparing other bio-inspired algorithms. By comparing the algorithms, we would come up with some kernel which is common in all the possible existing algorithms. We would intend to optimize the steps and uncover the basic common steps that have been used by the different algorithms.

References

1. Yeshurun, Schwartz, E.: Cepstral Filtering on a columnar Image Architecture: A fast Algorithm for binocular Stereo Segmentation. IEEE transaction on Pattern and Machine Intelligence 11(7), 759–767 (1989)
2. Ludwig, K.-O., Neumann, H., Neumann, B.: Local Stereoscopic Depth Image and Vision Computing, vol. 12, pp. 16–35 (1994)
3. Nomura, A., Ichikaw, M., Miike, H.: Reaction-diffusion algorithm for stereo disparity detection. Machine Vision and Application 20, 175–187 (2009)
4. Nomura, A., Ichikaw, M., Okada, K., Miike, H.: Stereo algorithm with reaction-diffusion equation. In: Asim Bhatti (ed.) Stereo Vision, pp. 259–272 (2008)

5. Nomura, A., Ichikaw, M., Okada, K., Miike, H.: Reaction-diffusion algorithm for vision systems. In: Obinata, G., Dutta, A. (eds.) Vision Systems: Segmentation & Pattern Recognition, ch. 4, pp. 61–80. i-Tech Education and Publishing, Vienna, Austria (2007)
6. Sanger, T.D.: Stereo disparity compuation using Gabor filters. Biol. Cybern. 59, 405–418 (1998)
7. Qian, N.: Computing Stereo disparity and motion with known binocular cell properties, vol.6 (3), pp. 390–404 (1994)
8. Qian, N., Mikaelian, S.: Relationship between phase and energy methods for disparity computation. Neural Comp. 12, 279–292 (2002)
9. Bardsley, D.: Stereo Vision for 3D Face Recognition, Year 1 Annual Review, PhD Report, University of Nottingham (2005)
10. Website, `http://www.middleburyedu/stereo`
11. Olison, T.J., Coombs, D.J.: Real Time Vergence Control for Binocular Robots, Technical Report 348, Dept of Computer Science University of Rochester (1990)
12. Ohzawa, I., DeAngelis, G.C., Freeman, R.D.: Stereoscopic depth discrimination in the visual cortex: Neurons ideally suited as disparity detectors. Science 249, 1037–1041 (1990)
13. Ohzawa, I., DeAngelis, G.C., Freeman, R.D.: Encoding of binocular disparity by simple cells in the cat's visual cortex. J. Neurophysiol. 75, 1779–1805 (1996)
14. Ohzawa, I., DeAngelis, G.C., Freeman, R.D.: Encoding of binocular disparity by complex cells in the cat's visual cortex. J. Neurophysiol. 77, 2879–2909 (1997)
15. Gabor, D.: Theory of Communication. J. Inst. Electr. Eng. 93 (1946)
16. Marcelja, S.: Mathematical Description of the Responses of Simple Cortical Cells. J. Opt. Soc. Am. 70 (1980)
17. Fleet, D.J., Jepson, A.D., Jenkin, M.: Phase-based disparity measurement. Comp. Vis. Graphics Image Proc. 53, 198–210 (1989)
18. Maimone, M.W.: Characterizing Stereo Matching Problems using stereo Spatial Frequency, PhD thesis (1996)
19. Stefano, L.D., Marchionni, M., Mattoccia, S., Neri, G.: A fast area-based stereo matching algorithm. In: 15th International Conference on Vision Interface, vol. 22, pp. 983–1005 (2004)
20. Scharstein, D., Szeliski, R.: A taxonomy and evaluation of dense two frame stereo correspondence algorithms. International Journal of Computer Vision 47, 7–42 (2002)
21. Lazaros, N., Sirakoulis, G.C., Gasteratos, A.: Review of Stereo Vision Algorithms: From Software to Hardware. International Journal of Optomechatronics 2, 435–462 (2008)

Analysis of Load Balancing Techniques in Grid

R. Venkatesan[1] and M. Blessy Rathna Solomi[2]

[1] Department of Information Technology, Karunya University, India
rlvenkei2000@gmail.com
[2] Department of Computer Science and Engineering, Karunya University, India
blessyrathna@karunya.edu.in

Abstract. Grid environment is the collection of independent systems which provide integrated computing facility. In a Grid infrastructure, some systems may be idle, while others are heavily loaded. This leads to an imbalance in load which results in under-utilization of resources, reduced throughput, and high response time. Several load balancing strategies are proposed to avoid the load imbalance. In this paper, the various load balancing models are discussed. The four load balancing models explored in this paper are graph-based, tree-based, agent-based and learning-based. Several load balancing techniques are described and discussed under appropriate category.

Keywords: Grid computing, Load balancing, Machine learning, Tree-based model, Graph partitioning, Software agents.

1 Introduction

Grid computing is a technology that enables resource virtualization, on-demand provisioning and large scale resource sharing. One of the substantial concerns of Grid is to utilize the resources efficiently and provide a cost effective infrastructure. This is commonly referred as load balancing problem. The main functionality of a load balancing technique is to enhance the performance by improving the throughput, optimizing the resource utilization and lowering the response time. For the past two decades, various techniques have been proposed to address load imbalance. This paper discusses some of the load balancing algorithms. The remainder of the paper is structured as follows: the load balancing is discussed in section 2. Section 3 describes the graph-based model. Tree-based model is elaborated in section 4. Section 5 gives the agent-based model. Section 6 discusses the learning-based model. The analysis of all the algorithms is given in section 7. Section 8 concludes.

2 Load Balancing

Load balancing is a methodology which distributes the processing among all the systems in a distributed system evenly. When a processor is overloaded, the requests are forwarded to another processor. Load balancing improves throughput and reduces response time. It enhances the resources and achieves high degree of parallelism.

V.V. Das and N. Thankachan (Eds.): CIIT 2011, CCIS 250, pp. 147–151, 2011.

Load balancing algorithms are classified into static and dynamic. It can further be classified into centralized or decentralized, based on their architecture. In static load balancing, load balancer makes the decisions at compile time, when the resource requirements are estimated [1]. Every time the system starts up, the job is assigned to the fixed resource. Static load balancing algorithms does not work properly when there is high variation in the load. Resource allocation is done when the job is started and it cannot be altered once the system is executing. In dynamic load balancing, the decisions to move the job requests from heavily-loaded systems to idle or lightly-loaded systems are made at runtime. The job information is not known previously. The reason that the dynamic load balancing has an edge over static load balancing is that it does not necessarily know the run-time requirements of the jobs.

The centralized approach performs the decision making in a single processor, to distribute the load evenly. The major drawback of the centralized algorithms is the single point of failure [2]. There is a bottleneck in the centralized system. The centralized load balancing algorithms are less reliable than the decentralized load balancing algorithms. The graph-based and learning-based algorithms discussed in sections 3 and 6 respectively are examples of dynamic centralized load balancing algorithms. The decentralized approach eliminates the use of a central processor for decision making. Decentralized algorithms are highly scalable and fault tolerant. But it suffers from communication overhead as the state of the processors has to be communicated frequently in the environment. The tree-based and agent-based algorithms discussed in sections 4 and 5 respectively are examples of dynamic decentralized load balancing algorithms.

3 Graph-Based Balancing Model

When the workload is not balanced, the graph which represents the Grid is partitioned and load balancing decisions are applied. In Improved Spectral Bisection Algorithm (ISBA) [3], the graph is divided into two parts which have equal weights. A hypergraph is formed, where an edge can connect to any number of vertices. This facilitates the mapping of hypergraph to Euclidean spaces. This algorithm yields high quality partitions compared to the Standard Spectral Bisection Algorithm. The drawback of this algorithm lies in its large execution time. In Repartitioning Hypergraph model (RHM) [4], the computational load information can be represented as a computational hypergraph. For the first epoch, the load balancing is performed by partitioning it. For the consecutive epoch, the load balancing cost between the previous and next epochs need to be included. This model minimizes both communication cost and job migration cost. However, the execution time is higher than the traditional graph partitioning methods.

Diffusion based Graph Partitioning Algorithm (DIBAP) [5] is a combination of two graph repartitioning methods BUBBLE-FOS/C and TRUNCCONS to partition the graph. DIBAP uses BUBBLE-FOS/C as a local improvement scheme. The partitions generated by BUBBLE-FOS/C are further improved locally by TRUNCCONS. DIBAP gives better partitions but the running time is high.

4 Tree-Based Balancing Model

To solve the load imbalance problem, the Grid architecture can be mapped into a tree-based model [6]. A tree is an aggregation of the grid manager in level 0, cluster managers in level 1 and nodes in level 2. In Hierarchical Tree-Based Strategy (LBSTRG) [6], there are two levels. First, in intra-cluster load balancing, cluster manager decides on the load balancing operation, depending upon its current workload. Second, in intra-grid load balancing, grid manager initiates the load balancing operation when any of the cluster managers fail to perform load balancing. This method is highly scalable since the nodes can easily be added or removed from the tree. The communication cost is less because of the intra-cluster load balancing. In Refinement-Tree based Partitioning Method (REFTREE) [7], the grid is partitioned into multiple grids and the load is distributed evenly when there is a load imbalance. There are two phases in this algorithm. In the first phase, each interior node is assigned a weight using depth first search of the REFTREE. In the second phase, the partitions are created using truncated depth first traversal of REFTREE. For two-dimensional grids, REFTREE partitioning method produces high quality partitions quickly. For three-dimensional grids, it becomes slow but the quality of the partitions is high. In Cluster-Aware Random Stealing Algorithm (CRS) [8], when a node becomes idle, it directly steals the job asynchronously from a node in a remote cluster. Until it receives a job, it synchronously steals a job from its own cluster. CRS algorithm is highly adaptable to the network and manual setting of parameters is not necessary.

5 Agent-Based Balancing Model

Software agents abstract a high level model of complex software systems. Each grid resource is represented by an agent. They communicate with each other to find suitable resource to distribute the load evenly. An agent-based system is coupled with a Performance-Driven Task Scheduler (PDTS) [9] to perform local load balancing. Local load balancing is achieved using an iterative heuristic algorithm based on the predictive performance data. This algorithm minimises the makespan and processor idle time. It also completes the execution of the jobs on time. The Messor System [10] is composed of a collection of interconnected Anthill nests configured to run the Messor software. A nest submits the job to the nest network. Jobs are executed by the nest on which the job resides. A job is said to be completed when its associated algorithm has been executed to completion. In Self-Organizing Agents (SOA) [11], load balancing is accomplished by an ant-like self-organizing mechanism in agent-based resource management system (ARMS). ARMS agents perform automatic balancing of batch jobs across multiple COSYs. Multiple agents improve the load balancing level and speed. However, they increase the communication overhead and cost.

6 Learning-Based Balancing Model

Machine learning is an approach which allows the computer to learn to recognize complex patterns and to make decisions on its own, based on the past data. The efficiency improves with experience. Multi-state Q-learning Approach [13] determines three parameters to balance the load – (a) the number of processors involved, (b) the load which is exchanged and (c) the type of load balancing algorithm [13]. The main feature of Q-learning algorithms is that the runtime and implementation overhead is low. But it is slow to converge and many times, the decisions made are not satisfactory. Machine Learning Approach [14] uses the data mining rules to make decisions. The job migration is done whenever there is a change in the load configuration. The initial parameters and the current parameters of load information are retrieved and load balancing decisions are made.

7 Analysis

ISBA [3] is better than the standard algorithm but its communication cost is high. RHM [4] results in less communication overhead but its execution time is high. DIBAP [5] yields better partitions but its running time is high. LBSTRG [6] addresses heterogeneity and scalability well but still its effectiveness is not measured. REFTREE partitioning method [7] yields high quality partitions but its running time is high for three dimensional grids. CRS algorithm [8] minimizes communication overhead but induces runtime overhead. PDTS [9] is highly scalable and gives high resource utilization. MESSOR [10] utilizes the computing power well but its security aspects need to be exploited. SOA [11] for load balancing poses high communication overhead. MSQL [13] learns from the Grid environment and selects the algorithm to be used and adjusts the parameters. It minimizes the communication cost and response time. Machine learning approach [14] reduces communication overhead and response time. The comparison of load balancing algorithms is presented in Table 1.

Table 1. Comparison of Load Balancing Algorithms

Algorithm		Architecture	Performance parameters			
			Communication Overhead	Response Time	Resource Utilization	Load Balance
Graph-based	ISBA	Centralized	High	High	n/a	Medium
	RHM	Centralized	Low	High	n/a	Medium
	DIBAP	Centralized	Medium	High	n/a	High
Tree-based	LBSTRG	Decentralized	Low	Medium	Medium	Medium
	REFTREE	Decentralized	Medium	Medium	n/a	Medium
	CRS	Decentralized	Low	Medium	n/a	Medium
Agent-based	PDTS	Decentralized	Medium	Medium	High	High
	MESSOR	Decentralized	Low	Low	Medium	Medium
	SOA	Decentralized	High	Medium	Medium	Medium
Learning-based	MSQL	Centralized	Low	Low	Medium	High
	ML	Centralized	Low	Low	Medium	High

8 Conclusion

In this paper, the problem of load balancing in Grid environment has been discussed. The classification of load balancing models are presented and four load balancing models are elaborated which includes graph-based, tree-based, agent-based and learning-based load balancing. The efficiency and performance of each model have been discussed. Machine learning approach proves to be promising in improving the efficiency in load balance and resource utilization. The future work will be focused on developing an efficient algorithm which addresses the issues of load imbalance and resource management using machine learning techniques.

References

1. Yagoubi, B., Slimani, Y.: Dynamic Load Balancing Strategy for Grid Computing. World Academy of Science, Engineering and Technology (2006)
2. Al-Azzoni, I., Down, D.G.: Decentralized Load Balancing for Heterogeneous Grids. In: Proc. of the 2009 Computation World: Future Computing, Service Computation, Cognitive Adaptive, Content, Patterns, pp. 545–550 (2009)
3. Van Driessche, R., Roose, D.: An Improved Spectral Bisection Algorithm and its Application to Dynamic Load Balancing. Parallel Computing 21, 29–48 (1995)
4. Catalyurek, U.V., Boman, E.G., Devine, K.D., Bozdag, D., Heaphy, R.T., Reisen, L.A.: A Repartitioning Hypergraph Model for Dynamic Load Balancing. Journal of Parallel Distributed Computing 69, 711–724 (2009)
5. Meyerhenke, H., Gehweiler, J.: On Dynamic Graph Partitioning and Graph Clustering using Diffusion. In: Dagstuhl Seminar Proceedings (2010)
6. Yagoubi, B., Slimani, Y.: Load Balancing Strategy in Grid Environment. Journal of Information Technology and Applications 1(4), 285–296 (2007)
7. Mitchell, W.F.: A Refinement-tree Based Partitioning Method for Dynamic Load Balancing with Adaptively Refined Grids. Journal of Parallel and Distributed Computing 67(4), 417–429 (2007)
8. van Nieuwpoort, R.V., Kielmann, T., Bal, H.E.: Efficient Load Balancing for Wide-Area Divide-and-Conquer Applications. In: Proc. PPoPP 2001, Snowbird, UT (2001)
9. Cao, J., Spooner, D.P., Jarvis, S.A., Saini, S., Nudd, G.R.: Agent-Based Grid Load Balancing Using Performance-Driven Task Scheduling. In: Proc. of 17th IEEE International Parallel and Distributed Processing Symposium (2003)
10. Montresor, A., Meling, H., Babaoglu, O.: Messor: Load-Balancing through a Swarm of Autonomous Agents. In: Proc. of the 1st International Conference on Agents and Peer-to-Peer Computing (July 2002)
11. Cao, J.: Self-Organizing Agents for Grid Load Balancing. In: Proceedings of 5th IEEE/ACM International Workshop on Grid Computing, pp. 388–395 (November 2004)
12. Zhu, X., Goldberg, A.B.: Introduction to Semi-Supervised Learning. In: Synthesis Lectures on Artificial Intelligence and Machine Learning. Morgan & Claypool Publishers (2009)
13. Meraji, S., Zhang, W., Tropper, C.: A Multi-State Q-Learning Approach for the Dynamic Load Balancing of Time Warp. In: IEEE Workshop on Principles (2010)
14. Revar, A., Andhariya, M., Sutariya, D.: Load Balancing in Grid Environment using Machine Learning – Innovative Approach. International Journal of Computer Applications 8(10) (October 2010)

Intermediate Population Based Differential Evolution Algorithm

Tarun Kumar Sharma and Millie Pant

Indian Institute of Technology Roorkee, India
{taruniitr1,millidma}@gmail.com

Abstract. In the present paper propose two novel variants of Differential Evolution (DE), named IP-OBL and IP-NSDE, have been proposed. In IP-OBL the initial population is generated by using the intermediate positions between the uniformly generated random numbers and opposition based numbers. While in case of IP-NSDE, the initial population is generated as an intermediate of uniform random numbers and numbers generated by Nelder Mead Method. The proposed algorithms are further modified by selecting best NP/2 individuals to perform in population evolution. The modified variants are termed as MIP-OBL and MIP-NSDE. The numerical results of 10 benchmark problems indicate the competence of the proposed algorithms.

Keywords: Differential Evolution, Opposition Based Learning, Nelder Mead.

1 Introduction

The focus of the present study is Differential Evolution (DE), which may be considered as an advanced version of another popular metaheuristic Genetic Algorithms (GA) [1][2]. Despite having several attractive features, DE is susceptible to a common drawback like slow convergence leading to long computational time. In order to overcome the drawback of DE, several modifications have been suggested in literature [3][4]. The focus of the present study is on the initial population generation that can affect the convergence speed and also the quality of the final solution. Here, the initial population is generated as the mean of uniformly generated random number and the random number generated using opposite based learning in one case and Nelder Mead (NM) method in other case. These algorithms are further modified by selecting best NP/2 individuals to attend population evolution. Mutation and Crossover is performed and then according to fitness value NP/2 individuals are selected from the offspring & parent. The modified versions are termed as MIP-OBL and MIP-NSDE. Remaining paper is organized as follows: brief overview of DE is given in section 2. OBL and NM methods are described in section 3. Proposed algorithms are given in section 4. Section 5 gives performance metrics and parameter settings. Simulation results and discussion are given in section 6. Finally the paper concludes with section 7.

V.V. Das and N. Thankachan (Eds.): CIIT 2011, CCIS 250, pp. 152–156, 2011.

2 Brief Overview of Differential Evolution

DE was proposed by Storn and Price in 1995 [5]. It starts with an initial population, randomly generated when no *a priori* knowledge about the solution space is available. Let $X_{i,\,G}$, $i=1, 2\ldots, NP$ be the solution vector, where i denote the population and G denote the generation to which the population belongs. The initial population should ideally cover the entire search space by randomly distributing each parameter of an individual vector with uniform distribution between the prescribed upper and lower parameter bounds x_j^u and x_j^i. At each generation G, DE employs mutation, crossover and selection operations to produce a trial vector $U_{i,G}$ for each individual vector $X_{i,G}$, also called target vector, in the current population.

Mutation: For each target vector $X_{i,G}$ at generation G , an associated mutated vector $V_{i,G} = \{v_{1,i,G}, v_{2,i,G,\ldots}, v_{n,i,G}\}$ can be generated using

$$V_{i,G} = X_{r1,G} + F(X_{r2,G} - X_{r3,G}) \qquad (1)$$

where r_1 , r_2 , $r_3 \in$ (1,2...,NP) are randomly chosen integers, different from each other and also different from the running index *i*. F is a real and constant factor having value between [0, 2] and controls the amplification of differential variation ($X_{r2,\,G}$ – $X_{r3,\,G}$).

Crossover: After the mutation phase, the "binominal" crossover operation is applied to each pair of the generated mutant vector $V_{i,G}$ and its corresponding target vector $X_{i,G}$ to generate a trial vector: $U_{i,G} = (u_{1,i,G}, u_{2,i,G}, \ldots, u_{n,i,G})$.

$$U_{i,j,G+1} = \begin{cases} v_{j,i} & \text{if } rand_j(0,1) \le Cr \forall j=k \\ x_{j,i} & \text{otherwi.} \end{cases} \qquad (2)$$

where $j = 1, 2,\ldots, n$ (n dimension problem), Cr is a user-specified crossover constant in the range [0,1] , $rand_j$ is a randomly chosen integer in the range [0,1] to ensure that the trial vector $U_{i,G}$ will differ from its corresponding target vector $X_{i,G}$ by at least one parameter and $k \in$ (1,2,...,D) is the randomly chosen index.

3 Brief Description of OBL and Nelder Mead Method

OBL: The concept of *opposition-based learning* (OBL) was introduced by Tizhoosh [6]. The main idea behind OBL is the simultaneous consideration of an estimate and its corresponding opposite estimate (i.e., guess and opposite guess) in order to achieve a better approximation for the current candidate solution. The concept of opposite numbers can be defined as:

Opposite Number: Let $x \in [a,b]$ be a real number. The opposite number $\breve{x}$ is defined by $\breve{x} = a + b - x$ .Similarly this definition can be extended to higher dimension.

Opposite Point: Let $P = (x_1, x_2, ..., x_D)$ be a point in D – dimensional space, where $x_1, x_2, ..., x_D \in R$ and $x_i \in \{1,2,...,D\}$. The opposite point $\breve{P} = (\breve{x}_1, \breve{x}_2, ..., \breve{x}_D)$ is completely defined by its components $\breve{x}_i = a_i + b_i - x_i$.

Nelder–Mead algorithm is a derivative-free optimization algorithm, utilizing a non-linear simplex to guide search directions. Proposed by Nelder and Mead in 1965 [7], it has gained vast applications due to its effectiveness and robust convergence. In most cases it could locate a greatly improved solution with much fewer function evaluations than its competitors.

4 Proposed Variants

The proposed IP-OBL algorithms starts with an intermediate initial population vector, which is the mean of randomly generated and opposition based learning. Similarly IP-NSDE initiates as the mean of randomly generated and points generated by Nelder Mead method, when no preliminary knowledge about the solution space is available.

In the proposed IP-OBL and IP-NSDE algorithm an attempt is made to generate better locations. The search space is contracted in the initial step consequently the population are able to locate the comparatively better solution space in a fewer number of generations. The potential solutions are produced in three easy steps.

1. Generate N uniformly distributed random numbers, say $N_{rand} = \{x_1, x_2, ..., x_n\}$

   In case of IP-OBL
2. Generate N opposite points using OBL, say $N_{OBL} = \{x_1^{'}, x_2^{'}, ..., x_n^{'}\}$

   In case of IP-NSDE
3. Generate N points using Nelder Mead method, say $N_{NM} = \{x_1^{'}, x_2^{'}, ..., x_n^{'}\}$
4. Find the intermediate locations

$$IP = \{(x_1 + x_1^{'})/2, (x_2 + x_2^{'})/2, ..., (x_n + x_n^{'})/2\} \tag{3}$$

Proposed MIP-OBL and MIP-NSDE versions

1. Initialize the P(0) individuals randomly, using Eq. (3)
2. Fitness is calculated. In each generation, the best individual is kept to mutate.
3. Select the best (fitness) 50% i.e NP/2, individuals to attend population evolution:
4. Perform mutation using: $V_{i,G} = X_{best,G} + F(X_{r2,G} - X_{r3,G})$ where Xbest denotes the best vector in the population giving the best objective value.
5. Perform crossover using Eq. (2)
6. Selection: According to the fitness value, NP/2 individuals are selected from the offspring and parents.

5 Performance Metrics and Parameter Settings

In the present study we have considered 10 benchmark problems from literature [8] given in the Appendix. The performance metrics used are:

1. Success rate (SR), to achieve the desired accuracy (ε).
2. Average number of function evaluations (NFE) of all successful runs.
3. The *acceleration rate* (AR) which is defined as follows, based on the NFEs is used to compare the convergence speeds.

$$AR = \frac{NFE_{one\ algo}}{NFE_{other\ algo}} \quad (4)$$

AR >1 means Algorithm is faster. Further, the *average acceleration rate* (AR_{ave}) over test functions are calculated as follows:

$$AR_{ave} = \frac{1}{n}\sum_{i=1}^{n} AR_i \quad (7)$$

n is number of problems and accuracy is defined by: $|(f - f^*)| < \varepsilon$, and ε is the considered threshold, *f** is the global minimum of the problem and *f* is the cost of the best point found by the algorithm.

Experimental Setting: Mutation strategy: DE/rand/1/bin, Population size NP = 100, Scaling factor (F) = 0.5, Crossover probability = 0.9, Maximum NFE = 10^6, Value to reach, VTR = 10^{-6}, Dimension for each problem are given in Table 1. All algorithms are executed on Pentium IV, using DEV C++. Random numbers are generated using inbuilt function *rand()* in DEVC++.

6 Simulation Results and Discussion

The numerical results for the proposed variants are given in Tables 1 and 2 in terms Number of Functions Evaluations (NFE) and Success Rate (SR). From the numerical results it can be clearly observed that the proposed versions are better or at par with basic DE and ODE in terms of all the performance criteria.

Table 1. Comparison of proposed variants with DE and ODE in terms of NFE and Average AR

Function	Dim.	DE	ODE	IP-OBL	IP-NSDE	MIP-OBL	MIP-NSDE
Sphere	30	28020	26912	24947	26718	23782	26119
Griekwank	30	54503	53711	51592	49871	49873	49912
Ackley	30	52474	51589	49302	50231	45092	48761
Restrigin's	10	382454	367150	270912	328839	268019	312898
Rosenbrock's	30	289121	285718	261781	251752	256729	*250091*
Michalewicz	10	39761	37192	32539	33463	36814	32985
Schawefel's	30	66154	63912	62920	62987	61256	62908
Quartic	30	26916	24756	23378	23730	22952	23001
Pathological	5	206219	175923	167298	170191	159642	167329
Colville	4	8105	7995	5929	6043	5479	5716
Average		115372.7	109485.8	95059.8	100382.5	92963.8	97972.0
AR_{ave}		1.24	1.18	1.02	1.08	---	1.05

Table 2. Success Rate (SR) and Average SR of the Algorithms

Function	DE	ODE	IP-OBL	IP-NSDE	MIP-OBL	MIP-NSDE
Sphere	1	1	1	1	1	1
Griekwank	1	0.82	0.84	0.84	1	0.74
Ackley	1	1	1	1	1	1
Restrigin's	1	0.80	0.76	0.82	1	0.86
Rosenbrock's	1	1	0.86	0.82	0.86	1
Michalewicz	0.74	0.68	1	1	1	0.64
Schawefel's	0.62	0.88	0.90	0.88	0.78	1
Quartic	0.54	1	1	1	0.72	0.94
Pathological	0.56	0.72	0.66	0.62	0.84	0.88
Colville	1	1	1	1	1	1
Av.	0.846	0.89	0.902	0.898	0.92	0.906

7 Conclusion

The proposed algorithms aim at locating the potential solutions in the beginning of the algorithm, by contracting the search space. The proposed versions are further modified that directed towards the best solution. Numerical results indicate that the proposed modifications help in faster convergence without compromising with the quality of solution.

References

1. Goldberg, D.E.: Genetic Algorithms in Search, Optimization, and Machine Learning. Addison-Wesley, Reading (1989)
2. Holland, J.H.: Adaptation in Natural and Artificial Systems. University of Michigan Press, Ann Harbor (1975)
3. Brest, J., Greiner, S., et al.: Self-adapting Control parameters in differential evolution: a comparative study on numerical benchmark problems. IEEE Transactions on Evolutionary Computation 10(6), 646–657 (2006)
4. Das, S., Konar, A., Chakraborty, U.: Two improved differential evolution schemes for faster global search. In: ACMSIGEVO Proceedings of GECCO, Washington, D.C, pp. 991–998 (2005)
5. Storn, R., Price, K.: Differential Evolution – a simple and efficient Heuristic for global optimization over continuous spaces. Journal Global Optimization 11, 341–359 (1997)
6. Tizhoosh, H.R.: Opposition-based learning: A new scheme for machine intelligence. In: Proc. Int. Conf. Comput. Intell. Modeling Control and Autom., Vienna, Austria, vol. I, pp. 695–701 (2005)
7. Nelder, J.A., Mead, R.: A simplex method for, function minimisation. The Computer Journal 7, 308–313 (1965)
8. Jia, L., Gong, W., Wu, H.: An Improved Self-Adaptive Control Parameter of Differential Evolution For Global Optimization. In: Cai, Z., Li, Z., Kang, Z., Liu, Y. (eds.) ISICA 2009. CCIS, vol. 51, pp. 215–224. Springer, Heidelberg (2009)

Interval Type-2 Fuzzy Set Extension of DEMATEL Method

Mitra Bokaei Hosseini and Mohammad Jafar Tarokh

Department of Industrial Engineering, K. N. Toosi University of Technology, Tehran, Iran
Mitra.bokai@sina.kntu.ac.ir, mjtarokh@kntu.ac.ir

Abstract. The purpose of this study was to extend the DEMATEL (Decision-Making Trail and Evaluation Laboratory) method based on the interval type-2 fuzzy sets to obtain the weights of criteria based on words. Generally most decision making methods consider the independency between criteria. DEMATEL method considers the inter-relations between criteria. Some decision making methods use words as the enabler of the decision making. These methods consider the perceptions of decision makers, the uncertainty assigned to each word and map the words into interval type-2 fuzzy sets (IT2 FSs). Therefore we extended the DEMATEL method to obtain the weights that can be used in decision making. The application of this method was proposed for six criteria.

Keywords: Decision making, DEMATEL, Interval Type 2 Fuzzy Sets (IT2 FSs).

1 Introduction

Many decision making methods are being proposed to facilitate the decision making process. The evaluation criteria are almost dependent based on the complexity and vagueness of the real world. The Decision-Making Trail and Evaluation Laboratory (DEMATEL) proposed by the Battelle Memorial Institute through its Geneva Research Centre [1]. This method considers the causal relationship between criteria.

Lin & Wu [2], proposed the fuzzy extension of DEMATEL method. The judges were based on the linguistic variables and triangular fuzzy numbers and the final weights of criteria are crisp numbers. In their approach all decision makers used specific words. Words mean different things to different people so are uncertain [3]. After Zadeh [4] introduced fuzzy set theory to deal with vague problems, linguistic labels have been used within the framework of fuzzy set theory. After he introduced the Type-2 fuzzy sets (FSs) the first concept of fuzzy set renamed to type-1 fuzzy sets (FSs) [4,5]. Zadeh proposed the paradigm of computing with words based on the T2 FSs that is a methodology in which the objects of computation are words and propositions drawn from a natural language [13]. Mendel [6,7,8] proposed the framework for perceptual computing based on the computing with words. Therefore, the aim of this study was the IT2 FS extension of DEMATEL method in order to obtain the criteria's weights based on the words. The rest of this paper is organized as follows. Interval type-2 fuzzy sets are introduced in section 2. The IT2 FS

V.V. Das and N. Thankachan (Eds.): CIIT 2011, CCIS 250, pp. 157–165, 2011.

DEMATEL is proposed in section 3. The application of this method is presented in section 4 and section 5 presents the conclusion of this study.

2 Type-1 Fuzzy DEMATEL Method

The DEMATEL method had been used successfully in many decision making problems. For example, Jassbi et al. [9] used fuzzy DEMATEL method for modeling cause and effect relationship of strategy map. Chang et al. [10] used fuzzy DEMATEL method for developing supplier selection criteria. Yang & Tzeng [11] proposed a combined MCDM model based on DEMATEL and ANP. Also Chen & Chen [12] used DEMATEL, fuzzy ANP and TOPSIS for evaluating innovation performance in Taiwanese higher education institutes.

3 Interval Type-2 Fuzzy Sets

Zadeh [13] proposed the paradigm of computing with words based on the T2 FSs that is a methodology in which the objects of computation are words and propositions drawn from a natural language. Words in the computing with words are modeled by T2 FSs that can model more uncertainties [14].
An IT2 FS $\tilde{A}$ is characterized by the MF $\mu_{\tilde{A}}(x,u)$, where $x \in X$ and $u \in J_x \subseteq [0,1]$, that is [3],

$$\tilde{A} = \{((x,u), \mu_{\tilde{A}}(x,u) = 1) | \forall x \in X, \forall u \in J_x \subseteq [0,1]\} \tag{1}$$

Equation (1) can be expressed as [6,15]

$$\tilde{A} = \int_{x \in X} \int_{u \in J_x \subseteq [0,1]} 1/(x,u) = \int_{x \in X} \left[\int_{u \in J_x \subseteq [0,1]} 1/u \right] / x \tag{2}$$

where x is called the primary variable with the domain of X. $u \in [0,1]$ is called the secondary variable, has domain $J_x \subseteq U = [0,1]$ at each $x \in X$; J_x, is called the primary membership (or the codomain) of x, and is in (2). The amplitude of $\mu_{\tilde{A}}(x,u)$, called a secondary grade of $\tilde{A}$, equals 1 for $\forall x \in X$ and $\forall u \in J_x \subseteq [0,1]$. The bracketed term in (2) is called the secondary MF, or vertical slice, of $\tilde{A}$, and is denoted $\mu_{\tilde{A}}(x)$, that is,

$$\mu_{\tilde{A}}(x) = \int_{u \in J_x \subseteq [0,1]} 1/u \tag{3}$$

so that $\tilde{A}$ can also be expressed in terms of its vertical slices as

$$\tilde{A} = \int_{x \in X} \mu_{\tilde{A}}(x)/x \tag{4}$$

Definition 1. Uncertainty about $\tilde{A}$ is conveyed by the union of all its primary memberships, which is called the footprint of uncertainty (FOU) of $\tilde{A}$ that is,

$$FOU(\tilde{A}) = \bigcup_{\forall x \in X} J_x = \{(x,u): u \in J_x \subseteq [0,1]\} \tag{5}$$

Definition 2. The $\mathrm{FOU}(\tilde{A})$ in equation (12) can also be expresses by (Mendel & Wu, 2010)

$$FOU(\tilde{A}) = \bigcup_{\forall x \in X} \left[\underline{\mu_{\tilde{A}}}(x), \overline{\mu_{\tilde{A}}}(x)\right] \tag{6}$$

The size of an FOU is directly related to the uncertainty that is conveyed by an IT2 FS.

Definition 3. The upper membership function (UMF) and lower membership function (LMF) of $\tilde{A}$ are two type-1 MFs that bound the FOU. $\mathrm{UMF}(\tilde{A})$ is associated with the upper bound of $\mathrm{FOU}(\tilde{A})$ and is denoted $\overline{\mu}_{\tilde{A}(x)}$, $\forall x \subseteq X$, and $\mathrm{LMF}(\tilde{A})$ is associated with the lower bound of $\mathrm{FOU}(\tilde{A})$ and is denoted $\underline{\mu}_{\tilde{A}(x)}$, $\forall x \in X$, that is,

$$UMF(\tilde{A}) \equiv \overline{\mu}_{\tilde{A}}(x) = \overline{FOU(\tilde{A})} \quad \forall x \in X \tag{7}$$

$$LMF(\tilde{A}) \equiv \underline{\mu}_{\tilde{A}}(x) = \underline{FOU(\tilde{A})} \quad \forall x \in X \tag{8}$$

UMF contains four digits and LMF contains five digits, the fifth parameter for the LMF is its height.

Definition 4. Let

$$\mathrm{FOU}(\tilde{A}) = \cup_{\forall\alpha}\left[\left[\overline{\alpha_1^\alpha}, \underline{\alpha_1^\alpha}\right], \left[\underline{\alpha_2^\alpha}, \overline{\alpha_2^\alpha}\right]\right] \quad \mathrm{FOU}(\tilde{B}) = \cup_{\forall\alpha}\left[\left[\overline{b_1^\alpha}, \underline{b_1^\alpha}\right], \left[\underline{b_2^\alpha}, \overline{b_2^\alpha}\right]\right]$$

and

and be to perfectly normal IT2 FN based on equation (13) [16,17]and $\circ = \{+, -, \times, \div\}$ then according to Wu & Mendel [18]:

$$FOU(\tilde{A})\circ FOU(\tilde{B}) = \begin{cases} \bigcup_{\forall\alpha} \alpha.\left(\left[\left[\overline{\alpha_1^\alpha}, \underline{\alpha_1^\alpha}\right] \circ \left[\overline{b_1^\alpha}, \underline{b_1^\alpha}\right], \left[\underline{\alpha_2^\alpha}, \overline{\alpha_2^\alpha}\right] \circ \left[\underline{b_2^\alpha}, \overline{b_2^\alpha}\right]\right]\right), if\ 0 \le \alpha \le \min(h_{\tilde{A}}, h_{\tilde{B}}) \\ \bigcup_{\forall\alpha} \alpha.\left(\left[\overline{\alpha_1^\alpha}, \overline{\alpha_2^\alpha}\right] \circ \left[\overline{b_1^\alpha}, \overline{b_2^\alpha}\right], if\ \min(h_{\tilde{A}}, h_{\tilde{B}}) < \alpha \le 1\right. \end{cases} \tag{9}$$

4 IT2 FS DEMATEL Method

The procedure of developing DEMATEL method by IT2 FSs is as follows.

Step 1: Identify the decision goals, criteria and group of experts
Step 2: develop linguistic codebooks for decision making

In this step a codebook is designed and decision makers are asked to define the interval end points for each word in the codebook. The codebook contains "very high influence", "high influence", "low influence", "very low influence", "no influence". The IA approach was used to map these intervals into IT2 FSs [19].

The DEMATEL method does not consider the difference between the levels of expertise for each expert, but in this paper we developed another codebook that considers level of expertise for each expert. This codebook contains three words (Low, Moderate, and High) [14].

Step 3: compute the linguistic weighted average of the assessments. To measure the weights and causal relations between the criteria $C = \{C_i | i = 1,2,\dots,n\}$, a group of p experts are asked to define the influence relation between criteria based on the codebooks in step 2. Therefore, p pair-wise comparison IT2 FSs matrices $\tilde{Z}^1, \tilde{Z}^2, \dots, \tilde{Z}^P$ are obtained. Linguistic weighted average (LWA) that was proposed by Mendel & Wu [14] was used to generate the IT2 FSs average matrix that is called initial-direct-relation IT2 FSs matrix.

Suppose k is the number of decision-makers ($k = 1,2,\dots,p$), and $\tilde{z}_{ij}$ is ijth entry of initial-direct-relation IT2 FS matrix $\tilde{Z}$. The LWA matrix $\tilde{Z}$ can be obtained from 10.

$$\tilde{z}_{ij} = \frac{\sum_{k=1}^{p} \tilde{Z}^k{}_{ij} \widetilde{W}_k}{\sum_{k=1}^{p} \widetilde{W}_k} \qquad (10)$$

Step 4: Establish the normalized initial-direct-relation matrix.

Let $\tilde{z}_{ij} = \left(\mathrm{UMF}(\tilde{Z}), \mathrm{LMF}(\tilde{Z})\right)$, and $\mathrm{UMF}(\tilde{Z}) = (a,b,c,d)$ and $\mathrm{LMF}(\tilde{Z}) = (e,f,g,i,h)$ the fifth element of $\mathrm{LMF}(\tilde{Z})$ is its height. Therefore, $\tilde{z}_{ij}$ can be defined by nine matrices, whose elements are crisp numbers [20].

$$Z_a = \begin{bmatrix} 0 & a'_{12} & \cdots & a'_{1n} \\ a'_{21} & 0 & \cdots & a'_{2n} \\ \vdots & \vdots & \ddots & \vdots \\ a'_{n1} & a'_{n2} & \cdots & 0 \end{bmatrix}; Z_b = \begin{bmatrix} 0 & b'_{12} & \cdots & b'_{1n} \\ b'_{21} & 0 & \cdots & b'_{2n} \\ \vdots & \vdots & \ddots & \vdots \\ b'_{n1} & b'_{n2} & \cdots & 0 \end{bmatrix}; \dots ; Z_h = \begin{bmatrix} 0 & h'_{12} & \cdots & h'_{1n} \\ h'_{21} & 0 & \cdots & h'_{2n} \\ \vdots & \vdots & \ddots & \vdots \\ h'_{n1} & h'_{n2} & \cdots & 0 \end{bmatrix}$$

Z_d contains the forth elements of $\mathrm{UMF}(\tilde{Z})$. All $\tilde{z}_{ij}$are normal IT2 FSs, therefore $\tilde{Z}_d$ contains the greatest elements in the initial-direct-relation matrix. The normalized direct-relation matrix can be defined as:

$$\tilde{X} = \begin{bmatrix} \tilde{x}_{11} & \tilde{x}_{12} & \cdots & \tilde{x}_{1n} \\ \tilde{x}_{21} & \tilde{x}_{22} & \cdots & \tilde{x}_{2n} \\ \vdots & \vdots & \ddots & \vdots \\ \tilde{x}_{n1} & \tilde{x}_{n2} & \cdots & \tilde{x}_{nn} \end{bmatrix} \text{ where } \tilde{x}_{ij} = \frac{\tilde{z}_{ij}}{s}$$

$$= \left(\frac{Z_a}{s}, \frac{Z_b}{s}, \frac{Z_c}{s}, \frac{Z_d}{s}, \frac{Z_e}{s}, \frac{Z_f}{s}, \frac{Z_g}{s}, \frac{Z_i}{s}, Z_h\right) \quad s = \max_{1 \le i \le n} \left(\sum_{j=1}^{n} X_{d_{ij}}\right) \qquad (11)$$

Note that the fifth element of $\mathrm{LMF}(\tilde{Z})$ (height) is normalized between 0 and 1, herefore there is no need to normalize this element.

Step 5: Computing the total-relation IT2 FS matrix $\widetilde{T}$

To compute the total-relation IT2 FS matrix $\widetilde{T}$, we have to ensure the convergence of $\lim_{l\rightarrow\cdot}\widetilde{X}^l = 0$. The elements of $\widetilde{X}^l$ are also IT2 FSs. $\widetilde{X}$ can be defined by 9 matrices and the elements of these matrices are all crisp numbers.

Theorem 1. Let

$$\widetilde{X}^l = \begin{bmatrix} \tilde{x}^l{}_{11} & \tilde{x}^l{}_{12} & \cdots & \tilde{x}^l{}_{1n} \\ \tilde{x}^l{}_{21} & \tilde{x}^l{}_{22} & \cdots & \tilde{x}^l{}_{2n} \\ \vdots & \vdots & \ddots & \vdots \\ \tilde{x}^l{}_{n1} & \tilde{x}^l{}_{n2} & \cdots & \tilde{x}^l{}_{nn} \end{bmatrix} \text{ where } \tilde{x}^l{}_{ij} = (a^l_{ij}, b^l_{ij}, c^l_{ij}, d^l_{ij}, e^l_{ij}, f^l_{ij}, g^l_{ij}, i^l_{ij}, h^l_{ij})$$

And further define eight matrices. There is no need to consider the 9th matrix that contains the heights of $\mathrm{LMF}(\widetilde{X})$.

$$\widetilde{X}^l{}_a = \begin{bmatrix} \tilde{a}^l{}_{11} & \tilde{a}^l{}_{12} & \cdots & \tilde{a}^l{}_{1n} \\ \tilde{a}^l{}_{21} & \tilde{a}^l{}_{22} & \cdots & \tilde{a}^l{}_{2n} \\ \vdots & \vdots & \ddots & \vdots \\ \tilde{a}^l{}_{n1} & \tilde{a}^l{}_{n2} & \cdots & \tilde{a}^l{}_{nn} \end{bmatrix}, \widetilde{X}^l{}_b = \begin{bmatrix} \tilde{b}^l{}_{11} & \tilde{b}^l{}_{12} & \cdots & \tilde{b}^l{}_{1n} \\ \tilde{b}^l{}_{21} & \tilde{b}^l{}_{22} & \cdots & \tilde{b}^l{}_{2n} \\ \vdots & \vdots & \ddots & \vdots \\ \tilde{b}^l{}_{n1} & \tilde{b}^l{}_{n2} & \cdots & \tilde{b}^l{}_{nn} \end{bmatrix}, \ldots., \widetilde{X}^l{}_i = \begin{bmatrix} \tilde{i}^l{}_{11} & \tilde{i}^l{}_{12} & \cdots & \tilde{i}^l{}_{1n} \\ \tilde{i}^l{}_{21} & \tilde{i}^l{}_{22} & \cdots & \tilde{i}^l{}_{2n} \\ \vdots & \vdots & \ddots & \vdots \\ \tilde{i}^l{}_{n1} & \tilde{i}^l{}_{n2} & \cdots & \tilde{i}^l{}_{nn} \end{bmatrix}$$

Proof: The proof is straightforward, all the eight matrices contain crisp values and the matrix multiplication is used to prove this theorem.

Lin and Wu [2] proved $\mathrm{limit}_{l\rightarrow\infty}\widetilde{X}^l{}_u = O$ and $\lim_{l\rightarrow\infty}(I + X_u + X_u{}^2 + \cdots + X^l_u) = (1 - X_u)^{-1}$ based on $\sum_{j=1}^{n} X_{u_{ij}} < s$ for triangular fuzzy sets. We used this theorem for IT2 FS matrix $\widetilde{T}$. Therefore, $\mathrm{limit}_{l\rightarrow\infty}\widetilde{X}^l{}_d = O$ and $\lim_{l\rightarrow\infty}(I + X_d + X_d{}^2 + \cdots + X^l_d) = (1 - X_d)^{-1}$ based on $\sum_{j=1}^{n} X_{d_{ij}} < s$ and $\widetilde{T} = \lim_{l\rightarrow\infty}(I + \widetilde{X} + \widetilde{X}^2 + \cdots + \widetilde{X}^l)$. Then the total-relation matrix $\widetilde{T}$ is acquired as follows:

$$\widetilde{T} = \begin{bmatrix} \tilde{t}_{11} & \tilde{t}_{12} & \cdots & \tilde{t}_{1n} \\ \tilde{t}_{21} & \tilde{t}_{22} & \cdots & \tilde{t}_{2n} \\ \vdots & \vdots & \ddots & \vdots \\ \tilde{t}_{n1} & \tilde{t}_{n2} & \cdots & \tilde{t}_{nn} \end{bmatrix}; \text{where } \tilde{t}_{ij} = (a^n_{ij}, b^n_{ij}, c^n_{ij}, d^n_{ij}, e^n_{ij}, f^n_{ij}, g^n_{ij}, i^n_{ij}, h^n_{ij}), \text{then } [a^n_{ij}] = X_a \times (1 - X_a)^{-1}, [b^n_{ij}] = X_b \times (1 - X_b)^{-1}, \ldots, [i^n_{ij}] = X_i \times (1 - X_i)^{-1}, [h^n_{ij}] = X_h \quad (12)$$

To acquire the importance weight of each criteria, we calculated $\widetilde{D}_i + \widetilde{R}_i$, where $\widetilde{D}_i$ shows the sum of the rows and $\widetilde{R}_i$ shows the sum of the columns of total-relation matrix $\widetilde{T}$, and can be obtained through equation 13 and 14.

$$D_i = \sum_{j=1}^{n} t_{ij} \quad (i = 1,2,\ldots,n) \quad (13)$$

$$R_j = \sum_{i=1}^{n} t_{ij} \qquad (j = 1,2,\dots,n) \tag{14}$$

Note that in 13 and 14, $t_{ij}, i, j = 1,2,\dots,n$ are IT2 FS, and their addition must be based on the 9.

Step 6: Decoding each IT2 FS into a word

The IT2 FSs obtained from the previous step were decoded into seven words, "Extremely low", "Very low", "Low", "Fair", "high", "Very high", "Extremely high". The decoder must compare the similarity between two IT2 FSs so that the output of step 5 can be mapped into its most similar word in the codebook. Several similarity measures are introduced for IT2 (Bustine [21], Gorzalczany [22], Mitchell [23], Wu and Mendel [18,24]). In this study we used jaccard similarity measure for IT2 FSs. Equation 15 is used to calculate the jaccard similarity measure for IT2 FSs.

In order to decode the IT2 FSs obtained from $\widetilde{D}_i + \widetilde{R}_i$, IT2 FSs must be mapped into [0 10]. For this reason we used min max normalization method defined in 16.

$$sm_j(\widetilde{A},\widetilde{B}) = \frac{\sum_{i=1}^{N} \min\left(\overline{\mu}_{\widetilde{A}}(x_i), \overline{\mu}_{\widetilde{B}}(x_i)\right) + \sum_{i=1}^{N} \min\left(\underline{\mu}_{\widetilde{A}}(x_i), \underline{\mu}_{\widetilde{B}}(x_i)\right)}{\sum_{i=1}^{N} \max\left(\overline{\mu}_{\widetilde{A}}(x_i), \overline{\mu}_{\widetilde{B}}(x_i)\right) + \sum_{i=1}^{N} \max\left(\underline{\mu}_{\widetilde{A}}(x_i), \underline{\mu}_{\widetilde{B}}(x_i)\right)} \tag{15}$$

$$v' = \frac{v - minA}{maxA - minA}(new - maxA - new - min\,A) + new - minA \tag{16}$$

5 Application of Proposed Method

Step 1: Identify the decision goals, criteria and group of experts

For evaluating knowledge management capability of organization based on words, we had to define weights for each criterion. A group of three knowledge management experts were asked to compare the criteria. Six criteria were chosen for this reason.

Step 2: develop linguistic codebooks for decision making

The codebook of words that was used for comparing the influence of criteria on each other is presented in table 1. The IA approach was used to map these intervals into IT2 FSs. The FOUs for each word is presented in table 2. The codebook used for the expertise weight is shown in the table 2.

Table 1. FOU data for all words in the influence codebook

Word	UMF	LMF
No influence	[0,0,0.137628,1.974745]	[0,0,0.091752,1.316497,1]
Very low influence	[0.37868,2,2.5,4.62132]	[0.585786,2.212445,2.212445,3.414214,0.849779]
Low influence	[2.37868,3.5,4.5,6.62132]	[2.792893,3.792893,3.792893,4.207107,0.585786]
High influence	[4.708759,7.770621,10,10]	[5.05051,8.724745,10,10,1]
Very high influence	[7.367007,9.816497,10,10]	[8.683503,9.908248,10,10,1]

Table 2. FOU data for all words in the expertise weight codebook

Word	UMF	LMF
Low	[0.085786,1.5,3,4.62132]	[1.792893,2.280847,2.280847,2.81066,0.404234]
Moderate	[3.585786,4.75,5.5,6.914214]	[4.858579,5.034231,5.034231,5.141421,0.273849]
High	[5.982233,7.75,8.6,9.517767]	[8.034315,8.357323,8.357323,9.165685,0.571004]

Step 3: compute the linguistic weighted average of the assessments. The initial direct-relation matrix can be computed using LWA. In this study we considered the equal expertise weights for the decision makers. Using 17, the linguistic weighted average was used to aggregate the influence matrices.

Step 4: Establish the normalized initial-direct-relation matrix. We used 16 to normalize the initial direct-relation IT2 FS matrix. The result is shown in the table 3.

Step 5: Computing the total-relation IT2 FS matrix $\tilde{T}$

Equation 19 was used to compute the total-relation IT2 FS matrix $\tilde{T}$. The result is shown in the table 4. $\tilde{D}_i + \tilde{R}_i$ can be computed from the 13 and 14, that is shown in the table 6.

Table 3. The normalized direct-relation IT2 FS matrix $\tilde{X}$

	C1	…	*C6*
C1	[0,0,0,0,0,0,0,0,0,0.2738]	…	[0.0602, 0.1224, 0.1420, 0.1777, 0.0984,0.1102, 0.1418,0.1480, 0.2738]
C2	[0.1025,0.1692,0.2177,0.2177,0.1099,0.1318,0.2177,0.2177, 0.2738]	…	[0.0082,0.0435,0.0544,0.1006,0.0128,0.0242,0.0659,0.0743, 0.2738]
C3	[0.1025,0.1692,0.2177,0.2177,0.1099,0.1318,0.2177,0.2177, 0.2738]	…	[0.1025,0.1692,0.2177,0.2177,0.1099,0.1318,0.2177,0.2177, 0.2738]
C4	[0.0231,0.0587,0.0778,0.1293,0.0961,0.0476,0.0766,0.0832, 0.2738]	…	[0.1025,0.1692,0.2177,0.21770.1099,0.1318,0.2177,0.2177, 0.2738]
C5	[0.4004,0.1017,0.1420,0.1777,0.06, 0.0780,0.1418,0.1480, 0.2738]	…	[0.1604,0.2137,0.2177,0.2177,0.1890,0.1963,0.2177,0.2177, 0.2738]
C6	[0.0691,0.1193,0.1622,0.1926,0.0847 0.1014,0.1525,0.1564,0.2738]	…	[0,0,0,0,0,0,0,0, 0.2738]

Table 4. The total-relation IT2 FS matrix $\tilde{T}$

	C1	…	*C6*
C1	[0.0296,0.1573,0.4131,1.2882,0.0546,0.0882,0.3857,0.4404,0.2738]	…	[0.0996,0.2912,0.5439,1.4252,0.1646,0.2083,0.5262,0.5869, 0.2738]
C2	[0.1209,0.2971,0.5852,1.4177,0.1467,0.1960,0.5745,0.6302,0.2738]	…	0.0501,0.2217,0.4716,1.3223,0.0837,0.1274,0.4796,0.5437, 0.2738]
C3	[0.1322,0.453,0.7340,1.6814,0.1603,0.2193,0.7058,0.7679, 0.2738]	…	[0.1476,0.3778,0.7504,1.6691,0.1814,0.2432,0.7345,0.7973, 0.2738]
C4	[0.0636,0.2460,0.5767,1.5072,0.0980,0.1473,0.5489,0.6103, 0.2738]	…	[0.1481,0.3678,0.7029,1.5614,0.1809,0.2403,0.6889,0.7447, 0.2738]
C5	[0.0759,0.2645,0.5504,1.4334,0.1218,0.1718,0.5325,0.5946, 0.2738]	…	[0.1865,0.3692,0.6065,1.4447,0.2416,0.2807,0.6007,0.6598, 0.2738]
C6	[0.0939,0.2672,0.5968,1.5117,0.1260,0.1742,0.5651,0.6256, 0.2738]	…	[0.0343,0.1803,0.4656,1.3369,0.0585,0.0952,0.4519,0.5110, 0.2738]

Table 5. FOU data for all words in the weight codebook

Word	UMF	LMF
Extremely low	[0,0,0.137628,1.974745]	[0,0,0.045876,0.658248,1]
Very low	[0.085786,1,2,3.414214]	[0.896447,1.353553,1.353553,1.603553,0.414214]
Low	[0.982233,2.75,3.75,4.81066]	[2.792893,3.353553,3.353553,4.207107,0.585786]
Fair	[2.87868,4.5,5.25,7.12132]	[4.292893,4.818667,5.207107,0.549337]
High	[4.585786,6,7.05,8.414214]	[5.792893,6.514348,6.514348,7.207107,0.573901]
Very high	[6.585786,8,9,9.789949]	[8.292893,8.630602,8.630603,9.207107,0.477592]
Extremely high	[7.367007,9.816497,10,10]	[9.473401,9.963299,10,10,1]

Table 6. The values of $\widetilde{D}_i + \tilde{R}_i$ and the decoded weights of criteria

	$\widetilde{D}_i + \tilde{R}_i$	Decode
C1	[0.0371,1.776,3.1255,9.3084,0.2876,0.5925,2.9490,3.3510,0.2738]	Low
C2	[0,1.1046,2.9316,8.9268,0.2499,0.5425,2.8212,3.2277, 0.2738]	Very low
C3	[0.1808,1.4706,3.6779,10,0.4287,0.7739,3.5119,3.9275, 0.2738]	Low
C4	[0.0060,1.0729,2.9632,8.9265,0.2190,0.5105,2.8278,3.2186, 0.2738]	Very low
C5	[0.1719,1.4384,3.4240,9.5869,0.4757,0.7974,3.3081,3.7270, 0.2738]	Low
C6	[0.1177,1.3616,3.4275,9.5949,0.3695,0.6949,3.3075,3.7258, 0.2738]	Low

Step 6: Decoding each IT2 FS into a word. The weights codebook was needed to decode the IT2 FSs obtained from the step 5 into words. A group of 30 people including the main decision-makers in the step 1 were asked to define endpoint intervals for the seven words in the codebook then the IA was used to map these intervals into IT2 FSs. FOUs for weights codebook is shown in the table 5. The result of decoder for each criterion is shown in the table 6.

6 Conclusion

To consider the inter-relations between decision making criteria in subjective judgments, we proposed interval type 2 fuzzy set extension of DEMATEL method. In this method we used the interval type-2 fuzzy DEMATEL to map the influence matrices defined by words into weights. IT2 FSs are able to show the uncertainty related to each word in the codebook. The DEMATEL method considers the inter-relations between criteria and defines weights based on these relations. Therefore, the IT2 FS extension of DEMATEL leads to decision making method that can consider the uncertainty related to decision making and also the inter-relations between criteria.

References

1. Gabus, A., Fontela, E.: Perceptions of the World Problematique: Communication Procedure, Communicating With Those Bearing Collective Responsibility (DEMATEL Report No. 1). Battelle Geneva Research Centre, Geneva, Switzerland (1973)
2. Lin, C.-L., Wu, W.-W.: A fuzzy extension of the DEMATEL method for group decision making. European Journal of Operational Research 156, 445--455 (2004)

3. Mendel, M.J., Wu, D.: Perceptual Computing: Aiding People in Making Subjective Judgments. Wiley-IEEE Press (2010)
4. Zadeh, L.A.: Fuzzy sets. Information and Control 8, 338--353 (1965)
5. Zadeh, L.A.: The concept of a linguistic variable and its application to approximate reasoning-1. Information Sciences 8, 199--249 (1975)
6. Mendel, J.M.: Uncertain Rule-Based Fuzzy Logic Systems: Introduction and New Directions. Prentice-Hall, Upper-Saddle River (2001)
7. Mendel, J.M.: An architecture for making judgments using computing with words. Int'l Journal of Applied Mathematics and Computer Science 12(3), 325--335 (2002)
8. Mendel, J.M.: Computing with words and its relationship with fuzzistics. Information Sciences 177, 988--1006 (2007)
9. Jassbi, J., Mohammadnejad, F., Nasrokkahzadeh, H.: A fuzzy DEMATEL framework for modeling cause and effect relationships of strategy map. Expert System with Application 38, 5967--5973 (2011)
10. Chang, B., Chang, C.-W., Wu, C.-H.: Fuzzy DEMATEL method for developing supplier selection criteria. Expert Systems with Applications 38, 1850--1858 (2011)
11. Yang, J.L., Tzeng, G.-H.: An integrated MCDM technique combined with DEMATEL for a novel cluster-weighted with ANP method, vol. 38, pp. 1417--1424 (2011)
12. Chen, J.-K., Chen, I.-S.: Using a novel conjunctive MCDM approach based on DEMATEL, fuzzy ANP, and TOPSIS as an innovation support system for Taiwanese higher education. Expert Systems with Applications 37, 1981--1990 (2010)
13. Zadeh, L.A.: From computing with numbers to computing with words---from manipulation of measurements to manipulation of perceptions. IEEE Trans. on Circuits and Systems-1, Fundamental Theory and Applications 4, 105--119 (1999)
14. Mendel, M.J., Wu, D.: Perceptual reasoning: A new computing with word sengine. In: Proc. IEEE Int'l Conf. on Granular Computing, Silicon Valley, CA, pp. 446--451 (2007)
15. Mendel, J.M., John, R.I.: Type-2 fuzzy sets made simple. IEEE Trans. on Fuzzy Systems 10, 117--127 (2002)
16. Hamrawi, H., Coupland, S.: Type-2 fuzzy arithmetic using alpha-planes. In: IFSA-EUSFLAT Conference (2009)
17. Kaufmann, A., Gupta, M.: Introduction to Fuzzy Arithmetic Theory and Applications. Van Nostran Reinhold Co. Inc. (1985)
18. Wu, D., Mendel, J.M.: Corrections to Aggregation Using the Linguistic Weighted Average and Interval Type-2 Fuzzy Sets. IEEE Transactions on Fuzzy Systems 16(6) (2008)
19. Mendel, M.J., Wu, D.: Perceptual reasoning for perceptual computing. IEEE Trans. on Fuzzy Systems 16(6), 1550--1564 (2008)
20. Liu, F., Mendel, J.M.: Encoding words into interval type-2 fuzzy sets using an interval approach, IEEE Trans. on Fuzzy Systems, vol. IEEE Trans. on Fuzzy Systems 16, 1503--1521 (2008)
21. Bustince, H.: Indicator of inclusion grade for interval-valued fuzzy sets. Application to approximate reasoning based on interval-valued fuzzy sets. International Journal of Approximate Reasoning 23(3), 137--209 (2000)
22. Gorzalczany, M.B.: A method of inference in approximate reasoning based on interval-valued fuzzy sets. Fuzzy Sets and Systems 21, 1--17 (1987)
23. Mitchell, H.B.: Pattern recognition using type-II fuzzy sets. Information Sciences 170(2-4), 409--418 (2005)
24. Wu, D., Mendel, J.M.: A comparative study of ranking methods, similarity measures and uncertainty measures for interval type-2 fuzzy sets. Information Sciences 179(8), 1169--1192 (2009)

Effective Resource Recommendations for E-learning: A Collaborative Filtering Framework Based on Experience and Trust

Pragya Dwivedi and Kamal K. Bharadwaj

School of Computer and Systems Sciences
Jawaharlal Nehru University, New Delhi, India
{pragya.dwijnu,kbharadwaj}@gmail.com

Abstract. A personalized e-learning recommender system can help learners in finding learning resources that suits their needs. Collaborative filtering (CF) generates recommendations to learners by leveraging the preferences of group of similar learners. In this paper, we put forward that in addition to the traditional similarity in recommending the E- learning resources (like book, subjects, teachers), other factors such as experience and trust have an important role in generating effective recommendations. So, we considered both experience and trustworthiness of learners to develop a collaborative filtering framework, called CF-EXP-TR scheme, for e-learning recommendations. A two level filtering methodology is proposed which shows that recommendation of learning resources is taken by those learners who are more experienced as well as high trustworthy. The experimental results show that incorporation of experience and trust concepts into collaborative framework, CF-EXP-TR indeed improves the recommendation accuracy and establishes that our scheme is better than traditional Pearson based collaborative filtering, CF-PR.

Keywords: Recommender System, Collaborative Filtering, E-learning, Trust.

1 Introduction

Effective e-learning provides to make information available to people without any time and space constraints. Nowadays availability of large amount of learning resources online, the learners puzzle to access these resources. They are enticed into spending more time on searching appropriate resources that suited their needs [6]. Recommender systems (RSs) are suitable tool to overcome the problem of information overload [1]. In E-learning environment, RSs deal with information about learners and learning activities and recommend resources such as books, subjects and other reading material which meet the pedagogical characteristics and interests of learners [5].Collaborative filtering (CF) as a classical method of information retrieval has been widely used in helping people to deal with information overload [2]. The most frequently technique used to measure the similarity between users is Pearson correlation coefficient. Recommendations are generated for active user with the help of these neighbors on the basis of Resnick formula[1].

V.V. Das and N. Thankachan (Eds.): CIIT 2011, CCIS 250, pp. 166–170, 2011.

Research has pointed out that person tends to believe more on recommendations from person they trust than on online recommender systems which generate recommendations based on anonymous person similar to them [4]. In this paper, we are interested in improving the ability of making accurate recommendations of resources in e-learning environment using collaborative filtering. However the Pearson similarity alone may not be sufficient to provide high quality recommendations. Therefore, there is a need to incorporate other factors like experience and trust to enhance the prediction accuracy. Our idea, in developing experience and trust based collaborative filtering framework CF-EXP-TR, is to enhance the quality of neighbors by relying only on those neighbors who are experienced and trustworthy.

2 Experience and Trust-Aware Recommendation Framework

In real life situation, we would like to take recommendation from those people who are similar, experienced and trustworthy. Sometimes persons are trustworthy but not experienced or vice-versa. So it may be better to take advantages of both the factors together for improving the recommendations.

2.1 Experience Computation

Experience is the effect on a person of anything or everything that has happened to that person. Experience of a learner can be computed on the basis of books, teachers and subjects chosen by the learner in e-learning environment. Let $L = \{l_1, l_2, l_3, \dots, l_k\}$ be the set of k learners in the system. Then experience E_i of learner l_i is computed as follows

$$E_i = \frac{H_i}{\max\{H_i \dots . H_k\}} \tag{1}$$

where H_i is the whole past history of learner l_i which includes number of books, subjects chosen by that learner and how many teachers have taught him.

In order to evaluate the importance of experience of learner l_i to an active learner l_j, an asymmetric function is defined as

$$f(x) = \begin{cases} E_i - E_j \, , E_i > E_j \\ 0, \quad E_i \leq E_j \end{cases} \tag{2}$$

Now a new metric of experience-based similarity, expsim( ) is established as given below in formula(3). The first component of this metric shows importance of experience while the second component refers to similarity between learners according to Pearson correlation formula.

$$\text{expsim}(i, j) = \left[\left(f(E_i, E_j)\right) . \text{sim}(i, j)\right] . \tag{3}$$

The value of expsim obtained between a pair of learners is utilized to obtain the desired k-neighborhood of each learner.

2.2 Trust Computation

Trust between two users u_a and u_b is computed as follows [7]:

$$T(u_a, u_b) = 1 - \frac{\sum_{i=1}^{n}\left(r_{u_a,i} - r_{u_b,i}\right)}{r_{max} * n} \tag{4}$$

Here n is defined as historical ratings of user u_a and r_{max} is maximum rating given in the system.

2.3 Proposed CF-EXP-TR Scheme

The proposed scheme obtains predictions for an active learner on unseen resources by incorporating experience and trust in collaborative framework. The main steps of our scheme are as follows:

Step 1: Compute the importance of experience of learners to active learner using formula (2).

Step 2: Compute the similarity expsim() using formula (3) and generate neighbors based on expsim() similarity.

Step 3: Find the trust values of these neighbors using formula (4) and extract more trustworthy neighbors among them.

Step 4: Predict the ratings for unseen resources for active learner using resnick formula

3 Experiments and Results

In order to evaluate the performance of proposed scheme incorporating experience and trust in collaborative framework, we conducted several experiments. The goal of these experiments is to demonstrate superior performance of our scheme as compared to traditional CF-PR scheme.

3.1 Experimental Setup

Since there is no well known dataset publically accessible for research [3] in the domain of e-learning RSs, we have mapped a well known MovieLens dataset from the RSs domain to e-learning RSs dataset (here after referred to as EL dataset) for our experimentation. We mapped movies as teachers, books and subjects and the ratings to movies are considered as ratings provided by learners to teachers, books and subjects. We randomly split dataset into three parts named as book-data (BK-data), subject-data (SB-data), teachers-data (TR-data) and whole-data (WL-data) for generating the effect on individual resource recommendation as well as randomly split the learners into subsets of 100,200 and 300 learners called EL100, EL200 and EL300 respectively. This is to illustrate the effectiveness of the proposed scheme under varying number of participating learners. Each of these sub datasets was randomly split into 60% training and 40% test data. For each dataset experiments were run 20 times to eliminate the effect of any bias in the data.

3.2 Performance Measurements

In order to test the performance of our scheme, we measure system accuracy using the mean absolute error (MAE) and coverage of the system. MAE is used to compute the accuracy of prediction. MAE measures the average absolute deviation of predicting rating of an item from the actual rating for the item. Coverage is measured as number of items for which RSs can generate prediction over total number of unseen items.

3.3 Results

Experiment 1
To demonstrate the performance of the system based on CF-EXP-TR scheme, we conduct experiments on different datasets keeping the neighborhood size fixed as shown in Table1 (i) and 1(ii).

Table 1. Comparison of MAE and Coverage% Between CF-EXP-TR and CF-PR using (i) EL100-EL300 (ii) BK-data, SB-data TR-data and WL-data.

Datasets	MAE		Coverage%	
	CF-EX-PR	CF-PR	CF-EX-PR	CF-PR
EL100	0.924	0.949	94.5	92.0
EL200	0.880	0.923	96.3	91.2
EL300	0.847	0.881	94.4	90.4

(i)

Datasets	MAE		Coverage%	
	CF-EX-PR	CF-PR	CF-EX-PR	CF-PR
BK	0.844	1.202	94.5	92.0
SB	0.842	1.212	96.3	91.2
TR	0.905	1.151	94.4	90.4
WL	0.842	1.216	96.9	84.0

(ii)

The results given in Table 1 clearly indicate the superiority of the proposed scheme CF-EXP-TR over CF-PR

Experiments 2
In order to observe the affect of neighborhood size on the performance, we conducted this experiment with varying neighborhood size from 5 to 30 with increment 1. Fig 1 shows the effect of neighborhood size on BK-data and SB-data for CF-EXP-TR and CF-PR scheme.

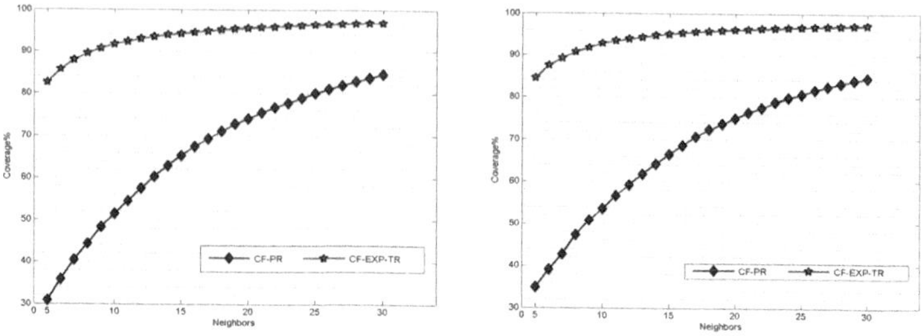

(a) (b)

Fig. 1. Effect of neighborhood size on coverage using datasets (a) BK data (b) SB data

4 Conclusions and Future Work

This paper proposed a scheme that takes advantages of experience and trust in collaborative filtering framework for recommendation of e-learning resources. A two level filtering is used to ensure that only experienced and trustworthy learners are involved in making recommendations to an active learner. Our experimental results clearly establish the superiority of the proposed scheme CF-EXP-TR over the traditional CF-PR scheme. In our future work, we plan to consider the sparsity issue in future and see how utilization of various sparsity measures[2] can further improve our e-learning recommender system CF-EXP-TR.

References

1. Adomavicius, G., Tuzhilin, A.: Toward the Next Generation of Recommender Systems: A Survey of the State-of-the-Art and Possible Extensions. IEEE Transaction on Knowledge and Data Engineering 17(6), 734–749 (2005)
2. Anand, D., Bharadwaj, K.K.: Utilizing Various Sparsity Measures for Enhancing Accuracy of Collaborative Recommender Systems Based on Local and Global Similarities. Expert Systems with Applications 38(5), 5101–5109 (2010)
3. Bobadilla, J., Serradilla, F., Hernando, A.: Collaborative Filtering Adapted to Recommender Systems of E-Learning. Knowledge-Based Systems 22, 261–265 (2009)
4. Carchiolo, V., Alessandro, L., MalGeri, M.: Reliable Peers and Useful Resources: Searching For the Best Personalised Learning Path in A Trust- and Recommendation-Aware Environment. Information Sciences 180, 1893–1907 (2010)
5. Chen, C.M., Lee, H.M., Chen, Y.H.: Personalized E-Learning System Using Item Response Theory. Computers & Education 44, 237–255 (2005)
6. Ghauth, I.K., Abdullah, A.N.: Measuring Learner's Performance in E-Learning Recommender Systems. Australasian Journal of Educational Technology 26, 764–774 (2010)
7. Lathia, N., Hailes, S., Carpa, L.: Trust Based Collaborative Filtering. In: Proceeding of the Joint iTrust and PST Conferences on Privacy, Trust Management and Security, pp. 167–182. Springer, Boston (2008)

Patellar Fracture Analysis Using Segmentation and Global Thresholding Techniques

Sarbani Datta and Monisha Chakraborty*

School of Bio-Science and Engineering, Jadavpur University, 188,
Raja S.C. Mallik Road, Kolkata, India
sarbanidatta.ju@gmail.com, monishack@school.jdvu.ac.in

Abstract. Radiologists identify abnormal pathologies including fractures with a high level of accuracy. However in some cases the examining reader accuracy may show high miss rate while reading X-rays containing abnormalities such as multiple patellar fracture. Accurate diagnosis of fractures is vital to the effective management of patient injuries. As a result, detection of patellar fracture is an important orthopedics and radiologic problem. In this paper, attempt has been made to develop an algorithm which will identify global thresholding ranges for different edge detection operators e.g. Sobel, Prewitt, Canny, Laplacian of Gaussian for analysis of fractured patella, which will help the orthopedic surgeons for analyzing the fracture in a better form than conventional method of diagnosis which is subjective, time consuming and tedious. The processing algorithms are developed on MATLAB 7.6.0 (R2008a) programming platform.

Keywords: X-ray image, patellar fracture, algorithms, segmentation, global thresholding.

1 Introduction

In current generation, large numbers of X-rays are being interpreted in hospitals especially for bone fractures. Computer aided system performs some intelligent task on these abnormal x-ray images and analysis is further needed in order to raise the accuracy and bring down the miss rate in hospital [1-2]. Conventionally, orthopedic surgeons examine the bone X-ray images based on their experience and knowledge for identification of the existence of fracture and even classify as in case of patellar fracture. This kind of manual inspection of X-rays consumes a lot of time and is subjective. The process itself is monotonous and tedious which might cause mistakes during the inspection [3]. If computer algorithm is developed then it will be a scale to compare the subjective result leading to reduction of miss rate and thus enhancing accuracy. Detection of fractures is an important orthopedic and radiologic problem and therefore it is proposed that our novel algorithm could improve the current manual inspection of X-ray images of patellar fracture. This paper discusses the development of an algorithm that detects the edges of the fractured patellar X-ray image to figure out the prominence of the fractured portions with a definite

* Corresponding author.

V.V. Das and N. Thankachan (Eds.): CIIT 2011, CCIS 250, pp. 171–179, 2011.

thresholding range, so that it can help orthopedic surgeons 1) during the study of the patellar structure, 2) identification of the fractured patella, 3) measurement of fracture treatment, 4) treatment planning prior to surgery. Patella is the largest sesamoid bone that improves the mechanics of the knee extension [4]. Fractures of such bones are common in males between the ages of 20 to 50 years. They are usually caused due to falling on the knee or sudden contraction of the quadriceps muscle which may lead to inability of walking [5].The fracture may be classified into a) transverse, b) lower pole, c) comminuted, d) vertical, and e) osteochondral patellar fracture. In case of sleeve or osteochondral patellar fracture it is difficult to recognize the fragments of the patella bone from the X-ray image. These fractures require tension band wiring or fixation by screws based approach for treatment [4-6]. X-ray bone segmentation is a vital step in X-ray image analysis techniques [7]. Segmentation is therefore an important task for medical imaging. It is considered as a challenging task because the bone x-ray images are complex in nature and the output of segmentation algorithm is affected due to closeness in gray level of different soft tissues [8]. Detection of the discontinuities in the X-ray images, different fragments of the fractured patella can be separated and identified. Edge detection operators look for discontinuities using the first-order-derivative or zero crossing in the second order derivative [9].

2 Materials and Methods

In order to detect the fractured patella, edge of patella features appears as a vital rule for the classification task [1]. Wide conventional edge detectors have been considered such as Prewitt, Sobel, Canny and Laplacian of Gaussian. Each of the mentioned edge detectors with a specific global thresholding range have been shown in the proposed algorithm to obtain the edge in an appropriate form for identification and classification of patellar fracture. The algorithms were developed on MATLAB version 7.6.0(R2008a) in Microsoft Windows XP operating system, with the processor 2.16GHz and 1.96GB of RAM.

2.1 Edge Detection

The edge detection process detects outline of an object and boundaries between objects and the background in the image. The basic edge detection operator shows a matrix area gradient operation that determines the level of variance between different pixels. The edge-detection operation is performed by forming a matrix centered on a pixel chosen as the center of the matrix area [10]. If the value of this matrix area is above a given threshold value, then the middle pixel is considered to be as an edge. Examples of gradient based edge detectors are Sobel, and Prewitt, operators. The gradient-based algorithms have kernel operators that calculate the strength of the slope in directions which are orthogonal to each other, commonly vertical and horizontal. Later, the different components of the slopes are combined to give the total value of the edge strength [11]. The first-order derivative of an intensity, f(x,y), of an image is the gradient. The gradient is defined as the vector,

$$\nabla f = \begin{bmatrix} G_x \\ G_y \end{bmatrix} = \begin{bmatrix} \partial f/\partial x \\ \partial f/\partial y \end{bmatrix} \quad (1)$$

The magnitude of the vector is,

$$\nabla f = \mathrm{mag}(\nabla f) = \left[G_x^{\ 2} + G_y^{\ 2}\right]^{1/2} = \left\{\left(\partial f/\partial x\right)^2 + \left(\partial f/\partial y\right)^2\right\}^{1/2} \quad (2)$$

The gradient vector points in the direction of the maximum rate of change of the 2-D function, f(x,y), of an image. The angle at which this maximum rate of change occurs is,

$$\alpha(x, y) = \tan^{-1}\left(G_y/G_x\right) \quad (3)$$

There are various approaches as mentioned in this section to determine the derivatives Gx and Gy digitally. The second-order derivatives of the intensity, f(x,y), of an image are computed using the Laplacian,

$$\nabla^2 f(x, y) = \frac{\partial^2 f(x, y)}{\partial x^2} + \frac{\partial^2 f(x, y)}{\partial y^2} \quad (4)$$

2.2 Sobel Operator

The Sobel operator performs a 2-D spatial gradient measurement on an image. It is used to find the approximate absolute gradient magnitude at each point in an input grayscale image [10]. Fig. 1 shows the 3x3 area representing the gray levels of an image. The operator consists of a pair of 3×3 convolution masks as shown in Fig. 2. One mask is simply the other rotated by 90° [10-12].

Z_1	Z_2	Z_3
Z_4	Z_5	Z_6
Z_7	Z_8	Z_9

Fig. 1. Image Neighborhood

-1	0	+1
-2	0	+2
-1	0	+1

Gx

+1	+2	+1
0	0	0
-1	-2	-1

Gy

Fig. 2. Sobel convolution masks

The detector uses the masks to compute the first order derivatives Gx and Gy,

$$Gx = Z7+2Z8+Z9 \quad (5)$$

$$Gy = Z1+2Z2+Z3$$

2.3 Prewitt Operator

The Prewitt operator as similar to the Sobel measures two components. The vertical edge component is calculated with kernel Gx and the horizontal edge component is calculated with kernel Gy

$$\begin{aligned} Gx &= (Z7+Z8+Z9)-(Z1+Z2+Z3) \\ Gy &= (Z3+Z6+Z9)-(Z1+Z4+Z7) \end{aligned} \tag{6}$$

In the mentioned formulation, the difference between the first and third rows of the 3x3 image region as show in Fig.1approximates the derivative in the x-direction, and the difference between the third and first columns approximates the derivative in the y-direction [11-12]. The Prewitt masks as shown in Fig. 3 are used to implement Gx and Gy.

-1	0	1
-1	0	1
-1	0	1

Gx

1	1	1
0	0	0
-1	-1	-1

Gy

Fig. 3. Prewitt masks

2.4 Canny Operator

The Canny edge detection algorithm is known as an optimal edge detector based on a set of criteria which include finding the most edges by minimizing the error rate, marking edges as closely as possible to the actual edges to maximize localization, and marking edges only once when a single edge exists for minimal response [13]. According to Canny, the optimal filter that meets all three criteria above can be efficiently approximated using the first derivative of a Gaussian function,

$$G(x,y) = \frac{1}{2\pi\sigma^2} e^{-\frac{x^2+y^2}{2\sigma^2}} \tag{7}$$

The first stage involves smoothing the image by convolving with a Gaussian filter. This is followed by computing the gradient of the image by feeding the smoothed image through a convolution operation with the derivative of the Gaussian in both the vertical and horizontal directions.

The 2-D convolution operation is described in the following equation,

$$I'(x,y) = g(k,l) \otimes I(x,y) = \sum_{k=-N}^{N} \sum_{l=-N}^{N} g(k,l) I(x-k, y-l) \tag{8}$$

-1	0	+1
-2	0	+2
-1	0	+1

Gx

+1	+2	+1
0	0	0
-1	-2	-1

Gy

Fig. 4. Canny convolution masks

where: g(k,l) = convolutional kernel, I(x,y) = original image, I'(x,y) = filtered image and 2N + 1 = size of convolutional kernel [10-13]. The non-maximal suppression stage finds the local maxima in the direction of the gradient, and suppresses all others, minimizing false edges. The Canny algorithm employs hysteresis thresholding. There are two threshold levels, th, high and tl, low where th > tl. Pixel values above the th value are immediately classified as edges. By tracing the edge contour, neighboring pixels with gradient magnitude values less than th can still be marked as edges as long as they are above tl [10].

2.5 Laplacian of Gaussian Operator

The Laplacian is a 2-D isotropic measure of the 2nd order derivative of an image. The Laplacian of an image highlights regions of rapid intensity change and is therefore often used for edge detection [11]. The Laplacian is applied to an image that has first been smoothed with Gaussian filter in order to reduce its sensitivity to noise. The operator takes a single graylevel image as input and produces another graylevel image as output.

0	1	0
1	−4	1
0	1	0

1	1	1
1	−8	1
1	1	1

−1	2	−1
2	−4	2
−1	2	−1

Fig. 5. Laplacian of Gaussian kernels

The kernels that are mentioned in Fig. 5 are used as discrete approximations to the Laplacian filter [11-12]. The 2-D LoG function centered on zero and with Gaussian standard deviation has the form,

$$\mathrm{LoG}(x,y) = -\frac{1}{\pi\sigma^4}\left[1 - \frac{x^2+y^2}{2\sigma^4}\right]e^{-\frac{x^2+y^2}{2\sigma^2}} \tag{9}$$

2.6 Thresholding

Segmentation involves separating an image into regions corresponding to objects. We identify contours by identifying differences between regions (edges). Natural way to segment regions is through thresholding, the separation of light and dark regions [14]. Thresholding creates binary images from grey-level ones by turning all pixels below some threshold to zero and all pixels about that threshold to one.

If g(x, y) is a thresholded version of f(x, y) at some global threshold T,

$$g(x,y) = \begin{cases} 1 & \text{if } f(x,y) \geq T \\ 0 & \text{otherwise} \end{cases} \tag{10}$$

The aim of our work is to identify a specific global thresholding range for each of the edge detection operators considered in this work. The operators are applied on patellar fracture X-ray images. The block diagram of our developed algorithm is shown in Fig. 6. The input X-ray images of fractured patella are taken from the websites e.g. boneandspine. com, joint-pain-expert. net, helmedica. gr, med-ed.virginia.edu, imaging.consult.com, gentili.net and from factotem.org. These images are processed on MATLAB 7.6.0 (R2008a) programming platform. An X-ray image of fractured patella (208 x 246 resolutions) has been taken using Canon PowerShot A400 camera as given in the website: www. boneandspine. com and it is shown in Fig. 6(a).

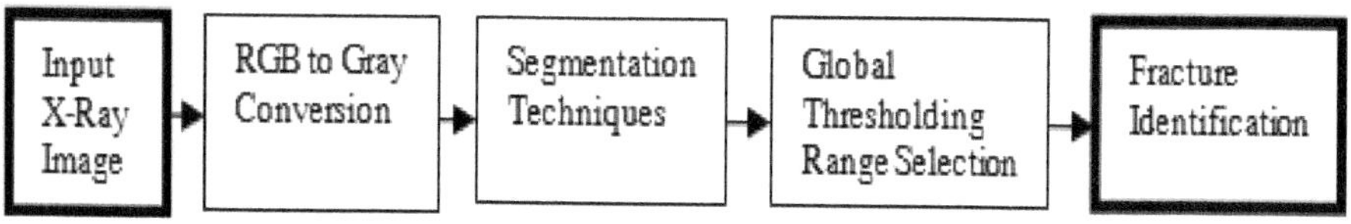

Fig. 6. System Block Diagram

3 Results and Discussion

The algorithm for patellar fracture detection with specific thresholding ranges is developed in this work and for these purpose a set of 20 X-ray images are collected. The global thresholding ranges identified from the developed algorithm for the edge detection operators are tabulated in Table 1.

Table 1. Thresholding range for each of the segmentation operators

Operators	Thresholding Range
Sobel	0.02-0.025
Prewitt	0.02-0.025
Laplacian of Gaussian	0.0015-0.0025
Canny	0.1-0.25

It is observed from Table 1, the range is similar for the Prewitt and Sobel operators, both the operators show almost the same result.

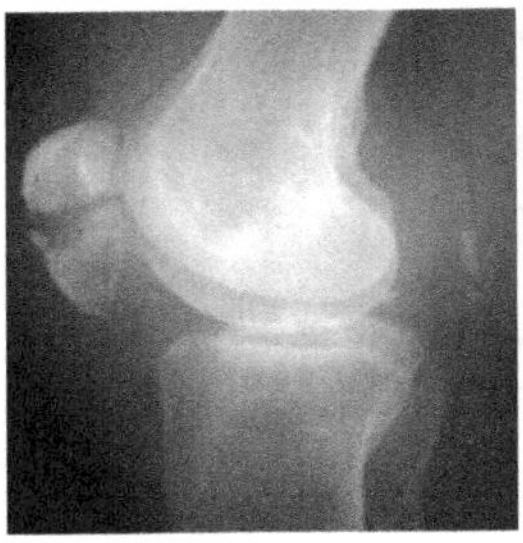

Fig. 7.(a). Fractured patella

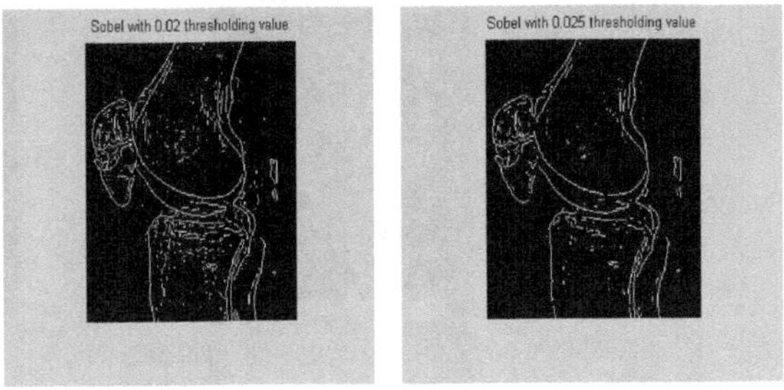

(**a**) Threshold = 0.02 (**b**) Threshold = 0.025

Fig. 8. Segmentation using Sobel operator

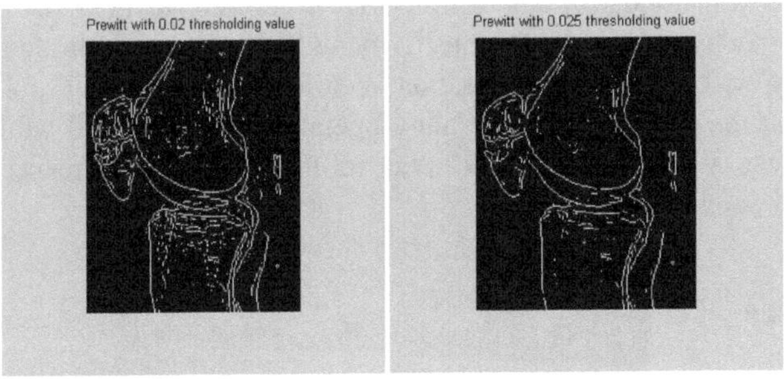

(**a**) Threshold = 0.02 (**b**) Threshold = 0.025

Fig. 9. Segmentation using Prewitt operator

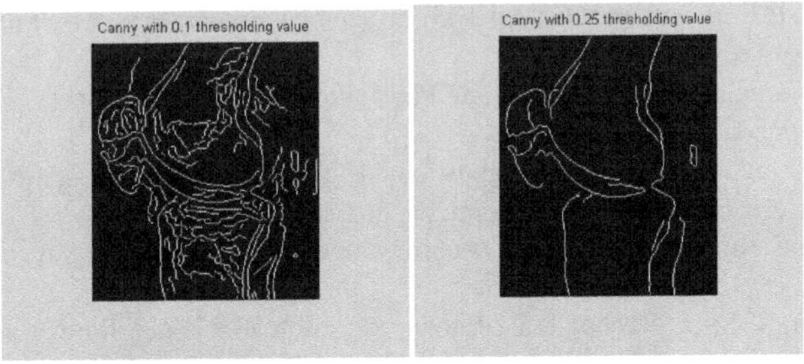

(**a**) Threshold = 0.1 (**b**) Threshold = 0.25

Fig. 10. Segmentation using Canny operator

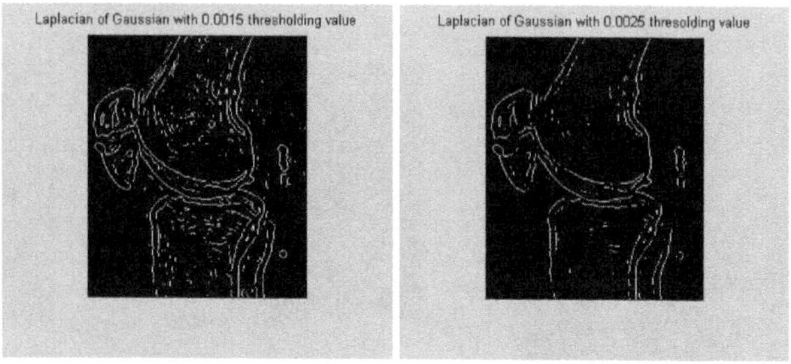

(**a**) Threshold = 0.0015 (**b**) Threshold = 0.0025

Fig. 11. Segmentation using Laplacian of Gaussian operator

4 Conclusion

The developed method will help orthopedic surgeons to identify the patellar fractures in a better way by reducing the subjectivity and miss rate in multiple patellar fractures and thereby will enhance the detection accuracy in less time. From this work, it is inferred that the performance of Canny operator with threshold value of 0.25 is the best amongst all other operators used in this work, with respect to automated detection of patellar fracture.

References

1. Chai, H.Y., Wee, L.K., Swee, T.T., Hussain, S.: Gray-Level Co-occurrence Matrix Bone Fracture Detection. Am. J. Applied Sci. 8, 26–32 (2011)
2. Pham, D.L., Xu, C., Prince, J.L.: Current Methods in Medical Image Segmentation. Annu. Rev. Biomed. Eng. 2, 315–337 (2000)
3. Neelgar, B.I., Benakop, P.G.: Analysis of Segmentation of Femur by Filtering Techniques. Ind. J. Sc. Tech. 1, 1–5 (2008)
4. Waugh, A., Grant, A.: Anatomy and Physiology in Health and Illness, 10th edn. Churchill Livingstone-Elsevier (2001)
5. Patella Fracture: Causes, Diagnosis and Treatment, `http://www.joint-pain-expert.net/patella-fracture.html`
6. Medscape Reference, `http://emedicine.medscape.com/article/394270-overview`
7. Mahendran, S.K., Baboo, S.S.: Enhanced Automatic X-ray Bone Image Segmentation using Wavelets and Morphological Operators. In: Int. Conf. on Information and Electronics Eng., pp. 125–129. IACSIT Press, Singapore (2011)
8. Chen, H.C., Wu, C.H., Lin, C.J., Liu, Y.H., Sun, Y.N.: Automated Segmentation for Patella from Lateral Knee X-ray Images. In: 31st Annu. Int. Conf. of the IEEE EMBS, pp. 3553–3556 (2009)
9. Meer, P., Georgescu, B.: Edge Detection with Embedded Confidence. IEEE Trans. on Pattern Analysis and Machine Intelligence 23, 1351–1365 (2001)
10. Nadernejad, E., Sharifzadeh, S., Hassanpour, H.: Edge Detection Techniques: Evaluation and Comparisons. Applied Mathematical Sciences 2, 1507–1520 (2008)

11. Gonzalez, R.C., Woods, R.E.: Digital Image Processing, 3rd edn. Prentice Hall (2001)
12. Moustafa, A.A., Alqadi, Z.A.: A Practical Approach of Selecting the Edge Detector Parameters to Achieve a Good Edge Map of the Gray Image. J. Comput. Sci. 5, 355–362 (2009)
13. Canny, J.: A Computational Approach to Edge Detection. IEEE Trans. on Pattern Analysis and Machine Intalligence 8, 679–714 (1986)
14. Sezgin, M., Sankur, B.: Survey Over Image Thresholding Techniques and Quantitative Performance Evaluation. J. Electronic Imaging 13, 146–165 (2004)
15. Tian, T.-P., Chen, Y., Leow, W.-K., Hsu, W., Howe, T.S., Png, M.A.: Computing Neck-Shaft Angle of Femur for X-Ray Fracture Detection. In: Petkov, N., Westenberg, M.A. (eds.) CAIP 2003. LNCS, vol. 2756, pp. 82–89. Springer, Heidelberg (2003)
16. Zahurul, S., Zahidul, S., Jidin, R.: An Adept Edge Detection Algorithm for Human Knee Osteoarthritis Images. In: Int. Conf. on Signal Acq. and Processing, pp. 375–379 (2010)

Intelligent Agent Based Architecture for Patient Monitoring in Bio Sensor Networks

Aloysius George

Managing Director, Griantek,
Chennai- 600 093, India
aloysiusgeorgephd@gmail.com

Abstract. Body Sensor networks are having wide range of applications in medical field; integration of biosensors with the wireless communication system has the potential to take the healthcare to the next level. With the implementation of the biosensor network system in health monitoring, it reduces the expense and the human body can be examined and abnormal medical conditions can be detected earlier. In this paper a new and effective Body sensor network monitoring method with real time positioning and tracking has been proposed. The intelligent agents used in this system provide continuous interaction between the patient, doctor and the hospital services. The main advantage of the proposed method is the positioning and tracking of the patient without the help of a mobile service provider. Mobile agent providing tracking and positioning is also employed for sending an ambulance to the patient in case of an emergency.

Keywords: Bio Sensor Networks, Wireless body area network (WBAN), Medical Server Agent [MSA], GSM, Bio Sensors.

1 Introduction

With the development of technologies in the field of healthcare services the cost has also increased drastically and it has lead to severe challenges for policy makers, hospitals, healthcare providers, insurance companies and the patients. Also the health related problems are increasing day by day demanding more facilities for patient's as a result. This challenge can be met by deploying an appropriate patient monitoring systems [1]. Wireless sensor networks can be effectively used in healthcare to enhance the quality of life provided for the patients. In case of emergency, the positioning systems are very useful which will help the ambulance to take the patient to the hospital [2]. A Body Sensor Network (BSN) (a.k.a. Body Area Network) is a device of wearable and implantable wireless sensors. These can be pervasive, long-term, and real time health management for the host or the patient on which it is deployed on. The data collected which may be either physiological (e.g. electrocardiogram (EKG), activity (e.g. walking), and environmental (e.g. ambient temperature) parameters from the host's body and its immediate surroundings; and can even actuate treatment (such as drug delivery). [3]. The patient's position location

V.V. Das and N. Thankachan (Eds.): CIIT 2011, CCIS 250, pp. 180–186, 2011.

or tracking has been always a key issue in using the above technology [4]. Chances for such conditions demands for an efficient method of tracking or positioning, so that an ambulance or doctor can reach to the patient for help. Other issues are high cost of operation for tracking of patient with the help of a service provider and method of communication between bio sensor network device and other related devices. In this paper, the Bio sensor network is integrated with intelligent agents that perform some automated works for transmitting data to other intelligent agents and the patient can be tracked or the real time position can be found with the help of a simple location based service without the help of a mobile service provider [5]. Also data transfer between agents is done as simple SMS via GSM network which reduces the operating cost. The proposed system is mainly divided into three intelligent agents: Sensor Agent, Mobile Agents and Medical server Agent. The information's from Mobile agents to Medical server agent is send via GSM network as simple SMS. [6]

2 Related Works

Radu Dobrescu et.al [7] have presented a hybrid wireless sensor network which contains both mobile and fixed nodes, which enables the monitoring of chronic patients and their home environment via normal or, if necessary, emergency communication with long distance transmitting system like Internet. Since the patient cannot be tracked and the communications had to be done via internet as a result it was not an effective method. Md.Asdaque Hussain and Kyung Sup Kwak [8] have proposed a different positioning system on the environment of wireless body area networks (WBAN). WBAN needed a technology that serves two way communication as well as positioning of the user and hence GSM technology is considered. Since the hospital personals should depend upon a service provider for positioning and tracking the patient, this method affect the security and privacy of the service also increase the cost of operation.

Kevin Miller and Dr. Suresh Sankaranarayanan [1] have proposed the technique of monitoring and notifying the health of patients using an intelligent agent, to the concerned hospital personnel. This approach reduces the hospital staffs to take care patients admitted in the hospital and it does not offer any service when the patient is discharged from the hospital. Rifat Shahriyar et.al [9] presented an intelligent mobile health monitoring system (IMHMS) that uses the Wearable Wireless Body/Personal Area Network. The patients will participate in the health care process by their mobile devices and thus can access their health information from anywhere any time. The system was effective for monitoring the conditions of the patient but it is not providing positioning and tracking of the patient which is the key issue and need. Kin-Yeung Wong and Yiu-Man Choi [5] proposed simple system providing location-based service. It can be easily implemented and maintained without the involvement of mobile network operators. This paper proposes a new idea for locating or positioning a PDA without the help of a service provider but it do not deals with the bio sensor body network or patient monitor system.

3 System Architecture

In this paper an effective and low cost way to monitor a patient using Bio sensors with real time positioning has been proposed. Real time positioning and path tracing without the help of a service provider is also made available in this proposed method. In this method the entire system has been divided into mainly three intelligent agents.

- Sensor Agent
- Mobile Agents
- Medical Server Agent

A basic diagram showing the flow of data between agents

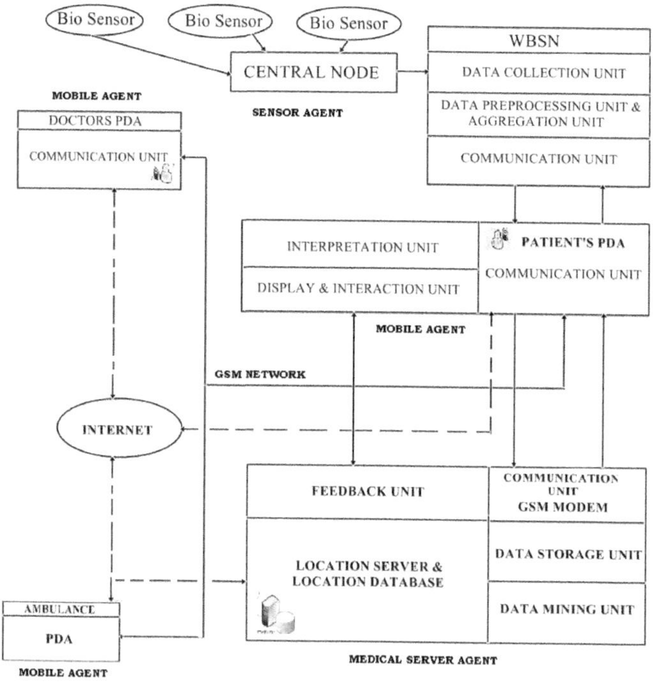

Fig. 1. System Architecture

3.1 Bio Sensor Agent

Bio sensor networks monitor the patient's entire body periodically. Bio sensor agent is installed in such a way that it can be made work automatically on pre set conditions. The agent collects all the necessary data from the patient's body. Each organ will be monitored by a group of sensors and the data is send to the group leader. Group leaders in each organ can communicate with each other and the aggregated information's from each group leader is send to the central controller. The central controller in the Sensor agent is the main communicating unit with the patient's

Mobile agent with the help of any of the three wireless protocols ZigBee, Bluetooth or WLAN (802.11). [9].

Sensor Agent Algorithm

- WBSN is activated and time interval for readings to be taken is set.
- Bio sensors collect the readings from patient's body in various intervals.
- Readings from each sensor is send to the CENTRAL NODE (here patient's body acts as the medium between BSs and Central node for communication and send as electromagnetic waves.)
- Central node collects and preprocesses the data and sends the data to patient's PDA using Bluetooth or Zigbee.

3.2 Medical Server Agent (MSA)

Mainly it has two sections:

- Location Server
- Medical storage and data mining

MSA includes central database, location server and location data base. The examination and treatment results of a patient are stored in the central database so that a Doctor or a specialist can examine these data whenever needed. The entire process of positioning is done separately in the Location server and the system includes mobile base station, mobile users, authorized mobile user, location server, and location database. Their roles are described as follows:

Mobile Base Station: All the mobile service provider's has given a unique ID for each mobile base station for station controlling on managerial purpose and it is used to link the mobile phones or the PDA with the GSM network for communication.

Location Database: It is a separate database for storing information's like details of the locations patient has traveled it is possible by recording the cell ID of the base station from which the PDA gets the signal from.

Location Server: It is linked with numerous of mobile agents which provide the proper information to the requested mobile agent. Location server consists of three processes such as location recording process, location reporting process and zone alerting Process.

Mobile User: Here patient's mobile agent is the mentioned mobile user. The application is stored in the mobile agent and it periodically requests the closest mobile station for cell ID and sends it to the MSA.

Authorized user: other mobile agents with doctor and ambulance are mentioned as authorized user. Authorized user includes two functions. One is to locate details of the specific patient and the path traveled by a patient.

Medical Server Agent Algorithm

- The IMS collects the data from the PDA with the help of a GSM modem.
- GSM modem decodes the data (patients ID, sensor readings and other information's such as time date etc).
- Data received is stored in a Data storage unit.
- Data stored is checked for any serious conditions by the operator.
- Data mining unit helps to check the data from the entire data base.
- The patient is informed about the conditions and the precautions to be taken by the feedback unit by SMS with the help of GSM modem.
- In case Doctor needs any past records of the Patient he can request to the IMS via SMS.

3.3 Mobile Agents

All the PDA's used in the system is a mobile agent each one having a specific work. Mainly we are considering three PDA's or mobile agents Patient's PDA, Doctor's and PDA provided in the ambulance. Mobile agent connected to the Sensor agent: Mobile agent receives information's send from the central controller of the sensor agent via Bluetooth or zigbee. Then the mobile agent sends the processed information's to the medical server agent. Mobile agents communicate with the MSA and other agents using GPRS/Edge/SMS. To send the information's between agents, a GSM modem is used in the Medical Server Agent to receive SMS and use EDGE or GPRS. [5].

3.4 Mobile Agent Algorithm

- Receives the data from central node
- The application installed in the PDA processes the data.
- It checks the data collected with the preset values (interpretation unit).
- If the collected value is beyond the set range the data is converted to SMS format.
- If not Data is deleted from the PDA.
- The readings beyond the range are sent to IMS (intelligent medical server) and Doctors PDA.

4 Algorithm

4.1 Algorithm for Positioning and Tracing the Patient

- All the PDA's are registered in the LOCATION SERVER and LOCATION DATABASE UNIT in the IMS.
- When the patients PDA send the readings collected by the BSN it sends the CELL ID of the mobile base station near by the patient.
- GSM modem decodes the data and the CELL ID of the base station is stored in the LOCATION DATABASE.
- LOCATION SERVER arranges the position of the patient in table with real time.

- LOCATION DATABASE has another table which stores location mappings between cell IDs and their related zone description, which helps to return comprehensive location to the operator or the user.
- The position of the patient can be monitored in the hospital from the LOCATION SERVER.
- If the Location Server receives the request from the doctor with only the keyword REQUEST, returns the most recent location of patient. The represent method of location depends on the Authorized User or the doctor. For text base, server directly sends the description of the location; for graphical base, server then sends the exact position where the Mobile User has located.
- Path tracing: the keyword REGUEST has another function: if Location Server receives the request from doctor with timestamp parameter following ID and the keyword REGUEST. Location Server search through all possible records from the table Record and reply them to Doctors PDA.
- Similarly the ambulance has an inbuilt module with GSM and GPS system on emergency reported from the IMS, it receives the real time position and path patient has traveled to the PDA. It can request for any update to the IMS via SMS or GPRS.

Fig 2 showing flow of Data between Agents:

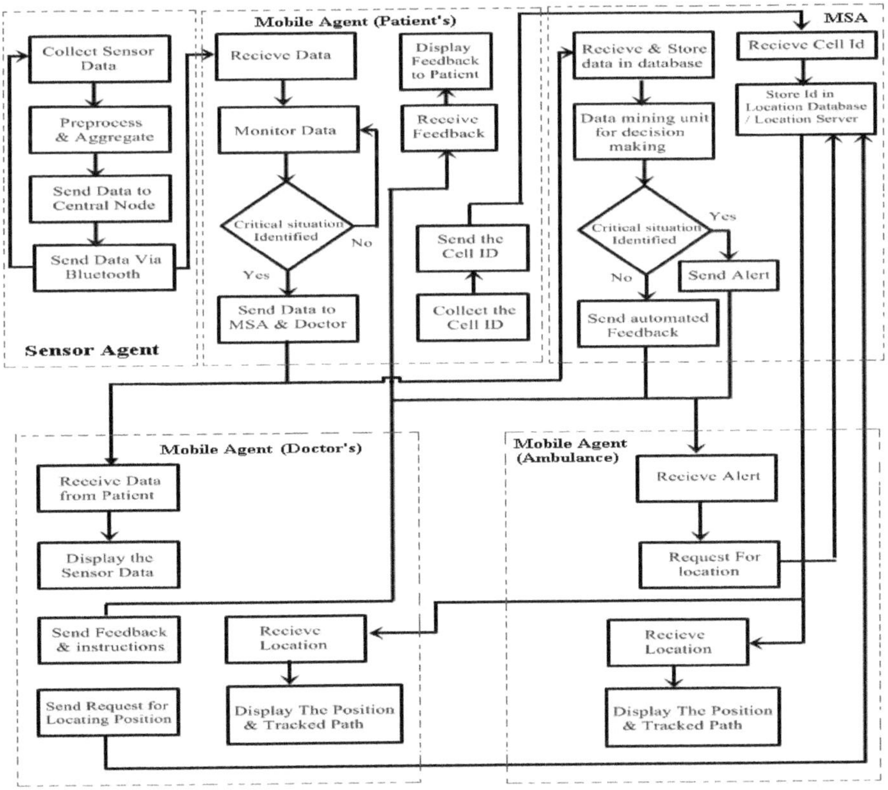

Fig. 2. Message Flow Between the agents

5 Conclusion

In this paper an effective way to monitor a patient continuously with real time positioning is proposed. Also a new method is designed in which the information's from different agents are send as simple SMS via GSM network and mainly a patient positioning and tracking system without the help of a service provider is explained. The whole system of Bio sensor network health care system places forward some future works such as finding the most effective method for ensuring security in biosensor network routing, finding of most reliable and energy efficient routing protocols and reducing the complexity of the entire system. As a future work, we will include some of the performance results by implementing this work using standard simulation tools like NS2 [10].

References

1. Miller, K., Sankaranarayanan, S.: Policy based Agents in Wireless Body Sensor Mesh Networks for Patient Health Monitoring. In: Intelligent Networking Group, Department of Computing, University of West Indies, Kingston, Jamaica
2. Khan, P., Hussain, A., Kwak, K.S.: Medical Applications of Wireless Body Area Networks. International Journal of Digital Content Technology and its Applications 3(3) (September 2009)
3. Tan, C.C., Wang, H.: Body Sensor Network Security: An Identity-Based Cryptography Approach. In: Proceedings of the First ACM Conference on Wireless Network Security (WiSec 2008), pp. 148–153 (2008)
4. http://en.wikipedia.org/wiki/Body_Area_Network
5. Wong, K.-Y., Choi, Y.-M.: A Simple Location-Based Service on Urban Area. International Journal of Computers 1(4) (2007)
6. Farooq, U., Haq, T.U., Amar, M., Asad, M.U., Iqbal, A.: GPS-GSM Integration for Enhancing Public Transportation Management Services. In: 2nd International Conference on Computer Engineering and Applications (2010)
7. Dobrescu, R., Popescu, D., Nicolae, M., Mocanu, S.: Hybrid wireless sensor network for homecare monitoring of chronic patients. International Journal of Biology and Biomedical Engineering
8. Hussain, A., Kwak, K.S.: Positioning in Wireless Body Area Network using GSM. International Journal of Digital Content Technology and its Applications 3(3) (September 2009)
9. Shahriyar, R., Bari, F., Kundu, G., Ahamed, S.I., Akbar, M.: Intelligent Mobile Health Monitoring System (IMHMS). International Journal of Control and Automation 2(3) (September 2009)
10. Network Simulator, http://www.isi.edu/nsnam/ns

Modeling k-Anonymity Framework for the Proximity-Based Privacy Protection in Context-Aware LBS

B.R. Rohini and B. Sathish Babu

Department of Computer Science and Engineering,
Siddaganga Institute of Technology, Tumkur-572103, India
rohini.br@gmail.com, bsb@sit.ac.in

Abstract. With the development of Context-aware location based services, there is a large scope for user's access to preference based services. One of the main research areas in context-aware location based services is proximity-based privacy protection for the users. The objective of our approach to proximity-based privacy protection is to deviate from the implementation of the centralized anonymizer and model the k-anonymity framework as a secure gateway in the context aware location service provider. Our design of privacy-protection is principled on guaranteed privacy protection rather than assuming the anonymizer to be a trusted third-party providing privacy protection. Using a symbolic model checker tool NuSMV, proximity based privacy protection has been modeled through the k-anonymity framework and it is observed that the system takes care of all the constraints by satisfying most of the specifications.

Keywords: Location based services, Context awareness, Model Checker, Symbolic Model Verifier, NuSMV.

1 Introduction

1.1 Importance of Context Aware Location-Based Services

The development in the field of mobile computing devices can be seen during the recent years. Need for user query based services provided on the mobile devices have increased rapidly. A special class of service among them is the Location Based Service (LBS) [1]. LBS is defined as an information and entertainment service, accessible with mobile devices through the mobile network and utilizing the ability to make use of the geographical position of the mobile device. The main promise of LBS is to provide services to customers based on the knowledge of their locations [2]. The mobile service providers provide various services to the user, some of the examples of services includes personalized shopping, real-time traffic information, digital map services which are delivered to mobile terminals according to users location requesting the nearest business or service (e.g., the nearest restaurant or cinema) [3].Unfortunately the current location based services are rigid as they cannot make good use of contextual information. For example in a restaurant finder application

V.V. Das and N. Thankachan (Eds.): CIIT 2011, CCIS 250, pp. 187–193, 2011.

users actually want to find the best restaurant according to their current preferences and context. Existing location-based services reduce the efficiency of the query result from best to only the closest details to the end user [4].The rigid nature of LBS is overcome by the introduction of Context-awareness in LBS. The use of context as a parameter in location bases services is important in user interactive applications where the users context is changing dynamically. Context Awareness is defined as any information that can be used to characterize the situation of an entity, where an entity can be a person, place, or physical or computational object [5]. Further context awareness or context-aware computing is defined as the use of context to provide task-relevant information and/or services to a user, wherever they may be [5]. While using context aware LBS, a user has much to gain by the effective use of implicitly sensed context where users requirement is serviced exactly. It allows an applications behavior to be customized to the users current situation and need. Thus the importance of context aware LBS leads to the system where the location service providers present the information and services to users where they can access preference based services at any place [6]. Context aware applications executing in mobile devices operating in LBS Scenario should address the following challenges for the efficient and practical realization of context aware location-based services (i).Context management a key requirement to build context-aware location based services includes context acquisition, context representation, context storage, context reasoning [7]. (ii) Service trigger mechanism provides user with comprehensive services even without any explicitly triggered command on the basis of context information [8]. (iii) Providing context and preference-based services is an important aspect of context awareness wherein preference acquisition method and preference usage are key issues where users preference in requesting the service is considered (iv) Proximity based privacy protection is a major concern in LBS where the release of user precise location information to untrust third parties should be protected [9].

1.2 Importance of Proximity Based Privacy Protection in Context Aware LBS

The importance of proximity-based privacy in Context aware LBS is providing users with privacy protection of their location information along with the access to preference based services [9]. Proximity based services are a special class of LBS in which the service adaptation depends on the comparison between a given threshold value and the distance between a user and other (possibly moving) entities. Research in privacy protection in LBS scenario requires a trusted third-party (anonymizer) or uses protocols that are computationally and communicationally expensive to provide security to users of Context-aware LBS. The following issues arise in designing LBS with privacy as a major concern: (i) LBS result accuracy depend on the context, such as population and road density, around a users location. (ii) an adversary may violate a users privacy based on the users location information and also based on the query request payload submitted to Location service provider (LSP) [10].We address the challenge of protecting users location information contained in the LBS query payload and his/her access to preference based services.

1.3 k-Anonymity Framework

The objective of a proximity based privacy-protection is to protect the privacy of a users location information while maintaining a high level of LBS accuracy. A k-anonymity based framework was proposed to protect location privacy by using a trusted third-party called the anonymizer. With this framework, user sends its service request to the centralized anonymizer, which subsequently model a k-anonymized cloaking region that covers not only this user, but also k-1 other users where k>1. Then, the anonymizer transmits the cloaking region to the LBS server as the constant in the LBS query, and forwards the query answer to the user. It prevents the location service provider from distinguishing a user among at least k-1 others users in the proximity of particular location [11].We advocate k-anonymity preserving management of location information by developing efficient and scalable system-level facilities for protecting the location privacy by ensuring location kanonymity Instead of assuming the anonymizer as a trusted third party providing privacy protection or the location service provider as semi-honest we model the k-anonymity framework as a secure gateway, in the context aware location service provider to ensure proximate based privacy protection.

1.4 Model Checking, NuSMV and Computation Tree Logic

Model checking is a technique to automatically analyze various types of computing systems, ranging from hardware to software. A System is said to be verified if it satisfies the specification defined by its designers. A specification is called a property [12]. For example in a context aware LBS where services are provided to users based on their request and users privacy is a concern could have the following property: where only authorized users are guaranteed with their access to preference based services. A model-checking algorithm takes in input (i) the representation of the system S to be analyzed and (ii) the property P. In more formal terms, S is defined as a finite state machine called a Kripke structure. A Kripke structure is a directed graph with nodes representing the possible states of the system and edges represent the transitions (or triggers) between states. NuSMV is a software tool for the formal verification of finite state systems [13].NuSMV allows us to check finite state systems against specifications in the linear temporal logic and Computation Tree Logic (CTL). In NuSMV a CTL specification is given as CTL formula introduced by the keyword SPEC. Whenever a CTL specification is processed, NuSMV checks whether the CTL formula is true in all the initial states of the model. If this is not the case, then NUSMV generates a counter-example,that is, a (finite or infinite) trace that exhibits a valid behavior of the model that does not satisfy the specification[14].

1.5 Organization of the Paper

The remainder of the paper is organized as follows. Section 2, discusses the related work. In Section 3 we formally specify the problem and present the architecture of modeling the kanonymity framework for proximity based privacy protection. The specifications of the formal verification are also mentioned in this section. In Section 4 we present the results of the NuSMV. Section 5 concludes the paper.

2 Related Works

Based on preserving location privacy, in LBS can be generally classified into two categories: trusted third-party based schemes and user based schemes. In a privacy-aware proximity based services user based schemes for location privacy protection has been proposed wherein privacy threats in LBS scenarios has been discussed, A centralized protocol is designed where privacy is achieved with respect to Service Provider and users. A hybrid approach is practiced in which a secure computation is performed only after a filtering step based on obfuscated locations. Three different privacy preserving protocols has been proposed the first of which is called Service Provider-Filtering and does not involve any communication between the users to evaluate their proximity. The other two, named HideSeek and HideCrypt, provide a more accurate estimation of the proximity by using Service Provider Filtering as the first step followed by a refinement step involving user to- user communication [9]. CAP, a Context-Aware Privacy-preserving LBS system provides integrated protection for data privacy and communication anonymity. CAP uses anonymity based approach for location privacy protection. CAP addresses protection of user location privacy from both location data and network communication perspectives [10]. Personalized k-anonymity model is developed for providing location privacy where, a trusted third-party called anonymizer is used to protect location privacy. This model allows mobile clients to define and modify their location privacy specifications at the granularity of single messages, including the minimum anonymity level requirement. The location service provider is assumed to be a semi-honest service provider and the anonymity server which performs location perturbation is assumed to be a trusted third party server [11].

3 Architecture Overview and Implementation

Fig.1 depicts the System Architecture. The user requests the Context aware LBS system to gain access for the services provided by the LSP. Due to privacy concerns, the user is unwilling to disclose its location to the LSP. The k-anonymity framework is a secure gateway which preserves users location privacy. Using a symbolic model checker tool called NuSMV, the k-anonymity framework is modeled and message exchange in the system is verified and observed that the system protects privacy related information in the users query for access to preference based services. Positioning and tracking devices are used to identify users location.

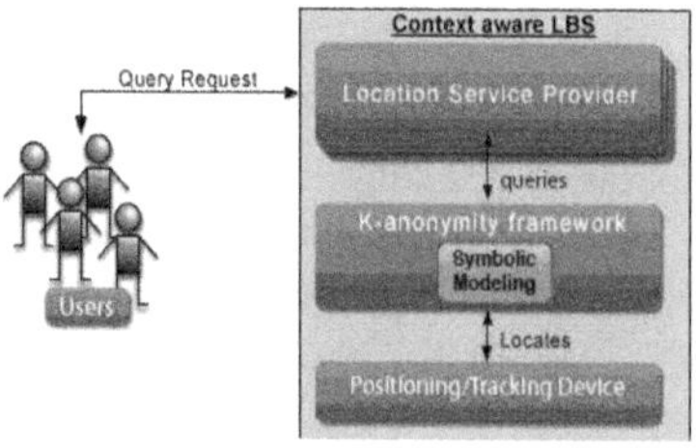

Fig. 1. Location Based Services with k-anonymity framework

Context aware LBS system is divided into different components which comprise of:

1) Location service provider: In Context aware LBS Location service provider handles request/response of user query. The user query requesting for access to preference based service is sent to LSP, LSP in turn redirects the query to k-anonymity framework to ensure the user location privacy. Legitimate users register themselves with a unique register-id with the LBS to gain access to the services provided by the LBS. Once the user query is confirmed as legitimate, LSP serves the users query request by providing access to preference based services.
2) k-anonymity framework: The user query is redirected from the LSP to the k-anonymity framework. The k-anonymity framework identifies the users location through the RFID or GPS schemes of location detection and also locates k-1 others users in proximity to the legitimate user requesting for services. LBS query is redirected to the LSP with the location co-ordinates of legitimate user along with k-1 users in proximity. The LSP does not distinguish the actual user from other users in proximity. Preference based services are rendered to the users without actually revealing the location information of the actual user sending request. The user request after going through the framework is marked as true to ensure that users location privacy is guaranteed.
3) Positioning/Tracking devices: Based on the user query sent from the k-anonymity framework the positioning device locates the user and other k-1 users in proximity and the location co-ordinates are returned. Using NuSMV, different states of the service provider are modeled through the CTL specifications and ensure user's location privacy.

4 Results and Discussions

The CTL specification for the LBS system can be given by:

AG(allusers)->AG(k_user->k-1_user)

The specification states that all users in a particular location are identified and LSP does not distinguish between k -1 user in proximity of the actual k user requesting for service. The specification resulting true

guarantees users location privacy.
AG(k user query)!AG(serviceavailable)

The specification depicts the scenario of all k user queries marked true by the k-anonymity framework gains access to the preference based services provided by the Context aware LBS.

This can be understood better with a help of Kripke structure as shown in Fig. 2. When user enters a particular location and query for services offered by the Context aware LBS, user query is redirected to the k-anonymity framework where the user is labeled as a legitimate user i.e, user query marked as true and only then the user has access to his preference based services hence user location privacy is protected.CTL specification are listed below in Table 1.

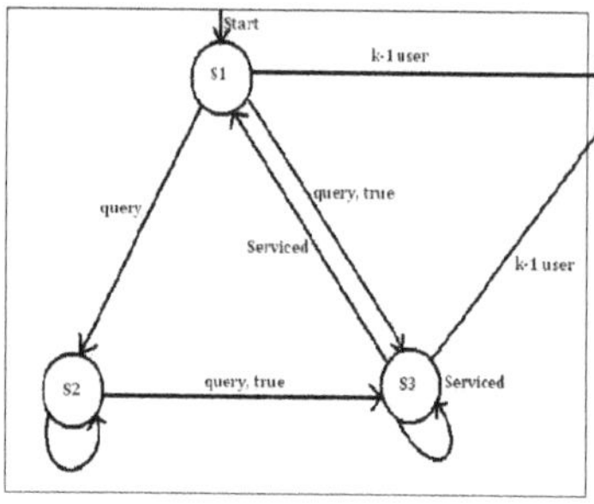

Fig. 2. Kripke structure for the entire LBS system

Table 1. Shows the various constraints placed on the system and results of the corresponding specifications

Sl.No.	Case	Specification
1	k_ reguser[1]=1 & k -1_unreguser[1]=1	True
2	k_ reguser _query[1][1]=1 & k_unreguser_ query[1][0]=0	False

1) The first specification in the table depicts the secure anonymity framework identifying the registered k user requesting for service and other k-1 unregistered users in proximity of a particular location. The state of the specification is proved true for all the traces since every k_reguser entering the location is identified along with the k -1_unreguser in proximity.
2) The second specification states that every registered user query (k_reguser_query) marked true is provided access to preferred services by the LSP protecting location privacy. The counter example is generated due to the falsity of the specification and proves location privacy of users. The service request from the unregistered user(k_unreguser_query) marked as false is denied by the LSP as location privacy is not preserved and the overall specification returns false as the unregistered users are not provided access to the services they request.

5 Conclusion and Future Work

In this paper, we have used symbolic model checking approach for proximity based privacy in the Context-aware Location Based Service systems. The tool NuSMV helps us to verify the constraints placed on the system by exploring the entire state space of the system. The various messages exchanged between the service provider and the registered user in the context-aware LBS environment is depicted. We have assumed the nature of the information in the Context-aware Location Based Services system to be static and modeled it accordingly to ensure location privacy in the system. The dynamic nature of the LBS location need to be taken into account and system specifications can be modeled.

References

1. Hoareau, C., Ichiro, S.: Query language for location-based services: A model checking approach. IEICE - Trans. Inf. Syst. E91-D(4), 976–985 (2008)
2. Moily, A., Prasanna, G., Shetty, K.S., Singh, S.: Model Checking Message Exchange in Location Based Services. In: Intl. Conf. on Computer Communication Technology, ICCCT (2010)
3. Asthana: An indoor wireless system for personalized shopping assistance. In: Proc. of the 1st Workshop on Mobile Computing Systems and Applications, pp. 69–74 (1994)
4. Zhu, T., Wang, C., Jia, G., Huang, J.: Toward Context- Aware Location Based Services. State Key Laboratory of Software Development Environment Beihang
5. Dey, A.K., Abowd, G.D.: Towards a better understanding of context and context-awareness. GVU Technical Report GITGVU- 99-22, College of Computing, Georgia Institute of Technology (1999)
6. Morse, D.R., Armstrong, S., Dey, A.K.: The What, Who, Where, When, and How of Context-Awareness. Graphics, Visualization and Usability Center, College of Computing, Georgia Institute of Technology
7. Chen, H., et al.: An Ontology for Context-Aware Pervasive Computing Environments. The Knowledge Engineering Review 18(3), 197–207 (2003)
8. Jang, S., Woo, W.: Ubi-UCAM: A Unified Context-Aware Application Model. In: Blackburn, P., Ghidini, C., Turner, R.M., Giunchiglia, F. (eds.) CONTEXT 2003. LNCS (LNAI), vol. 2680, pp. 178–189. Springer, Heidelberg (2003)
9. Mascetti, S., Bettini, C., Freni, D.: Privacy-Aware Proximity Based Services. In: Tenth International Conference on Mobile Data Management: Systems, Services and Middleware (2009)
10. Pingley, A., Yu, W.: CAP: A Context-Aware Privacy Protection System for Location-Based Services. In: 29th IEEE International Conference on Distributed Computing Systems (2009)
11. Gedik, B., Liu, L.: Protecting location privacy with personalized k-anonymity: Architecture and algorithms. IEEE Transactions on Mobile Computing 7(1), 1–18 (2008)
12. Clarke, E.M., Grumberg, O., Peled, D.A.: Model Checking. MIT Press (2000)
13. Cimatti, A., Clarke, E., Giunchiglia, E., Giunchiglia, F., Pistore, M., Roveri, M., Sebastiani, R., Tacchella, A.: NuSMV 2: An Open Source Tool for Symbolic Model Checking. In: Brinksma, E., Larsen, K.G. (eds.) CAV 2002. LNCS, vol. 2404, pp. 359–364. Springer, Heidelberg (2002)
14. Cavada, R., Cimatti, A., Keighren, G., Olivetti, E., Pistore, M., Roveri, M.: NuSMV 2.2 Tutorial ITCirst - Via Sommarive 18, 38055 Povo (Trento), Italy

A New Transferable Digital Cash Protocol Using Proxy Re-signature Scheme

M. Kavitha[1], N.R. Sunitha[1], and B.B. Amberker[2]

[1] Department of Computer Science and Engineering,
Siddaganga Institute of Technology, Tumkur, India
[2] Department of Computer Science and Engineering,
National Institute of Technology, Warangal, India
{kavitham,nrsunitha}@sit.ac.in, bba@nitw.ac.in

Abstract. Electronic payment systems have turned out to be a smart and convenient way of making payments. Digital cash is an electronic payment system which is modeled after our real cash system. If the digital cash is transferable then it allows the user to spend an e-coin received in a prior payment immediately without having to contact the bank, that is, the bank remains off-line. In the previous digital cash systems which supported transferability, the digital cash size was growing with each transaction. In this paper, we propose a new digital cash protocol which uses a Forward-Secure Multi-use Unidirectional Proxy Re-signature Scheme to achieve transferability, without any increase in the digital cash size with each transfer. Our scheme enables a secure off-line transaction, thus enforcing user anonymity and transferability. A Trusted Third Party is used to prevent the double spending of the digital coins.

Keywords: Transferability, Off-line, Anonymity, Forward-Secure Multi-use Unidirectional Proxy Re-signature, Double spending.

1 Introduction

In this current world of increased crime, it is not so easy and secure to carry the real cash. Even though the credit-based systems provide security, they won't protect people's privacy. Also, the bank needs to be on-line for these credit-based systems. Digital cash (Electronic cash or E-cash) is an electronic payment system which offers solution to the problems of real cash and today's credit cards. Lot of research work is going on to come up with an ideal digital cash system which works similar to the real cash system. Several challenges need to be addressed in the digital cash system such as maintenance of user anonymity, prevention of double spending of the digital coin. Along with providing security and privacy, the digital cash should be transferable i.e., it should allow the user to spend the digital coin received in the prior payment without contacting the bank. Several digital cash systems have been developed in the literature to provide the security and user's anonymity. But most of them do not provide transferability. Though few digital cash systems have been proposed to provide transferability, they are not efficient. The concept of anonymous off-line e-cash was first

V.V. Das and N. Thankachan (Eds.): CIIT 2011, CCIS 250, pp. 194–199, 2011.

introduced by D. Chaum using blind signatures and cut-and-choose methodology [2]. Brands presented a more compact way to represent e-cash using restrictive blinding with the help of representation problem in groups [9]. N. Ferguson published on single-term off-line anonymous e-cash which was the first practical e-cash [7]. This e-cash system's construction used blind signature and was inefficient to implement multi-spendable e-cash. Sebastiaan H., Von Solms and David Naccache pointed out that perfect anonymity enables perfect crimes, and thus suggested fair e-cash [10], where an authority can trace coins that were acquired illegally.

Tewari, Mahony and Peirce [4] introduced a scheme for transferable e-cash which used observer for coin refreshing. Other valuable contributions to transferable e-cash were made by C. G. Ma & Y. X. Yang [1], H. Wang & Y. Zhang [5]. D. Chaum and T. P. Pedersen [3] pointed out that the size of e-coins grows with the number of transfers. The focus of this paper is on introducing a new digital cash protocol which provides the transferability without any increase in the digital cash size with each transfer by using a Forward-Secure Multi-use Unidirectional Proxy Re-signature Scheme [8]. The rest of the paper is organized as follows: In Section 2, we explain how the Forward-Secure Multi-use Unidirectional Proxy Re-signature Scheme is used to provide transferability to the digital cash protocol; We have suggested further improvements for the proposed digital cash protocol in Section 3; conclusion is included in Section 4 and finally the references are listed.

2 Proposed Scheme

In our paper [6], we had presented Divisible and Transferable Digital Cash Protocol using a simple Verifiable Secret Sharing scheme and Trusted Third Party respectively. In this paper, we are using a new approach to achieve transferability. A Forward-Secure Multi-Use Unidirectional Proxy Re-signature Scheme [8] is used to incorporate transferability into the digital cash protocol presented in [6].

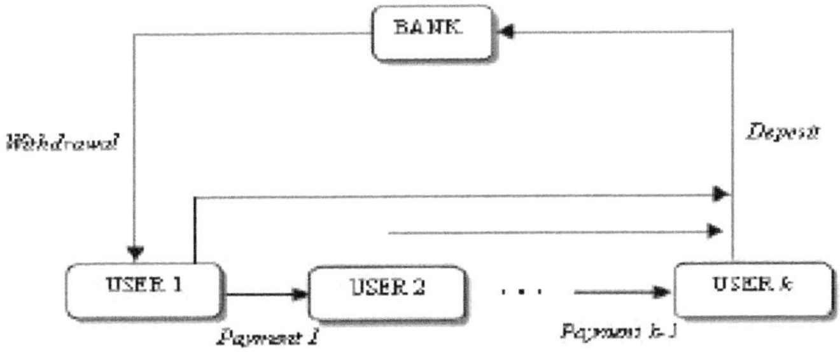

Fig. 1. Transferable Digital Cashprotocol

Let us consider three Users say, User A, User B and User C involved in the digital cash system. Each of the three Users will generate private key μA, μB and μC respectively. Now we shall see how the Forward-Secure Multi-use Unidirectional

Proxy Re-signature scheme[8] works for the transfer of sub-coin from User A to User B and then from User B to User C.

Initialization:

Key Generation Algorithm (KeyGen): Before the transfer process begins, each of the three users will run this algorithm only once to generate the keys for the first time. This algorithm takes as input the security parameter K, the number l of points in the keys and the number T of time periods over which the scheme is to operate. p, q are random distinct $K/2$ bit primes each congruent to 3 mod 4. $N \leftarrow p.q$. User A, User B and User C agree upon common N.

User A's keys: The base secret key $\mu A_0 = (\mu A_{1,0}, \ldots, \mu A_{l,0}, N, 0)$ (where $\mu A_{i,0} \xleftarrow{R} Z^*_N$ and N is a Blum-Williams integer). For verifying signatures, the verifier (User B) is given the public key I_A, calculated as the value obtained on updating the base secret key $T + 1$ times: $I_A = (UA_1, \ldots, UA_l, N, T)$where, $UA_i = \mu A_{i,0}^{2^{T+1}} \bmod N_A$, $i = 1, \ldots, l$.

Similarly User B's and User C's public keys are calculated.

Key Evolution: During time period j ($1 \leq j \leq n$; where, n can be fixed by Bank), the signer signs using key μ_j . This key is generated at the start of period j by applying a key update algorithm to the key μ_{j-1}. The update algorithm squares the l points of the secret key at the previous stage to get the secret key at the next stage.

Key evolution for User A: The secret key $\mu A_j = (\mu A_{1,j}, \ldots, \mu A_{l,j}, N_A, j)$ of the time period j is obtained from the secret key $\mu A_{j-1} = (\mu A_{1,j-1}, \ldots, \mu A_{l,j-1}, N_A, j-1)$ of the previous time period via the update rule: $\mu A_{i,j} = \mu A^2_{i,j-1} \bmod N_A$, $i = 1, \ldots, l$; $j = 1, \ldots, T$.

Similarly the secret keys of User B and User C are updated.

Sub-coin Transfer Process : Since, User A is transferring the sub-coin to User B and User B is in turn transferring the sub-coin to User C, the User A's signature must be translated to User B's signature and User B's signature must be translated to User C's signature respectively. Following are the steps involved in this signature translation process.

Step1: Signature Generation Algorithm (Sign*):* The User A generates her signature $(j, (Y, Z))$ by running this algorithm. It has as input, the secret key μA of the current period, the message M to be signed, and the value j of the period itself to return a signature $(j, (Y, Z))$ where Y, Z in Z^*_N are calculated as follows: $Y = R^{2^{(T+1-J)}} \bmod N$, where $R \xleftarrow{R} Z^*_N$ and $Z = R \prod_{i=1}^{l} \mu A_{i,j}^{c_i} \bmod N$, where $c_1, \ldots, c_l = H(j, Y, M)$ being the l output bits of a public hash function. When User A wants to transfer the sub-coin to User B then she transmits her signature to User B. User B will translate User A's signature into her own signature. The User B won't generate her signature when she wants to transfer the sub-coin to User C. In turn she will use the translated signature (i.e., User *B*'s signature which was obtained by translating User *A*'s signature into her own signature). This signature will be transmitted to User *C* who in turn translate User *B*'s signature into her own signature.

Step2: Re-Signature Key Generation Algorithm (ReKey): For transfer from User *A* to User *B*, this algorithm takes as input, the two secret keys $\mu A_j = (\mu A_{1,j}, \ldots, \mu A_{l,j}, N_A, j)$ and $\mu B_{j+1} = (\mu B_{1,j+1}, \ldots, \mu B_{l,j+1}, N_B, j+1)$, then computes the re-signature key, $rk_{A\to B,j} = (rk_{1,j}, \ldots, rk_{l,j})$ as $rk_{i,j} = \mu B_{i,j+1}/\mu A_{i,j} \bmod N$ where $i = 1, \ldots, l$; $j = 1, \ldots, T$ 1. Observe that the key $rk_{A\to B}$ can be securely generated as follows:

(i) The proxy (User *B*) sends a random $r \in Z_N$ to User *A*.
(ii) User *A* sends $(r/\mu A_{1,j}, \ldots, r/\mu A_{l,j})$ to User *B*.
(iii) User *B* computes $(r(\mu B_{1,j+1}/\mu A_{1,j}), \ldots, r(\mu B_{l,j+1}/\mu A_{l,j})$.
(iv) The proxy (User *B*) recovers $(\mu B_{1,j+1}/\mu A_{1,j}, \ldots, \mu B_{l,j+1}/\mu A_{l,j})$.

Similarly, *ReKey* algorithm is executed for transfer from User *B to* User *C*.

Step3: Signature Verification Algorithm (Verify): For transfer from User A to User B: On input of a re-signature key $\mathrm{rk}_{A\to B,j}$, a public key I_A, a signature (j,(Y,Z)), and a message M, User B verifies User A's signature by running this algorithm. User B checks if Verify (I_A, M, (j, (Y,Z))) = 1. User A's signature (j, (Y, Z)) for the message M in time period j is accepted (returns 1) if $Z^{2^{(T+1-j)}} = Y \prod_{i=1}^{l} UA_i^{c_i} \bmod N$ where $c_1, \ldots, c_l = H(j, Y, M)$, else rejected. Similarly, *Verify* algorithm is executed for transfer from User *B to* User *C*.

Step4: Re-Sign Algorithm (ReSign): For transfer from User *A to User B:* User *A* transmits her signature *(j, (Y, Z))* to User *B*. User *B* translates User *A*'s signature into her own signature *(j+*1*, (Y, Z'))* by running this algorithm. If User *A*'s signature is accepted then, User *B* sets $Z' = Z \prod_{i=1}^{l} rk_{i,j}^{c_i} \bmod N$, where $c_1, \ldots, c_l = H(j, Y, M)$ and outputs the signature *(j+*1*, (Y, Z'))*, otherwise outputs an error message. Similarly, *Re-Sign* algorithm is executed for transfer from User *B to* User *C*. Once the payee (*User B* in case of transfer from User *A* to User *B*; *User C* in case of transfer from User *B* to User *C*) translates payer's signature into her signature, she performs the following steps (These steps are explained considering transfer from User *A* to User *B*. Same procedure is followed for transfer from User *B* to User *C*):

1. User *A* transmits sub-coin X_i and sub-coin ID to User *B*.
2. User *B* verifies Bank signature (Refer [8]) using the bank's public key.
3. User *B* verifies whether sub-coin is valid or not (Refer [8]).
4. User *B* then transmits sub-coin ID to the TTP.
5 TTP searches for the ID (irrespective of *k*-bit counter value) in the database (Fig.2):
   a) If ID is not found then TTP stores ID in database & increments counter by one.
   b) If ID is found then TTP compares *k*-bit counter value of User *B*'s sub-coin ID with *k*-bit counter value of sub-coin ID stored in TTP's database.

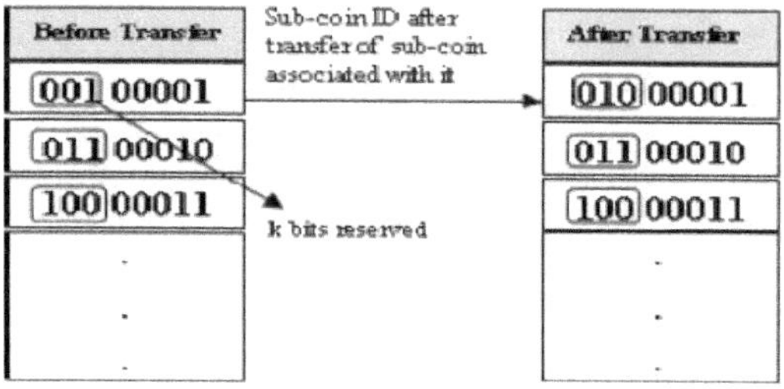

Fig. 2. Trusted Third Party Database (TTP)

- If values are not equal then TTP identifies that sub-coin is already transferred and hence intimates User *B* that sub-coin is invalid thereby preventing double spending by User *A*. User *B* rejects that forged sub-coin.
- If values are equal then TTP increments the counter of that sub-coin ID stored in database by one.

6. TTP transmits this new ID of the sub-coin and its' signature (r_t, s_t) to User *B*:

   rt = newIDg^{k_t} mod p and st = xtrt + kt mod p where, kt ∈ Zq , g is the generator ∈ Z*p and x_t is private key of TTP (Here, p and q are primes with q | p-1).
7. User *B* verifies TTP signature (r_t, s_t): $g^{-s_t} y_t^{r_t} r_t = newID \bmod p$ where, $y_t = g^{x_t}$ mod p is public key of TTP.

If verification holds then User *B* accepts the sub-coin. After 2^k-1 transfers of sub-coin, if a User wants to perform transfer operation and approaches TTP then TTP checks the *k*-bit counter value and identifies that no more transfers are possible and intimates the same to the User.

3 Further Work

There is potential for improvements to the proposed system in the following areas:

- Incorporation of transferability into the digital cash system without using a trusted third party.
- The number of transfers of the digital coins can be made unlimited as in case of the real cash.
- Improvement in complexity of the algorithm by using a better scheme than proxy re-signature scheme without compromising security.

4 Conclusion

With off-line digital cash systems, we can enforce user anonymity and we can have transferable e-coins. Our proposed digital cash protocol uses a proxy re-signature scheme to achieve transferability. This protocol enables a secure off-line transaction without revealing the payer's identity. We have also used a Trusted Third Party to prevent the double spending of the digital coins.

References

1. Ma, C.G., Yang, Y.X.: Transferable off-line electronic cash. Jisuanji Xue-bao (Chin. J. Comput.) 28(3), 301–308 (2005)
2. Chaum, D.: Blind signatures for untraceable payments. In: Advances in Cryptology: Proceedings of CRYPTO 1982, pp. 199–203 (1982)
3. Chaum, D., Pedersen, T.P.: Transferred Cash Grows in Size. In: Rueppel, R.A. (ed.) EUROCRYPT 1992. LNCS, vol. 658, pp. 390–407. Springer, Heidelberg (1993)
4. Tewari, H., O'Mahony, D., Peirce, M.: Reusable off-line electronic cash using secret splitting. In: Networks & Telecommunications Research Group, Computer Science Department, Trinity College, Dublin 2, Ireland
5. Wang, H., Zhang, Y.: A Protocol for Untraceable Electronic Cash. In: Lu, H., Zhou, A. (eds.) WAIM 2000. LNCS, vol. 1846, pp. 189–197. Springer, Heidelberg (2000)
6. Kavitha, Sunitha, M.N.R., Amberker, B.B.: A Divisible And Transferable Digital Cash protocol. IFRSA's International Journal of Computing 1(3), 407–413 (2011)
7. Ferguson, N.: Single Term Off-Line Coins. In: Helleseth, T. (ed.) EUROCRYPT 1993. LNCS, vol. 765, pp. 318–328. Springer, Heidelberg (1994)
8. Sunitha, N.R., Amberker, B.B.: Multi-use Unidirectional Forward-Secure Proxy Re-Signature scheme. In: IEEE Workshop on Collaborative Security Technologies, CoSec 2009, Bangalore, India, December 9 (2009)
9. Brands, S.: An efficient off-line electronic cash system based on the representation problem. Centrum voor Wiskunde en Informatica, Computer Science/Department of Algorithmics and Architecture, Report CS- R (1993)
10. Sebastiaan, H., Von Solms, Naccache, D.: On blind signatures and perfect crimes. Computers & Security 11(6), 581–583 (1992)

Hybrid Image Classification Technique to Detect Abnormal Parts in MRI Images

C. Lakshmi Devasena[1] and M. Hemalatha[2]

[1] Department of Computer Science,
Karpagam University, Coimbatore
[2] Department of Software Systems,
Karpagam University, Coimbatore – 641 021, India
devaradhe2007@gmail.com

Abstract. In Medical Diagnosis, Magnetic Resonance Images play a significant role. This work presents a hybrid technique to detect the abnormal parts in the magnetic resonance images of a human. The proposed technique consists of five stages namely, Noise reduction, Smoothing, Feature extraction, Dimensionality reduction or Feature reduction, and Classification. First stage obtains the noise reduced MR image using KSL (Kernel-Sobel-Low pass) Filter. In the second stage, smoothing is done by histogram equalization. Third stage obtains the features related with MRI images using discrete wavelet transformation. In the fourth stage, the features of magnetic resonance images have been reduced using principles component analysis to the more essential features. At last stage, the classifier based on K-means has been used to classify subjects as normal or abnormal MRI human images. Classification accuracy of 98.80% has been obtained by the proposed algorithm. The result shows that the proposed technique is robust and effective compared with other recent works.

Keywords: Discrete Wavelet Transform, K-Means, KSL Filter, PCA, Magnetic Resonance Images.

1 Introduction

MRI stands for magnetic resonance imaging. In actuality, the proper name for this study is a nuclear magnetic resonance image (NMRI), but when the technique was being developed for use in health care the connotation of the word "nuclear" was felt to be too negative and was left out of the accepted name. MRI is based on the physical and chemical principles of nuclear magnetic resonance (NMR), a technique used to gain information about the nature of molecules. It is a medical imaging practice used in radiology to envision detailed internal structures of the human body. Retrieving a high quality MR Image for a medical diagnostic is critical, because it injures human more if we pass high level Magnetic resonance sound to take the image. So denoising of magnetic resonance (MR) images and interpreting it into human understandable form is a challenging issue.

V.V. Das and N. Thankachan (Eds.): CIIT 2011, CCIS 250, pp. 200–208, 2011.

2 Related Works

An exploration of the applicability of the techniques in brain disorder diagnosis in MR images is given in [1]. Evaluation measures for patterns are described in [2] and [3]. A classification technique based on Least Squares Support Vector Machines (LS-SVM) using Radial Basis Function (RBF) kernels classifier is proposed in [4] & LS-SVM with RBF and Ada Boost is given in [16]. A hybrid classification of MRI brain Images is proposed in [5] using DWT, PCA and K-NN &A-NN. A method using wavelets as input to neural network SOM and SVM for classification of magnetic resonance (MR) images of the human brain is presented in [6]. A spectral-based classification technique to MR image using Vector Seeded Region Growing (VSRG) is proposed in [7]. A forward neural network (FNN) based method to classify a given MR brain image as normal or abnormal is proposed in [8] using a hybrid combination of DWT, PCA, FNN, and adaptive chaotic particle swarm optimization (ACPSO). A hybrid classification approach for of brain tissues in MRI images based on genetic algorithm (GA) and support vector machine (SVM) using spatial gray level dependence method (SGLDM) is proposed in [9]. A segmentation method for classification of MRI brain images by removal of artifact and noise in the first stage and applying Hierarchical Self Organizing Map (HSOM) for image segmentation is described in [10]. An algorithm for the automatic segmentation and classification of brain tissue from 3D MR scans using discriminative Random Decision Forest classification is presented in [11]. A method using both structural and functional MR images for brain disease diagnosis is presented in [12]. Pediatric brain tumor segmentation and classification of MRI images is established in [13] by fusing two novel texture features along with intensity in multimodal magnetic resonance (MR) images. A general method for segmenting brain tumors in 3D magnetic resonance images using fuzzy classification and symmetry analysis is presented in [14] and [15]. A method of k-Nearest Neighbor (k-NN) is proposed in [17] for abnormalities segmentation in Magnetic Resonance Imaging (MRI) brain images. A neuro-fuzzy segmentation process of the MRI data is presented in [18] to detect various tissues like white matter, gray matter, csf and tumor. A framework for automatic brain tumor segmentation from MR images using detection of edema based on outlier detection is proposed in [19]. Novel automatic brain tumor detection method that uses Gabor Wavelets to determine any abnormality in brain tissues is presented in [20].

3 Methodology and Design

3.1 The Model for the Proposed Hybrid Algorithm

The Fig. 1 explains the full-fledged model for the proposed algorithm. It has five stages namely, Noise reduction, Smoothing, Feature extraction, Dimensionality reduction or Feature reduction, and Classification to find the abnormal parts.

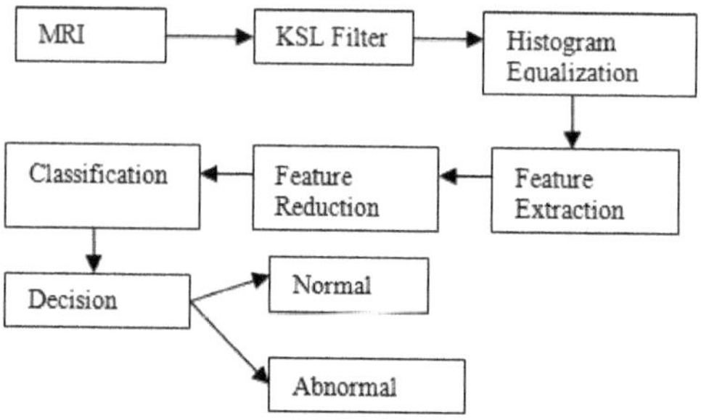

Fig. 1. Model for Proposed Algorithm

3.2 Techniques Used in Proposed Algorithm

3.2.1 KSL Filter for Noise Removal

This filtering technique with a nine step process applies the series of Kernel, Sobel and Low-pass filters to reduce the noise in the input MR image [21].

3.2.2 Histogram Equalization

To transfer the gray levels so that the histogram of the resulting image is equalized to be a constant.

$$h[i] = \text{constant}, \quad \text{for all } i. \tag{1}$$

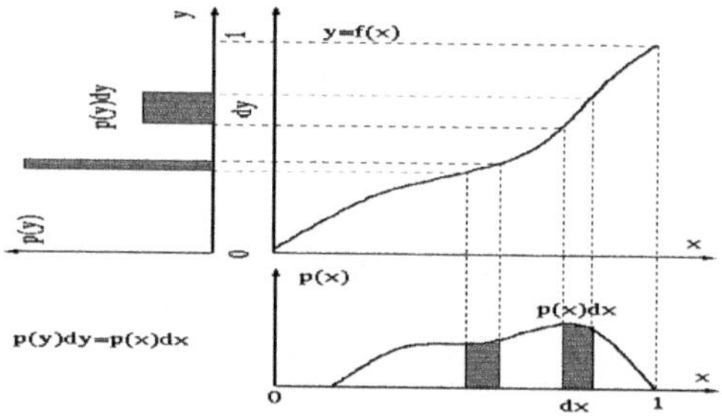

Fig. 2. Mapping Function between input and output

Fig 2 shows that for any given mapping function y = f(x) between the input and output images, the following holds: p(y) dy = p(x) dx i.e., the number of pixels mapped from to y is unchanged.

To equalize the histogram of the output image, we let p(y) be a constant. In particular, if the gray levels are assumed to be in the ranges between 0 and 1 (0 <= x <= 1, 0 <= y <= 1), then p(y) = 1. Then we have:

$$dy = p(x)dx, \text{ or } dy / dx = p(x) \tag{2}$$

i.e., the mapping function y = f(x) for histogram equalization is:

$$y = f(x) = \int_0^x p(u)du = P(x) - P(0) = P(x) \tag{3}$$

where $P(x) = \int_0^x p(u)du\ , P(0) = 0$ is the cumulative probability distribution of the input image, which monotonically increases.

3.2.3 Discrete Wavelet Transform

The input signal x(n) is decomposed into two sets of coefficients called approximation coefficients (denoted by ca) and detail coefficients (denoted by cd). These coefficients are obtained by convolving the input signal with a low-pass filter (for ca) or a high-pass filter (for cd) and then down sampling the convolution result by 2. The size of ca and cd is half of the size of the input signal. The filters are determined by the chosen wavelet. The DWT is computed by successive low-pass and high pass filtering of the discrete time-domain signal as shown in Fig 3. This is called the Mallat algorithm or Mallat-tree decomposition. Its significance is in the manner it connects the continuous-time multiresolution to discrete-time filters. In the figure, the signal is denoted by the sequence x[n], where n is an integer. The low pass filter is denoted by G0 while the high pass filter is denoted by H0. At each level, the high pass filter produces detail information, d[n], while the low pass filter associated with scaling function produces coarse approximations, a[n]. At each decomposition level, the half band filters produce signals spanning only half the frequency band.

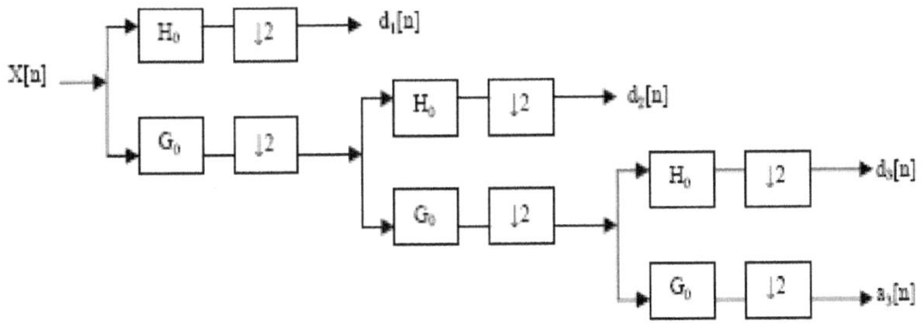

Fig. 3. Model for Proposed Algorithm

3.2.4 Principal Component Analysis

PCA is used for reducing the features which are required to find the abnormality in the MR image.

PCA algorithm:
Let an input data set be X (X: matrix of dimensions M X N). Perform the following steps:

1. Calculate the empirical mean

$$u(m) = (1/N)\sum_{i=1}^{N} X[m,n] \tag{4}$$

2. Calculate the deviations from the mean and store the data in the matrix B[M N]:, B=X-u.h, where h is a 1 x N row vector of all 1's: h[n] =1 for n=1....N.
3. Find the covariance matrix C.

$$C = (1/N)\ B.B^* \tag{5}$$

4. Find the eigenvectors and eigenvalues of the covariance matrix V-1CV = D, where V: the eigenvectors matrix, D: the diagonal matrix of eigenvalues of C, D[p,q] = λm for p=q=m is the mth eigenvalues of the covariance matrix C.
5. Rearrange the eigenvectors and eigenvalues $\lambda 1 \geq \lambda 2 \geq \lambda 3 \geq ... \geq \lambda N$.
6. Choosing components and forming a feature vector. Save the first L columns of V as the M x L matrix W: W[p,q]=V[p,q] for n=1....M, q=1....L where .
7. Deriving the new data set, the eigenvectors with the highest eigenvalues are projected into space, this projection results in a vector represented by fewer dimension (L < M) containing the essential coefficients.

3.2.5 Principal Component Analysis

K-means is the effortless unsupervised learning algorithms that work out the well known clustering problem. The procedure follows a trouble-free way to classify a given data set using a certain number of clusters fixed a priori. The main idea is to identify k centroids in each cluster. These centroids should be placed in an intelligent way because of different location causes diverse results. The next step is to take each point belonging to a given data set and associate it to the nearest centroid. When no point is pending, the first step is completed and an early groupage is done. At this point we need to recalculate k new centroids as barycenters of the clusters resulting from the previous step. After we have these k new centroids, a new binding has to be done between the same data set points and the nearest new centroid. A loop has been generated. As a result of this loop we may notice that the k centroids change their location step by step until no more changes are done. Finally, this algorithm aims at minimizing an objective function. The objective function is

$$J = \sum_{j=1}^{k} \sum_{i=1}^{n} \left\| x_i^{(j)} - c_j \right\|^2 \tag{6}$$

where $\left\| x_i^{(j)} - c_j \right\|^2$ is a chosen distance measure between a data point xi(j) and the cluster centre cj , is an indicator of the distance of the n data points from their respective cluster centers. The algorithm is significantly sensitive to the initial randomly selected cluster centers.

4 Experimental Results and Design

The proposed system has been implemented in Matlab. The main interface for the proposed algorithm is shown in Fig. 4. Here for discussion, two MR images are taken for classification. In that one is an abnormal MRI and another is a normal MRI. After doing the five stage image classification, in the abnormal MRI the abnormal parts are identified as shown in Fig. 5. The intermediate results of all the five stages are also shown. The input image, histogram of input image, results of Sobel, Kernel and Low-pass filters and the noise reduced image and its histogram are shown in the first (top) row. The second row shows the result of Histogram equalization, DWT, PCA and K-means. In the second row, right most image show the abnormal parts revealed in the MRI image. In similar way, the classification output of the normal MR image is shown in Fig. 6 and in that there is no abnormal parts are detected.

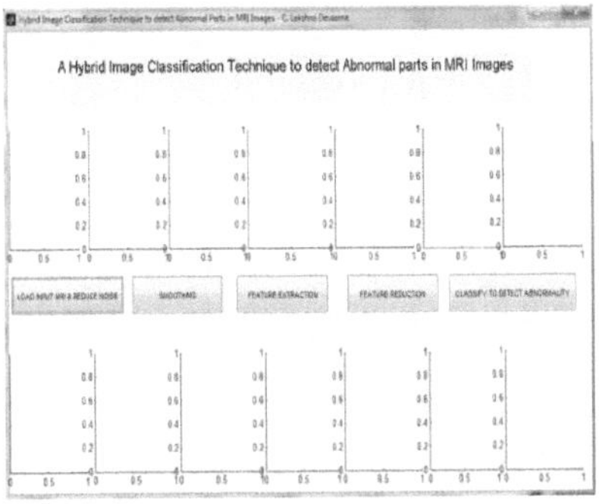

Fig. 4. Main Interface

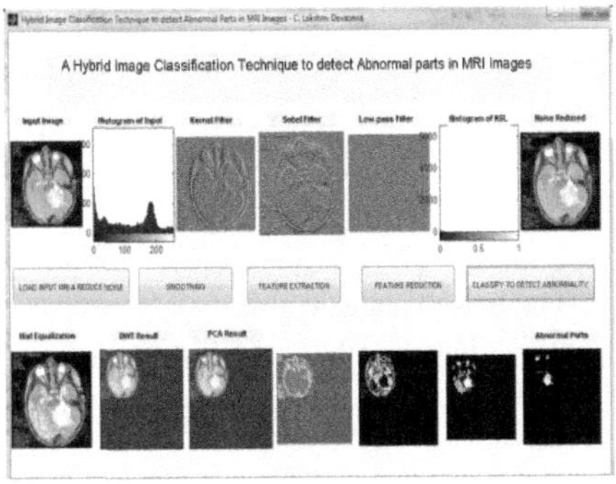

Fig. 5. Results of Abnormal MRI Input

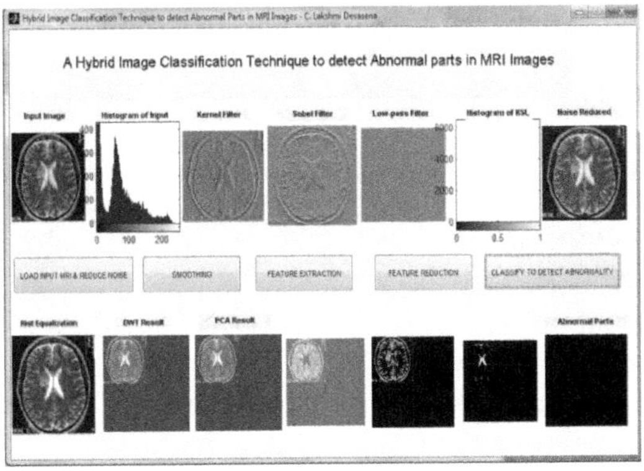

Fig. 6. Results of Normal MR Image

Performance Measures

All classification result could have an error rate and from time to time it will either fail to reveal an abnormality, or reveal an abnormality which is not present. It is usual to describe this error rate by the terms true and false positive and true and false negative as follows [1], [2]. The performance of the classifiers are measured using,

$$\text{Sensitivity} = TP/\ (TP+FN)\ *100\% \quad (7)$$

$$\text{Specificity} = TN/\ (TN+FP)\ *100\% \quad (8)$$

$$\text{Accuracy} = (TP+TN)/\ (TP+TN+FP+FN)*100\ \% \quad (9)$$

5 Comparison of Performance of Classifiers

In order to verify the effectiveness and robustness of proposed algorithm, experiments were performed on MR images. The confusion matrix of our method is listed in Table 1.The elements of the ith row and jth column represents the classification accuracy belonging to class i and is assigned to class j after the supervised classification.

Table 1. Confusion matrix of our Method (O denotes Output and T denotes Target)

	Normal (O)	Abnormal (O)
Normal (T)	99	1
Abnormal (T)	2	148

The results show that our method only misclassified 3 images out of 250 MR images. The whole classification accuracy is [99+148]/250=98.80%. Moreover, we compared our results with other results (DWT+PCA+ANN [5], DWT+PCA+KNN [5], DWT+SOM [6], DWT+SOM with linear kernel [6], DWT+SOM with radial basis function based kernel [6], Statistical Classifier KNN [4], DWT+PCA+ACPSO-FNN [8]) described in the recent literature that used the same MRI datasets, as shown in Table 2. It is very clear that our proposed hybrid technique earns the highest classification accuracy.

Table 2. Classification Performance (P) comparison of our Method with other recent works for the same MR images datasets

Technique	P (%)
DWT+PCA+ANN [5]	95.7
DWT + PCA + k-NN [5]	98.6
DWT+SOM [6]	94
DWT+SVM with linear kernel [6]	96.15
DWT+SVM with radial basis function based kernel [6]	98
Statistical Classifier KNN [4]	89.78
DWT+PCA+ACPSO-FNN	98.75
Our Technique KSLFilter+HE+DWT+PCA+K-Means	**98.80**

The other performance statistical measures such as sensitivity and of our method are

Sensitivity = 148 / (148+2) * 100 = 98.67%
Specificity = 99 / (99+1) * 100 = 99%

6 Conclusion

In this paper, the hybrid algorithm for automatic classification of MRI images of any part of human body to find the abnormality in that part is proposed. The implementation of the system is done in Matlab and tested with 250 normal and abnormal MR Images and produced excellence result. The performances of the classifiers in terms of statistical measures such as sensitivity, specificity and classification accuracy are analyzed. The results indicated that this hybrid approach yielded the best performance when compared to other classifiers. It suggests that this is a promising technique for image classification in a medical imaging application. It can be used in computer aided intelligent health care systems. This automated analysis system could be further used for classification of images with different pathological condition, types and disease status.

Acknowledgment. The authors thank the management of Karpagam University for their kind support to do this article successfully.

References

1. Jude Hemanth, D., Kezi Selva Vijila, C., Anitha, J.: A Survey on Artificial Intelligence Based Brain Pathology Identification Techniques in Magnetic Resonance Images. International Journal of Reviews in Computing, 30–45 (2009)
2. Theodoridis, S., Koutroumbas, K.: Pattern Recognition. Academic Press, San Diego (1999)
3. Polat, K., Akdemir, B., Gnes, S.: Computer aided diagnosis of ECG data on the least square support vector machine. Digital Signal Processing 18, 25–32 (2008)
4. Selvaraj, H., Thamarai Selvi, S., Selvathi, D., Gewali, L.: Brain MRI Slices Classification Using Least Squares Support Vector Machine. ICMED 1(1), 21–33 (2007)
5. El-Dahshan, E.-S.A., Salem, A.-B.M., Younis, T.H.: A Hybrid Technique For Automatic MRI Brain Images Classification. Studia Univ. Babes-bolyai, Informatica LIV(1), 55–67 (2009)
6. Chaplot, S., Patnaik, L.M., Jagannathan, N.R.: Classification of magnetic resonance brain images using wavelets as input to support vector machine and neural network. Biomedical Signal Processing and Control 1, 86–92 (2006)
7. Wang, C.-M., Chen, R.-M.: Vector Seeded Region Growing for Parenchyma Classification in Brain MRI. International Journal of Advancements in Computing Technology 3(2), 49–56 (2011)
8. Zhang, Y., Wang, S., Wu, L.: A Novel Method For Magnetic Resonance Brain Image Classification Based on Adaptive Chaotic PSO. Progress in Electromagnetics Research 109, 325–343 (2010)
9. Kharrat, A., Gasmi, K., Messaoud, M.B., Benamrane, N., Abid, M.: A Hybrid Approach for Automatic Classification of Brain MRI Using Genetic Algorithm and Support Vector Machine. Leonardo Journal of Sciences (17), 71–82 (July-December 2010) ISSN 1583-0233

10. Logeswari, T., Karnan, M.: An Enhanced Implementation of Brain Tumor Detection Using Segmentation Based on Soft Computing. International Journal of Computer Theory and Engineering 2(4), 1793–8201, 586-590 (2010)
11. Yi, Z., Criminisi, A., Shotton, J., Blake, A.: Discriminative, Semantic Segmentation of Brain Tissue in MR Images. Med. Image Comput. Comput. Assist. Interv., 558–565 (2009)
12. Fan, Y., Rao, H., Giannetta, J., Hurt, H., Wang, J., Davatzikos, C., Shen, D.: Diagnosis of Brain Abnormality Using both Structural and Functional MR Images. In: Conf. Proc. IEEE Eng. Med. Biol. Soc. Suppl., pp. 6585–6588 (2006)
13. Iftekharuddin, K.M., Zheng, J., Islam, M.A., Ogg, R.J.: Fractal-based brain tumor detection in multimodal MRI. Applied Mathematics and Computation. Elsevier (2008)
14. Khotanlou, H., Colliot, O., Atif, J., Bloch, I.: 3D brain tumor segmentation in MRI using fuzzy classification, symmetry analysis and spatially constrained deformable models. Fuzzy Sets and Systems 160, 1457–1473 (2009)
15. Khotanlou, H., Colliot, O., Bloch, I.: Automatic brain tumor segmentation using symmetry analysis and deformable models
16. Chandra, S., Bhat, R., Singh, H., Chauhan, D.S.: Detection of Brain Tumors from MRI using Gaussian RBF kernel based Support Vector Machine. IJACT 1(1), 46–51 (2009)
17. Khalid, N.E.A., Khalid, N.E.A., Haniff, P.N.M.M.: MRI Brain Abnormalities Segmentation using K-Nearest Neighbors (k-NN). International Journal on Computer Science and Engineering (IJCSE) 3(2), 980–990 (2011)
18. Murugavalli, S., Rajamani, V.: An Improved Implementation of Brain Tumor Detection Using Segmentation Based on Neuro Fuzzy Technique. Journal of Computer Science 3(11), 841–846 (2007)
19. Prastawa, M., Bullitt, E., Ho, S., Gerig, G.: A brain tumor segmentation framework based on outlier detection. Medical Image Analysis 8, 275–283 (2004)
20. Lashkari, A.: A Neural Network based Method for Brain Abnormality Detection in MR Images Using Gabor Wavelets. International Journal of Computer Applications 4(7), 9–15 (2010) ISSN: 0975 – 8887
21. Lakshmi Devasena, C., Hemalatha, M.: Noise Removal in Magnetic Resonance Images using Hybrid KSL Filtering Technique. International Journal of Computer Applications (0975–8887) 27(8) (August 2011)

A Secured and Fault-Tolerant Multipath Routing Protocols for WMN

Paramjeet Rawat[1], Meenakshi Soam[2], and Suraj Malik[1]

[1] Dept. of Computer Science, IIMT Engg College, India
[2] Dept. of Computer Science, RGGI College, India
{paramjeet.rawat,meenusoam}@gmail.com,
er_surajmalik83@rediffmail.com

Abstract. In recent years, Wireless Mesh Network (WMN) has become a compelling topic to many network researchers due to its simplicity in installation and robustness in operation. However, existing routing protocols designed for MANET can not work efficiently in WMN because backbone in WMN formed by Mesh Router has very low mobility and are not put under power and memory constraint. Even existing multipath routing protocols designed for WMN, do not consider all the issues of the network i.e. fault-tolerance, load-balancing, security, reliability etc. Each paper works on one or two issues of networking. In this paper, we basically tried to give solution to maximum problems of Wireless Mesh Networks rather than giving a solution to only one or two. Our work includes routing packets to the destination with minimum delay and minimum error rate considering security, congestion control and fault-tolerance so that it could be considered as a full proof protocol.

Keywords: congestion-aware, fault-tolerant, load-balanced, geographic, multipath, wireless, mesh, network.

1 Introduction

WMN has gained considerable attention in recent years not only due to its fast deployment, easy maintenance and low upfront investment compared with traditional wireless networks, but also its support of the existing wireless networks, such as wireless sensor networks, wireless fidelity network (Wi-Fi), and so on. WMNs are expected to improve significantly the performance of many ad hoc networks, including WLANs, WPANs, and WMANs. They are undergoing rapid progress and inspiring numerous deployments. WMNs will deliver wireless services in a large variety of scenarios of different scale, including personal, local, campus, and metropolitan areas. As WMN also provide the integration of the various different wireless networks, many challenges comes in its way. Out of which routing and security are one of the key problems. Due to the inherent and often quite fundamental differences among the various wireless networks, routing of packets and integration of the security schemes of those networks is not an easy task. To fulfill all such

V.V. Das and N. Thankachan (Eds.): CIIT 2011, CCIS 250, pp. 209–216, 2011.

demands, we propose a secured, fault-tolerant and load-balanced routing algorithm which reaches the destination with minimum delay and with minimum error rate.

2 Related Work

Our main aim is to take care of and improve maximum aspects of multipath routing for WMN, and we found various types of papers for different problems. Like topology control problem whose main purpose is to provide connectivity for wireless networks, with certain design criteria including power consumption [1], interference [2], quality-of-service (QoS) [3], antennas [4], and reliability [5]. In the literature, most studies on topology control focus on the characteristics of the resulting graph and skip the detail routing, scheduling schemes, which may affect the throughput and delay performance in wireless networks.

Another area of research is in the field of security, such as paper[6], [7], and [8] in which secure multi-path routing protocol were introduced. Kotzanikolaou et al presented Secure Multipath Routing (SecMR) [8] protocol to reduce the authentication cost. Paper [8] produces security approach better than paper [6] and [7]. However, due to the use of digital signature, the computation cost made this scheme inefficient. Paper [9], a security management mechanism for multipath utilizes efficiently the characteristics of WMNs, but this scheme uses Diffie-Hellman[12], which has a danger of man-in-the-middle attack, so we need a better approach. In [10] nodes are given differentiated security protection level based upon their type but the biggest drawback is that nodes cannot be protected against internal malicious node but rather from external malicious nodes. We also found several papers focusing on various aspects of a routing protocols like, Paper [17] focuses on interference aware routing, while paper [18] on load-balancing and [20] on Packet routing in an efficient way. These proposals give good solution for different problems but none of them focuses on all these issues. So, in our paper, we are proposing a secured geographic multipath routing protocol that considers all these aspects, such as topology construction for faster route discovery and re-discovery with minimum delay, minimum error rate, security, mobility and fault-tolerance.

3 Proposed Model

We propose a secured, efficient, simple, fast and fault-tolerant geographic multipath routing protocol for which we first constructed a topology, this topology uses virtual coordinates for packet transmission and by following our routing and security algorithms these packets reaches the destination safely, with minimum delay and complexity. For load balancing, a threshold is maintained at each node which alarms all its neighbors. This is done to reduce the control overheads.

Preliminaries

- Our whole network is divided into clusters in which the Gateway is placed at the center of each cluster. Default Gateway DG, indicates that the node and the

Gateway belongs to the same cluster. Each node is connected to six other node' s in hexagonal shape. We assume that each node has knowledge of all its six neighbors about their link and load status. Each node periodically sends beacon messages to all its neighbors to get their link status which is recorded by each node. They also have a record of how much hop away, they are from the gateway, as each hop is of same distance. In order to minimize the collision probability, each node should adjust its power to a level that is able to reach its six neighbors and no more. We also assume that the antenna's we are using at router level can work in two modes: omni-directional and directional[11]. If the node has nothing to transmit, then to detect any incoming signals, the antenna works in omni-direction and when the node need to transmit something to the other node, directional antennas are used so that data could be sent to only the one which is in desired direction with better signal quality.

- For security we assume that there is a Certification Authority (CA) in the WMN which is a trusted third party that can authenticate the digital certificates of the nodes. We also assume that a Social Security Number(SSN) which is used to identify the clients personal details containing his identity information (like name, father's name, address, passport number etc.) is maintained globally in all the countries wherever internet is accessed. It is an entry ticket to access the Internet. Any SSN can be used only by a single user i.e. simultaneously two persons cannot use the same SSN number.

3.1 Topology Construction and Coordinate Construction

We use a topology that can efficiently provide connectivity for the network in the absence of location information. We use the properties of a regular hexagon that says the sides and interior angles of a regular polygon are all equal as shown in Figure 1. Each node(mesh router), is placed at each vertex point. To construct virtual coordinates, we consider that the Gateway is placed at the center of each cluster which is marked as origin, i.e. 0,0 and let the radius to any of its vertex is 5, each neighbor of all the nodes are placed at the distance of 5. Now, all the coordinates of any node can be determined as: x coordinates as rcos30° and y coordinates as rsin30°. This way, all vertices are known, as shown in the Figure 2.

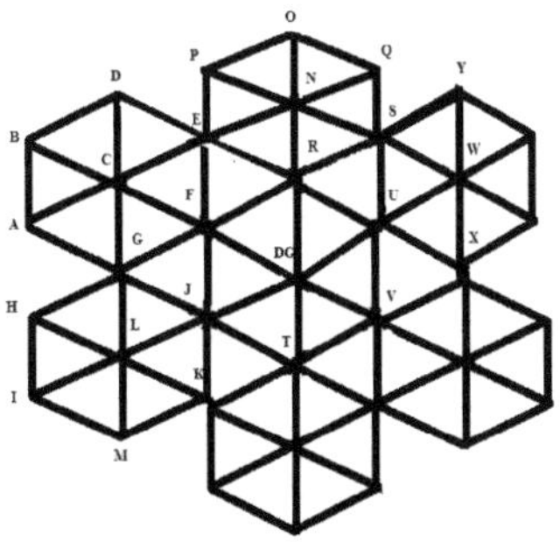

Fig. 1. Structure of a cluster

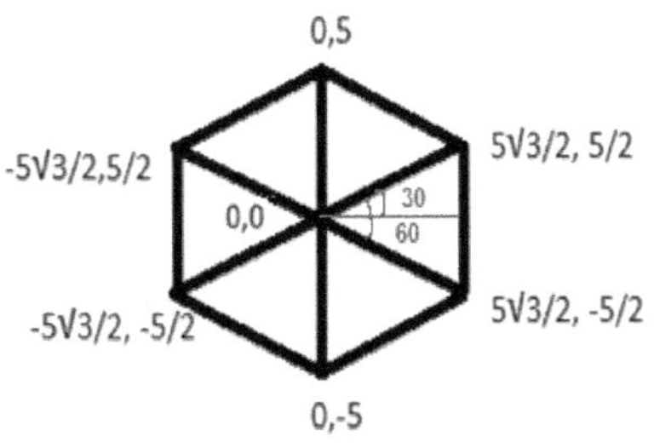

Fig. 2. Coordinate representation of the six nodes at origin

3.2 Packet Transmission

To discover the route, the protocol begins by determining the location of the destination. A packet is sent to the node which is in same direction as is the destination and is lightly loaded using directional antennas. The path once constructed is cached for further communication. Before sending any packet in the learnt path, each node checks the link and load status of next node in the path. If link to a node in the learnt path fails or is heavily loaded then, the intermediate node sends the packet to the surviving node using backup routes maintained at the time of route discovery. If the destination is a Gateway, then the node which has the minimum of both hop count and load is selected. If the whole network is heavily loaded, then only the location information is used for packet transmission and beacon packets are stopped. Only early link failure notification is used by taking feedback from physical layer of OSI model. For detailed algorithm refer to paper [13] by Paramjeet et al.

3.3 Load Sharing

We also introduced a congestion level threshold "μ" to determine whether a particular node in the network is congested[13] or not. The "μ" is the average queue length at a node in a particular path. A mesh router is said to be congested if its congestion level is greater than the threshold, i.e. $\frac{QLi}{tr} \geq \mu$, where QLi is the average queue length at a node in a particular path and tr is transmission rate at a node. We use "μ" to reduce periodic broadcasting of congestion information to the neighbors since if a node is not congested, communication with neighbors periodically results in the wasting the network bandwidth. Each node 'i' will compute its own congestion level periodically. If the ratio, $\frac{QLi}{tr}$ is less than 'μ' , then we assume that the node is lightly loaded. But if its congestion is greater than the threshold "μ", the node will send this information to all its six adjacent neighbors and no further messages will be sent to this nodes till the congested node reaches half of its threshold i.e. "μ".

At each mesh router i:

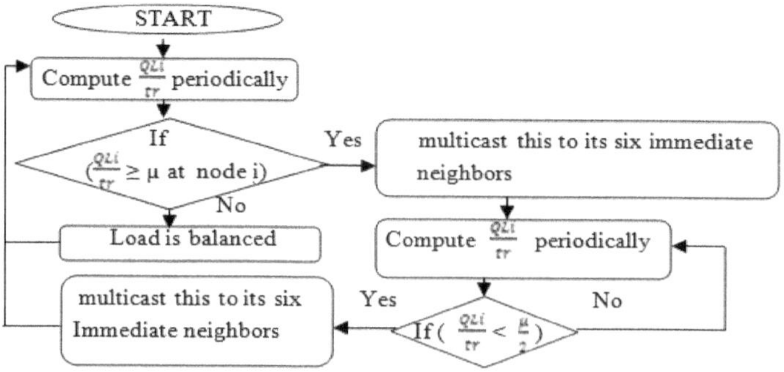

3.4 Fault Tolerance

In wireless mesh networks, where nodes tend not to move, route failure is most probably caused by power-off, system failure or poor signals. Under this circumstance, we may re-route to another alternate path stored as a backup in Route Discovery phase. During the route discovery procedure, a source can establish a primary path as well as several backup paths to the desired destination. Multipath can be used to reduce the delay in recovering from a failure, thus using the backup paths to switch the on-going traffic to these alternative paths, instead of shooting down the end to end connection, when the primary path fails. If there exists a situation where all the six neighbors of a node fails, it is called a Island node. As shown in Figure 3. However, if a station is unable to reach other nodes, it will have to increase its power level to find some neighbors. This situation is demonstrated in Figure 4, where red nodes demonstrate failed neighbors and blue nodes demonstrate new neighbors, found by increasing the power level of a Island node. Some island nodes might restore their power upon a new node's appearance, which could connect them to gateway in a normal mesh.

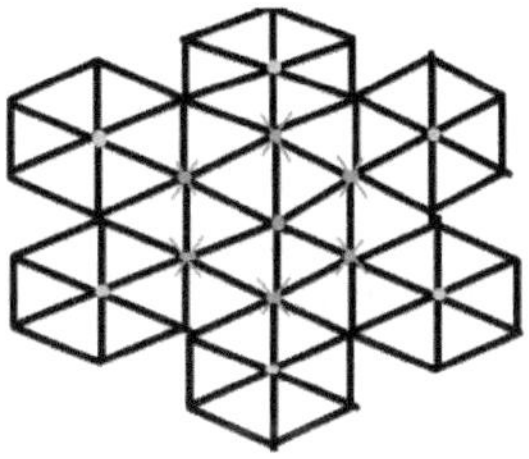

Fig. 3. Island Node

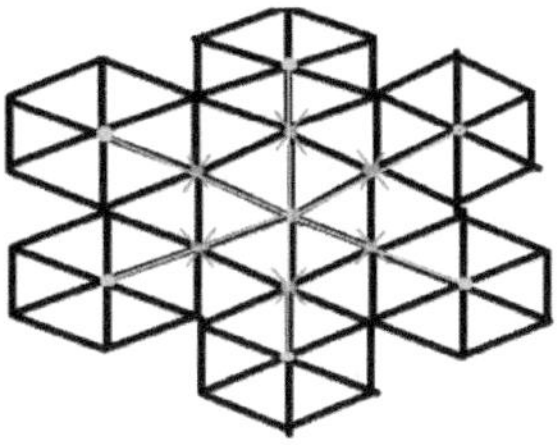

Fig. 4. Island node with its new neighbors

3.5 Security

To make our protocol work safely, a secured environment is needed. So to make our protocol secure, an efficient security algorithm is added to it. According to this algorithm[14] each mesh router is assigned a digital certificate by a CA which is used to authenticate the validity of a router. Whenever a new clients enters a network, he receives a digital certificate from its manager router to prove its validity. These certificate could be verified by contacting the CA. Thereafter, the client is asked to enter its SSN (Social Security Number) along with the password through SSL encrypted web page. After verification the captive portal (government authorized web server which keeps a record of SSN details) authorizes the client to network access and assigns him a UIDN (Unique Identification Number). The UIDN generated is used to keep a record of the client's SSN, IP address and its manager router (through which it received such information). In case some attack is detected in the network, this UIDN may be used to trace the person. The manager router stores the UIDN of the client along with a public key that will be sent to that client to ensure authenticity and integrity of the following messages. The router to router communication is also possible only after exchanging their corresponding digital certificates for the first time.

In the second step, both client node and its manager router encrypt the messages by their private keys before sending them to each other. This process authenticates both the nodes. Both of them can verify the authenticity of each other by contacting the CA. The secret public key which was sent at the time of assigning the UIDN is used to generate a key through Elliptic curve Diffie-Hellman(ECDH)[11] algorithm that can be used for further communication. ECDH provides desired security level with significantly smaller keys. Now, for future communication the secret keys need not be entered every time. This pair of secret keys is used to provide secure multi-path routing in WMN.

4 Simulation Analysis

The proposed simulation in NS2(NS2 2.29) [15] is implemented in Linux with some modification to support congestion-aware mechanism described in section 4. We consider the static wireless mesh network with a number of nodes arranged in the area of 1000x1000 m2. The topology is a hexagonal topology comprising of 36 nodes, in which each node is attached to six other nodes. The 802.11 MAC protocol is used in Data/Ack mode. Additionally, simulation uses a UDP traffic mode with a Constant Bit Rate (CBR) traffic. All MR has a fixed transmission range of 250m. In our simulation study, we compare our geographic routing protocol with the existing AOMDV and Packet Routing Protocol[19]. In order to compare with the other two protocols, the same traffic models were used. Source nodes are randomly selected among the common nodes at each runs. We basically study how the traffic is routed from the MR (mesh router) source to IGWs while traffic load gradually increases on a specific path. We also vary the traffic rates to measure throughput of these MRs by increasing number of flows along with time. We saw a big improvement in the throughput of nodes in our proposal (Figure 5) as compared to Packet Routing Protocol which incurs lot of control messages. In our design, each of examined MR can reach its maximum throughput due to the capability of predicting congestion risk and sharing load among multiple paths to protect links from overloaded. As for AOMDV, the throughput of the nodes which are far from IGW also degrades greatly because these nodes just forward packet hop-by-hop and are not aware of congestion when traffic is heavily loaded. In the Figure 6, we can see that PRP give a much better performance than pure AOMDV but still lower performance than our proposed protocol.

For checking the effectiveness of our secured routing we compared our security mechanism with the secure multi-path routing protocol of Burmester and Van Le [6], SecMR [8] routing protocols and SMRP[9]. We perform the simulation of each of these security schemes. The proposed scheme is implemented with AOMDV[16] which is a multi-path derivative of AODV. We have compared the routing overhead of these schemes and also the amount of energy consumed by these scheme at each node. The network model was consisted of 49 client nodes placed according to our proposed topology within an area of 1000 x 1000 m2. Each node has a propagation range of 150 meters with channel capacity 2 Mbps. The size of the data payload is 512. Each run of simulation is executed of 900 seconds of simulation time. The medium access control protocol used is IEEE 802.11 DCF. The traffic used is constant bit rate (CBR).

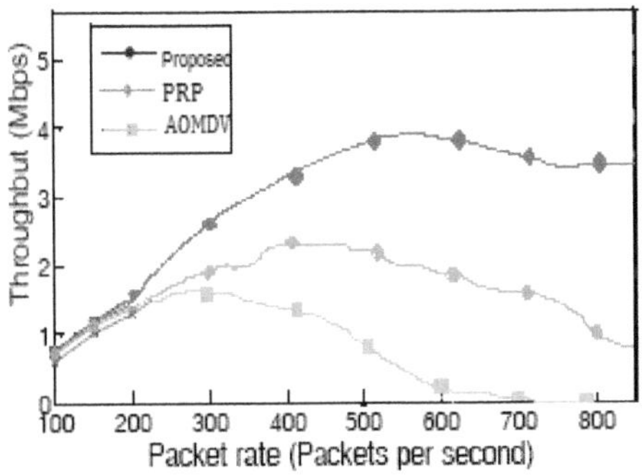

Fig. 5. Throughput analysis

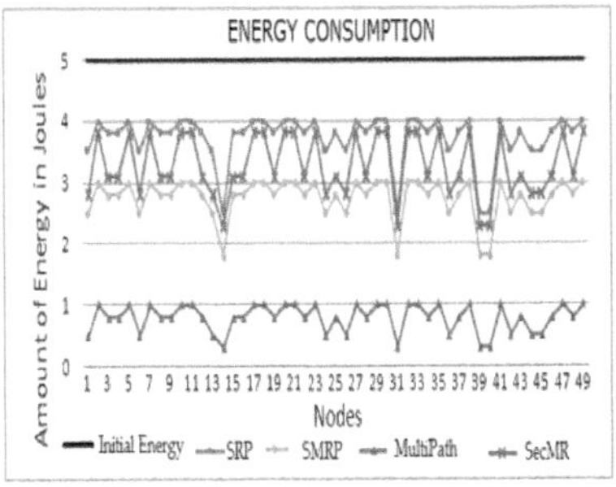

Fig. 6. Amount of Energy Left after 900s simulation

From the figures given above, we observe that SMRP works better than other schemes as it has less overhead and also consumes very little amount of energy. However, as there is a danger of man-in-the-middle attack in SMRP[9] so it do not provide appropriate security. In Scheme [8], SecMR shows high routing overhead as it contains the neighborhood information and digital signatures with the route request. Although the routing phase is separated from this authentication phase but this authentication is required after a constant interval, hence a considerable amount of energy is wasted in these periodic mutual authentications. Our security mechanism does not require this periodic authentication, instead it uses public key cryptography only once and secret keys are used for further communication. This secret key deployment is not periodic and done after the mutual authentication by using public key cryptography. This reduces the energy consumption at each node and the routing overhead is also less than the other schemes. However, as no such work is found which could be completely compared with our research as none of the paper highlighted all aspects a protocol, so no perfect comparison could be possible.

5 Conclusion

Routing in any network has a great impact on the overall network performance, thus a routing protocol or algorithm should be carefully designed, so we designed a fault-tolerant, load-balanced, secured geographic multipath routing protocol. Our philosophy is to perform whatever can be planned in advance to simplify the operation of WMNs, thus achieving efficiency and scalability. We design a mechanism to permit Mesh Routers to evaluate their consumed bandwidth to support Hop-Count based routing while being aware of congestion risk and security threats.

References

1. Ramanathan, R., Rosales-Hain, R.: Topology control of multihop wireless networks using transmit power adjustment, vol. 2 (2000)
2. Burkhart, M., Wattenhofer, R., Zollinger, A.: Does topology control reduce interference?, pp. 9–19. ACM Press, New York (2004)
3. Dai, F., Wu, J.: On constructing k-connected k-dominating set in wireless ad hoc and sensor networks. Journal of Parallel and Distributed Computing 66(7), 947–958 (2006)
4. Huang, Z., Shen, C.C.: Multibeam antenna-based topology control with directional power intensity for ad hoc networks. IEEE Transactions on Mobile Computing 5(5), 508–517 (2006)
5. Wang, F., Thai, M., Li, Y., Du, D.Z.: Fault Tolerant Topology Control for All-to-One and One-to-All Communication in Wireless Networks. IEEE Transactions on Mobile Computing 7(3), 322–331 (2008)
6. Burmester, M., van Le, T.: Secure multipath communication in mobile ad hoc networks. In: ITCC 2004. IEEE, Las Vegas (2004)
7. Weeks, M., Altun, G.: Efficient, Secure, Dynamic Source Routing for Ad-hoc Networks. Journal of Network and Systems Management 14(4), 559–581 (2006)
8. Kotzanikolaou, P., Mavropodi, R., Douligeris, C.: Secure multipath routing for mobile ad hoc networks. In: Proceedings of the WONSS 2005 Conference, St. Moritz, Switzerland, January 19-21, pp. 89–96. IEEE, Los Alamitos (2005)
9. Siddiqui, M.S., Amin, S.O., Hong, C.S.: On a Low Security Overhead Mechanism for Secure Multi-path Routing Protocol in Wireless Mesh Network. In: Ata, S., Hong, C.S. (eds.) APNOMS 2007. LNCS, vol. 4773, pp. 466–475. Springer, Heidelberg (2007)
10. Gamer, T., Völker, L., Zitterbart, M.: Differentiated security in wireless mesh networks. Security and Communication Networks (2009); published online in wiley interscience
11. Elliptic Curve Cryptography Lecture Notes on Computer and Network Security by Avi Kak (kak@purdue.edu)
12. Diffie, W., van Oorschot, P., Wiener, M.: Authentication and authenticated key exchange. Designs, Codes and Cryptography 2(2), 107–125 (1992)
13. Bedi, P.K., et al.: An Improved Hop-Count Metric for Infrastructural Wireless Mesh Network. International Journal on Computer Science and Engineering (IJCSE) 3(5), 1757–1763 (2011)
14. Rawat, P., et al.: Integrated Security Framework For Hybrid Wireless Mesh Networks (IJCSE) International Journal on Computer Science and Engineering 2(4), 1136–1141 (2010)
15. The ns Manual, formerly ns Notes and Documentation
16. Marina, M.K., Das, S.R.: On-demand Multi Path Distance Vector Routing in Ad Hoc Networks. In: Proceedings of IX International Conference on Network Protocols (2001)
17. A General Interference-Aware Framework for Joint Routing and Link Scheduling in Wireless Mesh Networks. IEEE Network (January-February 2008)
18. Choi, K.W., Jeon, W.S.: Efficient Load-Aware Routing Scheme for Wireless Mesh Networks. IEEE Transactions On Mobile Computing 9(9) (2010)
19. Koji, N., Ivan, M.Z.: Packet Routing in Wireless Mesh Networks. In: 10th Symposium on Neural (2010)

An Efficient Video Compression System Based on LSK Encoder

S. Anantha Padmanabhan[1] and S. Chandramathi[2]

[1] Department of Electronics
SEA College of Engineering, Bangalore, India
ananthapadmanbhanphd@gmail.com
[2] Department of Electronics
SRI Krishna College of Engineering and Technology, Coimbatore, India

Abstract. Video compression means reducing the size of data in order to represent the digital video images. The main goal of our research is to develop a robust video compression system. To begin with, wavelet decomposition is applied to the I-frame and using the Listless SPECK (LSK) algorithm, the resulting coefficients are quantized. Subsequently, an Adaptive Rood Search with Spatio-Temporal Correlation technique (ARS-ST) is employed for motion estimation. Finally, the difference between the original P-frame and the predicted P-frame is computed, which is referred as the residual. The proposed video compression technique is assessed by several videos and the effectiveness of compression is evaluated by measuring the PSNR values for the compression results.

Keywords: Video compression, Listless SPECK (LSK), motion estimation, Adaptive Rood Search with Spatio temporal Correlation (ARS-ST), Motion Vector Prediction.

1 Introduction

Image and video coding plays a significant role in several multimedia applications. Because of the popularity of the internet, there has been a tremendous increase in the use of video in digital form over the past few years [1, 2]. It is not possible to store the full digital video without processing, because the memory of the storage devices and the bandwidth of the transmission channel are not infinite to accommodate the very large quantity of digital video data [4, 9]. To circumvent these problems, and to decrease the number of bits required to represent a digital video data while maintaining an acceptable fidelity or video quality a series of techniques called video compression techniques have been proposed. The compression ratio quantifies their ability to perform this task [5, 11]. Video compression is a combination of spatial image compression and temporal motion compensation and it refers to decreasing the quantity of data required to represent digital video images. For the purpose of reducing the quantity of data and to provide the adequate quality several video compression algorithms have been developed. Effectively compressing the video is

V.V. Das and N. Thankachan (Eds.): CIIT 2011, CCIS 250, pp. 217–224, 2011.

the main objective of this research. In our proposed work, a transform coding technique LSK Listless SPECK (LSK) based on wavelets is used for compression of I-frame [8]. Here LSK is the enhanced version of Set Partition Embedded bloCK (SPECK). The rest of the paper is organized as follows: section 2 describes some of the recent related works. Section 3 briefs the proposed video compression process. Experimental results and analysis of the proposed methodology are discussed in Section 4. Finally, concluding remarks are provided in Section 5.

2 A Survey of Recent Research in the Field

In this section, a brief review of some important contributions from the existing literature is presented. Mohammed Benabdellah et al. [6] have investigated the selection of reference images in the process of video compression, by utilizing only the intra and predicted images which are extracted from sequences. Faber-schauder Multi-scale Transform (FMT) has been applied for intra and predicted image. Then, by subtracting the corresponding images transformed by FMT, each image has been compared with other images. Bruno Carpentieri et al. [7] have reviewed the Split-Merge technique that utilizes the temporal correlation between frames, retaining the spatial correlation between the elements of each frame. Their method has been based on segmentation of the frames into uneven sized regions known as super blocks Ilker Kilic et al. [10] have proposed a video compression algorithm at low bit rates, comparable to the standard techniques. The overlapping block motion compensation (OBMC) has been combined with discrete wavelet transform which was followed by Lloyd–Max quantization and Zero Tree Wavelet (ZTW) structure. Sudhakar Radhakrishnan et al. [12] have discussed that video coding schemes are highly important for low bit rates and the block transform employed, traditional coding schemes have blocking artifacts problems. Because they have proposed a wavelet transform based Video Codec, the performance of the coder has been superior to block transform based codecs. Esakkirajan Sankaralingam et al. [13] have proposed a new video coding method using multi wavelet transform and multi-stage vector quantization. Spatial, temporal and psycho visual redundancies have been the three types of common redundancies in video sequences. They have used the multi wavelet transform to minimize the spatial redundancy.

3 An Efficient Video Compression Based on LSK and ARS-ST

The video is a set of frames of size $M \times N$ that can be represented as $f_j(x, y) : j = 1,2,\cdots,N_f,\ x = 0,1,2,\cdots,M$ and $y = 0,1,2,\cdots,N$ where, N_f is the total number of frames present in the video.

3.1 Wavelet Based Compression of I-Frames Using LSK

A set of images representing a moving scene is a set of temporal samples The reference frames is the intra coded I-frame and the predicted frames are the P-frames [15]. LSK [20] represents Listless Set Partitioning Embedded block. Same block partitioning rules used by SPECK are also used by LSK. By placing markers at all initial pixels for all the sub-bands, partitioning of set 'I' into three 'S' sets is modified in the proposed algorithm [3]. Though the proposed LSK algorithm employs some minimum number of bits to specify the insignificant sub-band blocks in the initial passes, the required computational time and complexity are similar to that of SPECK [14]. This paper describes a new video codec called LSK that uses the Set Partitioning rules of SPECK, and does an explicit breadth first search without using lists.

In Storage and State table markers, the DC band, the number of coefficients is determined as $I_{dc} = R_{dc}C_{dc}$ where $R_{dc} = R2^{L}, C_{dc} = C2^{L}$, L is the number of sub-band decomposition levels. In order to keep track of the set partitions, the following markers are kept in the 2 bit per coefficient state table $mark$. Each element of mark indicates something about the corresponding element in the val image array, if it signifies a block. Each marker and its meaning are listed as MIP: The pixel is unimportant or untested for this bit-plane, MNP : The pixel is newly important, so it will not be refined for this bit-plane, MSP: The pixel is important and will be refined in this bit plane, $MS2$: The block is of size 2 × 2, i.e., 4 elements to be skipped.

In Initialization, Floating point transform coefficients are quantized to integers by performing a dyadic sub band transform on the image, with L=5 levels. After that, the transform is read into the linear array val. The entire two-dimensional transform matrix is mapped into one-dimensional array and it can be found for each (r,c) by bit interleaving and the corresponding coefficients can be moved. Each coefficient is marked with MIP and first element of every full sized block with MS^{*} markers to initialize the state table, i.e., $mark[i] = MIP$ and, $mark[i+j] = MS2$ Where, $j = 0,1,2,\ldots,e$ and $e\log_2(m/2^{L})$.

Encoder Algorithm

The main encoder algorithm performed for each bit-plane, b, starting with B and decremented to 0, or until a bit budget is met. There are three passes in the algorithm. They are 1) Insignificant Pixel pass 2) Insignificant Set pass 3) Refinement pass. For each bit-plane, the significance level is given by $S = 2^{b}$. In binary form, s has a single bit set, at a bit position b, the test to determine whether the coefficient $val[i]$ is newly significant is $d = Val[i] \text{AND} s$. The coefficient is newly significant if and only if its bth bit is set. If d is non zero, $val[i]$ significant. Start with Insignificant pixel pass, the new significant elements are identified and marked as the MNP. Then move to next element. This can be described as if $mark[i]==MIP$ then the elements in the state array is marked as MNP i.e., $\text{output}(d = S_b[\text{val}(i)])$ and $\text{mark}[i] = \text{MNP}$. Then start the Insignificant Set pass, the block significance can be checked in the state table mark. If the block is significant means it is split up into 4 children. Then check the block significance of the children. If the grand descendent block is significant we can further divide them into four. And check for the significance once again. In the Refinement pass, set $\text{mark}[i] = \text{MSP}$, and $i = i + 2^2 \text{cnt\_ms2}$. The same procedure followed by the encoder is also followed by the decoder but with a few low level changes.

3.2 Motion Estimation Based on Adaptive Rood Search with Spatio Temporal Correlation (ARS-ST)

The block matching is performed in two stages. In the first stage or the initial search stage, a new scheme is proposed is used for motion prediction, which chooses the candidate-neighboring block on the basis of temporal and spatial motion correlation between the blocks. After the initial search, the best matching block is found by repeatedly employing a fixed-size rood pattern. The following sequential steps summarize the ARS-ST [19] method. In our analysis, the MV measurements of the previous blocks are used to predict the MV for the current block using a linear predictor [17]. The predicted motion vector is computed as, $m\tilde{\vec{v}} = \sum_{i=1}^{M} s_i \vec{m}_{n-i}$, where $m\tilde{\vec{v}}$ is the expected current block motion $\vec{m}$, $\vec{m}_{n-i}$ is the vector obtained by block-matching in the raster scan order at the ith previous index and S_i, $i = 1,2,\ldots,M$ are the linear predictor coefficients of order M. Where the motion vector $\vec{m}$, is the assumed real motion of the block obtained using the block-matching algorithm.

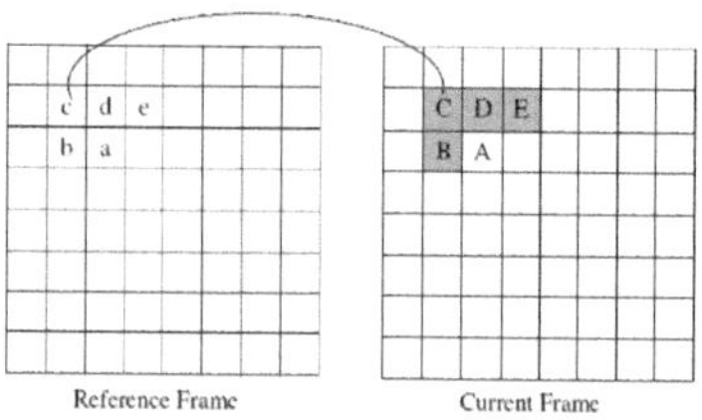

Fig. 1. The current block and its corresponding neighboring blocks in both current frame and reference frame

Temporal and spatial motion correlations between the blocks are used in our work for choosing the best candidate MV which is described in Fig.1. In our proposed method, the Mean Absolute Difference (MAD) between the Motion Vector of the two blocks is selected as the motion correlation between them and this can be represented in the following eqn.

$$\hat{D}_{ab} = \left|\left(\vec{M}_{ax} \;\; \vec{M}_{bx}\right) + \left(\vec{M}_{ay} \;\; \vec{M}_{by}\right)\right| ; \hat{D}_{ad} = \left|\left(\vec{M}_{ax} \;\; \vec{M}_{dx}\right) + \left(\vec{M}_{ay} \;\; \vec{M}_{dy}\right)\right| \quad (1)$$

Here $\hat{D}_{ab}$ is the MAD between the two blocks A and B Likewise the $\hat{D}_{ad}$ is the MAD between the two blocks A and D. To reduce the computational complexity, less number of candidate blocks is preferred for correlation comparison. By testing various video sequences, among the four candidate blocks "B", "C", "D", and "E", block "B" and "D" usually have more motion correlation with block "A" than the other two blocks and are more possibly to be selected as the best candidate neighboring blocks for MV prediction. The selection of best candidate block can be represented as If $\left(\left|\hat{D}_{ab}\right|\right) \le \left(\left|\hat{D}_{ad}\right|\right)$ is satisfied then assume $M_{prc} = \left[\vec{M}_{Bx}, \vec{M}_{By}\right]^T$ otherwise assume $M_{prc} = \left[\vec{M}_{Dx}, \vec{M}_{Dy}\right]^T$, where $\vec{M}_{Ax}$, $\vec{M}_{Ay}$, $\vec{M}_{Bx}$, $\vec{M}_{By}$, $\vec{M}_{Dx}$ and $\vec{M}_{Dy}$ are the horizontal and vertical components of the MVs of blocks "a", "b", and "d", respectively. Two stages, each stage adopting two search patterns are used to perform the block-matching method.

Adaptive Rood Pattern Initial Search with Predicted MV

In our analysis, a rood shaped pattern similar to the ARPS [16] is chosen for block matching. In our work, the search pattern is made more flexible by adjusting the horizontal and vertical arms individually, as follows,

$$R_h = \max\left\{\left|\vec{M}_{Bx}\right|, \left|\vec{M}_{Dx}\right|\right\} \; ; \; R_v = \max\left\{\left|\vec{M}_{By}\right|, \left|\vec{M}_{Dy}\right|\right\} \quad (2)$$

Here, Rh and Rv are the lengths of the two horizontal and two vertical arms, respectively. Rh and Rv have the same value for the blocks of the first column, and are determined from the MV components of their nearest top adjacent blocks using, Rh. In our method, we have selected a small diamond search pattern (SDSP) for the local search [18].In an unrestricted way, this fixed pattern is repetitively employed. The center of the rood is fixed as the point with the least matching error after each search, for the next search. The search is terminated; when the least error is found at the center of the rood, and the MV is determined from the location pointed by the least error point.

3.3 Video Encoder

The LSK algorithm is used to intra code the I-frame and after performing motion estimation the residual is encoded for the P-frame. Once the motion estimation is done using ARS-ST method, the P-frame is reconstructed using the motion vector calculated and the reference frame. The reconstructed P-frame is known as the Predicted P-frame. And the difference between the original P-frame and Predicted P-frame is called as the residual. This residual is transmitted along with the motion vector to produce good quality of predictive frames. The codec is tested at various rates of compression of the P-frame and generally as the rate of encoding increases the video quality also increases. In case of an I-frame the frame is intra coded using the LSK algorithm and in case of a P-frame motion estimation is done and the residual is encoded.

4 Results and Discussion

Our proposed Video Compression approach has been validated by experiments with a variety of video sequences. The proposed system has been implemented in Matlab (Matlab7.10). We report here some results obtained on a part of a video sequences utilized for compression. Here we use Akiyo video for compression. The gradual result obtained from the proposed system is given below. By employing this method, the motion block in P-frame are identified. This can be represented in Fig.2.

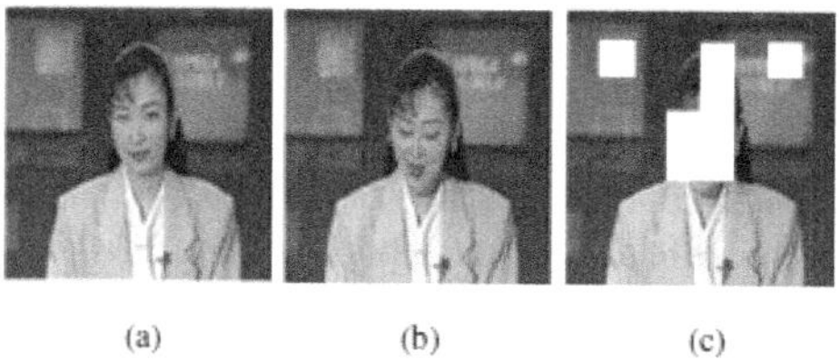

Fig. 2. The Sample output obtained from the motion estimation process in an akiyo video a) I-frame b) P-frame c) estimated motion in P-frame

Fig. 3 represents the decompressed frame for akiyo video. In this Figure, the proposed method is compared with the existing video compression scheme Fractal compression with Wavelet Sub trees (FCWS) [21].

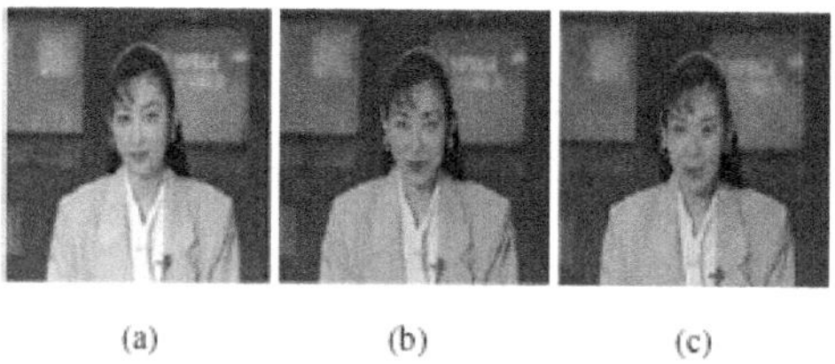

Fig. 3. The sample output obtained from the decompression process in an akiyo video a) Original frame b) Decompressed frame by proposed method c) Decompressed frame by FCWS video compression scheme

From this figure, we observe that the decompressed frame quality is better for proposed method than the FCWS. To analyze the result of our proposed system, the Compression Ratio (CR) and Peak Signal to Noise Ratio (PSNR) parameters are used. To evaluate the performance of the motion estimation technique in the proposed system, the Peak Signal to Noise Ratio (PSNR) is used as a quality measure For Akiyo video, the proposed system is compared with FCWS video compression scheme [21]. This can be represented in the following Fig.4. In this figure, the proposed system has high PSNR values when compared to the existing method.

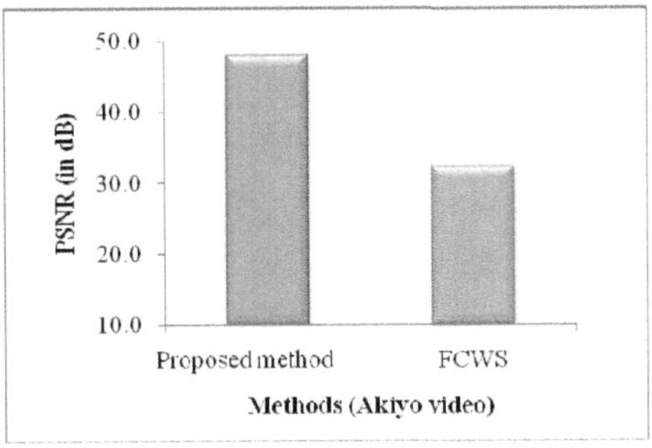

Fig. 4. PSNR comparison of proposed method vs FCWS method for Akiyo video

The PSNR for proposed method is 48.0293 but the PSNR for FCWS is 32.29. From Fig. 4, we observe that the proposed method has higher PSNR ratio than the existing video compression methods. The Compression Ratio (CR) for I frame is 1.7464 and P-frame is 8.5467. Thus the proposed method effectively compresses the video with better quality and high PSNR values when compared to the other methods.

5 Conclusions

In this paper, we have proposed a most promising video compression system using the fast block matching technique and compression method. Here, we have depicted a robust and efficient fast block matching technique based on adaptive rood pattern search (ARS-ST). Also, spatial and temporal correlations were employed for selecting the candidate-neighboring block for MV prediction. Only the residuals of motion vector predictor were sent as side information for reconstruction. Therefore, our proposed technique has better prediction as well as used very low side information. Experimental results have proved that the frames that are reconstructed by adaptive prediction are of high quality. Particularly, using the LSK technique, all decoded images for each bit-rate that were recovered from a single fidelity embedded encoded file, were truncated at desired bit rate.

Reference

1. Danyali, H., Mertins, A.: A 3-D virtual SPIHT for scalable very low bit rate embedded video compression. In: Proc. of the 6th international symposium on Digital Signal Processing for communication Systems (DSPCS 2002), pp. 123–127 (2002)
2. Sullivan, G.J., Wiegand, T.: Video Compression-From Concepts to the H.264/AVC Standard. Proc. of the IEEE 93(1), 18–31 (2005)

3. Leontaris, A., Cosman, P.C.: Video Compression with Intra/Inter Mode Switching and a Dual Frame Buffer. In: Proc. of the Data Compression Conference (DCC 2003), pp. 63–72 (2003)
4. Thamarai, M., Shanmugalakshmi, R.: Video Coding Technique Using Swarm Intelligence in 3-D Dual Tree Complex Wavelet Transform. In: Proc. of the Second International Conference on Machine Learning and Computing (ICMLC), Bangalore, pp. 174–178 (2010)
5. Abomhara, M., Khalifa, O.O., Zakaria, O., Zaidan, A.A., Zaidan, B.B., Rame, A.: Video Compression techniques: An Overview. Journal of Applied Sciences 10(16), 183–1840 (2010)
6. Benabdellah, M., Regragui, F., Gharbi, M., Bouyakhf, E.H.: Choice of Rererence Images for Video Compression. Applied Mathematical Sciences 1(44), 2187–2201 (2007)
7. Carpentieri, B.: Splits, Segs and Superblocks in Split-Merge Video Compression. International Journal of Computers 2(2), 158–164 (2008)
8. Pandit, A.K., Kant, A., Verma, S.: A Prune Modified Algorithm in Video Compression. Ubiqutious Computing and Communication Journal 3(5), 1–11 (2008)
9. Saran, R., Srivastava, H.B., Kumar, A.: Median Predictor-based Lossless Video Compression Algorithm for IR Image Sequences. Defence Science Journal 59(2), 183–188 (2009)
10. Kilic, I., Yilmaz, R.: A Hybrid Video Compression Based On Zerotree Wavelet Structure. The Arabian Journal for Science and Engineering 34(1B), 187–196 (2009)
11. Bakwad, K.M., Pattnaik, S.S., Sohi, B.S., Devi, S., Lohakare, M.R.: Parallel Bacterial Foraging Optimization for Video Compression. International Journal of Recent Trends in Engineering 1(1), 118–122 (2009)
12. Radhakrishnan, S., Subbarayan, G., Vikram, K.L.: Wavelet Based Video Encoder Using KCDS. The International Arab Journal of Information Technology 6(3), 239–245 (2009)
13. Sankaralingam, E., Thangaraj, V., Vijayamani, S.: Video Compression Using Multiwavelet and Multistage Vector Quantization. The International Arab Journal of Information Technology 6(4), 385–393 (2009)
14. Islam, A., Pearlman, W.A.: An Embedded and Efficient Low-Complexity Hierarchical Image Coder. In: Proc. of the Visual Communications and Image Processing (SPIE), vol. 3653, pp. 294–305 (1999)
15. Koga, T., Linuma, K., Hirano, A., Lijima, J., Ishiguro, T.: Motion Compensated Inter Frame Coding for Video Conferencing. In: Proc. of Natural Telecommunication Conference, New Orleans, pp. G5.3.1–G5.3.5 (1981)
16. Yao, N., Kuang, M.K.: Adaptive rood pattern search for fast block-matching motion estimation. IEEE Transactions on Image Processing 11, 1442–1449 (2002)
17. Shan, Z., Kuang, M.K.: A new diamond search algorithm for fast block matching motion estimation. IEEE Transactions on Image Processing 9, 287–290 (2000)
18. Makhoul, J.: Linear prediction: A tutorial review. Proceedings of the IEEE 63, 561–580 (1975)
19. Luo, Y., Celenk, M.: A new fast block-matching algorithm based on an adaptive rood pattern search using spatio-temporal correlation. In: Proc. of the 10th IASTED International Conference on Signal and Image Processing (SIP 2008), Hawaii (2008)
20. Latte, M.V., Ayachit, N.H., Deshpande, D.K.: Reduced memory listless speck image compression. Digital Signal Processing 16(6), 817–824 (2006)
21. Brijmohan, Y., Mneney, S.H.: Video Compression for Very Low Bit-Rate Communications Using Fractal and Wavelet Techniques. In: Proc. of the CD-ROM Southern African Telecommunication Networks and Applications Conference (SATNAC), vol. 1, pp. 39–44 (2004)

Towards Quantification of Information System Security

Sunil Thalia[1], Asma Tuteja[2], and Maitreyee Dutta[1]

[1] NITTTR, Chandigarh, India
[2] G D Goenka World Institute, Sohna, India
sunilthalia@rediffmail.com, asmatuteja@yahoo.co.in,
d_maitreyee@yahoo.co.in

Abstract. Quantification is a highly successful paradigm in many technical and engineering disciplines. Security quantification is the representation and analysis of information security in a quantitative manner. The exponential growth of information technology and the prospect of increased public access to the computing, communications, and storage resources have made these systems more vulnerable to attacks. The need to protect these systems is fueling the need of quantifying security metrics to determine the exact level of security assurances. This paper presents a quantitative framework based on Fuzzy Analytic Hierarchy Process (FAHP) to quantify the security performance of an information system.

Keywords: Information system, Security metrics, Fuzzy analytic hierarchy process.

1 Introduction

There are many ways to understand computer and information security. The idea of quantification has also been applied in various ways during the last two decades, under different names such as security metrics, security measures, operational measures, reliability/dependability metrics, risk analysis and similar terms. An IS metric/measure is a value, selected from a partially ordered set by some assessment process that represents an IS-related quality of some object of concern. It provides, or is used to create, a description, prediction, or comparison, with some degree of confidence [10]. The purpose of security quantification is to give an indication of how well a system meets specified criteria. Although security measurement and quantification is a stumbling block, yet to perform security cost-benefit analysis and statistically representation, reliable information security metrics do not exist. The vocabulary of information security is fraught with imprecision and overlapping meanings [1]. The main contribution of this paper is to introduce a security measurement framework based on Fuzzy Analytic Hierarchy Process (FAHP) [8, 2] to quantify the security performance of an Information System.

V.V. Das and N. Thankachan (Eds.): CIIT 2011, CCIS 250, pp. 225–231, 2011.

2 Background

Saaty [8] defined AHP as a hierarchical decomposing decision method for a complex multi-criteria decision problem. AHP is widely applied in the field of information systems [3]. Our earlier work includes an algorithm design to evaluate the security level of an Information System. In the beginning of this algorithm a high level information security goal are transformed in to low level security metrics using decomposition of goals that are then inserted into metrics templates to develop a perfect set of metrics aligned with the goals of the information system. In the middle, AHP is applied to identify the relative importance among sibling components and to evaluate their weight index. Finally, a quantitative approach is used to evaluate the security level of the information system [9]. The conventional AHP method is incapable of handling the uncertainty and vagueness involved in the mapping of one's preference to an exact number or ratio. The major difficulty with classical AHP is its inability in mapping human judgments. To address such uncertainties, Zadeh [4] for the first time introduced and used fuzzy sets theory. Because the real world is actually full of ambiguities or in one word is fuzzy, several researches have combined fuzzy theory with AHP. Laarhoven and Pedrcyz [6] propose the first method of implementing fuzzy AHP, which triangular fuzzy numbers (TFN) are compared according to their membership functions. In Fuzzy-AHP, pair wise comparisons are done using fuzzy linguistic preference scale ranging from 0 to 10. For simplicity, the reciprocal fuzzy numbers are replaced by individual TFN's in the pair wise comparison matrix. A triangular fuzzy number (TFN) is the special class of fuzzy number whose membership is defined by three real numbers, expressed as (l, m, u).

3 Proposed Framework

The proposed framework is divided into eight major steps; in the beginning of this framework, the security needs of the target information system are identified. These security needs constitute the security specifications for the target system and its environment, that are finally selected in terms of information security standards such as ISO/IEC 2700x series [11], NIST-800 series [7] etc., to achieve the defined security needs (See Fig.1).

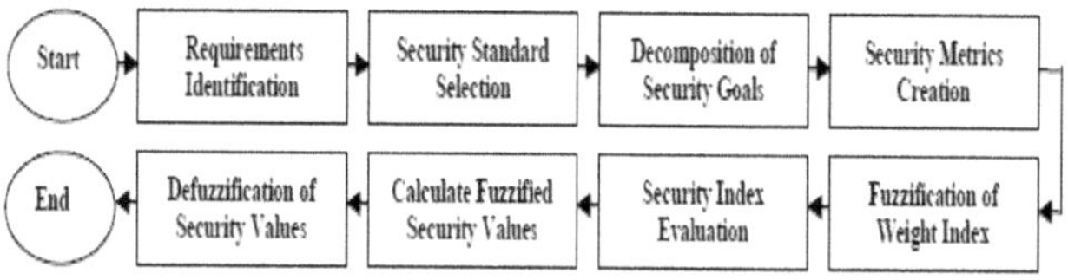

Fig. 1. Proposed Framework

After that this high level information security goal are transformed in to low level security metrics using decomposition of goals that are then inserted into metrics templates to develop a perfect set of metrics aligned with the security requirements of the information system. In the middle, FAHP is applied to fuzzifying the crisp pairwise comparison matrices (PCM) to fuzzy PCM and to evaluate fuzzified weight index. Finally, a defuzzification method is used to convert fuzzy data into crisp scores and on behalf of these crisp scores; security performance of the information system is evaluated.

1. Identification of Security Requirements: The framework is starts with a study of the information system's context and the identification of its components. In this step, the system and its environment are described, focusing on the sensitive activities related to information security. In the Context Study, the information system is studied, by analyzing its missions, its business, its own values, its constraints, its structure, the regulatory references applicable to the system, etc. The outcomes of this step are a description of the essential elements of the system (functions or information security sensitive) and second the determination of the entities or components of the underlying information system. A mapping is done between both of them. Thus, this step is further divided into the following five sub-steps.

    a. Identify critical assets
    b. Define security goal
    c. Identify threats
    d. Identify and analyze risks
    e. Define security requirements

    The security needs of the system are then defined. Based on asset/component identification, one needs to determine the security objectives to be reached. Security objectives are often defined in terms of confidentiality, integrity and availability properties of the assets.
2. Selection of Security Standard: In this step, the information system's security needs are compared with the identified threats. The risks are thus highlighted and can be treated by some security objectives. These security objectives constitute the security specifications for the target system and its environment. They must be consistent with all of the assumptions, constraints, regulatory references and security rules identified during the first step of the framework. The security requirements are finally selected in terms of information security standards such as ISO/IEC 2700x series [11], NIST-800 series [7] etc., to achieve the defined security objectives.
3. Decomposition of Security Goals: Decompose the target Goal into several sub-goals to generate a goal tree in following manner:

    i. If target goal is specific enough so that a set of simple measurements can show that it is fulfilled. Then stop the decompositions; Else go to step (ii).
    ii. Decompose the target goal in to sub goals that are more specific than the
    iii. original goal {maintain a record of the parent /child relation between goals.}
    iv. iii.Do step (i) for each of the sub goals from step (ii).

4. Security Metrics Creation: After these goals have been formulated a set of security related questionnaires to each goal is constructed where the answer to these

questions will show weather the goal is fulfilled or not. There is no any question asked for the internal nodes, as these nodes are used only for aggregate the information. But for terminal nodes, the questions asked should always be of the type that is answered by "yes" or "no". The metrics template is really two templates i.e. Security Metrics Template for Terminal Nodes (SMTTN) and Security Metrics Template for Internal Node (SMTIN), one for the internal nodes of the tree and one for the terminal nodes. When the third step of the framework, the decomposition step, is completed and a tree of goals has been created, the goals are inserted into one of the templates depending on what type of node the goal corresponds to. After a goal has been inserted the rest of the fields of the template are filled out [9].

5. Fuzzification of Weight Index (w_i): Apply Fuzzy Analytic Hierarchy Process (FAHP) [2, 6] to evaluate fuzzified weight index for each node (except root node) of goal tree.

   i. Take root node (parent node) as a final goal and make a pair wise comparison among its child nodes and decide the relative importance by ranking them as shown in Table-1 in following manner:

Table 1. Relative Importance (Ranking)

value $\tilde{a}_{ij}$	Comparison Description
(1,1,1)	Child "i" and "j" are of equal importance
(2,3,4)	Child "i" is weakly more important that "j"
(4,5,6)	Child "i" is strongly more important that "j"
(6,7,8)	Child "i" is very strongly more important that"j"
(7,8,9)	Child "i" is absolutely more important that "j"

   ii. Create an (n × n) comparison matrix ($\tilde{A}$) with respect to the parent node as follows:

      a. Let $\tilde{a}_{ij}$ = element of ith row and jth column, of the matrix.
      b. Then $\tilde{a}_{ji} = 1/\tilde{a}_{ij}$ and $\tilde{a}_{ii} = 1$.
      c. Create (n × n) comparison matrix ($\tilde{A}$)as shown below:

$$\begin{bmatrix} \tilde{a}_{11} & \tilde{a}_{12} & \dots & \tilde{a}_{1n} \\ \tilde{a}_{21} & \tilde{a}_{22} & \dots & \tilde{a}_{2n} \\ \cdot & \cdot & \dots & \cdot \\ \tilde{a}_{n1} & \tilde{a}_{n2} & \dots & \tilde{a}_{nn} \end{bmatrix}$$

   where $\tilde{a}_{ij} = (\tilde{a}^{l}_{ij}, \tilde{a}^{m}_{ij}, \tilde{a}^{u}_{ij})$ is the relative importance of each criteria in pair wise comparison and $\tilde{a}^{l}_{ij}, \tilde{a}^{m}_{ij}, \tilde{a}^{u}_{ij}$ are the minimum value, most plausible value & maximum value of the triangular fuzzy number.

   iii. Calculate fuzzy weight index (w_i) for each child node as follows:

      a) Sum each column of comparison matrix & get T_1, T_2,T_n as:

$$T_1 = \tilde{a}_{11} + \tilde{a}_{21} + \ldots + \tilde{a}_{n1} \quad (1)$$

$$T_2 = \tilde{a}_{12} + \tilde{a}_{22} + \ldots + \tilde{a}_{n2} \quad (2)$$

$$T_n = \tilde{a}_{1n} + \tilde{a}_{2n} + \ldots + \tilde{a}_{nn} \quad (3)$$

b) Divide each element of matrix with the sum of its column and obtain another (n x n) matrix with elements "b_{ij}".

c) Measure (w_i) of each child by averaging across the row,as:{$\sum (w_i)_n = 1.$}

$$(w_i)_1 = (b_{11} + b_{12} + \ldots + b_{1n})/n \quad (4)$$

$$(w_i)_2 = (b_{21} + b_{22} + \ldots + b_{2n})/n \quad (5)$$

$$(w_i)_n = (b_{n1} + b_{n2} + \ldots + b_{nn})/n \quad (6)$$

6. Security Index (s_i) Evaluation: To measure the security index(s_i) of all the terminal nodes, evaluate the answers (either in "yes" or "no") of all measurement questionnaires (related to the information system) for each node. The ratio of total number of questions answered by "yes" to the total number of questions asked for each terminal node will gives the value of security index (s_i) for that node.
7. Security Value (s_v) Calculation: Finally, at this stage the security values of all the nodes are calculated in a bottom-up manner by using the following formula:

$$(s_v) = (w_i) \times (s_i) \quad (7)$$

First, the security values $(s_v)_t$ of each terminal node is calculated by multiplying the weight index $(w_i)_t$ with their security index (s_i). Similarly, the security value $(s_v)_i$ of each internal node is calculated by multiplying the weight index $(w_i)_i$ to the security values (s_v) of all its child nodes. At last, the security value $(s_v)_r$ of root node is obtained by taking the sum of the security values (s_v) of all its child nodes. Now, on the behalf of the security value of root node i.e. $(s_v)_r$, security performance of the whole information system is calculated.

8. Defuzzification of Security Values: Now we need to defuzzify these fuzzy values in order to obtain a non-fuzzy form. This could be accomplished through utilizing the Best Non-fuzzy Performance (BNP) values defuzzification method [5]. The COA method's BNP value for triangular fuzzy performance score can be calculated as follows:

$$BNP = l + [(u - l) + (m - l)] / 3 \quad (8)$$

4 Test Case

Let we assume that at level-1, Factor A is weekly more important than Factor B; Factor C is strongly more important than Factor A; and Factor C is very strongly more important than Factor B.

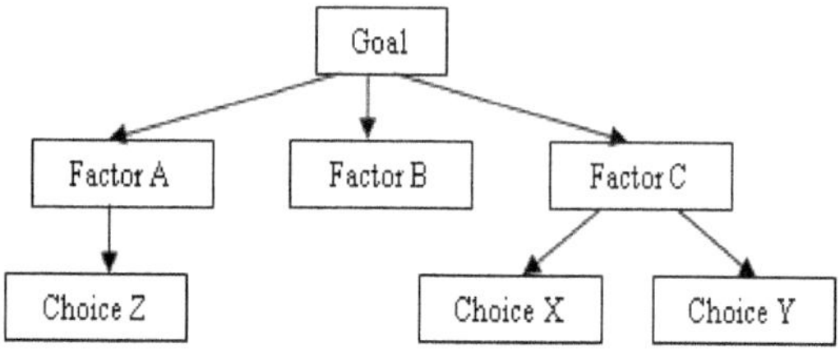

Fig. 2. Goal Tree [9]

	A	B	C
A	(1,1,1)	(2,3,4)	(1/6,1/5,1/4)
B	(1/4,1/3,1/2)	(1,1,1)	(1/8,1/7,1/6)
C	(4,5,6)	(6,7,8)	(1,1,1)

Similarly, at level-2, we assume that choice X is weekly more important than choice Y. Therefore, the comparison matrix for the Level-1 is generated as follows (See Fig.2): The fuzzified weight index of each node is calculated as following manner:

$(w_i)_A$= 0.1806, 0.1931, 0.2058
$(w_i)_B$= 0.0852, 0.0833, 0.0871
$(w_i)_C$= 0.7235, 0.7235, 0.7071
$(w_i)_X$= 0.7333, 0.75, 0.7333
$(w_i)_Y$= 0.2666, 0.25, 0.2666
$(w_i)_Z$= 1.0000, 1.0000, 1.0000

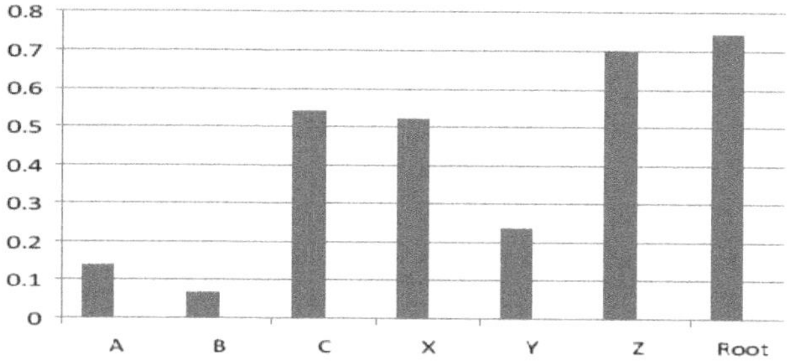

Fig. 3. Security Performance

In this manner, after calculating the security index of each node in the goal tree, fuzzified security value of every node is measured by applying the formula (mentioned in the framework) as follows:

Security Value $(S_v)_B$ of B = 0.06816, 0.06664, 0.06968
Security Value $(S_v)_Z$ of Z = 0.7,0.7,0.7
Security Value $(S_v)_X$ of X = 0.51331, 0.525, 0.51331
Security Value $(S_v)_Y$ of Y = 0.2399, 0.225, 0.2399
Security Value $(S_v)_A$ of A = 0.1264, 0.13517, 0.14406

Security Value $(Sv)_C$ of C = 0.5449, 0.54262, 0.53258
Security Value $(Sv)_{Root}$ = 0.7394, 0.74443, 0.7463

Now center of area (COA) method is applied for defuzzification. Thus, the security performance of information system is 0.7433 i.e. 74.33%. The security performance of all the factors and choices are shown in the figure 3.

5 Conclusion and Future Work

In this paper, a structured framework based on fuzzy analytical hierarchy process has been proposed to quantify the security performance of an information system, where Triangular Fuzzy numbers are utilized in collecting human judgments through linguistic variables. The extension of the efficient AHP into Fuzzy-AHP enables handling the vagueness associated with subjective assignments and comparisons. Further Analytical Hierarchy Process was used in generating criteria weights and sub criteria weights for the evaluation of alternatives. Although for simplicity less number of factors is taken but this model can be used in evaluating a number of factors. For the extension of this work, various methods of multi-criteria evaluation such as analytical network process (ANP) and fuzzy ANP which have the ability of considering interaction among factors and sub factors can be conducted in specific situations.

References

1. Geer Jr., D., Hoo, K.S., Jaquith, A.: Information Security: Why the Future Belongs to the Quants. IEEE Journal on Security & Privacy 1(4), 24–32 (2003)
2. Chang, D.Y.: Applications of the extent analysis method on fuzzy-AHP. European Journal of Operational Research 95(3), 649–655 (1996)
3. Salmeron, J.L., Herrero, I.: An AHP-based methodology to rank critical success factors of executive information systems. Computer Standards & Interfaces 28(1), 1–12 (2005)
4. Zadeh, L.A.: Fuzzy sets. Information and Control 8(3), 338–353 (1965)
5. Chen, M.F., Tzeng, G.H., Ding, C.G.: Combining fuzzy AHP with MDS in identifying the preference similarity of alternatives. Applied Soft Computing 8(1), 110–117 (2008)
6. Van Laarhoven, P.J.M., Pedrycz, W.: A fuzzy extension of Saaty's priority theory. Fuzzy Sets and Systems 11(1-3), 199–227 (1983)
7. Chew, E., Swanson, M., Stine, K., Bartol, N., Brown, A., Robinson, W.: NIST performance measurement guide for information security. Technical report, NIST (September 2008)
8. Saaty, T.: The Analytic Hierarchy Process. McGraw-Hill (1980)
9. Thalia, S., Tuteja, A., Dutta, M.: An algorithm design to evaluate the security level of an information system. In: Das, V.V., Stephen, J., Chaba, Y. (eds.) CNC 2011. CCIS, vol. 142, pp. 69–75. Springer, Heidelberg (2011)
10. WISSRR Workshop Proceedings, Security System Scoring and Ranking (May 2001)
11. Introduction to ISO 27004 / ISO27004, http://www.27000.org/iso-27004.htm

Accurate Image Retrieval Using Content Dissimilarity: Performance Enhancement by Indexing

Sonwane Priyanka[1] and S.G. Shikalpure[2]

[1]Faculty of Information Technology, Government polytechnic, Pune
priyankatarolkar@rediffmail.com
[2] Faculty of computer Engineering, Government Engineering College, Aurangabad
shikalpure@rediffmail.com

Abstract. This paper introduces the content dissimilarity measure, which significantly improves the accuracy of bag-of-features based image search. Our measure takes into account the local distribution of the vectors and iteratively estimates distance update terms in the spirit of Sinkhorn's scaling algorithm, thereby modifying the neighbourhood structure. Experimental results show that our approach gives significantly better results than a standard distance method. This paper also evaluates the impact of a large number of parameters, including the number of descriptors, the clustering method, the visual vocabulary size, and the distance measure. In particular, using a large number of descriptors is interesting only when using our dissimilarity measure. We have also evaluated two novel variants: multiple assignment and rank aggregation. They are shown to further improve accuracy at the cost of higher memory usage and lower efficiency. We also combine a indexing technique for achieving efficient and effective retrieval performance.

Keywords: Image retrieval, Distance regularization, Clustering, Indexing.

1 Introduction

In this paper, we address the problem of finding images of the same object or scene viewed under different imaging conditions. Initial approaches used simple voting-based techniques. More recently, they were extended based on a bag-of-features image representation. Our paper builds upon these approaches and presents methods to improve the accuracy. The main contribution of this paper is the content dissimilarity method (CDM), which takes into account the neighbourhood of a vector. This measure is obtained by iteratively regularizing the average distance of each vector to its neighbourhood. Intuitively, this phenomenon yields suboptimal accuracy, as will be confirmed in this paper. Experimental results show that the gain due to our Content dissimilarity method is significantly higher than the one obtained by a weighting scheme. The second proposed variant is rank aggregation, which has not been used in the context based image search before. The performance improves significantly and increases with the number of image search systems used in parallel. However, using several image search systems has a high cost in terms of memory and computation time.

V.V. Das and N. Thankachan (Eds.): CIIT 2011, CCIS 250, pp. 232–238, 2011.

2 The Image Search Scheme

In the following, we present steps of our image search framework.

Descriptors. N database images are described with local descriptors. We combine SIFT descriptor [1] with the affine Hessian region extractor[2].

Visual words. Visual words quantize space of descriptors..Assigning descriptors to visual words. Each SIFT descriptor of given image is assigned to closest visual word.

Weighting frequency vectors. The components of the frequency vector are weighted with a strategy similar to the one in [3]. The weighted component $w_{i;j}$ associated with image i is given by

$$w_{i,j}=f_{i,j} \log n/n_j \tag{1}$$

Distance. Given the visual word vector w_q of a query, similar images in the database are represented by vector(s) w_i minimizing $d(w_q,w_i)$,where relation $d(.,.)$ is a distance on the visual word vector space. It updates a given distance $d(.,.)$,

$$\text{CDM}\ (w_i,w_j)=d(w_i,w_j)\delta_i\ \delta_j \tag{2}$$

Efficient search. Distance computation is optimized with inverted file system exploiting the sparsity of visual vectors. Such an inverted file can be used for any Minkowski norm[3] when vectors are of unit norm. For huge vocabulary sizes, strategies in [3] and greatly reduce cost of assigning descriptors to visual words.

Rank aggregation. The idea is to use multiple visual vocabularies, i.e., to combine results of several image search systems where each one uses a different vocabulary.

3 Content Dissimilarity Method

This first step of this procedure, produces a new dissimilarity measure (noniterative approach). The proposed CDM is then obtained by iterating this update step until a stopping criterion is satisfied.

3.1 Nonreversibility of Neighborhood and Its Impact

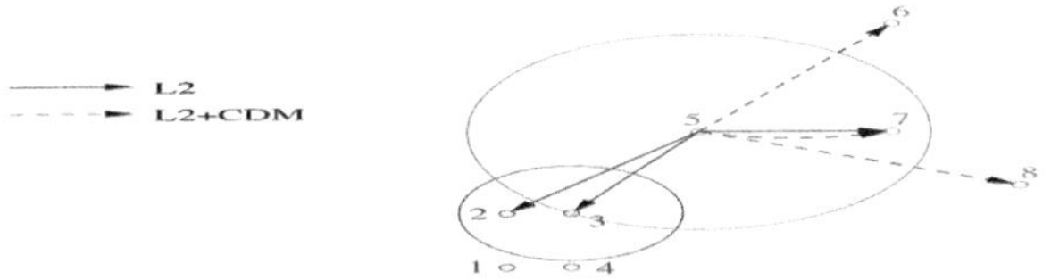

Fig. 1. The 3-nearest neighbours of vector 5 without (solid) and with CDM (dashed). The circles display the average distances of vectors 3 (blue) and 5 (red) to their neighbourhood. Vector 3 is a 3-nearest neighbor of vector 5, but converse is not true. In contrast, it is (trivially) the case for an ε-search, where the neighborhood of a vector q is defined as set of vectors x such that d(q,x)< ε. The neighborhood reversibility rate is then defined as :

$$\frac{1}{n} \sum_{w_i} \frac{1}{\#N(i)} \sum_{w_j} \text{revers}(w_i, w_j) \tag{3}$$

3.2 Noniterative Approach

Let us consider the neighborhood $N(i)$ of a given visual word vector w_i defined by its $\#N(i)=n_N$ nearest neighbors. We define the neighborhood distance as the mean distance of a given visual word vector w_i to the vectors of its neighborhood:

$$r(i) = \frac{1}{n_N} \sum_x d(w_i, x), \tag{4}$$

The quantity r(i)is shown in Fig. 1 by the circle radii. It is computed for each visual word vector and subsequently used to define a first dissimilarity measure d*(.,.)Between two visual word vectors:

$$d^*(w_i,w_j)= d(w_i,w_j) \frac{\bar{r}}{(r(i)r(j))^{1/2}} \tag{5}$$

3.3 Iterative Approach

The update of (5) is iterated on the new matrix of dissimilarities. The rationale of this iterative approach is to integrate the neighborhood modification from previous distance updates. Denoting with a superscript ^{k} the quantities obtained at iteration k, we have

$$d^{(k+1)}(w_i,w_j)= d^{(k)}(w_i,w_j) \frac{\bar{r}^{(k)}}{(r^{(k)}(i)r^{(k)}(j))^{1/2}}. \tag{6}$$

Let us define a small quantity $\varepsilon > 0$. As a stopping criterion, the algorithm terminates when the inequality $S^{(k)}-S^{(k+1)} > \varepsilon$ is not satisfied anymore. One has to maintain a cumulative distance correcting term $\delta_i^{(k)}$ during iterations as

$$\delta_i^{(k+1)} = \delta_i^{(k)} \left(\bar{r}^{(k)}/r^{(k)}(i) \right)^{1/2} \tag{7}$$

Denoting by δ_i the quantity $\delta_i^{(k-1)}$ when algorithm terminates, it is easy to show that

$$d^{(k)}(w_i,w_j) = d^{(k)}(w_i,w_j)\ \delta_i\delta_j \tag{8}$$

The k-nearest neighbors of a given query q are then the minima given by

$$NN(q)=k\text{-argmin}_j d(q,w_j)\delta_j. \tag{9}$$

Given original distance matrix and the parameters k(neighborhood) and ε , pseudo code for computing update terms of CDM is given by

Algorithm1.Compute CDM_update_terms (D, k,ε) , D: N $\times$ N matrix of vector distances , k: neighborhood size ε: convergence threshold
$\delta=(\delta_1,\delta_2,\ldots\delta_N):=(1,1,\ldots,1)$ repeat
% compute neighborhood average distances for i =1 to N do ,N(i):={k nearest neighbors of the ith vector } ,$r(i):=1/k\sum_j D(i,j)$ end for
% compute their geometric mean $\bar{r}:=(\prod_i r(i))^{1/n}$
% compute update terms for i =1 to N do $\delta_i=\delta_i(\bar{r}/r(i))^{1/2}$ end for
% update the pair wise vector dissimilarity measures
% diag(δ)is the diagonal matrix with diagonal δ D:=diag(δ)$\times$D$\times$diag(δ)
%test convergence $S_{old}:=S_{new}$,$S_{new}:=\sum_i |r_i-\bar{r}|$ until S_{old} _$S_{new} < \varepsilon$ return $(\delta_1,\delta_2,\ldots\delta_N)$

4 Basic Procedure

Procedure is: Distinguish special features among image in terms of descriptors, then Based on the descriptor value clustering is done. Since we group based on pixel values-(descriptor), we go for K - means clustering. After, all the above steps are over we compare the query image with our cluster in the database.

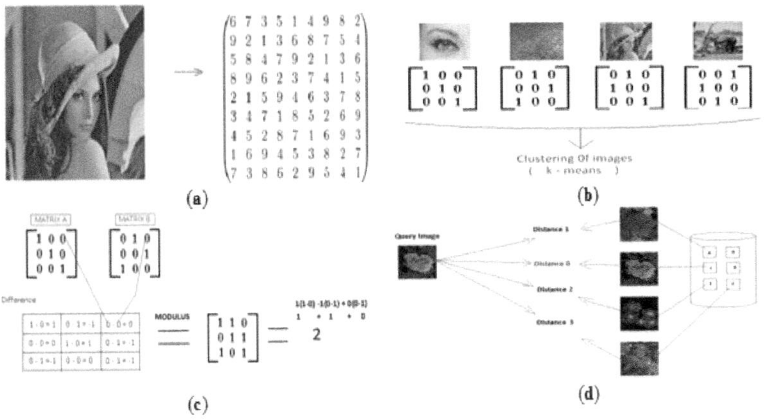

Fig. 2. (**a**) Extracting Features (**b**) Clustering of images (**c**) Calculating dissimilarity (**d**) Retrieval on the basis of minimum distance

5 Experiments

5.1 Data Sets and Evaluation Criteria

The evaluation is performed Niste´r and Stewe´nius (N-S) data set [6],. N-S data set is composed of 2,550 objects each of which is imaged from four different viewpoints..

For all the experiments, we used the Hessian-Affine detector [2]. Two different measures are used to evaluate the impact of the various parameters and variants: the average normalized rank (ANR) and, for the sake of comparison, the measure used by Stewe´nius and Niste´r [6]. For a given query image, the ANR [4] is given by

$$ANR = -\sum \frac{1}{n_q} \frac{1}{n_{rel(i)}} \left(\sum^{nrel(i)}_{j=1} rank(j) - \frac{n_{rel(i)}(n_{rel(i)}+1)}{2}\right) \quad (10)$$

where nq is the number of queries, n is the number of data set images, and $n_{rel(i)}$ is the number of images which should be retrieved for image

5.2 Impact of the Parameters and Variants

5.2.1 Number of Descriptors

Fig. 3 shows that the number of descriptors extracted for each image has a strong impact on accuracy. We can observe that accuracy increases up to a certain point only, i.e., using a too high number of descriptors decreases performance.

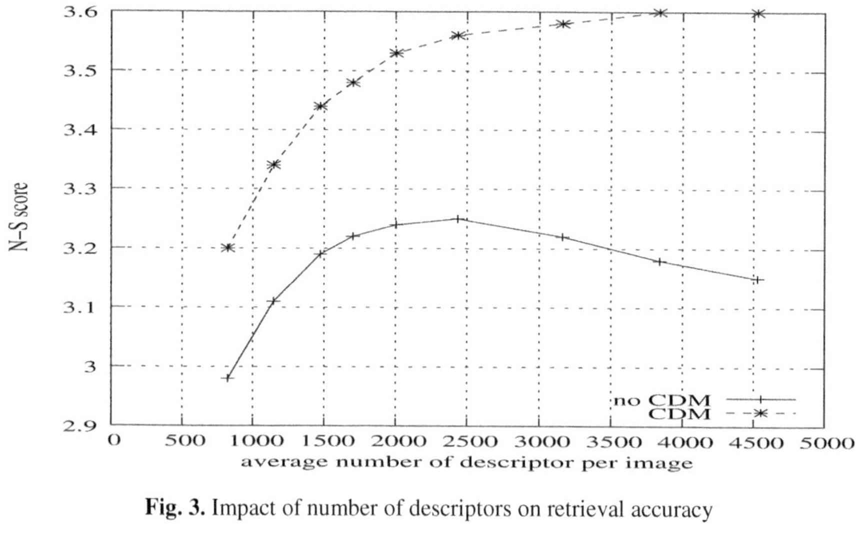

Fig. 3. Impact of number of descriptors on retrieval accuracy

5.2.2 Rank Aggregation

Table 1 presents the results obtained with rank aggregation method. Visual vocabularies have been obtained by modifying the seed of the random number generator. Results show that rank aggregation improves accuracy.

Table 1. N-S Data Set

No. of Distinct Visual Vocab.	1	3	5	9
Vocab. Size	1000 10000 30000	1000 10000 30000	1000 10000 30000	1000 10000 30000
N-S Score without CDM	2.91 3.16 3.26	2.93 3.20 3.29	2.94 3.21 3.31	2.95 3.22 3.32
N-S Score with CDM	3.49 3.57 3.57	3.54 3.63 3.63	3.55 3.64 3.65	3.56 3.65 3.67

Rank aggregation: Impact of the number of distinct visual vocabularies (1-9), learned here on the N-S data set itself.

6 Indexing

In content-based image retrieval systems, the content of an image such as color, shapes and textures are used to retrieve images that are similar to a query image. Most of the existing work focus on the retrieval effectiveness of using content for retrieval, i.e., studies the accuracy (in terms of recall and precision) of using different representations of content. By Indexing, we address the issue of retrieval efficiency i.e., study the speed of retrieval, since a slow system is not useful for large image databases. We use a multi-level R-tree index, called the Nested R-trees (NR-trees) and compare its performance with that of the R-tree. Our experimental study shows that R+-trees [8] can reduce the retrieval time significantly compared to R-tree, and facilitate similarity retrieval.

7 Conclusions

This paper introduces the contextual dissimilarity measure to compare frequency vectors of a bag-of-features image representation. This new measure is based on a distance regularization algorithm in the spirit of the Sinkhorn's algorithm. The performance of our approach has been demonstrated for a bag-of-features-based image search system. A large set of experiments shows that the accuracy is significantly and consistently improved by the CDM for two different data sets. We also analyze several variants and the impact of the main parameters of our image search system. Our final system also increases speed of retrieval of image by using indexing.

References

1. Lowe, D.: Distinctive Image Features from Scale Invariant Keypoints. Int'l J. Computer Vision 60(2), 91–110 (2004)
2. Mikolajczyk, K., Schmid, C.: Scale and Affine Invariant Interests. Int'l J. Computer Vision 60(1), 63–86 (2004)

3. Nistér, D., Stewénius, H.: Scalable Recognition with a Vocabulary Tree. In: Proc. IEEE Conf. Computer Vision and Pattern Recognition, pp. 2161–2168 (2006)
4. Sivic, J., Zisserman, A.: Video Google: A Text Retrieval Approach to Object Matching in Videos. In: Proc. IEEE Int'l Conf. Computer Vision, pp. 1470–1477 (2003)
5. Chopra, S., Hadsell, R., LeCun, Y.: Learning a Similarity Metric Discriminatively. In: Proc. IEEE Conf. Computer Vision and Pattern Recognition, pp. 539–546 (2005)
6. Stewénius, H., Nistér, D.: Object Recognition Benchmark (2008), http://vis.uky.edu/%7Estewe/ukbench/
7. Fagin, R., Kumar, R., Sivakumar, D.: Efficient Similarity Search and Classification via Rank Aggregation. In: Proc. ACM SIGMOD, pp. 301–312 (2003)
8. Kemper, A.: Algorithms and Datastructures for Database Systems. In: SS 2003 (2003)

A New Image Cipher Using Chaotically Twisted Maps

P. Devaraj

Department of Mathematics, College of Engineering Guindy,
Anna University, Chennai-25, India
devaraj@annauniv.edu

Abstract. This paper presents a new image encryption scheme that employs the Arnold cat map for total shuffling of the positions of image pixels and then uses two mixed chaotic maps twisted together to increase the key length and security. The states combination of two coupled chaotic systems are used to confuse the relationship between the plain-image and the cipher-image in a nonlinear fashion so as to resist against known plain-text and chosen plain-text attacks. In the diffusion process, the pixel values are altered sequentially. Various operations employed include nonlinear diffusion using the second chaotic key, random like diffusion of adjacent pixels and XORing with the third chaotic key. The security and performance of the proposed image encryption technique have been analyzed using statistical analysis, key sensitivity analysis, key space analysis, differential analysis and entropy analysis. The simulation shows that a single pixel difference of the plain-image will change almost all the pixels in the cipher-image (NPCR>99%), and the unified average changing intensity is high (UACI>33%). Since the entropy is found to be close to the theoretical value, we can observe that the information leakage is negligible and hence the scheme is highly secure. The experimental results demonstrate that the new algorithm has a low time complexity and the suggested encryption algorithm has the advantages of large key space and high security, and moreover, the distribution of grey values of the encrypted image has a random-like behavior.

Keywords: Twisted Chaotic Maps, Permutation, Byte Substitution, Nonlinear Diffusion, Random Diffusion.

1 Introduction

In recent years, the fast developments in digital image processing and network communications have created a great demand for real-time secure image/video transmission over the Internet and through wireless networks. Many applications like remote monitoring using CCTV, military image databases, confidential video conferencing, medical imaging system, cable TV, online personal photograph album, etc. require secure, reliable, fast and robust system to store and transmit digital images/videos over communication media, such as computer networks, mobile phones, cable TV, etc. Hence many applications require solutions for the problem of security in storage and transmission of confidential visual information. Most widely

V.V. Das and N. Thankachan (Eds.): CIIT 2011, CCIS 250, pp. 239–248, 2011.

used conventional ciphers, such as Data Encryption Standard (DES), International Data Encryption Algorithm (IDEA), Advanced Encryption Standard (AES), linear feedback shift register (LFSR), etc. have high computational security. They consider plain text as either block cipher or data stream and are not suitable for image/video encryption in real time because their speed is slow due to a large data volume and strong correlation among image pixels. To meet these security needs several encryption schemes (Refer [1-14] and references there in) have been developed. Among them some of the chaos based cryptosystems are seem to be suitable for the secure transmission of images due to the ergodic properties of chaos and its high sensitivity to initial conditions and parameters allow one to design encryption algorithms with good confusion and diffusion properties and are faster. Hence Chaotic encryption algorithms which use simple discrete systems have recently received much attention to generate chaotic keys. However some of the chaos based schemes [1, 2, 11] are weak against known plain text attack.

In this paper, chaos based image encryption scheme based on twisting two nonlinear chaotic maps is suggested to overcome the weakness of security level. The scheme resists against the attacks analyzed in [1, 2 and 11]. The algorithm uses significant features such as sensitivity to initial condition, permutation of keys, enhanced chaotic maps, nonlinear diffusion and Random diffusion. The nonlinearity is used to overcome the limitation of the other schemes like known/chosen plain text attack. The rest of this paper is organized as follows. Section 2 introduces the new twisted map. Sections 3 and 4 deal with the proposed image encryption/decryption scheme based on the new chaotic map. The security of the new algorithm is analyzed in Section 5. Finally, the conclusions are discussed in Section 6.

2 Proposed Non Linear Chaotic Maps

The proposed image encryption uses the following chaotic maps:

$$\begin{aligned} x_{n+1} &= (k_1 \times (x_n \times z_n + k_4 \times \sin(y_n))) \bmod 1 \\ y_{n+1} &= (k_2 \times y_n + x_{n+1} \times z_n) \bmod 1 \\ z_{n+1} &= (k_3 \times (x_{n+1} + z_n) \times (1 - z_n + y_{n+1})) \bmod 1 \end{aligned}$$

where $|k1|, |k2|, |k3|, |k4| > 2$ are used to increase the chaotic behaviors of the keys which is discussed in the key generation. Along with the key ki the distribution of the sequences becomes better. The distribution shown in Fig.1 shows that the common weaknesses in standard chaotic maps such as stable windows, blank windows, uneven distribution of sequences and weak keys are completely resolved.

Thus, the proposed nonlinear chaotic map does not have security issues which are present in the logistic map. Moreover, the resulting chaotic sequences are uniformly distributed and the key size has been increased greatly.

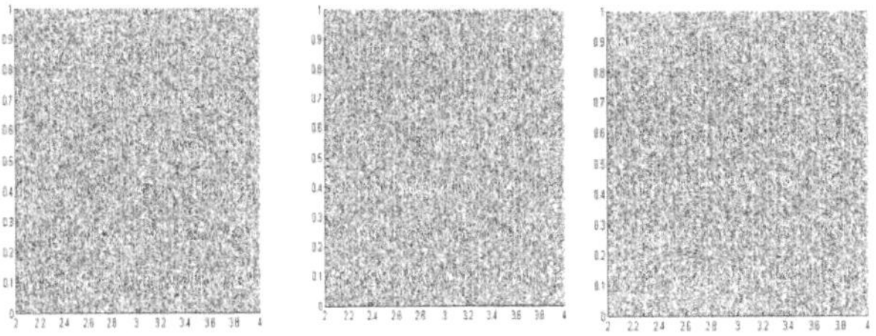

Fig. 1. Distributions of Co-Ordinate wise Projections of the new Map

3 Encryption Scheme

3.1 Key Generation

The discretized chaotic keys are generated using the three initial values x0, y0, z0 and four constants k1, k2, k3, k4 as follows:

```
x(1,1)=x0 and Xkey(1,1)=floor(x(1,1) × 256)
y(1,1)=y0 and Ykey(1,1)=floor(y(1,1) × 256)
z(1,1)=z0 and Zkey(1,1)=floor(z(1,1) × 256)
for i=1 to 255
  for j=0 to 255
    x(i+1,j+2)=k1 × (x(i+1,j+1))× z(i+1,j+1)+ k4 × sin(y(i+1,j+1)) mod 1
    y(i+1,j+2)=k2 × y(i+1,j+1)+x(i+1,j+2) × z(i+1,j+1) mod 1
    z(i+1,j+2)=k3 × (x(i+1,j+2)+z(i+1,j+1)) × (1-z(i+1,j+1)+ y(i+1,j+2)) mod 1
    Xkey(i+1,j+2)=floor(x(i+1,j+2) × 256)
    Ykey(i+1,j+2)=floor(y(i+1,j+2) × 256)
    Zkey(i+1,j+2)=floor(z(i+1,j+2) × 256)
  end
    x(i+2,1)=x(i+1,j+2)
    y(i+2,1)=y(i+1,j+2)
    z(i+2,1)=z(i+1,j+2)
end
```

3.2 Permutation

The confusion effect is obtained by permutation stage, while the diffusion effect is performed in the pixel value diffusion stage. Confusion makes the relationship between the key and the cipher text as complex as possible. The Arnold cat map is used for permutation. Assume that image is stored in an NxN array P of pixels with pixel coordinates $I=\{(i,j)/i,j=1,2,...,N\}$. The Arnold cat map is given by

$$\begin{bmatrix} i' \\ j' \end{bmatrix} = \begin{bmatrix} 1 & p \\ q & pq+1 \end{bmatrix} \begin{bmatrix} i \\ j \end{bmatrix} \bmod 256$$

The above map is used to permute the plain image pixel and the corresponding cipher image C is give by

$$C[i,j]=P[i',j'] \oplus Xkey[i,j].$$

One set of chaotic keys are XORed with the permuted pixel to attain the diffusion effect. This can greatly enhance the security of the scheme.

3.3 S-Box Substitution

The following S-box is used for byte substitution:

$$S = \begin{bmatrix}
2 & 4 & 3 & 5 & 7 & 8 & 9 & 10 & 11 & 12 & 13 & 14 & 15 & 16 & 1 & 6 \\
4 & 6 & 5 & 7 & 9 & 10 & 11 & 12 & 13 & 14 & 15 & 16 & 1 & 2 & 3 & 8 \\
12 & 14 & 13 & 15 & 1 & 2 & 3 & 4 & 5 & 6 & 7 & 8 & 9 & 10 & 11 & 16 \\
1 & 3 & 2 & 4 & 6 & 7 & 8 & 9 & 10 & 11 & 12 & 13 & 14 & 15 & 16 & 5 \\
5 & 7 & 6 & 8 & 10 & 11 & 12 & 13 & 14 & 15 & 16 & 1 & 2 & 3 & 4 & 9 \\
7 & 9 & 8 & 10 & 12 & 13 & 14 & 15 & 16 & 1 & 2 & 3 & 4 & 5 & 6 & 11 \\
8 & 10 & 9 & 11 & 13 & 14 & 15 & 16 & 1 & 2 & 3 & 4 & 5 & 6 & 7 & 12 \\
9 & 11 & 10 & 12 & 14 & 15 & 16 & 1 & 2 & 3 & 4 & 5 & 6 & 7 & 8 & 13 \\
10 & 12 & 11 & 13 & 15 & 16 & 1 & 2 & 3 & 4 & 5 & 6 & 7 & 8 & 9 & 14 \\
6 & 8 & 7 & 9 & 11 & 12 & 13 & 14 & 15 & 16 & 1 & 2 & 3 & 4 & 5 & 10 \\
3 & 5 & 4 & 6 & 8 & 9 & 10 & 11 & 12 & 13 & 14 & 15 & 16 & 1 & 2 & 7 \\
13 & 15 & 14 & 16 & 2 & 3 & 4 & 5 & 6 & 7 & 8 & 9 & 10 & 11 & 12 & 1 \\
14 & 16 & 15 & 1 & 3 & 4 & 5 & 6 & 7 & 8 & 9 & 10 & 11 & 12 & 13 & 2 \\
15 & 1 & 16 & 2 & 4 & 5 & 6 & 7 & 8 & 9 & 10 & 11 & 12 & 13 & 14 & 3 \\
16 & 2 & 1 & 3 & 5 & 6 & 7 & 8 & 9 & 10 & 11 & 12 & 13 & 14 & 15 & 4 \\
11 & 13 & 12 & 14 & 16 & 1 & 2 & 3 & 4 & 5 & 6 & 7 & 8 & 9 & 10 & 15
\end{bmatrix}$$

We split the pixel at (i,j)th position into two parts namely, left half and right half. These are denoted by p1ij and p2ij respectively.

Define

$$c^1_{ij} = S((y(i,j) \bmod 16)+1, p^1_{ij}+1)$$
$$c^2_{ij} = S((y(i,j) \bmod 16)+1, p^2_{ij}+1)$$
$$C(i,j) = (c^1_{ij} \| c^2_{ij}) \oplus Zkey(i,j)$$

where C(i,j) is the (i,j)th pixel in the cipher image. This substitution makes the process a non linear operation and confusion is also obtained as the byte is XORed with the key.

3.4 Random Diffusion

The image is stored in a two dimensional array P of pixels. The proposed diffusion process is given by:

```
temp=P(1,1)
for i=1 to 256
for j=1 to 256
C(i,j)=temp ⊕ (P(1+(1*i+p* j)) mod 256, 1+(q* i+(p*q+1)*j) mod 256) ⊕ Ykey(i,j)
temp=C(i,j)
end
end
```

The above process makes diffusion among the pixels in a random fashion and makes the scheme more secure.

3.5 Rounds

The scheme can be used without iteration. However the above set of operations 3.2-3.4 can be iterated from first to last at least twice so as to strengthen against the adversaries attack on key retrieval.

4 Decryption

The decryption is performed in the reverse order. Instead of S-box, SInv is used for substitution. Also for the inverse permutation, the inverse of the matrix AInv is used for decryption.

$$
SInv=\begin{bmatrix}
15 & 1 & 3 & 2 & 4 & 16 & 5 & 6 & 7 & 8 & 9 & 10 & 11 & 12 & 13 & 14 \\
13 & 14 & 15 & 1 & 3 & 2 & 4 & 16 & 5 & 6 & 7 & 8 & 9 & 10 & 11 & 12 \\
5 & 6 & 7 & 8 & 9 & 10 & 11 & 12 & 13 & 14 & 15 & 1 & 3 & 2 & 4 & 16 \\
1 & 3 & 2 & 4 & 16 & 5 & 6 & 7 & 8 & 9 & 10 & 11 & 12 & 13 & 14 & 15 \\
12 & 13 & 14 & 15 & 1 & 3 & 2 & 4 & 16 & 5 & 6 & 7 & 8 & 9 & 10 & 11 \\
10 & 11 & 12 & 13 & 14 & 15 & 1 & 3 & 2 & 4 & 16 & 5 & 6 & 7 & 8 & 9 \\
9 & 10 & 11 & 12 & 13 & 14 & 15 & 1 & 3 & 2 & 4 & 16 & 5 & 6 & 7 & 8 \\
8 & 9 & 10 & 11 & 12 & 13 & 14 & 15 & 1 & 3 & 2 & 4 & 16 & 5 & 6 & 7 \\
7 & 8 & 9 & 10 & 11 & 12 & 13 & 14 & 15 & 1 & 3 & 2 & 4 & 16 & 5 & 6 \\
11 & 12 & 13 & 14 & 15 & 1 & 3 & 2 & 4 & 16 & 5 & 6 & 7 & 8 & 9 & 10 \\
14 & 15 & 1 & 3 & 2 & 4 & 16 & 5 & 6 & 7 & 8 & 9 & 10 & 11 & 12 & 13 \\
16 & 5 & 6 & 7 & 8 & 9 & 10 & 11 & 12 & 13 & 14 & 15 & 1 & 3 & 2 & 4 \\
4 & 16 & 5 & 6 & 7 & 8 & 9 & 10 & 11 & 12 & 13 & 14 & 15 & 1 & 3 & 2 \\
2 & 4 & 16 & 5 & 6 & 7 & 8 & 9 & 10 & 11 & 12 & 13 & 14 & 15 & 1 & 3 \\
3 & 2 & 4 & 16 & 5 & 6 & 7 & 8 & 9 & 10 & 11 & 12 & 13 & 14 & 15 & 1 \\
6 & 7 & 8 & 9 & 10 & 11 & 12 & 13 & 14 & 15 & 1 & 3 & 2 & 4 & 16 & 5
\end{bmatrix}
\text{ and } AInv=\begin{bmatrix} pq+1 & N-p \\ N-q & 1 \end{bmatrix}
$$

5 Security and Performance Analysis

In this section, we discuss the results of the security and performance analysis done on the proposed scheme.

5.1 Key Space

The chaotic function used in the proposed scheme uses a set of three initial values x0, y0, z0 as keys. These are float numbers and can be treated as 64 bit keys. In addition to these numbers some of the control parameters can also be treated as keys. By taking all these parameters into account, the number of keys ranges from 2198 to 2396. With such a large key space, the scheme will be able to resist against brute force attacks.

5.2 Histogram Analysis

An image histogram shows how pixels in an image are distributed by plotting the number of pixels at each grey level.

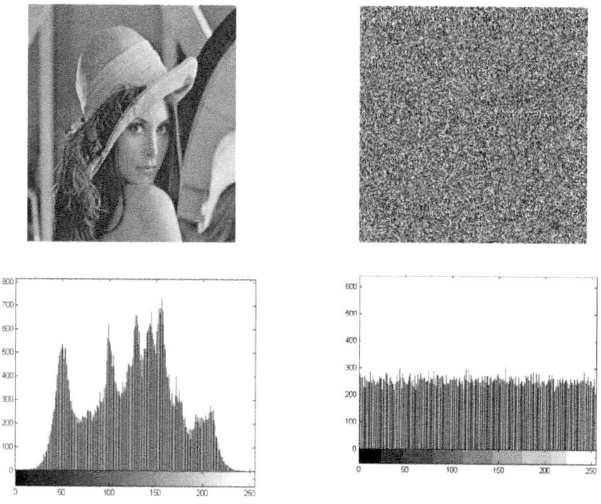

Fig. 2. Histogram of plain image Lena and its encrypted image

The Lena image is taken for analysis. The cipher image is created using the following set of keys: x0=0.41312738544343; y0=0.52625928350638; z0=0.98635737157599. The histograms of the original image and its corresponding encrypted image are shown in Fig. 2. It shows that the histogram of the encrypted image is fairly uniform and hence the scheme does not proved any clue to statistical attacks.

5.3 Correlation between Plain and Cipher Images

The correlation coefficient of the plain image and the corresponding cipher image is calculated as follows:

$$C = \frac{\frac{1}{H \times W}\sum_{i=1}^{H}\sum_{j=1}^{W}\left(P(i,j)-\bar{P}\right)\left(C(i,j)-\bar{C}\right)}{\sqrt{\left(\frac{1}{H \times W}\sum_{i=1}^{H}\sum_{j=1}^{W}\left(P(i,j)-\bar{P}\right)^{2}\right)\left(\frac{1}{H \times W}\sum_{i=1}^{H}\sum_{j=1}^{W}\left(C(i,j)-\bar{C}\right)^{2}\right)}}$$

where H and W are height and width of the image and P(i,j), C(i,j) denote the pixel values at position (i,j) in the original image and corresponding cipher image. We have used the float values x0=0.41312738544343; y0=0.52625928350638 and z0=0.98635737157599 as keys and then encrypted Lena image. The correlation coefficient between the original image and the corresponding cipher image is 0.0021. It is clear that the correlation coefficient is very small and hence there is no significant correlation between the plain image and corresponding cipher image.

5.4 Correlation of Adjacent Pixels

An ideal encryption scheme should produce the cipher images with no correlation in the adjacent pixels. If pi and ci denote the pair of horizontally/vertically adjacent pixels in an image, then the correlation between them is calculated using the following formula:

$$C = \frac{\frac{1}{N}\sum_{i=1}^{N}(p_i-\bar{p})(c_i-\bar{c})}{\sqrt{\frac{1}{N}\sum_{i=1}^{N}(p_i-\bar{p})^2\frac{1}{N}\sum_{i=1}^{N}(c_i-\bar{c})^2}}$$

where $\bar{p}$ and $\bar{c}$ are the averages of pi and ci respectively. The Lena image is taken for analysis and tested for horizontally and vertically adjacent pixels. The results are tabulated below:

Table 1.

	Original Image	Cipher Image
Horizontally Adjacent	0.9386	-0.0025
Vertically Adjacent	0.9689	-0.0075

Table 1 shows that the correlation of both horizontal as well as vertically adjacent pixels in the original image are closer to 1 but that of the encrypted image are very small. This shows that there is no correlation among horizontally/vertically adjacent pixels in the cipher image.

5.5 Differential Analysis

In order to perform either known plain text attack or chosen plain text attack, the adversary tries to make a slight change in the plain image and compares the corresponding cipher images. We have used the most common measures NPCR (Net Pixel Change Rate) and UACI (Unified Average Changing Intensity) to test whether there are any significant differences in the cipher images.

NPCR is defined as

$$NPCR = \frac{\sum_{i,j} D(i,j)}{W \times H} \times 100\%$$

where W and H are the width and height of two random images and D(i,j) is defined as

$$D(i, j) = \begin{cases} 0 \text{ if } C(i,j)=C'(i,j) \\ 1 \text{ if } C(i,j) \neq C'(i,j). \end{cases}$$

UACI is used to measure the average gray intensity difference between two cipher images C(i,j) and C'(i,j). It is defined as

$$UACI = \frac{1}{W \times H}\left[\sum_{i,j} \frac{|C(i,j)-C'(i,j)|}{2^L-1}\right] \times 100\%$$

where L is the number of bits used to represent the color component of red, green and blue respectively. The results of NPCR and UACI are presented in Table 2 for the different images.

Table 2. Sensitivity to cipher text

	NPCR %		UACI %	
Cipher Images	Proposed	Patidar et al[10]	Proposed	Patidar et al[10]
Lena	99.6132	99.0392	33.4291	33.4173
Baboon	99.6117	99.2676	33.4532	33.4292
House	99.6123	99.2676	33.4332	33.4292
Tree	99.6125	99.6084	33.4424	33.4365

In order to assess the influence of changing a single pixel in the original image on the encrypted image, the NPCR and the UACI are computed in the proposed scheme. It can be found that the NPCR is over 99% and the UACI is over 33%. The results show that a small change in the original image will result in a significant difference in the cipher-image, so the scheme proposed has a good ability to anti differential attack.

5.6 Information Entropy Analysis

Information entropy is one of the criteria to measure the strength of the cryptosystem in symmetric cryptosystem. The entropy H(m) of a message m can be calculated as:

$$H(m) = \sum_{i=0}^{2^{L-1}} p(m_i)\log\left(\frac{1}{p(m_i)}\right)$$

where p(mi) represents the probability of occurrence of symbol mi and log denotes the base 2 logarithm. If there are 256 possible outcomes of the message m with equal probability, it is considered as random. In this case, H(m)=8, is an ideal value. In the final round of proposed scheme, it is found that the value is 7.9974.

Table 3. The entropy analysis of the proposed and other schemes

Cipher	Proposed	Patidar et al.[10]
Lena	7.9974	7.9884

As shown in Table 3, we notice that the values obtained of our scheme are very close to the theoretical value of 8 than other schemes. This means that information leakage in the encryption process is negligible and the encryption system is secure upon entropy attack.

6 Conclusion

In this paper, a new image encryption scheme is proposed using twisted chaotic maps. The proposed cipher provides good confusion and diffusion properties that ensures high security. Confusion and diffusion have been achieved using permutation, byte substitution, nonlinear diffusion and random diffusion. This scheme is strong against various types of cryptographic attacks like known/chosen plaintext attacks and brute force attacks. The algorithm is tested for statistical analysis, key sensitivity analysis, key space analysis differential analysis and entropy analysis. Based on various analyzes, it is shown that the proposed scheme is more secure and fast and hence more suitable for real time image encryption for transmission applications.

References

1. Alvarez, G., Shujun, L.: Cryptanalyzing a nonlinear chaotic algorithm (NCA) for image encryption. Commun. Nonlinear Sci. Numer. Simulat. 14, 3743–3749 (2009)
2. Cokal, C., Solak, E.: Cryptanalysis of a chaos-based image encryption algorithm. Physics Letters A 373, 1350–1357 (2009)
3. Chen, G., Mao, Y., Chui, C.K.: A symmetric image encryption based on 3D chaotic cat maps. Chaos Solitons and Fractals 21, 749–761 (2004)
4. Fridrich, J.: Symmetric ciphers based on two-dimensional chaotic maps. Int. J. Bifurc Chaos 8(6), 1259–1284 (1998)
5. Guan, Z.H., Huang, F., Guan, W.: Chaos based image encryption algorithm. Phys. Lett. A 346, 153–157 (2005)
6. Li, C., Li, S., Lo, K.-T.: Breaking a modified substitution-diffusion image cipher based on chaotic standard and logistic maps. Commun. Nonlinear Sci. Numer. Simulat. (article in press), doi:10.1016/j.cnsns.2009.07.007
7. Li, C., Li, S., Alvarez, G., Chen, G., Lo, K.-T.: Cryptanalysis of two chaotic encryption schemes based on circular bit shift and XOR operations. Phys. Lett. A 369(1-2), 23–30 (2007)
8. Li, C., Li, S., Asim, M., Nunez, J., Alvarez, G., Chen, G.: On the security defects of an image encryption scheme. Image Vis. Comput. 27, 1371–1381 (2009)
9. Patidar, V., Pareek, N.K., Sud, K.K.: A new substitution diffusion based image cipher using chaotic standard and logistic maps. Commun. Nonlinear Sci. Numer. Simulat. 14(7), 3056–3075 (2009)

10. Patidar, V., Pareek, N.K., Purohit, G., Sud, K.K.: Modified substitution-diffusion image cipher using chaotic standard and logistic maps. Commun. Nonlinear Sci. Numer. Simulat. 15(10), 2755–2765 (2010)
11. Rhouma, R., Solak, E., Belghith, S.: Cryptanalysis of a new substitution-diffusion based image cipher. Commun. Nonlinear Sci. Numer. Simulat. 15(7), 1887–1892 (2010)
12. Shatheesh Sam, I., Devaraj, P., Bhuvaneswaran, R.S.: Enhanced substitution-diffusion based image cipher using improved chaotic map. In: Das, V.V., Vijaykumar, R. (eds.) ICT 2010. CCIS, vol. 101, pp. 116–123. Springer, Heidelberg (2010)
13. Sam, I.S., Devaraj, P., Bhuvaneswaran, R.S.: A novel image cipher based on mixed transformed logistic maps. In: Multimedia Tools and Applications. Springer, Heidelberg, doi:10.1007/s11042-010-0652-6
14. Xiaojun, T., Minggen, C.: Image encryption with compound chaotic sequence cipher shifting dynamically. Image Vision Comput. 26, 843–850 (2008)

Efficient Hardware Architectures for AES on FPGA

Nalini Iyer, P.V. Anandmohan, D.V. Poornaiah, and V.D. Kulkarni

BVBCET, Hubli, ECIL, Bangalore, ITI, Bangalore, Cg-coreel, Bangalore
nalinic@bvb.edu, anandmohanpv@hotmail.com,
poornaiah_dv@yahoo.co.in,
vdk@cg-coreel.com

Abstract. This paper presents design, implementation and comparison of highly efficient architectures for AES on FPGAS: Iterative architecture and pipelined architecture. The first design is optimized for area and the second one is optimized for speed. Implementation of AES algorithm involves design of two key functional operations namely Substitute Byte/InvSubstitute Byte and MixColumn/InvMixColumn in each round unit for encryption/decryption leading to area and speed bottlenecks.The suggested architectures exploit functional block resource sharing between encryption, decryption as well as on-the-fly key generation. Both designs use dedicated BRAM's for SubstituteByte/InvSubstituteByte functional blocks and combinational logic for MixColumn/InvMixColumn functions based on byte level decomposition. The two designs have been implemented on Xilinx Virtex II -XC2VP30 device. The Iterative architecture consumes 945 slices and 3 BRAM's and is more compact compared to the designs reported. The proposed pipelined architecture for improved throughput uses a total resource of 12556 slices and 100 BRAMs with a throughput of 47.7 Gbps , the fastest design reported so far. These designs cater to different applications from high performance e-commerce IPsec servers to low power mobile and home applications.

Keywords: Advanced Encryption Standard (AES), Cryptography, Rijndael, optimization, Field-Programmable Gate Array(FPGA), Block RAM(BRAM), Substitute Byte/Inverse Substitute Byte (SB/ISB), MixColumn/Inverse Mixcolumn (MC/IMC) , Shiftrow/InvShiftrow(SR/ISR).

1 Introduction

Data security is an important issue in many applications such as smart cards, hardware data encryptions and wireless communications. Rijndael's cipher developed by Joan Daemen and Vincent Rijmen accorded as standard for AES by (NIST) in November 2001, finds wide application in E-banking, Identity card, SIM card, network protocols, WWW servers and Automated Teller Machines (ATMs). The FPGA technology has much greater potential for providing higher security level because of its capability for dynamic reconfiguration. Many implementations have been carried out on FPGA for Rijndeal over recent years. Reported implementation of AES includes both iterative and pipelined structures.Zhang et al

V.V. Das and N. Thankachan (Eds.): CIIT 2011, CCIS 250, pp. 249–257, 2011.

[9], Hodjat and Verbauwhede [8] have reported pipelined architecture with 21.5Gbps throughput for high speed applications with high resources utilization. The on-the-fly implementation reported by Wang et al [6] utilized 5150 slices with increase in throughput to 9.72Gbps. The architecture suggested by Sklavas et al [3] used 2358 slices with reduced throughput of 259Mbps. The off-the-fly implementation suggested by Gaj et al[1] resulted in the area utilization of 2093 slices with increased throughput of 331Mbps. In this paper, two designs for AES, basic/iterative and pipelined architecture with encryptor/decryptor and on-the-fly key scheduler is proposed which exploits the use of embedded BRAMs to achieve high speed and compact size.

The main contribution of this paper can be summarized as follows. In this paper we exploit the implementation of two novel key operations, SB/ISB and MC/IMC operations in AES encryption and decryption resply with resource sharing.

SB/ISB operations using look-up tables is implemented on dedicated embedded block RAMs on a selected FPGA platform, as opposed to on-fly computation element using Galois field arithmetic. Similarly joint MC/IMC design is used for both encryption/decryption which leads to area reduction. AES SB/ISB-Box mapped to dual port BRAMs, reduces the area on device and results in less access time. In the present work, two types of architectures Iterative and Pipelined ,which exploits resource sharing between encryptor, decryptor and key scheduler and provides compact size and high throughput resply are proposed. The remainder of this paper is organized as follows. Section II, discusses the AES algorithm, section III proposed architectures for AES , section IV design of sub-functional unit and its optimizations. section V presents the implementation results and compare our results with existing ones, followed by conclusion.

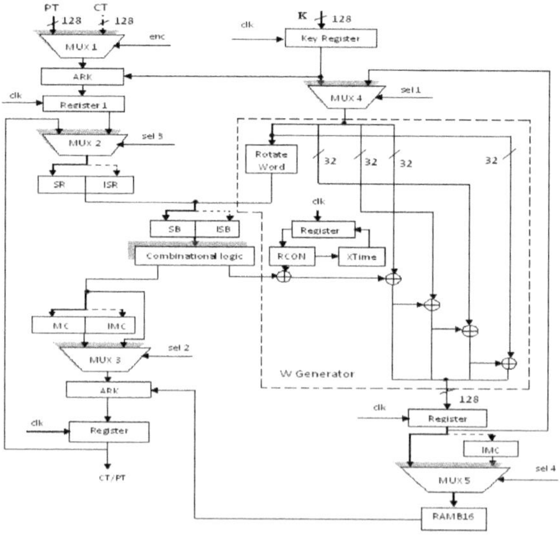

Fig. 1. Proposed Iterative AES Architecture with Encryptor, Decryptor and Key generator

2 AES Algorithm, Background

Rijndael algorithm is an iterated block cipher [1] supporting a variable data block and a variable key length of 128, 192 or 256 bits. The number of standard rounds depends on the data block and key length. If the maximum length of the data block or key is 128, 192 or 256, then the number of rounds is 10, 12 or 14, respectively. Each standard round includes four fundamental algebraic function transformations on arrays of bytes. These transformations are: byte substitution, shift row, mix column, and round Key addition. The final round of the algorithm is similar to the standard round, except that it does not have Mix Column operation. Decryption is performed by the application of the inverse transformations in the round functions, which are more complex than the corresponding transformation for encryption. The modified decryption process has the same sequence of transformation as that in the encryption process except for modified keys generated by applying additional Inverse MixColumn (IMC) transformations to the original round keys [2]. A generic Cores implemented from this architecture can perform both encryption and decryption catering to applications requiring different speed/area trade-offs.

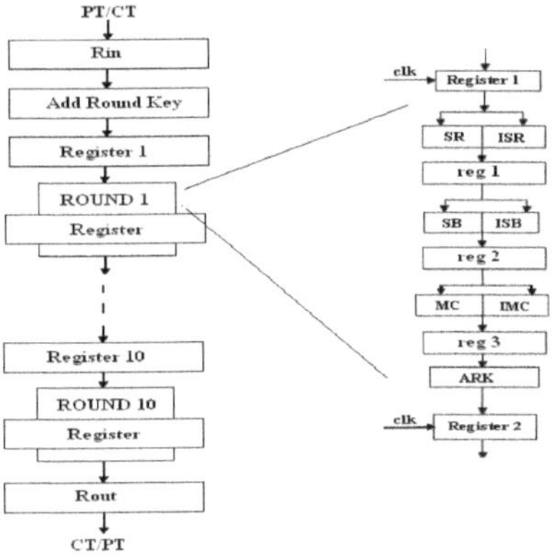

Fig. 2. Pipelined architecture showing the placement of registers between and within each round

3 Proposed Hardware Architectures

Two architectures are proposed for the Rijandael AES algorithm in order to reduce the required hardware resources and to obtain high speed performance. Both the architectures serve the encryption, decryption and key generation processes in the same hardware device.

Iterative Architecture: The compact architecture of AES proposed in this paper is an improved version of basic architecture suggested by [1]. The basic architecture unrolls only one full cipher round, and iteratively loops data through this round until the entire encryption or decryption transformation is completed. Only one block of data is processed at a time making it equally suited for feedback and non-feedback modes of operation. The structure of proposed architecture following the iterative looping and resource sharing between encryption/decryption and key generation is illustrated in fig 1. The architecture utilizes the pre-computed SB/ISB look-up table using BRAM's, SR/ISR using hardwiring and combined MC/IMC resulting in the resource sharing for both encryption and decryption

Path for encryption and decryption is differentiated by solid and dotted lines respectively as shown in fig 1. AES controller comprising of MUXs and Counters is used designed to generate select pins for the designed AES architecture.A multiplexer mux1 with select pin 'enc' is used to select the encryption/decryption path. The input 128 bit plain/cipher text is first XORed with the 128 bit input key K and stored in a 128 bit register 'Register 1'controlled by clock. Second multiplexer mux2 with select pin 'sel3' is used for iterative looping from round 1 to round 9. Initially sel3 is '0' till the completion of first round. Select pin 'sel3' is made high for rounds 2 to 9. The 128 bits from mux2 in each iteration undergoes the SR (ISR) transformation in encryption (decryption). In the proposed basic iterative architecture the same SB-Box is shared between AES encryptor and key generation module. This avoids using separate BRAMs for key generation and hence reducing the total number of BRAMs in the design making it more efficient for implementation. Combinational logic is a block which implements a counter. Since the BRAM used is a dual port and as we are using only one BRAM to implement SB/ISB-Box, time sharing has to be achieved to access different data from same output ports with respect to different counter values.All 16 bytes in AES cipher requires totally 8 clock cycles to get substituted with SB-Box, giving two bytes in each cycle as opposed to single port requiring 16 clock cycles with one byte in each clock cycle This is the advantage of using dual port than single port in BRAM and results in the reduction of clock cycles in the overall AES design, hence reducing the delay to generate cipher/plain text. The substituted values or SB(ISB)-box output undergo MixColumn (Inverse MixColumn) transformation. The multiplexer mux3 with select pin 'sel2' skips the MixColumn operation to perform the last round in the encryption/decryption. For AES from round 1 to 9, the sel2 is '0'. To perform the last round, sel2 is made high. In AES, MC and IMC are most complex transformations utilizing more hardware resources on FPGA in terms of slices and LUTs. The 128 bit result after this transformation is XORed with the corresponding keys computed and stored in RAMB16. The result after each round is stored in a 128 bit register. After the last round, the output register contains cipher/plain text.

Pipelined Architecture: The pipelining architecture offers the benefit of high speed performance. It unrolls the 10 AES rounds and pipelines them in order to optimize the frequency and throughput results. Pipelining can be explored in the proposed AES Architecture by duplicating the round architecture multiple times as demanded by optimum number of rounds (10 in this case) suggested in an algorithm to reduce the delay and hence increase the throughput at the cost of increase in area given in terms of resources required. Thus the proposed basic/Iterative Architecture shown in Fig.1 can be made fully pipelined by inserting registers between the rounds and also within the rounds, appropriately for each stage to store the intermediate results as illustrated in fig 2.

Key Generator: The Key Generator Module is responsible for generating the round keys and supplying these keys for the Encryption and Decryption. In the key scheduling data path, firstly the 128 bit key is separated into four 32-bit rows, and the lowest byte of each row is rotated and used as address to access the S-Box. Since the S-Box is not required in both encryption and key schedule simultaneously, it is possible to time share S-boxes between both circuits. This approach saves Block RAMs from being used in both circuits separately by having resource sharing. The returned 8-bit result from S-Box is XORed with the round constant RCON which is generated by RCON generator. This result is XORed with original lowest byte and sequentially each 32bit rows are XORed previous results. The unit that generates round keys is represented as W generator in Fig 1. The 128bit round key generated in each iteration is stored in a 128 bit register. In decryption, the round keys are obtained by applying the inverse Mix Column to the corresponding round keys of encryption. A multiplexer Mux5 with select pin 'sel5' is used to store the encryption and decryption keys in RAMB16. The advantage of storing round keys in BRAM than storing in registers is that the use of registers to store generated keys demands more number of slices thereby increasing the hardware resources on FPGA. The main advantage of this architecture is that the user can change the input keys depending on its application.

4 Design of Optimized Functional Operations

Substitute Byte/Inverse Substitute Byte Design

The substitute byte transformation uses SB-Box (ISB-Box) for encryption (decryption). In the proposed architecture, the Substitute Byte and Inverse Substitute Byte values are precomputed and directly mapped to the dedicated Block RAMs .The proposed architecture keep a good balance between utilization of LUTs and Block RAMs for the entire design, including combinational logic and memory on a target FPGA device. Each Block RAM represents a dual-port Memory of 1152 bits. Each port can be independently configured for different width and depth. We selected a dual port RAMB16 BRAM that provides access to the same memory space in the same way from both ports. A single Substitute Byte or Inverse Substitute Byte implementation requires a 256X8 ROM where 256 is the depth that is number of locations in BRAM and 8 is the data width. The S-Box values are stored from memory location 0 to 255 and inverse S-Box values from 256 to 511 .Each port has access to the entire memory space, and can perform a Substitute Bytes or Inverse Substitute Bytes transformation independently of each other. The Block RAM is a fully synchronous memory. Reading from it requires supplying the address one clock cycle before the data appears at the output. This feature can be viewed as a pipeline stage introducing a delay of one clock cycle.

Combined MixColumn/InverseMixColumn

Design Based on Byte Level Decomposition

In the proposed AES architecture an efficient MC/IMC implementation is derived by applying substructure sharing both to the computation within a byte and between the bytes in a given column of a MC/IMC state matrix Since Multiplication is distributive over addition in GF (28) we can decompose Mix column matrix as,

$$\begin{bmatrix} A_3 \\ A_2 \\ A_1 \\ A_0 \end{bmatrix} = \begin{bmatrix} 02 & 02 & 00 & 00 \\ 00 & 02 & 02 & 00 \\ 00 & 00 & 02 & 02 \\ 02 & 00 & 00 & 02 \end{bmatrix} \begin{bmatrix} B_3 \\ B_2 \\ B_1 \\ B_0 \end{bmatrix} + \begin{bmatrix} 00 & 01 & 01 & 01 \\ 01 & 00 & 01 & 01 \\ 01 & 01 & 00 & 01 \\ 01 & 01 & 01 & 00 \end{bmatrix} \begin{bmatrix} B_3 \\ B_2 \\ B_1 \\ B_0 \end{bmatrix}$$

$$a(x)*a^{-1}(x) = 1$$

$$a^{-1}(x) = a^{3}(x)$$

$$a\text{-}1(x) = a(x)*f(x)$$

$$f(x) = a^{2}(x) = \{04\}x^{2} + \{05\}. \tag{1}$$

Using the idea given in above Eq (1) suggested by Chowdeic et al [15] and Fischer et al [23], Inverse Mix column matrix can be decomposed in to product of MC and regular matrix consisting of variables {00},{05} and {04}, i.e.

$$\begin{bmatrix} c_3 \\ c_2 \\ c_1 \\ c_0 \end{bmatrix} = \begin{bmatrix} 02 & 03 & 01 & 01 \\ 01 & 02 & 03 & 01 \\ 01 & 01 & 02 & 03 \\ 03 & 01 & 01 & 02 \end{bmatrix} * \begin{bmatrix} 05 & 00 & 04 & 00 \\ 00 & 05 & 00 & 04 \\ 04 & 00 & 05 & 00 \\ 00 & 04 & 00 & 05 \end{bmatrix} \begin{bmatrix} B_3 \\ B_2 \\ B_1 \\ B_0 \end{bmatrix}$$

$$\begin{bmatrix} c_3 \\ c_2 \\ c_1 \\ c_0 \end{bmatrix} = \begin{bmatrix} A_3 \\ A_2 \\ A_1 \\ A_0 \end{bmatrix} \begin{bmatrix} 05 & 00 & 04 & 00 \\ 00 & 05 & 00 & 04 \\ 04 & 00 & 05 & 00 \\ 00 & 04 & 00 & 05 \end{bmatrix}$$

$$\begin{bmatrix} c_3 \\ c_2 \\ c_1 \\ c_0 \end{bmatrix} = \begin{bmatrix} 5A_3 + 4A_1 \\ 5A_2 + 4A_0 \\ 4A_3 + 5A_1 \\ 4A_2 + 5A_0 \end{bmatrix} \tag{2}$$

Using the following common sub expressions,
Z0 = 4(A3 + A1), Z1 = 4(A2 + A0), eq(2) can be written as

$$\begin{bmatrix} C_3 \\ C_2 \\ C_1 \\ C_0 \end{bmatrix} = \begin{bmatrix} A_3 + Z_0 \\ A_2 + Z_1 \\ A_1 + Z_0 \\ A_0 + Z_1 \end{bmatrix} \tag{3}$$

Multiplication by {02} and {04} can be implemented by X-Time and (X-Time)2 unit. Using the reduced expression for IMC given in (3),for a input state column with 4 bytes [B3 B2 B1 B0], Mixcolumn output is [A3 A2 A1 A0] and InvMixColumn output is [C3 C2 C1 C0] and is realized using 166 bit level XOR's with a critical path delay of 8XOR's as illustrated in Fig 3. MixColumn(InvMixcolumn) output is used for encryption(decryption) .

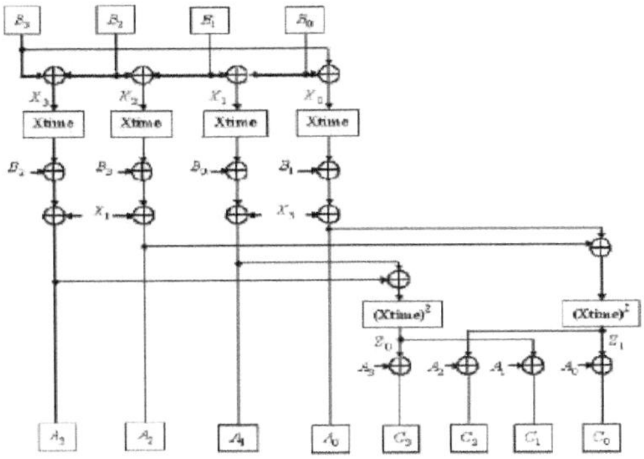

Fig. 3. Combined MC/IMC design with decomposition based on byte level resource sharing

5 Experimental Results and Comparison with Other Designs

The proposed designs have been implemented on Xilinx XC2VP30-5ff896 device and simulated and verified using ISE simulator in ISE 10.1 environment on Virtex II Pro FPGA Programmable platform. Different modes, different choices of operation such as encryption, decryption, key generation lead to different throughput and hardware overheads of a particular design in a particular device.Eventhough it is difficult to have fair comparison of the existing designs with our suggested design, we have attempted it relatively in terms of target devices, modes of operation and different choices of operation. In Table 1 and Table 2 we illustrate the comparative analysis of different existing architectures along with our suggested design for Iterative (Compact) and Pipelined (Fast) Architecture using Xilinx Virtex devices. The AES design using proposed iterative arch uses 945 slices (6%) and 3 BRAMs (2%) to achieve a throughput of 86Mbps with logical delay of 3.139ns and route delay of 3.881ns and is compact in size as compared to other similar reported designs. The design using pipelined structure uses 12556+100BRAM and provides a throughput of 47.74gbps and is the fastest among the reported designs so far.

Table 1. Comparison of proposed Iterative (Compact) Architecture with reported design

Design	Mode	Device	Freq(Mhz)	Throughput(Mbp)	Area(Slices)	Throughput/Slice
Rady [4]	E/D/K	XC3S400	45	10	2699+2BRAM	0.003
Gaj [1]	E/D	XCV1000	25.9	331	2902	0.14
Nazar [5]	E/K	XCV812	20.2	258.5	2744	0.09
Dandalis [2]	E/K	XCV1000	27.5	353	5673	0.06
Chitu [7]	E/D/K	XC2V1000	75	739	4325+1BRAM	0.17
Monjar[24]	**E/D**	XCV1000e-8	135	432	622	0.69
Proposed (Iterative)	E/D/K	XC2VP30	188	86	945+3BRAM	0.09

Table 2. Comparison of proposed Pipelined(Fast) Architecture with Reported Pipelined design

Design	Mode	Device	Freq(Mhz)	Throughput(Mbps)	Area(Slices)	Throughput /Slice
Mcloone [10]	E/K	XCV812E	54.3	6956	2222+100BRAM	3.1
Mcloone [11]	E	XCV812E	93.9	12020	2000+244BRAM	4.7
Tommiska [12]	E/K	XCV1000	129.2	16500	11719	1.4
Saggese [13]	E	XCV2000	158.5	20300	5810+100BRAM	3.4
Xhang [9]	E/D	XCV1000	168.4	21550	11022	1.95
Good [14]	E	XC2S15	72.3	218	122+2BRAM	1.78
Kaur [16]	E/D/K	XC2VP70	119.9	1180	6279+5BRAM	0.187
Standaert [19]	E/K	XCV1000	172	22000	17984	1.22
Wang [17]	E/D/K	XCV812E	61	1952	3046+280BRAM	0.64
Hodjat [18]	E	XC2VP20	169	21640	9446	2.29
Standaert [20]	E	XCV3200	145	18560	15112	1.288
Zambreno [21]	E/K	XC2V4000	184	23570	16938	1.3
Kotturi [22]	E/D	XC2VP70	125.3	16080	5408+200BRAM	2.97
Proposed (Pipelined)	E/D/K	XC2VP30	373	47744	12556+100BRAM	3.8

6 Conclusion

In this paper we presented a single chip encryptor/decryptor solution for AES using two architectures leading to compact size and high throughput resply.The design exploits the resource sharing by reutilizing the integrated blocks of SB/ISB, SR/ISR and MC/IMC. The architecture used the precomputed values of SB-Box and ISB-Box mapped to the BRAMs of FPGA.. The resulting implementation uses less area on FPGA making it more suitable for embedded applications.

References

1. Gaj, K., Chodowiec, P.: Comparison of the Hardware Performance of the AES Candidates using Reconfigurable Hardware. In: The Third Advanced Encryption Standard (AES3) Candidate Conference, New York, USA, pp. 13–14 (2000)
2. Dandalis, A., Prasanna, V.K., Rolim, J.D.P.: A Comparative Study of Performance of AESCandidates Using FPGAs. In: The Third Advanced Encryption Standard (AES3) Candidate Conference, New York, USA, pp. 13–14 (2000)
3. Sklavos, N., Koulopavlou, O.: Architecture and VLSI Implemenation of the AES-Proposal Rijindael. IEEE Transactions on Computers 51(12), 1454–1459 (2002)
4. Rady, A., El Sehely, E., El Hennawy, A.M.: Design and Implementation of area optimized AES algorithm on reconfigurable FPGA. In: IEEE ICM (2007)
5. Saqib, N.A., Rodriguez-Henriquez, F., Diaz-Perez, A.: AES Algorithm Implementation—An efficient approach for Sequential and Pipeline Architectures. In: Proceedings of the Fourth Mexican International Conference on Computer Science, ENC 2003 (2003)
6. Wang, S.-S., Ni, W.-S.: An Efficient FPGA Implementation of Advanced Encryption Standard Algorithm. In: ISCAS, vol. 2, pp. 597–600 (2004)
7. Chitu, C., Chien, D., Chien, C., Verbauwhede, I., Chang, F.: A Hardware Implementation in FPGA of the Rijndael Algorithm, vol. 1, pp. 507–510 (2002)
8. Hodjat, A., Verbauwhede, I.: A 21.54 Gbits/s fully pipelined AES processor on FPGA. In: Proc.12th Annual IEEE Symp: Field- Programmable Custom Computing Machines, FCCM, Napa,CA, USA, pp. 308–309 (2004)

9. Zhang, X., Parhi, K.K.: High-speed VLSI architectures for the AES algorithm. IEEE Trans. Very Large Scale Integration (VLSI) Syst. 12(9), 957–967 (2004)
10. McLoone, M., McCanny, J.V.: High performance single-chip FPGA rijndael algorithm implementations. In: Koç, Ç.K., Naccache, D., Paar, C. (eds.) CHES 2001. LNCS, vol. 2162, pp. 65–76. Springer, Heidelberg (2001)
11. McLoone, M., McCanny, J.V.: Rijndael FPGA implementation utilizing look-up tables. In: Proc. 2001 IEEE Workshop on Signal Processing Systems, SIPS 2001, Antwerp, Belgium, pp. 349–360 (September 2001)
12. Jarvinen, K.U., Tommiska, M.T., Skytta, J.O.: A fully pipelined memoryless 17.8 Gbps AES-128 encryptor. In: Proc. Int. Symp. Field-Programmable Gate Arrays (FPGA 2003), Monterey, CA, pp. 207–215 (February 2003)
13. Saggese, G.P., Mazzeo, A., Mazzocca, N., Strollo, A.G.M.: An FPGA-Based Performance Analysis of the Unrolling, Tiling and Pipelining of the AES Algorithm. In: Y. K. Cheung, P., Constantinides, G.A. (eds.) FPL 2003. LNCS, vol. 2778, pp. 292–302. Springer, Heidelberg (2003)
14. Chodowiec, P., Gaj, K.: Very Compact FPGA Implementation of the AES Algorithm. In: Walter, C.D., Koç, Ç.K., Paar, C. (eds.) CHES 2003. LNCS, vol. 2779, pp. 319–333. Springer, Heidelberg (2003)
15. Good, T., Benaissa, M.: Very Small FPGA Application-Specific Instruction Processor for AES. IEEE Transactions on Circuits and Systems 53(7) (July 2006); regular papers
16. Kaur, S., Vig, R.: Efficient Implementation of AES Algorithm in FPGA Device. In: International Conference on Computational Intelligence and Multimedia Applications 2007, pp. 179–187. IEEE Computer Society (2007)
17. Wang, J.-F., Chang, S.-W., Lin, P.-C.: A Novel Round Function Architecture for AES Encryption/Decryption utilizing Look-Up_Table, pp. 132–136. IEEE (2003)
18. Hodjat, A., Verbauwhede, I.: A 21.54 Gbits/s fully pipelined AES processor on FPGA. In: Proc. 12th Annual IEEE Symp. Field- Programmable Custom Computing Machines, FCCM 2004, Napa, CA, USA, pp. 308–309 (April 2004)
19. Standaert, F.X., Rouvoy, G., Quisquater, J.J., Legat, J.D.: A Methodology to Implement Block Ciphers in Reconfigurable Hardware and its Application to Fast and Compact AES Rijndael. In: Proc. of FPGA 2003, pp. 216–224. ACM (2003)
20. Standaert, F.-X., Rouvroy, G., Quisquater, J.-J., Legat, J.-D.: Efficient Implementation of Rijndael Encryption in Reconfigurable Hardware: Improvements and Design Tradeoffs. In: Walter, C.D., Koç, Ç.K., Paar, C. (eds.) CHES 2003. LNCS, vol. 2779, pp. 334–350. Springer, Heidelberg (2003)
21. Zambreno, J., Nguyen, D., Choudhary, A.K.: Exploring Area/Delay Tradeoffs in an AES FPGA Implementation. In: Becker, J., Platzner, M., Vernalde, S. (eds.) FPL 2004. LNCS, vol. 3203, pp. 575–585. Springer, Heidelberg (2004)
22. Kotturi, D., Yoo, S.-M., Blizzard, J.: AES Crypto chip Utilizing High Speed Parallel Pipelined Architecture, pp. 4653–4656 (2005)
23. Fischer, V., Drutarovsky, M., Chodowiec, P.: InvMixcolumn Decomposition and Multilevel Resource Sharing in AES Implementation. IEEE Trans. on VLSI Systems 13(8), 989–992 (2005)
24. Alam, M., Ghosh, S., RoyChowdhury, D., Sengupta, I.: Single chip Encryptor/Decryptor Core Implementation of AES Algorithm. In: Proc. 21st Int. Conf. on VLSI Design, pp. 693–698
25. Daemen, J., Rijmen, V.: AES submission document on Rijndael, Version 2 (September 1999), `http://csrc.nist.gov/CryptoToolkit/aes/rijndael/Rijndael.pdf`

Iris Recognition Using DCT

Rahesha Mulla and Amrita Manjrekar

Department of Computer Science & Technology, Shivaji University, Kolhapur, India
raheshamulla@gmail.com, amrita5551@gmail.com

Abstract. This paper presents an iris coding method for effective recognition of an individual. The recognition is performed based on a mathematical and computational method called discrete cosine transform (DCT). It consists of calculating the differences of discrete cosine transform (DCT) coefficients of overlapped angular patches from the normalized iris image for the purpose of feature extraction. DCT is used because it offers efficiency, it is much more practical and its basis vectors are comprised of entirely real-valued components.

Keywords: DCT (Discrete Cosine Transform), Iris, Recognition.

1 Introduction

Iris recognition belongs to the biometric identification. Biometric identification is a technology that is used for the identification an individual based on ones physiological or behavioral characteristics. Iris is the strongest physiological feature for the recognition process because it offers most accurate and reliable results. Iris recognition process mainly involves three stages namely, iris image preprocessing, feature extraction and template matching. In the pre-processing step, iris localization algorithm is used to locate the inner and outer boundaries of the iris. Detected iris region is then normalized to a fixed size rectangular block. In the feature extraction step, texture analysis method is used to extract significant features from the normalized iris image with the help of Discrete Cosine Transform (DCT) and Hanning window techniques. The matching step consists of the classification method, which is used to compare binary templates generated from the feature extraction method with existing one. Iris recognition technology combines computer vision, pattern recognition, statistical inference and optics. Its purpose is real-time, high confidence recognition of a person's identity by mathematical analysis of the patterns that are visible within the iris of an eye from some distance. Iris recognition technology covers broad areas of applications. Some of applications are as follows:

- Electronic commerce–On-line transactions
- Medical records and other personal information
- Security identification – Access control
- User verification – Computer security

This paper is subdivided into different sections as follows. Section 2 describes the iris recognition system comprising Localization and normalization, feature extraction and

V.V. Das and N. Thankachan (Eds.): CIIT 2011, CCIS 250, pp. 258–263, 2011.

template matching in order to accomplish an identification and recognition. Section 3 gives the experimental evaluation of the underlying system and Section 4 presents the conclusion of the organized work.

2 Iris Recognition Systems

Iris recognition system is used for personal identification or verification. The three main stages of an iris recognition system are localization and normalization, feature extraction, template matching. The block diagram of iris recognition system is given in figure 1.

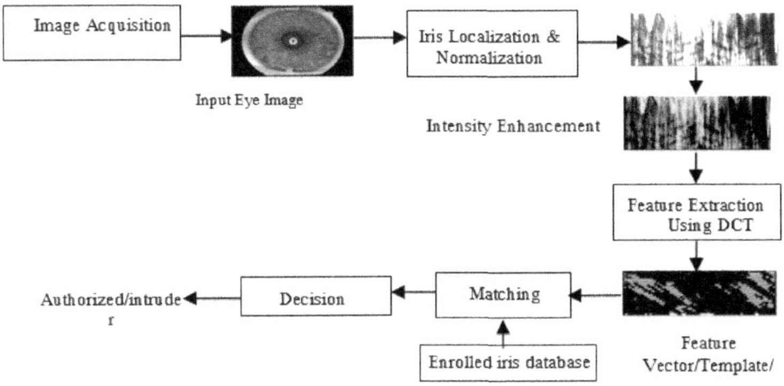

Fig. 1. Block diagram of Iris Recognition System

2.1 Iris Localization and Normalization

Iris image pre-processing basically consist of iris boundary detection (inner iris/pupil boundary and outer iris/sclera boundary) called as iris localization and then normalization. The Hough transform, standard computer vision algorithm is used for locating the iris. Canny edge detector is applied to a gray scale iris image to generate the edge map. The edge map is obtained by calculating the first derivative of intensity values and thresholding the results. Gaussian filter is applied for smoothing purpose. The voting procedure is used in order to search for the desired contour from the edge map. Each edge point on the circle casts a vote in Hough space. The center coordinate and radius of the circle with maximum number of votes is defined as the contour of interest. Gradient is biased in the vertical direction for the outer iris/sclera boundary. Vertical and horizontal gradient is weighted equally for the inner iris/pupil boundary giving required iris region [4]. Next step is to transform the obtained iris region to a rectangular representation with fixed dimensions. Such a transformation is referred to as normalization of the iris region. Normalization is performed to avoid the dimensional inconsistencies otherwise resulting deformation of the iris texture will affect the performance of subsequent feature extraction and matching stages of iris recognition [3].

Normalization is a process of remapping Cartesian coordinates *(x, y)* of iris region to its corresponding polar representation as:

$$I\big(x\,(r,\theta), y\,(r,\theta)\big) \rightarrow I\,(r,\theta) \tag{1}$$

with

$$\begin{aligned} x(r,\theta) &= (1-r)x_p\,(\theta) + r x_l\,(\theta); \\ y(r,\theta) &= (1-r)y_p\,(\theta) + r y_l\,(\theta) \end{aligned} \tag{2}$$

where, $I(x, y)$ is the iris region image, (x, y) are the original Cartesian coordinates, (r, θ) are the corresponding normalized polar coordinates, and x_p, y_p and x_l, y_l are the coordinates of the pupil and iris boundaries respectively along the Θ direction [2].

2.2 Feature Extraction Using DCT

Iris is coded based on zero crossing of the differences between one dimensional (1D) discrete cosine transform (DCT) coefficients of rectangular patches. This method gives low complexity and good interclass separation. Image patches are formed using bands of pixels along 45 degree lines through the image.

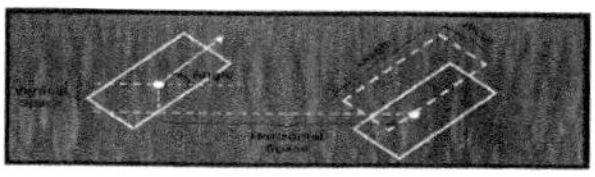

Fig. 2. Overlapped angular patches in normalized iris region [1]

Figure 2 shows overlapping angular patches in normalized iris region with different parameters. Idea is to slew each successive row of the image by one pixel compared to its predecessor. Patches are selected in 11 overlapping horizontal bands. Each patch has eight pixels vertically and 12 horizontally. In the horizontal direction, a weighted average under a 1/4 Hanning window is formed. In effect, the resolution in the horizontal direction is reduced by this step. Averaging across the width of the patch reduces the degrading effects of noise and the use of broad patches makes for easier iris registration. In the vertical direction (45 degrees from the iris radial), eight pixels from each patch form a 1D patch vector, which is then windowed using a similar Hanning window prior to application of the DCT in order to reduce spectral leakage during the transform[1]. A binary template is generated from the zero crossings of the differences between the DCT coefficients.

2.3 Template Matching

1) Hamming Distance: It is used as a template matching metric which gives the fractional measure of dissimilarity between two binary templates [3].It is defined as

HD = [M π ∑Nj=1 [subfeatures1ij XOR subfeature2 ij / N] 1/M (3)

Iris code is represented as a rectangular block of size $M \times N$. M is the number of bits per subfeature and N is the total number of subfeatures in a feature vector. Corresponding subfeature bits are XORed and the resultant N-length vector is summed and normalized by dividing by N. This is done for all M subfeature bits and the geometric mean of these M sums give the normalized HD lying in the range of 0 to 1. In case of perfect match, all M sums are 0 and so is the HD, while, for a total opposite, where MN/N^s are obtained with a final HD of 1. Since a total bit reversal is highly unlikely, it is expected that a random pattern difference should produce an HD of around 0.5. Using the HD of two bit patterns, a decision can be made as whether the two patterns were generated from different irises or from the same one [4]. Sample templates and corresponding HD is given below:

Template1:10 00 11 00 10 01	Template2:00 11 00 10 01 10	⇨	HD=0.83

As HD=0.83, person is recognized as an authorized one. The weighted Euclidean distance (WED) is also used as a classifier to compare two templates (integer/non binary data) to identify an iris. The WED is defined as,

$$WED(K) = \sum_{i=0}^{n} \frac{(fi - fik)^2}{(\delta ik)^2} \tag{4}$$

where, fi is the ith feature of unknown iris, f_i^k is the ith feature of iris template k and δ_i^k is the standard deviation of the ith feature in iris template k. When WED is a minimum at k, the unknown iris template is found to match iris template k.

2) Feature Fusion: The weighted Euclidean distance and the hamming distance are applied to the templates in order to match and classify based on threshold values. The expression of classifier fusion is

$$\text{Result} = \begin{matrix} 0 & WED \geq t1 \\ HD & t2 \leq WED \geq t1 \\ 1 & WED < t2 \end{matrix} \tag{5}$$

As value is between the threshold t1 and t2, local feature is considered to match for classification.

3 Experimental Evaluations

The experimental results presented here describe the steps in an iris recognition system. To determine the recognition performance of the system, database of 160 eye images were used. The system consists of segmentation using canny edge detection and Hough transform, to locate the circular iris and pupil region.

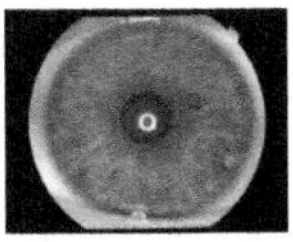

Fig. 3. Original iris image

Fig. 4. Canny edge detection

Fig. 5. Hough transform

The extracted iris region was then normalized into a rectangular block with constant dimensions.

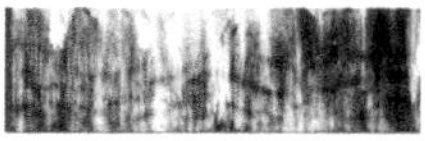

Fig. 6. Normalized iris region

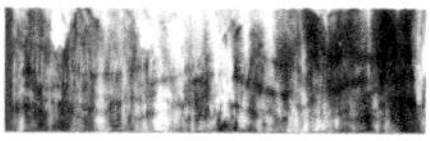

Fig. 7. Intensity Enhancement

Feature extraction method involves application of 1D DCT and hanning window to generate feature vector and encoding of the unique pattern into a template.

Fig. 8. Overlapped patches

Fig. 9. Hanning window (H)

Fig. 10. Hanning window (V)

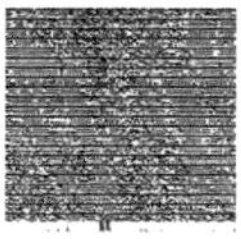

Fig. 11. 1D DCT difference o/p

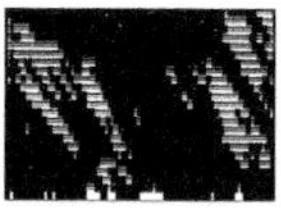

Fig. 12. Feature vector

The Hamming distance method was preferred for matching of iris templates and two templates were found to match if a test of statistical independence was failed. Perfect recognition was found on 140 iris images.

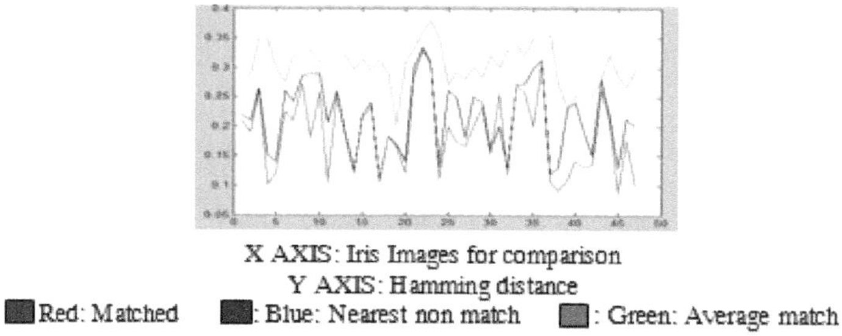

Fig. 13. Hamming Graph (Overall dataset)

4 Conclusion

In this paper we have presented DCT-based iris recognition system for identification and verification of a person for the security purpose. Proposed system makes use of effective and robust algorithms at various steps and is implemented on MATLAB platform. Template matching process is coded as a C program. From the results obtained we can conclude that the system presented is reliable, secure and can easily be implemented for highly secure and critical areas.

References

1. Monro, D.M., Rakshit, S., Zhang, D.: DCT-Based Iris Recognition
2. Masek, L.: Recognition of Human Iris Patterns for Biometric Identification
3. Ng, R.Y.F., Tay, Y.H., Mok, K.M.: Computer Vision and Intelligent Systems (CVIS) Group, University Tunku Abdul Rahman, Malaysia richng01@yahoo.com, A Review of Iris Recognition Algorithms
4. Gupta, S., Doshi, V., Jain, A., Iyer, S.: Iris Recognition System using Biometric Template Matching Technology
5. Khayam, S.A.: Department of Electrical & Computer Engineering Michigan State University, The Discrete Cosine Transform (DCT): Theory and Application (March 10, 2003)
6. Watson, A.B.: NASA Ames Research Center. Transform Mathematical Journal 4(1), 81–88 (1994): Image Compression Using the Discrete Cosine

Eye Dialing: A Comprehensive Approach towards Maximum Security

Mudit Srivastava[1] and Akansha Srivastava[2]

[1] Electrical and Electronics, BITS Pilani Hyderabad Campus, Hyderabad, India
mdt.srivastava@gmail.com
[2] Computer Science, TGT- BrightLand School, Ghaziabad, India
akanksha.sri23@gmail.com

Abstract. This paper presents a novel and practical approach towards attaining maximum security in case of high security zones where security breach is a concerning factor. This paper brings forth a completely new yet easily applicable product which has no loopholes of being cracked from an outsider. It uses the concept of tracking the movement of the eye over the sequence of generated password and comparison to the base image for password matching. The system involves more security by including the existing levels of security viz face recognition and retina scanning and then going for tracking eye movement. The system is assisted with random number generation algorithm which further advances the level of tight security.

Keywords: eye movement tracking, facial recognition, retina scanner, image processing, computer vision, random number generation, efficient security.

1 Introduction

Since the advancement in technologies there has been a major improvement on how to make things of high value more secure and less prone to any misuse. Thus security has been an area of maximum concern. But, no matter how highly secure a system can be made or developed; possibility of security breach [2] is always there. Our idea is to minimize this possibility as much as we can so that the resources of a country/organization can be well protected. Many advance technology based security system are in use now a days. UNICODE [3] is the most traditional and commonly used procedure where data is encoded with the help of special characters. But one of the biggest drawbacks with this is that its incorrect usage may expose the program or system to possible security attacks. Another technology is voice / speech recognition system [4], which is again commonly used due to its 'easy-to-implement' feature. But the key problem here is to maintain a huge amount of database. Also word error rates on some tasks are less than 1% and on others they can be as high as 50%. Sometimes it even appears that the performance is going backwards on harder tasks due to higher error rates.

Biometric security systems [5] are also getting recognition but they have not proved to be successful approach so far. This is because it is possible that the data

V.V. Das and N. Thankachan (Eds.): CIIT 2011, CCIS 250, pp. 264–269, 2011.

obtained during biometric enrollment may be used in ways for which enrolled individual has not consented. Second and most serious one is that there is always a danger to the owner of secured item. For instance in 2005, [1] Malaysian car thieves cut off the finger of a Mercedes-Benz S-Class owner when attempted to steal the car.

Our idea aims at developing a security system which authorizes a person and accepts the password by analyzing the movement of eyes. The system is provided with a chin-rest arrangement which would act as a fixed location from where our system will first scan the face then the eyes using the face detection and retina scanning algorithms. If these two input matches with that of an authorized user (from database) then system will ask to enter the password. If at any point, our system finds a mismatch or password entered by the user is in reverse order or password entered is that of system administrator, a security alarm will be send to control room. An authorized user is allowed three attempts to enter the password, after that the password will be locked and the user will have to contact the system administrator.

The best advantage of our system is its high level of security because system will authorize a person to get into the area if he has entered correct password through eyes. The password will be tracked with the help of movement of eyes and not just fixed eye. Secondly, if someone forces the user to enter the password, then he has an option to enter the password in reverse order which will send an emergency alarm to the control room. Our system will also overcome the disadvantage of biometric security system where there is always a danger for owner. In our system it will not work because no one can move a dead eye's eyeball. And even in any hypothetical situation the person makes the dead eye move by any modern technique; the person will not be able to open the security lock due to our 'random number generation algorithm'. This algorithm proves such beneficial in this context that even if the person gets to know the password by any chance; the person will not be able to open the security system by just tracking any eye over the same password.

2 Main Components of the System

Our idea is to provide maximum security and in order to provide this we require five main components. All these components play vital role in proper functioning of the system and are chosen among their alternatives because of their efficiency and accuracy in providing the results. We will now see how each of these components work individually, and how they are integrated together in the 'Working Mechanism' section.

2.1 Concave Panel

There will be a concave panel, with alphabets (a-z) and numbers (0-9) inscribed on it, which will act as a template to enter the password. A concave shaped panel is advisable because of our authorization process which deals with a security system that works on movement of the authorized person's eyeball. It will increase the binocular field (total area covered by human eyes at a point) of eyes and hence will help to increase the accuracy of our system.

2.2 High Definition (HD) Camera

We require a HD Camera with high display resolution (at least 1080 lines and above), good progressive scanning, which yields to good number of frames per second (1080p & higher are preferred). Since it plays a vital role in providing input to our system hence it should be fit even to work in low light & features like long zoom, optical zoom & image stabilization are must. The camera must also have auto-focus facility so as to execute the 'random number generation algorithm'.

2.3 Display Screen

Display screen is required to make our system more user- friendly. At the starting point it will display a message which will ask user to place his chin on the chinrest. Once the person has kept his chin on chin rest and passed the two levels of security viz. facial recognition and retina scanner; it will display message to "Enter the Password" and will continue to display different messages according to various inputs and will display the number of character entered through asterisk sign.

2.4 Memory

Memory in our system refers to physical device which will be used to store data and programs on a temporary or permanent basis for use in our security system. Data in our system will be a series of coordinates which will be required to identify the character or number which the user is viewing at the time of entering the password. This combination of coordinates will be unique for each random number in accordance with the 'random number generation algorithm'. Programs are sequence of instruction which our system has to follow while conducting an authorization process of the person.

2.5 Chin Rest Arrangement

Chin rest arrangement is the same which we all have seen in eye doctor's clinic, where we have to keep our chin so that doctor can inspect our eyes. This arrangement will give our camera a fixed and standard location, from where it can scan for eyes of the user and track its coordinates while moving the eyes on the panel.

3 Working Mechanism

3.1 When the eye-dialing security system is turned on, the initialization process occurs in which the chin-rest is opened at the specified distance and the camera is ready to capture the video feed.

3.2 As soon as the person rests his/her chin on the chin-rest, the system executes its face detection algorithm [7]. This face detection algorithm runs on Principle Component Analysis. Hence when the face is authenticated, a green LED blinks to signal the user for the second level of security.

3.3 The camera which has autofocus ability; now scans the retina of the eye and compares it with the earlier scanned images in the database using retina scanning technology[6]. If it matches, again a green LED blinks to allow the user to enter the password.

3.4 If any of the above mentioned security checks are failed; an emergency signal is being sent to the control station and other necessary security steps are taken. The concept of having chin-rest in the system is to ensure proper detection of the movement of the eye in real time during entering the password.

3.5 The [8] code for tracking the movement of the eye is based on tracking the coordinates of the eye. Every time the eyes roll to see the panel on the number palate. Hence this code depends upon the horizontal positioning of the eye as the datum level with respect to which the coordinates of the all the characters are fixed. While rolling the eye over the characters on the panel, its movement is tracked.

3.6 Since the panel is slightly concave in appearance, so for better results the complete panel is captured in panoramic view. This image serves as the "base image" for comparison. So when the camera tracks the coordinates of the pupil of the eye, those coordinates are being stored and are being compared from the predefined ones available in the database.

3.7 With acceptable tolerance, if the coordinates matches, a beep sound occurs and the tracked character is shown in asterisk form in the display screen. The user is required to roll over his eye on the required character in the time span of less than 1 second in order to maintain security. If the time exceeds 1 sec, the system takes it as a case of 'forgot password' or 'random entering'.

3.8 In such case, the system gives a long beep for 2 sec with the blinking of RED led and displays the error message to "reenter the password". The numbers of attempts are restricted to 'three' for security purposes. Beyond that the system gets locked and the warning signal is sent to control station.

3.9 For proper functioning, the user is required to focus on each character while rolling the eye during entering the password so that stray detection losses can be minimized.

3.10 The system is also designed with more advanced level of securities like if the person is forcefully made to enter the password, the person just needs to track the password through his/her eyes in exact opposite direction. In such case the system will open the vaults but also simultaneously will send an emergency situation message to the control station.

3.11 One very striking feature of our system design is the concept of 'random number generation'. In this algorithm, the system every time generates a new random number when someone comes to enter the password.

3.12 The utility of this 'random number generation' algorithm is that every time a new random number is generated; the camera which has autofocus capability focuses itself to a new horizontal position with respect to chin-rest. Since the coordinates of the character on the control panel which are to be tracked, depends upon the horizontal distance; hence for each random number a horizontal distance is fixed.

3.13 With respect to that horizontal distance the coordinates for all the character in the panel are stored in the database and are being retrieved for comparison for a particular random number during execution. Hence the system is designed to provide maximum security with no hit and trial algorithms and maximum precision.

4 Flowcharts

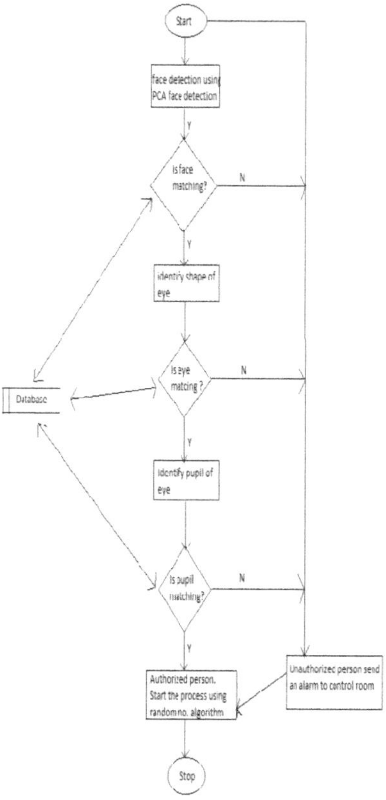

4.1 Levels of Entry

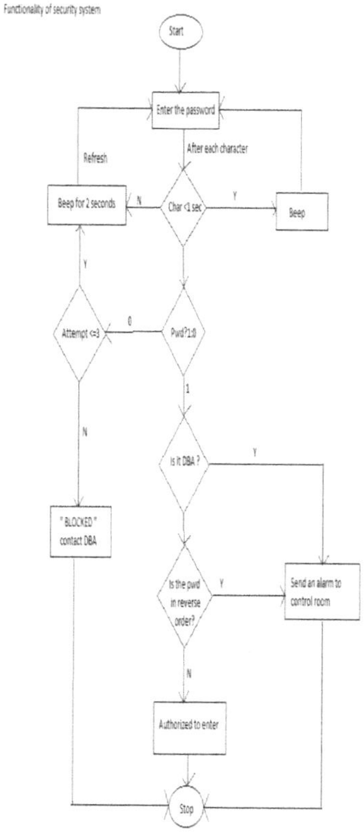

4.2 Authorization Process

5 Conclusion

This paper brings out an effective algorithm to attain highest level of security where security breach is still an area to be curbed. The paper brings forth the concept of tracking the movement of eye over the set of characters which form your password to pass a particular level of security and hence called eye dialing. The system is also integrated with already existing retina scanning and facial recognition technology to make system more secure and avoid any misuse. Also the system contains random number generation algorithm which makes it next to impossible for any person to track the password on the basis of coordinates even if the database is hacked. Some more advanced security features like entering of password in exact reverse manner will send and alert message is discussed. The system has been tested using system webcam with the algorithm implemented in visual c++. Further advancement in this system will add to its merits.

Acknowledgement. The authors want to thank Mr. Achintya Dixit, Mr. Shubhansh Srivastava and Mrs. Vimmi Srivastava for helping in catering through the loop holes at every stage of the project. The authors also wish to convey thanks to Mr. Zafar Savas, the developer of track eye demo software available on Code project.com for giving the required direction to work upon through this software. Lastly the authors wish to convey gratitude to their parents and god for making this project into reality.

References

1. Kent, J.: Malaysia car thieves steal finger. BBC Online (Kuala Lumpur) (March 31, 2005) (retrieved December 11, 2010)
2. http://www.businessdictionary.com/definition/security-breach.html
3. http://en.wikipedia.org/wiki/Unicode, http://unicode.org/standard/WhatIsUnicode.html
4. http://en.wikipedia.org/wiki/Speech_recognition
5. http://en.wikipedia.org/wiki/Biometrics1
6. Retina Scanning Anti-theft device. A Wolfsen - US Patent 5,845,733,1998 - Google Patents
7. Gottumukkal, R., Asari, V.K.: An improved face recognition technique based on modular PCA approach. Pattern Recognition Letters 25(4) (March 2004)
8. http://www.codeproject.com/KB/cpp/TrackEye.aspx

Enhancing Cloud Security through Policy Monitoring Techniques

B. Loganayagi[1] and S. Sujatha[2]

[1] Research Scholar (Full Time) in the Faculty of ICE
[2] Head of the Department, Department of MCA
Anna University of Technology Tiruchirappalli (Main Campus),
Tiruchirappalli, India
loks20@yahoo.com, ssujatha71@yahoo.co.in

Abstract. Cloud Computing is accessing Services through Internet based on pay per usage model. Software as a Service (SaaS), Infrastructure as a Service (IaaS) and Platform as a Service (PaaS) are available in Cloud. Cloud based products will eliminate the need to install and manage client rich applications. Cloud Service providers are helping companies to reduce the high cost infrastructure installation and maintenance cost. Besides having enormous useful features, cloud has some issues like security. This paper provides details about cloud computing issues, how policy monitoring techniques can be used to enhance the security of the cloud.

Keywords: Cloud Computing, IaaS, Paas, SaaS, Policy Monitoring.

1 Introduction

Cloud Computing is defined by a large-scale distributed computing paradigm that is driven by economies of scale, in which a pool of abstracted, virtualized, dynamically-scalable, managed computing power, storage, platforms, and services are delivered on demand to external customers over the Internet [1]. Cloud computing has the features of grid computing, cluster computing, service computing, and utility computing. End user has to run one time application, like tax calculation, can use cloud application as the best choice. End users can do their work or access services with thin client, no need to invest on resources. Instead they can rent/lease the resources. More over they can choose the best available computing platform, since many companies are going to offer cloud based applications in near future, like mobile services. Small companies, whose main business is not software related, can outsource their work to cloud providers, so that they can concentrate on such as application development only, instead of concentrating their focus on hosting environment. It is easy to scale if the application is deployed in cloud. It takes away all the risks of managing resources.

Cloud is providing preconfigured infrastructure at lower cost, which generally follows the Information Technology Infrastructure Library, can manage increased peak load capacity and moreover uses the latest technology, provide consistent performance that is monitored by the service provider. Dynamic allocation of the

V.V. Das and N. Thankachan (Eds.): CIIT 2011, CCIS 250, pp. 270–275, 2011.

resources as and when is needed. Cloud computing reduces capital expenditure (CAPEX) and it offers high computing at lower cost. Upgrading your hardware/ software requirement also easy with the cloud, without disturbing the current work. Scalability and maintenance is easy in the case of cloud. Easily user can rent/lease the services offered by cloud computing vendors. User will be charged as pay per usage like utility based services. Overall Cloud is giving good performance at lower cost instead of making more capital investment. The rest of the paper is organized as follows: Section 2 discusses about the Cloud providers. Section 3 discusses about the Cloud Issues and Proposed Solutions and Section 4 discusses about the Conclusion.

2 Cloud Providers

Cloud computing [7] [8] [13] [15] systems generally falls into three course grain categories. Infrastructure as a service (IaaS), Platform as a Service (PaaS), Software as a Service (SaaS). Many companies are offering services.

2.1 Infrastructure as a Service(IaaS)

Infrastructure as a Service (IaaS) provisions hardware, software, and equipments to deliver software application environments with a resource usage-based pricing model. Infrastructure can scale up and down dynamically based on application resource needs. Typical examples are Amazon EC2 (Elastic Cloud Computing) Service and S3 (Simple Storage Service) where compute and storage infrastructures are open to public access with a utility pricing model. This basically delivers virtual machine images to the IaaS provider, instead of programs, and the Machine can contain whatever the developer want. Example: Full virtualization (GoGrid, Skytap), Grid computing (Sun Grid), Management (RightScale), Paravirtualization (Amazon Elastic Compute Cloud).

2.2 Platform as a Service(PaaS)

Platform as a Service(PaaS) offers a high-level integrated environment to build, test, and deploy custom applications. Generally, developers will need to accept some restrictions on the type of software they can write in exchange for built-in application scalability. An example is Google's App Engine, which enables users to build Web applications on the same scalable systems that power Google applications, Web application frameworks, Python Django (Google App Engine), Ruby on Rails (Heroku), Web hosting (Mosso), Proprietary (Azure, Force.com).

2.3 Software as a Service (SaaS)

User buys a Subscription to some software product, but some or all of the data and codes resides remotely. Delivers special-purpose software that is remotely accessible by consumers through the Internet with a usage-based pricing model. In this model, applications could run entirely on the network, with the user interface living on a thin client. Salesforce is an industry leader in providing online CRM (Customer Relationship Management) Services. Live Mesh from Microsoft allows files and folders to be shared and synchronized across multiple devices. Identity (OAuth, OpenID), Integration (Amazon Simple Queue Service), Mapping (Google Maps, Yahoo! Maps), Payments (Amazon Flexible Payments Service, Google Checkout, PayPal), Search (Alexa, Google Custom Search, Yahoo! BOSS), Others (Amazon Mechanical Turk) Other than the listed above companies, many companies started offering cloud computing services.

3 Cloud Issues and Proposed Solution

Cloud Computing has some issues besides its nice features [6] [12]. The fig.1 shows the cloud challenges/issues, a survey taken by IDC in Aug 2008. Besides having nice features like Scalability, Availability, Performance, Cost-effective, Acquire resources on demand, Release resources when no longer needed, Pay for what you use, Leverage other's core competencies, Turn fixed cost into variable cost, security is the major issue [9] [13][14].

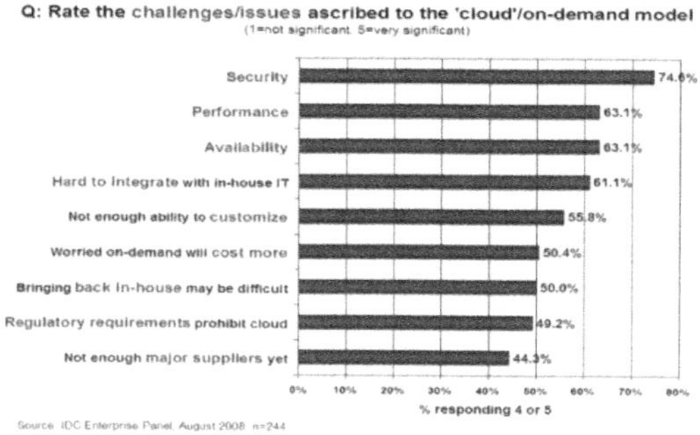

Fig. 1. Cloud Challenges/Issues by IDC Survey

Unless otherwise security is not there, which will raise problems in other feature also. so enhancing the security of the cloud is very much important to utilize all the nice features of cloud. The Proposed architecture is given in the figure.2. First layer consists of resources, second layer is the virtual management layer, third layer is Infrastructure as a Service Layer, fourth and fifth gives other types of cloud services such as Platform as a Service and Software as a Service and last one is where the end user connects with the cloud. Cloud Resources includes hardware, software, legacy application and network resources. Virtual management layer consists of virtual machines, VM management and deployment, a hypervisor, above that IaaS, PaaS, SaaS layers are there. Topmost layer is the one, where user applications can be run. Security and Compliances applicable to all the layers. Enhanced Cloud Protection System Model will be monitoring at the resources and virtualization layer levels.

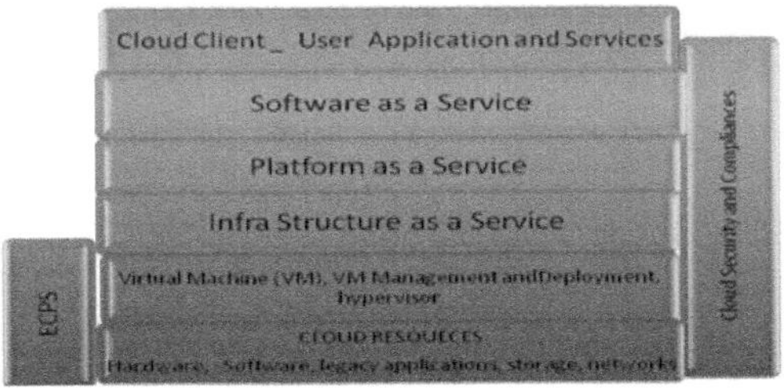

Fig. 2. Cloud Layers and Enhanced Cloud Protection System

To Deploy Web services, JDKTM 6 can be used. JDKTM 6 _Java EE 5 Development using GlassFish Application Server. GlassFish, allow application developers to develop and deploy Java EE-compliant applications such as Deploying Enterprise Applications, Web Applications, EJB module, Connector module, Life cycle Module, Application client module, Custom MBeans.

3.1 Policy Monitoring Techniques

Cloud Services are Services provided to the end user/ subscriber. Here there will be a Service Level Agreement between the Cloud Provider and the User. In General Security and compliances applicable to all the layers. Each layer level has its own security. When it comes to the topmost layer where applications are deployed and accessed will be coming under many security policy besides with firewall and service vulnerability monitoring, risk assessment and control management [3][4][5][10][11]. By using Java Authentication and Authorization Service (JAAS) can check who is accessing the service and whether they are authorized to access as per SLA. Now an interesting question arises before us. how policy can be enforced and how it can be monitored?. The Proposed Enhanced Cloud Protection System (ECPS) model is shown in fig.3.

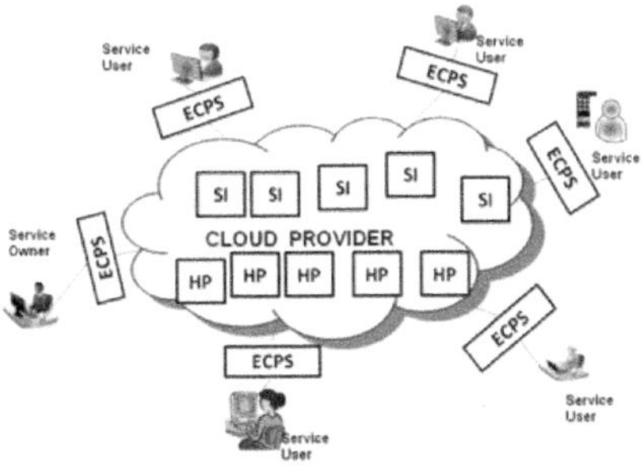

Fig. 3. Enhanced Cloud Protection Model

Here all the services are monitored continuously, vulnerability monitoring and risk assessment is made. Based on the Risk Assessment appropriate counter measures are applied to overcome the security problem [2]. ECPS has the sub modules as shown in fig. 4.

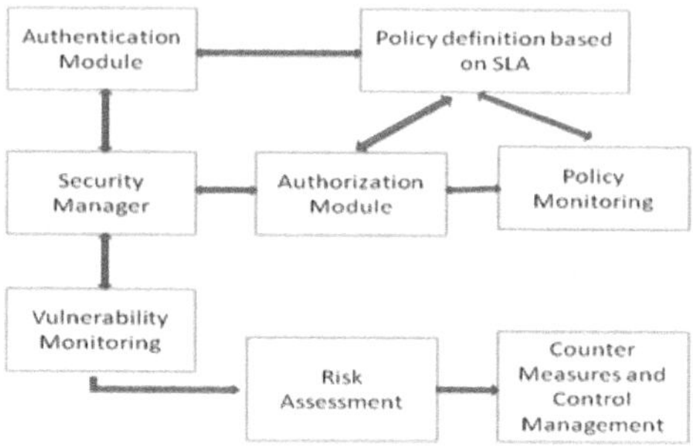

Fig. 4. Enhanced Cloud Protection System Method

Authentication module checks for who is accessing the service regardless of the service type and nature. Authorization module checks for whether the user is authorized to access the service based on Service Level Agreement. Policy is generated based on the SLA agreement between the user and the provider. Here policy varies with the price and other factor. Security manager will monitor for any vulnerability, risk assessment is made and based on the risk assessment, countermeasure steps are taken to overcome the security problem. Consider the following scenario, based an end user's requirement, whether it is a IaaS, PaaS, SaaS type of service, a single Virtual Machine is allotted for the user. Creation of Virtual Machine [7] and its images are taken based on their policy requirement. If suppose our monitoring report shows vulnerability, appropriate steps can be taken. Isolating Virtual Machines of each user is important which is done by the second layer with the help of a hypervisor. Snapshots can be taken. If it is intruded, necessary steps are taken to recover by forwarding request to the next VM which will be created with the help of images taken already. At worst case, the entire virtual machine can be destroyed and can be reconstructed immediately with the help of the images without affecting the regular workload of the user. Many Virtual Machines can be run on a single host machine itself. Proper updating of VMs Operating system, installing and updating the firewalls in VMs like the physical machine is important to ensure the security of the service. Based on the policy based risk assessment report generated, Virtual Machine maintenance is easy to achieve the enhanced security of the Cloud.

4 Conclusion

Even though Cloud has some serious issues like security, privacy, social and political issues [13], Cloud computing is going to be one of the venture technology in future. Cloud user should understand their own network, system, applications and data are moving to an unknown network which poses serious threat to security and privacy. So they have to vigilantly select Cloud Service Providers by checking their security service standards and compliances. Nowadays, Most of the vendors provide free usage to deploy their services in their cloud [8] with certain limits like hours of usage, or hard disk space, storage or data transfer or number of end users. As a cloud user or developer, they have to choose the vendor based on their Service Level Agreements. The above discussed policy based monitoring technique, which helps the provider to achieve full security of the virtual machine is possible. Since virtualization is the key technique of cloud computing, enhanced secure cloud service can be achieved with the help of policy monitoring techniques. In future like IaaS, PaaS and SaaS, Anything as a Service (XaaS) is going to be possible and can be achieved.

References

1. Foster, I., Zhao, Y., Raicu, I., Lu, S.: Cloud Computing and Grid Computing 360-Degree Compared. In: Grid Computing Environments Workshop, GCE 2008, November 12-16 (2008)
2. Peterson, G.: Don't Trust. And Verify: A Security Architecture Stack for the Cloud. IEEE Security and Privacy 8(5), 83–86 (2010)
3. Takabi, H., Joshi, J.B.D., Ahn, G.-J.: SecureCloud: Towards a Comprehensive Security Framework for Cloud Computing Environments. In: 2010 IEEE 34th Annual Computer Software and Applications Conference Workshops, Compsacw, pp. 393–398 (2010)
4. Takabi, H., Joshi, J.B.D., Ahn, G.-J.: Security and Privacy Challenges in Cloud Computing Environments. IEEE Security and Privacy 8(6), 24–31 (2010)
5. Li, H.-C., Liang, P.-H., Yang, J.-M., Chen, S.-J.: Analysis on Cloud-Based Security Vulnerability Assessment. In: 2010 IEEE 7th International Conference on e-Business Engineering, Icebe, pp. 490–494 (November 2010)
6. Xu, J., Yan, J., He, L., Su, P., Feng, D.: CloudSEC: A Cloud Architecture for Composing Collaborative Security Services. In: 2nd IEEE International Conference on Cloud Computing Technology and Science, cloudcom, pp. 703–711 (2010)
7. Loganayagi, B., Sujatha, S.: Creating virtual platform for cloud computing. In: 2010 IEEE International Conference on Computational Intelligence and Computing Research (ICCIC), December 28-29, pp. 1–4 (2010), doi:10.1109/ICCIC.2010.5705744
8. Loganayagi, B., Sujatha, S.: Cloud Computing in Stax Platform. In: IEEE International Conference on Computer Communication and Electrical Technology (IEEE-ICCCET 2011), March 18-19, pp. 1–5 (2011)
9. Harauz, J., Kaufman, L.M., Potter, B.: Data Security in the World of Cloud Computing. IEEE Security and Privacy 7(4), 61–64 (2009)
10. Zhou, M., Zhang, R., Xie, W., Qian, W., Zhou, A.: Security and Privacy in Cloud Computing: A Survey. In: 2010 Sixth International Conference on Semantics, Knowledge and Grids, SKG, pp. 105–112 (2010)
11. Bertram, S., Boniface, M., Surridge, M., Briscombe, N., Hall-May, M.: On-Demand Dynamic Security for Risk-Based Secure Collaboration in Clouds. In: 2010 IEEE 3rd International Conference on Cloud Computing, pp. 518–525 (2010)
12. Xue, J., Zhang, J.-j.: A Brief Survey on the Security Model of Cloud Computing. In: 2010 Ninth International Symposium on Distributed Computing and Applications to Business, Engineering and Science. Dcabes, pp. 475–478 (2010)
13. Mather, T., Kumaraswamy, S., Latif, S.: Cloud Security and Privacy. O'Reilly (2009)
14. Ritinghouse, J.W., Ransome, J.F.: Cloud Computing: Implementation Management and Security. CRC Press (2010)
15. Cloud General Information, `http://en.wikipedia.org/wiki/Cloud_computing`

EACS Approach for Grid Workflow Scheduling in a Computational Grid

E. Saravana Kumar[1] and A. Sumathi[2]

[1] Anna University of Technology, Coimbatore, TN, India
saraninfo@gmail.com
[2] Dept of ECE, Adhiyamaan College of Engineering, Hosur, TN, India
sumathi_2005@rediffmail.com

Abstract. Grid is a collection of heterogeneous resources for solving the complex computational problems. Workflow is a collection of atomic tasks. In this article we propose an Enhanced Ant Colony System (EACS) approach to solve grid workflow scheduling problem with two QoS parameters time and cost to minimize the makespan with low cost. We design a five heuristics for EACS approach and propose an adaptive scheme that allows ants to select heuristics in a quick convergence manner for mapping of tasks to resources based on the modified pheromone updating value. The experiment is done by the simulation with different tasks in various workflow applications and we achieve QoS as well as optimized performance.

Keywords: Ant Colony Optimization (ACO), Grid Computing, Workflow Scheduling.

1 Introduction

The popularity of the internet and availability of powerful computers and high performance networks as low cost commodity components are changing the way we use computers today. These technology advances have to led to the possibility of using geographically distributed and multi owner resources to solve large-scale problems in science [1]. To achieve the promising potentials of the large number of distributed resources, effective and efficient scheduling algorithms are fundamentally important. Grid supports sharing, interconnection and use of diverse resources, integrated in the framework of a dynamic computing system [2]. When processing a computing application in grids, the applications are called workflows. A workflow is a collection of atomic tasks that are processed in a specific order to accomplish a goal [3]. One of the most challenging problems in grid computing is to schedule the workflow to achieve high performance. Usually, a workflow is given a Directed Acyclic Graph (DAG) [4] in which the nodes represent individual application tasks and the directed arc stands for precedence relations between the tasks. The scheduler has to assign the tasks to heterogeneously distributed computing sites to process with the objective to achieve customers QoS requirements as well as to optimize the performance. As scheduling in a DAG is NP complete [5].

V.V. Das and N. Thankachan (Eds.): CIIT 2011, CCIS 250, pp. 276–280, 2011.

2 Related Work

In the past few years, researchers have proposed scheduling algorithms for parallel system [6] [7]. Grid resource management [8] was surveyed and analyzed based on classification of scheduler organization, system status, scheduling and rescheduling policies. Recently, many researchers have been studied several works on job scheduling on grid environment. Some of those are the popular heuristic algorithms, which have been developed, are min-min, the fast greedy, Tabu search [9] and an Ant System. The heuristic algorithms proposed for job scheduling in rely on static environment and the expected value of execution times. H. Casanova et al [10] and R. Baraglia et al [11] proposed the heuristic algorithms to solve the scheduling problem based on the different static data, for example, the execution time and system load. Unfortunately, all of information such as execution time and workload cannot be determined in advance of dynamic grid environments. In 1999, the Ant Colony Optimization (ACO) metaheuristic was proposed by Dorigo, Di Caro and Gambardella, which has been successfully used to solve many NP-problem, such as TSP, job shop scheduling, etc.

3 Proposed Work

Generally, workflow applications can be modelled as a directed acyclic graph (DAG) G = (V, A). Let n be the number of services in the workflow. The set of nodes V = {S1, S2, … , Sn} corresponds to the services of the workflow. The set of arcs A represents precedence relations. An arc is in the form of (Si,Sj), where Si is called the parent service of Sj, and Sj is the child service of Si. Typically in a workflow, a child service cannot be executed until all of its parent services have been completed. Each Task Ti ($1 \leq i \leq n$) has an implementation domain Si = { Si1, Si2,… Simi}, where Sij ($1 \leq j \leq mi$) represents a service instance provided by a owner and mi is the total number of available service instances for Ti. The properties of a service instance can be denoted as a group of four variables (Sij.g, Sij.t, Sij.c). Sij.g means that the owner of Sij. Sij.t and Sij.c stand for execution time, and cost of Sij respectively.

3.1 Algorithm Description

1. Set all pheromone values (PH) and parameters at the beginning of the algorithm
2. Selecting a path using random search (RAS)
   2.1 Forward ant selects the path in a precedence order
   2.2 Backward ant starts from end and the reverse directions of all arcs
3 For N number of ants constructs M number of solutions in parallel
   3.1 For each iteration different tasks are mapped to different service instances.
4. Enhanced pheromone updating rule (EPH) is applied for quick convergence of all the ants.

$$\tau ij = \frac{1}{(1-\rho)} \tau ij + \rho\tau_0 \quad (1)$$

5 Global pheromone updating value for construction of best feasible solution.
6 If the terminal test is completed, the algorithm will be ended. Otherwise, go to step(2) to begin a new iteration.

3.2 Pheromone and Heuristics Information

Pheromone and heuristic information are the most important factor to record the historical searching experiences and bias the ants' searching behaviour in future. As the scheduling problem is mainly to map all tasks in the abstract workflow to service instances to form a concrete workflow, we denote the pheromone value of mapping service instance S_i^j to task T_i as τ_{ij}, and the heuristic information value of mapping S_i^j to task T_i as η_{ij}.At the beginning of the algorithm, we set all pheromone values to an initial value τ_0 , i.e.,$\tau_{ij} = \tau_0,\ 1 \le i \le n,\ 1 \le j \le m_i$ .We defined five heuristics for the algorithm as follows.

1) Heuristic (TO): Time Optimization - The artificial ants to select the service instances with shorter execution time.

$$\eta_{ij} = TO = \frac{\max\_time_i - S_i^j.t + 1}{\max\_time_i - \min\_time_i + 1} \quad (2)$$

where $\min\_time_i = min_{1\le j\le m_i}\{S_i^j.t\}$ and $\max\_time_i = max_{1\le j\le m_i}\{S_i^j.t\}$ According to above equation, a service instance with shorter execution time will be associated with a higher heuristic value.

2) Heuristic (CO): Cost Optimization - The artificial ants to select the service instances with lower cost.

$$\eta_{ij} = CO = \frac{max\_cost_i - S_i^j.c + 1}{max\_cost_i - min\_cost_i + 1} \quad (3)$$

where $\min\_cost_i = min_{1\le j\le m_i}\{S_i^j.c\}$ and $\max\_cost_i = max_{1\le j\le m_i}\{S_i^j.c\}$ According to above equation, a service instance with lower cost will be associated with a higher heuristic value.

3) Heuristic (SB): Suggested Budget - The SB heuristic biases the artificial ants to select the service instances with just-within-budget cost.

$$\eta_{ij} = SB = \frac{\max\{|\max\_cost_i - SB_i|, |SB_i - \min\_cost_i|\} - |s_j^i.t - SB_i| + 1}{\max\{|\max\_cost_i - SB_i|, |SB_i - \min\_cost_i|\} + 1} \quad (4)$$

4) Heuristic (TC): Time/Cost - It integrates the TG heuristic with the CG heuristic. According to it, a service instance with shorter execution time and lower cost will be associated with a higher heuristic value.

$$\eta_{ij} = TC = \frac{1}{2}(TO_{ij} + CO_{ij}) \quad (5)$$

5) Heuristic (OP): Overall Performance - It unites the TO, and CO heuristics together.

$$\eta_{ij} = OP = \frac{1}{2}(TO_{ij} + CO_{ij}) \quad (6)$$

The algorithm uses different heuristics.1) If the objective is to optimize makespan, only the TO, CO and TC heuristics will be used to find the service instances with shorter execution time. The CO, TC heuristics are used to search for the service instances that satisfy the budget constraints. 2) If the objective is to optimize the cost, only the TO, CO, and TC heuristic will be used.

4 Experiments and Results

There are mainly three parameters in the algorithm: β and q_0 in the pseudorandom proportion selection rule and ρ in the pheromone updating rule. In our experiments, we set $\rho = 0.1$, which is the same as the suggestion given by the traditional ACS algorithm for travelling salesman problem (TSP). The EACS approach works by dividing the DAG into several partitions and each partition is assigned by some priority. This priority is based on completion time of the DAG job. Experiments are conducted on the five instances and different levels of QoS. The proposed EACS approach is a guided random search algorithm. Search the best instances, for the first iteration it will give the average value, in second iteration it will give the minimum value and the third iteration it will give the maximum value. The results are demonstrated in charts, it proves the effectiveness of the EACS approach.

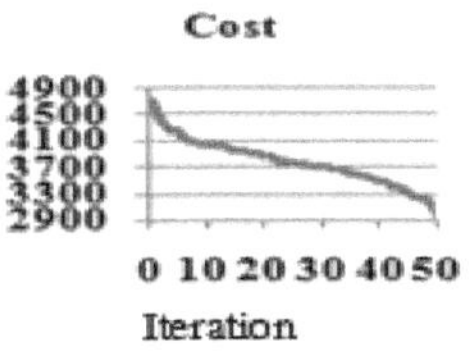

Fig. 1. (a)

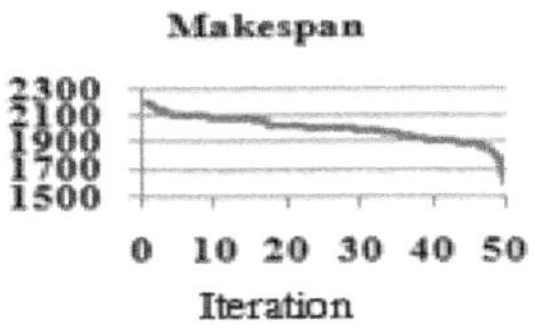

Fig. 1. (b)

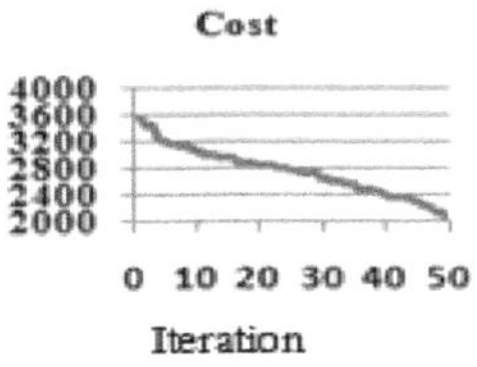

Fig. 2. (a)

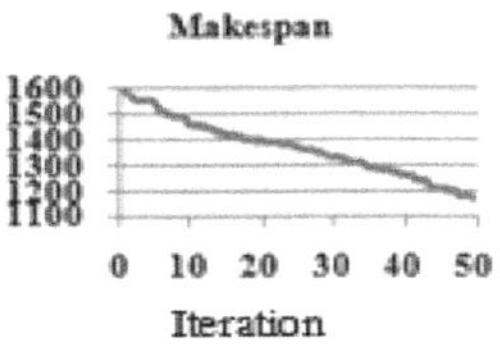

Fig. 2. (b)

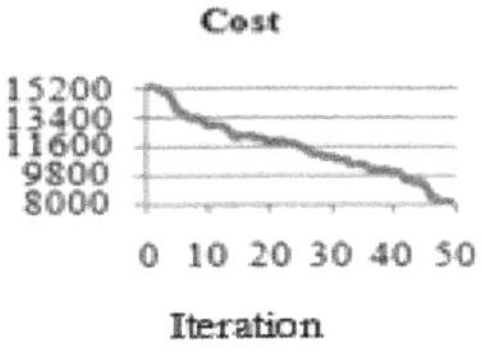

Fig. 3. (a)

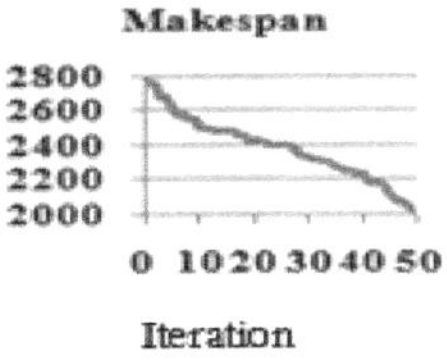

Fig. 3. (b)

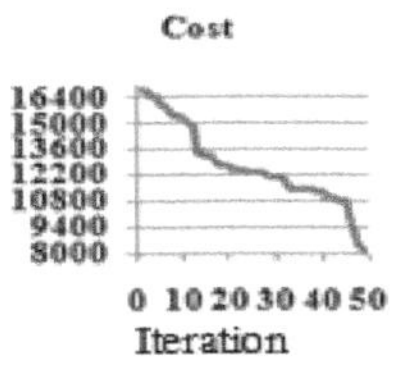

Fig. 4. (a)

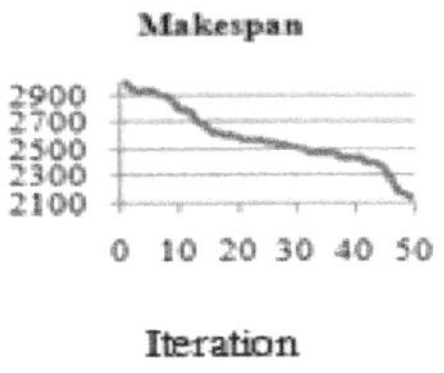

Fig. 4. (b)

Fig. 1. (a) and **Fig. 1.** (b) Performance of cost and Makespan in CO,
Fig. 2. (a) and **Fig. 2.** (b) Performance of cost and Makespan in TO,
Fig. 3. (a) and **Fig. 3.** (b) Performance of cost and Makespan in TO/CO,
Fig. 4. (a) and **Fig. 4.** (b) Overall Performance of cost and Makespan)

5 Conclusions

Enhanced Ant Colony Optimization with modified local pheromone updating rule for a large-scale workflow scheduling problem in computational grids has been proposed. In the algorithm, different QoS parameters are considered, including time, and cost. Users are allowed to define QoS constraints to guarantee the quality of the schedule. Moreover, the optimizing objective of the algorithm is based on the user-defined QoS preferences. We proposed five new heuristics for this problem. Experimental results demonstrate the effectiveness of the proposed algorithm.

References

1. Foster, I., Kesselman, C.: The Grid: Blueprint for a Future Computing Infrastructure. Morgan Kaufmann Publishers, USA (1999)
2. Foster, I., Kesselman, C., Tuecke, S.: The anatomy of the Grid: Enabling scalable virtual organizations. International Journal Supercomputer Applications 15(3) (2001)
3. Kyriazis, D., et al.: An innovative workflow mapping mechanism for grids in the frame of quality of service. Future Gen. Comput. Syst. (to be published)
4. Shi, Z., Dongarra, J.J.: Scheduling workflow applications on processors with different capabilities. Future Gen. Comput. Syst. 22, 665–675 (2006)
5. Garey, M.R., Johnson, D.S.: Computers and Intractability: A Guide to the Theory of NP-Completeness. Freeman, New York (1979)
6. Feitelson, K.D.G., Rudolph, L., Schwiegelshohn, U., Sevcik, K.C., Wong, P.: Theory and practice in parallel job scheduling. In: Feitelson, D.G., Rudolph, L. (eds.) IPPS-WS 1997 and JSSPP 1997. LNCS, vol. 1291, pp. 1–34. Springer, Heidelberg (1997)
7. Krallmann, J., Schwiegelshohn, U., Yahyapour, R.: On the design and evaluation of job scheduling algorithms. In: Feitelson, D.G., Rudolph, L. (eds.) JSSPP 1999, IPPS-WS 1999, and SPDP-WS 1999. LNCS, vol. 1659, pp. 17–42. Springer, Heidelberg (1999)
8. Li: Job scheduling and processor allocation for grid computing on Metacomputers. Journal of Parallel and Distributed Computing (2005)
9. Krauter, K., Buyya, R., Maheswaran, M.: A taxonomy and survey of Grid resource management systems for distributed computing. Software Pract. Exp. 2, 135–164 (2002)
10. Braun, T.D., Siegel, H.J., Beck, N., Bölöni, L.L., Maheswaran, M., Reuther, A.I., Robertson, J.P., Theys, M.D., Yao, B., Hensgen, D., Freund, R.F.: A Comparison of Eleven Static Heuristics for Mapping a Class of Independent Tasks onto Heterogeneous Distributed Computing Systems. Journal of Parallel and Distributed Computing 61(6), 810–837 (2001)
11. Casanova, H., Legrand, A., Zagorodnov, D., Berman, F.: Heuristics for Scheduling parameter sweep applications in Grid environment. In: Heterogeneous Computing Workshop 2000, pp. 349–363. IEEE Computer Society Press (2000)

Mobile Payment Security by Key Shuffle Mechanism in DES

V.B. Navya, R. Aparna, and G. Bhaskar

Siddaganga Institute of Technology, Department of Computer Science,
Tumkur 572102, India
navyavb@gmail.com, {raparna,bhaskar_gopal}@sit.ac.in

Abstract. Wide spread use of handheld devices extend possibilities of using mobile devices as universal payment mode. However, some issues constrain the widespread acceptance of mobile payment; for example: privacy protection, limited capability of mobile devices, and limited bandwidth of wireless networks. Due to the fact that wireless channel is an open medium to intruders, encryption is a crucial process to assure secure message exchange in the mobile payment systems. Several standard symmetric cryptographic algorithms such as DES and AES are widely used to solve the problem of communication over the insecure wireless channel in mobile payment systems. But intruders and hackers are devising new methods to decrypt the data. The effective key length of the DES is 56 binary digits (bits) and the straight forward "work factor" of the algorithm is 2^{56} (i.e., the number of keys that would have to be tried is 2^{56} or approximately 7.6 x 10^{16} times), hence the intruders and hackers can easily cryptanalyze.

Keywords: M-commerce, mobile payments, key-shuffle permutation array, DES.

1 Introduction

M-commerce is defined as using a mobile device for business transactions performed over a mobile telecommunication network, possibly involving the transfer of monetary values like the customer transaction details, marketing information and promotions and shopping order details [1] [2]. Business Transactions are given an opportunity for universal payment mode by "any time - anywhere payment" facility. Mobile phones and handheld devices are just not limited as end user devices but they extend their widespread usage in Business transactions. Transactions depend on the network technology used for transmission, the variation in the bandwidth capacity and security of the sensitive data transferred in the network from the customer to the gateway and/or merchant to gateway. Using a mobile device as a universal payment instrument in wireless medium, threat for sensitive data transactions increases which requires a strong security mechanism such as encryption of the data. Encryption is an essential process to assure confidentiality over wireless channels, because wireless channels are an open medium to intruders in which they can intercept and alter the contents of any transmitted information [3].

V.V. Das and N. Thankachan (Eds.): CIIT 2011, CCIS 250, pp. 281–285, 2011.

The Data Encryption Standard (DES) is a block cipher that uses shared secret encryption. It is based on a symmetric-key algorithm that uses a 56-bit key. Although DES is a safe encryption algorithm, the security issues of DES exist. First, the length of DES key is too short, because it includes 64 bits. Second, all the calculation of DES is linear besides the calculation of S box. Third, the weak links of DES are the protection and distribution of the key [4]. Once the key is lost, the whole system becomes worthless. Because the key of DES has some shortage, triple DES algorithm is brought up. Triple DES is more secure than DES but in triple DES two keys has to be shared between the users and hence length of the key to be shared increases. If the key is identified by cryptanalysis, the intruder can easily decrypt the message if it is either DES or triple DES as the algorithm is standard. This paper proposes an improvement over the Standard DES key generation methodology, which involves key mixing using the key-shuffle permutation array which changes the key for every chunk of 8 bytes of data. Together the Key shuffle permutation array and count of vowels generates intermediate keys which are different from the original key. The proposed algorithm transforms the DES encryption and decryption process to be more secure. The rest of the paper is organized as follows. In section 2, the proposed key generation algorithm for encryption and decryption with example and analysis is explained. Section 3 includes properties of the proposed algorithm and conclusions are drawn in section 4.

2 The Proposed Algorithm

The proposed key generation algorithm takes 8 bytes of the key and the key-shuffle order as inputs. The key is shuffled according to the shuffle order and new keys obtained are considered for sub keys generation. We have introduced novelty in key-shuffling by considering number of vowel's, 0's and 1's in the chunk which is very difficult for the adversary to get the information.

2.1 Key Generation Algorithm and Example for Encryption

The proposed key generation algorithm for encryption is described in the table 1.

Example: Suppose the original key "ABCDEFGH" and key-shuffle permutation array [3 6 8 4 5 1 2 7] are taken as inputs to the key generation algorithm. On permuting the original key with key-shuffle permutation array, we get "CFHDEABG". Consider this as one key to encrypt 8 bytes of data say "scenario". Count the number of vowel's, 0's and 1's which is C i.e., C = 4. If suppose data is "No.02315", then C = 3. Encrypt the data "scenario" using key "CFHDEABG". Now permute "CFHDEABG" with same key-shuffle permutation array, we get "HAGDECFB", use this key to encrypt next 8 bytes of data after taking the value of C. Similarly by permuting the key successively, we get "GCBDEHAF", "BHFDEGCA" and "FGADEBHC".

Table 1. Key generation algorithm for encryption

Step 1: Consider the symmetric key of 8 bytes called original key and random numbers from 1 to 8 which is called Key- Permutation array as inputs to key generation algorithm.
Step 2: The 8-bytes key is permuted according to Key-Shuffle permutation.
Step 3: Output of key-shuffle permutation is considered as one key to encrypt 8 bytes of data.
Step 4: Consider 8 bytes of data to be encrypted and count the number of vowels, 0's and 1's in the chunk, say C.
Step 5: Encrypt data using the obtained key after Step 3.
Step 6: Further this key is permuted with the same Key-Shuffle Permuted array. Repeat steps 2 through 5 until the original key is obtained.
Step 7: Take the count of the permuted keys obtained by shuffling the key, say K. If K > 8, compute modulus of 8 for K. Then K = K mod 8.
Step 8: Left Shift the original key K times.
Step 9: Now consider value of C and K from step 4 and step 7 respectively.
Step 10: Exchange the Kth and C^{th} place of the key-shuffle permutation array to obtain the new shuffle array.
Repeat Steps 1 through 10 till the end of encryption. Step 2 to Step 5 is carried out for every block of bytes of data. Step 7 to Step 10 is carried out every time after the original key is found by permuting the original key with key-shuffle permutation array.

Permuting "FGADEBHC" we get the original key "ABCDEFGH" which is discarded and we take K. Hence K=5. Suppose K>8, take K = K mod 8. Now consider original key and shift left 5 times, we get "FGHABCDE" and consider the obtained key as main key. Exchange 4th and 5th value in the key-shuffle permutation array "3 6 8 4 5 1 2 7" to get new key-shuffle permutation array i.e., 3 6 8 5 4 1 2 7. Now new original key and the new key-shuffle permutation array is "FGHABCDEF" and "3 6 8 5 4 1 2 7".

2.2 Key Generation Algorithm and Example for Decryption

The proposed key generation algorithm for decryption is described in the table 2.

Example: As DES is symmetric key algorithm, the same original key and key-shuffle permutation array is used in key generation algorithm for decryption. Hence "ABCDEFGH" as original key and [3 6 8 4 5 1 2 7] as key-shuffle permutation array are taken as inputs for key generation algorithm. On permuting the original key with key-shuffle permutation array, we get "CFHDEABG". Consider this as one key to decrypt first 8 bytes of encrypted data. Decrypt the first 8 bytes of encrypted data using key "CFHDEABG" and get the original data "scenario". Count the number of vowel's, 0's and 1's in the chunk of original data obtained which is C i.e., C = 4.

Now permute "CFHDEABG" with same key-shuffle permutation array, we get "HAGDECFB", use this key to decrypt next 8 bytes of data and take C from original data obtained. Similarly by permuting the key successively, we get "GCBDEHAF", "BHFDEGCA" and "FGADEBHC". Permuting "FGADEBHC" we get the original key "ABCDEFGH" which is discarded and we take K. Hence K=5. Suppose K>8, take K = K mod 8. Now consider original key and shift left 5 times, we get "FGHABCDE" and consider the obtained key as original key. Exchange 4th and 5th

value in the key-shuffle permutation array "3 6 8 4 5 1 2 7" to get new key-shuffle permutation array i.e., 3 6 8 5 4 1 2 7. Now new original key and the new key-shuffle permutation array is "FGHABCDEF" and "3 6 8 5 4 1 2 7".

Table 2. Key generation algorithm for decryption

Step 1: Consider the symmetric key of 8 bytes and the random numbers from 1 to 8 which is called Key-Permutation array as inputs to key generation algorithm.
Step 2: The 8-bytes key is permuted according to Key-Shuffle permutation.
Step 3: The output of the key-shuffle permutation is considered as one key to encrypt 8 bytes of data.
Step 4: Decrypt 8 bytes of data using the obtained key after Step 3.
Step 5: Take the count of vowel's, 0's and 1's from decrypted chunk of data, say C.
Step 6: Further this key is permuted with the same Key-Shuffle Permutation array. Repeat Steps 2 through 5 until the original key is obtained.
Step 7: Take the count of the permuted keys obtained by shuffling the key, say K. If K > 8, compute modulus of 8 for K. Then K = K mod 8.
Step 8: Left Shift the original key K times.
Step 9: Now consider value of C and K from Step 4 and Step 7 respectively.
Step 10: Exchange the Kth and C^{th} place of the key-shuffle permutation array to obtain the new key- shuffle permutation array.
Repeat Steps 1 through 10 till the end of decryption. Step 2 to Step 5 is carried out for every block of 8 bytes of data. Step 7 to Step 10 is carried out every time after the original key is found by permuting the original key with key-shuffle permutation array.

2.3 Analysis of the Proposed System

Cryptanalyzer needs 256 times to break the key in standard DES. In the proposed system along with original key, cryptanalyzer requires key-shuffle permutation array of length 8. For every 8 bytes of original data to be encrypted/decrypted, key-shuffle permutation array is required. We consider total length of the array, n=8 and total number of elements from the array r=8. Thus, we obtain different keys 8P8i:e:; 40320:

3 Properties of the Proposed System

The proposed key generation system has the following advantages:

1. The 8 bytes (64 bits) original key and the permutation array generate many other keys without repetition to use for encryption and decryption instead of using the original key. This would give 256*40320 trials instead of 256 [5].
2. The parameters number of keys generated by the key shuffle permutation array (K) and count of vowel's, 0's and 1's (C) helps in changing the original key and Key-shuffle permuted array so that unrepeated keys are generated. This makes cryptanalysis difficult even when the algorithm is known to the cryptanalyst.
3. This makes the differential cryptanalysis tedious as the key and key-shuffle array both keeps changing which in turn gives different keys for every chunk of the data to be encrypted or decrypted [6].

4. Randomly changing keys in the key generation system gives negligible chances for crypt analyzers to identify the key. By the time cryptanalyst identifies the key and the key-shuffle order, both would be changed.

4 Conclusion

Standard DES key generation can be cryptanalyzed with 256 maximum trails. We propose a novel key shuffle mechanism which increases the maximum number of trials and provides more security. Hence rendering the key generation technique tedious to cryptanalyzer using our key-shuffle permutation array. The drawback of the standard DES key generation mechanism is overcome by the proposed key generation algorithm by changing the original key for every 8 bytes of data to be encrypted or decrypted. In our scheme along with the original key the intruder also needs key-shuffle permutation array to cryptanalyze the message. The work factor of our key-shuffle permutation array mechanism is increased to 256*40320.

References

1. Beadle, H., Gonzalez, R., Safavi-Naini, R., Bakhtiari, S.: A Review of Internet Payments Schemes. In: Proceedings of the Australian Telecommunication Networks and Applications Conference (ATNAC 1996), Melbourne, Australia, pp. 486–494 (December 1996)
2. Kreyer, N., Pousttchi, K., Turowski, K.: Standardized Payment Procedures as Key Enabling Factor for Mobile Commerce. In: Proceedings of E-Commerce and Web Technologies: Third International Conference (2002)
3. Zibideh, W.Y., Matalgah, M.M.: Modified-DES Encryption Algorithm with Improved BER Performance in Wireless Communication. In: Proceedings of Radio and Wireless Symposium, RWS (2011)
4. Yang, K.-h., Niu, S.-j.: Data Safe Transmission Mechanism Based on Integrated Encryption Algorithm. In: Proceedings of International Conference on Computational Intelligence and Software Engineering, CiSE (2009)
5. Smid, M.E., Branstad, D.K.: The Data Encryption Standard Past and Future. In: Proceedings of the IEEE, vol. 76(5), pp. 550–559 (1988)
6. Eli, B., Adi, S.: Differential Cryptanalysis of DES-like Cryptosystems: The Weizmann Institute of Science. Department of Apllied Mathematics (1990)

Cepstral Smoothing for Convolutive Blind Speech Separation

Ibrahim Missaoui[1] and Zied Lachiri[1,2]

[1] National Engineering School of Tunis, ENIT, BP. 37 Le Belvédère, 1002 Tunis, Tunisia
[2] National Institute of Applied Science and Technology, INSAT,
BP 676 centre urbain cedex, Tunis, Tunisia
{brahim.missaoui,zied.lachiri}@enit.rnu.tn

Abstract. In this work, we have proposed an approach which combines two source separation techniques, convolutive blind source separation (BSS) exploiting the second-order non-stationary signals and binary time-frequency masking, together with a cepstral smoothing post-processing. The latter consists in smoothing of the estimated binary masks from the outputs of BSS algorithm in cepstral domain. The idea behind employing a cepstral smoothing of spectral masks is to improve the interference suppression and to reduce musical noise typically produced by time-frequency masking. Experimental results and the evaluation measurement prove the performance of proposed convolutive blind speech separation system.

Keywords: Cepstral smoothing, Ideal binary mask, Convolutive mixtures, Blind speech Separation.

1 Introduction

In the real world situation, the problem of blind separation of mixture signals measured by multiple microphones is usually modeled as convolutive. In which, the observed signal are formed by a filtered versions of the original signals. This case is viewed as a generation of instantaneous case. The classic example of this challenging is the cocktail-party problem that has been investigated and studied in extensive research work [1], [2]. Many algorithms have been proposed for the blind speech separation (BSS) of convolutive mixtures. These algorithms can be generally grouped into two categories [10]. The first tend to solve the BSS problem in the time domain, where generally it represents an extended of instantaneous domain algorithms to the convolutive mixture model [13],[3],[4]. However, this approach incurs a considerable computational cost for estimating the filter coefficients associated to the convolution operation. The second approach consists on decomposing the convolutive model into multiple instantaneous problems at each frequency bin [5], [6]. As a result, the frequency BSS approach is characterized by better convergence properties than temporal BSS and it has simpler implementation.

To perform the separation task, the convolutive BSS approach can use the higher-order statistics (HOS) [8],[18] or second-order statistics (SOS) [14], [15]. Although many convolutive BSS algorithms were proposed, there is still no reliable BSS

V.V. Das and N. Thankachan (Eds.): CIIT 2011, CCIS 250, pp. 286–293, 2011.

algorithm that can be used for the different convolutive mixture, especially for reverberant and noisy mixtures. For these cases, the separation performance of BSS algorithm is still limited and need further improvement.

Recently, a novel technique based on time-frequency masking has been proposed in computational auditory scene analysis (CASA) [11]. This technique, known as ideal binary mask (IBM), has been shown to be very well suited for speech separation. Indeed, it has shown promising properties as well in suppression interference as in improving intelligibility of target speech. IBM can be constructed by comparing the corresponding T–F units of target speech and background interference, where it is labeled with a value 1 if the target energy is stronger than the interference energy and with a value of 0 otherwise [11], [9]. However, the T-F masking generally caused temporal fluctuation artifact, so-called musical noise. In order to overcome this problem, a temporal cepstral smoothing of the ideal binary mask in cepstral domain is proposed in [16]. This step eliminates the random peaks in the time-frequency plane which can lead musical noise while preserving the speech structure of target speech.

The approach proposed in this paper is based on convolutive blind speech separation exploiting the second-order non-stationary signals and cepstral smoothing of binary masks. The estimated speech signals obtained using convolutive BSS algorithm proposed in [5] are then used to estimate the ideal binary masks. These masks are then smoothed in the cepstral domain and applied to estimated speech signals in order to generate the final separated signals. The organization of this paper is as follows: the section 2 introduces BSS problem in the convolutive case and describes the BSS algorithm used in our system. The cepstral smoothing of time frequency masking is presented in section 3. Section 4 exposes the experimental results and the evaluation measurements. Finally, Section 5 concludes our work.

2 Convolutive Blind Speech Separation

The convolutive BSS aims to extract the speech signals from theirs mixtures signals without referring to any information about the source or about the mixing model witch assumed to be convolutive. It can be modeled as follows:

$$x_m(t) = \sum_{n=1}^{N} \sum_{p=1}^{P} h_{mn} s_n(t-p+1) \tag{1}$$

Where h_{mn} is the impulse response of the mixing system, $x(t) = [x_1, .., x_M]^T$ is a vector of the mixtures signals $x_m(t)$ and $s(t) = [s_1, .., s_N]^T$ is a vector of unknown sources signals $s_n(t)$.

This model can be written using matrix notations as:

$$x_m(t) = \sum_{p=1}^{P} H_p s_n(t-p+1) \tag{2}$$

Taking a short-time Fourier transform (STFT) of the equation (1) the convolutive BSS problem is converted to multiple instantaneous problems in the frequency domain. This equation can be written as:

$$x_m(k) = H(k)S(k,m) \tag{3}$$

The objective of blind speech separation is to find a demixing filter $W(\tau)$ which is assumed to be invertible and time invariant. It is used to calculate the estimated signal $\widehat{s}(t)$ of source signals according to the following equation:

$$\widehat{s}(t) = \sum_{\tau=0}^{Q} W(\tau)x(t-\tau) \tag{4}$$

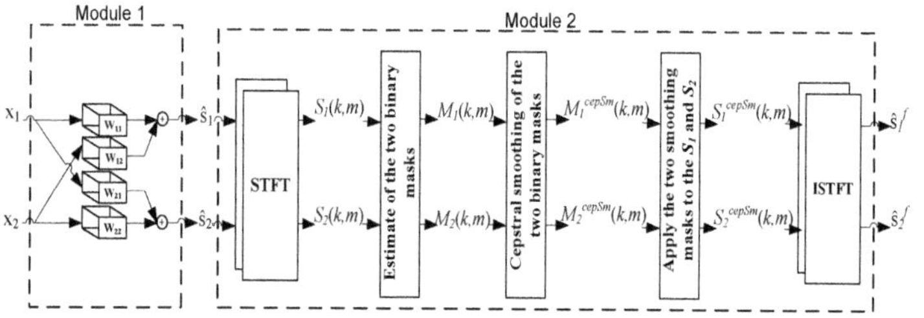

Fig. 1. The framework of proposed convolutive speech separation system

The proposed convolutive speech separation system, as illustrated in Figure 1, contains two modules shown in dotted boxes. In the first module, the separated signals are extracted using the convbss algorithm introduced by Parra and Spence [5]. This algorithm exploits the non stationarity structure of the speech signals. The separation task is done by performing a simultaneous diagonalization of cross-power spectrum and minimizing of a least squares cost function that leads to the estimation of the unmixing matrix $W(k)$. The separated signals are extracted by applying the unmixing filter to the mixtures signals.

$$\widehat{S}(k,m) = H(k)X(k,m) \tag{5}$$

The results signals $\widehat{S}(k,m)$ are then used to perform a cepstral smoothing step in the second module. In the first step of this module, two ideal binary masks are estimated using the obtained signals in the previous module. Then, temporal smoothing of these masks is done in the cepstral domain. Finally, the obtained masks are applied to the signals in order to generate the final estimated signals. The description of the cepstral smoothing module is given bellow.

3 Cepstral Smoothing of Time-Frequency Masking

3.1 Ideal Time-Frequency Binary Masking

The estimated speech signals $\widehat{s}_1$ and $\widehat{s}_2$ which were obtained in the last step are transformed into T-F domain using the STFT so that their spectrograms are obtained:

$$\begin{aligned} \widehat{s}_1 &\longrightarrow S_1(k,m) \\ \widehat{s}_2 &\longrightarrow S_2(k,m) \end{aligned} \tag{6}$$

Where k and m are respectively, the frequency and the time frame index.

The two ideal binary masks M1 and M2 are then determined by comparing the energy of each T–F unit of the two spectrograms as following:

$$\begin{aligned} M_1(k,m) &= \begin{cases} 1 & \text{if } |S_1(k,m)| \succ \tau |S_2(k,m)| \\ 0 & \text{otherwise} \end{cases} \\ M_2(k,m) &= \begin{cases} 1 & \text{if } |S_2(k,m)| \succ \tau |S_1(k,m)| \\ 0 & \text{otherwise} \end{cases} \end{aligned} \tag{7}$$

Where the threshold is chosen such τ=1.

3.2 Cepstral Smoothing of Spectral Masks

In order to reduce the musical artifact produced by the T-F masking, the binary masks are transformed into cepstral domain in which different cepstral smoothing level is done [16]. This smoothing procedure can reduce the musical noise while preserving the broadband structure and pitch harmonic information of the target speech signal [12],[16],[17]. The cepstral representation of each spectral mask is obtained as:

$$M_i^{cep}(l,m) = DFT^{-1}\left\{\ln\left(M_i(l,m)\right) /_{k=1,\dots K-1}\right\} \tag{8}$$

Where l and K are the quefrency bin index and the length of the discrete Fourier transform (DFT) respectively.

Then, a first order temporal recursive smoothing is applied to the result mask as:

$$\bar{M}_i^{cep}(l,m) = \beta_l \bar{M}_i^{cep}(l,m-1) + (1-\beta_l) M_i^{cep}(l,m) \tag{9}$$

Where the value of smoothing constants β_l are chosen separately according to the different values of the quefrency bins l as:

$$\beta_l = \begin{cases} \beta_{env} & \text{if } l \in \{0,..,l_{env}\} \\ \beta_{pitch} & \text{if } l = l_{pitch} \\ \beta_{peak} & \text{if } l \in \{(l_{env}+1),\dots,K\} \setminus l_{pitch} \end{cases} \tag{10}$$

For the low values of the quefrency bins ($0 \le l \le l_{env}$) which represent the spectral envelope of the mask $M_i^{cep}(l,m)$, the β_{env} is chosen to be a small value in order to maintain the speech onsets and the spectral envelope. Likewise, the regular structure of the pitch harmonics is protected by applying a low smoothing β_{pitch} for $l = l_{pitch}$. The rest of quefrency bins represents the fine structure of $M_i^{cep}(l,m)$ that contained the narrow spectral peaks with a high probability. This unwanted peak generally leads to the harmonic distortion. Therefore, a strong smoothing (a large value for β_{peak}) should be performed to these coefficients.

For each time-frame m, the pitch frequency l_{pitch} is calculated using the cepstral domain representation $sig^{cep}(l,m)$ of the estimated speech signals $\widehat{s}_1$ and $\widehat{s}_2$ as the following [16]:

$$l_{pitch} = \arg\max_l \left\{ sig^{cep}(l,m) \mid l_{low} \le l \le l_{high} \right\} \tag{11}$$

The two values of llow and lhigh are chosen so that possible pitch frequencies 50 to 500 Hz of human speech may be accommodated.

The mask $M_i^{cepSm}(l,m)$ is then determined by remaining symmetric half of cepstrum:

$$\overline{M}_i^{cep}(l,m) = \overline{M}_i^{cep}(K-l,m) \quad \text{for} \quad l \ge K/2 \tag{12}$$

The final smoothed spectral mask $M_i^f(l,m)$ is taken out as follows:

$$M_i^{cepSm}(k,m) = \exp\left(DFT\left\{ \overline{M}_i^{cep}(l,m) \mid_{l=0,\dots,K-1} \right\} \right) \tag{13}$$

These two obtained smoothed masks are then applied to the T-F representation $S_1(k,m)$ *and* $S_2(k,m)$ of two outputs estimated signals $\widehat{s}_1$ and $\widehat{s}_2$.

$$S_i^{cepSm}(k,m) = M_i^{cepSm} S_i(k,m) \tag{14}$$

Finally, the final estimated speech signals $\widehat{s}_1^f$ and $\widehat{s}_2^f$ are subsequently recovered in the time domain using inverse short time Fourier transform (ISTFT).

4 Results and Evaluation

In this section, we illustrate the performance evaluation of the proposed method. We have considered the convolutive case where the number of sources is equal to the number of mixtures. The experiments were done using two convolutive mixtures consisting of two speech signals. These speech signals were mixed together using a simulated room model [21]. The reverberation time (RT) was, respectively, chosen equal to 30, 50, 100, 150, 200 ms .The settings for all experiments are illustrated in the table 1.

Table 1. Parameter values for our experiments

DFT length= 2048	$B_{env} = 0$	l_{env}= 8
overlap factor=0.75	$B_{pitch} = 0.9$	l_{low}= 16
	$\beta_{peak} = 0.4$	l_{high}=120

To evaluate our BSS system, we have used different performance metrics including objective and subjective evaluations. We have exploited the ratio signal to interference ratio (SIR) as the objective evaluation. This reliable measurement was generated using the BSS evaluation toolbox [7],[20]. It can be expressed by the following equation:

$$SIR = 20\log \frac{\left\| s_{target} \right\|^2}{\left\| s_{interf} \right\|^2} \tag{15}$$

Where s_{target} and s_{interf} are, respectively, an allowed deformation of the target source si and an allowed deformation of the sources which takes account of the interference of the unwanted sources.

Table 2. The obtained SIR and SNR_i for different RT

RT		SIR		PESQ	
		Convbss	Proposed Method	Convbss	Proposed Method
30	y1	20.75	26.68	2.83	2.93
	y2	20.99	36.13	3.27	3.42
	Average	20.87	31.04	3.05	3.67
50	y1	21.08	26.88	2.57	2.62
	y2	17.93	29.15	3.22	3.34
	Average	19.50	28.01	2.89	2.98
100	y1	12.66	20.78	1.94	1.94
	y2	17.61	27.54	2.79	2.90
	Average	15.13	24.16	2.36	2.42
150	y1	13.83	29.10	1.71	1.68
	y2	2.33	8.64	2.50	2.65
	Average	8.02	18.87	2.10	2.16
200	y1	3.72	17.29	1.60	1.66
	y2	-0.72	7.51	2.36	2.42
	Average	1.5	12.4	1.98	2.04

Additionally, we have used the perceptual evaluation of speech quality PESQ as a subjective test. The PESQ measure, which is an objective method defined in the ITU-T P.862 standard [19], represents the equivalents of the subjective measure Mean Opinion Score (MOS). The experiment results of our convolutive BSS system has been compared to that of the convbss algorithm [5]. The results from the series of experiments are summarized in the table 2. It reports evaluation results for the separate performance measures including ratio SIR and PESQ obtained after separation by convbss algorithm and the proposed method. The results showed that our convolutive BSS approach has yielded a good performance for different values of RT. It can be observed that the best performance was obtained for the smallest value of RT and the performance of our proposed system was degraded gradually by increasing the RT from 30 to 200. However, these results seemed to be expected due to the augmentation of sound reflections for higher reverberation.

As reported in table 2, the proposed system was yielded interesting performance in comparison with convbss algorithm for different values of RT. We can see that the performance has improved considerably in terme SIR due to the cepstral smoothing step. For example, the SIR average obtained, where the simulated room RT=30, is 20.87 db for convbsss algorithm and 31.04 db for the poposed method.This improvement has been confirmed with the Perceptual Evaluation of Speech Quality (PESQ) measure, which represents as one of reliable methods of subjective test, was used to measure the quality of the separated speech signals. The PESQ measurement returns a score from 0.5 to 4.5. The results showed that our system has yielded remarkable results in terms of perceptual quality and still more effective than the convbss algorithm. For instant, in the experiment where the simulated room RT=30, we obtained PESQ equal to 2.93 for the proposed method and 2.83 for convbss algorithm.

5 Conclusion

In this paper, we have presented a blind speech separation system of convolutive mixtures. The proposed approach can be summarized in two essential steps. First, the speech signals were separated using convolutive BSS algorithm exploiting the second-order non stationary signals. Then, a cepstral smoothing of spectral mask as a post processing has done. This step consisted to smoothing the ideal binary masks which were estimated using the separated speech signals obtained in the first step. The experimental results and the evaluation measurement showed the efficiency of our BSS system for separating two signals sources using two microphone recordings.

References

1. Haykin, S., Chen, Z.: The cocktail party problem. Neural Computation 17, 1875–1902 (2005)
2. Asari, H., Pearlmutter, B.A., Zador, A.M.: Sparse Representations for the Cocktail Party Problem. The Journal of Neuroscience 26(28), 7477–7490 (2006)

3. Gorokhov, A., Loubaton, P.: Subspace based techniques for second order blind separation of convolutive mixtures with temporally correlated sources. IEEE Trans. on Circuit Systems I: Fundamental Theory and Applications 44(9), 813–820 (1997)
4. Douglas, S.C., Gupta, M., Sawada, H., Makino, S.: Spatio-temporal fastica algorithms for the blind separation of convolutive mixtures. IEEE Transactions on Audio Speech Lang. Processing. 15(5), 1511–1520 (2007)
5. Parra, L., Spence, C.: Convolutive blind separation of non-stationary sources. IEEE Trans. on Speech and Audio Processing 8(3), 320–327 (2000)
6. Makino, S., Sawada, H., Mukai, R., Araki, S.: Blind source separation of convolutive mixtures of speech in frequency domain. IEICE Trans. on Fundamentals of Electronics, Communications and Computer Sciences E88-A(7), 1640–1655 (2005)
7. Vincent, E., Gribonval, R., Fevotte, C.: Performance Measurement in Blind Audio Source Separation. IEEE Trans. on Audio, Speech, and Language Processing 14(4), 1462–1469 (2006)
8. Yellin, D., Weinstein, E.: Multichannel signal separation: methods and analysis. IEEE Trans. on Signal Processing 44, 106–118 (1996)
9. Wang, D.L.: On ideal binary mask as the computational goal of auditory scene analysis. In: Speech Separation by Humans and Machines. Springer, Heidelberg (2005)
10. Pedersen, M.S., Larsen, J., Kjems, U., Parra, L.C.: A survey of convolutive blind source separation methods. In: Handbook of Speech Processing. Springer, Heidelberg (2007)
11. Wang, D.L., Brown, G.J.: Computational Auditory Scene Analysis: Principles, Algorithms, and Applications. Wiley-IEEE Press, Hoboken, New Jersey (2006)
12. Oppenheim, A.V., Schafer, R.W.: Discrete Time Signal Processing, 3rd edn. Prentice Hall, New Jersey (2009)
13. Aichner, R., Buchner, H., Araki, S., Makino, S.: On-line time-domain blind source separation of non stationary convolved signals. In: 4th International Symposium on Independent Component Analysis and Blind Signal Separation, Japan, pp. 987–992 (2003)
14. Rahbar, K., Reilly, J.: Geometric optimization methods for blind source separation of signals. In: International Workshop on Independent Component Analysis and Signal Separation, Finland, pp. 375–380 (2000)
15. Chan, D., Rayner, P., Godsill, S.: Multi-channel signal separation. In: Proceedings of the IEEE International Conference on Acoustics, Speech, and Signal Processing, Georgia, pp. 649–652 (1996)
16. Madhu, N., Breithaupt, C., Martin, R.: Temporal smoothing of spectral masks in the cepstral domain for speech separation. In: Proceedings of the IEEE International Conference on Acoustics, Speech and Signal Processing, Las Vegas, pp. 45–48 (2008)
17. Jan, T., Wang, W., Wang, D.L.: A multistage approach for blind separation of convolutive speech mixtures. In: IEEE International Conference on Acoustics, Speech and Signal Processing, Taiwan, pp. 1713–1716 (2009)
18. Pesquet, J., Chen, B., Petropulu, A.P.: Frequency domain contrast functions for separation of convolutive mixtures. In: Proceedings of the IEEE International Conference on Acoustics, Speech, and Signal Processing, Salt Lake City, pp. 2765–2768 (2001)
19. ITU-T P.862, Perceptual evaluation of speech quality (PESQ), an objective method for end-to-end speech quality assessment of narrow-band telephone networks and speech codecs, International Telecommunication Union, Geneva (2001)
20. Fevotte, C., Gribonval, R., Vincent, E.: BSS EVAL toolbox user guide. Technical Report 1706, IRISA (2005)
21. Gaubitch, N.D.: Allen and Berkeley image model for room impulse response, Imperial College London (1979)

Comparison of Initial Solutions of Heuristics for No-wait Flow Shop Scheduling

Sagar Sapkal and Dipak Laha

Mechanical Engineering Department,
Jadavpur University, Kolkata 700032, India
sagar_us@indiatimes.com, dipaklaha_jume@yahoo.com

Abstract. No-wait flow shop scheduling problems have been proved to be NP-hard. Therefore, heuristics are considered as the most suitable ones for obtaining near optimal solutions and are generally developed in two phases namely, initial solution phase and improvement solution phase. We propose a method for obtaining the initial solution with a view to minimize total flow time. The exhaustive computational results reveal that the proposed method performs better than the existing heuristics with respect to both quality of solution and computational time.

Keywords: No-wait flow shop scheduling, Heuristics, Initial sequence, Total flow time.

1 Introduction

No-wait flow shop problems belong to the class of NP hard [1] and are commonly experienced in the industry and in many real-life applications. In these problems, each job is to be processed until completion without interruption either on or between machines. It is assumed that pre-emption is not allowed and the operation times on all machines are deterministic and known. A detailed survey of the methods and applications of these scheduling problems is given by Hall and Sriskandarajah [2]. Total flow time (TFT) is an important performance criterion in scheduling literature. Noteworthy heuristic algorithms for the no-wait flow shop with TFT criterion have been developed by Rajendran and Chaudhuri [3], Bertolissi [4], and Aldowaisan and Allahverdi [5]. In the present paper, we propose a method for obtaining the initial sequence for minimizing TFT in no-wait flow shop scheduling. We experimentally demonstrate that the proposed initial solution method performs significantly well compared to the initial solutions obtained by the currently popular heuristics.

2 The Problem Description

The problem is to determine a sequence of n jobs that minimizes the TFT criterion in no-wait flow shop scheduling. Let $\sigma = \{\sigma_1, \sigma_2, \ldots, \sigma_n\}$ represent the sequence of n jobs to be processed on m machines, and d(i, k) the minimum delay on the first

V.V. Das and N. Thankachan (Eds.): CIIT 2011, CCIS 250, pp. 294–298, 2011.

machine between the start of job i and the start of job k (required because of the no-wait restriction). Also, let $p(\sigma_i, j)$ represent the processing time on machine j of the job in the ith position of a given sequence, and $d(\sigma_{i-1}, \sigma_i)$ denote the minimum delay on the first machine between the start of two consecutive jobs found in the (i-1)th and ith position of the sequence. TFT of the sequence of n jobs in the no-wait flow shop scheduling is given by,

$$TFT = \sum_{i=2}^{n}(n+1-i)d(\sigma_{i-1},\sigma_i) + \sum_{i=1}^{n}\sum_{j=1}^{m}p(\sigma_i,j)$$

Where, the delay matrix of the d(i, k) values are calculated as in Bertolissi [4].

3 Initial Solutions Using Various Heuristics

Heuristics for these problems are generally developed in two phases namely, initial solution phase and improvement solution phase. It has been observed from scheduling literature [6] that the good initial solution helps in improving the quality of the final solution obtained by the improvement solution phase.

3.1 Initial Solution Phase of Rajendran and Chaudhuri Heuristics [3]

Rajendran and Chaudhuri [3] used two heuristic preference relations separately as the basis for selecting the initial sequence of jobs. Let $\mathrm{Ai} = \sum_{j=1}^{m}(m-j+1)p(i,j)$ and $\mathrm{Bi} = \sum_{j=1}^{m} p(i,j)$. For heuristic 1, the initial sequence is obtained by arranging the jobs in ascending order of the value of Ai. If any tie exists choose the job having the least value of Bi. For heuristic 2, the initial sequence is generated by arranging the jobs in ascending order of the value of Bi. If any tie exists choose the job having the least value of Ai.

3.2 Initial Solution Phase of Bertolissi Heuristic [4]

The main idea of the initial solution phase of Bertolissi heuristic [4] is to calculate the minimum apparent flow time of each pair of jobs and then to find the number of times of the starting jobs of the pairs, as marks. Next, by ordering the jobs in decreasing number of marks the initial sequence is created. To obtain the initial sequence of jobs, the heuristic consists of the following steps:

Step 1: Compute the flow times for each pair of jobs i, k by using the equation $F(i,k) = 2p(i,1) + \sum_{j=2}^{m} p(i,j) + R_{m(ik)}$, where $R_{m(ik)}$ is recursively computed as $R_{m(ik)} = p(k,m) + \max(R_{m-1(ik)}, \sum_{r=2}^{m} p(i,r))$, and $R_{1(ik)} = p(k,1)$.
Step 2: Compare each pair of flow times (F(i,k) and F(k,i)) and select the smallest one, and mark the starting job of the pair.
Step 3: Count the number of marks of each job and order the jobs in decreasing number of marks and use this ordering as the initial sequence of jobs.

3.3 Initial Solution Phase of Aldowaisan and Allahverdi Heuristic [5]

Aldowaisan and Allahverdi [5] developed the initial sequence gradually, by job insertion method comparing the total completion time at every partial sequence generated. To obtain the initial sequence of jobs, the heuristic consists of the following steps:

Step 1: Pick the job i with the smallest sum of processing times, i.e $\sum_{j=1}^{m} p(i,j) \leq \sum_{j=1}^{m} p(r,j) \ |\forall r = 1,2,\ldots n$ and insert it in the first position of the partial solution $\pi 1$. Let $\pi 2$ be the set of unscheduled jobs.
Step 2: For k = 2 to n, for each job $i \epsilon \pi_2$, insert it in position k of $\pi 1$ and compute the corresponding (partial) completion time. Among these, select job r yielding the minimum completion time. Remove it from $\pi 2$ and obtain a new partial sequence by inserting it in position k of current $\pi 1$. When k = n, corresponding $\pi 1$ is the initial sequence.

3.4 The Proposed Method

The well known Vogel's Approximation Method (VAM) is used for obtaining good initial solutions to transportation problems [7]. Simons [8] developed the heuristic for flow shop scheduling with sequence dependent setup times based on the application of the VAM to the travelling salesman problem. Similarly, we have made an attempt based on the principle of VAM to generate initial complete sequence of jobs in no-wait flow shop scheduling with TFT criterion. To obtain the initial sequence of jobs, the proposed method consists of the following steps:

Step 1: Calculate the delay matrix of d(i, k) values from the processing time matrix of n x m by using equation, $d(i,k) = \max_{1 \leq j \leq m}\{\sum_{r=2}^{j} p(i,r) + \sum_{r=2}^{j} p(k,r-1)\}, i \neq k$
Step 2: Using the delay matrix of n x n obtained from step 1, compute the row difference and the column difference by considering two lowest-valued cells in each row and each column. Pick up the pair of jobs at the intersection of the smallest cell value corresponding to the greatest value of row difference and column difference. Remove the cell values of row and column selected as pair, and cell value at the intersection of interchanged jobs pair selected, from the delay matrix.
Step 3: Repeat step 2 using current reduced delay matrix until all possible pairs of jobs are obtained. Otherwise, go to step 4.
Step 4: Arrange all the pairs of jobs combining each other to obtain a possible complete sequence of jobs. The complete sequence is then selected by breaking the chain at each possible point and implementing the sequence with the lowest TFT. This sequence of jobs with TFT value is considered as the output.

4 Computational Experience

The proposed method and the four existing heuristics considered for comparison have been coded in C and run on a PC having specifications as Intel Core 2 Duo, 2.93 GHz, 2 GB RAM. The processing times on machines were generated for each problem instance by using uniform random u(1 to 99) discrete distribution. Average relative percentage deviation (ARPD) from best heuristic initial solution is considered as performance measure and is given by,

$$\mathrm{ARPD} = \frac{100}{k}\sum_{i=1}^{k}\left(\frac{\mathrm{Heuristic}_i - \mathrm{Best}_i}{\mathrm{Best}_i}\right)$$

where, $\mathrm{Heuristic}_i$ is the initial solution value obtained for i-th instance, Best_i is the best initial solution value obtained for that instance, and k is the number of problem instances. The comparative results presented in the Table 1 reveal that the proposed method performs significantly better over the existing heuristics in almost all cases. The average computational times (in seconds) for the heuristics and the proposed method are reported in Table 2. The results show that the CPU time taken by the proposed method is better than those of the existing heuristics.

Table 1. ARPD of the heuristic initial solutions from the best solution (considering thirty number of instances for each problem size)

n	*m*	Rajendran-Chaudhuri Heuristic 1	Rajendran-Chaudhuri Heuristic 2	Bertolissi Heuristic	Aldowaisan-Allahverdi Heuristic	Proposed Method
10	5	7.8631	7.1924	5.1176	4.5140	3.2849
	10	5.5568	6.6705	3.4394	3.2284	2.6405
	15	5.4776	4.9307	3.0012	2.9579	1.1428
	20	4.1277	3.6793	2.7968	2.2029	2.2518
20	5	11.382	7.8077	8.0599	2.4521	0.7833
	10	11.379	9.4529	7.1394	2.7259	1.8087
	15	10.349	8.1420	8.3506	1.9984	1.7655
	20	10.930	6.9684	8.1605	1.6654	1.2927
30	5	14.747	10.319	10.286	1.8205	1.7393
	10	14.528	11.340	10.980	2.3936	0.5448
	15	14.536	10.939	12.950	2.2535	0.8579
	20	14.822	11.024	11.981	1.5540	1.1727
40	5	16.989	13.726	14.347	1.7723	0.6752
	10	18.517	14.236	14.904	1.7423	0.7744
	15	17.765	12.878	15.903	1.4992	0.4908
	20	18.897	13.806	15.360	2.1418	0.5786
50	5	17.537	13.986	15.958	1.1344	1.2048
	10	20.297	16.098	17.703	1.5160	0.8333
	15	21.155	14.896	18.815	1.4064	0.8896
	20	20.346	15.213	17.854	1.8200	0.6898
60	5	19.438	15.728	18.167	1.5634	1.1545
	10	22.354	18.207	19.281	1.3424	1.2765
	15	22.399	16.645	19.817	1.1305	0.8996
	20	22.236	16.888	20.066	1.9868	0.3680
Average		15.151	11.699	12.518	2.0343	1.2133

5 Conclusion

In this paper, we have presented a method based on the principle of well known Vogel's Approximation Method for generation of initial solutions for the no-wait flow shop scheduling for minimizing TFT criterion. The results show that the proposed method outperforms the existing heuristics. Also, the average computational times required are found to be comparable.

Table 2. Mean CPU times (in seconds) for the initial solutions of various heuristics

n	m	Rajendran-Chaudhuri Heuristic 1	Rajendran-Chaudhuri Heuristic 2	Bertolissi Heuristic	Aldowaisan-Allahverdi Heuristic	Proposed Method
10	5	0.0000	0.0000	0.0000	0.0000	0.0000
	10	0.0002	0.0002	0.0002	0.0002	0.0002
	15	0.0002	0.0004	0.0003	0.0004	0.0002
	20	0.0004	0.0004	0.0004	0.0004	0.0002
20	5	0.0002	0.0002	0.0002	0.0002	0.0004
	10	0.0004	0.0004	0.0004	0.0006	0.0004
	15	0.0010	0.0010	0.0010	0.0012	0.0006
	20	0.0016	0.0016	0.0018	0.0018	0.0006
30	5	0.0004	0.0004	0.0005	0.0006	0.0010
	10	0.0010	0.0010	0.0012	0.0012	0.0012
	15	0.0022	0.0022	0.0024	0.0026	0.0016
	20	0.0034	0.0036	0.0038	0.0040	0.0020
40	5	0.0006	0.0004	0.0008	0.0008	0.0022
	10	0.0018	0.0020	0.0022	0.0024	0.0026
	15	0.0038	0.0036	0.0040	0.0042	0.0034
	20	0.0062	0.0054	0.0064	0.0070	0.0040
50	5	0.0010	0.0006	0.0012	0.0016	0.0038
	10	0.0032	0.0030	0.0032	0.0040	0.0048
	15	0.0062	0.0060	0.0064	0.0070	0.0062
	20	0.0098	0.0096	0.0098	0.0112	0.0054
60	5	0.0014	0.0012	0.0018	0.0022	0.0052
	10	0.0050	0.0046	0.0052	0.0060	0.0060
	15	0.0076	0.0070	0.0080	0.0110	0.0072
	20	0.0150	0.0140	0.0160	0.0170	0.0084
Average		0.003025	0.002867	0.003217	0.003650	0.002817

References

1. Röck, H.: The three-machine no-wait flow shop is NP-complete. J. of Associate Computer Machinery 31, 336–345 (1984)
2. Hall, N.G., Sriskandarajah, C.: A survey of machine scheduling problems with blocking and no-wait in process. Operations Research 44, 510–525 (1996)
3. Rajendran, C., Chaudhuri, D.: Heuristic algorithms for continuous flow-shop problem. Naval Research Logistic Quarterly 37, 695–705 (1990)
4. Bertolissi, E.: Heuristic algorithm for scheduling in the no-wait flow-shop. J. of Materials Processing Technology 107, 459–465 (2000)
5. Aldowaisan, T., Allahverdi, A.: New heuristics for m-machine no-wait flowshop to minimize total completion time. Omega 32, 345–352 (2004)
6. Framinan, J.M., Leisten, R., Rajendran, C.: Different initial sequences for the heuristic of Nawaz, Enscore and Ham to minimize makespan, idletime or flowtime in the static permutation flowshop sequencing problem. Int. J. of Prod. Research. 41, 121–148 (2003)
7. Shore, H.M.: The transportation problem and the Vogel Approximation Method. Decis. Sci. 1, 441–457 (1970)
8. Simons Jr., J.V.: Heuristics in flow shop scheduling with sequence dependent setup times. Int. J. Mgmt. Sci. 20, 215–225 (1992)

An Efficient Forwarding Segmented and Backup Dependable Real-Time Communication in Multihop Networks

Shashikant Pandey[1], Anil Khandelwal[1], and R.K. Pandey[2]

[1] VNS Institute of Technology, Bhopal, M.P., India
{shashikant3017,Anilkhandelwalmt123}@gmail.com
[2] BU, Bhopal, M.P., India

Abstract. Multihop routing network with is to dynamically combine with frequency network is an emerging concept for improving the energy consumption and node reachability. Using wireless sensor networks (WSNs) to observe physical processes for control systems has attracted much attention recently. For some real-time control applications, controllers need to accurately estimate the process state within rigid delay constraints. By restricting the SFN sizes to a maximum number of nodes, the energy efficiency may be improved while the reachability is deteriorated. In this paper, we analyze several aspects of multihop networks with forward segmentation. For accurately estimating a process state as well as satisfying rigid delay constraints, we analyze an dependable segmented network estimation approach. Our network estimation operation performed at intermediate relay nodes which is interference-free, and able to aggregate as much estimate information as possible from a network to a sink within delay constraints. Several distributed real-time applications demand hard guarantees on the message delivery latency and the recovery delay from component failures. As these demands cannot be met in traditional datagram services, need to analyze several new aspects we delay backup segmentation with multihop network.

Keywords: SN, delay, backup channel, multihop network.

1 Introduction

The advent of multihop network with forwarding channel is most popular and new era in today's technology. Sensor data is shared between these sensor nodes and used as input to a distributed estimation system whose function is to extract the relevant information from the available data. Fundamental design objectives of sensor networks include reliability, accuracy, flexibility, cost effectiveness and ease of deployment. In wireless multi-hop Ad hoc networks, each node could be a router. Due to the contention for the shared channel, the throughput of each single node is limited not only by the raw channel capacity, but also by the transmissions in its neighborhood. A multihop traffic flow encounters contentions not only from other flows which pass by its neighborhood, but also from the transmissions of itself because the transmission at

V.V. Das and N. Thankachan (Eds.): CIIT 2011, CCIS 250, pp. 299–306, 2011.

each hop has to contend the channel with upstream and downstream nodes [1] [2]. There are several analysis which simplify multi-hop transmission into single-hop transmission [3] or an interference area [4] as their research issues. Single-hop fairness does not translate into multi-hop fairness because of the traffic dependency among different hops of a multi-hop flow.

Routing in sensor networks is very challenging due to several characteristics that distinguish them from contemporary communication and wireless ad hoc networks [5]. First of all, generated data traffic has significant redundancy in it since multiple sensors may generate same data within the vicinity of a phenomenon. Such redundancy needs to be exploited by the routing protocols to improve energy and bandwidth utilization. Second, sensor nodes are tightly constrained in terms of transmission power, on-board energy, processing capacity and storage and thus require careful resource management. All the sensor nodes cooperate with each other to feel, connect and deal with the data in the detected field, and then send the result to the observers [6][7]. The development of wireless sensor networks was originally motivated by military applications such as battlefield surveillance. Multihop routing is expected to be a key component in future wireless communication techniques such as mobile ad-hoc computer networking (MANET), WLAN mesh networks, wireless sensor-actuator networks (WSAN) and ultra-wideband (UWB) wireless-USB extension, and may also be useful in wireless digital radio and TV distribution. Currently, in the field of WSNs, the researches of state estimation and protocol design have remained largely separate. In the aspect of state estimation, estimation based on single sensor information over lossy networks has been extensively studied recently [8][9][10][11][12]. But these estimation techniques only view the network as a single end-to-end communication channel characterizing some data loss model and adapt to underlying communication protocols passively.

The communications schemes designed to tolerate faults can be broadly divided into proactive and reactive schemes. In the former, the failure-recovery process runs throughout the duration of the message transmission in anticipation of failures, while in the latter, the recovery process is initiated after detecting failure. In this paper we analyze several sympatric behaviors with the model which may be useful. The remaining of this paper is organized as follows. We discuss forwarding segmented backup scheme in Section 2. In Section 3 we discuss about SCR. The Evolution and recent scenario in section 4.In section 5 we discuss about model and problem formulation. The conclusions and future directions are given in Section 6. Finally references are given.

2 Forwarding Segmented Backup Scheme

When a fault occurs in a component in the network, all dependable connections passing through it have to be rerouted through their backup paths. This process is called failure recovery. This has three phases: fault detection, failure reporting and backup activation. The restoration time, called failure recovery delay, is crucial to many real time applications, and has to be minimized. One way of classifying backups is based on the architecture. That is, backups are classified in terms of the objects they deal with and the amount of awareness the backup application has of these objects.

2.1 Image- or Block-Level Backup

The backup application in this case deals with blocks of data. Typically, this kind of backup scheme needs all applications on the server to cease accessing the data that is being backed up. The application opens the disk to be backed up as a raw disk (ignoring the file locations) and literally does logical block-level read and write operations. The advantages of this kind of backup are that the backup and restore operations are very fast, and it can be a good disaster recovery solution. One disadvantage is that applications and even the operating system cannot access the disk while the backup or restore is happening.

2.2 File-Level Backup

With this type of backup, the backup software makes use of the server operating system and file system to back up files. One advantage is that a particular file or set of files can be restored relatively easily. Another is that the operating system and applications can continue to access files while the backup is being performed. There are several disadvantages as well. The backup can take longer, especially compared to an image-level backup. If a lot of small files are backed up, the overhead of the operating system and file and directory metadata access can be high. Also the problem of open files described earlier exists and needs to be solved.

2.3 Application-Level Backup

In this case, backup and restore are done at the application level, typically an enterprise application level—for example, Microsoft SQL Server or Microsoft Exchange. The backup is accomplished via APIs provided by the application. Here the backup consists of a set of files and objects that together constitute a point-in-time view as determined by the application. The main problem is that the backup and restore operations are tightly associated with the application. If a new version of the application changes some APIs or functionality of an existing API, one must be careful to get a new version of the backup/restore application.

2.4 Incremental Backup

An incremental backup archives only the changes since the last full or incremental backup. Again, the obvious advantage is that this backup takes less time because items not modified since the last full or incremental backup do not need to be copied to the backup media. The disadvantage is that a disaster recovery operation will take longer because restore operations must be done from multiple media sets, corresponding to the last full backup followed by the various incremental backups It is control by data center to confirm the backup scheme for the same concern.

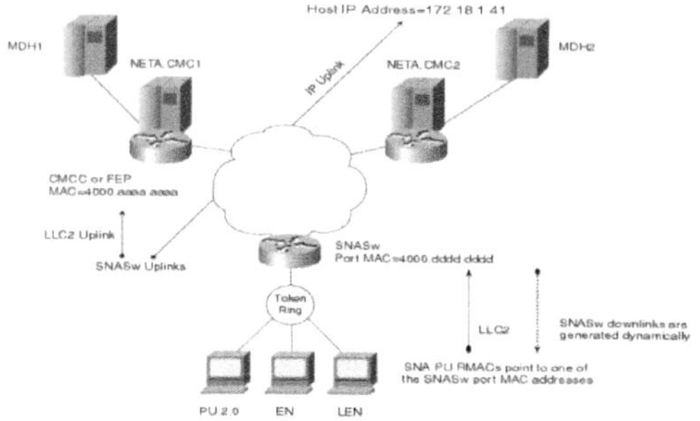

Fig. 1. Data Backup Center

It is possible to construct segmented backups optimized for different goals such as better resource utilization versus better failure-recovery delay. In this paper, we specifically provide algorithms for: 1) minimizing spare resources reserved by multiplexing segmented backups; and 2) constructing segmented backups that are optimal with respect to resource utilization. In forwarding backup scheme and its advantages over the end-to-end backup scheme. To establish dependable connections fault tolerant and real-time connections, earlier schemes have used end-to-end backups, backups that run from the source to the destination without sharing any components with the primary path. To establish forwarding scheme we taken the primary path with segmented backup. We find a backup path for each segment, which we call backup segment, independently. By segmented backup we refer to these backup segments taken together which is shown in fig2. The primary channel has three primary segments, each with its own backup segment.

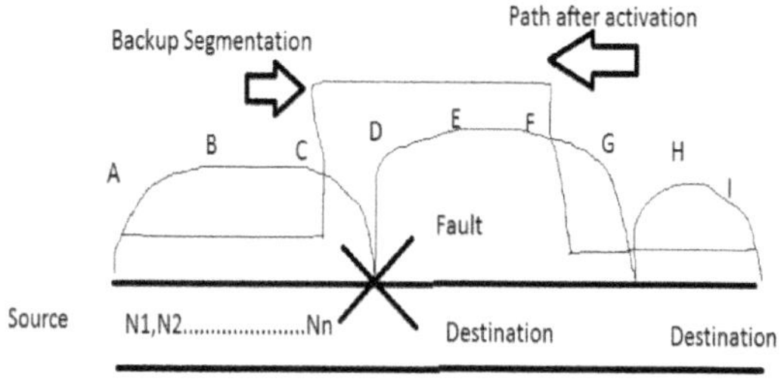

Fig. 2. Primary segmented Backup

These three backup segments together constitute the segmented backup for this primary path. In any network topology, whenever two disjoint paths exist between a pair of end nodes, backup segments are guaranteed to exist for any choice of a primary path between them. Similar guarantees cannot be provided on the existence of end-to-end backup.

3 Delay and Scalability

When a fault occurs in a component in the network, all dependable connections passing through it have to be rerouted through their backup paths. This process is called failure recovery. This has three phases: fault detection, failure reporting and backup activation. In Real Time Communication, it is essential to have the delays along both the primary and the backup channels to be as low as possible. Hence, we might have a restriction on the amount by which the delay along the backup exceeds that along the primary path. Adaptive QoS routing is a cross-layer optimization adaptive routing mechanism. The cross-layer mechanism provides up-to-date local QoS information for the adaptive routing algorithm, by considering the impacts of node mobility and lower-layer link performance. The multiple QoS requirements are satisfied by adaptively using forward error correction and multipath routing mechanisms, based on the current network status. The complete routing mechanism includes three parts: (1) a modified dynamic source routing algorithm that handles route discovery and the collection of QoS related parameters; (2) a local statistical computation and link monitoring function located in each node; and (3) an integrated decision-making system to calculate the number of routing paths, coding parity length, and traffic distribution rates.

The segmented backup scheme scales well since it does not demand global knowledge and does not involve any kind of broadcast. There is no necessity for a network manager and this scheme works well in a distributed network. For Backup Multiplexing each node needs to know the primary paths of the channels whose backups pass through it. This is easily accomplished if the information is sent along with the packet requesting the establishment of backup channel. Upon encountering faults, control messages are not broadcast, but sent only to a limited part of the network affected by the fault.

4 Evolution and Recent Scenario

In 2003, Mostafa I. Abd-El-Barr [13] analyzed about Wireless sensor networks (WSNs) which have a wide range of invaluable civil and military applications. Nodes in WSNs act as information sources, sensing and collecting data samples from their environment. They perform routing functions, creating multi-hop wireless networking fabric that conveys data samples to other sensor nodes. In 2010, Haitao Zhang et al. [13] proposed an in-network estimation approach which includes two coupled parts: the estimation operations performed at sensor nodes and an aggregation scheduling algorithm. Our in-network estimation operation performed at intermediate relay nodes not only optimally fuses the estimates obtained from different sensors but also predicts upper stream sensors' estimates which cannot be aggregated to the sink before deadlines. There estimate-based aggregation scheduling algorithm, which is interference-free, is able to aggregate as much estimate information as possible from a network to a sink within delay constraints. They prove the biasedness of in-network estimation, and theoretically analyze the optimality of our approach.

In 2010, Magnus Eriksson et al. [15] proposed about new approach to improving the energy consumption and node reachability of multihop networks is to dynamically combine multihop routing with single-frequency networks. Several nodes sending the same signal simultaneously over the same frequency channel. Four routing algorithms are suggested andevaluated for a broadcasting scenario. There Simulation results show that the best algorithm reduces the energy consumption by up to 42% in comparison to non-SFN multihop routing for the same node reachability. In 2010, Abdelhamid Eshoul et al. [16] present a comparative study between the dynamic survivability approaches in WDM mesh networks. They focuses on the diverse routing and the p-cycle approaches to protect mesh networks against single span failure under dynamic traffic. The computational complexity and the blocking performances of both approaches are analyzed and compared. Simulation results suggest that the p-cycle approach has better blocking performance than the diverse routing approach.

5 Model and Problem Formulation

We assume that the different channels experience independent fading. The system consists of subcarriers with total system power constraint. The power spectral densities of additive white Gaussian noise (AWGN) are equal at the source and the relay. The channel capacity of the subcarrier over the source-relay channel is given:

$$R_{s,i}(P_{s,i}) = \frac{B}{2N}\log_2\left(1 + \frac{P_{s,i}h_{s,i}}{N_0 B / N}\right),$$

where $P_{s,i}$ is the power allocated to the subcarrier i $(1 \le i \le N)$at the source, $h_{s,i}$is the corresponding channel power gain, N_0 is the power spectral density of AWGN, B is the total available bandwidth. Similarly, the channel capacity of the subcarrier j over the relay-destination channel is given:

$$R_{r,j}(P_{r,j}) = \frac{B}{2N}\log_2\left(1 + \frac{P_{r,j}h_{r,j}}{N_0 B / N}\right),$$

where $P_{r,j}$ is the power allocated to the subcarrier j $(1 \le j \le N)$ at the relay, $h_{r,j}$ is the corresponding channel power gain. When the subcarrier i over the source-relay channel is matched to the subcarrier j over the relay-destination channel, the channel capacity of this subcarrier pair is given:

$$R_{ij} = \min\{R_{s,i}(P_{s,i}), R_{r,j}(P_{r,j})\}.$$

Theoretically, the bits transmitted at the source can be reallocated to the subcarriers at the relay in arbitrary way. But for simplification in this paper, an additional constraint is that the bits transported on a subcarrier over the source-relay channel can be reallocated to only one subcarrier over the relay-destination channel, that is, only one-to-one subcarrier matching is permitted. This means that the bits on different subcarriers over the source-relay channel will not be reallocated to the same subcarrier at the relay.

For the optimally joint subcarrier matching and power allocation problem, we can formulate it as an optimization problem. The optimization problem is given.

$$\max_{P_{s,i},P_{r,j},\rho_{ij}} \sum_{i=1}^{N} \min\left\{R_{s,i}(P_{s,i}), \sum_{j=1}^{N} \rho_{ij} R_{r,j}(P_{r,j})\right\}$$

$$\text{subject to } \sum_{i=1}^{N} P_{s,i} + \sum_{j=1}^{N} P_{r,j} \le P_{tot}$$

$$P_{s,i}, P_{r,j} \ge 0 \quad \forall i,j,$$

$$\rho_{ij} = \{0,1\} \quad \forall i,j,$$

as

$$\sum_{j=1}^{N} \rho_{ij} = 1,$$

where P_{tot} is the total system power constraint, ρ_{ij} can only be either 1 or 0, indicating whether the bits transmitted on the subcarrier i at the source are retransmitted on the subcarrier j at the relay. The last constraint shows that only one-to-one subcarrier matching is permitted. By introducing the parameter C_i, the optimization problem can be transformed.

$$\max_{P_{s,i},P_{r,j},\rho_{ij},C_i} \sum_{i=1}^{N} C_i \quad \text{subject to } R_{s,i}(P_{s,i}) \ge C_i,$$

$$\sum_{j=1}^{N} \rho_{ij} R_{r,j}(P_{r,j}) \ge C_i,$$

$$\sum_{i=1}^{N} P_{s,i} + \sum_{j=1}^{N} P_{r,j} \le P_{tot},$$

$$P_{s,i}, P_{r,j} \ge 0 \quad \forall i,j,$$

$$\rho_{ij} = \{0,1\} \quad \forall i,j,$$

$$\sum_{j=1}^{N} \rho_{ij} = 1.$$

6 Conclusions and Future Directions

Multihop routing network with is to dynamically combine with frequency network is an emerging concept for improving the energy consumption and node reachability. Using wireless sensor networks (WSNs) to observe physical processes for control systems has attracted much attention recently. For some real-time control applications, controllers need to accurately estimate the process state within rigid delay constraints. Our network estimation operation performed at intermediate relay nodes which is interference-free, and able to aggregate as much estimate information as possible from a network to a sink within delay constraints. Several distributed real-time applications demand hard guarantees on the message delivery latency and the recovery delay from component failures. As these demands cannot be met in traditional datagram services, need to analyze several new aspects we delay backup segmentation with multihop network.In this paper we analyze several aspects with their advantages and disadvantages.

References

1. IEEE Computer Society LAN MAN Standards Committee. Wireless LAN Medium Access Protocol (MAC) and Physical Layer (PHY) Specification, IEEE Std 802.11-1997. The Institute of Electrical and Electronics Engineers, New York, NY (1997)
2. Zhai, H., Wang, J., Fang, Y.: Distributed Packet Scheduling for Multihop Flows in Ad Hoc Networks. In: Proc. IEEE WCNC (March 2004)
3. Li, B.: End-to-end fair bandwidth allocation in multi-hop wireless ad hocnetworks. In: Proc. of IEEE ICDCS, pp. 471–480 (June 2005)
4. Gambiroza, V., Sadeghi, B., Knightly, E.: End-to-end performance and fairness in multihop wireless backhaul networks. In: Proc. of ACM MobiCom, pp. 287–301 (September 2004)
5. Al-Karaki, J.N., Kamal, A.E.: Routing techniques in wireless sensor networks: a survey. IEEE Wireless Communications 11(6), 6–28 (2004)
6. Akyildiz, I.F., Su, W., Sankarasubramaniam, Y., Cayirci, E.: A survey on sensor network. IEEE Communications Magazine 40(8), 102–114 (2002)
7. Callaway, E.H.: Wireless Sensor NetWork: Architechture and Protocal, pp. 41–62. CRC Press LLC, Boca Raton (2004)
8. Sinopoli, B., Schenato, L., Franceschetti, M., Poolla, K., Jordan, M.I., Sastry, S.S.: Kalman Filtering With Intermittent Observations. IEEE Trans. on Automatic Control 49(9), 1453–1464 (2004)
9. Smith, S., Seiler, P.: Estimation with lossy measuraments:jump estimators for jump systems. IEEE Trans. on Automatic Control 48(12), 1453–1464 (2003)
10. Xu, Y., Hespanha, J.: Estimation under controlled and uncontrolled communications in networked control systems. In: 44th IEEE CDC-ECC, pp. 842–847 (December 2005)
11. Gupta, V., Spanos, D., Hassibi, B., Murray, R.M.: Optimal LQG control across packet-dropping links. Systems and Control Letters 56(6), 439–446 (2007)
12. Schenato, L., Sinopoli, B., Franceschetti, M., Poolla, K., Sastry, S.: Foundations of Control and Estimation over Lossy Networks. Proceedings of the IEEE 95(1), 163–187 (2007)
13. Abd-El-Barr, M.I., Youssef, M.A.M., Al-Otaibi, M.M.: Wireless Sensor Networks – Part I: Topology and Design Issues. IEEE, Los Alamitos (2005)
14. Zhang, H., Ma, H., Li, X.-Y.: Estimate Aggregation with Delay Constraints in Multihop Wireless Sensor Networks. IEEE, Los Alamitos (2011)
15. Eriksson, M., Mahmud, A.: Dynamic Single Frequency Networks in Wireless Multihop Networks. IEEE, Los Alamitos (2010)
16. Eshoul, A., Mouftah, H.T.: Performance comparison between dynamic protection schemes in Survivable WDM mesh networks. IEEE, Los Alamitos (2010)

Modified k-Means Clustering Algorithm

Vaishali R. Patel[1] and Rupa G. Mehta[2]

[1] SVMIT, Department of Computer Science and Engineering, Bharuch, Gujarat, India
[2] SVNIT, Department of Computer Engineering, Surat, Gujarat, India
vaishalirajpatel@gmail.com, rgm@coed.svnit.ac.in

Abstract. Clustering is the popular unsupervised learning technique of data mining which divide the data into groups having similar objects and used in various application areas. k-Means is the most popular clustering algorithm among all partition based clustering algorithm to partition a dataset into meaningful patterns. k-Means suffers some shortcomings. This paper addresses two shortcomings of k-Means; pass number of centroids in apriori and does not handle noise. This paper also presents an overview of cluster analysis, clustering algorithms, preprocessing and normalization techniques in modified k-Means to improve the effectiveness and efficiency of the modified k-Means clustering algorithm.

Keywords: Algorithm, Clustering, k-Means, Preprocessing, Normalization.

1 Introduction

Important pattern from various engineering fields can be extracted using different techniques like classification, clustering, prediction of data mining. Goal of clustering is to separate a finite unlabeled data set into a finite and discrete set of "natural," hidden data structures, rather than provide an accurate characterization of unobserved samples generated from the same probability distribution [1]. People always learn new object and properties of that object which can be comparable with other objects based on similarity or dissimilarity. Clustering is an unsupervised learning technique of data mining where huge collection of data is classified into clusters having similarity among data objects. Various clustering algorithms according to different techniques have been designed and applied to various data mining problems successfully. These algorithms promise to generate efficient and quality clusters, but the quality of clustering techniques depends on; similarity measure and technique used for implementation, ability to discover some or all hidden patterns, definition and representation of cluster chosen [2]. Accomplishment of clustering algorithms in many areas, it causes many precincts to the researchers when no or little information are available. There is also no universal clustering algorithm developed; that's why it is very crucial job to choose appropriate clustering technique and algorithm considering above precincts. A simple and commonly used algorithm for producing clusters by optimizing a criterion function; defined either globally or locally, is the k-means algorithm [5]. The k-Means algorithm [3], [4], [5], [6], [7] is effective in producing clusters for many practical applications. k-Means algorithm requires the number of centroids in the data set to be

V.V. Das and N. Thankachan (Eds.): CIIT 2011, CCIS 250, pp. 307–312, 2011.

define in advance. This algorithm results in different types of clusters depending on the random choice of initial centroids. Several attempts were made by researchers to improve the performance of the k-means clustering algorithm. This paper discuss cluster analysis, comparative analysis of clustering algorithms, result analysis of proposed modified k-Means clustering algorithm on various datasets from UCI data repositories.

2 Clustering Algorithms

Clustering problem is represented by different ways and different clustering algorithms are designed and apply to solve it. Table 1 summarizes different clustering algorithms and specific applications where clustering algorithms are applied.

Table 1. Comparison of Clustering Algorithms [8]

Cluster Algorithm	Complexity	Type, Size and Shape of Data	Application
k-Means	O(NKD) – Time O(N+K) – Space	Numerical, large size data of spherical shape	analyze student's result data-Nigeria [9]
PAM	O(K(N-K)2) – for each iteration	Numerical, small size Data of arbitrary shape	Circuit Partitioning using VHDL [10]
CLARA	O(K(40+K)2 + K(N-K)+ - Time	Numerical, large size of arbitrary shape	Image Information Mining [11]
CLARANS	Quadratic in total Performance/ O(N2)	Numerical, large size of arbitrary shape	Spatial Data Mining [12]
BIRCH	O(N) – Time	Numerical, large size Data of spherical shape	Filtering of real images [13]
ROCK	O(KN2)	Mixed, Graph, Large Size Data(Categorical Data)	Network Anomaly Detection [14]
Chameleon	O(N2) – Time	Discrete, High Dimensional Data of arbitrary shape	Gene clustering for biomedical literature [15]
DBSCAN	O(NlogN) - Time	Numerical, arbitrary of high dimensional Data	Network Traffic Classification [16]
OPTICS	O(NlogN) - Time	Numerical, arbitrary of high dimensional Data	Sequential Data [17]
STING	O(K)	Numerical, rectangular, Spatial Data	Spatial Data Mining
CLIQUE	O(NK+MK)	Numerical Data, arbitrary of high dimensional data	Automatic subspace clustering [18]
Wave Cluster	O(N)	Numerical, arbitrary of Spatial Data	Remote Sensing Image Retrieval [19]
COBWEB	O(AVB2logK)	sequence of simple and complex objects	Dynamic Web: Profile Correlation [20]
Fuzzycmeans	Near O(N)	Categorical Data	Image Segmentation

Partition based clustering technique partition data into number of subsets where each subset represents a cluster and each cluster must contain at least on object and each object must belongs to exactly one cluster. Well known partitioning algorithms are: k-Means, k-Medoids. k-Means algorithm is one of the most popular partition based clustering method. Yet it suffers from the some shortcomings; number of clusters and initial seed values must initialize in advance, it converges to local optima due to random initialization of seed values. Clustering techniques and algorithm are being applied in a wide variety of engineering disciplines. It can be argued that there will not be a universal clustering algorithm that could be applied to arbitrary data. It is therefore important to have a clear understanding of the requirements of a particular application and to choose the technique that best fits those requirements. k-Means is used in various application areas of software.

3 Proposed Work and Results

As k-Means's attractiveness lie in its simplicity and its local minimum convergence properties, yet it suffers from major shortcomings like; it scales poorly computationally means it is slow and scales poorly with respect to the time it takes to complete each iteration. The number of clusters k and initial seed values must to be supplied by the user, does not handle noise and outliers. This section address the shortcoming of k-Means to pass seed values in advance. Modified k-Means algorithm initialize seed values automatic and preprocess the data set using cleaning method and normalization approach with min-max, z-score and decimal scaling methods. Modified k-Means first preprocess the dataset with one of the minimum, constant, maximum, average, standard deviation options of cleaning method then normalization the dataset using min-max, z-score and decimal scaling techniques. Flow chart of proposed model "Modified k-Means Clustering Algorithm" is shown in Figure 1.

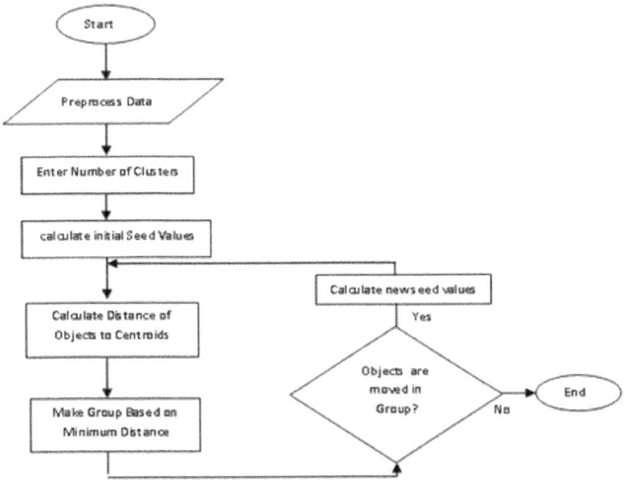

Fig. 1. Flow-Chart of Modified k-Means Clustering Algorithm

The proposed model is implemented using Visual Basic 6.0 and MS SQL Server 5.0 which prepare the data using different preprocessing techniques. First, Dataset is prepared by applying cleaning method which fill missing values with various options like average, maximum, minimum, constant and standard deviation and remove noise from the dataset. Once the noise is removed from the dataset, volume of data is reduced by applying different normalization approach. After data preparation, modified k-Means algorithm is applied computes sum of squared error of each cluster and mean of SSE. This section represents the performance evaluation of the proposed model on the River, Iris and datasets from UCI machine learning repository. During each iteration, the SSE of each cluster is computed. Finally, Mean of SSE (MSE) is computed for generated clusters which measure the accuracy of the generated clusters. Computed MSE for two clusters with different cleaning methods and normalization approaches; min-max, z-score and decimal scaling for above data sets is shown in Table 2.

Table 2. Computed Error in "Modified k-Means Clustering Algorithm"

1	2	3	4	5	6
Data	Cleaning Technique	Error Mk-Means	Error in Mk-means with Min Max Method	Error in Mk-means with z-score Method	Error in Mk-means with Decimal Scaling Method
River	Average	3.407	0.769	0	0.88
	Constant	8.758	0.433	0	1.729
	Maximum	3.407	0.769	0	0.885
	Minimum	7.775	0.769	0	0.912
	Stand. Devi.	3.407	0.44	0	1.611
Iris	Average	11.694	6.031	8.531	1.169
Breast Cancer	Average	156.483	8.856	9.267	1.159
Abalone	Average	17.129	7.849	8.242	2.267

4 Conclusion

Clustering is an important unsupervised technique in data mining. In clustering data are clustered based on certain criteria so data objects are closer to each other in a cluster than data objects in another clusters. Clustering algorithm never is universal to solve all problems as they are designed on certain assumptions. k-Means is popular for its favorable execution time having some shortcoming like pass number of seed values in advance, does not handle noise and outliers. This paper discuss cluster analysis, comparative analysis of clustering algorithms, k-Means algorithm and its shortcomings, proposed model for modified k-Means algorithm with data preparation which handle noise and reduce volume of the dataset by applying various cleaning method and min-max, z-score and decimal scaling methods of normalization approach. The result analysis is done using various datasets from UCI data repository. The proposed model suffers from shortcoming like more time complexity and number of clusters passes in advance. In future, we will try to remove this shortcoming of modified k-Means clustering algorithm.

References

1. Kaufman, L., Rousseeuw, P.: Finding Groups in Data: An Introduction to Cluster Analysis. Wiley, Chichester (1990)
2. Velmurugan, T., Santhanam, T.: Computational Complexity between K-Means and K-Medoids Clustering Algorithms for Normal and Uniform Distributions of Data Points. Journal of Computer Science 6(3), 363–368 (2010)
3. Jiawei Han, M.K.: Data Mining Concepts and Techniques. Morgan Kaufmann Publishers. An Imprint of Elsevier (2006)
4. Dunham, M.H.: Data Mining- Introductory and Advanced Concepts. In: Pearson Education 2006. Proceedings of the World Congress on Engineering, vol. 1 (2009)
5. McQueen, J.: Some methods for classification and analysis of multivariate observations. In: Proceeding 5th Berkeley Symp. Math. Statist. Prob., vol. 1, pp. 281–297 (1967)
6. Merz, C., Murphy, P.: UCI Repository of Machine Learning Databases, `ftp://ftp.ics.uci.edu/pub/machine-learning-databases`
7. Tan, P.-N., Steinback, M., Kumar, V.: Introduction to Data Mining. Pearson Education (2007)
8. Patel, V.R., Mehta, R.G.: Clustering Algorithms: A Comprehensive Survey. In: International Conference on Electronics, Information and Communication Systems Engineering, Jodhpur (2011)
9. Oyelade, O.J., Oladipupo, O.O., Obagbuwa, I.C.: Application of kMeans Clustering algorithm for prediction of Students' Academic Performance. International Journal of Computer Science and Information Security 7 (2010)
10. Sumitra Devi, K.A., Vijayalakshmi, M.N., Vasantha, R., Abraham, A.: Accomplishment of Circuit Partitioning using VHDL and Clustering Pertaining to VLSI design
11. Tilton, J.C., Marchisio, G., Koperski, K.: NASA's Intelligent Systems Program, NASA Headquarter Code R
12. Ng, R.T., Han, J.: CLARANS:A Method for Clustering Objects for Spatial Data Mining. IEEE Transaction on Knowledge and Data Engineering 14(5), 1003–1016 (2002)
13. Seidman, C.: Data Mining with Microsoft SQL Server 2000 Technical Reference, `http://amazon.com/Mining-Microsoft-Server-Technical-Reference/dp/0735612714`; ISBN:0-7356-1271-4
14. Noh, S.-K., Kim, Y.-M., Kim, D.K., Noh, B.-N.: Network Anomaly Detection Based on Clustering of Sequence Patterns. In: Gavrilova, M.L., Gervasi, O., Kumar, V., Tan, C.J.K., Taniar, D., Laganá, A., Mun, Y., Choo, H. (eds.) ICCSA 2006. LNCS, vol. 3981, pp. 349–358. Springer, Heidelberg (2006)
15. Sahay, S.: Study and Implementation of CHEMELEON algorithm for gene clustering
16. Erman, J., Arlitt, M., Mahanti, A.: Traffic Classification Using Clustering Algorithms. In: SIGCOMM 2006 Workshops, Pisa, Italy, September 11-15 (2006)

17. Santhisree, K., Damodaram, A.: OPTICS on Sequential Data: Experiments and Test Results. International Journal of Computer Applications 5, 1–4 (2010)
18. Agrawal, R., Gehrke, J., Gunopulos, D., Raghavan, P.: Automatic Subspace Clustering of High Dimensional Data for Data Mining Applications. Department of Computer Science, University of Wisconsin, Madison, WI 53706
19. Maheshwari, P., Srivastava, N.: WaveCluster for Remote Sensing Image Retrieval. International Journal on Computer Science and Engineering 3(2) (2011)
20. Scanlan, J., Hartnett, J., Williams, R.: DynamicWEB: Profile Correlation Using COBWEB. In: Sattar, A., Kang, B.-h. (eds.) AI 2006. LNCS (LNAI), vol. 4304, pp. 1059–1063. Springer, Heidelberg (2006)

Simulation of Multicarrier CDMA System in Rayleigh Channel

Sheetal Patil and U.V. Bhosle

Electronics Department, Vidyalankar Institute of Technology, Mumbai
sheetal.patil@vit.edu.in

Abstract. The combination of CDMA and OFDM that called "Multicarrier CDMA system" can reduce the interference and improve the performance of the system in fading channel. The conventional multicarrier CDMA system has three schemes. MC-CDMA, MC-DS-CDMA, MT-CDMA. The MC-CDMA transmitter spreads the original data stream over different subcarriers using a given spreading code in the frequency domain. The MC-DS-CDMA transmitter spreads the S/P converted data streams using a given spreading code in the time domain. The resulting spectrum of each subcarrier can satisfy the orthogonal condition with the minimum frequency separation. The MT-CDMA scheme uses longer spreading codes in proportion to the number of subcarriers as compared with a normal DS- CDMA scheme therefore the system can accommodate more users than the DS- CDMA scheme. MC- CDMA scheme can reduce interference and improve performance in fading channel.

Keywords: OFDM, CDMA, MC-CDMA, Rayleigh channel, modulation.

1 Introduction

The 4G systems will provide higher data rates and greater flexibility. This will necessitate the use a transmission scheme that can accommodate very high data rate transmission over the hostile wireless channel.

Although MC-CDMA resembles the signal structure for OFDM when the subcarriers are spaced as closely as possible, the manner in which the subcarriers are utilized is very different. In [16] OFDM is discussed as a means of decreasing the effective baud rate by transmitting different data symbols on different subcarriers. With MC-CDMA the same data bit is transmitted over all subcarriers without changing the original baud rate.

MC-CDMA takes the advantages of both OFDM and CDMA and makes an efficient transmission system by spreading the input data symbols with spreading codes in the frequency domain. It uses a number of narrowband orthogonal subcarriers with symbol duration longer than the delay spread. This makes it unlikely for all the subcarriers to be affected by the same deep fades of the channel at the same time thereby improving performance. Synchronization during transmission becomes easier with longer symbol durations [3].

V.V. Das and N. Thankachan (Eds.): CIIT 2011, CCIS 250, pp. 313–320, 2011.

2 MC-CDMA

MC-CDMA systems based on the combination of code-division multiple access (CDMA) and orthogonal frequency division multiplexing (OFDM) techniques, were proposed in 1993 [4]. The multicarrier CDMA schemes are categorized into two groups. One spreads the original data stream using given spreading code, and then modulates a different subcarrier with each chip, and other spreads the serial – to-parallel converted data using a given spreading code, and then modulates a different subcarrier with each of data stream[3]. These signals can be easily transmitted and received using the fast fourier transform (FFT) device without increasing transmitter and receiver complexities, and have the attractive feature of high spectral efficiency due to minimally densely subcarrier spacing [3]. Due to the attractive features like frequency diversity and high bandwidth efficiency [3], MC-CDMA outperforms direct sequence CDMA and MC-DS-CDMA in terms of BER performance over the downlink. Hence, MC-CDMA appears to be a suitable candidate for supporting multimedia services in mobile radio communications for the downlink [2].

2.1 Multicarrier CDMA

The serial input data stream is converted into parallel streams and are spread using CDMA spreading sequences in the frequency domain. This ensures frequency non-selective fading in the subcarriers.

The input data symbols, di[k], are assumed to be binary antipodal where k denotes the kth bit interval and i denotes the ith user. In the analysis, it is assumed that di[k], takes on values of -1 and 1 with equal probability. The number of subcarriers Nc can be equal to or greater than processing gain G_{MC}.

The generation of an MC-CDMA signal can be described as follows. A single data symbol is replicated into N parallel copies. The jth branch (subcarrier) of the parallel stream is multiplied by a chip, from a pseudo-random (PN) code or some other orthogonal code of length N and then BPSK modulated to a subcarrier spaced apart from its neighboring subcarriers by 1/Tb. The transmitted signal consists of the sum of the outputs of these branches. This process yields a multicarrier signal with the subcarriers containing the PN-coded data symbol. The transmitted signal corresponding to the jth data bit of the ith user is

$$s_i(t) = \sum_{j=0}^{N-1} C_i(j) d_i(k) \cos(2\Pi f_c t + 2\Pi jt / T_b) p_{Tb}(t - T_b) \tag{1}$$

where

Ci(j)=[1 -1], Spreading code for the ith user; fc =Centre Carrier frequency
Tb = Bit duration; di(j) = input data for the ith user

As seen from Equation (1), MC-CDMA shares same signal structure as OFDM and this can be achieved by performing IFFT. The spreading of data symbols is represented as

$$s = \sum_{j=0}^{N-1} d_i(j).C_i(j) = (S_0, S_2, ... S_{N-1})^T \tag{2}$$

where di(j) is the input data for the ith user and Ci(j)is the spreading code for the ith user.

3 System Design

The MC-CDMA system is design in three parts. The transmitter, The mobile radio channel, receiver.

3.1 MC-CDMA Transmitter

Multicarrier CDMA involves the concurrent transmission of identical data on multiple sub- carriers within an OFDM symbol. Orthogonality of each sub-carrier is achieved by making the carrier frequency spacing Δf, equal to the inverse of the active symbol period, T_a.

The MC-CDMA transmitter implemented is as shown in fig 1.

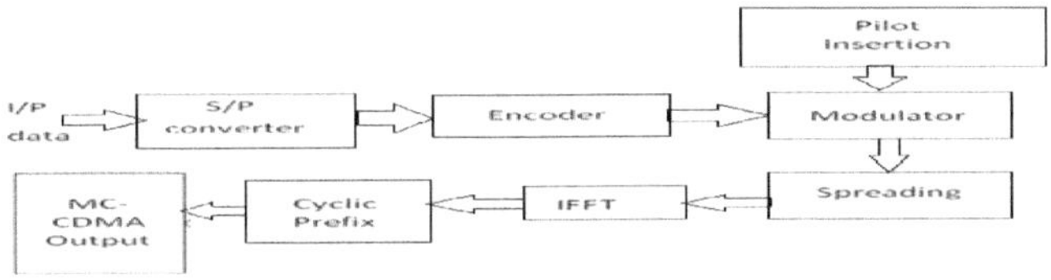

Fig. 1. MC-CDMA Transmitter

Forward Error Correction (FEC) coding through the application of a convoltional code has done. The modulation techniques used to simulate the BPSK, QPSK and 16-PSK modulation. Walsh-Hadmard sequences are bipolar spreading sequences that are used for channel separation in DS-CDMA. In this implementation length of the code is consider 32 as per the 802.11a standard of WLAN. [6] At the transmitter, the pilot symbols are inserted in the frequency domain at regular interval so when we interpolate at the receiver, the interpolation is the best possible everywhere.[7]

The number of pilot symbols is given by (FFT size * 1/8). Therefore, numbers of pilots are 512 *1/8.These pilot symbols are placed on every eighth subcarrier to give a subcarrier separation of 8 kHz. This system, therefore, has 64 subcarriers allocated to carry pilot symbols and 448 subcarriers allocated to carry spread data. Orthogonal modulation is achieved using a 512- point Inverse Fourier Transform. The OFDM symbol is generated in base band, which means that the first sub-carrier has frequency equal zero [1].

The addition of cyclic prefix of length 'FFT size/4' to the IFFT output ensures the orthogonality between the carriers and prevents Inter Carrier Interference (ICI) and the length of cyclic prefix is so chosen that it also remove Inter-symbol Interference (ISI). The modulated parallel data is converted into serial and transmitted over the channel.

3.2 Mobile Radio Channel

The mobile radio channel places fundamental limitations on the performance of wireless communication systems.

Time dispersion due to multipath causes the transmitted signal to undergo either flat or frequency selective fading. Flat fading channels are modeled as Rayleigh or Rician distributed channels.

Rayleigh fading occurs is present when there is no Line Of Sight (LOS) component available. The distribution describes the statistical time varying nature of a flat fading channel.

The signal arriving at the receiver is the sum of multiple, independent random variables. According to the Central Limit Theorem, the sum of these random variables converges under certain conditions to a Gaussian form. The envelope of this type of random variable represents a Rayleigh distribution. The pdf of the Rayleigh distribution is given by

$$p(r) = \begin{cases} \frac{r}{\sigma^2} \exp[-\frac{r^2}{2\sigma^2}] & 0 \le r \le \infty \\ 0 & r \le 0 \end{cases} \tag{3}$$

Where 'σ 'the rms value of the received voltage before envelope detection and 'σ 2' is the time-average power of the received signal before envelope detection.

If the channel possesses a constant gain and linear phase response over bandwidth that is smaller than the bandwidth of transmitted signal, then the channel creates frequency selective fading on the received signal. Under such conditions, the channel impulse response has a multipath delay spread which is greater than the reciprocal bandwidth of the transmitted message waveform. When this occurs, the received signal include multiple versions of the transmitted waveform which are attenuated (faded) and delayed in time, and hence the received signal distorted. Frequency selective fading is due to time dispersion of the transmitted symbol within the channel. Thus channel includes intersymbol interference (ISI).

To simulate the multipath behaviour of the channel, several Rayleigh fading simulators are used in conjunction.

The signal at the input of the receiver is a multipath signal consisting of a six ray Rayleigh faded signal with AWGN. Let $h[m]$ be the sampling version of the channel, then the output of the channel is:

$$\tilde{y}_n[m] = \sum_{l=0}^{Nc+L-1} \tilde{x}_n[l]h[m-l] \tag{4}$$

3.3 MC-CDMA Receiver

The basic block diagram of MC- CDMA receive3r is as shown in fig 2.

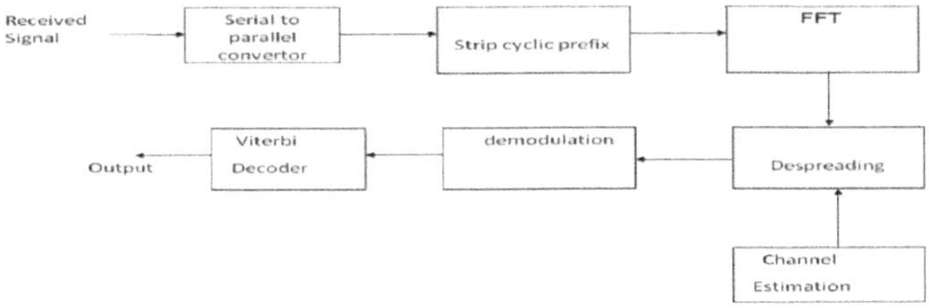

Fig. 2. Block Diagram of MC-CDMA Receiver

The signal is converted from serial to parallel format and then the cyclic prefix is stripped. OFDM demodulation is performed by taking FFT of the received signal. Then it is despread using the same 32-bit Walsh code as at the transmitter. Channel estimation is done and the closest estimate of the transmitted symbol is evaluated. This is followed by baseband demodulation. The subsequent utilization of soft decision Viterbi decoding in the receiver was considered. The Viterbi algorithm utilizes Minimum Likelihood Sequence Estimation (MLSE) metrics. [1]

The demodulation operation is a simple FFT according to the IFFT used as the OFDM modulation.

Then the demodulated output is

$$\tilde{Y}_n[k] = \left(\sum_{m=0}^{Nc-1} \tilde{x}_n[m] \exp\left(-2\pi jk \frac{m}{Nc} \right) \right) \Im(h[k]) \tag{5}$$

From equation 5 it is seen that simple division of demodulated signal by the channel frequency response gets back the transmitted signal.

$$\tilde{Y}_n[k] = \Im(x_n[k])\Im(h[k])$$
$$\tilde{Y}_n[k] = X_n[k]H[k] \tag{6}$$

The pilot symbols in the frequency-time domain at the transmitter are located at specific points. The location of these pilot symbols are also known in the receiver. The channel estimate at the pilot locations can be calculated as follows,

$$h_{n,r} = \frac{y_{n,r}}{x_{n,r}} \tag{7}$$

$h_{n,r}$ = impulse response at pilot positions; $x_{n,r}$ = input signal at pilot positions

$y_{n,r}$ = Corresponding received signal; n = subcarrier index ; r= OFDM symbol index

Channel estimates from different pilot locations can then be interpolated to obtain channel estimates at all values of n and r. In this receiver scheme, a time domain least squares (TDLS) method as described in [24, 25] was implemented in order to provide a more realistic channel estimation based on the training sequences and pilots inserted into the transmitted sequence. By this method estimated channel coefficients are in time domain therefore to obtain in frequency domain FFT has done.

3.4 System Software Design

An MC-CDMA system was modelled using Matlab to allow various parameters of the system to be varied and tested. The aim of doing the simulations was to measure the

BER performance of MC-CDMA system under different channel conditions and baseband modulations and to allow for variations in Doppler frequency to be tested.

The Simulation parameters considered for the MC-CDMA system implemented in this project are tabulated below.

Table 1. Simulation parameters

Freq of carrier	1GHz
Sampling freq	10Mbps
Bandwidth	4MHz
No of Carriers	512
Sub carrier spacing	8KHz
Useful symbol duration	125μs
Guard Time	31.25μs
Convolutional code generator polynomial	go=171, g1= 133 (octal)
Spreading & spreading sequence	Walsh code ,32 bt
Baseband modulation	BPSK/QPSK/16- PSK/16-QAM /64-QAM
Channel Model & multipath model	Rayleigh & 6 ray model

The speed of the vehicle considered as varying between 5.4Km/Hr to 200Km/Hr. The corresponding Doppler shift is calculated.

Table 2. Doppler frequency Vs Vehicle velocity

V Velocity Km / Hr	f_d Doppler frequency
5.4	5
60	55.56
120	111.1
200	200

4 Results

After simulation the following result has come.

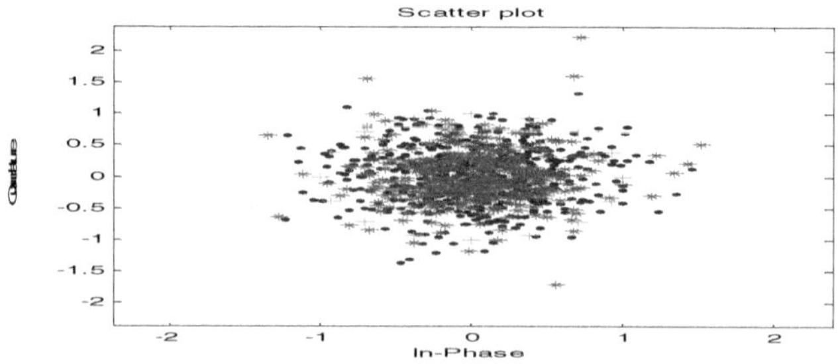

Fig. 3. Unequalized Received Data, Equalized Data, Constellation Diagram for 16-PSK Modulator in Rayleigh Channel

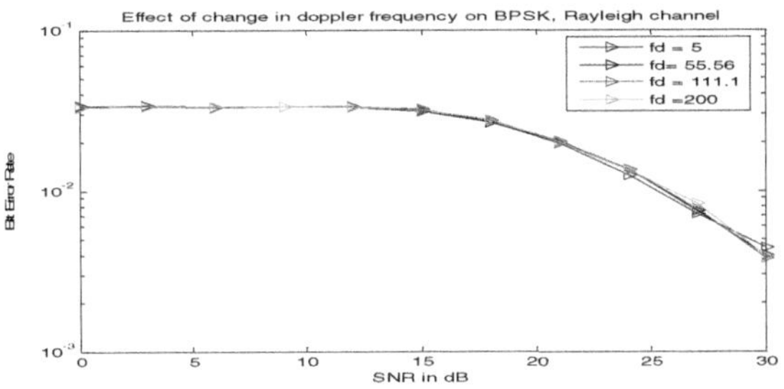

Fig. 4. Effect of Change in Doppler Frequency on BPSK Modulator in Rayleigh Channel Model

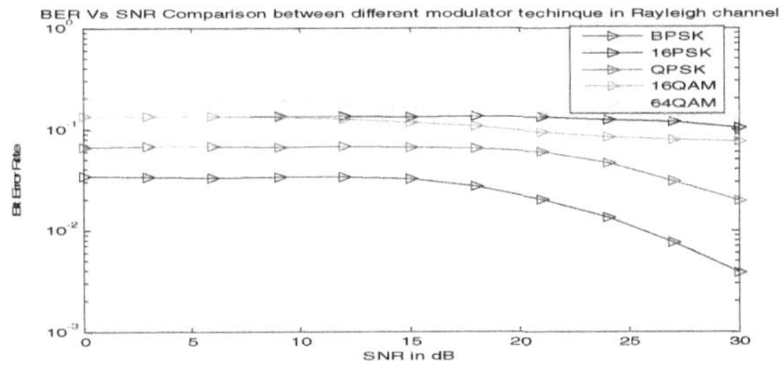

Fig. 5. Comparison for Different Modulation Technique When Channel Model is Rayleigh and f_d=111.1

5 Conclusions

Figure 3 shows output of 16 - PSK modulator with 512 points. It is seen that after equalization the some points remain scattered in Rayleigh channel model. The figure 3 also indicates constellation diagram for 16-PSK. figure 4 & 5 indicates that if SNR less than 15 db BPSK, QPSK performs same but after that as SNR increases BER reduces. 16-PSK, 16- QAM is almost having the same performance. If modulation technique is 64-QAM then it is possible to transmit more data at a time but BER is more although we increase SNR the BER is not affecting that much.

Although there is change in Doppler shift, the performance of system does not affect. For SNR above 15db for irrespective of change in Doppler shift the Baseband Modulation technique like BPSK and QPSK are more suitable.

With this, it is conclude that MC-CDMA can be consider as suitable modulation /multiple access technique in 4G mobile communication system.

Acknowledgment. I would profusely like to thank my Guide Dr. Udhav Bhosle, who has extended all valuable guidance, help and constant encouragement through the various difficult stages of project. I express my gratefulness towards my parents and my husband for their moral support and giving me the confidence and determination to work hard leading to the making of project work a big success.

References

1. Cooper, M.A., Armour, S.M.D., McGeehan, J.P.: Downlink Performance and Complexity Evaluation of Equalisation Strategies for an MC-CDMA '4G' Physical Layer Candidate. In: Proceedings Symposium IEEE Benelux Chapter on Communications and Vehicular Technology, Eindhoven (2003)
2. Hou, Z., Dubey, V.K.: BER Performance for Downlink MC-CDMA Systems over Rician Fading Channels. EURASIP Journal on Applied Signal Processing 5, 709–717 (2005)
3. Hara, S., Prasad, R.: Overview of Multicarrier CDMA. IEEE Communications Magazine, 126–133 (December 1997)
4. Yee, N., Linnartz, P.: Multi-Carrier CDMA in Indoor Wireless Radio Networks. In: PIMRC 1993, pp. 109–113 (1993)
5. Rappaport, T.S.: Wireless Communications, 2nd edn. PH (2004)
6. Proakis, J.G.: Digital Communications, 4th edn., pp. 483–492. MCGraw Hill
7. Molisch, A.F.: Wireless Communications. Wiley India Edition
8. Gemini Jr., L.J.: Analysis and Simulation of a Digital Mobile Channel Using Orthogonal Frequency Division Multiplexing. IEEE Transaction on Communication COM-33, 665–666
9. Alard, M., Lassalle, R.: Principles of Modulation and Channel Coding for Digital Broadcasting for Mobile Receivers. EBU Review - Technical 224, 168–190 (1987)
10. Hakin, S.: Communication System. Willey publications
11. Hu, Y., Zhu, J.: An Improved M-ary MC-CDMA for Mobile Communication System. IEEE (2004)
12. Hara, Y., Tsumura, S., Hara, S.: Performance Comparison of MC-CDMA and Cyclically Prefixed DS-CDMA in an uplink channel. IEEE (2004)
13. Paul, A.S.: Design and Performance of Multicarrier CDMA Systems in Frequency Selective Rayleigh Fading Channel
14. Chong, L.L., Milstein, L.B.: Multicarrier CDMA for Cellular Applications. final report 1998-99 for MICRO Project 98-105
15. Hathi, N.: Simulation of Multicarrier CDMA System for Future Wireless System
16. Litwin, L., Pugel, M.: The Principles of OFDM. RF Signal Processing
17. Richardson, K.W.: UMTS overview. IEE Electronics & Communications Engineering Journal, 93–100 (June 2000)
18. HIPERLAN Type 2 Technical Specification; Physical (PHY) Layer, (October 1999)
19. IEEE std 802.11a-1999, part 11: Wireless LAN Medium Access Control (MAC) and Physical Layer (PHY) specifications, High Speed Physical Layer in the 5 GHz Band
20. Doufexi, A., Armour, S., Karlson, P., Butler, M., Nix, A., Bull, D., Mc Geehan, J.: A Comparison of the HIPERLAN/2 and IEEE 802.11a Wireless LAN Standards. IEEE Communications Magzine 40(5) (May 2002)
21. Pereira, J.M.: Fourth Generation: Now it is Personal! In: PIMRC 2000, vol. 2, pp. 1009–1016 (2000)
22. Mahonen, P., Polyzos, G.C.: European R&D on Fourth Generation Mobile and Wireless IP Networks. IEEE Personal Communications Magazine 8(6) (December 2001)
23. Sklar, B.: Rayleigh Fading Channels in Mobile Digital Communication Systems Part II: Mitigation. IEEE Communications Magzine, 102–109 (July 1997)
24. Orfanos, G., Harbetha, J., Liu, L.: MC-CDMA Based IEEE 802.11 Wireless LAN
25. Metev, S.M., Veiko, V.P.: Laser Assisted Microtechnology, R. M. Osgood Jr., ed., 2nd edn. Springer, Berlin (1998)

Noise Cancellation Using Adaptive Filter for Bioimpedance Signal

Padma Batra[1], Rajiv Kapoor[2], and Rakhi Singhal[3]

[1] Mewar University, Chittorgarh
padmabatra61@gmail.com
[2] Delhi Technological University, Delhi
[3] Krishna Institute of Engineering and Technology, Ghaziabad

Abstract. This paper presents a new method for adaptive filtering of a signal obtained from measurement of bioelectrical impedance of the human muscles. In our application, four electrodes were used for detecting the changes in movement of muscles. A bioimpedance signal can be simulated by the combination of respiratory component and cardiac component. LMS algorithm for adaptive filtering is used to eliminate the noise from bioimpedance signal. Thereafter the rms value of the bioimpedance is calculated using MatLab.

Keywords: Electrical bioimpedance, Complex bioimpedance, signal processing, adaptive filtering, biomodulation, least mean square.

1 Introduction

BIOIMPEDANCE measurement for medical diagnosis purposes requires specific signal processing methods to reduce energy consumption and processing power requirements and to enhance the speed of digital processors. These requirements are particularly important when the miniaturized battery powered diagnosis devices are implantable or wearable. In this paper, we have described bioimpedance measurement basics as well as development tasks of the measurement setup to be designed.

1.1 Biompedance Measurement Basics

Electrical bioimpedance $Z = R + jX$ is determined by measuring a voltage response V to an excitation current I that is passed through some tissue or organ and is found as

$$Z = V / I$$

Fig.1 (a). Both the real Re and imaginary Im parts (R and X) of the complex impedance and its variations are to be measured using in-phase and quadrature (0° and 90°) relative to I synchronous demodulation (SD) [1]. The bioimpedance is the only exclusively electrically measurable tissue parameter of great diagnostic value. It reflects the state and structure of the tissue [Fig. 1(a)] through the equivalent circuit [Fig. 1(b)] and parameters of its component. To obtain complete information,

V.V. Das and N. Thankachan (Eds.): CIIT 2011, CCIS 250, pp. 321–325, 2011.

measurement of the whole frequency response of the complex impedance[Fig. 1(c)] is necessary[2].

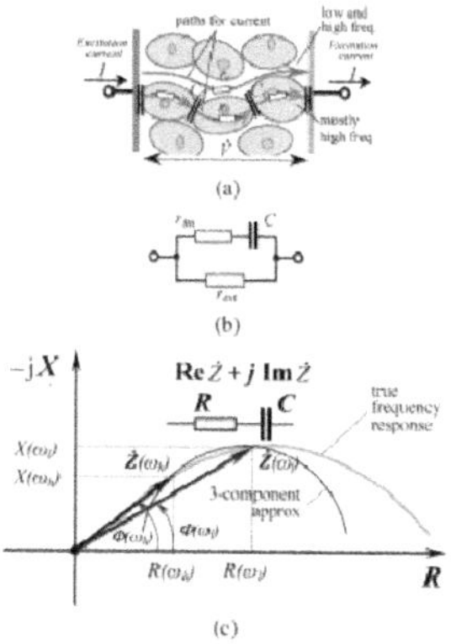

Fig. 1. Essentials of formation of (a) the electrical bioimpedance, (b) the three-component equivalent, and (c) the phasor diagram of static complex impedance between a pair of electrodes for two frequencies. Low ω_l and ω_h.

1.2 Model of Bioimpedance Signal

The model of bioimpedance signal is based on the approximation of the waveforms obtained from actual measurement of cardiac and respiratory signals[4]. Bioimpedance signal is the combination of cardiac output, which is a sawtooth waveform, and the respiratory output, which is a sinusoidal waveform. Therefore, in order to have a model for a standard bioimpedance signal for reference , we can combine the sine wave and sawtooth wave[fig.2].

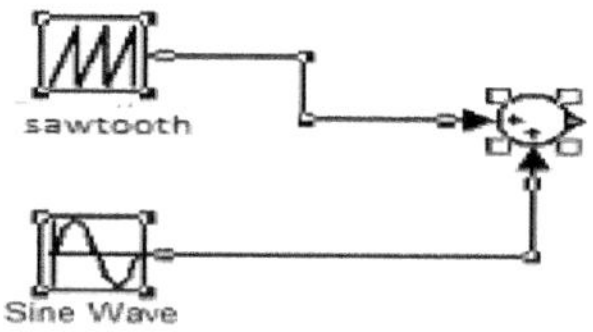

Fig. 2. Model of bioimpedance signal

2 Adaptive Filtering Technique

Adaptive filtering technique using neural networks has been shown to be useful in many biomedical application[3]. The basic idea behind adaptive filtering has been summarized by Widrow et al[5]. It reduces the mean square error between a primary input, which is noisy bioimpedance signal, and a reference input, which is correlated with the stadard bioimpedance signal[Fig. 3][6]. Adaptive filters permit to detect time varying potentials and to track the dynamic variations of the signal. These type of filters learn the deterministic signal and remove the noise. Therefore, they can detect shape variations in the ensemble and thus can obtain a better signal estimation. Different filter structures are presented to eliminate the diverse forms of noise. In this simulation work, sinusoidal (like power line interference) noise source is used to demonstrate the effectiveness of the adaptive filter[7] . The aim of the simulation is to design an adaptive filter and demonstrate its application in noise cancellation.The adaptive filter weights are updated by using Least Mean Square algorithm. The constructed filter is demonstrated with a single frequency noise source.

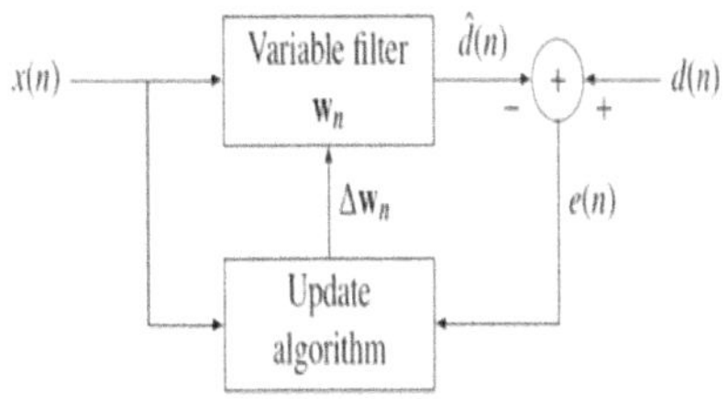

Fig. 3. Block diagram of adaptive filter

2.1 Adaptive Noise Cancellation

When the bioimpedance of a tissue is examined, there is a good chance that the bioimpedance signal has been contaminated by noise. To have a better understanding of the actual bioimpedance signal that has been obtained, we need to develop an adaptive filter to remove the contaminating signal from it.

2.1.1 The Least Mean Square (LMS) Algorithm

The LMS algorithm is an iterative technique for minimizing the mean square error (MSE) between the primary input and the reference signal. The adaptive filter weights are updated by using the LMS algorithm. The LMS algorithm can be written in matrix notation:

$$W(k+1)=W(k)+ 2\alpha.\ e(k)\ .pT(k) \quad (2.1)$$

$$\text{and } b(k+1)=b(k)+ 2\alpha\ .e(k) \quad (2.2)$$

where W(k) =[1 w(k) 2 w(k) ....i w(k)]T is a set of filter weights at time k, and i w(k) is the ith row of the weight matrix. PT(k) is the input vector at time k of the samples from the reference signal. The error is e(k)=t(k)– a(k) = (s(k)+m(k))- a(k) where t is the desired primary input to be filtered, and a(k) is the filter output that is the best least-squared estimate of t(k). For simplicity, we use a single sine wave noise source. In this case a neuron with two weights and no bias is sufficient to implement the adaptive filer. The inputs to the filter are the current and previous values of the noise source. Such a two-input filter can attenuate and phase shift the noise v in the desired way. The adaptive filter is shown in [Fig. 4].

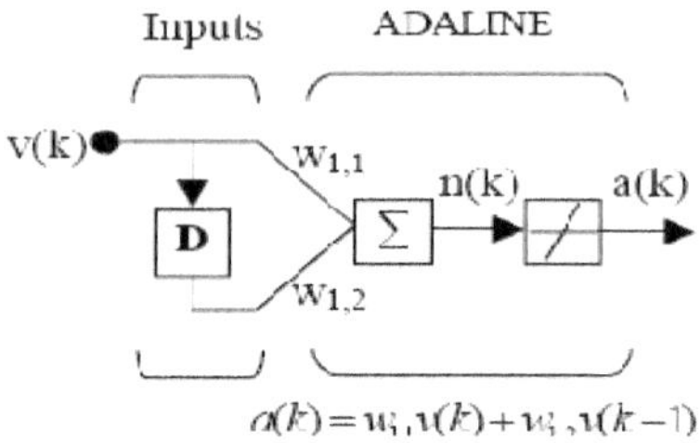

Fig. 4. Adaptive filter for sine wave noise source

2.2 Matlab Simulation

Bioimpedance measurement devices can be realised by using of the according analog conversion (modulation/demodulation) circuits, and micro controllers, or can be realised as analog and digital mixed signals. DSP based solutions compared with others are cost effective, precise, flexible and can include much functionality of measurement.

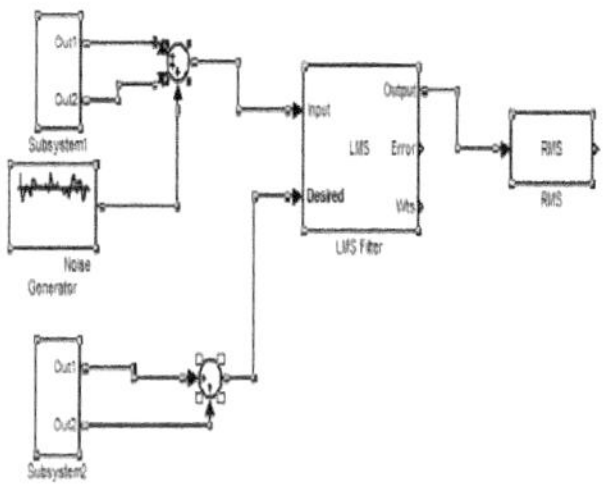

Fig. 5. Matlab simulation model

Fig.5 shows the matlab simulation model for adaptive filtering(LMS algorithm) of sinusoidal noise present in bioimpedance signal. After noise cancellation RMS value of the signal is calculated for better estimation of bioimpedance signal and further diagnosis purposes.

3 Results and Discussion

In this simulation work, first bioimpedance signal is generated by the combination of cardiac output of frequency 1 hz and respiratory output of frequency 0.5 hz, as shown in third subplot. This signal is applied as desired input to the LMS adaptive filter.After that a sinusoidal noise of frequency 2 hz is added to this bioimpedance signal,as shown in fifth subplot and applied as the actual input to LMS adaptive filter.

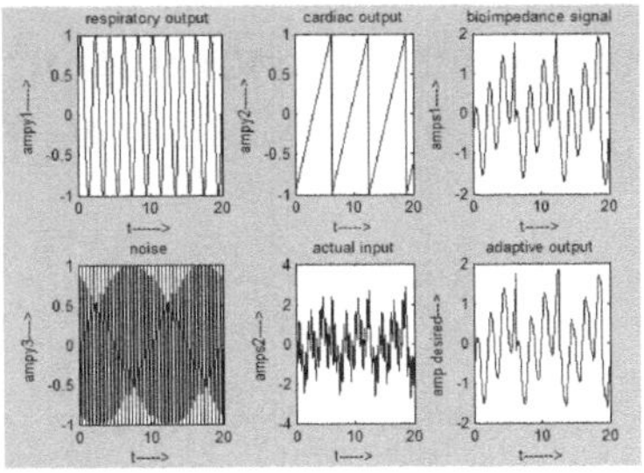

Fig. 6. Adaptive noise cancellation of bioimpedance signal

Then desired signal is compared with the actual signal and the signal is restored. This restored signal matches with the desired signal, as shown in sixth subplot. Results are shown in Fig.6.

4 Conclusion

In this paper, we have proposed a method to extract the original bioimpedance signal from the noisy signal obtained from human body. A reliable simulation model has been developed and designed. The filter does not need computation for error detection. As a result, it requires very little computational power or memory while still maintaining the ability to handle complex signal processing. Thus the adaptive filter approach as described herein can be applied to readily remove sinusoidal noise while minimally distorting the true bioimpedance signals.

References

1. Grimnes, S., Martinsen, O.G.: Bioimpedance and Bioelectricity Basics. Academic, San Diego (2000)
2. Nebuya, S., Brown, B.H., Smallwood, R.H., Milnes, P., Waterworth, A.R., Noshiro, M.: Measurement of high frequency electrical transfer impedances from biological tissues. Electron. Lett. 35(23), 1985–1987 (1999)
3. Cademartiri1, F., Mollet, N.R., Runza, G., et al.: Improving Diagnostic Accuracy of MDCT Coronary Angiography in Patients with Mild Heart Rhythm Irregularities Using ECG Editing. American Journal of Roentgenology 186, 634–638 (2006)
4. Krivoshei, A.: A Bio-Impedance Signal Synthesiser(BISS) for Testing of an Adaptive Filtering System. In: Proc.of Baltic Electronics Conference BEC 2006, Estonia, pp. 225–228 (October 2006)
5. Haykin, S.: Neural Networks: A Comprehensive Foundation, 2nd edn. Prentice Hall (1998)
6. Thakor, N.V., Zhu, Y.-S.: Applications of adaptive filtering to ECG analysis: Noise cancellation and arrhythmia detection. IEEE Trans. BioBiomed., Eng. 38, 785–789 (1991)
7. Tong, D.A., Bartels, K.A., Honeyager, K.S.: Adaptive reduction of motion artifact in the electrocardiogram. In: Proceedings of the Second Joint EMBS/BMES Conference, pp. 1401–1404 (2002)

Optimization Performance Evaluation of Evolutionary Algorithms: A Design Problem

M.A. Jayaram

Department of Master of Computer Applications,
Siddaganga Institute of Technology, B.H. Road
Tumkur-572103, Karnataka, India
jayaram_mca@sit.ac.in

Abstract. This paper provides a systematic comparison of four evolutionary optimization algorithms; elitism based genetic algorithm, particle swarm optimization, ant colony optimization and artificial bee colony optimization in terms of their performance with respect to population size, convergence, fitness evaluation and percentage error on an interdisciplinary problem. The case in point is optimized design of high performance concrete mix. The methodology consists of two stages. In the first stage, a huge data base of 450 mix designs garnered through standard research publications were statistically analyzed to elicit upper and lower bounds of certain range constraints and rational ratio constraints of functional parameters. In the second stage, the four algorithms were applied to find the optimized quantities of ingredients constituting the mix. The results indicated that GA was bit high on errors, the other three algorithms showed almost same percentage of error. The convergence of bee colony optimization algorithm was fast followed by particle swarm optimization.

Keywords: Evolutionary algorithms, mix design, high performance concrete, trial mixes, constraints.

1 Introduction

High-performance concrete (HPC) is rather new terminology in concrete construction industry, taking the place of the well-known high –strength concrete in recent years. In addition to the four basic ingredients of the conventional concrete, i.e., Portland cement, fine and course aggregates, and water, the making of HPC needs to incorporate the supplementary cementetious materials such as fly ash and blast furnace slag, and chemical admixtures such as superplasticizer [1]. Evolutionary algorithms (EAs) have become established as the method at hand for exploring the optimization problems that are too complex to be solved by exact methods, such as linear programming and gradient search. This is not only because there are few alternatives for searching intractably large spaces for multiple Pareto-optimal solutions. Due to their inherent parallelism and their capability to exploit similarities of solutions by recombination, they are able to approximate the Pareto-optimal front in a single optimization run [2].

V.V. Das and N. Thankachan (Eds.): CIIT 2011, CCIS 250, pp. 326–333, 2011.

2 Significance of Research

Most concrete design methods are fully experimental or semi-experimental. Often, special monograms are provided. Experimental or semi-experimental methods are reliable and accurate: however, they involve laboratory tests, and the effects of material prices are neglected [3]. Simon et al. [4] have reported the development of statically designed experiments named as response surface approach that facilitated increased efficiency in selecting optimum proportions for high performance concrete. Lim et al. [5] have reported the use of simple GAs for optimizing proportions of HPC. For this, the fitness function is developed by performing multiple regression analysis on 181 sets of mixtures. In some cases, it is the Contact Volume Editor that checks all the pdfs. In such cases, the authors are not involved in the checking phase. Maruyama et al. [6] have presented a Pareto optimality model for normal concrete mixture proportions according to the required performances. The formulations concerning rheological parameters of fresh concrete developed by various researchers have been used as objective functions for the algorithm. The author has developed a neuro-fuzzy hybrid model for the design of normal concrete mix [7]. Elitist GA models [8] developed for the optimized mix proportioning of HPC has shown a good estimate of quantities of ingredients of HPC with quantity of cement on a higher side when compared with the experimental results. With PSO the optimized values of HPC ingredients compared very well with experimental values [9]. In this paper, optimal mix proportioning for HPC using four EAs is presented. The methodology involves two steps:

- Perform statistical analysis of a large database and elicit the range of values for functional parameters as well as constraint ratios for different 28 days compressive strength ranges.
- Optimize the proportions of crucial ingredients viz., fly ash, cement, and water for maximum 28 days strength of concrete incorporating the constraints elicited in the first step.

Compare the four methods in terms of their behavior, convergence, fitness evaluation and percentage of errors in estimated quantities.

3 Optimization Formulation

The aim of the methodology is to find the optimum mix proportion for the given range of 28 days compressive strength. The analytical method used in this article is that of three constraints, better known as the constraints of available range, rational ratio, and absolute volume. The objective function used in this model is an estimation equation developed by Hwang et al. [10], which is concerned with the compressive strength development of concrete containing large volumes of fly ash. The equation incorporates the pozzolanic effect of fly ash with the aim of establishing a technique of proportioning concrete with high fly ash content. The equation is given as:

$$\text{Maximize } f_c(t) = A(t)\left(\frac{\alpha W_F + W_C}{W_W}\right) + B \quad (1)$$

Where A (t) is a coefficient, which indicates the strength development of concrete over time, and is expressed as;

$$A(t) = \frac{t}{a + bt} \tag{2}$$

In Eq. (2), t is the duration in days, a and b are experimental constants that depend on cement type, curing method, etc. From a large number of experimental observations, the constants a and b are given to be 0.049 and 0.0255,respectively [10]. The parameter B in Eq. (1) is judged as being constant regardless of age. For ordinary Portland cement, the value of B = −18.2 may be adopted [10]. The α in Eqn. (1) indicates fly ash's contribution to the strength. The objective function is subjected to the following constraints.

a) Available range constraints

$$W_C^{\min} < W_C < W_C^{\max} \tag{3}$$

$$W_F^{\min} < W_F < W_F^{\max} \tag{4}$$

$$W_W^{\min} < W_W < W_W^{\max} \tag{5}$$

$$W_{CA}^{\min} < W_{CA} < W_{CA}^{\max} \tag{6}$$

$$W_{FA}^{\min} < W_{FA} < W_{FA}^{\max} \tag{7}$$

$$W_{SP}^{\min} < W_{SP} < W_{SP}^{\max} \tag{8}$$

Where WC, WF, WW, WCA, WFA, WSP are weights of cement, fly ash, water, coarse aggregate, fine aggregate and super plasticiser respectively. The available range constraints reflect the regulation and experience of concrete mix design. They can reduce the search space and accelerate the optimization process.

b) Ratio constraints

$$R_1^{\min} \le R_1 \le R_1^{\max} \tag{9}$$

$$R_2^{\min} \le R_2 \le R_2^{\max} \tag{10}$$

$$R_3^{\min} \le R_3 \le R_3^{\max} \tag{11}$$

$$R_4^{\min} \le R_4 \le R_4^{\max} \tag{12}$$

Where,

$$R_1 = W_W / W_C \tag{13}$$

$$R2 = WW / (WC + WF) \tag{14}$$

$$R3 = WF / WC \tag{15}$$

$$R4 = WF / (WC + WF) \tag{16}$$

The rational ratios also contribute to reduction of search space and accelerate the search space.

c) Absolute volume constraint: The absolute volume equation represents a condition that the total volume of the components of concrete should correspond to the volume of one cubic meter of concrete:

$$\frac{W_C}{G_C} + \frac{W_F}{G_F} + \frac{W_W}{G_W} + \frac{W_{FA}}{G_{FA}} + \frac{W_{CA}}{G_{CA}} + \frac{W_{SP}}{G_{SP}} = 1000 \tag{17}$$

4 Implementation Details

Experimental data from 27 different sources were used to build the model [7]. About 350 concrete mixtures made with ordinary Portland cement and cured under normal conditions were evaluated. Table 1 presents the statistical details of the entire database of HPC concrete mixtures. The data were sorted for five different strength ranges, i.e., 30–35MPa, 35–40MPa, 40–50MPa, 50–60MPa, and 60–70MPa as the number of mixture proportion data available in these ranges were significant. Statistical analysis was performed on each of these sorted data to find the actual values for range constraints and ratio constraints to be used in all the algorithms. In order to have some commonality for the comparison of performance, following parameters were considered:

a) **Population size.** To find the appropriate positions of agents, computational experiments are conducted for different population sizes (with 20,25,30,35,40,50, 75, and 100).

b) **Constraint handling.** Penalty function method was adopted in order to handle the constraints. Initially, the penalty coefficient was taken as 108, and it was progressively reduced till the satisfaction of constraints. The detailed write up about the algorithms is beyond the scope of this paper. Interested readers may consult the enlisted references [11],[12],[13],[14],[15],[16],[17],[18]. Some specific details algorithmic parameters are in order.

4.1 Elitist Genetic Algorithm (EGA)

a) **Coding.** A variable length binary coding scheme has been used with 10 bits, 12 bits, and 8 bits, representing quantities of fly ash, cement, and water respectively.

b) **Fitness.** Equation (1) is taken as the objective function fi for the string i. The GA optimization problem is posed as that of determination of the string that maximizes the strength under given constraints.
c) **Crossover.** Although there are many forms of crossover, including two point cross over and uniform cross over, the simple single cross over is used. The crossover probability (pc) of 0.8 was adopted.
d) **Mutation.** Occasional random alteration of bits protects the GA process against premature loss of potentially useful genetic material. Each digit of the offspring's string is altered with a low probability (pm), usually held constant throughout the evolution. In this work, pm is set to 0.01.

4.2 Particle Swarm Optimization (PSO)

a) **The social (ν) and cognitive (μ) parameters.** After series of computational experiments, both the parameters were stood at a value of 1.
b) **Maximum velocity.** The maximum particle velocity was set to 0.5.
c) **The inertia weights (ω1, ω2).** The inertia weight parameters are adjusted dynamically during the optimization, as suggested by the researchers.

4.3 Ant Colony Optimization (ACO)

a) **The trail parameter.** At each time t, an ant has to choose the path it goes to, out of several paths available in search space. The probability of picking a certain path is biased by the distance between points and the amount of pheromone on the edge between these two points. Then the bigger the product of pheromone intensity and visibility the more likely it is that the path will be chosen. After a large number of computational runs, the weighted factor for trail (β) was found to be 10.
b) **The evaporation factor.** After all of the ants have completed their tours, the trail levels on all of the arcs need to be updated. The evaporation factor ρ ensures that pheromone is not accumulated infinitely and denotes the proportion of old pheromone that is carried over to the next iteration of the algorithm. Then for each edge the pheromones deposited by each ant that used this edge are added up, resulting in the pheromone- level-update. After repeated runs, this factor was found to be 0.8.

4.4 Honey Bee Colony Optimization (HBO)

a) **Number of food sources.** In the artificial bee colony algorithm [19], each food source is a possible solution for the problem under consideration and the nectar amount of a food source represents the quality of the solution represented by the fitness value. The number of food sources is same as the number of employed bees and there is exactly one employed bee for every food source. This is made equal to population sizes (20,25,30,35,40,50,75,and 100) to have uniformity across the four algorithms considered.
b) **Neighborhood patch limit.** If new fitness value is better than the best value achieved so far, then the bee moves to the new food source abandoning the old

one, otherwise it remains in its old food source. When all employed bees have finished this process, they share the fitness information with the onlookers, each of which selects a food source according to probability. With this scheme, good food sources will get more onlookers than the bad ones. Each bee will search for better food source around neighborhood patch for a certain number of cycle (limit), and if the fitness value does not improve, then that bee becomes scout bee. This limit was found to be 30 in this work.

Table 1. Statistical Details of 350 HPC mix design

Cement	206	384	118	198	155	54.74
Water	132	227	110	123	119	19.3
Fine aggregate	723	960	570	725	830	46
Course aggregate	1113	1334	920	1105	1100	86
Super Plasticiser	8.65	22.7	0	5.9	14.5	7.8
FlyAsh	200.6	311	35	211	211	45
W/C	0.67	1.258	0.349	0.69	0.7354	0.1351
W/(C+F)	0.334	1.68	0.194	0.3223	0.3278	0.0971
F/C	1.04	2.33	0.0025	1.009	1.000	0.357
F/(C+F)	0.507	1.732	0.100	0.510	0.500	0.134

5 Results and Discussions

For each of the four algorithms the optimization runs were done for five different strength ranges. For each model, the inputs are the bounds of variables as well as the constraints. The outputs are the optimized quantities of cement, fly ash, and water content. The variation of the fitness values of the objective function for different agent populations was found to be same by and large in all the cases except HBO. As far as HBO is concerned the fitness value almost stabilized for population strength of 25 this is followed by ACO, which stood at 30.This also pointed to a faster convergence of HBO and ACO to optimum values. To analyze the algorithms for their accuracy, the estimated values are compared with experimental values and the mean squared errors was calculated for quantities of cement, fly ash and water. This is shown in Figure 1.The mean squared error in optimized quantity of cement is found to be high in case of EGA (9-12 kg/cum), while other three algorithms showed lower error rate (5-9 kg/cum), PSO being the lowest. Same trend was seen in case of quantity of water with EGA showing the error range of 1.5 –3.5 kg/cum, while other three algorithms hovering around 1.5-2.5 kg/cum. Error rate in optimized quantity of fly ash was found to be low with EGA i.e. in the range 5-9 kg/cum, while other three algorithms showed higher error at 7-10 kg/cum, which is very marginal.

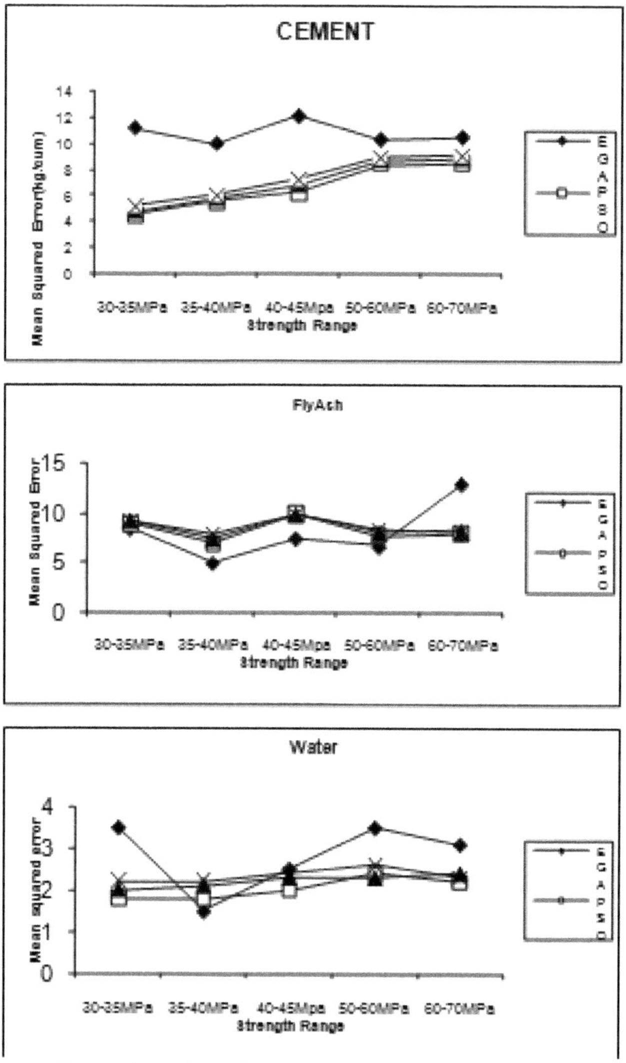

Fig. 1. Mean squared error in optimized quantities of cement, flyash and water by the algorithms considered

References

1. Alain, B., Malhotra, M.: High volume fly ash system: Concrete solution for sustainable development. ACI Materials Journal 97(1), 41–48 (2000)
2. Zitzler, E., Thailey, L., Deb, K.: Comparison of Multiobjective Evolutionary Algorithms: Empirical Results. Evolutionary Computation 8(2), 173–195 (2000)

3. Yeh, I.-C.: Design of high performance concrete mixture using neural networks and non-linear programming. Journal of Computing in Civil Engineering 13(1), 36–42 (1999)
4. Simon, M., Snyder, K., Fransdroff, G.: Advances in Concrete Mixture Optimization. In: Concrete Durability and Repair Technology Conference, pp. 21–32. University of Dundee, UK (1999)
5. Lim, C.-H., Yoon, Y.S., Kim, J.H.: Genetic algorithms in mix proportioning of high performance concrete. Cement and Concrete Research 34(4), 9–20 (2004)
6. Maruyama, I., Noguchi, T., Kanematsu, M.: Optimization of the concrete mix proportions centered on fresh properties using genetic algorithms. Indian Concrete Journal, 567–573 (2002)
7. Jayaram, M.A.: Innovative Methods and Applications of Soft Computing in Concrete Technology: An Interdisciplinary Approach, PhD Thesis, Visvesvaraya Technological University, Belgaum, India (2008)
8. Jayaram, M.A., Nataraja, M.C., Ravikumar, C.N.: Elitist Genetic Algorithm Models: Optimization of High Performance Concrete Mixes. Materials and Manufacturing Processes 24, 225–229 (2009)
9. Jayaram, M.A., Nataraja, M.C., Ravikumar, C.N.: Design of High Performance Concrete Through Particle Swarm Optimization. Journal of Intelligent Systems 19(3), 249–264 (2010)
10. Hwang, K., Noguchi, T., Tomosawa, F.: Prediction Model of Compressive Strength Development of Fly Ash Concrete. Cement and Concrete Research 34, 2269–2276 (2004)
11. Goldberg, D.E., Rundnick, M.: Genetic Algorithms and Variance of Fitness. Complex Systems 5(3), 265–268 (1991)
12. Ahn, C.W., Ramakrishna, R.S.: Elitism Based Compact Genetic Algorithms. IEEE Trans. Evolutionary Computtaion 7(4), 367–385 (2003)
13. Kennedy, J., Eberhart, R.: Particle Swarm Optimization. In: Proc. IEEE Int. Conf. On Neural Networks, pp. 1942–1948 (1995)
14. Shi, Y., Eberhart, R.: Parameter Selection in Particle Swarm Optimization. In: Proc. 7th Annual Conf. On Evolutionary Programming, pp. 591–600 (1998)
15. Dorigo, M., Maniezzo, V., Colorni, A.: Ant Colony System: Optimization by a Colony of Cooperating Agents. IEEE Trans. on Systems, Man and Cybernetics-Part B 26(1), 29–41 (1996)
16. Dorigo, M., Stutzle, T.: Ant Colony Optimization. The MIT Press, Massachusetts (2004)
17. Passino, K.M., Seely, T.D., Kirk Visscher, P.K.: Swarm Cognition in Honey Bees. Behav. Ecol. Sociobiol., 401–404 (2008)
18. Karboga, D., Basturk, B.: On the Performance of Artificial Bee Colony Algorithm. Applied Soft Computing 8(3), 687–697 (2008)

Evaluation of Short-Term Load Forecasting Methods Using Dynamic Neural Networks

C.G. Mallamma[1] and Sateesh Chandra Reddy[2]

[1] Dept. of CSE, SJCIT Chickballapur, India
mallammagoudar79@gmail.com
[2] Dept. of ISE, SJCIT Chickballapur, India
ssc_reddy@yahoo.com

Abstract. This paper presents forecasting of short-term electricity load using dynamic neural networks, DNN, and an assessment of the neural network stability to ascertain continued reliability. This includes an assessment and comparative study of three different neural networks, feedforward, Elman and the radial basis neural network. The performance and stability of each DNN is evaluated by means of an extensive simulation study using actual hourly load data. The neural networks weights are dynamically adapted. Stability for each of the three different networks is determined through Eigen values analysis. Evaluation of the neural network methods is done in terms of estimation performance, stability and the difficulty in training a particular network. The results show that the radial basis method performs better than the rest Eigen value analysis also shows that it is more reliable as it remains stable as the input varies.

Keywords: Dynamic Neural Networks, Short-term Load Forecasting, Stability, Eigen Values.

1 Introduction

Forecasting is a phenomenon of knowing what may happen to a system in the next coming time period. In electrical power system, there is a great need for accurately forecasting the load and Energy requirements because electricity generations as well as distribution are a great financial liability to the state exchequer. Accurate load forecast provides system dispatchers with timely information to operate the system economically and reliably. It is also necessary because availability of electricity is one of the most important factors for industrial development. Short-Term Load Forecasting (STLF) is aimed at predicting system load with leading times ranging from less than an hour to seven days ahead. STLF is a key component in system operations that allows operators to configure the system correctly in preparation for the next operating interval. There are two main approaches to SLTF. One is the simulation approach that requires a lot of information that is not always practically available when needed. The second approach involves use of recorded system load information and extraction and manipulation of the variation trends to predict the

V.V. Das and N. Thankachan (Eds.): CIIT 2011, CCIS 250, pp. 334–339, 2011.

likely future load values [1-5]. These include expert systems [6, 7], which are heuristic models that imitate the reasoning of a human expert operator, and neural networks. Expert systems approach presumes the existence of an expert capable of making accurate forecasts that will train the system. Neural networks do not rely on human experience, but the functional relationship between system inputs and outputs [7]. The development of an accurate, fast and robust short-term load forecasting methodology is of importance to both the electric utility and its customers.

1.1 Overview

Electricity demand forecasting is of great importance for the management of power systems. Short-term load forecasting is an essential action in electric power operations. Short-term load forecasting plays an essential role in power system planning and operation. The forecasts are important inputs to system analysis tools such as economic dispatch and short term unit commitment, used to maintain system reliability. The deregulation of the power system industry in the United States in recent years has made short term load forecasting increasingly important. In a deregulated, competitive electricity market environment, the ability to accurately forecast load in the short term is of interest not only to power system operators, but also to load serving entities, merchant plants or generators and other market participants. It is required for energy transfer scheduling and load dispatch and also required for the control and scheduling of power systems, also required by transmission companies when a self-dispatching market is in operation. With the emergence of load management strategies, the short-term forecast is playing a broader role in utility operations. Short Term Load Forecasting (STLF) is a key component in system operations that allows operators to configure the system correctly in preparation for the next operating interval. The development of an accurate, fast and robust short-term load forecasting methodology is of importance to both the electric utility and its customers.

1.2 Goal

In these dissertation dynamic neural networks for three different neural network architectures – feed forward (FFNN), Elman and the radial basis (RBF) neural networks, are set up. The DNN are initially trained on past demand data with network input vector being a moving window on the load time series. The networks that give acceptable forecasting error are retained. The main goal is,

- To evaluate the performance and stability of each DNN by means of an extensive simulation study using actual hourly load data.
- Evaluation of the networks by estimating performance, stability and the difficulty in training a particular network.

1.3 Motivation

In recent years, artificial intelligence (AI) techniques have captured the attention of power system researchers and operators as a potential load forecasting techniques. Some AI techniques that have been used include the expert system, the fuzzy-neural model, the artificial neural network (ANN) model and the genetic algorithm method. The artificial neural network (ANN) model is suitable for load forecasting due to its ability to model the nonlinear relationships between variables without making prior assumptions on the functional relationship among variables. An artificial neural network is a system based on the operation of biological neural networks, in other words, is an emulation of biological neural system. Neural networks do not rely on human experience, but the functional relationship between system inputs and outputs. A neural network can perform tasks that a linear program cannot. When an element of the neural network fails, it can continue without any problem by their parallel nature. A neural network learns and does not need to be reprogrammed. It can be implemented in any application.

2 Methodology

The proposed approach generally follows these steps.

i. Prepare input data – pre-process the raw data by removing mean and appropriate scaling.
ii. Train – configure the DNN and adjust the weights until error target is met.
iii. Test – Supply the DNN with test data and update the weights regularly.
iv. Represent the DNN as a system of linear difference equations and determine the coefficients.
v. Assess stability - Determine location of Eigen values. A discrete system is stable if all of its Eigen values lie inside the unit circle in the complex plane, and unstable if one or more of the Eigen values lie outside the unit circle. The structure of the DNN, setup for this study, does not allow for direct determination of its Eigen values, therefore it is represented as a system of linear difference equations, for which the Eigen values are then determined. Using an nth order identity matrix as input, the values of the coefficients in (1), a (a = [a1, a2, , , a_n,]) can be calculated.

$$y(t) = a_1 y(t-1) + a_2 y(t-2) + \ldots + a_n y(t-n). \tag{1}$$

3 Proposed System

In the proposed system, the networks were configured as in Figure 1, where y is the system load time series, being supplied to the network input through a tapped delay line. If m is the size of the input vector then y = [y(k), y(k-1), . . .y(k-m)] and y(k+1) is the future value to be forecasted. To facilitate the required evaluation several networks are setup and the block labeled NN is configured differently in each case with one of FFNN, Elman and RBF architectures. Training the FFNN involves adjusting the weights using the steepest descent algorithm that carries out a correction on the weight matrices, W(1) and W(2). Steepest descent method is an unconstrained method that relies on the idea of iterative descent in one form or another. Consider a cost function £(w) that is continuously differentiable function of some unknown weight vector w. the function £(w) maps the elements of w into real numbers. It is a measure of how to choose the weight vector w of an adaptive filtering algorithm so that it behaves in an optimum manner. Find an optimal solution w* that satisfies the condition £(w*)≤ £(w). That is, "Minimize the cost function £(w) with respect to the weight vector w". The necessary condition for optimality is ∇£(w*)=0. Where ∇ is the gradient operator.

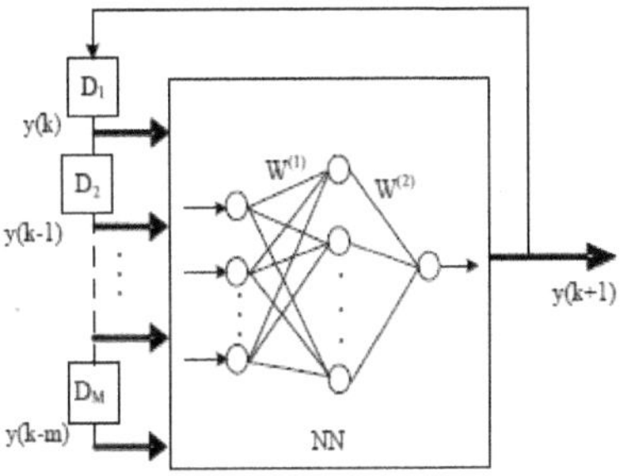

Fig. 1. DNN time delayed inputs

$$\nabla = \left[\frac{\partial}{\partial W1}, \frac{\partial}{\partial W2}, \ldots, \frac{\partial}{\partial Wm} \right]^T$$

and ∇£(W) is the gradient vector of the cost function.

$$\nabla £(W) = \left[\frac{\partial £}{\partial W1}, \frac{\partial £}{\partial W2}, \frac{\partial £}{\partial Wm3} \right]^T$$

A class of unconstrained optimization algorithms that is well suited for the design of adaptive filters is based on the idea of local iterative descent: "Starting with an initial guess denoted by w(0),generate a sequence of weight vectors w(1),w(2)….., such that the cost function £(w) is reduced at each iteration of the algorithm, as shown by £(w(n+1))< £(w(n)).Where w(n) is the old value of the weight vector and w(n+1) is its updated value. If e(k) is the output deviation from target t(k) , then the weights have to be adjusted by ΔWqj (1) and ΔWq (2) given in (3) and (4)[7].

$$E = 1/2 \sum_{k=1}^{Q} (e^{(k)})^2 = 1/2 \sum_{k=1}^{Q} (t^{(k)} - y^{(k)})^2 \qquad (2)$$

$$\Delta W_{qj}^{(1)}(k) = -\eta \frac{dE}{\delta \Delta W_{qj}^{(1)}} + \propto \Delta W_{qj}^{(1)}(k-1) \quad (3)$$

$$\Delta W_{q}^{(2)}(k) = -\eta \frac{dE}{\delta W_{q}^{(2)}} + \propto \Delta W_{q}^{(2)}(k-1) \quad (4)$$

Where, ή is learning rate (gain adjustment) and α is the momentum gain.

For the Elman network the weights are updated according to a second order Newton's method, the Levenberg-Marquardt (L-M) algorithm. The L-M weight update rule[7] is given in (5).

$$\Delta W = (JTJ + \mu I)\text{-}1JTE \quad (5)$$

Where J is the Jacobian matrix of derivatives of each error to each weight: I is the unity matrix, μ is a scalar and E is the error vector.

An RBF network is a two layer network whose hidden layer contains radial basis function neurons that most commonly use a Gaussian activation function, σ (x). The nodes take in as input the Euclidean distance between the centre of the function and the network input vector, and passes the result through the nonlinear function, σ (x).

$$\sigma_j(x) = \exp[-(x - \mu_j)/\grave{Y}^2_j]. \quad (6)$$

Where:

X is the input vector.
μj is the centre of a region called a receptive field.
Ỳj is the width of the receptive field.
σj(x) is the output of the jth neuron.

RBFNN performs a local mapping, meaning only inputs near a receptive field produce activation, in contrast FFNN performs a global mapping, meaning all inputs cause an output.Training the RBF network is different from that of the preceding networks in that the weight adjustments are done for zero error, that is, the weight giving the biggest error is replaced by the value of the signal causing the error. This is done incrementally as new training inputs are supplied and the number of weights is increased by a preset quantity at each step. Training stops when the overall output error falls within acceptable error limit or the number of hidden nodes reaches maximum allowed.

4 Performance Results

Networks with varying number of hidden nodes were setup for each of the three selected architectures. The networks were trained and tested using the same data sets. The forecasting accuracy and stability, for the networks are presented in Table I. The positions of the Eigen values for the RBF based load forecasting method show that it is much more stable compared to the other two architectures. The small values of the Eigen values show that the network can correct for any errors effectively and quickly retain to the desired operating, hence a much smaller prediction error.

Table 1. Performance of Selected DNN

N/N Type	Training Size	Training Error	Prediction Error	Eigen Values
FNN	5	0.623	0.013	0.326
	6	0.465	0.031	0.435
	7	0.847	0.019	0.337
	10	0.154	0.035	0.287
ELMAN	5	0.685	0.003	0.701
	6	0.638	0.060	0.549
	7	0.791	0.002	0.39
	10	0.772	0.013	0.478
RBF	5	0.608	0.003	0.008
	6	0.500	0.051	0.001
	7	0.773	0.034	0.007
	10	0.166	0.013	0.002

5 Conclusions

The proposed dynamic neural networks for short-term load forecasting were validated using out-of-sample data, i.e., data outside the training set. It has been shown that the future load values can be estimated within reasonable error limits. The estimation accuracy is comparable to that reported in previous research that used static networks. However, the dynamic neural network becomes a superior choice because they can be used perpetually as adaptation is inherent in their setup. Furthermore, an approach to ascertain the reliability of the networks has been shown here the network parameters, weights, are not symmetrical matrices. The RBF based method shows best overall performance. However, the training approach for RBF networks naturally results in a very large hidden layer because of the zero error targeting inherent in the training algorithm.

References

1. Zhao, F., Su, H.: Short-term load forecasting using Kalman Filter and Elman Neural Network. In: 2007 Second IEEE Conference on Industrial Electronics and Applications (2007)
2. Mandal, P., Tomonobu, S., Naomitsu, U., Toshihisa, F.: A neural network based several hours-ahead electric load forecasting using similar days approach. Electric Power and Energy Systems 28, 367–373 (2006)
3. Al-Hamadi, H.M., Soliman, S.A.: Short-term electric load forecasting based on kalman filtering algorithm with moving window weather and load model. Electric Power Systems Research 68, 47–59 (2004)
4. Tripathi, M.M., Upadhvay, K.G., Singh, S.N.: Short-term load forecasting using generalized regression and probabilistic neural networks in the electricity market. The Electricity Journal 21(9) (November 2008)
5. Moghram, S.R.: Analysis and evaluation of the short-term load forecasting techniques. IEEE Trans. Power Systems 4(4), 1484–1491 (1989)
6. Rahman, S., Bhatnager, R.: An expert system based algorithm for short-term load forecasting. IEEE Trans. PWRS 3, 392–399 (1988)
7. Hagan, M.T., Menhaj, M.B.: Training feedforward networks with Marquardt algorithm. IEEE Trans. Neural Netw. 5(6), 989–993 (1994)

Partition Sort and Its Empirical Analysis

Niraj Kumar Singh[1] and Soubhik Chakraborty[2,*]

[1] Department of Computer Science & Engineering, B.I.T. Mesra, Ranchi-835215, India
[2] Department of Applied Mathematics, B.I.T. Mesra, Ranchi-835215, India
{niraj_2027,soubhikc}@yahoo.co.in

Abstract. In the present paper we have introduced a new sorting algorithm named Partition Sort and performed its empirical study with necessary theoretical analysis. This algorithm was subjected to data coming from various standard probability distributions. Average Case analysis revealed that for some standard distributions it worked even more efficiently than the popular Hoare's quicksort algorithm. The relative order of execution time, for different distributions, in descending order came out to be: Discrete Uniform < Binomial < Poisson < Standard Normal < Continuous Uniform.

Keywords: Algorithmic complexity, empirical analysis, Partition Sort, statistical bound, empirical O, mathematical bound.

1 Introduction

Quicksort, Heapsort and Mergesort, all three are powerful and standard asymptotically fast sorting mechanisms. The mathematical bound for these methods exhibit almost similar behavior [$O(n\log_2 n)$] in best, worst and average cases, except for the quicksort which exhibit the running time of $O(n^2)$ with the worst possible arrangement of data. The worst case behavior of quicksort is attributed to its inability to partition the input list into almost equal halves. If a mid way partitioning could be ensured, then one would expect a better worst case bound even for quicksort. This motivated us to design PartitionSort.The mathematical bound analysis has its own limitations, which sometimes may create illusions especially in average case analysis. For instance, compare the behavior of mergesort with that of quicksort. In most of the analysis the key operations considered are comparison and assignment. In average case, quicksort performs almost 39 % more comparisons than the mergesort. Similarly the quicksort also requires almost 39 % more data assignments than that of mergesort [1]. Based on our assumption of key operations and the figure mentioned above we should prefer mergesort to quicksort. But this is not the scenario in practice, as experiments reveal that with average input quicksort is far better than the mergesort (is it? see [2]). It is known that the poor performance of mergesort is due to its requirement for an extra space proportional to the input size. But this measure was not taken into considerations as it was not a common requirement to both the approaches. This discussion reveals that something is wrong with our usual approach of analyzing

* Corresponding author.

V.V. Das and N. Thankachan (Eds.): CIIT 2011, CCIS 250, pp. 340–346, 2011.

the performance through mathematical bounds. A comprehensive literature has been given in [3] as to why should we prefer empirical analysis to mathematical one.

Sourabh&Chakraborty [2] in their empirical analysis questioned the robustness of the average complexity of quicksort on the ground that it does not get support from some of the standard probability distributions. However their empirical study on the robustness of average complexity for heapsort algorithm was a positive one in this direction [4]. In this paper we have introduced a new sorting algorithm, Partition Sort with $\Omega(n\log_2 n)$ best case count, which is same as that of standard sorting algorithms. However the worst case count of PartitionSort is $O(n\log_2^2 n)$ which is clearly a huge improvement over the worst case count of quicksort. This measure is however less efficient than the worst case count for mergesort and heapsort algorithms. The mid way partitioning in Partition Sort ensured that even with the worst possible arrangement of data its performance did not degrade to quadratic count as is the case with popular quicksort algorithm. Partition Sort like quicksort is a top to bottom approach. The Partition Sort algorithm is designed carefully by either including the merits or by excluding the demerits of the standard sorting algorithms.

2 The Algorithm

PartitionSort algorithm is based on divide and conquer paradigm. The function "partition" is the key sub-routine of this algorithm. The nature of partition function is such that when applied on input A[1.......n] it divides this list into two halves of sizes floor (n/2) and ceiling (n/2) respectively. The property of the elements in these halves is such that value of each element in first half is less than the value of every element in the second half. The PartitionSort routine is called on each half recursively to finally obtain a sorted sequence of data as required.

The functions Build-Max-Heap, Build-Min-Heap, Adjust_Max_Heap and Adjust_Min_Heap are the standard heap construction procedures (suggested by Floyd [5]) which are used as sub procedures in the PartitionSortalgorithm . The proposed algorithm is written in a hypothetical language which to some extent resembles the 'C' language.

Main_Procedure( )

{ /* A[ ] is the array of elements to be sorted, 'low' is the position of leftmost element in the list, initialized to 1,

and 'high' is the position of right most element in the list and is initialized to n.*/

```
PartitionSort( A, low, high )

}
PartitionSort ( integer A[], integer low, integer high )
{
     Integer mid;
     IF  low EQUALS high THEN RETURN
     ELSE {
          mid = (low + high) / 2
          Partition (A, low, high )
          Exchange(A[low], A[mid])
```

```
            PartitionSort ( A, low, mid-1 )
            PartitionSort ( A, mid+2, high )   }
}
 Partition(integer A[], integer low, integer high )
{
       Integer mid, maximum, minimum
        mid = (low + high) / 2
       /* This block is executed only once for  a
specific   pair of (low, high) values, rest of the
times  the alternative
              block contained in  immediate  ELSE section
is executed. */
                            IF (FLAG == FALSE) THEN {
                           maximum = Build-Max-Heap( A,
low, mid)
                           minimum = Build-Min-Heap(A,
mid+1, high)  }
                     ELSE  {
                          maximum= Adjust_Max_Heap(A, low,
mid)
                          minimum =
Adjust_Min_Heap(A,mid+1,high)   }

                    FLAG = TRUE
                    IF (maximum > minimum) THEN  {
                     Exchange (A[low], A[mid+1])
                     Partition ( A, low, high)   }
 } /* end of procedure 'Partition' */
```

2.1 Correctness of the Partitionsort Algorithm

We present the following arguments in favour of the correctness of our algorithm. Point(1): When the function "Partition" terminates, for an arbitrary sublist A[p, q], we obtained two partitions A[p, m] and A[m+1, q], where m is the floor{(p+q)/2}. An important feature of these partitions is that:

$$MAX\{A[p, m]\} <= MIN\{A[m+1, q]\}.$$

Point(2): The terminating condition in the function "PartitionSort" ensured that the recursive partitioning is desired only for those sub lists whose size is greater than or equal to two.

2.2 TheoreticalAnalysis of PartitionSort: Worst and Best Cases Only

The function Build_Max_Heap (Build_Min_Heap) constructed a max (min) heap for a random data set in O(n) time. Whereas the function Adjust_Max_Heap

(Adjust_Min_Heap) was used to restore the max (min) heap property of a structure whose nodes except the root follow the desired property. Time required by this function is $O(\log_2 n)$. The overall running time of this algorithm (in terms of number of comparisons as well as swappings) can be expressed through the recurrence relation: $T(n)=2T(n/2) + f(n)$,where $f(n)$ is the time incurred in partitioning the list into two equal halves. The worst case recurrence is : $T_{worst}(n) = 2T(n/2) + 2\{ (n/2) + (n/2)\log_2(n/2) \}$,which upon solving yielded $T_{worst}(n) = O(n\log_2^2 n)$, whereas the best case recurrence is : $T_{best}(n) = 2T(n/2) + \theta(1)$, which upon solving yielded a running time of $O(n\log_2 n)$.Instead of performing rigorous analysis (a less reliable approach as well [2]) to obtain the average case behavior we preferred to achieve it through the empirical study as suggested by [6] & [7]. For a comprehensive literature on sorting, see Knuth [8]. For sorting with emphasis on the input distribution, Mahmoud [9] may be consulted.

3 Average Case Analysis Using Statistical Bound Estimate or Empirical O

This section includes empirical results. The algorithm was run for data obtained from various probability distributions. The observed mean time (in sec) of 100 trials was noted in table (1). Average case analysis was done by directly working on program run time to estimate the weight based statistical bound over a finite range by running computer experiments [10] [11]. This estimate is called empirical O [3] [6] [7]. Here time of an operation is taken as its weight. Weighing permits collective consideration of all operations into a conceptual bound which we call a statistical bound in order to distinguish it from the count based mathematical bounds that are operation specific. The credibility of empirical O depends on the design and analysis of our special computer experiment in which time was the response. See [3] for more insight.

System Specification: All the computer experiments were carried out using PENTIUM 1600 MHz processor and 512 MB RAM.

Table 1. Observed mean times in seconds for PartitionSort algorithm

Array size N	Binomial (m=100. P=0.5)	Poisson λ =1	Discrete Uniform [1,2, ... k], k=2	Continuous Uniform [0,1]	Standard Normal (μ=0,σ =1)
10000	0.0266	0.0171	0.0162	0.0466	0.0531
20000	0.0354	0.0333	0.0284	0.1122	0.1157
30000	0.047	0.0482	0.0455	0.1875	0.1736
40000	0.0688	0.0655	0.0437	0.2497	0.245
50000	0.0796	0.083	0.0651	0.2641	0.2813
60000	0.1016	0.1221	0.0782	0.3247	0.3092
70000	0.1213	0.1362	0.0936	0.3704	0.3454
80000	0.147	0.1594	0.0182	0.4327	0.3984
90000	0.161	0.1797	0.1202	0.472	0.4266
100000	0.172	0.184	0.136	0.5063	0.4649

3.1 Average Complexity for Uniform and Non Uniform Distribution Inputs

A moment's reflection on fig 1 and 2 suggest that the average case O(nlogn) complexity is supported by experimental results both for uniform and non uniform inputs. For Binomial (m, p) inputs we took m=100 and p=0.5. For discrete uniform [1, 2...k] inputs we took k=2. We write $Y_{avg}(n)=O_{emp}(nlogn)$. See appendix for the definitions of a statistical bound and its estimate (empirical O).

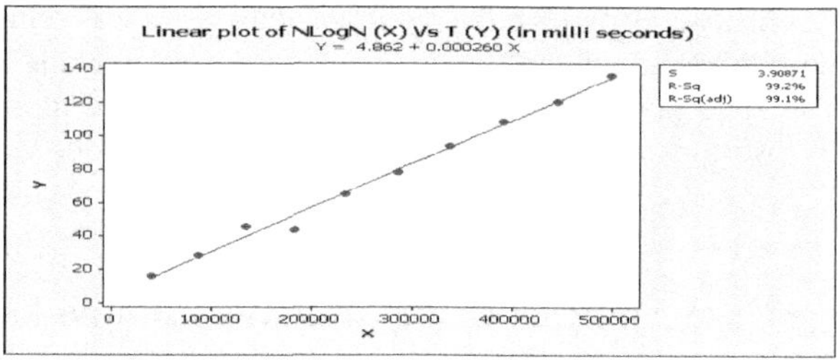

Fig. 1. Plot for Discrete Uniform input

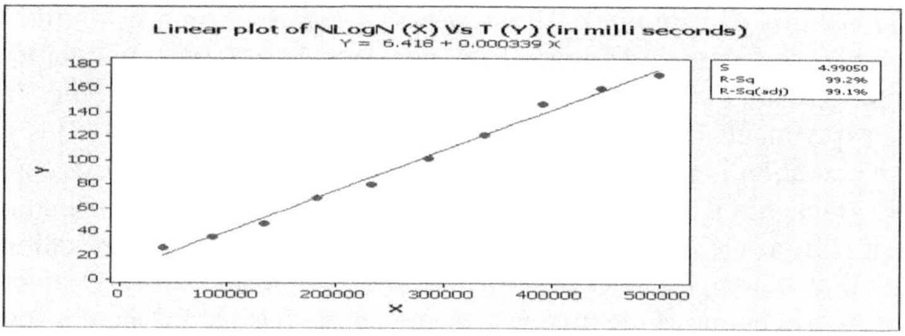

Fig. 2. Plot for Binomial Distribution inputs

4 Conclusion and Future Work

The experimental results revealed that among the five standard probability distributions examined in this paper, all were supporting the Oemp(nlogn) complexity. The relative order of execution time, for different distributions data, in descending order came out to be : Discrete Uniform < Binomial < Poisson < Standard Normal < Continuous Uniform.Our algorithm ,in average case could serve as a better choice for certain distribution data for which the popular quicksort algorithm is not an efficient choice[2]. It was observed that, contrary to quicksort, our algorithm is fastest for the Discrete Uniform Distribution data and slowest for the Continuous Uniform data [2]. Also it would be interesting to know the behavior of running times as a function of various distribution parameters which would be a rewarding study in parameterized complexity.

Remark: PartitionSort was found to be faster than the standard mergesort algorithm for majority of standard distributions discussed in this paper, over the range [10000 to 100000]. We omit the details.

Appendix

In the following definitions, the functions f and g are nonnegative functions. Definitions 1-3 are taken from [12].

Definition 1: [Big "oh"] The function f(n) = O(g(n)) (read as "f of n is big oh of g of n") iff (if and only if) there exists positive constants c and n0 such that f(n) <= c*g(n) for all n, n>= n0.

Definition 2: [Omega] The function f(n) = (g(n)) (read as "f of n is omega of g of n") iff there exist positive constants c and n0 such that f(n) >= c*g(n) for all n, n >= n0.

Definition 3: [Theta] The function f(n) = (g(n)) (read as "f of n is theta of g of n") iff there exist positive constants c and n0 such that c1g(n) <= f(n) <= c2g(n) for all n, n >= n0.

Definition 4: Statistical bound (non-probabilistic): If wij is the weight of (a computing) operation of type i in the j-th repetition (generally time is taken as a weight) and y is a "stochastic realization" (which may not be stochastic [3]) of the deterministic T= $\sum$ 1. wij where we count one for each operation repetition irrespective of the type, the statistical bound of the algorithm is the asymptotic leastupper bound of y expressed as a function of n where n is the input parameter characterizing the algorithm's input size. If interpreter is used, the measured time will involve both the translation time and the execution time but the translation time being independent of the input will not affect the order of complexity. The deterministic model in that case is T= $\sum$ 1. wij + translation time. For parallel computing, summation should be replaced by maximum. Empirical O (written as O with a subscript emp) is an empirical estimate of the statistical bound over a finite range, obtained by supplying numerical values to the weights, which emerge from computer experiments [3]. Empirical O can also be used to estimate a mathematical bound when theoretical analysis is tedious, with the acknowledgement that in this case the estimate should be count based and operation specific.

There is also another notion of a statistical bound which is probabilistic. In the words of Ferrari [13], a statistical bound means the following:-

"A client can specify a service requirement using the general form pred = TRUE, where some of the variables in the predicate pred can be controlled or influenced by the server. A simple and popular form of performance requirement is that involving a bound. A deterministic bound can be specified as (var<= bound) = TRUE or var<= bound, where variable var is server-controlled while bound is client-specified. The bounds in these expressions are upper bounds. If < is replaced by >, they become lower bounds. When the variable in the latter expression is a probability, we have a statistical bound and bound in that case is a probability bound; if the predicate is a deterministic bound, we have: Prob (var<= bound) >= probability-bound. In this requirement, the variable has an upper bound, and the probability a lower bound. Note that deterministic bounds can be viewed as statistical bounds that are satisfied with probability 1."

References

1. Kruse, R., Tondo, C.L., Leung, B.: Data Structures & Program Design in C. PHI, 2nd edn., p. 318
2. Sourabh, S.K., Chakraborty, S.: How robust is quicksort average complexity? arXiv:0811.4376v1 [cs.DS]. Advances in Mathematical Sciences Journal (to appear)
3. Chakraborty, S., Sourabh, S.K.: A Computer Experiment Oriented Approach to Algorithmic Complexity. Lambert Academic Publishing (2010)
4. Sourabh, S.K., Chakraborty, S.: Empirical Study on the Robustness of Average Complexity & Parameterized Complexity Measure for Heapsort Algorithm. International Journal of Computational Cognition 7(4) (December 2009)
5. Floyd, R.W.: Algorithms 245 (TREESORT). Communications of the ACM 7, 701 (1964)
6. Sourabh, S.K., Chakraborty, S.: On why an algorithmic time complexity measure can be system invariant rather than system independent. Applied Mathematics and Computation 190(1), 195–204 (2007)
7. Chakraborty, S., Modi, D.N., Panigrahi, S.: Will the Weight-based Statistical Bounds Revolutionize the IT? International Journal of Computational Cognition 7(3), 16–22 (2009)
8. Knuth, D.E.: The Art of Computer Programming. Sorting and Searching, vol. 3. Addison Wesely, Pearson Education Reprint (2000)
9. Mahmoud, H.: Sorting: A Distribution Theory. John Wiley and Son (2000)
10. Sacks, J., Weltch, W., Mitchel, T., Wynn, H.: Design and Analysis of Computer Experiments. Statistical Science 4(4) (1989)
11. Fang, K.T., Li, R., Sudjianto, A.: Design and Modeling of Computer Experiments. Chapman and Hall (2006)
12. Horowitz, E., Sahni, S., Rajasekaran, S.: Fundamentals of Computer Algorithms, Galgotia (2003)
13. Ferrari, D.: Client requirements for real time communication services, UC Berkeley, RFC 1193 (November 1990), http://www.faqs.org/rfcs/rfc1193.html

A Novel Image Retrieval Based on Multi Resolution Color and Texture Features of Image Sub-blocks

Ch. Kavitha[1], M. Babu Rao[2], B. Prabhakara Rao[3], and A. Govardhan[4]

[1] IT department, GEC, Gudlavalleru, Krishna (dist.), A.P., India
kavithachaduvula@yahoo.com
[2] CSE depatment, GEC, Gudlavalleru, Krishna (dist.), A.P., India
baburaompd@yahoo.co.in
[3] JNTUK, Kakinada, East Godavari(dist.), A.P., India
[4] JNTUHCE, Jagtial, Karimnagar(dist.), A.P., India

Abstract. In this paper we propose a new and efficient technique to retrieve images based on multi-resolution color and texture features of image sub-blocks. Firstly the image is divided into sub blocks of equal size in two resolutions. The size of the sub-block is fixed in two resolutions. Color of each sub-block is extracted by quantifying the HSV color space into non-equal intervals and the color feature is represented by cumulative histogram. Similarly the texture of the sub-block is extracted based on edge oriented gray tone spatial dependency matrix (GTSDM). An integrated matching scheme based on Most Similar minimum cost (MSMC) principle is used to compare the query and target image. The adjacency matrix of a bipartite graph is formed using the sub-blocks of query and target image. This matrix is used for matching the images. The experimental results show that the proposed method has achieved highest retrieval performance.

Keywords: Image retrieval, non-equal interval quantization, Cumulative color Histogram, edge image, GTSDM, integrated matching, MSMC.

1 Introduction

The need for efficient image retrieval is increased tremendously in many application areas such as medical imaging, military, digital library and computer aided design [1]. Color is one of the most reliable visual features. The advantage of HSV color space is its ability to separate chromatic and achromatic components. Therefore we selected the HSV color space to extract the color features according to hue, saturation and value. Non-interval quantized HSV cumulative color histogram is used to represent color of the sub-block. Texture may consist of some basic primitives, and may also describe the structural arrangement of a region and the relationship of the surrounding regions. In our approach we have used the statistic texture features of gray level edge image based gray-tone spatial dependency matrix (GTSDM). So, in this paper, we present a novel image retrieval based on multi-resolution color and texture of image sub-blocks.

V.V. Das and N. Thankachan (Eds.): CIIT 2011, CCIS 250, pp. 347–352, 2011.

2 Proposed Method

First the image is partitioned into equal sized non-overlapping sub-blocks in two resolutions. The color of each sub-block is extracted as a non-equal interval HSV cumulative color histogram and texture feature as statistic features of edge oriented GTSDM.

2.1 Grid

An image is partitioned into 24 (4 x 6 or 6 x 4) non overlapping sub-blocks. With the Corel dataset used for experimentation (comprising of images of size either 256 x 384 or 384 x 256), with 6 x 4 (or 4 x 6) partitioning, the size of individual sub-block will be 64 x 64. The choice of smaller sized sub-blocks than 64 x 64 leads to degradation in the performance. This tiling structure is extended to second level decomposition of the image. The image is decomposed into size M/2 x N/2, where M and N are number of rows and columns in the original image respectively. So, a two level structure is Grid.

2.2 Extraction of Color of an Image Sub-block

HSV image is quantized using the following quantization scheme where each component is quantized with non-equal intervals: H: 8 bins; S:3 bins and V:3 bins. Finally we concatenate 8X3X3 histogram and get 72-dimensional vector. To reduce the number of zeros in the histogram, we adopted the cumulative histogram.

$$H = \begin{cases} 0 \text{ if } h \in [316,20] \\ 1 \text{ if } h \in [21,40] \\ 2 \text{ if } h \in [41,75] \\ 3 \text{ if } h \in [76,155] \\ 4 \text{ if } h \in [156,190] \\ 5 \text{ if } h \in [191,270] \\ 6 \text{ if } h \in [271,295] \\ 7 \text{ if } h \in [296,315] \end{cases} \qquad S = \begin{cases} 0 \text{ if } s \in [0,0.2) \\ 1 \text{ if } s \in [0.2,0.7) \\ 2 \text{ if } s \in [0.7,1) \end{cases} \qquad V = \begin{cases} 0 \text{ if } v \in [0,0.2) \\ 1 \text{ if } v \in [0.2,0.7) \\ 2 \text{ if } v \in [0.7,1) \end{cases} \tag{1}$$

In accordance with the quantization level above, three- dimensional feature vector for different values of H, S, V with different weight to form one-dimensional feature vector named G:

$$G = QsQvH + QvS + V \tag{2}$$

Where Qs is quantified series of S, Qv is quantified series of V. Here we set Qs=Qv =3, then

$$G = 9H + 3S + V \tag{3}$$

In this way, three-component vector of HSV form One-dimensional vector, which quantize the whole color space for the 72 kinds of colors. Therefore, this paper represents the one-dimensional vector G by constructing a cumulative histogram of the color characteristics of image after using non-interval HSV quantization [4].

2.3 Extraction of Texture of an Image Sub-block

The edge image of the gray image sub-block is obtained using Prewitt's edge detection operator. GTSDM is constructed for edge oriented gray image. Elements in the GTSDM matrix are computed by the equation shown below:

$$P(i, j|d, \theta) = \frac{P(i, j|d, \theta)}{\sum_i \sum_j P(i, j|d, \theta)} \tag{6}$$

To reduce the computational complexity, we only select four of these features as retrieval feature: Contrast, Entropy, Energy, and Inverse difference moment.

$$Energy\ (E) = \sum_x \sum_y P(x, y)^2 \tag{7}$$

$$Contrast\ (I) = \sum \sum (x - y)^2 P(x, y) \tag{8}$$

$$Entropy\ (S) = -\sum_x \sum_y P(x, y) \log P(x, y) \tag{9}$$

$$InverseDifference\ (H) = \sum_x \sum_y \frac{1}{1 + (x - y)^2} P(x, y) \tag{10}$$

The texture features are computed for an image when d=1 and θ=00, 450, 900, 1350. In each direction four texture features are calculated.

2.4 Integrated Image Matching Based on Most Similar Minimum Cost Matching Principle

In our method, a sub-block from query image is allowed to be matched to any sub-block in the target image. However a sub-block may participate in the matching process only once. A bipartite graph of sub-blocks for the query image and the target image is built as shown in Fig. 1. The labeled edges of the bipartite graph indicate the distances between sub-blocks. A minimum cost matching is done for this graph.

To this effect, we have designed an algorithm for finding the minimum cost matching based on most similar minimum cost(MSMC) principle[3] using the adjacency matrix of the bipartite graph. The minimum distance dij of this matrix is found between sub-blocks i of query and j of target. The distance is recorded and the row corresponding to sub-block i and column corresponding to sub-block j, are blocked (replaced by some high value, say 99999). This process is repeated till every sub-block finds a matching. The complexity of the matching procedure is reduced from O(n2) to O(n), where n is the number of sub-blocks involved. The integrated minimum cost match distance between images is now defined as:

$$Dqt=\sum \sum dij,$$

Where i=1, 2,--n j=1, 2---n. And dij is the best-match distance between sub-block i of query image q and sub-block j of target image t and Dqt is the distance between images q and t.

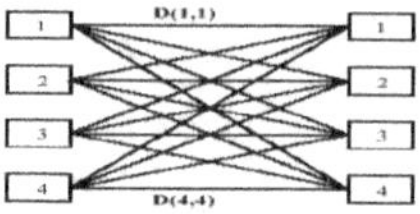

Fig. 1. Bipartite graph showing 4 sub-blocks of target and query images

3 Experimental Setup and Results

During the formulation of similarity measure, the appropriate weights are used to combine the distances between them in Euclidean measure.

$$D(A, B) = \omega 1 D(FCA , FCB) + \omega 2 D(FTA , FTB) \quad (7)$$

Here ω1, ω2 are the weight of color features and texture features, FCA and FCB represents the 72-dimensional HSV cumulative color Histogram features for image A and B. For a method based on Edge oriented GTSDM, FTA and FTB on behalf of 16-dimensional texture features correspond to image A and B. The value of ω through experiments shows that at the time ω1=ω2=0.5 has better retrieval performance. The distance between two images is computed as D = D1+ D2, where D1 and D2 are the distances computed by integrated matching scheme at two resolutions.

Table 1. Average Precision

	Average Precision		
Class	HSV color and GLCM texture of an image [2]	HSV color and GLCM Texture of image sub-blocks [5]	Proposed method
Africa	0.26	0.44	0.64
Beaches	0.27	0.5	0.542
Building	0.38	0.45	0.578
Bus	0.45	0.75	0.751
Dinosaur	0.26	0.61	0.989
Elephant	0.3	0.39	0.675
Flower	0.65	0.87	0.894
Horses	0.19	0.35	0.722
Mountain	0.15	0.34	0.584
Food	0.24	0.31	0.653
Average	0.315	0.501	0.7028

Fig. 2. The image retrieval results(dinosaurs) using different techniques (a) retrieval results based on HSV and GLCM texture of an image (b) retrieval results based on HSV color and GLCM texture of image sub-blocks (c) retrieval results based on Non-equal interval HSV cumulative color histogram and Edge oriented GTSDM texture features of image sub-blocks

The comparison of proposed method with other retrieval systems is presented in the Table 1 and in Fig. 2. The Fig. 3 shows the Average Precision with the number of returned images. Average precision decreases with increasing the number of returned images. And the Fig. 4 represents a graph showing the Average Recall with respect to number of returned images.

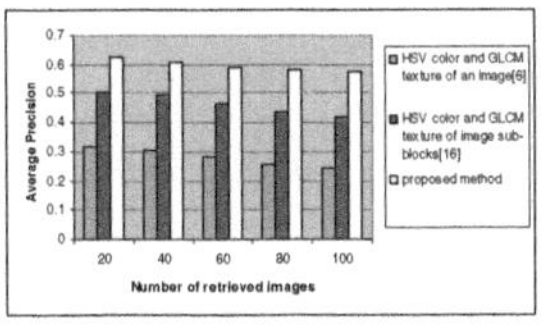

Fig. 3. Average Precision of various image retrieval methods

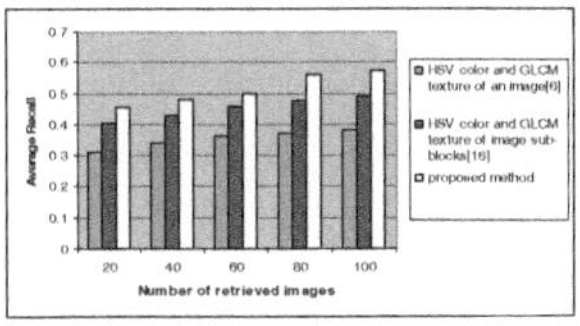

Fig. 4. Average Recall of various image retrieval methods

4 Conclusion

In this paper, a novel image retrieval technique has been proposed which uses the combination of Non-equal interval HSV cumulative color histogram and statistical features of gray level edge oriented gray tone spatial dependency matrix (GTSDM) for an image sub-block. An integrated image matching based on most similar minimum cost principle is used to match the database image with query image. Experimental results showed that the proposed method yielded higher average precision and average recall than the other techniques.

References

1. Datta, R., Joshi, D., Li, J., Wang, J.Z.: Image retrieval: ideas, influences, and trends of the new age. ACM Computing Surveys 40(2), 1–60 (2008)
2. Kong, F.-H.: Image Retrieval using Both color and texture features. In: proceedings of the 8th international conference on Machine learning and Cubernetics, Baoding, July 12-15 (2009)

3. Song, M., Li, H.: An Image Retrieval Technology Based on HSV Color Space. Computer Knowledge and Technology 3, 200–201 (2007)
4. Chen, Y., Wang, J.Z.: A Region-Based Fuzzy Fefature Matching Approach to Content-Based Image Retrieval. IEEE Trans. on PAMI 24(9), 1252–1267 (2002)
5. kavitha, C., Prabhakara Rao, B., Govardhan, A.: An efficient content based image retrieval using color and texture of image sub-blocks. International Journal of Engineering science and Technology (IJEST) 3(2), 1060–1068 (2011)

Content Based Image Retrieval Based on Dominant Color, Scan Pattern Co-occurrence Matrix of a Motif and Shape

M. Babu Rao[1], Ch. Kavitha[2], B. Prabhakara Rao[3], and A. Govardhan[4]

[1] CSE Department, GEC, Gudlavalleru, Krishna (dist.), A.P., India
baburaompd@yahoo.co.in
[2] IT Department, GEC, Gudlavalleru, Krishna (dist.), A.P., India
kavithachaduvula@yahoo.com
[3] JNTUK, Kakinada, East Godavari(dist.), A.P., India
[4] JNTUHCE, Jagtial, Karimnagar(dist.), A.P., India

Abstract. There is a great need of developing an efficient content based image retrieval system because of the availability of large image databases. A new image retrieval technique to retrieve the images using four features called dominant color (DC), scan pattern co-occurrence matrix of a motif (SPCMM), scan pattern internal pixel difference (SPIPD) and shape is proposed. Shape information is captured in terms of edge images computed using Gradient Vector Flow fields. Invariant moments are then used to record the shape features. Experimental results show that the proposed image retrieval is more efficient in retrieving the user- interested images.

Keywords: Image retrieval, Dominant Color, Texture, Motif Co-occurrence, Gradient vector flow.

1 Introduction

In CBIR system model, the images are indexed by their visual contents such as color, texture, shape, and color layout [1]. Huang and Dai [3] proposed a texture based image retrieval system which combines the wavelet decomposition and gradient vector. In Jhanwar et al. [4] the image retrieval system introduced is based on Motif co-occurrence matrix (MCM), which converts the difference between pixels into a basic graphic and computes the probability of its occurrence in the adjacent area as an image feature. To enhance retrieval performance, SPCMM, SPIPD, Dominant color and GVF are integrated to develop an image retrieval system based on texture, color and shape features.

2 Color Representation

DCD (Dominant color descriptor) [2] contains two main components: 1.representative colors 2.the percentage of each color. DCD can provide an effective, compact, and

V.V. Das and N. Thankachan (Eds.): CIIT 2011, CCIS 250, pp. 353–357, 2011.

intuitive salient color representation.First, the RGB color space is divided equally into 8 coarse partitions. Let X=(XR,XG,XB) represent color components of a pixel with color components Red, Green, and Blue, and Ci be the quantized color for partition i. The average value of color distribution for each partition centre can be calculated by

$$\overline{X}_i = \frac{\sum_{X \varepsilon Ci} X}{\sum_{X \varepsilon Ci} 1} \tag{1}$$

After the average values are obtained, each quantized color can be determined. i.e.

$$C_i = (\overline{X}_i^R, \overline{X}_i^G, \overline{X}_i^B)(1 \le i \le 8) \tag{2}$$

Where C_i is a 3D dominant color vector.

3 Scan Pattern Co-occurrence Matrix of a Motif and Scan Pattern Internal Pixel Difference

We have used a Scan pattern co-occurrence matrix of a motif (SPCMM) to represent the traversal of adjacent pixel color difference in an image. As each pixel corresponds to four adjacent pixel colors, each image can be presented by four images of motifs of scan pattern. A 3x3 convolution mask for each pixel G(x, y) can be generated as shown in Fig. 1. This 3x3 convolution mask can be further divided into four blocks of 2x2 grids (pixels) with each including pixel G(x, y). Here, we only consider the scan starting from the top left corner pixel p1 as shown in Fig. 1(a), because it represents a complete family of space filling curve, reducing the number of patterns to only 7 as shown in Fig. 2.

Let G(x, y): Nx x Ny→Z be the gray levels of an Nx x Ny image I for Z = {0, 1, . . ., 255}. to form four different motifs shown by number M of motif.

$$M_i(u,v) = M_i(u,v|\delta_x,\delta_y) = M_i(P_i[x,y], P_i[x+\delta_x, y+\delta_y]) \tag{3}$$

where Pi[x, y] = u, Pi[x + dx, y + dy] = v, 1≤ i≤ 4, 1≤ x≤Nx, 1≤y≤Ny, 1≤x + dx≤Nx, and 1≤ y + dy≤Ny. The co-occurring probabilities of the number i motifs of scan pattern matrix are determined by dividingMi (u, v) as shown below

$$m(u,v) = \frac{M_i(u,v)}{N_i} \tag{4}$$

Where

$$N_i = \sum_{u=0}^{6} \sum_{v=0}^{6} M_i(u,v) \tag{5}$$

and 1 ≤ i ≤ 4. As a result, there will be a 7 x 7 two-dimensional grids in total, which amounts to 7 x 7 = 49, with Nf = 49 is the total number of SPCMM attributes to be considered.

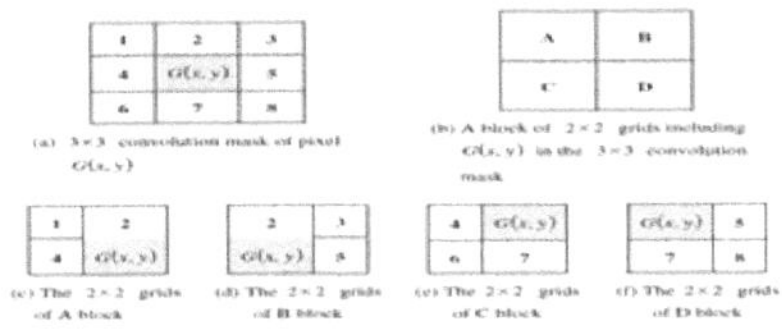

Fig. 1. The 3x3 convolution masksare divided into four 2x2 grids

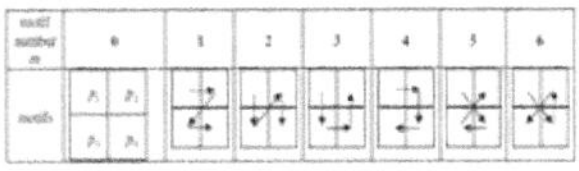

Fig. 2. Senen scan patterns

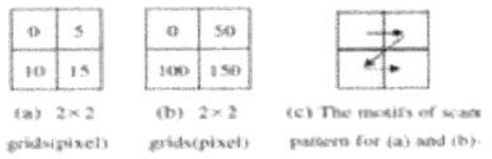

Fig. 3. The motifs of scan pattern for 2x2 grids

The SPCMM feature proposed above could effectively describe the direction of textures but not the complexity of textures. As shown in Fig. 3, the motif number in both Fig. 3(a) and (b) is 2, but the differences among the four pixels values are large. Therefore, we take the scan pattern internal pixel difference (SPIPD) as one of the texture features. Six basic motifs can be derived from MSPM as features of an image.The total pixel value difference of any coordinates (x, y) within the image is Δ(x, y).

$$
\begin{aligned}
\Delta^1(x,y) &= |p1-p2|+|p2-p3|+|p3-p4| \\
\Delta^2(x,y) &= |p1-p3|+|p3-p2|+|p2-p4| \\
\Delta^3(x,y) &= |p1-p3|+|p2-p4|+|p4-p2| \\
\Delta^4(x,y) &= |p1-p2|+|p2-p4|+|p4-p3| \\
\Delta^5(x,y) &= |p1-p4|+|p4-p3|+|p3-p2| \\
\Delta^6(x,y) &= |p1-p4|+|p4-p2|+|p2-p3|
\end{aligned} \tag{6}
$$

Where Δi(x, y) represents the total pixel value difference of all scan directions of ith motif number of any coordinates (x, y) within the image. The formula of i's motif number and p is shown in Fig. 3. Finally, we calculate the appearance rate of Δ(x, y) within the whole image as shown below:

$$
f_i = \frac{1}{N_i}\sum_{j=1}^{N_i} \Delta^i{}_j(x,y) \tag{7}
$$

Where i is the motif number and Ni is the total appearance of ith motif number within the whole image. Therefore, six SPIPD feature values can be obtained.

4 Shape

Shape information is captured in terms of the edge image of the gray scale equivalent of every image in the database. We have used gradient vector flow (GVF) fields to obtain the edge image. Translation, rotation, and scale invariant one-dimensional normalized contour sequence moments are computed on the edge image [5]. The gray level edge images of the R, G and B individual planes are taken and the shape descriptors are computed as follows:

$$F_1 = \frac{(\mu_2)^{1/2}}{m_1} \qquad F_2 = \frac{\mu_3}{(\mu_2)^{3/2}} \qquad F_3 = \frac{\mu_4}{(\mu_2)^2} \qquad \mu_r = \frac{1}{N}\sum_{i=1}^{N}[Z(i) - m_1]^r$$

$$F_4 = \overline{\mu_5} \quad \text{Where} \quad m_r = \frac{1}{N}\sum_{i=1}^{N}[Z(i)]^r \qquad \overline{\mu_r} = \frac{\mu_r}{(\mu_2)^{1/2}}$$

The Z(i) is the set of Euclidean distances between centroid and all boundary pixels of the digitized shape.

5 Image Retrieval Process

The image matching distance Δ^{SPCMM} between Q and D based on the CCM can be calculated via the following equation:

$$\Delta^{MCM} = \sum_{k=1}^{49} \left| \frac{m_k^q - m_k^d}{m_k^q + m_k^d + v} \right| \tag{8}$$

Where v is any small number that avoids denominator = 0.

Similarly
$$\Delta^{DBPSP} = \sum_{k=1}^{6} \left| \frac{f_k^q - f_k^d}{f_k^q + f_k^d + v} \right| \tag{9}$$

$$\Delta^{DDC} = \sum_{k=1}^{8} \left| \frac{c_k^q - c_k^d}{c_k^q + c_k^d + v} \right| \tag{10}$$

$$\Delta^{shape} = \sum_{k=1}^{15} \left| \frac{s_k^q - s_k^d}{s_k^q + s_k^d + v} \right| \tag{11}$$

Using such retrieval system, one can define the image matching distance $\Delta^{finaldiastance}$ between Q and D as

$$\Delta^{finaldistance} = W_1 X \Delta^{MCM} + W_2 X \Delta^{DBPSP} + W_3 X \Delta^{DDC} + W_4 X \Delta^{shape}$$

In this experiment, the values of the parameters are: spatial offset $(\delta_x, \delta_y) = (0, 1)$ and $W_1 = 0.2$, W2 = 0.3, $W_3 = 0.3$ and $W_4 = 0.2$.

6 Conclusion

The proposed system uses four image features namely SPCMM, SPIPD, shape and DC to characterize a color image for image retrieval. SPCMM and SPIPD can describe texture distribution, while shape and DC can describe color and shape features of the pixels in an image. DC is invariant to translation and rotation. Since these features can describe different properties of an image, the propose retrieval system integrates these four features to retrieve the images. The experimental results show that the proposed system outperforms Hung's and Jhanwar's methods.

Semantic name	proposed method	dominant color and Motif co-occurrence matrix[17]	Jhanwar et.al.[12]	Hung and Dai's [9]
African people	0.59 2	0.562	0.4525	0.424
Beach	0.53 6	0.536	0.3975	0.4455
Building	0.61	0.61	0.3735	0.4105
Buses	0.89 3	0.893	0.741	0.8515
Dinosaurs	0.98 4	0.984	0.9145	0.5865
Elephants	0.67	0.578	0.304	0.4255
Flowers	0.89 9	0.899	0.8515	0.8975
Horses	0.79	0.78	0.568	0.589
Mountain and glaciers	0.64	0.512	0.2925	0.268
Food	0.69 4	0.694	0.3695	0.4265
Average	0.730 8	0.7048	0.52645	0.53245

Fig. 4 The image retrieval results (Dinosaurs) using different techniques (a) N. Jhanwar et al.[4] (b) Hung and Dai et al.[3] (c) Dominant color and [illegible] pattern co-occurrence matrix [illegible] [illegible] proposed method

References

1. Datta, R., Li, J., Wang, J.Z.: Content-based image retrieval approaches and trends of the new age. In: Proceedings of the Seventh International Workshop on Multimedia Information Retrieval, Singapore, pp. 253–262 (2005)
2. Yang, N.-C., Chang, W.-H., Kuo, C.-M., Li, T.-H.: A fast MPEG-7 dominant color extraction with new similarity measure for image retrieval. Journal of Visual Communication and Image Representation 19(2), 92–105 (2008)
3. Huang, P.W., Dai, S.K.: Image retrieval by texture similarity. Pattern Recognition 36(3), 665–679 (2003)
4. Jhanwar, N., Chaudhurib, S., Seetharamanc, G., Zavidovique, B.: Content based image retrieval using scan pattern co-occurrence matrix. Image and Vision Computing 22, 1211–1220 (2004)
5. Lowe, D.: Distinctive image features from scale invariant keypoints. International Journal of Computer vision 2(6), 91–110 (2004)

Authenticate Program Complexity Metrics Using RAA

Abdul Jabbar and Sarala

Department of Information Technology, Bharathiar University,
Coimbatore, Tamil Nadu, India

Abstract. Complexity affects the productivity in the defined procedure to reduce the complexity of programs the various techniques have been analyzed. Complexity measure identifies the complex and error-prone area of code segment. It is based on indentation, naming convention, number of IFs, WHILEs, FORs the number of ANDs, ORs and NOTs in the code. Software metrics plays an important role in the software evaluation. In this work the adequacy of software metrics is validated by the proposed rule accuracy algorithm which is based on rule induction technique. In the context of predefined rules the efficiency and effectiveness of software metrics is also analyzed. The rules contain if and then clause which hold metrics excellence criterion. Information flow metrics used as data set for the adequacy evaluation. The evaluation processed with flexible outcome and it proves the Rule Accuracy Algorithm is an efficient validation technique.

Keywords: Fuzzy Rule System, Rule Induction, Ant Colony Algorithm, Rule Accuracy Algorithm, Software Metrics.

1 Introduction

The importance of software metrics in software development is renowned. With the assistance of metrics the developers gains various efforts in project development. To maintain the software quality, software metrics plays major scope which includes maintainability, effort and productivity. Predictive capability of software metrics is desirable, thus it is a significant factor to measure the productivity, quality and effort for cost estimation [2], [4], [5]. The validation of software metrics is highly complicated, moreover it has complex process. According to the existing work, a number of approaches have been developed for evaluation and validation of software metrics. Due to the lack of identifying efficient technique, the Rule Accuracy Algorithm (RAA) has been proposed. Rule induction is the common form of knowledge discovery in unsupervised learning systems [6], [16]. RAA allows for a more complicated evaluation of software metrics. From the given software metrics data set, the best metrics data are induced by RAA. A database creates, software metrics were the instances and the set of variable consisted from several programming module which provided by sourceforge, it is a web based open source code repository.

V.V. Das and N. Thankachan (Eds.): CIIT 2011, CCIS 250, pp. 358–362, 2011.

2 Mechanism in Existing Work

The evaluation performed in different ways which are analytical validation and empirical validation [7], [20]. In analytical validation the theoretical back ground of metrics as well as the attributes coverage associated with the parameters. Empirical validation is to identify precision and accuracy of software metrics on metrics association and the approaches of different client. In [20], the authors validate cohesion and information theoretic metrics which is used properties.In [3] indicates the validity has been to measure based on satisfying defined properties. Clearly, the most related work Elaine [21] has found in the literature. The described number of properties to validate the software metrics measures was depended only in the context of syntactic features of program. Taking properties as the relation between syntactical variations during the result formation, exactly 9 properties were discussed. Then, the response in validation these properties are distinguished on various complexity measures. It is argued that, as the reason of be unsuccessful to satisfy properties, most of the metrics being complex. Metrics validation is a difficult process, as the properties must confirm to the mathematical transparency in all perception. Since it is a difficult practice, it would be advisable to in a few measurements. This validation approach has been offering hopeful result but the result is not applicable in all case. Hence, it comprises an alternative to realize the complete effortless validation of metrics in all perspective. There for a new approach is proposed to validate metrics adequacy.

3 The Metrics Validation System

A rule induction approach use to validate metrics for adequacy. The predefined rules induce the best data from metrics data set which conform the integrity of the metrics. The rule induction is used in research for classification [6], [11], [12], [13], [14], [15]. In this work propose RAA classification algorithm, to perform the validation in advance. Given set of metrics, which validate whether the metrics is adequate or not. The fundamental issue is to begin the validation as the resolution of a rule optimization to find best rule. For this, rules formulate, and it organized by supervised classification method basis of improved Ant Colony optimization algorithm [9]. To define the ACO, the researchers consider how the almost blind ants found the shortest path to their feeding sources and rear. Basically, the phenomenon is that ants use pheromone for communication. The path of an ant lays a few of pheromone, which are detectable by other ants, along its path. Consequently, the ants can establish the shortest path to the feeding sources and back. Using this methodology the ACO finds the solution for various classification issues [8], [9], [10], [17], [18] and [19].

4 Rule Accuracy Algorithm

Based on rule induction technique s number approaches have been used to discover information from data base with good accuracy. The various if-then-rules are recognized based on adequacy criterion [13]. The *if-then rules* which is defined as, *rule1, rule2.....rule$_n$* holds the structural attributes of metrics, and thus it varied according to the characteristic of metrics. Consequently the RAA algorithm seems reliable. More precisely, the work concentrates on structural metrics, for each rule maximum parameters are considered. The parameters are acquired from a number of available source codes. The important issue of RAA is how to choose the preeminent rules from the rule set. The validation with all rules is big hazard; therefore it is optimized by ACO classification method. According to this, metrics adequacy factors distinguished the rules. In addition the adequacy factors which reflect on the source code behavior and measuring aspects. The quality coverage may vary considerably depending on the rules clarity. So as to avoid deceptive result, certain criteria are fixed for all rule definition. RAA algorithm is defined as the instances are selected according to the rules, which induced the data set and finds the accuracy. In the context of RAA algorithms with rules, induce the metrics data set, an individual from a metrics set m= (m_1, m2, m3...m_n) of a metrics set M = (M_1, M2,.M_n) and rule set R=(R1,R2,...Rn). Given rules of the best selection, R, and the preferred metrics, M, signify a data set, m. RAA estimate the metrics adequacy by each rule metrics values and parameters are examined. To facilitate the proposed RAA algorithm's steps are summarized as follows.

Rules Accuracy Algorithm(R, M, a)
Step1: Metrics Set M:={M1, M2,...... Mn}
Step2: metrics dataset from metrics set
Metrics dataset m=(m_1,m_2,m_3..m_n).
Step3: Rules Set R :={R1, R2,..........Rn}
Step4: check the metrics data M set is satisfied for each Rules R
Step5: Calculate aAccuracy and coverage of metrics.

Table 1. Henry and Kafura and IFC information flow metrics data set

Si No.	F-in	F-out	P-C	C-L	Henry and Kafura	IFC
1	463	320	40	1325	29085585920000	23.6377
2	2	3	1	13	468	0.3846
3	86	41	14	946	11761311496	1.8794
4	123	56	31	1256	59590347264	4.41799
5	108	30	19	1133	11893780800	2.31421

5 Experimental Results

Software metrics adequacy using RAA algorithm with rule induction technique is explained with distinct inputs. Initially, metrics data set is selected, followed by program analysis the value has been reflected with result. Henry Kafura information flow complexity metrics *length* (fan-in*fan-out)*^{2} and IFC *(Procedure call) *(fan-in +fan-out) / Code length*[1] are the metrics to prepare the database, which shows in table 1. RAA examine the data set which is previously selected best rules from the given set of rules. To be precise, each row in the table 1 that is M1, M2...Mn is validating in the best Rule set R. The rule is defined as to accomplish the each adequacy objective. However, broad realities of rules are possible for combining the RRA algorithm. Metric set M1 validate by rule set R that is M1 validate by each rule in Rule set R, nine rules are obtained after the ACO optimization. Following metrics are validated accordingly. Table 2 shows the result of the RAA. First column displays optimized rules, while the second validation result IFC and third validation result of Henry and Kafura respectively. The study restricted of the induction technique by setting maximum number of rules up to nine using ACO algorithm to ensure the reliability and efficiency. If the metrics M satisfy the rule R, RAA indicate either yes condition or no condition.

Table 2. IFC, Henry and Kafura Check bye optimized the all rules

No	Rules Accuracy Algorithm	IFC	Henry and Kafura
1	RULE 1	Yes	Yes
2	RULE 2	No	Yes
3	RULE 3	Yes	No
4	RULE 4	Yes	Yes
5	RULE 5	Yes	No
6	RULE 6	No	Yes
7	RULE 7	YES	NO
8	RULE 8	YES	YES
9	RULE 9	YES	NO
	Total	7	5

Accuracy of IFC information flow complexity metrics=77.7
Accuracy of Henry and Kafura information flow complexity metrics=55.5

6 Conclusions

Rule Accuracy Algorithm has been formulated with the selected data. RAA analyzed the metrics data set, state that the IFC is adequate. The processed data set shows in table 1, it illustrates examples of program metrics estimation. The optimized rules induced the metrics data set. In this work the efficiency of metrics is calculated. A number of metrics were analyzed based on rules induction approach. The Rule Accuracy Algorithm has determined that metrics evaluation is possible offered with best results. The Rule formation and selection in RAA algorithm gives an indication for the future enhancement. Rules formation and selection are very beneficial, both will improves the adequacy of measurement.

References

1. Sarala, S., Abdul Jabbar, P.: Information flow metrics and complexity measurement. In: 3rd IEEE International Conference on Computer Science and Information Technology, pp. 575–578 (2010)
2. Jabbar, A., Sarala, S.: Advanced Program complexity measurement. International Journal of computer Aplication, 29–33 (2011)
3. Nael, S.: Complexity metrics as predictors of maintainability and integrability of software components. Journal of Arts and Sciences, 39–50 (2006)
4. Sepasmoghaddam, A., Rashidi, H.: A Novel Method to Measure Comprehensive Complexity of Software Based on the Metrics Statistical Model, pp. 520–525. IEEE (2010)
5. Ma, Y., He, K., Du, D., Liu, J., Yan, Y.: A Complexity Metrics Set for Large-scale Object-oriented Software Systems. In: Proceedings of The Sixth IEEE International Conference on Computer and Information Technology. IEEE computer society (2006)
6. Tsumoto, S., Hirano, S.: Automated Empirical Selection of Rule Induction Methods based on Recursive Iteration of Resampling Methods and Multiple testing. In: IEEE International Conference on Data Mining Workshops, pp. 835–842 (2010)
7. MendoncËa, M.G., Basili, V.R.: Validation of an Approach for Improving Existing Measurement Frameworks. IEEE Transactions On Software Engineering, 484–499 (2000)
8. Ho, S.L., Yang, S., Wong, H.C., Cheng, K.W.E., Ni, G.: An Improved Ant Colony Optimization Algorithm and Its Application to Electromagnetic Devices Designs. IEEE Transactions On Magnetics, 1764–1767 (2005)
9. Dorigo, M., Birattari, M., Stutzle, T.: Ant Colony optimization. IEEE Computational Intelligence Magazine, 28–39 (2006)
10. Zhang, J., Chen, W.-N., Zhong, J.-H., Tan, X., Li, Y.: Continuous Function Optimization Using Hybrid Ant Colony Approach with Orthogonal Design Scheme, pp. 126–133. Springer, Heidelberg (2006)
11. Cohagan, C., Grzymala-Busse, J.W., Hippe, Z.S.: Mining Inconsistent Data with the Bagged MLEM2 Rule Induction Algorithm. In: 2010 IEEE International Conference on Granular Computing, pp. 115–120 (2010)
12. Tsumoto, S., Hirano, S., Abe, H.: Sampling from Databases for Rule Induction Methods based on Likelihood Ratio Test. In: Proc. 9th IEEE Int. Conf. on Cognitive Informatics, pp. 174–179 (2010)
13. Shadabi, F., Sharma, D.: Using Knowledge and Rule Induction Methods for Enhancing Clinical Diagnosis: Success Stories. In: International Conference on Future Computer and Communication, pp. 540–542 (2009)
14. Chaisorn, L., Chua, T.-S.: Story Boundary Detection In News Video Using Global Rule Induction Technique, pp. 2101–2104. IEEE (2006)
15. Bi, Y., McClean, S., Anderson, T.: Combining rough decisions for intelligent text mining using Dempster's rule, pp. 191–209. Springer, Heidelberg (2006)
16. Jiang, Q., Abidi, S.: From Clusters to Rules: A Hybrid Framework for Generalized Symbolic Rule Induction, pp. 219–228. Springer, Heidelberg (2006)
17. Chan, A., Freitas, A.: A New Classification-Rule Pruning Procedure for an Ant, pp. 25–36. Springer, Heidelberg (2006)
18. Chen, L., Tu, L.: Parallel Mining for Classification Rules with Ant Colony Algorithm, pp. 261–266. Springer, Heidelberg (2005)
19. Wang, Z., Feng, B.: Classification Rule Mining with an Improved Ant Colony Algorithm, pp. 357–367. Springer, Heidelberg (2004)
20. Barbara, P.: Problem Adopting Metrics from other Disciplines, pp. 1–7. ACM (2010)

Performance Comparison of AODV, AOMDV and DSDV for Fire Fighters Application

D. Annapurna[1], D. Shreyas Bhagavath[2], V. Gnanaskandan[2], K.B. Raja[3], K.R. Venugopal[3], and L.M. Patnaik[4]

[1] Department of Information Science and Engineering.
PES School of Engineering, Hosur Road, Bangalore 560100, India
[2] Department of Electronics and Communication Engineering
[3] Department of Computer Science and Engineering,
University Visvesvaraya College of Engineering, Bangalore University, Bangalore 560 001, India
[4] Defence Institute of Advanced Technologies, Pune, India
anusuresh111@yahoo.com

Abstract. Effective communication within the network is an important characteristic for a wireless network. A model with a combination of wireless sensor network and Adhoc network i,e Performance Comparison of Protocols for Firefighters (PCPFF) for fire rescue operation is proposed. This provides an effective interaction between the nodes to save the firefighters when they are in distress or when there is no lifeline. The model helps in effective area coverage by indicating the path that is already been used and provides a reliable lifeline to firefighters. It is observed that the performance of Adhoc On-Demand Distance Vector (AODV) is better when compared to Ad Hoc On-demand Multipath Distance-Vector Protocol (AOMDV) and Destination-Sequenced Distance-Vector Routing (DSDV).

Keywords: Firefighter, Lifeline, Routing Protocol, AODV, AOMDV, DSDV.

1 Introduction

An Adhoc network has mobile computing nodes distributed randomly in a specified area and are characterized by energy, node ID and node expiry time. The communication between nodes is based on wireless trans-reception without fixed infrastructure. The computing nodes are tiny devices having capability to measure and process the quantities of an environmental information and communicate to the information gathering centre to take approximate action. The sensing activity by the computing node are of two types viz.,(i) Periodic Sensing in which a node senses the environmental physical parameters such as temperature, humidity, nuclear radiations and electromagnetic radiations and (ii) Sporadic Sensing in which, the nodes are used to sense and measure physical parameters such as temperature of a furnace in an industry, stress on a structure and density of vehicles in a city to keep the measured values within the specified threshold level to avoid destructions and maintain the safety norms. The routing in Ad hoc network is dynamic and links changes randomly

V.V. Das and N. Thankachan (Eds.): CIIT 2011, CCIS 250, pp. 363–367, 2011.

An intelligent routing protocol is required to find the path as the Adhoc network is infrastructure less and network topology information of every node in the network is necessary for routing. The routing protocols[1] for Adhoc wireless network is classified on the basis of (i) Routing Information update mechanism [ii] Use of temporal Information for routing (iii) Routing Topology (iv) Utilization of specific resources. The routing information update mechanism is classified as (i) Table driven or proactive routing protocol: Routing table holds and maintains the topological information of the nodes. Routing Information is obtained by exchanging routing tables within the network and, path finding algorithm is used, to find the path. (ii)On demand or reactive routing protocols: The protocols do not maintain the network topology information. In order to find path, the connection is established. Hence periodical exchange of routing information among the nodes is not seen. (iii)Hybrid Routing Protocols: The protocols form the routing with a specified zone using proactive routing scheme and reactive routing scheme is used for nodes which are beyond the zone.

2 Literature Survey

Kulakowski et al., [2] illustrated spreading of fire model based on appropriate percolation theory. The network consists of sensors to gather temperature data and sending it to the control station to create a map of fire and to take necessary actions. Hady Abdel salam et al., [3] proposed an algorithm where firefighters are given support by increasing the life of the Wireless Sensor Network (WSN). This algorithm helps men at the fire area with sufficient and continuous information besides maintaining the energy of WSN. Ramesh V et al., [4] examined two routing protocols Destination Sequenced Distance Vector (DSDV) and Adhoc on Demand Distance Vector (AODV) and evaluated them on packet delivery fraction and average delay while varying the number of sources and pause time. AODV protocol is best suitable for UDP communication, while packet delivery fraction is very low for high mobility scenarios in case of DSDV. Daniele Miorandi and Eiton Altman E [5] explain the analysis of connectivity issues in one dimensional ad hoc networks. The model helps in the study of percolation problems in adhoc networks. It shows that node distribution is based on Poisson's distribution. Srdjan Capkun et al., [6] proposed a distributed infrastructure free positioning algorithm that does not rely on Global Positioning System (GPS).The algorithm uses the distance between the nodes to build a relative coordinate system in which the node positions are computed in two dimensions.

3 Proposed Model

The proposed model PCPFF is a combination of Wireless Sensor Network (WSN) and Mobile Ad Hoc Network (MANET). The concept is based on the fact that the firefighters are in motion for most part of the fire rescue operation. It is very important for the fire fighters to communicate with each other effectively as the fire fighters work in an environment that is continuously changing and complex. The visibility of the firefighters is usually impaired because of the smoke and fire hence cannot see all their fellow firefighters. Commanders stay outside the building while firefighters enter the building.

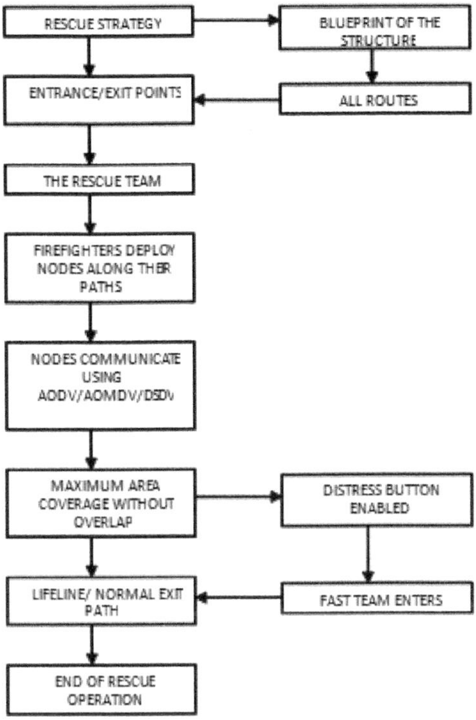

Fig. 1. Block Diagram of the proposed PCPFF model

The firefighters are part of the MANET, which serves as a medium of communication among the firefighters and the commanders, because they are in motion and need not always be in the radio range of the commanders. The information still reach all the firefighters even though they are not in the radio range of the sender. Since MANETS can act as routers and due to the multiple hops the information will reach the firefighter. The firefighters are provided with a device which has the capability to drop nodes at regular intervals of time inside the building and form a WSN. The nodes contain temperature sensors and transceivers. The transceivers are used to send and receive the temperature at each node. The device that the firefighters has also a display which shows positions of all the other firefighters along with the position of nodes which are dropped by that firefighter and fellow firefighters. The display has distress button. When the firefighter is in distress either due to asphyxiation or due to injuries, he initiates the distress signal. This intimates the incident commander to send the firefighters in each Rescue Team and Firefighter Assistance and Search team(FAST) to rescue the person in distress.

4 Performance Analysis

The Pause Time i,e., time for which simulation is run and has varied the pause time from 15sec to 190 sec and Packet delivery fraction (PDF) i,e., the ratio of number of packets received to the number of packets originated are used to evaluate performance of proposed algorithm. The graph in Figure 2 shows the variation of packet delivery fraction (PDF) with pause time. The movement of nodes starts at 25 seconds and ends at 125 seconds. Initially the PDF remains high for AODV and AOMDV because they are reactive protocols. Another reason is that the nodes are static at the start of simulation. Since DSDV is a table driven protocol, all the routes are not stored in the routing table, thereby justifying the low PDF. In the mid-region of the graph, that is, from 30 seconds to 125 seconds, the nodes are highly mobile. Since the topology changes are rapid, on demand routing performs better as the routes are determined every time a packet has to be sent to a destination. On the other hand, DSDV being table driven takes much longer to react to these rapid topology changes resulting in large packet loss. In the last part of the graph the nodes are almost static and hence the topology remains the same. In this region DSDV performs better because the route updates are less frequent. The routes remain same for almost all the destination nodes. However AODV and AOMDV take time to find routes to new destinations despite there being not much change in the topology of the network. In the 25 sec to 125 sec region of the graph AODV out performs AOMDV and DSDV with respect to PDF.

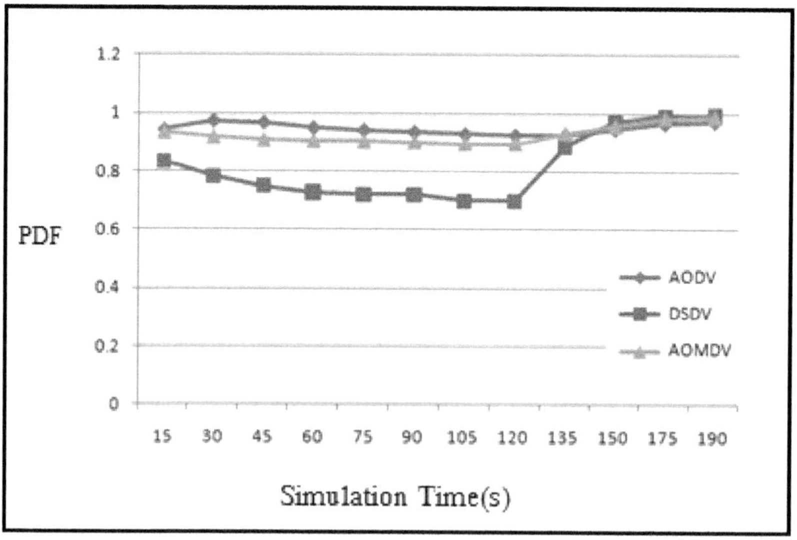

Fig. 2. Graph of PDF of AODV, AOMDV and DSDV with simulation time

5 Conclusions

The Adhoc network has a variety of applications, like in firefighting. Results clearly show performance of the three routing protocols. The packet delivery fraction remains high for AODV and AOMDV reactive protocols than DSDV a proactive routing protocol. These reactive protocols perform better where topology changes are rapid, as the routes are determined every time a packet has to be sent to a destination. DSDV justifies as proactive routing protocol with low packet delivery fraction. DSDV performs better for a network where the route updates are less frequent.

References

1. Siva Ram Murthy, C., Manoj, B.S.: Adhoc wireless networks: Blueprint for a Architectures and protocols. Pearson Education and Dorling Kindersley, South Asia (2004)
2. Pawel, K., Eusebi, C., Jose, M.L.: Sensors-Actuators Cooperation in WSANs for Fire Fighting Applications. In: IEEE International Workshop on Selected Topics in Mobile and Wireless Computing, pp. 726–732 (2010)
3. Salam, H.A., Syed Rizvi, R., Ainsworth, S., Olariu, S.: A Durable Sensor Enabled Lifeline Support for Firefighters. IEEE Autonomus Networked Sensor Systems (2008)
4. Ramesh, V., Subbaiah, P., Koteswar Rao, N., Janardhana Raju, M.: Performance Comparison and Analysis of DSDV and AODV for MANET. International Journal on Computer Science and Engineering 02(02), 183–188 (2010)
5. Daniele, M., Altman, E.: Connectivity in One-Dimensional Ad Hoc Networks, a Queueing Theoretical Approach. Institute National De Recherche En Informatique Et En Automatique (2004)
6. Capkun, S., Hamdi, M., Hubaux, J.-P.: GPS-Free Positioning in Mobile Ad Hoc Networks. In: Annual Hawaii International Conference on System Sciences (2001)

Robust and Energy Efficient Audio Watermarking Scheme Resilient to Desynchronizing Attacks

Reena Gunjan* and Priyam Pandia

Department of Computer Engineering, Malaviya National Institute of Technology, Jaipur, Rajasthan, India
{reenagunjan,priyampandia}@gmail.com

Abstract. With the advances of technology, security of the digital media has become a major challenge. Audio watermarking is the technique to embed some data into the audio signal for identifying the copyright ownership and preventing piracy. This energy based technique is different from others as it involves embedding the pre-processed image watermark in wavelet domain using mean quantization and patchwork methods. The low frequency wavelet coefficients are considered and they are further segmented into frames on the basis of the size of processed watermark. The frames, thus obtained are arranged in decreasing order of their energy and watermark processed with the synchronization code is hid in frames with highest energy thereby increasing the robustness against deliberate and non- deliberate attacks. The simulation results show that the implemented scheme is highly resistant to the signal processing and desynchronization attacks.

Keywords: Audio Watermarking, Desynchronization attacks, Mean Quantization, Patchwork method.

1 Introduction

With the rapid growth of technology, it is easier for digital data owners to transit multimedia files across the Internet. Thus, there is a huge increase in concentration over copyright protection of media. Digital audio watermarkingis the scheme of embedding some relevant information,watermark, into an audio signal so that a given piece of copyright information is permanently tied to the audio.This information can later prove the ownership, identify a misappropriating person, and trace the marked digital data disseminating through the network.The goal in this paper is to embed the watermark in the audio signal imperceptibly by the exploitation of the statistical and the objective properties of the cover signal. The low frequency region and the energy of the signal segments are considered in this regard. The organization of the paper is as follows. Section 2 reviews related works in this area, Section 3 describes the theory of techniques used, Section 4 discusses the implementation strategy, Section 5 shows results after applying various attacks to audio signal and Section 6 concludes the paper with a substance of future research in this method.

* Corresponding author.

V.V. Das and N. Thankachan (Eds.): CIIT 2011, CCIS 250, pp. 368–374, 2011.

2 Related Works

A technique proposed by Wang et al. [1] is based on information hiding where the Discrete Wavelet Transform (DWT) is applied on each segment of carrier audio. The secret bits are constructed by performing chaotic encryption on a combination of synchronizing codes and secret audio. These bits are then embedded into the low frequency coefficients of wavelet domain by quantization method. An audio watermarking technique proposed [2] uses two level DWT where the spectrum of the host audio signal is decomposed to find the appropriate regions to embed the image bits.Li [3] proposed a method in which the watermark sequence is first permuted and then encrypted using Arnold Transformation. The audio signal is divided into segments and Discrete Cosine Transform (DCT) and DWT is performed on each audio data segment and the watermark is embedded in the low frequency components.

Another approach [4] utilizes a multi-level DWT where the information is embedded a number of times into approximate coefficients of each level. A quantization based audio watermarking method is proposed [5, 6] which is based on DWT and DCT. The information is in the form of image which is encrypted using different techniques such as Arnold Transform and Linear Feedback Shift Register.Another approach [7] is based on an improved patchwork method in which two subsets in wavelet domain are considered. The watermark is embedded by the addition of a small value to one subset and subtraction of the same value from the other.A wavelet transform based approach [8] is considered in which the audio signal is decomposed into low frequency and high frequency components. The watermark is generated by pseudo random numbers. It is embedded into the approximate coefficients depending upon the binary values of a binary image.

3 Theoretical Foundations

Discrete Wavelet Transform. The signal is transformed by wavelet transforms using wavelet filters. The signal is decomposed into low frequencies (Approximation coefficients, W_{j_0}) and high frequencies (Detail coefficients,$W_{\Psi}(j,k)$) given as:

$$W_{j_0} = \frac{1}{\sqrt{M}} \Sigma_n f(n) \varphi_{j_0,k}(n) \quad (1)$$

$$W_{\Psi}(j,k) = \frac{1}{\sqrt{M}} \Sigma_n f(n) \Psi_{j,k}(n) \forall j \geq j_0 \quad (2)$$

The original signal isagain reconstructed by applying the inverse DWT defined as:

$$f(n) = \frac{1}{\sqrt{M}} \sum_k W_\varphi(j_0,k)\, \varphi_{j_{0,k}}(n) + \frac{1}{\sqrt{M}} \sum_{j=j_0}^{\infty} \sum_k W_\psi(j,k)\, \psi_{j,k}(n) \quad (3)$$

Mean Quantization Scheme. The implementation is by the following equations:

$$y = \begin{cases} q(x,D) + \frac{D}{4} if b = 1, \\ q(x,D) - \frac{D}{4} if b = 0 \end{cases}, \quad (4)$$

where x is the frame mean, b is the information bit, and $q(x, D)$ is the quantization function with D being the quantization step. The quantization function is given as:

$$q(x, D) = \left[\frac{x}{D}\right].D. \tag{5}$$

Where $[x]$ rounds to the nearest integer of x. Detection process is given as:

$$b = \begin{cases} 1 & if\ 0 < y - q(x, D) < D/4 \\ 0 & if\ -D/4 < y - q(x, D) < 0 \end{cases} \tag{6}$$

Patchwork Method. Patchwork method is used to store the mean of the frames in which image bits are embedded. These are added to mean of one patch of frame and subtracted from the other patch of frames.

$$a'(i) = a(i) + mean\ ,\ b'(i) = b(i) - mean \tag{7}$$

Where a(i) and b(i) are the coefficient values of each of the frames of the patches.

4 Energy Efficient Scheme

The essential features of the proposed algorithm are the use of statistical and objective features of the audio signal itself and the use of combined techniques of time and transform domain. The main advantage of the first strategy is that the use of statistical and objective features evenly distributes the embedding of the watermark over the complete signal. Not one part of the signal is crowded by the watermark bits which makes watermark detection nearly impossible for the attacker. Also the use of combined techniques of mean quantization and patchwork method in transform domain help achieve greater robustness and less algorithmic complexity as the time domain techniques are very simple to implement.

Preprocessing Watermark. To make the algorithm robust against de-synchronization attacks, the watermark is processed with the synchronization code. This code is a combination of 16 8-bit binary vectors which implies that each synchronization code is 8 bit long and 16 such codes are generated. Once the codes are generated they are added between the watermark bits. Once all the 16 codes are used, the next code used again is the first code which makes the cycle going on until all the watermark bits are put in the processed watermark as shown in figure 1. The steps involved for processing the watermark are defined as:

. . .	Synchronizing code	image bits	Synchronizing code	image bits	. . .

Fig. 1. Preprocessing of Watermark

1. Express the image as a two dimensional matrix whose size is N × N.
2. Convert the two dimensional matrix into one dimensional vector of length N × N.

3. Normalize the vector by dividing each entry by256 and round it to the nearest integer.
4. Embed the synchronization code in the vector such that before every two bits of the image vector is an 8 bit synchronization code which has a cycle of 16.

Embedding Strategy. The preprocessed watermark is further embedded in the audio signal by using the energy effective watermarking strategy shown in figure 2 which can be implemented by the following steps as:

1. Apply one dimensional DWT to the carrier audio signal.
2. Segregate the approximation coefficients and group them into frames. The size of each frame is governed by the size of image and size of the carrier audio signal.
3. Arrange the frames in the decreasing order of their energy by applying another level of wavelet decomposition
4. Embed the processed image vector containing the synchronization code in the ordered frames by mean quantization method.
5. Embed the locations of the frames in which the image bits are embedded in another groups of frames with lower energy values by patchwork method.
6. Reorder the frames to their exact locations thus, distributing the watermarked locations.
7. Apply inverse wavelet transform and reconstruct the audio signal containing the hidden image information.

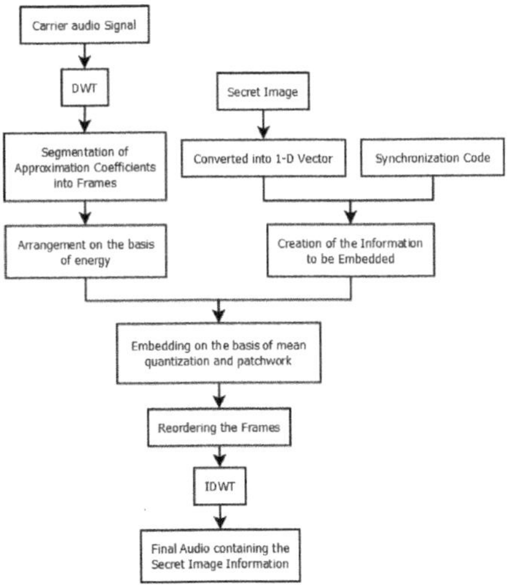

Fig. 2. Embedding Strategy

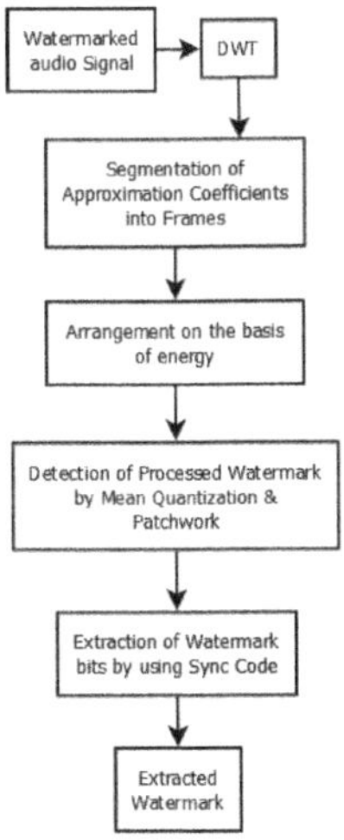

Fig. 3. Extraction

Extraction Strategy. The extraction procedure followed is exactly the reverse of the embedding procedure in which the DWT is applied to the watermarked audio signal then the approximation coefficients are grouped into frames and arranged according to their energy in the decreasing order. Then the watermark bits are detected by matching the synchronization code bits so as to guarantee the exact location of the watermark which is then cross checked by the values stored in the lower energy frames by patchwork method. This is schematically represented in figure 3.

5 Result Analysis

Audio signal used in this implementation strategy is shown in figure 4. It is a 16-bit mono audio sampled at 44100 Hz, sample size of 16 bits with duration 5 seconds. The watermark shown in figure 5 is a gray scale image of MNIT logo of size 32 × 32 and bit depth of 8 bits. Furthermore, CoolEdit Pro v2.1 has been used for audio editing and attacking in order to corrupt the watermark.

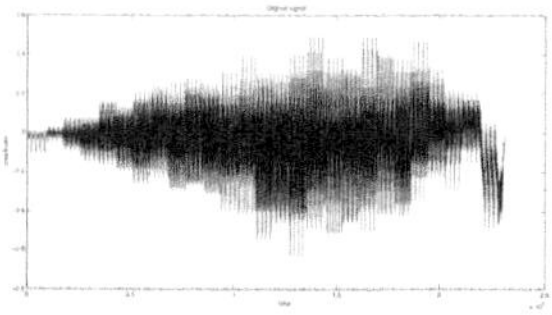

Fig. 4. Original Audio Signal

Fig. 5. Watermark

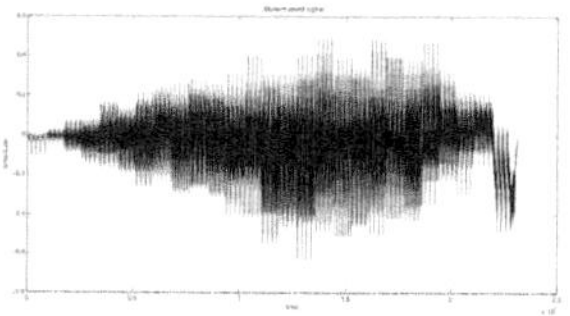

Fig. 6. Watermarked Audio Signal

The result Analysis is done by using two metrics: Similarity Factor (SM) and Bit Error Rate (BER).Similarity Factor (SM) is a measure to determine the similarity between the original and the extracted data. Its value ranges between 0 and 1.Bit Error Rate (BER) gives the percentage of the erroneous bits extracted and the total number of bits in the image.

It is seen that even after embedding the watermark in the audio signal, no visible difference is observed in the plots as shown in figure 6. The attacks implemented with low values of changes in amplitude or frequency performed to the signal are defined as *low intensity attacks* and those implemented without taking into account the extent of the changes in amplitude or frequency are called*high intensity attacks*. Robustness of the implemented strategy against signal processing and deliberate attacks from Stirmark Benchmark has been analyzed.

The table 1 displays the values of similarity measure for both high intensity and low intensity attacks. The Table 2 shows the comparison of the proposed strategy with the already implemented method ofBhat et al. [6] for the values of the similarity measure. The results thus computed display that the proposed watermark strategy is better than other already implemented strategies in this regard.

Table 1. Similarity Measure Values for low and high intensity attacks

Attacks	SM values for low intensity attacks	SM values for high intensity attacks
Re-Quantization	.9675	.5775
Re-Sampling	.9550	.5288
Amplification	.7865	.5784
Inversion	.8611	.5618
Noise Addition	.8995	.5513
Low Pass Filtering	.8981	.5073.
High pass Filtering	.9332	.5562
Cropping	.9895	.5345
Jittering	.9980	.5892
Pitch Shift	.8907	.5273
Time Stretch	.8437	.5012

Table 2. Similarity Measure Values for proposed algorithm and the reference

Attacks	Similarity Factor	
	Proposed Algorithm	Reference [6]
Re-Quantization	.9675	.9840
Re-Sampling	.9550	1
Noise Addition	.8995	.8110
LP filtering	.8981	.8860
HP filtering	.9332	.7510
Cropping	.9895	.999
Jittering	.9980	1

6 Conclusions

The proposed algorithm exhibits very low time complexity as there is no repetition of multiple transforms. The watermark is processed with the synchronization code to provide very high robustness against de-synchronization attacks. Also, if one part of the signal is destroyed by the attacks, some part of the watermark can be successfully extracted from the remaining signal by the algorithm thereby, serving the purpose of copyright protection. The watermark is up to 50% extractable even if the attacks of very high intensity are applied which result in the complete destruction of the signal.The main limitation of the proposed algorithm is that the similarity factor keeps decreasing if the intensity of attacks is increased. This can be improved by increasing the levels of DWT. Encryption or processing of watermark by other simple transforms like Arnold Transform, Hadamard Transform might increase the robustness of the algorithm and this area needs to be explored further.

References

1. Wang, J., Mo, Q., Mei, D., Yao, J.: Research for Synchronic Audio Information Hiding Approach Based on DWT Domain. In: International Conference on E-Business and Information System Security, EBISS 2009, pp. 1–5 (2009)
2. Al-Haj, A., Bata, L., Mohammad, A.: Audio Watermarking using Wavelets. In: First International Conference on Networked Digital Technologies, NDT 2009, pp. 398–403 (2009)

3. Li, D.: A New Algorithm of Self-adaptability for Digital Audio Watermark with Energy Quantization Circuits. In: Pacific-Asia Conference on Communications and Systems, PACCS 2009, pp. 559–562 (2009)
4. Datta, K., Sengupta, I.: A Redundant Audio Watermarking Technique Using Discrete Wavelet Transformation. In: Second International Conference on Communication Software and Networks, ICCSN 2010, pp. 27–31 (2010)
5. Ravula, R., Rai, S.: A Robust Audio Watermarking Algorithm Based on Statistical Characteristics and DWT+DCT Transforms. In: 6th International Conference on Wireless Communications Networking and Mobile Computing (WiCOM), pp. 1–4 (2010)
6. Bhat, K.V., Sengupta, I., Das, A.: Audio Watermarking Based on Quantization in Wavelet Domain. In: Sekar, R., Pujari, A.K. (eds.) ICISS 2008. LNCS, vol. 5352, pp. 235–242. Springer, Heidelberg (2008)
7. Jiang, J.-J., Pun, C.-M.: Digital Audio Watermarking using an improved Patchwork Method in Wavelet Domain. In: 6th International Conference on Digital Content, Multimedia Technology and its Applications (IDC), pp. 386–389 (2010)
8. Ercelebi, E., Batakci, L.: Audio Watermarking Scheme based on Embedding Strategy in Low Frequency Components with a Binary Image. J. Digital Signal Processing 19(2), 265–277 (2009)

Selection of Defuzzification Method for Predicting the Early Stage Software Development Effort Using Mamdani FIS

Roheet Bhatnagar[1], Mrinal Kanti Ghose[1], and Vandana Bhattacharjee[2]

[1] Department of Computer Science and Engineering,
Sikkim Manipal Institute of Technology,
Majitar, Rangpo, East Sikkim, India
{roheetbhatnagar,mkghose2000}@yahoo.com
[2] Department of Computer Science and Engineering,
BITEC, Lalpur, BIT Mesra, Ranchi, Jharkhand, India
vbhattacharya@bitmesra.ac.in

Abstract. The Soft Computing techniques presents an alternative to software development effort estimations and this paper is concerned with estimating the early stage effort estimations using student datasets. As we know, the output of fuzzy inference system depends on the selection of defuzzification method. This paper compares the outcomes of Mamdani Fuzzy Inference System (FIS) created using four different types of defuzzification methods namely centroid, bisector, Mean of Maximum (MOM) and Largest of Maximum (LOM). For this purpose a two inputs and one output Mamdani FIS was created using the above four defuzzification methods. The outputs (efforts) are evaluated using the standard performance evaluation metrics like Magnitude of Relative Error (MRE), Median of Magnitude of Relative Error (MMRE) etc. and it was found that the centroid method is the best and lom is worst among the defuzzification methods.

Keywords: Effort estimation, Soft computing, Mamdani FIS, defuzzification, metrics.

1 Introduction

One of the most critical and extremely crucial activities of any software development project is software effort and cost estimation and accurate estimation of a software development effort is critical for good management decision making [1]. If the effort requirements can be predicted accurately from the early phases of software development, then an efficient project development schedule can easily be prepared so as to complete the project well within the targeted time and budget constraints. This paper is based on a student dataset [2] prepared by us for carrying out the early stage software development effort estimation studies. A Mamdani FIS was created using the student dataset as given in Table - 3 of Appendix – I. The parameters *viz;* Total Count of Entities (TCOE) and Cumulative Grade Points Aggregate (CGPA) were chosen as two Inputs and the Redistributed Effort (RDE) was chosen to be one

V.V. Das and N. Thankachan (Eds.): CIIT 2011, CCIS 250, pp. 375–381, 2011.

output of the Mamdani FIS. Four different defuzzification methods namely centroid, bisector, mom and lom were used to create Mamdani FIS's and a comparison of effort estimations was carried out based on the standard performance evaluation criteria. Basically, defuzzification is a mapping from a space of fuzzy control actions defined over an output universe of discourse into a space of non fuzzy (crisp) control actions [3]. Nurcahyo et al. [4] had focused on the selection of the Defuzzification method to discover the most appropriate method for obtaining crisp values which represent uncertain data. Therefore this paper focuses on the defuzzification part of the Mamdani FIS [5], where the crisp values are obtained as outputs.

2 Experimental Methodology

Experiments have been conducted on a dataset which is created based on the Major Project reports of the B.Tech. students of Sikkim Manipal Institute of Technology [2] and is as given in Table 3 in Appendix - I. Mamdani type fuzzy inference system was implemented using Fuzzy Logic Toolbox, a GUI tool of Matlab. From the student dataset, we have taken TCOE and CGPA as two input variables and RDE as the output variable for preparing Mamdani FIS for estimating the effort required for software development. Two inputs and one output Mamdani FIS is as given in Fig.1. while the FIS specifications are as listed in the Table 1.

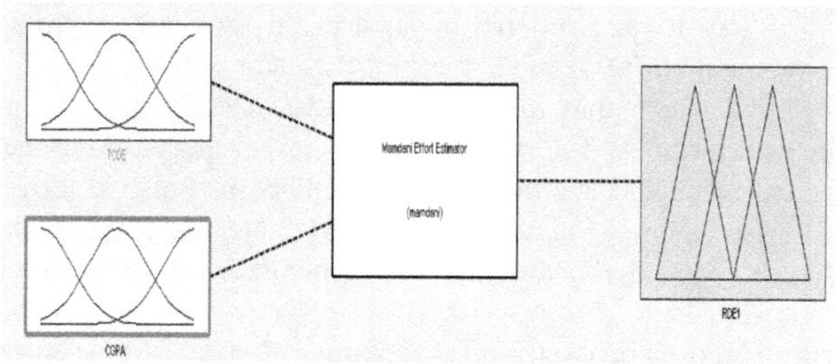

Fig. 1. Mamdani Model for Effort Prediction

Table 1. FIS Specifications

FIS Parameters	Specifications
Fuzzy Inference System Type	Mamdani
And Method	Min
Implication Method	Min
Aggregation Method	Max
Defuzzification	**Centroid**
Membership Function Type	Triangular

Figures 2, 3, and 4 shows the membership function for two input variables namely Total count of Entities (TCOE), Cumulative Grade Point Aggregate (CGPA) and one output variable as Redistributed Development Effort (RDE) respectively. TCOE has three linguistic values as Low, Medium and High, CGPA has Poor, Average and Excellent while RDE has Low, Medium and High.

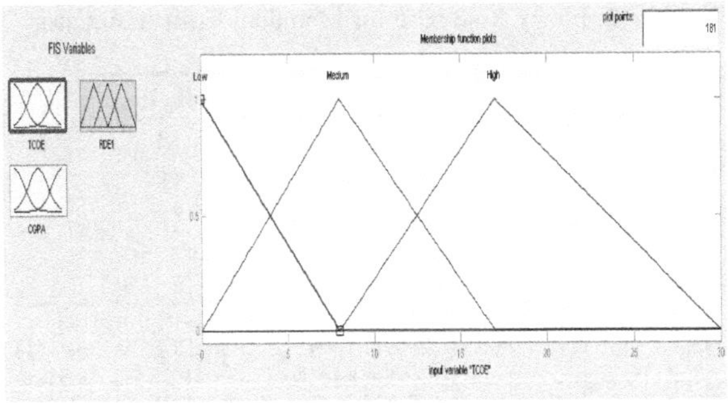

Fig. 2. Membership Function for TCOE

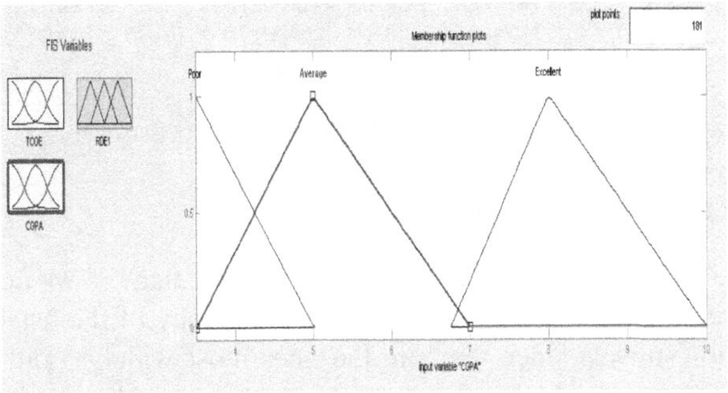

Fig. 3. Membership Function for CGPA

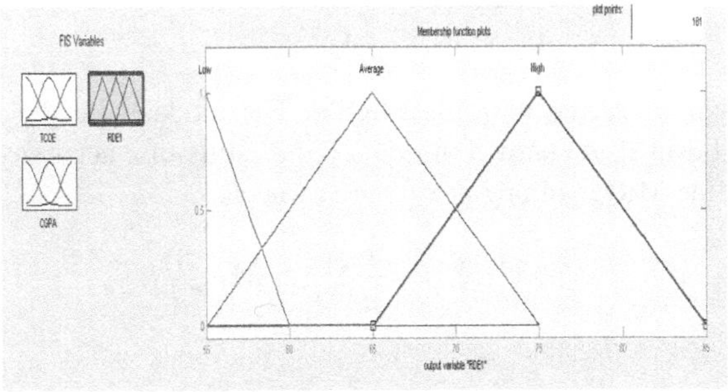

Fig. 4. Membership Function for RDE1

Once the inputs are fuzzified, the fuzzy rule base were applied to arrive at the fuzzy output. Fuzzy Inference Rule Base as shown in Table 2, comprises of different Fuzzy Rules (nine in numbers) which are shown in Fig.5. Mamdani FIS's were also created using other three defuzzification methods namely bisector, LOM (largest of maximum) and MOM (middle of maximum) [7] as well and the outputs were obtained as shown in Table 4 in Appendix – II.

Table 2. Fuzzy Rule base for Mamdani Effort Estimator

CGPA/TCOE	Poor	Average	Excellent
Low	L	L	M
Medium	L	M	H
High	M	H	H

1. If (TCOE is Low) and (CGPA is Poor) then (RDE1 is Low) (1)
2. If (TCOE is Low) and (CGPA is Average) then (RDE1 is Low) (1)
3. If (TCOE is Low) and (CGPA is Excellent) then (RDE1 is Average) (1
4. If (TCOE is Medium) and (CGPA is Poor) then (RDE1 is Low) (1)
5. If (TCOE is Medium) and (CGPA is Average) then (RDE1 is Average)
6. If (TCOE is Medium) and (CGPA is Excellent) then (RDE1 is High) (1)
7. If (TCOE is High) and (CGPA is Poor) then (RDE1 is Average) (1)
8. If (TCOE is High) and (CGPA is Average) then (RDE1 is High) (1)
9. If (TCOE is High) and (CGPA is Excellent) then (RDE1 is High) (1)

Fig. 5. Fuzzy Rules for Mamdani Effort Estimator

2.1 Evaluation Criteria Used

In this study, Mean Relative Error (MRE) and Median of Mean Relative Error (MMRE) were adopted as the indicators of the accuracy of the established software effort estimation models since they are the ones most widely used in the literature, thereby rendering our results more comparable to those of other work.

$$\mathrm{MRE}_j = \frac{|Y_j - \hat{Y}_j|}{Y_j} \tag{1}$$

The MMRE aggregates the multiple MRE's. The model with the lowest MMRE is considered the best [6]. As shown in Eq. (2), the estimation accuracy of the MMRE is the mean of all the MREs among n software projects.

$$MMRE = \frac{1}{n}\sum_{j=1}^{n} MRE_j \tag{2}$$

3 Results Discussion

Table 4 in Appendix - II contains the experimental results and shows the Redistributed Effort Estimations (RDE) obtained using the Mamdani FIS with four different defuzzification methods. The MRE values for each instances were calculated as shown in the Table 4 in respective columns namely MRE -1, MRE -2, MRE – 3 and MRE - 4. MMRE for each of the cases was calculated by summing up the MRE's and dividing the sum by 41 i.e. the total number of instances in the dataset. The MMRE value obtained is 0.0628 (MMRE % is 6.28) for COG method, 0.067 (MMRE % is 6.70) for bisector method, 0.070 (MMRE % is 7.0) for MOM method and 0.121 (MMRE % is 12.1) for LOM method.

4 Conclusion

MMRE as performance evaluation criteria analysis, shows that COG method is the best one for obtaining better crisp values for early stage effort estimations as compared to other defuzzification methods. It is evident from Table 4 in Appendix II, that MMRE in case of centroid defuzzification method is lowest and hence it is expected that *Mamdani FIS with COG defuzzification will produce better results.*

References

1. Wu, L.: The Comparison of the Software Cost Estimating Methods. In: MAART 1997, University of Calgary, Canada (1997)
2. Bhatnagar, R., Ghose, M.K., Bhattacharjee, V.: A Novel Approach to the Early Stage Software Development Effort Estimations using Neural Network Models-A Case Study. IJCA Special Issue on "Artificial Intelligence Techniques - Novel Approaches & Practical Applications (3) Article 5, 27–30 (2011)
3. Rao, D.H., Saraf, S.S.: Study of Defuzzification Methods of Fuzzy Logic Controller for Speed Control of a DC Motor. IEEE Transactions, 782–787 (1995)
4. Nurcahyo, G.W., Shamsuddin, S.M., Alias, R.A., Sap, M.N.M.: Selection of Defuzzification Method to Obtain Crisp Value for Representing Uncertain Data in a Modified Sweep Algorithm. JCS & T 3(2) (2003)
5. Mamdani, E.H.: Application of fuzzy algorithms for control of simple dynamic plant. Proc. IEEE 121(12), 1585–1588 (1974)
6. Shepperd, M., Schofield, C.: Estimating software project effort using analogies. IEEE Transactions on Software Engineering 23(12), 736–743 (1997)
7. Maraj, A., Shatri, B., Rugova, S.: Selection of Defuzzification method for routing metrics in MPLS network to obtain better crisp values for link optimization. In: Proceedings of the 7th WSEAS International Conference on System Science and Simulation in Engineering (ICOSSSE 2008), pp. 200–205 (2008) ISSN: 1790-2769 ISBN: 978-960-474-027-7

Appendix – I

Table 3. Student Dataset & Attributes for Early Stage Development Effort Estimations, TCOE: Total count of entities, TCOA: total count of attributes, TCOR: total count of relationships, CGPA: cumulative Grade Point Aggregate (parameter for judging academic excellence of students), RDE: Recalculated Development Effort in number of days.

Serial Number	TCOE	TCOA	TCOR	CGPA	RDE
1	24	70	29	6.219	75
2	24	70	29	8.012	75
3	24	70	29	7.733	75
4	10	56	9	7.564	70
5	5	44	5	5.519	55
6	19	47	11	7.507	70
7	8	33	9	6.171	75
8	8	33	9	6.705	75
9	17	53	7	7.629	75
10	9	37	7	8.130	70
11	10	36	8	8.083	65
12	10	36	8	8.126	65
13	10	36	8	7.202	65
14	5	17	5	8.417	65
15	5	16	7	7.757	70
16	4	26	4	7.431	70
17	4	26	4	7.121	70
18	4	26	4	7.660	70
19	7	34	6	8.017	75
20	7	34	6	9.076	75
21	7	27	5	7.550	70
22	6	37	5	6.583	65
23	6	27	12	7.276	65
24	6	27	12	8.124	65
25	5	26	4	6.530	75
26	5	26	4	6.685	70
27	6	28	6	7.843	65
28	7	38	9	9.160	70
29	7	38	9	8.617	75
30	6	18	3	8.719	80
31	4	22	3	8.860	65
32	5	18	5	7.664	75
33	16	85	15	6.795	65
34	16	85	15	6.757	65
35	9	36	9	6.207	70
36	9	36	9	6.636	70
37	9	36	9	6.790	70
38	8	24	7	8.095	65
39	20	115	22	7.990	75
40	20	115	22	8.095	75
41	15	60	9	6.340	75

Appendix – II

Table 4. RDE's using Mamdani FIS using all the FOUR defuzzification methods namely COG, bisector, MOM and LOM, with their respective MRE values calculated as MRE -1, MRE -2, MRE -3, and MRE – 4

Sl No.	TCOE	CGPA	Actual RDE	RDE using Mamdani FIS with Centroid Defuzzification	MRE - 1	RDE using Mamdani FIS with Bisector Defuzzification	MRE -2	RDE using Mamdani FIS with MOM Defuzzification	MRE - 3	RDE using Mamdani FIS with LOM Defuzzification	MRE - 4
1	24	6.219	75	75	0	75.1	0.001	75	0.000	80.8	0.077
2	24	8.012	75	75	0	75.1	0.001	75	0.000	80.2	0.069
3	24	7.733	75	75	0	75.1	0.001	75	0.000	80.2	0.069
4	10	7.564	70	75	0.071	75.1	0.073	75.1	0.073	78.4	0.120
5	5	5.519	55	64.3	0.169	64.3	0.169	64.9	0.180	68.5	0.245
6	19	7.507	70	75	0.071	75.1	0.073	74.9	0.070	78.7	0.124
7	8	6.171	75	65	0.133	64.9	0.135	64.9	0.135	70.6	0.059
8	8	6.705	75	65	0.133	64.9	0.135	64.9	0.135	73.3	0.023
9	17	7.629	75	75	0	75.1	0.001	75	0.000	77.8	0.037
10	9	8.13	70	75	0.071	75.1	0.073	75	0.071	76	0.086
11	10	8.083	65	75	0.154	75.1	0.155	75.1	0.155	77.2	0.188
12	10	8.126	65	75	0.154	75.1	0.155	75.1	0.155	77.2	0.188
13	10	7.202	65	75	0.154	75.1	0.155	75	0.154	81.1	0.248
14	5	8.417	65	71	0.092	72.1	0.109	75.1	0.155	78.7	0.211
15	5	7.757	70	71	0.014	72.1	0.030	75.1	0.073	78.7	0.124
16	4	7.431	70	70	0	70	0.000	70	0.000	79.9	0.141
17	4	7.121	70	70	0	70	0.000	70	0.000	82	0.171
18	4	7.66	70	70	0	70	0.000	70	0.000	79.9	0.141
19	7	8.017	75	73.4	0.021	74.2	0.011	75	0.000	76	0.013
20	7	9.076	75	72.8	0.029	73.6	0.019	75	0.000	80.2	0.069
21	7	7.55	70	73.2	0.046	73.9	0.056	75	0.071	78.4	0.120
22	6	6.583	65	64.4	0.009	64.3	0.011	63.9	0.017	72.7	0.118
23	6	7.276	65	71.3	0.097	72.1	0.109	75	0.154	80.5	0.238
24	6	8.124	65	72.1	0.109	73.3	0.128	75.1	0.155	77.5	0.192
25	5	6.53	75	64.4	0.141	64.3	0.143	63.7	0.151	72.4	0.035
26	5	6.685	70	64.5	0.079	64.6	0.077	64.2	0.083	73.3	0.047
27	6	7.843	65	72.1	0.109	73.6	0.132	75.1	0.155	77.5	0.192
28	7	9.16	70	72.7	0.039	74.2	0.060	75.1	0.073	80.8	0.154
29	7	8.617	75	73.3	0.023	73	0.027	75	0.000	77.8	0.037
30	6	8.719	80	71.9	0.101	70	0.125	75	0.063	78.4	0.020
31	4	8.86	65	70	0.077	72.1	0.109	70	0.077	79.9	0.229
32	5	7.664	75	71	0.053	70	0.067	75.1	0.001	78.7	0.049
33	16	6.795	65	70	0.077	70.3	0.082	70	0.077	83.8	0.289
34	16	6.757	65	70.4	0.083	66.4	0.022	75	0.154	83.5	0.285
35	9	6.207	70	67.1	0.041	67.9	0.030	65	0.071	70.9	0.013
36	9	6.636	70	68.6	0.02	70	0.000	65	0.071	73	0.043
37	9	6.79	70	70	0	75.1	0.073	70	0.000	83.8	0.197
38	8	8.095	65	75	0.154	75.1	0.155	75.1	0.155	75.4	0.160
39	20	7.99	75	75	0	75.1	0.001	75	0.000	77.2	0.029
40	20	8.095	75	75	0	75.1	0.001	75	0.000	77.2	0.029
41	15	6.34	75	71	0.053	71.5	0.047	75	0.000	81.4	0.085
Summation of respective MRE values					2.577		2.751		2.886		4.969
Respective MMRE values					0.062		0.067		0.070		0.121

Improved Normalized Least Mean Square Algorithm Using Past Weight Vectors and Regularization Parameter

Manish D. Sawale and Ram N. Yadav

Department of Electronics and Communication, Maulana Azad National Institute of Technology, Bhopal, India
{manish.sawale,rnyadav}@gmail.com

Abstract. In this paper we derive an improved minimization criterion for normalized least mean squares (NLMS) algorithm using past weight vectors and the regularization parameter. The proposed minimization criterion minimizes the mean square deviation (MSD) of currently updated weight vector and past weight vector. The result of the proposed NLMS algorithm approaches the conventional NLMS algorithm as the regularization parameter reduces to zero. The result also shows that as the regularization parameter decreases the convergence rate increases.

Keywords: Normalized least mean square algorithm, minimization criterion, regularization parameter, mean square deviation and weight vector.

1 Introduction

A wide variety of recursive algorithms have been developed for the operation of linear adaptive filters. The choice of one algorithm over another is determined by one or more of the factors such as, rate of convergence, misalignment, computational complexity [1-2]. Thus the desired objective can be achieved by altering the minimization criterion of an algorithm. The NLMS algorithm is designed to overcome the difficulty of gradient noise amplification problem suffered by Least Mean Square (LMS) algorithm. The conventional affine projection (AP) algorithm is modified using the set-membership affine projection (SM-AP) algorithm. The minimization criterion of SM-AP is derived using set-membership filtering to reduce the computational complexity of the conventional affine projection [3]-[4]. The modified criterion were developed for improving numerical stability using Leaky recursive least squares (LRLS) and leaky least mean squares (LLMS) algorithms [5].

In this paper, we develop an improved minimization criterion for the normalized least mean squares (NLMS) algorithm using the regularization parameter which minimizes the summation of each squared Euclidean norm of difference between the currently updated weight vector and past weight vectors. The proposed weight update formula which is derived from the proposed criterion has smaller misalignment than the conventional NLMS. A new update formula was designed called the momentum

V.V. Das and N. Thankachan (Eds.): CIIT 2011, CCIS 250, pp. 382–387, 2011.

LMS (MLMS) by adding a momentum term which contains previous weight vectors [6]. The method reduces the misalignment, but adding a momentum term is not based on a specific criterion. A modified NLMS was designed using a specific criterion [7], which suffers from low convergence speed. The new minimization criterion of our algorithm which is based on past weight vectors and regularization parameter shows improved convergence speed as the regularization parameter decreases. The MSD shows lower misalignment as the regularization parameter increases for a particular value of past weight vector, whereas MSD approaches conventional NLMS as the regularization parameter decreases to zero. It is also shown that proposed algorithm is a general case of conventional NLMS algorithm.

2 The Constrained Minimization Criterion of Conventional NLMS Algorithm

The NLMS algorithm is built around the transversal filter in which the filter coefficients or weights are updated at p+1 iteration with respect to the squared Euclidean norm of the input vector $\mathbf{x}(p)$ at iteration p. We assume the transversal filter as a finite impulse response (FIR) model wherein the impulse response sequence is defined as $\mathbf{w}^0$ called an R by 1 optimal vector. Thus, the measured output of the FIR model is expressed as follows [1]:

$$d(i) = y(i) + \eta(i) \tag{1}$$

where $y(i) = \mathbf{x}_i \mathbf{w}^0$, $\mathbf{x}_i$ is a 1 by R input vector, and $\eta(i)$ is noise measurement at time instant i. The value of R is of the same length as the impulse response sequence of the FIR model.

The conventional NLMS algorithm is a renowned adaptive filtering algorithm. The algorithm is derived from the following constrained minimization criterion:

$$\min_{\mathbf{w}_i} \| \mathbf{w}_i - \mathbf{w}_{i-1} \|^2 \qquad \text{subject to } d(i) = \mathbf{x}_i \mathbf{w}_i \tag{2}$$

where $\mathbf{w}_i$ is an estimated weight vector at time instant i.

The weight update formula is derived from the constrained minimization criterion by using the method of Lagrange multiplier [8],

$$\mathbf{w}_i = \mathbf{w}_{i-1} + \frac{\mathbf{x}_i^T}{\mathbf{x}_i \mathbf{x}_i^T} e(i) \tag{3}$$

where $e(i) = d(i) - \mathbf{x}_i \mathbf{w}_{i-1}$ and $(.)^T$ indicates the transpose operation.

3 The Proposed NLMS Algorithm

3.1 The Proposed Minimization Criterion and Update Formula

We propose an improved minimization criterion for the NLMS algorithm which reuses past n weight vectors, as follows:

$$\min_{\mathbf{w}_i} \sum_{k=1}^{n} \frac{\rho^{k-1}}{1+\rho^{k-1}} \| \mathbf{w}_i - \mathbf{w}_{i-k} \|^2 \quad \text{subject to } d(i) = \mathbf{x}_i \mathbf{w}_i$$
$$\text{where} \quad 0 < \rho < 1 \tag{4}$$

where ρ is the regularization parameter. Using the method of Lagrange multiplier, we rewrite the minimization criterion (4) as follows:

$$J = \sum_{k=1}^{n} \frac{\rho^{k-1}}{1+\rho^{k-1}} \| \mathbf{w}_i - \mathbf{w}_{i-k} \|^2 + \lambda g(i) \tag{5}$$

where $g(i) = d(i) - \mathbf{x}_i \mathbf{w}_i$ and λ is a Lagrange multiplier. By using the differential relationships of

$$\frac{\partial J}{\partial \mathbf{w}_i} = 2\sum_{k=1}^{n} \frac{\rho^{k-1}}{1+\rho^{k-1}} (w_i - w_{i-k}) - \lambda \mathbf{x}_i^T = 0 \tag{6}$$

and

$$\frac{\partial J}{\partial \lambda} = d(i) - \mathbf{x}_i \mathbf{w}_i = 0 \tag{7}$$

From (6), we get,

$$\mathbf{w}_i = \alpha \sum_{k=1}^{n} \left(\frac{\rho^{k-1}}{1+\rho^{k-1}} \right) \mathbf{w}_{i-k} + \alpha \frac{\lambda}{2} \mathbf{x}_i^T \tag{8}$$

where

$$\alpha = \left(\sum_{k=1}^{n} \frac{\rho^{k-1}}{1+\rho^{k-1}} \right)^{-1} \tag{9}$$

Substituting (8) into (7), we get,

$$d(i)-\mathbf{x}_i\left(\alpha\sum_{k=1}^{n}\left(\frac{\rho^{k-1}}{1+\rho^{k-1}}\mathbf{w}_{i-k}\right)+\alpha\frac{\lambda}{2}\mathbf{x}_i^T\right)=0 \tag{10}$$

Therefore,

$$\alpha\frac{\lambda}{2}=\frac{1}{\mathbf{x}_i\mathbf{x}_i^T}\left(d(i)-\mathbf{x}_i\alpha\sum_{k=1}^{n}\left(\frac{\rho^{k-1}}{1+\rho^{k-1}}\mathbf{w}_{i-k}\right)\right) \tag{11}$$

By substituting (11) into (8), the proposed NLMS algorithm becomes:

$$\mathbf{w}_i=\alpha\sum_{k=1}^{n}\frac{\rho^{k-1}}{1+\rho^{k-1}}\mathbf{w}_{i-k}+\frac{\mathbf{x}_i^T}{\mathbf{x}_i\mathbf{x}_i^T}\left(d(i)-\mathbf{x}_i\alpha\sum_{k=1}^{n}\left(\frac{\rho^{k-1}}{1+\rho^{k-1}}\mathbf{w}_{i-k}\right)\right) \tag{12}$$

We can write this as:

$$\mathbf{w}_i=\bar{\mathbf{w}}_{i-1,n}+\frac{\mathbf{x}_i^T}{\mathbf{x}_i\mathbf{x}_i^T}\left(d(i)-\mathbf{x}_i\,\bar{\mathbf{w}}_{i-1,n}\right) \tag{13}$$

where

$$\bar{\mathbf{w}}_{i-1,n}=\alpha\sum_{k=1}^{n}\left(\frac{\rho^{k-1}}{1+\rho^{k-1}}\mathbf{w}_{i-k}\right) \tag{14}$$

When ρ is one, the proposed NLMS algorithm simply becomes as follows:

$$\mathbf{w}_i=\bar{\mathbf{w}}_{i-1,n}+\frac{\mathbf{x}_i^T}{\mathbf{x}_i\mathbf{x}_i^T}\left(d(i)-\mathbf{x}_i\,\bar{\mathbf{w}}_{i-1,n}\right) \tag{15}$$

Comparing the conventional NLMS algorithm (3) with the weight update formula using regularization parameter (15), we find that the proposed algorithm is composed of the averaged past n weight vectors that need additional calculations. As the past weight vectors increases the number of calculations also increases but the additional calculations are not numerically complex and can be performed simply by addition and division operations. It can be seen that, when n=1, the proposed NLMS algorithm including the computational complexity, is identical to the conventional NLMS.

4 Results and Discussions

In this section, the simulation results of the proposed algorithm (13) are compared with the conventional NLMS algorithm (3). The channel is assumed as FIR model with channel length of 12, i.e., R is 12, and the channel is randomly generated. The performance is compared by evaluating the mean square deviation (MSD) defined as $E\|\mathbf{w}^0 - \mathbf{w}_i\|^2$ and then averaging over 250 independent trials.

The modified NLMS algorithm minimizes the variations between the currently updated vector $\mathbf{w}_i$ and previous weight vectors, i.e., $\mathbf{w}_{i-1},\cdots,\mathbf{w}_{i-n}$. Here n is taken as 1, 2 and 3 respectively, and the modified algorithm minimizes the summation of $\|\mathbf{w}_i - \mathbf{w}_{i-1}\|^2$, $\|\mathbf{w}_i - \mathbf{w}_{i-2}\|^2$ and $\|\mathbf{w}_i - \mathbf{w}_{i-3}\|^2$. Therefore the proposed NLMS algorithm has an effect by which it can prevent the updated weight vectors from heavily fluctuating especially in cases where noise measurement is high.

We calculate the MSD values over output signal-to-noise ratio (SNR) for 5dB. The input vector is chosen to be a random value.

Fig.1 and Fig. 2 show the effect of various values of regularization parameter when value of n is 2 and 3 respectively at 5dB. In general, we find that the MSD of the proposed NLMS becomes closer to the conventional NLMS as the value of ρ decreases to zero. The result shows that the MSD of newly updated NLMS algorithm is in general lower than the conventional NLMS and as the value of regularization parameter increases, the MSD of modified NLMS algorithm becomes much lower. The figures also show that as the regularization parameter decreases the convergence rate increases. Thus for a fixed value of n, the effect of the past weight vector reduces by decreasing the ρ .

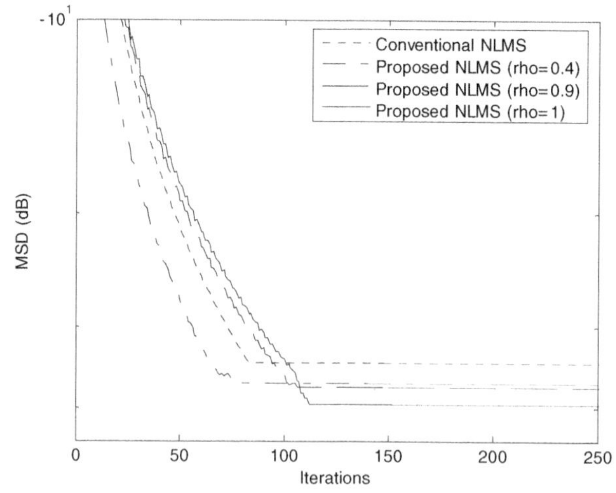

Fig. 1. MSD of the proposed NLMS with various ρ is compared with conventional NLMS at SNR 5dB and n=2

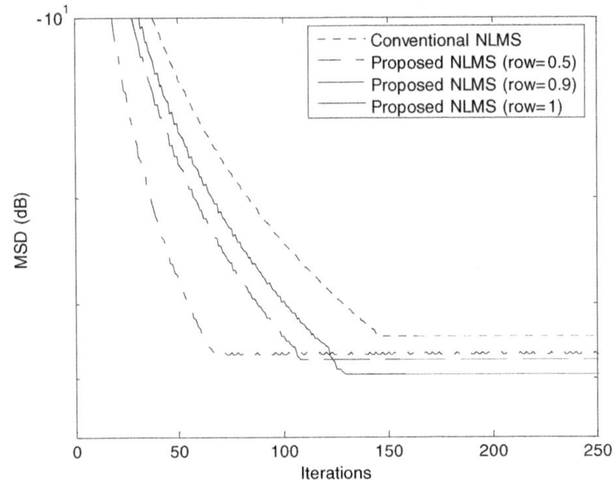

Fig. 2. MSD of the proposed NLMS with various ρ is compared with conventional NLMS at SNR 5dB and n=3

References

1. Sayed, A.H.: Fundamentals of Adaptive Filtering. Wiley, New York (2003)
2. Lee, C.W., Cho, H., Kim, S.W.: Comments on "Stereo echo cancellation algorithm using adaptive update on the basis of enhanced input signal vector". Signal Processing 88(4), 1079–1081 (2008)
3. Gay, S.L., Tavathia, S.: The fast affine projection algorithm. In: ICASSP, pp. 3023–3026. IEEE press Detroit, Michigan (1995)
4. Werner, S., Diniz, S., Kapoor, S., Huang, Y.F.: Set-membership affine projection algorithm. IEEE Signal Process. Letter 5(5), 111–114 (1998)
5. Horita, E., Sumiya, K., Urakami, H., Mitsuishi, S.: A leaky RLS algorithm: its optimality and implementation. IEEE Trans. Signal Processing 52(10), 2924–2936 (2004)
6. Roy, S., Shynk, J.J.: Analysis of the momentum LMS algorithm. IEEE Trans. Signal Processing 38(12), 2088–2098 (1990)
7. Cho, H., Lee, C.W., Kim, S.W.: Derivation of a new normalized least mean squares algorithm with modified minimization criterion. Signal Processing 89(4), 692–695 (2009)
8. Haykin, S.: Adaptive Filter Theory. Prentice-Hall, Upper Saddle River (2002)

Discussion on Impact of Carrier Sense Range on Available Bandwidth for IEEE802.11 Based Ad Hoc Networks

Neeraj Gupta

Hindu College of Engineering,
Sonepat, India
neerajgupta37@rediffmail.com

Abstract. Advances in wireless technology and portable computing along with demand for greater user mobility has provided a major impetus towards development of an emerging class of self organizing, rapidly deployable network architecture referred to as ad hoc networks. Lot of research work in estimating available bandwidth is carried out in last few decades. It has been shown that bandwidth consumption is not local concept but depends upon the transmission going in the channel itself. The link characteristic of channel plays an important role in this regard. The different sensing range affects the transmission of node. We present our study on how the carrier sense range affects the various parameters which are helpful in estimating available bandwidth.

Keywords: IEEE 802.11, NAV, Quality of Service, Ad hoc Networks, DIFS, Back off.

1 Introduction

The wireless communication was designed to provide location independent network access between various computational devices by using radio waves. IEEE 802.11 originally developed for Wireless LAN has now become de-facto standard. The ad hoc network can be differentiated from cellular network in the sense that routing and resource management are done in distributed manner in which all nodes coordinate to enable communication among themselves. The nodes in MANETs share the common radio channel and due to inherent nature of wireless communication one node in ad hoc network may consume the bandwidth of neighboring node. Link available bandwidth is one of the most important parameter and has received lot of attention in last decade. The term can be defined as maximum unused bandwidth at link or end-to-end in a network such that it does not disrupt any ongoing flow in the network between two peers, which depends not only on capacity but also the traffic load and is time varying metric. The estimation of available bandwidth is not a localized concept but is also dependent upon the state of its neighboring nodes in its transmission range as well as in carrier sense range [1].

V.V. Das and N. Thankachan (Eds.): CIIT 2011, CCIS 250, pp. 388–391, 2011.

Section II describes the IEEE802.11 MAC layer mechanism. The detailed survey on the effect of carrier sense range on MAC is presented in section III. Finally the remarks and proposed work is presented in section IV.

2 IEEE 802.11 MAC Sublayer

The IEEE 802.11 MAC sub layer defines two different access methods: Point Coordination Function (PCF) and Distributed Coordination Function (DCF). PCF is for infrastructure based network. DCF is based on carrier sense multiple access with collision avoidance (CSMA/CA). The nodes compete for channel in a distributed manner. This is accompanied through either physical carrier sensing (PCF) or optionally through virtual carrier sensing (VCS).In the physical carrier sensing, the backoff window, W, is initially set to CW_{min}. Whenever the node has data to send it senses the channel if the medium is free for specified time, the station is allowed to transmit the packet. The receipt of acknowledgement (ACK) for data packet ensures the successful transmission. In event of collision transmitter go in retransmission mode by increasing the backoff window based on exponential backoff algorithm. The fragment is thrown away after given number of retransmission. The above mechanism suffers from hidden terminal and exposed terminal problem. The solution for the problem comes in form of virtual carrier sensing (VCS). The VCS make use of request to send (RTS) and clear to send (CTS) control packets. In VCS, all station receiving either RTS or CTS will set their virtual carrier sense (called NAV, Network Allocation Vector) for a given duration. NAV along with PCS is indicated as busy state of medium. Between the transmission of control packets, data packets and ACK there are inter frame space time intervals which control the access to the wireless medium. These time intervals are mandatory and are essentially idle periods. A more detailed timing analysis of different timing parameter can be referred in [2] [4].

3 Effect of Carrier Sense Range

There are three different ranges in IEEE 802.11 MAC scheme.

- Transmission Range: range inside which nodes are able to receive or overhear the packet transmission successfully assuming there is no interference from other transmission.
- Carrier Sense Range: range inside which nodes are able to sense signal, even though the correct packet reception is not guaranteed. The busy state of channel is determined by the carrier sensing threshold (CST).
- Interference Range: The range inside which any new transmission by other transmitter will interfere with packet reception. This is not a fixed value and depends upon topology of the network.

It is generally assumed that transmission range is smaller than carrier sense range and interference range. In wireless communication all the node in the ad hoc network share the common channel. In collision model, all transmission including those that in carrier sense range is considered as interference to the receiver. Similarly, transmission by the carrier sense neighbours will interfere with the transmission of node even if they are not directly communicating. Thus while estimating the busy time of the node it is important to take care of theses contending nodes. In most of the cases the node's carrier sense is expressed in terms of number of hops [3] [5]. However these assumptions cannot be true in real scenarios. Many other methods [6] [5] were proposed but again these methods were either adding to network overheads and complexity or leads to misinterpretation of channel activity. In case of multi-hop ad hoc network interference range of nodes can overlap. This prevents the transmission of node while any path member of interference range is sending, leading to problem of intra-flow contention. It is necessary to identify all such contending nodes lying in the interference range of the node. In order for communication to happen medium should be available on both sender and receiver side thus we need to have some kind of synchronization between two. In multi-hop network the airtime synchronization poses another problem for us. Most of the above work assumed that transmission range and carrier sense range are fixed entities. The transmission range and capture threshold of transceiver are usually pre-determined by hardware specification and radio signal design. According to [7] carrier sensing range is tuneable parameter that can significantly affect the performance of system at MAC layer. Large value of carrier sense range leads to decrease in collision rate however smaller value leads to spatial frequency reuse but leads to higher collision rate. The concept of cost function was introduced such that the total reward of MAC scheme is defined as:

$$\eta = N_s - c\, N_d \tag{1}$$

Where N_s is channel throughput and N_d is the total amount of data is transmitted. For different values of c, the sensing range of node is tuned to maximize . Although RTS and CTS mechanism was deployed to solve the hidden terminal problem in ad hoc networks, in [8] it is claimed that VCS works only if every hidden nodes are within the carrier sense range of sender nodes. This is normally the condition for VCS mechanism to work. The interference range R_i of receiver with transmitter- receiver distance as d meters is:

$$R_i = 1.78 * d \tag{2}$$

When the distance d between the sender-receiver is larger than R_{tx} *0.56, where R_{tx} is transmission range, interference range exceeds the transmission range. It was concluded, RTS/CTS handshake is not sufficient enough to prevent the interference at receiver once the sender-receiver distance is greater than R_{tx} *0.56. It was suggested to limit the maximum distance between the nodes to value such that interference range equals to transmission range. The major disadvantage of the scheme was reduced transmission range. Since VCS is not effective in multi-hop outdoor scenario and is ineffective once interference range exceed the transmission range. In [4] authors proposes dynamic physical carrier sensing (DPCS). The authors propose to use PCS where the value of carrier sensing threshold (CST) is set in order to obtain the correct carrier sense range. The new value of CST can be written as:

$$CST_s = \frac{P_r}{(\sqrt[n]{SINR_{th}} + 1)^n} \tag{3}$$

Where n is generic signal attenuation coefficient, CST_s is optimal CST on the sender and P_r is power received at sender (the same at receiver). The above mechanism is based on the assumption of homogenous hardware and sets the CST according to received power level estimation.

4 Conclusion and Final Remarks

When multi-frames are received simultaneously at receiver, it calculates the ratio of strongest frame's signal strength to the signal strength sum of other frames. It is in this context that we should also consider minimum signal to interference and nose ratio (SINR). This means that a signal arriving at receiver is assumed to be valid only if packets signal strength is higher than SINR (the capture threshold); otherwise the packet is considered collided. The higher the signal to noise ratio the higher rate that packet can be reliably transferred. We must calculate carrier sense threshold form this value. For example in IEEE 802.11b standard which provides the transmission speed of 11 Mbps does not allow SINR below 10db.We can take into account SINR while calculating the value of CST. The estimation of available bandwidth is affected by collision probabilities and channel utilization. It is important to optimize the values of carrier sensing range such that total network throughput can be increased and decreasing the number of collisions before estimating available bandwidth in MANETs.

References

1. Prasad, R.S., Murray, M., Dovrolis, C., Claffy, K.C.: Bandwidth Estimation: Metric, Measurement Techniques and Tools. IEEE Networks (November-December 2008)
2. IEEE 802.11, Part II: Wireless LAN Medium Access Control (MAC) and Physical Layer (PHY) Specifications (August 1999)
3. Sarr, C., Chaudet, C., Chelius, G., Lassous, I.G.: Bandwidth Estimation for IEEE 802.11 Based Ad Hoc Networks. IEEE Transactions on Mobile Computing 7(10) (October 2008)
4. Valerio, D., De Cicco, L., M.S., Vacirca, V.: Optimization of IEEE 802.11 parameters for wide area coverage. In: Proceeding of MEDHOCNET 2006 (June 2006)
5. Yang, Y., Kravets, R.: Contention-aware Admission Control for Ad Hoc Networks. IEEE Transaction on Mobile Computing 4(4), 363–377 (2005)
6. de Renesse, R., Friderikos, V.: Cross-layer cooperation for accurate admission control decisions in mobile ad hoc networks. IET Communications, 577–586 (2007)
7. Deng, J., Liang, B., Varshney, P.K.: Tuning the Carrier Sense Range of IEEE802.11 MAC. In: IEEE Global Telecommunications Conference (November-December2004)
8. Xu, K., Gerla, M., Bae, S.: How Effective is IEEE802.11 RTS/CTS Handshake in Ad Hoc Networks. In: IEEE Global Communication Conference (2006)

Cloud Computing Resource Management for Indian E-Governance

Monali K. Patil and Roopali Lolage

Department of Information Technology
K.C. College of Engineering, Thane (E), India
mpp31_12_81@rediffmail.com
roopali.lolage@gmail.com

Abstract. The Today's Internet technology changing our lives in terms of the way we work, learn and interact. These changes naturally should reflect the way government functions in terms of the organization of the government, its relationship with its citizens, institutions and businesses and cooperation with other governments. Also, the increasing generalization of technology access by citizen and organizations brings expectations and demands on government. India is a country of 1.2 billion people, having 29 states, 6 union territories and 22 official languages. E-governance in such a big country is a challenging task in itself. The main objective of E-governance is to establish citizen transparent mechanism to provide easy and reliable access of its services of citizens and stakeholders.

Keywords: Information and communication technology, E- governance, cloud computing, G2G, G2B, G2C, G2E.

1 Introduction

Presently, all the government departments are creating their own infrastructure to deliver e-services to the citizen by computerizing and automating their office procedures. This requires large investment in the infrastructure, its maintenance and continual up gradation which leaves little time and money for improvement in the delivery of e -services. It has been reported that only 15% of the computing capacity in most of the government departments is utilized. The IT infrastructure created in this manner is too complex, difficult to sustain and expensive which require better management to bring down the costs. Cloud computing is an emerging technology which can play a vital role in effective implementation of E-governance of changing needs require on demand location independent computing services which include software, platform and scalable infrastructure. The cloud computing can provide such an environment for optimum utilization of resources [4]. It will minimize the duplication of efforts through centralization and standardization in ICT set up and reduce the overall cloud based infrastructure is also significantly lower as compared to conventional IT set up for E-Governance making it environment friendly and green technology cloud computing will also improve the information sharing among

V.V. Das and N. Thankachan (Eds.): CIIT 2011, CCIS 250, pp. 392–395, 2011.

different government agencies with similar platforms being in use. This paper systematically describes the importance of E-governance and the role of cloud computing in providing better services to the citizens and stake holders.

2 E-Governance

The E-governance is the application of information and communication technology (ICT) to provide and improve the government services, transactions and interactions with citizens, businesses, and other arms of government. Types of E-Governance: On the basis of interactions between government and different stake holders as shown in fig. 1, the E-Governance can be divided into following groups [1].

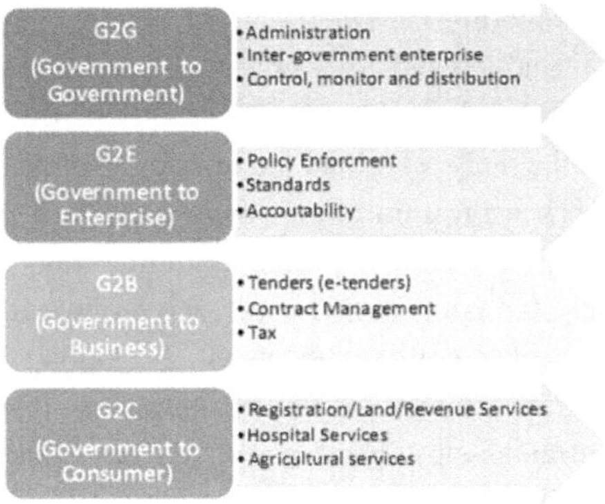

Fig. 1. Types of E-Governance

3 E-Governance with Cloud Computing

As we know that cloud computing is computing over a cloud, where a cloud consists of grids of commodity machines and a software layer (called Hadoop), which is responsible for distributing applications data across the machines, parallelizing and managing application execution across the machines, detecting and recovering from machine failures. We proposed a Hadoop which consists of four components. Each of components must have a specific job. The different components of Hadoop are shown in fig. 2.

Fig. 2. Proposed Components of Hadoop

where U.I is User Interface, A.C is Authentication Check, and W.S.M is Computational Web Service Mapping, J.S is Job Scheduler. Whenever user request for a E-Governance web service to Hadoop, the latter first checks the authenticity of the user after interfacing with Authentic Server then Hadoop refers "E-Governance Web Service Mapping" and maps to E-Governance web service existing at different locations and fetches the required E-Governance web service from it and submits it to "Job scheduler" of Hadoop which schedules the jobs to the Grid of volunteer commodity hardware. The idea behind volunteer computing is to allow ordinary users on the internet to volunteer their idle computers, processing powers (PCs, Clusters, Supercomputers, Mainframes etc., which as a whole make volunteer commodity hardware) towards solving computationally intensive tasks. The scheduler of Hadoop sends the jobs to idle volunteer commodity hardware, the sending jobs are loaded to these idle volunteer commodity hardware and when jobs get computed successfully they are pulled back by Hadoop and are sent to the required thin clients, mobile etc.

The load balancing of the idle volunteer commodity hardware is being done by the J.S of Hadoop. With the help of cloud computing, software applications can be accessed from a network using thin clients/mobiles (which are a lot cheaper).Thus cloud computing can help to make computing ubiquitous and bring it within the reach of the masses, especially the poor. In this paper, we propose a specific frame work of E-Governance based on clod computing, at which Hadoop is at the top, which is being accessed by thin clients or by commodity hardware(PCs, Clusters, Supercomputers, Mainframes etc). The Commodity hardware again is of two types: Active Commodity hardware- It needs E-Governance web-services. Idle Commodity Hardware- The idle Commodity hardware is used as volunteer computing commodity hardware. It is used for processing the web services and the processed web services are supplied to thin clients, active commodity hardware etc. Thus, Hadoop is connected with thin clients and commodity hardware. At a time all commodity hardware can not be busy, some may be idle and we have to use them in optimized order in order to enhance the cost/benefit analysis of cloud computing. By providing a simple interface to the user, Hadoop makes it possible to achieve super computing power as easily as one can get electric power through a wall socket. Again we intend to introduce an intelligent layer, with the help of which Hadoop would behave as an expert system on a specific domain. Here Hadoop would help E-Governance to address all types of users. Thus our cloud based expert e-Governance system would act as a human expert within one particular field of knowledge. The proposed expert E-Governance system embodies knowledge about one specific problem domain and possesses the ability to apply this knowledge to solve problems from that problem domain[2]. The proposed frameworks with hadoop are shown in fig. 3.

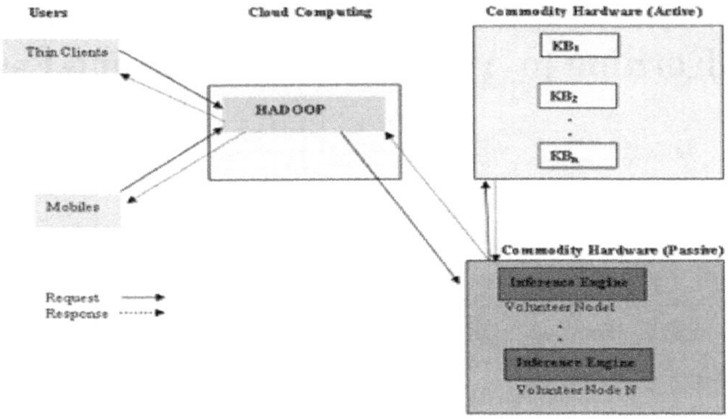

Fig. 3. Proposed frameworks with hadoop

4 Conclusion

Cloud architecture is playing important role by providing a shared and common infrastructure to the various government departments. Cloud provides a solid foundation for the introduction of widespread provision of services to various stakeholders. Applications designed using the principles of Service Oriented Architecture and deployed in cloud architectures will benefit the government in reducing operating costs and increasing the governance. With the help of grid and software layer (hadoop) cloud computing can make E-governance paperless and provide E services at affordable cost.

References

1. Vasudeva Varma, C.: Cloud Computing for E-Governance. Cloud Computing Group, International Institute of Information Technology, Gachibowli, Hyderabad (2010)
2. Mukherjee, K., Sahoo, G.: Cloud Computing: Future Framework for E-Governance. International Journal of Computer Applications 7(7), 0975–8887 (2010)
3. Kevin, L., Jackson, C.: Government Cloud Computing. Dataline, LLC (2009)
4. Andy Bechtolsheim, C.: Cloud Computing. Chairman & Co-founder, Arista Networks (November 12, 2008)

Introduction to Neural Network and Improved Algorithm to Avoid Local Minima and Faster Convergence

Ayesha Bari[1], Kavleen Bhasin[1], and Darshan N. Karnawat[2]

[1] College of Technology, G.B.P.U.A&T, Pantnagar (UA), India
[2] Electronics Dept., DKTE Society's Textile & Engineering Institute, Ichalkaranji, (MS), India

Abstract. Neural network is a massively parallel distributed processor inspired by the structure and functional aspect of biological neural network that employ learning algorithm, like back propagation for computation .back propagation follows supervised learning rule for processing data. The architecture is complex and processing confronts problems like local minima, slow convergence and premature saturation. We have introduced improved neuron model and learning rule like multiplicative neuron model using extra term in algorithm called a proportional factor. This along with other modifications in network architecture, that helps attain faster learning and accurate computation.

Keywords: Supervised Learning, Back Propagation Algorithm, Premature Saturation, Differential Adaptive Learning and Multiplicative Neuron Model.

1 Introduction

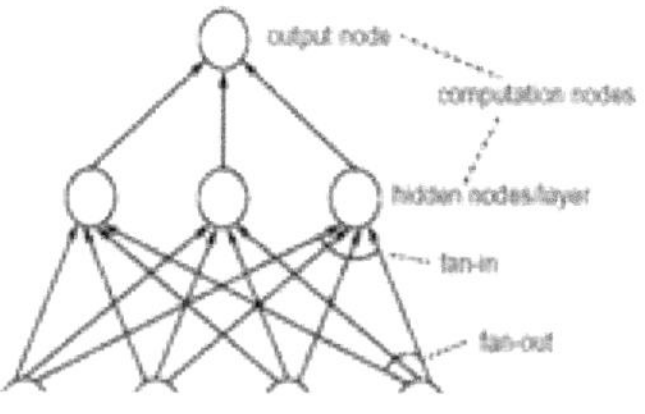

Fig. 1.1. Architecture of A Feed forward Network

Artificial neural networks are relatively crude electronic models based on the neural structure of the brains .They use connectionist approach as opposed to the cognitive approach used by computers for computation. They process by storing information as patterns, utilizing those patterns, and then solve problems. This field, as mentioned before, does not utilize traditional programming but involves the creation of massively parallel networks and the training of those networks through examples to solve specific problems [1]. Neural network is described by its architecture, neuron model and learning algorithm [2]. Architecture refers to a set of neurons and the weighted links connecting the layers of neurons. Neuron model refers to information processing unit of the neural network. A learning algorithm is used to train the NN by modifying the weights in order to model a particular learning task correctly on the training examples. Fig 1.1 shows the basic architecture of a neural network.

V.V. Das and N. Thankachan (Eds.): CIIT 2011, CCIS 250, pp. 396–400, 2011.

2 Learning in ANN

Learning is a fundamental and essential characteristic of ANN. The learning rules can be broadly classified as (i) supervised or 'teacher' approach and (ii) unsupervised or 'cluster' approach. Supervised learning rules require a 'teacher' to tell them what the desired output is given an input. The learning rules then adjusts all the necessary weights and the whole process starts again until the data can be correctly analyzed by the network [3]. Supervised learning rules include back-propagation and the delta rule. Tasks that fall within the paradigm of supervised learning are pattern recognition (also known as classification) and regression (also known as function approximation). The paper is organized in the following way. In next section we discuss supervised learning rule of back propagation. In section III we define the conventional issues during learning and their solutions. In section IV we introduce the improved algorithm using differential adaptive learning rate and multiplicative neuron model. In the section V we conclude the paper.

3 Back Propagation

The back propagation (BP) algorithm was developed by Rumelhart, Hinton and Williams in 1986.This algorithm is based on error based learning, where the actual response, which is the output of layer by layer propagation of signal called function signal in the network, is compared again desired output. The error signal then propagates backwards and the synaptic weights are adjusted accordingly. Back Propagation Learning Algorithm: The conventional neural network model which is based on the Mucculloch Pitt's neuron model uses the weighted sum of all signals coming to it to produce output signal. Fig 2.2 shows block diagram of computation for error gradient for hidden to output layer.

Table 1. Notation employed in the derivation of the back propagation learning algorithm [3]

	Hidden	Output
No. of neurons	q+1	p
Signal function	sigmoidal	sigmoidal
Neuron index range	h=0,......,q	j=1........,p
Activation	zh	yi
Signal	S(zh)	S(yi)
Weights(including bias)	Wih	Whj

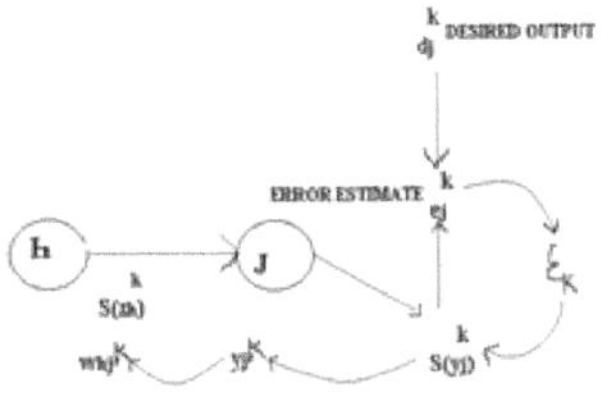

Fig. 2.2. Gradient Computation For

The error signal at the output of neuron j at iteration n (i.e. presentation of the nth training pattern) is defined by:

$$ej(n)=dj(n)-yj(n) \tag{2.1}$$

The instantaneous sum of squared errors of network at the output of neuron j can be written:

$$E(n) = ½ \sum c j^2 (n) \quad (2.2)$$

Where c is the set of all neurons on the output layer of the network. If N is the total number of patterns in the training set, the average squared error overall the pattern is given by:

$$Eav = 1/N \sum E(n) \quad (2.3)$$

Thus Eav represents the cost function of the learning process, which adjusts the free parameters of synaptic weights and thresholds so as to minimize the cost function. The training is done on the pattern by pattern basis and the error computed for each pattern presented to the network.

4 Problems in Processing and Their Solution

Premature Saturation: If the range of values of weights is too large, the system becomes stuck in a kind of saddle point, as activation function will saturate in the beginning, this phenomenon is premature saturation [4].It can be avoided by taking the initial weights and threshold levels of the network to be uniformly distributed inside a small range of values.. It is also maintained that premature saturation is less likely to occur when the number of hidden neurons is maintained low.

Local Minima: Gradient descent can also become stuck in local minima of the cost function. These are isolated valleys of the cost function surface in which the system may get "stuck" before it reaches the global minimum.The momentum term significantly accelerate the training time that is spent in a temporary minimum as it causes the weights to change at a faster rate

Symmetry Breaking Problem: It is important to note that if all the weights start out with equal values and the solution requires that unequal weights be developed, the system can never learn.. This means that all hidden units connected directly to the output units will get identical error signals, and since the weight changes depend on the error signals, the weights from those units to the output units must always be the same. This problem is known as the symmetry-breaking problem.

Slow Convergence: The convergence rate of back propagation algorithm is still too slow even if learning can be achieved. Furthermore the convergence behavior of back propagation algorithm depends very much on the choices of initial values of connection weights and parameters in the algorithm such as the learning rate and the momentum. Attempts to improve the performance of the original back propagation algorithm have concentrated on (i) selection of better energy function (ii) selection of dynamic learning rate and momentum.

Slow Learning: Plain back-propagation is terribly slow and it is desired to have faster training. There are a series of things that can be done to speed up training.First, fudging the derivative term. This is done by increasing the learning by rate η by 0.1 times the upper level η can check for both upper and lower level η values to the best results .This is known as differential step size method [3].Second, direct input output connections done when function to be approximated is almost linear. Last, a thumb rule generally followed is that total number of hidden neurons should be ⅔rd the total input output neurons i.e. best results on test are found with architecture having small number of hidden units [5].

5 Three Term Back Propagation in Multiplicative Neural Network

A method in the improved back propagation algorithm to reduce local minima using multiplicative neural network .In search for biologically closer models of neural interactions, neurobiologists have found that multiplicative like operations play important role in single neuron computation .Multiplication increases the computational power and storage capacity of neural networks is well known from extensions of ANN where the operation occurs as higher order units [6].

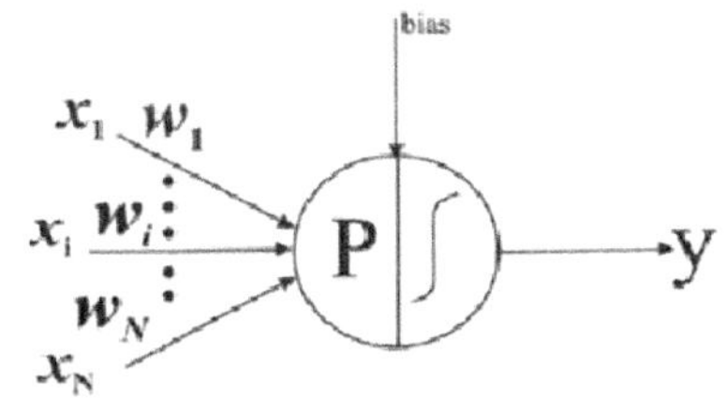

Fig. 4.2. Node Structure of Multiple Neural Network

The basic building block of an MNN is a single neuron or node as depicted in Fig 4.2. A node receives a number of real inputs n x1, x2, x3 ... , which are then multiplied by a set of weights n w1, w2, w3 ... , and bias terms n b1, b2, b3 ... , are added. The resultant values are multiplied to form a polynomial structure. This architecture has been shown in fig 4.2.This output of the node is further subjected to a nonlinear function f defined as:

$$U = \prod_{i=1}^{n} (WiXi + bi) \qquad (4.1)$$

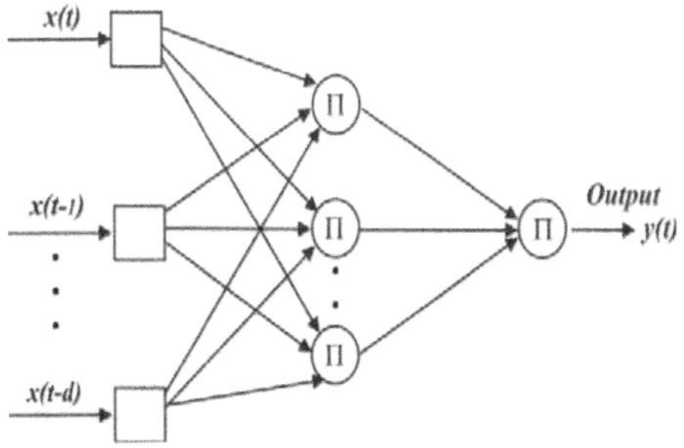

Fig. 4.2. Architecture of Feed Forward Network

This is subjected to the bipolar sig moidal activation function f is given by:

$$y = f(u) = (1-e^{\wedge}-u)/(1+e^{\wedge}-u) \qquad (4.2)$$

An error back propagation based learning rule is used for training. The MSE is given by:

$$E = \frac{1}{2} N \sum (y_p^i - y_d^i)^2 \tag{4.3}$$

Where p is the number of input patterns.

However simply following the standard learning techniques in multiple neuron models do not serve the purpose therefore, new learning algorithms have been developed. Therefore, the standard algorithm is further modified by adding the momentum term and proportional factor term[7].Momentum term is a fraction of the previous weight change, it prevents extreme changes in the gradient due to anomalies, suppresses error oscillation due to variations in the slope of error .the problem of slow convergence is solved by adding a term proportional to the difference between the output and the target [8]. The legitimate question is whether multiplicative units are actually needed in neural networks and weather their task cannot be done by some reasonably sized network of summing units? The answer is NO. The drawback with summing networks is that they grow in size, albeit polynomially with the number of bits required for the representation action of the number to be multiplied. Such quality is "certainly disastrous", when one would like to process real numbers with possibly infinite precision. Therefore, network of summing units do not seem to be an adequate substitute for genuine multiplication units.

6 Conclusion

In this paper we have introduced multiplicative neuron model that are capable of solving complex task in biologically plausible manner, and improved BP algorithm enhances the learning rate and helps overcome conventional problem faced during the processing in neural network.

References

1. Haykin, S.: Neural Networks: A Comprehensive Foundation. Prentice Hall, New Delhi (2006)
2. Edward, R.J.: An Introduction to Neural Networks. A White Paper, United States of America (2004)
3. Kumar, S.: Neural Network. A Classroom Approach. McGraw Hill, New Delhi (2004)
4. Wen, J.W., Zhao, J.L., Kuo, S.W., Han, Z.: Improvement of BP Neural Network Learning Algorithm. In: Proc. Of ICSP 2000, pp. 1647–1649 (2000)
5. Mass, W.: A Simple Model for Neural Computation in Neural system 9, 381–397 (1998)
6. Schnmitt, M.: On the Complexity of Computing and Learning with multiplicative Neural Network. Neural Computation 14(2), 241–301 (2002)
7. Wen, J.W., Zhao, J.L., Luo, S.W., Han, Z.: The improvements of BP neural network learning algorithm. In: Proc. of ICSP 2000, pp. 1647–1649 (2000)
8. Kaur, V.P.S., Manoria, M., Burse, K.: Improved Back Propagation Algorithm to Avoid Local Minima in Multiplicative Neuron Model. World Academy of Science, Engneering and Technology 72, 429–431 (2010)

Optimizing the Number of Decomposition Levels for a Novel Hybrid Multifocus Image Fusion

Sankalp Mohanty, Saurav Kumar Sahu, Jyoti Ranjan Swain, and Tapasmini Sahoo

ECE department, ITER, SOA University
Bhubaneswar, India
{sankalpmohanty2007,sauravsahu2009,jyotidon.swain1,
tapasmini.sahoo}@gmail.com

Abstract. The number of decomposition levels in the novel hybrid approach adopted for multifocus image fusion affects the fusion performance. Too few decomposition levels result in poor spatial quality in the fused images. On the other hand, too many levels induce distortion between the original and the fused images. In general, fusion of images with larger resolution requires a higher number of decomposition levels. In this paper, an optimization approach to determine the optimal number of decomposition levels is presented.

Keywords: Multi-Focus Image Fusion, DWT, Evaluation Metrics for Optimization.

1 Introduction

Image fusion is a process of integrating complementary information from multiple images of the same scene such that the resultant image contains a more accurate description of the scene than any of the individual source images. These kinds of images are useful in many fields such as digital imaging, microscopic imaging, remote sensing, computer vision and robotics. In the past decades, pixel-level image fusion has attracted a great deal of research attention. Generally, these algorithms can be categorized into *spatial domain fusion* and *transform domain fusion* [2]. The *spatial domain* techniques fuse source images using local spatial features, such as gradient, spatial frequency, and local standard derivation [1]. For the *transform domain* methods, source images are projected onto localized bases which are usually designed to represent the sharpness and edges of an image [2]. Recently, several methods based on multi-scale transforms have been proposed. To name a few, we have, Laplacian pyramid [3], morphological pyramid [4], discrete wavelet transform (DWT) [5-7], so on and so forth. Combining the efficacies of both transform (DWT) and spatial domain (sharpness based), an efficient and robust multi-focus image fusion method was proposed. Initially both the source images are processed through DWT to get their respective wavelet coefficients. Thereafter, sharpness based fusion rule was applied for each of the approximation and detail coefficients separately by dividing them into blocks and getting sharpest fused coefficients. Subsequently, using inverse transformation (IDWT), all the fused coefficients were recombined to get the final fused image.

V.V. Das and N. Thankachan (Eds.): CIIT 2011, CCIS 250, pp. 401–404, 2011.

2 Optimization of Decomposition Levels

The performance of wavelet-based multifocus image fusion depends on the number of decomposition levels in the wavelet transform. In order to obtain the optimal fusion results, we need to optimize the number of decomposition levels using optimization algorithms. As shown in Fig. 1, the flow is as follows:

1. Let the number of the decomposition levels for the wavelet-based multifocus image fusion is M. The value range of M is

$$0 \leq M \leq \log_2 N - 1 \,. \tag{1}$$

   where the size of original images is N by N.
2. Thereafter, DWT of both the source images A and B were found up to specified decomposition level and one approximation and 3 details were obtained. We have divided each coefficient sub-image into non-overlapping blocks with the size of m x n. The ith image blocks of A and B sub-images are referred to as A_i and B_i respectively.
3. The sharpness values of two corresponding blocks A_i and B_i, given by BSV_i^A and BSV_i^B are compared to determine the sharper image block and i th image block F_i of the fused image can be constructed as:

$$F_i = \begin{cases} A_i & \text{if } BSV_i^A > BSV_i^B \\ B_i & \text{if } BSV_i^A < BSV_i^B \\ (A_i + B_i)/2 & \text{otherwise} \end{cases} \,. \tag{2}$$

4. Subsequently, using inverse transform, all the fused coefficients are coupled to get final fused image employing hybrid approach and then optimization algorithms (explicitly defined in the figure shown below) using CC & PSNR are used to get the optimal level of decomposition.

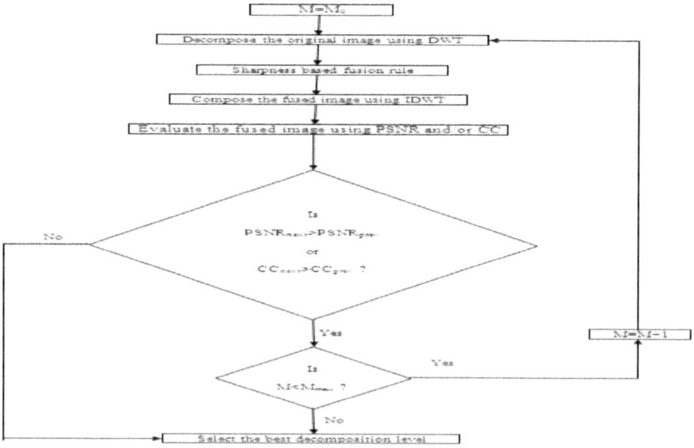

Fig. 1. Flowchart of hybrid image fusion decomposition level optimization

3 Objective Evaluation Metrics of Image Fusion

In this paper, we dealt with Correlation Coefficient (CC) and PSNR as the evaluation metrics, thus described in the following lines.

Correlation Coefficient (CC):

It reflects the correlation extent between the original and fused image. It's defined as

$$CC = \frac{\sum_{i=1}^{M}\sum_{j=1}^{N}(R(i,j)-\bar{R})(F(i,j)-\bar{F})}{\sqrt{\sum_{i=1}^{M}\sum_{j=1}^{N}(R(i,j)-\bar{R})^2\sum_{i=1}^{M}\sum_{j=1}^{N}(F(i,j)-\bar{F})^2}} \quad . \tag{3}$$

Peak Signal to Noise Ratio (PSNR):

This objective metric is used to measure quality of the fused image. PSNR is a metric for the ratio between the maximum possible power of a signal and the power of corrupting noise that affects the fidelity of its representation. It is defined as:

$$PSNR = 10\log_{10}\left[\frac{L^2}{\frac{1}{M\times N}\sum_{i=1}^{M}\sum_{j=1}^{N}(R(i,j)-F(i,j))^2}\right] . \tag{4}$$

Where, R(i, j)& F(i, j) are the pixel value of original image and fused, $\bar{R}$ & $\bar{F}$ are the mean values of the images & M &N are the number of rows& columns .

4 Experimental Results and Discussion

In this paper, we perform the experiments over 2 pairs of different source images, namely, book & clock (512×512), as shown in Fig. (2-3) & (6-7). By applying the optimization algorithm, we get 2 different sets of output fused images as shown in (Fig.4, 5) & (Fig.8, 9).

Fig. 2, 3, 4, 5. Left focused & Right focused source book images, fusion output images for $M = 1$ and 2

Fig. 6, 7, 8, 9. Left focused & Right focused source clock images, fusion output images for $M = 1$ and 2

The following Table 1 enumerates the experimental results of three pair of source images.

Table 1. Experimental results for Book and Clock images

Evaluation Metrics	Decomposition Levels (book)		Decomposition Levels (clock)	
	Level 1:	Level 2:	Level 1:	Level 2:
PSNR	36.8072	35.1863	35.6571	34.4566
CC	0.9970	0.9930	0.9926	0.9907

Smaller value of RMSE thereby leading to higher values of PSNR and Closer the correlation coefficient is to 1, indicates better fusion results as the information quantity increases and performance is improved. The comparing results show that the optimization up to first level of decomposition entailed higher PSNR and CC values.

5 Conclusion

This paper presented a new method for optimizing the number of decomposition levels in the multi-focus image fusion using novel hybrid approach. For each set of source images, initially, the wavelet coefficients were found out which were processed using sharpness based fusion rule, then reconfigured using inverse wavelet transformation to get enhanced fusion results. Thereafter, proposed optimization algorithm was carried out to obtain the optimal number of decomposition levels. The visual effect and the values of statistical parameters indicate that the performance of the new optimization algorithm was optimal up to first level of decomposition. During the process of optimization, the proposed algorithm not only preserves spectral information of the original multi-spectral image very well, but also enhances spatial detail information of the fused image greatly up to optimal decomposition level.

References

1. Goshtasby, S.A.A., Nikolov, S.: Image fusion: advances in the state of the art. Information Fusion 8(2), 114–118 (2007)
2. Mitianoudis, N., Stathaki, T.: Pixel-based and region-based image fusion schemes using ICA bases. Information Fusion 8(2), 131–142 (2007)
3. Burt, P.T., Andelson, E.H.: The Laplacian pyramid as a compact image code. IEEE Transactions on Communications 31(4), 532–540 (1983)
4. Toet, A.: A morphological pyramidal image decomposition. Pattern Recognition Letters 9(3), 255–261 (1989)
5. Li, H., Manjunath, B., Mitra, S.: Multisensor image fusion using the wavelet transform. Graphical Models and Image Processing 57(3), 235–245 (1995)
6. Pajares, G., Cruz, J.: A wavelet-based image fusion tutorial. Pattern Recognition 37(9), 1855–1872 (2004)
7. Yang, B., Jing, Z.L.: Image fusion using a low-redundancy and nearly shiftinvariant discrete wavelet frame. Optics Engineering 46(10), 107002 (2007)

Design of a Supplementary Controller for Power System Stabilizer Using Bacterial Foraging Optimization Algorithm

Mohammad Kiani, Hasan Nasiri Soloklo,
M. Ali Mohammadi, and Malihe M. Farsangi

Electrical Engineering Department, Shahid Bahonar University of Kerman, Kerman, Iran
{M.kiani1984,hasannasirisoloklo}@gmail.com,
{A_Mohammadi,mmmaghfoori}@mail.uk.ac.ir

Abstract. Power system stabilizers (PSSs) are the most efficient device to damp the power system oscillation. Recently designing of PSSs by heuristic algorithms is the conventional method for damping the power system oscillation. This work proposes a Bacterial Foraging Optimization algorithm (BFOA) to determine the PSS parameters to damp the power system inter area oscillation. The results are presented on a 2 area 4 machine system to feasibility of the proposed method. To show the effectiveness of the designed controller, a three phase fault is applied at a bus. The simulation results show that the designed controller by BFOA algorithm performs better than well known genetic algorithm (GA) in damping the power oscillation.

Keywords: Bacterial Foraging Optimization algorithm, Power System Stabilizer, supplementary control, Genetic Algorithm.

1 Introduction

Power system stability is a complex subject that has challenged power system engineers for many years. Poorly damped low-frequency oscillations are inherent in interconnected power systems. In the last three decades, the applications of Flexible AC Transmission System (FACTS) device for damping inter-area oscillations have been investigated and proven to have additional benefits for increasing system damping, in addition to their primary functions, for instance, voltage control and power flow control[1]. Power system stabilizers are a kind of FACTS device. PSSs are added to excitation system to enhance the damping of electric power system during low frequency oscillations. The generators are equipped with PSS, which provide supplementary feedback and stabilizes the signal in the excitation system [2]. Several methods are used for designing of power system stabilizers such as pole-placement, optimal control, adaptive control and variable structure control [3]-[4]. Tuning of supplementary controls for stabilizing system modes of oscillation has been the subject of much research during past 30 years [5]. In recent years, artificial intelligence played the important role in designing of PSSs parameters.

V.V. Das and N. Thankachan (Eds.): CIIT 2011, CCIS 250, pp. 405–410, 2011.

In this work, PSS structures are considered as lead-lag controller. Then Bacterial Foraging Optimization algorithm (BFOA) is used for determining PSSs parameters. The genetic algorithm is used for validate the achieve results of Bacterial Foraging Optimization method.

The paper is organized as follow: in section 2 the study system and problem formulation is described. In section 3 overview of Bacterial Foraging Optimization algorithm is explained. In section 4 simulation and results are presented. Finally In section 5, conclusion is presented.

2 Study System and Problem Formulation

In this paper, A 2-area-4-machine system is used. This test system is illustrated in Fig. 2. The sub transient model for the generators, and the IEEE-type DC1 and DC2 excitation systems are used for machines 1 and 4, respectively. The IEEE-type ST3 compound source rectifier exciter model is used for machine 2, and the first-order simplified model for the excitation systems is used for machine 3.

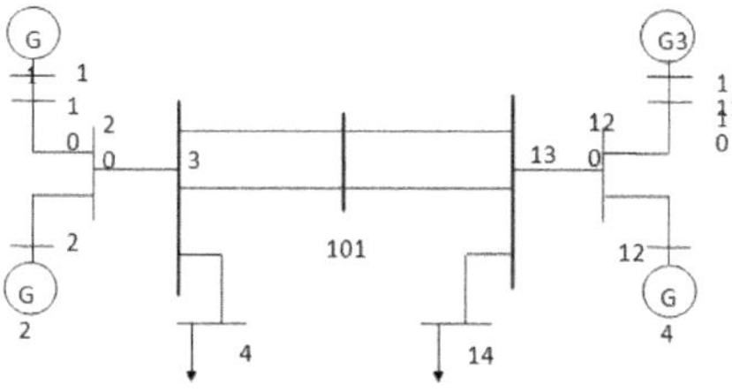

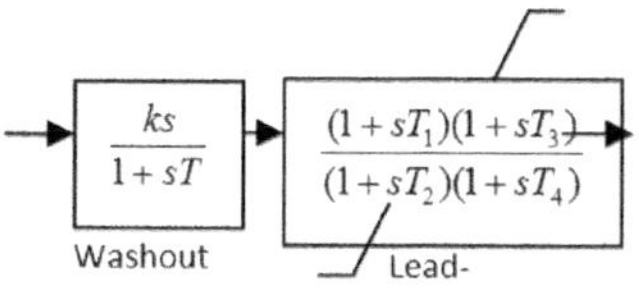

Fig. 1. Single-line diagram of a 2-area study **Fig. 2.** Conventional lead-lag supplementary system controller block diagram for PSS

Two PSSs are going to be designed for the above system and placed on Machines 2 and 3. The structure shown by Fig. 3 is used for each PSS where the input (u) to PSS could be generator speed (GS) or the generator electrical torque (GET). In this paper, the generator speed (GS) is considered as input.

The parameters of the PSSs, k, T, T_1, T_2, T_3, T_4, are determined by BFOA and GA by optimizing the following objective function:

$$f = \max(real(s) - \min(-\beta * abs(imag(s)/real(s)), \alpha)) \tag{1}$$

where in this study β is set to be 0.1. Also, a value α = - 0.2 is considered adequate for an acceptable settling time. This fitness function will place the system closed-loop eigenvalues in the D-shape sector [6].

Furthermore, the design problem can be formulated as the following constrained optimization problem, where the constraints are the supplementary controller parameter bounds:

$$Minimize\ f\ subject\ to \quad \begin{cases} 0 \le K \le 70 \\ 0 \le T \le 5 \\ 0 \le T_1 \le 2 \\ 0 \le T_2 \le 2 \\ 0 \le T_3 \le 2 \\ 0 \le T_4 \le 2 \end{cases} \tag{2}$$

The BFOA and GA are applied to solve this optimization problem.

3 Overview of Bacterial Foraging Optimization Algorithm

The BFOA was proposed by K.M.Passino and has three major operators: Chemotaxis, Reproduction and Elimination-dispersal. [7-8].

3.1 Chemotaxis

The behavior of the bacteria toward the nutrient sources is interpreted as chemotaxis. In fact bacterium tries to find nutrient-rich areas and stay away from toxic environments. An E.coli bacterium moves in two different ways: tumble and swim. Tumble is a unit walk in a random direction and always continues by another tumble or a swim. If random direction results in a better position, it will be followed by a swim, else another tumble will be taken. In fact swim is a unit walk in a previous random direction. In each tumble unit walk position of bacterium is updated based on (3):

$$\theta^i(j+1,k,l) = \theta^i(j,k,l) + c(i)\varphi(i) \tag{3}$$

Where i is the index of bacterium and $\theta^i(j,k,l)$ is the position of ith bacterium in the jth step of chemotaxis and kth stage of reproduction and lth stage of elimination-dispersal. C is the step size of chemotaxis operation. The cost function of the ith bacterium is determined based on its position and is represented with $J(i,j,k,l)$. $J_{\min}$ represents the minimum fitness value. In the swim stage if at $\theta^i(j+1,k,l)$ the cost function becomes better than $\theta^i(j,k,l)$ then another step will be taken in a same direction. This sequence will continue until N_s steps are taken in swim. In fact N_s is the upper band for the number of steps in swim. [7-8]

3.2 Reproduction

The basic idea of this operation is that nature tends to eliminate animals with poor foraging strategies and keep those which have better ones. In this operation all the population is sorted based on their fitness. (4) shows how the fitness functions sorted. Half of the population which has the worse cost function is eliminated. Each of the remained ones which have a better fitness is reproduced to two children bacteria to keep the population size.

$$J_{health}^{i} = \sum_{j}^{N_c+1} J(i,j,k,l) \quad (4)$$

3.3 Elimination and Dispersal

To increase the ability of bacteria for global searching and to prevent them from involving in local optimums, randomly some of the bacteria are eliminated and some of them are dispersed.[7-8].

4 Simulation and Results

In this work, the goal of the optimization is to find the best value for the supplementary controller, k, T, T_1, T_2, T_3, T_4 that by minimizing the objective function presented in (1) using BFOA, PSSs parameters are determined. Then for validating the obtained results by this method, same procedure is used by GA.

In table 1 and 2, obtained results by BFOA method and GA method for PSS1 and PSS2 are presented.

Table 1. The results obtained by BFOA and GA for PSS1

Algorithm	K	T	T1	T2	T3	T4
BFOA	30.80	0.09	0.62	0.16	0.84	2.44
GA	63.72	0.15	1.19	0.07	0.57	9.31

Table 2. The results obtained by BFOA and GA for PSS2

Algorithm	K	T	T1	T2	T3	T4
BFOA	48.1960	1.63371	0.81214	0.66123	1.25786	1.57184
GA	65.4369	0.6030	1.5832	1.0301	1.1422	5.9705

The obtained supplementary controller by BFOA and GA are placed in 2 area 4 machine system. A three phase fault is applied in one of the tie circuit at bus 3. Fault persisted for 70 ms; following this, the faulted circuit was disconnected by appropriate circuit breaker. The system operated with one tie circuit connecting buses 3 and 101. The dynamic behavior of the system was evaluated for 20 s. The voltage magnitude at fault bus and the machine angles, δ, with respect to a particular machine, were computed over the simulation period and shown in Figs. 3-5.

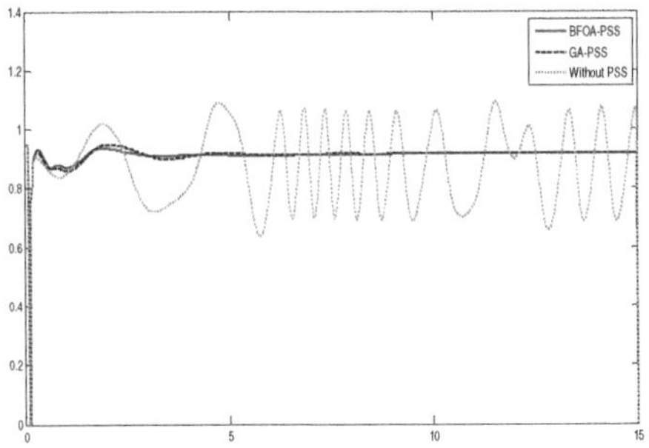

Fig. 3. The response of the system to a three phase fault at bus 3

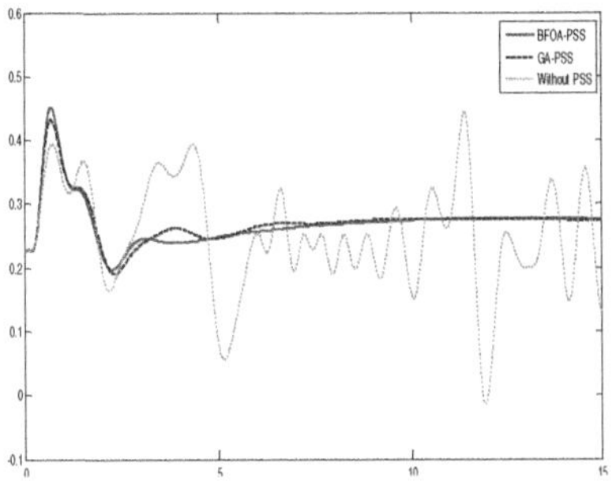

Fig. 4. The response of generator 3 to a three phase fault

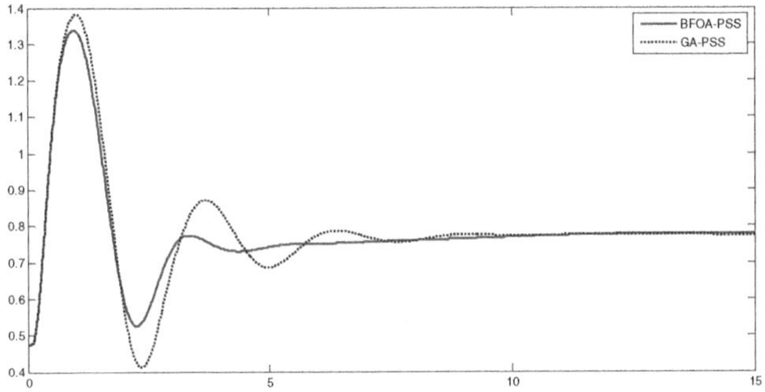

Fig. 5. The response of generator 4 to a three phase fault

5 Conclusion

In this paper a Bacterial Foraging Optimization algorithm is used to design supplementary controller of PSS to damp low frequency oscillation. The PSS parameters are determined by HS algorithm using an eigenvalue-based objective function. Genetic algorithm is applied to validate the results that achieved by Bacterial Foraging Optimization algorithm method. The results present in design supplementary control, the Bacterial Foraging Optimization algorithm method is slightly better than GA method.

References

1. Farsangi, M.M., Nezamabadi-pour, H., Lee, K.Y., Song, Y.H.: Placement of SVCs and selection of stabilizing signal in power systems. IEEE Trans. Power Systems 22(3), 1061–1071
2. Demello, F.P., Concordia, C.: Concepts of synchronous machine stability as affected by excitation control. IEEE Trans. Power App. Syst. 88, 316–329 (1969)

3. Chen, G.P., Malik, O.P., Hope, G.S., Qin, Y.H., Xu, G.Y.: An adaptive power system stabilizer based on the self-optimization pole shifting control strategy. IEEE Transactions on Energy Conversion 8(4), 639–644 (1993)
4. Samarasinghe, V., Pahalawaththa, N.C.: Damping of multimodal oscillations in power systems using variable structure control techniques. Proc. Inst. Elect. Eng. Gen. Transm. Distrib., 323–331 (1997)
5. Larsen, E.V., Swann, D.A.: " Applying power system stabilizers part- I: general concepts. IEEE Trans. On power Apparatus and systems PAS100(6), 3017–3024 (1981)
6. Kyanzadeh, S., Farsangi, M.M., Nezamabadi-pour, H., Lee, K.Y.: Design of a Supplementary Controller for SVC Using Immune Algorithm. In: Proceeding of the 17 th congress the IFAC, pp. 4583–4587 (July 2008)
7. Passino, K.M.: Biomimicry of bacterial foraging for distributed optimization and control. IEEE Control Systems Magazine 22, 52–67 (2002)
8. Liu, Y., Passino, K.M.: Biomimicry of social foraging bacteria for distributed optimization: Models, principles, and emergent behaviors. J. Optimization Theory Applicat. 115(3), 603–628 (2002)

Comparative Performance Analysis of Hysteresis Current Control and Direct Torque Control of 4 Phase 8/6 Switched Reluctance Motor Drive

P. Srinivas and P.V.N. Prasad

Department of Electrical Engg., University College of Engineering,
Osmania University, Hyderabad, Andhra Pradesh, India
srinivasp.eedou@gmail.com, polaki@rediffmail.com

Abstract. The Switched Reluctance Motor drives have been widely used in special applications like conveyer belts, compressors, vacuum cleaners etc., because of advantages like simple construction, no winding on rotor, high speed operation and high temperature handling capability. But its operation is not spread to the other applications because of presence of high torque ripple. The torque ripple can be minimized by adopting the Direct Torque Control Technique. In DTC technique, flux and torque are maintained within the set of hysteresis bands by applying suitable Space Voltage Vectors. This paper makes the comparative performance analysis of Switched Reluctance Motor drive with Hysteresis Current Control and Direct Torque Control techniques. The detailed simulation results based on MATLAB / SIMULINK is also presented.

Keywords: Direct Torque Control, Switched Reluctance Motor, Hysteresis Current Control.

1 Introduction

Switched Reluctance Motor drives have become popular in recent years because of simple mechanical structure, absence of winding on the rotor, high efficiency over a wide speed range, adaptable to harsh environment etc. But its applications are restricted to some areas because of its high ripple content in the torque due to double saliency structure [1]. The popularly used conventional control technique of SRM drives is Hysteresis Current Control [2],[3]. It has the disadvantage of high torque ripples. To minimize the torque ripple DTC technique is proposed in [4]. This paper which uses the concept of short flux pattern has the disadvantage of requirement of new winding topology. The new winding scheme is expensive and also inconvenient. In [5],[6] a novel DTC technique is applied to 3-phase 6/4 SRM. This paper has elaborately discussed the difference between conventional DTC applied to AC machines and the new DTC proposed to SR motor, showing experimental and simulation results. The performance of SRM using DTC applied to 3 phase 6/4 SRM is discussed in [7],[8]. DTC technique of 4 phase 8/6 SRM is analyzed in [9].

This paper compares the performance of 4 phase 8/6 SRM drive using Hysteresis Current control and DTC techniques.

V.V. Das and N. Thankachan (Eds.): CIIT 2011, CCIS 250, pp. 411–415, 2011.

2 Direct Torque Controller

The approximate equation for torque developed by the SR motor [5] is given by: $T \approx i\ \partial\psi(\theta,i)/\partial\psi(\theta)$, where $\psi(\theta)$ is the phase flux linkages as a function of rotor position θ and stator current i. The DTC technique for SRM is explained in [5].

Asymmetrical converter is popularly used for the SRM drives. As shown in Fig. 1, when both the switches are turned ON, the state is defined as 'magnetizing' (state 1). When one switch is turned ON and other is turned OFF, the state is defined as 'freewheeling' (state 0). When both the switches are turned OFF, the state is defined as 'demagnetizing' (state -1). The 4 phase Asymmetrical converter can have a total of 81 possible Space Voltage Vectors. But in order to apply DTC to SRM, eight Space Voltage Vectors that are separated by 45^0 are sufficient. The eight Space Voltage Vectors that lie in the center of eight sectors N = 1, 2…8, are shown in Fig. 2.

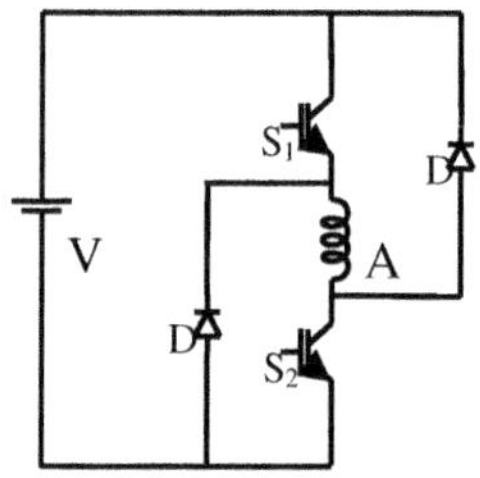

Fig. 1. Asymmetrical Converter

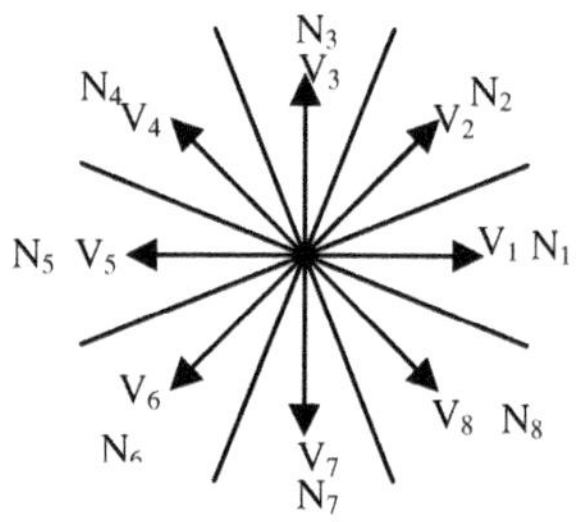

Fig. 2. Space Voltage Vectors for DTC

If the stator flux vector lies in the kth sector, the magnitude of the flux can be increased by using the Space Voltage Vectors V_{k+1} & V_{k-1} and can be decreased by using the vectors V_{k+2} & V_{k-2}. Hence, whenever the stator flux linkage reaches its upper limit in the hysteresis band, it is decreased by applying Space Voltage Vectors which are directed toward the center of the flux vector [5]. If an increase in torque is required, Space Voltage Vectors which accelerate the stator flux linkage vector are applied across the motor. Thus if the stator flux linkages lie in the kth sector, V_{k+1} and V_{k+2} Space Voltage Vectors are selected. If torque is to be decreased, voltage vectors which decelerate the stator flux linkage vector are applied to the motor. This corresponds to the vectors V_{k-1} and V_{k-2} in k^{th} sector [5]. Based on the output of the torque and flux hysteresis blocks, appropriate Space Voltage Vectors are selected.

3 DTC Implementation

The Block diagram of the DTC based 4 phase 8/6 SRM drive is shown in Fig. 3. The flux in each phase is calculated by flux linkage computation block. The output of the flux linkage computation block is given to the α–β block where the flux in 4 phases is converted into 2 phases. The magnitude Ψs and angle δ of the flux vector are calculated by flux vector calculation block. The flux vector magnitude Ψs and flux reference are fed to the flux hysteresis block. The flux hysteresis block compares the reference flux and the actual flux and outputs the flux increase or decrease Ψ_Q. The motor actual torque T and reference torque are fed to torque hysteresis block. The torque hysteresis block compares the reference torque and the actual torque and outputs torque increase or decrease T_Q. The switching table and Asymmetrical converter apply the suitable voltage vector to the SRM windings.

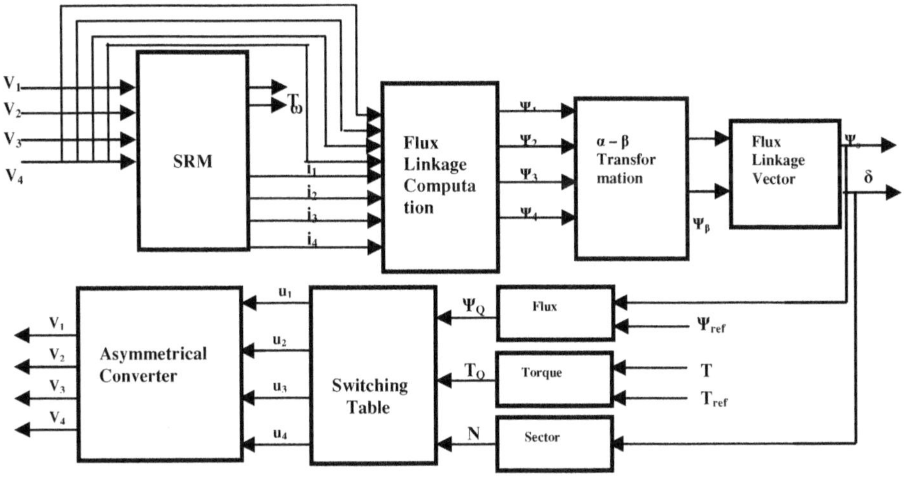

Fig. 3. Block diagram of DTC based SRM drive

4 Simulation and Results

The 4 phase 8/6 SRM drive is simulated in MATLAB/SIMULINK environment with Hysteresis Current Control and DTC methods. The DTC scheme is simulated by selecting the following set of 8 Space Voltage Vectors. V_1 = (-1010), V_2 = (-1-111), V_3 = (0-101), V_4 = (1-1-11), V_5 = (10-10), V_6 = (11-1-1), V_7 = (010-1), V_8 = (-111-1).

Fig. 4 shows the simulation waveforms of SRM drive with conventional Hysteresis Current Control technique for a Fan load of 4 Nm at a speed of 800 rpm. Fig. 4 (a) shows the current in four phases of the motor under steady state. The Hysteresis band of stator current in each phase is maintained at 1.0 A and the maximum current in each phase is 7.0 A. Fig. 4 (b) shows the flux linkages in all the four phases in steady state condition. The maximum flux in each phase is maintained at 0.20 Wb. Fig. 4 (c) shows the total torque developed by the motor. The torque ripple is 55.5%. It can be observed that the torque has high ripples. The speed waveform is shown in Fig. 4 (d). The steady state speed is 801 rpm.

Fig. 5 shows the simulation waveforms of SRM drive with DTC technique with same Fan load. Fig. 5 (a) shows the variation of stator current in all the four phases as a function of time. The maximum current drawn by each phase is 10.9 A, which is higher than the current drawn by each phase with Hysteresis Current Control method. Fig. 5 (b) shows the magnitude of the stator flux vector. The flux is maintained at the

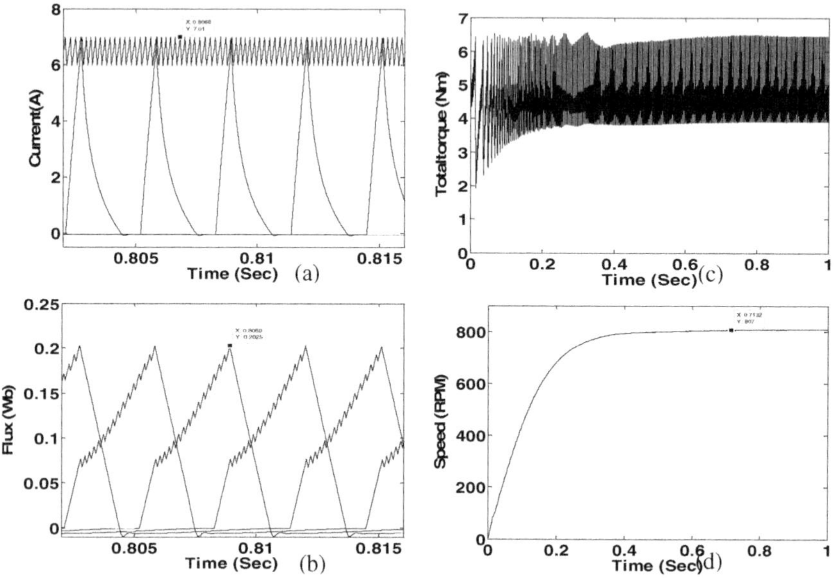

Fig. 4. Simulation waveforms of SRM with Hysteresis Current Control (a) Phase Currents in four phases (b) Fluxes in four phases (c) Total torque (d) Speed

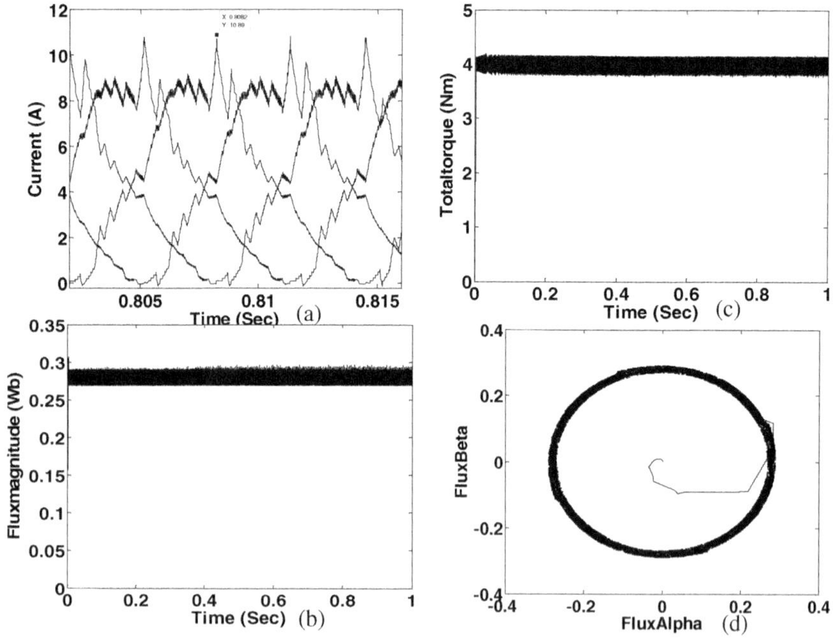

Fig. 5. Simulation waveforms of SRM with Direct Torque Control (a) Currents in 4 phases (b) Magnitude of flux vector (c) Total torque (d) Trajectory of fluxes

reference value of 0.28 Wb by following a hysteresis band of 0.02 Wb. Fig. 5 (c) shows the total torque waveform. It is observed that the torque is maintained within the hysteresis band of 0.29 Nm as against the set band of 0.2 Nm with DTC. The torque ripple is 8.9%. Fig. 5 (d) shows the variation of ψ_α with ψ_β. It can be seen that the trajectory of fluxes between α and β axes is circular in nature.

5 Conclusion

This paper compares the performance of SRM drive with conventional Hysteresis Current control and Direct Torque Control techniques. The performance is compared mainly in terms of torque ripple, phase current variations etc. with a Fan load. It is observed that with DTC technique the torque ripple is reduced by 84%. The torque and flux are maintained at their reference values by following the set hysteresis bands with DTC method. Though the current and flux in each phase with DTC are higher, the rate of change of current and flux are much lower when compared to Hysteresis Current Control method, causing drastic reduction in torque ripple.

References

1. Miller, T.J.E.: Switched Reluctance Motors & their Control. Magna Physics & Oxford (1993)
2. Srinivas, P., Prasad, P.V.N.: Voltage Control and Hysteresis Current Control of 8/6 Switched Reluctance Motor Drives. In: Proceedings of IEEE International Conference on Electrical Machines and Systems, pp. 1557–1562 (2007)
3. Srinivas, P., Prasad, P.V.N.: Torque Ripple Minimization of 8/6 Switched Reluctance Motor with Fuzzy Logic Controller for Constant Dwell Angles. In: Proceedings of the IEEE International Conference on Power Electronics Drives and Energy Systems (2010)
4. Jinupun, P., Luk, P.C.K.: Direct torque control for sensorless switched reluctance motor drives. In: Proc. 7th Int. Conf. Power Electron. Variable Speed Drives, pp. 329–334 (1998)
5. Cheok, A.D., Hoon, P.H.: A new torque control method for switched reluctance motor drives. In: 26 Annual Conference of the IEEE Industrial Electronics Society, pp. 387–392 (2000)
6. Cheok, A.D., Fukuda, Y.: A new torque and flux control method for switched reluctance motor drives. IEEE Trans. Power Electron 17, 543–557 (2002)
7. Guo, H.J.: Considerations of direct torque control for switched reluctance motors. In: Proceedings of the IEEE International Symposium on Industrial Electronics, pp. 2321–2325 (2006)
8. Song, G., Li, Z., Zhao, Z., Wang, X.: Direct Torque Control of Switched Reluctance Motors. In: Proceedings of the IEEE International Conference on Electrical Machines and Systems, pp. 3389–3392 (2008)
9. Jeong, B.H., Lee, K.Y., Na, J.D., Cho, G.B., Baek, H.L.: Direct Torque Control for 4-phase Switched Reluctance Motor Drives. In: Proceedings of the IEEE International Conference on Electrical Machines and Systems, pp. 524–528 (2005)

Adaptive Digital PID Controller Implemented on 32-bit ARM7 Microcontroller

Ali Hasanzade and S.M.A. Mohammadi

Department of Electrical Engineering, Shahid Bahonar University of Kerman, Iran
ali14hasanzade@gmail.com, a_mohammadi@mail.uk.ac.ir

Abstract. The variations of the process parameters is a strong reason to use adaptive controller. In this paper, the implementation of adaptive digital proportional-integral-derivative (PID) controller on 32-bit ARM7 microcontroller which is intended for general purpose applications is described. The controlled process is identified using recursive least squares algorithm, and the parameters of the PID controller are designed by the pole placement method on the basis of estimated plant coefficients. The system identification and controller designing are completely done in microcontroller. For to survey the effects of uncertainty on the process, a normalized model of a motor by MATLAB software is used. The connection between MATLAB and microcontroller is compatible with RS232 standard. The extensive studies carried out clearly proves that the proposed approach by the ARM microcontroller , is an excellent choice for control problems including adaptive control systems due to its high efficiency, speed and robustness.

Keywords: ARM microcontroller, Diophantine equation, Pole placement method, Reference model, RLS algorithm.

1 Introduction

Recently, very rapid progress in electronics and computer science has influenced all the areas of human activities. Production technology improvements of new microcontrollers lead to their miniaturization, increased central processor unit performance, decreased power consumption and price. Thus modern 32-bit one-chip microcontrollers not only have enough computing power for simple control loops consisting of fixed parameters controllers like PI or PID but also are able to handle tasks from the origin of modern control methods such as adaptive control.

This work presents the implementation of self-tuning digital PID controller on a member of wide family of 32-bit ARM microcontrollers which is an excellent candidate for control problems including adaptive control systems. The paper is organized as follows. In section 2, the implemented algorithms are briefly introduced. The hardware overview is presented in section 3. Section 4 appropriately introduces the implementation of the proposed controller on microcontroller. Experimental results are presented in section 5. In section 6, conclusions are drawn.

V.V. Das and N. Thankachan (Eds.): CIIT 2011, CCIS 250, pp. 416–420, 2011.

2 Implemented Algorithms

In this work we use the model reference adaptive system (MRAS) which was originally proposed to solve a problem in which the performance specifications are given in terms of a reference model. This model tells how the process output ideally should respond to the command signal. A block diagram of the system is shown in fig. 1-a. The key problem with MRAS is to determine the adjustment mechanism so that a stable system, which brings the error to zero, is obtained.

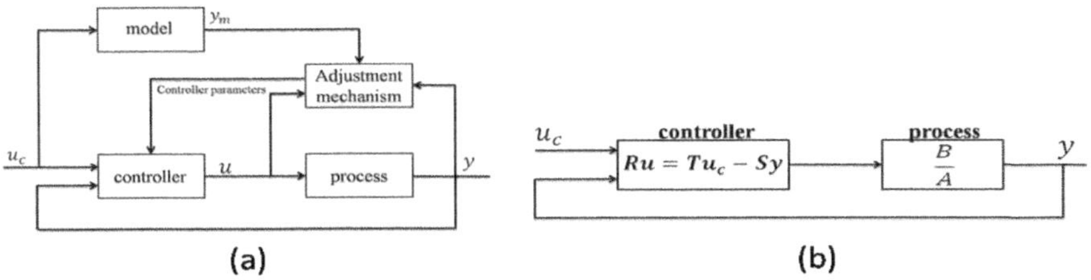

Fig. 1. a)Block diagram of a MRAS. b) A linear controller with two degrees of freedom.

2.1 Process Identification

For process identification was used recursive least square algorithm. Identified system is described by second order transfer Function(1).

$$G(q) = \frac{b_0 q + b_1}{q^2 + a_1 q + a_2} \tag{1}$$

Where q is forward shift operator.

The process identification with recursive least square(RLS) algorithm is described very well in literature [1,4], and, therefore, we will skip a detailed description of the whole RLS algorithm.

2.2 Digital PID Controller Designing Using Pole Placement Method

we can handle continuous systems simultaneously by writing the model :

$$Ay(t) = Bu(t) \tag{2}$$

where A and B denote polynomials in either the differential operator p = d/dt or the forward shift operator q.

A general linear controller can be described by :

$$\mathrm{Ru}(t) = \mathrm{Tu_c}(t) - \mathrm{Sy}(t) \tag{3}$$

where "R", "S" and "T" are polynomials. A block diagram of the closed-loop system is also shown in fig. 1-b.

we assume the reference model as follow:

$$H(q) = \frac{B_m(q)}{A_m(q)} = \frac{b_{m0} q}{q^2 + a_{m1} q + a_{m2}} = \frac{0.1761q}{q^2 - 1.3205q + 0.4966} \tag{4}$$

Then the parameters of controller calculate by solving Diophantine equation[1]:

$$s_0 = \frac{a_{m1} - a_1}{b_0}, s_1 = \frac{a_{m2} - a_2}{b_0} \tag{5}$$

The controller is thus characterized by the polynomials :

$$R(q) = q + \frac{b_1}{b_0}, S(q) = s_0 q + s_1, T(q) = \frac{b_{m0} q}{b_0} \tag{6}$$

The calculations, which were done above, give the control law :

$$u(t) = -r_1 u(t-1) + t_0 u_c(t) - s_0 y(t) - s_1 y(t-1) \tag{7}$$

The Controller Designing Using Pole Placement Method is described very well in literature [1,4].

3 Hardware Overview

Self tuning digital PID controller was implemented on At91sam7x256 by Atmel company. Atmel's AT91SAM7X256 is a member of a series of highly integrated Flash microcontrollers based on the 32-bit ARM RISC processor. It features a 256 Kbyte high-speed Flash and a 64 Kbyte SRAM, a large set of peripherals including an 802.3 Ethernet MAC and a CAN controller.

Development board photograph is in Fig. 2-a. the Board is equipped with a number of useful peripherals enabling comfortable development of new applications for this microcontroller. For example, for communication purposes, it provides a serial asynchronous communication interface RS232 with standard DB9-S connectors.

To process identification and controller designing a Program in C language in keil Compiler is written, and to upload the program into microcontroller SAM-PROG software is used. the connection between PC and microcontroller is compatible with RS232 standard.

4 Implementation of the Proposed Controller on Microcontroller

Flowchart of the proposed algorithm is depicted in Fig. 2-b. considering this figure in the first stage, we Initialize parameters. With respect to equation (1) two input-output pairs required at the beginning of each cycle. these pairs are acquired using sampling. The input signal for sampling is the controller output. In the next stage, the estimated output is gained using the value reached from RLS algorithm. Now, estimation error is calculated via the estimated and real output. If the error is more than a specific amount(parameter c), RLS algorithm is performed; otherwise, the values of RLS in the previous cycle is used. Then, the controller parameters are calculated using equations (5) to (7). in each cycle repetition, the system is identified, if necessary, so that In the case of any change, these changes are applied to the estimated transfer function, and consequently the controller is updated.

5 Experimental Results

To survey the effects of uncertainty on the process a normalized model of a motor in MATLAB software is used. connection between MATLAB and microcontroller is compatible with RS232 standard. Transfer function of motor is described by equation(8) and sampling rate is 42 hertz. The discrete transfer function is described by equation(9).

$$G(s) = \frac{1}{s(s+1)} \tag{8}$$

$$G(q) = \frac{0.0002812q + 0.000279}{q^2 - 1.976q + 0.9765} \tag{9}$$

Fig.s 3-a and 3-b respectively show the process output and the control signal when the command signal is a wry square wave. The output converges to the reference model output after an initial transient. The control signal has an oscillation ("ringing"). This is due to the cancellation of the process zero. The initial transient depends critically on the initial values of the estimator.

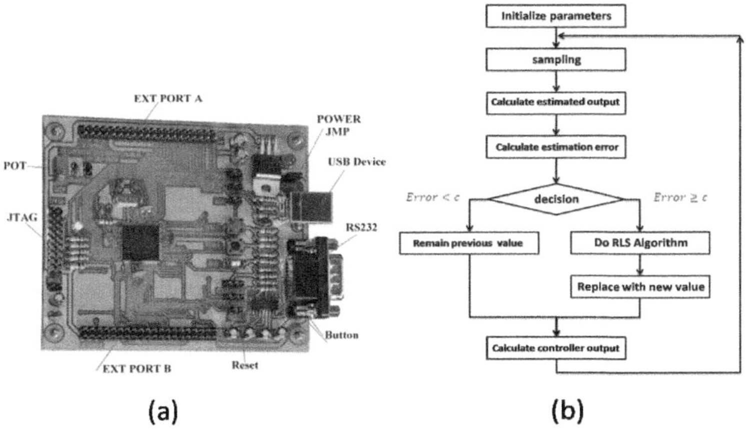

Fig. 2. a) Development board. b) Flowchart of the proposed algorithm

The parameter estimates are shown in Fig.3-c The behavior of the estimates depends critically on the initial values of the estimator. Notice that the estimates converge quickly. They are close to their correct values already at time t = 0.3 second.

To demonstrate adaptability of the system for changing parameters of the process, in the time 2.4 second, the parameter b_0 is multiplied by 11. figure 3-d shows the process output when the command signal square wave. It is evident that the output gets a desirable form after transient time.

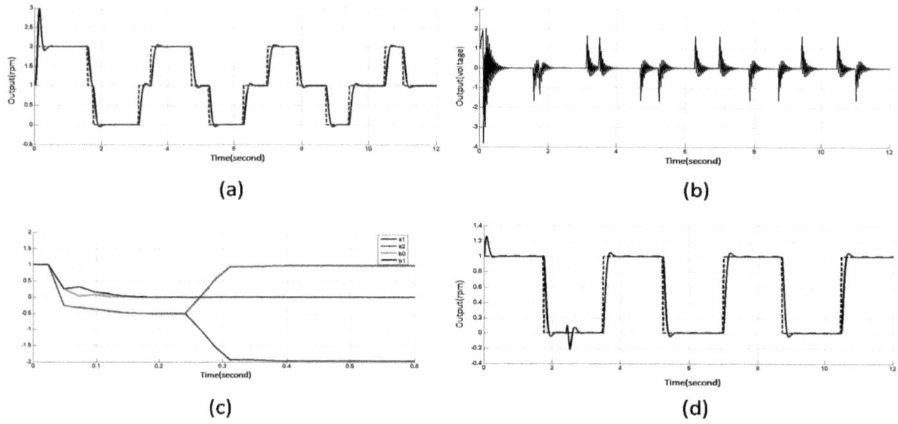

Fig. 3. a) process output when the command signal is a wry square wave. b) control signal when the command signal is a wry square wave. c) Convergence of parameters to true value. d) process output with suddenly change in b_o.

6 Conclusion

The Implementation of adaptive digital controller on microcontroller is shown to be feasible. The performance of system in the presence of noise and variation of the process model show that the ARM microcontroller can handle this work well. The capabilities of Arm microcontroller to operate at clock rates in the range of 10's to 100's of MHz provides plenty of processing capability. Furthermore, as the programming is in C language, complex mathematical calculation such as fuzzy and adaptive fuzzy controller can be easily managed.

References

1. Astrom, K.J., Wittenmark, B.: Adaptive control, 2nd edn. Wesley (1995)
2. Dostálek, P., Dolinay, J.: Self-tuning digital PID controller implemented on 8-bit free micro. International Journal of Mathematical Models in Applied Sciences, 274–281 (2010)
3. Oltean, S., Morar, A.: Direct digital self-tuning controllers with minimum variance. Acta Electrotehnica 47(3), 168–173 (2006)
4. Haykin, S.: Adaptive Filtering Theory. Prentice-Hall (2002)
5. Phillips, C.L., Nagle, H.T.: Digital Control System Analysis and Design. Prentice-Hall, Inc, Englewood Cliffs (1988)
6. Astrom, K., Hagglund, T.: PID Controllers: Theory, Design and Tuning, 2nd edn. Instrument Society of America, Research Triangle Park, NC (1995)
7. Huang, H.-P., Roan, M.-L., Jeng, J.-C.: On line Adaptive Tuning for PID Controllers. IEE Proceedings-Control Theory Applications 149(1), 60–67 (2002)
8. Leonhard, W.: Control of Electric Drives, 2nd edn. Springer, Germany (1997)

Feedback Control System for BioMEMS Application

Rupali Jumbadkar and Jayu Kalambe

Shri Ramdeobaba Kamla Nehru Engineering College, Nagpur, India
rupalijumbadkar@gmail.com, jayu_kalambe@rediffmail.com

Abstract. In this paper, we present the designing of control system for cantilever based biosensor. We propose to fabricate the digital feedback control system which will take care of providing the predeflection of the cantilever beam to maintain the constant gap between the electrodes which is the major problem in fabrication. The control system is carried out with digital modules and are implemented using SPARTAN II FPGA. Also an Analog circuit is designed on PCB and interfaced with FPGA.

Keywords: Biosensor, Microcantilever, Feedback system, FPGA.

1 Introduction

BioMEMS and devices have been used as biosensors. In the cantilever sensors, by stress sensing method, the bending of cantilever can be detected due to change in surface free energy. Since the stress detection method used with cantilevers is based upon a change in surface energy, it can be speculated that the DNA or protein layers are continuous over the area of gold-coated cantilevers, results in a uniform surface stress change, resulting in the cantilever bending [1]. Bending of the cantilever can be detected by various methods as optical reflection, piezoresistive, interferometric, piezoelectric, capacitive and electrical detection [2, 3, 4, 5]. From that various methods we are using electrical detection method.

The major problem related to fabrication is to achieve the gap between the cantilever and the electrode. To overcome this issue we are designing the Feedback controller for the system.

2 Cantilever Based Biosensor

Cantilever is used as nanomechanical Biosensor, microfabricated with the standard Si technology. There sizes are in micrometer or nm ranges.

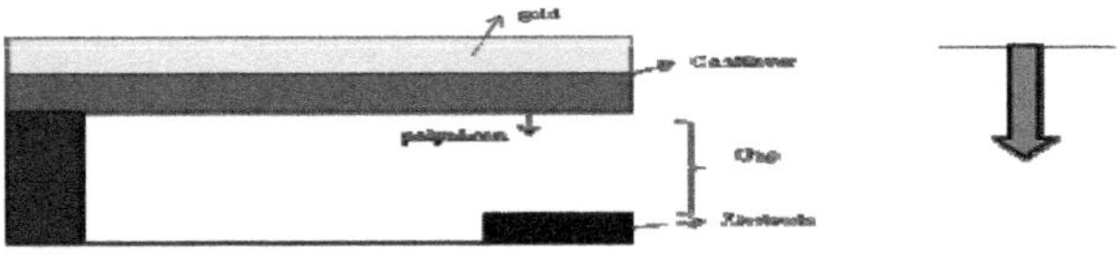

Fig. 1. Cantilever beam with biosensor

V.V. Das and N. Thankachan (Eds.): CIIT 2011, CCIS 250, pp. 421–423, 2011.

Figure 1 shows basic schematic diagram for cantilever based biosensor with electrode. When the deflection due to antibodies antigen interaction occurs, the cantilever beam touches the electrode, resulting in increasing current as the contact area between electrode and cantilever beam increases.

The surface stress is very small of the cantilever to the tune of a few tens of nanometer. The major issue for the device fabrication is the creation of gap between the electrodes of this order.

3 Design of Control System

The displacement of the cantilever is detected by an electrical method and the control voltage is applied to the cantilever by the feedback control system [6].

We will employ the control system for our sensor as in Figure 2.

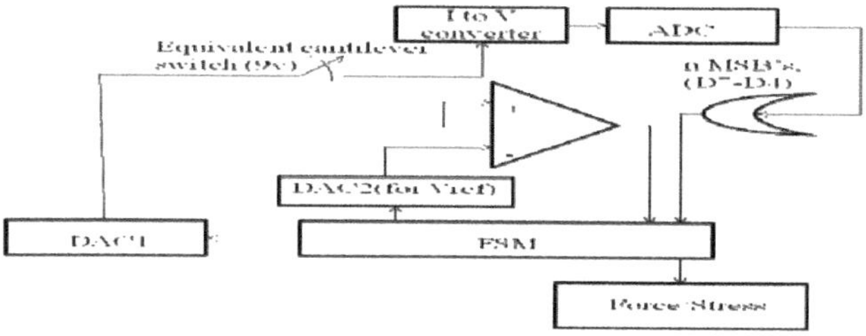

Fig. 2. Feedback Control System

3.1 Device Descriptions

FSM will supply the cantilever so as to make contact i.e. to close the sensor, it will increment the DAC1 input accordingly. This input value is then converted into analog voltage by DAC1 and applied to the cantilever sensor. Due to the applied voltage, the cantilever gets deflected and gap between cantilever and electrode get decreased. As the gap is not reduced to zero, current will be zero and the process gets repeated till the current starts flowing through the cantilever and the electrodes. When the current starts flowing through the cantilever sensor, that means the cantilever beam is attached to the electrode. The equivalent voltage will get generated through I to V convertor and is converted to digital value from ADC. The output of ADC given to OR gate will be equal to '1'given to FSM, will decrement the voltage at the cantilever. The cantilever will regain its original position, the current will reduce to zero. To avoid the noise we have to use MSB's of ADC output ignoring 2 or 3 LSB's.

When the current starts flowing through cantilever that voltage will decide the reference voltage for predeflection for cantilever sensor. Now, the predeflection reference voltage is applied to one input of comparator through the DAC2 for predeflection and second input will be the output of DAC1. Now, again we will increase the voltage across cantilever till we get the equivalent voltage of predeflection voltage value. So, we achieved the predeflection. FSM will switch to Force and will indicate that now we have to apply stress on cantilever beam by applying antibodies on it. As in Figure 2, we have used a switch of 9v for equivalent cantilever beam, which is decided by the coventor analysis for the system. In this analysis, the cantilever beam touches the electrode at the 9v and current flows through it.

4 Device Details

A digital circuit can be implemented using either DSP or FPGA platform for the above control system to minimize the above maintained problems. We will design an ASIC for feedback control system. We will use FPGA platform for digital circuit design. Also the PCB is designed to show practical implementation of the system. We will interface PCB with some digital modules to show the operation of the system. The PCB is designed using various IC's such as IC0808N for DAC and ADC, LF351 for I to V convertor, LM358 as comparator, IC74HCT541 octal buffer IC for level conversion for DAC and ADC.

Code is designed for FSM, Lookup table and OR gate. PCB is interfaced with FPGA by using 19 inputs from FPGA and giving 10 outputs to the FPGA.

5 Conclusion

We have designed Feedback control system for cantilever based biosensor. This method is used for all the readout methods where the gap between electrodes is very small. Our digital feedback control system will solve all the major fabrication issues. The gap between electrodes is adjusted by electrostatic actuation.

References

1. Abolfathi, N.: BioMEMS, Mechanical Engineering Department of North Dakota State University (April 2006)
2. Kale, N.S., Ramgopal Rao, V.: Design and Fabrication Issues in Affinity Cantilevers for BioMEMS Applications. Journal of Microelectromechanical Systems, 15(6) (December 2006)
3. Ansari, M.Z., Cho, C.: Design and Analysis of a high sensitive Microcantilever Biosensor for Biomedical Applications. In: 2008 International Conference on BioMedical Engineering and Informatics (2008)
4. Abdullah, M.F., Khuan, L.Y., Madzhi, N.K., Masrie, M., Ahmad, A.: Development of a Transduction Circuit for Piezoresistive MEMS Sensor for Biosensing. In: 2009 IEEE Symposium on Industrial Electronics and Applications (ISIEA 2009), Kuala Lumpur, Malaysia, October 4-6 (2009)
5. United states Patent, Patent no.: US 7,574,327 B2, Date of Patent: August 11 (2009)
6. Degen, C.L., Meier, U., Lin, Q., Hunkeler, A., Meiera, B.H.: Digital feedback controller for force microscope cantilevers. Review of Scientific Instruments 77, 043707 (2006)

Development of a Self-Tuning Fuzzy Controller through Relay Feedback Approach

A.K. Pal[1] and R.K. Mudi[2]

[1] Dept. of A.E.I.E, HIT, Kolkata, India
arabindakumarpal@gmail.com
[2] Dept. of I.E.E, Jadavpur University, Kolkata, India
rkmudi@yahoo.com

Abstract. A robust and simple self-tuning fuzzy PI controller (STFPIC) for high-order as well as non-linear dead-time processes is proposed. The output scaling factor (SF) of the STFPIC is updated by a fuzzy gain modifier (β), which is parameterized by the process ultimate gain (K_u) and ultimate period (P_u) obtained through relay feedback approach. Effectiveness of the propose STFPIC is demonstrated in terms of several performance indices.

1 Introduction

It has been reported that fuzzy logic controllers (FLCs) are suitable for high-order and non-linear systems and even with unknown structure [1]. But, the tuning of a large number of FLC parameters can be a difficult task and such problems may be eliminated by adopting self-tuning schemes [2-4]. Here, a self-tuning scheme is used to continuously update the controller gain with the help of fuzzy rules along with a process specific gain constant, which is obtained using relay feedback approach [5].

Generally a skilled operator always tries to manipulate the process input, usually by adjusting the controller gain based on the current process states. Following such an operator's policy, here, a simple but robust self-tuning scheme is proposed where an online fuzzy gain modifier β is determined by fuzzy rules defined on error (e) and change of error (Δe). The β is further augmented by a multiplicative factor α, which is directly related to the system dynamics and derived by relay feedback experiment. Thus, STFPIC uses process specific appropriate gain multiplicative factor instead of a fixed value (i.e., 3) used in [2, 3]. The propose STFPIC is used only 50 rules in place of 98 rules used in earlier works [2-4]. Robustness of the STFPIC is demonstrated for a wide range of processes with a considerable variation in dead-time. The rest of the paper is presented in the following three sections.

2 Development of Self-Tuning Fuzzy Logic Controller

The block diagram of STFPIC is shown in Fig.1. The output SF (G_u) is modified through β and α to implement the self-tuning mechanism.

V.V. Das and N. Thankachan (Eds.): CIIT 2011, CCIS 250, pp. 424–426, 2011.

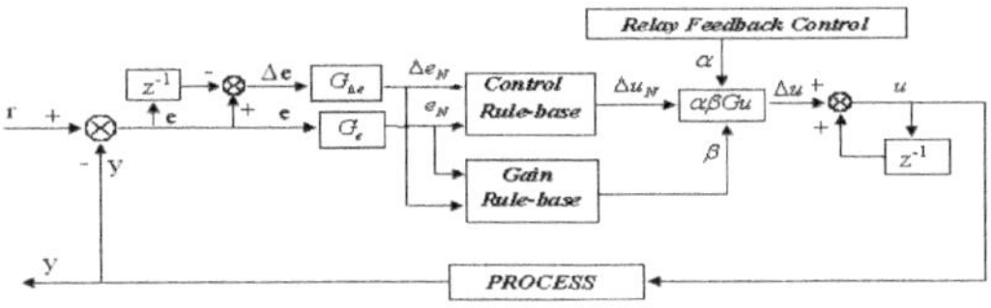

Fig. 1. Block Diagram of STFPIC

Fig. 2. MFs of E, ΔE and ΔU

Fig. 3. MFs of β

2.1 Fuzzy Membership Functions and Scaling Factor

Membership functions (MFs) for controller inputs e, Δe and output (Δu) are defined on the normalized domain [-1, 1], whereas the MFs of β is defined on [0, 1] as shown in Fig.2 and Fig.3. The term sets of e, Δe and Δu contain the same linguistic expressions for the linguistic values, i.e., $LE = L\Delta E = L\Delta U$ = {NB, NM, ZE, PM, PB} and represents the rule-base in Table1. The relationship between the SFs (G_e, $G_{\Delta e}$, G_u) and the input-output variables are: $e_N=G_e.e$; $\Delta e_N=G_{\Delta e}.\Delta e$; $\Delta u= (\alpha.\beta.G_u).\Delta u_N$.

Table 1. Fuzzy control rules for computation of Δu

Δe \ e	NB	NM	ZE	PM	PB
NB	NB	NB	NB	NM	ZE
NM	NB	NB	NM	ZE	PM
ZE	NB	NM	ZE	PM	PB
PM	NM	ZE	PM	PB	PB
PB	ZE	PM	PB	PB	PB

Table 2. Fuzzy rules for computation of β

Δe \ e	NB	NM	ZE	PM	PB
NB	VB	B	M	S	Z
NM	B	M	B	M	S
ZE	S	M	Z	M	S
PM	S	M	B	M	B
PB	Z	S	M	B	VB

2.2 Gain Updating Factor (β)

Membership Functions of β are mapped to the MFs {Z, S, M, B, VB} and represents the rule-base in Table2 in the form: *If e is E and Δe is ΔE Then β isβ*. This rule-base for β is designed in conjunction with Table 1. Basically the rule-base for β should be developed by the designer according to the type of response one wishes to achieve.

2.3 Computation of α

Earlier study [2, 3] reveals that a fixed value of α is considered irrespective of the type of system. Auto-tuner [5] is based on the observation that a feedback system in which output lags behind the input by –π radian will oscillate with a period P_u. For the computation of α, relay-feedback test [5] is performed on the individual processes to find out K_u and P_u and thus establish a relation: $\alpha = (K_u.P_u)/3$. From the same test Ziegler-Nichols (ZN) tuned parameters (Kc and Ti) of the PI controller (ZNPIC) are obtained.

3 Results

The performance of STFPIC is compared with other controllers for marginally stable system and non-linear system with different values of dead time. To establish the robustness of the proposed scheme, the same MFs (Fig.2 and Fig.3) and rule-bases (Table1 and Table2) for non-linear as well as marginally stable systems are used.

Marginally stable system: $G(s) = e^{-Ls} / (s^2 + s)$ (1)

The performance indices of process (1) are listed in Table3. From Fig.4 and Table3 it is observed that in each case the proposed controller outperforms the others.

Non-linear process: $d^2y/dt^2 + dy/dt + 0.25y^2 = u(t-L)$ (2)

Performance for this non-linear process (2) observed through Fig.5 and Table4 reveals that in this case also STFPIC exhibits superior performance.

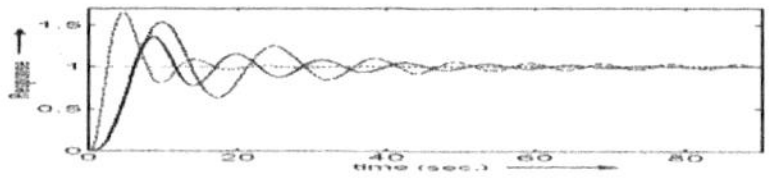

Fig. 4. Responses of process (1) with L=0.3 (PI-dotted, FPIC-dashed and STFPIC-solid)

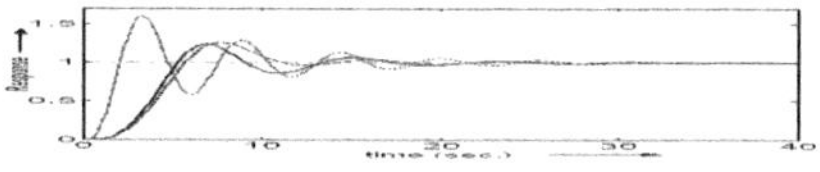

Fig. 5. Responses of process (2) with L=0.3 (PI-dotted, FPIC-dashed and STFPIC-solid)

Table 3. Performance of process (1)

L	Gu\Guα	FLC	%OS	t_r (s)	t_s (s)	ITAE	IAE	ISE
0.1	0.016	FPIC	44.62	6.1	41.2	87.15	8.1	3.71
	0.016α	STFPIC	27.43	6.0	32.9	46.15	5.89	2.98
0.2	0.016	FPIC	48.81	6.1	48	121.66	9.13	4.00
	0.016α	STFPIC	31.61	6.0	38.8	67.42	6.7	3.17
0.3	0.016	FPIC	53.64	6.1	82.9	187.18	10.89	4.49
	0.016α	STFPIC	36.21	6.0	54.3	100.33	7.65	3.37

Table 4. Performance of process (2)

L	Gu\Guα	FLC	%OS	t_r (s)	t_s (s)	ITAE	IAE	ISE
0.1	0.02	FPIC	22.66	5.5	12.5	15.31	4.2	2.61
	0.02α	STFPIC	19.78	5.1	16.0	14.33	3.97	2.42
0.2	0.02	FPIC	24.27	5.5	16.4	18.24	4.39	2.69
	0.02α	STFPIC	21.67	5.1	16.5	16.9	4.20	2.51
0.3	0.02	FPIC	25.98	5.6	17.0	23.87	4.65	2.78
	0.02α	STFPIC	23.86	5.2	20.2	20.48	4.48	2.61

4 Conclusion

The output SF of the STFPIC is updated online based on the process trend as well as the dynamics of the system. STFPIC with reduced rules has shown significantly improved performance compared to its conventional fuzzy and non-fuzzy controllers for high-order and non-linear systems with varying dead-time.

References

1. Sugeno, M.: Industrial Applications of Fuzzy Control. Elsevier, The Netherlands (1985)
2. Mudi, R.K., Pal, N.R.: A robust self-tuning scheme for PI and PD type fuzzy controllers. IEEE Trans. on Fuz. Sys. 7 (1999)
3. Pal, N.R., Mudi, R.K., Pal, K., Patranabis, D.: Rule Extraction through Exploratory Data Analysis for Self-Tuning Fuzzy Controller. Int. J. of Fuz. Sys. 6, 71–80 (2004)
4. Pal, A.K., Mudi, R.K.: Self-Tuning Fuzzy PI controller and its application to HVAC system. IJCC (US) 6 (2008)
5. Åström, K.J., Hägglund, T.: Automatic Tuning of Simple Regulators with Specifications on Phase and Amplitude Margins. Automatica 20, 645–651 (1984)

A GA Based Dynamic Bandwidth Allocation Scheme for Local Area Networks

Prashant Saxena and J.P. Misra

Birla Institute of Technology & Science, Pilani, Rajasthan - India
prashantsaxena@live.in, jpm@bits-pilani.ac.in

Abstract. With the ever increasing rate of internet traffic & limited bandwidth availability to support the same, efficient bandwidth allocation is becoming an indispensible requirement for wired & wireless local area networks. Our work proposes a novel scheme to allocate bandwidth amongst participating routers/switches within the IP network using Genetic algorithm framework. Proposed allocation scheme can be easily applied on wireless or wired networks. Simulation results show the effectiveness of the new bandwidth allocation mechanism.

Keywords: Modified genetic algorithm, Super chromosome, Dynamic bandwidth allocation, Request approval rate (RAR), Context aware mutation.

1 Introduction

Fair allocation of bandwidth among multiple users is an intuitively desirable property on Local Area Networks (LANs). A network with multiple intermediate routers starts with allotting a base bandwidth to all its participating routers, insuring that initial Quality of Service (QoS) assured to each user is met. As the time progresses, there is a possibility that a router/switch may be left with some free bandwidth after fully satisfying QoS requirement of its associated users. On flipside, a router may be overloaded, and hence, may require more bandwidth to serve its users. In such cases, lending and borrowing of bandwidth can increase overall QoS of the system. In our work, we try to redistribute the unused bandwidth amongst the participating routers by using modified genetic algorithm techniques. The rest of the paper is organized as follows. Section 2 describes our proposed GA-based allocation model. Simulation experiments are elaborated in Section 3. Section 4 presents a comparative analysis with standard Genetic algorithm techniques. Section 5 summarizes our work.

2 The Proposed Model

Our proposed model tries to allocate bandwidth between four intermediate routers which are connected to an edge router. The idea is to optimize overall Request Approval Rate (RAR) of the system using Genetic algorithm framework. RAR measures the ability of a router to meet the requests from its users. Each of the four intermediate routers serves users with different QoS requirements. Based on the

V.V. Das and N. Thankachan (Eds.): CIIT 2011, CCIS 250, pp. 427–432, 2011.

requirements, each router is statically assigned a base bandwidth. As the time progresses & the bandwidth is re-distributed, the proposed solution insures that the system returns to its base bandwidth distribution after a fixed time interval. Now, a router may operate in one of the following states.

State 1: A router has exactly the same bandwidth which is demanded by its users and hence it is able to utilize its allotted bandwidth completely.
State 2: A router is left with some free bandwidth after serving all its users.
State 3: A router is overloaded, and hence is unable to serve all the requests from its users.

A router in state 2 may dynamically lend its unused bandwidth to routers in state 3, and thereby increase the overall Request approval Rate (RAR) of system without significantly affecting the QoS requirements on individual routers.

2.1 Encoding Scheme

A chromosome defines one of the possible solutions to the problem. Data in chromosomes is stored in Genes. Each participating router is represented by a chromosome structure consisting of 9 genes. The detailed encoding scheme for a router R_i is shown below.

Gene 1: Number of active users
Gene 2: Avg. packet generation rate per user
Gene 3: Free Bandwidth
Gene 4: Bandwidth lended to R_{i+1}
Gene 5: Bandwidth lended to R_{i+2}
Gene 6: Bandwidth lended to R_{i+3}
Gene 7: Bandwidth borrowed from R_{i+1}
Gene 8: Bandwidth borrowed from R_{i+2}
Gene 9: Bandwidth borrowed from R_{i+3}

Lending and borrowing of bandwidth takes place based on pre-calculated fixed bandwidth quantum. A sample chromosome used in simulations is shown in figure 1. A set of four chromosomes, one for each participating router, when put together, forms a super chromosome as shown in Figure 2.A Super chromosome represents a possible solution to bandwidth allocation problem. Our method applies GA techniques on super chromosomes to obtain efficient allocation of bandwidth on each router.

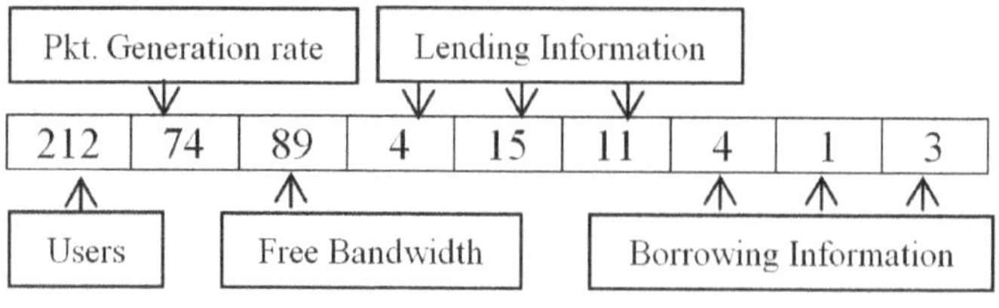

Fig. 1. Chromosome for Router R_1

117	53	93	16	17	0	2	4	3
136	61	88	13	1	8	20	17	6
212	74	89	4	15	11	4	1	3
243	83	84	2	11	8	4	20	9

Fig. 2. Super Chromosome

2.2 Proposed Optimization Scheme

Following symbols are used in formulating fitness function:
AB: Available Bandwidth
ABR: Aggregate Bandwidth Requested
FB: Free Bandwidth
B_i: Borrowed Bandwidth from router i
BB: Total Borrowed Bandwidth
U: Number of Users
P: Average packet generation rate per user
S: Average packet size
Request approval rate is defined as:

$$RaR = \frac{\mathrm{AB}}{\mathrm{ABR}} \quad (1)$$

For each router, the available bandwidth is the sum of its free bandwidth and the bandwidth which it has borrowed from other routers, i.e.

$$BB = \sum Bi \quad (2)$$

$$\mathrm{AB} = \mathrm{FB} + \mathrm{BB} \quad (3)$$

Aggregate bandwidth requested can be calculated using

$$\mathrm{ABR} = \mathrm{U} * \mathrm{P} * \mathrm{S} \quad (4)$$

Using above equations, we get

$$\hat{RaR} = \frac{\mathrm{FB+BB}}{\mathrm{U*P*S}} \quad (5)$$

Fitness value of chromosome is defined as

$$Fitness\ Value = \begin{cases} RaR, & if\ RaR \le 1 \\ 1, & Otherwise \end{cases} \quad (6)$$

Fitness value of super chromosome is defined as mean fitness value of chromosomes present in it.

2.3 Modules Used

All operations are performed on super chromosomes.

Selection Module: Selection Module prunes the current generation of chromosomes by eliminating the unfit ones. Chromosomes with low fitness value are eliminated from the mating pool.

Mutation Module: Mutation Module changes data stored in chromosomes. In standard GA techniques, this operation changes gene value to a new randomly selected value. But, such a change may bring inconsistency in our system by increasing/decreasing overall available bandwidth of the system. To mitigate this problem, we propose Context Aware Mutation step. In this scheme, a chromosome with access bandwidth may lend its bandwidth to others seeking bandwidth within the same super chromosome. Hence, instead of random shift in values, this scheme logically changes the value of genes within the super chromosomes. Lending & Borrowing again takes place in fixed size bandwidth chunks. Figure 3 gives illustrates this concept.

117	53	**93**	16	17	0	2	4	3
243	83	84	2	11	8	**4**	20	9

(a)

117	53	**83**	16	17	0	2	4	3
243	83	84	2	11	8	**14**	20	9

(b)

Fig. 3. Context aware Mutation, (a) Before mutation, (b) After Mutation

Crossover Module: This module performs crossover on two super chromosomes, exchanging their lending & borrowing information to generate two new super chromosomes. A sample crossover between two super chromosomes with 5 genes is shown in figure 4.

Superchromosome 1

117	53	2	4	3
136	61	20	17	6
212	74	4	1	3
243	83	4	20	9

Superchromosome 2

117	**53**	7	9	0
136	**61**	**13**	**6**	**12**
212	**74**	**7**	**5**	**2**
243	**83**	**18**	**13**	**4**

⟹

Offspring 1

117	53	**7**	**9**	**0**
136	61	**13**	**6**	**12**
212	74	**7**	**5**	**2**
243	83	**18**	**13**	**4**

Offspring 2

117	**53**	2	4	3
136	**61**	20	17	6
212	**74**	4	1	3
243	**83**	4	20	9

Fig. 4. Crossover in action

2.4 Algorithm

Following algorithm is used in the model.

1. Set Simulation parameters (Packet size, Channel Bandwidth, Maximum no. of Chromosomes allowed, maximum lending allowed, Maximum no. of mutations & crossover allowed in a generation, no. of Generations)
2. Generate Random population of chromosomes
3. Set Generation No = 1
4. Repeat step 5 to 8 till Generation No = Max Generation

5. Perform selection()
6. Perform mutation()
7. Perform crossover()
8. Generation No = Generation No +1

3 Simulation Experiments

The proposed model is tested against three loading conditions, i.e. under loaded, fairly loaded & over loaded system. In all simulations, initial population consists of 32 super chromosomes. Number of crossover & mutations in each generation is set to 20.Packet size is set to 100 bytes. Simulation algorithm is coded in C.

Case I) Over Loaded system
Channel Bandwidth = 1000 Bytes

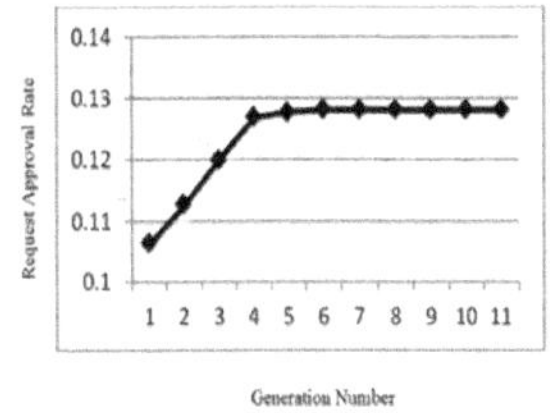

Case II) Moderately Loaded system
Channel Bandwidth = 5000 Bytes

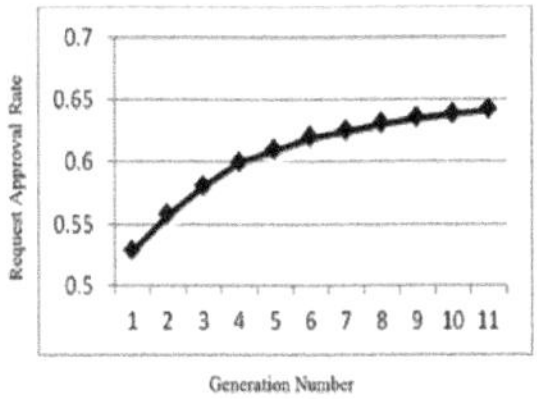

Case III) Under Loaded system
Channel Bandwidth = 10000 Bytes

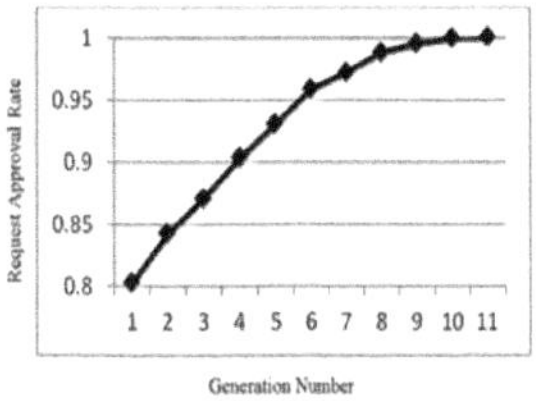

4 Comparative Analyses

In this section, we compare our modified GA based allocation scheme against conventional GA based methods.

Following abbreviations are used in Graphs
WDM : Without mutation
WM : With context aware mutation

Case I) Over Loaded system
Channel Bandwidth = 1000 Bytes

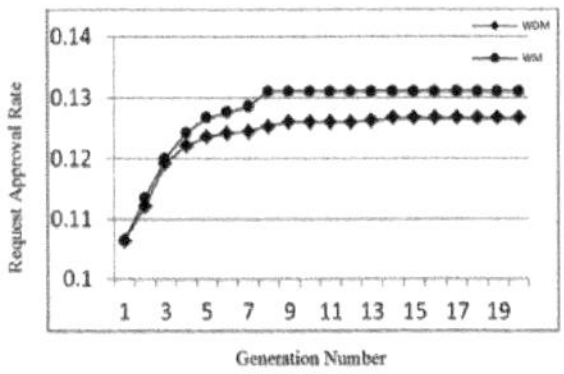

Case II) Moderately Loaded system
Channel Bandwidth = 5000 Bytes

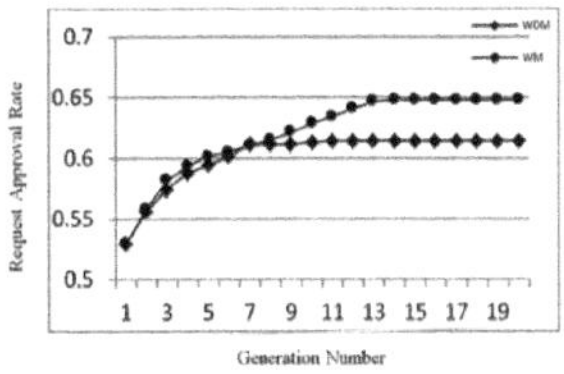

Case III) Under Loaded system
Channel Bandwidth = 10000 Bytes

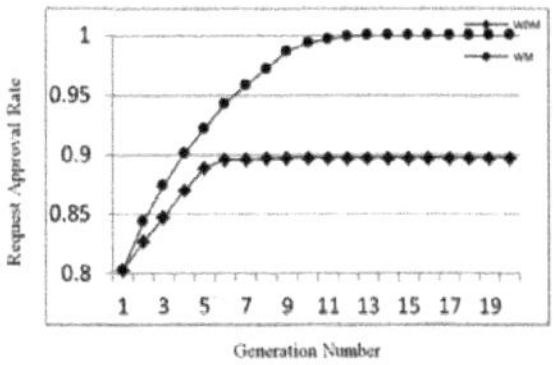

5 Observations and Conclusions

It can be concluded from the simulation results that the algorithm is able to generate a stable and optimal solution. In over loaded system, we observe that there is no significant increase in RaR after few generations. This is attributed to the fact that all the routers are in over loaded state, and hence no significant lending opportunity exists among the routers. On the contrary, significant improvement in RaR is obtained for moderately loaded and under loaded systems. RaR of under loaded system reaches its maximum value of 1. From the comparative analysis, it can be concluded that our modified GA based allocation algorithm promises a better solution to the dynamic bandwidth allocation problem than a conventional GA based method. Using context aware mutation step, the convergence rate to attain an acceptable solution is increased, and hence, optimal solution is obtained in lesser number of generations. The performance results strongly support the benefits of our algorithm to better support bandwidth redistribution problem without sacrificing on efficiency of the system as a whole. Even though we have focused on redistributing bandwidth on LAN's, our algorithm can be readily adapted for wireless, cellular & other networks.

References

1. Anbar, M., Vidyarthi, D.P.: GA-Based on Demand Bandwidth Reservation for Real-Time Traffic in Cellular IP Network. In: Fifth International Joint Conference on INC, IMS and IDC, NCM 2009, August 25-27, pp. 1935–1942 (2009), doi:10.1109/NCM.2009.280
2. Cooklev, T.: Dynamic bandwidth allocation and channel coding in providing QoS for wireless local area networks. In: 10th International Conference on Telecommunications, ICT 2003, Febuary 23-March 1, vol. 2, pp. 1388–1393 (2003), doi:10.1109/ICTEL.2003.1191637
3. Khanbary, L.M.O., Vidyarthi, D.P.: A GA-Based Effective Fault-Tolerant Model for Channel Allocation in Mobile Computing. IEEE Transactions on Vehicular Technology 57(3), 1823–1833 (2008)
4. Mitchell, M.: An Introduction to Genetic Algorithms, 1st edn., pp. 1–87. The MIT Press, Cambridge (1998)

A Simple and Improved Sensorless Control Technique for PMBLDC Motor

E. Kaliappan, C. Chellamuthu, and B. Balashankar

EEE, RMK Engineering College, Kavaraipettai, Tamilnadu, India

Abstract. This paper describes a simple and improved sensorless control technique for position and speed control of PMBLDC motor used in simple fan applications. In the proposed technique, instead of using the zero crossing time, the BEMF voltage at the middle of commutation period is used as a control variable, without using the motor neutral voltage, the BEMF of the floating phase which is detected during the PWM off time is used. The validity of this sensorless technique is confirmed by simulation and experimental results.

Keywords: PMBLDC motor, sensorless control, BEMF zero crossing.

1 Introduction

PMBLDC motors require an inverter and the rotor position information to perform electronic commutation as they are not self-commutating motorsA number of sensorless techniques have been developed for PMBLDC motor.[1][2] Some of the techniques available in the literature are based on position sensing using back EMF zero detection crossing or terminal voltage sensing, sensing from third harmonics of the motional EMF, back EMF integration, position sensing using induction variation, position sensing based on flux linkage variation, Extended Kalman filter estimation and detecting the freewheeling diode conduction in open phase[3][4].This paper presents a simple and improved sensorless control of PMBLDC motor to eliminate the above mentioned problems.

2 Proposed Simple and Improved Sensorless Technique

The following set of equation is valid for the presented topology, the voltage equations are expressed as

$$V_a = RI_a + (L - M)\frac{dI_a}{dt} + E_a \tag{1}$$

$$V_b = RI_b + (L - M)\frac{dI_b}{dt} + E_b \tag{2}$$

$$V_c = RI_c + (L - M)\frac{dI_c}{dt} + E_c \tag{3}$$

In this proposed technique using the detected back EMF from the terminal voltages, a virtual hall signal is produced. Using the comparator the back EMF's are compared to produce the position of the rotor. If a 60° period of conduction is given, it is relatively

V.V. Das and N. Thankachan (Eds.): CIIT 2011, CCIS 250, pp. 433–435, 2011.

easier for making a commutation. Then it resembles a hall signal which produces lesser loss with greater efficiency.

3 Simulated and Experimental Results

For the simulation of the proposed technique, the inverter and switching logic is implemented as a S-function that takes in the value of DC source voltage and the firing sequence from controller block. The firing signal include a chopping option that is the current in the two energized phases can be turned ON and OFF at any time during 60 degree interval. This feature is used in PWM control.

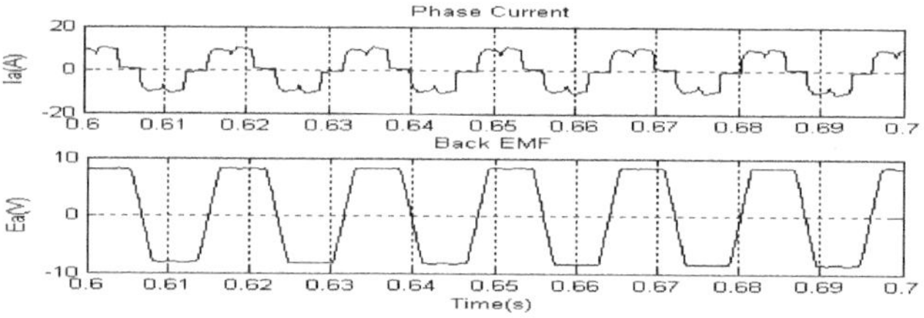

Fig. 1. Phase current and Back EMF waveform

The proposed technique is implemented using DSP F28335. Once the motor is turned on, the controller takes 0.85 secs for rotor positioning. Once it gets the rotor information, it starts the motor at 1.15 secs and subsequently the running mode is attained by 1.3 seconds. The phase current and speed of the motor on loaded condition is shown in Fig. 1, load is suddenly applied to the motor during the sensorless mode at 2 secs to test the dynamic programming of the proposed system. The motor continues to run sensorless even after sudden application of load is evident from Fig 2.

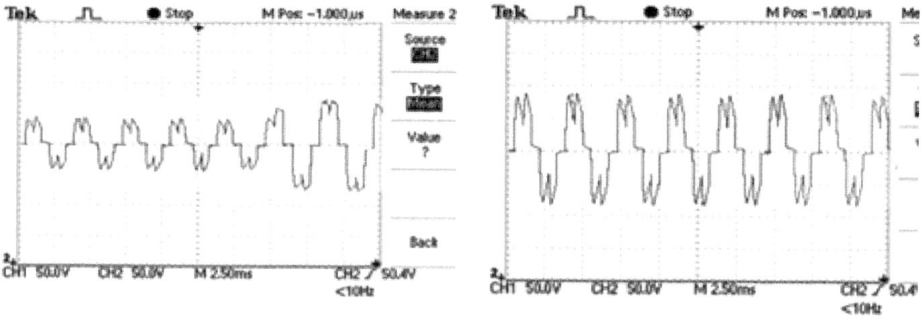

Fig. 2. Phase current under no load and Loaded conditions (Experimental)

The Zero Crossing information is obtained during the rising edge of the PWM i.e at the beginning of the PWM and also the end of the "off time" will latch the comparator output to capture the zero crossing information as shown in Fig.3. The motor terminal voltage is directly fed into the microcontroller (DSP) through current limit resistors. The commutation algorithm used is the standard BLDC motor control algorithm. Commutation happens 30 electrical degrees after the back EMF Zero Crossing. The ratings of the motor is: poles: 8, per phase resistance:0.6Ω, inductance:0.42mH,back emf constant:0.0002kg-m^2.

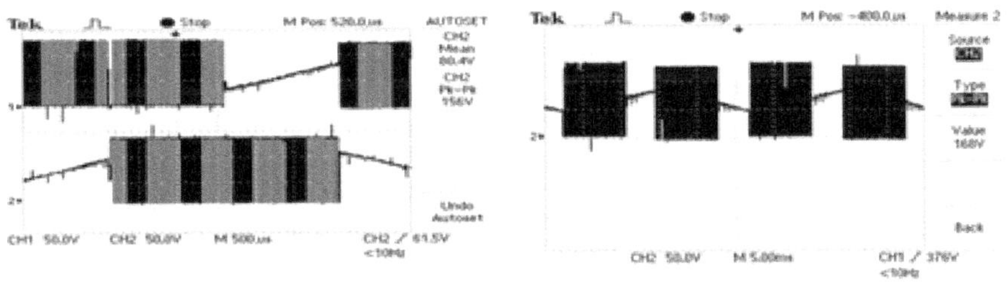

Fig. 3. Phase A terminal voltage with switching function at high speed and at lower speed (Experimental)

4 Conclusion

In the proposed sensorless technique, without using the motor neutral voltage, the BEMF of the floating phase which is detected during the PWM off time is used. Hence the proposed technique is very effective. This method can be used in home appliances like air conditioners, reciprocating compressor and refrigerators.

References

1. Acarnely, P.P., Watson, J.F.: Review of position – sensorless operation of brushless Permanent magnet machines. IEEE Trans. Ind. Electron. 53(2), 352–362 (2006)
2. Lai, Y.-S., Lin, Y.-K.: Novel Back-EMF Detection Technique of Brushless DC Motor Drives for Wide Range Control Without Using Current and Position Sensors. IEEE Transactions On Power Electronics 23(2), 934–940 (2008)
3. Damodharan, P., Vasudevan, K.: Sensorless Brushless DC motor drive based on the zero crossing detection of back emf from the line voltage difference. IEEE Trans. Engy. Conv. 25(3), 661–668 (2010)
4. Lin, C.-T., Hung, C.-W., Liu, C.-W.: Position Sensorless Control for Four-switch Three-Phase Brushless DC Motor Drives. IEEE Trans. On Power Electron. 23(1) (January 2006)

Evaluation of Electromagnetic Compatibility for GPS VTS Transmitter Board

Shreenivas Jog[1], Mukul Sutaone[1], and Vishweshwar Badawe[2]

[1] Department of E and TC, College of Engineering Pune, India
[2] BEPL, Pune, India
srjog_etc@rediffmail.com

Abstract. The main objective of this research proposal is to develop the strategic GPS based Vehicle Tracking System intended to be used in the stringent environment. The Electromagnetic compatibility for Global Positioning System (GPS) based Vehicle Tracking System (VTS) Transmitter Board has been evaluated. GPS VTS Transmitter Board was enclosed in specially designed EMI Enclosure. Radiated Emission (RE) for this board was measured for frequency range 100 KHz to 2.5 GHz. Conducted Emission (CE) for power supply lines of the board was also measured for frequency range150 KHz to 108 MHz. The tests were conducted in a national EMI test laboratory. The results of Radiated and Conducted Emission tests were compared with EMI/EMC test Standard MIL-STD-461E.

Keywords: GPS, VTS, RE, CE, Electromagnetic Compatibility.

1 Introduction

The Vehicle Tracking system, a module selected for research work has GPS VTS transmitter and receiver boards. GPS VTS transmitter board consists of GPS Module, GSM and Micro controller. The GPS module has been used to receive the information from the GPS satellites and to generate a 64Kbps data string of Latitude, Longitude, Date, Time, etc. [1] Micro controller and GSM Modem have been used to process this data string for further communication with remote VTS receiver by using SMS activation. VTS receiver board has GSM Modem and Microcontroller. The GSM Modem and Microcontroller in VTS receiver have been used to display this data on LCD or link it with PC / Laptop with local / Google Maps. The GPS VTS Transmitter Board with specially designed HE-30 Aluminum EMI enclosure is intended to be used for positioning and localization of vehicles in extreme climatic and dense EMI environment. [2]

2 GPS VTS System Compatibility Requirements

The proposed GPS VTS system has to be ruggedised /robust and it should be compatible with EMI/EMC standard MIL-STD-461E and Environmental standard MIL-STD-810. Electromagnetic Compatibility can be achieved by using techniques

V.V. Das and N. Thankachan (Eds.): CIIT 2011, CCIS 250, pp. 436–439, 2011.

like shielding, guarding, grounding, balancing, filtering, orientation and isolation. [3] Some of the techniques have been implemented in this system. The GPS VTS Transmitter board was enclosed in HE-30 Aluminum EMI Enclosure. This enclosure was sealed properly by using silver filled elastomer gaskets and Copper foil to cover openings and small gaps. [2] Shielded cables were used for antenna and power supply input connections.

The performance of this GPS VTS board shall be evaluated for different EMI/EMC tests and environmental tests like High and Low temperature, Humidity, Vibration, Bump, Shock, Corrosion, etc.

3 Conducted and Radiated Emission Measurement Test Set Ups

The Conducted and Radiated emission (CE and RE) measurement tests were conducted on GPS VTS Transmitter board with EMI Enclosure at Automotive Research Association of India (ARAI), Pune, a national EMI test laboratory. The tests were conducted in a shielded EMI test chamber. Fig.1 and Fig.2 show test set ups for Conducted and Radiated Emission respectively. [4], [5] Line Impedance Stabilization Network (LISN) was used in both the set ups for isolation of power supply noise. The graphs of Radiated and conducted Emission have been plotted in two different colours. The blue colour indicating peak values and green colour indicating average values of level measured.

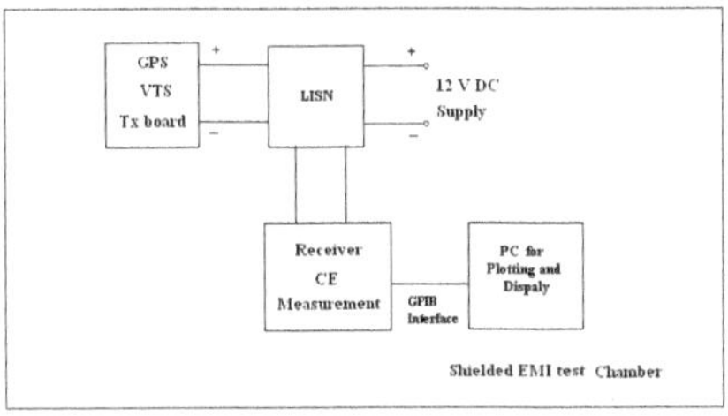

Fig. 1. CE measurement test set up

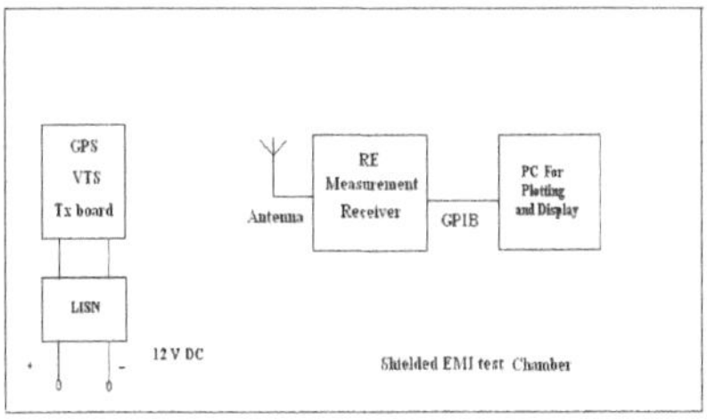

Fig. 2. RE measurement test set up

CE measurement Test Setup:-

Frequency Range:	150 kHz – 108 MHz
Receiver:	ESU 8
Hardware Setup:	CE_CISPR25_Voltage Method [5]

RE Measurement Test setup:-

Frequency Range:	25 MHz – 200 MHz
Antenna:	Biconical Antenna
Frequency Range:	200 MHz – 3 GHz
Antenna:	Log Periodic Antenna
Frequency Range:	150 kHz – 30 MHz
Antenna:	Monopole antenna
Receiver:	ESU 8 [in all frequencies]
Hardware Setup:	EMI radiated\RE_CISPR25 [5]

4 Observations / Results

The results of Radiated Emission level measured from GPS VTS Transmitter board with EMI Enclosure were compared with MIL-STD-461E standard for ground applications. The Radiated Emission levels in horizontal and vertical direction in the frequency range 30 MHz to 200 MHz (Figure 3 and Figure 4) were found to be within specified level of the standard. The Radiated Emission level between frequency range 200MHz to 2.5 GHz was also found to be within specified level and results have been published. [2] The RE level in frequency range 150 KHz to 30 MHz (Fig. 5) was just at the border of specified limits. This level may be reduced by using suitable magnetic shielding at these frequencies. [6]

Fig. 6 shows plot for Conducted Emission between the frequency range 150 KHz to 108 MHz. As compared to MIL-STD-461E, the emission level at frequency around 600 KHz was found to be slightly more than specified limits. The level can be reduced by using suitable RFI Filter in supply lines and improving magnetic shielding for frequencies up to 1 MHz. [6] Fig. 7 and Fig. 8 show specified limits for Radiated

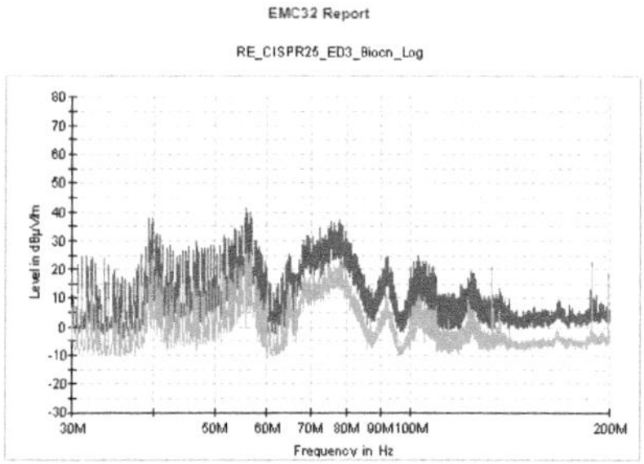

Fig. 3. Radiated Emission test (Horizontal direction), Frequency range-30 MHz to 200MHz

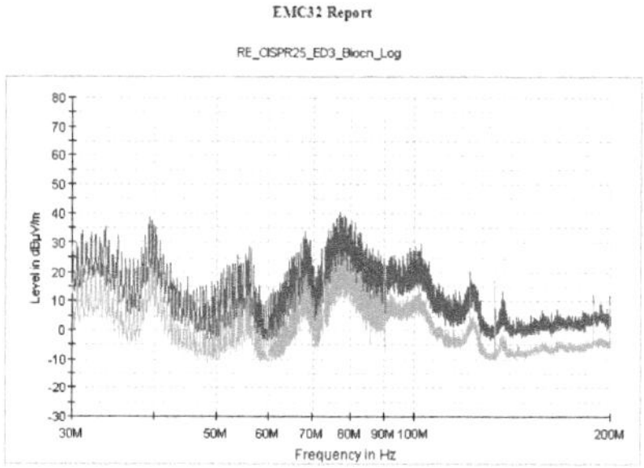

Fig. 4. Radiated Emission Test (Vertical direction), Frequency range- 30MHz to 200MHz

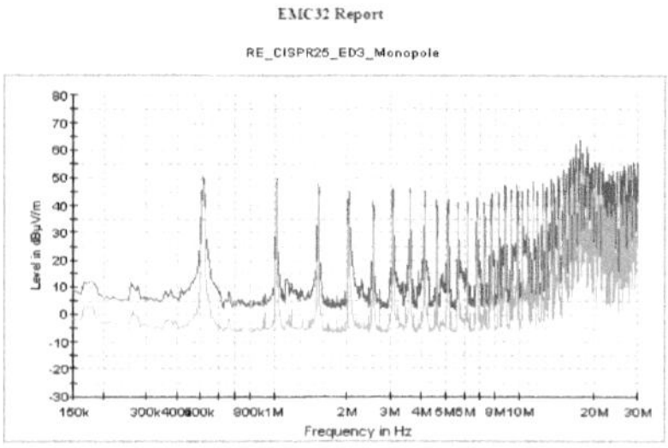

Fig. 5. Radiated Emission test (Horizontal direction), Frequency range-150 KHz to 30MHz

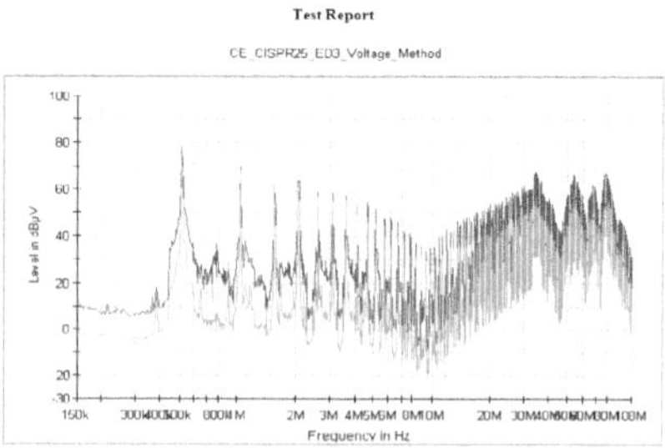

Fig. 6. Conducted Emission, Frequency range -150 KHz to 108 MHz

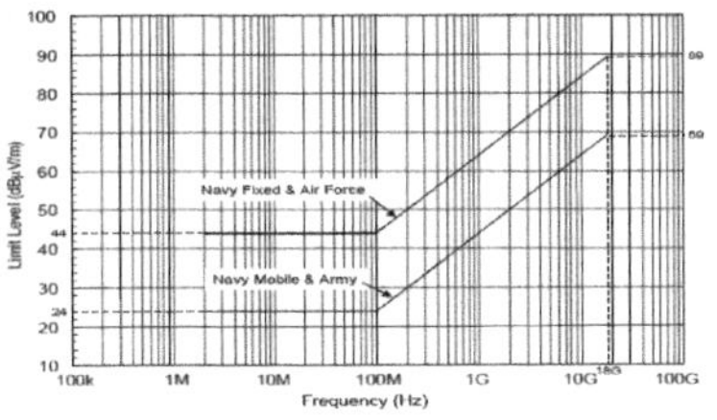

Fig. 7. MIL-STD-461E Radiated Emission limits [7]

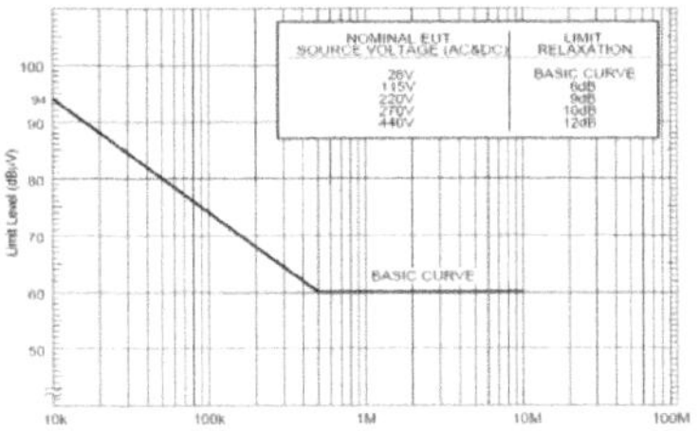

Fig. 8. MIL-STD-461E Conducted Emission limits [7]

and Conducted Emissions as per MIL-STD-461E. [7] The GPS VTS Board with EMI enclosure expected to meet Radiated and Conducted Susceptibility tests also as per MIL-STD-461E.

5 Conclusion

GPS VTS Transmitter board with EMI enclosure could meet the compatibility requirements for Radiated Emission limits as per MIL-STD-461E. However, the radiation level between frequency range 150 KHz to 30 MHz was found to be just at the border of the specified limits and it can be reduced by effective magnetic shielding. Conducted Emission level was found to be slightly above the specified limits at around 600 KHz. It can be reduced by using RFI Filter in power supply section and suitable magnetic shielding.

Acknowledgments. The authors would like to sincerely thank Automotive Research Association of India (ARAI), Padmashree Dr.D.Y.Patil Institute of Engineering Technology and University of Pune for their valuable support to this research work.

References

1. Datasheet and Technical Manual, Fastrax GPS IT03, `http://www.fastraxgps.com`
2. Jog, S., Sutaone, M.S., Badave, V.: HE-30 Aluminum Ruggedised EMI Enclosure for GPS based Vehicle Tracking System. In: IEEE International Conference on Wireless Communication, Vehicular Technology and Aerospace & Electronic System Technology (Wireless VITAE 2011), Chennai, India, February 28-March 3, pp. 1–5 (2011)
3. Boxleitner, W.: Electrostatic Discharge and Electronic Equipment: A Practical Guide for designing to prevent ESD Problems. Wiley- IEEE Press (October 1999)
4. Ott, H.W.: Noise Reduction Techniques in Electronic Systems. Wiley Interscience Publications (1987)
5. EMI/EMC test laboratory document: Test set up for Radiated and Conducted measurement, Automotive Research Association of India (ARAI), Pune, India.
6. Williams, T.: EMC for product design, 4th edn. Newness Publications (2007)
7. EMI/EMC Standard MIL-STD-461E, Revised (August 1999)

Development of Single Phase Z-Source Inverter Using ARM7 for Speed Control of Induction Motor

Pankaj Zope, K.S. Patil, and Prashant Sonare

JNU Jodhpur, India
phzope@gmail.com, prashantsonare@yahoo.co.in

Abstract. In this paper the performance of single-phase induction motor is studied with the control of single phase Z-source inverter using ARM-7. The LPC-2148 ARM-7 microcontroller senses the speed's feedback signal and consequently provides the pulse width modulated (PWM) signal that sets the gate voltage of the inverter, which in turn provides the required voltage for the desired speed. The proposed drive system is simulated using Matlab/Simulink. The simulation results were compared with the experimental results.

Keywords: LPC-2148 ARM-7 Microcontroller, Pulse width modulation, Single phase induction motor, Z-source inverter.

1 Introduction

The single-phase induction motors have been widely employed in low or middle power level fields. The speed control of such motors can be achieved by controlling the applied voltage on the motor by the use of power electronic devices [1]. The traditional voltage source inverter (VSI) and current source inverter (CSI) inverters are used for power control of single phase induction motor [2]. The use of microcontrollers, DSP processors [3],[4],[5],[6] has become very common to overcome the problem like, lagging power factor at the input side, delay in the firing angle, and high lower-order harmonic contents in both supply and load voltages and currents, over the past decade. ARM7TDMI-s LPC-2148 microcontroller has been chosen for implementation. It is used to sense and control the motor speed by supplying pulse width modulated signal for the operation of Z-source inverter. This paper describes the Matlab simulation and experimental analysis of single phase induction motor using Z-source inverter.

2 Methodologies

The block diagram of single phase Z-source inverter using ARM7 for speed control of induction motor is shown in figure 1. It contains following main section Z-source inverter, ARM 7 Processor, Driver section, Triggering circuit, speed control circuit. The Z-source inverter [7] is utilized to realize inversion and boost function. The Z-source inverter design and control is described in [8],[9]. The ARM 7 LPC-2148 microcontroller has been programmed to vary the PWM signal of the inverter

V.V. Das and N. Thankachan (Eds.): CIIT 2011, CCIS 250, pp. 440–443, 2011.

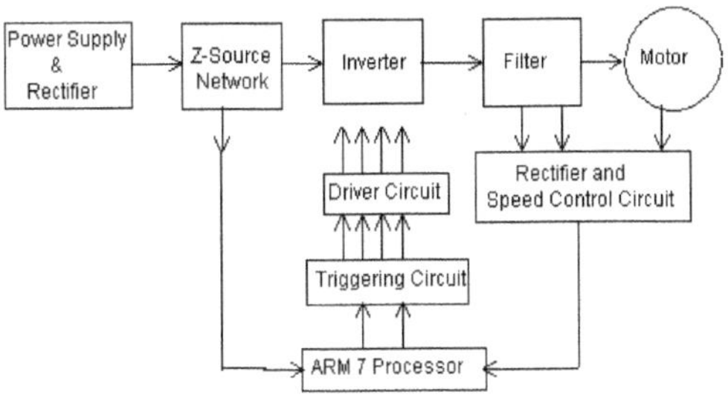

Fig. 1. Block diagram of the system

and converts it to ac power to feed the motor under control. Figure 1 shows the hardware circuit implemented for this work.

3 Model and Simulation of the System

The single phase Z-source inverter Matlab / Simulink model for speed control of induction motor is shown in figure 2, the design of Z-source network for simple boost control technique is described in [7], [8], [9]. The rectified DC pulsating signal is applied to the Z-source inverter then the output of the inverter is fed to the auxiliary winding and the motor's main winding is directly connected to the 110 V utility supplies. The reference value of the magnitude and phase of voltage applied to the auxiliary winding are computed by the reference voltage block. The voltage control loop uses a proportional-integral-derivative (PID) controller.

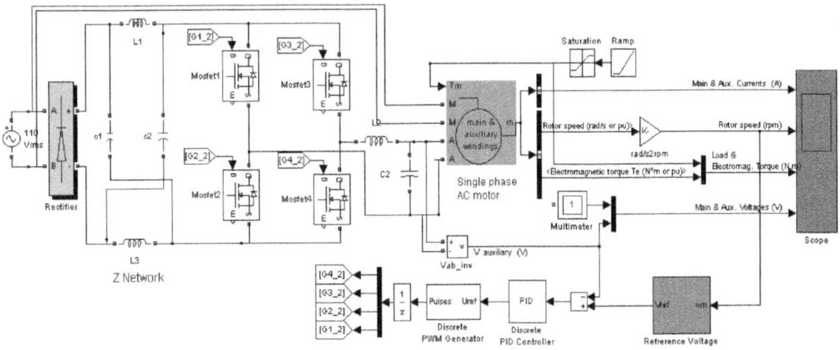

Fig. 2. Matlab/ Simulink model

The Matlab/ Simulink model is tested under input voltage *Vin = 110 Vrms,* shoot through duty ratio *D0 = 0.218,* and modulation index *M = 0.9, Vo = 210V.* The main and auxiliary winding voltages simulation and implementation response of single - phase induction motor is described in Figure 3 and 4.

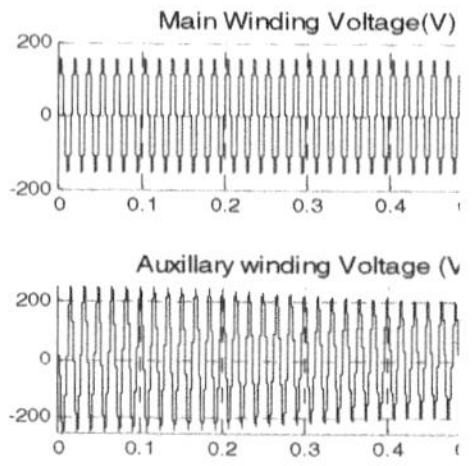

Fig. 3. Main and auxiliary winding voltage simulation result

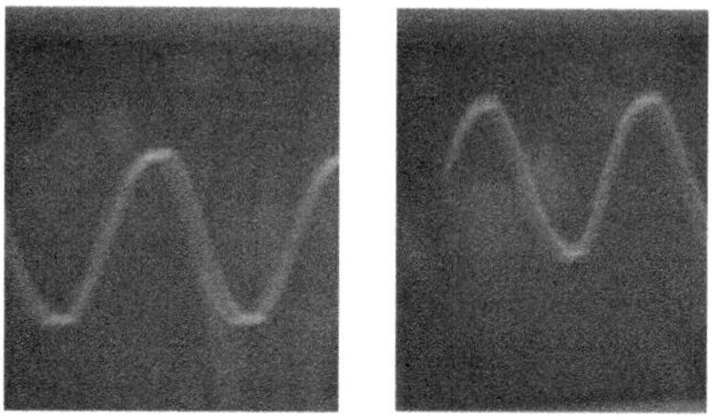

Fig. 4. Main and auxiliary winding voltage implementation result

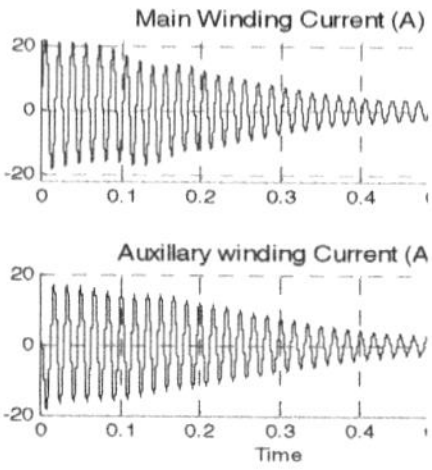

Fig. 5. Main and auxiliary winding current simulation result

Figure 5 show initially the rotor current fluctuates between 0 and 0.5 second then it is about 5A at 0.8 second. Figure 6 show the rotor speed is gradually increases to the rated speed. The rated speed is 1735 rpm and it is reached at nearly 0.5 second. Similarly the time response of electromagnetic torque of single-phase induction motor is variable between 0 to 0.5 second then it is nearly equal zero between 0.5-1.4 and at last the rated torque is 1.1N.m reached at 1.5 second. PWM technique has been employed in this inverter to supply the motor with ac voltage. The simulated and experimental PWM signal is shown in figure 7 and 8 they are used to switch the MOSFET's in inverter to drive the motor.

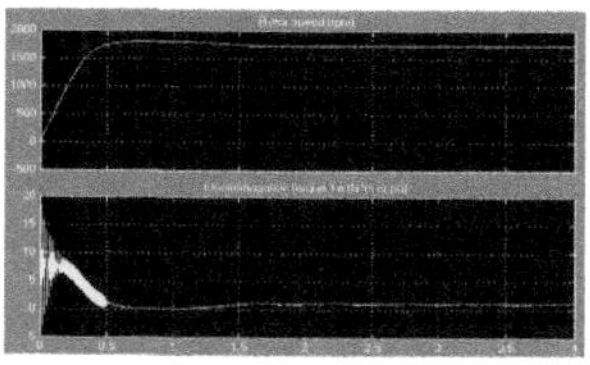

Fig. 6. Rotor-speed curve and electromagnetic torque simulation

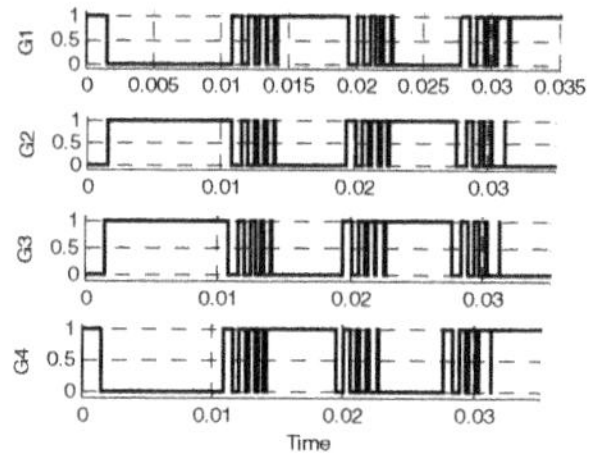

Fig. 7. PWM signal simulation result

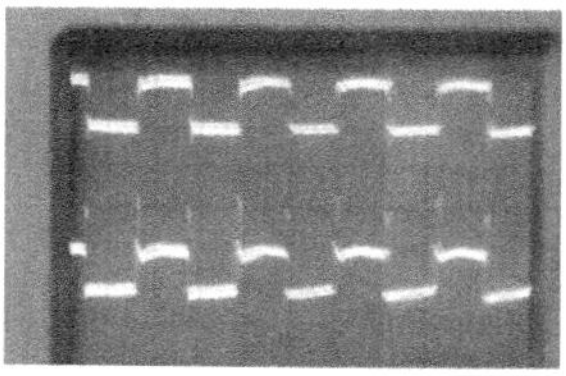

Fig. 8. PWM signal implementation result

4 Experimental Setup

The experimental set is developed using a LPC-2148 ARM-7 board shown in figure 9. The controller generates sinusoidal reference voltages which are needed for generating the PWM signals for driving the Z-source inverter. ARM-7 board is programmed to produce PWM signals by comparing a triangular carrier with reference sine waves. The designed controller shows good tracking with speed of the motor and efficiently reduces disturbance. The sensing, detecting, driving, switching, and

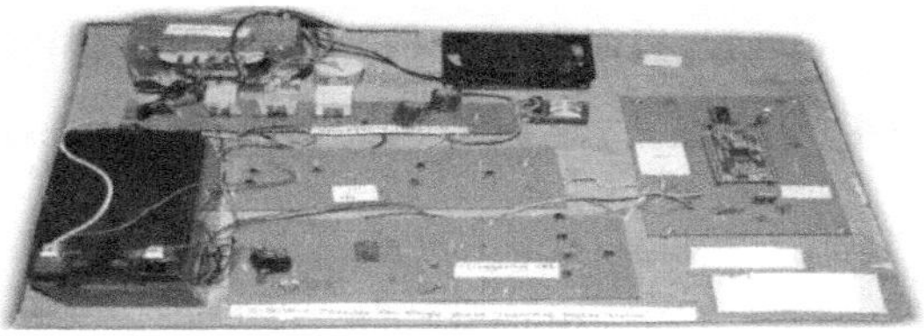

Fig. 9. Experimental setup

interfacing circuits are implemented by the hardware circuits; however, the maximum torque control algorithms are executed by the ARM-7 board.

5 Conclusion

In this paper the prototype of single phase Z-source inverter using ARM-7 for speed control of induction motor is successfully designed. The single-phase induction motor can be successfully driven from a voltage control and the motor's speed can be easily adjusted using the proposed drive system. The MATLAB simulink model for speed control of induction motor and the experimental results have been compared. The simulation results confirmed that the possibility of obtaining of the same results.

References

1. Anugrah, A., Sulaiman, M.B., Omar, R.: Space Vector Analysis In Electrical Drives For Single-Phase Induction Motor Using Matlab/Simulink. Journal of Theoretical and Applied Information Technology (July 2009)
2. Karuppanan, P., Mahapatra, K.K.: Operational Amplifier based control circuit for single phase multiple PWM inverter for Induction Motor Drive Application. In: ICAECT 2010, January 07-10 (2010)
3. Madi Ali, K.A., Salem Abozaed, M.E.: Microcontroller Based Variable Frequency Power Inverter. In: IMECS 2010, Hong Kong, March 17-19 (2010)
4. Bashi, S.M., Aris, I., Hamad, S.H.: Development of Single Phase Induction Motor Adjustable Speed Control Using M68HC11E-9 Microcontroller. Journal of Applied Sciences 5(2), 249–252 (2005)
5. Belhadj, C.A.: Simulation and Implementation of Soft-Started Residential Air Conditioner. In: IEEE International Symposium on Industrial Electronics (ISIE 2009), Seoul Olympic Parktel, Seoul, Korea, July 5-8 (2009)
6. Digital Signal Processing Solution for AC Induction Motor Application Note BPRA043, Texas Instruments Incorporated
7. Peng, F.Z.: Z-Source Inverter. IEEE Transactions on Industry Applications 39(2), 504–510 (2003)
8. Zope, P.H., Somkuwar, A.: Design and Simulation of Single phase Z-source inverter for utility interface. International Journal of Electrical Engineering & Technology 1(1), 127–143 (2010)
9. Zope, P.H., Patil, A.J., Somkuwar, A.: Performance and Simulation Analysis of Single-Phase Grid Connected PV System Based on Z-Source Inverter. In: IEEE PEDES 2010, December 20-23, pp. 1–6 (2010)

RTOS: A New Approach in Design and Organization of High-Speed Power Control Applications

Gupta Atul[1] and Uppuluri Srinivasa Venu[2]

[1] School of instrumentation, DAVV, Khandwa Road Campus,
Indore-452001, M.P., India
atulgupta2006@gmail.com
[2] CBIT, Mechanical Department, Osmania University,
Hyderabad-500075, A.P., India
venuuppuluri@gmail.com

Abstract. Real Time kernel has gained popularity over the years in designing advance software control algorithms coupled on powerful embedded processor cores. This paper discusses the importance of RTOS over generic OS, the pros and cons of using RTOS for microcontroller system development, and the benchmarking methods used for RTOS. Industries most advance RTOS are selected for performance benchmarking over different high-end microcontroller platform to fulfill the requirement of both control and connectivity imposed by digital high-speed power control applications.

Keywords: RT kernel, MQX, ThreadX, FreeRTOS, RTOS benchmarking.

1 Introduction

New emerging technologies in semiconductor industry offered the means to create high-performance digital components allowing implementation of more complex and sophisticated control algorithm applications. Embedded real-time (RT) control becomes a promising research domain to meet certain deadlines at the right time where the Hardware (HW) and Software (SW) components interact in order to perform the given task [1, 2].

Furthermore, control systems are commonly designed using a set of cooperating periodic sub modules where the system should meet timing constraints to ensure a correct behavior of the closed loop controller. This can be achieved by integrating an embedded Real-Time Operating System (RTOS) to provide support for such systems and to ensure RT specification. The proposed approach ensures high-level control application coding with RT performance. It can be readily applied to any other control system application using the same steps discussed below with minor adaptations.

1.1 RTOS vs. General-Purpose Operating Systems

General-computing non real-time operating systems (Windows, Unix or Linux) are not designed for deterministic. Their services can inject random delays into application

V.V. Das and N. Thankachan (Eds.): CIIT 2011, CCIS 250, pp. 444–449, 2011.

software and thus cause slow responsiveness of an application at unexpected times. The task switching time generally rises as a software system includes more tasks that can be scheduled. It might be well above or well below the time shown by the dashed line as shown in Fig. 1(a), extreme left.

On the other hand, real-time operating systems often go a step beyond basic determinism. For most kernel services, these operating systems offer constant load-independent and repeatable timing. The horizontal solid line shows the task switching time. It is constant, independent of any load factor such as the number of tasks in a software system. Most often, the RTOS will exhibit task-switching times much faster than its non real-time competitor when the number of tasks grows above 5 or 10.

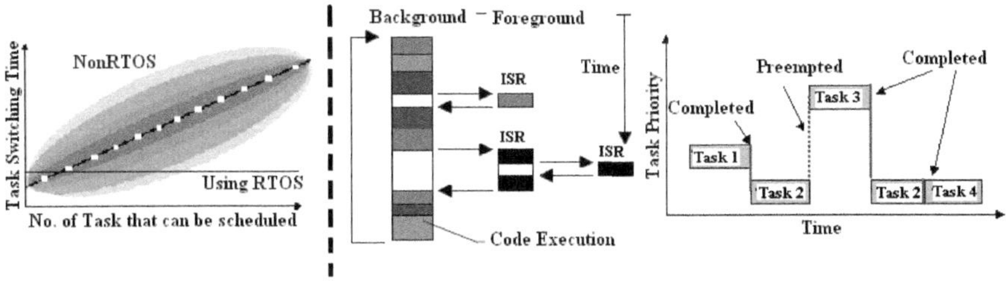

Fig. 1. **(a)** Comparison between General-Computer and RTOS. **(b)** Foreground/Background application. **(c)** RTOS based Preemptive Scheduling.

1.2 Foreground/Background

Systems, which do not use a RTOS, are generally designed as shown in Fig. 1(b), center. These systems are called foreground/background. An application consists of an infinite loop, which calls application modules to perform the desired operations. The modules are executed sequentially (background) with interrupt service routines (ISRs) handling asynchronous events (foreground). Critical operations must be performed by the ISRs to ensure that they are dealt with in a timely fashion. Because of this, ISRs have a tendency to take longer than they should. Information for a background module made available by an ISR is not processed until the background routine gets its turn to execute. The latency in this case depends on how long the background loop takes to execute.

1.3 Need and Advantages of Real-Time Kernel

Real-Time Programming is just a bunch of ideas, concepts, and techniques that allow us to divide complicated problems into smaller simpler tasks or threads. These more manageable units of code allow faster response to important events, while prioritizing the jobs to be done in a structured well-tested format. The kernel does the job of keeping the time, the peace between tasks, and keeping all the tasks' communication flowing. Thus, more activities can be performed in the same amount of time by allowing other tasks to work while other tasks are waiting for some event to occur. The scheduler keeps record of the state of each task and selects among them that are ready to execute and allocates the CPU to one of the ready task. A scheduler helps to maximize CPU utilization among different tasks in a multi-tasking program and to minimize waiting time. Priority-based preemptive scheduling requires control of the processor be given to the task of the highest priority at all time as shown in Fig. 1(c).

1.4 RTOS Disadvantages

There are certain disadvantages and concerns associated with using RTOS. Besides memory footprint, an RTOS also takes up additional CPU resource. Most RTOS require a periodic timer [3] to execute the scheduler and other relevant system services. RTOS services such as task synchronizations must have known execution time. Hence it is essential to understand the performance measurements and the benchmarking metrics among the RTOS.

2 RTOS Benchmarking

There are different approaches towards RTOS benchmarking: based on applications or based on the most frequently used system services. As there are various types of applications with each having very different requirements, benchmarking against any generic applications will not be reflective for the RTOS strengths and weaknesses.

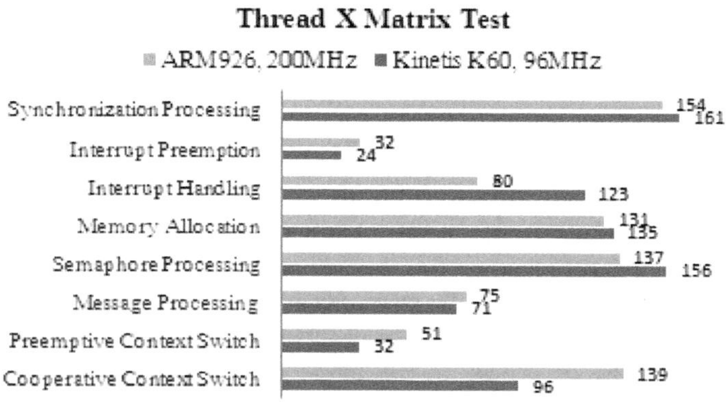

Fig. 2. ThreadX benchmarking Suite (TM Ratio) over ARM926 and Kinetis K60 (Cortex-M4)

There are various research publications related to benchmarking method based on frequently used system services [4, 5]. RTOS Performance is platform, processor, clock-speed, compiler-sensitive and design-sensitive. "Thread-Metric" [6] is a free-source benchmark suite for measuring RTOS performance. Fig. 2, shows the "Thread Metric" based ThreadX v5.4 RTOS performance comparison of Kinetis K60, 96MHz (Cortex-M4) over ARM929, 200MHz (ARM 9). Results show that most of system services timing offered by Cortex-M4 core is almost same as ARM9 even though there is significant difference of clock speed among them.

RTOS usage is gaining popularity in the past few years as clearly indicated in the EE Times embedded system survey for year 2011 [7]. There is another trend in RTOS selection - companies are moving towards open-source RTOS (mainly FreeRTOS) from 34% in current projects to 37% in the next projects in 2012 mainly on 10 - 99 MHz, 32bit ARM core based microcontrollers from TI (Concerto, C28x + Cortex M3), STMicro (CortexM3 - STM32F2X), NXP (43XX, CortexM4 + CortexM0), and Freescale (Kinetis, Cortex M4) etc. incorporated with DSP instructions, FPU and with advance connectivity options like USB 2.0, Ethernet (IEEE1588 compliant) etc.

3 RTOS for High Speed Power Control

Modern controllers that drive electrically commutated motors are hard real-time (HRT) systems. They are electrically commutated using a field oriented control or direct torque control system to calculate when to turn the inverter on and off for each phase of the motor. The complexity of the control system and the processing power required to implement it, increases as the simplicity of the motor and the efficiency goal increases. These hard real-time requirements must be satisfied to meet a diverse range of safety, energy and precision goals.

3.1 Control

Due to high schedule frequency of hard real-time of control loop in high-speed power control application, if the context switch is too time consuming; the overall load on CPU could have significant impact the on the performance of other soft real-time control loops. The time-jitter on hard real-time scheduling may result in performance degradation on control loops. Accidental task overtime or hard real-time missing schedule could cause malfunctioning or catastrophic failures on power sections. In past above problems were overcome by placing the hard real-time of control loop on timer driven fast interrupt service routine set outside RTOS with higher priority than RTOS tick, known as guerilla interrupt. The interrupt routine context switch is usually less time consuming than RTOS scheduled task context switch. Thus, this results in improvement of overall control system timing.

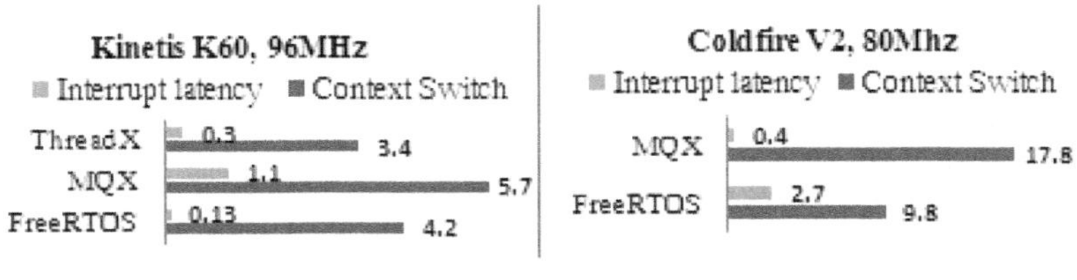

Fig. 3. Various RTOS performance (time in μs) on advance microcontrollers

Fig. 3 demonstrates industrial leading ThreadX, MQX and FreeRTOS performance over ARM (Cortex-M) based microcontrollers. These RTOS offers minimal Interrupt latency and context switching timing on these advance microcontroller platforms.

This offer flexibility to software architect to incorporate hard real-time control loop for high-speed power control within RTOS task with minimal CPU time overhead.

In Fixed-Priority Scheduling (FPS), each task has a fixed static priority, which is computed pre-run time. The tasks are executed in the order determined by their priorities. If all tasks (N) are periodic, a simple priority assignment can be done according to the statement: the shorter the period, the higher the priority. This approach is known as Rate Monotonic Scheduling (RMS) [8]. The schedulability analysis for this algorithm presumes that all tasks are pre-emptive, periodic with deadlines equal to the period (T_i) and independent (i.e. no task precedence between tasks exists). In this case the total utilization (U) has an upper bound given by

$$U = \sum_{i=1}^{N} \frac{C_i}{T_i} \leq N \cdot (2^{1/N} - 1) \qquad (1)$$

"C_i" is the worst-case execution time. This bound converges to 0.693 for n –›∞, to 0.88 when the periods are uniform and to 1.0 only when the periods are harmonics of the smallest period. Now days power control equipments rarely operate in isolation, as they are increasingly required to support a wide range of connectivity options such as ETHERNET, CAN, LIN, RS232, RS485 and USB.

3.2 Connectivity

In past, applications that requires diverse control, processing, and connectivity are served by a mixture of DSPs (High-level language programmable signal processing ability of a DSP), microcontrollers (the low cost and simple programming model) and FPGAs (fully flexible configurable I/O and interface Flexibility). Each device requires the developer to engage with a separate programming language, development environment, system peculiarities, board design and BOM requirements. In recent studies [9] it is found that new 32bits single/dual ARM based microcontrollers are more popular than FPGAs since they are remarkably better in terms of price, control peripherals, connectivity with ultra low power consumption. With integration of industries best RTOS (like FreeRTOS, ThreadX, MQX, µC-OS II/III) over them, we can easily overcome all limitation inherently required in high-speed power control.

4 Firmware Architecture

Threads can communicate and synchronize, so a PWM module running in one thread can be tightly synchronized with an ADC sample/hold point implemented in another thread. Multiple threads can share the same program in memory and pass ownership of data between them. Fig. 4. demonstrates how the whole system can be partitioned into RTOS tasks (white circles). The tasks are divided among two cores (Control/Connectivity) must be executed in isolation or their interferences must be time-bounded [10] and neutralizes fast messaging scheme to exchange critical data.

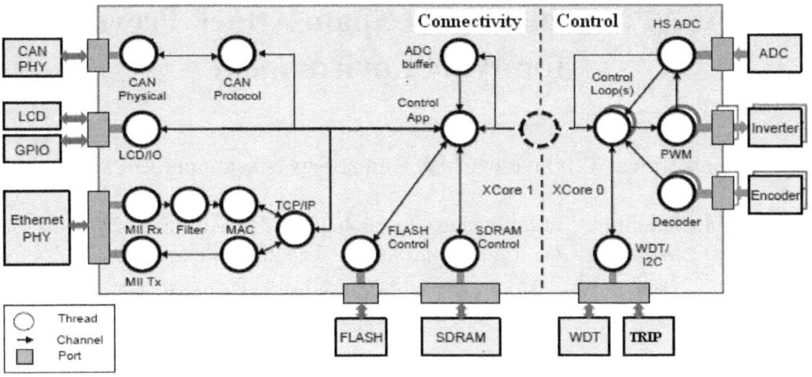

Fig. 4. Firmware architecture for Advance Power Control Embedded system

5 Conclusion

RTOS benchmarking have been carried out results show that each RTOS has different strengths and weaknesses. Results show, advance ARM microcontroller offer minimal Interrupt latency and context switching timing requirements imposed by high-speed HRT power control applications. Complete system firmware design is also presented to fulfill the need of both complex control and advance connectivity.

References

1. Anh, T.N.B., Su-Lim, T.: Real-Time Operating Systems for Small Microcontrollers. Micro IEEE (September-October 2009)
2. Ben Salem, A.K., Othman, S.B., Abdelkrim, H., Saoud, S.B.: RTOS for SoC embedded control applications. DTIS in Nanoscale Era, March 25-27 (2008)
3. Barry, R.: A portable, open source mini RT kernel (October 2007), `http://www.freertos.org/`
4. Kar, R.P., Porter, K.: Rhealstone: A real-time benchmarking proposal. Dr. Dobb's Journal (Febuary 1989)
5. Sacha, K.M.: Measuring the real-time operating system performance. In: Seventh Euromicro Workshop on Real-time Systems Proceedings, Odense, Denmark, pp. 34–40 (June 1995)
6. Lamie, W., Carbone, J.: Measure your RTOS's real-time performance. EDT
7. Wilson, R., Blaza, D.: Embedded Market Study. EDT and UBM Electronics (2011)
8. Singhoff, F., Plantec, A., Dissaux, P.: Can We Increase the Usability of Real Time Scheduling Theory? The Cheddar Project. In: Kordon, F., Vardanega, T. (eds.) Ada-Europe 2008. LNCS, vol. 5026, pp. 240–253. Springer, Heidelberg (2008)
9. Gupta, A., Chandra, A.: Fully Digital Controlled Front-End Converter Based on Boost Topology. CCPE, pp. 171–176. ACEEE (2010)
10. Wolf, J., Gerdes, M., Kluge, F., Uhrig, S., Mische, J., Metzlaff, S., Rochange, C., Cassè, H., Sainrat, P., Ungerer, T.: RTOS Support for Parallel Execution of HRT Applications on the MERASA Multi-core Processor. In: ISORC, pp. 193–201. IEEE CS (2010)

MASAP: Mobile Agent Spam Attack Prevention for WSN Environment

Sumit Kumar Tetarave[1], Ashish Kumar Srivastava[2], and Aditya Goel[2]

[1] Indian Institute of Information Technology, Jhalwa Allahabad-211012
[2] Manulana Azad National Institute of Technolog Bhopal-462051
{sumit.kr.iiita,akshere.ashish}@gmail.com,
adityagoel2@rediffmail.com

Abstract. Wireless sensor network (WSN) is prone to various security threats; one among them is anti sensor motes with existence of anti mobile agent in it, apart from jamming in WSN traffic it is also one kind of DoS (Denial of service Attack). They inject anti mobile agent to other motes to act as anti sensor motes thus spreading anti mobile agents clone among all neighboring motes and these clones send burst of sensed data to base station for exhausting the power of WSN. This process may continue till the entire WSN become dead. This paper focuses on miss use of power, memory and time consumption from mobile agents that leads to DoS spam mobile agent attack when they became anti mobile agents. We propose a novel Mobile Agent Spam Attack Prevention (MASAP) model to control this kind of DoS attack. Our simulation results validate this MASAP model which is able to stop spreading of anti mobile agent with very little energy, memory and time consumption and hence appropriate for WSN.

Keywords: Wireless Sensor Network, Anti Mobile Agent, Denial of Service Attack, MASAP model.

1 Introduction

The special features of sensor motes such as self organizing capability, continuous sensing, cooperative effort, etc make it a very powerful technology in almost all applications scenario of environment such as habitat monitoring, military applications, medical applications, etc [1]. Multi hop communication make less power consumption communication then traditional single hop network which is necessary requirement for WSN One of the unsolved research issue of Denial of Service attack [4] which is attempted in two different ways first, by injecting anti mobile agent motes into existing WSN and second, by injecting anti mobile agent programs into any existing mote of WSN. Anti mobile agent is silent spam attack which dispatches malicious code into a motes of WSN, where it continuously replicates to generate clone anti MAs, Then theses cloned anti MAs send sensed data to the base station and stay inside mote to consume mote's resources. For efficient WSN environment, we need to prevent this kind of unseen anti MA attack. Our paper focuses on the hazard

V.V. Das and N. Thankachan (Eds.): CIIT 2011, CCIS 250, pp. 450–452, 2011.

of anti MA attack and a novel prevention MA model to mitigation. Related work, proposed model, simulated results followed by conclusion and future scope is explained sequentially.

2 Literature Survey

The WSN technology exhibits many research issues, with mobile agent (MA) modular programming, capability it can solve many unsolved WSN research problems [1]. The middleware's can solve various challenging issues during developing WSN application. A powerful middleware "Agilla" uses mobile agent paradigm to perform different applications with supports of flexible reprogramming [2]. Various feature of mobile agent based computing motivated us to use in WSN environment over client-server based computing [3]. We will use this robust middleware Agilla for injecting mobile agents on TinyOS operating system with inbuilt simulation tool named Power Tossim for simulating WSN environment in our proposed model [5].Quarantine Region Scheme (QRS) against spam attack is proposed which separate those anti motes until they are not authenticate and this solution saves energy of non-quarantine region motes not on other nodes [6]. Mobile agents work in multi hop environment and dispatch with double direct-diffusion technique that are useful to reduce end to end latency delay, power consumption, and packet delivery ratio[7]. The sanctuary for Mobile Agents is present in [8].

3 Proposed Model Implementation and Simulation Results

Our proposed MASAP model has been divided into two life cycles phase, First phase is the initial setup of WSN environment and second phase will start when new agent is injected in any mote of WSN. Let the power consumed for migrating from one mote to another is $SPOW_{con}$, power consume for sending data is POW_C per iteration, memory consume per anti MA is MEM_C. Assuming that total battery power as P_{total}, total memory space as M_{total}, computational power taken by mote for anti MA is COM_{pow}, default memory space for other applications is DEF_{mcon}.

A mathematically equation for rejection of MAs request in a mote can be given as:

$$\sum_{i=0}^{n} POWcon + SPOW_{con} + COM_{pow} = P_{total} \tag{1}$$

$$\sum_{i=0}^{n} MEMcon + DEF_{mcon} = M_{total} \tag{2}$$

(Where n is the number of anti MA iterations) In this attacking scenario it is assumed that (m^m) maximum number of MA's clone will be created, where m is the number of motes in a WSN environment. The proposed model enables to prevent spreading of anti mobile agents and maximum $\mathbf{2 * m}$ clones will be created. The comparison of maximum number of clones will be created by SPAM MAs and our proposed model is mentioned in Table 1.

Table 1. Maximum number of created MA's clones between Spam attack and proposed model

Motes	SPAM Attack	Our Proposed Model
1	1	1
2	4	4
3	27	6
4	256	8
5	3125	10
6	46656	12
7	823543	14
8	16777216	16
9	387429489	18
10	10000000000	20

The MASAP mobile agent model proposes three types of reactions within it; they are Detector Mobile Agent (DMA) for checking authentication, Halt Mobile Agent (HMA) to kills MA that contain maximum cloned agent and Cleanser Mobile Agent (CMA) to clears all clones and their resources. HMA and CMA are register as reactions inside DMA mobile agent.

4 Conclusion and Future Scope

The paper gives awareness of silent MA spam attack in WSN; model is able to prevent DOS attack in WSN with minimum energy loss. Proposed model will also work in LAN, WAN or other networks after some modification.

References

1. Chong, C.-Y., Kumar, S.P.: Sensor Networks: Evolution, Opportunities, and Challenges, vol. 91(8), pp. 1247–1256. IEEE (2003)
2. Hadim, S., Mohamed, N.: Middleware Challenges and Approaches for Wireless Sensor Networks. Distributed Systems Online 7(3) (March 2006)
3. Qi, H., Xu, Y., Wang, X.: Mobile-agent-based collaborative signal and information processing in sensor networks, vol. 91(8), pp. 1172–1183. IEEE (2003)
4. Wood, A., Stankovic, J.A.: Denial of Service in Sensor Networks. IEEE Computer 35(10), 54–62 (2002)
5. Agilla with TinyOS, `http://mobilab.cse.wustl.edu/projects/agilla/`
6. Coskun, V., Cayirci, E., Levi, A., Sancak, S.: Quarantine region scheme to mitigate spam attacks wireless-sensor networks. IEEE Trans. On Mobile Computing 5(8), 1074–1086 (2006)
7. Chen, M., Kwon, T., Yuan, Y., Choi, Y., Leung, V.C.M.: Mobile Agent-Based Directed Diffusion in Wireless Sensor Networks. EURASIP Journal on Advances in Signal Processing, Article ID 36871 (January 2007)
8. Yee, B.S.: A Sanctuary for Mobile Agents. In: Ryan, M. (ed.) Secure Internet Programming. LNCS, vol. 1603, pp. 261–274. Springer, Heidelberg (1999)

Transformer Incipient Fault Diagnosis Using Artificial Neural Network

Nandkumar Wagh and Dinesh Deshpande

Electrical Engineering Department, Maulana Azad National Institute of Technology, Bhopal, M.P. India
nbwagh@gmail.com
dinesh_1949@rediffmail.com

Abstract. This paper presents the artificial neural network approach for incipient fault diagnosis of power transformers filled with oil.DGA data from reputed testing unit is obtained to deal with all possible faulty conditions in a power transformer. Well designed artificial neural network having the adaptive features and fast diagnosis capabilities are proposed and testing and training results of DGA samples made available are presented using neural network tool in Matlab 7.10. The diagnosis accuracy obtained during training and testing of samples is better. Programming features are incorporated proposing appropriate preventive maintenance action represented by a type of fault, so that the transformer in service can be saved.

1 Introduction

Power transformer is a major asset of transmission and distribution system and is vital to system operation and the techniques for diagnosis and detection of incipient faults are most valuable.

A power transformer is subjected to thermal and electrical stresses and could lead to the breakdown of insulating materials which releases the gases decomposition products. Arching, corona and overheating are the three primary causes of fault related gases. The gases dissolved in oil are hydrogen (H_2), carbon monoxide(CO), carbon dioxide(CO_2), ethane(CH_4), acetylene(C_2H_2), ethylene(C_2H_4), ethane(C_2H_6), nitrogen and oxygen. The analysis of dissolved gases is a powerful tool to diagnose developing faults in a power transformer. Many diagnostic criteria have been developed for the interpretation of dissolved gases. These methods would find the relationship between the dissolved gases and the fault conditions, some of which are obvious and some are hidden. New computer-aided techniques such as artificial neural networks, fuzzy sets and fuzzy rule base, expert system, evolutionary algorithms can be made use of in the diagnosis, but needs expertise to interpret the results correctly.

Although widely used by utilities, the IEC/IEEE DGA coding [1]-[3] is only the result of empirical evidence. Moreover, the DGA methods cannot provide a completely objective and accurate basis for all faults since the number of code combinations exceed that of fault types. Therefore no decision may follow from it, and diagnosis experts must determine the final possible faults. The diagnosis basis is

V.V. Das and N. Thankachan (Eds.): CIIT 2011, CCIS 250, pp. 453–459, 2011.

Roger's ratio codes shown in Tables 1, 2, 3, and IEC codes in Tables 4 and 5 along with fault classification.

Table 1. Gas Ratio Cod

Gas Ratio	Ratio Code
CH_4/H_2	I
C_2H_6/CH_4	J
C_2H_4/C_2H_6	K
C_2H_2/C_2H_4	L

Table 2. Roger's Ratio Codes

Ratio code	Range	Code
i	<=0.1	5
	>0.1,<1.0	0
	>=1.0,<3.0	1
	>=3.0	2
j	<1.0	0
	>=1.0	1
k	<1.0	0
	>=1.0,<3.0	1
	>=3.0	2
l	<0.5	0
	>=0.5,<3.0	1
	>=3.0	2

Artificial neural networks have been proposed [4]-[6] to tackle the transformer fault diagnosis, due to their accuracy and efficiency in numerical modeling problems and built in fault tolerance in practical applications. The ANNs can acquire new experiences by incremental training from newly obtained samples. The ANNs trained by an error back- propagation algorithm have good diagnostic accuracy. The adaptive ANN is proposed to tackle the problems such as local convergence and determination of network configuration and control parameters like momentum constant and learning rate using gradient decent approach and can become a useful diagnostic tool.

Table 3. Classification based on Roger's Ratio Codes

i	j	k	l	Diagnosis
0	0	0	0	Normal deterioration
5	0	0	0	Partial discharge
1-2	0	0	0	Slight overheating < 150^0 C
1-2	1	0	0	Overheating 150^0 -200^0 C
0	1	0	0	Overheating 200^0 -300^0 C
0	0	1	0	General conductor overheating
1	0	1	0	Winding circulating currents
1	0	2	0	Core and tank circulating currents, overheated joints
0	0	0	1	Flashover without power follow through
0	0	1-2	1-2	Arc with power follow through
0	0	2	2	Continuous sparking to floating potential
5	0	0	1-2	Partial discharge with tracking

Table 4. IEC Ratio Codes

Ratio Code	Range	Code
i	<0.1	0
	0.1-1.0	1
	1.0-3.0	1
	>3.0	2
j	<0.1	1
	0.1-1.0	0
	1.0-3.0	2
	>3.0	2
k	<0.1	0
	0.1-1.0	0
	1.0-3.0	1
	>3.0	2

2 Artificial Neural Network

Very complex systems [4] can be characterized with very little explicit knowledge using ANN. The relationship between gas composition and incipient fault condition is learned by ANN from actual training samples .Through training process ANN can reveal complex mechanism that may be unknown to experts.

An ANN design includes selection of input, output, network topology and weighted connection of nodes. Input feature selection constitutes an essentially first step. The feature space needs to be chosen very carefully to ensure that the input features will correctly reflect the characteristics of the problem. Fig.1 illustrates the overall design process with step by step adjustments to achieve desired structure and feature space .The corresponding connection weights are also determined in the process. In this paper, back propagation learning algorithm known as generalized delta rule is used for training ANN. In this paper a network having seven inputs and four outputs specifying the normal, overheating, corona and arcing is used.

Fig. 2 presents the Artificial Neural Network [7] proposed for fault diagnosis of power transformers, was constructed as three layer feed-forward structure with the input, hidden, and output layers. The nodes in each layer receive input signals from the previous layer and pass the output to the subsequent layer. The nodes of the input layer receive a set of input signals from outside system and directly deliver the input data to the input of the hidden layer by the weighted links. In the following computation, the subscripts n, h and k denote any node in the input, hidden, and output layers, respectively. The net input *net* is defined as the weighted sum of the incoming signal minus a bias term. The net input of node, h, net_h, in the hidden layer is expressed as follows:

$$net_h = \sum_n w_{hn} y_n - \theta_h \tag{1}$$

where y_n is the output of node *n* in the input layer, w_{hn} represents the connection weight from node *n* in the input layer to node, *h* in the hidden layer, and Θh is the bias of node *h* in the hidden layer. The tan sigmoid function is selected as the activation function in the proposed neural nets. Therefore, in the hidden layer, the output of node *h*, y_n , can be described as

$$y_h = f_h(net_h) = \frac{1}{1 + e^{-net_h}}. \tag{2}$$

Table 5. Classification based on IEC Ratio Codes

i	j	k	Characteristic fault
0	0	0	Normal ageing
*	1	0	Partial discharge of low energy density
1	1	0	Partial discharge of high energy density
1-2	0	1-2	Discharge of low energy(Continuous sparking)
1	0	2	Discharge of high energy(Arc with power follow through)
0	0	1	Thermal fault <150^0 C
0	2	0	Thermal fault 150^0-300^0 C
0	2	1	Thermal fault 300^0-700^0 C
0	2	2	Thermal fault>700^0 C

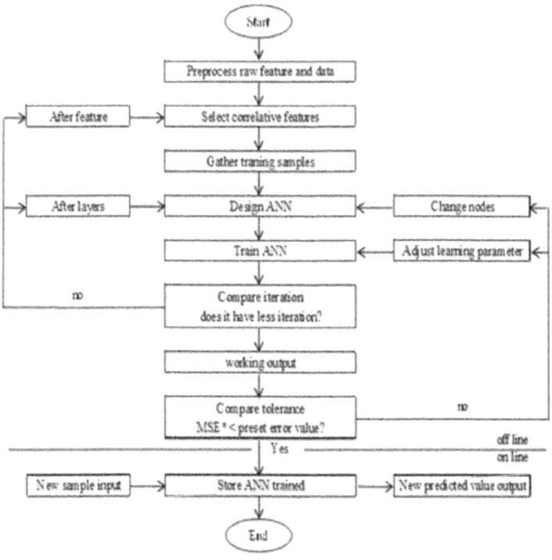

Fig. 1. Flow chart

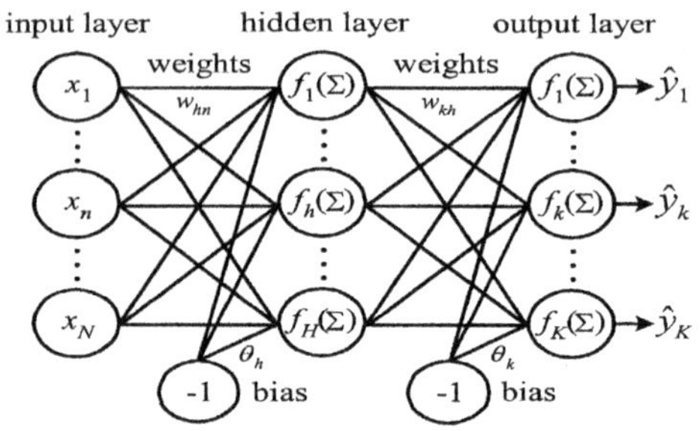

Fig. 2. Feed forward neural network

The output of the hidden nodes is then delivered to the nodes in the output layer via another set of connection weights. The output of node in the output layer can also be expressed as

$$net_k = \sum_h w_{kh} y_h - \theta_k \tag{3}$$

$$y_k = f_k(net_k) = \frac{1}{1 + e^{-net_k}} \tag{4}$$

Where Θ_k is the bias of node in the output layer. The parameters (connection weights and bias terms) must be determined by the learning process, before the neural nets can produce the desired outputs.

The generalized delta rule [14] is used to adjust the weights between the nodes by minimizing the following error function E:

$$E = \frac{1}{2} \sum_k (d_k - y_k)^2 \tag{5}$$

where d_k represents the desired output of node , and y_k is the computed output of node in the output layer. The weight w_{kh} is updated iteratively to minimize E for the training data by a gradient-descent technique.

$$w_{kh}(i+1) = w_{kh}(i) + \Delta w_{kh}(i) \tag{6}$$

$$\Delta w_{kh}(i) = \eta \delta_k y_k + \alpha \Delta w_{kh}(i-1) \tag{7}$$

$$\delta_k = (d_k - y_k) y_k (1 - y_k) \tag{8}$$

where i represents the iteration number, η is the learning rate, and α is the momentum constant. Similarly, the weight w_{hn} can be changed as follows:

$$w_{hn}(i+1) = w_{hn}(i) + \Delta w_{hn}(i) \tag{9}$$

$$\Delta w_{hn}(i) = \eta \delta_h y_h + \alpha \Delta w_{hn}(i-1) \tag{10}$$

$$\delta_h = y_h(1 - y_h) \sum_h \delta_k w_{hn}. \tag{11}$$

The bias terms Θ_k and Θ_h can be regarded as weights and iteratively altered in the same manner as the other weights. The output y_k of node k in the output layer implicitly includes the tunable parameters of the networks, the connection weights, and bias terms, in each node. In this paper, the connection weights and bias terms of the neural nets are automatically adjusted so as to avoid local convergence of parameters in ANNs trained by the gradient-descent approach.

3 Diagnosis Results and Discussion

In [4], two ANN's were used, one for major faults and another for checking paper insulation damage. In this paper, only one ANN with all seven gases including CO

Table 6. Diagnosis Results

		Training samples(90)				Testing samples(20)			
Sr.No.	Fault type	No. of cases	Samples correctly classified	Non diagnosed samples	%Success	No. of cases	Samples correctly classified	Non diagnosed samples	% success
1	Arcing (HEDA)	09	08	01	89%	04	03	01	75%
2	Conductor overheating	05	04	01	80%	---	---	--	--
3	Thermal fault >700^0 C	08	07	01	88%	05	05	---	100%
4	Partial Discharge with low energy(Corona)	22	22	-----	100%	07	05	02	70%
5	Healthy	36	34	01	97%	04	04	-----	100%
6	Filter oil (maint)	06	05	01	83%		----	--	--
7	Bad oil to be replaced(maint)	03	03	---	100%		----	---	---
8	Heated oil due to thermal effect >300^0	01	01	----	100%		-----	---	---

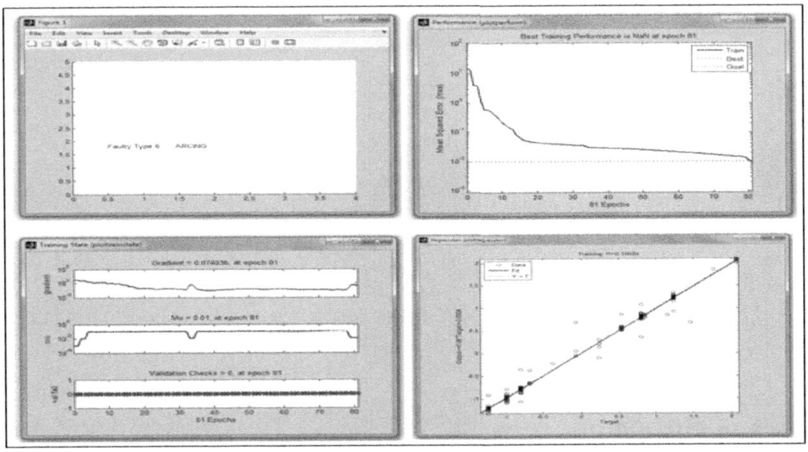

Fig. 3. Fault type 6- Arcing, network training performance in terms of gradient, mean squared error and validation check

and CO_2 is used for diagnosis. The main goal was to reduce the training error and number of iterations, so that the correct diagnosis of the fault can be made The proposed network system was then trained on 90 DGA samples, out of which 36were the healthy cases. The testing data base of 20 samples with main faults was used to test the validation. It was found that, the no. of iterations the network takes for training are less and the average error in training is also reduced to 0.009324.. The simulation results of some of the important faults like arcing and corona are presented as shown in fig.3 and 4 .The diagnosis results of various samples in training and testing in terms of accuracy in fault diagnosis obtained during training and testing are shown in Table 6.

The diagnosis accuracy can further be increased with more databases in training and testing.

4 Maintenance Actions Recommendation

Retest interval estimation is the key process of maintenance action recommendation and it is determined from both IEC codes and key gas DGA methods. Final recommendations are closely related to the retest interval output and basically the interval is modified based on the size and age of the transformer. The maintenance actions based on the sample test results like replacement of bad oil, filter oil with rehydration, normal ageing etc. were taken care of during diagnosis of oil samples and are considered to be most important for saving the costly device.

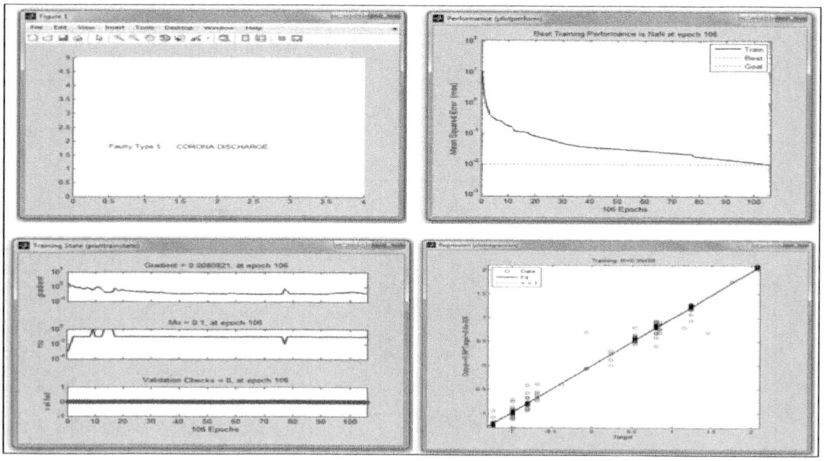

Fig. 4. Fault type 5 – Corona Discharge, network training performance in terms of gradient, mean squared error and validation check

5 Conclusion

The limitations of DGA methods with frequent non-decisions in case of multiple faults and boundary values of ratios are eliminated up to some extent by adaptive neural network used in the paper. It is found that, the adaptive neural network proposed for fault diagnosis improves the diagnosis considerably in terms of fault classification. The diagnosis accuracy and fast training of the proposed adaptive neural network were the key features revealed during study.

Acknowledgement. Authors are grateful to M/S. B.R.Industrial Services, Aurangabad (M.S.) India for providing database of transformer faulty cases which allowed us for diagnosis of incipient faults.

References

1. Interpretation of the Analysis of Gases in Transformer and other Oil-filled Electrical Equipment in service, IEC Publication 599 (1978)
2. Rogers, R.R.: IEEE and IEC codes to interpret incipient faults in transformers using gas in oil analysis. IEEE Trans. Electrical Insulation 13(5), 349–354 (1978)
3. IEEE Guide for the interpretation of Gases Generate In Oil-immersed Transformers, ANSI/IEEE std C57.104 (199, 1992)
4. Zhang, Y., Ding, X., Liu, Y., Griffin, P.J.: An Artificial neural network approach to transformer fault diagnosis. IEEE Trans. Power Delivery 11(4), 1836–1841 (1996)
5. Xu, W., Wang, D., Zhou, Z., Chen, H.: Fault diagnosis of power transformers: application of fuzzy set theory, expert systems and artificial neural networks. IEE Proceedings-Science Management and Technology 144(1), 39–44 (1997)
6. Wang, Z., Liu, Y., Griffin, P.J.: A Combine ANN and expert System tool for transformer fault diagnosis. IEEE Trans. Power Delivery 13(4), 1224–1229 (1998)
7. Huang, Y.-C.: Evolving Neural Nets for Fault Diagnosis of Power Transformer. IEEE Trans.on Power Delivery 18(3), 843–848 (2003)

A Personalised GA Technique for Estimating Maximum Loadability in Power Systems

R. Kanimozhi[1] and K. Selvi[2]

[1] Department of Electrical and Electronics Engineering,
Anna University of Technology-Tiruchirappalli,
Tiruchirappalli, Tamilnadu, India
kanimozhi_17@yahoo.com
[2] Thiagarajar College of Engineering, Madurai,
Tamilnadu, India
kseee@tce.edu

Abstract. The maximum loadability of power systems has been a topic of interest to both planners and operators for many years. A modest attempt can be made in this paper proposes an effective personalized Genetic Algorithm technique for the maximum loadability estimation of the transmission system. In connection with this, the objective function is formulated as a personalised GA with fitness of the objective function determined for every gene of the chromosomes. A pre-developed line based voltage stability index is utilized for calculating the fitness of the objective function. The proposed technique is validated on the IEEE 30 bus test system and it can be implemented for larger and practical systems.

Keywords: Voltage stability, transmission system, Personalised GA, FVSI, maximum loadability.

1 Introduction

The reactive power increases in transmission system until the system reaches the point of collapse which is the maximum loadability of the system. The estimation of maximum loadability is becoming an important task to predict the system collapse and to optimize the capital investment. Most of the literature agreed that maximum loadability depends on the solvability margin of the load flow .Many methods were proposed to determine maximum loadability viz. equality and inequality constraints [1], direct interior point algorithm [2], using elliptic properties of p-e curve [3]. The interior point algorithm was proposed to identify maximum loadability under contingency state [4]. Recently, evolutionary techniques have been developed to solve maximum loadability problem in power system. Evolutionary programming (EP) is an accelerated search technique for estimating maximum loadability [5].

This paper presents a personalized GA approach for estimating maximum loadability in transmission line. The newly developed personalised GA algorithm can also be executed for solving further optimization problem in power system. The value

V.V. Das and N. Thankachan (Eds.): CIIT 2011, CCIS 250, pp. 460–465, 2011.

of FVSI must be less than 1.00 in all the transmission lines to maintain a stable system. For maximum loadability estimation using personalised GA approach, maximum FVSI is set as 0.95 that is close to stability limit.

2 Personalised GA Algorithm

In general, the overall fitness was calculated for the generated chromosomes, but in the personalized GA, the fitness determined for each gene. The objective function was maximization of reactive power loading at each load bus separately. The fitness of every gene in random chromosomes was calculated by using pre-developed line based index termed as FVSI [6].

2.1 Generation of Chromosomes

Initially, N_p number of random chromosomes of length N_{l-1} was generated as in the equation (1).

$$\hat{\eta}^{(j)} = \left\{ \eta_0^{(j)}, \eta_1^{(j)}, \eta_2^{(j)}, \ldots, \eta_{N_{l-1}}^{(j)} \right\} ; \quad 0 \le j \le N_p - 1 \tag{1}$$

where, N_l be the number of load buses present in the transmission system and N_p be the population size.

2.2 Generation of Sweeping Chromosomes

The sweeping chromosomes were nothing but the detailed chromosomes, the Q_{sc} values which represent the receiving end reactive power of the transmission system. Based on this, the sweeping chromosomes are obtained as follows:

$$Q_{sc}^{(i)} = \left\{ \begin{array}{l} \left\{ q_{0-0}^{(j)}, q_{1-0}^{(j)}, q_{2-0}^{(j)}, \ldots, q_{n_k-0}^{(j)} \right\}, \left\{ q_{0-1}^{(j)}, q_{1-1}^{(j)}, q_{2-1}^{(j)}, \ldots, q_{n_k-1}^{(j)} \right\}, \ldots, \\ \left\{ q_{0-N_{l-1}}^{(j)}, q_{1-N_{l-1}}^{(j)}, q_{2-N_{l-1}}^{(j)}, \ldots, q_{n_k-N_{l-1}}^{(j)} \right\} \end{array} \right\} \tag{2}$$

where $q_{n_k-N_{l-1}}^{(j)}$ represents the receiving end reactive power of the transmission line connected between n_k and N_{l-1} buses of jth chromosome.

2.3 Determination of Gene Fitness

The FVSI used to determine the gene and it was computed for the kth gene of the jth random chromosome as follows,

$$f_{p-k}^{(j)} = \frac{4*(Z_{p-k})^2 * q_{sc_{p-k}}^{(j)}}{(V_{p-k}^{(j)})^2 * X_{p-k}} \quad (3)$$

Where Z - the line impedance, X - the line reactance, V_i - the sending end voltage, $q_{sc_{p-k}}^{(j)}$ - receiving end reactive power which was obtained from sweeping chromosome. After that, the random chromosomes has subjected to the genetic operations crossover and mutation to get new children chromosomes.

2.4 Crossover and Mutation

The two point crossover has been selected and the the two points C_1 and C_2 are determined using equation (4) and (5).

$$c_1 = \frac{|\eta^{(j)}|}{3} \quad (4)$$

$$c_2 = c_1 + \frac{|\eta^{(j)}|}{3} \quad (5)$$

Subsequently, the generated children chromosomes were subjected to mutation and then load flow analysis was conducted using the newly obtained chromosomes, then aforesaid procedure repeated once for getting best chromosome.

2.5 Generation of Shriveled Chromosomes

Once the genetic operations, crossover and mutation performs, N_p new children chromosomes were obtained for the corresponding N_p parent chromosomes. If the load increased at a particular bus influences FVSI value of more than one line which connected at that bus. The FVSI value of each gene in N_p parent and N_p children chromosomes are shriveled based on its highest value. From the $2\ N_p$ chromosomes, $N_p/2$ shriveled chromosome generated.

2.6 Selection and Termination Criteria

If all the genes fitness has 0.95 in the shriveled chromosome, or the generation reaches maximum, the process can be terminated. Otherwise shriveled chromosome was treated as random chromosome and remaining chromosomes generated randomly for further successive repetitions.

3 Results and Discussions

The personalized GA-based technique for estimation of maximum loadability has been tested in IEEE 30 bus system. This system has 24 load buses, 6 generator buses and 41 interconnected lines. All load buses were randomly chosen to find maximum reactive power estimation. In this, N_p=2 random chromosomes of length N_{l-1} generated. Each chromosome has the N_l-1=24genes; these genes have the load reactive power values of the load buses. These were subjected to load flow analysis for getting sweeping chromosomes which consist of receiving end reactive power and sending end voltages. The genes in sweeping chromosome were 41 and calculate gene fitness for all 41 genes .The random chromosomes have been subjected to the genetic

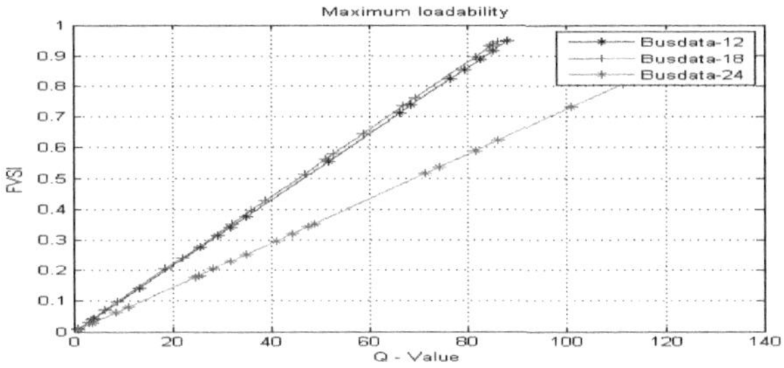

Fig. 1. Maximum loadability of load buses 12, 18, and 24

Table 1. Comparison between Personalised GA and VSA technique

Technique	Personalised GA(random search)			VSA technique		
Bus number	Q value (MVar)	FVSI	Voltage	Q value(MVar)	FVSI	Voltage
3	150.2371	0.95	0.8724	150.0	0.948	0.874
4	123.4180	0.95	0.9163	123.0	0.941	0.913
6	120.5430	0.95	0.8951	121.0	0.959	0.891
7	127.8500	0.95	0.7932	128.5	0.955	0.792
9	95.9812	0.95	0.8143	96.0	0.959	0.819
10	58.2243	0.95	0.9365	59.0	0.945	0.935
12	83.6523	0.95	0.8756	84.0	0.959	0.875
14	62.3450	0.95	0.7927	62.0	0.942	0.79
15	48.0113	0.95	0.9208	48.0	0.951	0.920
16	75.7650	0.95	0.7765	75.5	0.94	0.775
17	78.2301	0.95	0.8154	79.0	0.958	0.814
18	64.2560	0.95	0.7247	64.0	0.953	0.727
19	72.7825	0.95	0.6450	72.2	0.940	0.640
20	67.214	0.95	0.6827	70.0	0.984	0.68
21	108.5701	0.95	0.7331	108.0	0.945	0.731
22	90.3100	0.95	0.6675	88.0	0.920	0.665
23	70.2960	0.95	0.8166	73.6	0.956	0.816
24	61.5012	0.95	0.9356	60.7	0.941	0.956
25	44.5000	0.95	0.7923	45.0	0.956	0.793
26	28.3420	0.95	0.6024	30.3	0.969	0.624
27	48.4710	0.95	0.7540	51.0	0.967	0.74
28	88.8600	0.95	0.8670	90.0	0.957	0.870
29	33.1256	0.95	0.7081	31.9	0.946	0.681
30	26.4153	0.95	0.7652	25.9	0.946	0.760

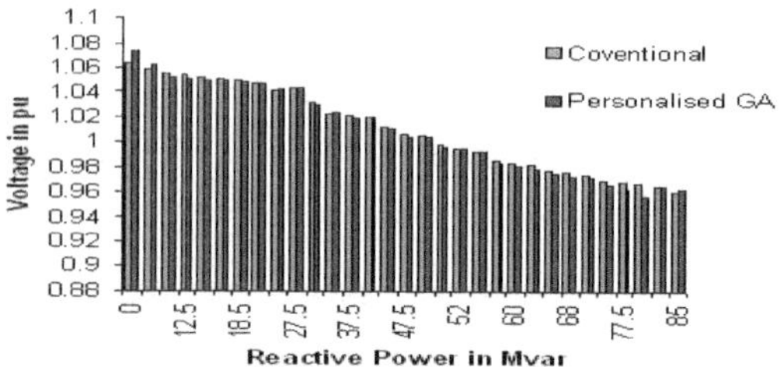

Fig. 2. Reactive load $Q_{j\ Vs}$ Voltage at bus 12

operations crossover, mutation and the selection of best chromosome. The crossover points as C_1=8 and C_2=16 and the N_{mp}=6 have been selected. The newly obtained chromosomes were subjected to load flow analysis and aforesaid procedure repeated once. Finally, 2 parent and 2 children chromosomes were available with all related values. The FVSI value of each gene in 2 parent and 2 children chromosomes were shriveled based on the highest value. From the 4 chromosomes one shriveled chromosome has been formed based on their highest FVSI value. If the FVSI value gets closer to $FVSI_{max}$, then the corresponding load reactive power value selected as the optimal value; if not, shriveled chromosome was consider as one random chromosome and another one random chromosome is generated and the process was repeated until all the genes obtained the optimal load reactive value. The developed personalised GA technique has tested on the IEEE 30 bus RTS and the results were tabulated in the table 1. The results obtained from the traditionally VSA technique are also tabulated the table for comparison purposes. In this algorithm, the generation completed the optimal load reactive powers for all the buses were obtained. Comparatively this technique can be able to produce more accurate results with short span of time. For the every odd generation, the shriveled chromosome considered as one of random chromosomes for next generation up to get optimized values. So this technique effectively helps to find the maximum reactive loading in transmission than other EP technique.

Table 1 also shows that the bus 30 has smallest maximum loadability 24.4153 Mvar and bus 7 has highest value 165.3500 Mvar. The bus 30 is considered as weakest bus and it needs proper monitoring so that the load connected to the respective bus will not exceed maximum value for maintaining stable system.

The Q value and the FVSI value of the load buses 12, 18 and 24 of the IEEE 30 bus system are plotted in the Figure 1. From the figure 1, it can be seen that the obtained reactive power values reaches very closer to the $FVSI_{max}$.

The voltage values obtained for various values of reactive power loading in conventional VSA technique is compared with personalised GA in Figure 2. This value decides the maximum loadability of the transmission system in an effective way.

4 Conclusion

This work has proposed an effective personalized GA to maintain stability by identifying the maximum loadability of the transmission line in power system. This was accomplished by fitness of the objective function determined for every gene of the chromosomes. An alternative to the earlier methods of calculating maximum loadability for individual load buses was proposed by considering several load buses simultaneously. This proves to be an approach which results in improved search technique for the determination of maximum loadability. The technique was tested on a 30 bus system by evaluating in MATLAB software.

References

1. Hiskens, I.A., Davy, R.J.: Exploring the power flow solution space boundary. IEEE transactions on power systems 16, 385–395 (2001)
2. Dai, Y., McCalley, J.D., Vittal, V.: Simplification Expansion and Enhancement of Direct Interior Point Algorithm for power system maximum Loadability. IEEE Transaction on Power Systems 15(3), 1014–1021 (2000)
3. Moon, Y.H., Choi, B.K., Cho, B.H.: Improved method of maximum Loadability Estimation in Power systems by Transforming the distorted p-e curve. In: Proce. IEEE on Power Engineering Society Summer Meeting, vol. 2, pp. 657–662 (2000)
4. Kubokawa, J., Inoue, R., Sasaki, H.: A Solution of Optimal Power Flow with Voltage Stability Constraints". In: Proce.International Conference of Power Systems Technology-Powercon, vol. 2, pp. 625–630 (2000)
5. Musirin, I., Rahman, T.K.A.: Evolutionary programming based optimization technique for maximum loadability estimation in Electric Power System. In: Proce. IEEE on National Power and Energy Conference Proceedings (2003), pp. 205–210 (2003)
6. Musirin, I., Abdul Rahman, T.K.: Estimating Maximum Loadability for Weak Bus Identification Using FVS. IEEE Power Engineering Review, 50–52 (November 2002)

Internet Connectivity between Mobile Adhoc Network Using Mobile IP

Sayali N. Mane [1] and A.R. Nigvekar [2]

Department of Electronics and Telecommunication
[1] D.Y. Patil College of Engg. Akurdi, Pune University, Maharashtra, India
sayalimane@rediffmail.com
[2] KIT, College of Engg., Kolhapur, Maharashtra, India
atulrn@indiatimes.com

Abstract. Mobile ad hoc networking allows nodes to form temporary networks and communicate beyond transmitter range by supporting multihop communication through IP routing. Routing in such networks is often reactive, i.e., performed on-demand, as opposed to Internet routing that is proactive. As ad hoc networks are formed on a temporary basis, any IP address should be allowed to appear in an ad hoc network. MIPMANET, a solution for connecting an ad hoc network, in which on-demand routing is used, to the Internet.MIPMANET, provides Internet access by using Mobile IP with foreign agent care-of addresses and reverse tunneling. This allows nodes to enjoy the mobility services of Mobile IP while at the same time the requirements on the ad hoc routing protocol are kept to a minimum. Simulations of MIPMANET have been performed in Network Simulator 2. The Ad hoc On-demand Distance Vector (AODV) routing protocol has been used for routing within the ad hoc network. These simulations show that the ability to choose the closest access point to the Internet is worth extra work, as less traffic is generated in the network resulting in lower delays and fewer dropped packets. This paper again tries to calculate nodal energy when packets are travel from source to destination under different conditions.

Keywords: MIPMANET, Mobile Ad Hoc Networks, Internet Access, Mobile IP, AODV.

1 Introduction

Mobile IP for Mobile Ad Hoc Networks (MIPMANET has been analyzed by means of simulations using Network Simulator 2. In the simulations the Ad hoc On demand Distance Vector (AODV [2], [5]) routing protocol has been used within the ad hoc network.

1.1 Mobile IP

Mobile IP solves the following two problems:

V.V. Das and N. Thankachan (Eds.): CIIT 2011, CCIS 250, pp. 466–468, 2011.

– If a node moves from one link to another without changing its IP address, it will be unable to receive packets at the new link; and
– If a node changes its IP address when it moves, it will have to terminate and restart any ongoing communications each time it moves.

Mobile IP allows mobile nodes that enter a foreign network to register with a foreign agent and obtain a care-of address (COA). This COA allows the mobile node to send and receive data packets from the networks other than its home network [6].

1.2 MIPMANET

MIPMANET is designed to provide nodes in ad hoc networks with access to the Internet and the mobility services of Mobile IP. The layering of Mobile IP and ad hoc routing functionality is illustrated in Fig. 1. By the use of tunneling, the ad hoc network becomes transparent to Mobile IP.

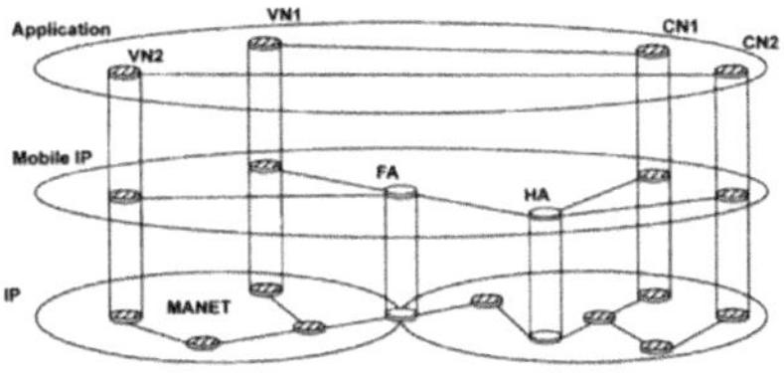

Fig. 1. Conceptual view of MIPMANET

2 Simulations

Since MIPMANET's only modifications to Mobile IP concerns the communication between the foreign agents and visiting nodes, focused on the wireless part of the scenario. Communication in the simulations is carried out between wireless visiting nodes and wired correspondent nodes. It is duplex; both the visiting nodes and their correspondent nodes are constant bit rate (CBR) sources. The mobility in the simulations is about 1.5 m/s; the nodes themselves move at random absolute speeds below 8 m/s.

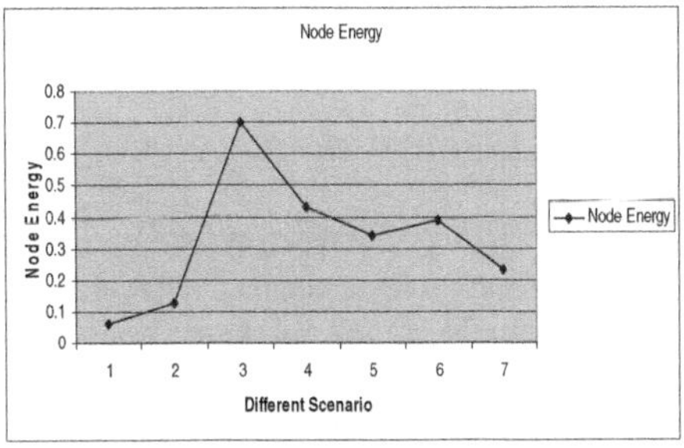

Fig. 2. One node with seven scenes

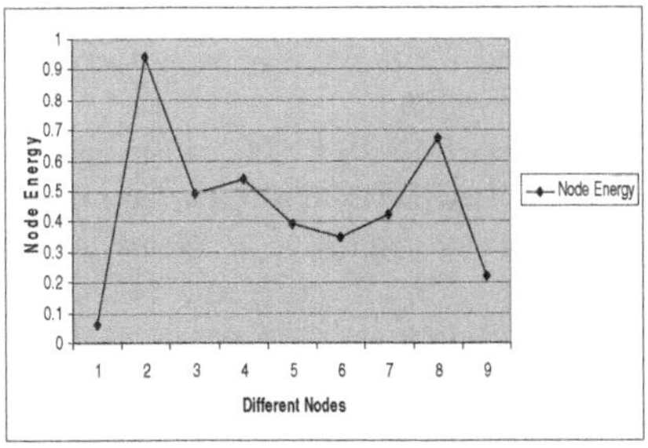

Fig. 3. One scene with ten nodes

The simulation study has evaluated what is the energy level of one node in the network while it come under different scenarios and what is energy level of 10 different nodes for the same scenario. For getting these points all trace files are observe. And the energy level chart of node/s with different scenarios shown above;

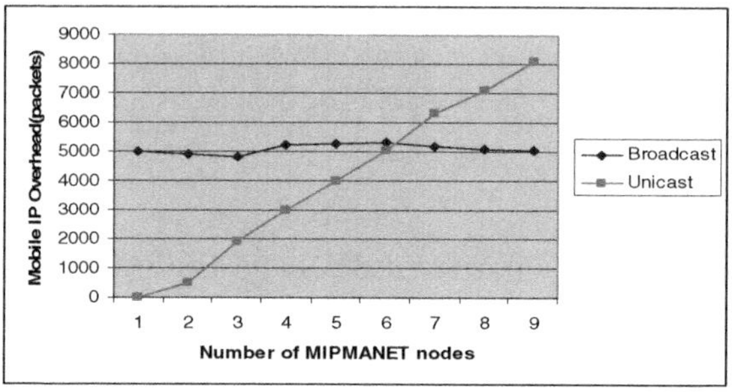

3 Conclusion

This paper has presented a solution of how to interconnect an ad hoc network with the Internet called MIPMANET. Ad hoc networking enables IP mobility within a network whereas Mobile IP enables IP mobility between networks. By combining these two, MIPMANET allows mobile nodes to enjoy extended IP mobility.

The simulation study has evaluated what is the energy level of one node in the network while it come under different scenarios and what is energy level of 10 different nodes for the same scenario. For getting these points all trace files are observe. Node energy at ten node setup will be more peaks are visible it seems that more drop in packet. Other hand we worked with 10 node configuration seems system little bit stable. This paper leads to give new exposure for mobile based system using MIPMANET to ensure the secure communication between the network entities.

References

1. The Internet Engineering Task Force (IETF), Webpage, http://www.ietf.org/
2. Perkins, C.E., Royer, E.M.: Ad-hoc on demand distance vector routing. In: Proceedings of the 2nd IEEE Workshop on Mobile Computing Systems and Applications, pp. 90–100 (Febuary 1999)
3. Perkins, C.E.: RFC 2002: IP mobility support, Updated by RFC 290. Status: PROPOSED STANDARD (October 1996)
4. Fall, K., Varadhan, K.: ns Notes and Documentation, The VINT Project, Work in progress
5. Perkins, C.E., Royer, E.M., Das, S.R.: Ad hoc on-demand distance vector (AODV)routing. Internet draft (work in progress), IETF Mobile Ad Hoc Networks Working Group (June 1999), draft-ietf-manet-aodv-03.txt
6. Lei, H., Perkins, C.E.: Ad hoc networking with Mobile IP. In: Proceedings of 2nd European Personal Mobile Communication Conference (September 1997)

Walsh Hadamard Transform Based Robust Blind Watermarking for Digital Audio Copyright Protection

Sunita V. Dhavale, R.S. Deodhar, and L.M. Patnaik

Defence Institute of Advanced Technology, Girinagar, Pune-411025, India
sunitadhavale75@rediffmail.com, {rsdeodhar,lalit}@diat.ac.in

Abstract. A blind audio watermarking algorithm based on mean quantization of Walsh Hadamard Transform (WHT) coefficients is proposed. The features of the proposed scheme are as follows: 1) data is embedded along with the synchronization codes in WHT domain to resist the synchronization attack more effectively; 2) the energy-compaction characteristics of WHT are used to improve the transparency of the digital watermark; 3) Fast Walsh Hadamard Transform Algorithm is used to reduce the computational time in searching the synchronization codes; 4) the watermark is embedded into the mean value of low sequency WHT coefficients of non-silent frames to take advantage of the perceptual properties of the Human Auditory System (HAS); 5) High data payload and efficient processing capability is achieved using small sized audio frames; and 6) the scheme can extract the watermark without the help of the original digital audio signal. Subjective and objective tests reveal that the proposed watermarking scheme maintains high audio quality and is simultaneously highly robust to pirate attacks, including MP3 compression, cropping, time shifting, filtering, resampling, and requantization.

Keywords: Audio watermarking, Walsh Hadamard Transform, Self Synchronization, Quantized Index Modulation, Robustness, Blind.

1 Introduction

Digital audio watermarking techniques can be successfully used for audio data copyright protection. Existing audio watermarking techniques are broadly categorized into time domain and transform domain techniques [1]. Time domain techniques are simple to realize, but they are less robust compared to transform domain techniques. Synchronization attack is one of the key issues of digital audio watermarking. In this paper a blind audio watermarking algorithm is proposed that can resist synchronization attack effectively along with providing reduced search time for detection of the synchronization codes. Here, we choose a set of binary logo images with size 32 x 32 pixels as a watermark. The binary logo image is first permuted using Arnold Transform in order to increase the secrecy of embedded watermark. To achieve robustness against cropping attacks, synchronizing codes are added along with the watermark bits. To achieve better error detection and correction capability, the combined watermark bit-stream is replicated according to the redundancy

V.V. Das and N. Thankachan (Eds.): CIIT 2011, CCIS 250, pp. 469–475, 2011.

factor (r) specified. Here, we apply Walsh Hadamard Transform (WHT) to the segmented audio frames, due to its simplicity and computation speed [7].We embed the watermark bits by modulating mean of WHT low sequency sub-band coefficients of non-silent frames; using QIM technique [5]. Instead of embedding data by modulating single WHT coefficient, mean value of several WHT coefficients in low sequency sub-band is modulated. This enhances robustness of the embedded data. As these WHT low sequency sub-band coefficients contain most of the signal energy, strong robustness can be achieved against common audio signal processing attacks; without degrading the acoustical quality of original host audio signals. For having low computational complexity against searching synchronization codes, we use Fast Walsh Hadamard Transform Algorithm (FWHT) [7-9]. The rest of this paper is organized as follows. Section 2 provides the outline of the proposed algorithm for embedding and extraction of binary image in an audio signal. Experimental results are compared with the results of previous works in Section 3; followed by the conclusions in Section 4.

2 Proposed Scheme

The proposed scheme consists of watermark processing stage and audio processing stage as shown in Figure 1 and the detailed procedure in case of watermark embedding process is as follows.

2.1 Watermark Embedding Process

Step 1: In watermark processing stage, the binary logo image is first permuted by the Arnold Transform in order to enhance the security of the system. Let W denote permuted binary watermark of size m x n representing the watermark logo.

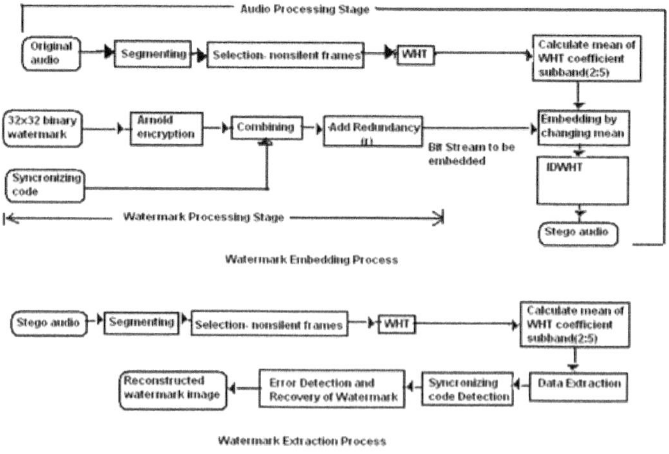

Fig. 1. Proposed system for audio watermarking

The resulting permuted binary image is converted into one dimensional array containing series of 0's and 1's (bits). To enhance the error detection capability of the system, this bit stream is replicated as specified by the redundancy factor (r). As time-scale or frequency-scale modification can cause false detection, synchronization code must be embedded robustly. False synchronization also depends on characteristics of the synchronization code chosen like the length of synchronization code, the probability of "0" and "1" in synchronization code [3]. The proposed scheme embeds 16 bit Barker code as synchronization code to locate the position of hidden informative bits, thus resisting the cropping and shifting attacks [3]. Barker codes are subsets of PN sequences and used for frame synchronization in digital communication systems. They have low correlation side lobes.

Step 2: In audio processing stage, the original host audio (X) is first segmented into non-overlapping audio frames of size 32 samples. Let Yk denotes the kth audio frame. The embedding capacity also depends on total number of segments, as each frame can embed one bit of watermark

Step 3: Skip silent audio frames that are present at beginning and end of audio signal. This also increases the robustness against the audio signal cropping attack, which is normally carried out during the start or end of an audio signal.

Step 4: Apply one dimensional Walsh Hadamard Transform (WHT) to each of the remaining non-silent frames.

Step 5: From each of the above processed frame, consider WHT coefficients in low-mid sequency band containing 2nd, 3rd, 4th and 5th WHT coefficients only. Due to energy compaction property of WHT, lower WHT sequency coefficients contain most of the energy in the frame. As these coefficients lie in low-mid sequency region, embedding watermark along with synchronization code in them will give good tradeoff between robustness and inaudibility. Calculate mean of these four coefficients. One bit of processed bit stream (containing watermark along with synchronization code) is embedded in each frame by modulating the mean Mk using quantization index modulation technique [3, 10] given by,

$$M_k{*}=\begin{cases} M_k - Mod\_(M_k,S) + \alpha_1 * S & if \quad w_i = 0 \\ M_k - Mod\_(M_k,S) + \alpha_2 * S & if \quad w_i = 1 \end{cases} \tag{1}$$

where,

$$Mod\_(M_k,S)=\begin{cases} M_k - \lfloor (M_k/S) \rfloor * S & if \quad M_k \geq 0 \\ M_k + (\lfloor (-M_k/S) \rfloor + 1) * S & if \quad M_k < 0 \end{cases} \tag{2}$$

where $\lfloor . \rfloor$ is the floor function and S denotes the embedding strength and α_1, α_2 are fractions ranging from 0 to 1 such that $\alpha_1 << \alpha_2$. The value of S should be chosen as large as possible to increase robustness under the inaudibility constraint. Then difference $Diff_k = M_k - M_k{*}$ is calculated and added to all the above four WHT coefficients, the mean of mid sequency coefficients also changes. This in turn affects every sample in that frame. Thus both watermark and synchronization code is embedded in frequency domain in a robust manner.

Step 6: Reconstruction:

The modified WHT coefficients are used in reconstruction process. Apply Inverse Walsh Hadamard Transform (IWHT) to embedded audio frames and combine them. The reconstructed audio signal is called as watermarked audio signal. The SNR of this audio signal with respect to the original audio signal is calculated and compared with the expected value of the SNR. The experimental results show that after embedding the watermarking information, the stego-audio signal gives SNR value more than 25dB.

2.2 Watermark Detection Process

The extraction algorithm consists of all the audio processing steps that are carried out at the time of embedding the WHT frames. First stego audio signal is segmented into non-overlapping frames of size 32 samples each. Then after selecting all non-silent audio frames, calculate mean of WHT mid sequency coefficient sub-band containing 2nd, 3rd, 4th and 5th WHT coefficients only and extract the watermark using the following equation,

$$w_k{}^* = \begin{cases} 1 & if \quad Mod(M_k{}^*, S) \geq S/2 \\ 0 & if \quad Mod(M_k{}^*, S) < S/2 \end{cases} \tag{3}$$

Once all the bits are extracted, the watermark logo image can be reconstructed by first detecting the synchronization codes. The original audio WHT coefficients are not required in the extracting process and thus the proposed algorithm is blind. The modification caused is not perceptually audible as only few WHT coefficients are modified from each non-silent frames. Experimental results show that four WHT coefficients per frame of 32 samples can be used without affecting the perceptual audio quality of the host signals. For the stereo audio signals, dual-channel signals are available for watermarking, while in case of a mono audio signals; only one single-channel signal is available for watermarking.

3 Experimental Results

3.1 Experimental Setup

To assess the performance of the proposed audio watermarking scheme, several experiments are carried out on different types of 250 mono audio signals of length 20 seconds each. These CD Quality audio signals are sampled at sampling rate 44.1 KHz with 16 bit resolution. These audio signals are categorized into following categories; the rock music (denoted by A1) that has very high signal energy, classical music (denoted by A2) and speech signal (denoted by A3) that has moderate signal energy.

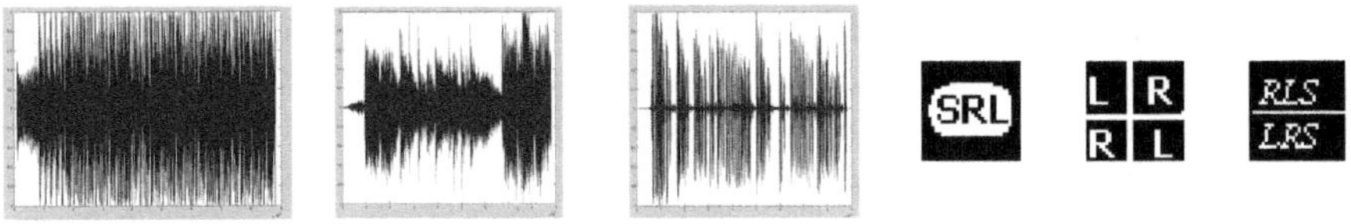

A1: Rock music | A2: classical music | A3: speech signal

(a) Original audio signals

(w1) (w2) (w3)

(b) 32x32 binary watermark images

Fig. 2. Original audio signals and binary logo watermark images

The ownership information is represented by a set of three different 32x32 binary logo images (denoted by w1, w2 and w3 respectively) as shown in Figure 2b. We use three different 32x32 binary logo images that represent the ownership information. The logo image is first permuted using Arnold Transform and converted into a one dimensional bit stream of 1's and 0's. After adding synchronization codes, it is replicated using redundancy factor r=3. The data payload (D) refers to the number of bits that are embedded into the audio signal within a unit of time. It is measured in the unit of bps (bits per second). It is measured as the ratio of the sampling rate of an audio signal to the frame size is Fs (i.e. number of samples per frame). For a frame containing 32 samples, the estimated data payload is 1378 bps. Without applying any redundancy, it needs an audio section about 0.7546 seconds in order to embed a 16 bit synchronization code (1111100110101110) along with a 32x32 binary watermark. With r=3, it needs an audio section about 2.2639 seconds. To achieve good robustness against different attacks, the value of embedding strength (S) is set to 500 for all audio files. To measure imperceptibility, we use signal-to-noise ratio (SNR) as an objective measure and a listening test based on Mean Opinion Score (MOS) as a subjective measure. The SNRs calculated are 29.49dB for A1, 26.92dB for A2 and 28.69dB for A3. The SNR is calculated only on the portion of an audio signal, where actual watermark bits are embedded. Ten listeners were involved in the actual listening test to estimate the subjective MOS grade of the watermarked audio signals. After presenting with the pairs of original audio signal and the watermarked audio signal, each listener was asked to report any difference detected between the two signals. The average grade for each pair from all listeners is found to be almost equal to 5.0 (where MOS grade=5.0 is the highest value that refers to total imperceptibility while MOS grade=0.0 is the lowest value that refers to very annoying quality of watermarked audio).

3.2 Robustness Test

Both Normalized Correlation (NC) and Bit Error Rate (BER) between the original watermark and the extracted watermark are used as an objective measure for the robustness. The watermarked audio signal is subjected to several standard audio processing attacks, in order to assess the robustness of the proposed watermarking scheme. The results are summarized in Table 1. We adopt the audio editing and attacking tool Stirmark for Audio, in order to carry out variety of different attacks. From the results, it can be seen that the proposed audio watermarking scheme is robust to most of the common audio processing attacks. Both rock audio signals (A1) and speech audio signals (A3) perform well compared to classical music (A2). In case of stereo audio signal, same watermark information or the meta data used during the embedding process (redundancy factor, length of watermark, Arnold Transform Frequency, value of S etc.), can be embedded in the second audio channel. This can also help receiver to retrieve and verify the watermark blindly. The performance of the proposed algorithm is also compared with the algorithms proposed by Wu, Huang, Daren and Shi, 2005 [6], Zhou and Lihau, 2007 [2] and Ravula and Rai,2010 [4]. The results are summarized in Table 2. The proposed algorithm gives moderate SNR values along with good amount of embedding capacity and lower bit error rates. The NC values are always above 0.9 for most of the common audio processing attacks.

Table 1. NC and BER values along with corresponding extracted watermarks for various attacks

Attack	BER (%)	NC (%)	Extracted watermark	Attack	BER (%)	NC (%)	Extracted watermark
No attack	0.0	1.00		Re-quantization (8 bit)	0.0	1.00	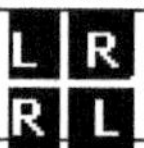
White noise (awgn)	0.0	1.00		Re-quantization (24 bit)	0.0	1.00	
Cropping (20%)	13.48	0.67		LPF (6 order Butterworth, 22.05 kHz)	6.54	0.84	
Re-sampling (22.05 kHz)	0.0	1.00		MP3 compression with the rate of 48 kbps	0.0	1.00	
Re-sampling (11.025 kHz)	0.19	0.99		MP3 compression with the rate of 32 kbps	0.68	0.98	
Re-sampling (8.00 kHz)	1.95	0.95		Amplitude (increased by 0.4)	0.0	1.00	

Table 2. Algorithm Comparison

Algorithm	Subj. Test Reported	Data Payload (bps) (approx.)	SNR (dB) (approx.)	NC UnderMP3 (96kbps) (approx.)	BER (%) Under MP3 (32kbps) (approx.)
Our Scheme	Yes	1378	26-30	0.99	0.39
[6]	No	172	29-30	Not Mentioned	24.18
[2]	No	1024	Not Mentioned	0.987	Not Mentioned
[4]	No	344	25-27	0.99	Not Mentioned

4 Conclusions

In this correspondence, we propose a novel blind audio watermarking scheme to provide a good amount of embedding data payload and high robustness along with required SNR. To increase the secrecy of watermark, the proposed scheme first permutes the watermark using Arnold Transform. To resist cropping attacks, watermark is embedded along with synchronization codes in the WHT domain. To take advantage of the perceptual properties of the Human Auditory System, watermark is embedding in non-silent audio frames by changing the mean value of few low sequency WHT coefficients. Adding redundancy to the watermark information provides error detection and correction capabilities. In order to improve the efficiency in searching synchronization codes, we use Fast Walsh Hadamard Transform algorithm. The experimental results show that the embedded watermark is perceptually transparent and the proposed scheme is robust against different types of attacks. For most of the attacks, the normalized correlation coefficient is more than 0.9. Small sized audio frames are used to provide high data payload along with efficient processing capability. In addition, the watermark can be extracted without the help from the original digital audio signal and can be easily implemented. Experimental results are analyzed by both the subjective listening test using MOS values and objective test using SNR values.

References

1. Acevedo, A.: Audio watermarking: properties, techniques and evaluation. In: Multimedia security: Steganography and Digital Watermarking Techniques for Protection of Intellectual Property, pp. 75–125. IGI Global (Idea Group Publishing), Pennsylvania (2005)
2. Zhou, Z., Zhou, L.: A Novel Algorithm for Robust Audio Watermarking Based on Quantification DCT Domain. In: 3rd International Conference on Information Hiding and Multimedia Signal Processing, vol. 1, pp. 441–444 (2007)
3. Wang, X., Zhao, H.: A novel synchronization invariant audio watermarking scheme based on DWT and DCT. IEEE Transactions on Signal Processing 54(12), 4835–4840 (2006)
4. Ravula, R., Rai, S.: A Robust Audio Watermarking Algorithm Based on Statistical Characteristics and DWT+DCT Transforms. In: Proceedings of Wireless Communications Networking and Mobile Computing (WiCOM), Chengdu, China, pp. 1–4 (2010)
5. Bhat K., V., Sengupta, I., Das, A.: Audio Watermarking Based on Quantization in Wavelet Domain. In: Sekar, R., Pujari, A.K. (eds.) ICISS 2008. LNCS, vol. 5352, pp. 235–242. Springer, Heidelberg (2008)
6. Wu, S., Huang, J., Huang, D., Shi, Y.Q.: Efficiently Self-Synchronized Audio Watermarking for Assured Audio Data Transmission. IEEE Transactions on Broadcasting 51(1), 69–76 (2005)
7. Beauchamp, K.G.: Applications of Walsh and Related Functions: with an Introduction to Sequency Theory, pp. 295–300. Academic Press, London (1984)
8. Zhihua, L., Qishan, Z.: Ordering of Walsh functions. IEEE Transactions on Electromagnetic Comupatibility, 115–119 (1983)
9. Brown, R.D.: A recursive algorithm for sequency-ordered fast Walsh transforms. IEEE Transactions on Computers, C-26(8), 819–822 (1977)

Bettering TCP Performance of Transient Mobile Nodes in 802.11 Networks by ACK Caching

Jansi Rani Sella Velusami[1], P. Narayanasamy[2], and Narendran Thangarajan[1]

[1] Department of CSE, SSN College of Engineering, Chennai, India
[2] Department of CSE, Anna University, Guindy, Chennai, India

Abstract. Transmission Control Protocol is the most widely used transport layer protocol in wired networks accounting to 95% of the Internet traffic. On wireless networks, TCP demands special focus. The TCP source in the wired domain is unaware of the vagaries of the lossy wireless domain and starts reducing the congestion window, which is the normal flow control mechanism of TCP. But this leads to a considerable degradation in TCP Performance in 802.11 WLAN networks. To address this issue, we propose a model which involves no change to the transient mobile node and to the wired host sending the Internet traffic. TCP performance is improved by introducing a cross-layer scheme accompanied by a buffer to cache ACKs and TCP packets. Then we have studied the TCP performance improvement in four of the TCP congestion control algorithms – NewReno and Linux.

Keywords: Transmission Control Protocol (TCP), Cross-Layer Scheme, Performance Enhancement, ACK Caching, Performance Comparison.

1 Introduction

The usage of wireless devices has increased manyfold over the past decade. But the inherent drawbacks in wireless networks like the high bit-error rate (BER) causing random loss, bursty traffic due to channel access asymmetry and disconnections due to handoffs and interferences, makes TCP performance in wireless networks a dubious concept. More specifically, timeouts and large, varying round-trip times have a notable impact on TCP's congestion control algorithms [6][7]. The wired host sending TCP traffic to the mobile node connected to the 802.11 network under investigation, cannot differentiate packet losses caused by congestion, from link errors. The wired host will assume that the packet loss is due to congestion and dissolves it by reducing the sender window size, thus drastically reducing throughput[3]. In this paper, we propose an idea wherein the base station acts proactively by using the Received Signal Strength (RSS) indication from the link layer after a frame from mobile node is received. This cross-layer interaction between the link layer of the base station and the transport layer is used to prevent the congestion control mechanisms from reducing the throughput of the transmission.

V.V. Das and N. Thankachan (Eds.): CIIT 2011, CCIS 250, pp. 476–478, 2011.

2 Related Works

The existing solutions could be categorized as:

1. End-to-end Schemes (Selective Acknowledgments, Explicit Loss Notification [1][8], Freeze TCP)
2. Link Layer Schemes (Snoop Protocol[4] and Delayed DupACKs)
3. Split Connection Schemes (Indirect TCP[5]).

The idea we propose in this paper belongs to the Split Connection Scheme and it involves no change to the TCP protocol stack of the sender or receiver.

3 ACK Caching and Pacing Mechanism

As a mobile node moves away from a base station, the RSS value of the received frame starts to drop. When the RSS value drops below a certain threshold, the link layer sends an alert to the TCP layer. This indication acts as a trigger causing the TCP layer of the base station to perceive that the transient mobile node is moving out. Then the ACKs received from the mobile node are stored until the transient mobile node is completely out of range of the base station. Then the accumulated ACKs are scheduled at a calculated pace so that the sender (wired host) is unaware of the fact that mobile has left the base station's coverage area. When the mobile node returns back to the same Basic Service Set (BSS), then the link layer identifies the presence of the node by detecting the signal strength and indicates it to the transport layer. The data hitherto cached in the base station is sent to the mobile node. Then the mobile node commences to acknowledge the TCP packets once again, thus maintaining almost the same throughput as observed before the mobile node's unavailability.

The ACK caching mechanism operates based on the following steps.

1. Calculate the estimate of RTT to the mobile and the fixed host.
2. Calculate the approximate RTO on the fixed host for the first packet whose ACK is cached.
3. Calculate the time at which the ACKs should be paced based on ACKs count and the approximate duration of mobile host unreachability.

The success of the above algorithm depends on the accuracy of the RTO chosen. The general formula for finding the RTO [2] is

$$RTO(n) = (7/8)^{(N-n)}\mu_n + 4(3/4)^{(N-n)}\sigma_n + [1-(7/8)^{(N-n)}]\Theta(n) + 8[(7/8)^{(N-n)}-(3/4)^{(N-n)}]|\mu_n - \Theta(n)| \quad (1)$$

In the above equation, N is the total number of ACKs stored by the base station, m denotes the number of ACKs made to wait since the start of the algorithm, Θ is the time between sending the ACKs and μ and σ being arbitrary constants. Using this formula, we could find an optimal interval T_i. The ACKs stored in the ACK buffer is scheduled and sent to the fixed host in equal intervals of T_i. Thus the congestion control mechanisms are not triggered due to this false positive occurrence.

4 Experimental Results

The proposed idea was implemented and the results were tracked using ns2. The results show a considerable improvement over the legacy TCP implementations. Fig 1 and Fig 2 show the throughput graphs when the proposed system was used with TCP/NewReno and TCP/Linux respectively.

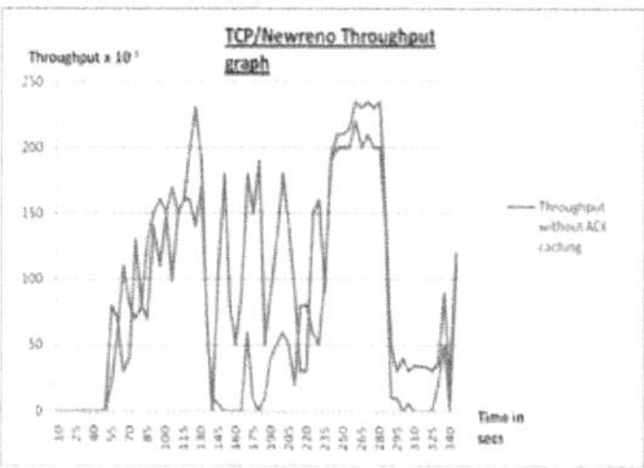

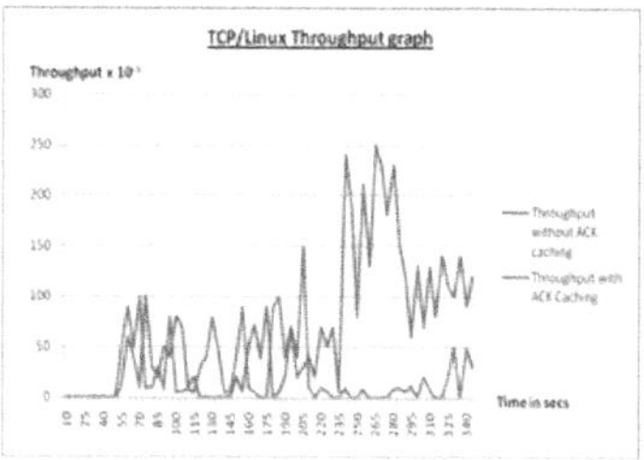

Fig. 1. TCP/Newreno Throughput Graph **Fig. 2.** TCP/Linux Throughput Graph

5 Conclusion

This paper proposes a premonitory scheme where data-link layer indicates the TCP layer about impending disconnections. The proposed system has been implemented and tested with TCP/NewReno and TCP/Linux algorithms using ns2 network simulator. In future, we are to implement the proposed system on a real base station as the test-bed and study the TCP flow in real-time scenarios.

References

1. Chawhan, M.D., Kapur, A.R.: TCP Performance Enhancement using ECN and Snoop Protocol for Wi-fi Network. In: Second International Conference on Computer and Network Technology (2010)
2. Bhutani, G.: A Near-Optimal Scheme for TCP ACK Pacing to Maintain Throughput in Wireless Networks. In: Proc. IEEE COMSNETS (2010)
3. Gopal, S., Paul, S.: TCP Dynamics in 802.11 Wireless Local Area Networks. In: Proc. IEEE Communications Society (2007)
4. Balakrishnan, H., Padmanabhan, V.N., Seshan, S., Katz, R.H.: A comparison of mechanisms for improving TCP performance over wireless links. IEEE/ACM Transactions on Networking, 756–769 (December 1997)
5. Bakre, A., Badrinath, B.R.: I-TCP: Indirect TCP for mobile hosts. In: ICDCS (1995)
6. Balakrishnan, H., Seshan, S., Amir, E., Katz, R.H.: Improving TCP/IP performance over wireless networks. In: Proc. ACM MOBICOM 1995 (1995)
7. Mondal, S.A.: Improving performance of TCP over mobile wireless networks. Springer Link (2007)
8. Balakrishnan, H., Katz, R.H.: Explicit loss notification and wireless web performance. In: Proceedings of IEEE GLOBECOM 1998 Internet Mini-Conferene, Sydney, Australia (November 1998)

Clustering Web Page Sessions Using Sequence Alignment Method

G. Poornalatha and S. Raghavendra Prakash

Department of Information Technology,
National Institute of Technology Karnataka (NITK), Surathkal,
Mangalore, India
poornalathag@yahoo.com, srp@nitk.ac.in

Abstract. This paper illustrates clustering of web page sessions in order to identify the users' navigation pattern. In the approach presented here, user sessions of variable lengths are compared pair wise, numbers of alignments are found between them and the distances are measured. Web page sessions are clustered by employing the modified k-means algorithm. A couple of web access logs including the well known NASA data set are used to illustrate the effectiveness of the clustering. R-squared measure is applied to determine the optimal number of clusters and chi-squared test is carried out to see the association between the various web page sessions that are clustered. These two measures show the goodness of the clusters formed.

Keywords: clustering, sequence alignment, web usage mining, R-squared measure, dynamic programming.

1 Introduction

The evolution of the internet along with the popularity of the web has attracted a great attention among the researchers to web usage mining. Web usage mining is the application of data mining techniques to usage logs of large data repositories maintained by the web servers [1]. A variety of approaches and models are discussed in the literature about the clustering and the distance measures used. Mojica et al. [2] clustered web pages by modifying gravitational algorithm. Yilmaz et al. [3] used ontology and sequence information for extracting behavior patterns from web logs. Oh [4] proposed the measure of similarity for effective hierarchical clustering. Yanchi et al. [5] focused on internal validation measures. Hay et al. [6] illustrated a method for mining navigation patterns using a sequence alignment method. They partition navigation patterns based on the order in which web pages are requested. The cluster analysis is done by the R-squared measure. George P. et al. [7] used model based clustering algorithm to group web user sessions and the clusters are validated by using statistical chi-square test. The work in [8] proposes an effective modified k-means algorithm based on variable length vector distance (VLVD) function. But, the order of page visits is not considered. For some applications like web page prediction the order information is essential. Hence the present work tries to deal with the order information. R-squared and chi-square measures are used to validate the clustering

V.V. Das and N. Thankachan (Eds.): CIIT 2011, CCIS 250, pp. 479–483, 2011.

done. The remainder of this paper is organized as follows. In section 2, method of finding distance between user sessions is discussed; in section 3, the outcome of the clustering and evaluation done is discussed followed by the conclusions in section 4.

2 Web Page Session Clustering

2.1 Sequence Alignment Based Distance

The similarity measure based on sequence alignment [9] is explained in this section. When any two sessions are considered, individual pair wise comparisons between them are required in order to get the distance. Here, two pages are said to be a match, if they are same. The mismatch results, if the pages are different. This indicates that either insertion, deletion or substitution operation is required to make both sessions exactly the same. The major steps of the algorithm used to find the distance between any two user's web sessions are given below:

Algorithm: Sequence Alignment Based Distance Measure (SABDM)

1. Consider two web sessions of length m and n respectively
2. Assign scores for match and mismatch suitably, say match=2, mismatch=-1. Initialize similarity count to zero.
3. Construct a score matrix of size (m+1, n+1) and initialize according to match or mismatch by comparing the pages of two sessions one by one in the order
4. Construct the distance and pointer matrix of size (m+1, n+1) and fill the distance matrix by using equation 1.

$$Dist(i,j) = \max\begin{Bmatrix} 0, \\ Dist(i-1,j) + mismatch, \\ Dist(i,j-1) + mismatch, \\ Dist(i,j) + score(i,j) \end{Bmatrix} \forall 0 \prec i \leq m+1, 0 \prec j \leq n+1 \tag{1}$$

5. Depending upon the value selected in step 4, update the pointer matrix to store the position, indicating whether the value taken for current cell is due to top/left/left-top cell
6. Find the cell in distance matrix with largest value, backtrack from that position with the help of pointer matrix and increment the similarity count whenever match is encountered
7. Stop the back tracking when cell with value zero is found in distance matrix or reached topmost row or left most column of distance matrix
8. Find the normalized distance value between two user sessions by using equation 2

$$dist = \frac{\max(m,n) - similaritycount}{\max(m,n)} \tag{2}$$

To illustrate the SABDM and compare with the SAM [6], consider the following: S1:p1,p2,p4,p7,p8,p9; S2:p1,p4,p7,p2,p8,p2; The distance between S1 and S2 is 4 in [6] whereas the distance is 2 by the SABDM method. Out of six pages of S1, four pages are aligned with S2. Here p2 and p9 are not aligned. Thus the normalized distance from S1 and S2 is 0.33 by the SABDM method. The method in [6] considers number of operations to be carried out to make both sessions equal as the distance, but, the SABDM method considers the alignments obtained for finding the distance.

2.2 Clustering

The web pages accessed by users in a session are clustered based on the order in which the pages are accessed by the user. The algorithm modified k-means for web session clustering [8] is used, but instead of using VLVD function, SABDM algorithm whose steps are given in section 2.1 is used. To decide the input 'k', the number of clusters, R-squared measure is used which is discussed in the section 3.2.

3 Results and Discussions

3.1 Data Sets and Navigation Patterns

Two data sets are considered for clustering: The first set is NASA log taken from http://ita.ee.lbl.gov/html/contrib/NASA-HTTP.html.The data is preprocessed and sessions are constructed. The different pages identified from this data set are 868. The second set is MSNBC data set taken from msnbc.com. Visits are recorded at the level of URL category. There are 30 categories of pages in NASA data set and 17 page categories in MSNBC data set as given in [9]. 5000 sessions are considered from each of the data sets for clustering. By observing the frequency of page categories in each cluster, the user navigation patterns of users are observed. Some of the patterns for the NASA data set are:

{/shuttle/missions/, /history/apollo/, /shuttle/countdown/},
{/elv/, /shuttle/missions/, /history/apollo/}
{/shuttle/missions/, /payloads/, /software/}
{/history/apollo/, /shuttle/missions/, /history/mercury/}
{/shuttle/missions/, /history/mercury/, /history/gemini/}

Similarly few of the patterns obtained from the MSNBC data set are:

{front page, news, sports}
{front page, misc, on-air}
{on-air, tech, msn-news}
{local, misc, front page}
{front page, business}

In [6] the number of clusters formed is 3 and in [7] the number of clusters is 5. When the number of sessions is more, it may not be possible to capture all the patterns of user navigation with only three or five clusters because human behavior pattern is dynamic in nature and due to the availability of various page categories with many pages in each category, wide variety of patterns is expected. Chances of obtaining majority of the sequential patterns is more, when the number of clusters are also reasonably more. Therefore, R-squared is used to decide the number of clusters.

3.2 R-squared Validation

R-squared is one of the widely used internal validation measure. It is the ratio of sum of squares between clusters to the total sum of squares of the whole data set. Given a model, the closer its R squared value is to one, the greater the reliability of a relationship identified by regression analysis. R-squared of 10% or 5% may be statistically significant in some applications [10]. If application is to predict human behavior, R-squared of 40% is also excellent [11]. Since the clusters of web page sessions is used to analyze the navigation pattern of users in a web site, 50% and above is considered as good here to decide the number of clusters. Thus the optimal number of clusters for NASA data set is 26 and 29 for the MSNBC data set. The Figure 1 shows the graph of R-squared values for various numbers of clusters ranging from 1 to 100 for the NASA data set.

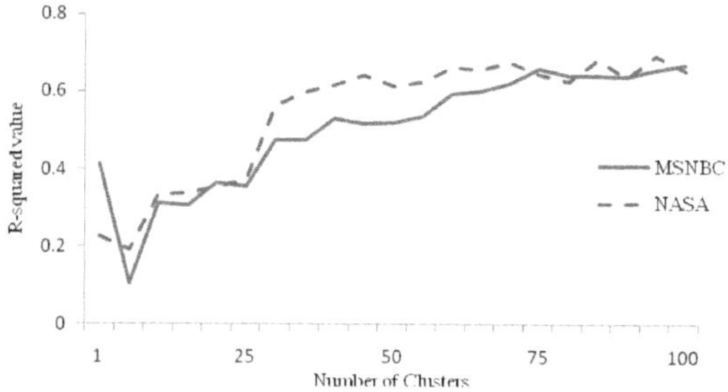

Fig. 1. R-squared v/s cluster number – NASA and MSNBC data set

The Figure 1 shows that, as the number of clusters increases, the R-squared increases up to some threshold. Here, at cluster number 26 the R-squared value reaches 0.6 for NASA data and beyond this, the increment is only in small quantities. Therefore, it can be inferred that, the number of clusters for this data set is 26. Similarly the number of clusters for MSNBC data set is 29.Thus using R-squared the number of clusters is decided and the graph is different for different data sets indicating that, R-squared depends on the individual data set.

3.3 Chi-squared Validation

In general, the chi-squared is a hypothesis test carried out to see the association between categorical variables. It is used to determine whether there is a significant difference between the expected frequencies and the observed frequencies in one or more categories. The Table 1 shows the results obtained by applying chi-square test. The chi-square value obtained is much higher than the critical value. Therefore, the null hypothesis H_0 is rejected and H_1 is accepted that indicates the goodness of the clustering done. The null hypothesis is "there is no association between the page categories and clusters" and an alternate hypothesis is "there is an association between the page categories and clusters".

Table 1. Chi- squared validation

Data set	Level of significance			Chi-square obtained
	0.05	0.01	0.001	
NASA	788.8	816.5	848.4	1443
MSNBC	498.3	520.5	546.2	20290

4 Conclusion

In this paper, an effective method for comparing pair wise web page sessions based sequence alignment is discussed. The clusters formed by this distance measure are validated by using two different statistical methods namely, R-squared and chi-square. The results obtained are encouraging in terms of the various navigation patterns obtained. The future work may use the resulting patterns in predicting the next page view of the user to further ensure the goodness of the clustering done.

References

1. Nina, S.P., Rahman, M., Bhuiyan, K.I., Ahmed, K.: Pattern Discovery of Web Usage Mining. In: Int. Conf. on Computer Technology and Development. IEEE (2009)
2. Mojica, J.A., Rojas, D.A., Gomez, J., Gonzalez, F.: Page Clustering Using a Distance Based Algorihm. In: 3rd Latin American Web congress, LA-WEB 2005. IEEE (2005)
3. Yilmaz, H., Senkul, P.: Using Ontology and Sequence Information for Extracting Behavior Patterns from Web Navigation Logs. In: IEEE Int. Conf. on Data Mining Workshops, pp. 549–556. IEEE (2010)
4. Oh, S.: Mining Clusters of Sequences Using Extended Sequence Element-Based Similarity Measure. In: 2nd Int. Conf. on Innovative Computing, Information and Control. IEEE (2007)
5. Yanchi, L., Zhongmou, L., Hui, X., Xuedong, G., Junjie, W.: Understanding of Internal Clustering Validation Measures. In: IEEE 10th Int. Conf. on Data Mining, pp. 911–916. IEEE (2010)
6. Hey, B., Wets, G., Vanhoof, K.: Mining Navigation Patterns Using a Sequence Alignment Method. J. Know. and Info. Systems, 150–163 (2004)
7. George, P., Lefteris, A., Anthena, V.: Validation and Interpretation of Web users' sessions clusters. J. Info. Processing & Mgmt. 43, 1348–1367 (2007)
8. Poornalatha, G., Raghavendra, P.S.: Web user session clustering using modified K-means algorithm. In: Abraham, A., Lloret Mauri, J., Buford, J.F., Suzuki, J., Thampi, S.M. (eds.) ACC 2011, Part II. CCIS, vol. 191, pp. 243–252. Springer, Heidelberg (2011)
9. Poornalatha, G., Raghavendra, P.S.: Alignment Based Similarity Distance Measure for Better Web Sessions Clustering. J. Procedia Computer Science 5, 450–457 (2011)
10. What's a good value for R-squared?, `http://www.duke.edu/~rnau/rsquared.htm`
11. How high, R-squared?, `http://cooldata.wordpress.com/2010/04/19/how-high-r-squared/`

Static Analysis of CPU Execution Time Using Implict Path Enumeration Techniques

T.K. Manjunath and Chidaravalli Sharmila

Amruta Institute of Engineering & Management Sciences,
Department of Computer Science and Engineering, Bengaluru-562109, India
manju_mist@rediffmail.com, c.sharmila11@gmail.com

Abstract. Static Analysis of CPU execution time using implicit path enumeration is an approach where translator predicts the execution time of a program. Basically translator is a System Software which converts computer languages to machine understandable formats. Generally these translators will not estimate the CPU execution time of a given program, because execution time usually depends on execution environment like user inputs, system status, and system architecture and so on. This paper provides approach of to predict the CPU execution time of a given program during translation process.

Keywords: Execution time, Path Analysis, Timing Analysis, Static Analysis, Object code.

1 Introduction

The execution time of a program that runs uninterrupted on a processor depends both on program characteristics and the hardware that executes the program. For a simple processor where single instructions have a fixed execution time, the program execution time is solely determined by the input data given to the program. The input data can influence the path taken through the program and the number of loop iterations done in loops and this causes the execution time to vary. For a more complex computer system execution time also depends on the previous programs that have executed on the processor, the *execution history* of the system. Also some single instructions can have an execution time that depends on the input data. A good example of the added complexity is to consider a data cache that holds recently fetched data from the main memory. A single load instruction that loads data from the memory executes fast if the data already exists in the cache (a cache hit) and slow if it must fetch data from memory (a cache miss). The outcome can depend both on the previous content of the data cache (the execution history) and the address used when accessing memory and this address can depend on the input data given to the program. The paper provides an approach to predict Execution Time of a program during translation Process. Various techniques and tools are available to analyze programs behavior using static and dynamic analysis. By predicting the execution paths using static analysis, during translation process it is possible to estimate execution time by accepting user inputs.

V.V. Das and N. Thankachan (Eds.): CIIT 2011, CCIS 250, pp. 484–488, 2011.

So, in order to find the CPU execution time, we must consider both the program characteristics, hardware characteristics and Timing factors.

Execution Time. Execution Time of a given Program depends on various factors like, System status, System architecture etc.

Elapsed Time. It is the time taken from start state (fetching an instruction) till completion of instruction execution (*disk and memory accesses, waiting for I/O, running other programs, etc.*) .Elapsed time is calculated by

Elapsed Time= CPU time + Wait Time

CPU Time. CPU Time does not count waiting for I/O or time spent running other programs. It can be divided into *user CPU time* and *system CPU time* (OS calls) .So CPU time is the time taken by User and the System given by

CPU time = User CPU time + system CPU time

Clock Cycles. Instead of reporting execution time in seconds our compiler predicts number of clock cycles for the given program. In modern computers hardware events progress cycle by cycle, in other words, each instructions/events, e.g., multiplication, addition, etc., is a sequence of cycles. By knowing number of clock cycles for a given program, compiler calculates execution time in seconds. For a program

CPU execution time = CPU clock cycles * clock cycle time

Our focus is to predict user CPU time (CPU execution time or, simply, execution time) time spent executing the lines of code that are generated by the compiler.

2 Proposed System

The proposed system, translator predicts CPU execution time of a program will identify the execution path during compilation process itself by accepting the user inputs and calculate CPU execution time of the predicted path. Proposed system will help the compiler to estimate execution time of a generated object codes. Finally compiler generates the target codes only for predicted execution path and same will be loaded for execution, by reducing loading time, space and execution time.

2.1 Structured Computer Organization

Programs will have many execution paths, based on the user inputs program may take any path during execution. In this regard many papers are published earlier to predict execution paths during compilation process itself. The proposed system accepts user inputs during compilation process and predicts CPU execution time of a given program as shown in Fig. 1. It is possible to identify execution paths during compilation process using static analysis by accepting user inputs. Compiler constructs the Abstract Syntax Trees for given program by performing Static Analysis on AST and finally it constructs CFG by accepting user inputs during compilation process and compiler predicts the execution path by using CFG. In our proposed system CPU execution time will be calculated for the Predicted Execution path using Timing Analysis. So

CPU execution time/program=(No. of cycles/program)*(seconds/cycle)+wait time

Wait Time=0 for ideal system, in a proposed System Timing analysis gives the number of clock cycles required to execute the instructions which come under predicted execution path. Execution path is collections of basic blocks; each basic block is a collection of instructions. Each instruction requires number of machine cycles to execute. Clock cycles for each instruction are different from instructions to instructions. Proposed system performs Timing analysis of the predicted Execution path and predicts the required number of clock cycles for the program.

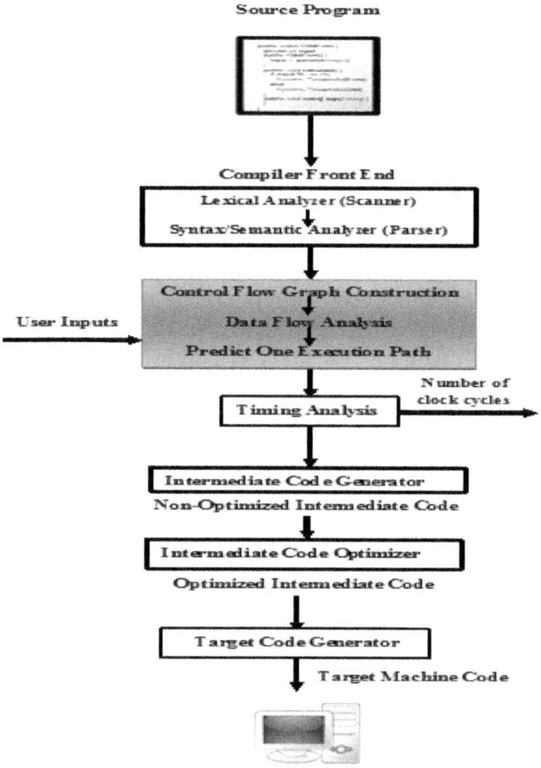

Fig. 1. Proposed System

2.2 Applications of the Proposed System

The proposed system will be applicable for the following applications:

Real Time Operating Systems.
CPU scheduling
Load and go compilers etc.

2.3 Limitations

The idea forwarded through this paper can cause overestimation of Execution Time due to two important reasons. First the analysis may include program paths that can never be executed regardless of the input data, usually referred to as infeasible program paths (Infeasible paths are sometimes called non-executable or dead program paths). Second, the timing model of the hardware platform may introduce overestimations of the Execution Time because of simplifying timing assumptions. To reduce overestimation, need to perform good path analysis as well as good timing analysis.

3 Expected Results

Consider a piece of code written in C Language and the same is converted into Assembly level language by the compiler. Assembly Level Language is generated for the X86 families.

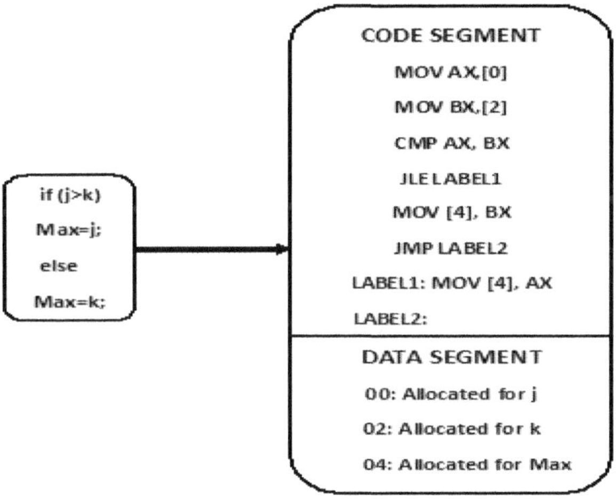

Fig. 2. Example showing how C code is translated to Assembly Level Language in X86 architecture machines

Compiler generates seven instructions for the above High Level Language program written in C language as shown in Fig. 2. Assuming each instruction will take 4 clock cycles executing in X86 architecture machines with 5 MHz speed, resulting with the CPU execution time of 5600 ns i.e.

$$\text{CPU execution time} = \text{CPU clock cycles} * \text{clock cycle time}$$

$$= 28 * 1/(5*10^6)*10^9$$

$$= 5600 \text{ nanoseconds}$$

4 Conclusions

The proposed system is based on static analysis and techniques; it predicts the CPU execution time by finding the execution path by using Path Analysis and Timing Analysis by accepting user inputs during translation process by the translator and generates the object codes for the predicted execution path. Thus automatically reduces the memory size and execution time.

References

1. Healy., C., Whalley, D.: Automatic Detection and Exploitation of Branch Constraints for Timing Analysis. IEEE Transactions on Software Engineering, 763–781 (August 2000)
2. Engblom, J., Ermedahl, A.: Modeling Complex flows for worst-case execution time analysis. In: Proceedings of 21st IEEE Real Time System Symposium, USA (2000)
3. Allen, F.E.: Control flow Analysis. In: Proceeding of a Symposium on Compiler Optimization, SIGPLAN Notices, pp.1–19 (July 1970)
4. Blieberger, J.: Discrete loops and worst case performance, 193–212 (1994)
5. Worst case Execution time Analyzers, http://www.ieuhsint.cr.in/ait

A Shape Representation Scheme for 2D Images Using Distributions of Centroid Contour Distances and Their Local Variations

T. Gokaramaiah[1], P. Viswanath[1], and B. Eswara Reddy[2]

[1]Dept. of Computer Science and Engineering,
Rajeev Gandhi Memorial College of Eng. and Tech., Nadyal-518501
tgokari@gmail.com, viswanath.p@ieee.org
[2]Dept. of Computer Science and Engineering,
JNTUA college of Engineering, Anantapur-515002
eswarcsejntu@gmail.com

Abstract. Content based image retrieval system (CBIR) retrieves images from a database based on the contents of the query image.Retrieval based on the shape of the 2D object present in the image is important in several applications. Shape of an objectis invariant to translation, scaling, rotation and mirror-reflection. Hence, the representation scheme which possesses all theseproperties is important. Signature histogram and k^{th} order augmented histogram have all invariance properties [17]. But,they are applicable only to convex shapes. This representation scheme assumes that centroid to contour distance is a functionof angle (with a predefined axis). This is not true for non-convex and open shapes, since for some angles there can be more than onecentroid to contour distance. The current paper does not make this assumption, but considers distribution of centroid tocontour distances. Further, to reduce the false positive rate, distribution of local variations of the centroid contour distancesare also considered. Experimental studies are done using a standard image database and handwritten symbols database. The present technique is comparedagainst a similar recent technique.

Keywords: Signature, Signature histogram, K^{th} order augmented histogram.

1 Introduction

Shape recognition has severalapplications, like content-based image retrieval [20], character recognition [4], object classification where input is image of an object [18], online hand-drawn text or shaperecognition [1], writer recognition [15], etc. In general, shape representation methods are categorized as (i) contour-based methods, and (ii) region-based methods. In contour based methods only the boundary is taken into account, whereas in region-based methods entire region is considered. Each category is further divided into global and structural approaches. Structural approach sees the object as consisting of several parts along with their relationships [10]. Some of the structural approaches are chain code representation [5, 6], polygon

V.V. Das and N. Thankachan (Eds.): CIIT 2011, CCIS 250, pp. 489–493, 2011.

decomposition [11, 12], smooth curve decomposition [2], *etc*. The other approach is called global which represents boundary as a whole. The area, circularity (ratio of squared perimeter and area), eccentricity (ratio of major axis' length and minor axis'length), major axis orientation, bending energy, *etc.*, [19] are some of simple global approaches. Shape signatures [14], boundary moments [13], etc. are other relevant global approaches. Elaborated reviews of several methods are given by Zhang *et. al.* [20].Shape signature is a one dimensional function which corresponds to the boundary points and there are several shape signatures like centroidal profile, complex coordinates, centroid distance, tangent angle, curvature, turning function, two segmented angle function [14, 20, 16]. The centroid distance signature [20] or centroid-contour distance (CCD) curve [18] is a function which is a mapping from a set of angles to a set of distances. Angle is taken between a predefined axis and the line joining centroid to a boundary point. Distance is the distance of the line joining centroid to the boundary point. In two segment turning function (2STF) [16] approach the angle between two consecutive segments is calculated. 2STF representation is calculated by traversing a polygon in anticlockwise direction and assigning certain value of 2STF for each linear segment curve. The x-value of step is equal to length of linear segment which is normalized with respect to the complete curve. The y-value is directional angle of the line segment with respect to its previous segment. We have compared our approach with 2STF.This is a generalization of our earlier shape representation method called signature histograms and k^{th} order augmented histograms [17] which are suitable only for convex shapes. The present paper proposes "a shape representation method using distributions of centroid contour distances and their local variations" which works for both convex and non convex shapes. The rest of the paper is organized as follows. Section 2 describes about the proposed shape representation method. Section 3 gives the kth order augmented representation method. Section 4 presents the hierarchical retrieval system which uses the proposed scheme. Section 5 gives the experimental details that were conducted to find the effectiveness of the proposed scheme against a similar method. Finally, Section 6 concludes the paper.

2 Distribution of Distances from Centroid to Boundary

Centroid distance signature fails for non convex shapes, because centroid distance signature function has more than one length for a same θ value. New signature is defined based on probability theory, which is called probability mass function (PMF) for shape. The lengths are taken from centroid to boundary with respect to the predefined horizontal axis. The lengths are normalized by dividing all lengths with the maximum length value, so that all the lengths are in the range *[0,1]*. Probability mass function for shape was derived from these lengths. The horizontal axis of PMF for shape is divided into equal intervals in the range *[0,1]*, each interval is called a bin. Ifa length falls within a particular bin, then count of that corresponding bin is incremented by one. This process has to be repeated for all lengths. The bin count indicates frequency of a particular length within a range. All bin count values are divided by total number of lengths, which gives probability mass function for shape(PMF for shape). This PMF for shape is invariant to rotation, scale, translation and flip. Let the set of contour points be $S = \{(x_1, y_1), (x_2, y_2), ... (x_M, y_M)\}$. We assume that this is an ordered set where the ordering is obtained as follows. Let (x_c, y_c) bethecentroid of the contour, i.e., mean of the points in S. The contour is translated such that centroid becomes the new origin. Starting from the nearest point to origin the contour is traversed in the anti-clockwise direction. The ordering of S is according to this ordering. The lengths $L = (l(\theta_1), l(\theta_2),..,l(\theta_M))$ are distances from centroid (x_c, y_c) to contour points. These lengths are normalized by dividing each length by the maximum length. The interval $[0,1]$ is divided into equi-width bins. Let the number of lengths falling into the ith bin be b_i. Then in the PMF for shape, the ith bin's probability is b_i/M.This PMF is called the 0th order PMF and is denoted by PMF_0.

The PMF_0 for any shape is invariant to translation, scale, rotation and flip.

3 3 k^{th} Order Augmented PMF for Shape

PMF for shape works for non convex shape but it has a drawback, namely it increases false positives. This problem was solved by taking into account the distribution of local variations of the centroid contour distances.

k^{th}order difference distance is defined as :

$$L^k(i) = \begin{cases} |l_i - l_{i+k}| & \text{for } i = 1 \text{ to } M - k \\ |l_i - l_{i+k-M}| & \text{for } i = M - k + 1 \text{ to } M \end{cases}$$

For $k = 1$ to $M-1$, PMFs are obtained similar to PMF_0. These PMFs are respectively denoted by PMF_1,PMF_2,…,PMF_{M-1}. A shape is represented by augmenting all these PMFs.That is the representation for the shape is $<PMF_0,PMF_1,\ldots,PMF_{M-1}>$, and this is called the kth order augmented representation .

4 Shape Based k^{th} Order Hierarchical Retrieval System

Shape based image retrieval system, retrieves similar images from database for given input image of an object. Each shape is represented by its kth order augmented representation. From a database of these representations, based on the query image, similar shaped objects are retrieved. The searching is done in a hierarchical way. That is, first only 0th order PMFs (i.e., PMF_0) are compared and a few matching images are stored. In our experiments, 25% of matching (i.e., nearest) images are retrieved. Then, from this subset of images, further filtering is done based on PMF_1. Likewise the searching is done and finally 5 images are presented the user.

5 Experimental Results

Proposed method PMF for shape was tested using leafs database available at the University of California Museum of Paleontology *(URL: http://www.ucmp.berkeley.edu/science/clearedleaf.php)*and a handwritten symbols database which consists of 16 handwritten symbols like +, @, #, etc.Leaves database consists of a total of 1500 images. For each image four more versions are created by applying transformations like rotation, scaling, translation, flip. So, a total of 6000 images is present in the leaves database. Out of this 300 images are randomly chosen for testing purpose. The handwritten symbols database consists of 1600 images, collected from ten different persons where each person is asked to draw the symbol on a writing pad for ten times (each time the writing pad is slightly rotated). Out of these 1600 symbols, 80 are chosen for the testing purpose. The results are summarized below which shows *recall rates* for each data set. Comparison is done with the 2STF method [16].

Table 1. Results showing recall rates

Method	Data Set	
	Leaf images	Handwritten symbols
2STF	0.55	0.67
The proposed method	0.81	0.84

6 Conclusions

This paper presented a new shape based representation method based on distribution of distances from centroid to contour which is invariant to translation, scale, rotation and flip which is simple to implement, but is effective at the same time. The proposed representation works for both convex, non-convex and open shapes. The proposed method is compared with a similar recent method and is shown to be effective.

Acknowledgments. The work is supported by an AICTE sponsored Project (under RPS Scheme). Ref: File No: 8023/BOR/RID/RPS-51/2009-10.

References

1. Artieres, T., Marukatat, S., Gallinari, P.: Online handwritten shape recognition using segmental hidden markov models. IEEE Transactions on Pattern Analysis and Machine Intelligence 29(2), 205–217 (2007)
2. Berretti, S., Bimbo, A., Pala, P.: Retrieval by shape similarity with perceptual distance and effective indexing. IEEE Transactions on Multimedia 2(4), 225–239 (2000)
3. Blum, H.: A transformation for extracting new descriptors of shape. In: Whaten-Dunn, W. (ed.) Models for the Perception of Speech and Visual Forms, pp. 362–380. MIT Press, Cambridge (1967)

4. Chakravarthy, V.S., Kompella, B.: The shape of handwritten characters. Pattern Recognition Letters 24, 1901–1913 (2003)
5. Freeman, H.: On the encoding of arbitrary geometric configurations. IRE Trans. Electron. Comput. EC-10, 260–268 (1961)
6. Freeman, H., Saghri, A.: Generalized chain codes for planar curves. In: Proceedings of the Fourth International Joint Conference on Pattern Recognition, Kyoto, Japan, November 7-10, pp. 701–703 (1978)
7. Fu, K.: Syntactic Methods in Pattern Recognition. Academic Press, New York (1974)
8. Gevers, T., Smeulders, A.W.: Combing color and shape invariant features for retrieval. IEEE Transactions on image processing 9(1), 102–119 (2000)
9. Gonzalez, R.C., Woods, R.E.: Digital Image Processing, 2nd edn. Pearson Education (2002)
10. Gorelick, L., Galun, M., Sharon, E., Basri, R., Brandt, A.: Shape representation and classification using the Poisson equation. IEEE Transactions on Pattern Analysis and Machine Intelligence 28(12), 1991–2005 (2006)
11. Groskey, W., Neo, P., Mehrotra, R.: Index-based object recognition in pictorial data managemenet. Computer Vision Graphics Image Processing 52, 416–436 (1990)
12. Groskey, W., Neo, P., Mehrotra, R.: A pictorial index mechanism for model-based matching. Data Knowlege Engineering 8, 309–327 (1992)
13. Sonka, M., Hlavac, V., Boyle, R.: Image Processing, Analysis and Machine Vision, 2nd edn. Chapman and Hall, London (1993)
14. Van Otterloo, P.J.: A Contour-Oriented Approach to Shape Analysis., 2nd edn. Prantice-Hall International(UK) Ltd, Englewood Cliffs (1991)
15. Srihari, S.N., Cha, S.-H., Arora, H., Lee, S.: Individuality of handwriting. Journal of Forensic Sciences 47(4), 1–17 (2002)
16. Starostenko, O., Cruz, C.K., Chavenz-Aragon, A., Contreras, R.: A novel shape indexing method for automatic classification of lepidoptera. IEEE Computer Society (2007)
17. Gokaramaiah, T., Viswanath, P., Reddy, B.E.: A novel shape based hierarchical retrieval system for 2d images. In: ARTcom 2010, pp. 10–14. IEEE Computer Society (2010)
18. Wang, Z., Chi, Z., Feng, D.: Shape based leaf image retrieval. In: IEE Proc.-Vis. Image Signal Process., vol. 150 (February 2003)
19. Yong, I., Walker, J., Bowie, J.: An analysis technique for biological shape. Computational Graphics and Image Processing 25, 357–370 (1974)
20. Zhang, D., Lu, G.: Review of shape representation and description techniques. Pattern Recognition 37, 1–19 (2004)

Illumination Compensation to Segment True Skin and Non-skin Regions for Skin Tone Images

H.C. VijayLakshmi[1] and Sudarshan PatilKulkarni[2]

[1] S J College Of Engineering, Mysore, India
vijisjce@yahoo.co.in
[2] J S S Research Foundations, Mysore
pk.sudarshan@gmail.com

Abstract. Skin segmentation is an important preprocessing step in detecting and localizing human faces. For indoor images under normal illumination condition, skin pixel segmentation using different color spaces segment the skin regions reasonably well. Outdoor images with skin tone region in bright sunlight calls for illumination compensation. In this paper we propose a wavelet texture energy based illumination compensation for segmenting the outdoor bright sunlight skin tone images.

Keywords: localizing, bright sunlight, illumination, wavelet, compensation.

1 Introduction

Face detection and localization is the task of checking whether the given input image or video sequence contains any human face, and if human faces are present, returning the location of the human face in the image. The face detection problem involves segmentation, extraction, and classification of the segmented and extracted region as face or non face irrespective of the background. Several researchers are at this task with different approaches, so that the machine detects and locates the faces efficiently as we human beings do in any complex scenarios. The faces play a major role in identifying and recognizing people. The area of face detection has gained considerable importance with the advancement of human-machine interaction as it provides a natural and efficient way to communicate between humans and machines. Face detection and localisation in image sequences has become a popular area of research due to emerging applications in intelligent human-computer interface, surveillance systems, content-based image retrieval, video conferencing, financial transaction, forensic applications, and many other fields.

2 Challenges

There are several challenges while detecting and locating faces in skin toned regions, refer [4]. In spite of using combination of different colour spaces during segmentation, it is tedious to demarcate region boundaries between skin and pseudo

V.V. Das and N. Thankachan (Eds.): CIIT 2011, CCIS 250, pp. 494–499, 2011.

skin regions and also eliminate these regions from searching process. The use of colour space alone sometimes fails to segment the boundary regions of the image. In order to overcome this problem combination of colour spaces for efficient skin segmentation followed by Canny and Prewitt edge detection to demarcate the region boundary is used for input image segmentation [4]. Due to variation in illumination, skin regions may not be properly identified as skin during skin segmentation. Locating faces in these circumstances is more complex as opposed to localizing faces with uniform, non skin-tone background. Face detection is a classification problem. It calls for classifying the selected segmented region as face or non-face. For efficient classification a robust feature set as well as robust classification method is very much essential. This calls for an efficient preprocessing, feature extraction followed by efficient classification method.

3 Preprocessing

Preprocessing step is the stage where the input image is processed to extract the regions and features of interest. The main task of this stage is to avoid processing regions which are not the candidate regions for the algorithm to process and eliminate these regions from further processing.

3.1 Need for Segmentation

Segmentation and feature extraction are the two important pre-processing steps that play a vital role in face detection and localisation Segmentation is a process that partitions an image into regions [8] of uniform texture and intensity. The extracted region should be uniform with respect to some measurable characteristics like intensity and texture, obviously regions adjacent to it should be different with respect to these characters. Region based image segmentation involves grouping adjacent areas with similar textural characteristics. With boundary based segmentation the goal is to find areas where textural properties change rapidly. In the problem of face detection, segmentation based on skin plays a major role in identifying the candidate face regions. Though there are different segmentation methods, segmentation based on colour is considered. For a detailed survey of colour spaces refer [7]. Segmentation of the input image is the most important step that contributes to the efficient detection and localization of multiple faces in skin tone colour images Skin segmentation of the input image based on skin pixel cue [1] combined with edges help to demarcate region boundaries and segment the image components efficiently [4]. Segmentation of an image based on human skin chromaticity using different colour spaces results in identifying even pseudo skin like regions as skin regions. Hence there is a need for further eliminating these pseudo skin regions Segmentation is a process that partitions an image into regions. In the problem of face detection, skin segmentation helps in identifying the probable regions containing the faces as all skin segmented regions are not face regions and aids in reducing the search space. Though there are different segmentation methods, segmentation based on colour is considered [9]. Precise segmentation of the input image is the most important step that contributes to the efficient detection and localization of multiple faces in skin tone colour images. There is a need for adaptive skin colour segmentation before detection.

3.2 Texture

Texture is the local intensity "pattern". It is one of the most important defining characteristics of an image. It is characterized by the spatial distribution of gray levels in a neighborhood. Texture analysis [2], classification and segmentation are of significance to researchers. Refer [1],[2] for detailed texture analysis. To accomplish texture analysis task, the first step is to extract texture features that most completely embody information about the spatial distribution of intensity variations in the textured image. Texture analysis has applications in image segmentation and classification, biomedical image analysis, and automatic detection of surface defects. When describing the content of a region, textures give a better understanding about the region as compared to intensity descriptors such as average gray-level, minimum and maximum gray level. The three common ways of analyzing textures are statistical, structural and spectral approaches. Smoothing is a preprocessing step to enhance the result of segmentation. Blurring is used in preprocessing steps, such as removal of small details from an image prior to object extraction and bridging small gaps in lines or curves. Random noise typically consists of sharp transitions in gray level, the most obvious application of smoothing is noise reduction. A major use of averaging filter is in the reduction of "irrelevant" detail in an image. By irrelevant we mean pixel regions that are small with respect to the filter mask. Smoothing based on texture energy image helps in illumination compensation and smooth segmentation.

3.3 Wavelets

The proposed methodology uses wavelets to generate texture image. Wavelets are mathematical functions that initially cutup the data into different frequency components and then study each component with a resolution matched to its scale. Thus wavelets analyze according to scale and self-similarity caused by scales and dilations. Wavelet algorithms process data at different scales or resolutions. The wavelet analysis procedures adopt a wavelet prototype function called an analyzing wavelet or mother wavelet [3]. Wavelets are centered around orthogonal decomposition to transform the given datasets into orthonormal datasets [3]. $\{R_{2k}V\}^{(N/2)-1}_{k=0} \cup \{\{R_{2k}U\}^{(N/2)-1}_{k=0}$ is considered as the first stage wavelet basis, consisting of collection of vectors V, U each of size N/2 rotated in steps that are multiples of two, to form the orthonormal basis for N dimensional vector space. The collection of vectors V generally contains the high frequency components and the collection U contains the low frequency components. This achieves frequency as well as spatial localization.

4 Proposed Methodology

The proposed methodology uses texture energy image generated for wavelet approximation image, addresses illumination compensation and results in smooth segmentation of the input image containing multiple objects. The algorithm is as follows.

Step1. Split the input colour image in to R, G, B channel images respectively.
Step2. Wavelet decompose each channel image up to third level.
Step3. For each channel third level approximation image, using a 3X3 image window a texture energy image is generated as shown in the following equation

$$t(x,y) = \frac{1}{th} * \sum_{s=-a}^{a} \sum_{t=-b}^{b} f(x+s,y+t) * f(x+s,y+t)$$

Here f(x, y) is the input image, s and t the size of the window, in our case 3X3 kernel is considered and t(x, y) is the weighted average texture image generated and 'th' is the threshold.
Step4. Using the texture energy image generated in step-3 in place of third level approximation image, reconstruct the image of each channel.
Step5. Combine all the three reconstructed RGB channel image into coloured texture image.
Step6. This coloured texture energy image is segmented further using the algorithm proposed by the authors [4].

5 Results

This paper is in continuation of the method used by the authors in [4]. The results of image segmentation using the proposed method and the method used by the authors in [4] are as shown in the following figures. The texture energy images generated in Figure2, Figure 6 and Figure 10 separates skin region from skin like regions. The corresponding segmented images are shown in Figure 4, Figure 8 and Figure 12. The segmentation using other method is shown in Figure 3, Figure 7 and Figure 11. The proposed method is found to perform better for images with skin tone background regions in bright sunlight. The texture image helps in demarcating skin region from pseudo skin regions. The results are tabulated in Table-1

Table 1.

Method	Image type	No of Input Images	Proper Segmentation
Proposed Method	Normal illumination condition	40	40
	Bright Sunlight	20	20
Combination of color spaces and Edges[4]	Normal illumination condition	40	40
	Bright Sunlight	20	10

Fig. 1. Input colour image in bright sunlight

Fig. 2. Texture energy image of figure1

Fig. 3. Skin segmented binary image of figure1

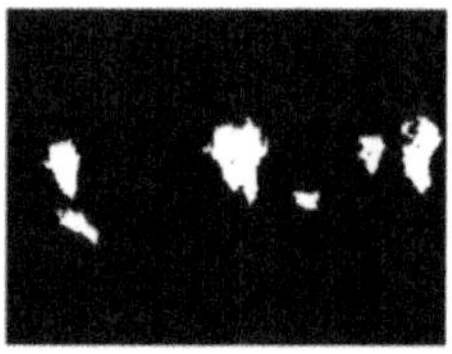

Fig. 4. Figure4 Skin segmented binary image of figure2

Fig. 5. Input colour image in bright sunlight

Fig. 6. Texture energy image of figure5

Fig. 7. Skin segmented binary image of figure5

Fig. 8. Skin segmented binary image of figure6

Fig. 9. Input colour image in bright sunlight

Fig. 10. Texture energy image of figure9

Fig. 11. Skin segmented binary image of figure9

Fig. 12. Skin segmented binary image of figure10

References

1. Haralick, R.M., Shanmugan, K., Dinstein, I.: Textural Features for Image Classification. IEEE Transactions on Systems, Man and Cybernetics 3(6), 610–621 (1973)
2. Tuceryan, M., Jain, A.K.: Texture Analysis
3. Frazier, M.W.: An Introduction to Wavelets through Linear algebra. Springer, Heidelberg (1999)
4. Vijaylakshmi, H.C., PatilKulakarni, S.: Segmentation Algorithm for Multiple Face Detection for Color Images with Skin Tone Regions. In: 2nd International Conference on Signal Acquisition and Processing, Bangalore, February 9-10, pp. 162–166 (2010)
5. Ming-Hsuan, Y., Kreigman, D.J., Ahuja, N.: Detecting Faces in images: a survey. IEEE Transactions on Pattern Analysis and Machine intelligence 24, 34–58 (2002)
6. Zhao, W., Chellappa, R., Rosenfeld, A., Phillips, P.: Face recognition:A literature survey. ACM Computing Surveys, 399–458 (2003)
7. Veznevets, V., Sazonov, V., Andreeva, N.: A survey on pixel-based skin color detection techniques. In: Proceedings Graphicon 2003, pp. 85–92 (2003)
8. Gonzalez, R.C., Woods, R.E.: Digital Image processing, 2nd edn. Prentice Hall India
9. Phung, S.L., Bouzerdoum, A., Chai, D.: Skin Segmentation Using Colour and Edge Information. In: Proc. Int. Symposium on Signal Processing and its Applications, Perth, Western Australia, Australia, Paris, France, July 1-4 (2003), doi:0-7803-7946-2/03

A Novel QoS Differentiation Framework for IEEE 802.11 WLANs: A Game-Theoretic Approach Using an Optimal Channel Access Scheme

Barsha Mitra, Debarshi Kumar Sanyal, Matangini Chattopadhyay, and Samiran Chattopadhyay

Jadavpur University, India
{mitra.barsha,debarshisanyal}@gmail.com,
chttpdhy@yahoo.com, samiranc@it.jusl.ac.in

Abstract. The ubiquity of multimedia applications and its sustenance with more traditional data services demand a Quality of Service (QoS) differentiation mechanism in telecommunications networks. This paper takes up a novel access method called Idle Sense developed to provide short-term fair high aggregate throughput to wireless stations in an IEEE 802.11 WLAN. We use a game-theoretic interpretation of the algorithm to determine how to incorporate QoS in the game. We show how the parameters in the algorithm may be tuned in order to achieve proportional throughput differentiation at the Nash equilibrium point of the game. Extensive numerical simulations performed for both IEEE 802.11b and 802.11g indicate that the traffic classes are indeed differentiated in terms of throughput.

Keywords: Quality of service, Nash equilibrium, Wireless networks, Throughput, Performance.

1 Introduction

Multimedia applications are ubiquitous in today's networks. Audio and video coexist with data traffic. While low throughput is tolerable for applications like web access, high throughput is necessary to sustain critical transmissions of data and multimedia. Thus Quality of Service (QoS) is an important requirement in today's network whether it is the Internet or a local area network. The DCF protocol defined in the IEEE 802.11 standard suffers from reduced throughput for large network sizes. Hence the Idle Sense access method [1] was developed. It assures optimal throughput equally distributed among the nodes even for large networks. In this paper, we use a recently developed game theoretic interpretation [3] of Idle Sense to support proportional QoS in WLANs. We show that simple tuning of the parameters used in the control algorithm of Idle Sense can support proportional throughput differentiation and hence QoS. It is noteworthy that our scheme is different from that in [2] where the contention window is directly manipulated.

2 Proposed QoS Differentiation Framework for WLANs

We consider an ad hoc wireless LAN of $\aleph$ nodes where all nodes can hear each other.

V.V. Das and N. Thankachan (Eds.): CIIT 2011, CCIS 250, pp. 500–502, 2011.

Node i accesses the channel with probability p_i which is, in general, time-dependent. We assume all nodes are permanently backlogged. In [1], the authors show that for equally divided high aggregate throughput, the mean number of idle slots between two transmission attempts approaches a constant as the number of nodes becomes arbitrarily large. This constant depends only on protocol parameters and is called the target number of idle slots. The Idle Sense access method uses this observation to formulate an additive-increase-multiplicative-decrease (AIMD) algorithm. If the mean number of idle slots between two transmission attempts is lower than the target, the channel access probability is reduced multiplicatively by b_i. If the mean is higher, the access probability is increased additively by a_i. In [3], the authors recover a non-cooperative game from this access method. The game played by the nodes is termed as the *IdleSense-Game* which is defined as $\left[\aleph, \times_{i\in\aleph} S_i, \{U_i\}_{i\in\aleph}\right]$ where $\aleph$ is the set of players (the nodes of the network), $S_i := \{p_i \mid p_i^{\min} \le p_i \le p_i^{\max}\}$ is the strategy set of player i, and $U_i(\mathbf{p})$ is the utility function that node i attempts to maximize. It may be noted that the strategy set of each player is the set of its channel access probabilities and $0 < p_i^{\min} \le p_i \le p_i^{\max} < 1$. In [3], the authors further prove that the game has a Nash Equilibrium (NE) in pure strategies and that under mild restrictions, the non-trivial NE in IdleSense-Game is unique. Here, we observe that at the unique non-trivial NE of the IdleSense-Game where node i has a channel access probability p_i^*, the channel access probabilities of the nodes depend on the AIMD parameters as:

$$\frac{p_i^*}{p_j^*} = \left(\frac{1-b_j}{1-b_i}\right)\frac{a_i}{a_j}$$

Thus if different nodes choose different (a_i, b_i), they enjoy different channel access probabilities and hence different throughputs at the NE. This is our proposed QoS model for proportional throughput differentiation. We validate it through numerical simulations in MAXIMA [4]. Both IEEE 802.11b (basic rate = 1 Mbps, data rate = 11 Mbps) and IEEE 802.11g (basic rate = 24 Mbps, data rate = 54 Mbps) style WLANs are simulated. We assume two traffic classes: I and II. Nodes are equally divided into the two classes. All nodes in each class choose the same (a_i, b_i) values. We plot aggregate throughput of each class against total number of nodes. Two cases are considered: (1) class I nodes choose $a_i = 0.002$ and class II nodes choose $a_i = 0.001$ while all nodes have same b_i. Here the throughput divides in 2:1 ratio. (fig. 1a and 1b) (2) class I nodes choose $b_i = 0.8$ and class II nodes choose $b_i = 0.4$ while all nodes have same a_i (fig. 2a and 2b). In this case, the throughput divides in 3:1 ratio.

3 Conclusions

We have presented a simple method using a non-cooperative game model to incorporate QoS at the MAC layer of an IEEE 802.11 based wireless LAN. We have shown that at the stable operating point of the protocol, the hosts can divide the aggregate throughput in a proportional manner.

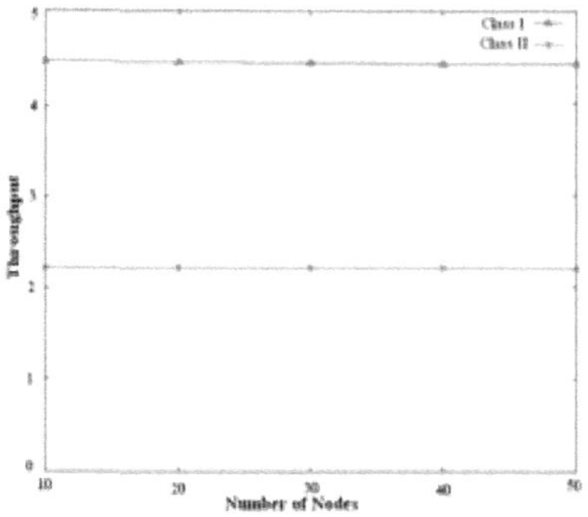

Fig. 1a. Varying a_i: Number of Nodes vs. Throughput for IEEE 802.11b Network

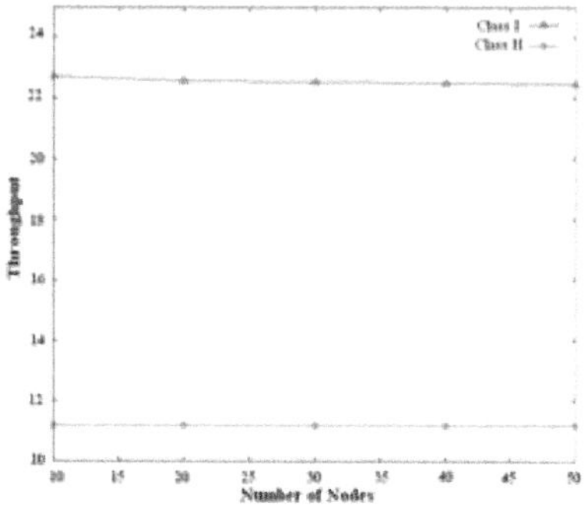

Fig. 1b. Varying a_i: Number of Nodes vs. Throughput for IEEE 802.11g Network

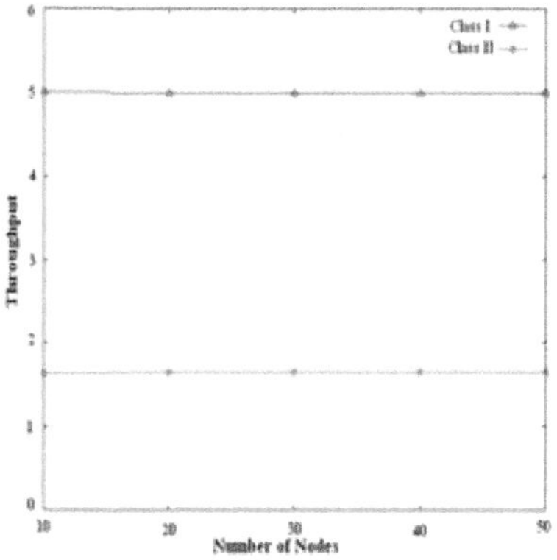

Fig. 2a. Varying b_i: Number of Nodes vs. Throughput for IEEE 802.11b Network

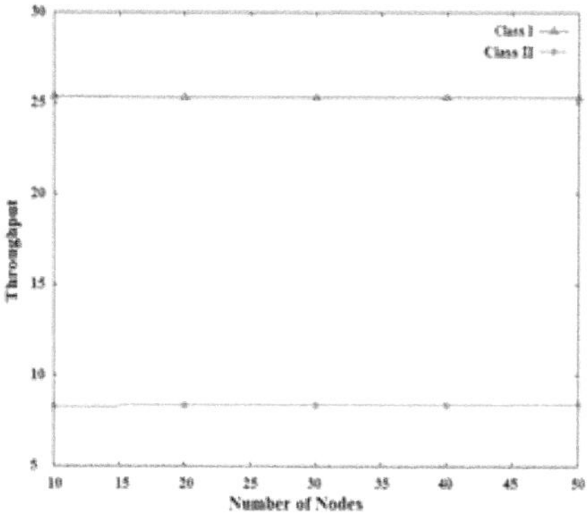

Fig. 2b. Varying b_i: Number of Nodes vs. Throughput for IEEE 802.11g Network

References

1. Heusse, M., Rousseau, F., Guillier, R., Duda, A.: Idle Sense: an Optimal Access Method for High Throughput and Fairness in Rate Diverse Wireless LANs. In: ACM SIGCOMM 2005 (2005)
2. Nassiri, M., Heusse, M., Duda, A.: A Novel Access Method for Supporting Absolute and Proportional Priorities in 802.11 WLANs. In: IEEE INFOCOM 2008 (2008)
3. Sanyal, D.K., Chattopadhyay, M., Chattopadhyay, S.: Recovering a Game Model from an Optimal Channel Access Scheme for WLANs. Telecommunications Systems (2011)
4. Maxima, `http://maxima.sourceforge.net/`

Dynamic Terrain Data Visualization Using Virtual Paging in Multi-threaded Environment

Sudhir Porwal and Virendra Singh Rathi

Image Analysis Center,
DEAL, Dehradun, India

Abstract. The realistic terrain visualization has been the requirement of many applications like flight simulator, land resource planning, fly-through etc. The requirement of real time frame construction for consistent performance has lead to development of numerous modeling & visualization techniques in past. In this paper, a novel-rendering algorithm is discussed based on tiled data modeling. It constructs the frame from 3D model of terrain in nearly constant time. The algorithm is well suited for handling large datasets using the virtual paging and thread level parallelism is used for rendering and selection of tiles.

Keywords: Terrain Visualization, DEM, Level of Details, Large dataset, multi-threading, tiling, GIS.

1 Introduction

The realistic visualization of large area of terrain has been a field of interest for researchers since last few decades. It is required in many civilian and military applications [1]. The primary input to terrain visualization system is **D**igital **E**levation **M**odel (DEM) that contains the elevation information of terrain in a rectangular grid fashion. Another model like **T**riangular **I**rregular **N**etwork (TIN) is also used to keep the elevation information of the terrain. It is found in literature [2] that DEM is best suited for large terrain data handling. The smooth rendering (0.066 sec/frame for 15 fps) during flythrough operation requires dynamic handling of terrain data using advanced algorithms for terrain data modeling & indexing, **L**evel **o**f **D**etails (LOD), culling and rendering. This paper discusses an efficient data layout & indexing scheme and the Index Generator Algorithm for construction of each frame in nearly constant time.

2 Previous Work

Many researchers have suggested different data indexing schemes like Bittener [3] has applied the BSP based technique to store the scene information. Jianjun [4] &Rotteger [5] has used the quad trees for terrain representation. Lindstorm [6] have used tiling method and reported its usefulness in GIS applications. The different methods for terrain modeling & indexing discussed above suites to different

V.V. Das and N. Thankachan (Eds.): CIIT 2011, CCIS 250, pp. 503–505, 2011.

applications. It was suggested by many researchers that tiling method is best for GIS applications handling very large datasets. LOD techniques [5] can also be used to further reduce the frame time.

3 Data Layout and Indexing Scheme

The tiled block representation is the most suitable representation of DEM grid data. The DEM layer and the texture layer (satellite or aerial imagery) are divided in to fixed size square tiles. The tile size can be chosen as power of two (2^n). If the tile size is 2^n x 2^n, it is observed that the seam of the adjacent tiles is not rendered properly and cracks appear on the screen. To avoid this problem, tile size is chosen as (2^n+1). Each tile is assigned a number starting from 1 and sequentially increasing. If number of tiles along x-axis areT_x and along y-axis are T_y then the tile number sequence ranges from 1 to $T_x \times T_y$. Each tile block will also store the normalized boundary co-ordinates for DEM and texture tiles.

4 Data Rendering

In the rendering process, the scene objects are approximated with triangle strips that requires less storage resulting in fast rendering. For view frustum culling, we have proposed an Index Generator Algorithm based on our data layout and indexing scheme and generates a list of tile numbers that are inside the view frustum.

4.1 Index Generator Algorithm

The proposed algorithm uses the view frustum parameters to compute the visible tiles The algorithm shows that it returns the index list of visible tiles always in constant time.The view frustum is shown in figure 1. The FOV is θ and the viewer is located at

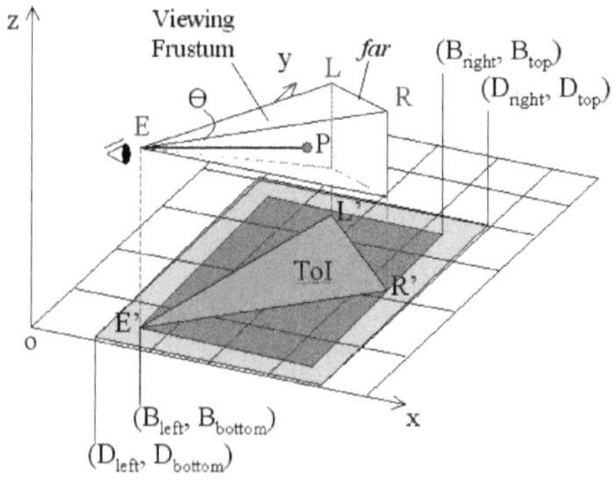

Fig. 1. View frustum and tile coverage

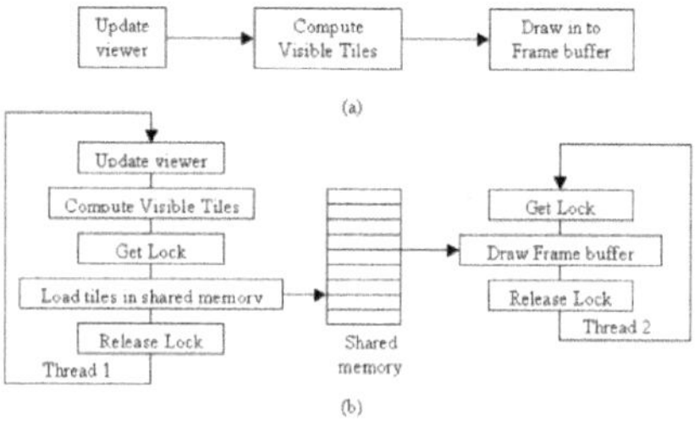

Fig. 2. (a): Serial implementation (b) Parallel implementation

the point E in the 3D space. The point P is the looked at point. The vector EP denotes the viewing direction. The projection of this view frustum on the xy-plane will be a triangle ΔE'L'R'. Let us call this triangle as Triangle of Interest (ToI). The minimum bounding rectangle (MBR) of ToI will be represented as (B_{left}, B_{bottom}, B_{right}, B_{top}). Since the MBR may or may not align with the tile boundaries so the tile boundaries aligned bounding rectangle (TABR) will be computed as (D_{left}, D_{bottom}, D_{right}, D_{top}). The tiles covered in TABR can easily be computed in constant time using the data layout and indexing scheme discussed in section 3.

4.2 Thread Level Parallelism

This frame construction time can further be reduced using thread level parallelism for compute and render stages of graphics pipeline. A block diagram is shown in figure 2 for illustration purpose. *Thread 1* is responsible for computing the visible tiles and updating the shared memory with those tiles that are not present in the shared memory. *Thread 2* keeps on reading the updated data from shared memory and draws in to the frame buffer.

5 Results and Conclusion

The proposed algorithm is implemented and executed on a different size datasets. It was recorded that the frame construction time in all the cases was 0.067 sec that is sufficient for smooth rendering of fly through application.

References

1. Cohen, D., Gotsman, C.: Photorealistic terrain imaging and flight simulation. IEEE Computer Graphics and Applications 14(2), 10–12 (1994)
2. Fan, M., Tang, M., Dong, J.: A review of terrain rendering techniques. In: Proceedings of IEEE conf. on computer supported cooperative work in design (2003)
3. Bittner, J., Wonka, P., Wimmer, M.: Visibility preprocessing for urban scene using line space subdivision. In: Proceedings of Pacific Graphics, Tokyo, Japan, October 16-18, pp. 276–284 (2001)
4. Li, J., Li, J., Hu, S., Ye, X., Li, Z.: A hybrid simplification algorithm for large scale terrain. In: Proceedings of ICSP (2006)
5. Röttger, S., Heidrich, W., Slusallek, P., Seidel: Real-Time Generation of Continuous Levels of Detail for Height Fields. In: Proceedings of WSCG, February 9-13, pp. 315–322. University of West Bohemia, Plzen (1998)
6. Lindstrom, P., Koller, D., Ribarsky, W., Hodges, L.F., Turner, G.A., Faust, N.: Real-time continuous level of detail rendering of height fields. In: Proceedings of the 23rd Annual Conference on Computer Graphics and Interactive Techniques, pp. 109–118. ACM Press, New York (1996)

A Multi Droplets Detection Technique for Single-Fault in Digital Micro-fluidic Biochip

Mukta Majumder, Shibotosh Ray, and Samir Roy

Department of Computer Science and Engineering,
National Institute of Technical Teachers' Training & Research, Kolkata,
Block-FC, Sec-III, Salt Lake City, Kolkata-700106, West Bengal, India
mukta_jgec_it_4@yahoo.co.in, sap.shibotosh@yahoo.com,
samir.cst@gmail.com

Abstract. With the recent advancement of micro-fluidic technology, application of digital micro-fluidic biochips have been rapidly increased in bio-sensing, clinical diagnostics and other laboratory works. As the bio-chips occasionally work on safety critical operations, correctness and dependability are important requirement for these devices. Therefore, these devices must be tested after manufacturing and during bioassay operations. We are proposing a novel multi droplets detection technique for single-fault in digital micro-fluidic biochips in this paper. The key idea is to manipulate multiple droplets in parallel to test the micro-array in a scan-like manner. The traversal of micro-array is carried out by scanning the intermediate cells and edges by a special type of movement pattern RURD (Right-Up-Right-Down) and the boundary cells and edges by anti-clockwise movement of the test stimuli droplets. The experimental results suggest that the proposed technique is an efficient one and show significant improvement in fault detection over existing methods.

Keywords: Biochip, Droplet, Lab-on-chip, Micro-fluidic technology, Start Electrode, Target Region.

1 Introduction

Now a day the digital micro-fluidic biochips have become very popular for biochemical analysis [1]-[3]. These biochips can also be well known as lab-on-a-chip or bio MEMS [2], [4]. It replaces highly repetitive laboratory tasks by removing traditional bulky lab equipments with composite micro-system. The advantages of these devices are design flexibility, higher sensitivity, and smaller size and lower cost [5]. These biochips are classified as traditional continuous flow based, carried out by using micro-pumps, micro-valves and micro-channels [6]-[8]; and discrete droplet based. The droplet based chip is referred as "Digital Micro-fluidic Biochip" [9] which is advantageous over the continuous flow Systems [10]. Testing of Micro-fluidic device is very much a new topic as the Micro-fluidic technology itself a new one. An excellent overview of previous works on the testing of micro fluidic biochips can be found in [11]. Fault modeling and fault simulation techniques for continuous-flow based micro-fluidic biochips have been described in [12], [13]. Defect classification, test planning, and test resource optimization techniques have recently been presented

V.V. Das and N. Thankachan (Eds.): CIIT 2011, CCIS 250, pp. 506–511, 2011.

for digital biochip. Defect classification and test application procedure are proposed in [5]. As faults are categorized as being either catastrophic or parametric, and techniques have been developed to detect these faults by electro statically controlling and tracking these droplets. Some efficient and effective test planning methods for the detection of catastrophic faults in digital micro-fluidic arrays have been investigated in [5], [14]. An optimal integrated testing and diagnosis technique for identifying defect in biochip has been shown in [15]. Fault detections in micro fluidic biochips with multiple droplets in parallel are being discussed in [6], [10], [16]. Hamiltonian paths have also used to detect catastrophic faults in micro-fluidic arrays [17] but checking the existence of Hamiltonian path in a given graph is NP-complete. An alternative method has been presented based on Euler paths in [18]. The remaining paper is organized as; Section two describes the basics of two dimensional micro-arrays, their faults and graph theoretic formulation. Section three discusses the proposed technique. Experimental results are explained at section four. And conclusions are drawn at section five.

2 Basics of Digital Micro-fluidic Biochip

Most digital micro-fluidic biochips are based on the manipulation of micro-nano liter droplets on a two dimensional electrode array using the principle of electro wetting - on-dielectric [19]. Basic structure of such a biochip is described below.

2.1 Structure of the Biochip

Most digital micro-fluidic devices consist of a two dimensional array of electrodes with one or more sources and sinks on the boundary and a droplet of some biochemical sample [10]. The bottom plate contains a patterned array of individually controllable electrodes, while the top plate is coated with a continuous grounded electrode. To decrease wet ability of the surfaces and increase capacitance between a droplet and a plate hydrophobic dielectric insulator is added to the plates. A droplet rests on a hydrophobic surface over an electrode, is sandwiched between two parallel glass plates [6], [10]. The droplet can be moved by applying a control voltage to an electrode adjacent to the droplet and at the same time, deactivating the electrode just under the droplet. It can achieve a speed up-to 20cm/s under a control voltage between 0 and 90V [12]. The basic cell of such a biochip is shown in Fig. 1.

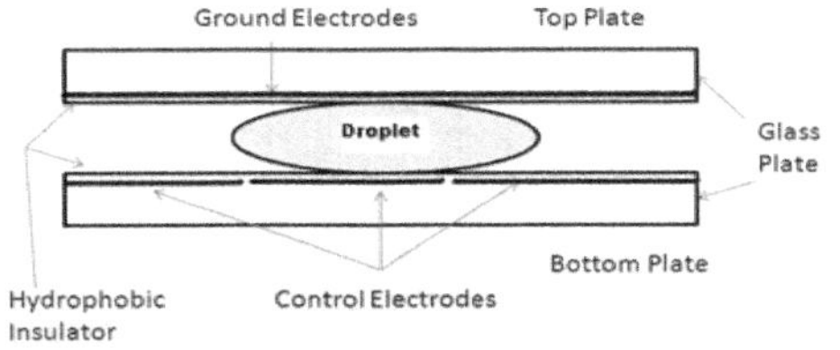

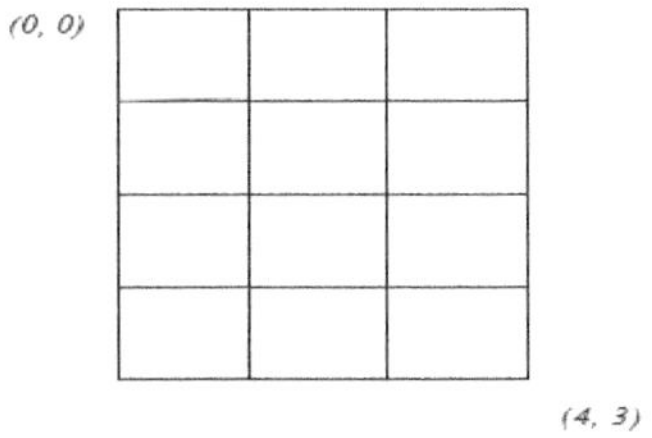

Fig. 1. Structure of a Digital Biochip **Fig. 2.** 5×4 micro-array, source *(0,0)* & sink *(4,3)*

2.2 Type of Faults in a Biochip

Fault can be categorized as either Catastrophic or Parametric in a Digital Micro-fluidic Biochip [6], [16], [20]. The Catastrophic or the hard fault which can not be recoverable causes complete break-down of the System. Most catastrophic faults result in a complete cessation of the droplet movement [13]. Thus, in a faulty system, the test droplet is stuck during its movement at the fault position. On the other hand Parametric or the soft fault does not causes system failure but it decreases system performance immensely by reducing droplet motion. In a fault-free system, all the test droplets can be seen to reach at the droplet sink in specified time by the capacitive detection circuit [5]. To find a fault, we have to traverse the entire biochip by moving the droplet to every cell and edge from source to sink. Source is the point where the droplet enters into the Biochip and sink is the point where it leaves the Biochip.

2.3 Graph Based Technique

Hence a Digital Micro-fluidic Biochip can be represented by an m×n array (matrix) where Cij denotes the cell at (i, j) position, and i=0 to m; j=0 to n. At any moment a droplet can be at any cell in the micro-array. Now a graph based technique can be used to detect the fault in it. Let us suppose the m×n micro-fluidic biochip can be represented in terms of a graph Gm×n. where m is the number of rows and n is number of columns. The above Fig. 2 shows a 5×*4* micro-fluidic array with source at *(0, 0)* and sink at *(4, 3)* position.

3 Proposed Technique

We are proposing a new advanced technique for detecting a single fault within a micro-fluidic array in this paper. The proposed technique is based on the graph based method. Here the key idea is to manipulate multiple droplets in parallel to test the micro-fluidic array in a scan-like manner. In this technique the entire biochip is traversed by the droplets in two steps.

3.1 First Step

In first step, droplets are distributed from the source reservoir to the start electrodes of their target regions. A target region for a droplet includes the cells that are traversed by this droplet [10]. Start electrodes are located on the array boundary, as in Fig.3.

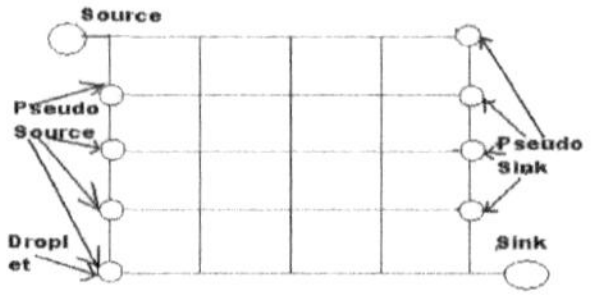

Fig. 3. Start electrode or pseudo-sources sink

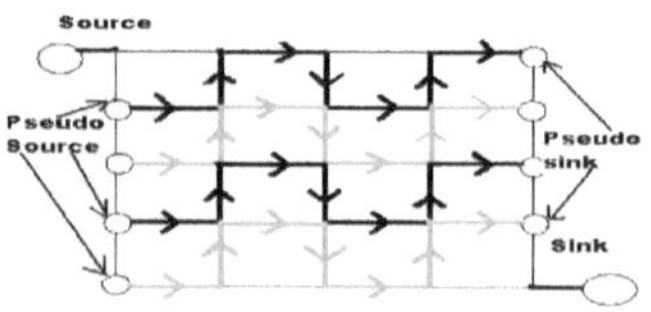

Fig. 4. Paths from pseudo sources to pseudo sinks

The start electrodes are referred as pseudo-sources as these act as droplet source for corresponding target region [10]. Starting from these pseudo-sources, droplets are routed in parallel to the electrode at the other end of the corresponding target regions. The end-points are referred as pseudo-sinks [10]. The traversal process is based on a special type of movement pattern RURD [6] which is shown in Fig.5. The above Fig.4 illustrates the paths from pseudo sources to pseudo sinks which are obtained through repeated application of this RURD movement. Such a path may not cover the entire graph. Finally, the test droplets are routed from pseudo sinks to the droplet sink reservoir. The path from pseudo sinks to droplet reservoir is shown in the Fig. 6. So after the first step all cells and edges of the micro-array are traversed at least once, except those which are on the boundary. The procedure for first step is given below.

Procedure for First Step
Begin.

1. Locate the start electrodes (pseudo sources) at column-wise from the droplet source reservoir.
2. **While** it is possible to move further from the pseudo sources.
3. **Repeat.**

By applying RURD movement pattern move the droplet from left to right, until the pseudo sinks at the last column are reached.
End While.

4. Move the droplet from pseudo sinks to the droplet reservoir sink.

End of procedure for first step.

3.2 Second Step

In second step starting from first row- first column a test stimuli droplet moves along the boundary line in anti-clock wise direction and backs again same location to traverse the cells and edges at the boundary of the biochip. The path of the second step is shown in Fig. 7. The procedure for second step is given below.

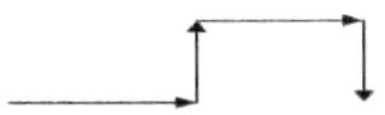
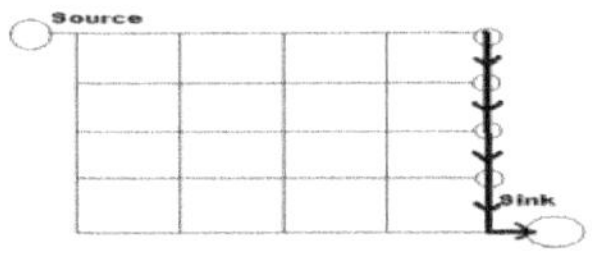

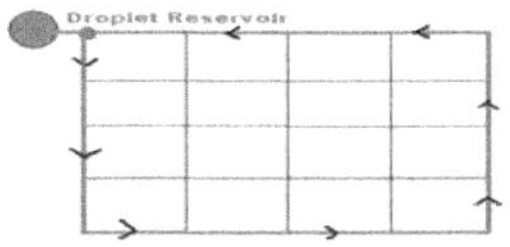

Fig. 5. RURD movement **Fig. 6.** Path from pseudo sink to reservoir **Fig. 7.** Path of second step

Procedure for Second Step
Begin.

1. **While** it is possible to move further at boundary wise.
2. Start traversing from source, first row, and first column.
3. Proceed along the boundary in anti-clock wise direction.
4. **If** it is the sink (again first row, first column) **then** stop.

End while.
End of procedure for second step.

After the completion of these two steps, there are no cells and edges left which are not traversed at least once. Therefore the traversal process is complete. Now we are taking that one edge movement is equivalent to one time unit. So if the process would carry out in sequential manner then the total time for traversing the micro-array will be the sum of the times of these two steps. But due to parallel execution of these steps, required time for traversing the biochip is the maximum time taken by a single step for its completion. Now we can detect that whither the droplet reaches the sink by capacitive detection circuit and the path from source to sink can also be identified.

4 Experimental Results

The experiment is done in Turbo C environment based on the following equation with a vast data set of micro-array from 4x3 to 10×10. A computer with 256 MB RAM, 40 GB Hard Disk and Pentium III processor is sufficient for experiment. The table below highlights that the proposed technique takes lesser time compared to the Existing technique [16]. Naturally the advantage of the proposed technique is justified in all aspects over the existing technique. In the table there are six columns which represent experiment serial number, size of biochip, total edges movement of the traversal, maximum edges movement in a single step as proposed, existing maximum edge movement in a single step and percentage of improvement respectively.

$$\%\,Improvement = \frac{\text{Existing Time} - \text{Proposed Time}}{\text{Existing time}} \times 100$$

Table 1. Experimental Result

SL No	Size of Biochip	Total Edge Movement	Max Edge Movement in a Step	Existing Max Edge Movement in a Step	% Improvement
1	5x6	49	18	19	5.263%
2	6x6	60	20	23	13.043%
3	7x5	58	20	24	16.667%
4	6x7	71	22	29	24.139%
5	6x8	82	24	35	31.429%
6	7x7	84	24	34	29.411%
7	7x8	97	26	41	36.585%
8	8x8	112	28	47	40.426%
9	8x9	127	30	55	45.455%
10	9x9	144	32	62	48.387%

5 Conclusions

An efficient and novel advanced single fault detection technique for digital micro-fluidic biochips has been presented. The proposed technique manipulates multiple droplets in parallel to test the micro-fluidic array in a scan-like manner. It is very much important to detect the fault in a micro-fluidic biochip because it operates on safety critical circumstances, as for example treating a diseased set of cells inside human body, massive parallel DNA analysis, automated drug discovery, air-quality monitoring, and food-safety testing etc. So, these devices must be fault free. The experimental results highlight that proposed method is efficient and shows significant improvement up-to 48.38% on fault detection over the existing methods and as the size of biochip is increased the percentage of improvement is also increasing rapidly.

References

1. Pollack, M., et al.: Electro wetting-based Actuation of Droplets for Integrated Microfluidic. Lab Chip 2, 96–101 (2002)
2. Pollack, M., Shenderov, A., Fair, R.B.: Electro wetting-based actuation of droplets for integrated micro-fluidics. Lab on a Chip 2, 96–101 (2002)
3. Su, F., et al.: Architectural-level synthesis of Digital Microfluidic based Biochips. In: Proc. IEEE Int. Conf. on CAD, pp. 223–228 (2004)
4. Srinivasan, V., Pamula, V., Fair, R.: An integrated digital micro-fluidic lab-on-a-chip for clinical diagnostics on human physiological fluids. Lab on a Chip 4, 310–315
5. Su, F., Ozev, S., Chakraborty, K.: Testing of Droplet-based Microfluidic Systems. In: Proc. IEEE Int. Test Conf, pp. 1192–1200 (2003)
6. Saha, S., Chakraborty, A., Roy, S.: An Efficient Single Fault Detection Technique for Microfluidic Based Biochip. In: International Conference on Advances in Computer Engineering (2010)
7. Schasfoort, R.B.M., et al.: Field-effect flow control for micro fabricated fluidic networks. Science 286, 942–945 (1999)
8. Paegel, B.M., et al.: Microfluidic devices for DNA sequencing: sample preparation and electrophoresis Analysis. Current Opinion Biotechnology 14, 42–50 (2003)
9. Fair, R.B., et al.: Electro wetting-based on-chip sample processing for integrated micro-fluidics. In: Proc. IEDM, pp. 32.5.1–32.5.4 (2003)
10. Xu, T., Chakraborty, K.: Parallel Scan-Like Testing and Fault Diagnosis Techniques for Digital Microfluidic Biochips. In: 12th IEEE European Test Symposium (2007)
11. Kerkhoff, H.G.: Testing of microelectronic-bio-fluidic systems. In: IEEED&T for Com. (2007)
12. Kerkhoff, H.G., Hendriks, H.P.A.: Fault modeling and fault simulation in mixed micro-fluidic microelectronic systems. JETTA 17, 427–437 (2001)
13. Kerkhoff, H.G., Acar, M.: Testable design and testing of Micro-electro-fluidic arrays. In: Proc. IEEE VLSI Test Symposium, pp. 403–409 (2003)
14. Su, F., Ozev, S., Chakraborty, K.: Test Planning and Test Resource Optimization for Droplet-Based Microfluidic Systems. In: 9th IEEE Euro. Test Symposium (2004)
15. Davids, D., Joshi, B., Mukherjee, A., Ravindran, A.: A Fault Detection and Diagnosis Technique for Digital Micro-fluidic Biochips
16. Majumder, M., Hansda, K., Roy, S.: A Novel Single-Fault Detection Technique of Digital Micro-Fluidic Biochip. In: International Conference on Advanced Computing, Communication and Networks 2011, pp. 247–250 (2011)
17. Su, F., Chakrabarty, K.: Defect tolerance for gracefully-degradable micro-fluidics-based biochips. In: Proceedings IEEE VLSI Test Symposium, pp. 321–326 (2005)
18. Itai, A., et al.: Hamilton paths in grid graphs. SIAM J. Comp. 11, 676–686 (1982)
19. Su, F., et al.: Testing and Diagnosis of Realistic Defects in Digital Microfluidic Biochip. In: Proc., Springer Science + Business Media (2007)
20. Su, F., et al.: Ensuring the operational health of droplet-based micro electro fluidic biosensor systems. IEEE Sensors 5, 763–773 (2005)

Competent Search in Blog Ranking Algorithm Using Cluster Mining

Robin Singh Bhadoria[1] and Rajaram Jaiswal[2]

[1] Samrat Ashok Technological Institute (Govt. Autonomous), Vidisha (MP)-India
ssr_robin@yahoo.co.in
[2] Dept. of Computer Science & Engineering, Sharda University, Greater Noida-India
rajaram.jaiswal@gmail.com

Abstract. In this paper, we focus on blogger search in blogs – in particular, who are the top authors for blogs of a particular topic. All blogs and their interconnections are collectively called the blogosphere. We emphasis on a new graph structure known as blogger graph, is proposed in the blogosphere based on the bloggers information.We concentrated on blogger search in blogs – in particular, who are the top authors for blogs of a particular topic. All blogs and their interconnections are collectively called the blogosphere. Results show that we can identify the top bloggers with a high precision.

1 Introduction

A blog (weblog) is a Web 2.0 communication tool, generally a website maintained by an individual user or by a group of users with regular entries of commentaries, descriptions of events, videos, etc. Most of the blogs provide commentary or news on a particular subject or topic. People mostly write about their personal life experiences, product reviews, technology trends, political opinions, etc. A typical blog entry contains text, images, videos and links to other blogs, web pages, and other media related to the blog topic. A blog reader can post her comments on the blog. This service makes the blogs a highly interactive discussion platform.

1.1 Blogosphere

Blogosphere continues to grow considerably, in 2006 around 35 million blogs was there, while in year 2007 this number reached to around 72 million. In 2008, around 184 million new users have started a blog, 346 million users read blogs,77% of active Internet users read blogs and 120,000 blogs were created every day[1].

V.V. Das and N. Thankachan (Eds.): CIIT 2011, CCIS 250, pp. 512–517, 2011.

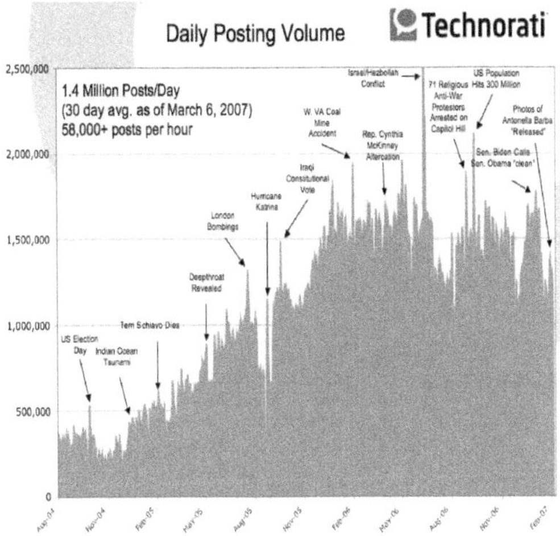

Fig. 1. Blogosphere Growth Taken From Technorati

2 Blogger Graph

In a blogger graph there is two components namely blogger graph node and blogger graph edge.

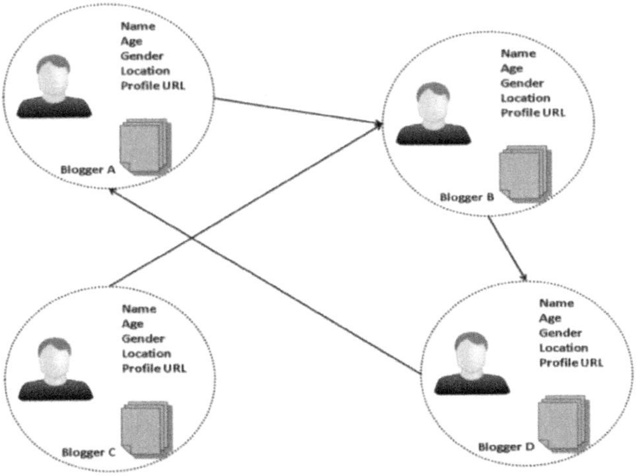

Fig. 2. Blogger Graph

This section explains the transformation of a post graph into blogger graph by an example. In post graph (Figure 2) in this example there are 3 bloggers and total 7 posts posted by these bloggers. So in post graph total 7 nodes are there and 5 edges between these posts. So the average links per node is 5/7 = 0.71.

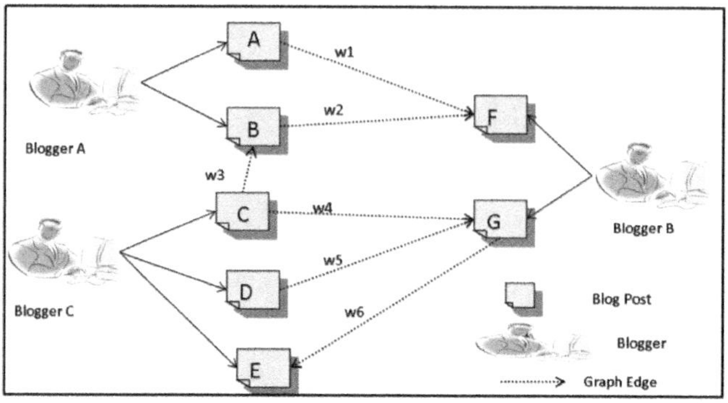

Fig. 3.

3 Blog Ranking Algorithm

Most of the ranking algorithms those using the interconnected graph.depends on the density of graph [9].But as already discussed that weblog graph is a sparse graph, so use of these web ranking algorithms give poor performance in the case of blogs. This is mainly due to the fact that bloggers usually write about their personal opinion on a topic without linking to the opinion of other bloggers.

3.1 Ontology

Ontology [14] is an explicit specification of a shared conceptualization. An ontology is a description of the concepts within a domain and relationships that can exist between those concepts. So an ontology can be used to describe a domain. Ontologies describe individuals (instances), classes (concepts), attributes, and relations. An ontology has many important components, few of them are following:-

3.2 Clustering Algorithms

The main objective of the clustering algorithm is to group the similar objects in the same cluster. If two objects lie in the same cluster then the similarity between these two objects should be more than the similarity between the objects of two different clusters.

4 Proposed System

Crawling Blog is a very different process than web crawling although blog is a subset of web. Because blogs are dynamic in nature so most of the blog storage services provide the Really Simple Syndication (RSS) feed of all the stored blogs. An RSS document may contain full or summarized text of the blog content, plus blog metadata. From this metadata we got the information about publishing date, author name, author profile, etc. There are some services like blog.gs and weblog.com that maintain a list of updated blogs.So, in case of blogs crawler we do not need to parse the HTML for getting outlinks information. Instead we fetched the updated blogs list and parsed this list using RSS XML parser. We used the weblogs.com to get the list of updated blogs. It provides two types of list of updated blogs URLs, one is last one hour updated blogs and other is last 15 minutes updated blogs.

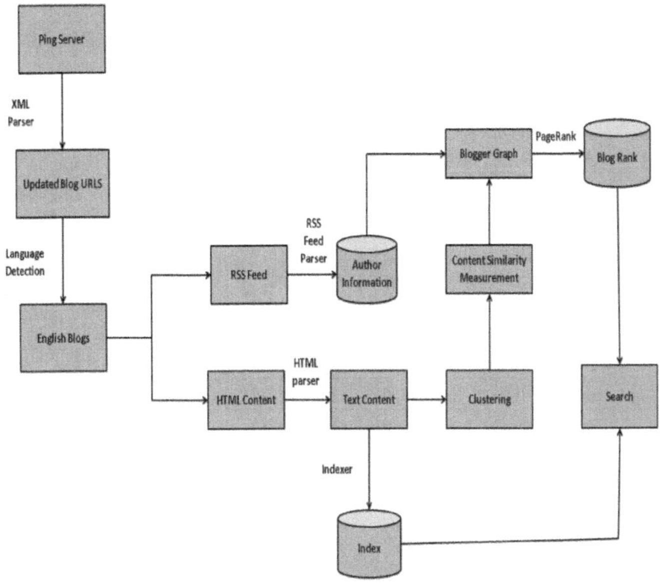

Fig. 4. Proposed System

To calculate dissimilarity between two blog posts we used the keywords extracted from the blog posts and the ontology. We first calculated the dissimilarity between each keyword pair of the two documents and used this for calculating the dissimilarity between the documents.

5 Clustering Results Analysis

We applied K-Means and PDDP clustering algorithm on the blog data. To measure the quality of a cluster we used the purity measurement. Purity of a cluster is defined as the fraction of blogs belonging to the dominant category in that cluster.

$$Purity(c_i) = \frac{max_j(|c_i|_{class=j})}{|c_i|}$$

where Purity (c i) is the purity of a cluster i.(|c i| class=j) denote number of items of class j assigned to cluster i.,|c i| size of cluster i.

Purity results of the 5 K-Means clustering are tabulated in Table1.

Table 1. Purity of K-Means Clustering

Experiment No.	Cricket Purity	Tennis Purity	Football Purity	Average Purity
1	84.44	70.15	81.25	78.61
2	83.25	72.39	79.86	78.5
3	81.96	73.43	80.95	78.78
4	80.64	71.42	83.46	78.51
5	85.43	70.15	78.72	78.1

Because in this case penalty score was assigned. In the last case when both the keywords were not present in the ontology the dissimilarity function value is more than the first three cases i.e. both the keywords are highly dissimilar.

Table 2. Dissimilarity Function Value for Different Keyword Pairs

Keyword 1	Keyword 2	Dissimilarity Function Value
SachinTendulkar Y)	Rahul Dravid (Y)	2
SachinTendulkar Y)	SaniaMirza (Y)	14
SachinTendulkar(Y)	Sonia Gandhi (N)	31
Aamir Khan (N)	Sonia Gandhi (N)	62

6 Conclusion

In this paper ,we proposed a new graph structure in blogs named as blogger graph. For building this graph we used the blogger information that is available in every blog post. This graph is denser then the post graph. To make the graph further denser we used the semantic similarity between the posts. We calculated semantic similarity between the blog posts using the ontology. Then we added the new edges in the graph based on the semantic similarity. Then we applied the PageRank algorithm on this modified graph.

References

[1] Blogosphere growth, `http://www.sifry.com/alerts/archives/000334.html`

[2] Kritikopoulos, A., Sideri, M., Varlamis, I.: Blogrank: ranking weblogs based on connectivity and similarity features. In: AAA-IDEA 2006: Proceedings of the 2nd International Workshop on Advanced Architectures and Algorithms for Internet Delivery and Applications, p. 8. ACM, New York (2006)

[3] Adamic, L., Adar, E., Zhang, L., Lukose, R.: Implicit structure and the dynamics of blogspace. Presented at the Workshop on the Weblogging Ecosystem at the 13th International World Wide Web Conference, New York (2004)

[4] Hearst, M.A., Hurst, M., Dumais, S.T.: What should blog search look like? In: SSM 2008: Proceeding of the 2008 ACM Workshop on Search in social media, pp. 95–98. ACM, New York (2008)

[5] Page, L., Brin, S., Motwani, R., Winograd, T.: The pagerank citation ranking: Bringing order to the web. Stanford InfoLab (November 1999)

[6] Kleinberg, J.M.: Authoritative sources in a hyperlinked environment. Journal of the ACM 46, 668–677 (1999)

[7] Haveliwala, T.H.: Topic-sensitive pagerank. In: WWW 2002: Proceedings of the 11th International Conference on World Wide Web, pp. 517–526. ACM, USA (2002)

[8] Massa, P., Hayes, C.: Page-rerank: Using trusted links to re-rank authority. In: WI 2005: Proceedings of the 2005 IEEE/WIC/ACM International Conference on Web Intelligence, pp. 614–617. IEEE Computer Society, Washington, DC, USA (2005)

[9] Langville, A.N., Meyer, C.D.: Deeper inside pagerank. Internet Mathematics 1 (2004)

[10] Kurland, O., Lee, L.: Pagerank without hyperlinks: structural re-ranking using links induced by language models. In: SIGIR 2005: Proceedings of the 28th Annual International ACM SIGIR Conference on Research and Development in Information Retrieval, pp. 306–313. ACM, New York (2005)

[11] Fujimura, K.: The eigenrumor algorithm for ranking blogs. In: Du, D.-Z., Jie, S. (eds.) Advances in Optimization and Approximation, Academic Publishers (2005)

[12] Kim, J.-H., Yoon, T.-B., Kim, K.-S., Lee, J.-H.: Trackback-rank: An e ective ranking algorithm for the blog search. In: IITA 2008: Proceedings of the 2008 Second International Symposium on Intelligent Information Technology Application, pp. 503–507. IEEE Computer Society, Washington, DC, USA (2008)

[13] Bansal, N., Koudas, N.: Blogscope: spatio-temporal analysis of the blogosphere. In: WWW 2007: Proceedings of the 16th International Conference on World Wide Web, pp. 1269–1270. ACM, New York (2007)

[14] Brewster, C., O'Hara, K., Fuller, S., Wilks, Y., Franconi, E., Musen, M.A., Ellman, J., Shum, S.B.: Knowledge representation with ontologies: The present and future. IEEE Intelligent Systems 19, 72–81 (2004)

[15] Kekalainen, J., Jarvelin, K.: Cumulated gain-based evaluation of in-formation retrival techniques. ACM Transactions on Information Systems 20(4), 422–446 (2002)

[16] Brooks, C.H., Montanez, N.: Improved annotation of the blogosphere via autotagging and hierarchical clustering. In: WWW 2006: Proceedings of the 15th International Conference on World Wide Web, pp. 625–632. ACM, New York (2006)

[17] Li, B., Xu, S., Zhang, J.: Enhancing clustering blog documents by utilizing author/reader comments. In: ACM-SE 45: Proceedings of the 45th Annual Southeast Regional Conference, pp. 94–99. ACM, New York (2007)

[18] Agarwal, N., Galan, M., Liu, H., Subramanya, S.: Clustering blogs with collective wisdom. In: ICWE 2008: Proceedings of the 2008 Eighth International Conference on Web Engineering, pp. 336–339. IEEE Computer Society, Washington, DC, USA (2008)

[19] Wu, S., Wang, J., Vu, H., Li, G.: Text clustering with important words using normalization. In: JCDL 2010: Proceedings of the 10th Annual Joint Conference on Digital Libraries, pp. 393–394. ACM, New York (2010)

Optimizing Frequent Pattern Mining through Elimination of Null Transactions

Binesh Nair[1] and Amiya Kumar Tripathy[2]

[1] SIES College of Science, Sion (west), Mumbai University, India
binesh5_nair@yahoo.com
[2] CSRE, Indian Institute of Technology Bombay, Mumbai, India
aktripathy@iitb.ac.in

Abstract. The mining of frequent itemsets is often challenged by the length of the patterns mined and also by the number of transactions considered for the mining process. Another acute challenge that concerns the performance of any association rule mining algorithm is the presence of null transactions. This work proposes a closed frequent itmeset mining algorithm viz., Closed Frequent Itemset Mining and Pruning (CFIM-P) algorithm using the sub-itemset pruning strategy. CFIM-P algorithm has attempted to eliminate redundant patterns by pruning closed frequent sub-itemsets. An attempt has even made towards eliminating the null transactions by using the vertical data format representation technique for finding the frequent itemsets.

Keywords: Data Mining, Frequent Pattern Growth (FP) Tree, Frequent Itemsets, Closed Itemsets, Frequent Pattern.

1 Introduction

Frequent itemset mining is an advancing area of research in the domain of data mining. Frequent Itemset mining leads to discovery of associations, correlations among items in large transactional or relational data sets. A typical example of frequent Itemset mining is market basket analysis [7]. Apriori and Frequent Growth Tree (FP-Tree) are two of the most popular mining approaches, to mine frequent itmesets. Apriori employs an iterative approach known as a level-wise search, where k-itemsets are used to explore $(k+1)$ itemsets [3]. Most of the frequent pattern mining algorithms are based on Apriori [1]. FP-growth mining algorithm offers better performance than Apriori algorithm as the former does not depend on candidate generation. Also, the database is fully scanned just twice. Thus, it more efficient and scalable compared to Apriori. Although, FP-tree is scalable and efficient, and many contemporary algorithms are based on FP-tree; its performance deteriorate as the length and number of the patterns increases, with most of the patterns being redundant [2], [5], [4], [5], [6], [8]. A severe challenge pertaining to the mining of frequent itemsets is the presence of null transactions. Null transactions are those transactions which provide no information for the mining of frequent itemsets. For instance, they contain either no frequent item or they contain just one item. The proposed work has made an attempt to overcome the drawbacks of FP-tree. Firstly, an algorithm is

V.V. Das and N. Thankachan (Eds.): CIIT 2011, CCIS 250, pp. 518–523, 2011.

introduced namely CFIM-P algorithm, which is based on closed frequent itemset mining. CFIM-P algorithm eliminates the redundant patterns thereby, attempting to minimize the depth of the tree, without losing any critical information. Also, before the mining process commences, the proposed framework through Vertical Data Representation technique for frequent itemsets, tracks the null transactions and filters them. Thus, the mining will be restricted just to the relevant set of transactions thereby, saving time and cost. The proposed framework has possible implications even in the mining of stream data, since, the only difference between data from a transactional database and stream data is the volume and the nature of data. Stream data grows exponentially and they are dynamic in nature. The main point of convergence for the sources of these data is the percentage of null transactions. Thus, the proposed framework may work fairly for optimizing the mining of stream data. This paper is an extension of our previous work [9]. In this, we provide a theoretical foundation for optimizing the mining of stream data using the proposed framework.

2 Methodology of the Proposed Framework

A major challenge in mining frequent Itemsets from a large data set is the fact that such mining often generates a huge number of Itemsets satisfying the minimum support threshold (min_sup), especially when min_sup is set low. This is because, if an Itemset is frequent, each of its subsets is frequent as well. A long Itemset will contain a combinatorial number of shorter, frequent sub-itemsets. Closed frequent Itemsets overcome this challenge by removing redundant patterns [3]. An Itemset *X* is closed in a data set *S* if there does not exists proper super-itemset *Y* such that *Y* has the same support count as *X*. An Itemset *X* is a closed frequent Itemset in set *S* if *X* is both closed and frequent in *S*.

2.1 Methodology

As shown in fig 1, the proposed framework consists of 3 phases; the first phase traces the null transactions and filters them for subsequent mining procedures. The second phase uses CFIM-P algorithm to find closed frequent itemsets. Finally, these closed frequent itemsets constitute to form patterns.

Fig. 1. Work flow diagram for mining frequent patterns

Table 1. Transaction Database (Modified from Han and Kamber, 2006)

TID	List of item-ID's
T100	I_1,I_2,I_5
T200	I_2
T300	I_2,I_3
T400	I_1,I_2,I_4
T500	I_1
T600	I_2
T700	I_2,I_1,I_5
T800	I_1,I_5
T900	I_6, I_7

Assuming that the minimum support is set to 2, the FP-tree while mining the frequent itemsets will have considered all the transactions. However, the proposed work considers transactions T200, T500 and T600 as null transactions, since they contain just 1-itemsets (TID stands for Transaction ID). These single itemsets apparently won't give any information for association, for the simple reason that they are not associated with any itemset in that particular transaction.

Screening Null Transactions: Null transactions may outweigh the non-null transactions in any real time merchandise. Null transactions also influence the various association and correlation measures [3]. Thus, in this proposed framework an attempt has been made to eliminate the null transactions thereby, attempting to reduce the processing time for finding frequent *k*-itemsets. Finding null transactions and later eliminating them from future scheme of things is the initial part of this proposed framework. This is achieved through Vertical Data Format of representation, wherein data is represented in the {item-set: Trans-ID} format.

Table 2. Transaction database of an electronic shop in Vertical Data Format

Item	Trans-ID's
I_1	T100,T400, T700, T800
I_2	T100,T300, T400,T700
I_3	T300
I_4	T400
I_5	T100,T700, T800
I_6	T900
I_7	T900

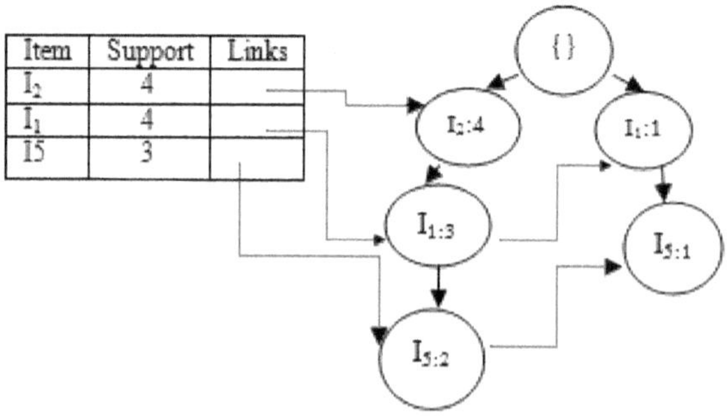

Fig. 2. FP-tree corresponding to table 2

Closed Frequent Itemset Mining-Pruning (CFIM-P) Algorithm: The proposed algorithm for finding closed frequent patterns by mining closed frequent itemsets (by sub-itemset pruning strategy) is given below.

```
CFIM-P (FP-tree, min-sup)
for each frequent single-itemset
construct conditional pattern bases, b = {b1, b2, b3, ...
, bn}
    for each bi  (where i = 1, 2, ..., n)
          if  bi  ≥  min-sup  and  support-count(bi)  >
    support-count(bj) , for i > j
insert bi to a set of frequent patterns
```

CFIM-P algorithm uses the sub-itemset pruning strategy of closed frequent itemset mining. If a frequent itemset X is a proper subset of an already found closed itemset Y and SupportCount(X) = SupportCount(Y), then X and all of X's descendents in the set enumeration tree cannot be frequent closed itemsets and thus can be pruned [3]. This will help in eliminating the redundant patterns and thereby, receiving refined patterns. CFIM-P algorithm mines closed frequent patterns from the FP-tree, constructed prior. With reference to table 1 and fig. 2, the closed frequent patterns will be {I2, I1: 3} and {I2, I1, I5: 2}; removing redundant patterns like, {I2, I1: 2}, {I2, I5:2}, {I1, I5:2} has been omitted; giving much refined patterns.

3 Theoretical Foundation for Optimizing the Mining of Stream Data Using the Proposed Framework

Generally, two main challenges for mining the stream data are designing faster mining algorithms and to promptly detect changing concepts and data distribution because of highly dynamic nature of data streams [10]. The proposed framework may enable faster processing of stream data since, only valid transactions are considered; transactions having just a single item are eliminated as null transactions and they are not considered for the mining process. This filtering is done during the preprocessing stage of the proposed framework. This would restrict subsequent scanning to the valid transactions. Finally, there may be an optimization in the memory usage since the focus is only on items which appear frequently with other items. This may help in effective management of the corresponding data structure.

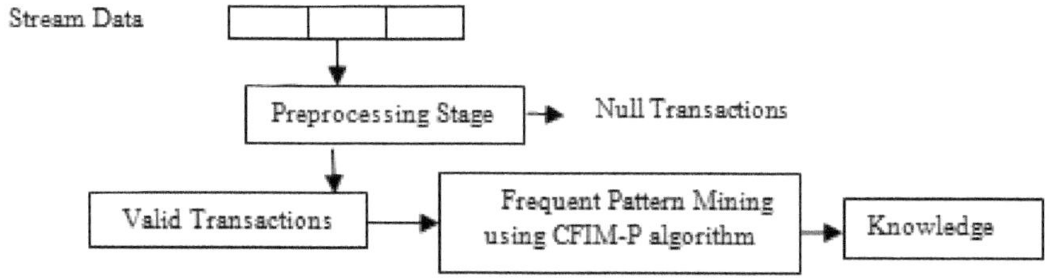

Fig. 3. Theoretical Framework for optimizing the mining of stream data

4 Experimental Observations

The real-time data has been collected from a local restaurant. The data collected consists of a set of transactions performed on one day. Each transaction has a transaction-id and an associated list of itemsets. The average length of itemsets for any transaction in the dataset is just under 3. The purpose of considering this dataset is that, it provides a good means to perform frequent pattern mining and at the same time helps to explain the effectiveness of the proposed work.

Experimental Analysis: The experiments have been based on a real life dataset based on a restaurant, which consists of 192 transactions and 64 itemsets.

Minimum Support	% of Null Transactions
0 %	32 %
4 %	37 %
7 %	41 %
10 %	54 %
14 %	55 %
18 %	55 %

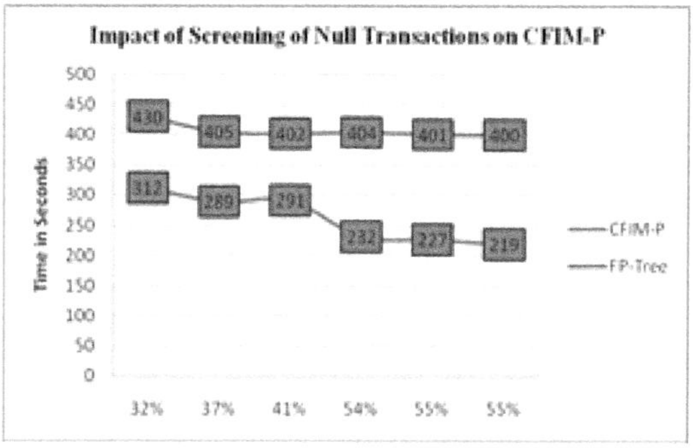

Fig. 4. Impact of elimination of null transactions in the performance of CFIM-P algorithm

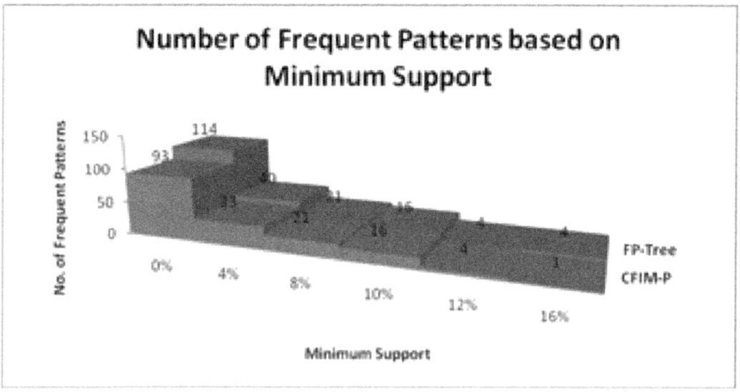

Fig. 5. Distribution of frequent patterns in both CFIM-P and FP-tree algorithms

Fig. 4 shows the impact of screening of null transactions in the performance of CFIM-P algorithm. With higher minimum support count, the number of frequent itemsets descends which in turn result in a greater ratio of null transactions in the dataset. These null transactions are ultimately eliminated in the proposed framework thereby, boosting the performance. Fig. 5 show the distribution of mined patterns across varying minimum support count with realtime dataset. It can be observed that, CFIM-P mines lesser number of patterns compared to that in FP-tree in each case.

5 Conclusion

The proposed work has attempted to resolve both these issues. From the experimental results, it has been observed that, CFIM-P algorithm performs better than the traditional FP-tree algorithm especially for higher minimum support count; since a higher minimum support result in a greater ratio of null transactions. Since, CFIM-P algorithm is based on Closed Frequent Itemset Mining; it even eliminates the redundant patterns thereby, giving refined patterns as compared to that obtained through FP-tree. It can be taken into consideration that, the proposed framework can be more efficient compared to the traditional FP-tree in mining massive, real-time merchandise dataset. Also, this framework may be helpful in the optimizing the mining of stream data by restricting the subsequent scanning to the set of valid transactions.

References

1. Agarwal, R., Ramakrishnan, S.: Fast Algorithms for Mining Association Rules. In: Proceedings of the 20th VLDB Conference, Santiago, Chile (1994)
2. Leung, C.K., Hao, S.B.: Mining of Frequent Itemsets from Streams of Uncertain Data. In: Proceedings of the 2009 IEEE International Conference on Data Engineering, Shanghai, China, pp. 1663–1670 (2009)
3. Han, J., Kamber, M.: Data Mining: Concepts and Techniques. Elsevier Publication, India (2006)
4. Ji, C.R., Deng, Z.H.: Mining Frequent Patterns without Candidate Generation. In: Fourth International Conference on Fuzzy Systems and Knowledge Discovery, Haikou, China, vol. 1, pp. 402–406 (2007)
5. Saravanabhavan, C., Parvathi, R.M.S.: Utility FP-Tree: An Efficient Approach to Mine Weighted Utility Itemsets. European Journal of Scientific Research 50, 466–480 (2011) ISSN 1450-216X
6. Yen, S.J., Lee, Y.S., Wang, C.K., Wu, J.W.: An Efficient Approach for Mining Frequent Patterns Based on Traversing a Frequent Pattern Tree. In: International Conference on Computer Science and Software Engineering, Wuhan, Hubei, China, pp. 354–357 (2008)
7. Liu, Y., Yong, G.: Application in Market Basket Research Based on FP-Growth Algorithm. In: Proceedings of the 2009 WRI World Congress on Computer Science and Information Engineering, Los Angeles, California USA, vol. 4, pp. 112–115 (2009)
8. Zhou, Z., Yang, B., Zhao, Y., Hou, W.: Research on Algorithms for Association Rules Mining Based on FP-tree. In: 2nd International Symposium on Systems and Control in Aerospace and Astronautics, Shenzhen, China, pp. 1–5 (2008)
9. Nair, B., Tripathy, A.K.: Accelerating Closed Frequent Itemset Mining by Elimination of Null Transactions. Journal of Emerging Trends in Computing and Information Sciences 2(7) (July 2011)
10. Kholghi, M., Keyvanpour, M.: An analytical framework for Data Stream Mining Techniques Based on Challenges and requirements. International Journal of Engineering Science and Technology 3(3) (March 2011)

Comparison on Multi-modal Biometric Recognition Method

Gandhimathi Amirthalingam[1] and Radhamani Govindaraju[2]

[1] Department of Computer Science, Bharathiar University, Tamil Nadu, India
[2] Department of Computer Science, Dr. G.R. Damodaran College of Science, Tamil Nadu, India
mathymca@yahoo.com, radhamanig@hotmail.com

Abstract. The biometrics` refers to the use of physiological or biological characteristics to recognize and verify the identity of an individual. In this paper, the recent multimodal biometric human recognition techniques are compared with parameters like combination scheme, description and limitation of the biometric sources. Methods that use multiple types of biometric sources for recognition purposes (multi-modal biometric) are reviewed. Evaluations of multi biometric technology that are used to improve the recognition are also presented along with the databases. The proposed comparison approach shows that the fusion of extracted face and ear images improves the human recognition.

Keywords: Face recognition, Ear recognition, biometric recognition, multi-modal recognition.

1 Introduction

A biometric recognition technique is a measurable physical characteristic or behavioral trait and is a more reliable indicator of identity than legacy systems [2]. A method of identification based on anthropometry of various parts of the human body had developed. Physiological biometrics is based on data derived from part of the human body with direct measurement. Behavioral biometrics is based on data derived from person or individual behavioral action. Verification compares the enrolled claim of identity against a face image of an unknown person, whether the person is claims to be. Identification compares the image of an unknown person against all records in a database of templates and the individual does not claim an identity.

2 Survey of Multi Modal Biometric

This literature survey deals with multi modal biometrics in order to improve robustness and accuracy of an existing single biometric method. The methodologies that use multiple types of biometric sources for recognition purposes are reviewed. A person identification system using two biometrics, face and ear, is presented by A.A. Darwish et al. [1]. PCA decorrrelate data in order to show difference and similarities

V.V. Das and N. Thankachan (Eds.): CIIT 2011, CCIS 250, pp. 524–526, 2011.

by finding the Eigen vectors of the covariance matrix. This system has implemented on MIT, ORL and Yale databases. The overall accuracy of the system is 92.24% with FAR of 10% and FRR of 6.1%. They concluded that the combined face and ear is a good technique because it offers a high accuracy and security. Cheng Lu et al. describe a multimodal biometric identification based on the face and palmprint [3]. The minimal distance rule (MDR) is applied at the matching score fusion level. In classification, city distance and square Euclidean distance are adopted to test the performance of nearest neighbor classifier. CIR can reach 100% based on ORL face database and PolyU palmprint database. Xu Xiaona et al. [8] proposed a novel kernel-based feature fusion algorithm method in combination of face and ear. This system analyzed with USTB database. The recognition rate for KPCA is 94.52% and KFDA is 96.84%. The experimental results show that the KPCA, KFDA method is efficient for fusion feature extraction. Muhammad Imran Razzak et al. [7] examine the face and finger veins. The scores of the face recognition are combined using weighted Fuzzy fusion to improve the system. The experimental results show that the proposed multimodal recognition system is very efficient in reducing the FAR 0.05 and increasing GAR 91.4. M. .H. Mahoor et al. [6] proposed a multi-modal biometric system comprised of 2D face and 3D ear recognition component. The system combined face and ear using the weighted sum technique. The result of rank-one identification and verification at FAR 0.01% shows that by combining multi-modal face and ear biometric, the performance of the system is increased to 100%; EER of the system is .01%. A face and speech information is proposed by Mohamed Soltane et al. [5]. The score level data fusion is proposed with finite GMM based Expectation Maximization (EM) estimated algorithm. Audio is extracted and fused with the face extraction to significantly achieve the recognition rate. The EER of the system is reduced to 0.087. Yan Yan et al. [9] formalized the framework for combining face and palm print biometric. The system proposed a Correlation Filter Bank (CFB) technique; the unconstrained correlation filter trained for a specific modality is designed by focusing on the overall origin correlation outputs. AR, FRGC and PolyU databases are used for the evaluation. The experiments are conducted on the non-real multimodal biometrics data for convenience and it shows the superiority of the novel method. Biological features of the face or other parts of the human have different properties for different sensors [4]. Reliable biometric system can be attained on what and how to combine multi biometric sources [3]. They are depends on the multiple samples, multiple matches, multiple snapshots, multiple sensors and the number of biometric features in the context of multi-biometric studies.

3 Multiple Biometric Using Face and Ear

Multimodal biometrics based on the combined two different biometric sources, face and ear may provide a new approach of non-intrusive biometrics authentication. The high performance of the system is to recognize faces in real time. Ear is a new class of human biometrics for passive identification with uniqueness and stability. In the absence of fingerprints, the ear shapes or marks are often used for the identification. It is more reliable due to lack of expressions and less effect of aging. The ear has information rich anatomical feature, its structure and pinna are distinctive. In [1,8,6], the fusion of face and ear biometric were used to perform the recognition.

4 Summary and Conclusion

This review studies the multi-modal combination scheme, number of samples, recognition rate and database used. Most of the studies in this review have work with a limited number of subjects and images in the performance evaluation dataset. The integration of multiple biometrics sources face and ear are discussed. The authors are working on the algorithm for multimodal face and ear to do best and produce better biometric recognition. Two images for a person, one for face and other for ear are considered separately. Each image will have to be classified correctly and apply a recognition algorithm to identify an individual. Among various multiple biometrics approaches considered in this paper, we found that person recognition with multiple biometric sources (face and ear) offers a high accuracy and security.

References

1. Darwish, A.A., Abd Elghafar, R., Fawzi Ali, A.: Multimodal Face and Ear Images. J. of Computer Science 5(5), 374–379 (2009)
2. Victor, B., Bowyer, K., Sarkar, S.: An Evaluation of Face and Ear Biometrics. In: Proc. 16th IEEE International Conference on Pattern Recognition (2002)
3. Lu, C., Wang, J., Qi, M.: Multimodal Biometric Identification Approach Based on Face and Palmprint. In: Proc. 2nd IEEE International Symposium on Electronic Commerce and Security, pp. 44–47 (2009)
4. Abdel-Mottaleb, M., Zhou, J.: A System for Ear Biometrics from Face Profile Images. International Journal on Graphics, Vision and Image Processing, 29–34 (2006)
5. Soltane, M., Doghmane, N., Guersi, N.: Face and Speech Based Multi-Modal Biometric Authentication. Int. J. of Advanced Science and Technology 21(8), 41–46 (2010)
6. Mahoor, M.H., Cadavid, S., Abdel-Mottaleb, M.: Multi-modal Ear and Face Modeling and Recognition. In: Proc. 16th IEEE International Conference on Image Processing, pp. 4137–4140 (2009)
7. Razzak, M.I., Yusof, R., Khalid, M.: Multimodal face and finger veins biometric authentication. Scientific Research and Essays 5(17), 2529–2534 (2010)
8. Xiaona, X., Xiuqin, P., Yue, Z., Qiumei, P.: Research on Kernel-Based Feature Fusion Algorithm in Multimodal Recognition. In: IEEE CS International Conference on Information Technology and Computer Science, pp. 3–6 (2009)
9. Yan, Y., Zhang, Y.-J.: Multimodal Biometrics Fusion Using Correlation Filter Bank. IEEE Press (2008)

An Efficient Weighted Median Filter for Impulse Noise Reduction Using Second Order Difference Based Detector

R. Rashidha and Philomina Simon

Department of Computer Science,
University of Kerala, Kariavattom, Thiruvananthapuram - 695 581, Kerala, India
rashidha_r@yahoo.com, philomina.simon@gmail.com

Abstract. This paper proposes a new efficient weighted median filter for the restoration of images corrupted by impulse noise. The proposed approach has two phases. Second order difference based impulse detector is the first phase and an Efficient Weighted Median (EWM) filter is the second phase. Uncorrupted pixels are preserved in this filter. The proposed method has been tested on benchmark images and obtained better performance than many of the existing methods.

Keywords: Image Denoising, Impulse Noise Detector, Second Order Difference.

1 Introduction

Digital images are corrupted by impulse noise by defective sensors or faulty channel during acquisition and transmission. Linear and Non linear filters can be used for removing impulse noise. But Linear filters give poor performance. Non linear filters such as Standard median [1], Weighted Median [2], Center Weighted Median are widely used for impulse noise reduction. In these filters some desirable details are lost and filtering is applied to all pixels without considering location of noise. A solution to this is the use of switching median filter [3], which applies filtering only to the noisy pixels. But these filters replace noisy pixel value without considering local characteristics.

Another approach for impulse noise reduction is Directional Weighted Median filter (DWM) [4], which uses information from four directions for detection and filtering. Even though good results are obtained, the computational overhead of this method is high. The impulse noise removal method in [5] uses the Second Order difference (SOD) for noise detection and a Directional Weighted Median (DWM) for filtering. Hence we call it SODDWM. The proposed method is a modification of SODDWM. SODDWM yield poor performance than DWM for high density noise. But the proposed method gives better performance than SODDWM and DWM for all noise models.

V.V. Das and N. Thankachan (Eds.): CIIT 2011, CCIS 250, pp. 527–530, 2011.

This paper is organized as follows. Section 2 explains an introduction about the impulse noise models. Section 3 discusses the proposed method and Section 4 describes the results and discussion. Section 5 concludes the paper.

2 Noise Models

In this section, four impulse noise models [6] are considered for examining the performance of the proposed filter. In Noise Model 1, pixels are randomly corrupted by two fixed extreme values, 0 for salt and 255 for pepper (for gray level image), generated with the same probability. Noise Model 2 is similar to Noise Model 1, but probabilities of salt and pepper are unequal. In Noise Model 3 salt and pepper have two fixed ranges of values at both ends with a length. Here noise density of salt and pepper are equal. Noise Model 4 is similar to Noise Model 3 but salt and pepper have different probabilities.

3 Impulse Noise Reduction Using EWM Filter - The Proposed Method

The proposed method EWM filter have two stages: a robust impulse noise detection stage and an Efficient Weighted Median filtering (EWM) stage to remove the impulse noise.

The detection algorithm is based on the Second Order Difference (SOD) [5] among pixels in a test window. SOD is used to determine the noise status of the central pixel. SOD has a stronger response to finer details such as edges and noise. For noisy pixels, the SOD value is high.

Consider a 3x3 window, W around a test pixel at (i, j) as

$$w=\{x(i+s, j+t) \ \mid -1 \leq s,t \leq 1\} \tag{1}$$

Edges aligned with four main directions are determined by computing SOD values in equation (2) corresponding to the directions shown in Figure 1.

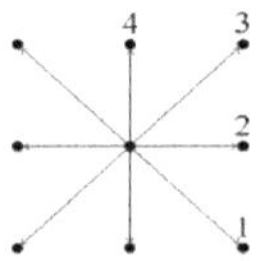

Fig. 1. Four directions of impulse detection

$$d_k = |x(i+u, j+t) + x(i-u, j-t) - 2x(i, j)| \tag{2}$$

where(k, u, v)={(1,1,1),(2,0,1),(3,-1,1),(4,-1,0)}. Minimum value from these four SODs is used for impulse detection, which can be denoted as d.

$$d = \min\{d_k \ : 1 \leq \mathrm{k} \leq 4\} \tag{3}$$

A small value of d implies the test pixel is uncorrupted and is on flat region. SOD of all directions is small for noise free pixel on flat region and the noise free pixels yield smaller SOD value along edges. If the test pixel is noisy, then it yields large SOD values in all directions resulting in larger value of d. The pixel can be classified as noisy or noise free by comparing the value of d with a threshold. If the value of d is greater than threshold, then it is considered as noise else noise free. Decision map is used in the filtering stage. Decision map entry for a pixel is defined as below.

$$N_{i,j} = \begin{cases} \text{noisy pixel} & \text{if } d > T \\ \text{noise free pixel} & \text{if } d \le T \end{cases}$$

After impulse noise detection stage, proposed EWM filter is applied. The EWM produces the restored image with more details than the SODDWM method. In EWM, more weight is given to all non noisy pixels in the 3X3 window so that it gives good performance for higher density noise also. In the noise filtering stage, noise only pixels identified in the detection are replaced based on the decision map. A 3x3 window, W around a central pixel position (i, j) is considered for filtering. The restored value for the selected window can be calculated as, $X_{i,j} = \text{median}\{w_{(i+s,j+t)} \lozenge x_{(i+s,j+t)} \mid -1 \le s,t \le 1\}$, where w is the weight assigned to pixels, symbol ◊ is used to represent repetition operator. and is defined as

$$w_{(i+s,j+t)} = \begin{cases} 3 \text{ if } x_{(i+s,j+t)} \text{ is non noisy} \\ 1 \text{ if} x_{(i+s,j+t)} \text{ is noisy} \end{cases}$$

4 Results and Discussion

The performance of the filter is analysed using PSNR, SSIM, IEF and IQI. Performance Evaluations using Lena, Boat, Peppers and Gold hill illustrated in this section. EWM filter is applied six to seven times iteratively with decreasing value of threshold to improve efficiency. In our experiment, we select $T_0 = 100$, $T_{k+1} = T_k * 0.8$ (k>0). All noise models described in the Section 2 are used for measuring the performance of the proposed filter.

Performance measures obtained for Lena image for Noise Model 1 is shown in Table 1.

Table 1. Performance measures obtained for lena image corrupted by Noise Model 1

Noise (%)	PSNR			SSIM			IEF			IQI		
	DWM	SODDWM	EWM	DWM	SODDWM	EWM	DWM	SODDWM	EWM	DWM	SODDWM	EWM
20	34.10	34.51	36.64	0.994	0.994	0.996	147.10	161.2	263.36	0.903	0.917	0.940
40	29.66	25.85	31.84	0.984	0.963	0.990	105.46	43.99	174.91	0.782	0.707	0.833
60	21.16	13.11	23.97	0.902	0.542	0.947	22.37	3.50	42.64	0.442	0.176	0.589

EWM has better performance than DWM and SODDWM for all performance measures. Restored images of Boat image is shown in figure 2. It shows that the proposed method, EWM produces image with better visual quality and edges are preserved.

Fig. 2. Boat image corrupted by the Noise Model 2 with 25%, noise, Images restored by SODDWM, DWM and EWM filter respectively

Fig. 3. Edge Map of peppers image and restored images corresponding to SODDWM, DWM, EWM filters

5 Conclusion

An efficient filter for impulse noise detection is proposed in this paper. The EWM filter improves the SODDWM based filter by giving more weight to all non noisy pixels in the test window. The proposed filter EWM preserves more details than SODDWM method. Experimental results have shown the superiority of the proposed method.

References

1. Pratt, W.K.: Digital Image Processing. John Wiley & Sons (1978)
2. Brownrigg, D.: The weighted median filter. Commun. Assoc. Comput. 27(8), 807–818 (1984)
3. Eng, H.-L., Ma, K.-K.: Noise adaptive soft-switching median filter. IEEE Trans. Image Process 10(2), 242–251 (2001)
4. Dong, Y., Xu, S.: A New Directional Weighted Median Filter for Removal of Random-Valued Impulse Noise. IEEE Signal Processing Letters 14(3), 193–196 (2007)
5. Dong, Y., Xu, S.: A New Directional Weighted Median Filter for Removal of Random-Valued Impulse Noise. IEEE Signal Processing Letters 14(3), 193–196 (2007)
6. Nair, M.S., Raju, G.: A new fuzzy-based decision algorithm for high-density impulse noise removal. Signal Image and Video Processing (2010), doi:10.1007/s11760-010-0186-4

Assessing and Improving Encapsulation for Minimizing Vulnerability of an Object Oriented Design

A. Agrawal and R.A. Khan

Department of IT, Babasaheb Bhimrao Ambedkar University,
Lucknow, India-226025
alka_csjmu@yahoo.co.in, khanraees@yahoo.com

Abstract. Like quality, proper blend of object oriented design (OOD) concepts may improve security of the software under development. The paper aims to find out the role of encapsulation in improving security of an OOD. A Vulnerability Confinement Capacity (VCC) metric is proposed to verify the vulnerability confinement strength of a class as well as of an OOD. The same is used to compare security of object oriented designs.

Keywords: Object Oriented Design, Design Phase, Software Security, Vulnerability, Security Metric,Encapsulation.

1 Introduction

Vulnerability can be defined as a defect which enables an attacker to bypass security measures [6]. Design phase is more responsible for vulnerable software than the other phases of software development life cycle [7].The approach proposed is a part of the research work which minimizes the vulnerability propagation by concentrating on OOD constructs such as inheritance, coupling, and encapsulation and examining which construct among all supports vulnerability propagation and which suppresses.

In previous work, it is proved that inheritance and coupling support vulnerability propagation and hence decreases security [1],[2],[3].Encapsulation improves quality of the software [4]. As security is an attribute of quality, a similar possibility is investigated in the research presented in this paper. Encapsulation is used to protect from unauthorized access [5]. This intuitively shows that encapsulation restricts propagation of vulnerability and hence improves security. Rest of the paper is organized as: next section introduces some new terminologies. Section 3 presents the approach for the development of vulnerability confinement capacity metric and the paper is concluded at section 4.

2 Terminology and Definition

Anything which is susceptible to attack is termed as vulnerable [6]. In addition, increasing availability of anything vulnerable (vulnerability propagation), would

V.V. Das and N. Thankachan (Eds.): CIIT 2011, CCIS 250, pp. 531–533, 2011.

increase its vulnerability [3] and increased vulnerability tends to reduce security. The development of VCC metrics introduces terminology as follows:

2.1 Vulnerable Attributes/ Methods/ Classes

In OOD, attributes and methods which represent assets or process confidential information or provide entry to the confidential information are termed as vulnerable attributes/ methods. A class containing vulnerable attributes or methods is called vulnerable class.

2.2 Vulnerability Confinement (VC)

VC in OOD context can be defined as confining the vulnerability of an attribute and its associated methods within the boundaries of its own class. With the increase in exposure of vulnerable attribute to other classes, vulnerability propagation increases [1], [2]. So VC is the phenomenon which restricts vulnerability propagation. A vulnerable class confines the vulnerability of its vulnerable attributes and their associated methods if it hides its identity, restricts accessibility to its vulnerable attributes and methods and provides them write protection.

This further introduces three terminologies as follows:

Hidden Identity (HI): In an OOD, class A knows that another class B exists by taking a parameter of its type, having a member of its type or returning its type from a method. A vulnerable class hides its vulnerable attributes if it hides its own identity.

Restricted Accessibility (RA): A class must not allow open access to its vulnerable attributes. There must be some restriction on accessibility of vulnerable attributes. A vulnerable class provides accessibility restriction to its vulnerable attributes if it provides service methods for them, hide their nature (type) or makes them private so that only the required information, not more than that, is disclosed to the client classes.

Write Protection (WP): A vulnerable attribute, if not write protected, has chances of damage. A class provides write protection to its vulnerable attributes if it associates only read methods with the attribute not write method, until necessary.

3 Vulnerability Confinement Capacity Measurement

In today's complex software which need enormous coupling and inheritance, it is not possible for a class to hide itself from the classes in the design. A completely hidden class will be useless. Hence, for computing VCC, a new term **'IdentityDisclosure'**, opposite to 'Hidden Identity' can be introduced. An identity disclosure happens whenever a class lets the other classes know that the class exists.Intuitively, a vulnerable class encapsulates its vulnerability more strongly if it does not let other classes in the design to know its existence. The more number of times it will disclose its identity, the less VCC it will have. In addition, increase in RA and WP of vulnerable attribute will increase VC. On the basis of the above discussion, VCC of a class and that of an OOD can be computed as:VCC of a class reflects how successfully a vulnerable class protects its vulnerable attributes. This may be defined as:VCC_VulClass =WPAR/ Total Identity Disclosure Count.

Total count of identity disclosure is the number of times vulnerable class breaks the rules given in the definition of 'Hidden Identity' when communicating with other classes. The WPAR can be computed as:WPAR=No. of Protected Vulnerable Attributes/ Total no. of Vulnerable Attributes in the Class.

VCC of an OOD is equal to the average of the VCC of all of its vulnerable classes.

$$\text{VCC\_OOD} = \sum \text{VCC\_VulClass}(i) / m$$

4 Conclusion

Quantitative estimation of security at design phase is almost missing [7]. No concrete conclusion can be drawn about the security of a software design in absence of quantitative measures. To bridge the gap, two vulnerability measures, VCC for a class as well as for an OOD are proposed.

Acknowledgments. This work is sponsored by University Grant Commission (UGC), New Delhi, India, under F. No. 34-107\ 2008(SR).

References

1. Agrawal, A., Khan, R.A.: Impact of Inheritance on Vulnerability Propagation at Design Phase. ACM SIGESOFT SEN 34, 1–5 (2009)
2. Agrawal, A., Chandra, S., Khan, R.A.: An Efficient Measurement of Object Oriented Design Vulnerability. In: IEEE Conference on Availability, Reliability and Security, pp. 618–622. IEEE Press, Japan (2009)
3. Agrawal, A., Khan, R.A.: A Vulnerability Metric for Design Phase of Object Oriented Software. In: IC3. CCIS, vol. 94, pp. 328–339. Springer, Heidelberg (2010)
4. Bain, S. L.: Encapsulation As a First Principle of Object Oriented Design, http://www.netobjectives.com/resources/articles/first-principle-object-oriented-design
5. Stroustrup, B.: What is "Object Oriented Programming"? (1991 revised version). In: 1st European Software Festival (1991)
6. Manadhata, P., Wing. J.M.: An attack surface metric. CMU-CS-05-155, (July 2005), http://www.cs.cmu.edu/%7Ewing/publications/CMU-CS-05-155.pdf
7. Alshammari, B., Fidge, C., Corney, D.: Security Metrics for Object-Oriented Design. In: 21st Australian Software Engineering Conference, pp. 55–64. IEEE Press (2010)

Formalizing Soft Trust Management

Priyanka Dadhich[1], Kamlesh Dutta[1], and M.C. Govil[2]

[1] National Institute of Technology, Hamirpur, India
prynkmshr@gmail.com, kd@nitham.ac.in
[2] Malviya National Institute of Technology, Jaipur, India
govilmc@yahoo.com

Abstract. Security plays very important role in distributed systems .Mobile agents allows us to gain greater access to hosts in these systems. But, the success of using mobile agent paradigm depends on the level of security that hosts offers it. We tried to put stress on social aspects related to security called soft trust to determine the intentions of hosts. Proposed model will help to move mobile agent through hosts by formulating their social behaviors, experience, recommendation and reputation.

Keywords: Mobile Agents, Security, distributed systems, soft trust.

1 Introduction

A mobile agent is an autonomous entity that can move from one host to another under self-control [6]. They move from one host to another in network to accomplish its tasks. Due to this, they are vulnerable to number of attacks in an open network. Mobile agent security issues include four aspects: protect hosts, protect agent, protect other agents and protect network [2]. So, the success of mobile agents depends on its security. The lack of comprehensive security solutions is a major concern that needs to be addressed before we see wide industry adoption of this new distributed computing paradigm. So to prevent these hindrances, we assume that there is a possibility to achieve better security solution through trust perspective [4].

The paper is organized as follows. Section two discusses related work in soft trust management. Section three enlightens differences between hard and soft trust. Section four proposes formalizing of experience and direct trust. Section five presents results and discussion. Section six gives conclusion.

2 Related Works

Trust model proposed by Marsh [3] concerned with soft trust that captures situational trust in different situations taking into account of trustor's own utility preferences. Then Abdul-Rahman et al [5] proposed a trust model along with a protocol for trust recommendation queries in distributed systems. Baolin Ma, Jizhou Sun [7] talks about trust based on reputation. Later, Maarof and Krishna [1] gave hybrid trust management model.

V.V. Das and N. Thankachan (Eds.): CIIT 2011, CCIS 250, pp. 534–536, 2011.

3 Hard Trust v/s Soft Trust

Hybrid Trust is a combination of hard and soft trust [1]. Hard trust symbolizes the trust relationships that can be derived from the underlying cryptography based security mechanisms, such as digital certificates, signatures and cryptographic checksums. Soft trust is based on trust relationships derived from localized and external observations of system entity behavior, through social control mechanisms such as direct experiences, recommendations or a combination of both.

Table 1. Results and Observations

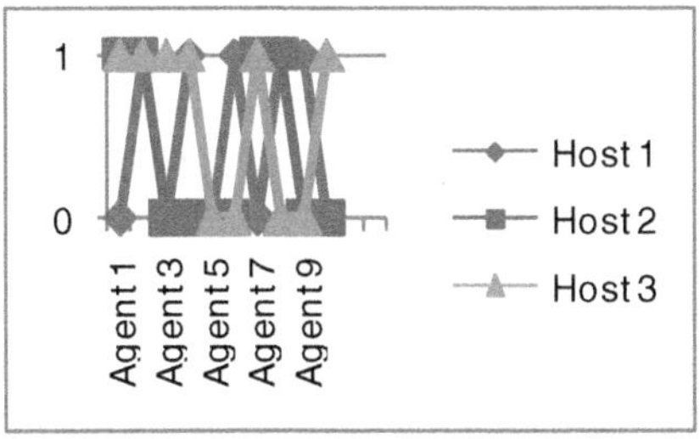

Result: Since Host 3 has more non-malicious points so it is highly trustworthy.

No. of Agents	Nature of actions taken by		
	Host1	Host2	Host3
1	0	1	1
2	1	1	1
3	0	0	1
4	1	0	1
5	0	0	0
6	1	0	0
7	0	1	1
8	1	1	0
9	1	0	0
10	0	0	1

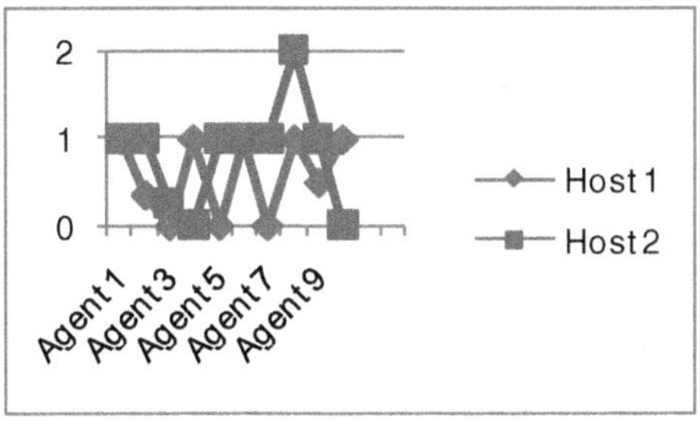

Result: Since Host 2 has more non-malicious points than Host 1. So, Host 2 is more trustworthy than Host 1.

No. of Agents	Nature of actions taken by	
	Host1	Host2
1	1	1
2	0.35	1
3	0	0.25
4	1	0
5	0	1
6	1	1
7	0	1
8	1	2
9	0.5	1
10	1	0

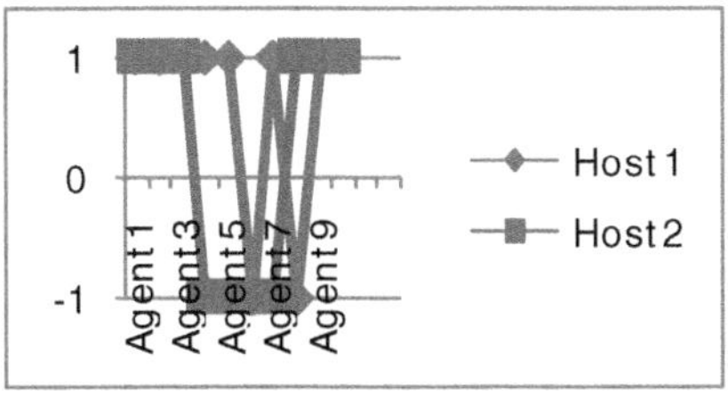

Result: Since host 1 has less malicious weight of rating of actions, so it is more trustworthy than host 2.

No. of Agents	Nature of actions taken by	
	Host1	Host2
1	1	1
2	1	1
3	1	1
4	1	-1
5	1	-1
6	-1	-1
7	1	-1
8	-1	1
9	1	1
10	1	1

4 Formalizing Trust Parameters

4.1 Experience Trust Rating (ET)

Rating is given to hosts according to their recent positive and negative transactions. Rating ranges from (-1 to 1). Weight is given to ratings accordingly. Rating to host (h_i) is given as follows: $R_i = +1$ (for recent positive transaction) ,$R_i = 0.5$ (for past recent positive transaction) $R_i = 0$ (for historic positive transaction),$R_i = -1$ (for negative action) $wt(R_i)=1$ if $R_i >=0$ and $wt(R_i)=-1$ if $R_i <0$.

4.2 Behavior Trust (BT)

Past behavior Trust (B_{pa}): na= number of negative transactions by , tot= total transactions by host h_i. $B_{pa}= 1-(na/tot)$ .Present behavior Trust(B_{pr}): SL= security level(SL) , V_a= value of action SL=1 if V_a= 1 or 0.5 , SL =2 if $V_a = 0$. $B_{pr} = (V_a)^{SL}$. Table 1 shows the results and observations.

5 Conclusion

Paper envisaged a paradigm shift from security-centric to trust-centric solutions that finally enabled better security decisions for agents against malicious hosts. Formulaic approaches are proposed to calculate soft trust factors. Observations are seen to conclude the results.

References

1. Maarof, A., Krishna, K.: A Hybrid Trust Management Model for MAS Based Trading Society
2. Dadhich, P., Dutta, K., Govil, M.C.: Security Issues in Mobile agents. International Journal of Computer Applications 11 (December 2010)
3. Marsh, S.: Formalizing trust as a computational concept. Ph. D. thesis, university of Stirling (1994)
4. Beth, T., Borcherding, M., Klein, B.: Valuation of Trust in Open Networks. In: Gollmann, D. (ed.) ESORICS 1994. LNCS, vol. 875, pp. 3–18. Springer, Heidelberg (1994)
5. Abdul- Rahman, A., Hailes, S.: Using Recommendations for managing Trust in Distributed Systems. In: Proceedings of IEEE Malaysia Int'l Conference on Communications (MICC 1997), Malaysia (1997)
6. Ma, L., Tsai, J.J.P.: Attacks and countermeasures in software system security. In: Handbook of Software Engineering and Knowledge Engineering
7. Ma, B., Sun, J.: Study on the behavior based Trust model in Grid Security System. In: IEEE Int'l Conference on Services Computing (2004)

Anomaly Detection in VoIP System Using Neural Network and Fuzzy Logic

Narendra Shekokar[1] and Satish Devane[2]

Department of Computer Engineering
[1] D.J. Sanghvi College of Engineering, Mumbai, India
[2] Ramrao Adik College of Engineering, Navi Mumbai, India
nshekokar@yahoo.co.in, satish@rait.ac.in

Abstract. As Voice over IP (VoIP) system is widely accepted by industries because of its economical benefit and its reach feature than traditional PSTN system. Most dominating session initialization protocol used by VoIP system is SIP, which is vulnerable to various threats like Denial-of-Service (DoS). The Intrusion Detection System (IDS) is use to identify to VoIP threats, but the current IDS system have fail to generate new rule set based on new signature of attack. We have proposed an Adaptive IDS using Artificial Neural Network (ANN) & Fuzzy Approximation technique to detect DoS attacks. Neural Network System is used to learn about new threats while Fuzzy System decides the severity of attack. Our experimental result shows that a combination approach of Neural Network and Fuzzy approximation proposed method have maximize detection rate and minimize false-positive rate.

Keywords: Denial-of-Service, Adaptive IDS, VoIP, ANN and Fuzzy logic, SIP.

1 Introduction

VoIP system uses increases gradually because of its rich feature and low communication cost. Due to its rapid growth of popularity, threats on VoIP are increases considerable these threats may cause a great loss of a company revenue.[1] With the growing number of computer networks in any organizations, Intrusion Detection System (IDS) has become a prime need to protect service, resources of organization [4]. Protocols in VoIP can be classified into signaling, media transport, and support protocols. Signaling protocols are responsible for call setup, tear down, and modification. Media transport protocols are involved in end-to-end transport of voice and multimedia data. Support protocols are used to enable services and features required for proper network operation. A major source of vulnerabilities in these protocols is that they transmit packet headers and payloads in clear text by default due to the absence of built-in authentication and encryption [5]. It is therefore easy for attackers to cause call termination and call flooding as well as to spoof caller ID or to exercise other attacks. As existing SIP security is not sufficient to protect from various threats, intrusion detection system (IDS) is needed to protect SIP communication.

V.V. Das and N. Thankachan (Eds.): CIIT 2011, CCIS 250, pp. 537–542, 2011.

IDS technique is divided into two main categories Signature Based Detection and Anomaly Based Detection. Based on deployment, IDS technique is further categories in two type i.e, Host-based systems and Network-based systems. Host-based monitor functions on a single host while Network-based systems monitor entire traffic over the network analyzing the stream of packets traveling across the network. Packets are captured through a set of sensors. Vulnerability assessment based IDS detects vulnerabilities on internal networks and firewall. Hybrid intrusion detection system uses both methods [2][3]. In this paper we have proposed a IDS technique using Neural Network and Fuzzy logic, Neural Network System is used to learn about new threats while Fizzy System decides the severity of attack. A combination approach of Neural Network and Fuzzy approximation will greatly reduce the false alarms. Our paper is organized as below. In section 2, we have discussed the analysis of SIP protocol and attack. In section 3, we have proposed a intrusion detection system using Neural Network. Experimentation and performance analysis of the proposed system is discussed in section 4. Finally, we have concluded paper in section 5.

2 SIP Protocol Analyses and Attacks

In VoIP system most dominating signaling protocol is SIP [5] , SIP is an application layer control (signaling) protocol responsible creating, modifying, and terminating VoIP session. SIP message exchange is given in figure 1.

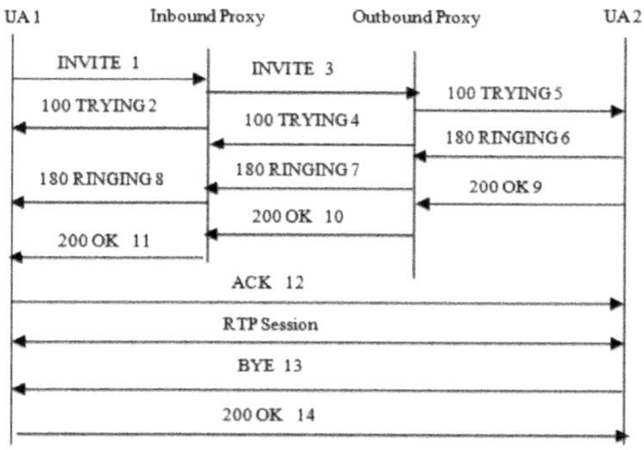

Fig. 1. SIP Message Flow

In SIP all signaling massage is exchange in clear text format, result of this is SIP base VoIP session is vulnerable to various threats. Most saviors threats is Denial of service attacks (DoS) can target the signaling plane elements (e.g. proxy, gateway, etc.) with the objective to take them down and produce havoc in the VoIP network.[12] Such attacks are launched by either flooding the signaling plane with a large quantity of messages, malformed messages. DoS attacks have been costing many high profile organization millions of dollars. Some of the most well known DoS attacks are discussed as below:

1) Land /Re-INVITE: Another name for this attack is Call Hijacking. SIP clients use Re-INVITE message if they want to move the phone call from one device to another without tearing down the session. This feature is called call migrating. An attacker can abuse this feature, taking advantage of the lack of authentication, by sending a Re-INVITE message to one of the parties involved in a session to fool it into believing that the other party is going to change its IP address to a new address. The new address is controlled by the attacker. This attack can be seen as a DoS attack. Furthermore, it breaches the privacy of the call since the attacker will be able to receive voice that is not meant for it. [7]

2) Teardrop/ BYE Attack: VoIP calls are terminated by one of the call participants sending a SIP BYE request. Many VoIP application servers and clients will process a BYE request without requiring authentication. This means that it is easy to construct a BYE request and send it to the application server, which will then terminate the call. [6] BYE attack is common in VoIP environments and is considered as a Denial of Service (DoS) attack.[7]

3) Cancel Attack: During the call setup , an attacker sends a crafted SIP packet with a "CANCEL" request to the proxy, which in turn cancel callee INVITE request. In order to perform these attacks, an attacker must have the necessary session information, such as caller IDs. To obtain said information attacker will plant a Trojan on vulnerable server through which they can attack the VoIP system.[8]

4) ICMP Flood/Smurf Attack: The Smurf attack is a way of generating significant computer network traffic on a victim network. This is a type of denial-of-service attack that floods a target system via spoofed broadcast ping messages. The attacker spoofs his source address as victim's address and sends ICMP echo requests the network router, which broadcasts this request. In turn every computer except the victim computer in the network will reply to the source address (victim's computer address) in the request packet, thus overwhelming the victim. [9]

5) Ping of Death: A ping of death (abbreviated "POD") is a type of attack on a computer that involves sending a malformed or otherwise malicious ping to a computer. A ping is normally 32bytes in size (or 84 bytes when IP header is considered); historically, many computer systems could not handle a ping packet larger than the maximum IPv4 packet size, which is 65,535 bytes. Sending a ping of this size could crash the target computer. [9]

3 Proposed Technique

We have proposed a IDS system using Neural network and Fuzzy logic to detect and learn from unknown attacks with a special focus on DoS attack. A neural network would be capable of analyzing the data from the network, even if the data is incomplete or unclear. In addition to this neural network also capable to process information from multiple source, it use backpropagation for training and testing of IDS. The fuzzy rules are generated from the proposed strategy can be able to provide better classification rate in detecting the intrusion behavior. Our Proposed IDS system will reside on a Proxy server. As a testing input to the neural network, the packet details are read from the connection database. The connection database is derived from captured packet.

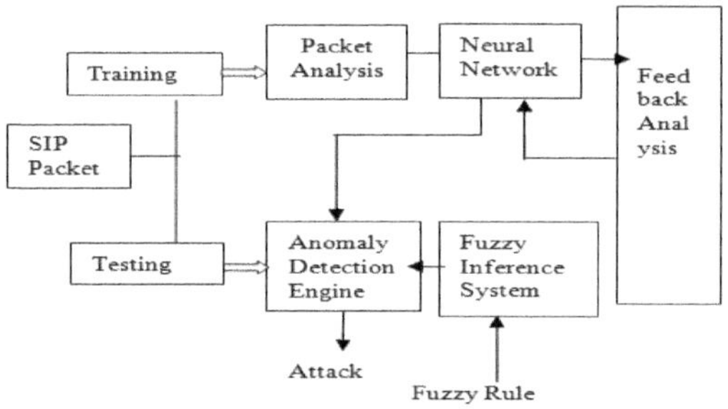

Fig. 2. System Architecture

3.1 Packet Analysis

Packet Analysis module is responsible for checking SIP packet format. To archive this it checks session description parameter SDP. If packet is not in appropriate format or non SIP packet then it will not forward to Neural network module for further processing.

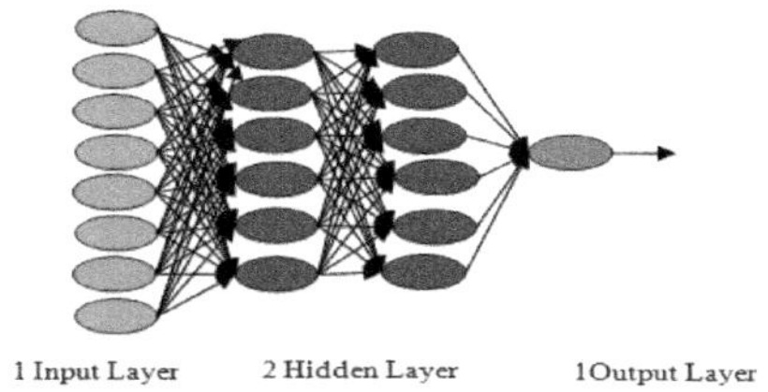

Fig. 3. General Architecture

3.2 Neural Network Learning

Our approach is to develop a machine learning algorithms to develop IDS. A salient feature of Artificial Neural Networks (ANN) is their learning ability. They learn by adaptively updating the synaptic weights to characterize the strength of the connection. The weights are updated according to the information extracted from training patterns. [10] An ANN based IDS need to train before testing it, To archive this IDS read input from the KDDcup99 database.[11].The figure 3 shows general architecture of feed forward neural network (FFNN). The feed forward neural network consist one input, two hidden and one output layer. The input layer consists of 8 neurons which represent 8 fields/characteristics of data set of SIP packets. The two hidden layers consist of 6 neurons respectively. The output layer consists of one neurons that classify DoS attack i.e Teardrop, Smurf, Ping of Death, Land and Back attacks. Initial weights were decided and the learning rate was maintained at 0.8.There is no accurate formula for the selection of hidden layers so we can make it by comparison and select which one is best [5]. Backpropagation is a very common method for training multilayered feedforward networks. Backpropagation can be used with any feedforward network that uses a activation function that is differentiable.

3.3 Fuzzy Approximation Technique

The attack detected by the neural system can be provided to the Fuzzy Logic controller which processes user-defined rules governing the system to identify the severity of the attack. For each type of attack detected severity is categorized using three levels namely trivial, warning and lethal. A rule set for each of the attack types is defined by us in separate rule file. For defuzziffication center of gravity (COG) method is applied.

4 Results and Discussion

After successful training of the Neural Network weight of neuron is frozen. Then system is ready for testing various attack, first we have attempt INVITE attack on system, which has given 100 % detection rate with 0 % false positive and false negative respectively After second and third attempts system has given similar result. In Teardrop /Bye attack detection ratio is 99.35 % while false positive and false negative is 0 % and 0.65 % respectively. In Cancle attack detection rate is improved by 0.49 % as compare to Teardrop / BYE attack . In Cancel attack ,We have observed no false negative detection but 0.16 % false positive detection. Both attack having similar behaviors, BYE attack is attempt after VOIP session initialization while Cancel attack is attempted during the session initialization. In case of Ping of death attack , system shows 97.61% detection rate with 1.6% of false positive rate and 2.03% as false negative rate. Our Proposed IDS technique gives average 98.865 % Detection rate which is promising value in case anomaly detection

Table 1. Experiment results

Attack name	False positives	False negatives
Land	0%	0%
Teardrop /BYE	0%	0.65%
Cancel	0.16	0
Ping of Death	1.6%	0.79%
Smurf	1.25%	2.03%

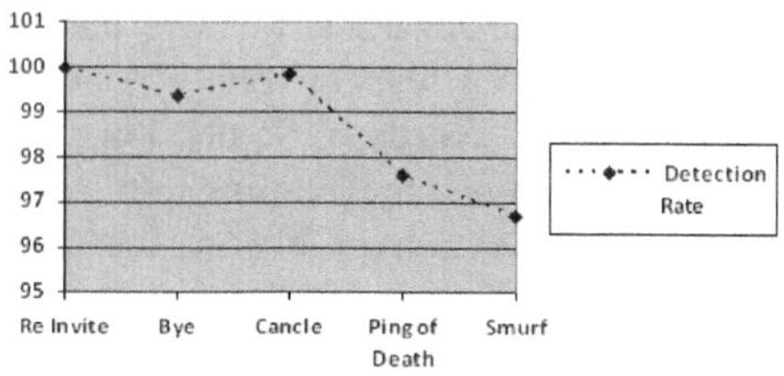

Fig. 4. Detection Accuracy of Various Attack

5 Conclusions

In this paper we have demonstrated the use of a feed forward neural network with back propogation technique for identification and classification of DoS attacks .We intend to overcome the major drawbacks of current IDS systems which is achieving greater accuracy thereby reducing false-positives and false-negatives. We have observed that Resilient back propagation with sigmoid function was the best one for classification. Using Fuzzy logic concept in proposed work we have also succeed to identify the severity of attack.

References

1. Riyad, A., Sumalee, S., Mohsen, T., Denis, R.: Using Neuro-Fuzzy Approach to Reduce False Positive Alerts. IEEE paper, Faculty Of Computer Science, Dalhousie University, Canada
2. Khattab Ali, M., Venus, W., Suleiman Al Rababaa, M.: The Affect of Fuzzification on Neural Networks Intrusion Detection System. IEEE Computer society (2009)
3. Jonsson, E., Valdes, A., Almgren, M. (eds.): RAID 2004. LNCS, vol. 3224, p. 102. Springer, Heidelberg (2004)
4. Ahmad, I., Abdullah, A.B., Alghamdi, S.: Application of Artificial Neural Network in Detection of Probing Attack. In: 2009 IEEE Symposium on Industrial Electronics and Applications (ISIEA 2009), Kuala Lumpur, Malaysia, October 4-6 (2009)
5. Rosenberg, J., Schulzrinne, H., Camarillo, G., Johnston, A., Peterson, J., Sparks, R., Handley, M., Schooler, E.: SIP: Session Initiation Protocol. RFC 3261, IETF Network Working Group (2002)
6. Shekokar, N.M., Devane, S.R.: Threats Analysis of VoIP System. In: 2010 3rd International Conference on Computer and Electrical Engineering, ICCEE 2010 (2010)
7. Barry, B.I.A., Anthony Chan, H.: A Signature Database for Intrusion Detection Systems Targeting Voice Over Internet Protocol Environments. In: IEEE Conf. (2008)
8. VoIP SECURITY Sample VoIP Attack, `http://www.apecsecurity.com/VoIPThreats/SampleVoIPAttacks/`
9. ICMP Attack, `http://www.javvin.com/networkSecurity/ICMPAttacks.htm`
10. Abraham, A.: Neuro Fuzzy Systems: Sate-of-the-Art Modeling Techniques. In: Mira, J., Prieto, A.G. (eds.) IWANN 2001. LNCS, vol. 2084, pp. 269–276. Springer, Heidelberg (2001)
11. KDD cup 99 Intrusion detection data set, `http://kdd.ics.uci.edu/databases/kddcup99/kddcup`
12. Al-Allouni, H., Rohiem, A.E., Hashem, M., El-moghazy, A.: VoIP Denial of Service Attacks Classification and Implementation. 26th NATIONAL

Knowledge-Based Systems, Problem Solving Competence and Learnability

D.P. Sharma[1] and Kapil Khandelwal[2]

[1] Maharishi Arvind Institute of Science & Management, Jaipur
[2] Dept. of Computer Science,
Suresh Gyan Vihar University, Jaipur
kapilusit@gmail.com

Abstract. Improved methods for development and maintenance of real world knowledge-based systems are strongly needed. It is a challenge for artificial intelligence research to develop methods that will make the building of such systems feasible. The work described in this paper is a contribution to that research. The problem addressed in this paper is that of developing a framework/system "X" which integrates problem solving with learning from experience within an extensive model of different knowledge types. "X" has a reasoning strategy which first attempts case-based reasoning, then rule-based reasoning, and, finally, model-based reasoning. It learns from each problem solving session by updating its collection of cases, irrespective of which reasoning method that succeeded in solving the problem.

1 Introduction

Information Retrieval. Information Retrieval system can be used to help in solving problems. But the IR system has no real model of the domain. It is doing little more than matching user keywords with keywords in an arbitrary collection of documents. In some cases, use might also be made of a thesaurus or of statistical properties of the documents (e.g. word frequencies).

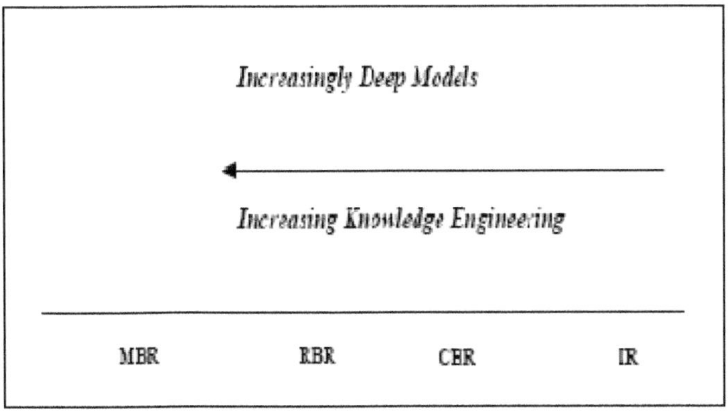

Fig. 1.

V.V. Das and N. Thankachan (Eds.): CIIT 2011, CCIS 250, pp. 543–547, 2011.

Case-Based Reasoning. CBR has quite shallow knowledge; it can even be used in domains where there is little or no understanding of the domain. Rule-Based Reasoning. Rule-based expert systems try to capture heuristic associations used by human experts.

Model-Based Reasoning. In model-based reasoning, the knowledge base contains a model of the system being reasoned about. The model captures the structure and/or behavior of the physical system. It uses deep knowledge from science and engineering, rather than an expert's heuristic associations.

The case-based method is the primary reasoning paradigm in "X", the other methods are used as separate reasoning methods - only if the case based method is unable to suggest a solution. The choice of reasoning method is made after the system has gained an initial understanding of the problem.

2 Functional Architecture of "X"

"X" integrates problem solving and learning into one architecture.

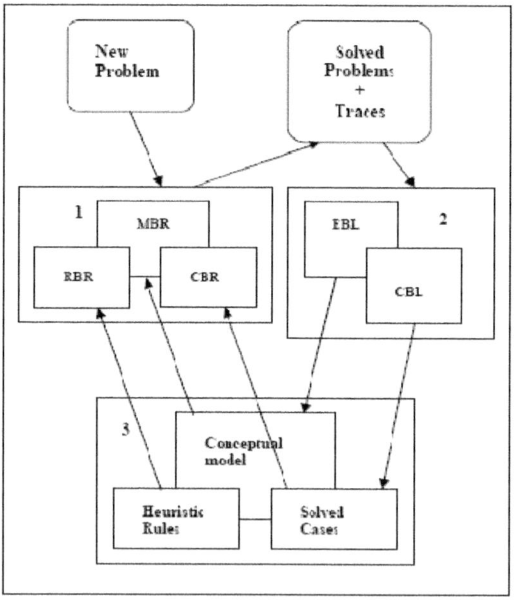

1. Combined Reasoning 2. Sustained Learning 3. Knowledge Base

Fig. 2. X's Functional Architecture

The flow of control and information between the knowledge base and the processes of problem solving and learning is shown in figure 2.

The figure 2. illustrates that problem solving in "X" is performed by a combination of model-based, case-based and rule-based reasoning (MBR, CBR and RBR, respectively). The learning combines case-based (CBL) and explanation-based (EBL) methods. The process of selecting the initial reasoning paradigm starts when a set of relevant features of a problem has been identified. This feature set typically contains input features as well as inferred features, i.e. features that the system derives from the input features by using its knowledge. If the set of relevant features gives a reminding to a previous case that is above a particular strength - called the *reminding threshold* - case based problem solving is tried, otherwise activation of the rule set is attempted. Relevant features may be input features or features inferred from the object domain model. If either the case base or the rule base fails to produce a result, the controller re-evaluates its previous decision, given the current state of the system. As more cases are added, the ratio of case-based to rule-based successes is likely to increase, and the system will gradually lower the threshold value. If a solution was derived by modifying a previous solution, a new case is stored and difference links between the two cases are established. A new case is also created after a problem has been solved from rules or the deeper knowledge model. Thus, the main target for the learning process in "X" is the case base. Heuristic rules are integrated within the conceptual model, and available for the same tasks as the conceptual domain model in general. A rule may be used to support learning.

3 Combined Reasoning in "X"

The case-based method is the primary reasoning paradigm in "X", the other methods are used - as separate reasoning methods - only if the case-based method is unable to suggest a solution. The choice of reasoning method is made after the system has gained an initial understanding of the problem. This initial understanding process (described in the next section) results in an activated problem context, including a set of relevant features for describing the problem, a structure of problem solving (sub) goals, and a hierarchy of possible faults. First, "X" will attempt to solve the problem by case-based reasoning. The relevant findings are combined into a set of remindings, where each reminding points to a case (or a class of cases) with a certain strength. If some cases are pointed to by remindings with strengths above the *reminding threshold*, the case most strongly reminded of is retrieved. If no such reminding is produced, the system may trigger its rule-based reasoning method. However, before doing that it will normally try to *elaborate* on the findings of the case most strongly reminded of. The purpose of this is to improve a weak match by looking for common states, constraints, etc., which will imply a stronger similarity than determined by the basic case retrieval method. Whether the elaboration on a weak match is attempted or not depends on the strength of the strongest reminding and the size and strength of the case base relative to the rule base. If an acceptable match is found, the case is used in the attempt to solve the problem. If not, rule-based reasoning is attempted1. If no cases were reminded of in the first place, "X" will also try its rule-based reasoning method, i.e. attempt to solve the problem by a combined forward chaining (from the relevant findings) and backward chaining (from the fault hierarchy) within the rule base.

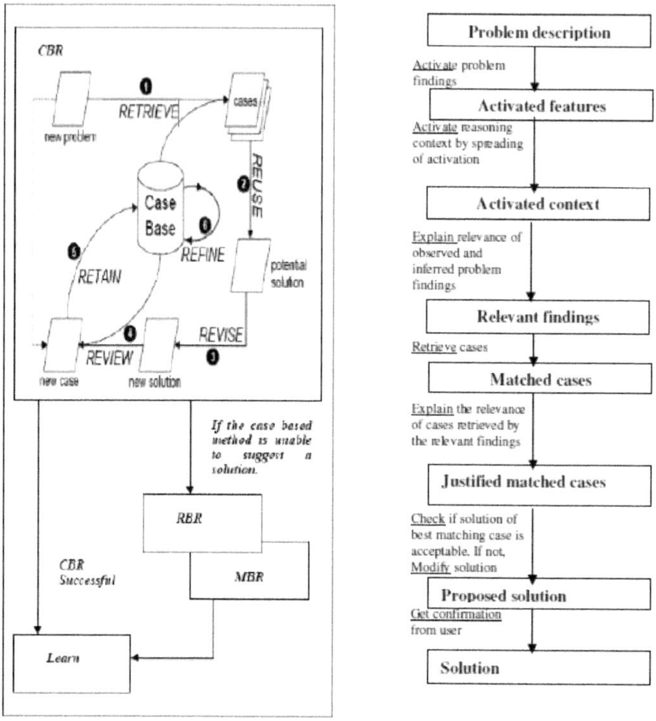

(CBR = Case-Based Reasoning, RBR = Rule-Based Reasoning, MBR = Model-Based Reasoning).

Fig. 3. (a) Combined Reasoning in "X" (b) Abstract structure of CBR in "X"

When a case is retrieved, the solution (fault and - possibly - treatment) is evaluated to see if it is acceptable for the current problem. If the system is unable to produce a good enough explanation to accept or reject the solution candidate, it is presented to the user for evaluation. If for any reason the solution is unacceptable, a check is performed to determine whether the solution would be accepted if slightly modified, in which case a modification is attempted. When no more modifications are relevant and no more new cases are available for use, "X" gives up case-based reasoning. The input to a reasoning process is a problem description. This may be a description of the user's problem, or a partial solution of this problem – for example a set of descriptors which includes a fault hypothesis, given as input to the retrieval of a case containing a suitable repair.

4 Conclusion

There is still a large number of important and challenging problems to be addressed in order to improved the quality and usefulness of expert systems for practical, real world problems. The research reported here has addressed the problem of how to achieve, and continually maintain, a higher level of competence and robustness in such systems than what they possess today. The problem has been approached from two sides:

- Strengthening of the problem solving capability by combining several reasoning paradigms within a knowledge-rich environment, focusing on case-based reasoning as the major method.
- Enabling a continually improvement of an incomplete knowledge base by learning from each problem solving experience, using a knowledge-intensive, case-based learning method.

The resulting framework, architecture, system design, and representation platform - i.e. the "X" approach - has been motivated and supported by relating it to strengths and weaknesses of other approaches.

References

1. Aamodt, A., Plaza, E.: Case-Based Reasoning: Foundational Issues, Methodological Variations and System Approaches. Artificial Intelligence Communications 7(1), 39–59 (1994)
2. Branting, L.K.: Building explanations from rules and structured cases. International Journal of Man-Machine Studies 34, 797–837 (1991)
3. Cheetham, W., Graf, J.: Case-Based Reasoning in Color Matching. In: Leake, D.B., Plaza, E. (eds.) ICCBR 1997. LNCS, vol. 1266, pp. 1–12. Springer, Heidelberg (1997)
4. Golding, A.R., Rosenbloom, P.S.: Improving rule-based systems through case-based reasoning. In: Proceedings of the Ninth National Conference on Artificial Intelligence, AAAI 1991, pp. 22–27. AAAI Press, Menlo Park (1991)
5. Hastings, J., Branting, K., Lockwood, J.: CARMA: A case-based rangeland management advisor. AI Magazine 23(2), 49–62 (2002)
6. Koton, P.: Reasoning about evidence in causal explanations. In: Proceedings of the Seventh National Conference on Artificial Intelligence (AAAI 1988), pp. 256–261. AAAI Press, Menlo Park (1988)
7. Montani, S., Magni, P., Bellazzi, R., Larizza, C., Roudsari, E.R.: Integrating model-based decision support in a multi-modal reasoning system for managing type 1 diabetic patients. Artificial Intelligence in Medicine 29(1), 131–151 (2003)
8. Porter, B.W., Bareiss, E.R., Holte, R.C.: Concept learning and heuristic classification in weak-theory domains. Artificial Intelligence 45(1–2), 229–263 (1990)
9. Sabater, J., Arcos, J.L., López de Mántaras, R.: Using rules to support case-based reasoning for harmonizing melodies. In: Freuder, E. (ed.) Multimodal Reasoning: Papers from the 1998 AAAI Spring Symposium, Technical Report WS–98–04. AAAI Press, Menlo Park (1998)
10. Budimac, Z., Kurbalija, V.: Case Based Reasoning – A Short Overview. In: Proceedings of the Second International Conference on Informatics and Information Technology, pp. 222–233
11. Watson, I.: Case-Based Reasoning and Knowledge Management: a Perfect Match? In: Proc. FLAIRS-2001. 14th Int. FLAIRS Conference, Key West Florida, May 21-23, pp. 118–123. AAAI Press, Menlo Park (2001)
12. Rissland, E.L., Skalak, D.B.: Combining Case-Based and Rule-Based Reasoning: A Heuristic Approach, pp. 534—530
13. Gebhardt, F., Voß, A., Gräther, W., Schmidt-Belz, B.: Reasoning with Complex Cases. Kluwer Academic Publishers, Boston (1997)

A Paradigm Shift from Legacy to AUTOSAR Architecture in Future Automotives

Rajeshwari Hegde[1], Mahesh Hegde[2], and K.S. Gurumurthy[3]

[1] BMS College of Engineering
rajeshwari.hegde@gmail.com
[2] Robert Bosch Business & Engineering Solutions
mahesh_hegde22@yahoo.com
[3] University Visvesvaraya College of Engineering, Bangalore, India
drksgurumurthy@gmail.com

Abstract. The modern automotive Electrical/Electronics (E/E) systems have reached a high level of complexity today, leading to a corresponding increase in the complexity of the deployed software. The increasing complexity of automotive embedded software increases the need for software reusability and shorter design cycle. These issues are addressed by *AUTOSAR* (AUTomotive Open System ARchitecture), an emerging technology in automotive software engineering that contributes to reuse and increased flexibility while preserving interfaces and system-level integrity. The AUTOSAR approach has much to offer software engineers working on embedded systems or model-driven development. In this paper, we explain the paradigm shift from a legacy architecture to the AUTOSAR architecture of ECU design, which eases the integration of ECUs supplied by different Tier1 suppliers.

Keywords: AUTOSAR, ECU, OEM, Run Time Environment(RTE), Virtual Functional Bus(VFB).

1 Introduction

The auto industry is facing a new era of significant change, based on challenges in consumer demands, technology development, globalization, integrated operations and collaboration strategies [1]. The complex automotive functions make the development of automotive electronics increasingly complex. The product's features and comfort requirements of the customers, as well as the increase of non-functional demand has aggravated the ECU development process complexity [2]. The increasing complexity of automotive embedded software, increasing needs for software reusability and shorter time to market, all require new software architecture standards [3]. The automotive engineers are facing numerous design challenges across a wide range of applications as a result of the complexity of ECUs in vehicles. In case of ECU centric approach (traditional method of ECU design), adding new software components to the existing software requires the redesign of the entire ECU, which leads to the increase in cost and time to market. AUTOSAR, an open system architecture tries to provide solution to these problems. In order to reduce the complexity of ECU software

V.V. Das and N. Thankachan (Eds.): CIIT 2011, CCIS 250, pp. 548–553, 2011.

development, AUTOSAR members develop a set of proven software architecture, which can be reused as the basis for the application. In current automotive systems, specific ECUs run specific functions or sets of functions such as body control ECU, powertrain ECU etc. These systems are specified by an OEM to run software written by the selected supplier or the OEM. As the ECUs contain more software-centric functionality, it is essential to design their software architecture in such a way that it will easily accommodate future changes driven by customer demands [4]. The rest of the paper is organized as follows. Section 2 discusses the current issues and provides background discussion as to why AUTOSAR compliant ECUs are required. Section 3 describes the architectural features of an AUTOSAR compliant ECU. Section 4 explains the Motivation for change from legacy to AUTOSAR compliant ECU. Paper is concluded in section 5.

2 Current Issues in Automotives

The typical embedded components in vehicles at present are centralized ECUs based on proprietary hardware and software components. Since each one has a different non-transferable function, adding new ECUs lead to higher susceptibility to failure. Due to the ever increasing processing power, more and more functional features are migrating from hardware to software. A paradigm shift from software centric to network centric ECU is occurring. Software is becoming the dominant automotive systems and the software components are no longer bound to specific hardware components, but can be executed on various units within the vehicles and even migrate during run-time[5]. In the current development environment, it is difficult to reuse automotive embedded software that is already developed for an ECU. Moreover, the complexity of the algorithms that reside on the ECU is being dramatically increased, and the trend of the integrated ECU is emerging. Managing the complexity is the one of the most important problems to achieve required reliability and performance [6]. Traditionally, the ECUs have been developed for OEM specific requirement and are highly customized proprietary solutions. New requirements such as integration across vehicles and OEM borders, greater flexibility in maintenance, scalability of functional features, reliability of the electronic system and most importantly hardware independence of the software , intensify the need to replace this ECU centered development approach by a functionally oriented approach[7]. Due to the increasing number of networked components, a level of complexity has been reached which is difficult to handle using traditional development processes [8]. Using the traditional, ECU-centric approach to design E/E-architectures, the vehicle manufacturer writes a specification of all the software involved, sometimes given to the supplier as an executable prototype. To ensure the interoperability of all functions, a communication matrix of all CAN messages is derived and given in parts to the appropriate supplier. Then, every supplier involved will start its own development cycle according to the V-model. An ECU centric approach prevents the reuse of functionality across different vehicle platforms[9]. The goal of the AUTOSAR standardization initiative has been to address these through a transition from customer-specific software to function oriented software [10]. In the AUTOSAR architecture, applications are decoupled

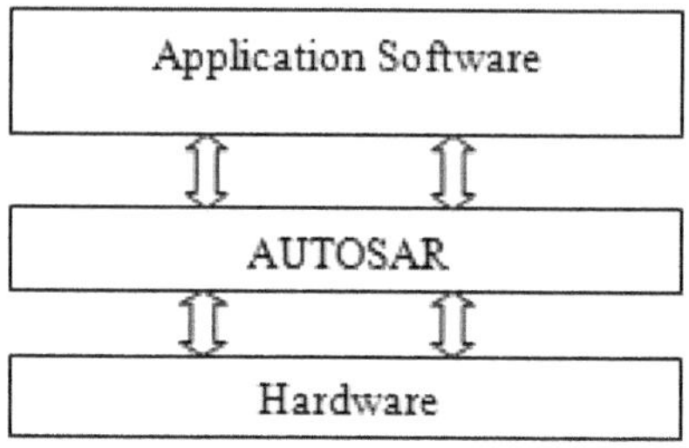

Fig. 1. AUTOSAR makes the application software independent from the hardware

from the hardware (Fig 1). With a standardized interface it would be possible to buy software and hardware from different manufacturers, and they would all work together. This would not be as smooth with the conventional solution as shown [11].

3 Architectural Features of AUTOSAR

The growing complexity of the electrical and electronic systems architectures and in-vehicle embedded technologies being deployed is directly reflected in the complexity of the application software that is required. AUTOSAR has been developed as a means of managing this complexity through a standardized architecture that separates an application software from its infrastructure. The AUTOSAR approach fosters tighter interaction between all the stakeholders in the development process, improving OEM-supplier development relationships. It also improves data exchange at the system level, not only placing higher quality and dependability at the forefront of concerns, but also allowing costs and complexity to be better managed [12]. Initiated in 2002, AUTOSAR mainly aims at (i) increasing the quality of automotive software, its maintainability, and its scalability, and at (ii) optimizing cost and time-to market [13]. The first cars that incorporate AUTOSAR-compliant ECUs are now reaching the market and most new development of embedded automotive software will in future be compliant with it, says Ingo Bruse from Geensoft.

The AUTOSAR architecture strictly separates the ECU software as

- Application: Interconnected software components that encapsulate complete or partial automotive functionality.
- Rune Time Environment (RTE): Provides means of data exchange between application and basic software.
- Basic Software (BSW): Provides the functionality of the ECU hardware and is necessary to run the functional part of the software.

The architectural concepts brought by AUTOSAR provide a wealth of new design choices to software engineers building distributed, communicating software systems. A key aspect of this architecture is a design abstraction called the AUTOSAR Virtual Function Bus (VFB) that allows the software systems to be designed without reference to target hardware and to defer the hardware allocation decision until later in the design process. The application software is divided into software components

(SW-Cs) [14]. Each SW-C can only interact with the other components and perform I/O through statically defined ports. Ports are defined to be well defined points of interaction which provide or require interfaces, thus a port may be of type require (R-port) or of type provide (P-port) [15]. Internally a SW-C is broken down into separate threads of control called "runnable entities". Runnable entities are responsible for handling communication on a SW-C's ports [16]. The separation of application from infrastructure enables the reuse of software in AUTOSAR architecture [17]. The main goal of AUTOSAR is to define a standard modular software infrastructure for application and basic software, which allows exchanging parts of the system's software. [18].

4 Motivation for Change from Legacy to AUTOSAR Compliant ECU

The current automotive electric/electronic (E/E) architecture landscape is characterized by proprietary solutions that seldom allow the exchange of applications between both automotive OEMs and their suppliers. A technological breakthrough is required in order to control the complexity of contemporary E/E architecture that is being driven by the introduction of innovative vehicle applications and increased passenger and legal requirements. This need is particularly effective for high-end, luxury vehicle manufacturers and their leading Tier 1 suppliers who are facing with often-conflicting requirements from

- Legal enforcement – key items include environmental aspects and safety requirements.
- Passenger convenience and service requirements from the comfort and entertainment functional domains.
- Driver assistance and dynamic drive aspects - key items include detection and suppression of critical dynamic vehicle states and navigation in high-density traffic surroundings [19].

Hence, motivation for change includes

1.Managing the growing complexity of automotive E/E systems.
2.Flexibility for product modification, upgrade and update.
3.Scalability of solutions within and across product lines.
4.Quality and reliability of E/E systems.

The standard for automotive software now under development will be a first step towards tackling these problems. The concept for the standard is a layered software architecture with standard APIs. Establishing a software standard will be a big step forward. In future, design engineers developing a new E/E architecture will adhere to the AUTOSAR design process. Introducing the AUTOSAR process would be a breakthrough in automotive E/E design. It would be a radical step and its repercussions would change the industry forever [20].

4.1 Migration to AUTOSAR

The introduction of the AUTOSAR standard in series development will unlikely occur in a single step. In order to secure existing assets, synchronize to vehicle development cycles and as a matter of risk minimization, a staged introduction and controlled maturation in any given development context will be preferable. Theoretically, automotive OEMs could attempt to integrate a fully AUTOSAR conformant electronic system in their next generation of cars. The cost and effort required to redevelop all components would be enormous, however, and the process would not be without risk. Modifications of conventional technology are therefore unavoidable when newly developed AUTOSAR components are added. Stepwise introduction of AUTOSAR -conformant software components into the overall architecture addresses this issue and is preferred by automotive OEMs since it offers better handling and greater validity. To work out a migration solution, one begins by comparing the existing custom software and the AUTOSAR architecture.

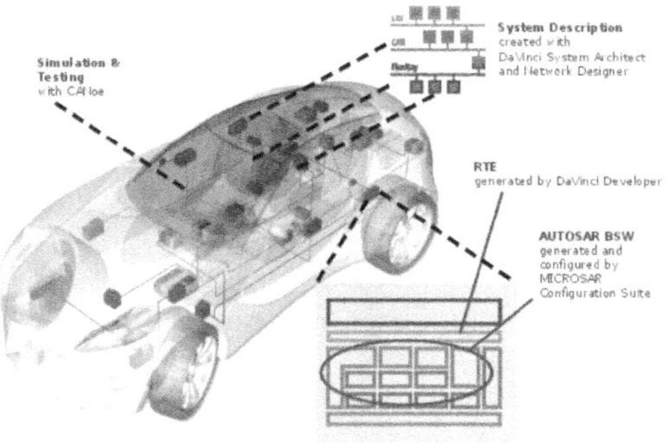

Fig. 2. The Vector AUTOSAR solution: From system description to standardized ECU software [21]

5 Conclusion

In this paper, the need for a paradigm shift from legacy to AUTOSAR architecture has been explained. AUTOSAR is described as the future of automotive E/E engineering as it offers new possibilities in reducing the complexity by decoupling the application software from the hardware infrastructure. This results in optimum utilization of resources and easier integration of ECUs.

References

1. Wang, D., Zheng, J., Zhao, G., Huang, B., Liu, S.: Survey of the AUTOSAR Complex Drivers in the Field of Automotive Electronics. In: 2010 International Conference on Intelligent Computation Technology and Automation (2010)

2. Casey, C., Grant, P.E.: Fire Fighter Safety and Emergency Response for Electric Drive and Hybrid Electric Vehicles, Final Report -The Fire Protection Research Foundation, Quincy, MA, USA
3. Wu, R., Li, H., Yao, M., Wang, J., Yang, Y.: A ierarchical Modeling Method for AUTOSAR Software Components. In: 2nd International Conference on Computer Engineering and Technology. IEEE (2010)
4. Rolina, T.: Past, Present and Future of Real-Time Embedded Automotive Software: A close look at basic concepts of AUTOSAR. In: SAE International (2005)
5. Anthony, R., Leonhardi, A., Ekelin, C., Chen, D., Törngren, M., de Boer, G., Jahnich, I., Burton, S., Redell, O., Weber, A., Vollmer, V.: A Future Dynamically Reconfigurable Automotive Software System, http://www.md.kth.se/RTC/ARTIST2/publications/ATT00014.pdf
6. Scharnhorst, T., Heinecke, H., Schnelle, K.-P., Bortolazzi, J., Lundh, L., Heitkämper, P., Leflour, J., Maté, J.-L., Nishikawa, K.: AUTOSAR – Challenges and Achievements 2005, VDI Berichte Nr. 1907 (2005)
7. AUTOSAR Migration, http://www.kpitcummins.com/downloads/autosar-migration-whitepaper.pdf
8. Fennel, H., Bunzel, S., Heinecke, H., Bielefeld, J., Fürst, S., et al.: Achievements and exploitation of the AUTOSAR development partnership. In: CTEA 2006 (2006)
9. Tracey, N., Lefarth, U., Wolff, H.-J., Freund, U.: ECU Software Module Development Process Changes in AUTOSAR. In: FKFSS Symposium, Stuttgart, Germany (2007)
10. Racu, R., Hamann, A., Ernst, R., Richter, K.: Automotive Software Integration. IEEE (2007)
11. Melin, J., Boström, D.: Applying AUTOSAR in Practice Available Development Tools and Migration Paths, Master Thesis, Computer Science, School of Innovation, Design and Engineering (2010)
12. Bruse, I., Fourgeau, E.: AUTOSAR: Setting the standard, http://www.automotive-electronics.co.uk/ArticleItem.aspx?Cont_Title=AUTOSAR%3A+Setting+the+standard
13. http://www.autosar.org
14. AUTOSAR – Enabling Technology for Advanced Automotive Electronics, http://www.autosar.org/download/AUTOSAR_long_en.pdf
15. Schreiner, D., Göschka, K.M.: A Component Model for the AUTOSAR Virtual Function Bus. In: 31st Annual International Computer Software and Applications Conference (COMPSAC 2007). IEEE (2007)
16. Specification of RTE Software, http://www.autosar.org/download/R2.0/AUTOSAR_SWS_RTE.pdf
17. Huang, B., Dong, H., Wang, D., Zhao, G.: Basic Concepts on AUTOSAR Development. In: 2010 International Conference on Intelligent Computation Technology and Automation. IEEE (2010)
18. Racu, R., Hamann, A., Ernst, R., Richter, K.: Automotive Software Integration. In: DAC 2007, June 4-8. ACM, San Diego (2007), doi:9781595936271/07
19. Heinecke, H., Schnelle, K.-P., Fennel, H., Bortolazzi, J., et al.: AUTomotive Open System ARchitecture - An Industry-Wide Initiative to Manage the Complexity of Emerging Automotive E/E-Architectures, Convergence Transportation Electronics Association (2004)
20. Why does the Automotive Industry need AUTOSART Today? http://www2.renesas.eu/applications/automotive/documents/AUTOSAR_2006.pdf
21. AUTOSAR on its Way to Production. Press Article (2008), http://www.vector.com/portal/medien/cmc/press/Vector/AUTOSAR_Elektronikpraxis_200802_PressArticle_EN.pdf

Harmony Search Algorithm for Feature Selection in Face Recognition

Dinesh Kumar and Shrutika

Department of Computer Science & Engineering,
Guru Jambeshwar University of Science &Technology, Hissar, Haryana -125001
{dinesh_chutani,jain.shrutika}@yahoo.com

Abstract. This paper presents a method for feature selection in face recognition using Harmony Search. The proposed method consists of two steps: Feature Extraction followed by Feature Selection. Principal Component Analysis has been used for the former while Harmony Search algorithm has been exploited for the latter. ORL face database has been used for experimentation. The results of the experiments demonstrate that the proposed method outperforms standard eigenfaces method for face recognition.

Keywords: Face Recognition, PCA, Harmony Search.

1 Introduction

A facial recognition system is a computer application for automatically identifying or verifying a person from a digital image or a video frame from a video source. It has become an important issue in many applications such as security systems, credit card verification, criminal identification etc [1]. Face Recognition involves capturing the face sample followed by feature extraction. Then comparison is done with a new sample and a decision is taken whether new samples is matched or not [12]. Appearance based approach is more popular than feature based face recognition approach [11]. Face images are high dimensional data. Mapping of high dimensional data to low dimension is done to reduce the memory space and to increase the computational speed. Dimensionality Reduction involves the process of feature extraction and feature selection. PCA is a common statistical technique for finding the patterns in high dimensional data [2] that has been used for feature extraction. There are many existing metaheuristic techniques which have been applied for feature selection in face recognition. Harmony Search is one such technique proposed by Lee and Geem [8]. Harmony Search technique has been exploited for feature selection in face recognition. In this paper, Section 2 briefly describes about Principal component analysis. Section 3 explains Harmony Search technique for face recognition. Section 4 demonstrates experimentation and results and the conclusions are covered in section 5.

2 Principal Component Analysis

Principal component analysis (PCA) [9, 13] involves a procedure that transforms number of possibly correlated variables into a smaller number of uncorrelated

V.V. Das and N. Thankachan (Eds.): CIIT 2011, CCIS 250, pp. 554–559, 2011.

variables called principal components. The algorithm used for Principal component analysis computes the covariance matrix C of a set of N face images from the training set. The matrix C is very large and determining the large number of eigenvectors and eigenvalues is computationally infeasible. By using the idea proposed by Turk and Pentland [2], we find the eigenvectors. Only N' $(N' < N)$ eigenvectors that correspond to the highest eigenvalues are retained. The classification is done using the Euclidean distance.

3 Harmony Search

Harmony Search (HS) was developed by Geem et al. in 2001 [8]. In the HS algorithm, each decision variable generates a value for finding a best global optimum value. This algorithm provides solution to different kinds of problems in different area of applications [3, 4, 5, 6, 7, 8].

3.1 Proposed Algorithm

The proposed algorithm contains three phases

Phase 1: Initialization
The solution of formulated problem is the index of N eigenvectors among the chosen eigenvectors after applying PCA. The number of solution vectors in Harmony Memory Matrix is the Harmony Memory Size (HMS). Each harmony vector is represented as $E^k = [e_1^k, e_2^k, \dots, e_N^k]$ where k=1, 2..., HMS. The FRR of each harmony vector is stored in Fitness matrix. Harmony Memory (HM) is an HMS×N augmented matrix:

$$HM = \begin{matrix} e_1^1 & e_2^1 \dots\dots & e_N^1 \\ e_1^2 & e_2^2 \dots. & e_N^2 \\ e_1^{HMS} & e_2^{HMS} \dots\dots & e_N^{HMS} \end{matrix}$$

and

$$Fitness = Max[FRR(E^1) \quad FRR(E^2) \dots \quad FRR(E^{HMS})]$$

The initial harmony memory is generated from the set of chosen eigenvectors N' .

For the formulated problem we considered HMS as 10. In order to use this memory effectively, the HS Algorithm adopts a parameter called Harmony MemoryConsidering Rate (HMCR). We assume HMCR as 0.9. The other components are the pitch adjustment, which is governed by Pitch Adjusting Rate (PAR), and bandwidth coefficient (BW). To achieve better results, we define lower limit and upper limit of the PAR and BW. These limits vary the value of PAR for each generation according to formula [6]

$$PAR(c) = PAR_{min} + \frac{(PAR_{max} - PAR_{min})}{maxitr} \times c \tag{1}$$

where c is current iteration and maxitr is maximum iteration. PAR_{min} and PAR_{max} are taken as as 0.4 and 0.9 respectively. In addition, BW is dynamically updated as follows [6]:

$$BW(c) = BW_{max} e^{\left(\frac{ln\left(\frac{BW_{min}}{BW_{max}}\right)}{maxitr} \times c \right)} \tag{2}$$

where BW(c) is the bandwidth for generation c, BW_{min} is the minimum bandwidth and BW_{max} is the maximum bandwidth, which is assumed as 0.001 and 1.0 respectively. The maximum number of searches (stopping criterion) is selected as 500. Further the bestfit, worstfit harmony vector are calculated over the harmony memory on the basis of maximizing fitness.

Phase 2: Improvise a new harmony

The improvisation of the HM is done by generating new harmony vector $e' = (e'_1 e'_2 \cdots e'_N)$. Each component of the new harmony vector e'_i is generated using following rule:

A random value is generated for each eigen variable of harmony vector. If this value is less than HMCR, one harmony vector is randomly selected from the HM by using given formula

$$Index = \left(round(rand(1) \times (HMS - 1) + 1)\right) \tag{3}$$

$$e'_i = HM(index, i) \quad where\ i = 1, 2 \dots, N \tag{4}$$

where Index is the number of harmony vector selected from the harmony memory. Otherwise the new eigenvector is randomly initialized. If e'_j is generated from theHM, then it is further modified or mutated according to PAR. A random value is generated and if it is less than PAR, then eigenvector index is modified according to given formula

$$e'_j = round\left(e'_j \pm rand(1) \times BW(i)\right) \tag{5}$$

Otherwise no modification is made to eigen vector. The generated harmony vector, $e' = (e'_1\ e'_2 \cdots e'_N)$ replaces the worst harmony in the HM, only if its fitness is better than that of the worst harmony. Further modify the bestfit and worsfit harmony vector.

Phase 3: Check the stopping criterion

Terminate when the maximum number of improvisations is reached. The current best solution is selected from the HM after the termination criterion is satisfied.

4 Experimental Results and Discussions

In this paper, ORL face database [10] has been used for experimentation. The original image was resized to 40×40 prior to further processing of the face images. The experiment was performed on three different sets. First, second and third sets consisted of five training and five test images, three training and seven test images, and seven training and three test images of each subject respectively. After feature extraction by using PCA, we choose 40% of total number of eigenvectors corresponding to highest eigenvalues.

Experiment 1: The first experiment was performed to find the face recognition rate of 10, 20 and 40 classes having training and testing image set of 50, 100 and 200 images (set-1) respectively. The results have been shown as figure 1. A close look at results reveals that the proposed method yields much better results in terms of recognition rate as compared to standard eigenface method.

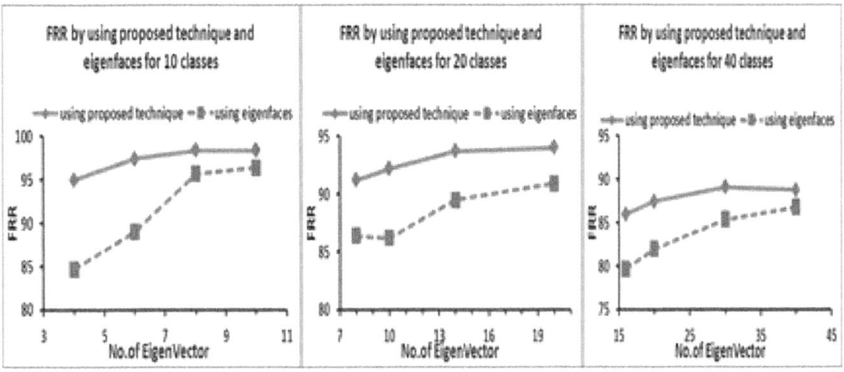

Fig. 1. FRR for 10, 20 and 40 Classes

Experiment 2: The next experiment was performed to find the face recognition rate for set-2 and set-3 for 10, 20 and 40 classes respectively. Again the total number of eigenvectors chosen was 40% of the total number of images in the training set. The results have been shown as figure 2 for set 2 and figure 3 for set 3.

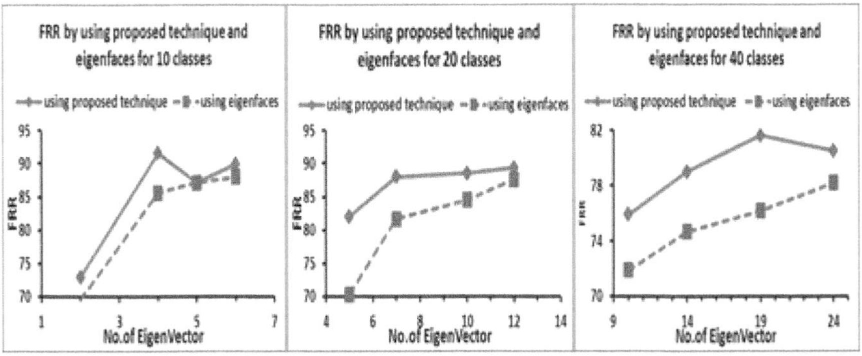

Fig. 2. FRR for 10, 20 and 40 Classes

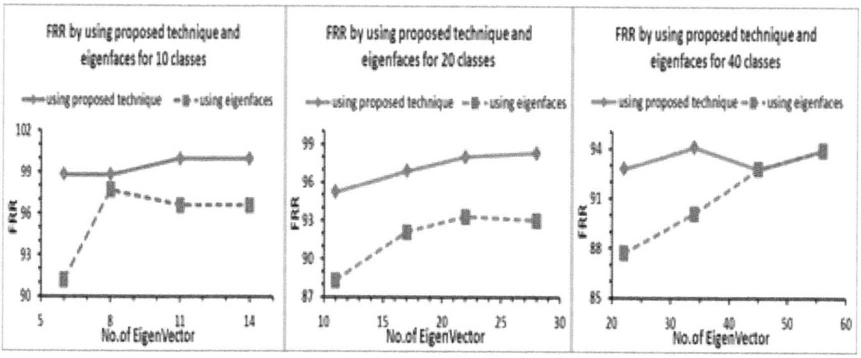

Fig. 3. FRR for 10, 20 and 40 Classes

The results demonstrate that the recognition rate decreases for same number of classes as the number of training images is decreased (set-2) whereas on the other hand, there is substantial increase in recognition rate when the number of training images is increased (set-3). The results depict that the proposed technique gives better performance as compared to eigenface method. From the results it was further observed that some eigenvectors are repeatedly selected by the algorithm amounting to much better recognition rate as compared to that where no repetition was allowed such as in Eigenface method.

5 Conclusion

This paper presents new approach for feature selection in face recognition by using combination of PCA and Harmony Search. The results show that the proposed technique gives much better results as compared to standard Eigenface method for face recognition. Even we have been able to get 100% recognition rate for only 11 numbers of features whereas Eigenface method yields only 96.6% recognition rate for the same number of features. We can say that the proposed method completely outperforms the standard eigenface technique. The results also depict that the recognition rate is increased when the number of training images is increased. By using proposed technique, we require less number of eigenfaces to get the same result as done by using Eigenface technique. Further it has been observed that the recognition rate decreases as the number of classes increase. This may be attributed to the fact that the chances of mismatch increase due to more similar faces.

References

1. Fromherz, T., Stucki, P., Bichsel, M.: A Survey of Face Recognition. MML Technical Report, vol. 97, pp. 1–18 (1997)
2. Turk, M., Pentaland, A.: Eigenfaces for Recognition. Journal of Cognitive Neuroscience 3(1), 71–86 (1991)

3. Alia, O.M., Mandava, R., Ramachandram, D., Aziz, M.E.: Dynamic Fuzzy Clustering using Harmony Search with Application to Image Segmentation. In: IEEE International Symposium on Signal Processing and Information Technology (ISSPIT), pp. 538–543 (2009)
4. Hoang, D.C., Yadav, P., Kumar, R., Panda, S.K.: A Robust Harmony Search Algorithm based Clustering Protocol for Wireless Sensor Networks. In: IEEE International Conference Communications Workshops (ICW), pp. 1–5 (2010)
5. Cobos, C., Leon, E., Mendoza, M.: A harmony search algorithm for clustering with feature selection. Rev. Fac. Ing. Univ. Antioquia (55), 153–164 (2010)
6. Mahdavi, M., Abolhassani, H.: Harmony K-means algorithm for document clustering. Applied Mathematics and Computation 188, 1567–1579 (2007)
7. Geem, Z.W., Fesanghary, M., Choi, J.Y., Saka, M.P., Williams, J.C., Ayvaz, M.T., Li, L., Ryu, S., Vasebi, A.: Recent Advances in Harmony Search. In: Advances in Evolutionary Algorithm, pp. 468–484 (2008)
8. Geem, Z.W., Kim, J.H., Loganathan, G.V.: A new heuristic optimization Algorithm: harmony search. Simulation 76(2), 60–68 (2001)
9. Latha, P., Ganesan, L., Annadurai, S.: Face recognition using Neural Networks. An International Journal of Signal Processing 3, 153–159 (2000)
10. `http://www.cl.cam.ac.uk/ORL face database`
11. Delac, K., Grgic, M., Liatsis, P.: Appearance-based Statistical Methods for Face Recognition. In: 47th International Symposium ELMAR-2005, pp. 151–158 (2005)
12. Lin, M., Hung, S.: An Introduction to Face Recognition Technology. Informing Science Special Issue on Multimedia Informing Technologies-Part2 3(1), 1–7 (2000)
13. Aishwarya, P.: Face Recognition using Multiple Face Eigen Subspaces. International Journal of Computer Applications 1(2), 89–91 (2010)

Block Modelling of SPIHT Algorithm: An Image Compression Approach for PSNR Analysis of Images

D.S. Chandak, P.H. Zope, and P.B. Shirude

dinesh.chandak1@gmail.com, phzope@indiatimes.com, p.shirude2@gmail.com

Abstract. This paper addresses the area of data compression as it is applicable to image processing. An analysis of SPIHT(set partitioning in hierarchical trees) image compression algorithm is examined for its relative effectiveness on several images. Here we have developed the block model of SPIHT image compression algorithm and the PSNR analysis with successive wavelet filtering is done. The results we quoted with the sample 5 images with different sizes and dimensions are varying and the simulation is also time taking. PSNR values are also studied to understand the reconstruction complexity of Image under processing.

Keywords: SPIHT, DWT, PSNR, Wavelet Decomposition.

1 Introduction

Image compression techniques, especially non reversible or lossy ones, have been known to grow computationally more complex as they grow more efficient. Image compression is one of the most visible applications of wavelets. The rapid increase in the range and use of electronic imaging justifies attention for systematic design of an image compression system and for providing the image quality needed in different applications.In this work we are introducing the block level coding and the modeling of the SPIHT(set partitioning in hierarchical trees) ,the workspace values of the original image and the SPIHT coded image are studied and the MSE[9] values or the peak signal to noise ratio(PSNR) is displayed. We use SPIHT algorithm for image compression[7] and tabulated the results for different 5 image files out of which 2 are live images and their parameters after recovery are also studied.

2 Experimental Work

The basic block diagram of experimental work is shown if Fig.1.We have created the image database in "MATLAB" with the different 5 images . These are the sample images, taken for the initial level and quoted the results in the form of PSNR and Compression ratio[2].

V.V. Das and N. Thankachan (Eds.): CIIT 2011, CCIS 250, pp. 560–563, 2011.

2.1 Block Diagram Description

Input image and its pre-processing. This block is directly available in the simulation environment which fetches the image from the desired location. In the pre-processing block if the input image is 3-color domain that is RGB image is pre-processed to pass further, it is converted into the intensity image with specified class and double data type for compatibility.[2]

Image Parameters and Frame conversion. In image parameter block, we are extracting the row and column vector parameters of an image and the maximum bits to represent the image used for the further processing. The Frame Conversion block does not make any changes to the input signal other than the sampling mode.

DWT of an Image. In the wavelet transform of the image it is decomposed in the pyramidal way with multi decomposition with the no. of significant and insignificant bits, here in our experiment we are using the 9/7 [9]filtering process in which out of every 9 coefficients 7 are significant. We are performing the 6-level decomposition of an image for better results.

SPIHT Encoder. In this block the image parameters in the form of block size , maximum bits and the input from the DWT block that is the wavelet coefficients and the decomposition level are combined to setup the SPIHT encoding describe in the SPIHT algorithm [7]. Initialization of coefficients, sorting and refinement is done based on these input parameters.

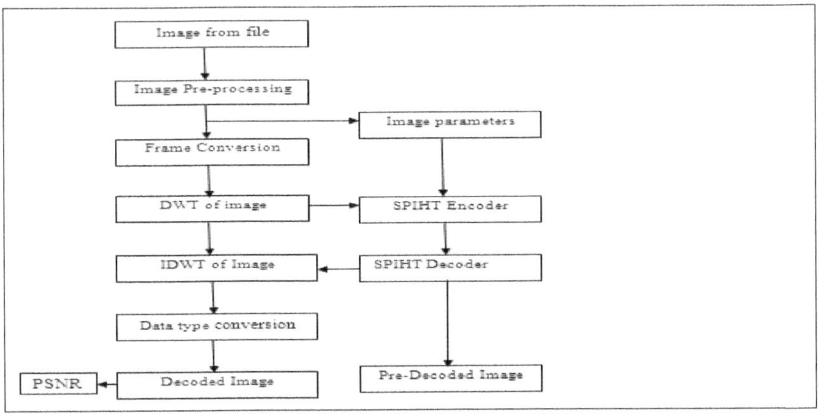

Fig. 1. Experimental Block Diagram

SPIHT Decoder. The encoded image obtained from the encoder block is decoded using the SPIHT decoding algorithm and the decoded wavelet components are generated for further processing.

IDWT of Image. In this block all the decoded wavelet components and the input from DWT are recovered. The IDWT parameters are passed through the data type conversion block to convert the output in double for compatibility.

Output Image. It displays the decoded and pre-decoded Image.

Experimental PSNR Calculation and Display. The quality of the decoded image is judge on the basis of the PSNR (Peak Signal to Noise Ratio) value[5].

3 Experimental Results

Here are the results of the experiment performed on 5 images. The table no. 1 shows the obtained results.

Fig. 2. Experimental Results

Where A - original image A'- pre-decoded image A'' – decoded image

Table 1. Experimental Analysis of 5 Images

Image	Size (In KB)	Dimension	PSNR	Compression Ratio
P	119	860×1146	37.41	0.36
Q	257	512×512	39.81	0.26
R	541	732×486	41.43	0.81
S	280	512×384	48.25	0.84
T	155	519×517	50.2	0.29

4 Conclusion

In this Paper we presented our experimental work to elaborate the SPIHT Algorithm for Image Compression by performing its block level simulation and the wavelet transformation of Image applicable for its compression. The results we quoted with the sample 5 images with different sizes and dimensions are varying and the simulation is also time taking. PSNR values are also studied to understand the reconstruction complexity of Image under processing. The compression ratio is calculated manually with the help of stored results in workspace of software. We hope that if the time constraints are overcome our model can be suited for the hardware designing of SPIHT algorithm for Image compression.

References

[1] Soman, K.P., Ramchandran, K.I.: Insight into WAVELETS. Prentice hall of India, New Delhi (2005)

[2] Gonzales, Woods: Digital Image Processing with MATLAB. Prentice hall of India, New Delhi (2004)

[3] Said, A., Pearlman, W.: A new, fast, and efficient image codec based on set partitioning in hierarchical trees. IEEE Trans. Circuit Syst. Video Technology 6, 243–250 (1996)

[4] Morales, A., Agili, S.: Implementing the SPIHT Algorithm in MATLAB. In: Proceedings of the 2003 ASEE/WFEO International Colloquium Copyright, American Society for Engineering Education (2003)

[5] Grgic, S., Grgic, M.: Performance Analysis of Image Compression Using Wavelets. IEEE Transaction on Industrial Electronics 48(3), 682–695 (2001)

[6] Grgic, S., KerS, K., Grgic, M.: Image Compression Using Wavelet. In: ISIE 1999-Bled, pp. 99–104. IEEE, Slovenia (1999)

[7] Wang, J., Zhang, F.: Study of the Image Compression based on SPIHT Algorithm. In: International Conference on Intelligent Computing and Cognitive Informatics, pp. 130–133. IEEE Computer Society (2010)

[8] Wang, J., Liu, B.: Modified SPIHT Based Image Compression Algorithm For Hardware Implementation. In: 2nd International Workshop on Computer Science and Engineering, pp. 572–576. IEEE Computer Society (2009)

Applying Mathematical Programming to Efficient Software Release Management

Fabrício Gomes de Freitas and Jerffeson Teixeira de Souza

Optimization in Software Engineering Group (GOES.UECE), State University of Ceará, Avenue Paranjana, 1700, Ceará, Brazil
fabriciogf.uece@gmail.com, jeff@larces.uece.br

Abstract. This paper presents a study on the theory and practice of the application of exact optimization in software engineering. A conceptual comparison of optimization approaches in the software engineering context is presented. Software requirements problem's aspects are analysed regarding suitability for use of exact techniques. The advantage is that such approach can provide the best solution. We aim to indicate the applicability of the technique and also its better behavior.

Keywords: Exact optimization, software engineering, software release.

1 Introduction

The Search Based Software Engineering (SBSE) field is focused on the formulation and resolution of software engineering problems by optimization techniques [1]. Aside the software engineering problems, an essential aspect of SBSE is the technique used for solving them, since it is the search method that provides the solution to be used. Thus far, SBSE works have mostly employed metaheuristic approaches, although such approach does not assure to find the best solutions.In this paper, the application of exact optimization in SBSE is investigated. Such optimization methods are disposed to find the best solution. This is decisive, since the solution's quality directly impacts on the process [2].Exact techniques have already been applied in software engineering problems. Previous works were focused on the solution of some instances, regardless the analysis of the method behaviour in different contexts. In [3], the requirements scheduling for release planning is tackled by an ILP approach. The problem formulation included different kinds of dependency among requirements, such as combination, implication, and exclusion, among others. The formulation for the problem considered the allocation of development teams. Experimental results revealed the validity of the approach in that context. Differently from the present work, the formulation in [3] was mono-objective. In addition, the work applied the ILP approach in only two small instances (9 and 99 requirements), and it has not analyzed the time efficiency of the application.The multi-objective next release problem was introduced in 2007 [4]. The authors considered two objective functions: maximize "score" and minimize "cost". Several experiments were performed in order to show the validity of the approach. The multi-objective metaheuristic NSGA-II outperformed other techniques in most cases. The problem instances had up to 200

V.V. Das and N. Thankachan (Eds.): CIIT 2011, CCIS 250, pp. 564–568, 2011.

requirements. In the present paper, beyond the use of exact optimization, larger instances are used.Papers [5] and [6] show others approaches to software release planning.In the present work, a theoretical and empirical study on the potential application of exact techniques on SBSE problems is carried out. In addition, to our knowledge, this is the first paper to propose and use exact techniques on the multi-objective context in the SBSE field. The main contributions of this paper are:

1 Conceptual analysis: The paper presents theoretical aspects regarding the methods and problems, showing the suitable scenarios for exact technique. This information may be used in future research as a basis for determining the applicability of exact optimization in SBSE.

2 Exact optimization applicability: Theoretical aspects on the application of exact method on SBSE are presented.

3 Execution time issue: From a series of comparison experiments, the execution time of the exact optimization approach is analyzed in various instances, in order to show its behaviour.

2 Conceptual Analysis of Methods and Problems Aspects

Metaheuristic approaches are categorized under the approximate methods, i.e., the method does not guarantee finding the best solution. Exact techniques, nonetheless, are able to find the optimal solution, and guarantee its optimality [7]. In an optimization approach, an optimization technique is assigned to supply the solution. Metaheuristics, given their non-deterministic aspect, may find different solutions among different runs. This aspect can negatively impact its reliability, given the lack of assurance in the outcome of the method. Given the previous discussion about accuracy and reliability, if a problem is suitable for exact methods, they may be more positively received in a context than metaheuristics.The execution time of exact optimization is generally higher than the presented by metaheuristics. However, this aspect must be taken in relation to the context of the problem. In real-time optimization problems, the execution time is of high interest, but in problems of planning activities for days, for example, if a solution can be found in seconds it still may be of practical use.As stated in [7], metaheuristics remain suitable even for problems with very large instances. The size of the problem instances can impact on the efficiency of the method. Exact technique Branch-and-bound, for example, is able to solve only small-middle size instances of general ILP problems in practical time. Therefore, it is necessary to study the behaviour of the method in different instance sizes in order to determine the size limits for a given problem in a certain context.The problem nature also has to be considered. For instance, problems with real variable decisions and only linear functions for both objective and constraints, linear programming, are efficiently solved by exact methods such as Simplex. However, the presence of nonlinearity, non differentiable functions, etc., require the use of generic optimization methods, such as metaheuristics. In the context of the present paper, the problem tackled is integer linear programming (ILP), for which Branch-and Bound technique have been successfully applied [8].

Metaheuristics able to deal with the multi-objective scenario have been proposed and successfully applied. An approach for solving multi-objective problems by exact techniques is the construction of the Pareto Front by multiple runs of the problem, each one with a defined scenario. One function remains as objective function to be optimized, and the others are treated as restrictions. By iteratively solving the problem with different scenarios, one can find the optimum value for each combination, and therefore find the true Pareto Front. This approach has as drawback the possible massive number of runs, if there are more than two functions. The approach can only be used if the functions used as restrictions have an integer domain.

3 Experimental Design

Displayed equations or formulas are centered and set on a separate line (with an extra The following research questions are covered:

- RQ1: Is exact optimization appropriate for SBSE problems?
  This question was partially addressed on the section 3 above. In addition, this work shows the first application of exact technique on a multi-objective problem in SBSE.
- RQ2: How does the execution time of exact method impact on its applicability? In order to analyse this aspect, instances with increasing sizes are used. The results are analysed mainly focusing on the SBSE context.

3.1 Problem and Intances

The Multi-Objective Next Release Problem (MONRP) [4] is composed by the set $R = \{r_1, \ldots, r_n\}$, which contains n requirements, each one with a cost of implementation. The set $C = \{c_1, \ldots, c_m\}$ with clients, each one with a value of importance to the company. An importance relation represents for each client the value of importance of each requirement. This way, each requirement has a score. Thus, in the MONRP, one wants to select the requirements with higher overall score and, simultaneously, lower cost.To perform the empirical study, we have generated 8 instances. The Table 1 indicates the configuration of each instance. The letter stands for the aspect which changes between the instances. 'I' relates to "instance", since instance I2 is twice as large as I1. 'C' stands for clients and 'R' for requirements. 'B' stands for boundary, since those instances were used to evaluate the methods in extreme scenarios.

Table 1. Instances used on the experiment

MONRP Instance	I1	I2	C1	C2	R1	R2	B1	B2
#Clients	100	100	200	400	100	100	200	200
#Requirements	100	200	100	100	200	400	400	800

3.2 Algorithm

The Branch-and-Bound (BnB) method works by iteratively solving the problem without the integer restriction. If the solution found has any variable decision that is not integer, then there is a branch on the variable, creating sub-problems for each configuration. The best objective found is stored, and used to skip branches. The process is repeated until all possible sub-problems are considered.

4 Results

Table 2 shows the execution time for the Branch-and-Bound approach in the 8 instances. The cost function was taken as restriction. We only show the time for the exact approach since the main aspect to be investigated regarding execution time is the behavior of the exact method with the increase of the sizes of the instances.

Table 2. Execution time for exact technique in seconds

Instance	I1	I2	C1	C2	R1	R2	B1	B2
BnB	33.30	201.74	59.18	98.85	126.96	508.41	855.63	4282.85

We observe that for Branch-and-Bound the increase in execution time between I1 and R1 was of 3.81 times. From R1 to R2, the increase was of 4.00 times. Then, when the number of requirements is doubled, the increase in execution time is about 4 times higher, indicating the exponential behaviour of the approach regarding the number of requirements. From I1 to C1, the increase factor was of 1.77, and between C1 and C2, it was 1.67. Then, the behaviour of exact technique regarding the number of clients is nearly linear. The limit of exact optimization can be analyzed in B1 and B2. For B1, with 400 requirements, the execution time was of 14.26 minutes, and for B2 (800 requirements) it reached 71,38 minutes. Then, the execution time of B2 was 5 times higher than B1, indicating an increase in the exponential behaviour of exact method.

5 Conclusions

The work proposes the application of exact optimization techniques in SBSE. Theoretical aspects on methods and problems indicate that exact optimization can be applied in software engineering problems, being able to find optimum solutions. As initial application, the multi-objective next release problem is tackled.Regarding the execution time of the exact method Branch-and-Bound, it can be concluded that for contexts with up to 200 clients and 400 requirements the approach is of practical use, since the true pareto front was found in less than 15 minutes. We also validated the exponential behavior of exact technique on the problem.

The work shows the application of exact technique in only one SBSE problem. Other problems that are also integer linear problems are expected to be studied in future works. Examples of such problems are the multi-objective test case selection, the staff allocation, among others.

References

1. Harman, M.: The Current State and Future of Search Based Software Engineering. In: Future of Software Engineering 2007, Minneapolis, pp. 342–357 (2007)
2. Yoo, S., Harman, M.: Pareto Efficient Multi-Objective Test Case Selection. In: 2007 International Symposium on Software Testing and Analysis, London, pp. 140–150 (2007)
3. Li, C., van den Akker, J.M., Brinkkemper, S., Diepen, G.: Integrated Requirement Selection and Scheduling for the Release Planning of a Software Product. In: Sawyer, P., Heymans, P. (eds.) REFSQ 2007. LNCS, vol. 4542, pp. 93–108. Springer, Heidelberg (2007)
4. Zhang, Y., Harman, M., Mansouri, A.: The Multi-Objective Next Release Problem. In: Proceedings of the 9th Annual Conference on Genetic and Evolutionary Computation, London, pp. 1129–1137 (2007)
5. Colares, F., Souza, J., Carmo, R., Pádua, C., Mateus, G.: A New Approach to the Software Release Planning. In: XXIII Brazilian Symposium on Software Engineering, pp. 207–215 (2009)
6. Ngo-The, A., Ruhe, G.: Optimized Resource Allocation for Software Release Planning. IEEE Transactions on Software Engineering 35(1), 109–123 (2009)
7. Talbi, E.: Metaheuristics: From Design to Implementation. Wiley (2009)
8. Michael, J., Stahl, B.: Branch-and-bound applications in combinatorial data analysis. Springer, Heidelberg (2005)

Color Image Segmentation Using Minimum Spanning Tree and Cycles

P.V.S.S.R. Chandra Mouli[1] and T.N. Janakiraman[2]

[1] School of Computing Science and Engineering, VIT University, Vellore, India
[2] Department of Mathematics, NIT Trichy, India
{mouli.chand}@gmail.com

Abstract. An unsupervised and robust algorithm for segmenting color images using graph theoretic concepts is proposed in this paper. A novel region growing procedure is proposed for cycle (segments) formation and cycle merging. Experiments were carried out on standard Berkeley Segmentation Database Set (BSDS) and other public domain images and the results show the efficacy of the proposed method.

Keywords: Color image segmentation, graph theory, minimum spanning tree, cycles.

1 Introduction

Human visual system plays an integral part in the theory of color. Color vision results from the action of three spectral sensitivities such as Red (R), Green (G) and Blue (B) of the visible light spectrum. Color is the complex perceptual phenomenon and the sensation of the color images arises due to the response of the threeneuro-chemical sensors or receptors in the retina to the visible light [1]. As color images are order of the day, their high prevalence motivated to extend the earlier work proposed on color images.

Color is a useful property which adds additional information to the images. The color perceived by human beings is a combination of three stimuli R, G and B which forms a color space. As compared to monochrome images, color images have information of brightness, hue and saturation for each pixel [2]. The color edge detection approaches are broadly classified into two categories.

(i) Synthetic approaches: The monochrome image edge detection method is applied to three color channels independently and the results are combined using certain logical operations.

(ii) Vector approaches: A color image can be viewed as 2D and 3-Channel vector field, where each pixel is defined by a 3D vector in a given color space. The edges are detected using different properties of space vector.

V.V. Das and N. Thankachan (Eds.): CIIT 2011, CCIS 250, pp. 569–575, 2011.

2 Background

Researchers have concentrated in the past few decades on devising algorithms for grayscale image understanding [3]. The major advantage of color is increase in quantity of information and it can be used for more accurate object location, preprocessing and the possibility of processing more complex images. A typical color image capturing system relies on a trichromatic input based on the additive primary colors red, green and blue [4-5]. In [6], an adaptive and unsupervised scheme for pixel clustering and color image segmentation was proposed. In [7], the authors dealt with region matching problem of a pair of color stereoscopic images. As a first step, the candidate selection which met relative position and overlapping constraints and in the second stage the correct match was determined based on cost function. In this paper, the work proposed in [8] was extended to color images after making substantial modifications.

3 Proposed Method

The steps involved in the proposed method are as follows: (i) Read the given image, (ii) Perform Gaussian smoothing (optional), (iii) Separate R, G and B channels and (iv) For each channel, do

a. Graph representation
b. Apply Hybrid MST algorithm
c. Call ADD_EDGE procedure
d. Call CYCLE_MERGE procedure.

3.1 Graph Representation

The input image is represented as a graph G= (V, E) where V represents the set of vertices and E, the set of edges. 8-connectivity of vertices is considered for edges. Thus, for a graph G of size $N \times N$ image, there will be N^2 vertices and $4N^2 - 6N + 2$ edges and looks like a grid graph.

3.2 Hybrid MST

The combination of Boruvka and Prim's algorithm called Hybrid algorithm has been chosen for generation of MST due to its lower time complexity $O(|N| \log \log |N|)$. Thus, the edge set is divided into two sets MST edges and non-MST edges.

$$E = E_1 \cup E_2 \tag{1}$$

3.3 Pseudo Code for ADD_EDGE

```
Algorithm: ALL_EDGE

Input: MST, E2; Output: Cycles

1. Sort E2 in non-decreasing order of weights
2. Cycles = {}
3. While E2 is not empty
   a. Extract an edge from E2 and store its end vertices
      in u and v respectively
   b. temp_path = BFS(MST,u,v); // Breadth First Search
   c. flag=check_constraint(temp_path)
   d. if(flag)
       i. MST=Union(MST,E2)
      ii. Cycles = Union(Cycles, temp_path)
   e. else
       i. Remove the extracted edge from E2
   f. end  // end of if
   g. end // end of while
```

Bubble sort is used in step-1 to sort the edges in non-decreasing order. In step 3b, there exists a unique path between any two vertices u and v in a tree, BFS is used to determine the corresponding path. Then the edge is added between u and v to form a cycle and is stored in Cycles vector. The pseudo code for sub procedure check_constraint given in step 3c is given below.

```
Algorithm: check_constraint

Input: temp_path, threshold_value; Output: Boolean

1. flag ← 1
2. T ← (maxv-minv)/2
   maxv and minv represents the max and min intensity
   vertices of temp_path
3. if T ≤ threshold_value
a. flag=0
```

3.4 Pseudo Code for CYCLE_MERGE

```
     Algorithm: CYCLE_MERGE
     Input: Cycles
     Output: Final_Segments
 1. for c = 1 to length(Cycles)-1
 a. search for common edge in the remaining cycles
 b. if common edge is found
 i. merge the two cycles and append the new cycle to
    Cycles vector
ii. remove the two cycles from Cycles vector
```

The adjacent cycles having common edge are merged to form bigger regions. Cycles having common vertex are retained as such to preserve the structure.

3.5 Fusion of Segments

The final_regions obtained from CYCLE_MERGE procedure for three channels are fused. The adjacent cycles having common edge are merged to form bigger regions. Cycles having common vertex are retained as such to preserve the structure. The similarity criteria is that the segment should be present in at least two of the three channels.

4 Experimental Results

The proposed method was tested on BSDS and the results show that the proposed method produced relevant segments compared to other methods. Quantitative results also exemplified the same. The results of segmentation were shown in grayscale images. Figures-1, 2 represent the output obtained for images in BSDS. In Figure-3, the results obtained for standard images are presented. The first and third columns represent the output obtained without Gaussian smoothing and the second and fourth columns represent the output with Gaussian smoothing.

4.1 Performance Evaluation

Martin [9] proposed the usage of precision and recall to characterize the agreement between the boundary elements of regions of two segmentations.

Fig. 1. Segmentation results –I for some sample images from BSDS

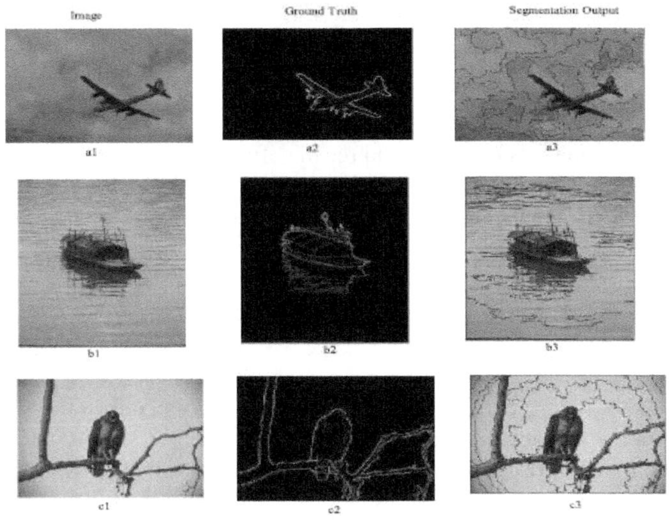

Fig. 2. Segmentation results – II for some sample images from BSDS

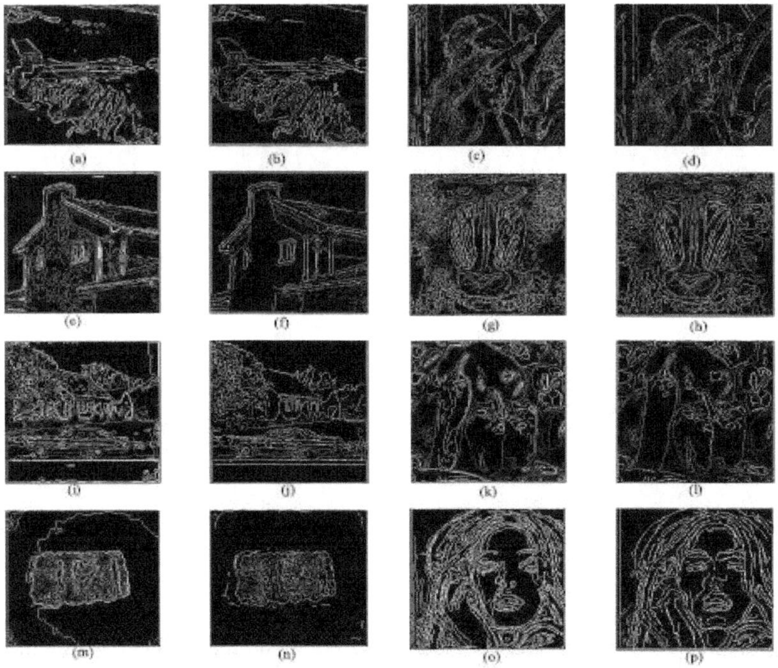

Fig. 3. Results of some standard benchmark images

Combining the both, the figure of merit (F) was defined as

$$F = \frac{PR}{\alpha P + (1-\alpha) R} \tag{2}$$

where P and R represents precision and recall defined as

$$\text{Precision} = \frac{Matched(S_1, S_2)}{|S_1|} \tag{3}$$

$$\text{Recall} = \frac{Matched(S_2, S_1)}{|S_2|} \tag{4}$$

where $|S_1|$ and $|S_2|$ represent the total number of boundary pixels in the result of any segmentation method and ground truth respectively.

For comparison of results, the recent works [10-12] were used using the F-measure defined in equation (2). Figure-4 shows the graphical representation of F-values of the proposed method and other methods.

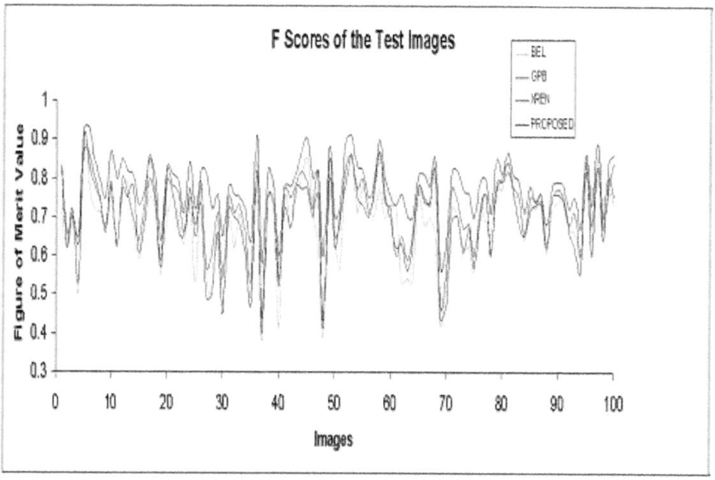

Fig. 4. Comparison of Figure of Merit values

5 Conclusion

In this paper, a novel algorithm for color image segmentation is proposed. The algorithm is unsupervised in nature due to the fact that segments are formed automatically without any input from the user about the number of segments. In addition, the algorithm guarantees to run in polynomial time and is applicable for any image domain.

References

1. Chanda, B., Mazumdar, D.: Digital Image Processing, 2nd edn. University of MMM, Chicago Press (2005)
2. Deshmukh, K., Shinde, G.: Adaptive Color Segmentation. Electronic Letters on Computer Vision and Image Analysis 5(4), 12–23 (2005)
3. Jain, A.K.: Fundamentals of Digital Image Processing. Prentice Hall, New Jersey (1989)
4. Gonzalez, R.C., Woods, R.: Fundamentals of Digital Image Processing, 3rd edn. University of MMM, Chicago Press (2005)
5. Pratt, W.: Digital Image Processing, 3rd edn. John Wiley & Sons (2001)
6. Yu, Z., Au, O., Zou, R., Yu, W., Ting, J.: An adaptive unsupervised approach toward pixel clustering and color image segmentation. Pattern Recognition Letters 43, 1889–1906 (2010)
7. El Mohammad, A., Lhoussaine, M., Abdelaziz, B.: A new region matching algorithm for color stereo images. Pattern Recognition Letters 28, 1679–1687 (2007)
8. Janakiraman, T.N., Chandra Mouli, P.V.S.S.R.: Image Segmentation using Minimal Spanning Tree and Cycles. In: Proceedings of International Conference on Computational Intelligence and Multimedia Applications, pp. 215–219 (2007)
9. Martin, D.: An empirical approach to grouping and segmentation, Ph.D. dissertation, University of California, Berkeley (2002)
10. Dollar, P., Zhuowen, T., Blongie, S.: Supervised Learning of edges and object boundaries. In: Proceedings of CVPR, pp. 1964–1971 (2006)
11. Maire, M., Pabalo, A., Fowlkes, C., Malik, J.: Using contours to detect and localize junctions in natural images. In: Proceedings of CVPR, pp. 1–8 (2008)
12. Ren, X.: Multi-Scale Improves Boundary Detection in Natural Images. In: Forsyth, D., Torr, P., Zisserman, A. (eds.) ECCV 2008, Part III. LNCS, vol. 5304, pp. 533–545. Springer, Heidelberg (2008)

Multi Agent System Architecture for Admission Control and Resource Allocation in Cellular Network

Megha Kamble and Roopam Gupta

Dept. Of Information Technology, UIT, RGTU, Bhopal
meghakamble@gmail.com, roopamgupta@rgtu.net

Abstract. In this paper, we present a multi agent system for resource allocation problem in cellular network. A multi agent system based approach is proposed by taking into consideration the concurrent nature of services and involvement of no. of participants in cellular network. This work emphasizes on enhancement of QoS using fundamental mechanism of call admission control as well as resource allocation as a additional measure. To meet the objective, this work proposes soft computing approach. This research paper presents the analysis of single parameter that is call dropping probability and the analysis has shown the enhancement over traditional approach.

Keywords: Cellular Network, Fuzzy Logic Control, Multi Agent System.

1 Introduction

Scarcity of resources as compared to increasing demand in cellular network is the key issue. With the help of available resources, cellular network is expected to provide guarantee Quality of Service(QoS). So resource management techniques are required to ensure QoS. Resource management functions are subdivided into two, call admission control(CAC) and resource allocation problem. CAC is to regulate the requests at the entry level and resource allocation is to support the ongoing call with proper resources without fail or with some delay. This work has combined fixed and dynamic channel allocation as hybrid channel allocation out of different strategies for channel allocation available in literature [1-4]. The main simulation technologies can be discrete event simulation and Multi-Agent System for performance analysis. Multi-agent system is suitable in this case for supporting real-time and concurrent events occurring in cellular network. Similarly decision making cannot be done by a single participant. Neighboring base stations have to participate for resource allocation. Figure 1 from [4] shows the layered architecture adapted for Multi Agent system.

1.1 Related Work

Parag Pendharkar[3] had implemented MAS using DCA and the results can be improved using HCA in place of DCA. E.L. Bodanase[1] had presented one of the early research about MAS in cellular network. Yao-Tien Wang [2] had implemented fuzzy logic for DCA. The framework presented in the literature was missing call admission decision at entry level so as to enhance QoS. Another is application of HCA in local planning layer which will improve the QoS.

V.V. Das and N. Thankachan (Eds.): CIIT 2011, CCIS 250, pp. 576–578, 2011.

2 Proposed Framework

2.1 Call Admission Decision in Reactive Layer

Fuzzy CAC scheme is explained in Figure 3[5]. This paper elaborates the fuzzificaton and defuzzification process to determine the time to buffer the call. Fuzzy rules from [5] are extended using more parameters like Network load, channel requirement.

Sample fuzzification of the variables as follows:

(a) Membership function for the network load

(b) fuzzification of traffic load

Fig. 1.

Crisp output of defuzzification (time to buffer the call) is determined using Mean of Maxima(MOM) method, MOM for every class is determined using the formula: $MOM=1/2(a_0+a_6)$ for a class over the interval [a0,a6]

$$f(x) = \sum_{k=1,i=1}^{n,c_{max}} \mu l * MOM\, c_l / \sum_{l}^{n} \mu l \quad (1)$$

2.2 Local Planning Layer

70 channels were used for simulation purpose in which 21:49 is the ratio for static and dynamic channels. Existing literature works for borrowing (DCA) using either search or update method. This work proposes identification of promising neighbor that is effective lender with the help of soft computing approach [2].

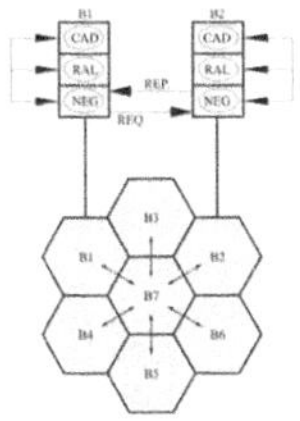

Fig. 2. Distributed Multi Agent System Architecture:7 cell cluster {B1..B7}

2.3 Agent Interaction

Fig. 2 shows distributed architecture of interaction amongst the agents. Each agent is a layered architecture[4], further represented by a set of processes for three layers vise {CAD,RAL,NEG} where CAD: call admission decision, RAL: resource allocation, NEG: Negotiation. The interaction is using interprocess communication[5].

3 Simulation Experiment

The simulation parameters used in this paper are similar to the ones used in [5]. Table 1 shows sample tabulated statistics for parameters NW=5.1(Network Load) Traffic Load(TL)=80 calls/hr (DYN)Dynamic Channel Requirement= 44 User Precedence=1. Table 2 states the percentage improvement seen in the QoS.

Table 1. Membership Grades Contributing to the fuzzy output Admission Decision

Rules	SA	WAB	WRB	WA
R1:min(0.0,0.0,0.0,1)	0.0			
R2: min(0.0,0.0,0.0,1)	0.0			
R3: min(0.0,0.0,0.0,1)	0.0			
R4: min(0.0,0.4,0.6,1)		0.0		
R5: min(0.0,0.4,0.0,1)		0.0		
R6: min(0.0,0.8,0.0,1)			0.0	

Table 2. The reduction of call drop probability

Call arrival rate (Erlangs)	At reactive layer	At local planning layer.
20	100%	100%
40	95%	96%
60	96%	96%
80	90%	92%
100	89%	90%

4 Conclusion

In this paper we presented a framework for call admission control and resource allocation using Multi-agent system. We have stated the results for enhancement of call dropping probability and further working to quantify the effect of the framework on resource utilization and call blocking probability using soft computing approach.

References

1. Bodanese, E.L., Cuthbert, L.G.: Application Of Intelligent Agents In Channel Allocation Strategies For Mobile Networks. In: IEEE International Conference On Communications, vol. 1, pp. 18–22 (June 2000)
2. Wang, Y.-T.: A Fuzzy-Based Dynamic Channel Borrowing Scheme for Wireless Cellular Networks. IEEE, 0-7803-7757-5/03/$17.K
3. Pendharkar, P.C., Harrisburg, P.S.: A Multi-agent Distributed Channel Allocation Approach For Wireless Networks. International Transactions In Operation Research 15(3), 325–337 (2006)
4. Kamble, M., Gupta, R.: DDCA in Cellular Network Using Fuzzy Rule Based Multi-agent System. IJCA(0975 - 8887) 1(17), 81–84 (2010)
5. Kamble, M., Gupta, R.: A new framework for call admission control in wireless cellular network. In: IEEE Int. Conf. ETNCC (April 2011) 978-1-4577-0239-6/178-181

A New Approach for Fractal Image Coding: Self-similarity at Smallest Scale

Ashish Awasthi and Manish Kumar

Dept. of Computer Application,
Shri Ramswaroop Memorial Group of Professional Colleges, Lucknow, UP, India
ashish3awasthi@rediffmail.com, dr.manish.2000@gmail.com

Abstract. Fractal image coding, the traditional approaches which are being used currently, based on dividing the images into blocks. These blocks are known as range blocks and domain blocks. In these of approaches after coding the image generally the decoding process is slow as extensive searching is required .In this paper we are going to present a scheme which uses the concept of self similarity at small scale that is at pixel level. Through this proposed scheme coding and decoding can be speed-up.

Keywords: Fractal image coding, Self-similarity, pixel etc.

1 Introduction

Fractal image coding (FIC) was introduced in 90's. Since then FIC methods have been studied in a variety of way. Fractal image coding is considered to be the 2nd generation of coding method [1]. In fractal image coding the concept of contractive transform and fixed point theorem is generally used. The first automatic scheme was introduced by A.E. Jacqin and Y. Fisher. In their scheme they modified the partition scheme and proposed a better scheme which is better in performance. In these schemes the original image is first partitioned in range and domain blocks and the process of matching from range to domain is implemented. Fractal image coding has many good features.

a. The first is resolution independence by which the decoded images of the larger size can be got without block effect.
b. The second is high coding ratio of 10000:1 was recorded in the article of Barnsley [2], who is the father of fractal image coding.
c. The third feature include two phase : coding and decoding, coding process include many ways to code image while decoding process is much faster than coding as employs generally an iterative process.

2 Previous Approaches

The previous approaches of fractal image coding schemes follow the following process:

V.V. Das and N. Thankachan (Eds.): CIIT 2011, CCIS 250, pp. 579–583, 2011.

(i) Partition of images based on range blocks
(ii) Pool of domain blocks
(iii) Types of transformation imposed on domain blocks
(iv) Search process to find appropriate domain block
(v) Transformation parameters representations

The above mentioned processes have the following schemes of partitions for fractal image coding

(i) **Fixed Size Square Block-**The simplest form of range partition consists of fixed size square blocks [3]-[5]).This type of block partition is very applicable in transform coding of these individual blocks.
(ii) **Quadtree-**This technique is a very well known image processing technique based on a recursive splitting of selected image quadrants[6]-[8].
(iii) **Horizontal-Vertical-**The horizontal-vertical partition produces a tree structured partition of the image. In this partition approach used is splitting of image in to two section one by horizontal line and other by vertical line. [9].
(iv) **Irregular Regions-**A tiling of image by right-angled irregular-shaped ranges may be constructed by a variety of merging strategies on a initial fixed square block. [10]- [13].
(v) **Polygon Blocks -**Polygonal partitions have been constructed by recursive subdivision of an initial coarse grid by the insertion of line segments at various angles [14], as well as by merging triangles, in a Delaunay triangulation, to form quadrilaterals [15].
(vi) **Overlapped Blocks -**Overlapping range blocks have been used to reduce blocking artifacts [16].

As a general concept the fractal image coding is done by using range blocks and domain blocks where an image is partitioned into the same sized range blocks and then some domain blocks are made from image.

3 Proposed Approach

As we know that an image in grey scale is stored in memory in double dimension array form where each location of 2d array represents a pixel value.

3.1 Proposed Process of Coding the Image

The proposed scheme uses a single dimension array, where each location of single dimension array represents an individual pixel color value of image now as we know that a same color pixel can be located at many places in the image so here we are storing the address of first occurrence of any individual color with help of linked list the process is as follows:

1. First take the grey scale image of 64 * 64 resolution
2. As per our concept first we define a 1-D array of 256 locations (as total numbers of grey levels are 256 including black and white-ranges between 0 - 255) and

linked list with each node having two parts one is info and other is next node address. Here info part contains the index for row and column. The each index of 1-D array contains the list of locations of pixel of corresponding grey level.

3. Here each index of 1- d array represents an individual grey level of image.(i.e. 0th index represents the o-level of grey code)
4. Now scan each pixel of image row wise and find the value (grey level value).
5. After finding the value of pixel go to the corresponding index number of defined 1-d array and save the location of scanned pixel value. This node will contain info and next node address (if any) –info parts have index value of pixel in 2-D array.
6. Similarly scan the whole 2-D array and put the each pixel value element at corresponding place in defined 1-D array.

3.2 Proposed Algorithm for Coding the Image

In the following Algorithm X is 2-D array of Input Image, P is a 1-D array having the index number according to the color code of grey level, i, j are two variables used to scan the 2-D array, N is a node of linked list having subscript value of 2-D array as info and address of next node.

```
Procedure (coding image)
begin
Let image is stored in variable x
Initialize 1-D array P with value 0
for each value of i  //loop for row of x
begin
for each value of j  // loop for column of x
begin
v=x[i][j];  // find the value of pixel which is index number of 1-D array P
if p[v] = 0
Create a node N with info part having x[i][j] and link part having null ; // first node
created for index P[v]
now assign the location of N in P[v];
else
traverse the previously existing list and add the newly created node at last;
end; //end of if
end ;//end of inner loop
end;//end of outer loop
end; // end of procedure
```

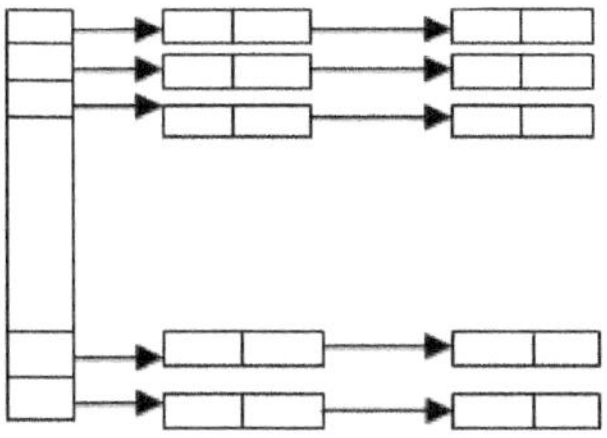

Fig. 1. Pictorial representation of the above mentioned process and algorithm {Left side of figure shows array and right side shows linked list}

3.3 Proposed Process of Decoding the Image

1. Scan the 1-D array P from index 0 sequentially.
2. If the value at index P[v] contains the address of a starting node of linked list then traverse that linked list till end and plot the values of pixels as stored in info part of each node.
3. Repeat the process in step 2 until all the locations of 1-D array and corresponding linked list are traversed.

3.4 Proposed Algorithm for Decoding the Image

Procedure (decoding)
begin
Take the created 1-D array P
for each value of v starting from 0 //loop for traversing 1-D array
begin
if P[v]=0
increase the value of v with 1 i.e. traverse next location of P
else
assign b=P[v]; and traverse the linked list till end and plot the pixel value of each node
end; //end of loop
end; //end of procedure

4 Conclusion and Future Scope

The concept of self similarity at pixel level that is at smallest scale is implemented in the proposed approach. This approach can be very useful for the small and fine grained grey scale images. Here after coding the image with this proposed approach the decoding process is very fast and the image can be decoded at a high speed and less searching. Presently this approach is applicable on grey scale image .Further this approach can be implemented on color images.

References

1. Zhao, Y., Wang, H., Yuan, B.: Advances in Fractal Image Coding. Acta Electronica Sinica 28(4), 95–101 (2000)
2. Barnsley, M.F., Sloan, A.D.: A Better Way to Compress Images. Byte, 215–223 (January 1988)
3. Oien, G.E., Lepsoy, S., Ramstad, T.A.: An inner product space approach to image coding by contractive transformations. In: Proc. IEEE Int. Conf. Acoustics, Speech, and Signal Processing,Toronto, Ont., Canada, pp. 2773–2776 (May 1991)
4. Monro, D.M.: Class of fractal transforms. Electron. Lett. 29, 362–363 (1993)
5. Thao, N.T.: A hybrid fractal-DCT coding scheme for image compression. In: Proc. IEEE Int. Conf. Image Processing, Lausanne, Switzerland, vol. 1, pp. 169–172 (September 1996)

6. Jacquin, A.E.: Fractal image coding based on a theory of iterated contractive image transformations. In: Kunt, M. (ed.) Proc. SPIE: Vis. Commun. Image Process., Lausanne, Switzerland, vol. 1360, pp. 227–239 (October 1990)
7. A novel fractal block-coding technique for digital images. In: Proc. IEEE Int. Conf. Acoustics, Speech and Signal Processing, Albuquerque, NM, vol. 4, pp. 2225–2228 (April 1990)
8. Image coding based on a fractal theory of iterated contractive image transformations. IEEE Trans. Image Processing 1, 18–30 (January 1992)
9. Saupe, D., et al.: Optimal hierarchical partitions for fractal image compression. In: Proc. IEEE Int Conf. Image Processing, Chicago, IL, vol. 1, pp. 737–741 (October 1998)
10. Thomas, L., Deravi, F.: Region-based fractal image compression using heuristic search. IEEE Trans. Image Processing 4, 832–838 (1995)
11. Saupe, D., Ruhl, M.: Evolutionary fractal image compression. In: Proc. IEEE Int. Conf. Image Processing, Lausanne, Switzerland, vol. I, pp. 129–132 (September 1996)
12. Tanimoto, M., Ohyama, H., Kimoto, T.: A new fractal image coding scheme Employing blocks of variable shapes. In: Proc. IEEE Int. Conf. Image Processing, Lausanne, Switzerland, vol. 1, pp. 137–140 (September 1996)
13. Ruhl, M., Hartenstein, H., Saupe, D.: Adaptive partitioning for fractal image compression. In: Proc. IEEE Int. Conf. Image Processing, Santa Barbara, CA, vol. II, pp. 310–313 (October 1997)
14. Reusens, E.: Partitioning complexity issue for iterated functions systems based image coding. In: Proc. Eur. Signal Processing Conf., Edinburgh, U.K., vol. 1, pp. 171–174 (September 1994)
15. Davoine, F., Svensson, J., Chassery, J.-M.: A mixed triangular and quadrilateral partition for fractal image coding. In: Proc. IEEE Int. Conf. Image Processing, Washington, D.C., vol. III, pp. 284–287 (October 1995)
16. Reusens, E.: Overlapped adaptive partitioning for image coding based on the theory of iterated functions systems. In: Proc. IEEE Int. Conf. Acoustics, Speech and Signal Processing, Adelaide, Australia, vol. 5, pp. 569–572 (April 1994)

Lossless Fractal Image Compression Mechanism by Applying Exact Self-similarities at Same Scale

Jeet Kumar and Manish Kumar

Shri Ramswaroop Memorial Group of Professional Colleges,
Luckow, Uttar Pradesh, India
jeetkm@sify.com, dr.manish.2000@gmail.com

Abstract. Almost all of the fractal image compression methods are lossy because the concept behind these traditional fractal compression methods is based on loose self-similarity, i.e., the transformation function applied on a domain block does not lead to exact matching with range block, instead the principle works on the minimum distance between transformed domain block and range block. Unlike the traditional fractal image compression methods the proposed mechanism does not partition the image into domain blocks and range blocks. Only a single partition of image serves the purpose. The proposed mechanism uses the concept that in most of the cases a small portion of an image is replicated in some other places of the same image; therefore need not to be stored more than once. The paper presents a novel algorithm to achieve lossless fractal image compression with less computation and fast compression and decompression process.

Keywords: Fractal, lossy compression, self-similarity, domain block, range block.

1 Introduction

An image can be thought of as a 2-dimensional array of pixels. A single partition of the image is needed in the proposed approach. The given image is partitioned into fix sized square blocks. Now the image is considered as a 2-dimensional array of blocks where each block is itself a 2-dimensional array of pixels. In the given approach we select one block and find the locations within the image where the selected block is replicated. Moreover we also find the locations where the selected block is replicated with some transformations. Only counter clock-wise rotation transformations are used with 90, 180, and 270 degrees. Since the given approach is based on same scale self-similarity, we do not require scaling transformations. The selected block is then stored in the block pool along with the list of locations where the block is replicated and the possible rotation transformation, if any. At the time of compression a pool of portions of images, called the blocks, is constructed. The pool contains a list of blocks. Each block is associated with one or more locations and the counter clock-wise rotation transformation code for each location. Therefore this approach does not store entire image pixel by pixel. The approach stores the image in the form of block pool. The block pool stores only selected portion of the image and the locations for their

V.V. Das and N. Thankachan (Eds.): CIIT 2011, CCIS 250, pp. 584–589, 2011.

replication. At the time of decompression, each block in the block pool is explored one by one and placed at the locations associated with that block in the block pool. The desired rotation transformation is also applied clock-wise, if applicable, before the placement of the block in the final reconstructed image. Since at the time of compression we need not to explore each domain block and all possible transformation functions for a given range block, therefore the compression process is considerably fast. Moreover since the pool of blocks contains the list of portions of images along with the direct indices of respective locations, the decompression process is also fast. Therefore the given approach does not suffer from slow speed of compression and decompression process as in traditional fractal image compression.

As far as the organization of the paper is concerned, the introduction section introduces the proposed concept and addresses the problems with existing approaches. After this the literature review section carried out the survey of related researches. The next section named as proposed mechanism contains the basic idea in detail along with the algorithmic implementation of the basic idea. At last conclusion and future scope section summarizes the work done and suggests some extension possibilities in the future.

2 Literature Review

Instead of storing an image bit by bit the idea to store the image in the form of contractive transformation was given by Michael Barnsley in 1988 [1]. Barnsley's graduate student Arnaud Jacquin implemented the first automatic algorithm in software in 1992 [2]. Since then the field of fractal image compression has evolved rapidly. Many ideas have been proposed till date towards the improvement of the image compression with fractal approach but still extensive computation requirement for compressing the image and closeness between domain and range blocks are the major issues. Traditionally an image is partitioned into non-overlapping range blocks and domain blocks (non-overlapping constraint is relaxed in domain blocks). Usually size of the domain blocks are larger than the range blocks to fulfil the contractive requirement. Some research work also advocated domain blocks of same size as that of range blocks to exploit self-similarity at same scale [3]. The size and shape of range blocks may vary to a great extent, but in many approaches square shaped range blocks are preferred. Although various mechanisms have been proposed for image partition. Some approaches like fixed size partition, quadtree partition, horizontal vertical partition and irregular partition fall under right angled partition category while other partition schemes like triangular and polygonal partition can be used [4]. Usually size of the domain blocks are larger than range blocks [5]. But most of the research is focussed on the fixed square shaped block of size B×B for range and 2B×2B for domain [6-8]. For each range block, i, every domain block is explored with all possible tranformations. Therefore this approach needs complete domain pool searching and applying all the transformations one by one which consumes much time. After this a best matched domain block is selected on the basis of minimum distance [9,10]. At last for each range block the location of the best matched domain block is stored along with the transformation applicable on the particular domain block. Therefore the image is stored as a list of domain block locations and corresponding transformations. The traditional fractal image compression method described in the previous paragraph is lossy. In fact most of the fractal image compression methods are lossy. Only very few methods are lossless, for example the method given by Korakot Prachumrak et. al. that makes extensive usage of simultaneous equations is lossless [11]. Proposed method gives a simplified algorithm with simple graphical transformations and lesser matching overhead.

3 Proposed Mechanism

3.1 The Basic Idea

The input image of size N×N is considered as a 2-dimensional array of pixels as shown below:

(1,1) , (1,2) , (1,3) , ……………………………, (1,N)
(2,1) , (2,2) , (2,3) , ……………………………, (2,N)
(3,1) , (3,2) , (3,3) , ……………………………, (3,N)
. .
(N,1) , (N,2) , (N,3) , …………………………., (N,N)

Where each location (i,j); $1 \leq i,j \leq N$ represents a pixel.

The input image is then partitioned into fix square sized blocks of size M×M. Now the image is considered as a 2-dimensional array of size N/M×N/M as shown below:

(1,1) , (1,2) , (1,3) , ……………………………, (1,N/M)
(2,1) , (2,2) , (2,3) , ……………………………, (2,N/M)
(3,1) , (3,2) , (3,3) , ……………………………, (3,N/M)
. .
(N/M,1) , (N/M,2) , (N/M,3) , ……………., (N/M,N/M)

Where each location (i,j); $1 \leq i,j \leq N/M$ represents a block of size M×M.

The key idea is to find the self-similar patterns within the image, and if more than one similar pattern is found, the pattern is stored once only. We store all the locations from the source image from where these similar patterns are found.

3.2 The Novel Algorithm

In this text the image is considered as a 2-dimensional array of blocks. For simplicity the 2-dimensional array blocks is processed as a single dimensional array, i.e., each row is processed one by one from top to bottom. The process described in the previous section can be summarized into following algorithm:

3.2.1 The Compression Procedure

```
Procedure compression (N×N Image)
begin
Partition the image into blocks of M×M; (M<N)
Keep each block unmarked initially;
For each unmarked block Bi (i=1 to N²/M²)
begin
```

```
Mark the block Bi;
  Add block Bi to the block pool;
Assign a unique sequence number to the block Bi;
Attach the indices for the location of Bi in the
source image with block Bi in block pool;
Attach '00' as transformation code with this location;
For each unmarked block Bj (j=i+1 to N²/M²)
Begin
If(Bi==Bj)
begin
Mark the block Bj;
Attach the indices for the location of Bj in the
source image with block Bi in block pool;
  Attach '00' as transformation code with this location;
  j=j+1;
exit and goto the inner for loop;
end;
If(Bi==RotateCounterClock90(Bj))
begin
Mark the block Bj;
Attach the indices for the location of Bj in the
source image with block Bi in block pool;
Attach '01' as transformation code with this location;
j=j+1;
exit and goto the inner for loop;
end;
If(Bi==RotateCounterClock180(Bj))
begin
Mark the block Bj;
Attach the indices for the location of Bj in the
source image with block Bi in block pool;
Attach '10' as transformation code with this location;
j=j+1;
  exit and goto the inner for loop;
end;
If(Bi==RotateCounterClock270(Bj))
begin
Mark the block Bj;
Attach the indices for the location of Bj in the
source image with block Bi in block pool;
Attach '11' as transformation code with this location;
j=j+1;
exit and goto the inner for loop;
end;
end;        //end of inner for loop.
i=i+1;
end;      //end of outer for loop.
Mark all the remaining unmarked blocks;
```

```
Append all the remaining blocks to the block pool;
Assign current sequence numbers to the blocks;
Attach the indices for the location of block in the
source image against each block in block pool;
Attach '00' as the transformation code against each
location of the blocks in the block pool;
Return total number of blocks in the block pool;
  end.      //end of procedure compression.
```

3.2.2 The Decompression Procedure

```
Procedure decompression (Block Pool, Number of Blocks)
begin
for each block Bi (i=1 to number of blocks in pool)
begin
for each location 'j' attached with the block Bi
begin
if(transformation code==00)
  begin
place the block Bi at the location 'j';
end;
if(transformation code==01)
begin
Ti=RotateClock90(Bi);
place the block Ti at the location 'j';
end;
if(transformation code==10)
begin
Ti=RotateClock180(Bi);
place the block Ti at the location 'j';
end;
if(transformation code==11)
begin
Ti=RotateClock270(Bi);
place the block Ti at the location 'j';
end;
end;        //end of inner for loop.
i=i+1;
end;        //end of outer for loop.
  end.      //end of procedure decompression.
```

4 Conclusion and Future Scope

The novel lossless fractal image compression method is discussed in the paper. The time taken by searching the best matched block is reduced. The work can be generalized to any arbitrary chosen block size as required by different types of images. Smaller block size results in high compression ratio at the expense of more computation.

References

[1] Barnsley, M.: Fractals Everywhere. Academic Press, Inc. (1988)
[2] Jacquin, A.E.: Image Coding Based on a Fractal Theory of Iterated Contractive Image Transformations. IEEE Transactions on Image Processing 1(1) (January 1992)
[3] Zhao, Y., Yuan, B.: A Novel Scheme for Fractal Image Coding. Institute of Information Science Northern Jiaotong University, Beijing, P.R.China (2001)
[4] Wohlberg, B., de Jager, G.: A Review of the Fractal Image Coding Literature (December 1999)
[5] Li, G.: Fast Fractal Image Encoding Based on the Extreme Difference Feature of Normalized Block. College of Computer Science & Technology, Southwest University for Nationalities, Chengdu, China (2009)
[6] Han, J.: Fast Fractal Image Encoding Based on Local Variances and Genetic Algorithm. Dezhou University, China (2009)
[7] Zhao, Y., Hu, J., Chi, D., Li, M.: A Novel Fractal Image Coding based on Basis Block Dictionary. School of Electronics and Information, Shanghai dian ji University, Shanghai, China (2009)
[8] Liu, Y., Sun, J.-g.: Face Recognition Method Based on FLPP. Liaoning Techinical University, Huludao Liaoning, China (2010)
[9] Loganathanff, D., Amudha, J., Mehata, K.M.: Classification and Feature Vector Techniques to Improve Fractal Image Coding. Electrical and Electronics Engineering, Amrita Institute of Technology and Science, Coimbatore, INDIA (2003)
[10] Furao, S., Hasegawa, O.: An Effective Fractal Image Coding Method Without Search, Japan (2004)
[11] Prachumrak, K., Hiramatsu, A., Fuchida, T., Nakamura, H.: Lossless Fractal Image Coding, Croatia (2003)

The Significant Parameter Measurement with the Analysis of Energy and Dynamic Power in Zigbee Based Wireless Sensor Node

R. Prabakaran[1] and S. Arivazhagan[2]

[1] Department of Electrical and Electronics Engineering,
Anna University of Technology, Tiruchirappalli, Tamil Nadu, India
[2] Department of Electrical and Electronics Engineering, Mepco Schlenk Engineering College, Sivakasi, Tamil Nadu, India
hiprabakaran@gmail.com, sarivu@yahoo.co.in

Abstract. In recent years, Wireless Sensor Networks (WSN) has found significant growth in embedded system technology, environmental monitoring, agriculture and industrial applications. The energy constraints of WSNs throw a challenge as of their limited processing, limited memory and battery operation. There are seldom attempts in modeling the energy consumption of WSN environment. Whereas, a good number of attempts focused only on the static behavior of WSN, this paper details with the modeling of energy consumption to explain stochastic behavior of the WSN with the different routing strategies and parameter based functioning of WSN. The WSN model is created and analyzed using the wireless protocol analyzer for the accurate results.

Keywords: Energy Estimation, Dynamic Power Consumption, Wireless Sensor Network (WSN), Sensor Node and Energy Modeling.

1 Introduction

The advancement in the wireless sensor technology is opening doors for a variety of potential applications in embedded system technology. It also provides an opportunity for the researchers in the development of protocols and modeling mechanisms. The sensor network constitutes thousands of sensor nodes to sense a physical parameter, analyze and monitor an application based scenario. The battery operation of a sensor node demands energy modeling and thereby increasing its lifetime of it. There are many methods available to enhance the lifetime of the sensor node. In this context it is worthwhile to mention that power management of the embedded device is categorized into two types, namely static and dynamic power managements. Static power management of the processor refers to shutdown of the peripherals of the processor (sleep state) and system in order to reduce the power when they are not in use. The dynamic power management on the other side is the scaling of frequency and voltage with respect application power requirement. Literature available regarding the methods of energy modeling, experimental approaches and their outcomes are outlined in the succeeding section.

V.V. Das and N. Thankachan (Eds.): CIIT 2011, CCIS 250, pp. 590–595, 2011.

2 Related Works

A set of previous attempts, model the energy consumption of sensor node only by characterizing the life time of the particular node. The life time of the sensor node depends on its physical characteristics, as well as several parametric issues like mobility, heterogeneity, application characteristics and Quality of Services (QoS). The authors in [1] presented the use of dynamic power management technique for a node and analyzed the power consumption of the radio device. The work presented in [2] details the energy consumption and its estimation for IEEE802.11 during data transmission. The contribution in [3] characterized the power consumption of the sensor node built with alternative energy source of solar cell and piezo electric crystals. In [4], life time of the sensor node is calculated by characterizing the transmitted and receiving powers of the radio and calculating sleep time to predict the power consumption of the sensor node. Experiment presented in [5] analyzed the power consumption model for major components and the effective range of the sensor node. In [6], the authors explained the effect of power transition from sleep state to wake up state. Researchers in [7], analyzed the energy of the battery in which will help to predict the life time of the senor node in the WSN. This paper aims to model the energy behavior of the sensor node with dynamic power management technique and analyze the network throughput, delay and the other network related parameters. Analysis of the sensor node's energy with the other network parameters is useful to increase the network life time and to reduce the fault occurrence in the network. Fig.1 shows a sensor node comprising of processing unit, radio unit, sensors, ADC and an optional module of actuators. The power of sensor nodes is limited, mostly battery operated. Systematic analysis of the sensor nodes will be helpful to identify the power dissipation of the different parts of the system, which can be extremely useful for designing optimized sensor node characteristics. A major amount of power dissipation of the sensor node is due to processing and data transmission. The following section explains the typical system entities and constraints of a sensor node that affect its energy consumption.

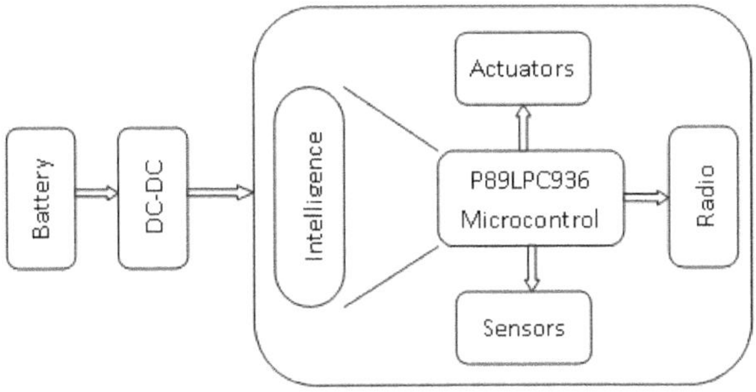

Fig. 1. Schematic of Sensor Node

3 Modeling of Energy Constraints of a Sensor Node

The modeling frameworks for energy consumption and fault analysis behavior significantly enhance the performance of the wireless sensor network [8]. In general microcontroller section of a sensor node will be helpful for the providing intelligence. Philips P89LPC936 microcontroller is used for the node with dynamic power management capability. This microcontroller receives the data from the sensor node through ADC channel, processes it and participates in data transmission through the radio channel. The received and processed data from sensor or from any other node is useful to provide the output through the actuator. The dynamic power management capability of the latest LPC900 series controller gives promising power reduction for low-end device applications.

Equation (1) shows the power relation among the characteristics of the processor [18]

$$P= CV^2f \tag{1}$$

In the above equation P indicates the power consumption of the processor which can be varied by three factors, namely total switching capacitance(C), Square of applied voltage (V) and clock frequency (f) respectively. Several commercial processors offer dynamic voltage and frequency scaling mechanism to reduce the power consumption. The main oscillator frequency (OSC_{CLK}) of the LPC936 can be scaled down to 510 times than that of the normal operating frequency [19].

$$C_{CLK} = OSC_{CLK}/2N \tag{2}$$

By configuring the 8 bit DIVM register (N), the output of the Core Clock (C_{CLK}) can be stepped down which is given by Equation [2].

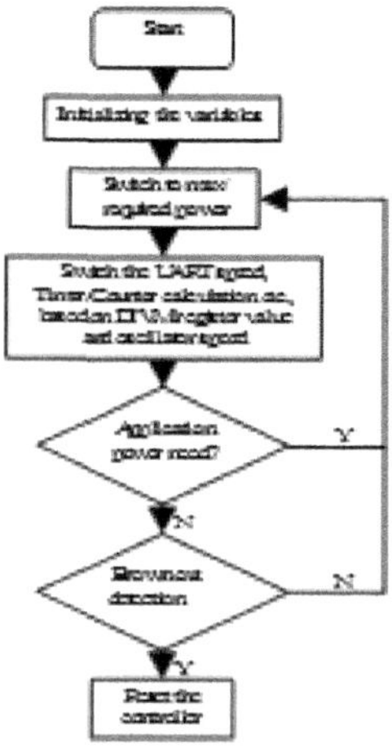

Fig. 2. Frequency Scaling Method

Fig. 3. Experimental Setup

3.1 Mechanism

The flow chart given below is an illustrative idea of how the low power consumption mechanism works out. When the program is initializes, the controller will be kept at the maximum frequency and starts processing. The peripheral values of the controller were set according to the clock speed of the controller, i.e., based on the CCLK value. Then the program checks for the application power needs which are based on the application power requirement. This mechanism also has additional feature of changing the speed of the controller by using the DIVM register value.

4 Experimental Setup

The experimental set up of our work uses a single sensor node constructed by using P89LPC936 microcontroller and XBee Zigbee module for data communication. The other XBee Zigbee module is connected with laptop through RS232 communication port. The Wireless protocol analyzer [16] is used to analyze the network parameters. Energy is measured using an integral type energy meter [17].

5 Result and Analysis

As a first attempt we tried the mechanism with the above mentioned experimental set up. The observations are made by varying the condition of DIVM. The condition of the delay and energy consumption of the sensor node during data communication by varying f_{CCLK} values is also observed in our work.

5.1 Delay, Throughput and Packet Loss Analysis

Node communication in wireless sensor network can also be analyzed using the delay parameter during packet transfer among nodes. Table 1 shows the results of energy, delay, packet loss and throughput for varied DIVM & f_{CCLK}. The results of delay analysis are illustrated in fig 4. Graphical observations reveal that delay is higher for lower amount of energy spent for communication and vice-versa. This result explains the conceptual understanding of dynamic power management for energy variations under frequency scaling technique.

Table 1. Delay, Throughput & Packet Loss Analysis

Idle Mode DIVM	f_{CCLK}	Energy (μJ)	Delay (ms)	Packet loss (213 packets)	Throughput
DIVM = 00h	11.059 MHz	32	1	4	98%
DIVM = 0Ah	553 kHz	19.9	2.6	14	93.5%
DIVM = 64h	55.3 kHz	4.6	2.75	16	92.5%
DIVM = FFh	21.7 kHz	4.5	2.9	16	92.5%

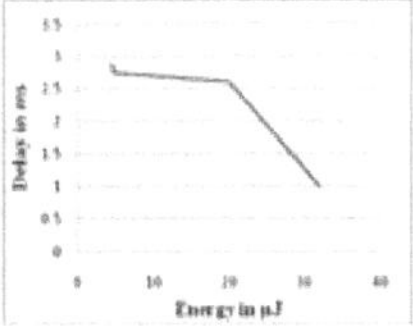
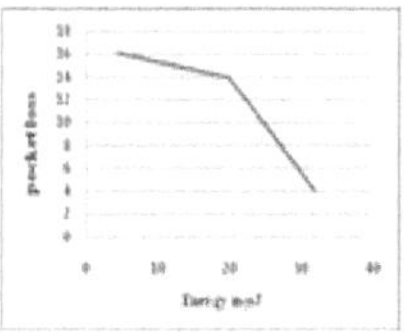
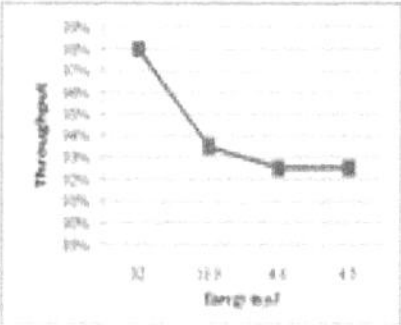

Fig. 4. Delay Vs Energy **Fig. 5.** Packet loss Vs Energy **Fig. 6.** Throughput Vs Energy

Fig. 6 shows the variation of throughput with energy. It can be found from the graph that higher energy spent over a node to communicate measures a higher throughput and a little reduction in throughput saves a higher amount of spent energy saved. From Fig 5, we observe that the packet loss is high for low energy and vice-versa. This result indicates the energy scavenging mechanism of our work. It also implies that this energy scavenging mechanism help dynamic power management of the node communication with not much variation of basic requirement of energy.

6 Conclusion and Future Scope

In this paper, we started with the aim of dynamic power management for an embedded device. We chose a sensor node as an example and conducted experiments for finding throughput, delay and packet loss for a selected communication process. The results of our experiment showed that the dynamic power management is an achievable phenomenon in an embedded environment. The proposed mechanism outperforms with respect to node and network parameters. The results also indicate the energy scavenging mechanism for a wireless sensor network environment. Our work measures the network and node parameters for a fixed node scenario and may be extended for scalability and random experimental conditions.

References

1. Min, R., Bhardwaj, M., Cho, S.-H., Shih, E., Sinha, A., Wang, A., Chandrakasan, A.: Low-Power Wireless Sensor Networks. IEEE (2000)
2. Feeney, L.M., Nilsson, M.: Investigating the Energy Consumption of a Wireless Network Interface in an Ad Hoc Networking Environment. In: Proceedings of Twentieth Annual Joint Conference of the IEEE Computer and Communications Societies, INFOCOM 2001, vol. 3, pp. 1548–1557. IEEE (2001)
3. Arms, S.W., Townsend, C.P., Churchill, D.L., Galbreath, J.H., Mundell, S.W.: Power Management for Energy Harvesting Wireless Sensors. In: SPIE Int'l Symposium on Smart Structures & Smart Materials, San Diego, CA, March 9 (2005)
4. Brownfield, M.I., Fayez, A.S., Nelson, T.M., Davis IV, N.: Cross-layer Wireless Sensor Network Radio Power Management. In: WCNC 2006 (2006)
5. Wang, Q., Hempstead, M., Yang, W.: A Realistic Power Consumption Model for Wireless Sensor Network Devices. In: 3rd Annual IEEE Communications Society on Sensor and Ad Hoc Communications and Networks, SECON 2006, pp. 286–295 (2006)

6. Alonso, J., Gómez, S., Alejandrez, M., Gil, M., Navarro, N.: Experimental Measurements of the Power Consumption for Wireless Sensor Networks June 26 (2006)
7. Behrens, C., Bischoff, O., Lueders, M., Laur, R.: Energy-efficient topology control for wireless sensor networks using online battery monitoring. Advances in Radio Science 5, 1–4 (2007)
8. Sarma Dhulipala, V.R., Aarthy, V., Chandrasekaran, R.M.: Energy and Fault Aware Management Framework for Wireless Sensor Network. In: Das, V.V., Vijayakumar, R., Debnath, N.C., Stephen, J., Meghanathan, N., Sankaranarayanan, S., Thankachan, P.M., Gaol, F.L., Thankachan, N. (eds.) BAIP 2010. CCIS, vol. 70, pp. 461–464. Springer, Heidelberg (2010)
9. Vijay, S., Sharma, S.C.: A Wireless Sensor Network for Distributed Fault Management in Power Systems. In: Proceedings of the World Congress on Engineering, WCE 2008, London, U.K, July 2-4, vol. III (2008)
10. Glaser, J., Weber, D., Madani, S.A., Mahlknecht, S.: Power Aware Simulation Framework for Wireless Sensor Networks and Nodes. EURASIP Journal on Embedded Systems, article ID 369178, 16 pages (2008), doi:10.1155/2008/369178
11. Santos, L.A.F., de Oliveira Marques, M., Bonatti, I.S.: Power-aware model for wireless sensor nodes
12. Khan, M.R.H., Passerone, R., Macii, D.: FZepel: RF-level Power Consumption Measurement (RF-PM) for Zigbee Wireless Sensor Network-Towards Cross Layer Optimization. In: IEEE International Conference on Emerging Technologies and Factory Automation, ETFA 2008, pp. 959–966 (2008)
13. Wang, X., Wang, S., Ma, J.-J., Bi, D.-W.: Energy-efficient Organization of Wireless Sensor Networks with Adaptive Forecasting. Sensors 8, 2604–2616 (2008)
14. Xing, G., Sha, M., Hackmann, G., Klues, K., Chipara, O., Lu, C.: Towards unified radio power management for wireless sensor networks. In: Wireless Communications and Mobile Computing. Wiley InterScience (2008)
15. Alippi, C., Anastasi, G., Di Francesco, M., Roveri, M.: Energy Management in Wireless Sensor Networks with Energy-hungry Sensors. IEEE Instrumentation & Measurement Magazine 12(2), 16–23 (2009)
16. `http://www.silabs.com/products/wireless/EZRadio/Pages/WirelessDevelopmentSuite.aspx`
17. Konstantakos, V., Kosmatopoulos, K., Nikolaidis, S., Laopoulos, T.: In-Chip Configuration for Monitoring Power Consumption in Micro-processing Systems. In: IEEE Workshop on Intelligent Data Acquisition and Advanced Computing Systems: Technology and Applications, Sofia, Bulgaria, September 5-7 (2005)
18. Chandrakasan, Sheng, S., Brodersen, R. W.: Low-power CMOS design. IEEE Journal of Solid-State Circuits, 472–484 (April 1992)
19. `http://ics.nxp.com/support/techdocs/microcontrollers/pdf/errata.p89lpc935.pdf`

Integrating Data Mining and AHP for Life Insurance Product Recommendation

Pradeep Kumar* and Dilbag Singh

Dept. of Computer Science & Application, Ch Devi Lal University, Sirsa (HR), India
pk_indya@yahoo.com

Abstract. Product recommendation is critical in attracting customers particularly in life insurance where the company has multiple options for the customer. Accordingly, improving the quality of a recommendation to fulfill customers' needs is important in competitive environments. Although various recommendation systems have been proposed, few have addressed the lifetime value of a customer to a firm. We developed a two-stage product recommendation methodology that combines data mining techniques and analytic hierarchy process (AHP) for decision-making. Firstly clustering technique was applied to group customers according to the age and income because these two are very important in deciding insurance product. Secondly the AHP was then applied to each cluster to determine the relative weights of various variables in evaluating the suitable product for them.

Keywords: Data mining, clustering, AHP, insurance.

1 Introduction

The life insurance company in India has multiple options for the customer. The insurance companies interacts the customer through its agent. The agent recommends the product on his own basis. But there is need to recommend right product to the customer as per their need.Recently, IT has been utilized to help companies maintain competitive advantage. Data mining techniques [12] are a widely used information technology for extracting marketing knowledge and further supporting marketing decisions [2, 3]. The applications include market basket analysis, retail sales analysis, and market segmentation analysis. Lin et al. [4] applied data mining techniques to extract inter-organizational retailing knowledge from POS information in retail store chains. Moreover, Hui and Jha[5] employed it to provide customer service support. The knowledge can support marketing decisions and customer relationship management.The buying patterns of individual customers and groups can be identified via analyzing customer data [6], but also allows a company to develop one-to-one marketing strategies that provide individual marketing decisions for each

* Corresponding author.

V.V. Das and N. Thankachan (Eds.): CIIT 2011, CCIS 250, pp. 596–602, 2011.

customer [7]. Recommender systems are technologies that assist businesses to implement such strategies. They have emerged in e-commerce applications to support product recommendation [8]. The systems use customer purchase history to determine preferences and identify products that a customer may wish to purchase. Generally, recommender systems increase the probability of crossselling; establish customer loyalty; and fulfill customer needs by discovering products in which they may be interested.Our work proposes a two-stage product recommendation methodology that combines data mining and AHP [1]. Since there are different segments of customers and each segment's customer need is different. Therefore clustering was applied to group customers based on their age and income. The analytic hierarchy process (AHP) [13] was applied to each cluster to evaluate the importance (weight) of each variable in evaluating the suitable product for them.

2 Techniques Used

2.1 Clustering

Clustering [10] seeks to maximize variance among groups while minimizing variance within groups. Many clustering algorithms have been developed, including K-means, hierarchical, fuzzy c-means, etc. We used the K-means method to group customers with similar age and income. K-means clustering [11] is a method commonly used to partition a set of data into groups. *K*-means clustering algorithm was developed by MacQueen and then by Hartigan and Wong. *K*-means is the simplest and most popular classical clustering method that is easy to implement. *K*-means clustering is an algorithm that classifies or groups objects based on attributes/features into *K* number of groups [12]. *K* is a positive integer. The grouping is done by minimizing the sum of squares of distances between data and the corresponding cluster centroid.

2.2 AHP

The Analytic Hierarchy Process (AHP) [9] is a structured technique for organizing and analyzing complex decisions. It has particular application in group decision making, and is used around the world in a wide variety of decision situations, in fields such as government, business, industry, healthcare, and education.

AHP is modeled into four steps

1. Structuring of the Decision Problem into a Hierarchical Model
2. Making Pair-wise Comparisons and obtaining the Judgmental Matrix
3. Local priorities and Consistency of Comparisons
4. Aggregation of Local Priorities

Step 1: Structuring of the Decision Problem into a Hierarchical Model -Most common models have at least three levels, although more levels could be included. The topmost level is the `focus' of the problem. The intermediate levels correspond to criteria and sub-criteria. The lowest level contains the `decision alternatives'.

Step 2: Making Pair-wise Comparisons and obtaining the Judgmental Matrix - The Elements of a particular level are compared pair-wise, w.r.t a specific element in the immediate upper level. Criteria are compared with respect to the focus first. Then alternatives are compared with respect to each of the Criteria.. A judgmental matrix, denoted as *A*, will be formed using the comparisons. Each entry a_{ij} of the judgmental matrix is formed comparing the row element A_i with the column element A_j. The semantic scale used in AHP is given below. "Of the two criteria Ci and Cj, which is more important with respect to a best product and how much more?" The scale is given in table 1.

Table 1. Semantic scale

Intensity of Importance	Definition
1	Equal Importance
3	Weak Importance of *Ci* over *Cj*
5	Essential or Strong Importance
7	Demonstrated Importance
9	Absolute Importance
2,4,6,8	Intermediate
Reciprocals of the above judgments	If *Ci* has one of the above judgments assigned to it when compared with *Cj*, then *Cj* has the reciprocal value when compared with *Ci*

Step 3: Local priorities (w^T) and Consistency of Comparisons-Local priorities are calculated by using Logarithmic Least Square Method (LLSM). In this we firstly compute the geometric mean of the elements of each row. After that we normalise the row geometric means (RGM). And finally the normalised geometric mean vector gives the local priorities. The consistency of the judgmental matrix can be determined by a measure called the consistency ratio (CR), defined in formula 1 below

$$CR= CI/RI \tag{1}$$

Where CI is called the Consistency Index and RI, the Random Index. CI is defined in formula 2.

$$CI= (\lambda_{max} - n)/(n-1) \tag{2}$$

Compute the product Aw^T. Compute λmax using the formula 3,

$$\lambda_{max} = \frac{1}{n}\sum_{i=1}^{n} \frac{i\text{th entry in } Aw^T}{i\text{th entry in } w^T} \tag{3}$$

RI is the consistency index of a randomly generated reciprocal matrix from the nine-point scale, with reciprocals forced. Saaty [9] has provided average consistencies (RI values) of randomly generated matrices for a sample size of 500. The RI values are given in table 2.

Table 2. RI values

Size	1	2	3	4	5	6	7	8	9	10
RI	0.00	0.00	0.58	0.90	1.12	1.24	1.32	1.41	1.45	1.49

Generally, a consistency ratio of 0.10 or less is considered acceptable. If the value is higher, the judgements may not be reliable and have to be elicited again.Step 4: Aggregation of Local Priorities -The Local priorities of elements of different levels are aggregated to obtain final priorities of the alternatives. The final priorities represent the rating of the alternatives in achieving the focus. Final Priority (F) can be calculated as given in formula-4.

$$F=\sum_i(\text{Local priority of Ci w.r.t. the goal*Local priority of product w.r.t. Ci}) \quad (4)$$

3 Methodology

3.1 Stage-I: Clustering

On the basis of interview of insurance agent 42 sample data was prepared on the basis of age and annual income of the customer. Data was classified by applying the clustering data mining techniques using SPSS. The clusters identified are mentioned in Table 3.

Table 3. Clustering of data

Cluster Number of Case			Age	Annual Income (Rs)
1	N	Valid	16	16
	Mean		25.38	3.32
2	N	Valid	14	14
	Mean		36.00	6.25
3	N	Valid	12	12
	Mean		46.00	8.77

Three clusters were identified with mean age 25.38, 36.00, 46.00 and mean income 3.32 Lakh, 6.25Lakh, 8.77 Lakh respectively. Out of 42 records 16 belongs to cluster-1, 14 belongs to cluster-2, and 12 belongs to cluster-3.

3.2 Stage-II: Appling AHP to Each Cluster

Step 1: As different customer had different needs, so there is need to apply AHP [14] for each cluster. The various levels for the selection of a particular life insurance product were identified by interviewing the agents. On the information collected, hierarchy (Fig-1) was built.

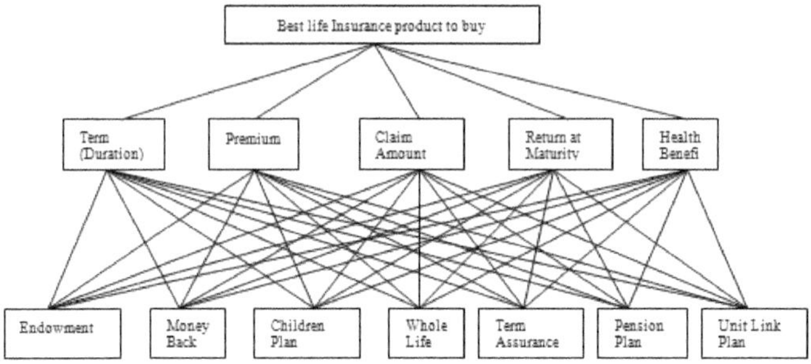

Fig. 1. Hierarchy for life insurance product

Cluster-1 (mean age 25.38 and mean income 3.32 Lakh)

Step-1 of AHP was common for the entire three clusters and has been described above.

Step 2&3: Eight insurance agents did the pair wise comparisons and filled judgmental matrix and their average rounded value were considered for final judgmental matrix. Local priorities were calculated and are mentioned in table 4 and 5.

Table 4. Judgemental matrix and local priorities for best insurance product

Best Product	Term	Premium	Claim Amt.	Return	Health Benefit	Local priorities
Term	1	0.333333	0.5	0.16666	0.5	0.064455
Premium	3	1	0.25	0.33333	2	0.132058
Claim Amt.	2	4	1	0.25	3	0.233951
Return	6	3	4	1	5	0.485532
Health Benefit	2	0.5	0.333333	0.2	1	0.0840037
	CR =0.090					

The consistency of the judgmental matrix were determined by a measure called the consistency ratio (CR) as described in formula-1.

Similarly the pair wise comparisons were done for criteria at middle level in the hierarchy and corresponding judgmental matrix were obtained. Local priorities and CR were calculated and are listed in table 5.

Table 5. Local priority and CR value of rest criteria

	Term (Duration)	Premium	Claim amt	Return at maturity	Health benefit
Local Priorities	0.125451	0.198739	0.172257	0.203503	0.172855
	0.216279	0.0527988	0.0772431	0.0988335	0.0701687
	0.102674	0.0630709	0.054902	0.0582797	0.115785
	0.052767	0.163669	0.210573	0.0480091	0.257145
	0.143411	0.29435	0.295833	0.0405656	0.114084
	0.073738	0.129384	0.105412	0.188869	0.209774
	0.285679	0.0979887	0.0837791	0.36194	0.060189
CR	0.093	0.090	0.080	0.051	0.080

Step 4: The Local priorities of elements at different levels are aggregated to obtain final priorities of the alternatives. As the final priority of **unit linked plan (ULIP) and endowment plans are higher**, so these are more suitable for them. Final results of this cluster are shown in table 6.

Table 6. Final Priorities of cluster-1

Best Product	Term	Premium	Claim Amount	Return at Maturity	Health Benefit	Final Priority
Endowment	(0.064*0.125)+(0.132*0.198)+(0.233*0.172)+(0.485*0.203)+(0.084*0.172)					0.187
Money Back	(0.064*0.216)+(0.132*0.052)+(0.233*0.077)+(0.485*0.098)+(0.084*0.070)					0.092
Childrn Plan	(0.064*0.102)+(0.132*0.063)+(0.233*0.054)+(0.485*0.058)+(0.084*0.115)					0.065
Whole Life	(0.064*0.052)+(0.132*0.163)+(0.233*0.210)+(0.485*0.048)+(0.084*0.257)					0.118
Term Plan	(0.064*0.143)+(0.132*0.294)+(0.233*0.295)+(0.485*0.040)+(0.084*0.114)					0.146
Pension Plan	(0.064*0.073)+(0.132*0.129)+(0.233*0.105)+(0.485*0.188)+(0.084*0.209)					0.155
Unit Linked	(0.064*0.285)+(0.132*0.097)+(0.233*0.083)+(0.485*0.361)+(0.084*0.060)					0.231

Similarly all the steps of AHP were applied for clusre-2 and cluster-3. Final results of these clusters are shown in table 7.

Table 7. Final Priorities of cluster-2&3

Best Product	Final Priority	Final Priority
Endowment	0.119	0.151
Money Back	0.064	0.068
Children Plan	0.183	0.142
Whole Life	0.195	0.138
Term Plan	0.220	0.155
Pension Plan	0.131	0.258
Unit Linked	0.085	0.084

As the final priority of the cluster-2 customers, **term, whole life and children plans are higher** than the others, so these can be recommended. Cluster-3 customers normally think about old age days. As per their need and requirements the **pension plan, term and endowment plans are more suitable**.

4 Conclusions

Our work involved the two-stage recommendation methodology that combines clustering and AHP methods. It clustered customers into segments according to their age and income. Moreover, clustering customers into different groups not only improves the quality of recommendation but also helps decision-makers identify market segments more clearly and thus develop more effective strategies. . AHP was then applied to determine the relative importance of variables and to calculate the local and final priorities. Unit linked and endowment plans are suitable for Cluster-1 type customers. Term, whole life and children plans are suitable for cluster-2 type customers. Pension plan, term and endowment plans are suitable for cluster-3 type customers.

References

1. Liu, D.-R., Shih, Y.-Y.: Integrating AHP and data mining for product recommendation based on customer lifetime value. Information & Management 42, 387–400 (2005)
2. Bose, I., Mahapatra, R.K.: Business data mining-a machine learning perspective. Information and Management 39(3), 211–225 (2001)
3. Brachman, R.J., Khabaza, T., Kloesgen, W., Simoudis, E.: Mining business databases. Communications of the ACM 39(11), 42–48 (1996)
4. Lin, Q.Y., Chen, Y.L., Chen, J.S., Chen, Y.C.: Mining inter organizational retailing knowledge for an alliance formed by competitive firms. Information and Management 40(5), 431–442 (2003)
5. Hui, S.C., Jha, G.: Data mining for customer service support. Information and Management 38(1), 1–13 (2000)
6. Wells, J.D., Fuerst, W.L., Choobineh, J.: Managing information technology (IT) for one-to-one customer interaction. Information and Management 35(1), 53–62 (1999)
7. Peppers, D., Rogers, M.: The One to One Future: Building Relationships One Customer at a Time. Bantam Doubleday Dell Publishing (1997)
8. Schafer, J.B., Konstan, J.A., Riedl, J.: E-commerce recommendation applications. Journal of Data Mining and Knowledge Discovery 5(1-2), 115–152 (2001)
9. Saaty, T.L.: Fundamentals of Decision Making and Priority Theory with the Analytic Hierarchy Process. RWS Publications, Pittsburgh (1994)
10. Punj, G.N., Stewart, D.W.: Cluster analysis in marketing research: review and suggestions for application. Journal of Marketing Research 20, 134–148 (1983)
11. MacQueen, J.B.: Some methods for classification and analysis of multivariate observations. In: Proceedings of the Fifth Berkeley Symposium on Mathematical Statistics and Probability, pp. 281–296 (1967)
12. Gupta, G.K.: Introduction to data mining with case studies. PHI private ltd. (2008)
13. Cheng, C., Chen, Y., Li, T.: An AHP Method for Road Traffic Safety. In: Fourth International Joint Conference on Computational Sciences and Optimization, pp. 305–308. IEEE (2011)
14. Ding, C., Li, L.: AHP Application in Objective Management of Coal Enterprises. In: 2010 International Conference on E-Business and E-Government, pp. 2635–2638. IEEE (2010)

Optimization of Conventional Bench through Skill Index Based Virtual Bench Approach

B.R. Shubhamangala and L. Manjunatha Rao

Dayananda Sagar Institutions, Bangalore-560078, Karnataka, India
brm1shubha@gmail.com, manjuarjun2004@yahoo.com

Abstract. In any Information Technology (IT) service organization up to 70% success of project is based upon the utilization factor of knowledge and experience of its niche technical staff. In IT organization, staff who does not have project on hand are moved to a reserve pool called 'bench'. Bench period of each benched employee varies from a few days to a couple of months. Bench period is non billable. Longer the bench period, greater is the threat to profitability of company. Longer bench period also results in staff attrition. Very short bench period encounters feeble staff availability which becomes peril towards organization's growth. Non filtering of niche employees from others and improper system to judge skills, uncertainty in job allocation date and uncertain bench duration for benched employees are creating employee dissatisfaction and staff attrition. Present IT industry requires a system which can optimize existing conventional bench and address the problems of bench effectively. Catering to the above stated requirement, this paper presents a new approach called "skill index based Virtual Bench", which addresses the conventional bench issues effectively. Staff index adaptively measures the knowledge and skills of staff and niche employees can be filtered. The approach has been validated through a case study in a medium size IT organization. Results are highly responsive towards the aim of approach. It can be concluded that virtual bench approach is viable to be implemented.

Keywords: Bench, Virtual Bench, Skill Index, Niche Employees.

1 Introduction

For any Information Technology (IT) service organization technical staffs are the prime asset apart from being the major part of work force [1]. In IT organization, the employees who get released from the project are moved to an internal resource pool called 'bench'. The staffs who are newly recruited and not been assigned to any project are also moved to bench. Hence bench possesses staffs those does not have project on hand. Bench serves as primary internal staff buffer. Whenever there is a need of staffing either towards a new project or towards current project, resource manager (RM)'s prime choice of staff allocation is primarily from bench. Always 6-10% of bench strength [2] is desirable for the stability of organization. Client is the critical stake holder [3] of the IT organization. Bench potential is one of the major factors considered in the project agreement between the client and organization.

V.V. Das and N. Thankachan (Eds.): CIIT 2011, CCIS 250, pp. 603–614, 2011.

Bench potential is critical focus domain of client before assigning project to company. Though bench sounds to be an asset, the current industry bench is resonating with certain issues. If these issues are not addressed properly, bench turns out to be a liability from being an asset to the organization.

1.1 Current Industry Issues with Bench

Up-to-date report visibility on benched staff skill, number and date of entry into bench is poor. Poor visibility is leading to ineffective resource management. Bench duration and date from which benched staff will be assigned to forthcoming projects is not assessed accurately, which is leading to staff attrition and uncertainty in job profile. Irrespective of performance level and skill level all employees who does not have project on hand are moved to bench. Due to non recognition of productive employees from others in the bench, employee dissatisfaction rate is increasing which is affecting the productivity of the company [4]. When niche employees are anchored to bench, though they are paid by the organization, the chance of quitting the organization is bright due to idle hours at bench. According to industry statistics 80% of company revenue and profit is produced by 20% of the workforce which is comprised by niche skilled employees [5]. The niche skilled staffs are the top revenue producers is an apparent fact in the IT industry and organization needs an approach which can ensure reduction in attrition rate especially of niche employees because of bench. Though there are existing tools and techniques such as the Project Evaluation and Review Technique (PERT), the Critical Path Method (CPM), Gantt diagrams, work allotment excel sheets and Earned Value Analysis, all of which can help to plan, track project milestones and staffing allotment, these tools and techniques have limitations in solving current bench issues such as

1. Assessing accurately the skill set of staff.
2. Efficient allotment of right skill set staff to right work.
3. Assessing accurately current and future bench strength.
4. Efficient handling of bench duration and strength.

This paper is divided into seven sections. The first one comprises this introduction. The second section gives a glimpse of related work in the area of our research. Section 3 focuses on problem definition and our approach to solve the problem. In Section 4 current bench functioning with its limitations are discussed. In Section 5 a unique way to calculate staff skill index which can assess staff in multi dimension is given. A new technique called virtual bench to address the limitations is explained in section 6. This section also showcases a graphical study which is being planned to evaluate the viability of the virtual bench approach. Finally, in Section 7 we present a case study, analysis of results and section 8 deals with conclusion.

2 Related Work

We could not find much research work related to the area of bench recourses in IT industry.

There have been a number of attempts to use skill set as one of the parameter in predicting project success rate. Shendil K, Madhavji N.H [6] to estimate human performance in the software process is studied using analytical model. In this paper personal skills are assessed only by line of code and percentage of errors. Critical qualities such as leadership, team work, efficiency which are the integral part of personal skill assessment have not been explored. James R. Rowland[7] have modeled the fine-grid model focusing on five component blocks to assess the overall continuous improvement of software project process, in multi disciplinary teams. The model does not address the important topic of individual student assessment for working on teams, but instead focuses on the overall process of multidisciplinary team experiences. Our work differs in a way that we have considered skill set matrix for each employee. Skill set matrix consists of parameters which focuses on essential skills apart from technical skills that an employee can possess to excel in the work performance. The parameters of skill set matrix are called competency parameters and are well aligned with business the motive of organization. Individuals are rated through competency parameters and awarded a value called skill index. An experimental study is taken up to substantiate all the above concepts we have presented in the paper.

3 Problem Definition

The prime issue addressed by this paper is how to revolutionize the conventional bench existing in the industry to suit the modern demanding needs of organization. This paper is focusing on other two issues which are aligned with prime issue. The first issue is to figure out niche skilled employees and their availability from the pool of large workforce. Second issue is how to avoid anchoring of niche employees to bench, so that attrition due to bench is reduced.

3.1 Approach

This paper introduces staff skill Index (SI) a new approach to assess, grade the entire workforce. Through SI niche skilled employees from workforce are figured out. Virtual bench technique is introduced to revolutionize the conventional bench. The novelty of the paper lies in contributing a novel approach called virtual bench. Case study is used to observe effects on benefit and operating margin in organization by adopting virtual bench.

4 Conventional Bench

In the existing IT scenario, upon the successful completion of the work assigned, staffs are moved to bench. Newly recruited staff, but not assigned to any project are also moved to bench. The resource manager, who is in charge of bench, allocates staff to different projects as per the need received from project managers. Staff allocation is based on general assessment and feedback from previous project. Once the work gets completed in current assigned project, again those staffs are moved to bench. This process is cumulative. The operation of conventional bench explained above is given in figure1.

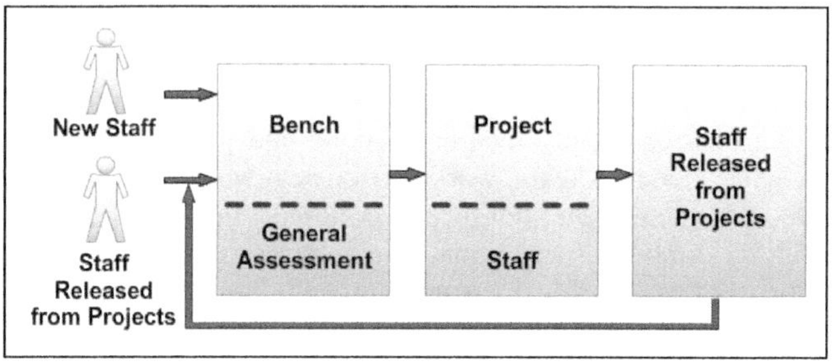

Fig. 1. Conventional Bench Operation

The "bench" is a business necessity in the IT industry to keep a skilled workforce ready for any immediate project requirement, quickly without waiting for recruitment. Although bench sounds as an asset to IT organization, it proves to be liability if not revived from current operational handling of benched employees. Bench duration varies from a few days to a couple of months. Longer the duration of bench, niche staffs who are in level 3 and level 4grade (according to staff skill index), may quit the organization creating skill drain. Long bench duration is also a threat to profitability of company, since bench duration is not billable. Very short bench period encounters feeble skilled staff resource which becomes peril to company for any immediate project requirement. Present IT service industry is trying to work out minimal, critical and highly fit bench strength. Industry is oriented towards a model bench which can retain good performers and niche skills on the bench. Bench must also be able to filter effectively, low performers or those who show no inclination to get themselves a billable role. Since low performers are a non-productive resource, such benched employees can be retrenched in an effort to reduce cost. Once the niche employees are figured out in the large workforce of the organization, the technological, managerial skills and over-all ability enhancement training can be implemented only for the niche benched employee for the forthcoming projects. Bench must also be able to forecast the number, skill index and date of staff entering into bench based on actual transactions in current project development and budgeted revenues. All the above stated requirements are addressed by optimizing the conventional bench through a new concept of bench, called "Virtual bench".

5 Staff Skill Index

Constantly changing market conditions demand proactive staff. When the skills, competencies and goals of high quality workforce are aligned with right task company wide, can enhance company brand by driving it to the pool of 'Best in Class' company cadre. Hence organization requires a technique to identify, track and rate high potential and high quality performers. This requirement can be achieved by a new concept called "Staff Skill Index", derived from skill set matrix. Skill set matrix consists of parameters, which identifies wide range of technology skills needed, apart from managerial skills and inter personal skills for an employee [8][9] to emerge as an efficient successful personality . Parameters are called as *competency parameters [10]*. Though staff skill matrix is very specific to the role of employee and project needs, skill matrix attributes can be tailor made by program manager, the chief of project under process for different cadres of employees namely developers, analysts, architects, test engineers..etc. In this paper we are considering skill set matrix comprising of fifteen competency parameters only for project managers and is given in table 1.

Table 1. Staff Skill Set Matrix

Technical skills	Business and leadership skills	Personal skills
Proficiency in project core technology	Business acumen and effective role model	Analytical and conceptual thinking
Initiate, plan, execute and control capability	Team motivation and mentoring ability	Customer service orientation
Process, product, patent and intellectual property knowledge	Leadership through vision and rapid team development.	Organizational awareness and commitment
Designing and goal setting ability, result orientation,	Align employee objectives with business objectives	Ability to address and anticipate issues
Ability to prepare comprehensive technical specifications	Business operations knowledge and collaborative team culture	Honesty, integrity, self aware and achievement orientation

The core skills needed for project manager is considered and categorized into three sections namely technical, personal, business and leadership skills as shown in table 1.

Table 2. Skill Index

	Level 0	Level 1	Level 2	Level 3	Level 4
Skill index	1-3	4-5	6-7.5	7.5-9	10
Category	Poor Performer	Awareness	Practitioner	Expert	Innovator
Description	Performance level not satisfactory	Inside learning and gaining experience cube.	Meets position requirements.	Exceeds position requirements	Exceptional. Exceed all requirements all the time

Each section has a list competency parameters, to judge the capability of the project manager under study Project managers are assessed against each parameter given, based on project performance and personality traits. The rating ranges from 1 to 10 numeric values, where rating 10 is the highest and rating 1 is the lowest, and is awarded for each parameter based on evaluation. Individual ratings for all 15 stated parameters are taken, summed up and average is calculated .The calculated average which is a numerical value is called" *Skill Index*". Skill index will be in the range of 0-10 numeric value and the range is divided into five different levels starting from level 0 to level 4 as depicted in table 2.Based on levels, project managers are classified into five different categories namely poor performer, awareness, practitioner [11], expert and innovator as given in table 2.For other staffs belonging to cadre of developers, architects, testers, analysis's..etc, project manager can set skill set matrix, rate and assign grades to them.

6 Virtual Bench

Consider the virtual bench model given in fig 2.The model includes skill assessment block, optimization block, virtual bench, and decision bench and organization policy block. Skill assessment block contains skill set matrix data base. The operational flow of the model is explained as below.

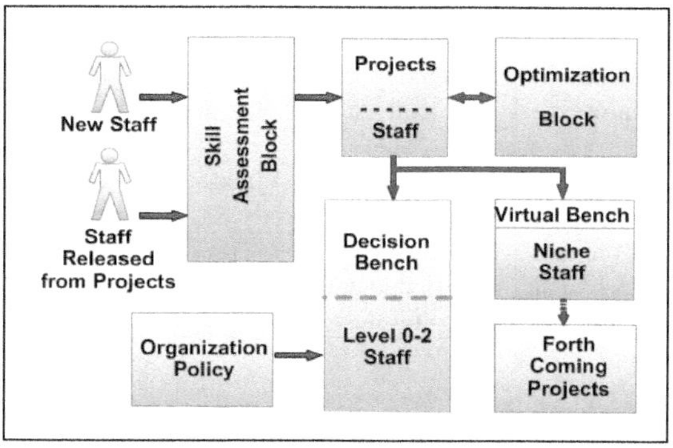

Fig. 2. Virtual Bench Model

Skill Assessment Block: Based on wide range of managerial, behavioral, technical and conceptual knowledge based skills which are crucial for successful achievement of goals in the organization, competency parameters are identified. Once competency parameters are identified, it is mapped to specific roles and responsibilities of employees in the organization, which gives raise to skill set matrix. Such cluster of skill set matrix specified for each role in the organization is stored in data base named skill set matrix database. The newly recruited staff and existing staff those have got released from project are moved to skill assessment block. Each employee in accordance with the role assigned is assessed based on skill set matrix and skill index is awarded. Based on skill index, as given in table 2 staffs are classified into level 0 to level 4 and classified data is fed to projects block.

Projects Block: Project block contains list of new projects. It also contains the number of staff required, optimum skill level, technical knowledge and other essential parameters such as scheduled time and cost allocation. etc to start the project. Requirements of the projects are mapped to the data fed by skill assessment block and staffs are assigned to projects. For each employee estimated time duration to complete the delegated work is noted. The estimated time duration is divided into three zones namely, ramp up, intermediate and ramp down. Time zone allotment is as shown in table 3. Ramp up zone is from 0 to 25%, intermediate zone is from 25% to 75% and ramp down zone is from 75% to 100% of estimated time respectively. Data containing particulars of staffs allotted to projects and estimated time is fed to optimization block.

Optimization Block: In this block employees work pattern and project progress is accounted. Successful completion of the project within the allotted time is the most critical factor which drives the project towards success and there by the organization. In the ramp up stage which is ranging from 0 to 25% of time, project progress will be slowly increasing and in the intermediate stage project progress must gain required momentum, in order for the project to get completed well within or at the end of ramp down stage. Hence it is essential to find the work completion percentage at the junction of intermediate stage meeting with the beginning of ramp down stage. Eventually this junction is at 75% of allotted time and this point is named as *threshold point*. . Whether the project will be completed within the allotted time or not can be assessed by taking work completion percentage at threshold point. At the threshold point if work completion percentage is in the range of 68-75% or above 75%of total allotted work, then it can be assessed that allotted work for that employee will be completed well within the allotted time and the employee is efficient and competent. To assess the project progress and successful completion, each employees work pattern is taken and plotted against the allotted time A sample graph of an employee work completion progress against allotted time zone is given in fig 3. At the threshold point, statistics comprising of percentage of completed work, staff release date, skill index in present project, exhibited proficiency, new technique learnt...etc for each employee is taken. Updated data is stored.

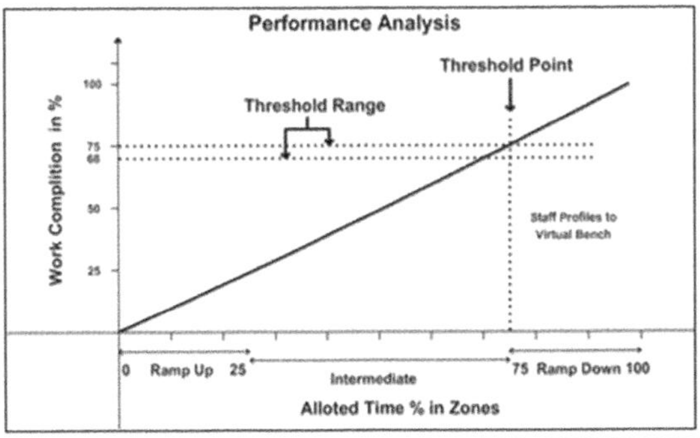

Table 3. Mapping of work performance against time zone

Work performance Percentage %	Time zone
0-25	Ramp up
25-75	Intermediate
75-100	Ramp down

Work Completion%	Allotted time in %	Work Completion%	Allotted time in %
10	11	75	64
20	23	80	73
40	33.5	85	82
50	44	90	91
60	54	100	98

Fig. 3. Sample graph of staff work completion against allotted time zone

Data regarding updated skill index and work completion percentage is taken. From the data, apart from assessing the project success, niche employees can be figured out by checking the data against two conditions namely Is skill index is greater than or equal to 7.5 (i.e skill grade level3 and level 4) and work completion percentage is falling in the range of 68- 75% or above. The staff those meet both the conditions are considered as niche employees. Thus niche employees who are the assets to company are caught. Once Niche employees are identified, they are moved to virtual bench block. The staff those who are not able to satisfy the, conditions to enter into virtual bench, are allowed to continue in the project and are moved to decision bench after the completion of current project.

Virtual Bench Block: Virtual bench block contains niche employees and they are allowed to continue with the current project till completion. By estimating the release date of such staff from current project, virtual bench strength, skill potential and availability date of niche employees is accurately estimated. This estimation helps to assign staffs to forthcoming projects in the pipeline without idle time. Thus forecasted project date, role and required skills are intimated to each niche employee well before the completion of current project. Once the current project gets completed, virtual bench staff is moved to the respective allotted projects without idle period. Required skill set of forecasted project against the current skill set of virtual benched staff is analyzed and if any skill gap is found, training to fill the gap can be implemented to such employees. This makes organization robust by equipping to take up any challenging projects and also drives the organization to be one of Class A cadre organizations.

Decision Bench and Organization Policy Block: Statistics for decision bench staffs are also taken and to which level (as stated in Table 2) they belong to is calculated. Organization policy block contains the policy of organization and policies are fed to decision bench block. Organization can handle such employees in its own way suiting to the requirements of organization according to the organization policy. Employees who need support and counseling at times can be identified by decision bench. This is the best phase when organizations can focus on soft skills, technical skills and personal skill enhancement trainings, so that their existing workforce in decision bench can also be enabled to move to virtual bench.

Table 4. Virtual Bench against Conventional Bench

Conventional Bench	Virtual Bench
Buffer which holds staff without on hand projects	Buffer which holds niche staff who are currently working on projects which are on the verge of completion.
Holds level 0 to level 4	Holds only niche performers
Highest ambiguity regarding future project work assignment.	Forthcoming project assignment date is delegated to staff well in advance while working on current project.
Bench duration cannot be assessed accurately. Prolonged bench duration	No idle duration
Work assignment based on general assessment.	Work assignment strictly based on skill index

By implementing virtual bench organization can hold only expert professional staff. This leads to tangible organization Cause and benefit analysis of implementing virtual bench. Virtual bench potential can be well understood by comparative study against conventional bench as given in table 4.

7 Case Study-Result and Analysis

Virtual bench approach was introduced in a medium sized product based software organization, for a period of three months with the aim of testing the viability and practical benefits of implementing the model. Projects were below $50, 00,000 budget. Team size was 14.Project budget type is fixed price project [12]. During this period effects of implementing virtual bench was studied. Profit (return on investment) for three projects were studied and compared to other projects where conventional bench was existing. Observed data of the projects is given in table 5and table 6.

Table 5. Analysis of projects embedded with Virtual bench against conventional bench

	Virtual bench			Conventional bench		
Projects →	P1	P2	P3	P4	P5	P6
Values in $ →	V1	V2	V3	V4	V5	V6
Total Billing	50,00,000	49,50,000	48,00,000	50,00,000	49,50,000	48,00,000
Operational Cost ↓						
Skill index & decision team effort	1,10,000	89100	1,03,200	1,03,950	1,04,370	1,01,920
Development cost	35,62,784	34,77,375	34,01,280	3,513,500	3475040	3582880
Risk factor	2,00,000	1,93,050	1,96,800	1,98,000	193550	205800
Training cost	1,02,400	1,01,600	1,01,600	1,00,765	107310	111230
Total cost	39,75,184	38,61,125	38,02,880	3916215	3880270	4001830
Gross Operating margin	10,24,816	10,88,875	9,97,120	1033785	1019730	898170
Effort saved due to early completion (VB gain)	1,90,840	209144.26	178260	0	0	0
Net operating Margin	12,15,216	1298019.3	1175380	10,33,785	1019730	898170
% profit	24.31%	26.22%	24.48%	20.88%	20.81%	18.33%

Metrics

Development cost	Prime cost+ overhead cost+ Direct cost+ infrastructure cost
Training cost	(Number of staff). Number of training hours.(staff billing rate per hour + trainer billing rate /hour)
Operating margin	Billing cost - Operating cost
Effort Saved	(Effort hours saved due to efficient reuse of module and technical expertise). Cost of production per hour
Attrition rate	(No of niche employees left /Total staff allotted for the project).100

7.1 Profit Analysis of Virtual Bench

Virtual bench(VB) is technology initiative. By practical results it is evident that VB yields tangible and non tangible benefits. To evaluate VB initiatives in terms financial value to the organization profit analysis is considered. Evaluation is based on cost, savings, strategic benefits and risks factors of projects under study. As there are different criteria to measure profit and multiple ways to quantify profit through calculation of operating margin [13], the measurement of profit vary from organization to organization. According to the organization specifications where experimental study on virtual bench was conducted, attributes for profit is taken and analysis is given in Table 6. Graph corresponding to profit analysis is given in figure 4.

Table 6. Comparison of profit for virtual bench and conventional bench approach

	Projects with Virtual Bench			Projects with Conventional Bench		
Projects	P1	P2	P3	P4	P5	p6
Total Billing in billion $	50	49.5	48	49.5	49	49
Profit %	24.3	26.22	24.48	20.88	20.81	18.33

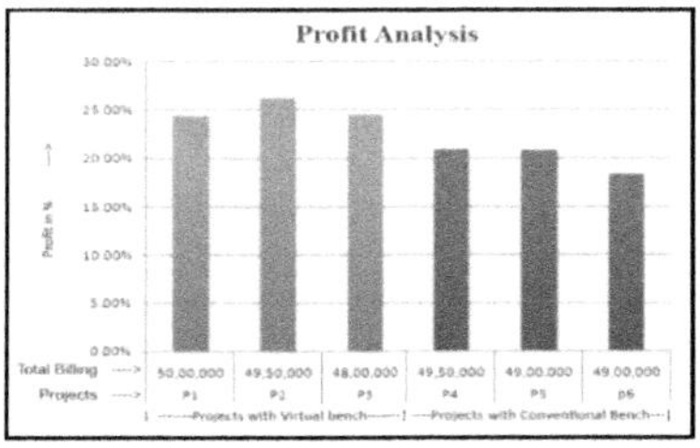

Fig. 4. Attrition Rate Analysis

From table 5,6 and figure 4, it is evident that projects embedded with virtual bench has more profit than

The projects embedded with conventional bench.

7.2 Attrition Rate

Attrition rate [14] was observed for a period of three months in three projects embedded with virtual bench and is compared with attrition rate of conventional bench projects. Remarkable reduction in niche staff attrition rate was observed after the implementation of virtual bench. The statistics are as given below in the table7.The analysis is presented through graph in fig 5. The return on investment is huge to IT organization, even if one attrition is reduced. From the table 7 it is evident that attrition rate of niche employees is reduced by 2.7% for a period of three months. The reduction in rate of attrition is remarkable and proves to be beneficial for organization's growth

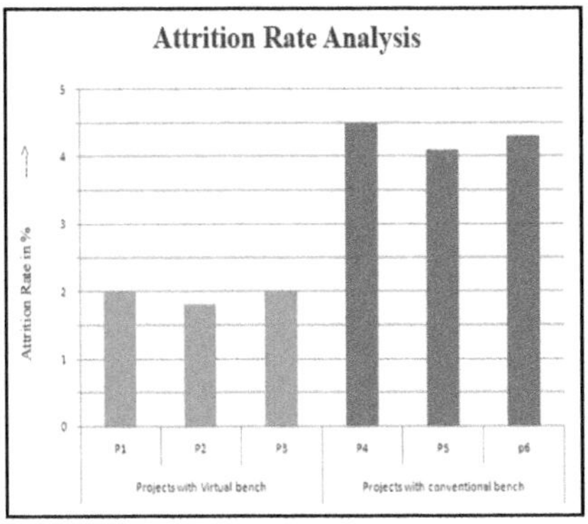

Fig. 5. Attrition Rate Analysis

Table 7. Attrition Rate Analysis

	Projects with Virtual bench			Projects with conventional bench		
Projects	P1	P2	P3	P4	P5	P6
Attrition Rate %	2	1.8	2	4.5	4.1	4.3
Attrition Rate %	1.6			4.3		

7.3 Benefits of Virtual Bench

The benefits of virtual bench can be listed as given below.

Tangible Benefits	Intangible Benefits
Improved return on IT investment	Staff motivation rate is high
Reduced staff attrition rate and Accurate assessment of each employee performance	Increased client and employee satisfaction rate
Increased efficiency and Risk quantification	Increase in technical competency
Increased project success rate	Increase in staff potential and overall development
Non billable hours are turned into billable hours	Highly disciplined and target oriented team

8 Conclusion

IT industry is a knowledge industry. Bench is very vital for IT industry. Conventional bench is having issues such as improper assessment of staff skill, uncertain bench duration, non billable hours at bench etc. This paper has proposed a novel approach to address above stated issues more effectively, through skill index based virtual bench approach. Challenging task of assessing employee skills accurately is achieved by skill index. Through skill index niche staffs are identified effectively and by virtual bench niche staffs are allocated to forthcoming projects. Due to virtual bench approach niche staff is avoided from entering the bench and organization also experiences the profit due to billable period of niche staff instead of unbillable period if conventional bench approach would have been used. Hence the resource utilization is maximum. Productivity is heavily dependent on quality of resource and experience of resource. Poor quality resource will directly increase the cost of IT organization by delivering less value comparatively for every dollar spent. Through our approach of virtual bench, organization can maximize productivity by figuring niche staff from large workforce. From case study it is evident that due to technical expertise and competency of niche staff, the projects are completed early, giving 2-3% profit hike compared to conventional bench approach. The success factor of projects is also raised. Niche staff attrition rate is reduced by 50% by adopting this approach. The practical case study with real-time observation reveals that virtual bench can be implemented. Virtual bench concept, is matching with the contemporary needs of IT service organization.

References

1. Gray, C.F., Larson, E.W.: Project Management: The Managerial Process, 2nd edn. McGraw-Hill (2008)
2. Barner, R.: Bench strength: Developing the depth and versatility of your organization's leadership talent. In: AMACOM, p. 245 (2006)
3. Barney, S., Aurum, A., Wohlin, C.: The relative imporatnce of aspects of intellectual capitol for software companies. In: 35 Euromicro Conference on Software Engineering and Advanced Applications, SEAA 2009, pp. 313–320 (2009) ISSN: 1089-6503
4. Kuni, R., Bhushan, N.: Wiprotechnologies: IT Application assessment model for global software development. In: International Conference ICGSE 2006, pp. 92–100 (2006) ISBN 07695-2663-2
5. Baron, J.: The people side of software. A lesson plan for establishing a sucessful training program. In: Appeared in ninth Conference on Software Engineering Education 1996 proceedings, pp. 184–198 (1996)
6. Shedil, K., Madhavji, N.H.: Personal 'progress Functions' in the software process. In: Process Appeared in Ninth International Software Process Workshop, p. 117 (1994)
7. Rowland, J.R.: A fine-grid model for evaluating multidisciplinary team experiences, fie. In: 31st Annual Frontiers in Education Conference 2001, vol. 1, pp. T4A-5–T4A8 (2001)
8. Lewis, P., Aldridge, D., Swamidass, P.: Assessing Teaming Skills Acquisition onUndergraduate Project Teams. Journal of Engineering Education 87(4), 149–155 (1998)
9. Downing, C.: Essential Non-Technical Skills for Teaming. Journal of Engineering Education 90(1), 113–117 (2001)
10. Bharat, E., Pahari, R.: Competency level of engineering graduates and quality of engineering education in Nepal. Journal of the Institute of Engineering 7, 1–11, TUTA/IOE?PCU
11. Grandon Gill, T.: Structural complexity and effective informing. Informing science: The International Journal of an Emerging Transdiscipline 11 (2008)
12. Fairley, R.E.: Managing and Leading Software Projects, p. 87. John Wiely&Sons, Inc., ISBN: 978-0-470-29455-0
13. Jhonson, G., Schles, K., Whittington, R.: Exploring corporate strategy: text and cases, edn. 7, pp. 685–690. Pearson Education Publishers
14. Madachy, R.J.: Software process dynamics, p. 258. Wiely-IEEE press (January 2008) ISBN: 978-0-471-27455-1

Design of an Analytical and Foresight Based Strategic Model for e-Governance in Public Transportation

Ajay Kumar Bharti and Sanjay K. Dwivedi

Department of Computer Science,
Babasaheb Bhimrao Ambedkar University, Lucknow, India

Abstract. India is a developing country with the huge potential for the fast paced development in e-Governance. Indian Transport sector is also severely affected by chronic corruption, inefficiency and overcrowded due to the poor planning. In this paper, we discuss about the definition and basic difference between e-government and e-Governance. Secondly, discuss current status of e-Governance in public transportation followed, the study about foresight and its functionality. On the basis of analysis performed on commuters and officials, the foresight is used as a tool to determine the appropriate strategies for the development of ICT enabled services for effective and efficient development of an e-Governance model for the public transportation. Therefore the implementation of e-Governance by using analysis and foresight as a tool can be able to improve the services in the public transportation sector.

Keywords: e-Governance, e-Government, ICT, Public Transportation, analytical, foresight, strategy, Strategic model.

1 Introduction: e-Government vs. e-Governance

According to world bank definition [1] "e-Government is the government owned or operated systems of information and communication technologies that transform relations with citizens, the private sector and/or other government agencies so as to promote citizens' empowerment, improve service delivery, strengthen accountability, increase transparency, or improve government efficiency." Where as e-Governance According to SpeG [2] "E-governance is the application of information & communication technologies to transform the efficiency, effectiveness, transparency and accountability of informational & transactional exchanges with in government, between govt. & govt. agencies of National, State, Municipal & Local levels, citizen & businesses, and to empower citizens through access & use of information". The relation between the e-government and the e-governance is explained in fig. 1. which describes People, Process, Technology and Resources are the four pillars of e-Governance and e-Government plays an intermediary role to manage the pillars in an effective way to provide effective services to their citizens. Therefore we can say that Government's foremost job is to focus society on achieving the public interest.

V.V. Das and N. Thankachan (Eds.): CIIT 2011, CCIS 250, pp. 615–620, 2011.

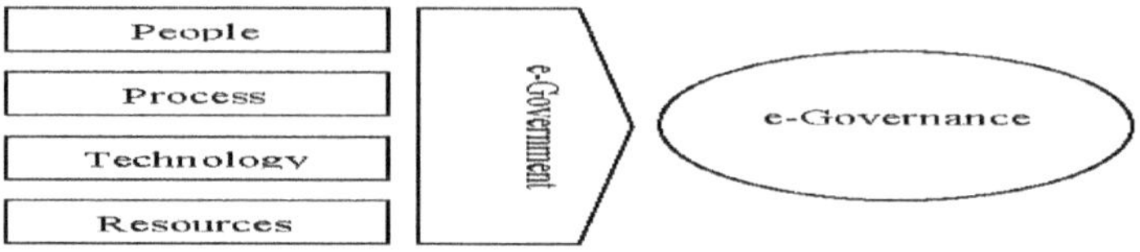

Fig. 1. Relation between e-government and e-Governance [3]

E-Governance is developed for the purpose of increasing transparency and accountability, allowing greater access to information about representatives, institutions, decisions, laws, regulations and project development. Therefore effective implementation of e-Government and e-Governance will be helpful to achieve efficiency in public transportation too.

2 Public Transportation

Public transport sector in developing countries like India carries more than 90 percent of passengers by buses and about 65 percent of freight [4], even though the sector faces severe problems such as lack of financial resources which restricts investment and up gradation of existing transportation system. Moreover the lack of proper and effective planning in public transport sector India has led to rapid growth in cars and two wheeler motor vehicle which causes congestion in roads that slows down the bus services, ultimately increases the operating cost and discourage the use of public transportations. Economical pressure and deficit budgets pressurises the public transport sector to improve operational effectiveness and efficient services. The public transport sector should use information and communication technology as a powerful tool to achieve operational effectiveness. Web technologies enabled government and administration to reduce efforts and costs for their services. Effective implementation of e-Governance in the public transport sector will be able to minimise the economical pressure.

3 Foresight

Foresight is a tool to determine appropriate strategies to meet with e-Government challenges. According to Martin [5] foresight is "the process involved in systematically attempting to look into the longer-term future of science, technology, the economy and society with the aim of identifying the areas of strategic research and the emerging generic technologies likely to yield the greatest economic and social benefits". The approach was developed after extensive consultation of US experts on technological forecasting in late 1960's which is based on four basic principles:

1) The forecast must include economic and social needs, as well as developments in science and technology.
2) The study must cover all of Science and Technology, to identify new fields is being formed by fusion of two or more previously separate research areas or technologies.

3) The study should evaluate the relative importance of different R&D tasks and determine priorities, so the results are useful policy purposes.
4) The forecast should have two complementary aspects of being (i) predictive i.e. forecasting what is likely to happen, and of being (ii) normative i.e. setting goals and associated time scales for what should happen in the future.

According to J. Voros, foresight was based on strategic planning which was given by their foresight framework in Voros forsight model [6] consists of four elements that are input, foresight, output and strategy. Input is collection of information and Foresight part can be visualized as comprising three subparts which are analysis, interpretation and prospection. Output is third part of Voros framework, consist tangible and intangible outputs. Strategy is last part of this framework. Strategy hands over for consideration by decision makers in making decisions for directing strategic actions for implementation. The result of strategy process should be fed back constantly into inputs.

4 Proposed Model for Public Transportation

On the basis of survey recommendations [7], and thorough study of foresight strategic models, a conceptual model for public transportation is proposed in Fig. 2., which have two blocks first block suggests strategies where as second part uses output of the first part to mechanise the e-Government to e-Governance. Voros model [6] and Kolsoom Abbasi Shahkooh [8] models are used to draw strategic conclusions form e-Government strategy foresight for public transportation on the basis of analysis, Interpretation and prospection on given parameters. Formulated strategies are further used by the Government for the process re-engineering to develop effective ICT enabled services to provide an effective e-Governance in the public transportation.

4.1 Input/ Data Collection

Data and information for future trends and ideas about e-Government is collected from a number of sources such as officials involve in planning, regulation and operation of public transportation, commuters, personal networks, government, other foresight and e-Government reports, research and surveys.

4.2 e-Government Foresight

Following are different stages of e-government foresight:-

a) Analysis to identify gap: On the basis of an extensive survey performed on commuters and officials of U.P.SR.T.C. [7], categorised them into following three parts to identify the gap between service providers and users of the services.

I. Awareness: There is general lack awareness found between users of the services or commuters and provider of those services or Officials.
II. Satisfaction level: Satisfaction level among commuters as well as officials strongly recommended for the implementation of an effective e-Governance in the Public Transport sector.

III. Need: According to commuters there are number of parameters such as Interconnectivity, use of ICT, on line information's and services, on which public transportation have to pay more attention to provide quality services to their users. On other hands official's needs are focused on interconnectivity private public partnership involvement for bridging the infrastructure gap, officials are also concern about some mechanism for tracking or locating the individual services.

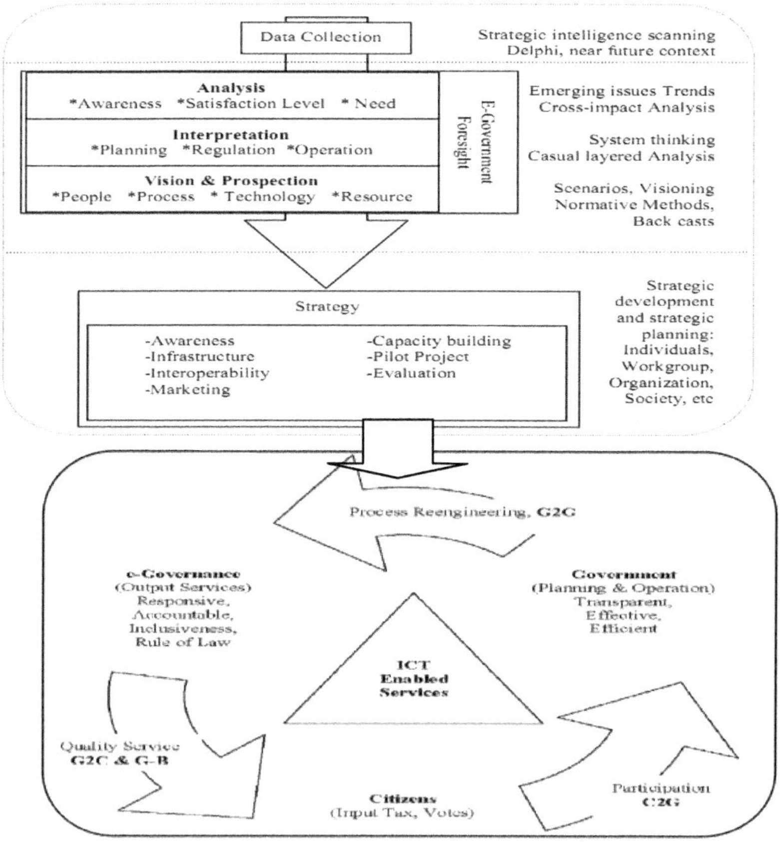

Fig. 2. Proposed Model for e-Governance in Public Transportation

b) Interpretation: The information collected from the survey was interpreted by using analytical tools on the basis of analysis to transform information into clear understanding priorities and objectives of the sector so that appropriate planning, regulative and operative issues can be foresighted considering past experiences and future vision.

c) Vision and Prospection: Alternative views of futures are explicitly examined considering the aspects like people, process, technology and resources. These are the focus points to foresight considering predictive and normative methods.

4.3 Strategies

The following strategies have to consider for e-Government foresight. This has to be considering in process reengineering of existing system to develop new ICT enabled public transportation to provide an effective and efficient services to their commuters.

Awareness: It was also one of the major issues identified by the survey result; therefore awareness raising is one of the strategy to improve the system.

Capacity building: For building eGovernance strategic capacity, strategic institutions has to be setup for development and implementation of framework and policies to provide consultancy and legislative, inputs to public transportation projects.

Infrastructure: Institution development to implement and maintenances of necessary infrastructure in the public transport sector.

Pilot Projects: Efforts should be consider for the priority the public transport sector with maximum citizens interface. An ABC analysis of the government services should be taken in consideration to arrive at the most functions of government.

Interoperability: While designing the e-Governance policy for public transportation, technical and standards interoperability must be consider to provide portability to the system.

Project Evaluation: Pilot projects evaluation is classified as success or failure according to desired output. Study should be carried out by independent agency because implementation agency will never identify project failure.

Marketing: Efforts should be focused on awareness of the online presence using the traditional Medias. Public transport sector should encourage their front line employees and government employees to promote their online business.

The out put of first block of model is the strategy formulation which is further used in the second part of model for effective and efficient implementation of e-Governance in the sector. Basically there are four important considerations of the e-Governance which is explained in the conceptual model for e-Governance in [9]

Government: The major actors of the administration are central government, sate government, local government or officials of public transportation. The involvement of Government is essentially required for the process re-engineering.

Process Reengineering: Study the existing system to identify the process, then on the basis of strategy recommendations for reengineering the process will be formulated accordingly.

Quality Service: It can improve the efficiency of government by streamlining administrative procedures (simplification and transparent) for effective communication within and outside government departments. E-governance not only reduces paper work, but also facilitates speedy communication and effective coordination.

Citizens: Participation of the stakeholders in policy formulation and implementation is very important for achieving good governance. E-governance enhances citizen participation in shaping the policies and improving service delivery.

Participation: ICT empowers citizens to have access to information related to government activities to monitor and judge government's performance.

ICT enabled Services: ICT enables efficiency in government management by staff and cost reduction. It increases efficiency and ensures responsive and transparent administrative environment.

5 Conclusions

With the advancement of e-Government and e-Governance the quality and effective services will be provided to the citizens, public transportation is not the exception too. But the services in public transportation lag behind because of ineffective planning therefore an effective e-Governance model is required by the public transport sector. In this paper several models on various parameters are reviewed to design an effective e-governance model for public transportation. The foresight application is used as a tool to draw strategic conclusion for the e-Government on the basis of Analysis, Interpretation and Prospection considering various parameters. These strategy output is considered as input for process reengineering to provide e-Governance to the citizens. Therefore an analytical and foresight based strategic model for e-governance in public transport sector is proposed. This may helpful to provide quality services to their commuters.

References

1. World Bank, LAC PREM – Issues Note: E-Government and The World Bank. November 5 (2001)
2. SpeG A society for promotion of e-Governance, `http://www.egovindia.org/egovernancepaper.doc`
3. Mohanty, P.K.: Using e-Tools for Good Governance & Administrative Reforms, `http://www.cgg.gov.in/workingpapers/eGovPaperARC.pdf`
4. India Transpor Sector - Roads, `http://web.worldbank.org/WBSITE/EXTERNAL/COUNTRIES/SOUTHASIAEXT/EXTSARREGTOPTRANSPORT/0,contentMDK:20703625~menuPK:868822~pagePK:34004173~piPK:34003707~theSitePK:579598,00.html`
5. Martin, B.R.: Foresight in Science and Technology. Technology Analysis & Strategic Management 7(2), 139–168 (1995)
6. Voros, J.: A generic foresight process framework. Foresight 5(3), 10–21 (2003)
7. Bharti, A.K., Dwivedi, S.K.: Proceedings of ICSCA-2011. In: IPCSIT, vol. 9, pp. 7–12 (2011) ISSN 2010-460X
8. Shahkooh, K.A., Abdollahi, A., Fasanghari, M., Azadnia, M.: Foresight based Framework for E-government Strategic Planning. Journal of software 4(6), 544–549 (2009)
9. Dwivedi, S.K., Bharti, A.K.: e-Governance in India – Problems and Acceptability. Journal of Theoretical and Applied Information and Technology (JATIT) 17(1), 37–43 (2010) ISSN 1992-8645

Novel Approach for Segmentation of Handwritten Touching Characters from Devanagari Words

Akshata Doiphode[1] and Leena Ragha[2]

[1] K.C. College of Engineering, Thane, Maharashtra, India
akshatadoiphode@gmail.com
[2] Ramrao Adik Institute of Technology, Nerul, Navi Mumbai, Maharashtra, India
leenaragha@gmail.com

Abstract. Segmentation in image processing refers to the process of partitioning a digital image into multiple segments. This paper makes an attempt to segment the handwritten Marathi words using Devanagari script. Segmentation of handwritten words into characters is a challenging task primarily because of complexity of structural features of the script and varied writing styles. Without dissecting these touching characters, we cannot recognize the individual characters, hence arises the need for segmentation of touching characters in a word. Paper proposes a technique which performs necessary pre-processing of a word, finds joint points in the word, identify vertical and horizontal lines and finally dissect touching characters by taking into account its dimensions namely height and width of bounding box.

Keywords: Structural features, Segmentation, Vertical bar, Joint points.

1 Introduction

Optical Character Recognition (OCR) is the process of converting scanned images of machine printed or handwritten text into a computer process able format. OCR is one of the most challenging topics in the fields of pattern recognition. Recognition is impossible without proper segmentation of words. Segmentation of handwritten text in Devanagari script is a difficult task. The challenge is to take into account structural features of the script and varied writing styles. The homogeneity and uniformity of header lines, vertical and horizontal parts in printed text make use of histograms possible. However histograms are of little help for segmentation of handwritten words because of lack of uniformity at every level. In this paper, we propose a system for segmentation of handwritten touching characters from Devanagari words.

2 Literature Review

Very few papers are available on segmentation of handwritten characters from word. No work for touching handwritten Devanagari character segmentation is found so far to the best of our knowledge. Veena Bansal et al [1], Veena Bansal et al [2], M. Hanmandlu et al [3], Naresh Kumar Garg et al [4] made an attempt to segment handwritten or printed Indian languages.

V.V. Das and N. Thankachan (Eds.): CIIT 2011, CCIS 250, pp. 621–623, 2011.

3 Devanagari Language

Devanagari has been script of Indian Aryan languages. It is used as script by Sanskrit, Hindi, Marathi and Nepali languages. We are considering Devanagari script for Marathi. Devanagari is the most popular script in India. It has 11 vowels and 33 consonants. All the characters have a horizontal line at the upper part, known as shirorekha or headline. In continuous handwriting, from left to right direction, the shirorekha of one character joins with the shirorekha of the previous or next character of the same word. Figure 2 shows how Devanagari characters of word touch each other.

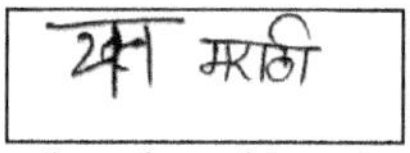

Fig. 1. Examples of touching characters in word

4 Proposed Work Flow

4.1 Structural Properties of the Devanagari Script and Characters

There are three classes [1] of core characters based on presence and position of vertical bar.

End bar characters	अ ख घ च ज झ ञ त थ ध न प ब भ म य ल व ष स
Middle bar characters	क्ष क फ
Non bar characters	इ उ ऊ ए छ ट ठ द ड ढ द र ह श

Fig. 2. Visually extracted properties of Devanagari characters

4.2 Workflow

For touching handwritten character segmentation we are giving word image as input, perform many pre-processing techniques then word processing and finally processing of character will be done.

Pre-Processing Stage. The input image is first binaries and complemented. After this make thinning to remove unnecessary pixels for making further processing possible. Finally we will get pre-processed input image. The words are dilated to allow formation of bounding boxes only around words so that each word gets separated.

Word Processing stage on pre-processed word

Joint point detection and removal from thinned image. The sum of 3 x 3 matrixes (minus centre pixel) around each pixel is found. If this sum is equal to or more than 3

then the pixel is considered as a joint point. Also the terminating points are found which have only one pixel in the surrounding. Remove all detected joint points and form bounding box.

***Shirorekha* detection and removal.** Horizontal rectangles are rectangles having width-height ratio more than or equal to 3:1. Rectangles having most number of pixels are considered as parts of *shirorekha*. **Vertical bar detection and removal** Vertical rectangles are rectangles having width-height ratio less than or equal to 1:3. In the vertical rectangles percentage of white pixels (which are parts of vertical bars) is found. If this percentage is more than 60% then the rectangle contains a vertical bar. Max row equal to last row of these BB will be considered as baseline.

Character Processing Stage on *shirorekha* and vertical bar removed image. Procedure to find cut positions:-Form Bounding Box around *shirorekha* and vertical bar removed image.Find width of Bounding Box (BB).

Category 1: Segmentation of side bar character touching to another character.

Bounding Box width is not equal on both sides of removed vertical bar, make cut after each vertical bars.

Category 2

i) Segmentation of middle bar character touching to another character. If width of BB is greater than single character width then make cut at first joint point from left of BB.

ii) Another way of middle bar touching character.

If width of bounding Box is equal on both the sides of vertical bar (i.e. character is middle bar) make cut after right bounding box of vertical bar.

Category 3: Separated characters without vertical bar (Non Bar).

If character without VB then make cut at the right of Bounding Box.

5 Conclusion

We are able to detect vertical lines and horizontal lines (i.e. *shirorekha*) satisfactorily without skew correction by using bounding box method based on that cut points will be computed for segmentation of Devanagari handwritten touching characters.

References

1. Bansal, V., Sinha, R.M.K.: Integrating Knowledge Sources in Devanagari Text recognition System. IEEE Transactions on Systems, Man, and Cybernetics—Part a: Systems and Humans 30(4), 500–505 (2000)
2. Bansal, V., Sinha, R.M.K.: Segmentation of Touching and fused Devanagari Characters. Pattern Recognition 35, 875–893 (2002)
3. Hanmandlu, M., Agrawal, P.: A Structural Approach for Segmentation of Handwritten Hindi Text. In: Proceeding of the International Conference on Cognition and Recognition, Mandya, Karnataka, India, December 22-23, pp. 589–597 (2005)
4. Garg, N.K., Kaur, L., Jindal, M.K.: Segmentation of Handwritten Hindi Text. 2010 International Journal of Computer Applications (0975 – 8887) 1(4), 19–23 (2010)

A Comparative Study on IPv6 Based Mobility Management Protocols

Arun Kumar Tripathi[1], J.S. Lather[2], and Ramaswami Radhakrishnan[3]

[1] Krishana Institute of Engg. and Tech-Ghaziabad
[2] National Institute of Technology-Kurukshetra
[3] Inderprastha Engineering College-Ghaziabad
{mailtoaruntripathi,jslather,ramaswamiradhakrishnan}@gmail.com

Abstract. Mobile IP is the current standard proposed by IETF for mobility management in IP networks. Mobility management becomes a critical issue to track mobile user's current location and to efficiently deliver secure services to them when they are away from their home network. Handover latency is the primary cause of packet loss resulting in performance degradation of Mobile IPv6. In this paper we have performed comparative study of existing Mobile IPv6 schemes on parameters such as packet loss, handover latency, registration overhead, location privacy etc.

Keywords: Mobility, MIPv6, HMIPv6, PMIPv6, Handover latency.

1 Introduction

The tremendous advancements in the field of communication and information technology over the last decades have influenced our lives greatly. IP-based next-generation wireless networks are widely adopted for transporting media such as voice, data, etc. Mobile IP is the mobility protocol widely used for Internet and standardized by Internet Engineering Task Force (IETF). Mobile IP has two different versions Mobile IP version 4 (MIPv4) and Mobile IP version 6 (MIPv6). The IP based protocol, Mobile Internet Protocol version 6 (MIPv6) [1] has been proposed to solve the problem of mobility in the new era of Internet by handling routing of IPv6 packets to mobile nodes that have moved away from their home network. This allows users to seamlessly move from one location to another and stay connected to the Internet. As mobility increases across networks, handovers will significantly impact the quality of the connection and user application. This paper is organized as follows. Section 2 deals with classification of IPv6 based mobility management protocols. Section 3 describes host-based mobility management protocols while section 4 deals with network-based mobility management protocol. Section 5 details comparative analysis among various mobility management protocols based on IPv6. Conclusion is made in Section 6.

2 Classifications of Mobility Management Protocols

Mobility management protocols are broadly classified into host-based mobility and network-based mobility management protocols [2]. Initially IETF standardized

V.V. Das and N. Thankachan (Eds.): CIIT 2011, CCIS 250, pp. 624–629, 2011.

mobility management protocol known as host-based mobility protocol. In this system most of the efforts are made by the Mobile Node (MN) to detect a new network, request a Care-of Address (CoA) and send information about the CoA to the Home Agent (HA). This causes high amount of latency. Recently IETF and Network-based Localized Mobility Management (NetLMM) standardized a network-based mobility management protocol known as Proxy Mobile IPv6 (PMIPv6). Network-based mobility uses a Mobile Access Gateway (MAG) and a Local Mobility Anchor (LMA) to allow hosts to move around within a domain while keeping their address stable. PMIPv6 improves handover performance in terms of handover delay and packet loss as well as maintains minimal control signaling overhead in the air interface. The left hand side of Fig. 1 represents host-based mobility and right hand side represents network-based mobility. In RFC-3775 Network Working Group suggested first host-based mobility management protocol as MIPv6. As an extension to it Fast Mobile IPv6 (FMIPv6), Hierarchical Mobile IPv6 (HMIPv6), Fast Hierarchical Mobile IPv6 (FHMIPv6) etc. are proposed. Proxy Mobile IPv6 (PMIPv6), Fast Proxy Mobile IPv6 (FPMIPv6) etc. come under the category of network-based mobility.

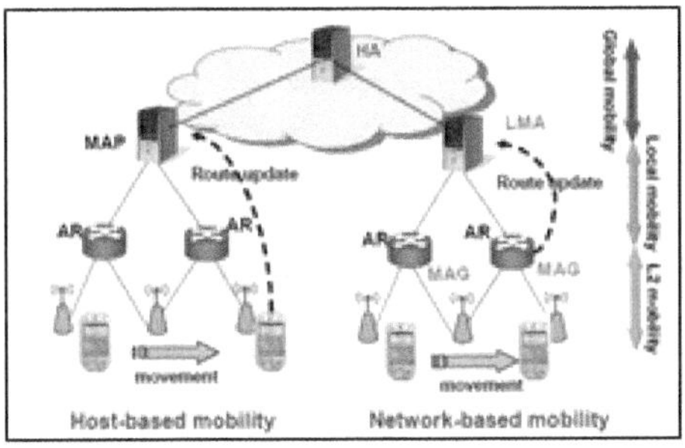

Fig. 1. Types of Mobility management

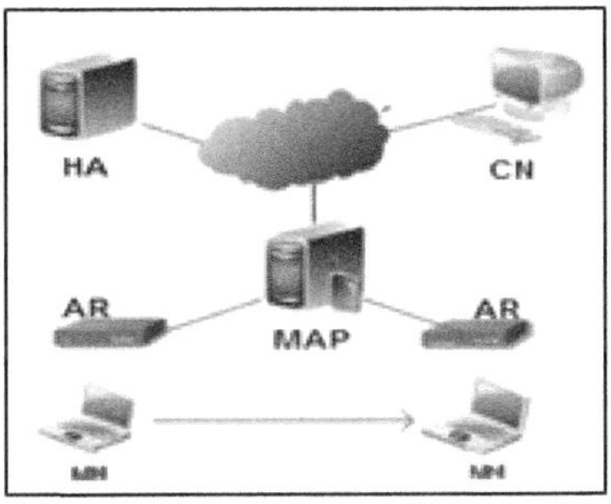

Fig. 2. MIPv6 Architecture

In host-based mobility management protocol MN is directly involved in movement detection and mobility signaling.

2.1 MIPv6 Protocol

Mobile IPv6 (MIPv6) provides transparent mobility to MN. This is done with the help of two addresses: A permanent address known as Home Address (HoA) provided by its HA and a temporary address that represents current location of MN, known as CoA. The HoA remains fixed, while the CoA changes according to the location of the node. MIPv6 provides a mechanism to map between the two addresses dynamically. The architecture of MIPv6 domain is shown in Fig 2. Each Correspondent Node (CN) can have its own binding cache where (HoA, CoA) pairs are stored. To keep these mappings up-to-date, MN has to periodically inform its Home Agent (HA) and CN(s) about its new CoA via Binding Update (BU) message. The registration process involves Duplicate Address Detection (DAD) [3]. If registration is successful Binding Acknowledgement (BA) [4] sends back to MN. When a CN has recent registration information for a MN, it can send packets directly to the MN. Otherwise, it sends packets to the MN's HoA, the MN's HA will then forward them to the MN. A MN may change its point of attachment very frequently. Therefore, it has to register both the HA and the CN each time. This causes registration overhead and takes longer delay. Hence increases packet loss as well as handover latency. Each time in registration process control signal are transferred that causes air interface traffic overhead.

2.2 HMIPv6 Protocol

Hierarchical mobile IPv6 (HMIPv6) [5] was proposed to reduce signaling load and improve handoff latency [6]. It is accomplished with the help of Mobility Anchor Point (MAP) [8], [9] which is located in between MN and HA. The basic task of MAP is assigning and managing a Regional Care-of Address (RCoA) for each mobile node, binding the RCoA to the subnet On-Link CoA (LCoA) [10], and managing the traffic between the RCoA and LCoA.

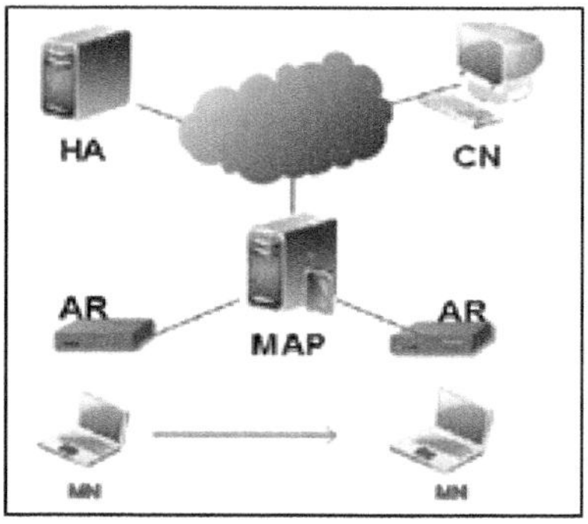

Fig. 3. HMIPv6 Architecture

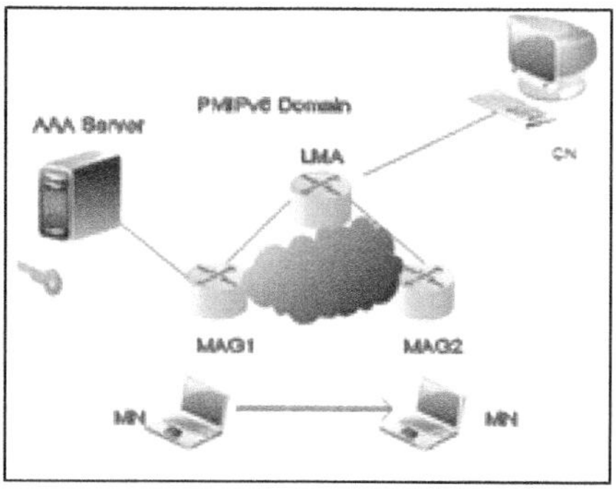

Fig. 4. PMIPv6 Architecture

The architecture of HMIPv6 domain is shown in Fig 3. A mobile node entering a MAP domain will receive Router Advertisements (AR) containing information on one or more local MAPs. The MN can bind its current location i.e. LCoA with an address on the MAP's subnet (i.e. RCoA). Acting as a local HA for MN, the MAP intercepts all packets addressed to MN and tunnels [7] them to the corresponding LCoA of MN. If MN changes its location within the boundary of MAP domain, it only needs to register new LCoA with the MAP. If MN changes its location across MAP domain boundary and enters to a new MAP domain, it acquires an RCoA and LCoA. The MN then uses new MAP address as RCoA, while LCoA address can be formed as stated in [5]. After forming the RCoA and LCoA, the MN sends a regular BU to MAP. Now MAP performs DAD for RCoA and then binds RCoA and LCoA to MN. If successful, the MAP sends a BA to MN indicating successful registration. After successful registration with the MAP all packets sent by the MN are tunneled to the MAP. MN will also register new RCoA with its HA as well as CN by sending another BU. HMIPv6 overcomes from problems associated with MIPv6 as follows: Since intra-domain handoffs are performed locally therefore HMIPv6 reduces signaling overhead by involving only MAP. Hence, decreases registration overhead as well as packet loss. It also reduces air interface traffic overhead by transferring less control data as compare to MIPv6.

3 Network-Based Mobility Management Protocols

Network-based mobility management enables IP mobility for a host without requiring its participation in any mobility-related signaling. The network is responsible for managing IP mobility on behalf of the host. The mobility entities in the network are responsible for tracking the movements of the host and initiating the required mobility signaling on its behalf.

3.1 PMIPv6

PMIPv6 [11] is a network-based mobility protocol. It reuses and extends concepts of MIPv6. All mobile nodes in PMIPv6 are identified by a network access identifier (NAI), which has an associated set of information stored on the network, including a profile containing the home prefix. PMIPv6 introduces two entities Mobile Access Gateway (MAG) and Local Mobility Anchor (LMA) [11]. The main function of the MAG is to detect the MN's movements and initiate mobility related signaling with the MN. On the other hand LMA acts as HA of MN in PMIPv6 domain and maintain reachability to the MN address when it moves within a PMIPv6 domain. The architecture of PMIPv6 domain is shown in Fig 4. As soon as mobile node moves from one MAG and attach to another MAG. The authentication procedure is called up by MAG. After successful authentication, the MAG sends the Proxy Binding Update (PBU) message to the LMA. When the LMA receives the PBU message, it stores the profile of the MN in Binding Cache Entry (BCE), and sends a Proxy Blinding Acknowledge (PBA) message including home network prefix (HNP) [11] of the MN to the corresponding MAG. The MAG that has received the PBA message sends the Router Advertisement (RA) message including the HNP to the MN. After this procedure, the MN configures its Home Network Address (HoA) using the received HNP. In PMIPv6 network element performs mobility related signaling on behalf of the MN. This helps in reducing binding update delay by decreasing the round-trip time. Therefore, handover latency is also reduced. Location privacy is maintained by PMIPv6 because it doesn’t allow changing in IP address as MN moves across the link. Air interface traffic overhead is very less because control signals are transferred during the handover process.

4 Comparative Analysis among Existing MIPv6 Based Mobility Management Protocols

We have done comparative study among MIPv6, HMIPv6 and PMIPv6 mobility management protocols, as shown in Table 1, based on features such as packet loss, multi-homing, air interface traffic overhead, tunneling overhead at MN, handover latency etc.

Table 1. Comparative analysis among Mobility Based Protocols

Features	MIPv6	HMIPv6	PMIPv6
Mobility Region	Global	Local	Local
Packet loss in Handover	High	Average	Low
Multi-homing	No	Yes	Yes
Terminal Modifications	Yes	Yes	No
Air interface Traffic overhead	High	Average	Low
Required infrastructure	HA,AR	HA, MAP	LMA, MAG
Route Optimization	Support	Support	Support
Handover latency	Bad	Moderate	Good
Mobility Management	Host-Based	Host-Based	Network-Based
Router Advertisement	Broadcast	Broadcast	Unicast
Tunneling Overhead at MN	Yes	Yes	No
Packet reordering method	Sequence Number	Sequence Number	Time Stamp
Binding Cache lookup Key	MN-Host Address	MN-Host Address	MN-HNP
Protocol layers	L3	L3	L3
Mobility Stack on MN	Yes	Yes	No
Mobility Stack on CN	Yes	Yes	No
Location Privacy	Low	Average	High
Registration overhead	High	Average	Low
Buffering Maintained by	HA	MAP	MAG
Secure key distribution method	Internet key exchange (IKE)	IKEv2	IKEv2
Energy Consumption	High	Average	Low

5 Conclusion

In this paper, we have discussed host-based and network-based mobility management protocols. In comparative study we found that host-based protocols, such as MIPv6 and HMIPv6, are much complex and suffer from drawbacks such as high signaling overhead, more packet loss, high handover latency, high energy consumption, broadcasting of router advertisement packets etc. On the other hand network-based protocols, such as PMIPv6, overcome from most of the drawbacks associated with host-based protocols. PMIPv6 is adopted by 3rd Generation Partnership Project (3GPP) as well as non-3GPP service providers and well suited for transporting voice and data.

References

1. Perkins, D.J., Arkko, J.: Mobility Support in IPv6. Internet Engineering Task Force, Request for Comment 3775 (June 2004)
2. Al-Surmi, I., Othman, M., Ali, B.M.: Review on mobility management for future-IP-based next generation wireless networks. In: 12th International Conference on Advanced Communication Technology (ICACT), pp. 989–994 (2010) ISBN: 978-1-4244-5427-3
3. Moore, N.: Optimistic Duplicate Address Detection (DAD) for IPv6 Network Working Group, Request for Comment 4429 (April 2006)
4. Pack, S., Lee, B., Kwon, T., Choi, Y.: Taekyoung Kwon and Yanghee Choi:A pointer forwarding scheme with mobility-aware binding update in Mobile IPv6 networks. Published by Computer Communications Journal 31(5), 873–884 (2008)
5. Soliman, H., Castelluccia, C., Malki, K. E., Bellier, L.: Hierarchical Mobile IPv6 mobility management (HMIPv6). Internet Engineering Task Force RFC 4140 (August 2005)
6. Wu, X., Nie, G.: Comparison of different mobility management schemes for reducing handover latency in Mobile IPv6. In: International Conference on Industrial Mechatronics and Automation (ICIMA 2009), pp. 256–259. IEEE Xplore (2009) ISBN: 978-1-4244-3817-4
7. Le, D., Chang, J.: Tunnelling-based route optimization for Mobile IPv6. In: IEEE International Conference on Wireless Communications, Networking and Information Security (WCNIS), pp. 509–513. IEEE Xplore (2010) ISBN: 978-1-4244-5850-9
8. Pack, S., Nam, M., Kwon, T., Choi, Y.: An adaptive mobility anchor point selection scheme in Hierarchical Mobile IPv6 networks. Computer Communications journal 29(16), 3011–3340 (2006)
9. Kusin, Z., Zakaria, M.S.: The Future Enhancements of Mobile Ipv6 Micro-Mobility Management. In: Second International Conference on Network Applications Protocols and Services (NETAPPS), pp. 193–197. IEEE Xplore (2010) ISBN: 978-1-4244-8048-7
10. Pérez-Costa, X., Marc, T.M., Hartenstein, H.: A Performance Comparison of Mobile IPv6, Hierarchical. Mobile IPv6, Fast Handovers for Mobile IPv6 and their Combination. In: ACM SIGMOBILE Mobile Computing and Communications Review. 7(4), pp. 5–19. IEEE Xplore (2003) ISSN: 1559-1662
11. Gundavelli, S., Leung, K., Devarapalli, V., Chowdhury, K., Patil, B.: Proxy Mobile IPv6. Network Working Group, Request for comment 5213 (2008)

Discrete Binary Honey Bees Mating Optimization with Capability of Learning

Vahid Azadehgan[1], M.R. Meybodi[2], Nafiseh Jafarian[1], and Farshad Jafarieh[1]

[1] Department of Information Technology, Sufi Razi Institute of Higher Education, Zanjan, Iran
[2] Soft Computing Laboratory, Department of Computer Engineering and Information Technology, Amirkabir University of Technology, Tehran, Iran
{V.Azadehgan,N.Jafarian,F.Jafarieh}@sufi.ac.ir,
MMeybodi@ce.aut.ac.ir

Abstract. Honey Bees Mating Optimization (HBMO) is a novel developed method used in different engineering areas. Optimization process in this algorithm is inspired of natural mating behavior between bees. In this paper, we have attempted to create a reciprocal relation between learning and evolution which can produce an algorithm with the power of dominating local optimums and finding global optima. In the proposed model, a set of learning Automata, which can produce reinforcement signal by obtaining feedback from queens, is attributed to each drone. Simulation and comparisons based on several well-studied benchmarks demonstrate the effectiveness, efficiency and robustness of the proposed algorithms.

Keywords: Honey Bees Mating Optimization, Learning Automata, Function Optimization.

1 Introduction

A very interesting swarm in nature is honey bee swarm that allocates the tasks dynamically and adapts itself in response to changes in the environment in a collective intelligent manner [1]. Honey Bees Mating Optimization (HBMO) algorithm is a typical swarm-based approach to optimization, in which the search algorithm is inspired by the honey bees mating process. The Honey Bees Mating Optimization Algorithm was first presented in [2], [3], and since then it was used on a number of different applications [4][5][6]. HBMO is an evolutionary computation algorithm which simulates the mating process of the queen of the hive. The mating process of the queen begins when the queen flights away from the nest performing the mating flight which the drones follow the queen and mate with her in the air .Learning Automaton (LA) is a general-purpose stochastic optimization tool, which has been developed as a model for learning systems. They are typically used as the basis of learning systems, which through interactions with a stochastic unknown environment learn the optimal action for that environment. The learning automaton tries to determine, iteratively, the optimal action to apply to environment from a finite number of actions that are available to it. The environment returns a reinforcement signal that shows the relative

V.V. Das and N. Thankachan (Eds.): CIIT 2011, CCIS 250, pp. 630–636, 2011.

quality of action of the learning automaton. This signal is given to learning automaton and learning automaton adjusts itself by a learning algorithm [7][8]. In this paper, we have suggested a discrete optimization model based on mating action between honey bees and learning Automata. We have tried to consider evolution and learning in proposed algorithm. various researches have been done on evolutionary algorithms by using learning automata such as using learning automata to determine parameters in particle swarm optimization [9], presenting a new swarm optimization model based on learning automata [10]and also inducing A New Evolutionary Computing Model based on Cellular Learning Automata [11]. In our proposed algorithm a set of learning automata has been attributed to each drone and the algorithm attempts to produce better drones for mating with queen by getting feedback from the queens. To show the effectiveness and efficiency of the proposed algorithm we test the algorithm on several function optimization problems. The results of computer simulations show that the proposed algorithm attains better solutions in a faster way for most of the problems. The rest of this paper is organized as follows: In the next section a short review of the bees mating algorithms is presented, Section 3 describes the Learning Automata. In Section 4, a proposed algorithm is described in detail. Section 5 presents results on the benchmark optimization functions. Section 6 contains the concluding remarks and the future work.

2 Honey Bees Mating Optimization

A very interesting swarm in nature is honey bee swarm that has been considered significantly by wide range of researchers. Honey bee has remarkable characteristics in nature which make it considerable as an intelligent model. these characteristics consist of task division, individual and group communications. Honey bee mating in nature is one of the most notable things that scholars have marked lately and it has been able to develop optimization models. The mating between honey bees includes three different bee categories: queen bee, drones and workers. Queen bee is the only egg-laying female who is the mother of all the members of the colony. The queen usually mates only once in her life and she stores sperms in spermatheca and use them to produce broods. Drones are the fathers of the colony. Drones die after they mate with the queen. This process has been simulated in the model as a search of global optima. Workers are responsible for conserving the produced bees during mating process between queen and drones. Workers search on produced answers locally in simulated model. The main process in honey bees mating is mating flight. it begins with a dance of queen. During the flight the drones follow the queen and mate with her in the air. Sperm of the drones will be deposited and accumulated in the queen's spermatheca to form the genetic pool of the potential broods to be produced by the queen.

2.1 Honey-Bees Modeling

The mating flight may be considered as a set of transitions in a state-space where the queen moves between the different states in some speed and mates with the drone encountered at each state probabilistically. At the start of the flight, the queen is initialized with some energy content and returns to her nest when her energy is within some threshold from zero or when her spermatheca is full. In developing the algorithm, the functionality of workers is restricted to brood care, and therefore, each worker may be represented as a heuristic which acts to improve and/or take care of a set of broods. A drone mates with a queen probabilistically using an annealing function as [2][3]:

$Prob(Q,D) = e^{-\frac{\Delta(f)}{S(t)}}$ where *Prob(Q, D)* is the probability of adding the sperm of drone D to the spermatheca of queen Q ; $\Delta(f)$ is the absolute difference between the fitness of D and the fitness of Q ; and $S(t)$ is the speed of the queen at time t. It is apparent that this function acts as an annealing function, where the probability of mating is high when either the queen is still in the start of her mating flight and therefore her speed is high, or when the fitness of the drone is as good as the queen's. After each transition in space, the queen's speed, $S(t)$, and energy, $E(t)$, decay using the following equations:

$$S(t+1) = \alpha \times S(t)$$
$$E(t+1) = E(t) - \gamma$$

Where α is a factor $\in$ [0, 1] and γ *is* the amount of energy reduction after each transition.

3 Learning Automata

Learning Automata are adaptive decision-making devices operating on unknown random environments. The Learning Automaton has a finite set of actions and each action has a certain probability of getting rewarded by the environment of the automaton. The aim is to learn to choose the optimal action through repeated interaction on the system. If the learning algorithm is chosen properly, then the iterative process of interacting on the environment can be made to result in selection of the optimal action. Learning Automata can be classified into two main families: fixed structure learning automata and variable structure learning automata (VSLA) [6][7]. In the following, the variable structure learning automata is described. A VSLA is a quintuple $<\alpha,\beta,p,T(\alpha,\beta,p)>$, where α, β, $p$are an action set with s actions, an environment response set and the probability set p containing s probabilities, each being the probability of performing every action in the current internal automaton state, respectively. The function of T is the reinforcement algorithm, which modifies the action probability vector p with respect to the performed action and received response. Let a VSLA operate in an environment with $\beta=\{0,1\}$. Let $t \in N$ be the set of nonnegative integers. A general linear schema for updating action probabilities can be represented as follows. Let action i be performed. If $\beta(t)=0$ (Reward),

$$p_i(t+1) = p_i(t) + \alpha[1 - p_i(t)]$$
$$p_{j\neq i}(t+1) = (1-\alpha)p_j(t)$$

If $\beta(t)=1$ (Penalty),

$$p_i(t+1) = (1-b)p_i(t)$$
$$p_{j\neq i}(t+1) = \left(b/_S - 1\right) + (1-b)p_j(t)$$

Where a and b are reward and penalty parameters. When $a=b$, automaton is called L_{RP}.

4 Honey Bees Mating Optimization Based on Learning Automata

In this section, the new DHBMO based on learning automata is suggested. In this model, each drone has been attributed to a set of learning automata which are responsible for producing better drones. In this algorithm each drone consists of two parts, Model genome and string genome. Model genome is a set of learning automata. The set of actions selected by the set of learning automata determines the second component of the genome called string genome which a reinforcement signal is produced after mating flight and replacing queens with better broods for every automaton. Each learning automaton based on the received signal update its internal structure according to a Learning algorithm. Then each drone generates a new string genome and compares its fitness with the fitness of the string genome of the drone. If the fitness of the generated genome is better than the quality of the sting genome of the drone, the generated string genome becomes the string genome of that drone. This process of generating string genome by the drones is iterated until a termination condition is satisfied. Proposed algorithms as the one described algorithm in this paper can be used in any arbitrary finite discrete search space. In order to use the algorithm for the optimization function f first a set of learning automata is associated to each drone. The number of learning automata associated to a drone is the number bits in the string genome representing points of the search space of f. Each automaton has two actions called action 0 and 1. After each mating flight, these set of steps are done:

1. Every automata in a drone i chooses one of its actions using its action probability vector
2. drone_i generates a new string genome, new_i, by combining the actions chosen by the learning automata of drone_i . The newly generated string genome is obtained by concatenating the actions of the automata (0 or 1) associated to that drone. This section of algorithm is equivalent to learning from previous self-experiences.
3. Every drone_i computes the fitness value of string genome new_i ; if the fitness of this string genome is better than the one in the drone then the new string genome new_i becomes the string genome of that cell. That is

$$\xi_{t+1}^{i} \begin{cases} \xi_t^i & f(\xi_t^i) \leq f(\text{new}_{t+1}^i) \\ \text{new}_{t+1}^i & f(\xi_t^i) > f(\text{new}_{t+1}^i) \end{cases}$$

4. Se queens of the hive are selected. This Selection is based on the fitness value of the queens in hive.

5. Based on selected queens a reinforcement vector is generated. This vector becomes the input for the set of learning automata associated to the drones. This section of algorithm is equivalent to learning from experiences of others. Let Q_s be set selected queens :

$$Q_j(k) = \sum_{l \in Q_s} \delta(\xi_t^{l,j} = k) \quad \text{Where} \quad \delta(\exp) = \begin{cases} 1 & \text{exp is true} \\ 0 & \text{othewise} \end{cases}$$

$\beta^{i,j}$, the reinforcement signal given to learning automaton j of drone i, is computed as follows:

$$\beta_n^{i,j} = \begin{cases} u\left(Q_j(1) - Q_j(0)\right) \text{if } \xi_t^{i,j} = 0 \\ u\left(Q_j(0) - Q_j(1)\right) \text{ if } \xi_t^{i,j} = 1 \end{cases} \quad \text{Where u(.) is a step function.}$$

5 Experimental Setting and Results

In this section, the efficiency of proposed algorithm is presented. For this purpose, Standard functions borrowed from reference [12] are used to show proficiency of suggested algorithm. In the below table, functions with their characteristics are described.

Table 1. Benchmark functions and their characteristics

Function	Formulation	Range	Optimum
De Jong	$f_1(\vec{x}) = x^2 + y^2$	[-30,30]	0
Rastrigin	$f_2(\vec{x}) = 20 + x^2 + y^2 - 10\cos(2\pi x) - 10\cos(2\pi y)$	[-30,30]	0
Ackley	$f_3(\vec{x}) = 20 + e - 20\exp\left[-0.2\sqrt{\frac{1}{2}(x^2 + y^2)}\right] - \exp\left[\frac{1}{2}(\cos(2\pi x) + \cos(2\pi y))\right]$	[-32,32]	0
Easom	$f_4(\vec{x}) = -\cos(x)\cos(y)\exp\left[-((x-\pi)^2 + (y-\pi)^2)\right]$	[-100,100]	-1
Schwefel	$f_5(\vec{x}) = -(x\sin(\sqrt{\lvert x\rvert}) + y\sin(\sqrt{\lvert y\rvert}))$	[-500,500]	−837.9658
Shubert	$f_6(\vec{x}) = \left[\sum_{i=1}^{n} i\cos(i + (i+1)x)\right]\left[\sum_{i=1}^{n} i\cos(i + (i+1)y)\right] \; n = 5$	[-10,10]	−186.7309

The parameters used for LA-DHBMO and DHBMO consist of the number of queens set to 7, the spermatheca size set to 5, the maximum number of produced broods set to 30, and also the number of workers suggested in paper[2][3] set to 4.

Table 2. Results of 50 independent runs on DHBO and LA-DHBMO within 500 mating-flights in each run

Function	Algorithm	Best	Worst	Mean
f_1	DHBMO	0	20.46119	2.627948
	LA- DHBMO	0	0	0
f_2	DHBMO	0	15.19747	2.197145
	LA- DHBMO	0	0	0
f_3	DHBMO	$4.44E^{-16}$	11.64061	3.104444
	LA- DHBMO	$4.44E^{-16}$	$4.44E^{-16}$	$4.44E^{-16}$
f_4	DHBMO	$-1.60E^{-01}$	$-8.66E^{-7}$	$-1.00E^{-02}$
	LA- DHBMO	-0.9991	-0.7969	-0.9367
f_5	DHBMO	-837.816	-323.863	-664.774
	LA- DHBMO	-837.96	-833.019	-837.046
f_6	DHBMO	-180.9998	-172.4213	-178.8839
	LA- DHBMO	-186.7306	-184.717	-186.451

A setting for LA-DHBMO includes a kind of learning automata, L_{RP} with reward and penalty parameters set to 0.01 and 0.0.1 respectively, and a selection of all queens of hive are used to produce reinforcement signal. In the table below, the results of 50 independent runs within 500 mating-flights in each run are shown which demonstrates high proficiency of LA-DHBMO in comparison with standard algorithm.

6 Conclusion and Future Work

In this paper, we have developed a new optimization method with capability of learning. The results of experiments demonstrate the efficiency of algorithm in comparison with original algorithm. As it is shown in results, the new algorithm has a power of conquering local minimums and it is able to converge to global optima. As a consequence, the proposed algorithm may be a promising and viable tool to deal with complex numerical optimization problems. The future work includes the studies on how to extend it to handle multi objective optimization problems. It is desirable to further apply it to solve those more complex real-world optimization problems.

References

1. Karaboga, D., Akay, B.: A survey: algorithms simulating bee swarm intelligence. Artif. Intell. Rev., 61–85 (2009)
2. Abbass, H.A.: Amonogenous MBO approach to satisfiability. In: Proceeding of the International Conference on Computational Intelligence for Modelling, Control and Automation, CIMCA 2001, Las Vegas, NV, USA (2001)

3. Abbass, H.A.: Marriage in honey-bee optimization (MBO): a haplometrosispolygynous swarming approach. In: The Congress on Evolutionary Computation (CEC 2001), Seoul, Korea, pp. 207–214 (May 2001)
4. Afshar, A., Bozog Haddad, O., Marino, M.A., Adams, B.J.: Honey-bee mating optimization (HBMO) algorithm for optimal reservoir operation. Journal of the Franklin Institute 344, 452–462 (2007)
5. Fathian, M., Amiri, B., Maroosi, A.: Application of honey-bee mating optimization algorithm on clustering. Applied Mathematics and Computation, 1502–1513 (2007)
6. Marinakis, Y., Marinaki, M., Dounias, G.: Honey Bees Mating Optimization Algorithm for the Vehicle Routing Problem. NICSO, 139–148 (2007)
7. Narendra, K.S., Thathachar, M.A.L.: Learning Automata: An Introduction. Prentice-Hall Inc. (1989)
8. Thathachar, M.A.L., Sastry, P.S.: Varieties of learning automata: an overview. IEEE Transactions on Systems, Man, and Cybernetics, Part B, 711–722 (2002)
9. Hashemi, A.B., Meybodi, M.R.: A note on the learning automata based algorithms for adaptive parameter selection in PSO. Appl. Soft Comput., 689–705 (2011)
10. Rastegar, R., Meybodi, M.R., Badie, K.: A new discrete binary particle swarm optimization based on learning automata. In: ICMLA, pp. 456–462 (2004)
11. Rastegar, R., Meybodi, M.R.: A New Evolutionary Computing Model based on Cellular Learning Automata. In: CIS, pp. 433–438 (2004)
12. Yang, X.-S.: Test problems in optimization. In: Engineering Optimization: An Introduction with Metaheuristic Applications. John Wiley & Sons (2010)

An Evolutionary Optimization Approach to Software Test Case Allocation

Camila Loiola Brito Maia, Thiago Ferreira do Nascimento,
Fabrício Gomes de Freitas, and Jerffeson Teixeira de Souza

Optimizattion in Software Engineering Group (GOES.UECE), State University of Ceará,
Fortaleza, Ceará, Brazil
{camila.maia,thiagonascimento.uece,fabriciogf.uece,
prof.jerff}@gmail.com

Abstract. The problem of allocating test cases can be considered difficult because of the large number of possible solutions and the many factors that can influence the search for these solutions. There are several studies that use optimization techniques in finding solutions to difficult problems in software engineering in a recent research field called Search-Based Software Engineering (SBSE). Within this context, this paper proposes a multi-objective approach to the problem of allocating test cases. Two experiments were designed and implemented, and demonstrate the applicability and competitiveness of multi-objective algorithms in relation to the results generated by human users.

Keywords: Software testing, software engineering, optimization.

1 Introduction

In software engineering, aside problems related to the software specification and implementation, several other problems can be considered hard to solve. Those problems, such as task allocation, requirements prioritization, and selection of test cases, are in general complex to solve given their structure, high number of possible solutions, and context restrictions. This paper proposes a multi-objective evolutionary approach to solve the problem of allocating test cases. The purpose of test case allocation is to distribute the test cases among the available testers. The main research questions covered are as follows:

- Q1. How can the test case allocation problem be mathematically modeled?
- Q2: Which metaheuristic is the most suitable for the problem?
- Q3: Is optimization competitive to human test managers?

In the literature, many works deal with tasks allocation though mathematical optimization techniques. However, a specific optimization formulation for the allocation of test cases was not found. In the following are described some related works to the present paper.

V.V. Das and N. Thankachan (Eds.): CIIT 2011, CCIS 250, pp. 637–641, 2011.

The authors of [1] investigate two allocation problems of module testing (unit testing): minimizing the number of undetected faults in the system after the resources allocation, and minimizing the resources allocated (number of test cases, CPU time), given a number of undetected faults after the testing process. Two heuristics are proposed to solve the problems.

In [2], the impact of the Brooks' Law [Brooks 1975] on the allocations of a project is explored. The approach is based on genetic algorithms, and it analyses the effect of communication overhead of the project team, both in the completion time and in the people allocation in teams.

One approach based on dependencies, fragmentation, conflict and specialization is described in [3]. The metaheuristics used to evaluate the approach were Simulated Annealing, GA and Hill Climbing.

2 The Approach

The approach considers the testers' ability, their preferences for test cases, the execution history of the testing process, the minimal skill required to run each test case, and an ordered set of test cases. The following sets compose the formulation:

Test Cases. Let C be the set of all test cases. C has m test cases, i.e., $C = \{C_j \mid j = 1, \ldots, m\}$. Each test case has the following attributes: $requiredExperience_j$ and $precedence_j$.

System Testers. Let T be the set of all available testers. The set T has p testers, i.e., $T = \{t_w \mid w = 1, \ldots, p\}$. Each tester has an $experience_w$ level, which is the experience of the tester.

System Testers vs Test Cases. Each tester w has a preference level for each test case j (preferencew, j). In addition, the number of executions of the test case j by the tester j is also considered (numberOfExecutionsw,j).

Allocations. An allocation is the assignment of a test case for a tester. The solution is represented by a vector of integers, called ATC in the approach, in which **each** cell has the tester assigned for the correspondent position in the vector. For example, if the vector is "3,2,3,1", the first test case should be run by the tester 3; the second test case by tester 2; and so on.

The following aspects are considerd for the allocation: $numberOfExecutions_{ATC}$ (the sum of $numberOfExecutions_{w,j}$ for the testers), $preference_{ATC}$ (the sum of $preference_{w,j}$ for the testers), and $experience_{ATC}$ (the sum of $experience_w$ for the testers). In the proposed approach, it is possible to associate a test case to a tester that does not have the minimum experience required for it, however, in these cases, a penalty should be applied in order to decrease the value of $experience_{ATC}$. The penalty function is represented by $penalty_{w,PTCa}$, where w is the tester and $PTCa$ is the test case in test suite represented by PTC, where test cases are already ordered for the execution.

Given the aspects considered, the proposed optimization formulation of the test case allocation problem is defined as:

1) $Min\ numberOfExecutions_{ATC} = \sum_{w=1}^{P} \sum_{a=1}^{Y.lenght} numberOfExecutions_{w,PTC_a} * isAllocated_{w,PTC_a,ATC}$

2) $Max\ preference_{ATC} = \sum_{w=1}^{P} \sum_{a=1}^{PTC.lenght} preferences_{PTC_a,w} * isAllocated_{w,PTC_a,ATC}$

3) $Max\ experience_{ATC} = \sum_{w=1}^{P} \sum_{a=1}^{PTC.lenght} (experience_w - penalty_{w,PTC_a}) * isAllocated_{w,PTC_a,ATC}$

Subject to:

4) $\forall\ t_{j1},\ t_{j2} \in C,$

$$\left(\left(precedence_{t_{j2}} = t_{j1}\right)\ and\ (isAllocated_{w,t_{j2},ATC} = 1)\right) \rightarrow (isAllocated_{w,t_{j1},ATC} = 1)$$

Equation 1 aims at assigning to a tester the test cases that he performed less often. The equation 2 is set to assign testers to test cases that they prefer to run the most. Equation 3 wants to allocate test cases to testers who have a minimum experience required by each test case. All function use the *isAllocated* procedure, which is a boolean value for whether the test case is allocated or not to a tester. The equation 4 is a problem restriction used to ensure that the precedence relation between test cases is respected. When a test case is allocated to a tester Y, its predecessor should be allocated to the same tester Y.

3 Experiments

The first experiment regards the application of optimization techniques, where three multi-objective metaheuristics and a random method are applied to the problem. The comparison among the techniques is performed through the use of the hypervolume indicator [4]. The second experiment is applied to investigate whether the approach is human competitive, where the responses of the multi-objective algorithms are compared with the solutions of potential users of the proposed approach (human test analysts). The algorithms used in the experiments are: NSGA-II [4], MOCell [5] and SPEA2 [6], all based on genetic algorithms, but multi-objective. These algorithms were chosen for their good performance in comparison with other multi-objective algorithms, as can be seen in [5], [6]. To perform the experiment, 29 random instances were created.

3.1 Application of the Techniques

The metaheuristics and the random algorithm were applied to all instances (indicated by #). The main results of these experiments are presented in the Table 1 below, which shows the values for the hypervolume metric, for each instance and algorithm.

Table 1. Hypervolume for the techniques

#	NSGA-II	MOCell	SPEA2	Rand	#	NSGA-II	MOCell	SPEA2	Rand
A	0.00078	**0.00079**	0.00081	0.00043	P	0.00012	0.00012	**0.00015**	0.00001
B	**0.00004**	0.00004	0.00004	0.00001	Q	0.00017	0.00017	**0.00017**	0.00005
C	0.00039	0.00040	**0.00046**	0.00014	R	0.00078	0.00056	0.00069	**0.00370**
D	0.00012	0.00016	0.00020	**0.01355**	S	0.00008	0.00010	**0.00012**	0.00004
E	0.00011	0.00009	**0.00014**	0.00004	T	**0.00017**	0.00012	0.00011	0.00011
F	**0.00038**	0.00027	0.00025	0.00005	U	0.00027	0.00024	**0.00030**	0.00000
G	0.00018	**0.00025**	0.00012	0.00001	V	0.00013	0.00014	**0.00014**	0.00004
H	0.00003	0.00002	**0.00006**	0.00000	W	0.00012	**0.00014**	0.00009	0.00003
I	0.00032	0.00033	**0.00035**	0.00002	X	0.00016	0.00015	0.00018	**0.00020**
J	**0.00011**	0.00006	0.00009	0.00000	Y	0.00045	0.00037	0.00052	**0.00150**
K	0.00009	0.00008	**0.00011**	0.00000	Z	0.04777	0.03750	0.04630	**0.06080**
L	**0.00029**	0.00020	0.00028	0.00006	1	0.00028	0.00028	0.00030	**0.00091**
M	**0.00015**	0.00012	0.00014	0.00006	2	0.00019	0.00016	**0.00030**	0.00000
N	0.00006	0.00005	**0.00008**	0.00005	3	0.00005	0.00013	**0.00026**	0.00000
O	**0.00065**	0.00047	0.00050	0.00015					

In general, SPEA2 had the best hypervolume values overall, with the best values for this metric in 44.82% of the instances.

3.2 Human Comparison

Some potential users solved the problem. The users were of software engineer, about 60% having testing experience. Figure 1 shows the comparison of human solutions to the solutions obtained by multi-objective metaheuristics.

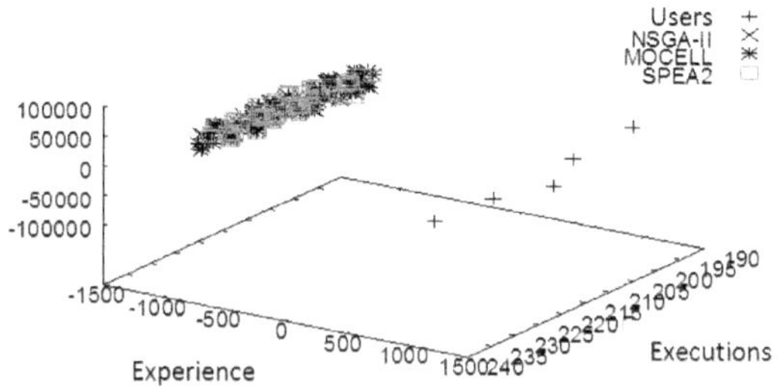

Fig. 1. Solutions of the algorithms and from human experts

As can be seen, the values of the solution provided by the human are worse than the ones from the metaheuristics. This indicates that the problem, given its complexity, should be solved by the proposed approach in the present paper.

4 Conclusion

About question Q1, the allocating test cases problem can be mathematically formulated as the approach proposed in this paper. The proposed approach is multi-objective, taking into account three important factors when choosing which testers to perform which test cases. The Q2 question was answered by an experiment. The aim was to know which of the three chosen techniques was the most appropriate. Overall, the results of the experiment showed that the algorithm SPEA2 performed better in relation to the hypervolume metric. Most of the solutions generated by this algorithm are in the Pareto optimal front, formed by the best solutions of the three algorithms.

To answer question Q3, a second experiment was conducted. As can be seen in the figure generated by the experiment (Figure 1), the solutions generated by users are far from the Pareto optimal front. There are four limitations to this approach. The first limitation is the absence of an interface for data entry. Given the amount of data, a person without a graphical interface is hard to input. A tool to generate text files in the format read by the tool is also need. The second limitation is the time to acquire the values of each input parameter of the proposed approach, since as you increase the number of requirements and test cases; it increases the amount of data to be informed. The third limitation is concerned on the objectives chosen by the approach, not contemplating goals that could be important. Finally, the fourth limitation is the use of randomly generated data in the approach evaluation, rather than actual project data.

We can cite two threats to the validity of the results generated by the experiments. The first threat is the configuration of the algorithms, as regards the rates of mutation and recombination, as well as other methods of recombination and mutation. The second is the use of data generated, since the algorithm that randomly generated the data may have done so in a bias manner.

References

1. Rou, R.H., Kuo, S.Y., Chang, Y.P.: Needed resources for software module test, using the hyper-geometric software reliability growth model. IEEE Transactions on Reliability 45(4), 541–549 (1996)
2. Di Penta, M., Harman, M., Antoniol, G., Qureshi, F.: The effect of communication overhead on software maintenance project staffing: a search-based approach. In: IEEE International Conference on Software Maintenance, pp. 315–324 (2007)
3. Di Penta, M., Harman, M., Antoniol, G.: The use of Search-Based Optimization Techniques to Schedule and Staff Software Projects: an Approach and an Empirical Study. Software – Practice and Experience (2009)
4. Deb, K., Agrawal, S., Pratap, A., Meyarivan, T.: A Fast Elitist Non-Dominated Sorting Genetic Algorithm for Multi-Objective Optimization: NSGA-II. In: Deb, K., Rudolph, G., Lutton, E., Merelo, J.J., Schoenauer, M., Schwefel, H.-P., Yao, X. (eds.) PPSN 2000. LNCS, vol. 1917, pp. 849–858. Springer, Heidelberg (2000)
5. Nebro, A.J., Durillo, J.J., Luna, F., Dorronsoro, B., Alba, E.M.: A cellular genetic algorithm for multiobjective optimization. International Journal of Intelligent Systems 24(7), 726–746 (2009)
6. Zitzler, E., Laumanns, M., Thiele, L.: SPEA2: Improving the Strength Pareto Evolutionary Algorithm (2001)

Lung Cancer Diagnosis from CT Images Using Fuzzy Inference System

T. Manikandan[1] and N. Bharathi[2]

[1] Rajalakshmi Engineering College, Chennai-602 105
[2] Velammal Engineering College, Chennai-600 066
mani_stuff@yahoo.co.in, rathiraj_2000@yahoo.com

Abstract. The Fuzzy Inference System (FIS) plays a vital role in the medical field to provide medical assistance to the radiologist to diagnose the abnormality in the medical images. This paper presents a scheme to improve the efficiency of the lung cancer diagnosis system by proposing the segmentation of the suspected lung nodules by region based segmentation and cancer identification by FIS. The proposed method is implemented in two phases. The first phase carries pre-processing for primary noise removal by wiener filter followed by region growing to segment the suspected lung nodules from CT lung images. The second phase carries the classification of the segmented nodules as either benign (normal) or malignant (cancerous) by extracting the features like diameter, shape and intensity values and given as the input to the FIS. The Fuzzy system finds the severity of the suspected lung nodules based on IF-THEN rules. The sensitivity of the proposed system is 92.3%, which show that the proposed work can help the radiologists to increase their diagnostic confidence.

Keywords: Computed Tomography (CT), Segmentation, Region growing, and Fuzzy Inference System (FIS).

1 Introduction

Lungs are the essential organs for respiration (inspiration and expiration) situated at thoracic cavity. Today, the lung cancer is serious disease in the world causing large number of deaths [1]. The cells of all living organisms normally divide and grow in a control manner. When this control process is lost and tissues start expands then the situation is called cancer. Among the various cancers like bone cancer, breast cancer, blood cancer etc., the lung cancer is the most deadly one. The causes of lung cancer are cigarette smoking, inhalation of tobacco, lung diseases, air pollution etc. The research shows that smoking of cigarette is the leading cause of lung cancer (90%) in the world. The people they don't smoke (non-smokers) also get's lung cancer, however the chance of risk is 10 times lesser than the smokers. The most preferred option for treating the lung cancer in the final stage is surgical removal of the diseased lung. Hence it is necessary to detect the lung cancer at an early stage to limit the danger. In this paper, lung cancer diagnosis system based on Fuzzy logic is proposed

V.V. Das and N. Thankachan (Eds.): CIIT 2011, CCIS 250, pp. 642–647, 2011.

to detect the lung cancer at the early stage. The proposed system first segments the suspected lung nodules from the input lung image and classifies either benign or cancerous based on the feature extraction. Then the extracted features are given to the input of FIS. The Fuzzy Inference System makes the decision based on IF-THEN rules. This paper is organized as follows: Section 2 describes the related works, Section 3 deals the proposed work. Section 4 gives the experimental results and finally section 5 draws the conclusion and Future work.

2 Related Work

2.1 Artificial Neural Networks

The Artificial Neural Networks (ANN) refers to computing systems whose central theme is borrowed from the analogy of biological neural networks. Neural networks can be configured in various arrangements to perform range of tasks such as machine vision, pattern recognition, data mining, text mining, classification and optimization. The most commonly used Neural Networks (NN) are feed forward and back propagation NN. The ANN consists of three layers namely input layer, hidden layer and output layer. The ANN is trained with the set of feature vectors. The training may be of any one of the following: supervised learning, unsupervised learning and reinforcement learning. In the literature there are number of proposals for diagnosing the cancerous nodules from lung images. To assess the benefit of ANN for diagnosing lung cancer the systematic review was conducted by N.Ganesan et. al [2]. The CAD system to diagnose the lung cancer based on ANN to assist radiologists in distinguishing malignant from pulmonary nodules was proposed by Yongjun et. al [3]. In neural network based classifier, the difficult task is designing of ANN structure. To provide the solution for the above problem Genetic algorithm (GA)-ANN hybrid intelligence was described by Fazil Ahmad et. al [4]. In their approach GA was used to select significant features simultaneously as input to ANN and optimal number of hidden node is determined automatically. Every intelligent technique has particular computational properties that make them suited for particular problems and not for others. For example, the NN are good at recognizing patterns, they need more processing time and lot of past data to make the decision.

2.2 Fuzzy Logic

Fuzzy logic is a rule based system it uses if-then rules. Fuzzy logic has been found applications in many areas from control theory to artificial intelligence. An automated method to detect the lung nodules based on wavelet transform, bi-histogram equalization, morphology filter and Fuzzy logic was proposed by C.Clifford Samuel et. al [5], however in their work the bronchovascular details are also detected as nodules. M.A.Saleem Durai et. al [6] described the technique to determine disease name, stage and diagnostic treatment of the cancer patient using Fuzzy rules but the diagnosis were complex because of the analysis of all the information gathered about the symptoms. To overcome the drawbacks of ANN and existing Fuzzy systems the new system is proposed to diagnose the lung cancer.

3 Proposed Work

The proposed work is carried in two phases. In first phase the suspected lung nodule are segmented. In the second phase the Fuzzy Inference System makes the diagnosis from the extracted features from the suspected nodules. The flow diagram of the proposed method is shown in Fig. 1. The proposed method consists of three steps. They are pre-processing, suspected lung nodule segmentation and feature extraction and Fuzzy Inference System.

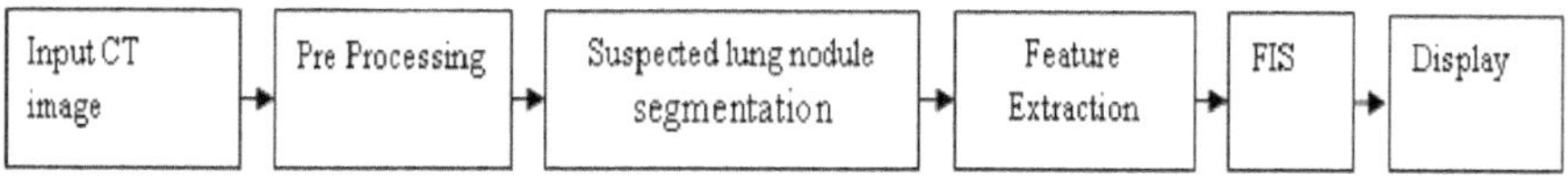

Fig. 1. Flow diagram of the proposed method

3.1 Pre -processing

The pre-processing aims to reduce the noise in the input CT lung images. The pre-processing is achieved by suppressing the noise. The noise distribution in CT images follows the Gaussian distribution therefore Wiener filter is employed to remove the noise. The Wiener filter is an optimum filter which minimizes the means square error hence it maximizes the image quality. In order to balance between the noise removal and over blurring the size of the Wiener filter is selected as 3x3. The metrics used to evaluate the performance of filters are Mean Square Error (MSE) and Peak Signal to Noise Ratio (PSNR). The PSNR is a measure of the peak error whereas the MSE is the cumulative squared error between the filtered and the original image. The mathematical formulae for the above two are,

$$MSE = 1/MN\{ [g(x, y) - g'(x, y)]^2 \} \quad (1)$$

$$PSNR=20*\log_{10} [255/sqrt(MSE)] \quad (2)$$

Where, g(x, y) is the original image, g'(x, y) is the filtered image and M, N are the dimensions of image.

3.2 Suspected Lung Nodule Segmentation and Feature Extraction

The next step after pre-processing is the segmentation of the suspected lung nodules from the CT images. The suspected lung nodules are segmented by region based segmentation. In segmentation technique, the complex image is divided into small sub images. The segmentation should be stopped when the Region of Interest (ROI) of a particular application is isolated. The ROI in CT image is usefully a cluster of pixels that appears to be dense mass. The region based segmentation uses region growing technique, which is based on the similarity approach to segment the suspected lung nodules. The region growing starts with set of seed points. The region is allowed to grow by appending the neighbouring pixels that have properties similar to the seed such as specific gray level. Thus the region based segmentation segments the suspected lung nodules from the input CT lung images. The selectivity of the cancer detection depends on the ability to segment the suspected nodules from the lung images. The various features like diameter, shape and intensity are extracted for the suspected lung nodules. These features are the input to the Fuzzy Inference System.

3.3 Fuzzy Inference System

Fuzzy inference is the process of formulating the mapping from a given input to an output using Fuzzy logic. The mapping then provides a basis from which decisions can be made. The overall name for a system is, that uses fuzzy reasoning to map an input space into an output space. Fuzzy logic is a rule based system it uses if-then rules. The Fuzzy logic is proved to be a potential tool for decision making systems such as pattern recognition and expert systems. FIS is used to recognize the nodules depending on the input, output Fuzzy membership functions. Extracted features like diameter, shape and intensity are the input to the Fuzzy system. Based on the extracted features the FIS can classify whether the suspected nodules are normal or cancerous one. The cancerous nodules have greater diameter and intensity than the normal lung nodules. Further the cancerous nodules will have irregular shape. The severity of the detected nodule is computed using Fuzzy rules framed relating to the extracted features. The rules used in FIS to diagnose the lung cancer (based on the observation of the radiologists and field experts) is as follows,

IF (Diameter>10pixels, Intensity>240) and
IF (Shape is irregular?) THEN
Disease = Cancer
Else
Normal cells are found.

4 Experimental Results

The lung cancer diagnosis using FIS is shown in Fig. 2.The input lung image acquired from CT image [see Fig. 2(a)] is first pre-processed by Wiener filter to remove the noise. After the removal of noise the PSNR value is calculated as 40.6 decibels. Hence the Wiener filter maximizes the quality of the input image and reduces the means square error of the counterpart. The filtered image is given in Fig. 2(b). After pre-processing, the region growing technique is applied on the input lung image to segment the suspected lung nodules. The region growing is shown in Fig. 2(c).

The segmented suspected lung nodules are shown in Fig. 2(d), which show that they are cluster of pixels that appears to be dense mass. The suspected lung nodules may be benign or malignant. The various features are extracted for the suspected

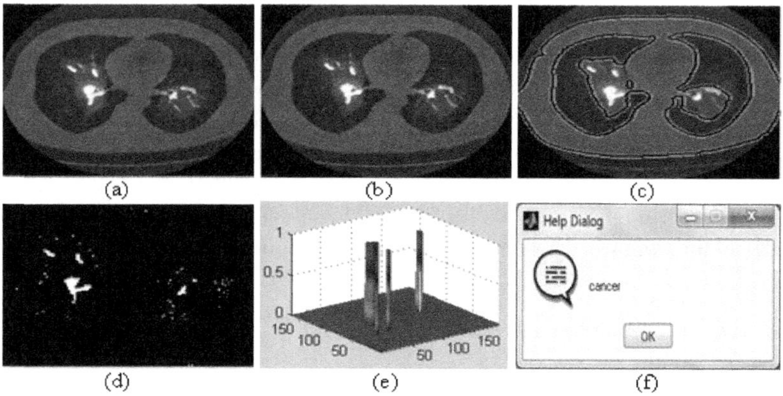

Fig. 2. Lung cancer diagnosis using FIS (a) Input CT image (b) Filtered image (c) Region growing (d) Suspected lung nodules (e) 3D view of malignant nodules (f) Dialog box displaying the result

nodules and given as input to the FIS. Based on the extracted features, the Fuzzy Inference System classifies whether the suspected nodules are benign or malignant. The 3D views of malignant nodules are given in Fig. 2(e). The dialog box displays the output of FIS is given in Fig. 2(f). The obtained results are compared with the radiologists for sensitivity, which is computed using the equation,

$$\text{Sensitivity} = TP / (TP + FN) \quad (3)$$

Where TP is the True Positive nodules and FN is False Negative nodules. The test is carried out for 50 patient's data sets, out of which 25 patients data sets are taken with normal condition and 25 patient's data sets are taken with cancerous condition. The output of the FIS for the sample data sets are given in table 1. The sensitivity of the FIS is compared with the various existing methods, which is shown in table 2. The obtained results show that the sensitivity of the proposed method is higher than the other methods.

Table 1. Output of FIS for sample data

Patient's test data	Output of FIS	
	Positive	Negative
Positive (25 data)	True Positive (TP)=24	True Negative (TN)=1
Negative (25 data)	False Negative (FN)=23	False Negative (FN)=2

Table 2. Quantitative comparison of FIS with other methods

Method	Sensitivity	Data Used
Yongjun et. al [3]	84.6%	117 cases
Kenji Suzuki et. al [7]	82.4%	91 cases
Ayman El-Baz Et. al [8]	91.5%	27 cases
Ganesan et. al [2]	87%	20 cases
Proposed FIS	**92.3%**	**50 cases**

5 Conclusion and Future work

In this paper, the lung cancer diagnosis system based on FIS is proposed. The proposed system consists of pre-processing, segmentation of the suspected nodules and classification to detect the lung cancer. The sensitivity of the system is calculated as 92.3%, which is higher than the existing methods. Therefore the lung cancer diagnosis system based on FIS can be useful for the radiologists to diagnose the lung cancer at the early stage. However in future, the sensitivity of the proposed system may improve by using the hybrid systems i.e., combining either Neural Network with Fuzzy logic (Neuro-Fuzzy network) or Fuzzy logic with Neural Network (Fuzzy-Neural) network.

References

1. Asbestos cancer resource, `http://www.asbestos.net/lung-cancer/lung-cancer-facts`
2. Ganesan, N., Venkatesh, K., Rama, M.A.: Application of Neural Networks in diagnosing cancer diseases using Demographic data. International Journal of Computer Applications 1, 76–82 (2010)
3. Wu, Y., Wang, N., Hongshezhang: Application of Artificial Neural Networks in the Diagnosis of Lung Cancer by Computed Tomography. In: Sixth International Conference on Natural Computation, China, pp. 147–153 (2010)
4. Ahmad, F., Mat-Isa, N.A.: Genetic algorithm-Artificial Neural network Hybird intelligence for cancer diagnosis. In: Second international Conference on Computational Intelligence, Communication Systems and Networks (2010)
5. Clifford Samuel, C., Saravanan, V., Vimala Devi, M.R.: Lung nodule diagnosis from CT images using fuzzy logic. In: International Conference on Computational Intelligence and Multimedia Applications (2007)
6. Saleem Durai, M.A., Iyengar, N.C.S.N.: Effective analysis and diagnosis of lung cancer using Fuzzy rules. International Journal of Engineering Science and Technology 2(6), 2102–2108 (2010)
7. Suzuki, K., Shairaishi, J.: False-Positive reduction in computer-aided diagnostic scheme for detecting in chest radiographs by means of massive training artificial neural network. IEEE Transaction on Medical Imaging 24, 1138–1143 (2005)
8. El-Baz, A., Falk, R.: Promising results for early diagnosis of lung cancer. IEEE transactions on Medical imaging, 1151–1154 (2008)

Template Matching Approach for Printed Kannada Numeral Recognition

Ravindra S. Hegadi

Department of Computer Science, Karnatak University,
Dharwad-580003, India
ravindrahegadi@rediffmail.com

Abstract. In this paper a simple template matching method based on correlation coefficient is proposed to recognize the printed Kannada numerals. Here the scanned printed Kannada numeral documents are preprocessed and each numeral is extracted by first performing the line segmentation and then segmenting each numeral from the segmented line. Each segmented object is resized to a predefined size. The correlation coefficient is computed between the image under consideration and stored numeral image data. A high value of correlation coefficient will indicate the successful match. The proposed algorithm is invariant to size of the numerals since segmented objects are resized in the preprocessing stage. Experimentation is carried out on 30 different fonts of Kannada numerals generated from Nudi 4.0 software. The results are encouraging.

Keywords: Kannada Numerals, Template matching, correlation coefficient.

1 Introduction

The problem of Kannada numeral recognition falls under character recognition, which is a sub problem of document image analysis. The document image analysis can be categorized in to two groups, namely, text processing and graphical processing. In text processing the characters, including numerals and special characters, are processed [1]. Many commercial OCR are available for English, most of the European languages, Chinese and Japanese languages with good level of accuracy. Few works are reported for Indian as well as Kannada languages in recent years. A neural network based classifier proposed by R. S. Kunte et. al. [4] uses the wavelet coefficients as features for character recognition. The drawback of this method is, it fails to recognize the similar characters and it requires very large database. A template matching based Kannada OCR was proposed by Ashwin et. al. [5] in which SVM is used as classifier. This method is very sensitive to the fonts and malfunctions for different character sizes. Recognition of isolated Kannada handwritten numerals using image fusion method [6] uses the nearest neighborhood classifier for numeral pattern matching. In this paper a template matching method based on correlation coefficient computation is proposed for the recognition of printed Kannada numerals. The methodology of the proposed work is discussed in section 2. The experimentation is discussed in

V.V. Das and N. Thankachan (Eds.): CIIT 2011, CCIS 250, pp. 648–651, 2011.

section 3. In this section the detailed analysis of failures in recognition of different numerals is also presented. Finally, in section 4 conclusions are drawn and future work is proposed.

2 Proposed Method

The input images are preprocessed to eliminate noise and resized to a standard size. Each image template is matched with the stored numeral image data in the database. The description of these processes is given in the following sub sections.

2.1 Image Preprocessing

Kannada language has ten basic numerals (Figure 1). The scanned image document containing Kannada numerals is converted to binary image by applying thresholding. The preprocessed image will contain the data in multiple lines, each line containing multiple numerals. The document is scanned from the top-left corner of the image and when a pixel is found, its corresponding bottom-right point is located. The rectangle formed with the help of these points is extracted, which will be one line of text containing numerals. The image document may contain many such lines. The extracted line is segmented into individual numeral image by identifying the connected components and drawing the bounding box for each connected component. They are resized to a standard size of 42×24 pixels before further processing.

೧ ೨ ೩ ೪ ೫ ೬ ೭ ೮ ೯ ೦

Fig. 1. Printed Kannada numerals

2.2 Template Matching

A training data set for each numeral is created using Nudi 17 K font and stored in the database. The numerals in this data set will have a size of 42×24. For each character a bounding box is drawn and the content within this box is stored. A correlation coefficient is computed between the segmented image and every numeral image data in the database. The correlation coefficient is a real value between -1 and 1. As the strength of the relationship between the predicted values and actual values increases so does the correlation coefficient. A perfect fit gives a coefficient of 1.0. The mathematical formula for computing correlation coefficient value, r is

$$r = \frac{n\sum xy - \left(\sum x\right)\left(\sum y\right)}{\sqrt{n\left(\sum x^2\right) - \left(\sum x\right)^2}\sqrt{n\left(\sum y^2\right) - \left(\sum y\right)^2}} \tag{1}$$

where n is the number of pairs of data, x and y are the training and testing numeral image data. Higher the value of r, the correlation coefficient, more will be match between the numeral with the template from the database. For each numeral from the input image ten correlation coefficient values are generated with each value corresponding to numerals from 0 to 9. The maximum highest correlation coefficient value among these will show the matching numeral from the database.

3 Experimental Results

Experimentation is carried out on thirty different fonts of Kannada numerals generated from Nudi 4.0 Kannada scripting software. Figure 2 shows an input scanned image containing some Kannada numerals in two rows. The segmented numeral images are resized to 42×24 pixels as shown in Figure 3. The correlation coefficient is computed between the training numeral image data sets with the testing numeral image data. One such results of a particular font are recorded as shown in Table 1. In this table *x* represents the training numeral image data and *y* represents the testing numeral image data. From this Table it can be seen that there is a very high correlation between training and testing image data corresponding to same numeral.

Fig. 2. Input image containing Kannada numerals

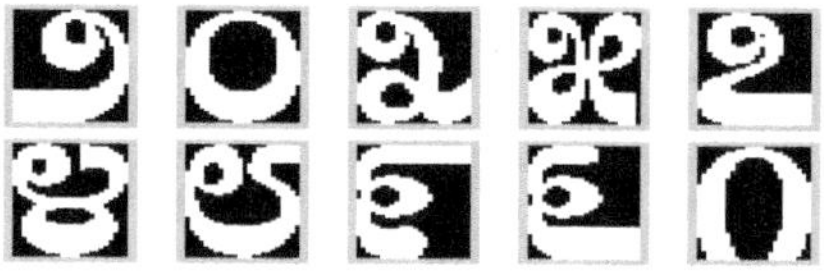

Fig. 3. Segmented numeral images

Table 1. Correlation coefficient values between training and one set of testing data

x	-	1	2	3	4	5	6	7	8	9	0
	1	0.97	0.04	-0.08	0.01	0.07	0.02	0.01	0.12	-0.09	0.53
	2	0.02	0.95	-0.04	0.13	0.02	0.15	0.24	0.25	0.09	0.21
	3	-0.08	-0.05	0.90	0.06	0.26	0.35	0.38	0.04	0.06	-0.09
	4	0.01	0.19	0.05	0.90	0.30	0.14	0.03	0.31	0.15	0.33
y	5	0.05	0.04	0.25	0.32	0.92	0.22	0.12	0.08	0.17	0.00
	6	0.04	0.14	0.35	0.16	0.22	0.95	0.55	0.13	0.57	0.20
	7	0.01	0.25	0.37	0.10	0.11	0.57	0.92	0.17	0.24	0.11
	8	0.10	0.25	0.02	0.33	0.09	0.13	0.13	0.93	0.17	0.43
	9	-0.07	0.08	0.03	0.20	0.18	0.54	0.21	0.18	0.92	0.07
	0	0.52	0.23	-0.08	0.34	0.01	0.19	0.11	0.45	0.06	0.96

The above experimentation is carried out on numerals belonging to thirty different fonts, generated using Nudi software. The number of correct and false detection for these numerals is as shown in Table 2. It can be noticed that two numerals, namely, 2 and 9 are detected with 100% accuracy. The worst detection rate is shown by numeral

3 with an accuracy of 76.67%. The overall accuracy of all the numerals using the proposed method is 91%.

Table 2. Rate of accuracy in detecting numerals using proposed method

Numerals	1	2	3	4	5	6	7	8	9	0
Correct detection	29	30	26	29	28	27	27	28	30	27
False detection	1	0	4	1	2	3	3	2	0	3
Rate of accuracy	96.67	100	76.67	96.67	90	86.67	86.67	90	100	86.67

4 Conclusion

Even though the template matching algorithm is old and well known, here an attempt is made to implement this algorithm based on the correlation coefficient to recognize and classify the printed numerals. The main characteristic of the Kannada numerals is their shapes, which are mostly formed with curves. Most of the failures in recognition are due to either selection of fonts which display numerals with sharp edges and corners, or breaking of a character making it as separate multiple numerals. The fonts selected for the experimentation cover almost all the computer generated fonts using very popular and widely used Kannada word processing software, Nudi. The performance of the proposed algorithm can be improved by considering more features like topological properties of numerals, curvature, etc.

References

1. Gorman, L.O., Kasturi, R.: Document image analysis. IEEE Computer Society Press (1995)
2. Choudhary, B.B., Pal, U.: An OCR system to read two Indian language scripts: Bangla and Devanagari. In: Fourth Int. Conf. Doc. Ana. Rec., pp. 1011–1015 (1997)
3. Sinha, R.M.K., Mahabala, H.: Machine recognition of Devanagari script. IEEE Trans. Sys., Man, Cybern. 9, 435–449 (1979)
4. Kunte, R.S., Samual, R.D.S.: An OCR system for printed Kannada text using two-stage Multi-network classification approach employing Wavelet features. In: Int. Conf. Computational Intel. Multimedia Appl., pp. 349–455 (2007)
5. Ashwin, T.V., Sastry, P.S.: A font and size independent OCR system for printed Kannada documents using support vector machines. Sadhana 27(1), 35–58 (2002)
6. Rajput, G.G., Hangarge, M.: Recognition of Isolated Handwritten Kannada Numerals Based on Image Fusion Method. In: Ghosh, A., De, R.K., Pal, S.K. (eds.) PReMI 2007. LNCS, vol. 4815, pp. 153–160. Springer, Heidelberg (2007)
7. Yuhai, L., Jian, L., Jinwen, T., Honbo, X.: A fast rotated template matching based on point feature. In: Proc. SPIE, vol. 6043, pp. 453–459 (2005)

Feature Selection Using Various Hybrid Algorithms for Speech Recognition

Manisha Pacharne[1] and Vidyavati S. Nayak[2]

[1] Defence Institute of Advance Technology (DU), Pune-411025, India
[2] Armament Research & Development Establishment, Pashan, Pune-411021, India
manishapacharne@gmail.com, vidyavatinayak@diat.ac.in

Abstract. Feature selection aims at selection of relevant features by applying certain selection criteria leading to high classification performance. Many practical problems consist of number of features, which makes classification as challenging task. With all these features system load and computation time will increase. Various feature selection and ranking methods are available to eliminate irrelevant features. In this paper the dataset used is available in analog form, which is converted into digital form for feature extraction and the obtained dataset is used to perform the experiments. Various algorithms like Minimum Redundancy Maximum Relevance (MRMR), Correlation based Feature Selection (CFS), t-Test, Chi Square, Fast Correlation Based Feature selection (FCBF), Fisher Score, Gini Index, Information Gain, Krushkal Wallis and BlogReg are used to rank and select features from speech dataset. These algorithms are combined with genetic algorithm; this hybrid approach minimizes the selected features. SVM is used for classification and prediction of data for selected features. The classification accuracy of dataset with reduced features obtained using above mentioned algorithms and hybrid approach is compared.

Keywords: Support Vector Machine (SVM), Genetic Algorithm (GA), Weka, Feature Extraction, Feature Selection, Speech Recognition.

1 Introduction

Feature selection techniques are used to select optimal subset of features and improve classification accuracy. It also helps to reduce training and testing time, storage requirements and facilitates data understanding, thus improves classifier performance. Features are ranked based on their influence towards the final classification. Many methods are available for feature selection, among them feature ranking approaches are particularly attractive because of their simplicity, scalability. Various issues like [1] definition of various types of speech classes, speech representation, feature extraction techniques, speech classifiers are consider for design of speech recognition system. Speech signal is in analog form, which is converted in to digital form for feature extraction. From each audio file 109 features are extracted and important features are selected which are more effective for classification using various feature ranking and selection algorithms. Further the hybrid approach is used to reduce the features, some

V.V. Das and N. Thankachan (Eds.): CIIT 2011, CCIS 250, pp. 652–656, 2011.

features may be redundant they are also eliminated. The paper is organized as follows. First is introduction section. Section 2 gives the brief about the features extracted for further analysis. Section 3 presents the various feature selection and ranking algorithms used for feature selection. Section 4 gives hybrid algorithms for feature selection; here various feature selection and ranking algorithms are combined with genetic algorithm. Section 5 gives brief about SVM as classifier. Section 6 presents experimental results and then finally we conclude our work in the last section.

2 Feature Extraction

Audio feature extraction plays an important role in analyzing and characterizing audio content, where a segment of audio is characterized into a compact numerical representation. Audio data to be classified cannot be represented as raw audio data. Hence, some form of parameterization is required. Parameterization of audio data is based on audio analysis. For analysis of speech signal, the signal is digitized, some features like zero crossing, bits per sample, mean, median, standard deviation, average magnitude, average power, sound pressure level, magnitude are computed using digitized value of speech signal. Discrete wavelet transform is used to calculate the wavelet coefficients of the input signal. There are thousands of coefficients of an audio signal; among them randomly hundred are selected as input features to perform further analysis.These extracted features are converted into vector form to perform its classification.

3 Feature Ranking and Selection Algorithms

Feature selection [2] improves classification by searching for the subset of features, which best classifies the training data. In our approach various data mining techniques used for feature ranking and selection are discussed here. Minimum Redundancy Maximum Relevance (MRMR) is an incremental feature selection algorithm, selects top ranking features based on mutual information. It is used to select features having maximum relevance and redundant features are eliminated [3]. Firstly, the mutual information (MI) between the candidate variable and the target variable is calculated (the relevance term). Then the average MI between the candidate variable and the variables that are already selected is computed (the redundancy term). In this method, the redundancy among the features is minimized while the relevance is maximized. The Waikato Environment for Knowledge Analysis (Weka) is used to select the features using Correlation based Feature Selection (CFS) [4], the Chi Square statistic, Information Gain and Fast Correlation Based Feature selection (FCBF) [5]. The other algorithms such as t-Test [6], Fisher Score [7], Gini Index [8], Krushkal Wallis [9] and BlogReg [10] are implemented in MatLab. t-Test is the statistical hypothesis where weight of each feature is calculated and used to rank the features. Fisher Score is used for determining most relevant features for classification. It uses discriminative methods and generative statistical model. Gini index is used as a measure for feature ranking and it is a statistical measure of dispersion. Krushkal Wallis is a test of variance using population variance among groups and BlogReg algorithm is an implementation of Bayesian logistic regression method.

4 Hybrid Algorithms Using GA

The basic idea of a Genetic Algorithm [11] is to search a hypothesis space to find the best hypothesis. A pool of initial hypotheses called a population is randomly generated and each hypothesis is evaluated with a fitness function. Hypotheses with greater fitness have higher probability of being chosen to create the next generation. Some fraction of the best hypotheses may be retrained into the next generation, the rest undergo genetic operations such as crossover and mutation to generate new hypotheses. The size of population is same for all generations in our implementation. This process is iterated until either a predefined fitness criterion is met or the preset maximum number of generations is reached. In our approach two stage selection [12] algorithm by combining all above mention algorithms with GA is used. In the first stage any one of the above mention algorithm is used to filter noisy and redundant genes in high dimensional microarray data. In the second stage, selected features are given as input to GA and then GA and SVM work together for selecting the highly discriminating genes.

5 Classification Using Support Vector Machine (SVM)

SVM is a classifier, performs classification by constructing hyperplanes in a multidimensional space that separates cases of different class labels. To reduce the error in the classifications it uses kernel functions like polynomial, radial basis function etc. The user may provide any of these functions at the time of training the classifier, the experiments are carried out using RBF kernel function. SVM classify data by using support vectors, which are members of the set of training inputs that outline the hyper plane in feature space. The advantages of SVM are low expected probability of generalization errors, its speed and scalability. LibSVM [14] tool is library for SVM. Classification model is build using training data by LibSVM and used for performing binary classification.

6 Experimental Result

For performance evaluation of various feature selection methods, the audio dataset [15] used in our work is drawn from closed set of talkers available in .wav format. The dataset consist of 1000 record (audio files) and each record is having 109 features. The features are extracted from each .wav file and used to create new dataset in vector form. The features and class labels are represented by numeric values.

Various feature ranking and selection algorithms as mention in Section 3 on the dataset and then performed binary classification using LibSVM using RBF kernel function and the optimal kernel parameters such as c(error cost) = 1.0 and g(gamma)

= 3.05175e-05 are selected using 10 fold cross validation. In 10 fold cross validation the data is randomly split into 10 mutually exclusive subsets of approximately equal size. A learning algorithm is trained and tested 10 times; each time it is tested on one of the 10 folds and trained using remaining 9 folds. Thus we obtain cross validation accuracy of speech data set. The cross validation estimate of accuracy is the overall number of correct classification, divided by the number of examples in the data. The reduced feature subset is given as input to genetic algorithm to obtain optimal feature subset. Thus we obtain another 10 fold cross validation accuracy of optimal feature subset. The comparison of classification accuracy for different feature subsets using various algorithms is shown in Table 1.

Table 1. Classification accuracy for various feature subsets

Feature Selection Algorithms	Features Obtained from various Algorithms	Accuracy(%)	Features Obtained from GA	Accuracy
SVM	109	49.1	45	50.2
MRMR	62	54.1	30	64.8
CFS	30	69.8	11	62
t-Test	30	64	13	63.1
Chi Square	30	69.2	19	63.3
FCBF	30	66.4	18	66.4
Fisher Score	30	68.4	19	65.4
Gini Index	30	63.1	18	60.5
Information Gain	30	64.2	14	62.3
Krushkal Wallis	30	49	13	62.4
BlogReg	11	71.2	5	65.7

The first column of Table 1 shows various feature ranking and selection algorithms used. Second column gives the total number of features that are selected after applying these algorithms. These features are selected based on the rank assigned to them. BlogReg and MRMR are feature selection algorithms while SVM considers all the features in the first stage before combining it with GA and remaining other algorithms are feature ranking algorithms. Third column gives the classification accuracy in percentage obtained using SVM classifier. The features listed in second column are given as input to genetic algorithm which gives the optimal features displayed in fourth column. The forth column represents the number of features that are selected as output of hybrid algorithms, and fifth column represents the classification accuracy in percentage using SVM classifier.

7 Conclusion

The reduced subsets of the features were obtained using various feature ranking and selection algorithms. Optimal subsets of features were obtained using hybrid algorithms. We have compared the performance of various subsets of features obtained from the feature selection methods over generated dataset. Experimentally as shown in Table 1, we find that after applying GA on data containing all features and feature selected using MRMR, Krushkal Wallis algorithm recognition accuracy is increased with the reduced features. While in case of FCBF classification accuracy remained unchanged with reduced features and for other remaining algorithm there is reduction in classification accuracy with reduced features. MRMR, Krushkal Wallis algorithm performs better after combining with GA instead of individually. And we can also conclude that accuracy of SVM using feature selection usually outperforms than without feature selection.

References

1. Anusuya, M.A., Katti, S.K.: Speech Recognition by Machine: A Review. J. IJCSIS 6(3), 181–205 (2009)
2. Guyon, I., Elisseeff, A.: An Introduction to Variable and Feature Selection. Journal of Machine Learning Research 3, 1157–1182 (2003)
3. Elakadi, A., Amine, A., Elouardighi, A., Aboutajdine, D.: A New Gene Selection Approach Based on Minimum Redundancy Maximum Relevance (MRMR) and Genetic Agorithm (GA). In: ACS/IEEE International Conference on Computer Systems and Applications, pp. 69–75 (2009)
4. Michalak, K., Kwasnicka, H.: Correlation Based Feature Selection Strategy in Classification Problems. IJAMCS 16(4), 503–511 (2006)
5. Yu, L., Liu, H.: Feature Selection for High Dimentional Data: A Fast Correlation-Based Filter Solution. In: 10th International Conference on Machine Leaning (ICML 2003), Washington, D.C, pp. 856–863 (2003)
6. Zhou, N., Wang, L.: A Modified T-test Feature Selection Method and Its Application on the HapMap Genotype Data. Genomics, Proteomics & Bioinformatics 5(3-4), 242–249 (2007)
7. Duda, R.O., Hart, P.E., Stork, D.G.: Patteren classification, 2nd edn. John Wiley & Sons, New York (2001)
8. Shang, W., Huang, H., Zhu, H., Lin, Y., Qu, Y., Wang, Z.: A Novel Feature Selection Algorithm for Text Categorization. J. Expert System with Applications 33, 1–5 (2007)
9. Wei, L.J.: Asymptotic Conservativeness and Efficiency of Kruskal-Wallis Test for K Dependent Samples. Journal of the American Statistical Association 76(376), 1006–1009 (1981)
10. Cawley, Gavin, C., Talbot, Nicola, L.C.: Gene Selection in Cancer Classification using Sparse Logistic Regression with Bayesian Regularization. J. Bioinformatics 22(99), 2348–2355 (2006)
11. Sivanandam, S.N., Deepa, S.N.: Introduction to Genetic Algorithms. Springer, Heidelberg (2008)
12. Michael, L., Raymer, W.F., Punch, E.D., Goodman, L.A., Leslie, A.K., Jain, A.K.: Dimensionality Reduction using Genetic Algorithm. IEEE Transaction on Evolutionary Computation 4(2), 164–171 (2000)
13. LibSVM (A library for Support vector machine), `http://www.csie.ntu.edu.tw/cjlin/libsvm/`
14. Cooke, M., Te-won: Speech Separation Challenge, `http://staffwww.dcs.shef.ac.uk/people/M.cooke/SpeechSeparationChallenge.htm`

Refinement of the Test Bed Using Various Prioritization Techniques for Assuring Software-Quality

Rajat Sheel Jain[1] and Amit Gupta[2]

[1] Department of Information Technology, Institute of Management Studies, Noida, India
jainrajatsheel@gmail.com
[2] Maharaja Agrasen Institute of Management Studies, New Delhi, India
amitgupta21@gmail.com

Abstract. Test development is an expensive technique. Test suite saving for the software application by which test cases from the suite can be used for the software maintenance. We propose to develop Specification Analyzer that accepts specification like statement coverage, code coverage for the generation of efficient test cases from test suite. The Specification Analyzer compares the information about the techniques like Precision, Efficiency, Inclusiveness and Generality. The Fault detection capability tool provides the minimized size of test suite which satisfies the above criteria. By reducing the test suite size, we can reduce the execution cost and time, validation and management of the test cases from the suite for future releases of the software and able to maintain the fault detection capability by reusing the refined test cases. The prioritization method will increase time-effectiveness in detecting the faults. An improved rate of fault detection can provide faster feedback of the system under test.

Keywords: Regression Testing, Regression Test Selection, Linear Equation, Symbolic Execution, Data Flow Techniques, Prioritization.

1 Introduction

Software Testing is the practice that we do with the intention to find out the errors in applications. Regression Testing is the process of validating modified software to detect whether the new errors have been introduced into the previously tested codes and provide confidence that the modifications are correct. Since the regression testing is an expensive process, researches have proposed regression test selection techniques as a way to reduce some of this experience. These techniques attempt to reduce the costs by selecting and running subsets of the test cases in the program's existing test suites. However it is difficult to compare and evaluate these techniques because they can be used to solve the different problem goals.

A typical selective retest technique proceeds as follows:

1) Select $T^1 \subseteq T$, a set of tests to execute on P^1.
2) Test P^1 with T^1, to establish the correctness of P^1 with respect to T^1.
3) If necessary, create T^2, a set of new functional or structural tests for P^2.
4) Test P^1 with T^2, to establish the correctness of P^1 with respect to T^2.
5) Create T^3, a new test suite and test history for P^1 from T, T^1 and T^2.

V.V. Das and N. Thankachan (Eds.): CIIT 2011, CCIS 250, pp. 657–661, 2011.

All code-based regression test selection techniques attempt to select a subset T^1 of T that will be helpful in establishing confidence that P^1 was modified correctly and that P's functionality has been preserved where required. In this sense, all code-based test selection techniques are concerned, among other things, with locating tests in T that expose faults in P^1. Thus, it is appropriate to evaluate the relative abilities of the techniques to choose tests from T that detect faults.

2 Regression Test Selection Techniques

There are three categories for the regression test selection techniques: Linear Equation, Symbolic Execution and Data Flow Technique.

A. Linear Equation Techniques

A selective re-tests technique that uses a system comprising of linear equations to select test suites that yield segment coverage of modified code. Linear equation techniques use systems of linear equations to express relationships between tests and program segments. The techniques obtain systems of equations from matrices that track program segments reached by test cases, segments reachable from other segments, and (optionally) definition-use information about the segments. Linear equation techniques are automated. When the techniques operate as minimization techniques, they return small test suites and thus reduce the time required to run the selected tests. However, Fischer states that due to the calculations required to solve systems of linear equations the techniques may be data and computation intensive on large programs. In fact, the underlying problem is NP-hard, and all known 0-1 integer programming algorithms may take exponential time. Despite this possible worst-case behavior, 0- 1 integer programming algorithms exist that can obtain solutions, in practice, in times that may be acceptable.

B. Symbolic Execution Techniques

A selective re-tests technique that uses input partitions and data-driven symbolic execution to select and execute regression tests. Initially, the technique analyses code and specifications to derive the input partition for a modified program. Next, the technique eliminates obsolete tests, and generates new tests to ensure that each input partition class is exercised by at least one test. Given information on where code has been modified, the technique determines edges in the control flow graph for the new program from which modified code is reachable. The technique then performs data driven symbolic execution, using the symbolic execution tree to symbolically execute all tests. When tests are discovered to reach edges from which no modifications are reachable, they need not be executed further. Tests that reach modifications are symbolically executed to termination. The technique selects all tests that reach new or modified code. However, the technique also symbolically executes these selected tests, obviating the need for their further execution.

C. Data Flow Technique

Several selective retest techniques are based on dataflow analysis and testing techniques. Dataflow test selection techniques identify definition-use pairs that are new in, or modified for, P', and select tests that exercise these pairs. Some techniques also identify and select tests for definition use pairs that have been deleted from P. Two overall approaches have been suggested. Incremental techniques process a single change, select tests for that change, incrementally update dataflow information and test trace information, and then repeat the process for the next change. Non-incremental techniques process a multiply-changed program considering all modifications simultaneously.

3 Proposed Specification Analyzer Approach

In this paper we propose to implement the Incremental algorithm which selects the test cases from test suite T whose outputs may be affected by the modifications made to the programs. The algorithm exploits the following observations:

1. Not all statements in the program are executed under all test cases.
2. If a statement is not executed under a test case, it cannot affect the program output for that test case.
3. If a statement is executed under a test case, it does not necessarily affect the program output for that test case
4. Every statement does not affect every part of the program output.

The Specification Analyzer will work as a parser. The test cases from the test suite pass to the Analyzer where these cases will be observed in terms of the statement coverage and costs-benefits. Applying the algorithm to parse which decomposes the program and selects test cases to ensure that there is no linkage between the modified and unmodified code.

4 System Architecture

The framework analyses the test cases on the basis of the four properties i.e. Inclusiveness, Precision, Generality and Efficiency. Inclusiveness measures the extent to which a technique chooses tests that will cause the modified program to produce different output than the original program, and thereby expose faults caused by modifications. Precision measures the ability of a technique to avoid choosing tests that will not cause the modified program to produce different output than the original program. Efficiency measures the computational cost, and thus, practicality, of a technique. Generality measures the ability of a technique to handle realistic and diverse language constructs, arbitrarily complex code modifications, and realistic testing applications.

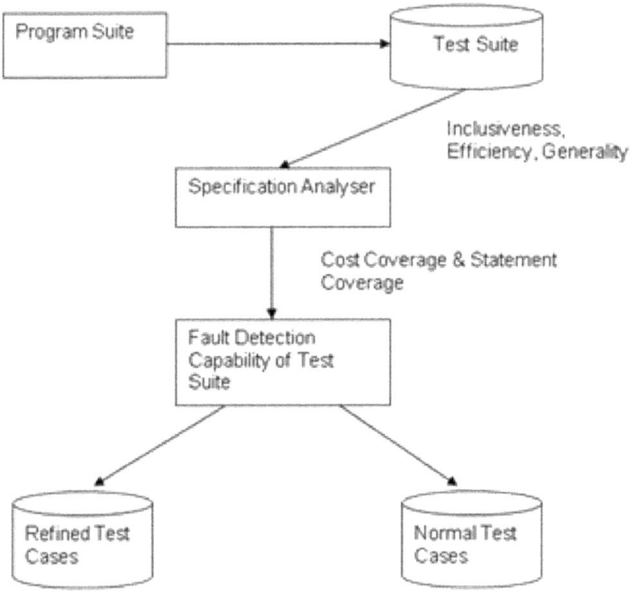

Fig. 1. System Architecture

5 Results and Discussions

The fault detection capability tool may refine those test cases that perform for the maximum statement coverage and having the minimum cost. The cost could be found on the fact that, if there are hundred test cases in a test pool and only 30% test cases satisfy the criteria for statement coverage and efficiency cannot be affected due to any modifications made to the program. The main benefit of our framework is to evaluate each and every test case from the test suite on the given criteria basis and compare them with the manual test cases that can be directly given to the tool. The tool helps us to evaluate which test cases are more efficient: either manual test cases or those that would be analyzed by the Specification Analyzer through the different properties.

6 Conclusions and Future Scope

A. Conclusions

This paper focuses that the proposed frame work is used to identify the strengths and the weaknesses of those test cases that cannot help for the minimization of the test pool and may affect their fault detection capability. Our evaluation indicates that despite of different goals of the various properties, the effectiveness of the fault detection can be compared and understood if our framework is used for the industrial purposes and applied for the same.

B. Future Scope of the work

We propose a pre-emptive designing "Evaluation of the Fault Detection Capability of the Test Suite" for the future work on the given hypotheses:

(a) How the minimization is fair in terms of costs and benefits when the coverage of test suite is adequate?
(b) If the test suite size increases then how the fault detection effectiveness should be affected?

Acknowledgment. The author express his sincere gratefulness to Mr. Rajeev Kumar Gupta, The President, Institute of Management Studies, Noida, India for his encouragement and support throughout the work of this wish and also for facilitating technical and literature facilities, required in the development of this work. One of the authors (Rajat Sheel Jain) expresses his thanks to Mr. Alok Agrawal, Advisor, Institute of Management Studies, Noida, India for his valuable suggestions and encouragement.

References

1. Rothermel, G., Harrold, M.: Analyzing regression test selection techniques. IEEE Trans. On Softw. Eng. 22(8), 529–551 (1996)
2. Wong, W.E., Horgan, J.R., Mathur, A.P., Pasquini, A.: Test set size minimization and fault detection effectiveness: A case study in a space application. In: Proc. of the 21st Annual Int'l. Comp. Softw. & Appl. Conf., pp. 522–528 (1997)
3. Agrawal, H., Horgan, J.R., Krauser, E.W., London, S.A.: Incremental regression testing. In: Proceedings of the IEEE Software Maintenance Conference, pp. 348–357 (1993)
4. Rothermel, G., Harrold, M.J.: A Comparison of Regression Test Selection Techniques. Tech. Rep., Department of Computer Science, Clemson University, Clemson, SC (1994)
5. Kim, J.-M., Porter, A., Rothermel, G.: An empirical study of regression test application frequency. In: Proc. of the 22nd Int'l. Conf. on Software Eng. (2000)
6. Rosenblum, D., Rothermel, G.: A comparative study of regression test selection techniques. In: Proc. of the 2nd Int'l. workshop on Empir. Studies of Softw. Maint. (1997)
7. Rothermel, G., Harrold, M.J.: A safe, efficient algorithm for regression test selection. In: Proceedings of the IEEE Software Maintenance Conference, pp. 358–367 (1993)
8. Wong, W.E., Horgan, J.R., London, S., Mathur, A.P.: Effect of the Test Set Minimization on Fault Detection Effectiveness. In: Proc.17th Int'l Conf. Software Eng., pp. 41–50 (1995)
9. Rothermel, G., Harrold, M.J.: Selecting Tests and Identifying Test Coverage Requirements for Modified Software. In: Proc. of Int'l Symp. Software Testing and Analysis, pp. 169–184 (1994)

Correlation of Alerts Using Prerequisites and Consequences for Intrusion Detection

Sanoop Mallissery[1], K. Praveen[2], and Shahana Sathar[2]

[1] Department of I&CT, MIT, Manipal University, Karnataka, India
sanoop.m@manipal.edu
[2] TIFAC Core in Cyber Security, Amrita School of Engineering, Coimbatore, India
{praveen.cys,shahanasathar}@gmail.com

Abstract. Alert Correlation is a process that analyses the alerts produced by one or more Intrusion Detection Sensors and provides a clear picture of occurring or attempted intrusions. Even though the correlation process is often presented as a single step, the analysis is actually carried out by a number of components, each of which has a specific goal. The idea of prerequisites of an intrusion, that is the necessary condition for the intrusion to be successful and the possible outcomes of intrusion is the consequences. This method also help us to correlates two alerts if the consequence of the earlier alert prepares for the prerequisites of the later one. In this system, before alert classification we are performing normalization, pre-processing, and alert correlation. In correlation phase there are two types of correlation, which are duplicate removal (alert fusion) and consequence correlation. Thus the resulting alert set is clustered. Based on this analysis of the alert set, the prioritization component assigns an appropriate priority to every alert. This priority information is important for quickly discarding information that is irrelevant or of less importance. The second way of prioritizing is based on the number of alerts coming from the networked systems.

Keywords: IDS, Alert Fusion, Alert Correlation.

1 Introduction

In order to alleviate some of the problems of intrusion detection systems, alert correlation systems have been proposed. Correlation systems collect the alerts from a number of sensors and process these alerts in order to generate a high-level view of the current security status of the network. The main goal of a correlation system is to reduce the number of alerts a system administrator has to manually process. The correlation system achieves this by identifying and suppressing false alerts, grouping alerts that refer to the same incident together, and prioritizing the alerts.No correlation system currently exists that enables integration of multiple alert correlation techniques. Existing systems are not easily extended, and they only operate in real-time when processing datasets with a low alert-rate. This project work is a modular framework for intrusion detection alert correlation. The framework supports the

V.V. Das and N. Thankachan (Eds.): CIIT 2011, CCIS 250, pp. 662–666, 2011.

integration of multiple alert correlation techniques and enables easy implementation of new components. The framework introduces minimal processing overhead and enables the construction of a correlation system. A set of correlation components is implemented using the framework. The components utilize multiple correlation techniques, which together form a complete correlation system.

2 Related Work

Most of the previous works on alert correlation has mostly focused on one of three types of correlation techniques: multi-step, fusion-based, and filter-based [1]. Multi-step correlation relies on the fact that complex attacks are usually executed in several phases or steps, where the first steps prepare for the attacks executed in the later steps. This approach is usually based on a function that calculates the similarity between any two pairs of alerts. If this similarity score exceeds some threshold, the alerts are correlated. Filter-based approaches either identify alerts that are irrelevant or assign a priority to each alert [2, 3]. Priorities are usually assigned to alerts depending on how important the attacked assets are.

3 Correlation Components and Process

Inspecting thousand of alerts per day is not feasible, especially if 99% of them are false positives [4]. This issue has motivated the researcher to do research on correlation of alert produce by intrusion detection sensor and heterogeneous log resources [5].Alert can be produced from various types of sources and it may cause multiple stages of attack [6]. Alert correlation is multi-step processes that receives alerts from one or more IDS as input and produce a high-level description of the malicious activity on the network [7]. Fig. 1 gives a graphical representation of the integrated correlation process that we implemented. Table 1 shows the prerequisites and consequences of some alerts that specify one event should be followed by another type of event [9]. It will link together alerts that are sequential in nature.

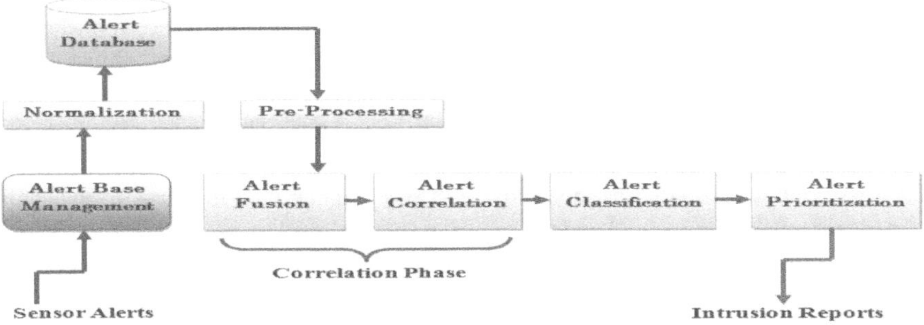

Fig. 1. Correlation Process Overview

Table 1. Examples of Prerequisites and Consequence

Alert Name	Prerequisite	Consequence
ICMP_PING_NMAP	ExistService(DestIP,DestPort) AND VulnerableAuthenticate(DestIP)	{ExistHost(DestIP)}
SCAN_NMAP_TCP	ExistHost(DestIP)	{ExistService(DestIP,DestPort)}
IMAP_Authen_Overflow	ExistService(DestIP,DestPort) AND VulnerableAuthenticate(DestIP)	ExistService(DestIP,DestPort) AND VulnerableAuthenticate(DestIP)
FTP Glob Expansion	ExistService(DestIP,DestPort) AND VulnerableFTPRequest(DestIP)	{GainAccess(DestIP)}
Email_Almail_Overflow	ExistService(DestIP,DestPort)AND VulnerableAlMailPOP3Server(DestIP)	{GainAccess(DestIP)}
SadmindBufferOverflow	ExistHost (VictimIP) AND VulnerableSadmind (VictimIP)	{GainRootAccess (VictimIP)}
TooltalkBufferOverflow	ExistHost (VictimIP) AND VulnerableTooltalk (VictimIP)	{GainRootAccess (VictimIP)}
RPCBufferOverflow	ExistHost(VictimIP)AND VulnerableRPC (VictimIP)	{GainRootAccess (VictimIP)}
DNS_HInfo	ExistService(DestIP,DestPort)	{GainOSInfo(DestIP)}
FTP_Syst	ExistService(DestIP,DestPort)	{GainOSInfo(DestIP)}
FTP_User	ExistService(DestIP,DestPort)	{GainOSInfo(DestIP)}
FTP Pass	ExistService(DestIP,DestPort)	{GainOSInfo(DestIP)}

4 Experimental Results

The network-based sensor has little idea of the security state of the host it is protecting. The alert set may have an enormous amount of alerts that are not caused by real attacks, known as false alerts. These alerts may be false positives or false negatives. We have to make these alerts in format that consist of date, time, attack name etc. Then it will be easy to understand by a normal user or to the administrator. After that we have to go through different process like normalization, pre-processing, fusion etc, before correlating the alerts.We are first normalizing the alerts in the dataset into the same format, because we are collecting the alerts from different IDS sensors. So we have to make this into a generalized format known as the Intrusion Detection Message Exchange Format (IDMEF) [8]. After this we are fusing the alerts. Alert fusion component is to combine alerts that represent the independent detection of the same attack occurrence by different intrusion detection systems. The decision to fuse two alerts is based on the temporal difference between these attack names. When a new alert arrives, it is compared to the alerts in the alert dataset. A match is found if the attack name attribute are equal and the new alert is produced by a sensor different from the sensors already associated with the alert being matched. Hence the duplicates will be removed (fusion).We are using this fused alert set for correlation, which is correlating the alerts generated by IDSs using prerequisites and consequences of the corresponding attacks. Most of the alerts like SadmindBufferOverflow, TooltalkBufferOverflow, and RPCBufferOverflow will results to same consequence that is gain access to root. For these attacks the prerequisites and the consequence are same. So we can correlate these attacks to anyone of the attack. Here we correlate these attacks to VulnerableRPCService. Similarly we can correlate all the alerts that the consequence will be same. Thus we can again reduce the number of alerts in the dataset. That is alert correlation is based on the observation that in series of attacks, the component attacks are usually not isolated, but related as different stages of the attacks, with the early ones preparing for the later ones. For example, an attacker needs to install the Distributed Denial of Service (DDOS) daemon programs before he can launch a DDOS attack. Intuitively, the prerequisite of an attack is the necessary condition for the attack to be successful. For example, the existence of a vulnerable service is the prerequisite of a remote buffer overflow attack against the service. Moreover, an attacker may make progress (e.g., discover a vulnerable service, install a Trojan horse program) as a result of an attack. Informally, we call the possible outcome of an attack the (possible) consequence of the attack. In a series of attacks where attackers launch earlier ones to prepare for later ones, there are usually strong connections between the consequences of the earlier attacks and the prerequisites of the later ones. Then we are classifying these correlated alerts into different files, based on the alert type, IP address, port and protocol. That if we are classifying based on alert types there will be different categories like bad unknown, successful admin. Policy violation, misc activity, attempted recon, unknown, trojan activity etc. Similarly we are classifying all alerts based on the IP address as public or private, then based on the port as privileged or not, and based on the protocol of the service that was attacked (TCP, UDP, ICMP etc). Then based on the impact of attack we are prioritizing the alerts that we classified. Alert prioritizing relies on meta-information about the nature of the attack to determine if one alert or meta-alert should be considered more critical than another. Thus, unless a precise description of how to prioritize alerts is provided (in addition to the alert dataset), it is difficult to evaluate the effectiveness of this component. We developed a very simple alert prioritization policy just to give an estimate of how much reduction this step could achieve. It is purely based on Snort rule base. Number 1 is the highest priority. So we can discard the alert information that is irrelevant or of less Importance from the important ones. The second way is based on the how many alerts are there from different systems in the network. For example from 172.17.128.72 if we get 100 alerts and from 172.17.128.73 only 5 alerts, then based on that it will be prioritized.

5 Conclusions and Future Works

In this study, we implemented an alert correlation technique to overcome some of the IDS's problems and an improved solution for alert correlation technique based on some capability criteria, like capability to do alert reduction, capability to do alert classification, capability to correlate alerts based on prerequisites and consequences and capability to reduce false alert. That is we implemented a component-based correlation system. The system utilizes multiple techniques to provide a complete correlation solution. The system can be extended by creating new correlation components, and it can be tailored to a protected network by selecting what components to use and configuring each individual component's parameters.The approach has the ability to fuse alerts for which the match is good but not perfect. We used the approach for alert correlation, is prerequisites and consequences of attacks. The approach was based on the observation that in a series of attacks, the attacks were usually not isolated, but related as different stages, with the earlier stages preparing for the later ones. Thus these correlated alerts are classified and then prioritized for generating better intrusion reports.Several issues are worth future research that is to develop better ways to specify hyperalert types, especially how to represent predicates to be included in their prerequisite and consequence sets to get the best performance for alert correlation. Further improvement should be done on the possible ways to integrate our method to get performance metrics, which reports the reduction rate achieved along with performance metrics for each component .In particular, we are interested in methods that can better tolerate false alerts and missing detections typically seen in current IDSs and also for real time datasets. In general, we would like to develop a suite of comprehensive techniques that facilitate the analysis and management of intensive intrusion alerts.

References

1. Cuppens, F., Miege, A.: Alert Correlation in a Cooperative Intrusion Detection Framework. In: IEEE Proceedings Security and Privacy, pp. 202–215 (2002) ISSN: 1081-6011
2. Anderson, D., Fong, M., Jonsson, E., Valdes, A.: Heterogeneous Sensor Correlation: A Case Study of Live Traffic Analysis. In: The Proceedings of IEEE Assurance and Security Workshop (2002)
3. Yusof, R., Selamat, S.R., Sahib, S.: Intrusion Alert Correlation Technique Analysis for Heterogeneous Log. International Journal of Computer Science and Network Security 8(9) (2008)
4. Julisch, K.: Clustering Intrusion Detection Alarms to Support Root Cause Analysis. ACM Transactions on Information and System Security 2(3), 111–138 (2003)
5. Yusof, R., Selamat, S.R., Sahib, S.: Intrusion Alert Correlation Technique Analysis for Heterogeneous Log. IJCSNS International Journal of Computer Science and Network Security 8(9) (2008)
6. Ning, P., Xu, D., Healey, C.G., Amant, R.S.: Building Attack Scenarios through Integration of Complementary Alert Correlation Method. In: NDSS (2004)
7. Valeur, F., Vigna, G., Krügel, C., Kemmerer, R.A.: A Comprehensive Approach to Intrusion Detection Alert Correlation. IEEE Transactions, Dependable Secure Computing 1(3), 146–169 (2004)
8. Curry, D., Debar, H.: Intrusion Detection Message Exchange Format: Extensible Markup Language (XML) Document Type Definition. draft-ietf-idwg-idmef-xml-10.txt (January 2003)
9. Cheung, S., Lindqvist, U., Fong, M.: Modeling Multistep Cyber Attacks for Scenario Recognition. In: Proceedings of the DARPA Information Survivability Conference and Exposition (DISCEX III), pp. 284–292 (2003)

Heterogeneous Network Architecture for Habitat Monitoring

Raghavendra Ganiga, Sanoop Mallissery, and Santhosha Rao

Department of I&CT, MIT, Manipal University, Karnataka, India
{raghavendra.n,sanoop.m,santhosha.rao}@manipal.edu

Abstract. Habitat and environmental monitoring represent a class of sensor network applications with enormous potential benefits for scientific communities and society as a whole. Habitat monitoring permits researchers to obtain detail measurements of a particular environment in an unobtrusive manner. Sea bird colonies are notaries for their human disturbances. Sensor networks represent a significant advance over traditional invasive methods of monitoring. In our system we used heterogeneous network architecture for habitat monitoring. The architecture has been tested and analyzed by using the discrete event simulation framework called QualNet 4.5.1. In this architecture we are using the present wireless technologies like Wi-Fi, WiMax and ZigBee network. We designed the heterogeneous network and developed a traffic generator protocol for the sensor network called sensor bit rate (SBR).Which is stochastic traffic generation models are used to analyze the performance and behavior of the SBR traffic in habitat monitoring architecture.

Keywords: Wi-Fi, WiMax, ZigBee, CBR, SBR.

1 Introduction

Recent advances in wireless communications and electronics have enabled the development of low-cost, low-power, multi-functional sensor nodes that are small in size and communicate in short distances. These tiny sensor nodes, which consist of sensing, data processing, and communicating components, leverage the idea of sensor networks [1], [2], [3]. Sensor networks represent a significant improvement over traditional sensors. Wireless sensor networks are becoming a prevalent technology providing a broad variety of uses and benefits. A sensor network is composed of a large number of sensor nodes that are densely deployed either inside the phenomenon or very close to it. The position of sensor nodes need not be engineered or predetermined. This allows random deployment in inaccessible terrains or disaster relief operations. On the other hand, this also means that sensor network protocols and algorithms must possess self-organizing capabilities. Another unique feature of sensor networks is the cooperative effort of sensor nodes. Sensor nodes are fitted with an onboard processor. Instead of sending the raw data to the nodes responsible for the fusion, they use their processing abilities to locally carry out simple computations and transmit only the required and partially processed data.

V.V. Das and N. Thankachan (Eds.): CIIT 2011, CCIS 250, pp. 667–672, 2011.

2 Related Works

One of the earliest deployments of a larger sensor network was carried out in the summer of 2002 on Great Duck Island [4], located in the gulf of Maine, USA. The island is home to approximately 5000 pairs of Leach's Storm Petrels that nest in separate patches within three different habitat types. Seabird researchers are interested in questions regarding the usage pattern of nesting burrows with respect to the microclimate. As observation by humans would be both too costly and might disturb the birds, a sensor network of 43 nodes was deployed for 4 months just before the breeding season. The nodes had sensors for light, temperature, humidity, pressure, and infrared radiation and have been deployed in a single hop network. Each sensor node samples its sensors every 70 seconds and sends its readings to a solar-powered gateway. The gateway forwards the data to a central base station with a database and a two-way satellite connection to the Internet. During the 123 days of the experiment, 1.1 million readings have been recorded, which is about one sixth of the theoretical 6.6 million readings generated over this time. The most loss of data was caused by hardware-related issues. Several nodes stopped working due to water entering the sensor node casing. As all sensors were read out by a single analog to digital converter, a hardware failure of one of the sensors caused false readings of other sensors. Due to the transparent casing of the sensor nodes, direct sun light could heat the whole sensor node and thus lead to high temperature readings for nodes which are deployed above ground [5, 6].

3 Existing System Architecture

In the existing system architecture for habitat monitoring, the sensor nodes may be deployed in dense patches that are widely separated [7]. The sensor nodes transmit their data through the sensor network to the sensor network PAN (Personal Area Network). The PAN coordinator is responsible for transmitting sensor data from the sensor patch through a local transit network called Wi-Fi to the remote base station (WiMax) that provides WAN connectivity and data logging. The base station connects to database and from database required information for the end user spread across the internet. The full architecture of the existing architecture is shown in Fig. 1.

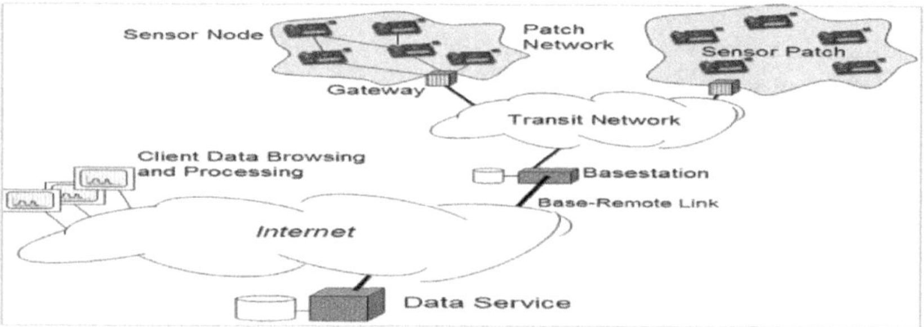

Fig. 1. Existing Architecture

4 Proposed Architecture

In our heterogeneous network architecture wireless sensor network is deployed over a region where some phenomenon is to be monitored shown in Fig. 2. As an example, a large quantity of sensor nodes could be deployed over a habitat region to detect the presence of birds. When the sensors detect the event being monitored (heat, pressure, sound, light, vibration), the event needs to be reported to one of the base stations, which can take appropriate action (e.g., send a message on the internet or to a satellite). We divide the sensor network nodes into 3 categories like PAN coordinator, coordinator and sensor nodes. Wireless Personal Area Networks (WPANs) senses the data from surrounding and sends it to the coordinator node. The coordinator node collect the information from the sensor node those who are in its neighborhood and send it to the PAN coordinator. Here PAN coordinator will act as a gateway between sensor networks and external networks. To nullify the congestion at the PAN coordinator, we are sending all traffic data to the coordinators and then to PAN coordinator. The traffic data collected by the PAN coordinator is sent to a Wi-Fi network. In Wi-Fi network many number of wireless stations are associated to an AP (Access Point). All communications take place through the AP. The collected information from AP is forwarded to WiMax Network. The data stored in Subscriber Station (SS) of WiMax network is delivered to the end user through Wi-_Fi as depicted in Fig. 2. SS database can be used in research work pertaining to habitat activities.

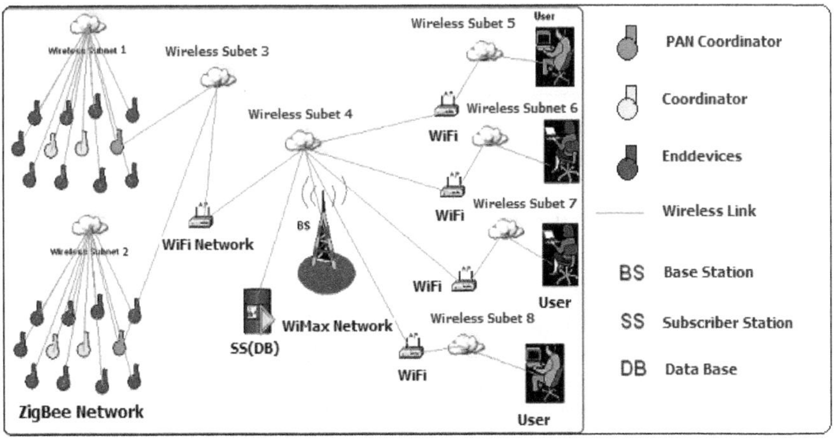

Fig. 2. Proposed Architecture

5 Wireless Channel Assignments

Channel masks are used in multi-channel wireless simulations to specify the channels that nodes in the simulation are able to listen to, and the ones they are currently listening to. PHY-LISTENABLE-CHANNEL-MASK specifies the channels that a node is able to listen to, whether it is configured to do so, or not. It is assumed that the network interfaces on this node allow it to be able to listen on these channels. This parameter is static throughout the simulation duration, and the number of digits in the mask must match the number of defined channels. A node can change the channels that it is currently listening to, during the course of the simulation. Any channels specified as "1" in this mask must also be specified as "1" in the PHY-LISTENABLE-CHANNEL-MASK parameter, and the number of digits in the mask must match the number of defined channels as well. Channel masks are used in multi-channel wireless simulations to specify the channels that nodes in the simulation are able to, and the ones they are currently listening to. Configured channel mask in such a way that each subnet in the network should not interference with each other. In our architecture, we assigned the channel for each network by setting the PHY-LISTENING-CHANNEL-MASK and PHY-LISTENABLE-CHANNEL-Mask in '.config' file. Setup the channel mask for each network given below using the different cases that shown in Fig. 3.

CASE 0:	Channel assignment for the ZigBee Subnet 0. Listenable Channel Mask: 11000000 Listenable Channel Mask: 10000000	CASE 4:	Channel assignment for the Wi-Fi Subnet 4. Listenable Channel Mask: 00011111 Listenable Channel Mask: 00001000
CASE 1:	Channel assignment for the ZigBee Subnet 1. Listenable Channel Mask: 11000000 Listenable Channel Mask: 01000000	CASE 5:	Channel assignment for the Wi-Fi Subnet 5. Listenable Channel Mask: 00011111 Listenable Channel Mask: 00000100
CASE 2:	Channel assignment for the WiMax Subnet 2. Listenable Channel Mask: 00100000 Listenable Channel Mask: 00100000	CASE 6:	Channel assignment for the Wi-Fi Subnet 6. Listenable Channel Mask: 00011111 Listenable Channel Mask: 00000010
CASE 3:	Channel assignment for the Wi-Fi Subnet 3. Listenable Channel Mask: 00011111 Listenable Channel Mask: 00010000	CASE 7:	Channel assignment for the Wi-Fi Subnet 7. Listenable Channel Mask: 00011111 Listenable Channel Mask: 00000001

Fig. 3. Channel Assignments

6 Traffic Generating Protocols

Traffic-generating protocols simulate the traffic generated by a real network application. QualNet 4.5.1 provides a large number of traffic generating protocols [8]. While some protocols are used directly as applications, such as FTP and Telnet, others are used to simulate real network applications. Applications such as CBR (Constant Bit Rate) can be configured to simulate a large number of real network applications by mimicking their traffic pattern. For example, audio traffic and old video codec's infuse traffic at a constant rate into the network and can be accurately simulated by appropriately configuring the CBR application in QualNet. The Traffic generator protocol CBR supports individual packet size of 512 bytes only. So we developed a new protocol named, SBR (Sensor Bit Rate) that supports individual packet size of 70 bytes. Because of this we are able to send low data rate traffic packets from sensor networks to end user.

7 Experimental Results

We have designed the habitat monitoring architecture by using the network simulator called QualNet 4.5.1. Testing is conducted by the simulation mode for the habitat monitoring architecture. However simulation isn't always viewed as valuable or viable tool for comprehensive performance testing and evaluation, as there are vast differences in model fidelities and levels of abstraction between the actual system and the simulated model. In simulation, the model is often simplified or abstracted, which can mask the very phenomena (e.g., adaptive behavior) that are captured during testing on physical test beds. We compared our results with the existing system architecture. Our architecture showing more accuracy while receiving the traffic and reduced the percentage of missing the traffic packets. Simulated result for existing architecture and proposed architecture by sending high number of packets shown in the Fig 4. We tested our proposed architecture by sending 43,199 packets and compared with the existing architecture. While reception of the traffic in proposed architecture is having more accurate results and reduced the loss of packets compared to existing architecture that shown in Table 1 and the sending and reception of packets in SBR client and server side shown in Fig. 4.

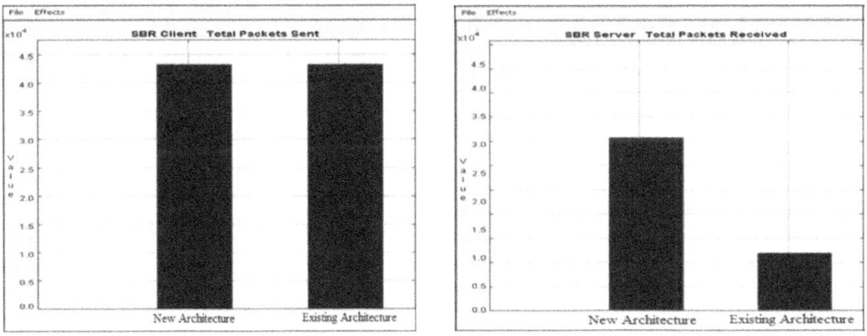

Fig. 4. Simulated result for existing and proposed architecture by sending high number of packets

Table 1. Experimental Results

Existing Architecture				Proposed Architecture			
Packets Send	Packets Received	Packet Received (%)	Packet Lost (%)	Packets Send	Packets Received	Packet Received (%)	Packet Lost (%)
43,199	14,676	33.97	66.03	43,199	30,270	56.89	43.11

8 Conclusions and Future Works

The newly created architecture uses the present wireless technology and increases the diameter of the network using the coordinator in between the PAN coordinator. The major objectives of the new system architecture are Eliminates wired network, reduces invasion of bird habitat, can have more nodes than existing one so it's more scalable, can be deployed across habitats, better use of resources, very economical and it nullify the congestion at the PAN coordinator, that helps in achieving better results. Work is ongoing to develop more advanced analysis tools in QualNet 4.5.1 to support troubleshooting along with network testing and evaluation and allow for sending videos as well as human interaction to enable evaluation of imaginary scenarios using the real-time emulation based test bed.

References

1. Zhao, F., Guibas, L.: Wireless Sensor Networks: An Information Processing Approach. The Proceedings of Morgan Kaufmann Networking Series. Elsevier (2004) ISBN: 978-1-55860-914-3
2. Akyildiz, I.F., Su, W., Sankarasubramaniyam, Y., Cayirci, E.: A Survey on Sensor Networks. IEEE Communications Magazine (8), 102–114 (2002) ISSN: 0163-6804
3. Chong, C.Y., Kumar, S.P.: Sensor Networks: Evolution, Opportunities and Challenges. The Proceedings of IEEE 91(8), 1247–1256 (2003)
4. Polastre, J., Szewczyk, R., Mainwaring, A., Culler, D., Anderson, J.: Analysis of Wireless Sensor Networks for Habitat Monitoring. In: Wireless Sensor Networks. Kluwer Academic Publishers (2004) ISBN: 1-4020-7883-8
5. Szewczyk, R., Polastre, J., Mainwaring, A., Culler, D.: Lessons from a Sensor Network Expedition. In: Karl, H., Wolisz, A., Willig, A. (eds.) EWSN 2004. LNCS, vol. 2920, pp. 307–322. Springer, Heidelberg (2004)
6. Woo, A., Tong, T., Culler, D.: Taming The Underlying Challenges of Reliable Multihop Routing in Sensor Networks. In: The Proceedings of 1st ACM Conference on Embedded Networked Sensor Systems, pp. 14–27. ACM Press (2003)
7. Mainwaring, A., Polastre, J., Szewczyk, R., Culler, D.: Wireless Sensor Network for Habitat Monitoring. In: The Proceedings of Inter Research Berkley (2002) IBR-TR-02-006
8. QualNet 4.5 Programmer's Guide

Design and Implementation of High Speed Signed Digit Adder

Varsha M. Muragod[1] and J.M. Rudagi[2]

[1] VLSI, Dept. of Electronics & Communication,
KLE's College of Engineering & Technology, Belgaum-590008, India
varsha.muragod@gmail.com
[2] Dept. of Electronics & Communication,
KLE's College of Engineering & Technology,
Belgaum-590008, India
js_itti@)yahoo.co.in

Abstract. Signed digit number representation limit the carry propagation to one position to the left during the operation of addition and subtraction. Carry-free addition for signed digit number systems is primarily a three-step process. The special case of maximally redundant signed digit number systems leads to more efficient carry-free addition. Conventional Signed Digit Adder is implemented for radix 16 symmetric numbers. A new Speculative Adder is designed which is 10% faster and 22% less area than Conventional SD Adder. The register transfer level (RTL) description is done in verilog and the functionality is verified using Xlinx9.2i.

Keywords: Redundant numbers, signed digit, redundancy index, maximal redundancy.

1 Introduction

Addition is considered as the fundamental operation in digital arithmetic. Normally one or more add operations are embedded in the implementation of other arithmetic operations. For example, subtraction is essentially a special case of addition, multiplication is normally a process of multi-operand addition. Finally, division algorithms are based either on iterative subtractions or converging multiplications [1]. Therefore, any improvement in the addition speed potentially reduces the latency of other digital arithmetic operations.

The signed-digit (SD) number system offers fully redundant parallel carry-free addition. A radix – r redundant signed digit number system is based on digit set: $S = \{-\beta, -(\beta-1)\ldots-1, 0, 1\ldots\alpha\}$, where $1 \leq \beta, \alpha \leq r-1$[3]. A special case of redundant signed digit representation is maximally Redundant Signed Digit adder (MRSD). The *MRSD* number system provides symmetric representation.

This paper will focus on comparing conventional signed digit adder with new designed SD adder for two radix-16 signed digit operands. The rest of the paper is organized as follows: In section 2 conventional signed digit algorithm is discussed. In section 3 the design of new maximally redundant signed digit adder is discussed. Here

V.V. Das and N. Thankachan (Eds.): CIIT 2011, CCIS 250, pp. 673–676, 2011.

transfer values are computed using logical equations. In section 4 comparisons between the two adders is done in terms of delay and area.

2 Conventional Signed Digit Adder (CSD)

A general carry-free addition scheme for radix-2^h SD number systems with digit set [−α, α], is described by Algorithm as in [5], where $\alpha > 2^{h-1}$.

2.1 Algorithm for Conventional SD Adder

1. Digit parallel additions of $pi = xi + yi$ for each i in the range [0, n-1].
2. Comparison of pi with α to obtain the value of the transfer $ti+1 \in \{-1,0,1\}$.Calculation of the sum digit wi, by adding r or $-r$ to pi, according to the transfer: $wi = pi - ti+1 \times r$
3. Parallel addition of $si = wi + ti$ in each position without any carry propagations.

Example:

Inputs: Two operands each of 4 digits, each digit is of 5bit.
Output: sum of 5 digits. An example of signed digit adder is shown in fig.1.

	i	4	3	2	1	0	Numerical decimal value
	x_i		F	C	-E	-2	16^3F+16^2C-16E-2=64286
	y_i		3	-F	-7	8	16^3*3-16^2F-16*7+8=8344
Step I	p_i		18	-3	-21	6	72630
Step II	w_i		2	-3	-5	6	7350
	t_i	1	0	-1	0		65280
Step III	s_i	1	2	-4	-5	6	72630

Fig. 1. Example of CSD Adder

3 Experimental Work

In this architecture three sums are calculated as in [4]. Depending on the transfer values one sum is selected. This scheme use h+1-bit sign-magnitude encoding of the signed digits and rely on triple active hardware redundancy on concurrently computing w_i-1, w_i, and w_i+1 in anticipation of the coming transfer value from position i−1. It was observed that the h least significant bits of the interim sum w_i are the same as the corresponding bits of p_i and the transfer bits may be computed by combinational logic.

$$t_0^{i+1} = \overline{p_4^i}\ \overline{p_3^i p_2^i p_1^i p_0^i} \quad (1)$$

$$t_{-1}^{i+1} = p_5^i \overline{p_4^i}\ p_3^i p_2^i p_1^i p_0^i + p_5^i p_4^i \quad (2)$$

$$t_1^{i+1} = \overline{p_5^i p_4^i} p_3^i p_2^i p_1^i p_0^i + \overline{p_5^i} p_4^i \quad (3)$$

Hardware requirements for new adder is shown in fig.2 containing 3 Adders, one combinational logic and multiplexer.

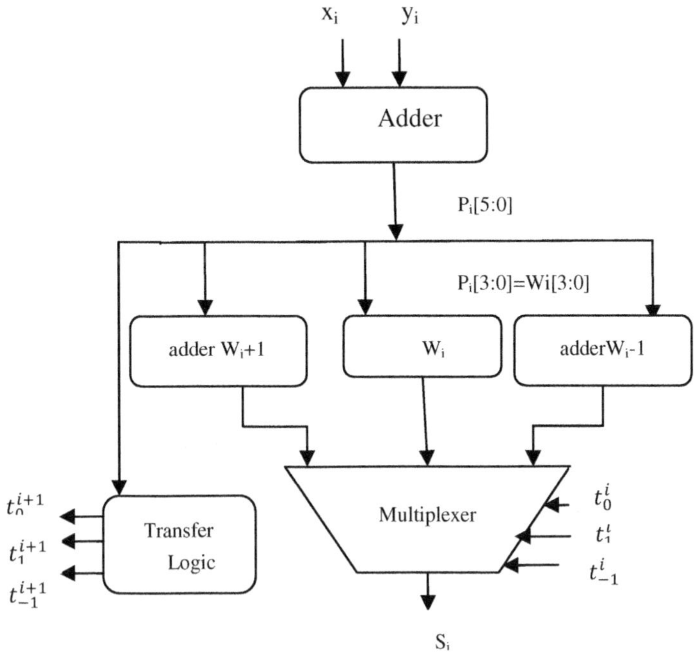

Fig. 2. New Speculative MRSD Adder

3.1 Algorithm for New Speculative Adder

Input: Two 4-digit radix-2^4 SD numbers $X = x_{n-1}\ldots x_0$ and $Y = y_{n-1}\ldots y_0$, where $-15\leq xi, yi \leq 15$

Output: An 5-digit radix-2^4 SD number $S = s_n\ldots s_0$, where $-14 \leq S \leq 14$

1. Compute the n-digit radix-2^4 SD number $P = p_{n-1}\ldots p_0 = X + Y$, by digit-parallel computation of $p_i = x_i + y_i$ for $0 \leq i \leq 3$, where $-30 \leq pi \leq 30$.
2. The last 4 bits of w_i is same as p_i ,i.e $p_i[3:0] = w_i[3:0]$ and $w_i[4]=pi[5]$.Transfer values are calculated using equations 3,4,5.In this step three sums are computed w_i,w_i+1.w_i-1.
3. Depending upon the transfer value one sum will be selected. i.e w_i is selected when $t_0^{i+1} = 1$,w_i+1 is selected when $t_1^{i+1} = 1$,w_i-1 is selected when $t_{-1}^{i+1} = 1$.

4 Results and Discussion

The Adders are simulated on XILINX ISE simulator and Implemented on Spartan 3 FPGA board for the example shown in fig 3. The register transfer level (RTL) description is done in verilog. The following details are obtained from the synthesis report as illustrated in table 1 below.

Table 1. Comparision of Two Adders

Adders	Delay(ns)	Power(mw)	PDP(ns)	No of Slices	No of IOS	No of boundedIOs
Conventional SD adder	29.865	56	1.52	155	65	65
New Speculative SD Adder	26.512	56	1.48	122	62	62

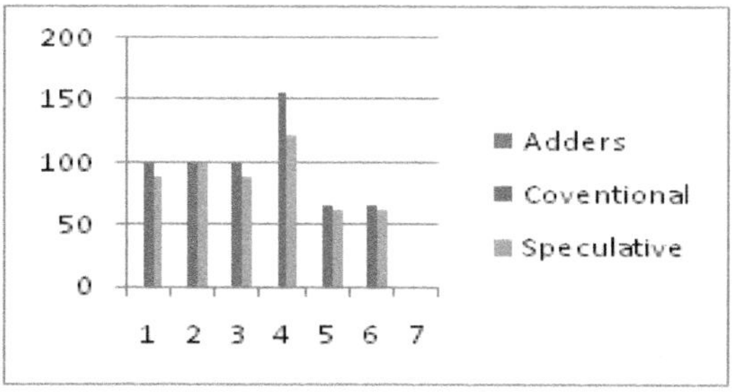

Fig. 3. Comparisons of three adders

5 Conclusions

Sign Digit Adder is represented using a redundant digit set. Having the output in redundant representation will reduce the addition time by reducing the length of the maximum carry propagation-chain. From the above results it is clear that Speculative SD Adder is 10% faster than Conventional SD Adder and 22% less in area than CSD.

References

1. Parhami, B.: Computer arithmetic: algorithms and hardware designs, Oxford (2002)
2. Avizienis: Signed-digit number representations for fast parallel arithmetic. IEEE Transactions on Electronic Computers EC-10, 389–400 (1961)
3. Parhami: Generalized signed-digit number systems: a unifying framework for redundant number representations. IEEE Transactions on Computers 39, 89–98 (1990)
4. Fahmy, H.A.H., Flynn, M.J.: The case for a redundant format in floating point arithmetic. In: Proceedings of the 16th IEEE Symposium on Computer Arithmetic, Sanntiago de Compostela, Spain (June 2003)
5. Jaberipur, G., Ghodsi, M.: High radix digit number system: representation paradigms. Scientia Iranica 10, 383–391 (2003)

Performance Evaluation of Mobile Communication in an Hierarchical Cellular Systems with Different Schemes

Kashish Parwani, G.N. Purohit, and Geetanjali Sharma

Banasthali University, AIM & ACT, Banasthali-304022, India
kparwani1@yahoo.com, gnpurohit_jaipur@yahoo.co.in,
geetanjali.bu@gmail.com

Abstract. This paper develop analytical models for calculating the blocking probabilities of two low layers (picocell and femtocell) of hierarchical cellular networks providing integrated services of mobile users. The analytical models are based on continuous time multi dimensional birth death approach having two layers cellular architecture with reserved number of channels to give the priority to handoff calls. These reserved channels may also be allocated to new calls if reserved channels are free. The two lower layers architecture is based on picocell and femtocell and cellular network consists of two types of subscribers in the system, high mobile subscribers (HMS) and low mobile subscribers (LMS).The channel assignment scheme based on new call bounding, cutoff priority and sub-rating are suggested in cellular network for both type of layers. All the schemes are compared in terms of blocking probability by providing numerical results.

Keywords: Hierarchical Cellular Network (HCN), New Call Bounding (NCB1), Cut-Off Priority (COP1), Sub-rating.

1 Introduction

In cellular network, it is estimated that 2/3 of calls and over 90% of the data services occur indoors. it is extremely important for cellular operator to provide good indoor coverage for not only voice but also video and high speed data services [1]. It is very expensive to provide indoor coverage using an "outside in" approach. Hence, how to provide good indoor coverage, in particular for high speed data services, is a big challenge for the operator. Recently, the development of femtocells provides a good opportunity for low cost indoor solutions for such scenarios. Femtocells, also known as "home based station", are cellular networks access points that connect standard mobile devices to a mobile operator's networks using residential DSL, cable broadband connections, optical fibers or wireless last-mile technologies. In this paper, two lower layers are used for indoor networks i.e. picocell and femtocell. These layers cover a small area of hierarchical cellular network (HCN) and usually used in residential areas (home, office, shopping malls, railway station etc).Its coverage areas are of as little as 200 meters.

V.V. Das and N. Thankachan (Eds.): CIIT 2011, CCIS 250, pp. 677–683, 2011.

2 Related Work

In July 2007, the Femto Forum [2] was founded to promote femtocells standardization and deployment world wide. Hou J et al. [3] proposed mobility-based call admission scheme which provided services to multiple classes of mobile users (i.e. pedestrians and vehicular travelers). Li et al. [4] gave a new channel assignment schemes called sub-rating schemes. Fang et al. [5] discovered call admission control schemes and performance analysis in wire mobile network. Li et al. [6] studied PCS network, which deals with Markovian Arrival Process (MAP) having correlation of the inter-arrival times among new and handoff calls by employing spitted sub-rating scheme. Jain M et al. [7] studied channel assignment schemes based on new call bounding, cutoff priority and sub-rating. Jain et al. [8] proposed channel assignment schemes for PCS with cut off priority and sub rating. In [9], a microcell and macrocell cellular architecture for low and high mobility wireless users has been developed.

3 System Description

There are two low layers of HCN. (i) Pico layer, that is the outer layer and (ii) Femto layer, that is the inner layer. The outer layer has connection to subscribers and receives fresh traffic destination for the networks whereas the inner layer only deals with traffic inside the networks structure. Some models developed here. New calls of both LMS and HMS and handoff calls of LMS are to be admitted to femtocell. There is provision of reserved channels of handoff calls of LMS whereas handoff calls of HMS are to be admitted in picocell. Two layers cellular architecture models with sub-rating is proposed in one model. The reserved channels of femto cellular cells may be splitter into two half rate channels. The channel holding time for new calls and handoff calls are assumed to be different in all the models. A cellular networks, which is a cluster of K hexagonal cells of uniform size having C pico layer. As shown in fig. 4(a) each layer has N_j (j=1,2,.... K) numbers of femto cells in the pico cellular layer. The pico layer has connection to subscriber and receives fresh traffic for the network whereas the femto layer only deals with the traffic inside the network structure. Let c_j (j=1, 2 ....K) be the numbers of channels allocated to each femtocell in its coverage area. In each cell, a fixed number of channels r_j is reserved to give priority to handoff call. Thus s_j are the number of channels which serve both type of calls. The calls arrival to the LMS and HMS follow poisson distribution with different arrival rates, λ_{Ln} (λ_{Hn}) is the arrival rates of new calls for LMS (HMS), λ_{Lh} (λ_{Hh}) is the arrival rates of handoff calls of LMS(HMS). So,

$$\lambda_n = \lambda_{Ln} + \lambda_{Hn}, \qquad \lambda_h = \lambda_{Lh} + \lambda_{Hh}$$

Aggregate arrival rate of calls, $\lambda = \lambda_n + \lambda_h$. The call holding time for new (handoff) calls are $1/\mu_o$ ($1/\mu_h$).$P_{(0,0)}$ steady state probability that there is no call in cell j. $P_{(m,n)}$ the steady state prob. that m channels are occupied by new calls and n channels are occupied by the handoff calls in femtocell. B_n, is the blocking probability of new calls in cell j (j=1,2....K).B_{Lh} is the blocking probability of handoff calls at LMS in cell j.

B_{Hh}, is the blocking probability of handoff call at HMS in cell j. Here q_i is the steady state probabilities that i channels are busy with handoff calls of HMS in picocell. B is the overall blocking probability. Traffic intensities of new calls and handoff calls for LMS (HMS) are:

$$\rho_{Ln} = \frac{\lambda_{Ln}}{\mu_o}, \quad \rho_{Hn} = \frac{\lambda_{Hn}}{\mu_o}, \quad \rho_{Lh} = \frac{\lambda_{Lh}}{\mu_h} \quad \rho_{Hh} = \frac{\lambda_{Hh}}{\mu_h}, \quad \rho_n = \frac{\lambda_n}{\mu_o}, \quad \rho_h = \frac{\lambda_h}{\mu_h}$$

4 Analysis

In this section, describe four types of channel assignment schemes without and with sub-rating for analyzing the performance of cellular mobile system. We propose four schemes for two low layers of HCN; (i) New Call Bounding, (ii) Cut-off Priority, (iii) New Call Bounding with Sub-rating and (iv) Cut-off Priority with Sub-rating.

4.1 Two Layer Cellular Models without Sub-rating

4.1.1 New Call Bounding Scheme (NCB1)

Consider the two low layer of hierarchical cellular network (HCN) with threshold limit t, i.e. if the number of new calls in the cell exceeds t, the new call will be blocked. Otherwise it will be admitted. The hand off call is rejected only when all channels in the cell are used up. Fig. 1(a) shows the state transition diagram.

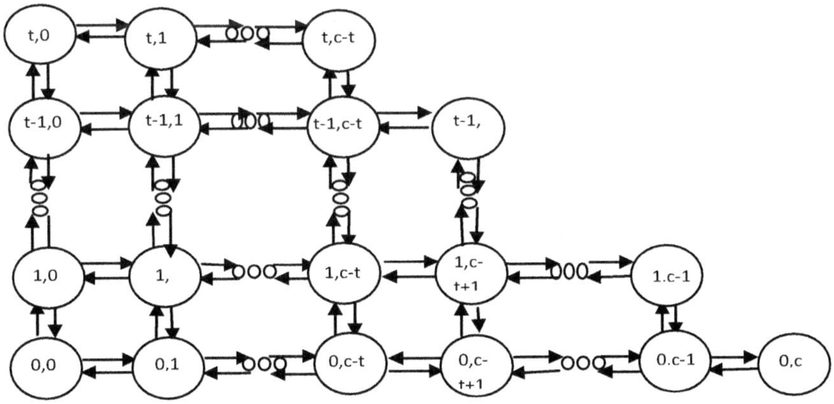

Fig. 1(a). State transition diagram of new call bounding scheme

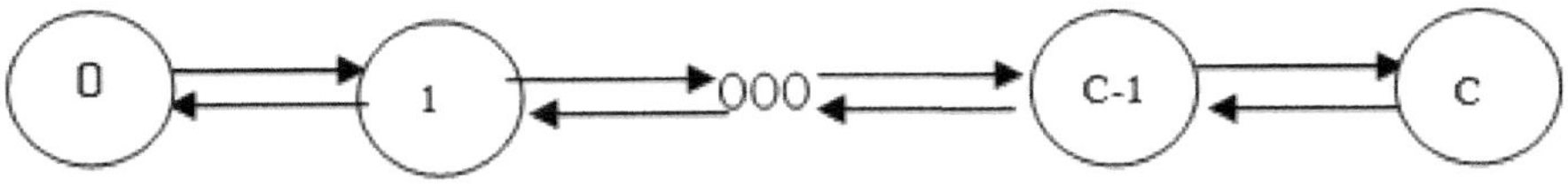

Fig. 1(b). State transition diagram of new call bounding scheme for picocell

The steady state probability is

$$P_{(mn)} = \frac{\rho_n^{\ m}}{m!}\frac{\rho_{Lh}^{\ n}}{n!}P_{(0,0)}, \qquad 0 \le m \le t, \qquad m+n \le c, n \ge 0 \tag{1}$$

Using Normalization condition $$P_{(0,0)} = \left[\sum_{m=0}^{t}\sum_{n=0}^{c-m}\frac{\rho_n^{\ m}}{m!}\frac{\rho_{Lh}^{\ n}}{n!}\right]^{-1} \tag{2}$$

Blocking probability of new call

$$B_n = \frac{\sum_{n=0}^{c-t}\frac{\rho_n^{\ t}}{t!}\frac{\rho_{Lh}^{\ n}}{n!} + \sum_{m=0}^{t-1}\frac{\rho_n^{\ m}}{m!}\frac{\rho_{Lh}^{\ c-m}}{(c-m)!}}{\sum_{m=0}^{t}\sum_{n=0}^{c-m}\frac{\rho_n^{\ m}}{m!}\frac{\rho_{Lh}^{\ n}}{n!}} \tag{3}$$

Blocking probability of handoff calls of LMS,

$$B_{Lh} = \frac{\sum_{m=0}^{t}\frac{\rho_n^{\ m}}{m!}\frac{\rho_{Lh}^{\ c-m}}{(c-m)!}}{\sum_{m=0}^{t}\sum_{n=0}^{c-m}\frac{\rho_n^{\ m}}{m!}\frac{\rho_{Lh}^{\ n}}{n!}} \tag{4}$$

Blocking probability of hand off call of HMS

$$B_{Hh} = \frac{(N.\rho_{Hh})^C}{C!} \tag{5}$$

The overall blocking probability of the calls in cellular networks

$$B = \frac{\lambda_n B_n + \lambda_{Lh} B_{Lh} + \lambda_{Hh} B_{Hh}}{\lambda} \tag{6}$$

4.1.2 Cut off Priority Scheme (COPI)

In this scheme, if the total number of busy channels exceeds a threshold limit s, and a new call arrives, the new call will be blocked; otherwise it will be admitted. The handoff call is rejected only when all channels in the cell are used up. Now, if there is no new call bounding but r= c-s channels are reserved to give priority to handoff traffic in femto cell. Then the steady state probabilities are obtained as

$$P_i = \begin{cases} \frac{(\rho_n + \rho_{Lh})^i}{i!} P_0, & 0 \le i \le s \\ \frac{(\rho_n + \rho_{Lh})^s \rho_{Lh}^{\ i-s}}{i!} P_0, & s+1 \le i \le c \end{cases} \tag{7}$$

Where, P_0 is obtained by using normalization condition i.e. $\sum_{i=1}^{c} P_i = 1$

Similarly, we can easily obtain B_n, B_{Lh}, and B_{Hh}.

4.2 Two Layer Cellular Models with Sub-rating

All the c channels are busy in a femto cell and a handoff calls of LMS arrives, splitting a reserved channel into two half rated channels creates a channel. In the pico layer, if all the C channels are busy in the picocell and a handoff call of HMS arrives, then this call is allowed to wait in finite buffer of size Q. The two schemes for channel assignment with the provision of sub-rating are suggested as follows.

4.2.1. New Call Bounding Scheme with Sub-rating (NCB2)

We can obtain the steady state probabilities as:

$$P_{(m,n)} = \frac{\rho_n^{\ m}}{m!}\frac{\rho_{Lh}^{\ n}}{n!}P_{(0,0)},\quad 0 \le m \le t,\ m+n \le 2c - m,\ n \ge 0 \tag{8}$$

For the normalization eq. we get,

$$P_{(0,0)} = \left[\sum_{m=0}^{t}\sum_{n=0}^{2(c-m)}\frac{\rho_n^{\ m}}{m!}\frac{\rho_{Lh}^{\ n}}{n!}\right]^{-1} \tag{9}$$

Similarly, we can obtain B, B_n, B_{Lh}, and B_{Hh} .

4.2.2 Cut-Off Priority with Sub-rating (COP2)

In this section, priority is given to handoff calls and more handoff calls can be accommodated by sub-rating the channels already occupied by handoff calls. The steady state probabilities can be obtained by examining the inflow rates and outflow rates for each state. Now,

$$P_i = \begin{cases} \dfrac{(\rho_n + \rho_{Lh})^i}{i!}P_0, & 0 \le i \le s \\[2ex] \dfrac{(\rho_n + \rho_{Lh})^s \rho_{Lh}^{\ i-s}}{i!}P_0, & s+1 \le i \le 2c - s \end{cases} \tag{10}$$

$$P_0 = \left[\sum_{i=0}^{s}\frac{(\rho_n + \rho_{Lh})^i}{i!} + \sum_{i=s+1}^{2(c-s)}\frac{(\rho_n + \rho_{Lh})^s \rho_{Lh}^{\ i-s}}{i!}\right]^{-1} \tag{11}$$

Similarly, we can obtain B, B_n, B_{Lh}, and B_{Hh}.

5 Numerical Result and Discussions

Comparison of various performance indices i.e. blocking probability of new call, and blocking probability of high mobile subscribers and low mobile subscribers, overall blocking probability, obtained by using different schemes i.e. (NCB1),(COP1),(NCB2) and (COP2). The coding of computer program is done using MATLAB software. In this numerical illustration, we have constant default parameters N=3, c=10, C=15, t=4. Fig(a) and fig(b) show the overall blocking probability (B) with the variation in λ_{Hh} λ_{Lh}, for the different schemes. In fig.(2) overall blocking probability(B) of (HMS) increases with the increase in λ_{Hh} for all schemes and show that NCB2 is much better than other three. The reason for this is due to fact that the buffer is present in NCB2. In fig(3) Overall blocking probability of low mobile subscriber (LMS) decreases with the increase in arrival rate λ_{Lh}. In this figure, NCB2 schemes are more beneficial for handoff calls as there is slow blocking probability. Fig(4) shows the blocking probability of handoff call for (LMS) varying the reserved channels (r). In this fig, B_{Lh} increases in three schemes (NCB1, COP1, COP2) but decreases in NCB2 because of used buffer in NCB2 schemes. Blocking probability of new calls in fig(5) decreases with NCB2 when varying r. For the new calls NCB2 is better than others i.e. NCB1, COP1 and COP2. The reason for this is due to fact that the handoff calls are added. So NCB2 gives the lesser result in the all figures.

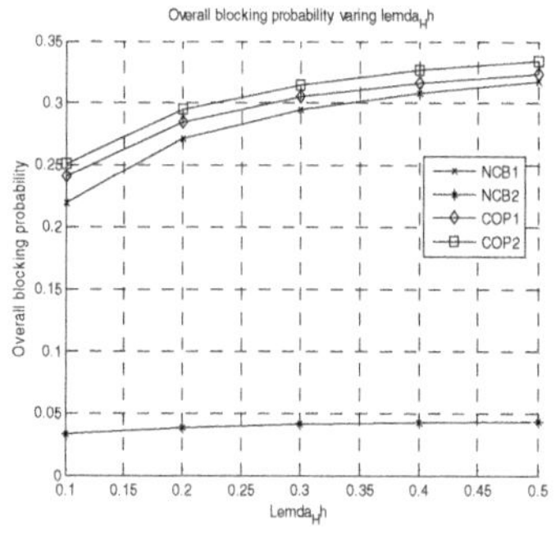

Fig. 2.

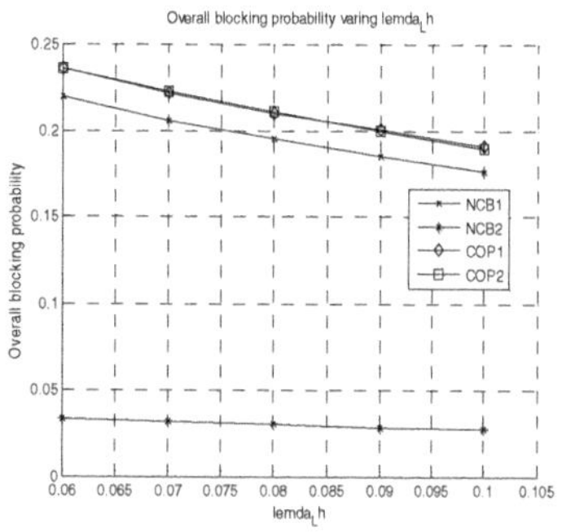

Fig. 3.

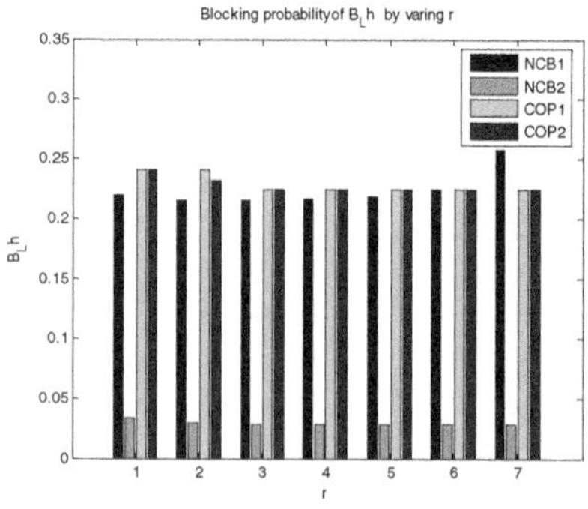

Fig. 4.

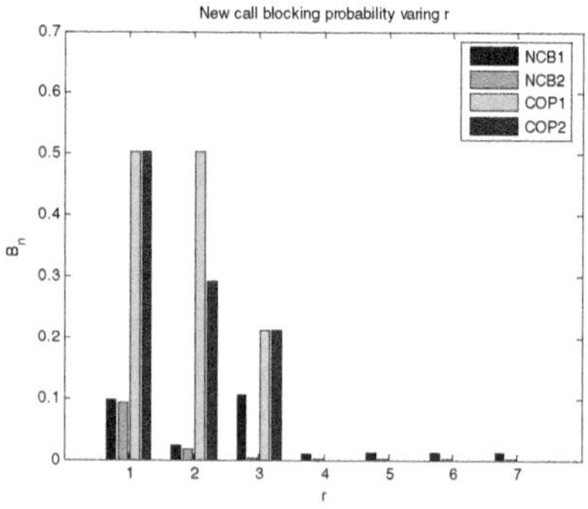

Fig. 5.

Table 1. Overall Blocking Probability for HMS(B)

λ_Hh	NCB1	NCB2	COP1	COP2
0.1	0.2193	0.0335	0.2410	0.2410
0.2	0.2712	0.0387	0.2849	0.2849
0.3	0.2951	0.0411	0.3051	0.3051
0.4	0.3088	0.0425	0.3167	0.3167
0.5	0.3177	0.0434	0.3242	0.3242

Table 2. Blocking Probability for New Calls(B_n)

r	NCB 1	NCB 2	COP 1	COP 2
1	0.0972	0.0939	0.5015	0.5015
2	0.0232	0.0176	0.5015	0.3433
3	0.0106	0.0026	0.2112	0.2112
4	0.0098	3.2650e-004	0	0
5	0.0103	3.27206e-005	0	0
6	0.0105	4.6450e-005	0	0
7	0.0105	9.3779e-005	0	0

6 Conclusion

In this paper, we proposed the call admission schemes i.e. (NCB1), (COP1), (NCB2), (COP2) for the two low layers of HCN. The numerical results show that (NCB2) much better than other schemes. The blocking probabilities can be determined to evaluate the optimal number of channels allocated to femtocells and picocells and optimal number of reserved channels in a particular cell based on traffic load.

References

1. Zhang, J., et al.: Femtocell technology and deployment. A John Wiley and Sons, Ltd. (2010)
2. `http://www.femtoforum.org`
3. Hou, J., Fang, Y.: Mobility-based call admission control schemes for wireless mobile networks. Wireless Communications and Mobile Computing 1, 269–282 (2001), doi:10.1002/wcm.18
4. Li, B., Lin, C., Chanson, S.: Analysis of a hybrid cutoff priority scheme for multiple classes of traffic in multimedia wireless networks. ACM/Baltzer J. Wireless Networks 4(4), 279–290 (1998)
5. Fang, Y., Zhang, Y.: Call admission control schemes and performance analysis in wireless mobile networks. IEEE Trans. Veh. Technol. 51(2), 371–382 (2002)
6. Li, W., Alfa, A.S.: A PCS with correlated arrival process and splitted-rating channels. IEEE Journal on Selected Area in Commun. 17(7), 1318–1325 (1999)
7. Jain, M., Agarwal, N.: Allocation scheme for multi-layer cellular network with integrated traffic. Journal of theoretical and applied information technology (2010)
8. Jain, M., Sharma, G.C., Saraswat, V.K.: Channel assignment schemes for PCS with cutoff priority and sub-rating. Int. Jour. Inform. Comp.Sci. 6(2), 46–56 (2003)
9. Chambers, D.: Femtocell primer (2008)
10. `http://www.Thinkfemtocell.com/website`
11. Parwani, K., Purohit, G.N.: Performance Measures of Mobile Communication in a Hierarchical Cellular System IEEE Xplore. In: ICDeCOM International Conference (2011)

Using Pattern Discovery Method and Position Details with Tree Matching for Extracting Information from Template Based Web Pages

B. Venkat Ramana[1] and A. Damodaram[2]

[1] Faculty, Department of Computer Science, MIPGS, Hyderabad, India
venkatbhavanasi@gmail.com
[2] Department of Computer Science, JNTUH, Hyderabad, India
damodarama@jntuh.ac.in

Abstract. To extract structured data from web sites we recommend a new method for information extraction from web, which effectively uses content redundancy on the web. This new method finds the matching pattern between the attribute values of the two sites and ignores unwanted portions of the attribute. Automatic pattern discovery along with position details method with tree matching is used as structured data extraction method. The main advantage of the method is that it requires less human intervention. In this paper we will discuss the implementation of the extractor using that method and then the approach is evaluated in terms of correctness. Experimental results show that almost all extraction targets can be successfully extracted by the developed extractor.

Keywords: Information Extraction; Template WebPages; Pattern Matching; Tree Matching; Data Position; Content Matching.

1 Introduction

Automatic data records extraction by computer can help human to gather information from web. Web pages can be broadly classified as static and dynamic pages [10]. The content and style of static pages does not change often. Where as the dynamic pages are generated when they are requested and change their content very often. Now a day's most pages on the web are generated by loading fixed page templates with data from a backend database. Previous studies estimate that as high as 45-55% of the content on the web is template content [1].

2 Ease of Use

The data region of a web page is a collection of similar data records that exist on contiguous part of a web page. In our approach, we populated the seed database S of records, from a few initial sites. By using wrapper learning method human editors

V.V. Das and N. Thankachan (Eds.): CIIT 2011, CCIS 250, pp. 684–686, 2011.

annotate attribute values in a sample page for each site. Since the sites are template based, a new site Xi which belongs to the group of similar sites, X will have same type of entities that are there in the seed database. Now we can scan the new site to find values that match attribute values of the records. The matching values are used to learn wrappers that are subsequently used to extract records from remaining other pages. This process is repeated for other new sites. By continuously expanding the seed database it ensures that sufficient overlap between the seed database and new sites. We can use Jaccard coefficient [3] to measure the similarity between attribute values, where each value is treated as a block of words with space as a delimiter. Our new extraction approach uses content redundancy over the websites and structural similarity among template based pages to extract attribute values with high precision and with minimum human intervention.

3 Experimental Evaluation

Table 1 shows the experimental results of the data records extraction for each input web page. Table 1 shows that from 40 pages, incorrectly extracted actual data records are found only in three input pages.

Table 1. Data Records Extraction Results

NO	I/P Pages	ACT	COR	WRG	MISS	FOU
1	www.jobitcom.com	14	14	0	0	149
3	www.jobindo.com	10	10	0	0	52
5	www.jobsdb.com	50	50	0	0	152

Table 2 describes the value of precision and recall of the data records extraction and data items alignment resulting from the extraction of the 40 web sites.

Table 2. Precision & recall of the data records extractions and data items alignments

NO	I/P Pages	ACT	COR	WRG	MISS	FOU
1	www.jobitcom.com	19.23	100	100	92.31	100
3	www.jobindo.com	32.89	100	100	81.82	100
5	www.jobsdb.com	19.23	100	100	100	100

Table 3 it can be seen that weak similarity computation dominates the execution time despite the use of prefix filtering [4] in our implementation. A complete run

Table 3. Running Time (Hrs) of the different steps for the two data sets

Stage	Restaurant	Bibliography
Weak similarity	23987	17488
Strong Similarity	163	15
Multi- attribute Matching	22	5
Extraction	65	26
Total	24237	17534

involving all the stages can be done on a 1000 CPU cluster in 1 day for the restaurant dataset and in 0.73 days for the bibliography dataset. Note that the execution time for the restaurant dataset is more than that for the bibliography dataset.

4 Conclusion and Future Work

To extract structured data from web sites we recommend a new method for information extraction from web, which effectively uses content redundancy on the web. We extract records from the initial web sites and populate the seed database with the records. For a new extracted record, our method will compare it with the already available records in the seed database. We also developed an Apriori-style algorithm for efficiently enumerating attribute positions with matching values in a sufficient number of pages. In our experiments our techniques were able to extract records with > 95% precision and > 80% recall. An important direction for future work involves extending our methods to handle non-text numeric (e.g., price) and image (e.g., ratings) attributes.

References

1. Agichtein, E., Ganti, V.: Mining reference tables for automatic text segmentation. Proceeding of SIGKDD 20(1), 152–187 (2004)
2. Agichtein, E., Gravano, L.: Snowball: extracting relations from large plain-text collections. In: Proceedings of the 5th ACM International Conference on Digital Libraries (ACM DL), pp. 85–94 (2000)
3. Agrawal, R., Srikant, R.: Fast algorithms for mining association rules. In: Proceedings of SIGMOD-VLDB 1994, pp. 487–499 (1994)
4. Chaudhuri, S., Ganti, V., Kaushik, R.: A primitive operator for similarity joins in data cleaning. In: Proceedings of ICDE (2006)
5. Koudas, N., Sarawagi, S., Srivastava, D.: Record linkage: Similarity measures and algorithms. SIGMOD (Tutorial) 3(3), 975–3397 (2011) ISSN: 0975-3397
6. Manning, C., Raghavan, P., Schutze, H.: Introduction to IR. In: First IEEE International Conference on Semantic Computing, pp. 19–26. Cambridge University Press (2008)
7. Sarawagi, S., Bhamidipaty, A.: Interactive deduplication using active learning. In: SIGKDD, EDBT, pp. 450–461 (2009); SIGKDD Explorations 6(2), 61–66 (2004); (2002)
8. Breuel, T.M.: Information Extraction from HTML Documents by Structural Matching. In: Proceedings of the 2nd International Workshop on Web Document Analysis (WDA 2003). PARC, Inc., Palo Alto (2003C)
9. Yeonjung, K., Jeahyun, P., Taehwan, K., dan Joongmin, C.: Web IE by HTML Tree Edit Distance Matching. In: Proceedings of the International Conference on Convergence Information Technology (ICCIT 2007), Washington, DC, US (2007)
10. Zhai, Y., Liu, B.: Structured Data Extraction from the Web Based on Partial Tree Alignment. IEEE Transaction on Knowledge and Data Engineering 16(12), 1614–1628 (2006C)
11. Dewanto, S., Mustofa, K.: IE using Automatic pattern discovery based on tree matching, Computer Science Department, GM University (2011)

A Survey of Release Planning Approaches in Incremental Software Development

Amir Seyed Danesh

Department of Software Engineering,
Faculty of Computer Science and Information Technology,
University of Malaya, 50603, Kuala Lumpur
amir_s_d@siswa.um.edu.my

Abstract. In Incremental Software Development today, consecutive series of releases are generated with adding and changing some features in the process of development. Release planning is in fact prioritizing and assigning the features for different releases and deciding which features to be included in every future release to satisfy the stakeholders. There are several different methods to solve the problems in release planning for new products in industry and each one has their own benefits. In this study we investigate which release planning approaches have been proposed, their degree of empirical experience, and their factors for requirements selection. In this paper, we are studying current approaches in and investigate their weakness and strength by analyzing each of them.we conclude that many approaches are related to each other and use similar techniques to address the release planning challenges.

Keywords: Release planning, Software development, Methods.

1 Introduction

Large-scale software systems go through many changes during their evolution. These changes can be addition of new features or change in the existing features. Through different releases, new features are demanded by the stakeholders and making decision about which feature to be included in every release is what we call release planning. The decision making process can be very complicated when stakeholders have different preferences, resources are limited and there are lots of constraints. Therefore, the need for an intelligent decision support in release planning is felt. Several approaches and methods have been present for better release infrastructure that some of them are based on re-planning for new releases. Release planning is a company-wide optimization problem involving many stakeholders in which the goal is to maximize utilization of the often limited resources, such as budget and developers, of a company and turn them into business benefit [1].in this paper we are going to study current release planning methods and a hoped this survey can be useful to better understating of release planning challenges.

V.V. Das and N. Thankachan (Eds.): CIIT 2011, CCIS 250, pp. 687–692, 2011.

2 Current Release planning Methods

Today, large software companies in software development face to many problems for their new releases. Various methodologies aimed at addressing the release planning challenges have been used in industry and many more approaches have been proposed in academic research. Although there are various methods and approaches to develop a new release, a new version has always its own problems and challenges. The next section of this paper studies and reviews these available methods.

2.1 Ad Hoc (Non-plan) Approach

Some of the organizations do not see release planning activity as independent, and they think basic decisions in theirs organization are based on business rule and needs and once. Most part of the decision-making process is haphazard with an emphasis on guessing, discussion, business rules, and customers' needs instead of a systematic way based on formulation and quantitative ways. In Ad-hoc approach that is the easiest form to practice, for scheduling, planning and prioritization of requirements there is no clear order and findings are manual and usually based on negotiation but Anton in[2] reported that a complex project will likely fail without a plan. Many release plans focus only on the target release contents[3], rather than on defining incrementally releasable products. Ruhe in[4] did a comparison between Ad hoc planning and Systematic planning to know the level of reliability and trust of their research and found out Systematic planning based on tools is more reliable than Ad hoc planning. The Ad-hoc manner is more common and maybe suitable for a relatively small in-house project that includes a few of features and no serious constraints. We can say that prioritization in this approach is based on many things such as judgment of project manager and ideas of stakeholders. Therefore, this approach depends more on individuals.

2.2 Planning Game Approach

The planning game (PG) refers to the process of planning and deciding what to develop in extreme programming (XP) projects[5]. The main goal of XP is to lower the cost of change in software requirements[5]. With traditional system development methodologies, like the Waterfall Methodology, the requirements for the system are determined often at the beginning of the project .The first Extreme Programming project was started March 6, 1996. Extreme Programming is one of several popular agile development processes. It has already been proven to be very successful at many companies of all different sizes and industries worldwide. Extreme planning [6]conducts release planning by performing planning games techniques. It has been very successful at many companies of all different sizes and industries worldwide. Extreme Programming is successful because it emphasizes on customer satisfaction. The aim is to deliver maximum value to the customer in the least time possible. Customers write story cards describing the features they want and developers assign important features and estimate the value of time required to develop those features.

The customers then choose the most promising story cards for the next release by either setting a release date and adding the cards until the estimated total matches the release date, or selecting the highest value cards first and setting the release date based on the estimates given on the cards. PG's strength is in the simplistic and straightforward approach it adopts, which works well in smaller projects. However, as the size and the complexity of the projects increases, the decisions involved in planning releases become very complex.

According to [3], XP (and thus PG) does not provide guidance on some key issues. XP does not:

- address how a development group should interact with key stakeholders
- describe how to produce consistent features and priorities that satisfy multiple stakeholders
- provide a suggested technique to balance conflicting demands of multiple stakeholders
- Provide a technique for managers to assess the value of proposed features.

2.3 Incremental Funding Method (IFM)

These days, software companies for investigation in software development need to return in much shorter time and take more revenues. These companies do not invest in software development without clear returns. It means first they look at market and demands and based on that they start their developments. IFM is a financially informed approach to software development, designed to maximize returns through delivering functionality in 'chunks' of customer valued features, carefully sequenced so as to optimize Net Present Value (NPV)[7]. The Incremental Funding Method is a software engineering methodology that emphasizes financial consideration in a software project. The method is introduced by Mark Denne and Jane Huang. This method decomposes the system into units of customer-value functionality known as minimum marketable feature that can be delivered quickly and that provide market value to the customer[8]. An MMF's value is typically measured in terms of both tangible and intangible factors such as revenue generation, cost savings, competitive differentiation, brand-name projection, and enhanced customer loyalty. MMFs are identified by customers, developers, and business stakeholders according to the adopted software development process[9].

2.4 Optimization-Based Techniques

Considering the complex nature of RP, several studies have modelled the problem of selecting release features as a specialized optimization problem. In formulating an optimization model for RP, Bagnall et al. [10] assign weights to customers based on their importance to the software company. The objective is to find a subset of customers whose features are to be satisfied within the available cost. Ho-Won Jung [11] follows a similar footing with a goal of selecting features that give maximum value for minimum cost within allowable cost limits of a software system.

These optimization approaches cope better with larger problem sizes, but customers are not given an opportunity to participate in RP decisions. The importance of customers to a company is not the only issue RP should seek to satisfy. Most of the problems discussed for "planning games" above arise equally here.

2.5 Hybrid Intelligence Approach

The hybrid intelligence approach for RP proposed by Ruhe et al. [12] is an extension of the optimization-based techniques. The belief that computational intelligence cannot replace a human decision maker was the driving force of this approach. A synergy between the two decision strategies was explored. The overall architecture of this approach called EVOLVE* [12] is designed as an iterative and evolutionary procedure mediating between the real world problem of software RP, the available tools of computational intelligence for handling explicit knowledge and crisp data, and the involvement of human intelligence for tackling tacit knowledge and fuzzy data. At all iterations of EVOLVE*, three phases are passed: modelling, exploration, and consolidation. We will later illustrate the approach in a case study example.

2.6 Lightweight Re-planning

Lightweight re-planning first time was intruded by Thamer AlBourae in[13] and emphasizes in re-planning by adding new features. In fact in the process model old features are compared with newly added ones by using Analytical hierarchy process. In Incremental software development changes are very important and new change requests arrive during the process. These changes imply the modification or some features or the addition of new ones. The main goal of this light re-planning model is to develop a new product plan that achieves higher stakeholder satisfaction. Figure 1 shows a generic process model that is describing main release re-planning activities incusing their input and output. In this model three main roles are considered, including: *Product manager*, who is responsible for the whole development process; *Stakeholders*, which include any team member who are concerned with the product development; and *the supporting environment*, which facilitates the achievement of the processes goals.

In the next section, we explain each activity in detail. Main steps[13]:

New features: When the developments are going to start, the new features are collected. The change requests received are added to the old sets of features and directed to be categorized by the feature categorization process.

Feature categorization: Adopted framework changes requested should be categorized to distinguish between duplicated features, ongoing of new added ones.

Stakeholders' voting: Stakeholders are people that are effective in development process and can include different levels such as managers, developers or end users.

Resource estimation: Resources capacities are one of the boundaries that should be considered when re-planning product releases. The main aim is to determine the likely usage of effort Effort (*fi*), and time Time (*fi*) for each feature *fi* for the next release.

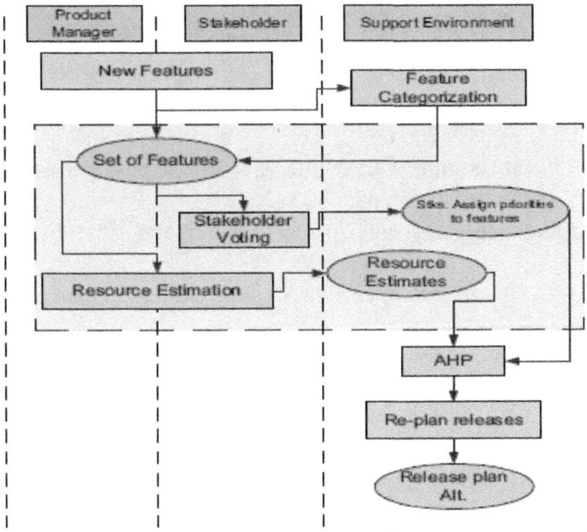

Fig. 1. Generic process model for the Light-Weight Re-planning

3 Conclusion

Different methods and approaches are presented in Release Planning of which each has particular advantages and disadvantages. These methods can be effective in developing a new Release and big software companies can use these patterns to create and develop new Releases. To study and identify effective factors on these methods can play a significant role in having better Releases and consequently in developing more efficient software. Today, most companies are aimed at studying and analyzing these methods to achieve a final product desired for the customer. In the present article, a set of Release Planning methods is studied and reviewed.

References

1. Ruhe, G., Saliu, M.O.: The art and science of software release planning. IEEE Software 22(6), 47–53 (2005)
2. Anton, A.I.: Successful software projects need requirements planning. IEEE Software 20(3), 44–46 (2003)
3. Nejmeh, B., Thomas, I.: Business-Driven Product Planning Using Feature Vectors and Increments. IEEE Softw. 19(6), 34–42 (2002)
4. Du, G., McElroy, J., Ruhe, G.: Ad Hoc Versus Systematic Planning of Software Releases – A Three-Staged Experiment. In: Münch, J., Vierimaa, M. (eds.) PROFES 2006. LNCS, vol. 4034, pp. 435–440. Springer, Heidelberg (2006)

5. Ruhe, G., Saliu, M.O.: The Science and Practice of Software Release Planning. Technical Report TR-SEDS 23/2004, University of Calgary (2005)
6. Beck, K.: Extreme Programming Explained. Addison Wesley (2001)
7. Denne, M., Cleland-Huang, J.: The incremental funding method: data-driven software development. IEEE Software 21(3), 39–47 (2004)
8. Denne, M., Clelang-Huang, J.: Software by Numbers: Low-Risk, High-Return Development. Prentice-Hall (2003)
9. Denne, M., Cleland-Huang, J.: The Incremental Funding Method. Data Driven Software Development 21(3), 39–47 (2004)
10. Bagnall, A.J., Rayward-Smith, V.J., Whittley, I.M.: The next release problem. Information and Software Technology 43(14), 883–890 (2001)
11. Jung, H.-W.: Optimizing Value and Cost in Requirements Analysis. IEEE Software 15(4), 74–78 (1998)
12. Ruhe, G., Ngo, A.: Hybrid Intelligence in Software Release Planning. Int. J. Hybrid Intell. Syst. 1(1-2), 99–110 (2004)
13. Albourae, T., Ruhe, G., Moussavi, M.: Lightweight Replanning of Software Product Releases. In: International Workshop on Software Product Management, IWSPM 2006 (2006)

Evaluation of Protocols and Algorithms for Improving the Performance of TCP over Wireless/Wired Network

V. Vasanthi[1], N. Ajith Singh[1], M. Romen Kumar[1], and M. Hemalatha[2]

[1] Department of Computer Science, Karpagam University
[2] Dept. of Software Systems, Karpagam University, Coimbatore - 21
{vasarthika,ajithex,hema.bioinf}@gmail.com,
romen_kumar.2007@yahoo.com

Abstract. Transmission Control Protocol (TCP), it is an Internet Protocol which is designed for relatively reliable wire line network; it has another name called Transfer Control Protocol. It is known to perform poorly in the presence of wireless links because of its basic assumption that *any* loss of a data segment is due to congestion and consequently it invokes congestion control measures. However, in wireless access links a large number of losses are occurred due to wireless link errors or host mobility. For this reasons, many researchers are working to improve TCP performance in such environment. In this paper WTCP's performance is compared with TCP and WAP, Vegas showed a better performance in WTCP over TCP algorithms Vegas and New Reno. This results show that WTCP significantly improves the throughput of TCP connections due to its unique feature of hiding the time spent by the base station.

Keywords: WAN, WTCP, TCP/IP, UDP.

1 Introduction

Technology advances in communication, hardware and software, and the ever increasing the need for accessing the Internet and Intranet which has been created for a new for wireless data communication. In recent years usage of wireless wide-area networks (wwans) are grown longer such as CDPD, RAM and Ardis, with industry projections topping $5.7 billion by the year 2009. In the typical WWAN use scenario, a mobile user connects over the WWAN network to a dedicated replacement in the business backbone, which then acts as the service point for all the requests from the mobile user [9]. Providing efficient and reliable connectivity between the proxy and the mobile host over commercial wide-area wireless networks is thus becoming a vital issue.

2 Related Works

In Wireless/wired there are many approaches have been proposed to improve TCP performance over these networks. Those approaches are divided into two major categories i.e. transport level and others is link level. In Transport level proposals include

V.V. Das and N. Thankachan (Eds.): CIIT 2011, CCIS 250, pp. 693–697, 2011.

Indirect-TCP (I-TCP) [1], Freeze-TCP [8], Explicit Bad State Notification (EBSN) [2], and fast-retransmission [6]. I-TCP splits the transport link at the wire line–wireless border. The base station maintains two TCP Connections, i.e. fixed and wireless link. This way, the poor quality of the wireless link is hidden from the fixed network. By splitting the transport link, I-TCP does not maintain end-to-end TCP semantics, i.e. I-TCP relies on the application layer to ensure Reliability upon detecting a poor signal strength, Freeze-TCP [8] at the mobile host throttles the sender by advertising a receive window size of zero. This causes the sender to enter persist mode and freeze all the timers and window sizes. This way, the mobile host can prevent the sender from taking any congestion control measures. Freeze-TCP requires TCP code modification at the mobile host.

3 About the Wireless Networks

3.1 Transmission Control Protocol

TCP is the protocol that major Internet applications such as the World Wide Web, email, remote administration and file transfer rely on. Other applications, which do not require reliable data stream service, may use the User Datagram Protocol (UDP), which provides a datagram service that emphasizes reduced latency over reliability. TCP controls segment size, flow control, the rate at which data is exchanged, and network traffic congestion.

3.2 The Wireless Application Protocol (WAP)

It is technical standard for accessing information over a mobile wireless network. A WAP browser is a web browser for mobile devices such as mobile phone that uses a protocol [15].

3.3 Wireless Transmission Control Protocol (WTCP)

- WTCP receives data segment from source
- WTCP sends data segments to mobile host
- WTCP receives acknowledgement from mobile host.

3.4 Necessity to Improve the Performance of TCP in a Wireless Environment

When used in wireless environment, the TCP developed for fixed networks with relatively reliable links wrongly assumes segment loss due to wireless link errors to be a sign of network congestion and invokes congestion control mechanisms that curb the flow of segments on that connection, because of which the throughput is affected badly.

Venturi Transport Protocol (VTP) is a patented proprietary protocol that is designed to replace TCP transparently in order to overcome perceived inefficiencies related to wireless data transport [13].

About TCP Vegas and New Reno algorithms

Vegas are a TCP congestion avoidance algorithm that emphasizes packet delay, rather than packet loss, as a signal to help determine the rate at which to send packets. It was developed at the University of Arizona by Lawrence Brakmo and Larry L. Peterson. TCP Vegas detects congestion at an incipient stage based on increasing Round-Trip Time (RTT) values of the packets.

TCP **New Reno** improves retransmission during the fast recovery phase of TCP Reno. During fast recovery, for every duplicate ACK that is returned to TCP New Reno, a new unsent packet from the end of the congestion window is sent, to keep the transmit window full. New Reno performs as well as SACK at low packet error rates, and substantially outperforms Reno at high error rates.

4 Evaluation of Tcp, Wap and Wtcp

To evaluate the performance TCP algorithms such as New Reno and Vegas are used. The simulation programs were written in Maisie, a parallel-programmable simulation language. The proposed work compared WTCP with TCP and WAP. It shows the throughput as the performance measurement: the total number of transmitted packets over the total elapsed time. The simulation was based on the following parameters:

Parameter	values
Error bit rate on the wireless link	1/64 K, 1/128 K, 1/256 K, ..., 1/8 M, and 1/16 M.
Packet size	1024 bytes
Total amount of transport data	5 M bytes-namely 5,000 packets.
Size of sliding window	64 Kbytes
Propagation delay –Wireless Network	5 time units
Propagation delay-Wired Network	Random-6 to 9 simulation time units.
Number of iterations	1/64 K to 1/16 M
Round trip time (RTT)	20

The simulation results are summarized in Tables and charts below. Note that here the diagrams shows only the averaged number of received packets versus time for the cases in which the error bit rate was 1/64 K, 1/512 K, and 1/4 M in table (a), (b), and (c) respectively. In figure 1, summarize the throughput versus the error bit rate of the wireless link for all cases. The throughput is defined as the average number of packets received per time unit. It clearly shows that the WTCP achieves maximum channel utilization with both the bandwidth values and that the utilization of New Reno and Vegas are very much below the maximum possible value. In fact, the figure indicates that for a 50Kbps channel with an error rate of 6%, WTCP provides about 200% improvement in performance over the other versions of TCP it have considered.

Table (a), (b), (c) represents the Throughput versus the Error Bit Rate of the Wireless Link was 1/64, 1/512, 1/4 MB respectively.

Time Taken	TCP	WAP	WTCP
1/64 kbits			
248	400	375	1200
495	650	600	2200
742	1100	1000	3800
969	1300	1200	5000
1236	2000	1600	5400
1483	2200	2000	5500

Time Taken	TCP	WAP	WTCP
1/ 512 Kbits			
105	200	600	200
209	650	600	1200
313	1000	900	2100
417	1200	1000	3100
525	1800	1500	3800
625	2400	1800	5000

Bytes	WAP	TCP	WTCP
64KB	80	100	220
128 KB	85	95	420
256 KB	120	180	580
512 KB	160	220	660
1 MB	260	460	780
2 MB	440	680	800

Time Taken	TCP	WAP	WTCP
1/4 MB			
57	700	300	700
100	1000	800	1200
133	1100	1000	1300
166	1400	1200	1560
190	1900	1600	2000
232	2100	1800	2300

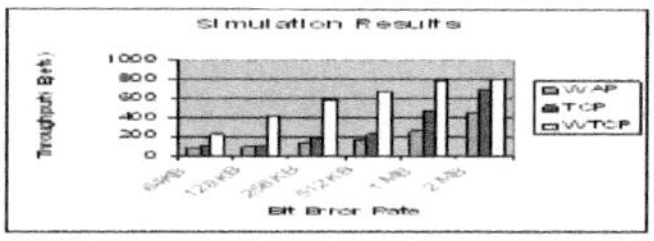

Fig. 1. Overall Simulation Result

Performance Analysis of WTCP with TCP New Reno and TCP-Vegas
Table e, f & Figure 2 Bandwidth of 50 and 19.2Kbps

Time in sec	WTCP	Vegas	new Reno
500	2000	1500	1200
1000	4000	2700	2000
1500	6000	3600	3200
2000	8000	5500	5000
2500	11500	7800	6200

Time in sec	WTCP	Vegas	New Reno
500	5000	1500	1200
1000	10000	3500	2500
1500	17000	4200	3500
2000	23000	7000	4500
2500	30000	9000	6200

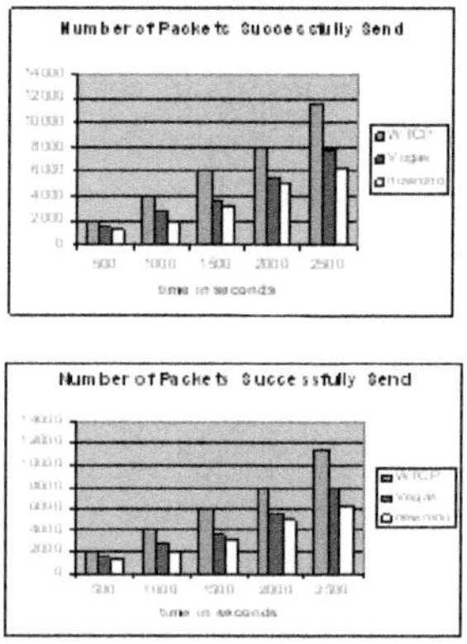

Fig. 2.

From the above figures and tables e, f it is concluded that the Vegas is outperforms than new Reno among WTCP algorithms respectively.

5 Conclusion

WTCP performed better than TCP and WAP in all the simulated cases. The main reason is that WTCP uses fast acknowledgement, which hides the wireless environment from the sender. In the cases with high error bit rates, the throughput difference between WTCP and the other two protocols was higher compared to it. This implies that the WTCP protocol is suitable for wireless/wired internetworking.

Acknowledgement. We thank Karpagam University for motivating and encouraging doing our Research work in a Successful.

References

[1] Sinha, A.: Study of Proposed Methods for Improving TCP Performance over Wireless Links (March 2003)
[2] Brakmo, L., Peterson, L.: End to end congestion avoidance on a global internet. IEEE JSAC 13(8) (October 1995)
[3] Floyd, S., Henderson, T.: The new Reno modification to tcp's fast recovery algorithm, Internet Request for Comments 2582 (April 1999)
[4] Lakshman, T.V., Madhow, U.: The performance of TCP/IP for networks with high bandwidth-delay products and random loss. IEEE/ACM Trans. Networking (June 1997)
[5] Sinha, P., Venkitaraman, N., Siva Kumar, R., Bharghavan, V.: WTCP: A Reliable Transport Protocol for Wireless Wide-Area Networks. In: Proc. of ACM Mobicom 1999 (August 1999)
[6] Bakre, A., Badrinath, B.R.: I-TCP: Indirect TCP for Mobile Hosts.DCS-TR-314, Rutgers University (October 1994)
[7] Bakshi, B.S., Krishna, P., Vaidya, N.H., Pradhan, D.K.: Improving Performance of TCP over Wireless Networks. Texas A & M University, technical report TR-96-04 (May 1996)
[8] Amir, E., Balakrishnan, H., Srinivasanseshan, Katz, R.H.: Efficient TCP over Wireless Links. In: Hot Topics in Operating Systems (HotOS-V) (1995); Proceedings of Fifth Workshop on IEEE Explore (August 06, 2002)
[9] Ratnam, K., Matta, I.: WTCP: An Efficient Transmission Control Protocol for Networks with Wireless Links. Technical Report NU-CCS-97-11, Northeastern University (July 1997)
[10] Vaidya, N., Mehta, M., Perkins, C., Montenegro, G.: Delayed Duplicate Acknowledgements, A TCP-Unaware Approach to Improve Performance of TCP over Wireless. Technical Report 99-003 (February 1999)
[11] Agosta, J., Russle, T.: CDPD: Cellular Digital Packet Data Standards and Technology. McGraw Hill, New York (1997)
[12] Pawlan, J.: The World of Mobile and Stationary Devices (August 2000)
[13] Pawlan, M.: Introduction to Wireless Programming with the MID Profile (September 2000)
[14] Mahmoud, Q.: Wireless Application Programming (February 2003)
[15] Information on WAP & WAP TCP/IP, `http://www.W3schools.com`

Service Oriented Requirements Engineering – A New Dimension

Jaya Vijayan[1] and G. Raju[2]

[1] Department of Computer Science, Rajagiri College of Social Sciences, Kalamassery, Cochin, India
[2] Department of Information Technology, Kannur University, Kannur, India

Abstract. This paper proposes a new approach for service oriented requirements Engineering (SORE). It also differentiates traditional requirements engineering and Service Oriented Requirements Engineering (SORE). SORE is different from traditional RE process in various aspects. The paper progress through a four step approach for service oriented requirements engineering. Further as a next step the method need to be simulated using a case study and also need to be tested in the industry.

Keywords: SOA, SORE, Requirements Engineering, Services, Business Process Modeling.

1 Introduction

"The software architecture of a program or computing system is the structure or structures of the system, which comprise software components, the externally visible properties of those components, and the relationships among them." [4]. Service-oriented architecture is a special kind of software architecture that has several unique characteristics. It is important for service designers and developers to understand the concepts of SOA, so that they can make the most effective use of Web services in their environment.SOA is a relatively new term, but the term "service" as it relates to software service has been around since at least the early 1990s, when it was used in Tuxedo to describe "services" and "service processes" [7]. Service consumers view a service simply as an endpoint that supports a particular request format or contract. Service consumers are not concerned with how the service goes about executing their requests; they expect only that it will. Consumers also expect that their interaction with the service will follow a contract, an agreed-upon interaction between two parties. The way the service executes tasks given to it by service consumers is irrelevant. The service might fulfill the request by executing a servlet, a mainframe application, or a Visual Basic application. The only requirement is that the services send the response back to the consumer in the agreed-upon format. Service Oriented Architecture (SOA) is a way of developing distributed systems where the components of these systems are stand alone services. These services may execute on geographically distributed computers. Standard protocols have been designed to support service communications and information exchange.

V.V. Das and N. Thankachan (Eds.): CIIT 2011, CCIS 250, pp. 698–704, 2011.

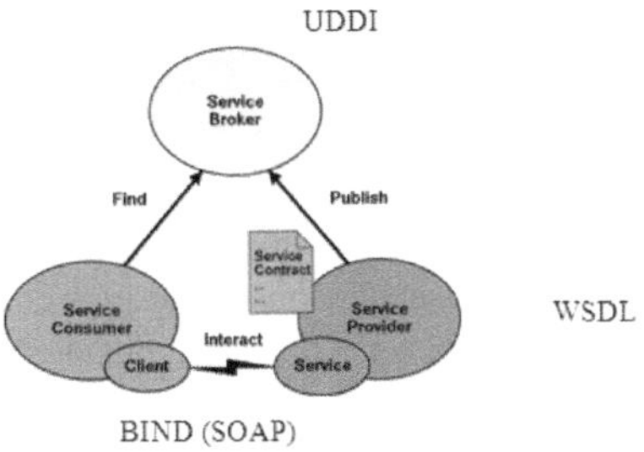

Fig. 1. SOA Architecture

Service providers design and implement services and specify these services in a language called Web Services Description Language (WSDL).They also publish information about these services in a generally accessible registry using a publication standard called Universal Description Discovery & Integration (UDDI).

Service Requestors, who wish to make use of a service, search the UDDI registry to discover the specification of that service and to locate the service provider.

2 Service-Oriented Requirement Engineering (SORE)

SORE differs from traditional requirement engineering as it assumes that the concerned application will be developed in an SOA framework running in an SOA infrastructure. Many SOA infrastructure systems are developed on top of an OO infrastructure e.g. C# is both an OO language as well as an SOA language because it has classes and methods. While SORE involves many activities commonly in traditional requirement engineering, the entities identified and the process used are different and the way models are used in the development process are different. SORE focuses on identifying "Services" and "Workflows". A dynamic SOA application may change its services, workflows, user interfaces, and policies, data and data Schema based on the system status as well as new user needs. [1]

3 SOA Lifecycle Model (IBM Foundation)

SOA lifecycle model consists of two development activities and two operation activities. The two development activities are :

1 **Model** – During the model phase architects and other members of the organization gather business requirements and design optimal business processes to meet these requirements.
2 **Assemble** – The optimized business processes are realized in the assemble phase by combining new and existing services to form composite applications.

The two operation activities are :

1 **Deploy** – In the deploy phase, these assets are then deployed into a secure and integrated environment that leverages specialized services. These services help the organization integrate people, processes and information.
2 **Manage** – During the manage phase, the entire service model is managed and monitored from both an IT and a business perspective. Information gathered during this phase is used to gain real-time insight into business processes, enabling better business decisions and feeding information back into the life cycle for continuous process improvement.

The four phases are performed iteratively. The entire process will be controlled and orchestrated by the governance policies. One distinction is that the SOA lifecycle includes an explicit process of discovering reusable assets such as services and workflows. [1]

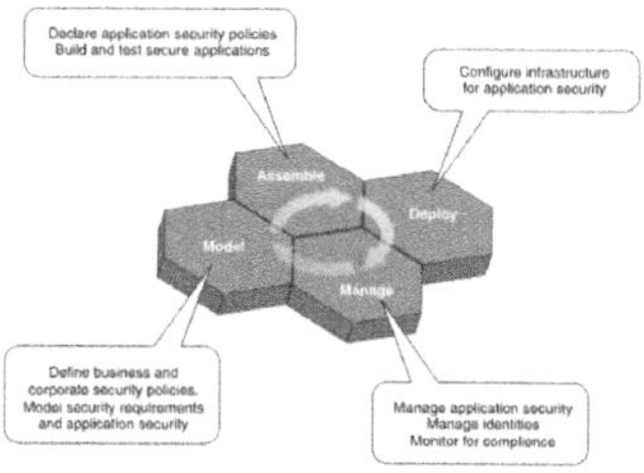

Fig. 2. IBM SOA Foundation Architecture

4 Sore Framework

SORE assumes an SOA framework will be used, thus some design decisions are made before even starting any requirement analysis. This is different from traditional requirement engineering where analysis and design are often separate activities, with design following requirement analysis, probably in an iterative manner. SORE has the following major features.

a. Reusability-Oriented and Cumulative
b. Domain-Specific
c. Framework-Oriented Analysis
d. Model-Driven Development
e. Evaluation-based.

5 Traditional versus SORE

5.1 Requirements Engineering Process

The concepts of requirement and requirements engineering are core for the software engineering discipline. The set of all requirements forms the basis for subsequent development of the system or system component. A full Requirements Engineering process (REP), when it is conducted with sufficient detail, is similar to a full software development lifecycle. Traditionally, a REP is performed in the beginning of the system development lifecycle. Therefore, a REP is an incremental and iterative process, where more detail is addressed in each iteration. In complex systems, a REP can be extended until the Analysis and Design phases. The correct selection of a REP depends on several attributes: particular organization, particular systems engineering and software development process, and particular type of software developed, among others [9]. Usually a good requirements engineering process includes the following activities:

- Requirements elicitation, where the system requirements are discovered.
- Requirements analysis and negotiation, where the requirements are analyzed in detail and accepted by the stakeholders.
- Requirements validation, where the consistency and completeness of the requirements is checked.[2]

5.2 Service-Oriented View of Requirements Engineering

There are several concepts which are the building blocks for a modern Requirements Engineering. Such concepts are: (i) software as a service, (ii) business process modeling, (iii) service-oriented design, and (iv) IT service management, (v) methods and techniques of RE and BPM, (vi) services classification, and (vii) basic Requirements Engineering Process Model to Service-oriented Software Systems Development.

5.2.1 Software as a Service

"Software as a Service now defines those services relating to the delivery to and remote access of software applications via web browser". Software as a service (Saas) can be broken down into three main types of service:

(i) **on demand software purchasing,** where individual users or organizations try, buy, download or rent a personal, workgroup, or enterprise full software across the internet;
(ii) **on demand IT service-oriented architecture** (SOA), where an IT system and application processing is defined and developed as a set of own organizational packages of services that can interoperate and exchange information with each other; and

(iii) **on demand application services**, where individual user or organizations pay external third-party providers for the service [2].

5.2.2 Business Process Modeling

In general, a model is something that functions as a representation of something that we wish to understand. An important goal of business process modeling is its use as a tool for requirements engineering. Many businesses face the problem to support their processes by new technology. The first step in these projects is to understand how their processes work. Disciplines such as Information Systems Development, Workflow Automation, and the selection of Enterprise Resource Planning (ERP) utilize business process modeling to understand the business processes that are supported by the technology that is introduced in the organization [8].

5.2.3 Service-Oriented Design

Service-oriented Design is needed to aid in the communication between application architects as well as between application and enterprise architects. It is also needed to verify the conformance of services to their requirements and to enable a model-driven approach to service development and composition. It follows that the design of services is a complex activity. It involves reconciling disparate aspects such as the involved providers and consumers, their interfaces, interactions, and collaboration agreements, their internal business processes, data, and (legacy) applications.

5.2.4 IT Service Management

IT Service Management refers to the planning, design, building-transition, operation and continuous improvement of IT services in an organization. In the Software Engineering domain, a service at most can be a full software application, but in the IT domain, it is only considered a part of the full service, which is finally delivered for a service systems comprised of people, technology and processes .In order to support IT Service Management, a number of service-oriented frameworks and themes have been developed, however, these guidelines lack some of the key principles, phases, and steps available in traditional systems development frameworks. A further poorly addressed area in existing guidelines is the elicitation and determination of provider and customer service requirements.[10].

6 Proposed Method Overview

As from literature we know that there is a basic difference between traditional requirements engineering and service oriented requirements engineering. The proposed method focus on service oriented requirements engineering. The SORE activities are divided into phases as follows

1 Business process modeling
2 Stakeholder analysis
3 Service Identification
4 Requirements Elicitation & Specification.

6.1 Business Process Modeling

The business goals and business processes are identified and understood, as a result of the activities of this face a high level model of those business goals and processes is generated. The analysts have to start identifying the business goals, understanding them and helping the stakeholders to define the business processes that have to support the business goals success.

6.2 Stakeholder Analysis

Identify the individuals or groups that are likely to affect or be affected by the system. A list of the stakeholders and their roles are generated too. Identifying the stakeholders will help the analyst to identify the type of services and the various Characteristics the stakeholders will need for the services.

6.3 Service Identification

Service identification is one of the major part of this method. Here the analyst has to identify the various services the software is going to provide for the end-users. Three main types of services are as follows:

a. **On demand software purchasing**, where individual users or organizations try, buy, download or rent a personal, workgroup, or enterprise full software across the internet.
b. **On demand IT service-oriented architecture** (SOA), where an IT system and application processing is defined and developed as a set of own organizational packages of services that can interoperate and exchange information with each other.
c. **On demand application services,** where individual user or organizations pay external third-party providers for the use of packages of services for their own application.

The analyst has to clearly identify the categories of services that is involved in software based on the above classification. Once the services are correctly identified it leads to an effective requirement elicitation & Specification phase.

6.4 Requirements Elicitation and Specification

In this face analysts analyze the outcomes from the previous phases. Once the stakeholders and the services they want are known the analyst can proceed to a detailed requirements elicitation phase .Here a novel method of Paper prototyping can be used for effective requirements elicitation. Paper prototyping is a cost effective method of elicitation. It is mainly used in user interface testing. This is an iterative process. Once requirements are stable the analyst can do the specification activity. These specifications must include the components of software needed to develop the software system required .For each component, the analysts have to make an

"Operational Level Agreement, an OLA is a technical document that specifies in a detail way the functional requirements that a software component must fulfill; a set of OLAs form an "Service Level Agreement (SLA). Some of the key concerns here are (i) relevance of knowledge about the business goals and business process (ii) suitable modeling techniques etc.

7 Conclusion

This paper proposes a new approach for service oriented requirements engineering which is a very simple four step approach. It is very systematic approach for finding the business goals, identifying the stakeholders, identifying the services& requirements and specification of requirements. In this paper we have elaborated a conceptual method of requirements engineering for service oriented architecture which need to be simulated further. As a future work the implementation part of the approach can be simulated using a case study. This method need to be tested for industry projects for further results.

References

1. Tsai, W.T., Jin, Z., Wang, P., Wu, B.: Requirements in Service –Oriented system Engineering. In: ICEBE 2007, Proceedings of the IEEE International Conference on e-Business Engineering (2007)
2. Mejía, F.F., Tavarez, J.M.M.: From Requirements Engineering to Service-Oriented Requirements Engineering: An Analysis of Transition. In: Thirtieth International conference on Information Systems, Phoenix (2009)
3. Summerville, I.: Software Engineering, 8th edn.
4. Bass, L., Clements, P., Kazman, R.: Software Architecture in Practice. Addison-Wesley (1997)
5. Bieber, G., Carpenter, J.: Introduction to Service-Oriented Programming (Rev. 2.1), http://www.openwings.org/download/specs/ServiceOrientedIntroduction.pdf (accessed October 2002)
6. Garlan, D.: Software Architecture: A Roadmap. ACM Press (2000)
7. Herzum, P.: Web Services and Service-Oriented Architectures. Executive Report, 4(10), Cutter Distributed Enterprise Architecture Advisory Service (2002)
8. Hommes, B.: The Evaluation of Business Process Modeling Techniques. Doctoral Thesis, Delft Technical University, The Netherlands (2004)
9. Sommerville, I., Sawyer, P.: Requirements Engineering: A Good Practice Guide. Wiley, Chichester (1997)
10. Lichtenstein, S., Nguyen, L.: Issues in IT Service-Oriented Requirements Engineering. Australasian Journal of Information Systems 13(1), 176–190

An Efficient PANN Algorithm for Effective Spatial Data Mining

N. Naga Saranya[1], S. Megala[1], P. Revathi[1], G.V. Nadiammai[1], S. Krishnaveni[1], and M. Hemalatha[2]

[1] Karpagam University, Coimbatore -21, India
[2] Dept. Software System, Karpagam University, Coimbatore - 21, India
{nachisaranya01,hema.bioinf}@gmail.com

Abstract. Spatial Data mining is one of the challenging field in data mining. The explosive development of spatial data and common use of spatial databases highlight the need for the automated detection of spatial knowledge. Extracting interesting and useful patterns from spatial datasets is more difficult than extracting the corresponding patterns from traditional numeric and categorical data due to the complexity of spatial data types, spatial relationships, and spatial autocorrelation. Remote sensing is the one of the area very much depend on sophisticated data clustering and classification algorithms. In this research first we elaborate a study on data clustering, particularly on spatial data clustering. Some of the existing classical clustering algorithm and the proposed PANN were tested with UCI repository datasets for spatial data clustering and classification. Several tests were made on the system and overall significant results were achieved. The average accuracy of classification is defined by the Rand index as well as Sensitivity, Specificity and Accuracy. Proposed method is an influential tool for the classification of multidimensional spatial data sets.

Keywords: Spatial Clustering Techniques, Spatial Land sat Data, Artificial Neural Network (ANN), and Principal Component Analysis (PCA).

1 Introduction

The Landsat satellite data is one of the many sources of information available for a scene. The interpretation of a scene by integrating spatial data of diverse types and resolutions including multispectral and radar data, maps indicating topography, land use etc. is expected to assume significant importance with the onset of an era characterized by integrative approaches to remote sensing. Clustering of data is a difficult problem that is related to various fields and applications. Challenge is greater, as input space dimensions become larger and feature scales are different from each other. Existing statistical methods are ill-equipped for handling such diverse data types such as spatial data. Note that this is not true for Landsat MSS data considered in isolation. This data satisfies the important requirements of being numerical and at a single resolution, and standard maximum-likelihood classification performs very well. Consequently, for this data, it should be interesting to compare

V.V. Das and N. Thankachan (Eds.): CIIT 2011, CCIS 250, pp. 705–709, 2011.

the performance of other methods against the statistical approach. Major drawbacks have to be tackled, such as curse of dimensionality and initial error propagation, as well as complexity and data set size issues. So in this research, we are going to study the performance of some of the classical clustering algorithm for spatial data clustering and will derive a hybrid model for better spatial data clustering.

2 Recent Works in Spatial Data Mining

Kharin. Y. S, zhuk. E. E. [1], were investigated the problem of cluster analysis of discrete (multinomial) random observations, assuming the presence of outliers in the sample. MATHER. L. A. [2], an application of linear algebra to text clustering, a metric for measuring cluster quality was described.

Vaithyanathan [5], presented an approach to model-based hierarchical clustering by formulating an objective function based on a Bayesian analysis. Polanco. X [6], suggested using artificial neural networks for mapping of science and technology as a multi-self-organizing maps approach.

Cluster-Rasch models for micro array gene expression data were developed by Li, Hongzhe And Hong, Fangxin [7]. Dudoit [8], devised a prediction-based resampling method for estimating the number of clusters in a dataset. Paulo Gonçalves [9], the goal is to achieve an automatic pixel level classification using a Support Vector Machine (SVM) learning approach.

3 Proposed System Design

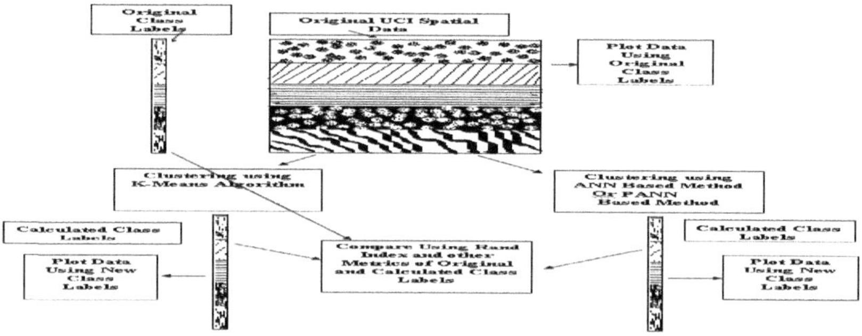

Fig. 1. Proposed Evaluation Strategy

3.1 Steps to Follow the Algorithm

K-means based Spatial Data Clustering Algorithm

Step1: Prepare D_n € C_c

Step2: Apply K-Means clustering algorithm and classify the Original N data and this will give a set of new class labels L2.

Step3: Compare the Class labels L1 and L2 with Rand Index and Other Metrics and evaluate the accuracy of clustering.

Step4: Classify the N UCI Test data using the previously calculated cluster centers.
Step5: Compare the Class labels with Rand Index and Other Metrics and evaluate the accuracy of classification.
Step6: Repeat the above steps for Different values of N for studying the performance with different number of records.

ANN based Spatial Data Clustering Algorithm
Step1: Prepare D_n € C_c
Step2: Create a neural network with D number of inputs and C number of outputs.
Step3: Train the network with N Number of records.
Step4: Test the Network with the Training data or Testing Data and Find the new Class label L2.
Step5: Compare the original Class labels L1 and calculated class label L2 with Rand Index and Other Metrics and evaluate the accuracy of Classification.
Step6: Repeat the above steps for Different values of N for studying the performance with different number of records.

PANN based Spatial Data Clustering Algorithm
Step1: Prepare D_n € C_c
Step2: Reduce the Diminution of input Data using Principal Component Analysis. This will give a reduced d dimensional data.
Step3: Create a neural network with D number of inputs and C number of outputs.
Step4: Train the network with N Number of records.
Step5: Test the Network with the Training data or Testing Data and Find the new Class label L2
Step6: Compare the original Class labels L1 and calculated class label L2 with Rand Index and Other Metrics and evaluate the accuracy of Classification.
Step7: Repeat the above steps for Different values of N for studying the performance with different number of records.

4 Implementation and Results

The proposed system has been implemented and the performance of the classification algorithm was tested with the spatial dataset called "UCI Landsat Multi-Spectral dataset".

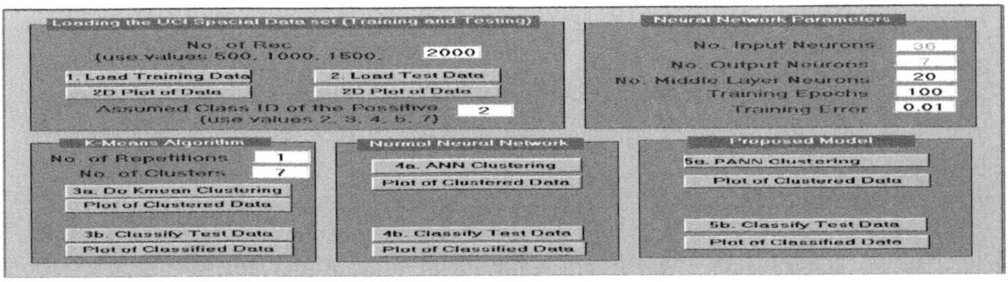

Fig. 2. Main Interface Design

4.1 Evaluation Results

Step 1: loading the Training and Testing Data
Loading the Training data (Loaded Records: 500)
Step 2: Clustering and Classification using k-means
The Accuracy of Clustering (Time Taken: 1.1250 sec): 94.80
Classifying the Testing Data using previous Cluster Centers
The Accuracy of Classification (Time Taken: 0.0150 sec): 97.80
Step3: Clustering and Classification using ANN
The Accuracy of Classification with ANN (Time Taken: 7.2190 sec): 99.40
Testing the ANN with testing Data
The Accuracy of Classification with ANN (Time Taken: 1.2500sec): 99.00
Step 4: Clustering and Classification using PANN
The Accuracy : 99.20
Testing the Model with testing Data
The Accuracy of Classification with PANN: 99.00

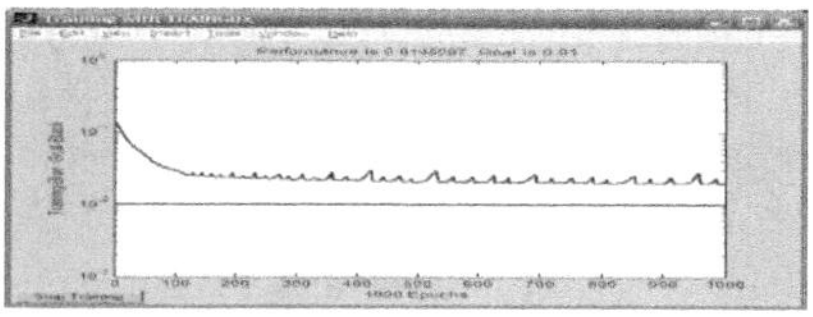

Fig. 3. Clustering and Classification using ANN

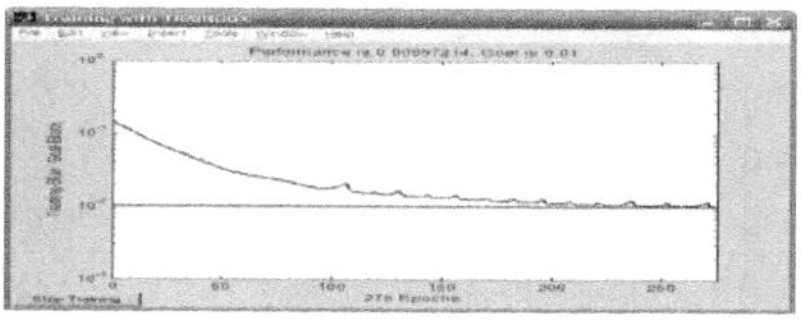

Fig. 4. Clustering and Classification using PANN

4.2 Comparative Results

Table 1. Rand Index

Sl.No	No. of Records	Rand Index		
		kmeans	ANN	PANN
1	500	0.90	0.90	0.94
2	1000	0.82	0.86	0.89
3	1500	0.83	0.79	0.82
4	2000	0.78	0.79	0.81
Avg Performance		0.8325	0.835	0.865

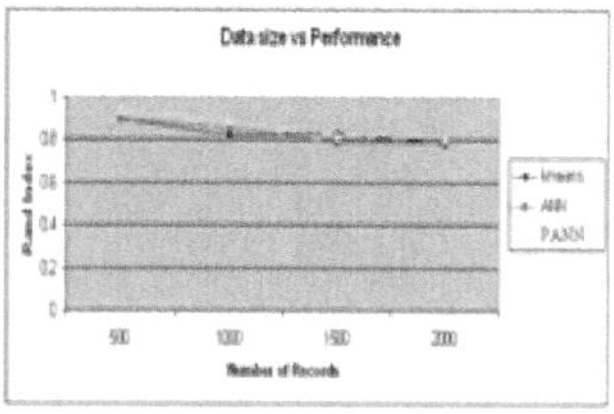

Fig. 5. Data vs. Performance

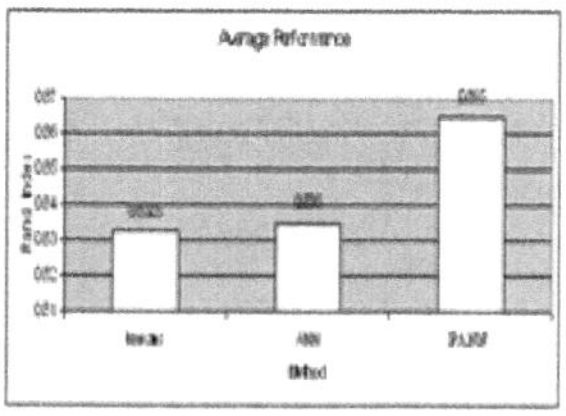

Fig. 6. Average Performance

5 Conclusion

The average accuracy of classification has been measured using the metrics Rand index as well as Sensitivity, Specificity and Accuracy. As shown the performance graphs in the previous section, the transformation of data using principal component analysis leads to better accuracy of clustering and classification with neural network. The results proves that the traditional methods like k-means clustering will not give better accuracy in the case of spatial data due to its nature of complexity and dimensionality. The arrived results were significant and comparable. This makes the proposed method as a simple and powerful tool for the classification of multidimensional spatial data sets.

Acknowledgments. We are very thankful to our Karpagam Unniversity for the encouragement to do this research as a successful one.

References

1. Vaithyanathan, S., Dom, B.: Model-Based Hierarchical Clustering. In: Proc. 16th Conf., Uncertainty in Artificial Intelligence (2000)
2. Polanco, X., Francois, C., Lamirel, J.C.: Using artificial neural networks for mapping of science and technology: A multi-self-organizing-maps approach. Scientometrics 51(1), 267–292 (2001)
3. Koren, Y., Harel, D.: Clustering of spatial data using random walks. In Proc. KDD, Arnetminer, pages 6 (2001)
4. Dudoit, S., Fridlyand, J.: Prediction-based resampling method for estimating the number of clusters in a dataset. Genome Biol. 3(7), research0036.1–research0036.21 (2002); published online (June 25, 2002)
5. Song, J.-W., Whang, K.-Y., Lee, Y.-K., Lee, M.-J., Han, W.-S., Park, B.-K.: The clustering property of corner transformation for spatial database applications. Information and Software Technology 44(7), 419–429 (2002)
6. Vishwanathan, S.V.N., Murty, N.M.: Kernel Enabled K- Means Algorithm (2002)
7. Madhubala, M., Mohan Rao, S.K., Ravindra Babu, G.: Classification of IRS LISS- III Images by using Artificial Neural Networks. IJCA Journal (3), article 2 (2010)
8. Xu, R., Wunsch, D.: Survey of Clustering Algorithms. IEEE 16(3), 645–678 (2005)
9. Dong, G., Xie, M.: Color Clustering & Learning for Image Segmentation Based on Neural Networks. IEEE 16(4), 925–936
10. Accelerating the pace of engineering and science, Multilayer Neural Network, http://www.mathworks.com
11. Naga Saranya, N., Hemalatha, M.: Potential Research into Spatial Cancer Database by Using Data Clustering Techniques. International Journal of Computer Science and Information Security (IJCSIS) 9(5), 168–173 (2011)
12. Naga Saranya, N., Hemalatha, M.: A Recent Survey on Knowledge Discovery in Spatial Data Mining. International Journal of Computer Science Issues (IJCSI) 8(3,2), 473–479 (2011) ISSN (Online): 1694-0814

Optimizing Quality of Service Parameter of Multimedia Traffic on IPV6 Enabled Linux Kernel Based Scheduling Parameters and Algorithms for HPN

Hitesh Nimbark[1], Paresh Kotak[2], Shobhen Gohel[3] and Rajkamal[3]

[1] B H Gardi College of Engineering and Technology, Rajkot, Gujarat, India
hitesh.nimbark@gmail.com
[2] A V Parekh Technical Institute, Rajkot
kotakp2003@yahoo.com
[3] Govt. Poly Technique, Jamnagar
{shobhen.ce,rajkamal}@gmail.com

Abstract. Current era is the era of Multimedia traffics. This paper investigates into the scheduling aspects of real time multimedia streams with a real time test-bed environment. This will include the Operating System Scheduling Issues, as well as Routing at the Network Layer. An Ipv6 enabled distributed system is designed for priority based scheduling of Multimedia stream generated by VideoLAN Software. The Multimedia Applications must adhere to stringent real-time constraints and Quality-of-Service (QoS) requirements. A DiffServ based, QoS management approach is developed using a new developed kernel level module to parse the network packets and identify the DSCP value, which is marked during multimedia streaming at the source. This paper also highlights several other approaches and comparison that can be implemented for QoS based scheduling of multimedia traffic.

Keywords: Quality-of-Service, Traffic Control, Integrated services, Differentiated services, XORP, ZEBRA, Forwarding Engine Abstraction.

1 Introduction

Real Time Linux operating system scheduling demands the setup of a distributed infrastructure. The proposed architecture is inspired from a Video On Demand (VOD) Server based application. The system includes one Real Time Linux server where files are stored. The client requests for a particular multimedia file from a remote host. The file is streamed on the server and sent to the client side. The server and the client lie on different networks. Hence routers come into picture and the multimedia traffic needs to be routed, with Quality of Service parameters. The routers used in the setup is XORP [3,4,5], a software based router. There are at least four routers each configured for different network is used. This forms the middleware of the implementation. Most of the results derived are for unicast transmission of data. The protocol stack on which the architecture is implemented is IPv6 [1], since Ipv6 has

V.V. Das and N. Thankachan (Eds.): CIIT 2011, CCIS 250, pp. 710–715, 2011.

got inherent support for real time applications and multimedia communications. Here the client side could be a Windows based system also. But the source server and the software routers are all implemented on XORP router running over RTLinux3.1 kernel, further configured on Red Hat Linux or Fedora Core 6 nodes. The main objective of the paper is to study and configuration of software based routers (XORP, ZEBRA)[3] and implements various methods for QoS [6] based routing of Multimedia IP Traffic in IPV6 and implementation of a kernel level module to read/set the DSCP value in the Traffic Class of IPv6 header and TOS field of Ipv4 field. The UDP traffic that is generated by streaming a multimedia file is to be scheduled as per the DiffServ[2] architecture frame work. Finally, test the performance of the network in routing of multimedia traffic, with the developed module on the experimental test-bed. With a heavy traffic is generated artificially using traffic Generation Tool.

2 Project Architecture

As shown in above Figure 1, The experimental set up created for the implementation of priority based scheduling of multimedia traffic through a real time Linux operating system, and routing the stream through software based routers; required tremendous effort.

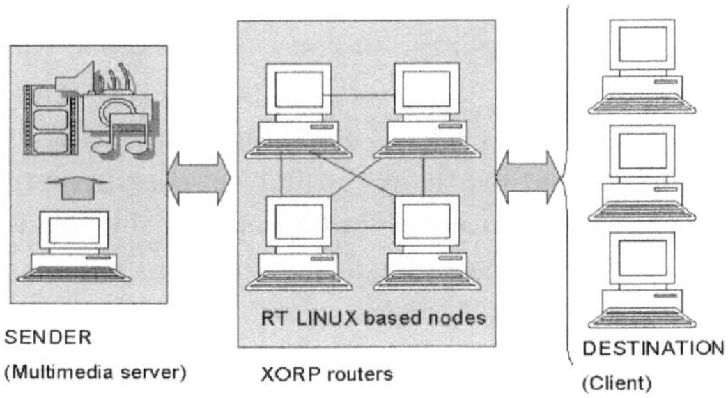

Fig. 1. Project Architecture (Higher Level)

Because of scarcity of space we are not including the following points of installation and configuration of this paper work eg. RTLinux 3.1 with Linux Kernel (2.6.26) [6] with IPv6 support, Ipv6 Layer Kernel Configuration as Router IPv6 To IPv4 Tunneling, kernel parameters Configuration at runtime, Streaming with Ipv6 support on RTLinux, XORP, ZEBRA configuration and IPV6 support, Forwarding Engine Abstraction of ZEBRA, Enable QoS support in Linux Kernel etc. The core part of the implementation was development of a module at the kernel level, which gets invoked, which is event driven and gets invoked when there is a packet at the network interface. The module parses the packets and reads the DSCP[22] value. A DSCP value of 16 is identified as a high priority multimedia traffic and if put in the High Priority queue. The other traffic, which is mostly TCP traffic is kept in the Low

Priority queue. The packets are released to the XORP router. On the routers, the DSCP value is checked propagated to the Routing Information Base (RIB)[3] at the Router. The RIB, in turn notifies this to the forwarding plane and release the traffic at a high priority.

A process on one end writes to a FIFO, which appears as a normal file, while another one reads from the other end. With RTLinux[6], the reader might be a real-time process, while the writer is a user-space program shuttling directives to the real-time code through the FIFO or vice versa. In either case, the FIFO devices are normal character devices (/dev/rtf*), and both ends can interact with the device through normal POSIX calls, such as open(), close(), read() and write(). In this implementation, the User Space code comprises of a program to read the configured network interface for outgoing packets. This is done using the pcap utility available in the pcap.h header file. The module is inserted at all the computers where XORP is running. The above implementation adds Priority based Scheduling or Class based Scheduling, which was otherwise lacking in XORP. The traffic is generated to create a real time scenario of loads of traffic in network, with different bandwidth and delay requirements; within a Computer Lab. The traffic was generated using the Multi-Generator (MGEN) tool. The Measurement tools have been chosen keeping in mind their open-source origins and flexibility of use. Ex OpenIMP, MGEN, Ethereal, Ping.

3 Test-Bed

This experiment was conducted using 2 streams, of which one was multimedia traffic while the other was normal periodic traffic. The bandwidth required is 120Mbps which is greater than 1OOMbps link. The multimedia traffic being Periodic with regular bursts, it was expected the delays would increase abruptly at burst instances when the traffic bandwidth required would be much greater than that available [14]. The queuing delays increase and average delay shoots up. Table 1 describes the traffic profile of the multimedia traffic's characteristics.

Table 1. Profile for Traffic Generation for both IPv6 and IPv4 network

Stream	Type	Rate (packet/Sec)	Size In bytes
Multimedia	Periodic Bust	4500	1024
UDP	Every 4.5 Sec	4500	1024
Normal TCP	Periodic	3000	1024

Table 2. Comparison of IPv4 and IPv6

	Packet Loss(%)	Average Jitter(msec)	Max jitter(msec)	Average receive time(msec)
IPV4	5	40	81	98
IPV6	1	21	65	20

The IPv6 network showed a better quality, as compared to the IPv4 network. Also the bandwidth consumption of the IPv6 network is much more stable as compared to the IPv4 network. This is shown in the Figure 2. Also, the UDP foreground traffic, Ex. multimedia traffic, suffers less packet loss with respect to the TCP background traffic (generated artificially through MGEN Traffic Generator Tool). The results derived after the experiment was used to display packet loss, delay and latency as shown in Figure 3.

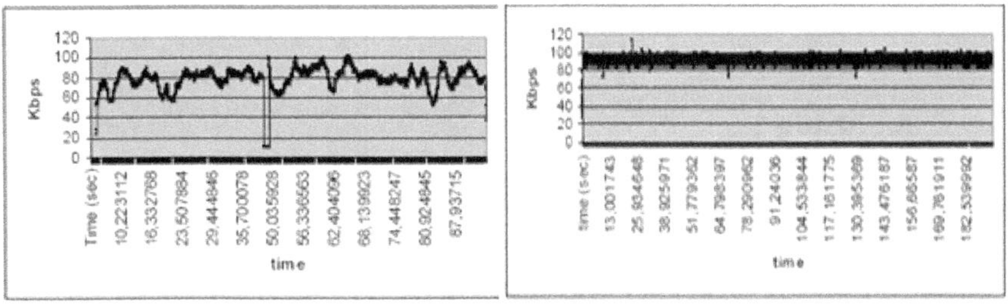

Fig. 2. (a) IPV4 (b) IPV6 bandwidth Consumption

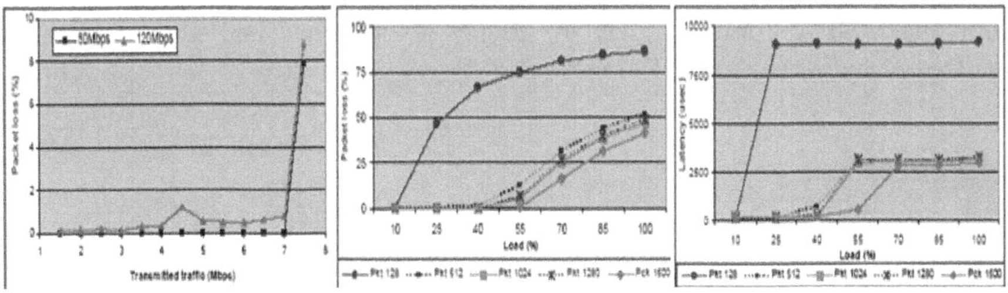

Fig. 3. Packet Loss for the (a) High Priority Multimedia Traffic (b)Different Packet Sizes (c) Latency for Different Packet Sizes

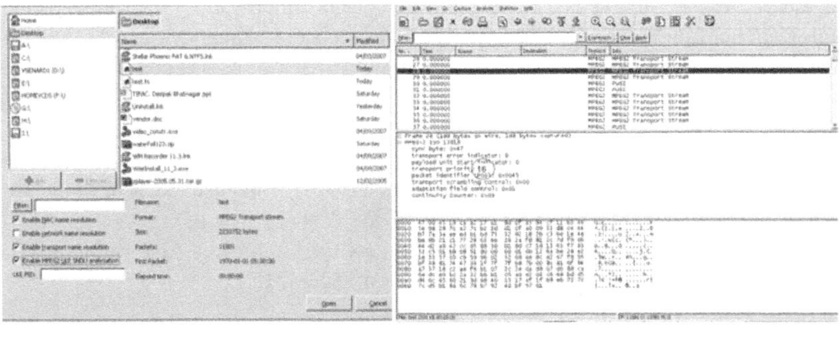

Fig. 4. (a) Ethereal's Open page for Transport stream file (b) showing a High Transport priority

The MPEG-2 TS (Transport Stream) dissector for Ethereal can display transport stream and section heading information, reassemble the sections and analyze the PSI (Program Specific Information) data. Open the .ts file (created through VideoLAN), from Ethereal (version 0.10.8). There are two possibilities to dissect MPEG 2 ULE (Unidirectional Lightweight Encapsulation), we will use etherial "Enable MPEG2 ULE SNDU analyzation" option as shown in Figure 4. If these settings are wrong the analysis will be incorrect. The Figure 4 shows the Transport priority marked with red circle. The experimental results indicated that priority based IPv6 traffic has less of packet loss, latency and jitter problems as compared to the normal IPV6/IPv4 network.

4 Conclusion

The complete architecture and configurations was considered more preferable due to its extensibility features, powerful API, event driven approach etc. The proposed module implemented to gives the priority to multimedia traffic gives significant improvement in multimedia streaming application. Table 2 conforms that if we can release router to priority of Multimedia Streaming data through kernel level IPV6 field modification then the user can get waste differentiated performance and QoS parameter optimization in the output. Also, the experimental results indicated that priority based IPv6 traffic has less of packet loss, latency and jitter problems as compared to the normal IPV6/IPv4 network.

References

1. Deering, S., Hinden, R.: RFC 2460 Internet Protocol, Version 6 (IPv6) Specification (December 1998)
2. Mahajan, M., Parashar, M.: Managing QoS for Multimedia Applications in the Differentiated Services Environment, The Applied Software Systems Laboratory (TASSL), 94 Brett Road, Piscataway, New Jersey (October 2004)
3. XORP, `http://www.xorp.org/`, `http://www.zebra.org`
4. Nimbark, H., et al.: Proxy Based TCP/IP Stack Modification to Support QoS. In: International Conference on Computer Engineering and Technology (2010), 10-981-4289-67-1(PBK)
5. Chimata, A.K.: A Route Control Platform using XORP Design Considerations (July 27, 2006)
6. Ferguson, P., Huston, G.: Quality of Service: Delivering QoS on the Internet and in Corporate Networks. Wiley Press, New York (1998); Almquist, P.: RFC1349: Type of Service in the Internet Protocol Suite (July 1998)
7. Nimbark, H., et al.: Sundry Path Routing Protocol for Multimedia Application in Wireless Networks (2011), ISBN Online: 2230-9039, Print: 2231-2153

8. Nimbark, H., et al.: Optimizing TCP Quality of Service Parameter Using Linux Kernel based Tuning Parameters for HPN. In: International Conference on Computer and Network Technology. World Scientific Press (2009) 13-978-981-4289-67-2(PBK)
9. Nimbark, H., Gohel, S., Doshi, N.: Width of a General Tree for Packet Routing. In: Das, V.V., Stephen, J., Chaba, Y. (eds.) CNC 2011. CCIS, vol. 142, pp. 322–324. Springer, Heidelberg (2011)
10. Nimbark, H., Gohel, S., Doshi, N.: A Novel Approach for Matrix Chain Multiplication Using Greedy Technique for Packet Processing. In: Das, V.V., Stephen, J., Chaba, Y. (eds.) CNC 2011. CCIS, vol. 142, pp. 318–321. Springer, Heidelberg (2011) ISSN: 978-3-642-19541-9

Future System: Using Manet in Smartphones the Idea the Motivation and the Simulation

Mustafa Abdulkadhim and K.S. Korabu

I.T. Department, Sinhgad College of Engineering, Pune University, Pune, India
{mstfkadum,kitri_korabu}@yahoo.com

Abstract. In the present time, the tremendous growth of mobile use made it an indispensable device in the daily life, in many instances the call that we made or we expect to receive control the way in which our day will be, because humans tend for communicate and the mobile phones in this time is the way of communication it becomes very important to ensure the availability of the signal wherever the person goes. In this paper we will take a live example for the out of coverage phenomena which is the sub-way station. Because once the people enter in the sub-way it become very difficult to reach or to be reached from outside, this encouraged me to find a solution and to make use of an existing technology to solve. As one of the critical issues in the mobile phones devices is its battery level as a metric for its availability, for that reason the EEAODV "Energy Efficient AODV" protocol will be suggested as the primary protocol that the devices (nodes) will operate on. The EEAODV protocol will be simulated as a way for reliable communication based on the power level for mobile devices. This protocol will be the major part in the new system.

Keywords: MANET, Subway Station, AODV, Mobile Device, Node, Energy Efficient.

1 Case Studies on the Sub-ways

Million and a half people annually ride the New York City subway system, which comprises 468 stations to form the largest subway complex in the world. The diverse human conglomerate of cultures and lifestyles that inhabit NYC's subway though, share at least one common trend: a lack of mobile coverage – a rather serious, both economic and social issues. Thus, a daily influx of 5,042,263 potential customers is practically lost for mobile companies. Not to mention the irritating circumstance that in a world of otherwise global communications one is forced to spend significant periods of time without a connection signal. From that reason a need arises for a solution to this problem, many solutions have been considered before; the common problem regarding these solutions is the cost of implementation represented by time and money.

2 The Core Idea

The suggested system relies on smart software installed on mobile phones that will convert an extended group of nearby phones into a fast-changing ad hoc network,

V.V. Das and N. Thankachan (Eds.): CIIT 2011, CCIS 250, pp. 716–721, 2011.

with communications packets being passed down this network to reach the intended recipient phone. Hence, true to the MANET paradigm, the individual mobile device would act both as a receiver and dispatcher of signal... Social phenomena and behaviors can be used in favor of disseminating network coverage. Thus the signal coverage will depend on social communities. The peoples "nodes", the sub-way and the path of a call is shown in fig 1 below.

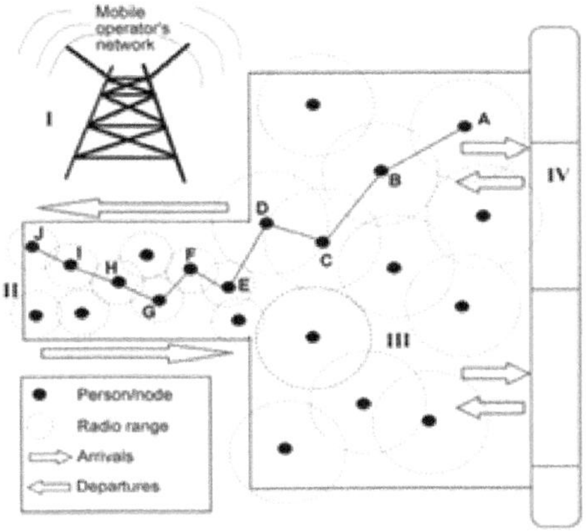

Fig. 1. Scenario for call transmission in sub-way. Types of lines. Elements of the figure described in the caption should be set in italics, in parentheses, as shown in this sample caption.

3 Energy Efficient AODV Routing Protocol

The energy-saving routing algorithm which is adopted in Maximum Energy Level Ad Hoc Distance Vector protocol (MEL-AODV) has enhanced the RREQ handling process. MEL-AODV considers node remaining energy as a routing metric. The development process of the MEL-AODV to achieve higher energy efficiency is as below. Here NS2 simulator is used for development. NS2 is a discrete event, object oriented, simulator developed by the VINT project research group at Carnegie Mellon University [6] which includes: nodes mobility, a realistic physical layer that includes a radio propagation model, radio network interfaces and the IEEE 802.11 Medium Access Control (MAC) protocol using the Distributed Coordination Function (DCF). NS2 is one of the most popular network simulator tools worldwide. The NS2.34 was installed under Linux Redhat 9.0 as a simulation platform. After the development of our energy efficient protocol "EEAODV", a comparison will be made with the original AODV from performance point of view as shown in section 4.

In order to develop a new routing protocol in ns2 we need to understand the file hierarchy of the protocol and its interactions in ns2. Below is how AODV file design looks like in ns2.34.

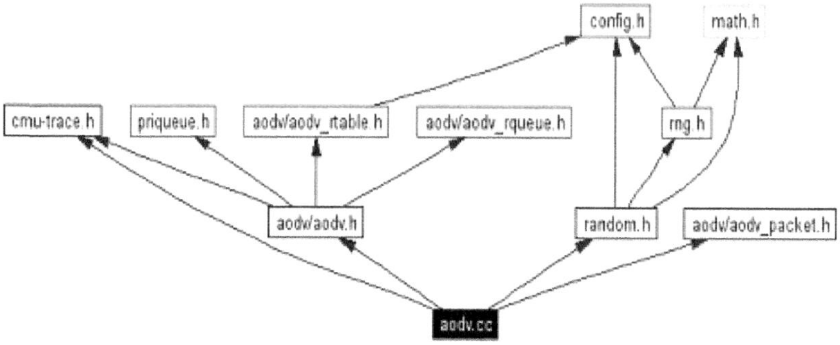

Fig. 2. AODV File Hierarchy

3.1 AODV File Modification

Major changes are highlighted here in the process of the new protocol development. These changes are listed below:

- Energy initialization: by default energy access of AODV in ns2 is not activated so the first step is to activate the energy and initialize it.
- Accessing and recording the node's energy: in order to manipulate the energy or perform energy decision making actions we need to access the energy of the nodes in aodc.cc file. Also the index of the nodes is saved in order to perform individual processing and manipulation.
- Energy Decision-based modification: according to our algorithm if the node on the path that receives RREQ message has energy less than a pre-defined threshold then it drops the RREQ packet and it can't be considered as a member of the route discovery process.

3.2 UMTS Mobile Node Design

To simulate the UMTS 3G network an additional package should be installed to ns2. The EURANE1.12 ns2 extension package was installed under Linux Redhat 9.0. in order to give our node the UMTS characteristics and functionalities and to simulate the 3G network part of the project.

4 Simulation and Analysis

A graphical user interface is designed in Linux in order to contain the simulation material. Figure 4.1 shows the GUI of the project. As shown in fig 3.

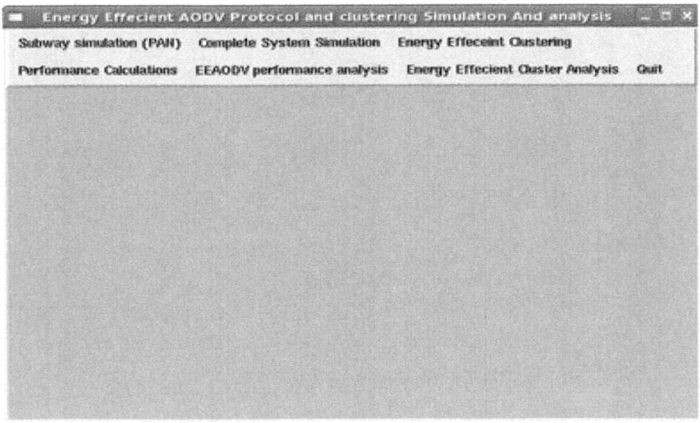

Fig. 3. The Simulation GUI

According to the GUI we have 7 tabs to consider:

1. Subway simulation: in this tab the subway environment is simulated with a PAN "Personal Area Network" configuration using the 802.14.5 MAC protocol.
2. Complete system simulation: in this tab we have 10 sub tabs that represents 10 different simulations with 10 20 30 40 50 60 70 80 90 and 100 nodes. The simulation represents the integrated 3G-MANET network with the modified EEAODV "Energy Efficient AODV" being applied.
3. Energy efficient clustering: in this simulation program an energy efficient cluster-based formation is developed. With our modified AODV working we have done two-level development on two different layers. The routing layer development represented by the EEAODV in one hand (backend C++ development) and the cluster formation developed in the application layer (frontend Tcl development).
4. Performance calculations: in this tab we have the awk program used for analyzing the data generated at the end of the simulation.
4. EEAODV Performance analysis: in this tab we have 4 graphs generated from the collected data at the end of the simulation to evaluate the new protocol.
5. Energy efficient cluster analysis: to evaluate the energy conservation of a selected cluster.
6. Quit: to exit the GUI.

4.1 Complete System Simulation

In this tab we have 10 sub tabs that represent 10 different scenarios. As shown in fig 4.

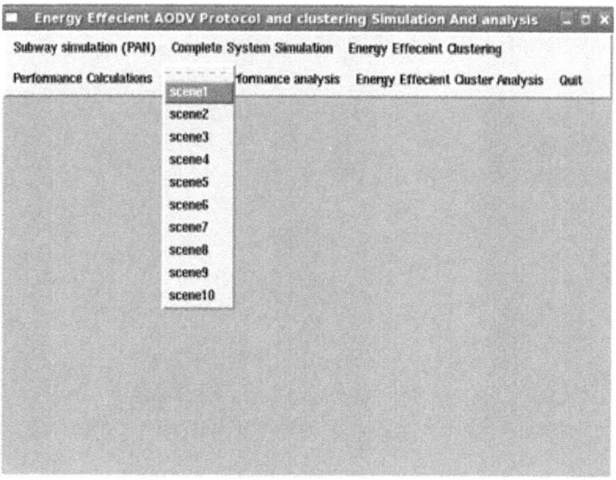

Fig. 4. Main simulation scenes

4.2 EEAODV Performance Analysis

After analyzing the trace files generated from running our scenarios 4 graphs were generated to compare the original AODV routing protocol with our EEAODV routing protocol.

The metrics being used for the performance analysis are:

1. Energy: the two routing protocols were compared from their energy consumption point of view.
2. Communication Load (overhead): the two protocols were compared to show which protocol put an extra load on the network than the other.
3. Throughput: a very important metric as it shows the capability of the network for packet delivery.
4. Network lifetime: also called the survivability of the network that measures thetime the network still in operation and stay "alive". The four metrics evaluating AODV and EEAODV are shown in the next figures.

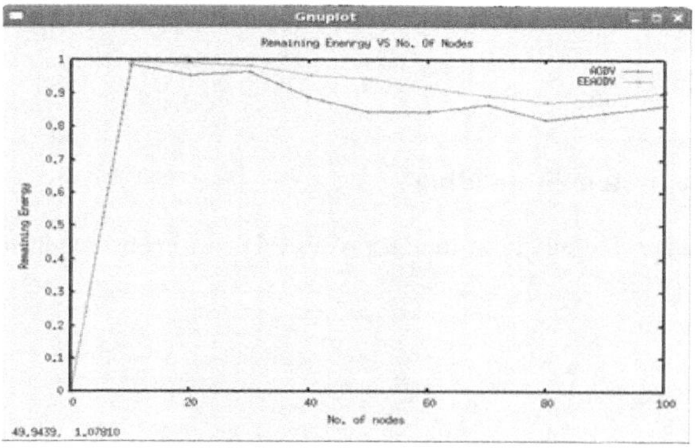

Fig. 5. Remaining Energy VS No. of Nodes

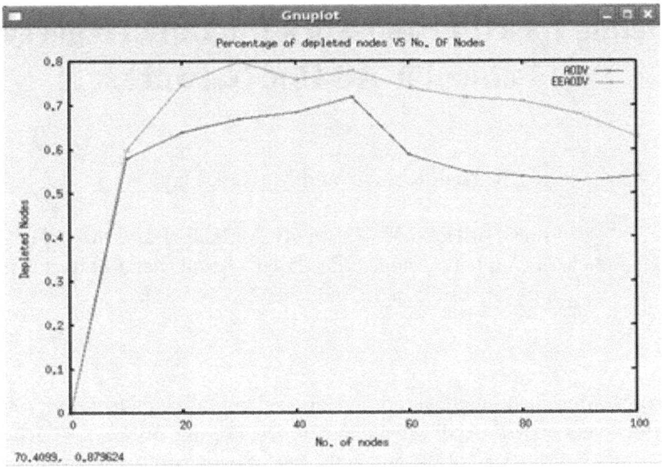

Fig. 6. Network Lifetime

5 Conclusion

From the figures shown. We notice that the performance of our new EEAODV according to the selected metrics is improved. And we have also studied the possibility of applying this protocol to our problem in hand which is the sub way – out of coverage - problem.

References

1. Tie, T., Eng, C.: alternate link maximum energy level ad hoc on demand distance vector scheme for energy efficient ad hoc networks. In: ICCCE 2010 (2010)
2. Tarik, S., Hussein, T.: An efficient energy aware Clusterhead formation Infrastructure protocol for MANETs. In: Eighth IEEE International Symposium (2006)
3. Hafiz, M., Tareq, S.: Power and Delay Analysis of the WEAC Protocol Based MANET under Video Transport. In: 21st International Conference on Advance Networking and Applications (2007)
4. Tareq, S., Hussain, M.: A Comparative Study of on-demand and Cluster-based Routing Protocols in MANETs (2006)
5. Gupta, P., Kumar, P.: critical power for asymptotic connectivity in wireless Networks. Berkhauser, Boston
6. The Network Simulator – ns-2, `http://www.isi.edu/nsnam/ns/`

Knowledge Based Framework for Data Aggregation in Vehicular Ad Hoc Networks

Rakesh Kumar[1] and Mayank Dave[2]

[1] Department of IT, M.M. University, Mullana, Haryana, India
[2] Department of Computer Engineering, N.I.T., Kurukshetra, Haryana, India
{raakeshdhiman,mdave67}@gmail.com

Abstract. Most data aggregation and dissemination techniques for Vehicular Ad Hoc Networks (VANETs) attempt to create and utilize a structure for collecting information. Conventional data aggregation schemes are not appropriate for mobile network. In this paper, we design a cooperative model to facilitate the aggregation of adjacent traffic reports. The idea behind this work is that we can adaptively change the forwarding delay of individual reports in a manner that a report can have a better chance to meet other reports. Simulation results based on realistic map data and traffic models demonstrate that proposed scheme can effectively reduce communication overhead with acceptable delay.

Keywords: VANET, Information Dissemination, Data aggregation, Routing.

1 Introduction

VANETs are self-organized networks formed by vehicles and road-side units and are used to provide drivers with advance notification of traffic congestion or hazard events using wireless communication. In this type of networks, warning messages affect the decisions taken by drivers so that a timely message can reduce transportation times, fuel consumption, environmental contamination, impact of road constructions, and less traffic accidents. Other practical applications of VANETs are, for instance, to provide the ability to find free parking spaces. Bandwidth limitation and channel collision are two serious problems for VANET communications. Data aggregation is an approach to relieve this problem. It consists of a variety of adaptive methods that can merge information from various data sources into a set of organized and sophisticated information. The process of data aggregation can be performed in-network so that communication overhead can be efficiently reduced soon after redundant information is generated. It can be applied to any distributed information collection application, such as sensor networks and vehicular networks.

2 Related Work

In the past few years, data aggregation schemes for VANET have received much attention. Most of the VANET aggregation mechanisms are targeted towards one

V.V. Das and N. Thankachan (Eds.): CIIT 2011, CCIS 250, pp. 722–727, 2011.

specific use case, often dissemination of average speeds on road segments, while mentioning applicability to other use cases, as well. Similarly, generic modeling schemes for network data have been proposed in the different research domains.

Wischhof et al. introduced the Self Organizing Traffic Information System (SOTIS) [3]. The protocol uses periodic beaconing for exchange of traffic information. Each road is divided into segments and received data is aggregated. For each segment, the average speed is calculated and later forwarded. Although the authors argue that information precision should decrease with increasing distance but they do not discuss how exactly an increase in the segment size depending on distance can be realized in practice. A more advanced system is TrafficView [4]. Similar to SOTIS, it disseminates information about the average speed of vehicles on the road. In contrast to SOTIS, TrafficView is node-centric, rather than space-centric. That is, reports generated by the nodes which are close to each other are aggregated by averaging their current speed and position. Lochert et al. [5] take a hierarchical approach on aggregating free parking slots using globally known map data for segmentation. One major advantage of their system is the usage of an adapted version of Flajolet-Martin sketches to achieve a probabilistic but duplicate insensitive sum of free parking spaces. Aggregates can therefore be arbitrarily combined without counting free parking slots multiple times.

Van Eenennaam et al. [6] use run length encoding to achieve efficient data compression scheme. Instead of averaging information about road segments, only the most relevant information items for a given segment is communicated. Ibrahim and Weigle [7] present a cluster based aggregation scheme suitable for dissemination of vehicle speeds. Contrary to the previously presented models, the CASCADE system employs only syntactic, lossless compression of data. At local scope only single reports are disseminated and collected using geo-broadcast. This local view is then clustered using flat size segments and differential coding is applied. Dietzel et al. [2] describe an aggregation scheme that focuses on flexible decision metrics. Fuzzy logic rules are employed to base aggregation decisions on qualitative metrics, such as induced quality loss due to aggregation. The resulting scheme aggregates data more where the road network state is homogenous, yet allows more bandwidth to stretches with high state entropy. Scheuermann et al. [8] provide a theoretical scalability bound for aggregation protocols in VANETs. The main result is that the data rate must be reduced asymptotically faster than the squared distance to the information source (i.e., $O(1/d^2)$) to be able to scale to larger deployments. Also, the authors provide a construction framework for a mechanism achieving the claimed rate.

3 Proposed Approach

Our goal is to propose a framework that takes the generic applicability for in-network data aggregation in VANETs where nodes only have a partial knowledge of the whole network state. Such a model can easily be used to make existing aggregation schemes more compatible and help in the design of suitable comparison metrics. Fig. 1 shows the flow of information in a given data aggregation system. At conceptual level aggregation system has to decide whether two items of information are similar enough to be aggregated or not. Segment-oriented aggregation systems base this decision on the fact that two information items fit into the same spatial segment. Once the decision to aggregate two data items has been reached, a defined algorithm may easily be applied to combine them. In the proposed approach we have assumed that each vehicle is equipped with an on-board computing device, a GPS device, a wireless radio, and digital maps. Timings in different vehicles can be synchronized by using GPS technologies. For neighbor discovery, each vehicle periodically broadcasts beacons to make other aware of its speed and location.

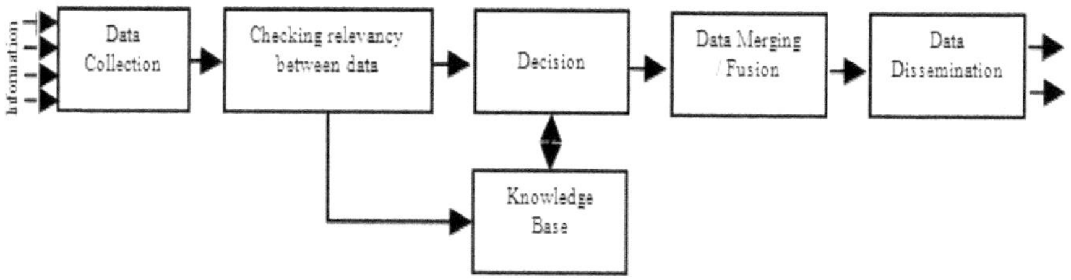

Fig. 1. Information Flow in Data Aggregation

Algorithm: -

1. Each vehicle maintains a local knowledge base that is updated by its own information and the information received by other vehicles.
2. As soon as a vehicle detects an event occurred in its given range it collects the information in its database and waits for a random amount of time.
3. If any other vehicle broadcasts the same message in a given time period then it simply discards that message and stores the decision (and related parameters like vehicle identity, distance, response time, vehicle speed etc.) in the database. Otherwise it disseminates the same information and updates the knowledge base.
4. The intermediate node that receives the broadcasted message also looks into the knowledgebase and tries to increase the chances of meeting more number of reports at the next node by variably changing the speed of message i.e. either by inserting the delay in sending the report or by sending the report earlier.
5. The decision taken by the vehicle is stored in its own knowledge base. Also it is communicated to its neighbors.
6. After regular interval each vehicle communicates the information in terms of decision taken by itself to all its neighbors.

4 Evaluation

A. Analysis

Estimation is done to find the average number of vehicle records (NoVR) that any node can obtain through beaconing. The number of records depends upon the communication radius R, and for a given node on a highway the maximum reach in both directions is 2R. The number of vehicles within this reach depends on the average vehicle speed v and the vehicle arrival rate λ, so the formula is:

$$NoVR = 2R\frac{\lambda}{v} - 1 \tag{1}$$

Under ideal circumstances, when the density of vehicles is high the underlying approach can maximize its reach under the specified communication radius R, NoVR should be doubled, thus representing the local view for a given vehicle by:

$$NoVR = 4R\frac{\lambda}{v} - 1 \tag{2}$$

We assumed the distance between the vehicles conforms to a Poisson - distribution:

$$f(x) = C\lambda e^{-\lambda x} \tag{3}$$

where λ represents the arrival rate of vehicles per meter. The normalization constant C is calculated by forcing the condition that the probability needs to be equal to unity on the interval from the minimum distance (0 m) to the maximum distance (1/λ m) between two consecutive vehicles, so the final expression for the probability function:

$$f(x) = \frac{1}{(e-1)}\lambda e^{1-\lambda x} \tag{4}$$

B. Simulation and Results

To evaluate the proposed algorithm for data aggregation in VANET, we implemented the scheme in network simulator NS2. In the beginning of the simulation, nodes are placed randomly in the simulation area. Transmissions are received by all nodes within transmission range. We have assumed that a packet transmission takes exactly one time unit. A node can either send or receive only one packet in single time unit.

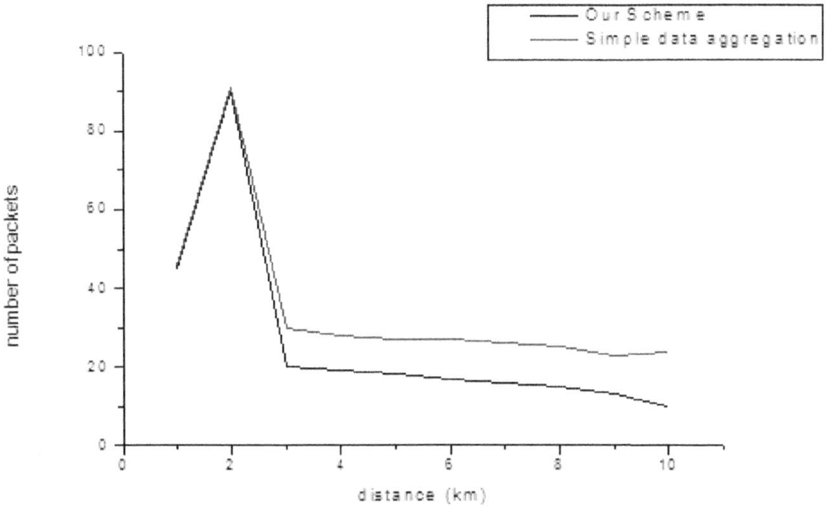

Fig. 2. Number of packets vs. distance

For network traffic, we assumed that each node has one packet to broadcast to all the nodes in the network. All of these packets are generated at the beginning of the simulation, and after that the simulation continues to run without inserting further new packets until all the packets are delivered to the entire network. Fig. 2 clearly shows that initially when the distance is less both the schemes perform equivalently but as the distance increases the number of packets transmitted is quite less after employing the proposed scheme as compared to the simple data aggregation approach.

5 Conclusion and Future Work

According to the literature, efficient and accurate aggregation in VANETs is possible without the need of pre-defined road segments. Knowledge base reasoning enables us to employ natural language rules to make aggregation decisions. A flexible, relevance based dissemination approach enables to disseminate those aggregates that are likely to have the highest benefit for the surrounding vehicles. Evaluation has shown that the proposed data aggregation scheme using knowledge base intelligence clearly outperforms the flooding of exact information in terms of bandwidth consumption. Moreover, especially if the beginning or end of an event like traffic congestion does not coincide with a fixed segment border, proposed structure-free system's accuracy is significantly better than that of segment based aggregation approaches. Our future work will try to strengthen the system by securing it against data integrity attacks and to propose an approach to secure aggregation against forgery or defective sensors.

References

1. Schoch, E., Kargl, F., Weber, M., Leinmuller, T.: Communication patterns in Vanets. IEEE Communications Magazine 46(11), 119–125 (2008)
2. Dietzel, S., Bako, B., Schoch, E., Kargl, F.: A fuzzy logic based approach for structure-free aggregation in vehicular ad-hoc networks. In: The Proceedings of Sixth ACM International Workshop on VehiculArInterNETworking, pp. 79–88. ACM Press, USA (2009)
3. Wischhof, L., Ebner, A., Rohling, H., Lott, M., Halfmann, R.: SOTIS-A Self-Organizing Traffic Information System. In: 57th IEEE Vehicular Tech. Conf., pp. 2442–2446 (2003)
4. Nadeem, T., Dashtinezhad, S., Liao, C., Iftode, L.: TrafficView: Traffic data dissemination using car-to-car communication. ACM SIGMOBILE Mob. Comp. and Comm. Review 8(3), 6–19 (2004)
5. Lochert, C., Scheuermann, B., Mauve, M.: Probabilistic aggregation for data dissemination in VANETs. In: Proceedings of the Fourth ACM International Workshop on Vehicular Ad Hoc Networks, pp. 1–8. ACM Press, New York (2007)
6. van Eenennaam, M., Heijenk, G.: Providing Over-the-horizon Awareness to Driver Support Systems. In: Proceedings of 4th IEEE Workshop on V2V Communications (2008)
7. Ibrahim, K., Weigle, M.C.: CASCADE: Cluster-Based Accurate Syntactic Compression of Aggregated Data in VANETs. In: IEEE Globecom Workshops, pp. 1–10 (November 2008)

8. Scheuermann, B., Lochert, C., Rybicki, J., Mauve, M.: A fundamental scalability criterion for data aggregation in VANETs. In: Proceedings of the 15th Annual International Conference on Mobile Computing and Networking, pp. 285–296. ACM Press, USA (2009)
9. Ding, Z., Güting, R.H.: Modeling Temporally Variable Transportation Networks. In: Lee, Y., Li, J., Whang, K.-Y., Lee, D. (eds.) DASFAA 2004. LNCS, vol. 2973, pp. 154–168. Springer, Heidelberg (2004)

On-Line Automatic Measurement of Contact Resistance of Metal to Carbon Relays Used in Railway Signaling

Hemant Kagra[1] and Prashant Sonare[2]

[1] Indian Railways, Mumbai, India
hemantkagra@yahoo.co.in
[2] SSJCET, Asangaon, Mumbai
Mumbai, India
prashantsonare@yahoo.co.in

Abstract. The contact resistance of metal to carbon relays is a vital quality parameter. The manual measurement system is tedious, error prone and involves lot of time, effort & manpower. Besides, it is susceptible to manipulation and this may adversely affect the functional reliability of relays. To enhance the trustworthiness of CR measurement, an On-line automated measurement system having a testing jig attachment and specially designed software was developed. When the relay was fixed on the testing jig, the software measured the CR and results were ported on an internet website. Thus, accurate & reliable CR values were available in real time, easily and swiftly.

Keywords: Metal to Carbon relays, Railway signaling, Contact Resistance, BDE, On-line testing.

1 Manual Measurement System and Limitations Therein

The Contact Resistance (CR) of *Silver (metal)* and *Silver Impregnated Graphite (carbon)* contacts [1] of Metal to Carbon relays used in railway signaling systems plays a vital role in their reliability performance [2]. The CR was measured manually with non-automated equipment. The relay, whose CR is to be measured, was plugged in standard relay base and power is applied across the coil / contacts and the resistance of various contacts are measured [3]. Manual measurement using numerous meters and recording multiple results involves a lot of time, effort and manpower. The measurement of CR is very critical as it is susceptible to get merged with the wiring & termination resistances. Due to human, instrumental & systemic errors, the accuracy of manual test results was only approx. 98% [4]. With the manual system, only 300 relays could be tested per day and it was susceptible to manipulation. This had an adverse effect on their reliability.

2 Automated Measurement System

The microprocessor based On – Line Automated measurement system for CR consisted of a testing jig having relay plug-board fixture, as per the relay configuration, connected to an Industrial computer, as shown in Figure 1.

V.V. Das and N. Thankachan (Eds.): CIIT 2011, CCIS 250, pp. 728–730, 2011.

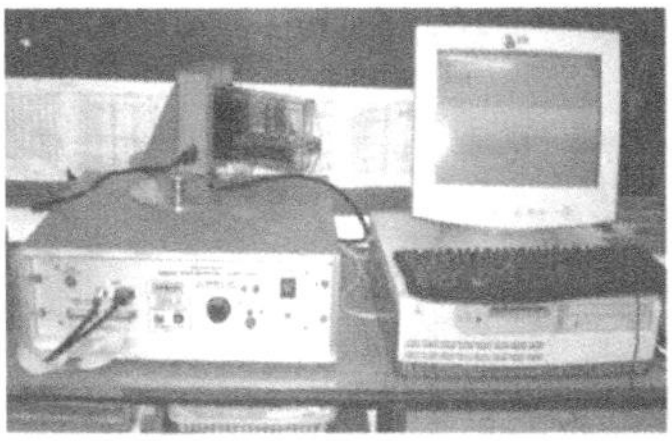

Fig. 1. Automatic Measurement Setup

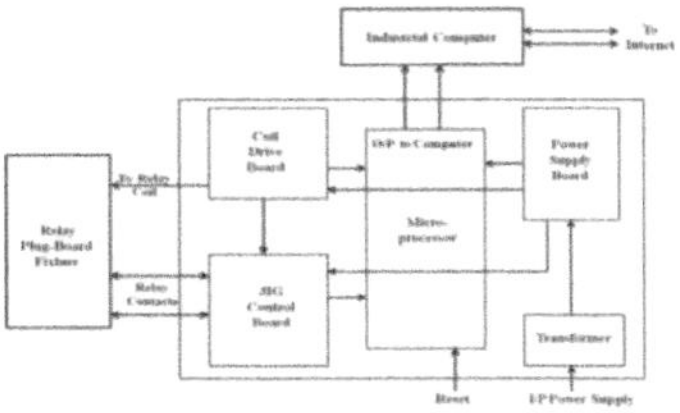

Fig. 2. Schematic dia. of measurement setup

2.1 System Configuration and Philosophy

The details of the test setup are as depicted in figure 2. The test jig consists of a coil drive board & Jig control Board wired to relay plug-board fixture. Working on 230 V AC, the microprocessor controlled the operation and sent the output to the COM port of a dedicated Industrial computer through a RS 232 C connection. The application software works on MS-Windows and the data storing was done with Borland-Delphi database engine. The database files were ported onto the internet through FoxPro & JavaScript. The relay plug-board fixture jigs were made as per the relay type / configuration and had gold contacts to reduce wear. For the signal relays having many contacts, the wiring, crimping & termination resistances also get added to the CR value while testing. To avoid this error, four terminals – two current connections (CDLO & CD1) and two voltage connections (CSH1 & CSL1) were connected separately to a set of contact as shown in figure 3. The system measured the CR of each contact by applying 100 mA current across the contact and measuring the voltage drop across the contact. The measurement resolution was 0.1 mOhm with an accuracy of +/- 0.5% +/- 0.1mOhm.

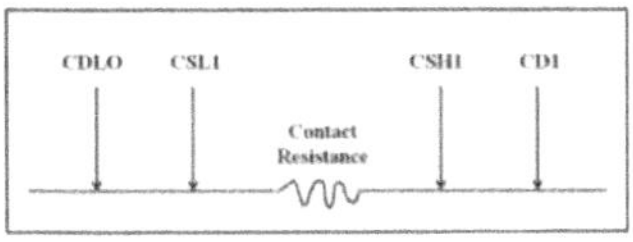

Fig. 3. Kelvin test method

2.2 Measurement Process

For measuring the CR, relay was fixed on plug board fixture, the ID no. of relay was filled in and the testing was started by pressing the start button. The micro-processor scanned all the relay contacts, measured & displayed the CR and also saved the values in the database. The comparator software compared the measured values with the standard values and if all the values were within the specified range of CR, then the system indicated that the relay is *Pass* i.e. the quality of relay was acceptable.

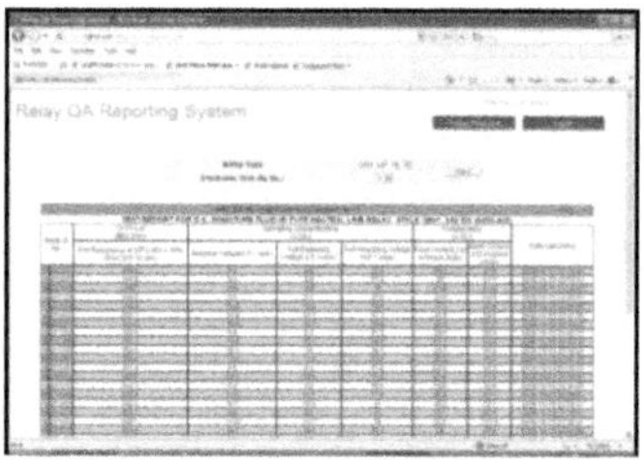

Fig. 4. On-line display of CR

For on-line monitoring, *'Relay QA Reporting System'* was developed which was installed on an internet website. The software was designed in FoxPro & JavaScript and it picked up the values from the database files and displayed the CR in real time, as shown in figure 4.

3 Benefits

The automatic test process was simple, fast and required less manpower. With this system, CR of approx. 800 relays could be measured per day and the accuracy increased to 99.95%. The system was completely manipulation proof and hence more reliable. The test results could be observed on-line, at any location, away from the production area, and thus, the overall quality of relays could be easily monitored.

4 Conclusion

The automatic On-Line measurement system for metal to carbon signaling relays has proved to be very useful in substantiating the trustworthiness of measurement of CR & has made the process faster. The system has certainly enhanced the reliability of metal to carbon relays.

Acknowledgement. Sincere thanks are due to research guide Dr. Prashant Sonare and quality & production team of M/s. Crompton Greaves, Indore, for their support.

References

1. Metal-to-carbon Relay specification No. RDSO/SPN/84/88, Indian Railways, India
2. A Signaling Circuit Handbook, Indian Railways, India,
3. The Manufacturing Process Sheets for relays. M/s. Crompton Greaves Limited, India
4. The Quality Assurance Plan for relays. M/s. Crompton Greaves Limited, India

Comparative Performance Analysis of MANET Routing Protocols Using NS2 Simulator

S. Mohapatra and P. Kanungo

Department of Electronics and Telecommunication Engineering
C.V. Raman College of Engineering, Bhubaneswar, Odisha, India
{selimohapatra,pkanungo}@gmail.com

Abstract. In the routing strategic approach, mostly in wireless scenario, primary emphasis is given on path routing and routing protocol selection. Again in Mobile Ad hoc Network (MANET) a routing protocol is to be selected in such a way that the network can be suitably designed to give best data delivery as well data integrity. So performance analysis of the protocols is the major step to select these protocols. In this paper comparative performance analysis like delay, throughput, control overhead, and PDR is done over protocols like Ad hoc On demand Distance Vector (AODV), Optimized Link State Routing (OLSR), and Destination Sequenced Distance Vector (DSDV) in NS2 Simulator. Based on these parameters a proper protocol can be designed for an efficient MANET.

Keywords: Mobile Adhoc Network, Routing protocols, NS2.

1 Introduction

Ad hoc networks consist of hosts interconnected by routers without a fixed infrastructure and can be arranged dynamically. Considerable work has been done in the development of routing protocols in different types of ad hoc networks like MANETs, WMNs, WSNs, and VANETS. In recent years, the interest in ad hoc networks has grown due to the availability of wireless communication devices that work in the ISM bands. While designing an ad hoc network in particular we are concerned with the capabilities and limitations that the physical layer imposes on the network performance. Since in wireless networks the radio communication links are unreliable so it is desirable to come up with an integrated design comprising of physical, MAC and network layers [1]. Routing protocols in MANETs were developed based on the design goals of minimal control overhead, minimal processing overhead, multi hop routing capability, dynamic topology maintenance and loop prevention [2]. According to routing strategy the routing protocols can be categorized as table-driven or proactive and source-initiated or reactive or on-demand routing. Each of these types of protocols behaves differently on different wireless conditions. Hence the performance analysis of these protocols is a must task to know its behavior and work in that environment accordingly. The factors like node mobility, network size, control overhead and traffic intensity along with inherent characteristics of ad hoc networks may result in unpredictable variations in the overall

V.V. Das and N. Thankachan (Eds.): CIIT 2011, CCIS 250, pp. 731–736, 2011.

network performance. The primary objective of this paper is to evaluate and quantify the effects of the above factors that may influence network performance. In section 2 we briefly reported the overview of the protocols we considered for performance analysis, followed by the simulations and performance analysis using NS2 in section3 and Conclusion and future works in section 4.

2 Overview of Routing Protocols

In this section we briefly describe the key features of the AODV, OLSR and DSDV routing protocols studied in our simulations.

Ad-hoc On-demand Distance Vector(AODV): AODV is a combination of on-demand and distance vector i.e hop-to-hop routing methodology [3].When a node needs to know a route to a specific destination it creates a ROUTE REQUEST. Next the route request is forwarded by intermediate nodes which also create a reverse route for itself for destination. When the request reaches a node with route to destination it creates again a REPLY which contains the number of hops that are require to reach the destination. In literature [4-9] reported the performance analysis of AODV.

Destination Sequenced Distance Vector(DSDV): DSDV is a hop-by-hop distance vector routing protocol requiring each node to periodically broadcast routing updates based on the idea of classical Bellman-Ford Routing algorithm [10]. Each node maintains a routing table listing the "next hop" for each reachable destination, number of hops to reach destination and the sequence number assigned by destination node. The sequence number is used to distinguish stale routes from new ones and thus avoid loop formation. In literature many articles [4][5][8][9] reported about the performance of DSDV in their respective literature.

Optimized Link State Routing (OLSR): OLSR is an optimization of pure link state algorithm [11], uses the concept of Multi point Relays (MPR) for forwarding control traffic, intended for diffusion into the entire network. The MPR set is selected such that it covers all nodes that are two hops away. Due to proactive nature, OLSR works with a periodic exchange of messages like *Hello* messages and Topology Control *(TC)* message only through its MPR.

3 Simulations and Performance Analysis

In this work, we used the discrete event simulator NS2 (version 2.34) [12] and the performance analysis were conducted using AWK script. Each run of the simulator accepts as input a scenario file that describes the exact motion and position of each node using Random Waypoint Mobility model. For the evaluation of a particular factor we considered the average value of the performance results of 10 random scenario patterns. In all our simulations we considered five sample points of a particular factor (Throughput, Routing overhead, Delay and Packet Delivery Ratio) and compared in three environments (AODV, OLSR and DSDV).The above performances were analyzed under following scenarios: (i) varying the number of nodes (ii) varying the pause time (iii) varying the network area.

Network Load Analysis: In this analysis we varied the number of nodes from 10 to 50 with an increment of 10 nodes, whereas we fixed the pause time to 30s, network size to 600x600 sq.m and the simulation duration to 150s. Other parameters of network are same as described above. From the performance plots shown in Fig.1(a), (b) and (c) we observed that the DSDV protocol outperforms the AODV and OLSR in terms of average throughput, routing overhead and average delay. Though the OLSR has maximum routing overhead the data integrity (PDR) is better as compared to AODV and DSDV as shown in Fig.1(d).

Mobility analysis: In mobility analysis we consider the following pause times: 0s, 30s, 90s, 120s, and 150s. The mobility of the network varied from high mobile condition (0s pause time) to static condition (150s pause time). The maximum speed is fixed at around 10m/s and the total number of nodes is fixed at 30 for each scenario of different pause time by keeping all other parameters fixed. From Fig.2(a) and (b) we observed that DSDV is better in terms of average throughput for different pause time and has lowest routing overhead. From Fig.2(c) we observed that from 90s pause time to 150s pause time AODV, OLSR and DSDV have almost same performance in terms of average delay but, in case of high mobility condition i.e 0s and 30s pause time DSDV has lowest in comparison to AODV and OLSR. Whereas, in terms of average PDR as shown in Fig.2(d), OLSR is better than AODV and DSDV. Hence, we found that OLSR is the most suitable protocol for high mobility node network.

Network Size Analysis: We considered 200x200, 400x400, 600x600, 800x800, and 1000x1000 sq.ms. for the study of network size. The number of nodes for different network size is 30 and the pause time of 30s. From Fig.3 (a) we observed that if the size of the network increases the average throughput decreases for all the three protocols whereas the DSDV has the highest average throughput. In the same time from Fig.3(b) we observed that the routing overhead increases for increase in area. It is clear that AODV and OLSR have nearly same routing overhead for area 400x400 sqm and above. It is obvious that AODV and OLSR having higher average delay because of the higher routing overhead which is presented in Fig.3(c). As per the PDR performance in Fig.3 (d) OLSR is better than AODV and DSDV whereas the PDR decreases as network size increases but, for higher size of the network with fixed number of nodes the rate of fall of PDR performance is faster than AODV and OLSR.

4 Conclusion and Future Work

In this paper we evaluated the four performance measures i.e. average throughput, routing overhead, average delay and average PDR with different number of nodes, different speed of nodes and different size of network. From the results reported in Section 3 we concluded that OLSR for high mobility condition of nodes OLSR gives better packet delivery rate than other protocols, making it suitable for highly mobile random network. Similarly for network size analysis it is observed that all three protocols behave almost same in packet delivery fraction whereas, if the data delivery is more important in some applications then the DSDV is the better choice. In future, utilizing these performances we can design such a protocol that can be suitably provide data integrity as well as data delivery in highly random mobility network.

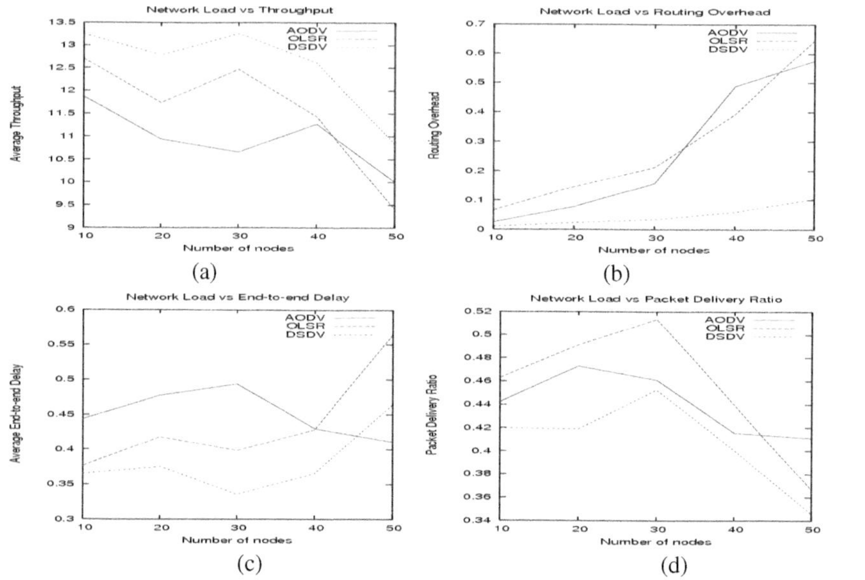

Fig. 1. Performance analysis varying no. of nodes **(a)** Variation for throughput **(b)** Variation for routing overhead **(c)** Variation for delay **(d)** Variation for PDR

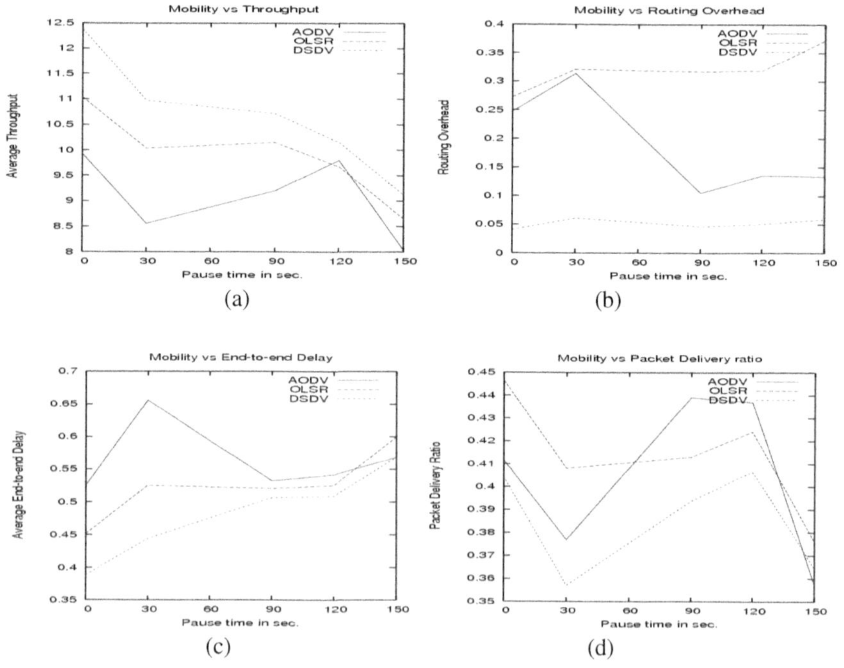

Fig. 2. Performance Analysis varying pause time: **(a)** Variation for Throughput **(b)** Variation for routing overhead **(c)** Variation for delay **(d)** Variation for PDR

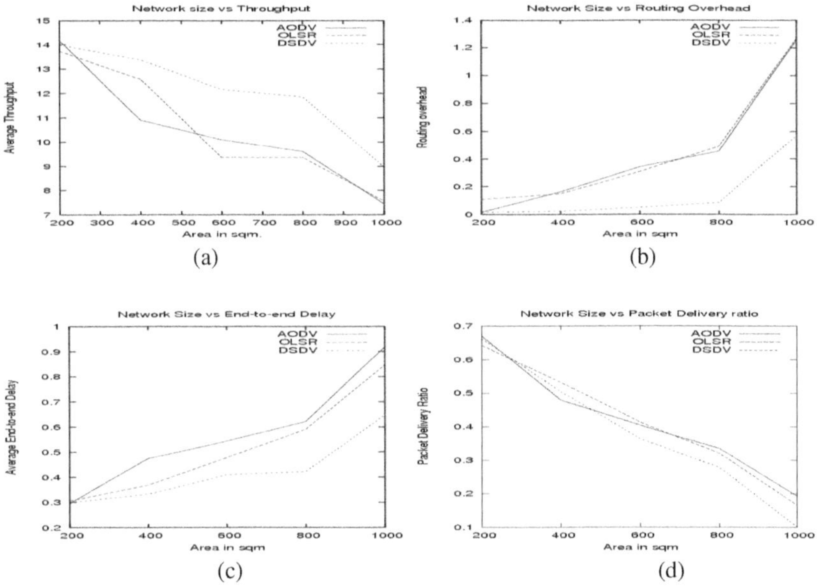

Fig. 3. Performance analysis varying network size. **(a)** Variation for throughput **(b)** Variation for Routing overhead **(c)** Variation for Delay **(d)** Variation for PDR.

References

1. Sarkar, S.K., Basavaraju, T.G., Puttamadappa, C.: Ad hoc Mobile Wireless Networks: Principles, Protocols and Applications. Auerbach Publications (2008)
2. Royer, E.M., Toh, C.: A review of current routing protocols for adhoc mobile wireless networks. IEEE Personal Communications, 46–56 (1999)
3. Perkins, C.E., Royer, E.M., Das, S.: Ad-hoc On-demand Distance Vector Routing, draft-ietf-manet-aodv-13.txt. RFC 3651 (July 2003)
4. Tuteja, A., Gujral, R., Thalia, S.: Comparative performance analysis of DSDV, AODVand DSR Routing protocols in MANET using NS2. In: 2010 International Conference on Advances in Computer Engineering, pp. 330–333. IEEE Comp. Society (2010)
5. Broch, J., Maltz, D.A., Johnson, D.B., Hu, Y., Jetcheva, J.: A Performance comparision of Multihop Wireless Ad-Hoc Network Routing Protocols. In: 4th ACM/IEEE Int.Conf. MOBICOM (1998)
6. Boukhalkhal, A., Yagoubi, M.B., Djoudi, M., Ouinten, Y., Benmohammed, M.: Simulation of Mobile Ad hoc Routing Strategies. In: 4th Int. IEEE Conf. IIT 2007, 128–132 (November 2007)
7. Karthiga, G., Christinal, J.B., Moses, J.C.: Performance analysis of various adhoc routing protocols in multicast environment. IJCST 2(1), 161–164 (2011)
8. Singh, Y., Chaba, Y., Jain, M., Rani, P.: Performance evaluation of Ondemand multicasting routing protocols in Mobile adhoc networks. In: ICRTITC, pp. 298–300. IEEE Comp. Society (2010)

9. Sarevski, F., Ognenoski, O., Gavrilovska, L.: Performance analysis of routing protocols in adhoc and sensor networking environments. Telfor 1, 10–13 (2009)
10. Perkins, C.E., Bhagwat, P.: Highly dynamic Destination-Sequenced Distance-Vector Routing (DSDV)for Mobile Computers. SIGCOMM ACM, 234–245 (1994)
11. Clausen, T., Jacquet, P.: RFC 3626-Optimized Link State Routing Protocol (OLSR) (2003)
12. Fall, K.: The ns manual US Berkerley LBL USC/ISI and Xerox PARC (2010)

Faults Classification for Voltage Sag Causes Based on Empirical Mode Decomposition with Hilbert Transform

Manjula Mane[1], A.V.R.S. Sarma[1], and Sukumar Mishra[2]

[1] Department of Electrical Engineering, Osmania University, Hyderabad, Andhra Pradesh, India
{manjulamane04,avrs2000}@yahoo.com
[2] Department of Electrical Engineering, IIT Delhi, India
sukumar@ee.iitd.ac.in

Abstract. This paper presents a novel method of classifying the power system faults for obtaining the information on the causes of voltage sags. Empirical Mode Decomposition (EMD) with Hilbert Transform (HT) is used to detect voltage sag causes. The voltage sags are mostly due to short circuit faults. The techniques employed for analyzing the fault data require the information about the underlying event i.e. the fault type. The key feature of EMD is to decompose a non stationary signal into mono component signals called Intrinsic Mode Functions (IMFs). Further the Hilbert transform provides the magnitude and phase of these IMFs. The characteristic features of the first three IMFs of each phase are used as inputs to the classifier, Probabilistic Neural Network (PNN) for identification of fault type. Simulation results show that the classification accuracy is high for each of the fault type.

Keywords: Empirical mode decomposition, faults, hilbert transform, intrinsic mode functions, power quality, probabilistic neural network, voltage sag causes.

1 Introduction

Voltage sag is one of the most disturbing power quality problems. The voltage sags are mostly due to short circuit faults [1]. They have drawn the attention of the customers as well as the power engineers due to the problems they cause to the different equipment is not the same. The characteristics of voltage sags are defined by the sag magnitude, its phase angle and duration [2]. The faults are either symmetrical or asymmetrical. In order to mitigate and find a solution, it is required to detect and identify the source of the problem. Thus a technique is required which has the capability to extract the features of the fault data and do the classification [3]. This paper presents the Empirical Mode Decomposition (EMD) [4-5], together with Hilbert transform for extracting the features and Probabilistic Neural Network (PNN) [6] is used to classify the faults. The advantage of this method is that it does not require any predetermined set of functions but allows projection of a non stationary signal onto a time -frequency plane using mono component signals called the IMF. As these IMFs are obtained from the original signal, thus making it adaptive in nature.

V.V. Das and N. Thankachan (Eds.): CIIT 2011, CCIS 250, pp. 737–740, 2011.

The rest of the paper is organized as follows: In section 2 Empirical mode decomposition method is discussed for extracting mono component and symmetric components from the non stationary signals by sifting process. Section 3 explains the features extracted from the respective IMFs and the PNN classifier. In section 4, the results are discussed and finally section 5 gives the conclusions.

2 Empirical Mode Decomposition

Empirical mode decomposition is a method which extracts mono component and symmetric components from the non linear and non stationary signals by sifting process. These are called as Intrinsic Mode Functions. Any oscillating wave is defined as an IMF, if it satisfies the following two conditions:

(a) For a data set, the number of extreme and the number of zero crossings must either be equal or differ at most by one.
(b) At any point, the mean value of the envelope defined by the local maxima and the local minima is zero.

2.1 Hilbert Transform

The Instantaneous frequency of each IMF is calculated by using the Hilbert Transform. The Hilbert Transform of a real valued time domain signal x(t) is another real valued time domain signal, denoted by $\hat{x}(t)$, such that $z(t) = x(t) + j\hat{x}(t)$ is an analytic signal. From z(t), one can define a magnitude function A(t) and a phase function $\theta(t)$, where the A(t) describes the envelope of the original function x(t) versus time and $\theta(t)$ describes the instantaneous phase of x(t) versus time.

3 Feature Extraction for Fault Classification

Faults are either symmetrical or asymmetrical. Depending on the type of fault the magnitudes of the voltage sag of each phase are equal or unequal. Here four types of faults are considered i.e. Phase to ground (LG), Phase to Phase (LL), Double Phase to ground (LLG) and Three phase short circuit (LLL). The faults are applied on a 11kV power system network for different values of fault resistance, the duration of fault applied and time of application are varied.

3.1 Phase to Ground Fault

The three phase voltage waveforms and its RMS magnitude for phase to ground fault are shown in Fig. 1(a) and (b). The magnitude plot of Hilbert transform of the first IMF detects the event as shown in Fig. 2(a). Fig. 2(b)-(d) are the waveforms of the first three IMFs of the signal.

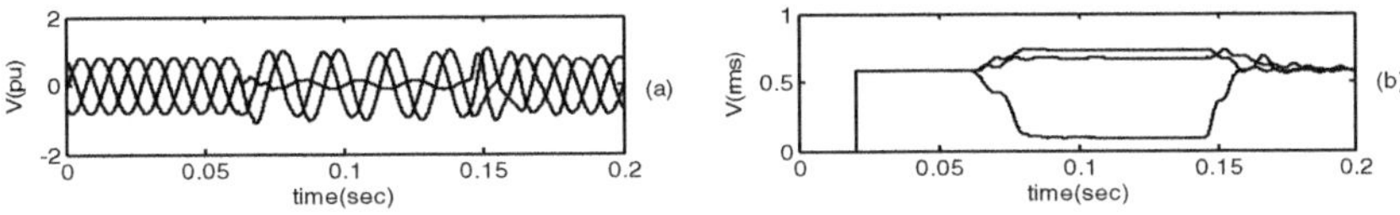

Fig. 1. (a). Waveform of voltage sag due to LG fault, **(b)** Voltage sag (rms)

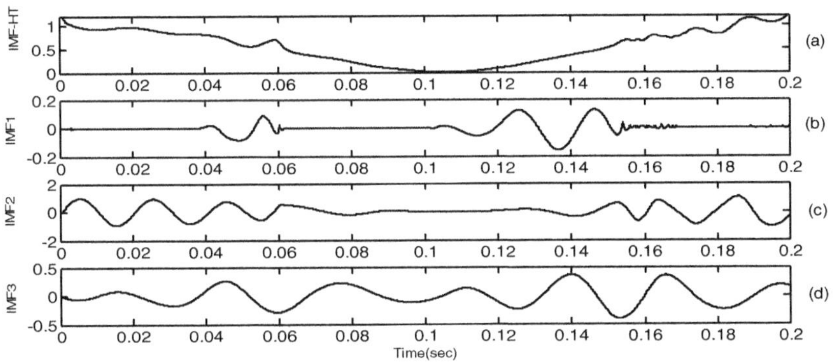

Fig. 2. (a). Magnitude plot of the HT of IMF1, **2(b)-(d)** Intrinsic Mode Functions(IMF1-IMF3)

Similarly the IMFs are extracted for other three faults i.e. LL, LLG and LLL. The first three IMFs are considered for the feature extraction. The following three features (1) Energy distribution, (2) Standard deviation of the amplitude and (3) Standard deviation of the phase are taken. Thus, we have nine features from the three IMFs from each phase. These are inputs to the probabilistic neural network for training used for classification.

4 Results and Discussion

EMD decomposes any complicated signal into finite number of IMFs. These IMFs define the local properties of the signal. For a LG, LL and LLL faults the IMFs are six, where as for LLG fault the total IMFs are seven. Simulations are performed to generate 428 signals, 308 data sets are used for training the PNN classifier and 120 are used for testing. The classification result using the method is shown in Table 1. When PNN is trained, the spread factor is tuned by trial and error method to 0.08, which has given better results. As shown in the Table 1 the overall efficiency of the EMD method is 93.15%. The reason for better classification accuracy of disturbances by EMD method lies in the fact that it is a sieving process of the signal where the IMFs are extracted and they are associated with different intrinsic time scales. The extraction of Instantaneous frequency by the application of Hilbert transform over the IMFs gives a better time frequency distribution for non stationary signals. Hence, EMD method with Hilbert transform is better suited for non-stationary signals like faults.

Table 1. Percentage Classification Accuracy of Probabilistic Neural Network

EMD Method	LG	LL	LLG	LLL	Classification Efficiency (%)	Overall Efficiency
LG	26	-	4	-	86.6	93.15%
LL	-	30		-	100	
LLG	2	-	28	-	93	
LLL	-	-	2	28	93	

5 Conclusions

In this paper probabilistic neural network combined with EMD and Hilbert transform is used to classify the type of faults (voltage sag causes). EMD method is used to decompose the original signal into mono component signals called the IMFs. Hilbert transform is used to extract the feature information from first three modes of oscillation. The results show that the overall classification accuracy is 93.15% indicating that the method is efficient in classifying the faults. Thus, making it a better method in assessing power system faults.

References

1. Das, B.: Fuzzy Logic based fault type identification in unbalanced radial power distribution system. IEEE Trans. Power Delivery (2006)
2. Carpinelli, G., Di Perna, C., Verde, P.: Methods for assessing the robustness of electrical power systems against voltage dips. IEEE Trans. Power Delivery (2009)
3. He, Z., Fu, L., Lin, S., Bo, Z.: Fault Detection and Classification in EHV Transmission Line Based on Wavelet Singular Entropy. IEEE Trans. Power Delivery (2010)
4. Huang, N.E., Shen, Z., Long, S.R., Wu, M.C., Shih, H.H., Zheng, Q., Yen, N.C., Tung, C.C., Liu, H.H.: The empirical mode decomposition and hilbert spectrum for nonlinear and non stationary time series analysis. Proceedings of the Royal Society, London A454, 903–995 (1998)
5. Shukla, S., Mishra, S., Singh, B.: Empirical-Mode Decomposition With Hilbert Transform for Power-Quality Assessment. IEEE Trans. Power Delivery (2009)
6. Specht, D.F.: Probabilistic neural networks. Neural Networks 3(1), 109–118 (1990)

Design of a Feedback Compensator for Electric Vehicle Based on Indian Road Conditions

Poorani Shivkumar

Sona college of Technology /EEE Department, Salem, India
drpooranieee@gmail.com

Abstract. A Novel approach of designing a feedback compensator for the Electric Vehicle Drive based on Indian Road conditions is dealt here. The performance analysis of PI controller as well as compensator design for the developed transfer function has been done.

Keywords: Electric Vehicle, Transfer function, PI controller, Indian Road conditions, Feedback compensator, Bode plot.

1 Introduction

The search for vehicles with improved fuel economy, reduced emissions, and affordable cost without sacrificing the performance, safety, reliability and other attributes of a conventional vehicle has made the Electric Vehicle Technology (EVT) [1,8] as one of the challenges for the automotive industry. The focus of this research is to develop a compensator for the developed transfer function for the electric vehicle that includes vehicle dynamics, road dynamics and motor parameters. The performance of controller like PI has been dealt. In order to improve the performance specifications, the compensator design has been done. The paper is organized as follows: Section 2 provides the design of compensator for Indian road conditions and the Section 3 conclusions.

2 Design of Feedback Compensator

The electric vehicle transfer function developed based on motor parameters, rolling resistance and the vehicle parameters [5] has been taken here along with PI controller performance [2,3,5]. Compensator an additional component is inserted into the Electric Vehicle system [3] to compensate for the deficient performance of the PI controller. The compensator design methodology [6] such as bode plot requires a linear plant model, since the Electric Vehicle system model taken into account is nonlinear. It must be linearized before designing the compensator for it. As a result, the design of good compensators relies on a good linearization. The operating point of

V.V. Das and N. Thankachan (Eds.): CIIT 2011, CCIS 250, pp. 741–743, 2011.

a dynamic system defines its overall state at a given time. A linearized model is an approximation that is valid in a small region around the operating point of the system. Near the operating point the approximation will be good, while far away it will be poor. Then the compensator design [6,9] has been done for the transfer function model of the three terrains namely Concrete, Medium Hard and Sand [4] by selecting the same operating point and further tuned by graphical analysis to obtain the compensator design response. The tuning is done and the gain margin and phase margin is obtained as shown in Figure 1.With the final tuned compensator design the whole control loop is executed and the result is obtained for the concrete terrain as shown in Figure 2. The Table 1depicts the performance criteria of the three terrains for the PI controller and the Compensator.

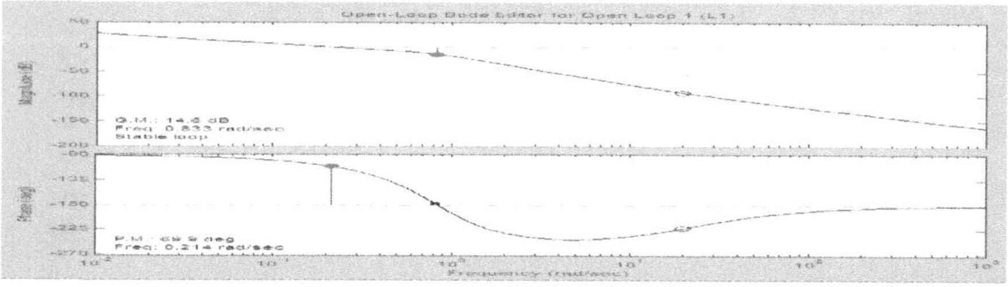

Fig. 1. Response of the control loop of PI controller for the concrete terrain compensator design using bode plot –analysis

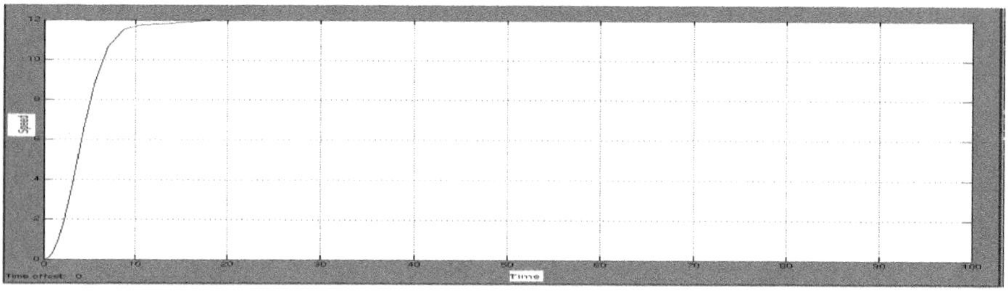

Fig. 2. Response of the control loop of PI controller for the concrete terrain with Compensator

3 Conclusion

From the performance criteria stated in Table 1, it is clearly depicted that comparative to PI controller the compensator designed for the three terrains is found to be efficient and can be further optimized in future to get the better results.

Table 1. Performance Criteria's of Controllers

S.No	Types of Terrain	Performance Criteria	PI controller	Compensator
1	Concrete	Rise time (t_r)	1	0.01
		Settling time (t_s)	37	19
		Peak Time (t_p)	5	10
		Max peak Overshoot (M_p)	12.8	1.1
		Delay Time (t_d)	0.01	0.001
		Steady State error (e_{ss})	0	0
2	Medium hard	Rise Time (t_r)	0.8	0.001
		Settling Time (t_s)	21	11
		Peak Time (t_p)	3	11
		Max peak Overshoot (M_p)	12.7	1.3
		Delay Time (t_d)	0.001	0.001
		Steady State error (e_{ss})	0	0
3	Sand	Rise Time (t_r)	0.9	0.0001
		Settling Time (t_s)	16	12
		Peak Time (t_p)	6	15
		Max peak Overshoot (M_p)	12.6	1.5
		Delay Time (t_d)	0.1	0.001
		Steady State error (e_{ss})	0	0

References

1. Chan, C.C.: An overview of electric vehicle Technology. Proceedings of IEEE 81(9), 1202–1213 (1993)
2. Ho, W.K., Hang, C.C., Zhou, J.H.: Performance and gain and phase margins of well known PI tuning formulas. IEEE Transactions on Control Systems Technology 3(2), 245–248 (1995)
3. Nandam, P.K., Sen, P.C.: Analog and Digital speed control of DC Drives using proportional-integral and integral-proportional control techniques. IEEE Transactions on Industrial Electronics, IE 34(2), 227–233 (1997)
4. Gillespie, T. D.: Fundamentals of Vehicle Dynamics. Society of Automotive Engineers Group (1999)
5. Poorani, S., UdayaKumar, K., Renganarayanan, S.: Design of a fuzzy based controller for Electric Vehicles on Indian roads. Proceedings of the Institution of Mechanical Engineers, Part I, Journal of Systems and Control Engineering 221(1), 61–74 (2007)
6. Dorf, R.C., Bishop, R.H.: Modern Control Systems, 8th edn. Addison-Wesley (1998)
7. Sciarretta, A., Back, M., Guzzella, L.: Optimal control of parallel hybrid electric vehicles. IEEE Trans. on Control Systems Technology 12(3), 352–363 (2004)
8. Serrao, L., Hubert, C., Rizzoni, G.: Dynamic modeling of heavy duty hybrid electric Vehicles. In: Proceedings of the 2007 ASME International Mechanical Engineering Congress and Exposition (2007)
9. Bertsekas, D.: Dynamic Programming and Optimal Control. Athena Scientific, Belmont (1995)

Diagnosis of Alzheimer's Disease from 3D MR Images with Statistical Features of Hippocampus

M.M. Patil[1] and A.R. Yardi[2]

[1] Department of Electronics and Telecommunication, College of Engg. Pandharpur , Dist. Solapur, Maharashtra, India
mns.patil@gmail.com
[2]Department of Electronics, Walchand College of Engg, Sangli, Maharashtra, India
aryardi@yahoo.com
"and the Alzheimer's Disease Neuroimaging Initiative*"

Abstract. Alzheimer's disease (AD) is the most common cause of dementia with a progressive course, beginning with neuronal dysfunction, and evolving to irreversible loss of neurons. Early AD detection and treatment allow better clinical results, preserving the loss of cognitive functions for longer periods, with great social economical impact. [2].Subtle hippocampus atrophy can be observed even in early AD, becoming an important biomarker for the disease, especially with disease progression. Volumetric MRI studies already indicate small volume loss of those anatomical structures and, hippocampus appears to shrink. However, there is recent evidence that this shrinkage can be reversed and perhaps prevented in people with depression and bipolar disorder, with effective treatment if timely diagnosed. This paper is on detection of AD from AD, MCI and Normal based on statistical features of Hippocampus derived using MIPAV and further classified by ANN. Our primary goals are: (1) Locate VOI (Volume of Interest) for Hippocampus on 3D MRI. (2)Extract features from this VOI (3) Construct feature vector (4) Train ANN (5) Test ANN. We developed feed forward back propagation neural network in Matlab and trained. Testing of trained ANN revealed the overall accuracy of 80%. VOI analysis is performed using MIPAV. MR Images used are from (ADNI database). 30 AD and 30 Normal images were used for investigation.

Keywords: Neuro-degeneration, 3DMRI, AD, MCI, ANN, Hippocampus, MIPAV, Matlab.

* Data used in preparation of this article were obtained from the Alzheimer's Disease Neuroimaging Initiative (ADNI) database (www.loni.ucla.edu/ADNI). As such, the investigators within the ADNI contributed to the design and implementation of ADNI and/or provided data but did not participate in analysis or writing of this report. A complete listing of ADNI investigators can be found at:
http://loni.ucla.edu//ADNI//Collaboration//ADNI_Authorship_list.pdf

V.V. Das and N. Thankachan (Eds.): CIIT 2011, CCIS 250, pp. 744–749, 2011.

1 Introduction

The portion of the brain that helps the names get into memory in the first place, is hippocampus, part of temporal lobe of brain. It's an inside fold, see Fig.2 purple part at the bottom, that's the hippocampus. It is the innermost fold of the temporal lobe. This part of the brain appears to be absolutely necessary for making new memories.

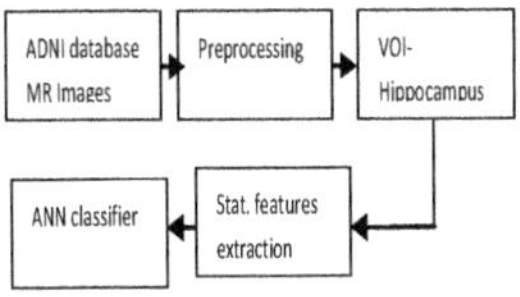

Fig. 1. Overall System

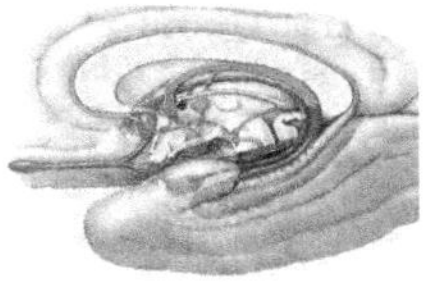

Fig. 2. Inside of brain temporal lobe

And this is common: Alzheimer's disease affects the hippocampus first and severely, [1]. As described in Fig. 1 this paper discusses volume of interest analysis of 3D MR images of ADNI database for hippocampus feature extraction. Feature vector divided in training and testing sets further used for ANN classifier design. Regarding related works, Flavio Luiz Seixas et al. [3] analyzed three medical image analyzing tools, Freesurfer, IBASPM and FSL, in order to identify the best method for hippocampus volumetric assessment. Marie Chupin et al. [5] proposed a fully automatic method using probabilistic and anatomical priors for hippocampus segmentation. S. Li et al. [6] analyzed regional changes of bilateral hippocampi and were characterized using computational anatomic mapping methods Liana G. Apostolova et al. [8], analyzed baseline regional hippocampus atrophy. Simon Duchesne et al [14] used methodology of Jacobian determinants. Yong Fan et al [15] made used of computational neuroanatomy to analyze brain regions. J. Ramirez et al [16] proposed approach based on image parameter selection and support vector machine (SVM) classification. Xiangbo LIN et al [17] proposed a new registration method to segment the hippocampus. Benoit Magnin et al [18] used three-dimensional T1-weighted MR images and ROI. Jie Wu et al [19] proposed a new texture feature-based seeded region growing algorithm. J. Rajeesh et al [20] proposed a new approach to segment the hippocampus from the MRI.

2 Method

We selected subjects from Normal and AD categories. MRI pre-processing was done using statistical parametric mapping software (SPM5; Welcome Department of Cognitive Neurology, Institute of Neurology, London,UK, http://www.fil.ion.ucl.ac.uk/spm/) website accessed on 21 November 2010) with the VBM tool Updated version VBM5.1 toolbox Published by Christian Gaser on May 13, 2009. Jena script http://dbm.neuro.uni-jena.de/vbm.html; in MATLAB. Image by image VBM image segmentation is carried out. VBM calculates the bias-corrected whole brain image in normalized space (wm*).

Authors already published paper on VBM pre-processing [11]. For VOI analysis, MIPAV (Medical Image Processing, Analysis and Visualization) is used. [7]. To generate statistics about hippocampal region following steps are are performed: 1.Open pre-processed 3D MR image.2.Contour and save VOI for hippocampus as shown in Fig.3 3.Select the VOI, click on propagate VOI to all slices to select the same VOI on all slices in 3D MR image.4.Select VOI > Properties. 5.Right-clicked inside the VOI, which automatically selected it. Then selected Properties on the menu. The VOI Statistics dialog box opened.6. Chosen the following properties of statistics to calculate.

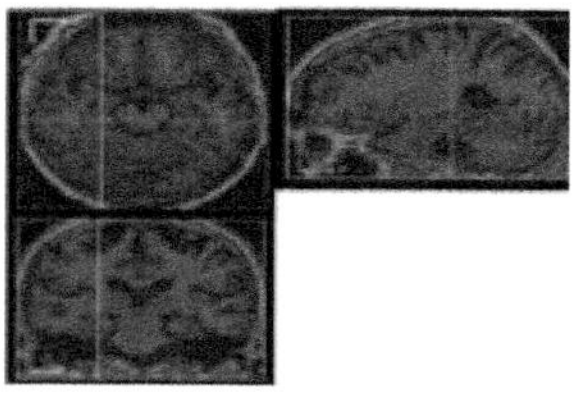

Fig. 3. VOI contour for hippocampus

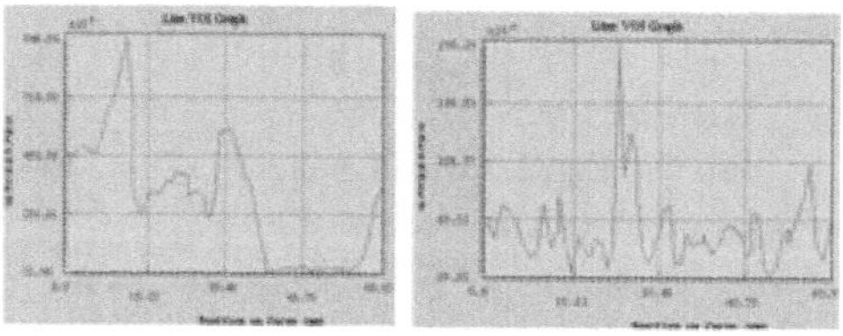

Fig. 4. Intensity graph for Normal and AD

Volume, Area, Perimeter, Max. Intensity, Average voxel intensity, Std. dev. of voxel intensity. Process is repeated for every MR image in study, in order to construct a feature vector. Validity of selected Intensity features can be observed from 3D intensity maps for same VOI on one AD and one Normal image as in Fig.4. Features are derived for 30 AD and 30 Normal 3D MR Images. Then divided into training set (25-25) and test set (5-5). Out of the several features derived, only those features which show maximum changes are selected for ANN training can be seen from fig. 6. ANN [12], [13] training is carried out in Matlab. Feed forward networks have one-way connections from input to output layers. Training algorithms used are gradient descent (GD) method and the Levenberg-Marquardt algorithm (LM). Radial basis networks provide an alternative, fast method for designing nonlinear feedforward networks. Used here for comparison of results. During the training phase, the network is presented with sets of pairs (input and desired output). The network is iteratively updated to reach a desired Mean—Squared—Error (MSE) and optimally provide generalization for test inputs. Tab. 1 and Fig.5 give all the details of FFNN used.

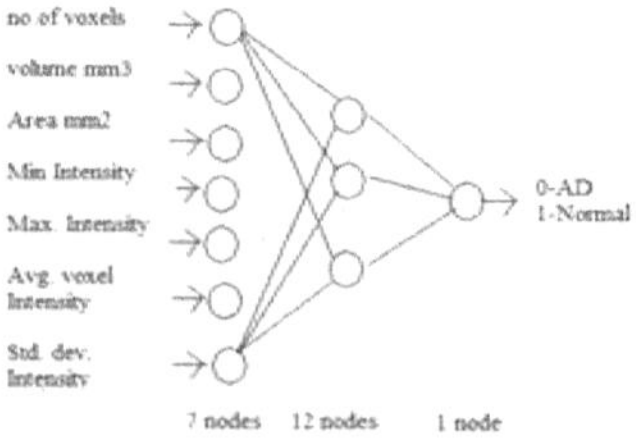

Fig. 5. Feed forward neural network architecture used

Table 1. ANN architecture used

FFNN parameter	Detail
NETWORK TOPOLOGY	FEEDFORW BACKPROPAGATION
TRAINNING FUN	TRAINLM
TRANSFER FUNCTION	TANSIG-LOGSIG-PURELIN
LEARNING FUNCTION	LEARNGDM
PERFORMANCE	MSE
LEARNING RATE	0.001
NO. OF LAYERS	3
LAYER1	7 NODES
LAYER2	12 NODES
LAYER3	1
EPOCHES	1000

3 Results

Feed forward neural network is used. Training experimentation is carried out several times by varying various ANN parameters like number of hidden neurons, activation functions, training function, learning rate. Final training curve is as shown in Fig.6. Performance is evaluated every time by applying several test cases and comparison is made with other classifiers by computing the percentages of Sensitivity (SE), Positive Predictivity and Accuracy (AC) as given in Tab. 2, using the following formulae, Where, the confusion matrix used is [4],

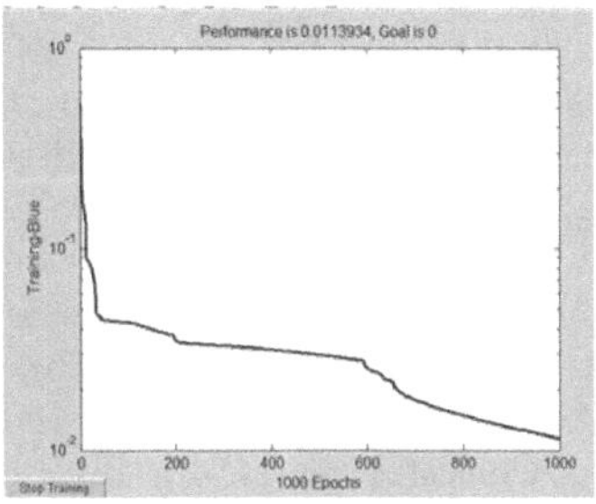

Fig. 6. FFNN training curve

Table 2. ANN performance

Classifier	Training	Test
FFNN	100%	70%
RBF	100%	86%

4 Conclusion and Discussion

In this paper, the computer based technique for automatic classification of 3D MR Image as normal or Alziemers Disease with Hippocampus as VOI feature using FFNN classifier is proposed. The performances of the classifiers in terms of statistical measures such as sensitivity, positive predictivity and classification accuracy are analyzed. The results indicated that the FFNN with Trainlm as training function yielded the better performance when compared to other classifiers. It suggests that FFNN is a promising technique for image classification in a medical imaging application.

Acknowledgement. Authors are thankful to Alzheimer's disease Neuroimaging Initiative (ADNI) database (www.loni.ucla.edu/ADNI). Authors are also thankful to Center for Information Technology (CIT), National Institutes of Health (NIH), an agency of the United States Public Health Service (PHS) within the Department of Health and Human Services (DHHS) for software support MIPAV.

References

1. Seixas, F.L., de Souza, A.S.: Memory, Learning, and Emotion. Anatomical Brain MRI Segmentation Hippocampus, Psycheducation.org
2. Methods: Volumetric Assessment of the Hippocampus. In: Proceedings of 17th International Conference on Systems, Signals and Image Processing, IWSSIP 2010, pp. 247–251 (2010)

3. Seixas, F.L., de Souza, A.S.: Anatomical Brain MRI Segmentation Methods: Volumetric Assessment of the Hippocampus. In: IWSSIP 2010 - 17th International Conference on Systems, Signals and Image Processing, pp. 247–252 (2010)
4. Selvaraj, H., Thamarai Selvi, S., Selvathi, D., Gewali, L.: Brain MRI Slices Classification Using Least Squares Support Vector Machine. J. IC-MED 1(1), 21–33
5. Chupin, M., Gérardin, E., Cuingnet, R., Boutet, C., Lemieux, L., Lehéricy, S., Benali, H., Garnero, L., Colliot, O., The Alzheimer's Disease Neuroimaging Initiative: Fully Automatic Hippocampus Segmentation and Classification in Alzheimer's Disease and Mild Cognitive Impairment Applied on Data from ADNI. Hippocampus 19(6), 579–587 (2009), doi:10.1002/hipo.20626
6. Li, S., Shi, F., Pu, F., Li, X., Jiang, T., Xie, S., Wang, Y.: Hippocampal Shape Analysis of Alzheimer Disease Based on Machine Learning Methods. AJNR Am. J. Neuroradiol. 28, 1339–1345 (2007)
7. Bazin, P.-L., Cuzzocreo, J.L., Yassa, M.A., Gandler, W., McAuliffe, M.J., Bassett, S.S., Phama, D.L.: Volumetric neuroimage analysis extensions for the MIPAV software package. Journal of Neuroscience Methods 165, 111–121 (2007)
8. Apostolova, L.G., Dutton, R.A., Dinov, I.D., Hayashi, K.M., Toga, A.W., Cummings, J.L., Thompson, P.M.: Conversion of Mild Cognitive Impairment to Alzheimer Disease Predicted by Hippocampal Atrophy Maps. Arch. Neurol. 63, 693–700 (2006)
9. Li, L., Wang, J.Z., Chahal, D., Eckert, M.A., Lozar, C.: Detection of Mild Cognitive Impairment Using Image Differences and Clinical Features. In: IEEE International Conference and Symposium on Bioinformatic and Bioengineering, pp. 106–111 (2010)
10. Jude Hemanth, D., Kezi Selva Vijila, C., Anitha, J.: A survey on Artificial intelligence based brain pathology identification techniques in amgnetic resonance images. International Journal of Reviews in Computing E-ISSN: 2076-331X
11. Patil, M.M., Yardi, A.R.: "VBM based MR Imaging Volumetric Analysis of AD and MCI" Paper on VBM based MR Imaging Volumetric Analysis of AD and MCI. IJCA 13(2), 1749–2383, `http://www.ijcaonline.org/archives/volume13/number2/1749-2383`
12. Tandon, R., Adak, S., Kaye, J.A.: Neural networks for longitudinal studies in Alzheimer's disease. Artificial Intelligence in Medicine 36, 245–255 (2006)
13. Cuingnet, R., Gerardin, E., Tessieras, J., Auzias, G., Lehéricy, S., Habert, M.-O., Chupin, M., Benali, H., Colliot, O.: Automatic classification of patients with Alzheimer's disease from structural MRI: A comparison of ten methods using the ADNI database. NeuroImage (2010), doi:10.1016/j.neuroimage.2010.06.013
14. Duchesne, S., Caroli, A., Geroldi, C., Barillot, C., Frisoni, G.B., Louis Collins, D.: MRI-Based Automated Computer Simon Duchesne Classification of Probable AD Versus Normal Controls. IEEE Transactions On Medical Imaging 27(4), 509–520 (2008), doi:10.1109/TMI.2007.908685
15. Fan, Y., Batmanghelich, N., Clark, C.M., Davatzikos, C., Alzheimer's disease Neuroimaging Initiative: Spatial patterns of brain atrophy in MCI patients, identified via high-dimensional pattern classification, predict subsequent cognitive decline. Neuroimage 39(4), 1731–1743 (2008), doi:10.1016/j.neuroimage.2007.10.031
16. Ramirez, J., Gorriz, J.M., Salas-Gonzalez, D., Romero, A., Lopez, M., Alvarez, I., Gomez-Rio, M.: Computer-aided diagnosis of Alzheimer's type dementia combining support vector machines and discriminant set of feature. Information Sciences (2009), doi:10.1016/j.ins.2009.05.012

17. Lin, X., Qiu, T., Morain-Nicolier, F., Ruan, S.: Automatic Hippocampus Segmentation from Brain MRI Images. International Journal of Computer Information Systems and Industrial Management Applications (IJCISIM) 1, 239–248 (2009), http://www.mirlabs.org/ijcisim, ISSN: 2150-7988
18. Magnin, B., Mesrob, L., Kinkingnehun, S., Pelegrini-Issac, M., Colliot, O., Sarazin, M., Dubois, B., Lehericy, S.: Habib Benali Support vector machine-based classification of Alzheimer's disease from whole-brain anatomical. MRI Neuroradiology 51, 73–83 (2009), doi:10.1007/s00234-008-0463-x
19. Wu, J., Poehlman, S., Noseworthy, M.D., Kamath, M.V.: Texture feature based automated seeded region growing in abdominal MRI segmentation. J. Biomedical Science and Engineering 2, 1–8 (2009), http://www.scirp.org/journal/jbiseJBiSE
20. Rajeesh, J., Moni, R.S., Palanikumar, S., Gopalakrishnan, T.: Knowledge Based Automatic Segmentation of Hippocampus in Wave Atom Preprocessed MRI 2(3), 409–418 (2010) ISSN 0975 - 6450

Analysis of Pole Placement Problem in Control Systems Using State Derivative Feedback

Saurav Malviya[1], Yogesh V. Hote[2], P.K.V. Kishan[1], and Siddharth Malhotra[1]

[1] Division of Instrumentation and Control Engineering,
Netaji Subhas Institute of Technology, Class of 2010
[2] Department of Electrical Engineering,
Indian Institute of Technology, Roorkee
{malviya.saurav,parasu.kishan,sid.siddharth}@gmail.com,
yhotefee@iitr.ernet.in

Abstract. In this paper, we have designed a state derivative feedback controller for inverted pendulum. The presented approach is based on results reported by Abdelaziz and Valášek[1], [2] which shows that for some class of control system problems, state derivative feedback gives smaller gain in comparison to traditional state feedback. This paper pointed out the physical interpretation of the result obtained by previous authors about energy required by state derivative feedback and state feedback. The results are verified in Matlab environment.

Keywords: State Derivative feedback, Pole placement, Stability, State feedback.

1 Introduction

The pole placement method is a widely used mathematical tool to design linear control systems[1], [2], [3], [4], [5], [6], [15], [17]. In this paper, we investigate the state derivative feedback approach of solving the pole placement problem[1], [2], [4], [7], [11]. The tendency of state derivative feedback control systems to result in singularity in case the original system ceases to be state variable system has been overcome recently by employing traditional state feedback approach which provides a solution to both the threat of singularity and to more general time-varying systems[1]. The inspiration for the approach followed in [1] came from controlled vibration absorbers[12]. Due to the specific nature of such systems, use of state derivative feedback is a natural and powerful way to design controllers for them.

The motivation for this paper stems from the possibility of reduced energy consumption of the controller when designed using state derivative feedback for a given level of stability. This would expand the scope and range of possible applications of state derivative feedback and provide a new method for generating more energy efficient control system designs.

In [1] the scope has been kept limited to developing the theoretical and mathematical analysis of the state derivative feedback approach. Extending the study, in this paper, the feedback controller is designed for the inverted pendulum[18] using both the traditional full state feedback, which is the Ackermann's formula[8], [9], [13],

V.V. Das and N. Thankachan (Eds.): CIIT 2011, CCIS 250, pp. 750–754, 2011.

[14] and the state derivative feedback. The resulting feedback gain matrix elements from both the approaches are compared, with a lower value in case of state derivative feedback indicating lesser energy consumption than state feedback. Furthermore, we explore the reason behind the observed trend.

2 Solution of Pole Placement Problem by State Derivative Feedback for Linear Time-Invariant System

The pole placement problem is solved using state derivative feedback by the method given in [1].

2.1 The Pole Placement Problem

The single input linear time-invariant system with nth order differential equation is given by:

$$\dot{x}(t) = Ax(t) + Bu(t), x(t_0) = x_0 . \tag{1}$$

Where $A(n \times n)$ is the system matrix and $B(n \times 1)$ is the control gain matrix. The closed-loop characteristic equation is then given by:

$$Det[sI - (I + Bk)^{-1}A] = 0 . \tag{2}$$

When equation (2) is evaluated, this yields an nth order polynomial in s-plane containing the gains $k_1, k_2, \ldots , k_n$. The control law design then consists of choosing the gains so that the roots of equation (2) are at desired locations. To solve the pole placement problem, instead of using the direct approach, which often results in iterative optimizations, the system is transformed into Frobenius canonical form and the poles are then placed at the desired locations.

2.2 Solution of Pole Placement Problem for Linear Time-Invariant System by State Derivative Feedback[1]

The solution of the pole placement problem proposed by Abdelaziz and Valášek is given below. The Frobenius canonical form of the system is given by:

$$\dot{z} = A_F z + B_F u . \tag{3}$$

$$z = Q^{-1}x . \tag{4}$$

Where,
$A_F = Q^{-1}AQ$, and $B_F = Q^{-1}B$.
And, $Q = [q_1\, q_1A \ldots q_1A^{n-1}]$,

While, $q_1 = (e_n^T)R^{-1}$.
R is the controllability matrix of the system, given by, $R = [B\ AB\ A^2B \ldots A^{n-1}B]$ and $e_n = [0\ 0 \ldots 1]^T$ (a unit vector).
The expression of state derivative feedback gain matrix is hence given by,

$$K = \left(\frac{a_0}{d_0}\right) e_n^T (AR)^{-1} D(A) \ . \tag{5}$$

Where,
a_0 =Constant term in open loop characteristic polynomial of the system.
d_0 =Constant term in desired closed loop characteristic polynomial of the system.
$D(A) = [A^n + d_{n-1} A^{n-1} + \ldots + d_1 A + d_0 I]$
When the system matrix A is singular, then, from the discussion above, it follows,

$$K = e_n^T D^{-1} \ . \tag{6}$$

Equation (5) is similar to the Ackermann's formula given by:

$$K = e_n^T U^{-1} D(A) \ . \tag{7}$$

Where, $U = [B\ AB \ldots A^{n-1}B]$.

3 Comparison of State Feedback and State Derivative Feedback in Control System Problems

3.1 The Pole Placement Problem

The state space model of the inverted pendulum is given by,

$$\dot{x}(t) = \begin{bmatrix} 0 & 1 & 0 & 0 \\ 0 & \frac{-(I+ml^2)b}{I(M+m)+Mml^2} & \frac{m^2gl^2}{I(M+m)+Mml^2} & 0 \\ 0 & 0 & 0 & 1 \\ 0 & \frac{-mlb}{I(M+m)+Mml^2} & \frac{mgl(M+m)}{I(M+m)+Mml^2} & 0 \end{bmatrix} x(t) + \begin{bmatrix} 0 \\ \frac{I+ml^2}{I(M+m)+Mml^2} \\ 0 \\ \frac{ml}{I(M+m)+Mml^2} \end{bmatrix} u.$$

Where,

M = Mass of the base (on which the pendulum is pivoted), m = Mass of the pendulum, b = Friction of the base with respect to the stationary ground, l = Length to pendulum centre of mass, I = Inertia of the pendulum, F = Force applied to the base, x = Base position coordinate.
$u(t)$ = Control input.

$$x(t) = \begin{bmatrix} x \\ dx \\ \theta \\ d\theta \end{bmatrix}.$$

M = 0.5kg; m = 0.2kg; b = 0.1N/m/sec; I = 0.006kgm^2; g = 9.8m/s^2 ; l = 0.3m. The open loop poles of this system come out to be 0, -5.6130,-0.1429 and 5.5741. The desired closed loop poles are chosen to be -5 ± 5i and -1 ± i. By applying the mathematical process used to arrive at (5), a MATLAB simulation was performed with initial conditions $x(t_0)$ = $[0.05\ 0.05\ 0.2\ 0.2]^T$ to get the state derivative feedback gain matrix, given by,

$$K = [-0.0184 \quad -0.0004 \quad 0.0340 \quad 0.0007]\,. \tag{8}$$

The feedback gain matrix computed using Ackermann's formula is given by,

$$K = [-1.8449 \quad -3.7067 \quad 118.5980 \quad 18.5577]\,. \tag{9}$$

As evident from (8) and (9), the derivative feedback gains are smaller than state feedback gains in magnitude. Hence, the control system designed with state derivative feedback will require lesser power to achieve the desired gains than its state feedback counterpart. State Derivative Feedback technique was applied to a variety of systems such as controlled vibration absorber[1], magnetic levitation[10] and servomechanism[16], yielding lesser feedback gains than traditional State Feedback approach.

4 Physical Interpretation of the Results

In [1], as well as in the above examples, it has been noted that for some systems, the feedback gain matrix elements in case of state derivative feedback are lower in magnitude than those in case of state feedback. This in turn results in lower gain for the feedback amplifier, resulting in a reduction in overall energy consumption. One way to explain this outcome is that a definite amount of effort is required to stabilize an unstable system. In case of state feedback, this effort is provided by just the feedback gain, while in state derivative feedback, a portion of the effort is shared by the derivative part of the feedback. Hence, the corresponding feedback gains in state derivative feedback are smaller. In other words, due to the presence of a derivative in the feedback, the rate of change of the state contributes towards stabilizing the system. This can be verified by the fact that within the same system, the differences between state and state derivative feedback gain constants for different states vary in proportion to their respective rates of changes.

5 Conclusion

In this paper, we have explored the possibilities of using state derivative feedback as an effective tool for designing energy efficient control systems. We have seen that by using state derivative feedback to solve the pole placement problem, the elements of feedback gain matrix are less in magnitude than those of feedback gain matrix obtained from state feedback. This results in reduction of energy consumption of the controller, thereby improving the overall energy efficiency of the control system.

References

1. Abdelaziz, T.H.S., Valášek, M.: Pole placement for SISO linear systems by state-derivative feedback. IEE Proc.-Control Theory Appl. 151(4), 377–385 (2004)
2. Abdelaziz, T.H.S.: Pole assignment by state-derivative feedback for single-input linear systems. In: Proc. IMechE. J. Systems and Control Engineering, vol. 221, part I (2007)
3. Valášek, M., Olgac, N.: An efficient pole-placement technique for linear time invariant SISO systems. IEE Proc., Control Theory Appl. 142(5), 451–458 (1995)
4. Abdelaziz, T.H.S., Valášek, M.: Direct Algorithm for Pole Placement by State-Derivative Feedback for Multi-Input Linear Systems - Nonsingular Case. Kybernetika 41(5), 637–660 (2005)
5. Valášek, M., Olgac, N.: Efficient eigen value assignments for general linear MIMO systems. Automatica 31(11), 1605–1617 (1995)
6. Valášek, M., Olgac, N.: Pole-placement for linear time-varying nonlexicographically fixed MIMO systems. Automatica 35(11), 101–108 (1999)
7. Moreira, M.R., Mainardi Jr., E.I., Esteves, T.T., Teixeira, M.C.M., Cardim, R., Assunção, E., Faria, F.A.: Stabilizability and Disturbance Rejection with State-Derivative Feedback. Mathematical Problems in Engineering 2010, article ID 123751 (2010)
8. Gopal, M.: Control Systems (Principles and Design). Tata McGraw Hill (2008)
9. Ogata, K.: Modern Control Engineering. Phi Learning (2010).
10. Wong, T.: Design of magnetic levitation system-an undergraduate project. IEEE Transactions on Education 29, 196–200 (1986)
11. Lewis, F.L., Syrmos, V.L.: A geometric theory for derivative feedback. IEEE Trans. Autom. Control 36(9), 1111–1116 (1991)
12. Kejval, J., Sika, Z., Valasek, M.: Active vibration suppression of a machine. In: Proc. Conf. on Interaction and Feedback, UT AV Praha, CR, pp. 28–29 (2000)
13. Choudhary, D.R.: Modern Control engineering. Prentice and Hall (2005)
14. Dorf, R.C., Bishop, R.H.: Modern Control Engineering, 8th edn. Addison-Wesley (1999)
15. Mehrmann, V., Hongguo, X.V.: Analysis of the pole placement problem. Electronic Transactions on Numerical Analysis 4, 89–105 (1996)
16. Desoer, C.A., Wang, Y.T.: Linear time-invariant robust servomechanism problem - A self contained exposition. In: Control and Dynamics Systems, pp. 89–129. Academic Press, Inc., New York (1980)
17. Kautsky, J., Nichols, N.K., Van Dooren, P.: Robust pole assignment in linear state feedback. International Journal of Control 41, 1129–1155 (1985)
18. Bugeja, M.: Non-Linear Swing-up and stabilizing control of an Inverted Pendulum sytem. In: Eurocon, IEEE Region 8, vol. 2, pp. 437–441 (2003)

Investigation of Breast Cancer Detection Based on Tissue Sensing Adaptive Radar (TSAR)

Harish Kumar[1], V.N. Pandey[1], Manish Kumar[1], D.K.P. Singh[2], and M.D. Upadhayay[3]

[1] Bhagwant Institute of Technology Muzaffarnagar, India
[2] GL Bajaj Institute of Technology, Greater Noida, India
[3] IIT Delhi, India,
{hc78,madhur_deo}@rediffmail.com, singhdkp@gmail.com

Abstract. This work present an analysis of breast cancer is the commonest cancer in urban and rural areas in India and accounts for about 20% to 25% of all cancers in women. And also investigation of breast cancer detection is based on differences in electrical properties between healthy and malignant tissues. Tissue sensing adaptive radar (TSAR) has been proposed as a method of microwave breast imaging for early tumor detection. TSAR senses all tissues in the volume of interest and adapts accordingly. In this paper, the second generation experimental system for TSAR is presented. Materials with electrical properties similar to those in the breast are used for the breast model. A resistively loaded Wu–King monopole antenna is fabricated, and reflections from the breast model over the frequency range of 1–10 GHz are recorded.

Index Terms*:* Breast cancer detection, experimental verification, microwave imaging, tissue sensing adaptive radar.

1 Introduction

It is very evident from the various statistics, that the incidence of breast cancer is rapidly rising, amounting to a significant percentage of all cancers in women. Breast cancer is the commonest cancer in urban and rural areas in India and accounts for about 20% to 25% of all cancers in women. If these percentages are converted into actual numbers, the numbers are very high. breast cancer is a significant health issue for women and affects one in every seven women in world [1]. The current method of detection is mammography, which involves X-ray imaging of a compressed breast. X-ray mammography creates images of the density of breast tissues and the images are used to locate suspicious areas. Although mammography is the gold standard, concerns related to the false-positive and false-negative rates exist [2]. There is need for a complementary, safe, and reasonably priced method [3]. Microwave breast cancer detection has been introduced as a complementary method for breast cancer detection. Microwave breast cancer detection relies on differences in electrical properties between malignant and fatty tissues as summarized in [4]. Microwave breast imaging methods include hybrid, passive, and active approaches. Hybrid

V.V. Das and N. Thankachan (Eds.): CIIT 2011, CCIS 250, pp. 755–758, 2011.

methods include thermo acoustic tomography, which use microwaves to selectively heat tumors and ultrasound approaches to create images [5]–[7]. One passive approach, microwave radiometry, measures the increased temperature of the tumor compared to the normal tissue [7]–[9]. Active microwave approaches include tomography and radar-based imaging. Microwave tomography records the transmission of waves through the breast and creates an electrical property map of the region of interest [7].

2 Experimental Setup

The experimental system is shown in Fig. 1. The system is composed of a Plexiglas tank, immersion liquid, ground plane, antenna, and breast phantom. The top of the tank is a ground plane, which is implemented to simplify the antenna design. This places limitations on the imaging capabilities of the system; however, this setup is similar to preliminary simulations in [10] In all experiments, reflections from the antenna (S_{11}) are recorded with an 8719ES vector network analyzer (VNA) (Agilent Technologies, Palo Alto, CA) connected to a 50-Ω coaxial cable. Data are recorded at 1601 frequency points and 16 samples are averaged at each frequency. The frequency range over which data are acquired is from 1 to 10 GHz. In the experiment phantom plate (Fig. 2) is rotated in increments of 22.5 or 45.

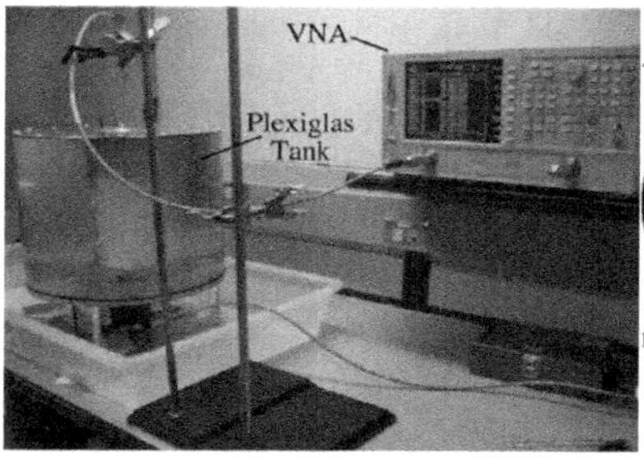

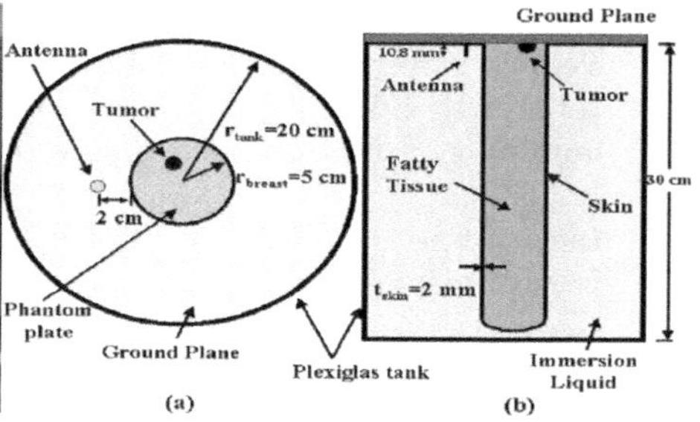

Fig. 1. TSAR experimental system. The tank is shown on the left and the VNA is on the right. The coaxial cable is held with stands to reduce flex and movement.

Fig. 2. Test setup with a monopole antenna, immersion liquid, and breast phantom. (a) Top-down view. (b) Slide view.

2.1 Phantom Materials

Fig 2 shown ,an immersion liquid is needed to improve the match between interior and exterior of the breast. Therefore, the tank is filled with an immersion liquid of canola oil ($\epsilon r = 2.5$ and $\sigma = 0.04$ S/m). Canola oil is similar to the liquid investigated in [8], which provides excellent tumor detection and localization. Additionally, fewer antennas are required to scan a even volume than with a higher permittivity liquid [7-8]. Furthermore, canola oil is minimally dispersive over the frequency range of interest and has low loss.

2.2 Antenna Fabrication

The antenna used to illuminate the breast model is a resistively loaded Wu–King monopole [9]. The monopole has length of 10.8 mm and is designed in a lossless liquid similar to oil with Єr = 3.0. The design and characterization of the antenna are outlined in [8] and [18]. The antenna is fabricated using high-frequency chip resistors (Vishay 0603- HF) (Malvern, PA) soldered to a high frequency substrate (Rogers RO3203 series) (Rogers Corporation, Chandler, AZ). The substrate (Єr = 3.02 and σ = 0.001 S/m) has electrical properties similar to those of the canola.

3 Results and Discussion

Three antennas are fabricated with the same profile and compared to simulations to confirm correct operation. The impedance of the simulated antenna in [8-9] is converted to represent a monopole. The theoretical impedance is calculated from . The voltage standing wave ratios (VSWRs) for the fabricated, simulated, and theoretical antennas are shown in Fig. 3 and 4. The results demonstrate a good match between all fabricated antennas and the simulated antenna. The VSWR is below 2 between 7–10 GHz. The poor VSWRs at lower frequencies are expected as matching to 50Ω were not a design goal.

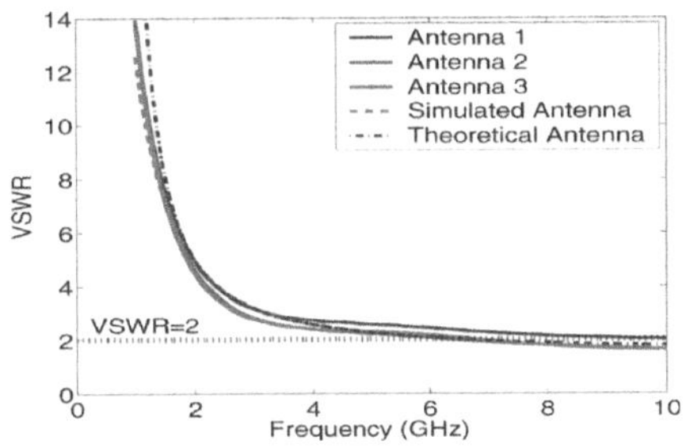

Fig. 3. Experimental, simulated, and theoretical VSWR calculated from the reflection coefficient

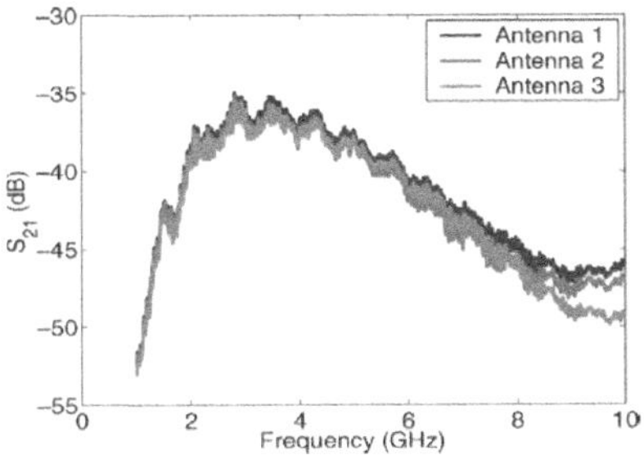

Fig. 4. Transmission between two antennas (S_{21})

The signal-to-clutter ratios for each of the three experiments are shown in Table 1.

Table 1. Signal-To-Clutter Ratios For Each Breast Model

Tumor Size (cm)	Tumor Only (dB)	Skin Tumor (dB)	Skin – Fat - Tumor (dB)
1	7.20	14.37	10.40
2	8.20	14.50	13.74

As expected, the signal-to-clutter ratio decreases as the tumor size decreases. The tumor-only simulations have low signal-to-clutter ratios compared to the skin tumor case as only eight antenna positions are used to create an image. Finally, as the complexity of the system increases, the signal-to-clutter ratios decrease.

4 Conclusion

This paper presents the second-generation TSAR experimental system. Furthermore, this is the most complex breast model currently under investigation for radar-based tumor detection. An improved antenna is under development, and improved performance and directivity are expected. This should increase the tumor detection capabilities of the TSAR system. The materials and methods reported here may be used to develop this realistic model. Finally, a scanning system must be developed to scan the improved antenna around the new model. This may involve a vertical scan in addition to the rotation of the model reported here. Therefore, this paper with a simple model provides a foundation for expansion to a 3-D system.

References

1. Gandhi, O.P., Lazzi, G., Furse, C.: Electromagnetic Absorption in human head and neck for mobile telephones at 835 and 1900 MHz. IEEE Trans. Microwave Theory Tech. 44(10), 1884–1897 (1996)
2. Mammography and Beyond: Developing Technologies for the Early Detection of Breast Cancer. Inst. Med., Nat. Academy Press, Washington, DC (2001)
3. Saving Women's Lives: Strategies for Improving Breast Cancer Detection and Diagnosis. Inst. Med., Nat. Academy Press, Washington, DC (2004)
4. Fear, E.C.: Microwave imaging of the breast. Technol. Cancer Res. Treat. 4(1), 69–82 (2005)
5. Kruger, R.A., Kpoecky, K.K., Aisen, A.M., Reinecke, D.R., Kruger, G.A., Kiser Jr., W.L.: Thermo acoustic CT with radio waves: A medical imaging paradigm. Radiology 211(1), 275–278 (1999)
6. Wang, L.V., Zhao, X., Sun, H., Ku, G.: Microwave-induced acoustic imaging of biological tissues. Rev. Sci. Instrum. 70(9), 3744–3748 (1999)
7. Fear, E.C., Hagness, S.C., Meaney, P.M., Okoniewski, M., Stuchly, M.A.: Enhancing breast tumor detection with near-field imaging. IEEE Micro 3(1), 48–56 (2002)
8. Sill, J.M., Fear, E.C.: Tissue sensing adaptive radar for breast cancer detection: A study of immersion liquid. Electron. Lett. 41(3), 113–115 (2005)
9. Sill, J.M., Williams, T.C., Fear, E.C.: Tissue sensing adaptive radar for breast tumor detection: Investigation of issues for system implementation. In: Int. Zurich Electromagnetic Compatibility Symp., Zurich, Switzerland, pp. 71–74 (February 2005)
10. Fear, E.C., Stuchly, M.A.: Microwave system for breast tumor detection. IEEE Microw. Guided Wave Lett. 9(11), 470–472 (1999)
11. Sill, J.M.: Second generation experimental system for tissue sensing adaptive radar, M.S. thesis, Univ. Calgary, Calgary, AB, Canada (2005)

Segregation of Colored Objects Using Industrial Robotic Arm

Manish Chhabra, Abhishek Gupta, Anubhav Mangal and Parminder Singh Reel

Electronics and Communication Engineering Department
Thapar University, Patiala -147001, India
{manish_chh,anubhav965}@yahoo.co.in,
{abhishek.gupta0211,parminder.reel}@gmail.com

Abstract. There is a great need of reducing human effort in each and every span of industrial engineering. The paper deals in a robotic arm that fetches objects from a conveyor belt and does some dedicated work say packing the objects in the same color of packaging as that of object or segregating the objects on the basis of color or geometry. An overhead camera is mounted perpendicular to the belt at some specified height which would be sending recorded images to the processing unit and processing unit would be instructing the robotic arm to pick up some objects. The processing unit uses image processing to instruct the arm.

Keywords: Color detection, watershed, threshold, robotic arm, MATLAB GUI.

1 Introduction

Robotics can not only affect labor of unskilled workers but have a significant influence on professional engineers and managers of production. The day is not far when the use and involvement of robotics in each and every field would be so prominent as that of mobiles or computers in today's world. We are living in an era in which technology has given us the choice to replace the past long system of manual labor and switch towards the world of robotics.

2 Robotic Arm Basics

The robotic arm's main components are the arm itself, which may have several segments; the joints (called axes), which are located between segments; the "hand" (called the end effecter or end-of-arm tooling); and software that tells the arm what to do. The robotic arm is mounted on a base that can be installed on the floor, ceiling, or wall or in a metal framework — whatever best suits your plant layout. The arm also has a power source, most commonly an electric motor, and it has wiring and various electrical and electronic components that allow it to perform its functions, direct it, and enable operators to interact with it[1].

V.V. Das and N. Thankachan (Eds.): CIIT 2011, CCIS 250, pp. 759–761, 2011.

2.1 Working of Image Processing

In the proposed algorithm the robotic arm must pick up any specified color object for instance let's take the case of picking up of balls say blue in color.

Image Processing Algorithm: The image acquired from the capturing device is fed in the image processing algorithm running in the microprocessor unit [2]. The basic information to extract from the image is the color detection and the co-ordinates of the required object. Color is detected by using HSV color detection algorithm.

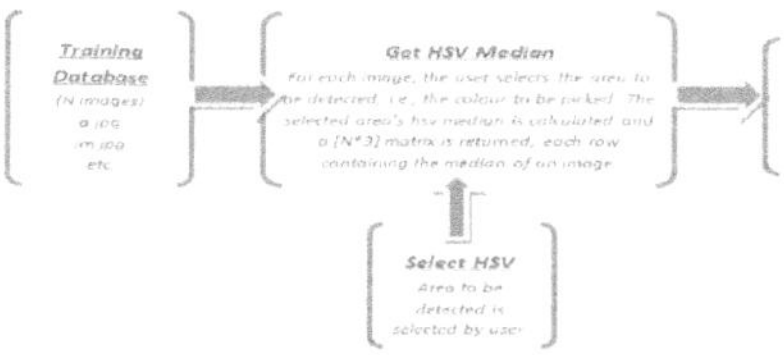

Fig. 1a. Training of the system with HSV values of the required pixels/color

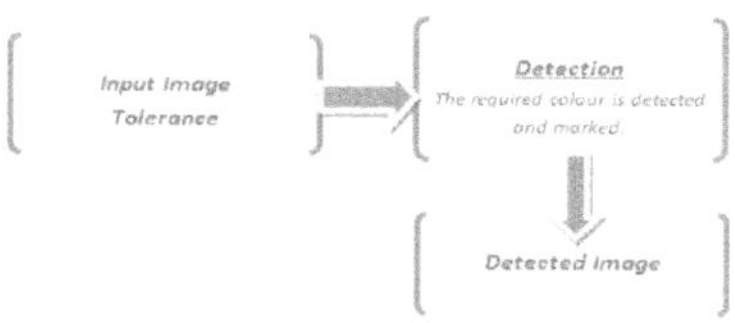

Fig. 1b. Detection of required pixels/color

Now grain boundaries function is used to calculate the centroid of this blue ball. Once its generated, calculations are done to get the time for which actuators are to be powered to generate the required motion. Once the centroid and other properties are detected to position the object, distance is calculated between the present position of arm and the position desired to pick the object.

$$Distance = \sqrt{(x_2 - x_1)^2 + (y_2 - y_1)^2} \tag{1}$$

The distance is calculated between pixels and then converted into real dimensions.

2.2 GUI (Graphical User Interface)

A GUI is made for the operation of the robotic arm. The arm is completely autonomous but in case of any problem, the user can interrupt its algorithm by using the GUI. The GUI displays the video of live camera. The motion of conveyor belt and arm can be seized by using STOP button[3]. Then the arm can be navigated by using emergency controls and the object can be gripped or cab be freed from the grip by using PICK/DROP button. Also, if the algorithm is not trained properly for the color then user can input the RGB values of the required color which are converted in HSV by following relations:

M=max(R,G,B)
m=min(R,G,B)
r=(M-R)/(M-m)
g=(M-G)/(M-m)
b=(M-B)/(M-m)
Value Calculation
[V](range 0 to 1)
V = max(R,G,B)
Saturation
Calculation [S]
(range 0 to 1)
if M = 0 then S = 0
and H = 180 degrees
if M <> 0 then S =
(M - m) / M
Hue Calculation [H]

(hue range of 0 to
360)
if R = M then H =
60(b-g)
if G = M then H =
60(2+r-b)
if B = M then H =
60(4+g-r)
if H >= 360 then H =
H - 360
if H < 0 then H = H
+ 3

2.3 Watershed Algorithm

With the repaid advancement of computer technology, the use of computer-based technologies is increasing in different fields of life. Image segmentation is an important problem in different fields of image processing and computer vision. Image segmentation is the process of dividing images according to its characteristic e.g., colour and objects present in the images. Different methods are presented for image segmentation. This is done by watershed algorithm[4].

3 Observation and Analysis

The overall algorithm was tested and analyzed under two conditions, i.e., with and without watershed to distinguish overlapping objects and HSV training of the algorithm to detect colour. A table is formulated for the same elaborating different parameters thus obtained. According to table.1, although the time required evaluating single frame is more with complex algorithm but the effectiveness has a spectacular increase thus overshadowing the increase in run time

Parameters	Without Watershed and HSV training	With Watershed and HSV training
Successful objects detected (out of 10)	5	8
Error in position detection (x-coordinate, y-coordinate respectively)	3.8%, 4.25%	1.2%, 1.7%
Distinguish between overlapping objects	No	Yes
Colour detection success rate (out of 10)	4	9
Overall time required for execution of one frame	548 ms	673 ms
Overall effectiveness of algorithm	67%	89%

Table 1. Observations

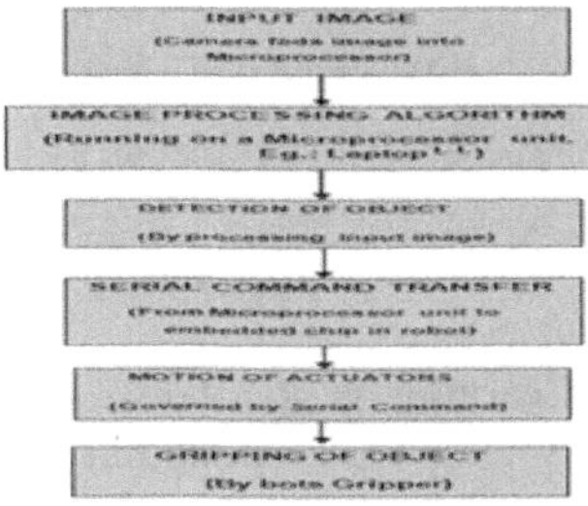

Fig 2. Algorithm

References

1. Ferrarini, L., Veber, C.: Design and implementation of distributed hierarchical automation and control systems with IEC 61499. In: 3nd IEEE Int. Conf. on Industrial Informatics (INDIN 2005), Perth, Australia (August 2005)
2. Papanikolopoulus, N.P., Khosla, P.K., Kanade, T.: Visual tracking of a moving target by a camera mounted on a robot: a combination of control and vision. IEEE Trans. on Robotics and Automation 9, 14–35 (1993)
3. Adaptive technique for human face detection using HSV color space and neural networks, ISSN: 1110-6980, Print ISBN: 978-1-4244-4214-0
4. Bencina, R., Kaltenbrunner, M., Jorda, S.: Improved topological fiducial tracking in the reactivision system. In: Proceedings of IEEE Conference on Computer Vision and Pattern Recognition, vol. 3, pp. 99–106 (2005)

Social Networking: A New Vision of E-Learning

Manish Chhabra[1], Abhishek Gupta[1], Anubhav Mangal[1], Prateek Mehrotra[2], and Parminder Singh Reel[1]

[1] Electronics and Communication Engineering Department
Thapar University, Patiala -147001, India
[2] Jaypee University of Information Tech., Waknaghat, Distt. Solan.
{manish_chh,anubhav965}@yahoo.co.in,
{abhishek.gupta0211,prtkmehrotra,parminder.reel}@gmail.com

Abstract. The paper aims at promoting e-learning through most popular websites of the era, better known as Social Networks. The focus of the research is to build a common platform where every individual be it be a technician or an industrialist or may be a student can share their ideas and resources with an ease of troubleshooting and problem handling. In addition to it, the help fetched from the server can facilitate video call support to enhance the overall scenario.

Keywords: e-learning, social networking, domain, knowledge, website.

1 E-Learning: Introduction

E-Learning is a kind of learning that comes from involvement and interaction between people through an electronic medium whose domain would be worldwide. It helps and encourages the people to share their ideas and help the people who are in a dilemma The reason for this is that now the profession of teaching is taken by a few people due to less salary, monotonous work, etc. So it is mandatory to increase the number of e-learning sites which can educate people. Online courses allow students to learn at their own pace[1]. Professors could conceivably be shared in an inter university environment, freeing up knowledge resources, reducing travel time and expense, and even alleviating the need for classroom space[2].

2 Social Networking

Social networking is the alignment of persons into specific groups, like small rural communities or a neighborhood subdivision, if you will. Depending on the website, many of these online community members are differentiated on the basis of common interests in hobbies, religion, or politics[3]. One of the many benefits to social networking online is that you can make friends, join communities which interest you, can chat with the people who are your friends, etc. The advantage to social networking in not restricted to making friends but can also help the persons to exchange their cultures. As mentioned, social networking often involves grouping specific individuals or organizations together[4]. This can easily be done by

V.V. Das and N. Thankachan (Eds.): CIIT 2011, CCIS 250, pp. 762–764, 2011.

performing a standard internet search. Your search will likely return a number of results, including MySpace, FriendWise, FriendFinder, Yahoo! 360, Facebook, Orkut, and Classmates[5].

3 Our Prospective

The main aim is to use social networking as a tool for e-learning in a specific manner by building up a platform for all the existing professional and technical fields, including almost all the age groups. Also, they are equipped with very limited flexibility and lacks in user interaction. The main feature of this upcoming e-learning domain would be:

3.1 Includes All the Professions, Researches and Studies

The domain is intended to sub-divide itself into different fields of interest of all the target audience. The individual will categories himself in his specific fields and so will get all the updates and posts from his realm of interest.

3.2 Ease to Join the Domain

If any individual is a member of any of the existing social networking site, his database will be extracted from that server after fetching proper privileges from the user and an automatic profile for that individual will be created on this domain.

3.3 Source of Employment

From this domain/platform; teachers, professionals, experts and trainers from different fields can be employed.

3.4 The Share and Access Flexibility

One of the basic features of this domain is that people can share notes, audio/video lectures, live webinars and links to databases.

4 Website

A prototype website is made on local area network and tested. Some screenshots are given below. The site is named as SOCNET. Fig. 2(a) shows the main page of the site. A person can select his field of interest from this page.

Fig.2(b) shows the shared notes of a profile. Anyone can comment on the shared documents and download to use them. Fig.2(c) shows the audio video chatting zone. Here any person can chat and seek help from his friends or friends of friends. One can even make a conference call or chat to make the session more interactive. Fig.2(d) gives the screenshot of the discussion blog of the site.

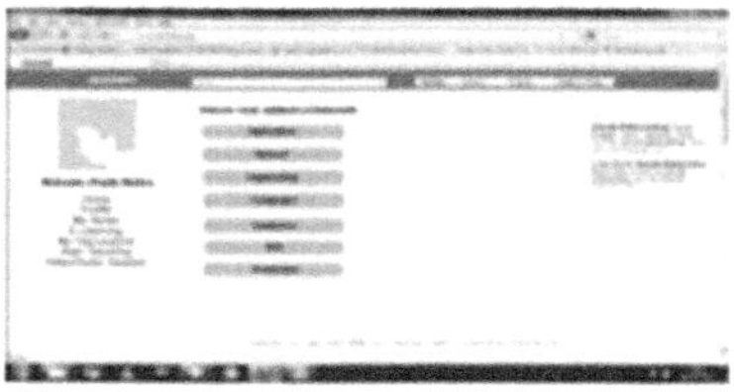

Fig.2(a) Main page of the site

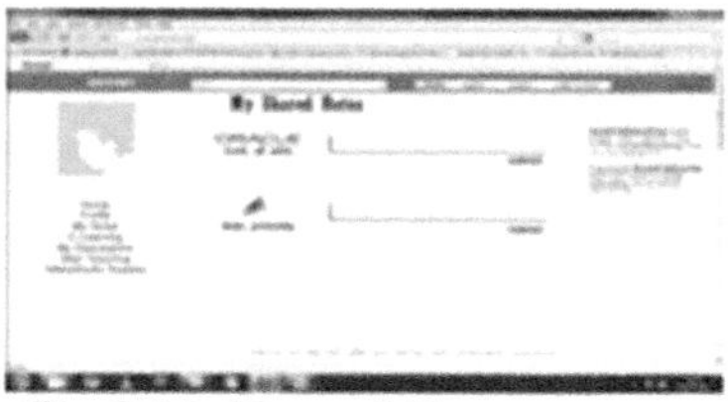

Fig.2(b) Shared Documents

Fig.2(c) Audio/Video Chatting Zone

Fig.2(d) Discussion

5 Conclusion

The proposal of this domain will bridge up the gap between different fields and will out stretch the realms of knowledge for everyone associated through it. As many developing countries have a huge illiteracy rate, so such kind of approach can be of a big help. Not only it wide spreads literacy but also generates employment and revenue.

References

1. Nazir, A., Raza, S., Chuah, C.N.: Unveiling Facebook: AMeasurement Study of Social Network Based Applications. In: Proceedings of the 8th ACM SIGCOMM Conference on Internet Measurement. ACM (2008)
2. Brown, B.C.: The Secret Power of Blogging: How to Promoteand Market Your Business. Atlantic Publishing Group, Inc. (2007)
3. Harrison, R., Thomas, M.: Identity in online communities: Social networking sites and language learning. International Journal of Emerging Technologies and Society 7(2), 109–124 (2009)
4. Huang, D.C., Behara, R.S.: Outcome-driven experimental learning with web 2.0. Journal of Information Systems Education 18(3), 329–336 (2007)
5. Kaplan, A., Haenlein, M.: Users of the world, unite! The challenges and opportunities of social media. Business Horizons 53(1), 59–68 (2010)

A Covariance Matrix Adapted Evolution Strategy Based Solution to Optimal Power Flow Plus Transmission Charging

J. Bastin Solai Nazaran[1] and K. Selvi[2]

[1] Department of Electrical and Electronics Engineering, Syed Ammal Engineering College, Ramanathapuram, Tamilnadu, India

[2] Department of Electrical and Electronics Engineering, Thiagarajar College of Engineering, Madurai, Tamilnadu, India

Abstract. The main objective of the paper is to minimize the overall operating cost while satisfying the power flow constraints, system security and equipments operating limits. The operating cost includes generation cost, transmission cost and consumer benefit. CMAES (Covariance matrix adapted evolution strategy) algorithm has been used as optimization tool to solve the problem. Newton Raphson's method is used to calculate power mismatch, loss and bus voltages. Power flow tracing method is used to find transmission cost. A nine bus, three generator power system is taken as test system.

Keywords: CMAES, optimal power flow, power flow tracing, transmission charging.

1 Introduction

The objective of optimal power flow is to find the optimal settings of a given power system that optimizes the system objective functions such as total generation cost, system loss, bus voltage deviation, emission of generating units, number of control actions, and load shedding while satisfying its power flow equations, system security, and equipment operating limits. Different control variables, such as generators ' real power outputs and voltages, transformer tap changing settings, phase shifters, switched capacitors, and reactors, are adjusted to achieve an optimal setting based on the problem [1]. The power system must be secure to withstand the loss of some or several transmission lines, transformers or generators, such events are often termed as *credible* contingencies. To determine the credible contingencies, in this paper a contingency ranking is used [2]. Combining the previous two problems is termed the optimal power flow with security constraints (OPF-SC). Through an optimal power flow formulation, a method for computing the optimal pre- and post-contingency operating points is presented. Nowadays, with the electrical power industry deregulation, the transmission system can be considered as an independent transmission company that provides open access to all participants. Fair allocation of transmission cost is expected. Different methods to allocate transmission costs among network users have been applied worldwide [3,4]. This paper employs a power flow

V.V. Das and N. Thankachan (Eds.): CIIT 2011, CCIS 250, pp. 765–769, 2011.

tracing based transmission pricing scheme [5,6] to estimate the actual contribution of generators to each flow in the branches. Conventional methods used to solve OPF-SC ended with local optimum due to their initial guess. The theoretical assumptions behind such algorithms may be not suitable for the OPF-SC formulation. Optimization methods such as evolutionary programming (EP), genetic algorithms (GA) and particle swarm optimizer (PSO) have been employed to overcome such drawbacks. For solving the OPF-SC, a particle swarm optimizer with reconstruction operators (PSO-RO) is proposed [7]. For handling constraints, such reconstruction operators plus an external penalization are adopted. In this paper a CMAES algorithm based optimal power flow with transmission cost solution is proposed. CMAES is becoming popular in recent times for solving non-convex / non-smooth engineering optimization problems [8].

2 Objective Function

2.1 Objective Function

In this paper, the minimization of the total cost includes the pre contingency cost (C^0) besides each credible contingency cost (C^k). Thus, the objective function is comprised by three terms: (i) the generating costs, (ii) the transmission costs, and (iii) the consumer benefit

$$F = \min\left\{C^0 + \sum_{k=1}^{K} C^k\right\} \tag{1}$$

$$C^0 = \sum_{i=1}^{NG} f\left(P_{Gi}^0\right) + TC^0 - \sum_{j=1}^{ND} B(P_{Dj}^0) \tag{2}$$

$$C^k = \sum_{i=1}^{NG} f\left(P_{Gi}^k\right) + TC^k - \sum_{j=1}^{ND} B(P_{Dj}^k) \tag{3}$$

where k is the total number of credible contingencies; C^0 represents the base case operating cost; NG is the total number of available generators; $f(P_{Gi}^0)$ i-th generator's function cost ; P_{Gi}^0 active power supplied by the i-th generator at the pre-contingency state, TC^0 pre-contingency transmission cost, ND total number of load buses, $B(P_{Dj}^0)$ is the consumer benefit curve for j-th load; P_{Dj}^0 pre-contingency active power consumption at the j-th load; C^k credible contingencies' cost; P_{Gi}^k active power supplied by the i-th generator at the post-contingency state , P_{Dj}^k post-contingency active power consumption at the j-th load; TC^k post-contingency transmission cost.

$$TC_i = \sum_{m=1}^{nlines} c_m(MW_{gi,m}) L_m MW_{gi,m} \tag{4}$$

where, $c_m(\cdot)$ cost per MW per unit length of line m; L_m length of line m in miles; $MW_{gi,m}$ flow in line m, due to the i-th generator.

2.2 Constraints

2.2.1 Equality Constraints

This is the set of nonlinear power balance equations that govern the steady-state power flow formulation, both at pre- and post-contingency state, defined as follows

$$\sum_{i=1}^{NG} P_{Gi} - \sum_{j=1}^{ND} P_{Di} - P_{loss} = 0 \tag{5}$$

$$\sum_{i=1}^{NG} Q_{Gi} - \sum_{j=1}^{ND} Q_{Di} - Q_{loss} = 0 \tag{6}$$

2.2.2 Inequality Constraints

(i) Active power Generation of each units must be within limits

$$P_{Gi\_\min} \le P_{Gi} \le P_{Gi\_\max} \tag{7}$$

(ii) Voltage at load buses must be within limits

$$V_{j\_\min} \le V_j \le V_{j\_\max} \tag{8}$$

(iii) The active power flow through each branch of the network must satisfy the security limits

$$Flow_{ij} \le Flow_{ij\_\max} \tag{9}$$

3 Transmission Cost Allocation

To allocate transmission cost power flow tracing method proposed by Bialek [5] is used. This method uses a topological approach to determine the contribution of individual generators or loads to every line flow based on the calculation of topological distribution factors. In this method, it is assumed that nodal inflows are shared proportionally among nodal outflows. This is known as proportional sharing principle and proved on game theoretic background. This tracing method can deal with both DC-power flow and AC power flows; that is, it can be used to find contributions of both active and reactive power flows. Proportional sharing principle considers i) two flows in each line, one entering the line and the other exiting the line ii) generation and load at each bus.

4 Covariance Matrix Adapted Evolution Strategy

CMAES is proposed by Nikolaus Hansen and Ostermeier in1996 [9]. CMAES algorithm is derived from the concept of self-adaptation in evolution strategies. The basic Evolutionary Strategy generates solutions around the parents, but CMAES keeps track of the evolution path. For every generation it updates mean location of the population, covariance matrix and the standard deviation of the sampling normal distribution. The solutions are ranked. Solutions contribute according to their ranks to the updating of the mean position, covariance matrix, and the step-size parameter. Covariance analysis finds the interactions among the parameters. For detailed explanation refer [9].

5 Proposed Methodology

Step 1: Create Random candidate solutions within limits.
Step 2: For each candidate solution perform a NR power flow
Step 3: Apply power flow tracing method to find contribution of generators to lines and find transmission cost
Step 4: Calculate Fitness function value for the solution using (1)
Step 5: Apply CMAES algorithm steps to obtain best fitness and its solution.

6 Test System and Results

The proposed solution is implemented in MATLAB and the nine bus system [10] is used to validate the result and its single line diagram is shown in Fig.1. Line outage $L_{8\text{-}9}$ is considered as contingency. Results for pre contingency and post contingency cases are tabulated in Table 1&2.Standard deviation for control variables lay between

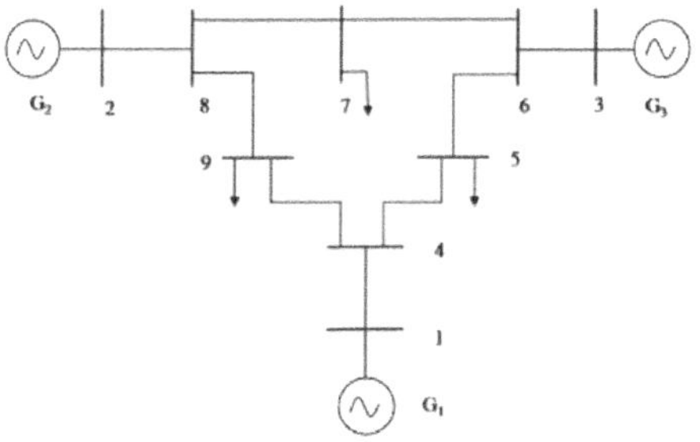

Fig. 1. Single line diagram of nine bus Test System

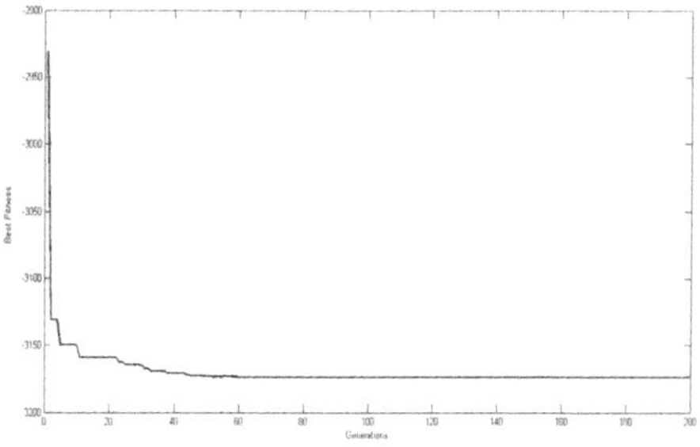

Fig. 2. Convergence characteristics of CMAES algorithm for nine bus system

Table 1. Share of Transmission Cost on post contingency using Power Flow Tracing

Line m	Line cost $	$MW_{G1,m}$	$MW_{G2,m}$	$MW_{G3,m}$	TC_{G1}	TC_{G2}	TC_{G3}
$L_{1\text{-}4}$	0.60	203.0845	0	0	121.8507	0	0
$L_{4\text{-}5}$	2.40	97.0434	0	0	232.9042	0	0
$L_{5\text{-}6}$	2.80	0	0	22.5995	0	0	63.2786
$L_{3\text{-}6}$	1.20	0	0	81.9084	0	0	98.2901
$L_{6\text{-}7}$	0.30	0	0	59.3089	0	0	17.7927
$L_{7\text{-}8}$	2.40	0	25	0	0	60	0
$L_{8\text{-}2}$	0.60	0	25	0	0	15	0
$L_{8\text{-}9}$	2.80	0	0	0	0	0	0
$L_{9\text{-}4}$	0.30	106.0411	0	0	31.8123	0	0
Transmission Cost for each Generators $					386.567	75	179.361
Total Transmission Cost $					640.928		

Table 2. Optimal Generation and Fitness value

	Pre contingency	Post contingency $L_{8\text{-}9}$ out
P_{G1} MW	202.43	203.08
P_{G2} MW	25.00	25.00
P_{G3} MW	82.27	81.91
P_{loss} MW	3.19	3.48
Transmission Cost $	640.856	640.928
Fitness $	-3173.7	

1.2e-8 & 4.7e-4. From the table 1 it is observed that each line gets its contribution from single generator. Generator 2 contributes only for $L_{7\text{-}8}$ and $L_{8\text{-}2}$ power flow and transmission cost for this generator is low due to line outage.

7 Conclusions

The given problem is a complex problem which includes both normal and credible contingency cases. This objective function minimizes overall cost of operation. A fair allocation of transmission cost is performed using power flow tracing method instead of embedded cost methods. CMAES algorithm is used to solve the problem because of its good convergence characteristics. The Results shows consistency over different runs.

References

1. Zhu, J.: Optimization of Power System Operation. John Wiley & Sons, New York (2009)
2. Wood, A.J., Wollenberg, B.: Power Generation Operation and Control, 2nd edn. John Wiley & Sons, New York (1996)
3. Shahidehpour, M., Yamin, H., Li, Z.: Market Operation in Electric Power Systems. John Wiley & Sons Inc., New York (2002)
4. Junqueira, M., Da Costa, L.C., Barroso, L.A., Olivera, G.C., Thomé, L.M., Pereira, M.V.: An Aumann–Shapley approach to allocate transmission service cost among network users in electricity markets. IEEE Transactions on Power Systems 22, 1532–1546 (2007)
5. Bialek, J.: Tracing the flow of electricity. IEE Proceedings Generation Transmission and Distribution 143, 313–320 (1996)
6. Kirschen, D., Allan, R., Strbac, G.: Contribution of individual generations to loads and flows. IEEE Transactions on Power Systems 12, 52–60 (1997)
7. Pablo Onate, Y., Ramirez, J.M., Coello, C.A.C.: An optimal power flow plus transmission costs solution. Electric Power Systems Research 79(8), 1240–1246 (2009)
8. Visalakshi, S., Baskar, S.: Covariance matrix adapted evolution strategy based decentralized congestion management for multilateral transactions. IET Generation, Transmission and Distribution 4(3), 400–417 (2010)
9. Hansen, N.: The CMA evolution strategy: a comparing review. Studies in Fuzziness Soft Comput. 192, 75–102 (2006)
10. Anderson, P.M., Fouad, A.A.: Power system Control and Stability, 1st edn. Iowa state university press (1977)

Real Time Online Banking Fraud Detection Using Location Information

Nadeem Akhtar and Farid ul Haq

Department of Computer Engineering, Aligarh Muslim University,
Aligarh, India
{nadeemalakhtar,faridulhaq}@gmail.com

Abstract. This paper presents a location based approach for user authentication in online banking environment. The physical location of the user is identified using two different methods. Firstly, IP geo-location of user's computer system is used. Secondly, User is assumed to have a mobile device, which is used to identify the current physical location of the user. Both locations are used to determine whether mobile device or user is near to the computer system, which is being used for transaction. Based on this information, legal user is authenticated implicitly.

Keywords: Location based Authentication, IP geo-location, GPS, Online Bank Fraud.

1 Introduction

The amount of money lost to online banking fraud is continuously increasing every year. According to financial fraud action UK [1], the amount of money lost to online banking fraud last year rose by 14%. Total losses on UK cards fell by 28% between 2008 and 2009. Most of the banks generally use one of the three types of authentication methods: First," What you know" type of authentication requires a username and associated password. Second, "What you have" type of authentication requires some kind of card. Third, "Who you are" type of authentication require some biometric information like facial or fingerprints. In this paper, a new method based on "Where you are" type of authentication method, although very simple but promising, is proposed to identify potential frauds. This technique exploits the fact that almost every bank customer possesses a mobile phone.

2 Literature Review

Recently, location information has started to be used for authentication purpose. Some banks and online retailers use a kind of location based authentication that use IP geo-location of the computer system to detect possible credit card fraud by comparing the user's location to the billing address on the account or the shipping address provided. In [2], a puzzle-based authentication scheme is implemented. In this scheme, the server asks dynamic location-based questions and the client answers them based on

V.V. Das and N. Thankachan (Eds.): CIIT 2011, CCIS 250, pp. 770–772, 2011.

the proposed route of travel. In [3], two new space-time authentication techniques are proposed. First technique called STAT I uses GPS system and the second technique (STAT II) uses proprietary communication technology IQRF for position determination.

3 Proposed Method

In the proposed method, Location of the customer is identified in two different ways. First approach identifies the customer location using customer computer system IP. Second approach exploits the fact that almost all the online banking and card users own some kind of mobile phone. Mobile phone may be a smart phone, personal digital assistant (PDA) or a simple cellular phone. These mobile devices are used to identify present location of customer. These two approaches are explained below.

3.1 IP Geo-Location

Geo-location technology provides the absolute geographic location by IP address of the computer system from which the transaction is made in real-time. By using the IP-Location database, location of the customer is known after the IP address is transformed into physical location. There are a number of free and paid subscription geo-location databases, ranging from country level to state or city - including ZIP/post code level - each with varying claims of accuracy. Some services that make use of IP-location database are available online provided by companies [4].

3.2 Mobile Phone Location

In the second way, location of the user is identified using mobile phone. Three types of connection can be used to identify the location of mobile device: Global Positioning System (GPS), Wi-Fi triangulation and cellular triangulation. All the personal digital assistants (PDA) and smart phones support GPS and Wi-Fi. A GPS receiver uses information transmitted by three or four satellites which continuously transmit their orbital position and the time of transmission. The receiver uses the messages it receives to determine the transit time of each message and computes the distance to each satellite. These distances along with the satellites' locations are used to compute the position of the receiver [5]. There have been several companies like Skyhook Wireless [6] that offer Wireless Positioning Services that uses signal strength from various Wi-Fi hotspots to access a database of known locations of access points. Wi-Fi triangulation can give better results than GPS in urban areas where GPS signals find it difficult to penetrate into high buildings. For simple cellular phones, several techniques are available that use received signal strength (RSS) from the mobile phone [7]. These techniques exploit the fact that a mobile phone always communicates wirelessly with one of the closest base stations. Any one of the above method can be used to find the location depending on the type of mobile phone. GPS can be combined with Wi-Fi or cellular triangulation to achieve more accurate results in urban areas.

3.3 Comparison of Both Locations

Both of the user locations are compared and accordingly actions may be taken. If both locations are same then user is authenticated. Otherwise, security risk on the basis of difference between both locations is calculated. On the basis of security risk calculated, user may be abandoned or other security measures may be taken to authenticate the user. Accuracy of the proposed location based authentication system depends on the level of location details that is found using IP geo-location and mobile phone. Mobile phone with GPS can provide exact location in the range of 10 meters. Wi-Fi and cellular signals can also provide good location within the range of 100 meters in urban areas using triangulation of multiple receivers (access points or base stations). It may not always be possible to locate the user computer system exactly using its IP address. Sometimes it may provide location details up to city level. So it is necessary to define the level of sameness of the two obtained locations. Depending upon the level of sameness security risk associated can be calculated.

4 Conclusions and Future Work

In this paper, a simple location based authentication method is proposed for banking environment that utilises user computer system IP and mobile phone. The authentication process can be used for online banking, credit and debit card processing where a computer system is being used. This system cannot be used in circumstances where user uses his PDA or smart phone for banking transactions because two different locations cannot be obtained then.

References

1. Financial Fraud Action UK Report (2010), `http://www.financialfraudaction.org.uk/financial-landing.asp`
2. Sharma, Seema: Location Based Authentication. University of New Orleans Theses and Dissertations. Paper 141 (2005)
3. Jaros, D., Kuchta, R.: New Location-Based Authentication Techniques in the Access Management. In: 2010 6th International Conference on Wireless and Mobile Communications, Valencia, Spain, September 20-September 25 (2010)
4. `http://www.maxmind.com/app/ip-location`
5. Zur Bonsen, G., Ammann, D., Ammann, M., Favey, E., Flammant, P.: Continuous Navigation Combining GPS with Sensor-Based Dead Reckoning. GPS World (April 01, 2005), `http://www.skyhookwireless.com/`
6. Wang, S., Min, J., Yi, B.K.: Location Based Services for Mobiles: Technologies and Standards. In: IEEE International Conference on Communication (ICC), Beijing, China (2008)

Matlab Based Modelling of Body Sensor Network Using ZigBee Protocol

G.R. Kanagachidambaresan[2], V.R. Sarma Dhulipala[1,*], D. Vanusha[2], and M.S. Udhaya[2]

[1] Centre for Convergence of Technologies,
[2] Pervasive Computing Technologies
Anna University of Technology, Tiruchirappalli
{kanagachidambaresan,dvrsarma,d.vanusha.cse, udhayacse23}@gmail.com

Abstract. This paper presents the Matlab based modelling of Body Sensor Network (BSN). The body sensor network helps in monitoring the patient remotely without disturbing the activity of the patient. The EEG signal, heart beat and pulse rate are mathematically derived and the signal is transmitted using IEEE 802.15.4 ZIGBEE protocol. The Percentage rms difference between the send and the received signal is calculated. The EEG, heart beat and pulse rate are being simulated using Matlab 7.10 version.

Keywords: Body Sensor Network, ZigBee, Modelling, Matlab.

1 Introduction

Body sensor network is developing in the modern era for the monitoring of many applications. The body sensor network is especially used for monitoring the patient in the hospital. This technology enables the healthcare and diseases to be detected in advance and helps the patient early discharge from the hospital and enables continuous monitoring even out of hospital [1-5]. The development of wireless body sensor networks offers a tool to establish, surgical and post surgical monitoring and represents the remote diagnostic tool. BSN patient monitoring systems will provide information that is likely to be important and that is to be continuously monitored using ZigBee. [6-8].

2 Proposed Model

The heartbeat, pulse rate, and EEG signals are developed using the time domain analysis, the derived mathematical equation is used in Matlab to generate the EEG, HB and Pulse rate signal. The generated analog signal is converted to digital signal and transmitted using IEEE 802.15.4 ZIGBEE protocol. The physiological signal and the mathematical description of the sensor node as follows. Time Domain Analysis of heart beat and pulse rate.

* Corresponding author.

V.V. Das and N. Thankachan (Eds.): CIIT 2011, CCIS 250, pp. 773–776, 2011.

$$HB_{\Psi}(t,\text{a}) = \frac{1}{a}\int_{-\infty}^{-\infty} s(t)\Psi(t-t_a)dt \quad (1)$$

Where
$\Psi(t)$- width of order of scale
a → order of scale
t_a → Centred at line
s(t) → Time Services
Solving the above equation

$$HB_{\Psi}(s,\text{a}) = \frac{1}{2a}[\text{S(s)}.\Psi(s)] \quad (2)$$

$$PR_{\Psi}(s,\text{a}) = \frac{1}{2a}[\text{S(s)}.\Psi(s)] \quad (3)$$

Equations (1),(2) & (3) are used to generate Hear Beat, Pulse Rate, EEG in Matlab. The modelled equations are being simulated using matlab software. The output signal is being sent via the ZigBee communication module as shown in the figure 1. True Time simulator is used in simulation of ZigBee for communicating the signal wirelessly. The signals are fused and sent through the transmitter. The receiver receives the signal and the received signal is reconstructed.

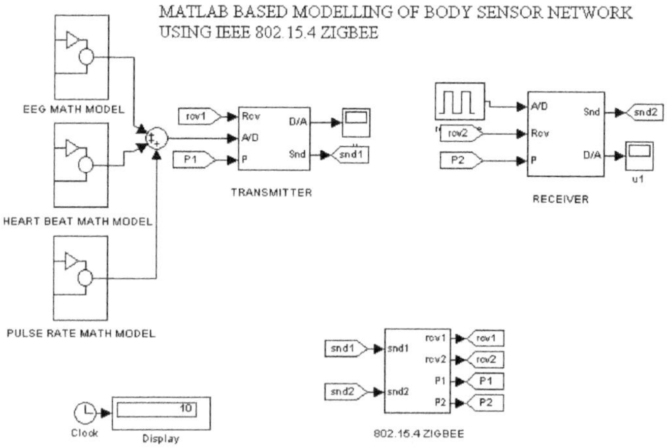

Fig. 1. Matlab simulation diagram IEEE 802.15.4 ZIGBEE Protocol

2.1 Percentrms Difference

Following equation represents the percentage rms difference from [9],

$$\text{PRD} = \sqrt{\frac{\sum_{1=0}^{N-1}(x(i)-x\hat{}(i))^2}{\sum_{1=0}^{N-1}(x(i)-\mu)^2}} \text{ x } 100\% \quad (4)$$

Where
PRD- Percent rms Difference
x(n)- rms signal sensed by the bio sensors
x^(n)- rms signal of the reproduced waveform.
μ- Base line value of analog to digital conversion
equation 4 is used to represent the rms difference of sent and received signal.

3.2 Results and Discussion

The Peak rms difference between the sent and received signal is tabulated and shown in Fig 2. The error during transmission of the Heart Beat, Pulse Rate and EEG signals are calculated using the equation 4. The Percent rms difference indicates the rms difference between sent and received signal. The future work of this paper can include more physiological signals.

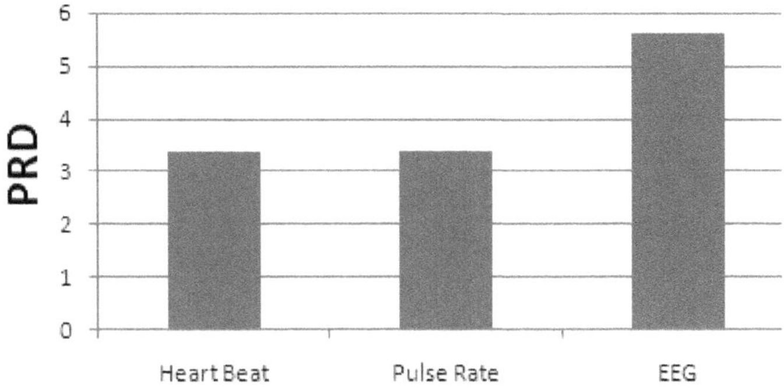

Fig. 2. PRD of the generated and received signal

References

1. Martin, T., Jovanov, E., Raskovic, D.: Issues in wearable computing for medical monitoring applications: A case study of a wearable ECG monitoring device. Presented at the Int. Symp. Wearable Computing, Atlanta, GA (October 2000)
2. Janani, K., Sarma Dhulipala, V.R., Chandrasekaran, R.M.: WSN based framework for Human Health Monitorings. In: Proceedings of IEEE International Conference ICDeCoM – 2011, Mesra, Ranchi, India (2011); doi: 10.1109/ICDECOM.2011.57384530, Print ISBN: 978-1-4244-9189-6
3. Milenkovic, A., Otto, C., Jovanov, E.: Wireless sensor network for personal health monitoring: Issues and an implementation. J. Comput.Commun. 29(13/14), 2521–2533 (2006)
4. Rasid, M.F.A., Woodward, B.: Bluetooth telemedicine processor for multi-channel biomedical signal transmission via mobile cellular networks. IEEE Trans. Inf. Technol. Biomed. 9(1), 35–43 (2005)
5. Blasi, D., Cacace, V., Casone, L., Rizzello, M., Rotolo, S., Bononi, L.: Ad hoc wireless sensor networking: Challenges and issues. ST J. Res. 4(1), 19–32 (2006)
6. Yang, G.–Z.: Body sensor network. Springer, Heidelberg (2006) ISBN-978-1-84628-272-0

7. Solomides, T., McClatchey, R., Breton, V.: From Grid to Healthgrid. IOS Press (2005) ISBN-1-58603-510-X
8. Barcelo, D., Diedrich Hansen, P.: Biosensors for the Environmental Monitoring of Aquatic System. Springer, Heidelberg (2009) ISBN-978-3-540-00278-9
9. Filho, E.B.L., Rodrigues, N.M.M., da Silva, E.A.B., de Carvalho, M.B., de Faria, S.M.M., da Silva, V.M.M.: On ECG Signal Compression With 1-D Multiscale Recurrent Patterns Allied to Preprocessing Techniques. IEEE (2009)

Forensic Analysis on QEMU

N. Chandra Shekar and Wilson Naik Bhukya

Department of Computer and Information Sciences,
University of Hyderabad, Hyderabad, AP, India
chandrashekar512@gmail.com, naikcs@uohyd.ernet.in

Abstract. QEMU is a generic and open source machine emulator and virtualizer. Snapshots in Qemu are stored inside the image itself where the guest OS is installed. Patches have been submitted for qemu to store the snapshot file in the home directory. In this paper we have explained the modifications done to the qemu source code by which snapshots can be stored in the user specific location in the computer for forensic analysis. In this paper we also discussed about snapshot comparisons.

Keywords: virtual machines, Qemu, emulator, snapshots.

1 Introduction

A virtual machine monitor (VMM) allows a single computer to run two or more operating systems at the same time. VMMs are relatively simple and are typically built to high assurance standards, which mean that the quality of isolation provided by a virtual machine monitor is usually greater than that which can be achieved with a general-purpose operating system. QEMU is a processor emulator [3] that relies on dynamic binary translation to achieve a reasonable speed while being easy to port on new host CPU architectures. In conjunction with CPU emulation, it also provides a set of device models, allowing it to run a variety of unmodified guest operating systems; it can thus be viewed as a hosted virtual machine monitor

2 Snapshots

Snapshot saves the current state of the virtual machine [4], so we can return to it at any time. When a snapshot is created, the original disk becomes read-only, and a separate delta file is created that contains all the disk changes that are made thereafter. The delta file does not contain an ongoing history or transaction log of all the changes to data on the disk; it simply updates disk blocks as they are changed. Snapshot contains Memory state, Settings state and Disk state. At any time, we can revert back to that original configuration, losing all changes we made since that snapshot was taken. This is very helpful when we want to test specific scenarios over and over again without having to reinstall the operating system. In virtualization software's such as Vbox and VMware the snapshots are stored in the same directory where the software is installed. As a result applications such as CompareVMwareSnapshot [2] can be used and forensic analysis

V.V. Das and N. Thankachan (Eds.): CIIT 2011, CCIS 250, pp. 777–781, 2011.

such as finding hidden files hidden by any particular malware can be identified by comparing the snapshots of the same virtual machine. Many patches[21] have been submitted for bringing the snapshot outside the image file and these patches does not provide the functionality of storing the snapshots in desired location. We have modified Qemu source so as to store the snapshot in desired location.

3 Limitation of Current Scenario on Storing Snapshots

In Qemu snapshots are stored as image file that is the reason the snapshots are not accessible outside the image file. The main disadvantage is the storage process by which the snapshots are not possible to backup. And if the snapshots are modified or deleted then the complete set of data is lost and not recoverable.

4 Our Approach for Capturing Snapshots in Qemu

We have proposed a solution through which the snapshots files are stored at the user specified location in the local system. We have modified savevm.c file and added two new commands savevm_file and loadvm_file which takes arguments as file name and location where the snapshots are to be stored, and passes this arguments to script file present in the folder where the Qemu is installed and it stores the snapshot to the desired location.

5 Experiment Setup

- Qemu 0.10.6
- Ubuntu 10.04 is used as host OS.
- Windows XP is used as guest OS.
- Patch[1] applied to Qemu.

6 Steps for Installing the Patch

- Download the patch[1] and save it as foo.patch in the same directory where Qemu is installed.
- In the terminal use the following command patch -p1 < foo.patch.

Patch[1] adds two more commands “savevm_file” and “loadvm_file” and the qemu files that are modified by this patch is “savem.c” and “sysemu.h” and the functions “void do_savevm_file” and “void do_loadvm_file” are added in the savevm.c file.

Patch[1] adds the functionality of storing the snapshots in the folder where the qemu is installed and also once the snapshot is stored the VM halts and needed to be restarted. After applying the patch we have modified the “void do_savevm_file” and “void do_loadvm_file” functions so that snapshots can be stored to the desired location in the local system. “savevm_file” and “loadvm_file” commands usage are changed because of the modifications that we have done to the source code of qemu.

Figure-2 shows the pictorial representation of the flow in which snapshots are stored to the desired location.

7 Modified Commands for Snapshots in Qemu

Syntax for storing snapshots is changed as,

- Run Guest OS and access the Qemu monitor by pressing Ctrl+2 and Ctrl+1 to return to Guest OS.
- "info snapshots" gives the list of all snapshots already saved. In general typing only info in Qemu monitor lists all the commands that can be used inside Qemu monitor.
- The Commands "savevm_file snapshotname-locationofsnapshot" and "loadvm_file snapshotname-locationofsnapshot" are used to save and load the snapshot from a specified location.

8 Forensic Snapshot Analysis

Once the snapshots are stored to the desired location they can be compared. Comparison is useful when we want to check the changes made after previous snapshot was taken. This may lead to identification of any unnecessary files or any malware has installed in the system. The software used to compare the two snapshots is "comparesnapshots[2]". Commands such as strings and grep can be used for finding the strings inside the snapshot file whose contents are in hexadecimal format. Comparesnapshot software identifies all the processes and the length of that string which was found in the hex file and also gives the offset address of the processes.

9 Observation through Case Studies

9.1 Loading the Snapshot of One Guest OS on the Other Guest OS

Loading the snapshot of one guest OS onto other guest OS is useful when the main source guest image file is not present and we want to know the previous state of that guest OS and we only have the snapshot of that guest OS.

Experimental Setup

- Ubuntu 10.04 is used as host OS.
- Windows xp is used as guest OS.
- We have installed Windows xp as two images namely "windows1.img" and "windows2.img".
- The snapshot "one" is the snapshot of windows1.img", which is loaded onto "windows2.img".
- "Windows2.img" contains snapshot "two which we have used to get back to previous good state if any problem occurs to "windows2.img".

After loading the snapshot "one" of "windows1.img" or guest OS1 onto other guest OS2 first it loads successfully and then "disk read error" occurs and the "windows2.img" halts. So to get back to the safe state we access Qemu monitor on guest OS2 or "windows2.img" and load the snapshot "two" and the previous safe state is restored back.

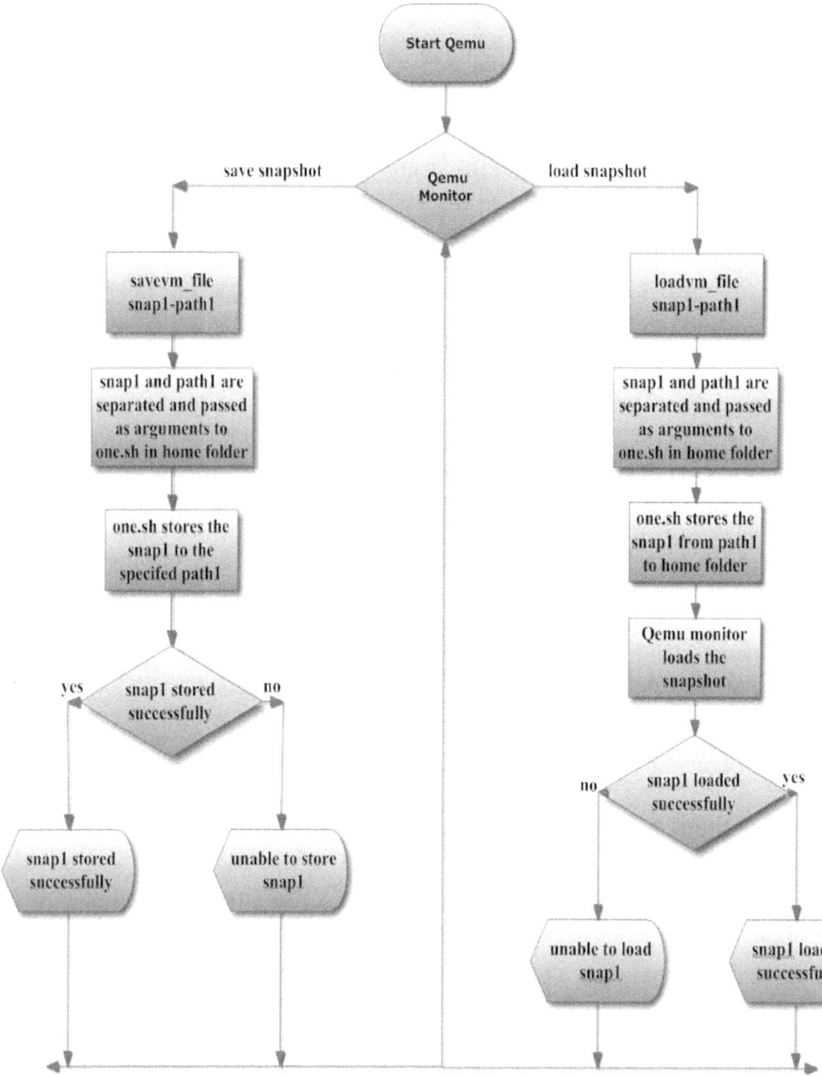

Fig. 1. Flowchart showing how snapshots are stored to desired location

10 Conclusion and Future Work

We have modified Qemu source code and added the functionality of storing the snapshot at the desired location in the local system as a result of two new commands savevm_file and loadvm_file. we have also showed how to add the patch manually to the qemu source code as part of enhancing the functionality of Qemu. We have also compared snapshots of the same Guest OS for forensic analysis and highlighted the differences in files and processes utilized by the Guest OS at different times. In future work we would like to work on storing the snapshots through network at different locations. And also identifying the malware activities inside the Guest OS, analyze the core dump of the guest OS and trace back the malware to its origin.

References

1. Qemu Snapshot patch, `http://copilotco.com/mail-archives/qemu.2009/msg01213.html`
2. Compare Snapshot Software, `http://zairon.wordpress.com/2007/08/31/find-out-hidden-files-comparing-vmwares-snapshots/`
3. Qemu Manual, `http://wiki.qemu.org/`
4. Qcow image format, `http://people.gnome.org/markmc/qcow-imageformat.html`
5. Hu, Y., Jin, H., Yu, Z., Zheng, H.: An Optimization Approach for Qemu. In: Information Science and Engineering (ICISE 2009) (2009)
6. Golden, B., Scheffy, C.: Virtualization for Dummies. Wiley Publishing, Inc., Hoboken (2008); Kroeker, K.L.: The evolution of virtualization
7. Kirch, J.: Virtual Machine Security Guidelines (September 2007)
8. Understanding Full Virtualization, Para virtualization and Hardware Assist (November 15, 2007)
9. Understanding Full Virtualization, Para virtualization and Hardware Assist (November 15, 2007)
10. Kroeker, K.L.: The Evolution of Virtualization
11. Nance, K., Hay, B., Bishop, M.: Investigating the Implications of Virtual Machine Introspection for Digital Forensics, Department of Computer Science University of Alaska Fairbanks and Computer Science Department University of California Davis (2009)
12. Henskens, F., Huebner, E.: The Role of Operating Systems in Computer Forensics, University of Western Sydney and University of Newcastle, Australia
13. Collier, G., Plassman, D., Pegah, M.: Virtualizations Next Frontier: Security, Ringling College of Art and Design, Sarasota
14. Barham, P., Dragovic, B., Fraser, K., Hand, S., Harris, T., Neugebauer, R., Pratt, I., Warfield, A.: Xen and the Art of Virtualization (October 2003)
15. Sailer, R., Valdez, E., Jaeger, T., Perez, R., van Doorn, L., Griffn, J.L., Berger, S.: Secure Hypervisor Approach to Trusted Virtualized Systems. Thomas J.Watson Research Center, Yorktown Heights, NY
16. Goldberg, R.P.: Survey of Virtual Machine Research. IEEE Computer Magazine (1974)
17. Quist, D., Smith, V.: Detecting the Presence of Virtual Machines Using the Local Data Table
18. Kirch, J.: Virtual Machine Security Guidelines (September 2007)
19. Dolan-Gavitt, B.: Forensic analysis of the Windows registry in memory
20. Hyde, D.: A Survey on the Security of Virtual Machines
21. Qemu snapshot, `http://lists.nongnu.org/archive/html/qemu-devel/2010-09/msg01662.html`

Hand Gesture Recognition System for Numbers Using Thresholding

Bhavsar Swapna[1], Futane Pravin[1] and V. Dharaskar Rajiv[2]

[1] Sinhagad college of engineering, Pune UniversityPune, India
[2] Research Center Amravati University Amravati, India
swapna.s.bhavsar@gmail.com, prfutane.scoe@sinhgad.edu,
rvdharaskar@rediffmail.com

Abstract. An efficient human computer interaction is assuming utmost importance in our daily lives. Human beings can communicate mainly by vision and sound. Human can recognize the meaningful expressions of motion using hand gesture. Hand Gesture is the most important to exchange ideas, messages, thoughts etc among deaf and dumb people. This paper discusses a simple recognition algorithm that recognizes the numbers from 0 to 10 using thresholding. The overall algorithm has three main steps: image capture, apply threshold and recognizing the number. The assumption is made that user must wear color hand gloves.

Keywords: Thresholding, Segmentation, Hand Gesture Recognition.

1 Introduction

Recognition of sign languages is one of the major concerns for the international deaf community [6]. Sign Language spotting is the task of detecting and recognizing signs in a signed utterance, in a set vocabulary. The difficulty of sign language spotting is that instances of sign vary in both motion and appearance. The hands express our thoughts and feelings. This is done in communication with one another. The hands move, appearing to further communicate what one is speaking. The hands also move reflecting the state of mind even when one isn't speaking [1].Gesture recognition is a topic in computer science and language technology with the goal of interpreting human gestures via mathematical algorithms. Gestures can originate from any bodily motion or state but commonly originate from the face or hand. Current focuses in the field include emotion recognition from the face and hand gesture recognition. Many approaches have been made using cameras and computer vision algorithms to interpret sign language. Generally, hand gestures can be classified into hand postures and dynamic gestures. The first one focuses on hand shape and position, while the second one intends to convey the meaning of hand movements of people [6]. In the present day, there are different tools for gesture recognition, based on the approaches ranging from statistical modeling, computer vision and pattern recognition, image processing. In our life everyday hand gesture plays an important role in human communication. Hand gesture has been the most common and natural way for human to interact and communicate with each other. Hand gesture provides expressive means

V.V. Das and N. Thankachan (Eds.): CIIT 2011, CCIS 250, pp. 782–786, 2011.

of interactions among people that involves hand postures and dynamic hand movements [8]. A hand posture represents static finger configuration without hand movement, whereas dynamic hand movement consists of a hand gesture with or without finger motion. The ability to detect and recognize the human hand gesture posed many challenges to researchers throughout the decades. Hand Gesture recognition can be applicable for teleconferencing, for controlling household electronic appliances. Gesture recognition can be conducted with techniques from computer vision and image processing. In Human Computer Interaction, gesture based interface gives a new direction towards the creation of a natural and user friendly environment [3].Segmentation is a process of grouping image pixels into units that are homogeneous with respect to one or more characteristics. There are many segmentation techniques like thresholding, boundary based, region based, hybrid based. Thresholding is the segmentation technique which is based on intensity and variance [5]. Otsu method is one of the threshold selection methods which are based on variance and intensity [11].This paper is organized as follows, in section II related work is presented. Section III describes the main method with its architecture and Section IV includes experimental results.

2 Related Work

To recognize the sign language or numbers, the trackball, the joystick, and the mouse are successful devices for and based computer input. Devices such as the Data glove can be worn which sense hand and finger positions and thenlanguage and numbers can be recognized. Using shape based analysis [8] sign language or numbers can be recognized. Hand shape analysis can be useful whenever it is difficult to analyze hand feature directly from images with low resolution [2] .Static Hand Gesture Recognition (S-HGR) assumes a certain hand pose or configuration which has to be recognized using appropriate techniques [4]. Research on hand gestures can be classified into three categories. The first category, glove based analysis, employs sensors (mechanical or optical) attached to a glove that transduces finger flexions into electrical signals for determining the hand posture. The relative position of the hand is determined by an additional sensor. This sensor is normally a magnetic or an acoustic sensor attached to the glove. The second category, vision based analysis, is based on the way human beings perceive information about their surroundings, yet it is probably the most difficult to implement in a satisfactory way. Several different approaches have been tested so far. One is to build a three-dimensional model of the human hand. The model is matched to images of the hand by one or more cameras, and parameters corresponding to palm orientation and joint angles are estimated. These parameters are then used to perform gesture classification. The third category, analysis of drawing gestures, usually involves the use of a stylus as an input device. Analysis of drawing gestures can also lead to recognition of written text. The vast majority of hand gesture recognition work has used mechanical sensing, most often for direct manipulation of a virtual environment and occasionally for symbolic communication. Sensing the hand posture mechanically has a range of problems, however, including reliability, accuracy and electromagnetic noise. Visual sensing has the potential to make gestural interaction more practical, but potentially embodies some of the most difficult problems in machine vision. The hand is a non-rigid object and even worse self-occlusion is very usual. In some interactive applications, the computer needs to track the position or orientation of a hand that is prominent in the image. Relevant applications might be computer games, or interactive machine control [10].

3 Method

Hand Gesture Recognition System for numbers using thresholding has three main steps to recognize the number from 0 to 10: Image capture, Apply thresholding, and recognition of the number. There is setup required to recognize the number like web camera up to 5 MP, background with black color, and color glove (with red, green, blue, pink, and yellow colored on the finger tip). The architecture of the proposed system is shown in Fig 1 and the Outline of the proposed method is shown in Fig 2.

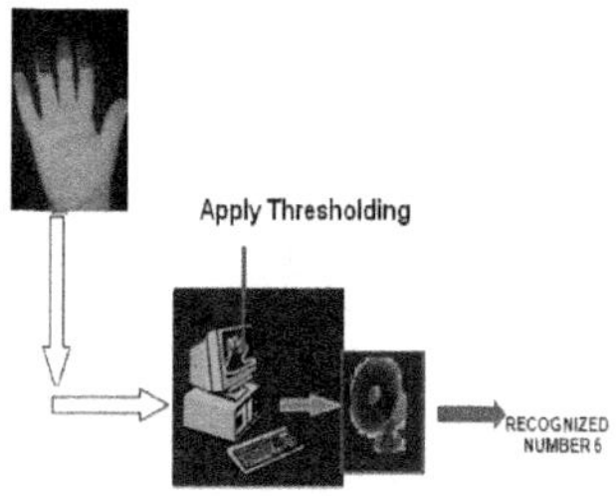

Fig. 1. Architecture of the proposed method

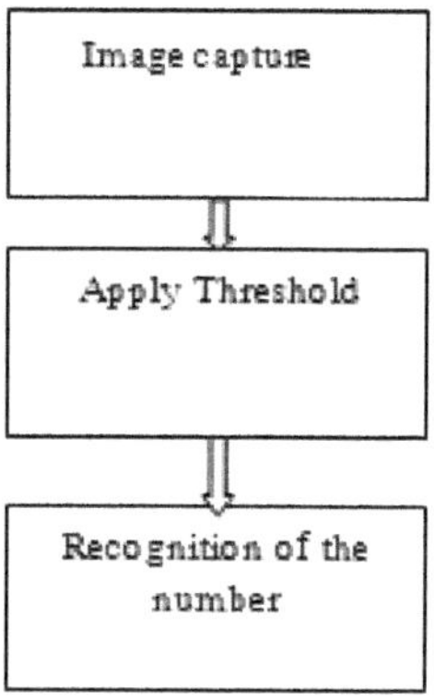

Fig. 2. Outline of the proposed method

A.Image Capture: Web camera is connected to the machine. RGB image (image of hand) is captured by the camera.The algorithm which has applied on captured image calculates the distance for all colors i.e. black (background), white (glove), and red, green, blue, yellow, pink.As we are focusing on colors for recognizing the numbers so initially the count for colors (Rcnt, Gcnt, Bcnt, Ycnt, Pcnt) isset to zero. Vertical and horizontal scanning is done on captured image.

B.Apply Threshold: We have declared threshold value which is fixed. Thresholding is the simplest method of image segmentation. On an image, thresholding is applied five times to know how many colors are present whether it is red, green, blue, pink or yellow. And according to colors we get count of particular color. Using the count value of colors next step is executed.

C. Recognition of the Number: If the color count is more than threshold value then that color is identified. Finally according to the conditions the number is recognized.

Conditions are given as below.

1.If count value of all five colors is greater than threshold value then that number is 5.

2 If count value of four colors (red, green, blue, pink) is greater than threshold value then that number is 4.

3.If count value of three colors (Red, green, yellow) is greater than threshold value then that number is 3.

4.If count value of three colors (Red, Green, Blue) is greater than threshold value then that number is 6.

5.If count value of three colors (Green, Blue, Pink) is greater than threshold value then that number is 9.

6.If count value of three colors (Red, Green, Pink) is greater than threshold value then that number is 7.

7.If count value of three colors (Red, Blue, pink) is greater than threshold value then that number is 8.

8.If count value of two colors (Red, Green) is greater than threshold value then that number is 2.

9.If count value of color (Yellow) is greater than threshold value then that number is 10.

10.If count value of color (Red) is greater than threshold value then that number is 1.

11. If count value of all five colors is less than threshold value then that number is 0.

If the above conditions are false then image is recognized as invalid image.

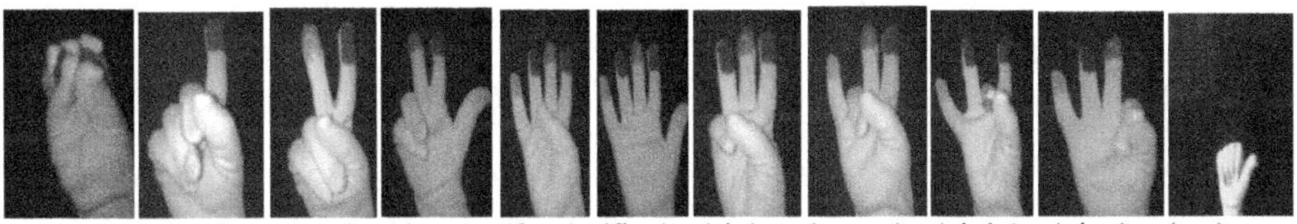

(zero) (one) (two) (three) (four) (five) (six) (seven) (eight) (nine) (ten)

Fig. 3. Input Hand Gesture for Numbers

4 Experimental Results

For recognition of the numbers from 0 to 10 we have tested many images dynamically. Table 1 shows recognition ratio of the given input which is number.

Input Number	Recognition Ratio(%)	Input Number	Recognition Ratio(%)	Input Number	Recognition Ratio(%)
0	98	4	85	8	80
1	90	5	90	9	85
2	92	6	85	10	90
3	99	7	85		

5 Conclusion

There are many approaches to recognize hand gesture like glove based, sensor based, shape based analysis and each has its own strengths and weaknesses. The algorithm which is explained in this paper also has some strength and some weaknesses. The strength of the method is that according to intensity values number is recognized easily and there are no limitations like to check angle, scaling etc. but the weakness of the method is that user has to wear color glove with only five restricted colors. Second limitation is that background should be black. It does not matter whether the hand is vertical or horizontal, numbers are being recognized. Several part of the proposed method can be improved for more robust recognition.If the alignment is not proper still captured number is being recognized. So there is possible direction to improve the current method. In future, method will be implemented in such a way that alignment of hand will be proper, then and then number will be recognized.

References

1. Futane, P.R., Dharaskar, R.V.: "Hasta Mudra" An Interpretation Of Indian Sign Hand Gestures. In: 2011 3rd International Conference on Electronics Computer Technology (ICECT 2011), vol. 2, pp. V377–V380 (2011)
2. Bilal, S., et al.: Vision-based Hand Posture Detection and Recognition for Sign Language-A study. In: 2011 4th International Conference on Mechatronics (ICOM), Kuala Lumpur, Malaysia, May 17-19 (2011)
3. Bhuyan, M.K., Neog, D.R., Kar, M.K.: Hand Pose recognition using geometric features. IEEE (2011)
4. Vieriu, R.-L., Goraş, B., Goras, L.: On HMM static Hand Gesture Recognition. IEEE (2011)
5. Nimbarte, N.M., Mushrif, M.M.: Multi-Level Thresholding For Color Image Segmentation. In: 2010 Second International Conference on Computer Engineering and Applications, pp. 231–233 (2010)
6. Rokade, R., et al.: Hand Gesture Recognition by Thinning Method. In: International Conference on Digital Image Processing, pp. 284–287. IEEE (2009)
7. Elmezain, M., Al-Hamadi, A., Jorg, Appenrodt, Michaelis, B.: A Hidden Markov Model Based continuous gesture recognition system for Hand motion Trajectory. IEEE (2008)
8. Mitra, S.: Gesture Recognition: A survey. IEEE Transactions on Systems, Man, And Cybernetics—Part C: Applications And Reviews 37(3), 311–324 (2007)
9. Jinda-apiraksa, A., Pongstiensak, W., Kondo, T.: A Simple Shape-Based Approach to Hand Gesture Recognition
10. Ray Lockton Balliol College, Hand Gesture Recognition Using Computer Vision
11. http://en.wikipedia.org/wiki/Otsu%27s_method

Automatic Text Summarization

S. Soumya, Geethu S. Kumar, Rasia Naseem, and Saumya Mohan

Department of Computer Science, College of Engineering Munnar, Idukki, Kerala
{ps.soumya02,geethuskumar14,rasianaseem,saumyamohan89}@gmail.com

Abstract. AutomaticText Summarization is a Natural Language Processing task which has experienced great development in recent years, mostly due to the rapid growth of the Internet. Therefore, we need methods and tools that help users to manage large amounts of information. Text Summarization aims to condense the information contained in one or more documents and present it in a more concise way, can be very useful for this purpose. It is the creation of a shortened version of a text by a computer program. The product of this procedure still contains the most important points of the original text.

Keywords: nlp, summarization, Stanford dependency, lucene, word frequency.

1 Introduction

Automatic text summarization is the technique, where a computer summarizes a text. A text is entered into the computer and a summarized text is returned, which is a non redundant extract from the original text[3].

2 The Proposed Work

Our proposed work includes two types of summarization namely rule based summarization and keyword based summarization. Rule based summarization is abstraction based technique. It uses Stanford Depedency parser. The lexicalized probabilistic parser implements a factored product model, with separate PCFG phrase structure and lexical dependency experts, whose preferences are combined by efficient exact inference, using an A* algorithm[6]. The second type keyword based summarization is almost purely a syntactic approach of summarization. The summarizer used here is lucene summarizer. It is based on the extraction of keywords from the document and identifying the sentences containing them.

3 Rule Based Summarization

The Stanford typed dependencies represents all sentence relationships uniformly as typed dependency relations between pairs of words. [1]. In our algorithm initially there would be a number of rules which consists of inputs and expected outputs all parsed using Stanford parser and stored in text files, one text file for each input and

V.V. Das and N. Thankachan (Eds.): CIIT 2011, CCIS 250, pp. 787–789, 2011.

another text file for corresponding output. When the text to be summarized is given as input to the algorithm, it tokenizes the document into paragraphs and then each paragraph into sentences. Each sentence is then parsed using Stanford parser. The result is then matched with each of the rule file contents. If any of the rules matches exactly in number and order of dependencies, then the corresponding result file is searched for in the database and retrieved. The differences are observed when rule was converted into result. The same differences are obtained in the input text by eliminating the dependencies that were eliminated from rule to get the result. This algorithm is applied to each of the sentences and the words are reordered using the word position returned by the parser. After reordering the sentences are concatenated to form the summary.

3.1 Definitions of Stanford Typed Dependencies

The current representation contains 55 grammatical relations. The dependencies are all binary relations: a grammatical relation holds between a governor and a dependent. A few grammatical relations are defined below, in alphabetical order according to the dependency abbreviated name (which appears in the parser output). The definitions make use of the Penn Treebank part-of-speech tags and phrasal labels.[1][4] A few examples for the grammatical relations are Abbrev : abbreviation modifier, Appos : appositional modifier, Cc : Coordination, Conj : Conjunct etc.

4 Keyword Based Summarizer

Lucene based summarizer tokenizes a document into paragraphs and paragraphs into sentences, then builds a in-memory lucene index for the document with sentences as fields in single-field Lucene documents with index time boosts specified by the paragraph and sentence number. Extracts the top terms from the in-memory index and issue a Boolean OR query to the index with these terms, then return the top few sentences found ordered by Lucene document id.

The main components of the algorithm are

Analyzer. In our prposed work we use a text file stopwords.txt as the analyzer which contains a pool of all the stopwords to be eliminated from the summary.

NumSentence. The number of sentences required in the summary. Default is 2.

ToptermCutoff. This value specifies where to cut off the term list for query. The topTermCutoff is a ratio from 0 to 1 which specifies how far to go down the frequency ordered list of terms. The terms considered have a frequency greater than(topTermCutoff*topFrequency).TopTermCutoff a ratio specifying where the term list will be cut off.

SentenceDeboost. An index-time deboost is applied to the sentences after the first one in all the paragraphs. The first paragraph is not deboosted at all. For the second and succeeding paragraphs, the deboost is calculated as (1 - sentence_pos * deboost) until the value reaches sentenceDeboostBase (default 0.5) or less, and then no more deboosting occurs.It Must be between 0 and 1.

SentenceDeboostBase. This value defines the base until which deboosting will occur and then stop. Default is set to 0.5 if not set. Must be between 0 and 1.

In-memory Lucene Index. An in-memory index of the sentences in the text is built with the appropriate document boosts if specified.

The algorithm computes a term frequency map for the index at the specified location. The frequency of a term is the product of TF(Term frequency) and IDF (Inverse Document Frequency) .

Then

$$(\text{tf-idf})_{i,j} = \text{tf}_{i,j} \times \text{idf}_i$$

The term map is then sorted by frequency descending frequency order. The algorithm builds a Boolean OR query out of the "most frequent" terms in the index and returns it. "Most Frequent" is defined as the terms whose frequencies are greater than or equal to the topTermCutoff * the frequency of the top term. Here ramdir the directory where the index is created.The query is executed against the specified index, and returns a bounded collection of sentences ordered by document id (so the sentence ordering is preserved in the collection). [5]

References

1. de Marnee, M.-C., Manning, C.D.: Stanford Typed Dependencies manual (2010)
2. Martins, D., Dartis, A.F.T.: A Survey on Automatic Text Summarization, Language Technologies Institute (2007)
3. Hassel, M.: Evaluation of Automatic Text Summarization, A practical Implementation (2004)
4. de Marnee, M.-C., Manning, C.D.: The Stanford typed dependencies representation. In: COLING Workshop on Cross-Framework and Cross-Domain Parser Evaluation (2008)
5. Natural Language Processing Research at Columbia University, `http://www.cs.columbia.edu/nlp/newsblaster`
6. Stanford Natural Language Processing Group, `http://nlp.stanford.edu/software/lex-parser.shtml`

Efficient Fuzzy Clustering Based Approach to Brain Tumor Segmentation on MR Images

Megha P. Arakeri and G. Ram Mohana Reddy

National Institute of Technology Karnataka, Surathkal, Karnataka, India
{meghalakshman,profgrmreddy}@gmail.com

Abstract. Image segmentation is one of the most vital and significant step in medical applications. The conventional fuzzy c-means (FCM) clustering is the most widely used unsupervised clustering method for brain tumor segmentation on magnetic resonance (MR) images. However, the major limitation of the conventional FCM is its huge computational time and it is sensitive to initial cluster centers. In this paper, we present a novel efficient FCM algorithm to eliminate the drawback of conventional FCM. The proposed algorithm is formulated by incorporating distribution of the gray level information in the image and a new objective function which ensures better stability and compactness of clusters. Experiments are conducted on brain MR images to investigate the effectiveness of the proposed method in segmenting brain tumor. The conventional FCM and the proposed method are compared to explore the efficiency and accuracy of the proposed method.

Keywords: Segmentation, Magnetic resonance image, Fuzzy c-means clustering, Brain tumor, Efficiency.

1 Introduction

Brain tumor is one of the major causes of death among adults and children [1]. Magnetic resonance imaging is the commonly used method for brain imaging. It gives the cross sectional images of the brain in several slices by using magnetic field and radiofrequency waves [2]. Image segmentation techniques can aid the radiologist in tumor volume analysis, surgical planning and in knowing the severity of the cancer. The unsupervised FCM clustering is the most extensively used method for segmenting brain tumor on MR images. The main characteristic of FCM clustering is to allow pixels to belong to multiple classes with certain degree. This can effectively process MR images where uncertainty, limited resolution and noise are present. But the conventional FCM algorithm consumes lot of time to partition the image into desired number of clusters and is sensitive to initial cluster centres values leading to local minima results [3]. There exist several improvements to conventional FCM in the literature. Kannan [4] improves the segmentation efficiency of the FCM algorithm by silhouette method based on cluster center initialization instead of random initialization. The FCM algorithm has been also improved using parallel processing [5]. Even though it provides high speed processing, the hardware implementation is

V.V. Das and N. Thankachan (Eds.): CIIT 2011, CCIS 250, pp. 790–795, 2011.

not effective. Weiling et al [6] presents generalized framework for FCM clustering which guarantees robustness to noise and preserves edge details. Mohammed et al. [7] improved FCM clustering by eliminating those points with membership value smaller than a threshold value. The choice of appropriate threshold was not automatic but based on experiments. Rogerio et al. [8] reduced the number of iterations of FCM algorithm required for convergence by presenting a new equation to calculate cluster centres. Though the method could reduce total iterations, there was not much improvement in the efficiency of the algorithm. Bin et al. [9] presents improved model to FCM algorithm using membership smoothing constraint. The algorithm uses the spatial information of image and improves accuracy of segmentation. But the main drawback is that it computes neighbourhood term in each iteration, which is very time consuming. Snehashis et al. [10] proposed semi automatic fuzzy clustering method to classify tissues in brain MRI by incorporating the compactness term into traditional FCM. Most of the methods in the literature attempt to speed up the fuzzy clustering process but not concentrating on the compactness and well separation of clusters. Computed aided diagnosis in medicine expects the algorithms to be automatic, efficient and accurate to provide the better diagnosis of diseases [11][12]. Accordingly this paper proposes a novel efficient FCM based approach to brain tumor segmentation which partitions the image into well separated clusters and gives global optimal solutions.

3 Proposed Methodology

The proposed approach provides efficient segmentation of brain tumor on MR images by using wavelet and modified FCM clustering. In the first step, image is decomposed by applying wavelet transform and in the next step modified FCM algorithm is applied to segment the approximate image in the highest wavelet level. Operating on a low resolution image helps in reducing the computational complexity of the process and in restraining noise. Then the low resolution segmented image is projected on to the full resolution image by inverse wavelet transform.

3.1 Wavelet Decomposition

The discrete wavelet transform (DWT) is a linear transformation which operates on a data vector transforming it into numerically different vector of same length. DWT can be expressed as [13]:

$$DWT_{x(n)} = \begin{cases} d_{j,k} = \sum x(n) h_j^* (n - 2jk), \\ a_{j,k} = \sum x(n) g_j^* (n - 2jk). \end{cases} \tag{1}$$

The coefficient $d_{j,k}$ refer to the detail components in signal $x(n)$,where as $a_{j,k}$ refer to the approximation components in the signal. The functions $h(n)$ and $g(n)$ represent the coefficients of high-pass and low-pass filters respectively. The parameters j and k refer to the wavelet scale and translation factors. By using wavelets, the given image can be analysed at various levels with resolution matched to its scale [14].

3.2 Modified FCM

In traditional FCM clustering, time of segmenting the image is dependent on the image size. Hence, it takes more time to converge [15]. The proposed modified FCM considers image gray levels *(g)* instead of pixel intensities as number of gray levels is less than number of pixels in the image. This leads to improved complexity of *O(gcI)*. Accordingly, the new cluster centres and membership function are calculated as:

$$u_{ig} = \frac{\left(g - v_i\right)^{-\frac{2}{m-1}}}{\sum_{j=1}^{c} \left(g - v_i\right)^{-\frac{2}{m-1}}} . \quad (2)$$

$$c_i = \frac{\sum_{g=0}^{L-1} h(g) u_{ig}^{m} g}{\sum_{g=0}^{L-1} h(g) u_{ig}^{m}} . \quad (3)$$

Where *L* is the maximum gray level in the image and *h(g)* is the probability that the pixels have gray level *g*. The clustering should partition the given data into desired number of clusters such that the distance between the data points and the cluster centre should be minimized within the cluster and also the distance between the clusters should be maximized. Accordingly the objective function is defined as:

$$J = \sum_{i=1}^{c} \sum_{g=1}^{L-1} u_{ij}^{m} h(g) \left\| g - v_i \right\|^2 - \frac{1}{c(c-1)} \sum_{i=1}^{c} \sum_{k=1}^{c} \left\| v_i - v_k \right\|^2 . \quad (4)$$

The modified FCM algorithm effectively reduces the computation time and also ensures compact and well separated clusters.

4 Experimental Results

The proposed method is simulated using MATLAB. All the experiments were simulated on a personal computer with 1.5MHz Pentium processor and 2GB of memory running under Windows XP operating system.. The effectiveness of the proposed method was tested by experimenting on several MR images of the brain tumor. The MR images used in this study were acquired from Shirdi Sai Cancer Hospital, Maniapal. Each image was digitized to 512×512 size with each pixel representing 0.624mm×0.624mm of the actual size. All the images were in gray color with intensity ranging from 0 to 255. Fig.1 shows the original MR image of brain.

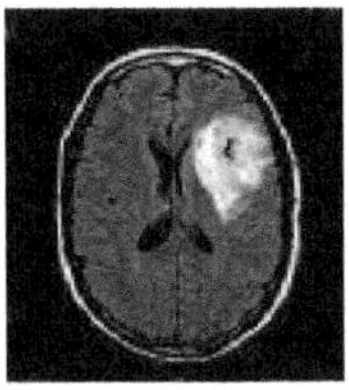

Fig. 1. Original MR brain image

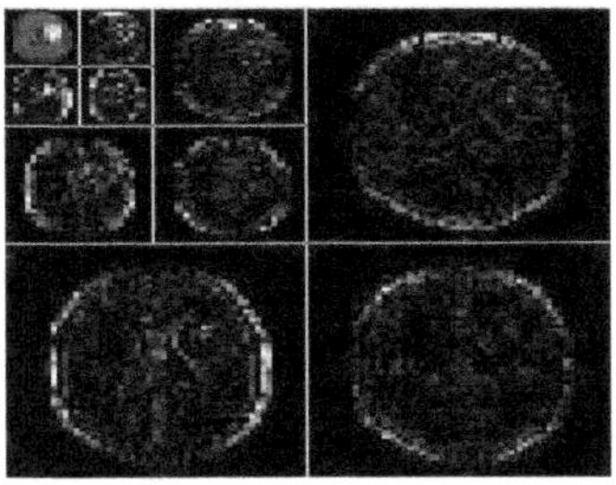

Fig. 2. Wavelet decomposition

Fig.2 shows the brain MR image decomposition using discrete wavelet transform. After creating the pyramid representation of the image by wavelet transform, the wavelet decomposed LL sub band image at the third level is segmented through application of modified FCM clustering algorithm on the image. The brain image is partitioned into four clusters such as white matter, gray matter, cerebrospinal fluid and fourth cluster represents brain tumor and skull region as shown in Fig.3, Fig.4, Fig.5 and Fig.6 respectively.

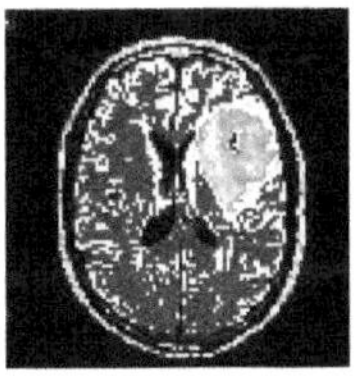

Fig. 3. White matter

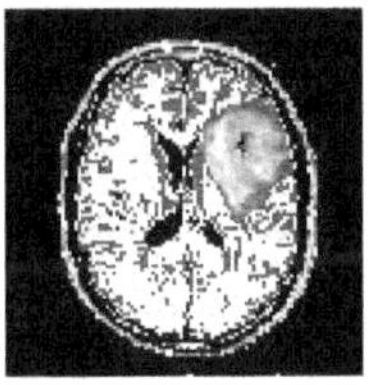

Fig. 4. Gray matter

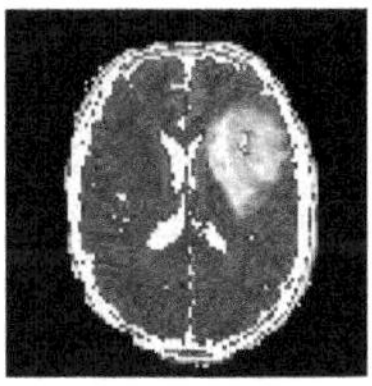

Fig. 5. Cerebrospinal fluid

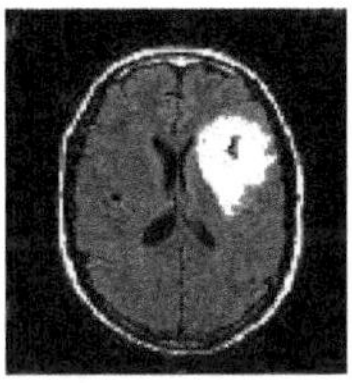

Fig. 6. Tumor and skull

During the initial stages of the experiments, the FCM produced considerably varied results on each run. Due to this finding, we used 10^{-7} as the minimal amount of improvement for the experiments. It was found that the performance of FCM improved and always achieved stable clustering results. As shown in Fig.6 tumor and skull are in same cluster. Thus skull is removed from the image by applying morphological operators on the binary image in Fig.7. The result of morphological processing is shown in Fig.8 and the boundary of the segmented tumor is marked on the original image by using 4-connected neighbours as shown in Fig.9.

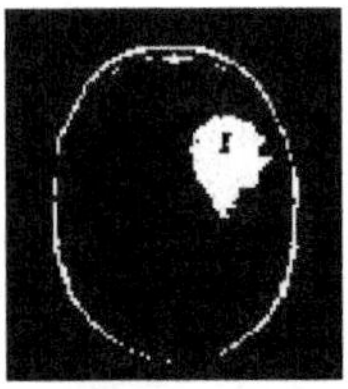

Fig.7. Tumor cluster in binary

Fig.8. Morphology processing

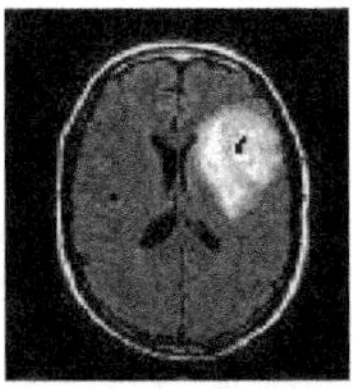

Fig.9. Segmented brain tumor

To validate the clustering and test its quality, we have used Davies-Bouldin index and Xie-Beni index [16] which are defined in (5) and (6) respectively.

$$DB = \frac{1}{c}\sum \max_{i \neq l}\left\{\frac{d_w(v_i) + d_w(v_l)}{d_b(v_i, v_l)}\right\}. \tag{5}$$

$$XB = \frac{\sum_{i=1}^{c}\sum_{k=1}^{N} u_{ik}^{2}\left\|v_i - x_k\right\|^2}{N\min_{i,k}\left\|v_i - v_k\right\|^2} . \tag{6}$$

Where d_w indicates within cluster distance and d_b indicated between cluster distance.The valid clustering procedure should make DB and XB value as low as possible. Table.1 presents the comparative analysis of conventional FCM and the proposed modified FCM based on execution time and cluster validity indexes.

Table 1. Performance comparision of fuzzy clustering algorithms

Method	DB index	XB index	Execution time (sec)
FCM	0.6513	0.46	1.320
Modified FCM	0.6301	0.41	0.521

5 Conclusion

The proposed method overcomes the drawback of conventional fuzzy clustering algorithm by improving its efficiency. The wavelet transform gives the low resolution images for analysis in the subsequent stages. The modified FCM has a good efficiency and also gives compact and well separated clusters by introducing a new objective function. The proposed method effectively segments the brain tumor from magnetic resonance images and thus can play a vital role in computer aided diagnosis of brain tumors enabling the radiologists to provide more accurate and faster diagnosis.

References

1. World health organization cancer fact sheets (2010), `http://www.who.int/mediacenter/factsheets/fs297/en/index.html`
2. Zulaikha Beevi, S., Mohamed Sathik, M.: An effective approach for segmentation of MRI images: combining spatial information with fuzzy c-means clustering. European Journal of Scientic Research 41(3), 437–451 (2010)
3. Hou, Z., Qian, W., Huang, S., Hu, Q., Nowinski, W.L.: Regularized fuzzy c-means method for brain tissue clustering. Pattern Recognition Letters 28, 1788–1794 (2007)

4. Kannan, S.R., Ramathilagam, S., Pandiyarajan, R., Sathya, A.: Fuzzy clustering approach in segmentation of T1-T2 brain MRI. International Journalof Recent Trends in Engineering 2(1), 157–160 (2005)
5. Murugavalli, S., Rajamani, V.: A high speed parallel fuzzy c-mean algorithm for brain tumor segmentation. BIME Journal 6(1) (2006)
6. Cai, W., Chen, S., Zhang, D.: Fast and Robust fuzzy c-means clustering algorithms incorporating local information for image segmentation. Pattern Recognition 40, 825–838 (2007)
7. Belal, M., Hudaib, A., Al-Shboul, B.: A Fast Fuzzy Clustering Algorithm. In: WSEAS International Conference on Artificial Intelligence. Knowledge Engineering and Databases, pp. 28–32 (2007)
8. de Vargas, R.R., Bedregal, B.R.C.: A comparative study between fuzzy c-means and ckmeans algorithms. In: Fuzzy Information Processing Society, IEEE North American Annual Meeting, pp. 1–6 (2010)
9. Li, B., Chen, W., Wang, D.: An improved FCM algorithm incorporating spatial information for image segmentation. In: IEEE International Symposium on Computer Science and Computational Technology, pp. 493–495 (2008)
10. Ray, S., Agarwal, H., Carass, A., Bai, Y.: Fuzzy c-means with variable compactness. In: IEEE International Symposium on Biomedical Imaging:From Nano to Macro, pp. 452–455 (2008)
11. Fujita, H., Zhang, X., Kido, S., Hara, T.: An introduction and survey of computer aided detection/diagnosis. In: IEEE International Conference on Future Computer, Control and Communication, pp.200–205 (2010)
12. Uchiyama, Y., Yokoyama, R., Fujitha, H.: Computer aided diagnosis scheme for detection of lacunar infarcts in MR images. Academic Radiology 14, 1554–1561 (2007)
13. Bouchaffra, D., Tan, J.: Structural hidden markov models for biometrics:fusion of face and fingerprint. Pattern Recognition 41, 852–867 (2008)
14. Kocionek, M., Materka, A., Strzelecki, M., Szczypinski, P.: Discrete wavelet transform-derived features for digital image texture analysis. In: International Conference on Signals and Electrical Systems, Poland, pp. 163–168 (2001)
15. Shasidhar, M., Sudheer Raja, V., Vijay Kumar, B.: MRI brain image segmentation using modified fuzzy c-means clustering algorithm. In: IEEE International Conference on Communication Systems and Network Technologies, pp. 473–478 (2011)
16. Srivastava, A., Asati, A., Bhattacharya, M.: A fast and noise adaptive rough fuzzy hybrid algorithm for medical image segmentation. In: IEEE International Conference on Bioinformatics and Biomedicine, pp. 416–421 (2010)

Using KNN Algorithm for Text Categorization

M.A. Wajeed[1] and T. Adilakshmi[2]

[1] SCSI, Sreenidhi Institute of Science & Technology,
Ghatkesar, Hyderabad, AP India
wajeed.mtech@gmail.com
[2] Vasavi College of Engineering,
Ibrahimbagh, Hyderabad AP India
t_adilakshmi@gmail.com

Abstract. Today much data is generated through electronic devices in large scale. This is due to the electronics devices having the ability of automated computing facilities. The data generated could be in textual format, and if one wish to analyze the generated textual data then data mining techniques of numerical type (data) cannot be applied so the need to transform the textual data into the numerical format is deemed necessary, thus opening the scope of textual data mining making inevitable as a different area to explore. Classification has been an important area in data mining, but in this paper an attempt to classify documents, based on the contents of the data is made, the content being in textual type. A common application with binary textual classification is to classify the mails into spam and hams (legitimate mails), but considering a case where the documents (mails) are to classified based on the contents into multi-class (say mails to be forwarded to the respective section from a single mail-id, for multiple departments) instead of binary classification is explored in the paper. In this paper K-Nearest Neighbors algorithm is employed which has given good results.

Keywords: legitimate mails, spam, text classification, confusion matrix, mean square-root normalization.

1 Introduction

In the process of data classification commonly two approaches are adapted supervised classification, un-supervised classification. In supervised classification, based on the training data an attempt to build a model is made such that the unseen data can be classified based on the learning achieved through the training data. Emphasis needs to be given to choose the best features from the training data and discard the non-relevant features from the training data [10]. While un-supervised classification makes an attempt to form clusters with a property such that the inter-cluster similarities are almost zero and intra-cluster similarities are maximized. As substantial portion of the information is stored in text databases so the need of classify the textual data becomes inevitable.

In this paper supervised textual data classification is explored. [1] provides the disadvantages of manual classification, making automatic text classification indispensable. This paper is organized as follows. In section-2 we propose different

V.V. Das and N. Thankachan (Eds.): CIIT 2011, CCIS 250, pp. 796–801, 2011.

vector generation techniques, with/without normalization. Detailed discussed of the same are furnished. Section-3 deals with experiment implementation details, it also includes the results obtained, and finally at the end of the paper in section-4 conclusions and future work are provided.

2 Transformations

This section deals about the transformation techniques where textual data is mapped to the numerical data. In this process we assume the appearance of words, i.e. the order of the words as unimportant. Binary vectors are the vector which maps the documents and can have on/off bit values only. If the corresponding word, which is represented by the column is present in the document then the corresponding bit is 'on' so has a value 1, otherwise the bit is 'off', which is represented by taking the value 0. Using the above rules of binary vector generation 5485 rows (for 5485 documents) with 14,822 (lexicon size) columns was generated. In the Frequency vector generation process the number of times the word appeared in each of the document is considered. So the components of the vector have values in the range 0 through n, for some value of 'n'. In the process of textual categorization using frequency vectors which aims in finding the impact of each words, no: of times its occurrences rather than just taking into consideration the words presence or absence in the document.

2.1 Normalization

Attribute need to be normalized by scaling its values so that they fall within a small range such as **[new_min$_A$:new_max$_A$]**. Normalizing the attributes aims in speeding up the learning phase [8], also attribute with large range may dominate when compared to attributes with smaller range, so normalization is applied. There are many techniques to normalize the data.

2.1.1 Length Normalized Binary Vector with Unique Words. This is very important normalization technique in the textual data classification, as it aims in normalizing the variation in the lengths of the documents. More the length of document, larger would be the probability of (all the) word (or more words) appearing. In order to overcome this, binary vector obtained is normalized by diving each component of the vector by the number of unique words in the document.

2.1.2 Length Normalized Binary Vector with all Words. In order to understand the distribution of words in the document, normalization of binary vector was done by taking length normalized with all words. Another variation to this normalization is done by dividing the elements of the vector by all words, instead of dividing the vector elements by all unique words.

2.2 Frequency Based Vectors

In addition to the above process of normalization treatment to the binary vector, we adapted few more normalization techniques for frequency vector.

2.2.1 Min-Max Normalization. Min-max normalization performs a linear transformation on the original data [6]. Suppose that min_A and max_A are the existing minimum and maximum values of some attribute say A, Min-max normalization maps a value 'v', to v' in the new range [new_min_A : new_max_A] by computing, using the formula

$$v' = (v - \min_A) / (\max_A - \min_A) * (new\_\max_A - new\_\min_A) + new\_\min_A \quad (1)$$

Min-max normalization preserves the relationships among the original data values. This normalization is cannot be applied to binary vector, as the min_max normalization when applied with the new_min_A and new_max_A as 0 and 1 respectively to binary vector, we obtain the input values itself as the output.

2.2.2 Length normalized Frequency Vector with Unique Words. Similar procedure as that of binary vector normalization, frequency vector normalization is done taking all unique words into consideration. So the numerator of the binary vector normalized with unique words is changed while the denominator is untouched. So both the numerator as well as the denominator considers the number of occurrence of words, in the numerator the occurrence of a particular word in a document under consideration is taken, and denominator has the number of unique words in that document.

2.2.3 Length Normalized Binary Vector with all Words. In the process of obtaining length normalized frequency vector with all words, we divide the frequency vector elements with the number of words in that document. This is because as the size of the document increases the probability of inclusion of (all) the word also increases, so to normalize the increase in the probability, length normalized frequency vector with all words is considered.

2.2.4 Root Mean-Square Frequency Normalization. It is also called as sum of squares normalization, where the numerator represents the frequency of the word in the document while the denominator is the under square-root, sum of squares of all the components of the vector.

3 KNN Implementation

A K-Nearest Neighbor algorithm is also called as instance based learning algorithm [4]. Nearest Neighbor classifier are based on learning by analogy, that is by comparing a given test tuple with training tuples that are similar to it. Each tuple represents a point in an n-dimension pattern space. When given an unseen tuple, a K-nearest neighbor classifier searches the pattern space for different values of K (which can take any value 1 through some arbitrary number) the training tuples that are closest to the unseen tuple. Depending on the value of K, K training tuples are used which are near to the unseen tuple. The Euclidean distance between two points or tuples say X_1 and X_2 which have 'n' component elements is used to find the similarity (closeness) between the tuples using the Euclidean distances. The test data consists of 2189 documents, the distance between the training and a particular test document is measured, the class with the smallest distance in the training data is taken as the class of the test data, as here K value in K-NN is 1. In case of K value 2, we take 2 smallest distances, and if both belong to same class than the test tuple is considered to belong to the same class as of the training document class, in case of tie an arbitrary consensus is used to resolve the conflict [5]. Based on the distance between the training and test tuples we obtain confusion matrix. A confusion matrix is used to evaluate the performance of a classifier in supervised learning. It is a matrix with the predicted versus the actual classes as given in [3]. For m classes, a confusion matrix is a table of m by m. An entry $CM_{i,j}$ in the first m rows and m columns indicates the number of tuples of class *i* that are labeled by the classifier as class *j*. For a classifier to have good accuracy, ideally most of the tuples along the diagonal of the confusion matrix should have values and rest of the elements close to zero. The experiment was repeated for different value of k ranging from 1 through 100. Figure 1 gives the results obtained for K value 1 through 10 in for different binary vectors and we find that inv_freq vector gives very poor results, while bin_binc vector which is binary normalized with unique words and binary vector gives best result and both these vectors coincides with each other in the results. Freq_binc which is binary normalized with frequency vector results are in-between the bin_binc, binary and inv_freq vector. Figure 2 gives the results for K value 10 through 100 for binary vector. Figure -2 depicts that bin_binc which is binary normalized with unique words is better, which is followed by binary normalized with frequency count (freq_binc). Figure 3 gives the text classification results for frequency vectors for K value varying from 1 to 10. We find from figure 3 that bin_freq which is frequency normalized with unique words is the best which is followed by frequency normalized to min_max normalized (freq_min_max) with the range [0, 1]. The next vector better to freq_min_max is freq_min_max is frequency normalized with normal (freq_sqrt). Figure 4 gives the results obtained for frequency vectors for K value in the range 10 to 100, and we find that feq_min_max is the worst and the best being the freq_sqrt.

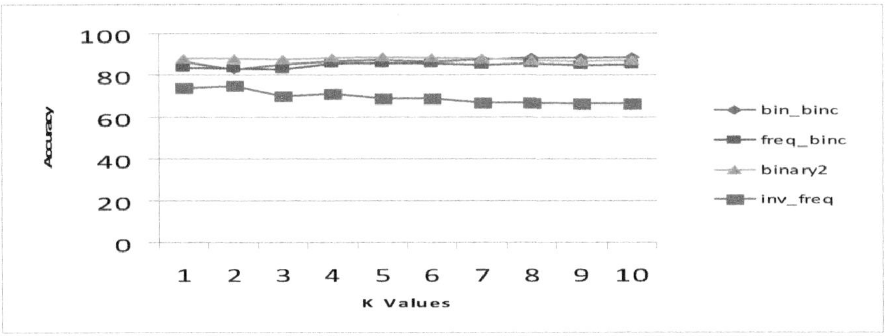

Fig. 1. Different binary vectors for K value 1 to 10

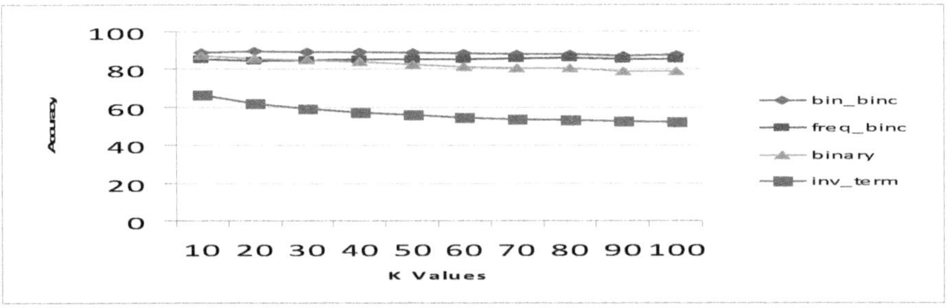

Fig. 2. Different binary vectors for K value 10 to 100

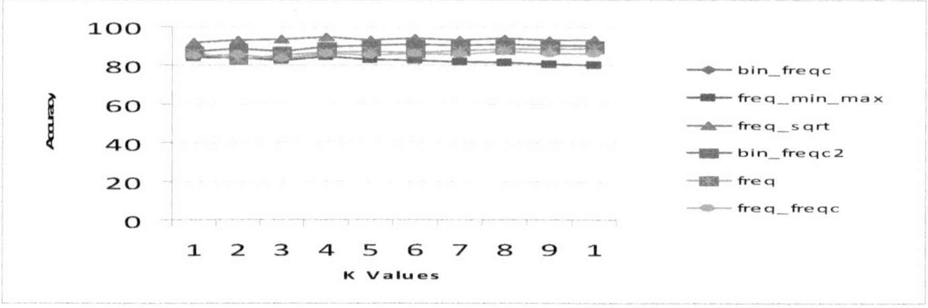

Fig. 3. Different frequency vectors for K value 1 to 10

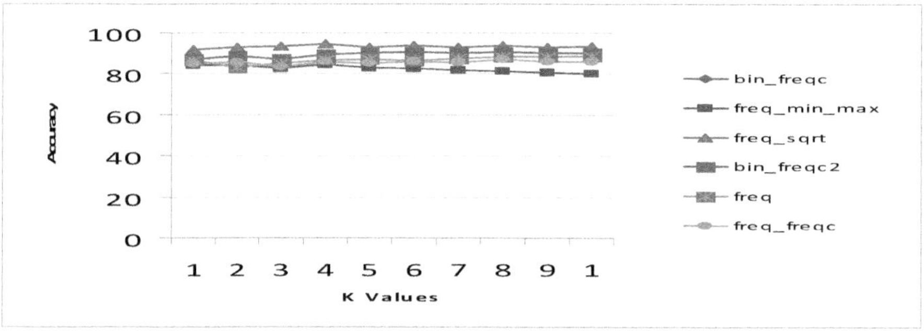

Fig. 4. Different frequency vectors for K value 10 to 100

4 Conclusion

Text classification is very much indispensable in present times due to large electronics data processing. As it generate information that is stored in electronics form, which can also be textual format. To organize this and reuse the generated data classification has to be done. The paper attempts in one such classification. The experiments conducted depicted that mean square root results are better when compared to all other vectors. More ever we could also find that as the K value increases the classifier accuracy decreases, but for large k values also we found that the classifier accuracy was never below 55% for different (all) vector types. As a further expansion to the work carried out, we wish to reduce the feature sets and perform the experiments and see how the classifier performs, with feature reduction.

References

1. Wajeed, M.A., Adilakshmi, T.: Text Classification Using Machine Learning. Journal of Theoretical and Applied Information Technology 7(2), 119–123 (2009)
2. http://www.daviddlewis.com/resources/testcollections/reuters21578/

3. Cunnigham, P., Delany, S.J.: k-Nearest Neighbour classifiers. Technical Report UCD-CSI 2007-4
4. Aha, D.W., Kibler, D., Albert, M.K.: Instance-based learning algorithms. Machine Learning 6, 37–66 (1991)
5. Au Yeung, C.-m., Gibbins, N., Shadbolt, N.: A k-Nearest-Neighbour Method for Classifying Web Search Results with Data in Folksonomies. In: 2008 IEEE/WIC/ACM International Conference on Web Intelligence and Intelligent Agent Technology, wi-iat, vol. 1, pp. 70–76 (2008)
6. Data normalization, `http://abbottanalytics.blogspot.com/2009/04/why-normalization-matters-with-k-means.html`
7. `http://tartarus.org/~martin/PorterStemmer`
8. Sebastiani, F.: Text classification, automatic. In: Brown, K. (ed.) The Encyclopedia of Language and Linguistics, 2nd edn., vol. 14, Elsevier Science, Amsterdam (2004)
9. Debole, F., Sebastiani, F.: Supervised Term Weighting for Automated Text Categorization. In: Proc. 18th ACM Symp. Applied Computing (SAC 2003), pp. 784–788 (2003)
10. Shankar, S., Karypis, G.: A Feature Weight Adjustment Algorithm for Document Classification. In: Proc. SIGKDD 2000 Workshop Text Mining (2000)
11. Kim, J., Kim, M.H.: An Evaluation of Passage-Based Text Categorization. J. Intelligent Information Systems 23(1), 47–65 (2004)

Energy Efficient Node-Disjoint Multipath Route Discovery Mechanism for Wireless Sensor Networks

G. Shiva Murthy[1], R.J. D'Souza[1], and G. Varaprasad[2]

[1] Department of Mathematical and Computational Sciences,
National Institute of TechnologyKarnataka,
Surathkal, India
kgshivam@gmail.com
[2] Department of Computer Science and Engineering,
BMS College of Engineering, Banaglore, India

Abstract. To increase the operational lifetime of the wireless sensor network is the major objective of energy efficient routing protocols. Mutlipath routing protocols enhance the lifetime of the wireless sensor network by distributing the traffic among multiple paths instead of single optimal path. This Work proposes a low control overhead route discovery mechanism for Energy Efficient Node-disjoint Multipath Routing Protocol. The number of control messages used in the route construction is minimized. The energy spent on the route discovery mechanism is also minimized.

Keywords: Wireless Sensor Networks, Multipath Routing, Low Control Overhead, Route Discovery.

1 Introduction

Routing the sensed data from the source to sink node in a resource constrained environment in Wireless Sensor Network (WSN) is still a challenge. There were many attempts are made to route the data in the resource constrained scenarios. Optimal path between the source and destination is selected by the routing protocols to satisfy the resource constraints such as energy, bandwidth and computation power. The routing protocols take into account the metrics like minimum hop, minimum transmission cost, high residual energy etc. to route the data. Many routing protocols attempt to reduce the energy usage in the nodes to increase the network life time. This provides an optimal path between source and destination. Selecting an optimal path between the source and destination and sending the data through that path may not increase the life time of the network. The energy usage in such an approach is not as efficient as that in multipath approach.The multipath routing protocols select the available possible paths between the source and destination. The data is distributed among the multiple paths and the usage of the energy for the data transmission is spread among the number of nodes on multiple paths. The transmission delay is reduced as portion of the data is being sent in different paths. The multipath routing protocols provide the effective load sharing among the multiple paths to satisfy the resource constraints and to meet the requiredquality of service in the wireless sensor

V.V. Das and N. Thankachan (Eds.): CIIT 2011, CCIS 250, pp. 802–807, 2011.

networks. The multipath routing increases the probability of reliable data delivery. In multipath routing, the energy cost overhead for data retransmission due to link failure or node failure and alternate path constructions are minimized. In this work it is proposed to minimize the number of control messages needed for the route discovery so that the energy spent on route discovery is also reduced. The rest of this paper is organized as follows. In section 2, the existing work is discussed. In section 3, the energy efficient node disjoint multipath route discovery mechanism is proposed. In section 4 results and discussions are provided and conclusions are drawn in section 5.

2 Related Works

Ad Hoc On-Demand Multipath Distance Vector Routing (AOMDV) is a reactive and source initiated routing protocol [1]. Route discovery is initiated by broadcasting the route request (RREQ) packets to its neighboring nodes. Source node waits for the route reply (RREP) packet from destination node or intermediate node which has the valid route to the destination. The intermediate node receiving the RREQ packets sets up a reverse path to the source using the previous hop of the RREQ as next hop on the reverse path. As AOMDV is reactive protocol and most of the wireless sensor networks are static in nature, route discovery process has to initiate by sensor nodes, when it wants to send the data to the sink node. The message overhead in the route discovery is high for the wireless sensor networks. Ke Guan et al [2] proposed Energy-Efficient Multi-Path Routing Protocol for Wireless Sensor Networks. It is a reactive routing protocol. In the network, every node may act as a source and a sink node. The assumption of the common base station is eliminated. The route discovery mechanism provides the multiple paths between source and destination using shared nodes in the query tree and search tree. The number of control messages used in the multiple route construction is high, because, to construct query tree and search tree, query messages and search messages are to be broadcast in the network. These messages are sent from the sink and source nodes respectively.Choon-Sung Nam et al [3] proposed an efficient path setup and recovery in wireless sensor networks. The mechanism is a sink initiated, query based routing protocol. It is a variant of directed diffusion routing protocol. This mechanism finds the optimal path between source and destination based on minimum number of hops. However, the route set up is efficient, setting up of the multiple paths are not shown. Marjan Radi et al [4] proposed Low-Interference Energy-Efficient Multipath Routing (LIEMRO) for wireless sensor networks. It is a source initiated event-based, reactive routing protocol. LIEMRO finds the multipath between the source and destination. However, these multipaths exclude the node disjoint property. LIEMRO proposes the load balancing algorithm. Load balancing is done based on the, average interference level, average residual battery and estimated transmit energy (ETX) value of each path.Power aware node-disjoint multipath source routing [5] (PNDMSR) is a reactive, source initiated routing protocol. The route discovery in PNDMSR is similar to route discovery in dynamic source routing (DSR)[6]. In PNDMSR, only the destination node is allowed to send the route reply to source node, while in DSR, the route replyis sent by the intermediate and destination node. The node cost field is added in the RREQ packet and carries the cumulative cost. The proposed routing protocol is a sink initiated proactive protocol. The protocol finds the multiple paths between source and destination based on residual energy of the node and rate of energy consumption in the node. The protocol reduces the control overhead in the route discovery.

3 Energy Efficient Node Disjoint Multipath Route Discovery Mechanism

The energy efficient node-disjoint multipath routing protocol (EEMRP) assumes the wireless sensor network into number of stages based on the number of hops between source and destination. The sink is stage 0 node. Every node that can communicate with sink node is in stage 1. We assume that stage s node can communicate with nodes on the same stage and next s+1 stage but cannot communicate with the s-1 stage nodes. This back communication prevents the formation of loop paths.

3.1 The Format of the Route Construction Packet

The route construction packet has following components: type of the packet, forwarding node type and its id, number of hops away from the sink, residual energy of forwarded node and packet traversed from sink to that packet received node as shown in the Fig 1.

Packet Type	Hop Count	Forward ID	Threshold Energy value	Route
1 byte	2 byte	2 byte	4 byte	2 byte

Fig. 1. Format of the route construction packet

3.2. Route Construction Phase

The sink node initiates the route construction by broadcasting the route construction packet to its neighbouring nodes. The neighbouring nodes receive the route construction packet. If route construction packet is not received by any of its neighbouring nodes, the packet is received from the s-1 stage and if its residual energy is above the threshold value, it receives the packet and updates its routing table. Otherwise it discards the packet.

Node ID	Hop Count	Node Weight	Residual Energy	Node Disjoint Paths

Fig. 2. Format of the Routing Table

The node that received the route construction packet updates the packet information with the its information such as, its type, packet type, hop count, its id, and its residualenergy and appends its node id to path and broadcasts to its neighbouring nodes. Routing table contains node id, number of hops away from the sink, node weight, residual energy and possible disjoint paths between that node to the sink node. The format of the routing table is shown in the Figure 2. The route construction packet is forwarded until all the nodes generate its routing table.

4 Results and Discussion

The route construction phase of the EEMRP is simulated using Network Simulator 2.34. The EEMRP is compared with the AOMDV. The objective of the comparison between EEMRP and the AOMDV is to identify number of control messages and total node energy being used in the route construction phase. The network simulator setup is as follows:

Table 1. Simulation Parameters

Sl.No	Parameter	Values	Sl.No	Parameter	Values
1	Simulation area	200 m x200 m	6	Energy Threshold Value	5 Joules
2	Network size	10 to 100 nodes	7	Data Rate	2 MBPS
3	Transmission range	15 meters	8	Traffic type and packet size	CBR, 512 Bytes
4	Transmission Power	0.036 J	9	Simulation time	150 sec
5	Initial Energy	100 Joules	10	Topology	grid
	Reception Power	0.036 J			
	Idle Power	1μJ			

The number of control messages considered in EEMRP is less than the control messages used in AOMDV for the route construction. When the number of nodes in the network is 100, the control messages used in the route construction is 100 and 152 messages in EEMRP and AOMDV respectively as shown in the Figure 3. In EEMRP, every node rebroadcasts the receicved valid route construction packets to its neighbours once after incrementing its hop count. When all the neighbouirng nodes of a node which receives the route construction packet has generated the routing table, then that node stops rebroadcasting route construction packet. All the nodes in the network construct their routing table and generate their node-disjoint paths to the sink node in the same iteration of route construction phase. The new routing table is constructed by all the nodes only when there is no node-disjoint paths are available between any source node, which wants to send the sensed data to the sink node. The reactive protocl nature of the AOMDV makes each source node to initiate the multiple route construction, whenever it requires to send sensed data to the sink node. The number of control messages used and energy spent in the route construcion is also more compared to EEMRP as shown in the Figure 3 and Figure 4 respectively.

There is a reduction of 34.7% control messages and 29.9% energy used in the route construction phase.In AOMDV, each intermediate node sends the route reply to its previous hop and destination node sends the multiple route reply messages to source node. EEMRP is a sink initiated proactive routing protocol. The route reply messages are avoided in the EEMRP.

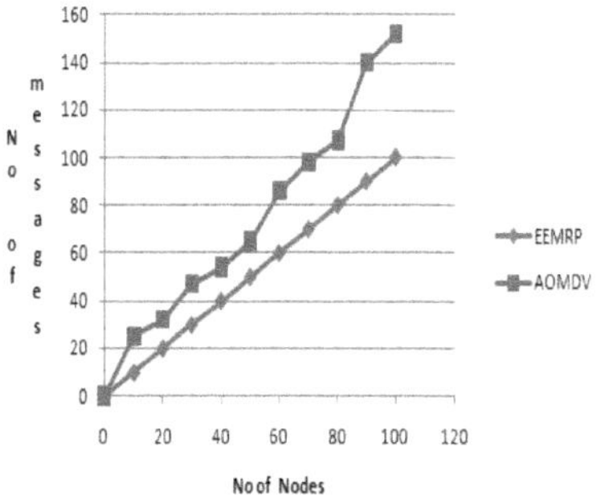

Fig. 3. No of control messages Vs No of nodes

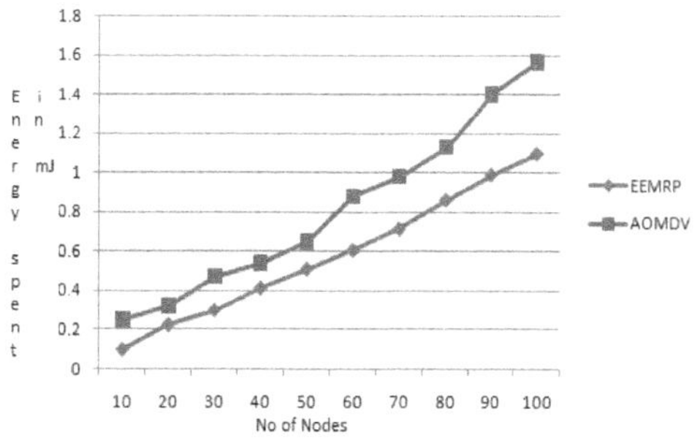

Fig. 4. No of nodes Vs Energy used in milli Joules

5 Conclusion

Increasing the network life time in the resource constrained sensor networks is the major concern of this work. The work proposes low control overhead route discovery mechanism for node disjoint multipath protocol. The number of control messages used in EEMRP is less than the control messages used in AOMDV for the route construction. There is a reduction of 34.7% control messages and 29.9% energy used in the route construction phase.Three different node-disjoint path selection criteria are proposed. The energy minimization in the route construction phase will increase the operational lifetime of the wireless sensor network.

References

1. Marina, M., et al.: On-Demand Multipath Distance Vector Routing in Ad hoc Networks. In: The International Conference for Network Protocols, pp. 14–22 (2001)
2. Guan, K., et al.: A Novel Energy-Efficient Multi-Path Routing Protocol for Wireless Sensor Networks. In: International Conference on Communications and Mobile Computing, pp. 214–218 (2010)
3. Nam, C.-S., et al.: Efficient Path Setup and Recovery in Wireless Sensor Networks by Using the routing table. In: 2nd International Conference on Education Technology and Computer (ICETC), pp. V4156–V4159 (2007)
4. Radi, M., et al.: LIEMR, A Low- Interference Energy-Efficient Multipath Routing Protocol for Improving QoS in Event-Based Wireless Sensor Networks. In: Fourth International Conference on Sensor Technologies and Aplications, pp. 551–557 (2010)

5. Naidu, B.M., et al.: Power- Aware Node-Disjoint Multipath Source Routing Low Overhead in MANET. Int. J. Mobile Network Design and Innovation 3(1), 33–45 (2009)
6. Broch, J., Johnson, D., Maltz, D.: Dynamic Source Routing Protocol for Mobile Ad Hoc Networks. IETF Internet draft (2004)
7. Abbas, A.M., et al.: An Analytical Framework for Disjoint Multipath Routing in Mobile Adhoc Networks. In: The IFIP International Conference on Wireless and Optical Communications, pp. 5–8 (2006)

Artificial Neural Networks and Fuzzy Logic in Process Modeling and Control

Smarti Reel[1] and Ashok Kumar Goel[2]

[1] Electronics and Communication Engineering Department, Thapar University, Patiala–147001, India
kotwalsmarti@gmail.com
[2] M M Group of Institutions, V.P.O. Sadopur, Distt. Ambala – 134003, India
ashokkgoel@rediffmail.com

Abstract. This paper presents a review on application of Artificial Neural Network and Fuzzy Logic in process modeling and control. The intelligent control techniques are rapidly replacing the conventional control due to their abilities like learning, function approximation, associative memory, prediction, combinatorial optimization and non-linear system modeling etc. In this paper, research work done in process modeling and control using conventional techniques, Artificial Neural Networks, Fuzzy Logic and Neuro-Fuzzy paradigms is discussed. For each control methodology its corresponding limitations are also presented. An outline of recent alternative approaches for process modeling and control are also included.

Keywords: Artificial-Neural-Networks, Fuzzy-Logic, Neuro-Fuzzy-Systems.

1 Introduction

The developments in artificial intelligence appear promising when applied to real world intelligent task [1]. Artificial Neural Networks (ANNs) find a wide variety of applications in control [2]. Neural networks have greatest promise in the field of nonlinear control problems. This stems from their theoretical ability to approximate arbitrary non-linear mappings [3]. Goel et al. has proposed Modified Functional Link ANN based controller for thermal processes [4]. Fuzzy logic is best used for controlling nonlinear processes. Assilian and Mamdani developed the first fuzzy controller for controlling a steam engine [5]. Khalid et al. presented a fuzzy controller for a laboratory process model of a Water Bath System [6]. Lee and Takagi proposed a method of determining all parameters simultaneously using Genetic Algorithms (GAs) for a Takagi-Sugeno type of FLC [7]. A hybrid fuzzy logic and neural network algorithm was proposed for robot motion control by Huang and Lian [8]. Seng et al. presented a neuro-fuzzy controller based on RBF nets whose parameters and rule base are tuned automatically using GAs [9]. A Neuro-Fuzzy controller with a simplified architecture was designed by Bordon et al. [10].

V.V. Das and N. Thankachan (Eds.): CIIT 2011, CCIS 250, pp. 808–810, 2011.

2 Artificial Neural Network Based Control

There are several learning architectures proposed whereby the neural network may be trained [11]. Astrom and Wittenmark, and Narendra et al. proposed many adaptive control techniques to replace the conventional classical methods [12], [13]. Khalid and Omatu have trained neural network as an inverse dynamic model of a temperature control system and then configured it as a direct controller to the process. Water Bath Temperature Control System has been taken as an example [14]. Luiz et al. proposed a neural network based direct inverse control for active control of vibrations of mechanical systems [15]. Goel et al. proposed a novel, computationally efficient ANN controller for industrial temperature control system using direct inverse control [16].

3 Fuzzy Logic Control

Lofti A. Zadeh first proposed Fuzzy Logic in 1965. Zadeh stated that the fuzzy reasoning method adopted by humans is an effective way to get at the solution to the problem [17]. There have been studies where neural network based control systems have been compared to fuzzy and adaptive control systems [18]. An interesting application is also introduced by Pan Lian et al. for combustion automatic control system for reheating furnace using hybrid fuzzy control formula [19]. Viana et al. has also recently proposed a management intelligent system that acts in the controllers of Direct current machine (DC) and thermoelectric control systems drives [20].

4 Conclusions

In the last couple of decades, Neural Networks and allied fields like Fuzzy Logic and Genetic Algorithms have been most widely applied field of research. Consequently, these artificial intelligent techniques are being widely appreciated in the field of modelling and control. Neural networks have attained wide exposure in the control industry. Therefore, novel ANN architectures are being developed for specific applications in process modelling and control. Hybrid controllers built by combining Fuzzy logic and allied technologies like Neural Networks and Genetic Algorithms are being applied for effective desired dynamic performance of complex control applications. Thus, has resulted in possible implementation of new resources for better and efficient control.

References

1. Rumelhart, D.E., Hinton, G.E., Williams, R.J.: Learning internal representations by error propagation. In: Rumelhart, D.E., McClelland, J.L. (eds.) Parallel Distributed Processing: Explorations in the Microstructure of Cognition, pp. 318–362. MIT Press, Cambridge (1986)
2. Narendra, K.S., Parthasarathy, K.: Identification and Control of Dynamical Systems Using Neural Networks. IEEE Transactions on Neural Networks 1, 4–27 (1990); Kaufman, C.J.: Rocky Mountain Research Lab., Boulder, CO, Private Communication

3. Hornik, K., Stinchcombe, M., White, H.: Multilayered Feed-forward Networks are Universal Approximators. Neural Networks 2, 359–366 (1989)
4. Goel, A.K., Saxena, S.C., Bhanot, S.: Modified Functional Link ANN Based Controller for thermal Processes. IETE Technical Review 23(1), 81–92 (2006)
5. Mamdani, E.H., Assilian, S.: An experiment in linguistic synthesis with a fuzzy logic controller. International Journal of Machine Studies 7(1) (1975)
6. Khalid, M., Omato, S., Yusof, R.: Temperature regulation with neural networks and alternative control schemes. IEEE Transactions on Neural Networks 6(3), 572–582 (1995)
7. Lee, M.A., Takagi, H.: Integrating design stages of fuzzy systems using genetic algorithms. In: Proc. Second IEEE Int. Conference Fuzzy Systems, pp. 612–617 (1993)
8. Huang, S.-J., Lian, R.-J.: A hybrid fuzzy logic and neural network algorithm for robot motion control. IEEE Transactions on Industrial Electronics 44(3), 40–41 (1997)
9. Seng, T.L., Khalid, M., Yusof, R.: Tuning of a Neuro-Fuzzy Controller by Genetic Algorithms with an Application to a Coupled-Tank Liquid-Level Control System. Engg. Applications of Artificial Intelligence 11(4), 517–529 (1998)
10. Bordon, M.E., da Silva, I.N., Avolio, E.: Design of a Neuro-fuzzy controller with simplified architecture. Department of Electrical Engineering, State University of Sao Paulo, Bauru, Sao Paulo, Brazil (2001)
11. Psaltis, D., Sideris, A., Yamamura, A.: A Multilayered Neural Network Controller. IEEE Control Syst. Mag. 10(3), 44–48 (1989)
12. Astrom, K.J., Wittenmark, B.: Adaptive control. Addison-Wesley, Reading (1989)
13. Narendra, K.S., Ortega, R., Dorato, P.: Advances in adaptive Control. IEEE Press, New York (1991)
14. Khalid, M., Omatu, S.: A neural network controller for a temperature control system. IEEE Control System Mag. 12(3), 58–64 (1992)
15. Luiz, G., de Abreu, C.M., Teixeira, R.L., Ribeiro, J.F.: A Neural Network-Based Direct Inverse Control for Active Control of Vibrations of Mechanical Systems: sbrn. In: VI Brazilian Symposium on Neural Networks (SBRN 2000), p. 107 (2000)
16. Goel, A.K., Gill, N., Sharma, M.: ANN Controller for industrial Temperature Control System. Journal of the Instrument Society of India 35(1), 48–53 (2005)
17. Zadeh, L.A.: Fuzzy sets. Information and Control 8(3), 338–353 (1965)
18. Kraft, L.G., Campagna, D.P.: A Comparison Between CMAC Neural Network control and Two Traditional Adaptive Control Systems. IEEE Control System Mag. 10(3), 36–43 (1990); Proc. 4th Annu. Allerton Conf. Circuits and Systems Theory, New York, pp. 8–16 (1994)
19. Lian, P., Junjie, S.: The Research of Fuzzy Nerve Network Control System on Steel Rolling Heating Furnace, Implementation of Steel Rolling Heating Furnace Adopting Fuzzy Nerve Network Control System. In: 2010 International Conference on Electrical and Control Engineering (ICECE), June 25-27, pp. 2407–2410 (2010)
20. Viana da-Fonseca Neto, J., de Andrade, G.A.: Design of Decision Making Unit for Neuro-fuzzy Control of Dynamic Systems. In: 2011 UkSim 13th International Conference on Computer Modelling and Simulation (UKSim), March 30-April 1, pp. 116–121 (2011)

Lazy-Parallel Function Calls for Automatic Parallelization

Soumya S. Chatterjee and R. Gururaj

Dept. of Computer Science and Information Systems, BITS-Pilani, Hyderabad Campus
500 078, Hyderabad, Andhra Pradesh, India
soum@live.in, gururaj@bits-hyderabad.ac.in

Abstract. When using traditional imperative languages for parallel programming, language guarantees like order of change of program state cease to exist making it harder to reason about correctness of the program. As a result, compilers mostly cannot help with the parallel constructs. We propose a mechanism, Lazy-Parallel Function Calls, which allows programs written with lazy evaluation semantics to be automatically parallelized and retain same behavior under both sequential and parallel execution. The analysis and the transformation the compiler needs to do is presented here.

Keywords: Lazy evaluation, automatic parallelization, compiler optimization.

1 Introduction

Mainstream programming languages has only rudimentary support for parallel programming but without any semantic guarantees from the language to mask the issues arising out of non-determinism in order of execution [1], leaving the developer to deal with the parallel constructs. Designing an automatically parallelizing compiler is a long sought-after goal, but a general purpose solution is evasive. But there are concepts in functional programming languages which could help with that. This research tries to adapt those for imperative programming and establish how the compiler will use those semantic guarantees to automatically parallelize the code. The background of the work is discussed in Section 2, followed by the proposals, prototype implementation and results in Sections 3, 4 and 5, respectively. The paper ends with future directions and conclusions in Section 6 and references in Section 7.

2 Background

Functional programming languages like Haskell are *Lazily Evaluated* [1][2]. When a function is called, the body of the function is wrapped in a *closure* [2], with the variables of the function replaced by their value at that instant, and returned to the caller without being evaluated. When the result is needed, the closure is accessed, in turn triggering the evaluation of the result. With this, functions are evaluated only if needed, and the results are cached to prevent redundant evaluations [2]. It also means

V.V. Das and N. Thankachan (Eds.): CIIT 2011, CCIS 250, pp. 811–816, 2011.

data is not modified in program order anymore, but this non-determinism does not lead to wrong results as all data structures are *persistent* and *immutable* [2][3]. *Immutability* means that the data structure is read-only; any change creates a new copy with the changes applied. *Persistent* means that once a change is made, both the old and the new revisions are available. A lazily evaluated closure is created with the *persistent identity* [2] of the variables at that instant, so that even if the variables change before the closure is executed, the result of the closure does not change.

3 Proposal

We propose a new function call mechanism called *Lazy-Parallel Function Calls (L-P Calls)*, which abstract parallelism using lazy evaluation semantics. On doing so, the code can exhibit same behavior under both serial and parallel evaluation. In addition, the compiler itself can generate code necessary for either execution model. L-P calls can be used in garbage collected imperative languages like C# and Java. When a function is called with these semantics, the parameters are cached and a closure is created with the cached values. The closure is returned to the caller, and the caller proceeds normally. In addition, the closure starts executing in a background thread simultaneously. On completion, the result is placed in the closure object itself, where it is accessed. If the result is not yet ready when the closure is accessed, the caller is blocked temporarily. From the programmers' perspective, it is just like using lazy evaluation but the parallel execution of the closure ensures higher performance. If the parameters are restricted to be immutable, the non-determinism due to parallelism will not lead to incorrect results or race conditions. Each L-P call creates a closure to be executed in parallel. But we cannot use OS-threads to schedule them as they will be too heavy-weight. Instead Nano-threads [4][5] are used. Nano-threads are constructs to queue up small units of work [6] and schedule them using a user-mode non-pre-emptive scheduler onto OS-threads.

3.1 Compiler Analysis

The compiler has to decide which function calls to be replaced with L-P calls so that there is enough work for the parallel threads to do, and ensure that the overhead of threading does not outweigh the performance gains. We propose two analysis methods – *Call Graph Analysis*, suitable for latency-sensitive scenarios like JIT compilers, and *Weighted Control Flow Graph*, a more exhaustive analysis.

Call Graph Analysis (CGA). Consider the following snippet of (pseudo) code given in Fig. 1. Assume it starts execution at *A*. For each node, we calculate the depth, which is the number of nodes till the farthest leaf node in that branch is reached. The node where the depth reaches a pre-determined threshold is to be replaced with an L-P Call. In the example, the branch from *B* has a depth of 3 whereas the one from *C* has a depth of *1*. If the threshold is 3, the initial call to *B* will be an L-P Call.

```
function A() {
    return B() + C();
}
function B() {
    return D();
}
function C() {
    return 1;
}
function D() {
    return E();
}
```

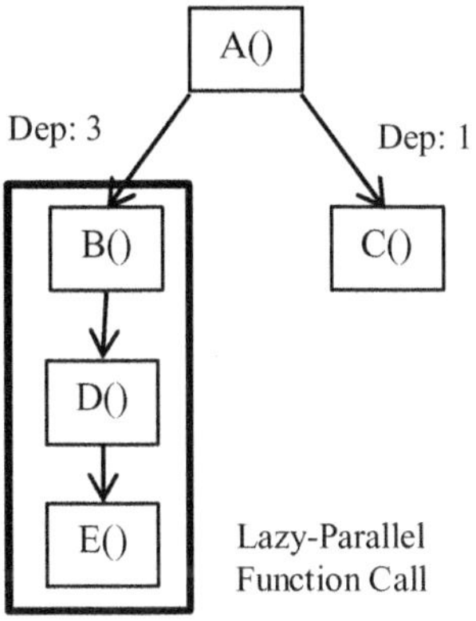

Fig. 1. A sample code snippet and the associated call-graph generated from the code snippet

So the Call-Graph Analysis algorithm can be summarized as follows:

- For root node, depth $\delta = 0$, for other nodes calculate depth δ as:

  $$\delta(\text{Node}) = \text{Max}(\delta(\text{Childnode}_1), \ldots, \delta(\text{Childnode}_n) + 1$$

- Do a depth-first traversal; at a node if $\delta(\text{Node}) >$ threshold †, the call to Node should be a Lazy-Parallel call.
- If the call is a part of a recursion chain, only the initial call should be a Lazy-Parallel call.
- Once the call to a certain node is replaced with a Lazy-Parallel function call, consider its depth as 1 and repeat the procedure for the rest of the call graph.
- Continue iterating until there no changes are made.

Weighted Control Flow Graph (WCFG). The CGA method described previously has very low overhead but ignores the cost of functions. The *Weighted Control Flow Graph* method takes the cost of individual functions into account, but takes more effort to compute. In this, we start with the set of methods identified by CGA, and for each of the method, we compute the *control flow graph* [8][9] starting from the identified method and including all the methods that can be reached starting from the identified method. For example, consider the following control flow graph given in Fig. 2., where each of the boxes represent a basic block, which is a straight run of code from a branch in to a branch out. Please note that the control flow is important here, not the actual code. The weights (cost) of each of the blocks are computed as the number of low-level intermediate language instructions [7] (such that which have a one-to-one correspondence with machine language) in each (represented in the figure as *B1, B2 … B5*). If the block is a part of the loop or recursion, the weights are then again multiplied by the number of times the loop runs (identified in the figure as *B1 * 2* etc). There are three conditional statements (*if-else* statements) identified as *C1* and *C2*.

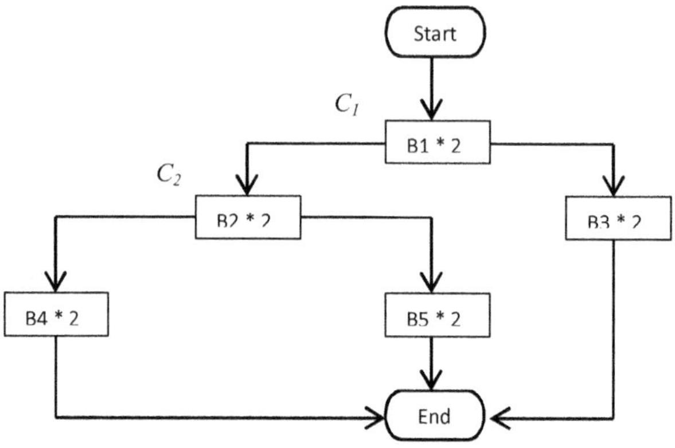

Fig. 2. A sample control flow graph, where the boxes represent the basic blocks. The three conditional statements are represented as C1 and C2.

From the control flow graph, we can see that there are four possible paths of execution, ψ_1 to ψ_4, each consisting of a series of basic blocks:

$\psi_1 \rightarrow \{B1, B3\}$ where ψ_1 = C1
$\psi_2 \rightarrow \{B1, B2, B5\}$ where ψ_2 = !C1 && C2
$\psi_3 \rightarrow \{B1, B2, B4\}$ where ψ_3 = !C1 && !C2

The cost of each path is the summation of the weights of all the blocks in the path. For example,

$$\text{Cost, } \mathfrak{c}(\psi_1) = \mathfrak{c}(\text{B1}) + \mathfrak{c}(\text{B3})$$

The ψ conditions specify which path to actually execute. The runtime can use *pattern matching* [10] – efficient implementations of which are available for functional languages – to calculate which path to actually take. If the cost of the path is greater than some threshold $\dagger$, the function should be invoked as Lazy-Parallel. Profiling information can be used to make the decision at compile time.

4 Implementation

A prototype demonstrating the Lazy-Parallel Call mechanism has been implemented in C#. It uses a library based approach, using *reflection* to bind to the methods. The compiler analysis has not been implemented yet.

The API requires an object of type Evaluator<TResult> be created, specifying the required call semantics – regular function call, lazily evaluated call or a Lazy-Parallel call. The Evaluate() method is then called on the object:

```
public void Evaluate(string function,
  Type containingType,
  dynamic containingInstance,
params dynamic[] arguments)
```

The following arguments are to be provided to the Evaluate() function:

- *function*: The case-sensitive name of the function to bind to and invoke.
- *containingType*: The type containing the function to bind to.
- *containingInstance*: The object the function will bind against.
- *arguments*: The arguments that the bound function expects.

For closure creation, if the object implements the ISnapshottable<T> interface, it is assumed that it returns a persistent revision. Else, it is cloned using *serialization*.

5 Results and Discussion

It is necessary to guarantee the transformations produce the same results as without the changes as well as there is significant speedup. To verify that, consider the following snippet for the easy to parallelize N-Queens problem for a 13x13 board.

```
var evaluators = new List<Evaluator<int>>();
for (int i = 0; i < BoardSize; i++)
  var b = new int[BoardSize];
  var e = new Evaluator<int>(Mode.LazyParallel);
  e.Evaluate("PrtlSln", typeof(Q), this, b, 0, i);
  evaluators.Add(e);
}
return evaluators.Select(S => S.Result).Sum();
```

For a hard to parallelize problem, consider the following sort where the list of numbers is split into smaller lists, sorted in parallel and merged back. The merging part is not parallelized here.

```
subLists = Partition(nums, count, PartitionSize);
foreach (var l in subLists) {
  var e = new Evaluator<List<int>>(Mode.LazyParallel);
  e.Evaluate("Sort", this.GetType(), null, l);
  evals.Add(e);
}
```

When run, the N-Queens program gives close to 2x speedup, whereas the hard to parallelize sorting code gives a non-trivial 1.65x speedup on a dual-core system.

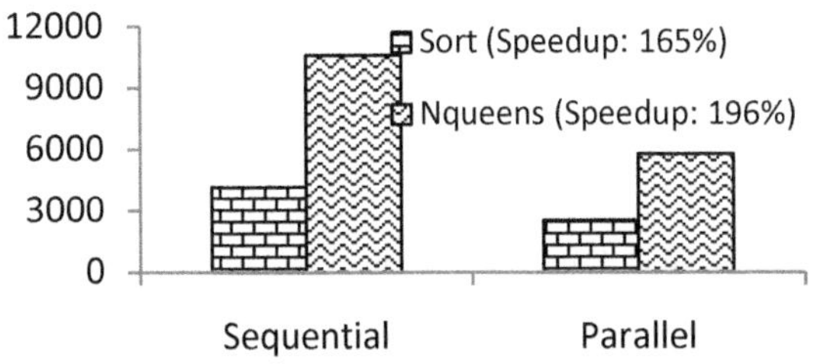

Fig. 3. Comparing the respective performances of sequential & parallel executions

The results shown graphically in Fig. 3 show that there is indeed significant speedup. Also changing the execution mode does not change the results, thereby proving correctness. But to bring it to mainstream programming languages, there are many barriers to overcome. Serialization is a costly way of caching parameters. So, we need to provide a library of immutable data structures, but keeping track of unused revisions is cumbersome. So garbage collection to remove unused revisions is a must to keep memory usage in check. And the compiler must ensure that only methods working with such data structures are considered for automatic parallelization. It should be noted that such functions can use regular data structures internally, but at function call boundaries it should only use immutable data structures.

6 Conclusions and Future Work

Techniques like lazy evaluation and immutable data structures fit nicely with the parallel programming model. This paper presents the techniques for adapting them to imperative languages. The results have been verified using a prototype implementation and are promising. It is time to implement the ideas into a real compiler by modifying the Mono C# compiler to include the code analysis and generation techniques presented here and use the prototypes to determine the cost threshold values and determine if any language extensions are needed.

References

1. Chris, O.: Purely Functional Data Structures. Carnegie Melon University
2. Launchbury, J.: A Natural Semantics for Lazy Evaluation. In: Proceedings of the 20th ACM SIGPLAN-SIGACT symposium on Principles of Programming Languages, pp. 144–154
3. Peschanksi, F.: Parallel Computing with the π-Calculus. Université Pierre & Marie Curie UPMC - LIP6 - Paris, France
4. Polychronopoulost, E.D., Martorell, X., Nikolopoulos, D.S., Labarta, J., Papatheodorou, T.S., Navarro, N.: Kernel Level Scheduling for Nano-Threads Programming Model. University of Patras, Greece
5. Dubois, M.: Fighting the Memory Wall with Assisted Execution. University of South California
6. Mohr, E., Kranz, D.A., Halstead, R.H.: Lazy Task Creation: A Technique for Increasing the Granularity of Parallel Programs. Yale University, MIT and Cambridge Research Lab
7. Chen, J.: A Typed Intermediate Language for Supporting Interfaces. Microsoft Research
8. Joisha, P.G., Schreiber, R.S., Bannerjee, P., Boehm, H.J., Chakrabarti, D.R.: A Technique for the Effective and Automatic Reuse of Classical Compiler Optimizations on Multithreaded Code. Hewlett-Packard Laboratories
9. Gao, L., Li, L., Xue, J., Ngai, T.-F.: Loop Recreation for Thread Level Specification. Microprocessor Technology Lab, Intel
10. Syme, D., Neverov, G., Margeston, J.: Extensible Pattern Matching Via a Lightweight Language Extension. In: Proceedings of the 12th ACM SIGPLAN International Conference on Functional Programming, pp. 29–40

Image Retrieval Using Shape Feature: A Study

Padmashree Desai[1], Jagadeesh Pujari[2], and Shweta Parvatikar[1]

[1] CSE Department, BVBCET, Hubli, Karnataka, India
[2] SDM college of Engg. & Tech., Dharwad, Karnataka, India
padmashri@bvb.edu, jaggudp@yahoo.com,
shwetaparv@gmail.com

Abstract. As the network and development of multimedia technologies are becoming more popular, users are not satisfied with the traditional information retrieval techniques. So now a day the Content Based Image Retrieval (CBIR) is becoming a source of exact and fast retrieval. There are four important feature components for content-based image retrieval: colour, texture, shape, and spatial relationship. Among these features, shape contains the most attractive visual information for human perception. The main purpose of this paper is to discuss issues and challenges in CBIR systems, the importance of shape feature in image retrieval and proposing a new method for image retrieval using wavelet based shape feature.

Keywords: CBIR, shape, colour, texture, wavelet.

1 Introduction

Because of recent advances in computer technology and the revolution in the way information is processed, increasing interest has developed in automatic information retrieval from huge databases. In particular, content-based retrieval has received considerable attention and consequently improving the technology for content-based querying systems becomes more challenging [1]. There are four important feature components for content-based image retrieval: color, texture, shape, and spatial relationship. Among these features, shape contains the most attractive visual information for human perception. Different methods [2]-[6] have been proposed for feature extraction and shape representation. P Liu, K. Jia, Z. Wang and Z. Lv explained a new and effective image retrieval method based on combined features [3]. Jeong-Yo Ha, Gye-Young Kim, and Hyung-Il Choi discussed the content-based image retrieval method using multiple features [4]. Ryszard S. Choras, Tomasz Andrysiak, and Michal Choraś discussed integrated color, texture and shape information for content-based image retrieval [5].An important step before shape extraction is edge point detection. Many edge detection methods have been proposed [7]-[14]. D.N. Verma, Vrinda Mar and Bharti explained an efficient approach for colour image retrieval using Haar wavelet [7]. J. Pan has proposed an edge detection combining wavelet transform and canny operator based on fusion rules [11]. Most of these research results show that they are robust but fail in one or the other aspect of

V.V. Das and N. Thankachan (Eds.): CIIT 2011, CCIS 250, pp. 817–821, 2011.

shape extraction. Using this literature survey, we propose an efficient method to solve the image retrieval problem. This paper is organized as follows: In Section 2, we bring up principles of CBIR and different commercially available CBIR systems, its advantages, disadvantages and motivation for the study of this paper. Section 3 concentrates on different conventional edge detectors, their advantages and disadvantages. Section 4 proposes a new method using wavelets decomposition for edge detection and shape representation that is invariant to translation, rotation, and scaling. Section 5 makes the conclusion on proposed work.

2 Principles of CBIR

A typical CBIR system as shown in Fig.1., automatically extract visual attributes (colour, shape, texture and spatial information) of each image in the database based on its pixel values and stores in a different database within the system called feature database. The feature data for each of the visual attributes of each image is very much smaller in size compared to the image data. Thus the feature database contains an abstraction (compact form) of the images in the image database; each image is represented by a compact representation of its contents (colour, texture, shape and spatial information) in the form of a fixed length real-valued multi-component feature vectors or signature. The users usually formulate query image and present to the system. The system automatically extract the visual attributes of the query image in the same mode as it does for each database image, and then identifies images in the database whose feature vectors match those of the query image, and sorts the best similar objects according to their similarity value.

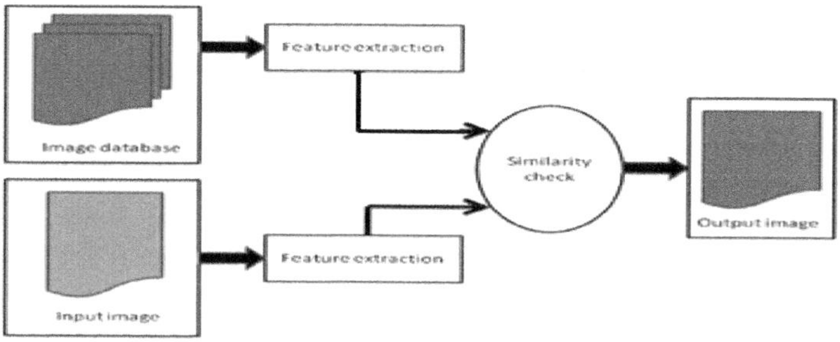

Fig. 1. CBIR System

2.1 Different CBIR Systems

A considerable number of image retrieval systems [4] have been developed for commercial use and demonstrations versions are in existence in the academic world. Some of the systems include QBIC, VIR, Photobook , VisualSEEK , MARS and NETRA. A total of fifty-eight CBIR systems were reviewed in. Virtually all the systems incorporate colour in their feature extraction. Merely more than fifty percent of the systems use texture feature. Shape features are utilized in half of the systems reviewed. Most of the shape features are the simple ones, for example, eccentricity, area and orientation. Less than half of the systems use spatial information. Shape descriptors adopted are not much effective because they are prone to noise. According to [5] the frequency of usage of the feature descriptors is inversely proportional to the computational complexity involved in extracting the features.

Remarkable observations in the review of related works are as follows:

- Current CBIR systems use the combination of texture, shape and spatial information for retrieval. Fourth feature is added usually colour to improve its efficiency.
- Shape with other low level features give better results.
- Many systems lack the combination of edge detectors for finding the edge map of the image and also the use of wavelets in edge detection.
- Many systems lack the use of fuzzy techniques for the shape extraction and representation.

Literature review shows that combination of feature that is shape as a main feature with colour and texture as other low level features gives better results. So these are the motivations for this study paper. Edge detection is an important step for efficient shape representation. Edge detection has attracted many researches to provide different techniques for edge detection.

3 Edge Detection

Edges are curves that follow a path of rapid change in intensity. In image processing, an edge is often interpreted as one class of singularities and they can be characterized easily as discontinuities where the gradient approaches infinity.

Conventional edge detection mechanisms [9] examine the pixels where the first derivative of the intensity is larger in magnitude than some threshold, or finding places where the second derivative of the intensity has a zero crossing. Traditional edge-detection algorithms usually belong to -Gradient-based edge detectors, Laplacian of Gaussian (LOG), Zero crossing and Canny edge detector. Although canny's method is known to many as the better edge detector than the gradient-based, LoG, and zero-crossing methods, it still suffers from some practical limitations.

3.1 Edge Detectors with Wavelets

To overcome the disadvantages of the edge detectors, more edge detecting or generally singularity investigation techniques are developed. The Fourier transform is one of them. It was viewed as the main mathematical tool for analyzing singularities. It is hard to find the location and spatial distribution of singularities using Fourier transform. The wavelet transform, on the other hand, is a local analysis. It is more suitable than the Fourier transform for the time-frequency analysis, which is essential for singularity detection including edges and corners etc.

4 Proposed Method

Studying the different edge detection and shape descriptors we propose new technique for image retrieval using wavelet based shape features as shown in Fig. 2.

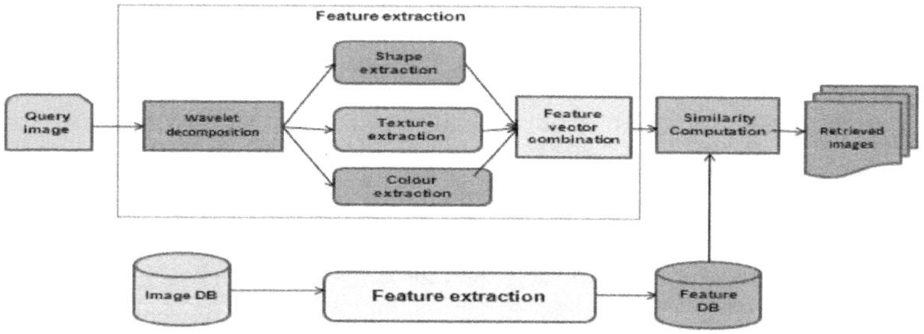

Fig. 2. Image retrieval using wavelet decomposition

A 2-D image is processed and the wavelet analysis is performed separately for the horizontal and the vertical directions. Thus, the vertical and the horizontal edges are detected separately. The 2D discrete wavelet transform (DWT) decomposes the images into sub-images, 3 details and 1 approximation. The approximation looks similar to the input image but only 1/4 of original size. The results of 2-D DWT decomposition results sub-images (a single iteration of the DWT) as LL (the approximation or we say the smoothing image of the original image which contains the most information of the original image), LH (preserves the horizontal edge details), HL (preserves the vertical edge details), and HH (preserves the diagonal details which are influenced by noise greatly) as shown in Fig. 3. The pixel information obtained from sub bands are used to extract shape, texture and color information.

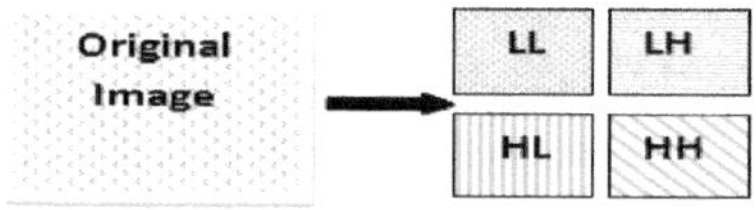

Fig. 3. Wavelet decomposition of an image

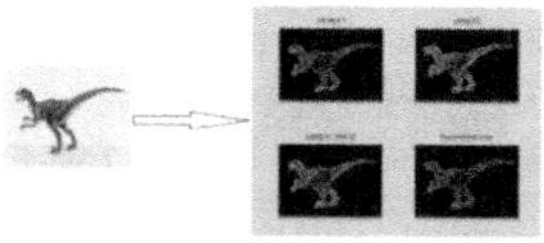

Fig. 4. Edge maps of an input image

The proposed work uses Daubechies wavelets (db2) for image decomposition. Input query image is converted to grayscale image. The resulted grayscale image is decomposed into 4 components as Approximation, Horizontal, Vertical component and Diagonal component. In the wavelet decomposition process, only alternative rows and columns of the input image are present in approximation component. Other prominent edge information is obtained from different components. To get all strong and weak edge information, all four components are used. Four edge maps are obtained by multiplying four masks with the approximation component as shown in Fig. 4 .Moment invariants are applied on these edge maps to obtain feature vector. The process is repeated for creating Feature Database of Image Database. Similarity measure is done based on Canberra distance measure and similar images are retrieved.

5 Conclusions

This paper presented a new technique for image retrieval using wavelet based shape features which addresses challenges and issues of current CBIR systems. The key contribution of this paper is to make of multi resolution wavelets for identifying the edges of an image and achieve better image retrieval efficiency. Performance of the CBIR system is improved to achieve better results in different applications. The experimental results demonstrate the efficiency and robustness of proposed system.

References

1. Ritendradatta, Dhirajjoshi, Li, J., Wang, J.Z.: Image Retrieval: Ideas, Influences, and Trends of the New Age. ACM Computing Surveys 40 (2) (April 2008)
2. Wu, Y., Wu, Y.: Shape-based Image Retrieval Using Combining Global and Local Shape Features. In: IEEE 2nd Conference on Image and Signal Processing, CISP 2009 (2009)
3. Liu, P., Jia, K., Wang, Z., Lv, Z.: A New and Effective Image Retrieval Method Based on Combined Features. In: Proc. IEEE Int. Conf. on Image and Graphics, vol. I, pp. 786–790 (August 2007)
4. Ha, J.-Y., Kim, G.-Y., Choi, H-Il.: The content-based image retrieval method using multiple features. In: IEEE Fourth International Conference on Networked Computing and Advanced Information Management, NCM 2008, vol. 1, pp. 652–657 (2008)
5. Choraś, R.S., Andrysiak, T., Choraś, M.: Integrated color, texture and shape information for content-based image retrieval. Pattern Analysis & Applications 10(4), 333–343 (2007)
6. Adnan, A., Gul, S., Ali, M., Dar, A.H.: Content Based image Retrieval Using Geometrical-Shape of Objects in Image. In: IEEE Conference on Emerging Technologies, ICET 2007 (2007)
7. Verma, D.N., Mar, V., Bharti: An Efficient Approach for Color Image Retrieval Using Haar Wavelet. In: International Conference on Methods and Models in Computer Science (2009)
8. Goh, Y.Z., Teoh, A.B.J., Gog, M.K.O.: Wavelet Based Illumination Invariant Preprocessing in Face Recognition. In: Proceedings of the 2008 Congress on Image and Signal Processing, vol. 3, pp. 421–425. IEEE Computer Society (2008)
9. Akansu, A.N., Serdijn, W.A., Selesnick, I.W.: Wavelet Transforms in Signal Processing: A Review of Emerging Applications. Physical Communication 3(1), 1–18 (2010)
10. Wenchang, S., Jianshe, S., Lin, Z.: Wavelet Multi-scale Edge Detection Using Adaptive threshold. In: IEEE 5th International Conference, WiCom 2009 (2009)
11. Pan, J.: Edge detection combining wavelet transform and Canny operator based on fusion rules. In: IEEE Proceedings of the 2009 International Conference on Wavelet Analysis and Pattern Recognition (July 2009)
12. Sur, Patra, N., Chakraborty, S., Saha, I.: A new wavelet based edge detection technique for iris imagery. In: IEEE IACC (2009)
13. Brannock, E., Weeks, M.: Edge detection using wavelets. In: ACMSE (March 2006)
14. Wang, X.: Image edge detection based on lifting wavelet. In: IEEE International Conference on Intelligent Human-Machine Systems and Cybernetics (2009)

An Effective Technique to Identify River's Stage through Satellite Images by Means of RBFNN

R. Kalaivani[1] and P. Thangaraj[2]

[1] Department of Computer Science and Engineering, Institute of Road and Transport Technology, Erode, 638 316, Tamilnadu, India
[2] Department of Computer Science and Engineering, Bannari Amman Institute of Technology, Sathyamangalam, Tamilnadu, India
kalai_nandhu@yahoo.com, ctptr@yahoo.co.in

Abstract. Today, a significant role is played by satellite image processing in the research improvement of various subject of analysis such as Astronomy, Remote Sensing, GIS, Agriculture Monitoring and Disaster Management. Forecasting natural disasters so that necessary safety measures can be taken to safeguard the surroundings is the objective behind the utilization of remote sensing images in most of the researches. In this paper, the stage of a river is predicted utilizing satellite images of the river. Initially, in the preprocessing phase, the image is filtered and then converted to the LAB color space for acute analysis. Subsequently, the segmentation process is carried out using the designed Radial Basis Function Neural Network (RBFNN) and then morphological operation are performed on the image. After that in the testing phase, the segmented image is analyzed and the stage of the river is identified as either normal or flood or draught using the designed RBFNN.

Keywords: Remotely Sensed Image, Radial Basis Function Neural Network, River Water Level, Morphological operation, Water Region.

1 Introduction

Feature extraction from remotely sensed imagery has been a field of active research in computer vision and digital photogrammetry, for the previous few decades [1]. Several environmental applications like earth resources tracking, geographical mapping, agricultural crops prediction, urban development, weather, flood and fire control etc use images obtained by satellites [2]. In this paper, we propose an effective mechanism to predict the stage of the river by analyzing its water level using its satellite image.

1.1 Radial Basis Function Neural Network

In recent years, the ANN has attracted substantial interests from various fields. Capability to learn from sample sets is the most important property of ANN models [3][6]. RBF's are implemented in a two layer neural network, where a radial activated

V.V. Das and N. Thankachan (Eds.): CIIT 2011, CCIS 250, pp. 822–825, 2011.

function is implemented by each hidden unit. A weighted sum of hidden unit outputs is implemented by the output units. A linear output is obtained from the RBF network by giving it a non-linear input [4]. The radial basis function (RBF) the value of which is dependant only on the distance from the origin is a real-valued function. If a function 'h' is a radial function if it satisfies the property h(x) =h (||x||). Monotonically decreasing or increasing response with distance from a central point is their characteristic feature[5].

2 Proposed Mechanism to Identify the Stage of the River

2.1 Preprocessing Phase

Initially, the input image is filtered to sluice the noises and then the denoised river image is put into the further process. The denoising process has been carried out to acquire the acute information of the river.

Let D be the database of river images and let the dimension of each image I be $M \times N$ and p_{ij} be the number of pixels of the image. Before commencing the identification of watered regions, the preprocessing steps have been taken.

$$D_k = \{I_0, I_1, I_2 \cdots, I_{N_I - 1}\} \qquad 0 \le k \le N_I - 1 \tag{1}$$

Initially the image is filtered to remove the noises from it and then the denoised image is converted to the LAB color space which is utilized to identify the acute information from the image. A Lab color space is a color-opponent space with dimension L for lightness and a and b for the color-opponent dimensions, based on nonlinearly compressed CIE XYZ color space coordinates. The following eqn (2) details the process.

$$\begin{bmatrix} X \\ Y \\ Z \end{bmatrix} = \begin{bmatrix} 0.412453 & 0.357580 & 0.180423 \\ 0.212671 & 0.715160 & 0.072167 \\ 0.019334 & 0.119193 & 0.950227 \end{bmatrix} * \begin{bmatrix} r \\ g \\ b \end{bmatrix} \tag{2}$$

$$L = \begin{cases} 116 * (Y / Y_n)^{1/3} - 16, & for \;\; Y / Y_n > 0.008856 \\ 903.3 * Y / Y_n, & otherwise \end{cases} \tag{3}$$

$$a = 500 * (f(X / X_n) - f(Y - Y_n)) \tag{4}$$

$$b = 200 * (f(Y / Y_n) - f(Z - Z_n)) \tag{5}$$

where $f(t) = \begin{cases} t^{1/3} & for \;\; t > 0.008856 \\ 7.787 * t + 16/116 & \text{otherwise} \end{cases}$.

Here X_n, Y_n and Z_n are the tri-stimulus values of the reference white. In the pre processing phase the steps carried out are Segmentation, Binarization, applying morphological operation and thresholding.

2.2 Training Phase

The water regions presented in the river images which are selected manually is utilized on this network to train this RBFN network with Bayesian regulation back propagation.

Step 1: The input layer has a single neuron to accept the different length input vector L, and the output layer also must have of a single neuron to interpret the change in water level and provide the status weight as the output. The hidden layer must have N_{hd} numbers of hidden neurons and a bias neuron.

Step 2: Set up the input weights and bias for the designed NN. Assign weights only to those neurons that are present in the hidden and output layer.

Step 3: The basis function and the activation function which are chosen for the designed NN is given below.

$$Y_n = \tau + \sum_{m=0}^{N_{hd}-1} w_{mn} \varphi(\|l_{mn} - u_{mn}\|) \tag{6}$$

$$\varphi(\|l_{mn} - u_{mn}\|) = \exp\left[-\eta \|l_{mn} - u_{mn}\|^2\right] \tag{7}$$

The above eqns (6) and (7) which are the activation and the basis functions and u_{mn} is the center vector for the neuron. τ, η are bias and w_{mn} is the weight assigned for the neuron.

Step 4: The learning error is determined for the NN as follows

$$Err = \frac{1}{N_{hd}} \sum_{x=0}^{N_{hd}-1} D_x - Y_x \tag{8}$$

Here, Err is the error in the designed RBFN network NN, D_x is the desired output and Y_x is the actual output.

3 Results and Discussion

The proposed mechanism to predict the river water level changes was implemented in the working platform of MATLAB (version 7.10). The proposed mechanism was evaluated through the river image database used to design the network and the input river image of Amo river was analyzed. The stage of this river was obtained through the step by step process and the results attained by this proposed mechanism are given below.

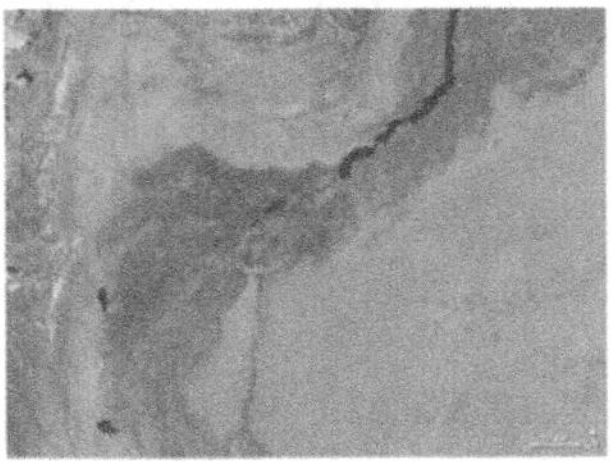

Fig. 1. Watered regions marked in the original image

4 Conclusion

In this paper, an effective mechanism to predict the stage of water level was proposed. The proposed mechanism, initially trained two neural networks one to identify the water regions and the other to determine the stage of the river from its water level. The raw input image of Amo river was de-noised and then it was segmented into different regions with the aid of the designed RBFNN. Finally the stage of the river was identified as 'draught' stage. The results proved the proficiency of the proposed method in determining the status of a river from its satellite image.

References

[1] Ye, F.-M., Su, L., Tang, J.-L.: Automatic Road Extraction UsingParticle Filters from High Resolution Images. Journal of China University of Mining and Technology 16(4), 490–493 (2006)

[2] Qiaoping, Z., Couloigner, I.: Automatic road change detectionand GIS updating from high spatial remotely-sensed imagery. Geo-Spatial Information Science 7(2), 89–95 (2004)

[3] Dhubkarya, Nagariya, D., Kapoor, R.: Implementation of a radialbasis function using VHDL. Global Journal of Computer Science and Technology 10(10), 16–19 (2010)

[4] Yang, G., Zhang, K., Wu, Q.: Modeling Technique for RFMEMS Phase Shifter Based on Artificial Neural Network. I. J. Wireless and Microwave Technologies 1, 60–67 (2009)

[5] Baragada, S.R., RamaKrishna, S., Rao, M.S., Purushothaman, S.: Implementation o Radial Basis Function Neural Network for Image steganalysis. International Journal of Computer Science and Security 2(1), 12–22 (2008)

[6] Kalaivani, Thangaraj: An Efficient Mechanism to Predict the Stage of River using Artificial Neural Network in Satellite Images. European Journal of Scientific Research 50(3), 380–394 (2011)

An Integrated Approach to Capture Semantics of Requirement Conflicts

Kiran Khatter[1] and Arvind Kalia[2]

[1] Ansal Institute of Technology, Indraprastha University, Delhi
[2] Deptt. of Comp. Science, Himachal Pradesh University, Shimla
{kirankhatter,arvkalia}@gmail.com

Abstract. Conflict Identification is one of the critical areas in software engineering. It is very important to understand the semantics of conflicts among non-functional requirements for conflict resolution task. In this paper a framework is provided to understand the nature of conflicts among non-functional requirements using the integrated analysis of functional requirements, non-functional requirements, internal constraints and external constraints. The output of proposed model is a conflict tree that refines conflicts among non-functional requirements from one level to another level. Finally a case study on monitoring and controlling system of a manufacturing firm is discussed to understand the nature of conflicts among non-functional requirements.

Keywords: Conflict Analysis, Non-Functional Requirements, Internal Constraints, External constraints, Strategy vs. Requirement Matrix.

1 Introduction

Functional requirements address specific problems where as non-functional requirements define global constraints [13] on software development process or on a software system. Since most of requirement analysis methods do not consider non-functional requirements, which leads to serious software development problems [16][11][8][10]. The problems faced because of negating non-functional requirements are more severe than the problems of functional requirements omissions [8]. Problems due to negligence of NFRs are the most difficult problems to solve [13][7]. Several reports show that improper handling of NFRS lead cons. The paramax systems corp. faced major deadline problems and cost overrun problems in the development of a real time system, which put the deployment on risk [14]. We have well known problem of software development in *London Ambulance Service* Report. *London Ambulance System* was failed due to negligence of non-functional requirements (reliability, usability and performance) [2] [4]. Therefore it is important for software development process to accommodate non-functional aspects also. For a system to perform in real-time, the complete system has to be designed to meet not only

V.V. Das and N. Thankachan (Eds.): CIIT 2011, CCIS 250, pp. 826–831, 2011.

functional requirements but non-functional requirements also. Bosch [6] suggested an approach which focus on designing functionality based architecture and then applying architectural transformations to satisfy non-functional requirements. Bruin [5] focused on a composition technique to derive software architecture by using a recursive approach. Functional requirements are never conflicting to each other but conflicts arise when non-functional requirements behave opposite to each other. For example: Satisficing security might call for the use of fingerprint or multilevel authentication. But multi-level authentication might conflict with usability requirement. There are varieties of models for the conflict identification in the literature. Poort [17] provided a framework known as non-functional decomposition to resolve conflicting requirements in a system. Gebhardt used Meta model for analyzing conflicts among requirements [9]. Boehm [3] proposed a software cost option strategy to deal with cost factors and risks among requirements. Xiaoqing Frank Liu [19] suggested a framework, which is based on the relationship among system requirements and constraints to deal with conflicts. Bertagnolli [18] used aspect-oriented software engineering for handling of requirements. Egyed [1] proposed a model for the identification of conflicts with the help of automated traceability. In and Kim [12] proposed a QoS (Quality of Service) resource conflict identification model for situation-aware middleware to identify trade-offs among requirements. After studying available literature, it was found some of the approaches failed to understand the nature of conflicts and some approaches did not clearly mention conflict-detection approach. Therefore we developed a framework, which analyzes and detects conflict using Strategy vs. Requirement matrix and then represent those conflicts in conflict tree to understand the hierarchy of non-functional requirements.

2 Proposed Model

The proposed model uses Strategy vs. Requirement matrix, which starts with the descriptions of visualized system to understand structural properties and architectural requirements of the system. Conventional techniques tend to suppress conflicts with the consideration of conflict resolution and development as two separate tasks. If the conflicts are resolved separately, it could not be done at appropriate time and could lie outside the software development framework leading to an untraceable resolution. Therefore this matrix considers conflict detection and overall development process both in parallel. Proposed matrix starts with the descriptions of visualized system to understand structural properties and architectural requirements of the system. This requires consideration of various factors such as development process, design strategies, a decomposition strategy, implementation strategies and system functionality. Matrix visualizes two dimensions intersections. One dimension is the strategy and other dimension is requirements. The cell of this matrix contains strategies from each of three strategy dimensions satisfying each of the four types of requirements. We categorized requirements into functional requirements, non-functional requirements, internal constraints and external constraints. Strategies to satisfy above-mentioned requirements are categorized on three criteria: Choice of development process, Design and Implementation.

Strategy

Requirements	Choice of Development Process	Design	Implementation
Functional	Traditional Development Methods	Database normalization, Choice of Programming Language	Implement required functionality such as audit trailing, printing facility, online help
Non-Functional	Capability Maturity Model, Agile Data Models, Object Oriented S/W Process, Test Driven Methods	Level of Granularity, Choice of multi-tier architecture, Choice of DBMS	Access control List, Encryption Key, Backup
Internal Environment Constraints	Time boxing, Prototyping, Incremental Development approach	Rapid application development /Prototyping	Make or Buy decision, Reuse of software components
External Environment Constraints	Available Hardware Resources, Available network Resources	Different releases of software	Available Hardware Resources, Available network Resources

Fig. 1. Conflict detection using Strategy versus Requirements Matrix based on the relationship between requirements and architecture

As a result, Choice of development process strategy results in the best choice to achieve system requirements and satisfy environment constraints. Design strategy gives structural solutions for system requirements and environment constraints. The combination of implementation strategies provides overall system functionality. Proposed model emphasizes conflict detection at a high level non-functional requirement based on the relationship among functional requirements, non-functional requirements and constraints. When a conflict is detected at a high level non-functional requirement, Non-functional requirement is then refined into low-level non-functional requirements and again conflict is detected using requirement Strategy vs. Requirement matrix. Above steps are repeated until high-level conflicts are analyzed and transformed into low-level conflicts. These conflicts are represented in conflict tree to understand the hierarchy of non-functional requirements with conflicts.

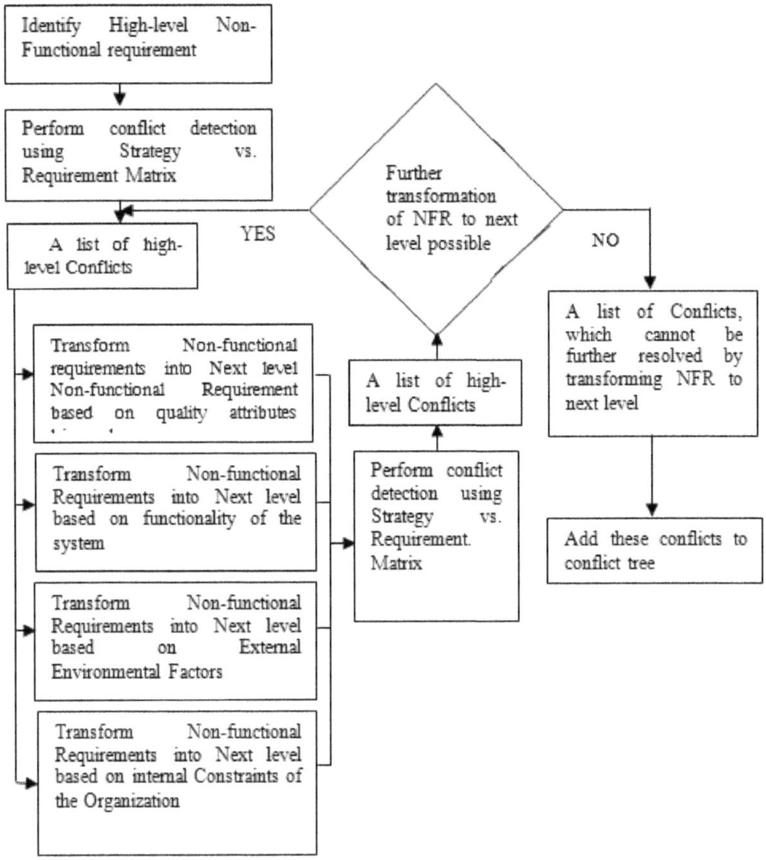

Fig. 2. Model for understanding semantics of conflicts using integrated analysis

3 A Case Study

The case is a monitoring and control system of a manufacturing firm. System aims at monitoring of the working of machines and controlling the manufacturing process. We identified two low-level non-functional requirements Reliability and Efficiency in order to achieve high-level non-functional requirement quality but this gives rise to a conflict C1. Reliability is furthermore refined into Maturity and Recoverability and Efficiency into Time Economy and Resource Economy. On comparison of quality attributes in Maturity, Recoverability, Time Economy and Resource Economy, we found Resource Economy conflicts with Recoverability and this conflict is denoted by C1.1, which is further transformed to Workload distribution of machines, Capacity of machines, Fault Recovery and Fault Prevention requirements. Quality attributes in Time Economy and Maturity Requirements generate conflict C1.2. Now C1.2 is further refined to another level of non-functional requirements Response time, Workload, Mean time between failure and Mean time to failure. If there is any fault during manufacturing process, Response time depends upon Recovery Process, which gives rise to another level conflict C1.2.1. One of the Fault Prevention techniques is removal of service with fault, which may delay the completion of task assigned to a machine. That is another conflict C1.2.2. Response time depends upon the complexity of task and the start up time of task. Here we got the transformation of conflict C1.2.1. to start time, task, Redundancy and Rollback functionalities. But these transformations produce another level of conflicts denoted by C1.2.1.1 and C1.2.1.2. This process continues until we get a list of conflicts that cannot be further resolved by transforming non-functional requirements to the next level. All conflicts are represented using conflict tree, which shows abstract and low-level conflicts.

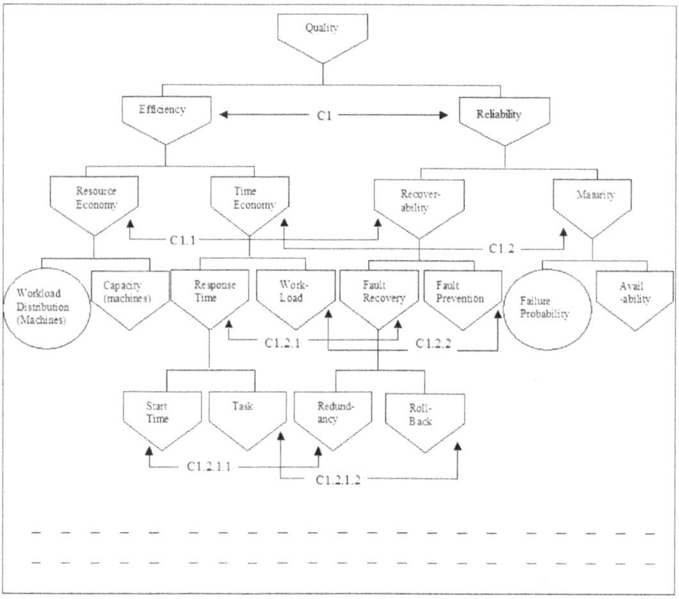

Fig. 3. Conflict Tree representing the hierarchy of non-functional requirements with conflicts

This conflict tree represents high level conflicts using symbol . Solutions to a conflict which can be implemented is shown using symbol . At the lowest level, all non-functional requirements are compared again and detected whether there is another conflict.

4 Conclusion

The proposed model not only focus on the identification of conflicts among non-functional requirements, also focus on the analyzing of conflicts by transforming high-level conflicting quality attributes to low level functional requirements. This paper attempts to focus on the conflict detection using integrated analysis of functional requirements, non-functional requirements, internal constraints and external constraints by the means of Strategy versus Requirement matrix. After detection of conflicts, it proposed a framework for understanding the semantics of conflicts based on the integrated analysis.

References

[1] Egyed, A., Grunbacher, P.: Identifying Requirement Conflicts and Cooperation: How Quality Attributes and Automated Traceability can Help. IEEE Software 21(6), 50–58 (2004)
[2] Finkelstein, A., Dowell, J.: A comedy of Errors: The London Ambulance Service Case Study. In: Proceedings of the Eighth International Workshop on Software Specification and Design, pp. 2–5. IEEE Computer Society Press (1996)
[3] Boehm, B., In, H.: Conflict Analysis and Negotiation Aids for Cost Quality Requirements. Software Quality Professional 1(2), 38–50 (1999)
[4] Breitman, K.K., Leite, J.C.S.P., Anthony, F.: The World's Stage: A Survey on Requirements Engineering Using a Real-Life Case Study. Journal of Brazilian Computer Society 1(6), 13–37 (1999)
[5] de Bruin, H., van Vliet, H.: Top-down composition of software architectures. In: Proceedings of the 9th annual IEEE International Conference on the Engineering of Computer Based Systems (April 2002)
[6] Bosch, J.: Design and Use of Software Architectures. Addison Wesley (2000)
[7] Cysneiros, L.M., Leite, J.C.S.P.: Integrating Non-Functional Requirements into data model. In: 4th International Symposium on Requirements Engineering, Ireland (June 1999)
[8] Ebert, C.: Dealing with Nonfunctional in Large Software Systems. Annals of Software Engineering 3, 367–395 (1997)
[9] Gebhardt, M., Jacobs, S., Jarke, M., Nissen, H.W.: Conflict Analysis Across Heterogeneous Viewpoint: Formalization and Visualization. In: HICSS 1996 Proceedings of the 29th Hawaii International Conference on System Sciences. Collaboration Systems and Technology, vol. 3. IEEE Computer Society, Washington, DC, USA (1996)
[10] Kotonya, G., Sommerville, I.: Requirements Engineering: Processes and Techniques. John Willey & Sons (1998)
[11] Roman, G.-C.: A Taxonomy of Current Issues in Requirements Engineering. IEEE Computer 18(4), 14–22 (1985)
[12] In, H., Kim, C.H., Yun, U., Yau, S.S.: Q-MAR: A QoS resource Conflict Identification Model for Situation-Aware Middleware. In: Proc. 9th IEEE Workshop Computing Systems (FTDCS 2003). IEEE Computer Society (2003)
[13] Mylopoulos, J., Chung, L., Nixon, B.: Representing and Using Non-functional Requirements: A Process-Oriented Approach. IEEE Trans. on Software Eng. 18(6), 483–497 (1992)
[14] Wiegers, K.: Software Requirements, 2nd edn. Microsoft Press (2003)
[15] Paech, B., Detroit, A., Kerkow, D., von Kenthen, A.: Functional requirements, non-functional requirements and architecture should not be separated- a position paper. REFSQ, Essen, Germany (September 2002)
[16] Yeh, R., et al.: Software Requirements: New Directions and Perspectives. In: Handbook of Software Engineering, pp. 519–543 (1984)
[17] Poort, E.R., de With, P.H.N.: Resolving Requirement Conflicts through Non-Functional Decomposition. In: Fourth Working IEEE/IFIP Conference on Software Architecture (WICSA 2004), p. 145 (2004)
[18] Bertagnolli, S.C., Lisboa, M.L.B.: The FRIDA Model (2000)
[19] Sadana, V., Frank Liu, X.: Analysis of Conflicts among Non-Functional Requirements Using Integrated Analysis of Functional and Non-Functional Requirements. In: Proceedings of the 31st Annual International Computer Software and Applications Conference on COMPSAC 2007, vol. 01. IEEE Computer Society, Washington, DC, USA (2007)

Active Queue Management Based Congestion Control for Unresponsive Flows

G. Thiruchelvi[1], J. Raja[2], and M. Saravanan[1]

[1] Department of Computer Science and Engineering, Periyar Maniammai University, Thanjavur, Tamil Nadu, India
[2] Department of Electronics and Communication Engineering, Anna University of Technology, Trichirapalli, Tamil Nadu, India
{thiruchelvi2000,saran84gct}@gmail.com, raja@tau.edu.in

Abstract. The Quality of Service (QoS) requests from network users expand greatly with ever fast development of the network technology as well as new network applications. In order to support a number of predicted communication products to the future, it is essential to develop a network infrastructure which can provide a greater bandwidth with better control of quality of service (QoS). In this paper we propose a new active queue management technique ICU (Isolate and Control Unresponsive Flows) which effectively controls the unresponsive flows, based on the network load status. First, a flow isolator isolates the unresponsive flows from the traffic mix of responsive flows and unresponsive flows, using the traffic arrival rate and loss ratio of the incoming flows. Then it checks for load un-balance of the network and automatically triggers the adaptive packet dropping policy wherein the unresponsive flows are shifted to a drop window. For every small interval, depending on the status of load un-balance, the size of the drop window is incremented or decremented. If the size of the window increases beyond a threshold value the packets will be dropped. By our simulation results, we show that our proposed algorithm achieves less loss.

Keywords: Active Queue Management, Congestion Control, Unresponsive flows.

1 Introduction

Although the majority of the traffic over the Internet is still TCP-based, applications such as voice over IP and video-conferencing are changing this very rapidly. Due to the increasing demand for applications running over Packet networks [1], congestion occurring at the intermediate nodes can be a serious problem which causes the bad effects such as long delays, large delay variation and high packet loss rates and unfairness. During the last several years, a number of mechanisms have been proposed to minimize undesired effects mentioned above. Some of them are aimed at solving the problem from inside the network, and some of them are focusing on developing a responsive or a TCP-congestion-control-compatible protocol to be

V.V. Das and N. Thankachan (Eds.): CIIT 2011, CCIS 250, pp. 832–837, 2011.

employed at traffic sources and destinations. However, most of the solutions are either too complex to execute in real life or not applicable to a random network topology.

1.1 Active Queue Management

Active Queue Management (AQM) mechanisms are router-based algorithms and are deployed inside the network, i.e. in the routers, to regulate the flows. By sending congestion signals in a proactive manner, an AQM technique makes attempt to prevent congestion and control the queue length. This would finally cause the senders to reduce the sending rates. An AQM scheme may mark or drop the packets depending upon the policy at the router.

An AQM scheme can detect congestion based on

- The queue length at the link
- The arrival rate of the packets at the link
- Combination of both

In addition to this, most of the AQM schemes include adapting the marking probability in some other way. The design of robust AQM schemes is an active research area in the Internet community. Some of the proposed AQM schemes consists of RED [2], SRED [3], Blue [4], REM [5], Proportional Integral (PI) controller [6], An Adaptive Virtual Queue (AVQ) [7] among others. In the next section we present other related works done on the active queue management technique. Although the above papers have made significant progress towards improving the fairness of the Internet and suppressing the unresponsive flows, the respective problems of unresponsive flow detections and their impact on the performance of AQM still leave space for further developing in this research direction. So it is required to develop a new active queue management technique which effectively controls the unresponsive flows, based on the network load status.

2 Related Work

To achieve fairness several per-flow packet scheduling mechanisms have been proposed. Because of the scalability and complexity issues they have not been widely implemented. A complex less practical approach is to use a packet dropping policy. There are several newer packet dropping schemes that focus on tracking and regulating only high bandwidth or misbehaving flows rather than monitoring every active flow. To monitor large flows to examine whether they consume more bandwidth than a value computed from the TCP bandwidth equation at steady state [8] , Floyd et.al have proposed a mechanism where the accuracy depends heavily on some parameters unknown to the router such as flows round trip time [9]. In CHOKe [10] the router randomly selects a packet from the queue at each packet arrival. Both packets are dropped if they belong to the same flow. Since High bandwidth flows have high probability of having more packets in the buffer space it is assumed here that if the incoming packet and the packet selected from queue belong to the same flow they are considered as unresponsive. However in CHOKe, a high bandwidth unresponsive flow still can gain much more bandwidth than the fair share. Stochastic Fair Blue [11] on the other hand utilizes a bloom filter with multiple hashing to detect misbehaving flows. SFB limits them to a fixed amount of bandwidth. In practice setting the bandwidth limit effectively is a difficult task as a fair bandwidth level may be unknown to an SFB router. Jun Zheng et al [12] have proposed new AQM algorithm- Clue in order to strengthen the robustness of Internet against unresponsive flows. As a sort of the scheduling algorithm, Clue relies on the detection and punishment of unresponsive flows and gets the elastics control of unresponsive flows, which benefit the buffer queue with the high performance. By their simulation results they have proved that Clue can detect and restrain unresponsive flows more accurately compared to other AQM algorithms. The objective of this paper is to propose a router mechanism called ICU (Isolate and Control Unresponsive flows) to protect TCP flows from unresponsive flows. The rest of the paper is organized as follows. Section 3 describes in detail about ICU algorithm. The evaluation of ICU and comparison with other schemes are discussed in section 4. Finally conclusion is presented in section 5.

3 The ICU

3.1 Detection of Unresponsive Flows

The main cause of congestion is only a small number of connections that consume large bandwidth. Dropping the packets from these flows at the router could lessen congestion more effectively. The edge-to-edge probing detects excessive packet loss inside of a network domain and the cause behind the loss. We use back to-back probe packets for a small sample interval of *TS* seconds to infer a link loss by computing the correlation of a packet loss within a set of probe packets at different destinations. Packet loss ratios due to probe packets and actual flow are found. At the egress routers the difference between the loss ratios is calculated and used as one of the two factors to identify unresponsive flows. Probe packets are used to estimate the initial loss incurred in the network. According to unresponsive flow feature of high rate of sending data, there is a high probability that the loss is mainly due to unresponsive flows and it is high during congestion Hence the loss difference between probe packets and actual flow (unresponsive flow) will be high and that is used as a classification factor. Flow arrival rate (r_i) is calculated and used as a second factor. These two factors together determine the unresponsiveness when they exceed certain threshold values. The value of the threshold (T1) for the difference between loss ratios can be selected between 0 and 1 and we assume the initial value of 0 and it can be set based on the minimum value of the difference between loss ratios. The value of the threshold (T2) for the flow arrival rate can be fixed based on link fair rate. As per CSFQ, all flows that are bottlenecked by a router will have same output rate when Max min Bandwidth allocations are achieved. This rate is the link fair share rate. Each flow i will receive service at a rate given by min(r_i, fair share rate).

Algorithm

D = ALRq – LRq , where Rq is any given path
If (D > T1) and (r_i^{new} > T2), then
Flow_status = Unresponsive.
Else
Flow_status = Responsive.
End if.

where ALRq is the loss ration due to actual flow, LRq is the Loss ratio due to probe packet and r_i^{new} is the arrival rate of the packet.

3.2 Checking Load Balancing Condition

The triggering policy raises the Adaptive Dropping Policy when the system is unbalanced. If the current queue length Q_{len} of node is more than the threshold Q_{th} (which is 70% of the maximum size), then the system is considered as unbalance and the load balancer is invoked.

3.3 Isolate and Control of Unresponsive Flows

The detected unresponsive flows are isolated and rate limited for a short duration (*limiting time*). The unresponsive flows will be depressed excessively and cannot obtain fair share of bandwidth if the value of *limiting_time* is too big. On every packet arrival the packets of these unresponsive flows are shifted to a drop window of size DW. It checks the status of load un-balance for every small interval d, and then increments the size of the drop window by D_{incr}. thereby permitting more unresponsive packets to enter the drop window. If the size of D_{win} increases beyond a threshold value D_{thr}, then the packets will be dropped. On the other hand, if the load balance is being attained at an interval d_k, then the size of Drop window will be reduced by D_{decr}. thereby releasing packets from the drop window to pass through the bottleneck link and also to provide additional space for new packets to enter drop window during next interval if there is load unbalance . -If the packet is dropped successfully, the next incoming packet is processed. Otherwise we will check that if the queue length Q_l is more than threshold Q_{th}. If it is true, again the flow is checked whether it is an unresponsive flow. Otherwise, this incoming packet could be permitted to enter the buffer.

Algorithm

If interval < limiting_time, then
rate limit the unresponsive flow
Else if interval > limiting _time
shift the flow to Dwin
If load is unbalanced, then
Dw = Dw + Dincr

If Dw > Dthr, then

Drop the flow
If load is balanced, then
Dw = Dw – Ddecr
Process next packet
If Ql > Q_{thr}, then
Check for unresponsive flow
Repeat from rate limited

4 Simulation and Results

In this section, we examine the performance of our Isolate and Control Based Active Queue Management technique (ICU) with an extensive simulation study based upon the ns-2 network simulator [19]. We compare our results with AQM techniques such as REM [5], VQ [7], RED [2] and Drop Tail. The topology used in our experiments is depicted in Figure 1. We kept Packet size: 512 bytes, Bottleneck link is between R1 and R2. Bottleneck Bandwidth: 5 Mb, No. of TCP flows : 4 and No. of UDP flows: 4

In our simulation, we vary the rates as 100 Kb, 200 kb… 500Kb in order to find the packet loss .We have taken the traffic as a mix of TCP and UDP flows. If we increase the sending rate of a flow, more packets enter the bottle neck router. As the bottleneck bandwidth is fixed (5 Mb) between R1 and R2, some of these packets may get lesser chance to pass the bottleneck. This introduces increased packet loss at higher sending rates. Due to the introduction of the drop window wherein the unresponsive flows are delayed for *limiting time* period during congestion, the loss is minimum compared to other mechanisms (Figure 2).

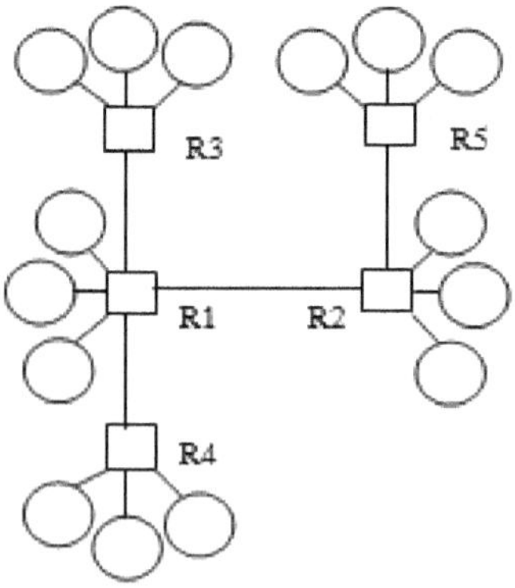

Fig. 1. Simulation Topology

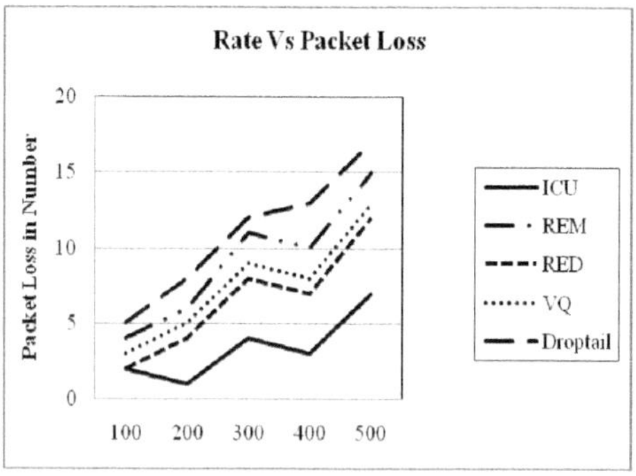

Fig. 2. Rate vs Packet Loss

5 Conclusion

In this paper we have proposed an active queue management system for controlling unresponsive flows based on an adaptive dropping policy. For detecting unresponsive flows we have used packet loss ratio and flow arrival rate as two factors In adaptive dropping policy the detected unresponsive flows are isolated and shifted to Drop Window of size DW that can be increased or decreased based on network load status. The packets will be dropped when Drop window size exceeds a threshold value. By our simulation results, we have shown that our proposed algorithm achieves minimum loss.

References

1. Akin, O.: Active Queue Management and Scheduling Methods for Packet-Switched Networks, Electrical and Computer Engineering, NC State University, Raleigh
2. Floyd, S., Jacobson, V.: Random early detection gateways for congestion avoidance. IEEE/ACM Transactions on Networking (August 1993)
3. Ott, T.J., Lakshman, T.V., Wong, L.H.: SRED: Stabilized RED. In: Proceedings of INFOCOM, New York, NY (March 1999)
4. Feng, W., Kandlur, D., Saha, D., Shin, K.: Blue: A new class of active queue management schemes, Technical Report, CSE-TR-387-99, U. Michigan (April 1999)
5. Lapsley, D., Low, S.: Random early marking for Internet congestion control. In: Proceedings. of Conf. on Global Telecommunications, vol. 3, pp. 1747–1752 (1999), doi:10.1109/GLOCOM.1999
6. Hollot, C.V., Misra., V., Towsley, D., Gong, W.-B.: On Designing Improved Controllers for AQM Routers Supporting TCP Flows. In: Proc. of Annual Joint Conf. of IEEE Computer and Communication Societies, Anchorage, USA, vol. 3, pp. 1726–1734 (2001), doi:10.1109/INFCOM.2001.916670
7. Srisankar, S., Kunniyur Srikant, R.: An Adaptive Virtual Queue (AVQ) Algorithm for Active Queue Management. IEEE Transactions on Networking 12(2) (April 2004)
8. Floyd, S., Fall, K.: Promoting the use of End to End Congestion Control in the Internet, IEEE? ACM Trans. Networking 7(4), 458–472 (1999)
9. Ott, T.J., Kemperman, B., Mathis, M.: The stationary Behaviour of Idealised TCP Congestion Behaviour. Computer Communication Review 23(3) (July 1997)
10. Pan, R., Prabhakar, B., Psounis, K.: CHOKe. A Stateless Active Queue Management Scheme For approximating Fair Bandwidth Allocation. In: Proceeding IEEE INFOCOM 2000, pp. 942–951 (2000)
11. Feng., W.-C., Kandlur., D.D., Saha., D., Shin, K.G.: Stochastic Fair Blue: A Queue Management Algorithm for Enforcing Fairness. In: Proc. of INFOCOM 2001 (April 2001)
12. Zheng, J., Zhao, L., Zhang, T.: Improving Unresponsive Flow Control by Active Queue Management Algorithm. In: Proc. of IEEE Intl. Conference on Wireless Communication an Networking, Kowloon, March 11- 15, pp. 4360–4364 (2007), doi:10.1109/WCNC. 2007.795

SNS: Privacy at Stake

Rajneeshkaur Bedi and V.M. Wadhai

Computer Engineering Department, Pune University
MIT College of Engineering, Pune, India
meenubedi@hotmail.com
wadhai.vijay@gmail.com

Abstract. Nowadays all Internet savvy people knows the buzzword social networking sites (SNS) like Facebook, LinkedIn, Orkut etc, On these SNS we provide our personal data which we share among our group contacts. To maintain our personal data as private even in shared environment, data privacy is an indispensable security requirement. In this paper we discussed various provisions for data privacy from technology and government laws point of view. In addition we proposed our architecture to implement data privacy along with Watermarking.

Keywords: Social networking, Privacy, watermarking, encryption, RDBMS.

1 Introduction

Popularity of social networking site is more than ever due to its various features. All age group people those who want to stay connected with their friend and relatives on internet got their profiles on social networking sites. This information revealing can be helpful to other unethical users, hackers, or terrorists, companies and third parties. They use this data source for all good and bad reasons like marketing, data mining etc. Social network site (SNS), [1] proposed, can be separated into nine kinds: business, common interests, dating, face-to-face facilitation, friends, pets, and photos. Individual identity safety and security should be the topmost concerns of today's user while creating account on the social networking site that are currently used. The issue of copyright of digital content is taken at priority by owner who provides these data due intellectual property rights. Protection of this asset demands for watermarking it for the copyright and intellectual protection. Watermarking is a process of embedding information in the original content Digital watermarking [2] must have atleast three properties: Robust, value should not be lost, both the copy should be perceptually identical. Along with watermarking our personal data some part of very sensitive data also need to encrypt for privacy and security reasons. Our focus is on ECC rather than RSA due to speed and smaller keys or certificates from the comparisons[3]. Apart from making provisions in technology the government of various countries are taking efforts for safeguarding online privacy.

V.V. Das and N. Thankachan (Eds.): CIIT 2011, CCIS 250, pp. 838–843, 2011.

2 Government Laws

We are presenting provisions made by India, U.S and U.K referring to [4] and [5].

Indian Law: The Personal Data Protection Bill, 2006: To provide for protection of personal data and information of an individual collected for a particular purpose by one organization, and to prevent its usage by other organization for commercial or other purposes. Provisions contained in this Act are relating to nature of data to be obtained for the specific purpose and the quantum of data to be obtained for that purpose.

U.K. Law: Act is basically instituted for the purpose of providing protection and privacy of the personal data of the individuals in UK. The Act covers data which can be used to identify a living person. As per the Act, the persons and organizations which store personal data must register with the information commissioner, which has been appointed as the government official to oversee the Act. This put restrictions on collection of data.

U.S. Law: Though both U.S and the European Union focus on enhancing privacy protection of their citizens, U.S takes a different approach to privacy from that of the European Union. US adopted the sectoral approach that relies of mix of legislation, regulation, and self regulation. In U.S, data are grouped into several classes on the basis of their utility and importance. Thereafter, accordingly a different degree of protection is awarded to the different classes of data.

3 Related Work

A literature survey presented by [6] has investigated a privacy of social network sites. Two main ways of obtaining private information on social network sites were summarized as based on privacy disclosure and attack technique. One essential type of privacy attacks is identified [7]: neighborhood attacks. We are suggesting for this is to encrypt data and share the key only among the trusted. Another way for privacy is given [8] they pointed to the centralized architecture of existing on-line social networks as the key privacy issue and suggest a solution that aims at avoiding any centralized control. Their solution is an on-line social network based on a peer-to-peer architecture. Here we also briefly discuss the previous approaches related to work for watermarking relational databases and also the approaches by researchers for watermarking text data. Watermarking relational database for numeric data was first proposed [9] to flip specific least significant bit 0 to 1 or 1 to 0 based on the value of hash function on selected tuple. An [10] approach is to append a new attribute which will serve as a watermark containing checksum of all other attributes and an aggregate value for any one of the numeric attribute. An [11] approach inserts new tuples that are not real and called them "fake" tuples, to the relation as watermarks, which increases the size of database. The approach proposed [12] for content authentication and integrity of text document where these authors contributes a novel secure and efficient algorithm using the mathematical concept of Eigen values for text watermarking. This concept motivated use to create tuple Relation matrix which we have used in our study [13,14] proposed approach and later on we implemented. Text based to prove the authenticity of text document is proposed [15]. Access control schemes [16], to address the problem of tracing unauthorized distribution of sensitive intelligence documents. The concept of watermarking an object based text document where proposed [17] where each and every text string is entertained as a separate object having its own set of properties which motivated us to consider it for every attributes. A survey[21] has given very latest comparison and classification on his latest survey for watermarking techniques for relational database has helped us to understand various changes taken place in research for watermarking of relational database. The tutorial given [18] helps us to understand various cryptography techniques in a unified way, including classical and recent algorithms. The concept of joint watermarking and encryption is studied [19], so as to include encryption of secret key in our approach. Other approach given [20] system allows to watermark encrypted data without requiring the knowledge of the original data and also to cipher watermarked data without damaging the embedded signal is for our future scope.

4 Proposed Architecture

Survey: User Approach towards Data Revealing Online: Our proposed architecture is based on the survey we conducted for understanding the user approach towards data submitting while creating the user profile. This survey is based on [1] paper results. We have done our survey in Pune city in all age groups and gender to understand the Indian people attitude in providing the information. We have listed all the attributes which is generally available in social networking sites, like, Name, DOB, City, School, The data we gathered are summarized low and high impact attribute. This survey work has allowed us to categories the attributes those need to be handle with watermarking and encryption either jointly or separately. We segregate these attributes as low impact (LI) and high impact (HI). Low impact attributes are the one which can be altered little bit like one special character, number and will be used to inset watermark like address, interest, school / college name etc. The high impact attributes like name, city, friends, groups etc are very sensitive for any changes so these attributes will not be used for watermark insertion whereas they will contribute to generate secrete key and there data will be encrypted. Even when these attribute data is shared in group, based on the group preference the data is available in actual form or it will remain in encrypted format only.

Architecture: In existing client-server architecture we found following problems. 1. User provides his personal data on client side is unsafed till IPsec protocol comes in picture. Attack like Man-in-the-Browser. 2. On server side generally data will encrypted / watermark with single key on entire tuples by the DBS and stored in database. 3. On the fly, the intruder may sniff each packet data to be transferred or may alter the packet data. So this modified data get stored in database. Based on the above problems and attribute studies we proposed our architecture as given in figure 1. Here, we recommend that when user is registering himself same time the watermark key will be evaluated, watermark will be generated and high impact attribute will be encrypted with the same key and in low impact attribute the watermark will be inserted. These also include encryption of the form data before sending it on internet. Now this data with watermark and encryption will travel the network layer and in the same format it will be saved in database. So, data sniffing, packet alteration, code injection, Cryptanalysis and many client side web application attack can attack will be avoided by taking its care on client side. For watermarking we will first generate a secrete key (K_w) based on high impact non numeric attribute data like count vowel, consonant, special character number etc., of each attribute

$$K_w = Key(HI,mateval(V,C,S,N)) \tag{1}$$

and using this key K_w watermark will be generated using the function

$$W = insert(LI, K_w) \tag{2}$$

and inserted in low impact attribute at the same time high impact attribute data is encrypted E by

$$E = encrypt(HI, K_e) \tag{3}$$

To the database administrator also this data is not available in original format as every tuple attribute is marked and encrypted with different key only. When user logs in next time along with is login name and password he also needs to submit his secrete key which will display his encrypted data in decrypt form as shown in figure 2. If the user needs to share his data with other user then he also needs to share his public key with him. The problem we detected in this architecture is the time requirement. But for cost high level of privacy it's negligible.

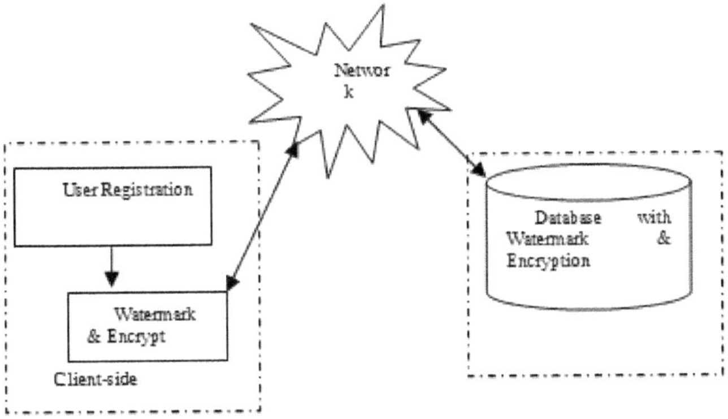

Fig. 1. Proposed Architecture

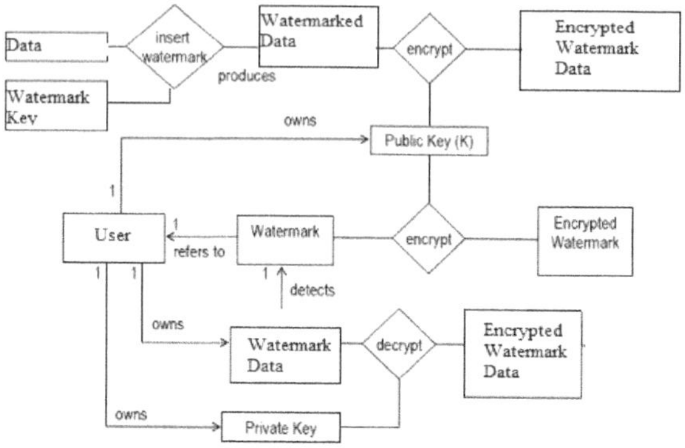

Fig. 2. Watermarking and Encryption jointly

5 Conclusion

We consider the problem of ensuring an individual's data anonymity while releasing person-specific data on social networking sites. We pointed out that the previous work is based on separate parts of data flow like database, text of blogs, network etc. Information specific to individuals are watermarked and encrypted based on the attribute impact. Also for encryption a small key size algorithm is selected and is also fast in processing. This joint effort of encryption and watermarking helps to make our architecture strong: encryption guarantees the access control keeping away malicious eavesdroppers and robust watermarking concept implicitly increases the data integrity protection on the key as well as data. It can also scale for large data set.

References

1. Gross, R., Acquisti: Information revelation and privacy in online social networks. In: Proceedings of ACM Workshop on Privacy in the Electronic Scoiety, pp. 71–80 (2005)
2. Qadir, M.A., Ahmad, I.: Digital Text Watermarking: Secure Content Delivery And Data Hiding In Digital Documents. In: Proceedings of 39th Annual International Conference on Security Technology, pp. 101–104 (2005)
3. Balitanas, M., Robles, R., Kim, N., Kim, T.: Crossed Crypto-scheme in WPA PSK Mode. In: Symposium on Bio-inspired Learning and Intelligent Systems for Security, pp. 102–106. IEEE Computer Society (2009)
4. http://www.legislation.gov.uk/ukpga/1998/29/contents
5. http://www.legalserviceindia.com/article/137-Data-Protection-Law-in-India.html
6. Chen, X., Shi, S.: A Literature Review of Privacy Research on Social Network Sites. In: IEEE International Conference on Multimedia Information Networking and Security, pp. 93–97 (2009)
7. Zhou, B., Pei, J.: Preserving privacy in social networks against neighborhood attacks. In: Proceedings of IEEE 24th International Conference on Data Engineering, pp. 506–515

8. Cutillo, L., Molva, R., Strufe, T.: Privacy Preserving Social Networking Through Decentralization. In: Proceedings of 6th IEEE International Conference on Wireless On-Demand Network System and Services, New Jersey, USA, pp. 145–152
9. Agrawal, R., Kiernan, J.: Watermarking Relational Databases. In: Proceedings of the 28th Very Large Data Bases, pp. 155–166 (2002)
10. Prasannakumari, V.: A Robust Tamperproof Watermarking for Data Integrity in Relational Databases. Research Journal of Information Technology 1(3), 115–121 (2009)
11. Pournaghshband, V.: A New Watermarking Approach for Relational Data. In: Proceedings of the 46th Annual Southeast Regional Conference, pp. 127–131 (2008)
12. Rethika, T., Prathap, I., Anitha, R., Raghavan, S.V.: A Novel Approach to Watermark Text Documents Based on Eigen Values. In: Proceedings of International Conference on Network and Service Security, pp. 1–5 (2009)
13. Bedi, R., Wadhai, V.M., Sugandhi, R., Mirajkar, A.: Watermarking Social Networking Relational Data using Non-numeric Attribute. International Journal of Computer Science and Information Security (IJCSIS) 9(4), 74–77 (2011)
14. Bedi, R., Thengade, A., Wadhai, V.M.: Article: A New Watermarking Approach for Non-numeric Relational Database. International Journal of Computer Applications (IJCA) 13(7), 37–40 (2011)
15. Abdulla, M., Wahab, F.: Key Based Text Watermarking of E-Text Documents in an object Based Environment Using Z-Axis for Watermark Embedding. World Academy of Science, Engineering and Technology 46, 199–202 (2008)
16. Cheung, S., Dickson, K., Ho, C.: The use of Digital Watermarking for Intelligence Multimedia Document Distribution. Journal of Theoretical and Applied Electronic Commerce Research 3(3), 103–118 (2008)
17. Jalil, Z., Mirza, A.M., Sabir, M.: Content based Zero-Watermarking Algorithm for Authentication of Text documents. International Journal of Computer Science and Information Security 7(2), 212–217 (2010)
18. Desoky, A.: Cryptography: Algorithms and Standards. In: Proceedings of 5th IEEE International symposium on Signal Processing and Information Technology, pp. 924–929
19. Merhav, N.: On Joint Coding for Watermarking and Encryption. IEEE Transactions on Information Theory 52(1), 190–204 (2006)
20. Battisti, F., Cancellaro, M., Boato, G., Carli, M., Neri, A.: Joint Watermarking and Encryption of color images in the Fibonacci-Haar Domain, Research Article. EURASIP Journal on Advances in signal Processing 2009, 1–13 (2009)
21. Halder, R., Pal, S., Cortesi, A.: Watermarking Techniques for Relational Databases: Survey, Classification and Comparision. Journal of Universal Computer Science 16(21), 3164–3190 (2010)

Performance Comparison of Reconfigurable Low Complexity FIR Filter Architectures

J.L. Mazher Iqbal[1] and S. Varadarajan[2]

[1] Rajalakshmi Engineering College, Chennai, 602 105, India
[2] Sri Venkateswara University, Tirupati, 517 502, India
{mazheriq,varadasouri}@gmail.com

Abstract. This paper compares three architectures of low complexity digital finite impulse response (FIR) filters for high-performance applications. The design of three reconfigurable architectures includes two fully programmable MAC-based filter processor and one dedicated architecture where the filter coefficients are fixed before synthesis. The proposed MAC-based FIR Filter architecture uses two different multipliers for higher order and lower order filters. The multipliers specifically targets on computation re-use in vector-scalar products and can be effectively used in the low complexity programmable FIR filter design. The proposed MAC based filter architecture with different multiplier blocks are capable of operating for different word length filter coefficients at a high speed clock frequency of 109.7 MHz based on Virtex 2v3000ff1152-4 field-programmable gate array.

Keywords: Common Sub expression Elimination (CSE), FIR filters, Reconfigurability, Multiplier Block, Computation Sharing Multiplier (CSHM), Canonical Signed Digit (CSD), Processing Element (PE).

1 Introduction

Digital Finite Impulse Response (FIR) filters are essential building blocks in most Digital Signal Processing (DSP) systems. Large application areas of digital FIR Filters are mobile communication systems and multimedia applications. The characteristics of FIR filtering can be expressed as a sequence of multiplication and addition operations. Multiplication can be computationally expensive in FIR filtering hence simplifying the multiplication operations is highly desirable for low-complexity design. The approach is based on CSE identification in the context of operation minimization multiple occurrences of identical bit patterns that are present in the CSD representation of coefficients, and eliminate these redundant multiplications [3]. The reconfigurable multiplier blocks reduce the complexity of the FIR filter implementations effectively, by exploiting the redundancy of the multiple constant multiplications. In this paper, we compare different implementation approaches for high-performance and low-power design for FIR filter with programmable coefficients and fixed coefficients which are reconfigurable and less complex. The architecture with programmable coefficients focuses on direct implementation of FIR filter using one of the two dedicated MB

V.V. Das and N. Thankachan (Eds.): CIIT 2011, CCIS 250, pp. 844–849, 2011.

(MB-1, MB-2). The architecture with fixed coefficients focuses on synthesis of FIR Filter using multiple adder graphs for a coefficient.

2 Programmable FIR Filter Architecture

The structure of the proposed FIR filter is shown in Fig. 1. The Reconfigurability of the FIR filter is achieved by reconfiguring the MB (PE). The proposed FIR Filter architecture can obtain a high area efficiency and high performance. The basic modules of the filter architecture consist of two PEs (PE-1 & PE-2), Memory Elements, and Interconnection Networks [1]. The PEs are capable of performing addition (inc. carry) and multiplication, with two inputs and one output. The signal s1 and s2 are control signals based on these control signals, the PEs act as either MB or Accumulation Block. In this Section, we present two different low complexities MB (PE) for the proposed FIR Filter architecture shown in Fig.1.

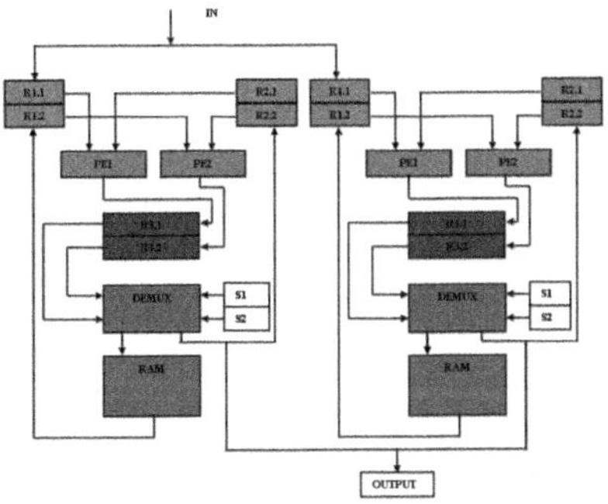

Fig. 1. FIR filter architecture [1]

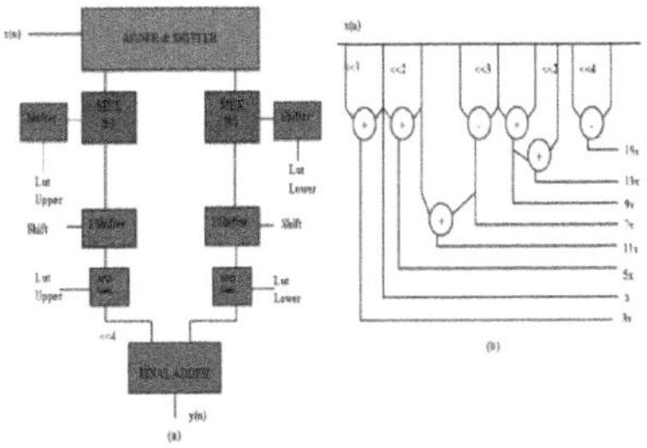

Fig. 2. Reconfigurable MB-1(a) 8 bits (b) Shift and add unit

2.1 Reconfigurable MB-1

The Reconfigurable MB-1 is shown in Fig.2. It consists of an adder and shifter unit, multiplexer unit and final adder (S&As) [4]. The adder and shifter unit performs the multiplication of alphabets with input x. The adder and shifter unit generates eight {1,3,5,7,9,11,13,15} alphabets. The multiplexer unit is composed of shifter, mux(8:1), ishifter, and and gate. To find the correct alphabet, shifters perform the right shift operation until they encounter 1 and send an appropriate select signal to muxes (8:1). Shifters also send the exact shifted values to ishifters. The muxes (8:1) select the correct answer among the eight precomputer outputs from adders and shifters unit. Ishifters simply inverse the operation performed by shifters. When the coefficient input is 0000, we cannot obtain a zero output with shifted value of the pre computer outputs. Simple AND gates are used to deal with the zero (0000) coefficient input. The final adder unit adds the outputs of the multiplexer unit to obtain the final multiplication output. For example, a simple vector scaling operation $[c_0, c_1].x$,

c_0=11001011, c_1=11001110, can be decomposed as $c_0.x=2^6.(0011).x+(1011).x$, $c_1.x=2^6.(0011).x+2^1(0111).x$. if x, (0011).x, (1011).x and (0111).x are available, the entire multiplication process is significantly reduced to a few add and shift operations. We will call these chosen basic bits of information as alphabets. In this example, (0011).x is computed once and the result is shared to calculate both $c_0.x$ and $c_1.x$, which show the concept of computation sharing in the vector scaling operation.

2.2 Reconfigurable MB-2

The Reconfigurable MB-2 is shown in Fig.3. The MB-2 integrates reconfigurability and low complexity to realize FIR filters for higher order. It consists of adder and shifter unit, multiplexer unit, final shifter and final adder unit [2]. The operation of the MB-2 (PE) can be explained with the help of an 8-bit coefficient h = "11101001. In this case, n = 8, and therefore the number of multiplexers required is 3. The output $y = h*x$ is expressed as, $y = (11,101,001)*x$, $y = (11*2^6*x) + (101*2^3*x) + (001*x)$, Consider x=0010, $y = (11*2^6*0010) + (101*2^3*0010) + (001*0010)$; y=111010010.

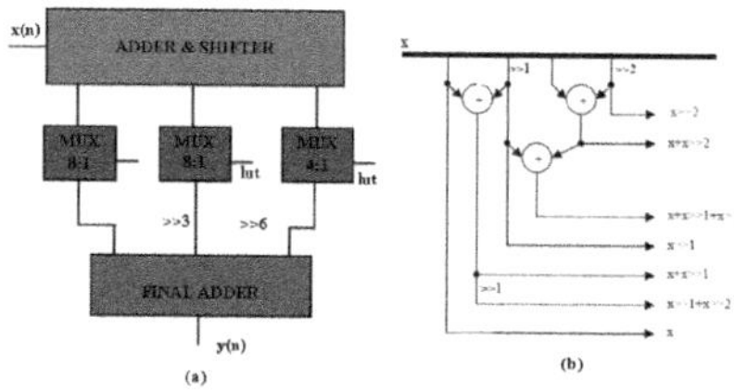

Fig. 3. Reconfigurable MB-2 (a) 8 bits (b) Shift and add unit

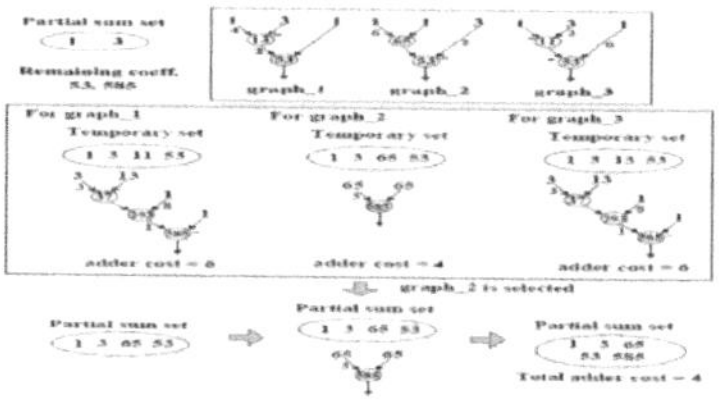

Fig. 4. Synthesis procedure for a coefficient set {3, 53, 585} [5]

3 FIR Filter Architecture for Fixed Coefficients

In this section, a FIR digital filter synthesis algorithm is presented which consider multiple adder graphs for a coefficient. If we consider multiple candidates adder graphs and then selects an adder graph that can be shared maximally with the remaining coefficients, the total adder cost can be reduced. Fig. 4. illustrates an example of the adder graph generation process for a coefficient set {3, 53, and 585} [5]. Three adder graphs are possible for 53, the total adder cost of each graph is examined first, and then the algorithm selects a proper graph (graph 2 in this case) that minimizes the total adder cost. The partial sums of graph 2 are inserted to the current partial sum set. In this case, the use of one additional adder to synthesize 585 the total adder cost becomes 4.

4 Experimental Results and Discussion

In this section, the synthesis and design results of proposed FIR Filter architecture using reconfigurable MB-1 and MB-2 are presented. We have used Xilinx 9.1i ISE for synthesizing purposes. The synthesis has been done on Xilinx's Virtex-II family

2vp2fg256-6. The simulation and floor plan result of a Reconfigurable FIR Filter using MB-1 and MB-2 for a coefficient word length of 8 bit is shown in Fig. 5. and Fig. 6. The performance of two MBs in terms of the basic design metrics are tabulated in Table 1 and Table 2. We have also analyzed the effect of the MB-1 and MB-2 for different filter coefficient word lengths of 8, 12, and 16 bits. The results are shown in Table 3 and Fig.7. It is noted that as the precision of the coefficients is made high, the consumption area is increased and the speed of operation is reduced. Thus, by choosing the appropriate filter coefficient word length, it is possible to obtain reduced area as well as increased speed for the FIR Filter architecture. The proposed FIR Filter architecture with MB-1 is appropriate for lower order filter while architecture with MB-2 is appropriate for higher order filter. The fixed coefficient FIR Filter is used in many applications.

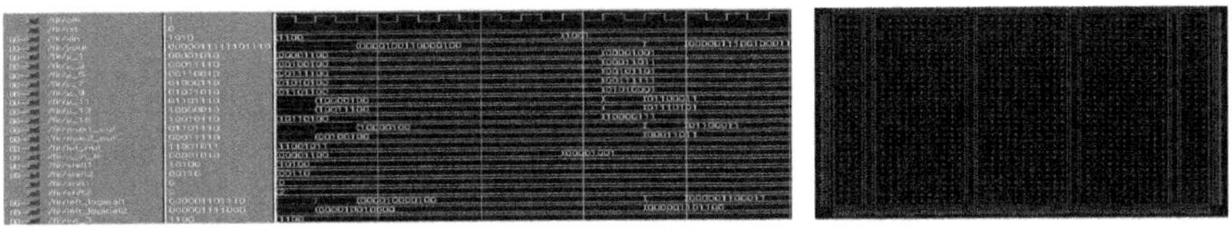

Fig. 5. Simulation Result and Floor Plan of a Reconfigurable FIR Filter using MB-1

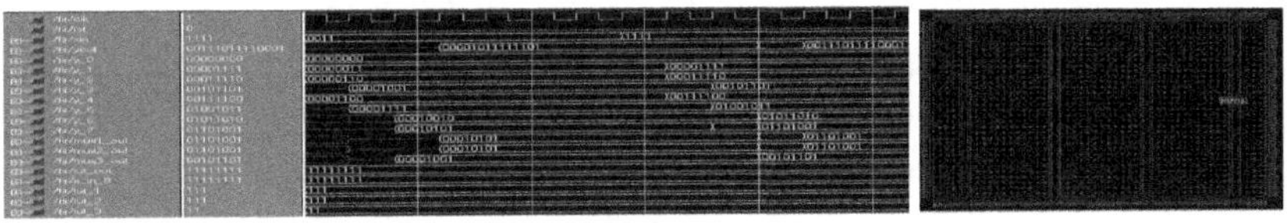

Fig. 6. Simulation Result and Floor Plan of a Reconfigurable FIR Filter using MB-2

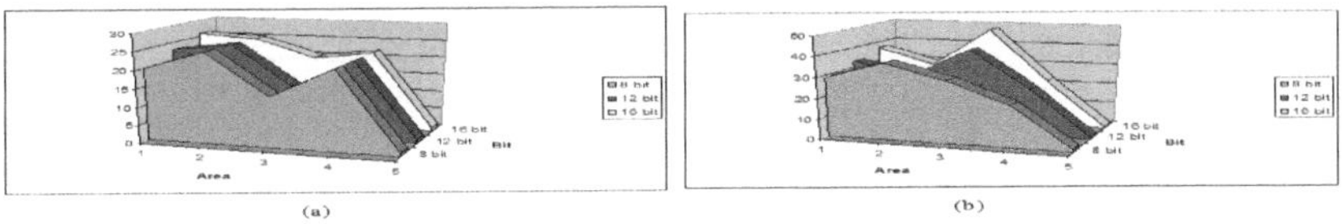

Fig. 7. Synthesis Results for (a) MB-1 and (b) MB-2 of the proposed FIR Filter Architecture

Table 1. Comparison of synthesis Result for Reconfigurable FIR Filter architectures

2vp2fg256-6	MB-1	MB-2
Number of Slices	20 out of 1408	29 out of 1408
Number of Slice Flip Flops	25 out of 2816	37 out of 2816
Number of 4 input LUTs	14 out of 2816	30 out of 2816
Number of bonded IOBs	22 out of 140	20 out of 140
Number of GCLKs	1 out of 16	1 out of 16
Minimum Period	3.082ns	3.206ns
Minimum input arrival time before clock:	3.677ns	1.543ns
Maximum output required time after clock	5.927ns	8.040ns

Table 2. Macro Statistics

2vp2fg256-6	Macro Statistics	
	MB-1	MB-2
Multiplexers	# Multiplexers : 3 12-bit 4-to-1 multiplexer: 1, 8-bit 8-to-1 multiplexer: 2	# Multiplexers : 3 8-bit 4-to-1 multiplexer : 1 8-bit 8-to-1 multiplexer : 2
Registers	# Registers: 10 8-bit register: 10	# Registers : 10 8-bit register :10
Adders /Subtractors	# Adders/Subtractors : 8 16-bit adder: 1, 8-bit adder: 4, 8-bit subtractor: 3	#Adders/Subtractors : 5 11-bit adder : 1,14-bit adder : 1, 8-bit adder : 3

Table 3. Synthesis Results for MB-1 and MB-2 with Different Coefficient Word length

2vp2fg256-6	8 bit	12bit	16 bit
MB-1			
Number of Slices	20 out of 1408	23 out of 1408	26 out of 1408
Number of Slice Flip Flops	25 out of 2816	25 out of 2816	25 out of 2816
Number of 4 input LUTs	14 out of 2816	14 out of 2816	20 out of 2816
Number of bonded IOBs	22 out of 140	22 out of 140	22 out of 140
Number of GCLKs	1 out of 16	1 out of 16	1 out of 16
MB-2			
Number of Slices	29 out of 1408	33 out of 1408	37 out of 1408
Number of Slice Flip Flops	37 out of 2816	27 out of 2816	29 out of 2816
Number of 4 input LUTs	30 out of 2816	41 out of 2816	48 out of 2816
Number of bonded IOBs	20 out of 140	23 out of 140	23 out of 140
Number of GCLKs	1 out of 16	1 out of 16	1 out of 16

5 Conclusion

In this paper, dynamically reconfigurable FIR filter architectures based on CSHM is proposed. It is based on the CSE technique. The MB-1 (PE) is suitable for lower order filter and the MB-2 is suitable higher order filter. The MB-2 ensures constant shifts and hence faster shifting. The CSHM architectures ensure low complexity as well as reconfigurability. We have implemented the architectures on Virtex 2 xc2vp2-6fg256 FPGA and synthesized using 0.18 μm CMOS technology. The results show a significant reduction in hardware necessary to implement those operations combined with satisfactory runtimes.

References

1. Mazher Iqbal, J.L., Varadarajan, S.: High Performance Reconfigurable Balanced Shared Memory Architecture For Embedded DSP. International Journal of Computer Science & Information Security 8(4), 198–206 (2010)
2. Mahesh, R., Vinod, A.P.: New Reconfigurable Architectures for Implementing FIR Filters with Low Complexity. IEEE Transactions on Computer-Aided Design of Integrated Circuits and Systems 29(2), 275–288 (2010)
3. Mahesh, R., Vinod, A.P.: A New Common Subexpression Elimination Algorithm for Implementing Low Complexity FIR Filters in Software Defined Radio Receivers. In: Proc. IEEE Int. Symp. on Circuitsand Systems, pp. 4515–4518 (2006)
4. Park, J., Jeong, W., Mahmoodi-Meimand, H., Wang, Y., Choo, H., Roy, K.: Computation sharing programmable FIR filter for low-power and high-performance applications. IEEE J. Solid State Circuits 39(2), 348–357 (2004)
5. Han, J.-H., Park, I.-C.: FIR Filter Synthesis Considering Multiple Adder Graphs for a Coefficient. IEEE Transactions on Computer-Aided Design of Integrated Circuits and Systems 27(5), 958–962 (2008)
6. Shyu, J.-J., Pei, S.-C., Chan, C.-H., Huang, Y.-D., Lin, S.-H.: A New Criterion for the Design of Variable Fractional-Delay FIR Digital Filters. IEEE Transactions on Circuits And Systems—I: Regular Papers 57(2), 368–377 (2010)
7. Mahesh, R., Vinod, A.P.: A new common subexpression elimination algorithm for realizing low complexity higher order digital filters. IEEETrans. Comput.-Aided Design Integr. Circuits Syst. 27(2), 217–219 (2008)
8. Benkrid, K.: High Performance Reconfigurable Computing: From Applications to Hardware. IAENG International Journal of Computer Science 35(1) IJCS_35_1_04 (2008)
9. Chen, K.H., Chiueh, T.D.: A low-power digit-based reconfigurable FIR filter. IEEE Trans. Circuits Syst. II 53(8), 617–621 (2006)
10. Meribout, M., Motomura, M.: A combined approach to highlevel synthesis for dynamically reconfigurable systems. IEEE Trans.Comput. 53(12), 1508–1522 (2004)
11. Vinod, A.P., Edmund, M.K., Lai: An Efficient Coefficient-Partitioning Algorithm for Realizing Low-Complexity Digital Filters. IEEE Transactions on Computer-Aided Design of Integrated Circuits and Systems 24(12), 1936–1946 (2005)
12. Vinod, A.P., Edmund, M.K., Lai: Low Power and High-Speed Implementation of FIR Filters for Software Defined Radio Receivers. IEEE Transactions on Wireless Communications 5(7), 1669–1675 (2006)
13. `http://www.xilinx.com`

HyberFast: An Effective Way to Save/Resume Processes with Prevention of Real-Time Data Loss

Bhaskar Bandyopadhyay, Raju Neyyan, and Uddhav Arote

Fourth Year Computer Engg., VCET, PREC, VCET
University of Mumbai, Pune, Mumbai
{bhaskarsuper9000,neyyanraju,aroteuddhav}@gmail.com

Abstract. A technique by which the process of hibernation can be sped-up is presented. During normal hibernation, the contents of the entire RAM are stored in the hard disk. However, as the number of running processes increase, the amount of RAM being used also increases and consequently more time is required to store its contents. In the proposed technique, the focus is only on the storage of that data which is critical to resume a running process after hibernation. This reduces the amount of memory required to be stored before hibernation, which in turn will reduce the time required for hibernation. This may also prevent real time data loss.

Keywords: hibernation, real-time data loss, OS (Operating System), critical data, RAM, processes.

1 Introduction

Hibernation is a feature of many computer operating systems where the contents of RAM are written to non-volatile storage such as a hard disk, as a file or on a separate partition, before powering off the computer[1].Going into hibernation requires no user interaction. On the other hand, shutting down the computer, either requires the user to save the data and close the running programs manually or pre-emption by the OS. As the number of running processes increase, greater amount of memory is required for storage, thereby increasing the time required for hibernation. The problem with the current method of hibernation is that, the content of the entire RAM has to be saved, which is a lot of data. The proposed technique minimizes the amount of data that is needed to be saved during hibernation. It does so by allowing the application programmer to specify a certain portion of data as critical data. This critical data saved by the OS is then made available to the application program during resumption. The space required to store it is very small. Hence the hibernation time is reduced, and it is aptly termed ‘HyberFast’.

2 Analytical Study

The results of an analytical study carried out to check the time required for hibernation while different amounts of RAM were in use are shown in Fig 1.

V.V. Das and N. Thankachan (Eds.): CIIT 2011, CCIS 250, pp. 850–854, 2011.

The following graph shows that, larger the amount of RAM being used more is the time required for hibernation.

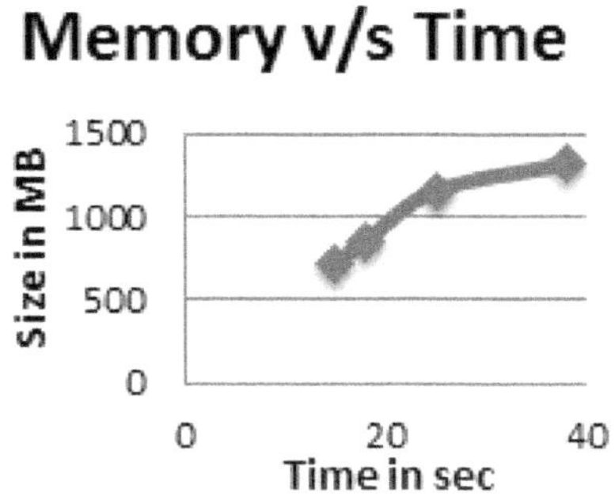

Fig. 1. Graph showing memory v/s time plot

3 Implementation

For efficient implementation on different platforms using different languages a standard is required. A framework for such standardization is suggested below.

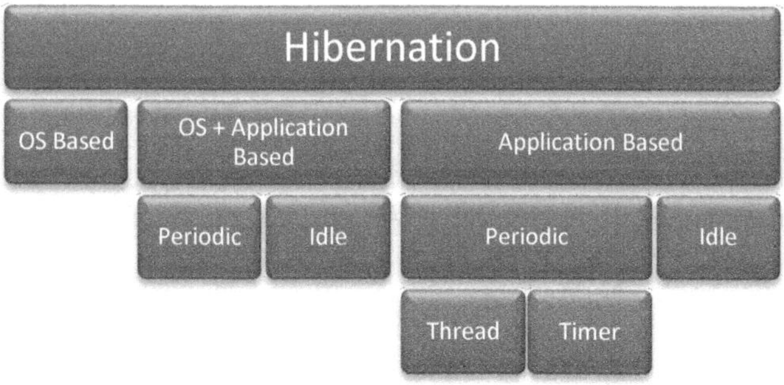

Fig. 2. Classification of the Hibernation techniques used

Techniques for implementation of hibernation have been classified into 3 broad categories (Fig. 2) as OS based, OS + Application based and Application based and further classified as Periodic and idle. In application based implementation the periodic method can be implemented by using thread or timers.

3.1 OS Based

This is the current technique used for hibernation. Here the OS is unaware about the type of application program or the critical data which it needs to save. Therefore the only steps are:

1. All the programs are suspended.
2. The snapshot of the RAM is copied into the hard-disk.
3. Status of CPU as well any other devices, if required, are saved.

3.2 OS + Application Based (HyberFast)

This is the best technique for saving the context of a running process. It requires combined efforts from both, OS developers and application developers. The OS is notified about the critical data of every process. Instead, the OS selectively saves the critical data of independent processes, as and when required. Since this technique requires a combined effort, it has to be standardized as under:

1. Critical data of the application has to be identified by the programmer.
2. A call-back function which returns the critical data/context as a stream.
3. This function has to be registered with the OS.
4. Another call-back function which restores the .
5. This function also has to be registered with the OS.

The following call-back functions have to be defined by the application programmer. Integer return type of the resume_app() indicates that it should return an integer indicating success or failure. The function rhh(), meaning register hibernate handler, has to be created by the OS developer. This function registers the above two functions with the OS. Its definition is given below.
Function prototypes in C:

```
char* get_critical_data();
int resume_app(char* s);
void rhh(char*(*gcd)(),int(*ra)(char*));
```

3.3 Application Based

Application programs like Mozilla Firefox use this technique for saving their critical data. There is no intervention by the OS. Ideally, in this technique, the application should handle the ACID properties of the critical data while saving it. This makes it possible to resume the application even in case of failures. The only difference is that the user has to re-initiate the application after failure. Few guidelines for the application based technique are suggested below:

1. Identify critical data enough to resume the application
2. Create two functions, to save the critical data to a file and to recover it.
3. ACID properties of the data has to be maintained.

Two functions to save the critical context and resume the application have to be created by the application programmer. Since this is at the discretion of the programmer, he/she can modify the definition as required. The programmer should call the resume function during application initialisation phase. The resume function should check the stored flag to determine whether the application had properly terminated during its last run.

Function prototypes in C:

```
void save_to_file();
int resume_from_file();
```

By using technique 3.2 and 3.3 for hibernation, some amount of real-time data loss can be avoided. Technique 3.1 can be used only for hibernation. Technique 3.2 can be used to restore and resume the system if it needs to hibernate or encounters a sudden failure. Technique 3.3 may only be used to recover from a system failure.

4 Demonstration

A program demonstrating technique 3.3 has been made using Java. The program is basically a factorial generator which finds factorials from one to three. It is forcibly stopped by CTRL + C and run again. This time, it resumes at the previously interrupted point and hence calculates the factorial of three. To achieve this the function saveToFile saves the critical data to a specific file and the function resumeFromFile reads the same file and resumes the program.

Method prototypes in Java:

```
void saveToFile();
void resumeFromFile();
```

The function resumeFromFile() is called during initialisation which helps it to read the valid critical data. If it is found, the program resumes from the instant where it ended otherwise it begins execution from start.

```
C:\Seminars + Workshop\Papers\Self\Hyberfast\program>java Test

======Program to demonstrate hibernation======
The output is in the format <number>:<factorial>

1:1
Press 1 to continue :1
2:2
Press 1 to continue :Exception in thread "Thread-0" java.util.NoSuchElementExcep
tion
        at java.util.Scanner.throwFor(Scanner.java:897)
        at java.util.Scanner.next(Scanner.java:1520)
        at java.util.Scanner.nextInt(Scanner.java:2150)
        at java.util.Scanner.nextInt(Scanner.java:2109)
        at SampleApp.run(Test.java:206)

C:\Seminars + Workshop\Papers\Self\Hyberfast\program>java Test

======Program to demonstrate hibernation======
The output is in the format <number>:<factorial>

3:6
Press 1 to continue :1

C:\Seminars + Workshop\Papers\Self\Hyberfast\program>_
```

Fig. 3. Screenshot of the program used for demonstration

5 Advantages and Applications of Hyberfast

There are few advantages of Hyberfast. One of the advantages is avoidance of real time data loss. By saving the critical data periodically we can resume the application even in case of Power failure. The OS should ensure that the ACID properties are maintained while saving the critical data to ensure that the data is error-free. Other advantage is User behaviour tracking. As the critical data is saved from time to time, research can be done to enhance the user experience. Also less storage space and fast hibernation is possible using this method as only the critical data is saved so very less amount of memory is required for most of the programs to hibernate. Saving of critical data of programs can be prioritized as per their criticality.

6 Limitations

Extra code to be written by OS and application developers increases overhead. As only the critical data is saved, some programs may take more time to start-up

7 Conclusion

HyberFast is a technique by which the process of hibernation can be sped-up. It provides a solution to prevent real-time data loss.

8 Future Work

Newer magnetic storage disks that save data at incredible speeds coupled with HyberFast can provide a foolproof solution to enterprises, servers, etc where data loss is not an option.

Acknowledgment. The authors would like to acknowledge Mozilla Firefox which implements the application based technique to recover from failure. The idea that the other applications could do the same was the basic inspiration for this research paper.

References

1. Hibernation basics (2011), `http://www.en.wikipedia.org/wiki/Hibernation_(computing)`
2. Boot-Process (2011), `http://www.tar.hu/wininternals/ch05lev1sec1.html`

Hashed-K-Means: A Proposed Intrusion Detection Algorithm

Samarjeet Borah, Saugat P.K. Chetry, and Pramod Kr Singh

Department of Computer Science & Engineering
Sikkim Manipal Institute of Technology, Majitar, East Sikkim, 737136
samarjeetborah@gmail.com, saugat_chetry@yahoo.com,
pramodkr.singh@hotmail.com

Abstract. Intrusion Detection Systems detect the malicious attacks which generally include theft of information or data. It is found from the studies that clustering based intrusion detection methods may be helpful in detecting unknown attack patterns compared to traditional intrusion detection systems. In this paper a new clustering algorithm is proposed to work on network intrusion data. The algorithm is experimented with KDD99 dataset and found satisfactory results.

Keywords: Intrusion Detection, Clustering, IDS, K-Means, AIM, Training Data Set.

1 Introduction

Now-a-days computer network provides usefulness in many ways to mankind. It becomes an integral part of daily life. However, ease of access, outward anonymity, and wide prevalence of saving sensitive information on computers has attracted a large number of criminals and hacker hobbyists. So it is impossible for any computer system to be claimed resistant to network intrusion. Since there is no perfect solution to prevent intrusions from happening, it is very important to be able to detect them at the first moment of occurrences and take actions to minimize the possible damage.

2 Introduction

Intrusion Detection [1] is the process of detecting the malicious attacks or threats to any computer or network. The basic task of Intrusion Detection is to audit the log data of a computer which includes network as well as host based data. Intrusion detection process helps to make the network more secure for data transmission. An Intrusion Detection System (IDS) helps to determine the attackers and ensures secure transmission of data. It also facilitates to stabilize and increase the lifetime of the network.

V.V. Das and N. Thankachan (Eds.): CIIT 2011, CCIS 250, pp. 855–860, 2011.

3 Clustering

Clustering [2], [3] can be considered as one of the widely used unsupervised learning process. Clustering algorithms may play a vital role in developing efficient intrusion detection algorithms. These algorithms are able to detect important patterns in huge amount of data. Again, they are having the potential to detect new types of network attacks without any prior knowledge of their existence. Thus clustering techniques are best suited for designing anomaly detection models, means they can deal with new type of attacks. In the following section some clustering algorithms that are used in intrusion detection are discussed briefly.

4 Clustering Algorithms for Intrusion Detection

4.1 Y-Means Algorithm

Y-Means [7] is based on the K-Means Algorithm [4]. In this algorithm partition of the data takes place automatically. It classifies the normal and the abnormal or intrusive clusters. The iteration will continue until there is no empty cluster. Outliers of clusters are removed to form new cluster. If instances are more similar to each other, then the clusters will overlap each other. At last, population ratio of one cluster is above the given threshold all the instances in the cluster will be classified as normal labeled as intrusive.

4.2 Intrusion Detection Using Unlabelled Data Technique [8]

This approach groups similar data instances into clusters together and then uses distance metrics on clusters to trace out the anomalies. The assumptions for this technique to work are: data instances having same type should be close to each other in feature space under some reasonable metric, while instances with different types must be far apart. The data instances having normal type must be in majority in the training set. It creates clusters from its input data, then labels these clusters as either normal or anomaly and then uses these clusters to classify unseen network data instances as either normal or anomalous.

4.3 Hybrid Intrusion Detection System [9]

The Hybrid system is built using two basic models, anomaly detection and misuse detection. Anomaly detection consists of a Rule-Based model of normal behavior, against which the detected behavior is compared. It has a high detection rate, but the false positive rate is also high. The misuse detection model is built to classify the attack type by comparison with the known types of attack behavior. It has high accuracy, but the detection rate is lower. By combining features of both the models, the Hybrid system gains advantages of both the models.

5 Hashed-K-Means: The Proposed Algorithm

As it is found from the studies that the K-means [2] algorithm can be adopted to apply in different application areas, one attempt has been made in this paper to adopt this algorithm for intrusion detection. This proposed algorithm is not user dependent as it is using AIM [5] module for finding out the number of clusters to be generated. The algorithm has two phases, namely: cluster formation and anomaly detection. The KDD99 [6] dataset is used as training dataset for hashed-k-means algorithm.

5.1 Methodology

Let the dataset be represented as $X = \{x_i, i = 1,2 \ldots N\}$ which consists of N data objects$x_1, x_2 \ldots x_N$, where each object has M different attribute values corresponding to the M different attributes. The value of i-th object can be given by: $X_i = \{x_{i1}, x_{i2} \ldots x_{iM}\}$.

In the first phase the AIM algorithm is applied to find out the value automatically in prior to partition the dataset into k disjoint subsets. The initial mean set will be generated by the AIM algorithm based on the following distance measures:

$$Distance - Threshold\ (D_x) = \mu \pm 1\alpha \tag{1}$$

$$\text{Where } \mu = \frac{\sum_{i=1}^{n} x_i \overline{M_\iota}}{\sum_{i=1}^{n} x_i} \quad \text{and} \quad \alpha = \sqrt{\frac{\sum_{i=1}^{n} (x_i - \overline{M_\iota})^2}{n-1}}$$

where X_i is the $i - th$ object of the dataset $X, i = 1,2 \ldots 3$. $\overline{M_\iota}$ is the mean of $i - th$ object of X, μ is the grand mean and α is the standard deviation of the dataset X.

$$Average - Distance\ (A_{dx}) = \frac{1}{m}\left(\sum_{i=1}^{m} d(Marr_i, m_c)\right) \tag{2}$$

where $Marr_i$ is the set of initial means, m_c and is the candidate for new cluster mean.

The hash value is calculated based on the training dataset. It is found that the value will be different for normal as well as different attack types. A hash table is maintained for all types of known attack types. In the next phase the dataset is partitioned based on the initial mean set. Mean and standard deviations are calculated on the training dataset. The last field in the dataset is replaced by the product of the standard deviation and the number of instances of each type thereby, providing each type with a new value. Then, based on the Euclidean distance of the points in the modified training dataset, clusters are formed. These clusters are used as base for classification of the testing dataset.

Cluster Formation & Training Phase: In this phase, the KDD99 dataset for intrusion detection is used to train the system. The number of instances for each type of connection is calculated along with the mean and the standard deviation. The hash value is generated as mentioned above. Then the last field is replaced with its hash value and process of cluster formation is carried out.

The Detection Phase: After the cluster formation is over the next step is to check whether the system is able to detect the intrusion on the system or not. It is done by taking a testing dataset and matching it with the cluster formed already in the training phase.

Algorithm

```
Algorithm HASHED-K-MEANS ()
Input:
   //Input Dataset
K //Number of desired clusters obtained from the method.
Output:
   // Set of clusters
START
Calculate number of instances of each type, the mean and
standard deviation of the input.
Replace the last field of the labels in the training data
with the product of the standard deviation    and the no
of instances.
Assign initial values for means m1, m2.... mk;
Repeat
  Assign each item ti to the cluster which has the closest
  mean;
  Calculate new mean for each cluster;
Until convergence is met;
STOP
```

6 Results and Discussion

6.1 The Initial Clusters Formed

The figure (Fig. 1) below shows the one of the initial clusters formed after the training of the system with the Kdd99 dataset. It is found that the normal instances making their own clusters while the other type of connections making their own clusters based on the hash values and the Euclidean distances.

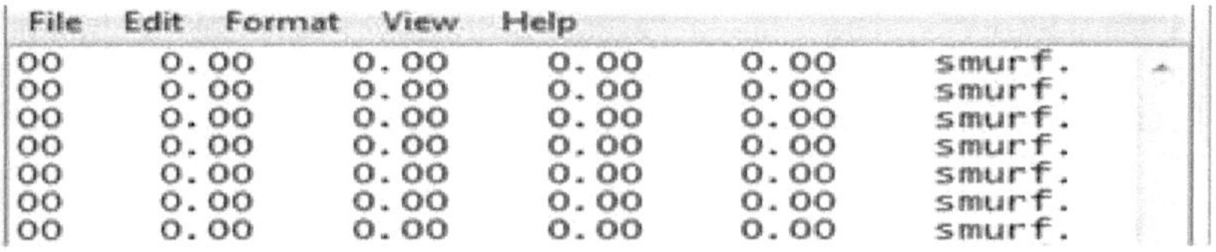
File Edit Format View Help

00	0.00	0.00	0.00	0.00	smurf.
00	0.00	0.00	0.00	0.00	smurf.
00	0.00	0.00	0.00	0.00	smurf.
00	0.00	0.00	0.00	0.00	smurf.
00	0.00	0.00	0.00	0.00	smurf.
00	0.00	0.00	0.00	0.00	smurf.
00	0.00	0.00	0.00	0.00	smurf.

Fig. 1. Initial Cluster 2

6.2 The Detection Phase

This figure shows the different threats detected which were present in the testing dataset. The proposed algorithm is able to detect unknown type of connections present in the testing dataset.

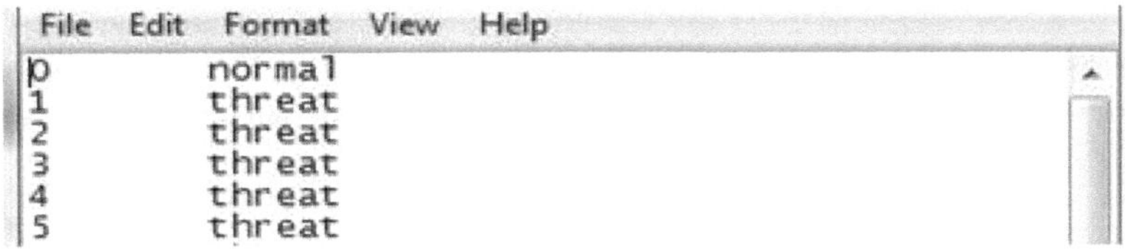

Fig. 2. Detection Phase

6.3 Comparative Analysis on Inter-Cluster Distance

The inter cluster distance of the clusters formed is calculated by finding the Euclidean distance between the cluster means and the clusters members of all the clusters formed. A graph is plotted to study the variations of the clusters formed. A larger inter-cluster distance would mean clusters are more distinct and tight.

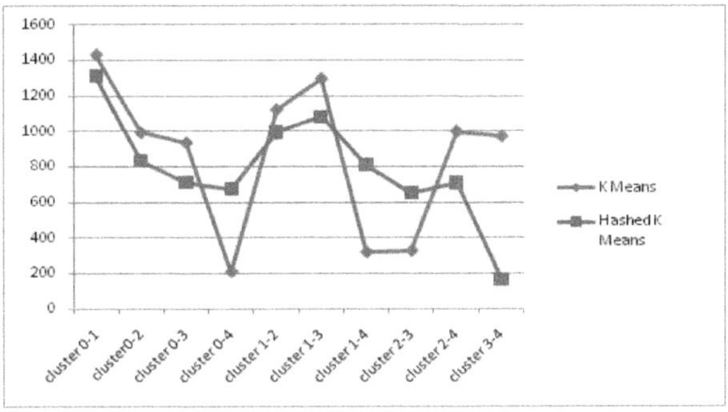

Fig. 3. Inter cluster distances for K means and Hashed K means Algorithm

The above graph shows the inter-cluster distances of the clusters formed by the K-Means and Hashed K-Means algorithms. It can be seen that the clusters formed by the Hashed-K-Means show better and distinct results as compared to normal K-Means algorithm.

7 Conclusion

In this paper a new clustering algorithm is proposed which is based on K-means and AIM method. The efficiency of the algorithm with which intrusions are detected is around 90%-95%. The accuracy of this algorithm depends on the training data taken. If the number of instances of a particular type is equal to that of the other then there is a chance that a particular normal instance might be considered as an abnormal / attack type rather than a normal instance. The algorithm can detect new types of attacks but its classification would be a difficult task because it's not present in the training data.

References

1. Sabahi, F., Movaghar, A.: Intrusion Detection: A Survey. In: The Proceedings of 3rd International Conference on Systems and Networks Communications, ICSNC 2008. IEEE (2008) ISBN: 978-0-7695-3371-1
2. Han, J., Kamber, M.: Data Mining Concepts and Techniques, 2nd edn. Elsevier ISBN: 81-312-0535-5
3. Kaufman, L., Rousseeuw, P.J.: Finding Groups in Data: An introduction to Cluster analysis. John Wiley, New York (1990) ISBN 0-471-85233-3
4. McQueen, J.B.: Some methods for classification and analysis of multivariate observations. In: Proceedings of the Fifth Berkeley Symposium on Mathematical Statistics and Probability, vol. 1, pp. 281–297. Univ. of California Press, Berkeley (1967)
5. Samarjeet Borah, Ghose, M.K.: Automatic Initialization of Means (AIM): A Proposed Extension to the K-means Algorithm. International Journal of Information Technology & Knowledge Management 3(2), 247–250 (2010) ISSN: 0973-4414
6. Dataset is, `http://kdd.ics.uci.edu/databases/kddcup99/kddcup99.html`
7. Guan, Y., Ghorbani, A., Belacel, N.: Y-means: A Clustering Method for Intrusion Detection. In: Proceedings of Canadian Conference on Electrical and Computer Engineering, Montreal, Quebec, Canada, May 4-7, pp. 1083–1086 (2003)
8. Portnoy, L., Eskin, E., Stolfo, S.: Intrusion Detection with Unlabeled Data Using Clustering. In: Proceedings of the ACM CSS Workshop on Data Mining Applied to Security (DMSA 2001), Philadelphia, PA, November 5-8 (2001)
9. Yan, K.Q., Wang, S.C., Liu, C.W.: A Hybrid Intrusion Detection System of Cluster-based Wireless Sensor Networks. In: Proceedings of the International Multi-Conference of Engineers and Computer Scientists, IMECS 2009, Hong Kong, March 18 - 20, vol. I (2009)

Implementation of Zigbee Based Power Management System

Prashant Aher, Auna Adhav, Falguni Adbe, Dhanashri Gawali, and Y.V. Chavan

Electronics and Telecommunication Department,
M.A.E. Alandi(D), Pune, India
{prashantaher07,adbe89fal,dhanashree.gawali,
chavan.yashwant}@gmail.com

Abstract. The power management scenario in India, is not efficient. To conserve energy, government applies power cuts, resulting in lot of inconvenience as even the essentials are cut off. Another way to save power is to train the staff to use power efficiently. This is again a method which is neither foolproof nor easy to monitor. This paper describes a proposed system which helps use the available energy efficiently. A Controller system has been developed that manages efficient utilization of power over an electrical network and helps conserve energy by making authorities keep a check on energy usage. To demonstrate this wireless sensor network have been developed which consists of number of nodes. ZigBee protocol has been used for the wireless communications. The main advantage of using ZigBee protocol is low power requirement which result in longer battery life. As a proof of concept ARM based prototype of proposed system is designed and developed for small application.

Keywords: Power Management, Energy Management, Zigbee, Wireless sensor network.

1 Introduction

Generating power from within Power loss in its distribution and transmission still touches a whopping figure of 29% in India! Being a developing country with limited financial resources, India cannot afford this kind of loss (International statistics) and the situation is further compounded by power thefts and poor state of infrastructure. The power management scenario in India, today, is not as efficient as it can be. To conserve energy, power cuts are applied resulting in lot of inconvenience. Another way to save power is to train the staff to use power efficiently, which is neither foolproof nor easy to monitor. Some industries like the Indian cement industry have their own power plants to meet their energy requirements. This paper describes a proposed system which helps use the available energy efficiently. With this system available power may be used in such a way that only low power devices like Tubes, Fans etc. which are primary needs should be allowed and high power devices like heater, pump-set, A.C. etc should not be allowed for particular time period [2]. To achieve this, system should be able differentiate between high power and low power devices at every node and allow only low power devices to be ON [5]. A Controller

V.V. Das and N. Thankachan (Eds.): CIIT 2011, CCIS 250, pp. 861–864, 2011.

based system has been developed that manages efficient utilization of power over an electrical network and helps conserve energy by making authorities keep a check on energy usage. To demonstrate this wireless sensor network have been developed which consists of number of nodes. These nodes communicate with each other in full duplex mode. The communication consists of data transfer, controlling node operations. ZigBee protocol has been used for the wireless communications. The main advantage of using ZigBee protocol is that the nodes require very less amount of power to provide longer battery life. As a proof of concept a prototype of proposed system is designed and developed for small application.

2 Design of Proposed Sensor Network

This section presents various design aspects of proposed sensor network for power management. For proposed system the area over which the electrical network resides and needs to be managed, is divided into number of parts. Each part is treated as a node. Each node consists of an end device connected to respective electrical network part. Thus interconnection of these nodes forms a wireless mesh network. The central node called controller, monitors and controls the activities of all nodes. In proposed system the chief node i.e. the controller block shall calculate the threshold values for the different blocks based on inputs received from central authority.

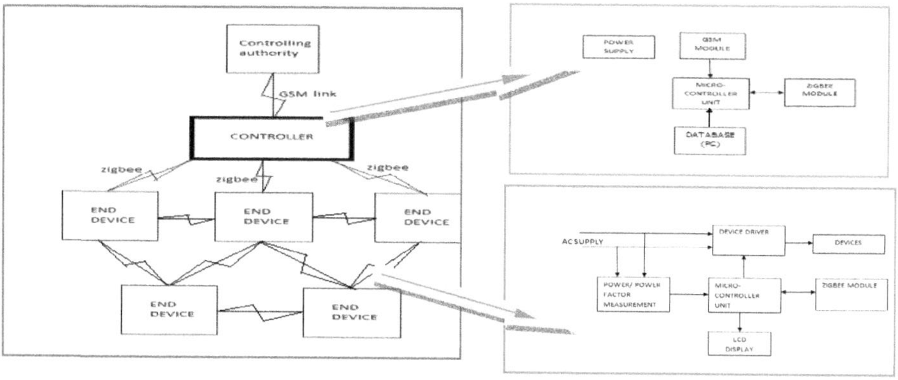

Fig. 1. System block diagram

To enable the central authority to send the information required from any location a GSM link is provided. Controller sends the thresholds to the respective nodes. The data sent by the controller reaches the target unit through the zigbee modules. As shown in figure 1 microcontroller on sensor node receives the threshold value from controller wirelessly through Zigbee module. Whenever any device is switched on through the device driver, the power factor measuring IC measures the power factor of the same and sends the value to the microcontroller which compares the value to the threshold stored and checks it with the priority list to decide if it must be allowed to switch on or not. LCD display is used to show the status of various devices connected. Central node also decides which nodes to keep in wakeup mode or in sleep mode depending on the requirement.

3 Implementation

A prototype of proposed system has been implemented for demonstration of a small application. Considering the computational requirement of the system ARM 7 microcontrollers LPC2138 has been selected for prototype implementation [11]. The system needs 5V and 3.3 V power supply for its working.

Fig. 2(a). The controller

Fig. 2(b). End device (Node)

Considering the system specification ZigBee module JN 5139 was selected, however due to unavailability XBee Module manufactured by digicom has been used [9]. For power measurement ADE7756 IC has been used. The GSM module is interfaced with the controller to receive the message send by the controlling authority. The relay driving circuit is interfaced to switch ON/OFF the device.

4 System Testing and Results

Different sensor nodes are used to setup a wireless sensor network to measure the power required by that section (node). For demonstration we have used only one node to test the communication between controller and node and then the power management part at the node. Power required is compared with the threshold given to that node to automatically manage the available power among different devices depending on strategy (high, low power/ priority). For demonstration 3 loads D1, D2, D3 have been connected to a node. All the loads (devices) are of different power requirements; D1=100W, D2= 60W and D3=40W. For the various cases result was obtained. It is shown in the following table. Demonstration was done in order to certify the nodes communication ability, power regulation and management.

Table 1. Node's power management performance

Sr.No.	Case	Power available at controller (W)	Threshold Given to Node 1 (W)	Power required at Node 1 (W)	Device Status(On/Off) D1	D2	D3
1	Wth > Preq	800	266.6	200	On	On	On
2	Wth < Preq	500	166.6	200	Off	On	On
3	Wth < Preq	250	83.33	200	Off	Off	On

5 Conclusion and Future Scope

Sensor networks are the key to gathering the information needed by smart environments, whether in buildings, utilities, industrial, home, shipboard, transportation systems automation, or elsewhere. A ZigBee based Power Management system has been developed for an educational institute. The system can be applied to industry, hospitals, residencies, stadiums & theatres for energy management. Successful implementation of ZigBee based Power Management system provides a solution for convenient deployment and thus saving energy, as well as cost. The proposed system can be modified to be used for three phase systems as well. The basic hardware can further be extended to include number of nodes with a mesh network topology. Routing protocols may be implemented for further optimization.

References

1. Lam, K.L., Tsang, K.F., Tung, H.Y.: Energy management using zigbee. In: Third International Conference on Next Generation Mobile Applications, Services and Technologies, pp. 412–415. IEEE (2009)
2. Pritam Shah, K.G., Shaikh, T., Shilasakar, S.: Power management using zigbee wireless sensor network. In: First International Conference on Emerging Trends in Engineering and Technology, pp. 242–245. IEEE (2008)
3. Hou, J., Gao, Y.: Greenhouse wireless sensor network monitoring system design based on solar energy. In: International Conference on Challenges in Environmental Science and Computer Engineering, pp. 475–479. IEEE (2010)
4. Han, D.-M., Lim, J.-H.: Design and implementation of smart home energy management systems based on zigbee. In: Third International Conference on Next Generation Mobile Applications, Services and Technologies, NGMAST 2009, pp. 412–415. IEEE (2009)
5. Wadhawa, C.L.: Generation, Distribution and Utilization of electrical system. New age International publication (2000)
6. Thareja, B.L.: A Text of Electrical Technology. In: S.I. Units, 3rd edn., vol. 2, S. Chand Publication (1999)

Design and Analysis of Downlink Scheduling for Network Coverage for Wireless Systems

Harish Kumar, Pushpneel Verma, V.K. Sharma, and Mohit Kumar

Member, IEEE
Department of ECE&CSE, Bhagwant Institute of Technology,
Muzaffarnagar, UP India
hc78@rediffmail.com, pushpneelverma@gmail.com

Abstract. In this paper, we shall focus on the downlink scheduling design optimized for network coverage for wireless systems with multiple antennas. & proposed a wireless system consisting of a base station (with n_T transmit antennas) and K client mobiles (each with single antenna). with multiple antennas, we have additional degrees of freedom for *spatial multiplexing* and *spatial diversity,* to include the spatial multiplexing into the framework, we first extends the conventional concept of network coverage to a more general *utility-based network coverage* to deal with the possibility of allocating resource to multiple users at the same time. consider the *network centric utility* and the *user centric utility* as two examples of the utility based coverage concept. raised on the generalized concept of network coverage, we proposed a systematic frame-work based on information the critical approach and formulate the scheduling design as a mixed convex and combinational optimization problem.

Keywords: *MIMO,* Coverage-capacity tradeoff, Cross layer, Wireless.

1 Introduction

In this paper, we consider a wireless system consisting of a base station (with n_T transmit antennas) and K client mobiles (each with single antenna). with multiple antennas, we have additional degrees of freedom for *spatial multiplexing* and *spatial diversity* to include the spatial multiplexing into the framework, we first extends the conventional concept of network coverage to a more general *utility-based network coverage* to deal with the possibility of allocating resource to multiple users at the same time. We consider the *network centric utility* and the *user centric utility* as two examples of the utility based coverage concept[1-2]. Raised on the generalized concept of network coverage, we propose a systematic frame-work based on information the critical approach and formulate the scheduling design as a mixed convex and combinational optimization problem

1.1 Overview of System Model with Multiple Transmit Antennas

1.1.1 Downlink Channel Model

The fig 1 shown, a communication system with K mobile users having single receive antenna and a base station with n_T transmit antennas. The microscopic channel fading

V.V. Das and N. Thankachan (Eds.): CIIT 2011, CCIS 250, pp. 865–869, 2011.

between different users and different antennas is modeled as i.i.d. complex Gaussian distribution with unit variance. Furthermore, it is assumed that the encoding and decoding frame are short bursts which are much shorter than the coherence time of the fading channel.

Let Y_k be the received signal of the k-th mobile. The K x 1 dimension vector of received signal **Y** at the K mobile stations is given by

$$Y = \begin{bmatrix} Y_1 \\ . \\ . \\ . \\ Y_K \end{bmatrix} = \begin{bmatrix} \sqrt{L_1} H_1 \\ . \\ . \\ . \\ \sqrt{L_K} H_K \end{bmatrix} X + \begin{bmatrix} Z_1 \\ . \\ . \\ . \\ Z_K \end{bmatrix} \tag{1}$$

where **X** is the n_T x 1 transmit symbol from the base station to the K mobiles, Z_k is the complex Gaussian noise with variance σ_z^2, $\mathbf{H}_k$ is the 1 x n_T dimension channel matrix between the n_T transmit antennas (at the base station) and the k-th mobile and L_k is the path loss between the base station and the k-th mobile[4]

1.1.2 Multi-user Physical Layer Model

Before we could discuss the scheduling optimization problem, it is very important to define the physical layer model because different physical layer implementations will definitely affect the system level performance. To isolate the physical layer performance from specific implementation details (such as channel coding and modulation, multiple access schemes like TDMA, FDMA, CDMA), and information theoretical approach is adopted Specifically[5]. The maximum achievable rate at the physical layer (with arbitrarily low error probability) is given by the Shannon's capacity and is realized by random codebook and Gaussian.

1.1.3 MAC Layer Model

The scheduling algorithm in the MAC layer is responsible for the allocation of channel resource at every fading block. The system resource is partitioned into short frames. We assume time division duplexing (TDD) systems so that channel reciprocal holds. At the beginning of every frame, the base station estimates the channel matrix from the participating mobile users. The uplink channel estimation is used as the downlink channel information. Due to short burst transmissions, the channel estimation is used as the downlink channel information. Due to short burst transmissions, the channel fading remains the same across the entire burst duration. The estimated CSI is passed to the scheduling algorithms in the MAC layer.

1.2 General Formulation of the Downlink Scheduler Design

Before we proceed with the scheduler design, it is important to quantify what is meant by *system performance*. In multi user systems. the system performance is can be defined by an *instantaneous utility* $G(r_1,...r_K)$ where r_k is the instantaneous data rate of the k-th user. For meaningful optimization. we have

$$\frac{\partial G}{\partial r_k} > 0 \forall r_k \geq 0 \tag{2}$$

1.2.1 Utility-Based Network Coverage

Consider a sequence of N realization of fading blocks, the instantaneous achievable data rate (s) of a scheduled mobile user (s) are random variables (functions of the specific fading realization) in that fading block. In conventional wireless systems where the scheduling is constrained to select one active user at any scheduling instance (fading block), *outage* is defined as the event that the instantaneous data rate of the scheduled user is below a target data rate R_0. *Outage probability* is defined as the likelihood of the outage event.

2 Numerical Results and Discussions

In this section, we shall compare the performance of the downlink schedulers optimized for utility-based coverage, we shall investigate the contributions of multi-user selection diversity and spatial multiplexing to the network coverage. To highlight the contribution of multi-user selection diversity, we compare the coverage with respect to the random scheduler, where n_T users are randomly selected irrespective of their channel matrices at every fading block[6-7]. In the simulation, each data point consists of 5000 realizations of channel fading. Channel fading of the K users are generated based on independent complex Gaussian distribution (with unit variance). We assume 0dB antenna gain in the transmit and receive antenna. The carrier frequency is assumed to be 2GHz. Data rate is expressed in terms of bits per second per Hz.

2.1 Contribution of Spatial Multiplexing/Spatial Diversity to Network Coverage

Figure 3 and 4, illustrates the *network centric* coverage versus the network capacity (network loading) of the coverage-optimized scheduler at N_T = 1.2, 4. We observe that a significant gain in network coverage is achieved by increasing the number of transmit antenna n_T at high SNR and this illustrates the contribution of spatial multiplexing to network coverage. For example, in Figure 3, there are 50% and 90% area coverage gain at target network capacity of 5b/s/Hz comparing relative to $N_T=1$ for n_T=2,4 respectively. On the other hand, Figure 4 illustrates the user-centric utility $G_{user}(r_1,..r_K) = \min_{k\in A} r_k$ threshold versus cell radius at various Q=1,2...., 5 and n_T=5 where Q=|A|.

2.2 Contribution of Multiuser Selection Diversity to Network Coverage

Figure 6, illustrates the capacity versus coverage between optimal scheduling and random scheduling at n_T = 1.4. For example, there is 3.2 times are coverage gain between the optimal scheduler and the random scheduler at n_T=4 and target network capacity of 2 b/s/Hz. This illustrates that multi-user selection diversity contributes significantly to coverage area gains[8]. Fig 6 illustrates the performance of the genetic algorithm. The genetic algorithm has relatively small performance loss compared with the optimal scheduler.

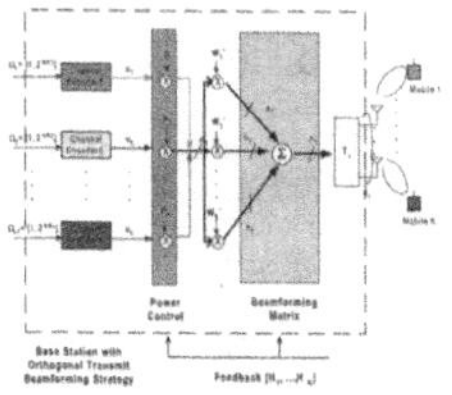

Fig. 1. Orthogonal Transmit Beam-Forming strategy with multiple antennas.

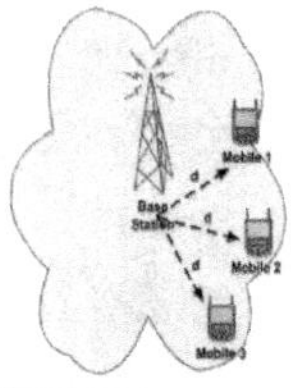

Fig. 2. Illustration of worst-case outage.

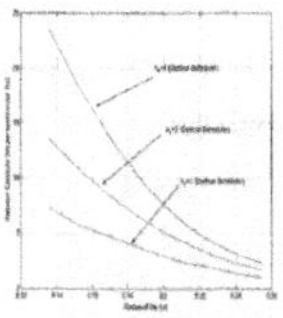
Fig. 3. Network coverage (km) versus network capacity (b/s/Hz) of coverage-optimized scheduler at $n_T = 1, 2, 4$. Total transmit power of the base station is 30dBm. Path loss exponent is 4. Total number of users is 10. The network coverage refers to the *network centric coverage* at a target outage of 1%.

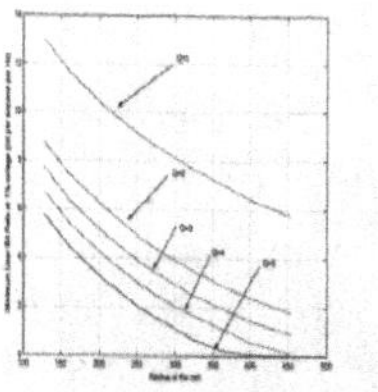
Fig. 4. Minimum scheduled data rate (b/s/Hz) versus cell coverage (m) at various $Q = 1, ..., 5$ where $Q = |A|$. Total transmit power of the base station is 30dBm. Path loss exponent is 4. Total number of users is 10. The cell coverage refers to the *user centric coverage* at a target outage of 1%.

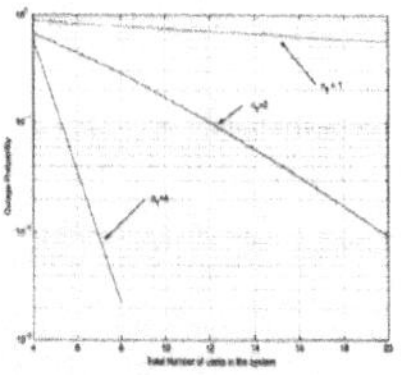

Fig. 5. Outage Probability versus Number of users K. Target network capacity is 7.0 b/s/Hz. Cell radius is 0.19 km. The transmit power at the base station is 30 dBm. The outage event refers to the *network centric utility* at a target outage of 1%.

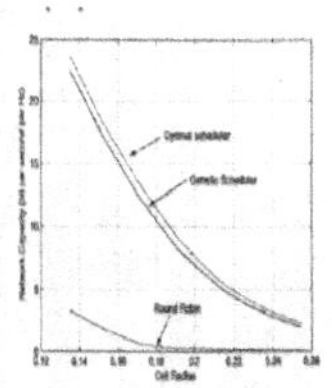

Fig. 6. Coverage (km) Performance of Genetic Downlink Schedulers at $n_T = 4$. Base station transmit power is set at 30dBm. Path loss exponent is 4. The network coverage refers to the network centric coverage at a target outage of 1%.

3 Conclusion

In this paper, we focus on the design of *coverage-optimized* downlink scheduler for systems with multiple antennas. A systematic framework is proposed for the scheduler design Problem based on information theoretical approach. There are K mobiles with single receive antenna and one base station with n_T transmit antennas. We proposed a generalized definition of network coverage, namely the *utility-based coverage*. The contributions of *multi-user selection diversity* and *spatial multiplexing* to the network coverage are analyzed. While the optimal scheduler delivers the best coverage, the computation complexity is huge. A real-time genetic algorithm is proposed, which offers enormous computational savings compared with the optimal algorithm and is an attractive candidate given it's performance complexity tradeoff.

References

1. Jalali, A., Padovani, R., Pankaj, R.: Data through put of CDMA. HDR a high efficiency-high data rate personal communication wireless. System. IEEE Trans. Veh. Technol. 28(1) (January 2000)
2. Lau, K.N., Liu, Y.J., Chen, T.A.: Optimal space-time scheduling for wireless communications with partial power feedback. Bell Labs Technical J. (November 2002)

3. Yu, W., Rhee, W., Cioffi, J.M.: Optimal power control in multiple acess fading channels with multiple antennas. In: Proc. ICC 2001 (2001)
4. Chen, C.J., Wang, L.C.: Coverage and capacity enhancement in multiuser MIMO systems with scheduling. In: Proc. IEEE Clobecom 2004, pp. 1024–1038 (2004)
5. Lau, K.N.: Optimal down space time scheduling for wireless systems with multiple antennas. IEEE Trans. Veh. Technol. 54, 1322–1333 (2005)
6. Rappaport, T.S.: Wireless Communications: Principles and Practice. Prentice Hall (1996)
7. Kumar, H., Sharma, V.K., Verma, P., Venkat Babu, G.: Analysis of a New Base Station Receiver for Increasing Diversity Order in a CDMA Cellular System. In: Das, V.V., Stephen, J., Chaba, Y. (eds.) CNC 2011. CCIS, vol. 142, pp. 104–110. Springer, Heidelberg (2011)

HVS Based Enhanced Medical Image Fusion

A. Gayathri and V. Nandhini

MNM Jain Engineering College, Tamilnadu, India
{gaybalahari,nandhu.velu}@gmail.com

Abstract. Medical image fusion will help the physicians to extract the features visible in images by different modalities. In this paper, a novel discrete wavelet transform (DWT) based technique for medical image fusion is presented. Firstly, the medical images to be fused are extracted .Secondly conversion into grayscale is carried out before decomposition by the DWT. Then by considering the characteristics of human visual system (HVS) and the physical meaning of the wavelet coefficients, new different fusion schemes are performed on low frequency and high frequency bands separately, i.e. Visibility Based Scheme for the low frequency coefficients and Variance Based Scheme for the high frequency coefficients are applied. Finally, the fused image is constructed by the inverse discrete wavelet transform (IDWT) with all the combined coefficients.

Keywords: Discrete wavelet transform (DWT), Inverse discrete wavelet transform (IDWT), Human Visual system (HVS).

1 Introduction

In order to better support more accurate clinical information for physicians to deal with medical diagnosis and evaluation, multimodality medical images are needed, such as X-ray, computed tomography (CT), magnetic resonance imaging (MRI), and positron emission tomography (PET) images. These multimodality medical images usually provide complementary and occasionally conflicting information. Therefore, the fusion of the multimodal medical images is necessary and it has become a promising and very challenging research area in recent years. For medical image fusion, the fusion of images can often lead to additional clinical information not apparent in the separate images. Another advantage is that it can reduce the storage cost by storing just the single fused image instead of multi-source images. So far, many techniques for image fusion have been proposed in the literature and a thorough overview of these methods can be viewed in reference. Since the real-world objects usually contain structures at many different scales or resolutions, multi resolution techniques for medical image fusion have become very essential.

1.1 Fusion Techniques

A generic categorization of image fusion methods is the following: 1) linear superposition 2) nonlinear methods 3) optimization approaches 4) artificial neural

V.V. Das and N. Thankachan (Eds.): CIIT 2011, CCIS 250, pp. 870–872, 2011.

networks 5) image pyramids 6) wavelet transform 7) generic multi resolution fusion scheme.

1.2 Wavelet Transform

A signal analysis method similar to image pyramids is the Discrete Wavelet Transform. The main difference is that while image pyramids lead to an over complete set of transform coefficients, the wavelet transform results in a non redundant image representation. The discrete 2-dim wavelet transform is computed by the recursive application of lowpass and high pass filters in each direction of the input image (i.e. rows and columns) followed by sub sampling. Details on this scheme can be found in the reference section[2]. One major drawback of the wavelet transform when applied to image fusion is its well known shift dependency, i.e. a simple shift of the input signal may lead to complete different transform coefficients. This results in inconsistent fused images when invoked in image sequence fusion. To overcome the shift dependency of the wavelet fusion scheme, the input images must be decomposed into a shift invariant representation. There are several ways to achieve this: The straightforward way is to compute the wavelet transform for all possible circular shifts of the input signal.

2 Proposed System

In this system after decomposition by DWT, the coefficients of low frequency portions and high frequency portions are processed with different fusion schemes providing enhanced visual information. The image reader used is based on Sinkhorn scaling algorithm which makes the system flexible to the size of the input image[1]. The multimodal medical images usually contain complementary and conflicting medical information, i.e., the same object in the multimodal medical images may appear very distinctly. Hence, when the source images are decomposed by wavelet transform, the approximation images (low frequency band) and the detail images (high frequency bands) must have quite different physical meaning in different images. On the other hand, as we know in most applications, the ultimate user or interpreter of the fused image is a human. So the human perception should be considered in theimage fusion. According to the theoretical models of the HVS, we know that the human eyes have different sensitiveness to the wavelet coefficients of low resolution band and high resolution bands[5]. Based on the above analysis, this paper presents a new fusion rule which treats the low frequency band and high frequency bands with different schemes separately.

Step 1: Image Extraction using Sinkhorn Scaling Algorithm
Step 2: Gray scale conversion
Step3: Performing discrete wavelet transform
Step4: Fusion schemes
Step5: Fused image creation by IDWT

3 Conclusion

Thus a novel DWT based technique for medical image fusion is presented. The method is developed by not only considering the characteristics of HVS but also considering the physical meaning of the wavelet coefficients. Different fusion schemes are then performed on the coefficients of the low frequency band and high frequency bands with simultaneous computation of IDWT. We have compared the proposed method with some existing fusion approaches.Our application is intended to be useful for physicians who need to fuse multi-modality images for support in diagnosis. We can integrate the fusion process into a distributed Application. As technology keeps developing new and efficient filters can be used to obtain better fusion results through z-transform, Laplace transform or DWT. Instead of performing multilevel DWT which can affect the overall processing speed we can apply other methods that yield an equivalent result in a single level of decomposition. We can also use the simple Haar'stransform to obtain efficiency.

References

[1] Yang, Y.: Multimodal Medical Image Fusion Through a New DWT Based Technique. School of Information Technolog. Jiangxi University of Finance and Economics, Nanchang, China (2010)

[2] Cheng, S.L., He, J.M., Lv, Z.W.: Medical Image of PET/CT Weighted Fusion Based on Wavelet Transform. In: Proceedings of the 2nd International Conference on Bioinformatics and Biomedical Engineering, pp. 2523–2525 (2008)

[3] Sabalan, D., Hassan, G.: MRI and PET images fusion based on human retina model. Journal of Zhejiang University SCIENCE A 8(10), 1624–1632 (2007)

[4] Zhu, Y.M., Cochoff, S.M.: An object-oriented framework for medical image registration, fusion, and visualization. Computer Methods and Programs in Biomedicine 82(3), 258–267 (2006)

[5] Pajares, G., Cruz, J.M.D.L.: A wavelet-based image fusion tutorial. Pattern Recognition 37(9), 1855–1872 (2004)

Web Service Composition through BPEL Using Intalio

Rajat Bhandari[1], Ugrasen Suman[2], and A.K. Ramani[2]

[1] Venkteshwar Institute of Technology, RGPV University,
Indore (MP), India, 2006
bhandari@gmail.com
[2] School of Computer Science and IT, Devi Ahilya University, Indore (MP), India
{ugrasen123,ramaniak}@yahoo.com

Abstract. Web service is an emerging technology in recent years due to its open standard specification. The World Wide Web Consortium (W3C) defines a web service as a software system designed to support interoperablemachine-to-machine interaction over a network [11]. These web services can be composed together with the help of composition operation called web service composition. The web service composition can be achieved with the help of Business Process Execution Language (BPEL). In this paper, we have proposed an architecture for web service composition through Intalio business process designer.

Keywords: Web service, Web service composition, Business processes, Service composition, BPEL.

1 Introduction

The current enterprise is focusing on the development of platform independent software components called, web services. The web service is a self-contained function, which depends on Service Oriented Architecture (SOA) for its design, development and deployment as per W3C proposed guideline [1]. The web services which follow the SOA architecture can be composed through the process of web service composition [5]. The web services can be created with the help of Jdeveloper, Eclipse, NetBeans etc. There exist various tools for web service composition such as, Intalio business process designer, Microsoft Biztalk server and Bea weblogic [5].Web service composition can be achieved in two ways, i.e. static and dynamic [4]. The dynamic composition is achieved with the help of OWL-S language and semantic mechanism whereas, in static composition, the web services can be composed using BPEL or BPEL4WS language and with Orchestration and Choreography mechanism. There are two main approaches for web service composition, i.e., industry approach and semantics approach [4]. In industry approach, the WSDL file can be created for each web services and perform the composition of the services. Whereas the semantic approach mainly focuses on semantics of services or keyword based searching. There are various composition languages such as, Web Service Choreography Interface, Business Process Modeling Language, BPEL and Darpa Agent Markup Language [6].

V.V. Das and N. Thankachan (Eds.): CIIT 2011, CCIS 250, pp. 873–876, 2011.

The web services can be composed in sequential as well as in parallel manner. There exists different architecture for sequential composition of web services [12]. In sequential composition, a web service will not start its execution until the previous web service will finish its processing. But in parallel web service composition, set ofweb services can be processed at the same time in an independent manner [12]. Thus, there is a need of combing set of web services in parallel as business processes to fulfill business requirements. We have proposed an architecture for web service composition with the help of Intalio business process designer. The proposed framework will helps the end user to evaluate the functionality of different web services at the same time. The set of web services can interact at run time in order to complete the service request. The rest of the paper is organized as follows. The web service composition architecture involving BPEL will be discussed in Section 2. The working example of business process and web service composition will be illustrated in Section 3. Finally, conclusion and future research directions will be described in Section 4.

2 Web Service Composition Architecture

The architecture for web service composition is proposed, which is developed with the help of Intalio business process designer. The working model of web service composition is illustrated in Fig. 1. The BPEL process is published over central repository so that it could be available for service consumers publicly. The central repository is having collection of web services or business processes, which are categorized on their domain. The set of domains related to different fields are managed in central repository such as entertainment, education, jobs, crimes etc. The central repository used in the proposed framework is Universal Description Discovery and Integration (UDDI). The set of UDDIs are available in private and public domain of internet as a freeware or on payment basis.

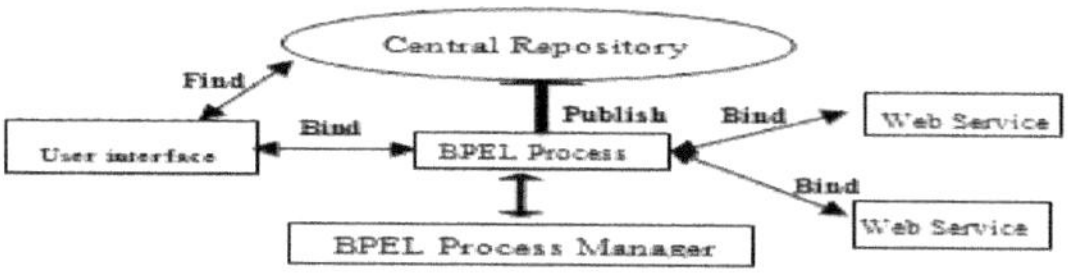

Fig. 1. Web Service Composition Architecture

Also, we have focused on the development of user interface for providing the interaction with BPEL process. The user interface can be used by service consumers to access all the available BPEL processes in public domain. The working of central repository is such that the service consumer will search BPEL process in UDDI on the basis of their respective domain and the available processes or services will be provided to the consumers. Finally, service consumer will start interaction with the BPEL process directly and use the functionality of web services through business processes. The BPEL process manager manages the BPEL processes that can interact with different web services, which may be developed by different service providers.

3 Working Example

The proposed architecture is illustrated for two web services, i.e., PVR_WS and INOX_WS for different multiplexes. Once the web service is developed, we have managed WSDL files for each web service because WSDL files will work as interface for web services. Thereafter, business process will be developed from different web services, which will be responsible for interaction with the web services and retrieving movie time in parallel, and make available the coming outputs to the service consumer.

3.1 Implementation

The Jdeveloper is a tool used for deployment and development web services with the help of SOA architecture. The PVR web service (PVR_WS) and INOX web service (INOX_WS) are demonstrated in Fig. 2 and Fig. 4, respectively. The Fig. 3 and Fig. 5 are providing the tested output.

Fig. 2. PVR_WS Deploy **Fig. 3.** PVR_WS Result **Fig. 4.** Inox_WSDeploy **Fig. 5.** Inox_WS Result

The business process diagram is developed in Intalio business process designer as shown in Fig.6. Web services are called here with the help of Invoke1 and Invoke2 operations of BPEL process. The client application is also developed for invoking BPEL process. Each invoke operation will call the different web services.

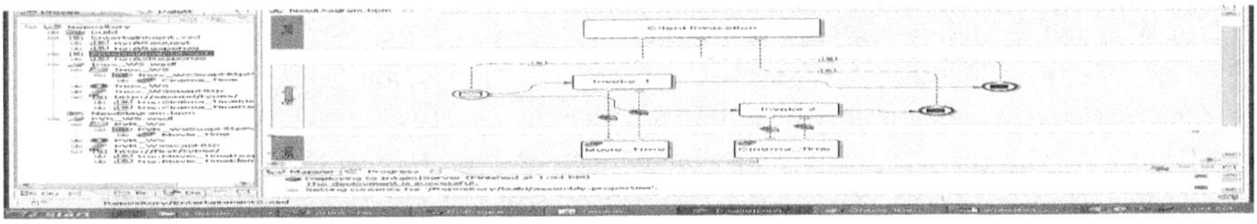

Fig. 6. Web Service Composition through Intalio

3.2 Testing and Deployment

BPEL is deployed on Intalio server for testing of above illustration. For testing, the movie name is provided as input to the BPEL process available on Intalio server. These BPEL process will call different web services such as PVR_WS and INOX_WS, respectively for same input as shown in Fig. 7. The output coming from business process through PVR and INOX web services is shown in Fig. 8 and Fig. 9, respectively. We have two different outputs corresponding to the different web services, which are composed by BPEL process. These outputs are having time of movie currently running in both the multiplexes.

Fig. 7. BPEL Testing

Fig. 8. BPEL Output 1

Fig. 9. BPEL Output 2

4 Conclusion and Future Work

The paper has focused on development and deployment of BPEL processes with the help of Intalio business process designer. The developed BPEL process is having movie time running in different theaters through different web services. The BPEL process requires process manger for processing the different BPEL processes. The BPEL process manager does not have support for security issues [8][9]. The future research will focus on the development of secure framework for BPEL processes, which will provide the support for authorization, XML encryption and XML decryption etc.

References

[1] Gunzer, H.: Introduction to web service, Online Document at Borland, pp.1–17 (2002), http://archive.devx.com/javasr/whitepapers/borland/12728JB6/webservwp.pdf

[2] Bhandari, R., Thakar, U., Dagdee, N.: Web service based campus recruitment process National level Conference Proceeding at KCET, pp.1–6 (2008)

[3] Wang, H., Zhexue Huang, J., Qu, Y.: Web services: problems and future directions. Journal of Web Semantics, 309–320 (2004), http://www.sciencedirect.com

[4] Srivastava, B., Koehler, J.: Web service composition: current solutions and open problems. In: Proceedings of ICAPS, Workshop on Planning for Web Services, vol. 35, Key: citeulike: 7026122 (2003)

[5] Dustdar, S., Schreiner, W.: A survey on web services composition. International Journal of Web and Grid Services 1, 1–30 (2005)

[6] Gnesi, S., Bucchiarone, A.: A survey on services composition languages and models. In: International Workshop on Web Services Modeling and Testing, WS-MaTe 2006 (2006)

[7] Peltz, C.: Web services orchestration and choreography. Journal Computer 36(10), 46–52 (2003), http://portal.acm.org/citation.cfm?id=1437007

[8] IBM, Oracle, Adobe, BEA: Business process limitation (2007), http://www.ibm.com/developerworks/webservices/library/specification/ws-bpel4people/

[9] Business process limitation, http://download.oracle.com/docs/cd/B31017_01/integrate.1013/b28982/security.htm#CDDJIAEC

[10] Bhandari, R., Suman, U., Ramani, A.K.: Generalized Framework for Secure Web Service Composition. In: IEEE Xplore, ICNCC 2011 (2011)

[11] Lande, N.: Basics of web services (2007), http://www.codeproject.com/KB/XML/Defining_Web_Services.aspx

[12] Antonio, F., Carlos, J., Souto, N.: Improving Transparent Adaptability in web service composition. In: IEEE International Conference on Service Oriented Computing and Application, pp. 80–87 (2007)

Author Index

GPSR Compliance

The European Union's (EU) General Product Safety Regulation (GPSR) is a set of rules that requires consumer products to be safe and our obligations to ensure this.

If you have any concerns about our products, you can contact us on ProductSafety@springernature.com

In case Publisher is established outside the EU, the EU authorized representative is:

Springer Nature Customer Service Center GmbH
Europaplatz 3
69115 Heidelberg, Germany

Batch number: 10844611

Printed by Printforce, the Netherlands